MW00534116

The Essential Goethe

The Essential

Goethe

JOHANN WOLFGANG VON GOETHE

Edited and Introduced by

MATTHEW BELL

PRINCETON UNIVERSITY PRESS
Princeton & Oxford

COPYRIGHT © 2016 BY PRINCETON UNIVERSITY PRESS

Faust translation copyright © John R. Williams 1999 and 2007.
First published by Wordsworth Editions 1999 and 2007.

Requests for permission to reproduce material from this work
should be sent to Permissions, Princeton University Press

PUBLISHED BY PRINCETON UNIVERSITY PRESS
41 William Street, Princeton, New Jersey 08540

IN THE UNITED KINGDOM: PRINCETON UNIVERSITY PRESS
6 Oxford Street, Woodstock, Oxfordshire OX20 1TR

press.princeton.edu

All Rights Reserved

FRONTISPIECE: 1791 engraving of Johann Wolfgang von Goethe,
by Johann Heinrich Lips.

Second printing, and first paperback printing, 2018
Paper ISBN 978-0-691-18104-2

The Library of Congress has cataloged the cloth edition as follows:
Goethe, Johann Wolfgang von, 1749–1832.
[Works. Selections. English]
The Essential Goethe / Johann Wolfgang von Goethe ; edited
and introduced by Matthew Bell.
pages cm
ISBN 978-0-691-16290-4 (hardcover : acid-free paper)
1. Goethe, Johann Wolfgang von, 1749–1832—Translations into English.
I. Bell, Matthew, 1964– editor. II. Title.
PT2026.A2B44 2015
838'.603—dc23
2015007997

British Library Cataloging-in-Publication Data is available

This book has been composed in Adobe Garamond Pro and Gulden Draak

Printed on acid-free paper. ∞

PRINTED IN THE UNITED STATES OF AMERICA

5 7 9 10 8 6 4

Contents

Introduction

Reading a French translation of his drama *Faust* in 1828, Goethe was struck by how "much brighter and more deliberately constructed" it appeared to him than in his original German. He was fascinated by the translation of his writing into other languages, and he was quick to acknowledge the important role of translation in modern culture. Literature, he believed, was becoming less oriented toward the nation. Soon there would be a body of writing—"world literature" was the term he coined for it—that would be international in scope and readership. He would certainly have been delighted to find that his writing is currently enjoying the attention of so many talented translators. English-speaking readers of *Faust* now have an embarrassment of riches, with modern versions by David Luke, Randall Jarrell, John Williams, and David Constantine. Constantine and Stanley Corngold have recently produced versions of *The Sorrows of Young Werther*, the sentimental novel of 1774 that made Goethe a European celebrity and prompted Napoleon to award him the Legion d'Honneur. Luke and John Whaley have done excellent selections of Goethe's poetry in English.

At the same time the range of Goethe's writing available in English remains quite narrow, unless the reader is lucky enough to find the twelve volumes of Goethe's *Collected Works* published jointly by Princeton University Press and Suhrkamp Verlag in the 1980s. The Princeton edition was an ambitious undertaking. Under the general editorship of three Goethe scholars, Victor Lange, Eric Blackall, and Cyrus Hamlyn, it brought together versions by over twenty translators covering a wide range of Goethe's writings: poetry, plays, novels and shorter prose fiction, an autobiography, and essays on the arts, philosophy, and science. Its size made the Princeton edition more suited to the library than the general reader's bookshelf. There has long been demand for an edition of the collected works that offers the reader a similar breadth of coverage in a more manageable format. The present volume satisfies that demand. Drawing on the twelve Princeton volumes, it offers readers a representative picture of Goethe's writing in a single self-contained and relatively portable volume. (We have made one exception to the rule of only using versions from the Princeton/Suhrkamp collection: the version of *Faust: Part One* by Stuart Atkins that originally appeared in Volume II of the collection is replaced here by John Williams's excellent version, originally published by Wordsworth Classics.) It contains a broad selection of Goethe's writing in different genres—lyric, drama, prose, autobiography—as well as a range of essays on cultural, philosophical, and scientific subjects. We believe that it is the most comprehensive and representative selection of Goethe's writing that has ever been made available to the English-speaking reader in a single volume.

The volume has been produced first and foremost with the general reader in mind, though we hope it will also prove useful for students of European and comparative literature, where Goethe is an important but often inaccessible figure. Readers will find many of Goethe's canonical works here. There is a selection of poems in various forms from the full span of his career, including several of the remarkable lyrics that were set to piano accompaniment by Schubert and others. Music lovers will also be familiar with operatic versions of *Faust* by Gounod, Berlioz, and others, as well as the overture and incidental music that Beethoven composed for *Egmont*. This latter play is rarely seen in English translation, though it is central to the German canon of Goethe's writings. Also hard to find in English translation are his neo-classical dramas *Iphigenia in Tauris* and *Torquato Tasso* and the novel *Wilhelm Meister's Apprenticeship*, which stands at the head of the important German tradition of the *Bildungsroman* (novel of education) and influenced, though invisibly to most Anglophone readers, the "art novel" tradition of George Eliot, Henry James, Thomas Mann, and James Joyce. One aim of this volume, then, is to present a broader picture of Goethe than is usually seen in the English-speaking world—a Goethe as he has been read both in Germany and in the wider non-Anglophone world.

We also felt it was important to include a wide selection of the nonliterary essays, with special emphasis on his writings on art and science. As well as providing a context for his literary works, these essays have much intrinsic value, even if Goethe's place in the history of science is controversial. Like his father, Goethe took academic study and scholarship very seriously, and both were avid art collectors. Goethe was well read in art history and aesthetics, philosophy, theology, and science. He firmly believed that any creative work, even the very direct and life-oriented poetry that is one of his hallmarks, had to be informed by ideas from these fields; in this broad sense he was a determinedly philosophical writer. This is the Goethe whom the reader will meet in these pages: a lover, a thinker, a scholar, a practical man, a controversialist, a writer of very diverse moods and urges.

"I came into the world in Frankfurt am Main on the stroke of 12 midday on 28 August 1749. The stars were set fair." So begins Goethe's autobiography, *From My Life: Poetry and Truth*. It might seem odd for a poet to characterize himself as lucky, but Goethe certainly was a lucky poet. Apart from a few episodes of illness, he enjoyed good health and a long and active life, so that even in his last years, before his death at the age of eighty-two, he was producing works of a quality to match anything he had written earlier in his life, poetry of startling beauty and subtlety. His material circumstances were comfortable. He did not have to support himself by his writing: he was the master of his pen, not its slave. He lived in the manner of a gentleman, traveling to Italy on the Grand Tour, albeit somewhat late in life, and amassing expensive collections of art, books, majolica pottery, coins, and minerals. (It is reckoned that he possessed the largest private collection of minerals in the world at the time.) To the end he maintained a remarkable work ethic, complemented happily by a belief that "the whole man is to move together," as Richard Steele put it in the *Spectator* in 1711. All the faculties of mind and body must be exercised in the service of the public good. Aside from his writing, Goethe worked as a lawyer, public intellectual, scientist, minister of state (with responsibility for all arms of government), diplomat, theater director, and university administrator. To say the times he lived through were interesting would be a gross understatement; many of the philosophical and political ideas we think of as distinctively modern were formulated and put into practice during his lifetime, in the years either side of the French Revolution. He was in close contact with some of the finest minds of his generation, men like Herder, Wieland, Schiller, Fichte, and Schelling, who, like Goethe, shaped the intellectual and cultural revolution that we now call Romanticism. But having grown to manhood under the ancien regime, Goethe was not formed by the French Revolution or Romanticism; rather he reacted to them as an engaged and critical observer.

He was born into a well-to-do family, to parents of contrasting character and stock. The money came from a wine merchant business that his paternal grandfather, originally a master tailor, had built up after he acquired the ownership of one of Frankfurt's smartest hostelries through his second marriage. The family wealth enabled Goethe's father, Johann Caspar Goethe, to study law and aspire to a career in the politics of the Holy Roman Empire, a path Goethe was destined to follow. The timing of Johann Caspar's entry into politics was a mixed blessing. In 1740 the Holy Roman Emperor Charles VI died, leaving no adult male heir. The obvious Habsburg successor was Maria Theresa, but ancient Salic law forbade female succession. The Habsburgs had sought to circumvent the ban by means of the Pragmatic Sanction of 1713, but when the time came, the sanction proved ineffectual. The Bavarian Prince-Elector Charles Albert, supported by the French, renounced the sanction and invaded the Habsburg territories. In 1742 he was crowned king of Bohemia and unanimously elected Charles VII as Holy Roman emperor. The tide of war soon turned against Charles. An Austrian invasion of Bavaria forced him to abandon his dynastic lands and settle in Frankfurt, where during the following two years Goethe's father seems to have made a good impression on the displaced emperor, and he was permitted to buy the honorary title of Imperial councilor. In 1744 Charles returned to Bavaria in poor health, and when he died the following year, the Imperial throne reverted to the Habsburgs. As supporter of the Bavarian usurper, Goethe's father's hopes for advancement in Imperial politics were dashed.

Instead, Johann Caspar turned to local Frankfurt politics and in 1748 married Catharina Elisabeth Textor, the gregarious, down-to-earth daughter of Frankfurt's chief administrator. Neither the Goethes nor the Textors were members of the local patriciate that dominated Frankfurt's oligarchical government. Despite this handicap, Catharina's father, Johann Wolfgang Textor, was appointed to the city council before he had even been granted citizenship of Frankfurt, and though he remained a controversial figure, he became a senator and senior city mayor, a position he occupied three times, and in 1747 was elected lifelong chair of the city's judicial bench. Yet while the Textors were assimilated into the city's ruling elite, Goethe's father was not—an abiding source of resentment. He devoted the remainder of his life to his collection of books and art and the education of his children.

Frankfurt was proud of its historic commercial success and political status—favorably situated on the River Main near its confluence with the Rhein in an ancient wine-growing region, and recognized since 1220 as a self-governing free Imperial city. By the middle of the century, both the commercial and political freedoms of Frankfurt were coming under threat. Frankfurt had traditionally hosted Germany's biggest book fair. Publishers and booksellers met each spring to exchange the products of the flourishing literary culture. By 1750 the book fair in Leipzig, in the territory of the much larger electoral duchy of Saxony, had overtaken Frankfurt's book fair. Germany was divided into over 350 separate polities, each with its own economic and fiscal governance, forming a patchwork of local trade and tariff arrangements. Small polities like Frankfurt were at the mercy of the protectionist economic policies of the bigger states.

They were equally at the mercy of larger political upheavals. The War of the Austrian Succession had an unforeseen consequence that would shape German politics for the next forty years: it initiated a period of rivalry and sometimes outright hostility between the two greatest German powers, Austria and Prussia, that would last until the French Revolution. Goethe was born in the years of peace between the end of the war in 1748 and the beginning of the Seven Years' War in 1756, when Prussian King Frederick the Great, seeing himself encircled by a new alliance of Austria, France, and Russia, invaded Saxony. As a free Imperial city, Frankfurt was obliged to side with the Austrian emperor who guaranteed the city's ancient but fragile freedoms, but Goethe's father, alienated within his home city and no friend of the Habsburgs, sided with Prussian Fritz. In a painful irony, when the French army occupied Frankfurt in 1759, the civilian commander of the French garrison, Comte de Thoranc, was billeted in the Goethe household, a double-edged recognition of Johann

Caspar's ambiguous standing in Frankfurt and of the improvements he had made to the family home, which had turned the rambling and characterful half-timbered house of Goethe's early childhood into an elegant neo-classical establishment. The French occupation had its compensations. The troops garrisoned in the city brought their culture with them; a French theater was established, which the young Goethe visited with Thoranc's encouragement.

Aside from the French occupation and the inevitable tragedies of sibling childhood mortality, Goethe's upbringing was for the most part ordinary. He received private tutoring in the conventional subjects—the Bible, Latin, and French—and in accomplishments that might embellish a young man of high rank: dancing, music, drawing, and English. Goethe's father made use of his ample free time to teach the boy geography, law, and the history of the city of Frankfurt, as well as inflicting on him the turgid memoire of his travels in Italy. It may be that his abortive political career made Johann Caspar anxious to map his son's academic and professional path to a leading role in Frankfurt's government. On this point, as on several others, there was friction within the family. Goethe wanted to study classical philology at the new English-oriented University of Göttingen, where an enlightened and energetic classicist, Christian Gottlob Heyne, was modernizing the discipline. Goethe's father prevailed: Wolfgang was dispatched to study law at the University of Leipzig, "the Little Paris" of Saxony, with its broad avenues and tidy neo-classical facades. There followed several years of academic foot-dragging. Goethe enjoyed his time in Leipzig too much. Culturally rich, the city's literary scene had been dominated by two figures: the rhetorician, critic, and playwright Johann Christoph Gottsched, an arch systematizer and modernizer, and the more emollient Christian Fürchtegott Gellert, moral philosopher and author of popular verse fables and a fashionable sentimental novel. The influence of both men was, however, waning, and by his third semester, Goethe had instead attached himself to Adam Friedrich Oeser, the recently appointed director of the new Art Academy. It was Oeser who introduced Goethe to the writings of the newest and brightest star in German intellectual life, the great historian of ancient art Johann Joachim Winckelmann, who would exercise a profound influence on Goethe's thought.

In July 1768, still with no degree to his name after three years' half-hearted study, Goethe suffered an acute illness of the lungs that left him bedridden for weeks. As soon as he was able, on his nineteenth birthday, he returned to Frankfurt to convalesce. During his recovery he briefly (and for the only time in his life) flirted with organized Christian religion, albeit in the not very organized form of the local Frankfurt brand of Pietism, a mystical enthusiastic faith that melded adoration of Christ's wounds with arcane alchemical beliefs. A second attempt to graduate as a lawyer began in Strasbourg in April 1770. Again cultural life proved more attractive than the law. Goethe's first significant essay on the arts, "On German Architecture" (pp. 867–872), was inspired

INTRODUCTION

by the Strasbourg minster. Probably written in stages from 1770 to 1772, the essay enunciates a striking new aesthetic. In keeping with the half-finished form of the Strasbourg minster—only one of the two spires was completed— Goethe rejects the standard eighteenth-century formal definitions of beauty. Instead beauty reveals the soul of the artist. Great art—he terms it "characteristic art"—is forged in the artist's struggle for self-expression, in this case a struggle against the gloom of medieval Christianity. (Goethe had declared himself a non-Christian as early as 1768.) The more direct and the less self-reflective the creative drive, the more powerful will be the result. Part of this project, which echoes Rousseau's celebration of a humanity uncorrupted by modern urban life, is to rescue the culture of nations and historical periods that the Enlightenment disdained, including "primitive" non-European cultures. Modern Europe's inflated image of itself as the apogee of civilization is to be punctured.

Goethe would not have arrived at these ideas had he not become friends with Johann Gottfried Herder, one of the most flexible and fertile thinkers of the late eighteenth century. Herder and Goethe set out on horseback through the villages around Strasbourg to find evidence of the region's authentic culture, in particular its popular song (*Volkslied*). The results were poems such as "Rosebud in the Heather" (p. 2), whose superficial simplicity recalled popular song, but whose sinister psychology—the poem brings to light the violence and guilt in male sexual desire—expresses Goethe's aesthetics of "characteristic art" and its focus on deep psychology. The 1771 poem "Welcome and Farewell" (p. 1) portrays the feverish anticipation of a young lover riding through the night to meet his beloved, and his guilt on leaving her in the morning. (What happens between the "welcome" and the "farewell" is glossed over.) The guilt is in fact a product of Goethe's rewriting of the poem in the mid-1780s (the version printed here); in the original version, it is the girl who leaves the boy struggling to rescue some sense from his short-lived bliss.

In summer 1771, Goethe at last submitted his doctoral dissertation, on the relation between church and state and the secular origins of church law. The Strasbourg theological faculty deemed it unfit to publish, which was a requirement for graduation. There was worrying talk of Goethe's "insane mockery of religion." Instead of rewriting the thesis and meeting the full requirements for the doctorate, Goethe elected to defend a series of theses in public examination and thereby attain the lesser qualification of the licentiate. Though the licentiate conventionally carried the title "doctor," as it happened the title was not recognized in Frankfurt—a further source of friction between Goethe and his father. On his twenty-second birthday, he applied for permission to practice as an advocate in Frankfurt, though it was the city's literary life that commanded his attention. From this period comes the first evidence of his intense and lifelong, though typically idiosyncratic, interest in Shakespeare. The rhapsodic

"Shakespeare: A Tribute" (pp. 872–875) was written to celebrate Shakespeare's name-day. Ungratefully repaying the cultural gifts of the French occupation of Frankfurt, Goethe contrasts the heroic Shakespeare with the pathetic efforts of French theater to emulate Greek tragedy. Shakespeare is no feeble imitator; he is a truly national poet who magically condenses his nation's history into the narrow frame of the stage. He is the original "characteristic" artist. His strength of personality expresses itself in his heroic characters, great loners admirable more for their self-reliance than for their moral qualities—for the central insight of the "Tribute" is that the Shakespearian hero embodies good and evil inseparably. The role of the national poet—a role Goethe rightly saw as his own—was to render the ambiguity of human nature and its striving for independence amid the press of historical events.

Goethe's return to Frankfurt saw a rush of creative energy. He sketched plans for a series of works on self-reliant loners: Julius Caesar, Prometheus, the rebel knight Götz von Berlichingen, Ahasverus the Wandering Jew, the Dutch freedom-fighter Egmont, and the sixteenth-century German magus Faust. Some were plotted in detail and included whole monologues that he would dazzlingly perform from memory for his friends. Of these embryonic works, only the Götz drama was completed in the early 1770s. Some of the projects came to nothing. The composition of others stretched over decades: Goethe continued to work on *Faust* until shortly before his death in 1832. Of the Prometheus project, all that survives is a poetic monologue (pp. 2–4). Superficially an outspoken rebellion against monotheistic religion, the poem conceals a more subtle reflection on the psychological harm caused by religious enthusiasm, indeed the very pietism Goethe had flirted with during his convalescence. The same theme of excessive enthusiasm pitching suddenly into bleak cynicism appears in the early parts of *Faust*.

The play *Egmont*, substantially written in the 1770s but only completed in the late 1780s, embodies Goethe's most sustained reflection on politics. Through its portrayal of the revolt of the Low Countries against Spanish rule, it argues for the kind of local self-determination enjoyed by Frankfurt. Among the characters belonging to the play's ruling elite, only its hero Egmont is not in some sense foreign, and only he enjoys a direct connection with the people of the Low Countries, not least through his affair with a bourgeois girl Clara. Even though Egmont catastrophically misjudges the cynical intentions of the Spanish occupiers, only he (and Clara) can motivate the Dutch to rebel against the Spaniards. His success as a symbol draws on another feature of his character: politics holds no interest for him, indeed he misjudges the Spaniards' intentions because he resents the intrusion of *Realpolitik* into his life, unlike his Machiavellian ally the Duke of Orange—who plays Cassius to Egmont's Brutus. (The play contains several allusions to Shakespeare's *Julius Caesar*.) But his insouciance is also a source of Egmont's charisma; his weakness as a politician is also his strength. What is more troubling is that Clara is bewitched by Egmont's charm into joining him as a martyr for the Dutch cause. (Inventing the character of Clara was Goethe's most egregious departure from the historical record: the real Egmont was married and had eleven children.) As the play reaches its climax, it moves into an increasingly stylized and artistic mode. Egmont and Clara become works of art—the hero and heroine as artistic and political symbols.

In Goethe's version, the Dutch were provoked to revolt by the Holy Roman Empire's failure to protect them. Aside from the (relatively benign) occupation of Frankfurt by the French, Goethe had his own reasons for skepticism about the empire's institutions. From May to September 1772, he attended the Imperial law courts in Wetzlar, a small medieval town not far from Frankfurt. The courts were notoriously inefficient, and there were stories of legal backlogs longer even than the Jarndyce case in Charles Dickens's *Bleak House*. The structure of the empire was partly to blame, for the majority of cases brought before the court involved either disputes between the member states of the empire or disputes between subjects and their rulers. In neither type of case was there much prospect of enforcing an agreeable settlement, not least because obstructive lobbying by the resident ambassadors of the territorial states on one side or the other led to almost interminable delays.

Goethe seems to have left Wetzlar even more disaffected with the empire. In the spring before his departure to Wetzlar, he had joined his Frankfurt literary friends in taking over the editorship of a local review journal. During their short tenure, they turned the journal into an organ of Enlightenment thought. Goethe was particularly fascinated by the philosophy of Spinoza, one of the instigators of the Enlightenment and another heroically self-reliant figure who had been expelled from his local synagogue as an atheist. After Wetzlar Goethe continued to practice half-heartedly as an advocate in Frankfurt while pursuing his literary interests. His life lacked any kind of stability. He was developing an unfortunate gift for entering into complicated emotional attachments that left him with feelings of guilt and a countervailing need to protect himself, by flight if necessary. In Wetzlar he became infatuated with a young woman, Lotte Buff, who was already betrothed—his hasty departure from Wetzlar seems to have been an attempt to avoid causing further damage, though paradoxically he later fictionalized the relationship in *The Sorrows of Young Werther*. Another botched relationship, with the Frankfurt banker's daughter Anne Elisabeth ("Lili") Schönemann, was broken off in 1775. Escape from his turbulent life in Frankfurt was beckoning, perhaps to Italy, though an altogether different opportunity soon presented itself. While staying in Karlsruhe, Goethe encountered the young Duke Karl August of Sachsen-Weimar-Eisenach. An invitation from Weimar followed, and in the face of his father's opposition, Goethe moved to Weimar in November 1775.

Weimar enticed Goethe with a role entirely different from legal practice in Frankfurt and a more direct route to political influence. As companion and favorite of the recently married eighteen-year-old duke, Goethe was entrusted with mentoring the ruler of a sovereign territory, even if an insignificant and indebted one. The town of Weimar, dominated by the ducal residence, was a mere village compared to Frankfurt. Soon after arriving in Weimar, Goethe wrote to his friend Merck:

> My situation is favourable enough, and the Duchies of Weimar and Eisenach are in any case a stage on which I can find out whether a role in the political world suits me. I'm not in any rush, and freedom and comfort will be the main conditions of my new situation, even if I'm more than ever in a position to see the thoroughly shitty state of this our temporal majesty.

Unpromising though the outlook might have been, a territorial state promised greater dynamism than stodgy, tradition-bound Frankfurt, as well as more independence from Imperial law. During the next decade, Goethe shouldered more responsibilities in Weimar: first the reopening of the disused silver mines at Ilmenau (ill fated, as it turned out) and later forestry, highways, and war. By the early 1780s, he was running most of the ducal government, and in 1782 he took over the presidency of the ducal chamber. In the same year, thanks to his grateful employer, he was ennobled by the emperor and could move into a smart premises in the center of town.

There was a high price attached to the freedoms of Weimar, for no matter how culturally or intellectually enlightened it was, the ducal court was still a court, with all the petty formalities demanded of minor royalty in the eighteenth century. In light of these circumstances, it should not surprise that Goethe clutched at any opportunities for private human warmth. Within weeks of arriving in Weimar, he struck up a close friendship with the evidently fascinating Charlotte von Stein, seven years his elder and married to the duke's chief equerry. The nature of their relationship has been the subject of endless and probably empty speculation. Goethe certainly found it bewildering. The poem "Why confer on us the piercing vision" ("To Charlotte von Stein," pp. 6–8), which he sent to Charlotte in a letter of April 1776, suggests that there was some profound spiritual connection between them that tantalizingly eluded rational analysis: "You're the wife, the sister I forgot." The confident conjecture belies a telling ambiguity: for she cannot have been both wife and sister, and it surely matters which she was. Beneath its urgent and seemingly formless surface, the poem presents a mind disoriented by the dissonance of appearance and reality and teetering on the brink of disintegration. This sense of an enticing but threatening mystery reappears in other poems of the period, such as the brilliantly haunting ballad "Erlkönig" (pp. 16–17) or the equally perfect "The Fisherman" (pp. 12–13). Few poets have distilled the conflicts of reason and desire into more powerful and finely balanced forms.

Amid the tedious formalities and private desires of his first decade in Weimar, Goethe remained conscious of his national mission as a poet. The literary project that preoccupied him was the semiautobiographical novel *Wilhelm Meister*, which, like most of his longer works, had to wait over a decade for completion. Its working title was "Wilhelm Meister's Theatrical Mission," but after a change in direction in the 1790s, it was published under the title *Wilhelm Meister's Apprenticeship*. A novel of the theater morphed into a novel of education. The early chapters charmingly portray domestic life in a German city during the Seven Years' War. Haphazardly and reluctantly, Wilhelm's childhood passion for the theater develops into a budding career as a writer and actor. The dilemma of the modern artist that Flaubert would later identify—"to live like a bourgeois and think like a demi-god"—finds perhaps its earliest expression in the novel's portrayal of the hand-to-mouth existence of traveling theater troupes. The undertone is unmistakably skeptical. In his "Tribute," Goethe acclaimed Shakespeare's stage as the crucible of national identity. *Wilhelm Meister* examines the stage's more ambitious aspiration to educate the nation and finds it wanting, for the novel concurs with the cynical conclusion of Rousseau's "Letter to Monsieur D'Alembert" (1758) that the theater is mired in vanity. The more Wilhelm recognizes this, the less satisfaction he takes from his theatrical successes and the more he retreats into his private relationships, in particular with the mysterious androgynous child Mignon.

Writing to Charlotte von Stein in 1782, Goethe announced that he was revising *Egmont*'s "all too unbuttoned and student language, which contradicts the dignity of the subject matter." He did the same to *Wilhelm Meister* when he rewrote it in the 1790s, imposing a higher stylistic register and a more detached irony. Two verse plays conceived in the late 1770s and finished ten or more years later, *Iphigenia in Tauris* and *Torquato Tasso*, traced a similar arc, albeit from less demotic beginnings. When they were finally published, in polished blank verse and a neo-classical register, Goethe's readers were shocked. The popular playwright Iffland found in *Iphigenia* "a supposed Hellenic simplicity that often degenerates into triviality—bizarre syntax, strange vocabulary, and instead of sublimity the coldness of a minister's speech at the mines in Ilmenau." Both are in fact deeply personal plays grounded in Goethe's perplexing experience of the Weimar court. In both there is a reckoning with the ambition of society—a society dominated by men in *Iphigenia* and by aristocrats in *Tasso*—to possess and control the individual. The language is part of the problematic. Iphigenia and Tasso both speak openly and freely when it is impolitic to do so.

In Euripides' *Iphigenia among the Taurians*, the matricide Orestes rescues his sister from the barbarian King Thoas. Orestes receives an oracle of Apollo that directs him to cure his inherited curse by stealing the holy statue of Apollo's sister Artemis. Thanks to Iphigenia's cunning plan, the Greeks are on the verge of absconding with the statue, a symbol of Taurian national identity. Thoas is prevented from pursuing them by the sudden appearance of the goddess Athena, who rebukes him with a stern reminder of Greek cultural superiority. Goethe's adaptation of Euripides' play contains a stroke of genius. Instead of having Orestes steal the statue and humiliate the Taurians, the play turns the oracle of Apollo—the command to "steal the sister"—into a riddle that can only be interpreted by someone capable of renouncing the old religion and making a dangerous leap into enlightened humanity. The "sister" of the oracle is not the statue of Apollo's sister Artemis—a mere religious symbol—but Orestes' sister Iphigenia, a human, indeed a humane being. So the Taurians keep their holy statue, and the Greeks part from them as equals. No *deus ex machina* appears to impose Greek supremacy. Instead the play renounces all the dogmas of the old religion (and Greek imperialism) in a thoroughly Spinozist spirit. Through her own agency Iphigenia lifts the curse of the Tantalids (read: Christian original sin). Instead of conniving with Orestes and his cousin Pylades to deceive the Taurians and steal the statue, she performs an "unheard-of deed" by revealing the Greek plan to Thoas. In her humane openness, Iphigenia proves herself not only equal but superior to her Greek and Taurian male counterparts, whose first instinct is always deceit or force. The play is both a vivid enactment of Spinozist Enlightenment humanism and arguably one of the most insightful accounts of the social plight of women by any male writer before the nineteenth century.

Torquato Tasso deals more directly with Goethe's troubles as a court poet, and it is remarkable that Goethe wrote it at all, particularly in the face of Duke Karl August's understandable opposition. Tasso's circumstances bore obvious similarities to Goethe's in Weimar: both were court poets dependent on a noble patron. In traditional accounts of his life, Tasso went mad and was incarcerated. The play presents a moment shortly before his incarceration. Given the tragic arc of Tasso's biography, it is hard not to read the play for signs of his future madness or, more controversially, its causes in courtly life. Tasso is on the verge of finishing his epic poem *La Gerusalemme liberata*. (Goethe's inability to finish his own longer works was another painful parallel.) Tasso hopes that by leaving Ferrara for the wider world he will learn what an epic poet needs to know, but the duke fears that in letting Tasso take the manuscript away, he will lose the poem he has been subsidizing. The main agents of Tasso's descent into madness are in fact two women, the duke's sister and Leonore Sanvitale: the former dotes platonically and unhealthily on him, the latter hopes to poach him for her own court. Both are also in their own way victims, especially of their own vanity, which loves to see itself mirrored in Tasso's verse. The play is full of sinister psychological manipulation. In seeking to control him, the court infantilizes him. A poet needs freedom to invent and speak the truth, but the manipulation of Tasso causes his poetic inventiveness to bleed into delusion and paranoia. This becomes clear in the contrast between Tasso and the diplomat Antonio—a recapitulation of the contrast of Egmont and

Orange. Both are bourgeois in an aristocratic world. Tasso demands absolute poetic freedom at the cost of his liberty; Antonio subordinates his liberty to the game of politics. The play ends ambivalently with their reconciliation but without any hope of a future for Tasso at court.

The first sign of a change in Goethe's sense of his poetic mission comes in a Pindaric ode, "Winter Journey in the Harz" (pp. 9–11), written in 1777, three years before he began to write *Tasso*. In oracular mode it presents a journey away from the poet's past (the young poet of *Werther*) and his present (the court poet). The destination is obscure: the clouded summit of the mysterious Brocken mountain, traditionally the site of witches' gatherings. The poet's aim and the revelation he receives, like Moses on the mountaintop, is to replace folklore with science. The mountain is to yield up its geological secrets, the veins of silver running through it that enrich the surrounding territories. The poet has become a scientist. The poem was prompted by the decision to re-open the disused silver mines in Ilmenau, which Goethe was to supervise. He took his responsibilities earnestly and embarked on reading the latest scholarly treatises on geological stratigraphy. The idea that humans were simply the latest products of an immensely slow process of creation, far slower than a literal reading of scripture would allow, appealed to Goethe, as is evident in the essay "On Granite" (pp. 913–915). The essay may belong to a larger project for a "Novel on the Universe" that Goethe began to plan in 1781. In the same year he turned his thoughts to anatomy, where he found more evidence of nature's evolving forms and of the thought that "we were once plants and animals," as Charlotte von Stein summarized the thrust of a new book that Herder was writing. Goethe was jubilant when in 1784 he thought he had discovered evidence of the intermaxillary bone in humans—the absence of which was the slender thread on which some orthodox-minded anatomists hoped to hang a distinction between man and the other primates. Goethe followed the great Swedish naturalist Linnaeus in holding that no such distinction existed. On a smaller scale, he spent long hours observing microscopic organisms cultured in water. These were the cause of much excitement at the time: did they prove that there was no absolute boundary between plants and animals? Again Goethe was interested in breaking down boundaries and seeing how natural forms bled into one another.

Goethe's interest in science was grounded in two beliefs. First, nature was characterized by constant and steady change: "nature makes no leaps," as Linnaeus put it. Second, underlying these changes were law-like principles intrinsic to nature itself and requiring no external (divine) hand to shape them. There is no role for God in science. In 1784 he returned to the study of Spinoza (pp. 916–917), though the infamous Dutch philosopher had in fact never been far from his thoughts. Egmont is a good Spinozist: he disavows free will to follow his own fate. Also in the spirit of Spinoza, Iphigenia rejects human sacrifice in favor of humanity. Also pervaded by Spinozism are the poems of

INTRODUCTION

the late 1770s and early 1780s, such as the complex and deceptive "The God-like" (pp. 13–15), which ostensibly presents the orthodox view that humans are made in the image of God, but in fact argues the reverse: the gods are how we make them, the products of our moral imagination. Spinoza's significance to Goethe has been much debated and often underestimated. In the 1780s, discomfited by his turbulent and troubled life in Weimar, Goethe developed a settled picture of the world and his place in it. Nature offers compensation for human inconstancy. The highest we can hope for is insight into natural regularities, and this is where we find God, if anywhere. Art provides the best evidence of this truth, for great art reflects natural regularities in its own structures (pp. 875–878). The scientist and the artist are (or should be) brothers in arms. Goethe would continue to develop variations on this idea through the 1790s and beyond.

To put these ideas into practice required time and energy, which Goethe lacked, while he continued to run the impoverished duchy. Eventually he felt he had done enough. On September 3, 1786, just one week after his thirty-seventh birthday, Goethe suddenly vanished. He had been staying at the spa town of Carlsbad (Karlovy Vary) and stole away at night by coach toward Bavaria. Within three days, he was in Munich and on September 8, traveling under the assumed identity of Phillip Miller, German painter, he crossed the Brenner Pass into Italy. Like his father, he kept a meticulous travel journal, which he would later rework and publish as his *Italian Journey* (pp. 751–866). It is full of detail, sometimes mundane but always conveying genuine inquisitiveness and wonder, not only at the great art and architecture of Italy, but also at Italian manners and social life, the climate, vegetation, geology, and weather. If to some extent he was his father's son, he also followed in the footsteps of Winckelmann, who had left Germany to make his name in Rome. Winckelmann's understanding of ancient art far outstripped that of any modern before him, though it was not free of paradoxes. On the one hand, he was the first to set out, in laboriously detailed accounts of the representation of fingers and toes, the subtle shifts in style between the different periods of ancient art, sculpture in particular. The greatest art, which Winckelmann saw was produced in fifth-century BC Athens, was a product of its place and time. The Athenians inhabited a mild climate, lived their lives outdoors, were devoted to the cultivation of the body in (naked) athletics and of the mind in philosophy, and were fortunate to live in a democratic polity. The best ancient sculpture reflects this unconstrained physical and mental freedom. However, classical Greek art does not merely reflect nature. It idealizes; it aspires to reflect the Platonic forms of which all bodies are (so Plato) mere imitations, and it is motivated by desire, as was obvious to readers of Winckelmann's homoerotic descriptions of classical statues. In Italy Goethe felt liberated; he was able to devote himself to objects—an exotic and ancient palm fern in the botanical gardens of Padua (which still stands today), the Roman amphitheatre at

Verona, the coolly beautiful villas of Palladio, and of course the sculptures in the great Roman collections. Whether or not the story of an affair with a Roman widow is true, the poetry Goethe wrote after his return to Weimar in 1788, especially the extraordinary sequence of *Roman Elegies* (pp. 17–21), make the Winckelmannian connection between art and sexual desire, and they do so, as Winckelmann argued, as great art must: through an enthusiastic, personal emulation of ancient culture, in this case the love poetry of first-century BC Rome.

If Goethe's friends were upset by his sudden and unannounced flight to Italy, what he did on his return to Weimar was downright scandalous. In July 1788 he was approached by a young woman, Christiane Vulpius, with a request for help on behalf of her brother, a struggling author of popular novels. Goethe and Christiane became lovers. In December 1789 she bore their first son, August. The Vulpius family had fallen on hard times. The father had been dismissed from his post in the duchy's archives, and Christiane was obliged to take a sinecure position with a local manufacturer. In any case, the family was not aristocratic, so there was no question of Goethe and Christiane marrying. From this point on, Goethe led a happy domestic existence quite disconnected from his life at court. By escaping to Italy, he had erected a wall between himself and the Weimar court; on his return to Weimar, the wall was renewed and buttressed, and Christiane was firmly on its Italian side.

During his Italian furlough Goethe finished *Egmont* and *Iphigenia* and made progress with *Tasso* and *Faust*. In doing so, he reengaged with the literary world from which he had partially withdrawn during his first ten years in Weimar. However, it was a reengagement on his terms. He no longer had any interest in pandering to the sentimental tastes of the German reading public. As he wrote to Schiller in 1795, "I know the charade that is authorship in Germany inside and out; one must simply play the game, there's nothing more to be said on the subject." There was a rich supply of things to disagree with. His new neo-classical view of the arts was at odds with the sentimentalism of much German culture, and worse was to follow when the Romantic movement began in the late 1790s and then made a turn toward Catholicism. Goethe got on well with some of the young Romantics for a while, as he did with the radical young idealist philosophers Fichte and Schelling. His interest was short lived, not for any lack of patience on his part. Matters of fundamental importance alienated him from the new trends. He was committed to his own rather idiosyncratic version of scientific realism, and he soon came to the view that idealism had little to offer him as a scientist. What alienated him most was the French Revolution. Goethe had devoted his early Weimar years to making the ancient regime work for the good of society as a whole, or so he thought. The later books of *Wilhelm Meister's Apprenticeship*, written after the revolution, are concerned with these questions: of what use is the aristocracy? How can it benefit and integrate with the rest of society? Goethe's politics are hard to define. He believed in Enlightened progress; he tried to reduce the expenditure of the Weimar court and to develop the local economy. But he also subscribed to the overriding aim of all ancien regime governments, which was to maintain public order, even if that required unpalatable measures. The revolution initiated a period of disorder that was anathema to him, and this was his chief objection to it. Having said that, his stance was a more nuanced view than he is usually given credit for. Two of his *Venetian Epigrams* express these conflicts. One bemoans the revolutionary "apostles of freedom" who have no understanding of the responsibilities of government. The other acknowledges that although what they say might be insane, the revolutionaries are at least free, whereas slaves are merely silent. For all that he abhorred chaos, he knew it could be creative. For an opponent of the revolution, he invested a remarkable amount of creative energy into trying to come to terms with it. What alienated Goethe most from his fellow Germans was the advent of Napoleon, whom Goethe admired and the young generation of German nationalists demonized. But Goethe had long since abandoned any thoughts of German nationhood or even a unified national culture. After Italy, Europe and the wider world mattered more to him.

Goethe was interested in philosophy in a broad sense, but not in the academic debates about epistemology and moral agency that dominated the early years of post-Kantian idealism. Kant had argued that in the realm of observable phenomena, science was the only authoritative source of knowledge. Kant's scientific realism appealed strongly to Goethe; it confirmed his devotion to Spinoza and reinforced his view of himself as a "child of the world" (*Weltkind*). In the essay "The Experiment as Mediator between Object and Subject" (pp. 940–947), Goethe tried to square his own empiricist science with the Kantian framework. The other side of Kant's philosophy—the attempt to ground ethics in rigorous and self-denying duty—affronted Goethe's Rousseauian belief in the intrinsic goodness of human nature. In the *Critique of Judgement*, Kant tried to build a bridge between the realm of phenomena and the realm of ethical ends by means of an investigation of art and biological forms. Goethe found this much more to his liking, though as the later essay "The Influence of Modern Philosophy" (pp. 983–986) makes clear, he found it congenial to remain at a distance.

In any case, in the summer of 1794 a far more congenial presence interposed itself between Goethe and the young Kantian philosophers. Some fourteen years previously, Friedrich Schiller (1759–1805) had exploded onto the literary scene with his chaotic "Storm and Stress" drama *The Robbers*, which was not at all to Goethe's taste. By 1794 the career of Germany's most exciting young dramatist had run into the sand. He had struggled for years with a vast verse drama *Don Carlos*. Thanks to Goethe's recommendation, he was appointed to a chair in history at the University of Jena, and he enjoyed great success as a lecturer, though the financial rewards were meager and the study of history was only ever a means to an artistic end. In the early 1790s, he took a sabbatical and spent two years studying Kant. He approached Goethe in 1794 with an invitation to contribute to a new literary journal. A close friendship and creative partnership rapidly developed, indeed one of the most intimate working relationships between two great poets in literary history. Goethe and Schiller found that they shared fundamental beliefs about the nature of literature, about the ways writers are molded by tradition and their political and social circumstances, in particular the national context, which in Germany's case meant political fragmentation, the lack of a cultural center such as Paris or London, and a consequent tendency for taste to seek out the lowest level ("Response to a Literary Rabble-Rouser," pp. 878–881). In a conscious act of resistance to the national misery, Goethe and Schiller encouraged, inspired, and competed with each other. In 1795 they collaborated on a controversial collection of epigrams, and in 1797 they wrote a series of ballads (e.g., "The Bride of Corinth," pp. 21–26). It was Schiller who insisted Goethe publish the *Roman Elegies*; he pushed Goethe to complete *Faust* and looked over Goethe's shoulder during the completion of *Wilhelm Meister's Apprenticeship*. In Italy Goethe had hoped to complete his major unfinished works and be reborn as a writer. It was thanks to Schiller that the promise of Italian rebirth was fully realized in the 1790s. When Schiller died in 1805, Goethe wrote to his friend Zelter that he felt he had lost half of his own existence.

Goethe had begun work on the *Meister* novel in the winter of 1775–76, and in fits and starts the novel had slowly taken shape. By 1786 he had written a total of 90 chapters in six books narrating Wilhelm's development from childhood to his engagement by a professional theatrical company managed by his friend Serlo. The novel's tortuous, punctuated genesis had resulted in a certain unevenness of style and compositional method. The direction of the novel was not at all clear: at the end of Book VI, Wilhelm joined Serlo's company, but with serious misgivings about his own aptitude and the very possibility of making a success of a theatrical company in the current German climate. Goethe hesitated to resume work on the novel. In 1791 he wrote some plans for its completion. In 1793 he had a fresh copy made of the manuscript. Only in 1794 did he take the decisive step of agreeing to a contract with the publisher Unger in Berlin. Still he needed the help of a critical and judicious reader to guide him toward his goal. He asked Herder to help, but the sexual content of Book I elicited a caustic response from his acerbic old friend. Then the friendship with Schiller blossomed unexpectedly, and with Schiller's critical encouragement, Goethe was able to complete the novel in 1796.

The six books of the *Theatrical Mission* were distilled into the first four books of the new novel, *Wilhelm Meister's Apprenticeship*. The narrative became more ironic and distanced, while the account of Wilhelm's childhood, which in the original drafts was presented by a third-person narrator, was now recast as a retrospective narrative by Wilhelm himself. The effect of all this is to intensify the difficulties already evident in Wilhelm's theatrical misadventures. In Book V Wilhelm begins the thankless task of turning Serlo's company into a vehicle for national renewal, with mixed results. A haphazardly prepared performance of *Hamlet* enjoys a rapturous first-night reception, but catastrophe follows when the theater burns down. Wilhelm is also troubled by Serlo's sister, the suicidal Aurelie. When she dies, he sets off to find the man he holds responsible for ruining her life. Book VI, the seemingly irrelevant "Confessions of a Beautiful Soul," forms an intermezzo between the theatrical part of the novel and its concluding two books. The Beautiful Soul is in reality a troubled soul; she passes through a series of emotional and religious stations, never quite reaching contentment until she finally withdraws from social life. The book is based on the lost autobiography of a Frankfurt family friend of the Goethes, the Pietist Susanne von Klettenberg, and it reminds us of the national religious context, one of the main obstacles to Germany's renewal. The other chief obstacle is the social divide. In Books VII and VIII, Wilhelm turns his back on the theater and becomes part of a group of reform-minded aristocrats, with whom he has an obscure connection via his grandfather's art collection—an allusion to Goethe's own and his father's compulsive art collecting, both worthy attempts at bourgeois self-education of taste. Against this amateurism is set the more educated Palladian taste of the Beautiful Soul's uncle. The seemingly self-indulgent discussions of art are in fact germane to the novel's political concerns, in the same way as Schiller's *Letters on Aesthetic Education* (1795) uses art as a way of thinking about politics. It is unclear how a bourgeois, whose natural milieu is our modern statistical world, can be an artist: in the bourgeois world, money is king. It is equally unclear how a leisured aristocrat, though he may have the disposition of an artist, can be useful to society. Cultural renewal, so Goethe's argument runs, can only come from an alliance between a culturally aware bourgeoisie and a reformist aristocracy, and that is what Book VIII hesitantly and with evident misgivings sketches out. Finally Wilhelm is betrothed to the aristocratic Natalie, though there is something purposely contrived about the *mésalliance*, and the need for a sequel is clearly signaled.

Having helped Goethe to finish the *Meister* novel, Schiller now pressed him to solve the enigma that was *Faust*. The composition of this massively rich and barely performable poetic drama spanned Goethe's entire adult life. Part One was written between the early 1770s and 1800. Its genesis was convoluted, and the shifts in direction that each new layer of material brought have given rise to much scholarly debate. The text was composed in three phases. The Faust of the first phase, before Goethe's move to Weimar, is a self-reliant hero, as delineated in the Shakespeare "Tribute": a titan composed equally of good and evil. Faust sets himself against small-minded academia and the triviality of what commonly passes as knowledge. Instead of tradition, Faust will rely on his own resources. His pedantic assistant Wagner cannot accept Faust's skepticism about university learning and begs him to acknowledge that at least we can understand the human mind. Faust's answer is melodramatic and unsettling:

WAGNER. Yes—but the world! The human heart and mind!
　We all seek knowledge, surely, in this sphere?
FAUST. Why, yes, however knowledge is defined.
　But who will dare to speak the truth out clear?
　The few who anything of truth have learned,
　And foolishly did not keep truth concealed,
　Their thoughts and visions to the common herd revealed,
　Since time began we've crucified and burned. (pp. 263–264, lines 586ff)

There are profound truths, but the visionaries who have seen them have ever been branded as heretics: Socrates, Christ, the Protestant reformer Jan Hus, and of course Spinoza, who was excommunicated by his synagogue. Faust's attitude to knowledge is not always so bleak. From the very beginning of the *Urfaust*, he is skeptical, but also grimly proud of his own skepticism, his ability to unmask the vanity of ordinary knowledge. In the first scene, "Night" (pp. 258–259), he alternates between a melancholic acceptance of our limitations and a euphoric quest for deeper knowledge. The latter drives him into the arms of magic. Just before the scene with Wagner, Faust summons a mysterious Earth Spirit, hoping to hear from it the very reassurance Wagner will demand of Faust. The Earth Spirit spurns Faust with the perplexing response: "You match the spirit that you comprehend, / Not me!" (p. 262, lines 512–513). Following the Wagner scene, the tragedy of the scholar breaks off, with the tension between vaulting ambition and desperate melancholia unresolved.

We next meet Faust in the company of Mephistopheles; presumably this is who the mysterious Earth Spirit had in mind. However, the summoning of the devil and the traditional pact scene are missing. This is the so-called "great lacuna" in the original version, the *Urfaust*; Faust is pitched from his study directly into the bourgeois world where he meets a young girl Margarete (Gretchen). With Mephistopheles' fiendish help he wins her affection, but it is a *mésalliance*. A young petit-bourgeois girl is beguiled by a charismatic and socially superior man, and just as in *Egmont*, it can come to no good. Goethe's portrayal of Gretchen going half-knowingly to her fate, innocent and insightful in equal measure, is one of his great achievements. Gretchen's monologue at the spinning wheel and her song of the King of Thule, set as songs by Schubert, have become canonical. As for Faust, he is too much a slave to his own desire to be able to act on his scruples. The fragment ends with the trauma of Gretchen in prison, maddened by guilt, like Ophelia. Faust makes a tardy bid to rescue her, but this only serves to wake her out of her delirium into the clarity of guilt. She now sees that execution is the proper penance for her infanticide and the murder of her mother. Uncomprehending, Faust is whisked away by Mephistopheles. For Anglophone readers coming to

Goethe's play from Marlowe's *Dr Faustus*, which contains nothing remotely like it, the Gretchen plot is an unforgettable dramatic shock.

Goethe returned to *Faust* in Rome in 1787. Among the material he added to the Gretchen tragedy is a striking passage in which, contrary to the rebuff he receives from the Earth Spirit, Faust seems to have learned from the Spirit about the interrelatedness of biological species:

> You gave me, sublime Spirit, gave me all
> I asked of you; and it was not in vain
> You turned your face upon me in the fire.
> You gave me glorious nature as my kingdom,
> The power to feel it and delight in it.
> No cold encounter, no mere spectacle
> You granted me, for nature's very heart
> Is like the bosom of a friend revealed.
> Creation's ordered scale of life you've shown me;
> I learn to know my brother creatures here
> In quiet woods, in streams and in the air. (pp. 331–332, lines 3217ff)

No longer the disaffected professor of the early scenes, Faust is now a modern scientist. The talk of "brother creatures" sounds remarkably like the protoevolutionary view of species that we know Goethe and Herder held in the 1780s. Goethe projects his own scientific interests onto Faust, and it now becomes clear why Goethe had found the pact scene impossible to write. Although in the early 1770s Goethe could be outspokenly skeptical about university scholarship, he was bookish like his father, and he maintained a fascination with science and the natural world throughout his life. How then could he write about a scholar and scientist whose very lust for knowledge drove him into a pact with the devil?

Another concern was the gap between the tragedy of the scholar and the tragedy of Gretchen: how does a crabbed and jaded scholar end up falling in love with a simple bourgeois girl? Also in Rome he wrote the scene in the witches' kitchen. Here the weary Faust is offered a potion that is supposed to rejuvenate him, but in fact will make him fall in love with the next woman he sees: Gretchen. It is a mechanical device and fails to resolve the underlying problem, which continued to exercise Goethe when, under friendly pressure from Schiller, he resumed work on Faust in 1797. Three pieces of prefatory material were now added, all standing outside Part One proper (pp. 249–257). The poem "Dedication" presents a very personal rationale for the play. The other two pieces are more substantial. A scene in the theater invites us to imagine a poet, a theater manager, and a comic actor debating the play that is about to be written—again a form of rationale, this time matching the play to the needs and demands of the late eighteenth-century German theater and its audiences. What emerges is full of irony and compromise, above all a sense that this may in fact *not* be a play that Germans will want to see. The last prelude is the "Prologue in Heaven," which pits God against Mephistopheles in a debate about human nature and leads to what appears to be a wager between them.

In 1797 Goethe resolved the problem of the pact. The resumption of work on *Faust* coincided with his producing Mozart's *Così fan tutte* for the Weimar court theater. In Da Ponte's libretto, translated for the production by Christiane's brother, Ferrando and Guglielmo agree to a wager with the mysterious Don Alfonso to test the fidelity of their lovers Fiordiligi and Dorabella. Faust's deal with Mephistopheles is also a test and a wager. What is at stake is Faust's conviction that nothing the devil can offer him will give satisfaction. The wager expresses Faust's melancholy sense that the world is worthless. But what may seem like a fit of melancholia in Faust is also a test for humanity, and modern humanity in particular. Faust commits himself to ceaseless striving and so to one of the great ideas of Enlightenment Europe: never-ending progress. The scholar's tragedy and the Gretchen tragedy now fit together. For Gretchen is to be a counter in the great game and eventually a martyr to the ambivalent dynamic of modernity. While on one level the wager tests Faust's ability to live up to his own self-image, on another level it raises a moral question: is progress for its own sake morally acceptable? The form of the wager adds a further degree of complexity. Mephistopheles evidently thinks that he has come away with the traditional prize of such contracts, a human's immortal soul, and yet Faust gives quite a different impression:

FAUST. If I should ever choose a life of sloth or leisure,
 Then let that moment be my end!
 Or if you can beguile or flatter me
 Into a state of self-contented ease,
 Delude me with delight or luxury—
 That day shall be my last. These
 Are my terms.
MEPHISTOPHELES. It's done!
FAUST. So let it be:
 If I should bid the moment stay, or try
 To hold its fleeting beauty, then you may
 Cast me in chains and carry me away,
 For in that instant I will gladly die. (pp. 290–291, lines 1692ff)

Faust seems to think that losing the wager will mean losing his life. There is no mention here of his soul. Mephistopheles asks for a contract signed in blood, which Faust energetically rebuts, and we do not see such a document or learn of its contents. Faust and Mephistopheles are clearly at cross purposes, and the wager arises out of a debate that contains more heat than light. Goethe was enough of a lawyer to know how problematic contracts can be.

Completed in 1801, Part One of *Faust* is a huge rambling lyrical drama, forbiddingly diverse in its forms and moods and containing some of Goethe's most outrageous experimentation. Around 1800 he started work on Part Two, which would occupy him up to 1806 and then again from 1825. It was published posthumously in 1832, a baffling and outrageous bequest to his countrymen. Part One was finally published in 1808, delayed by illness and war. From the invasion of France by the armies of the First Coalition in 1792 to the defeat of Napoleon at Waterloo in 1815, war was a near-constant threat, even if Weimar itself was only once affected directly. In October 1806 Napoleon's armies delivered a humiliating defeat to the Prussians on Weimar's very doorstep at the Battle of Jena-Auerstedt. Orders were given for Goethe's house to be spared by the marauding French troops, but the orders arrived late, and Christiane is said to have kept the soldiers at bay for a time. She and Goethe hurriedly married a few days later.

The first years of the new century were a precarious turning point in Goethe's life. He suffered a near-fatal bout of shingles in January 1801, and in the following years what must have seemed like a generation of German writers passed away: Herder and Klopstock (1803), Kant (1804), and then Schiller (1805). There could be no more painful reminder of the need to secure his legacy, and this explains his turn to reflective autobiography, a mode that had hitherto made him uneasy. Goethe is a remarkable case of a creative figure who experiences a distinct "late" phase of creativity, only with Goethe the late phase began nearly thirty years before his death, and though undoubtedly overshadowed by death and the need to preserve the past, it was tremendously vigorous and productive. He continued to insist on the perfection and humanity of classical art. In the year of Schiller's death, he published a collection of letters from Winckelmann to his friend Berendis. The short accompanying homage to Winckelmann (*Winckelmann and His Age*, pp. 881–903) defends pagan humanism against Romantic religiosity and includes a remarkably open acknowledgment of Winckelmann's homosexuality. In 1813 he wrote a short essay that attempts to reconstruct a lost work by the Greek sculptor Myron of Eleutherae ("Myron's Cow," pp. 903–908), still guided by the Platonic spirit of Winckelmann: "the Greeks' goal is to deify man, not humanize Gods." But the next year he was reading Joseph von Hammer-Purgstall's new German translation of the *Divan* of the medieval Persian poet Hafiz, which inspired him to embark on his own collection of poems in the Persian style, the *West-Eastern Divan*. In later life he became interested in Chinese literature. He also coined the influential term *Weltliteratur* ("world literature"): "National literature is no longer of importance; it is the time for world literature, and all must aid in bringing it about" (p. 908).

Another legacy Goethe was anxious to secure in these troubled times was his contribution to science. Since the early 1790s he had been engrossed in the study of colored light. In the same way as he believed the leaf to be the building block of all plant life, its *Urphänomen* ("primal phenomenon"), he thought white light was the source of all color effects. This brought him into conflict with Newton's discovery that white light is composed of the rainbow spectrum. Goethe believed that colors were instead the product of the inter-action of light and its absence. In terms of physics, this was a dead end. Other aspects of the project did bear fruit. Goethe was among the first to explore the physiology of color vision, in particular the ways in which our vision deals with contrasts between light and dark, and in this field his intuition about the generation of color led to productive hypotheses. He also investigated the emotional effects and artistic uses of color; indeed, his interest in color origi-nated under the azure skies of Italy and among the radiant paintings of the Venetian school. The resulting work, the *Theory of Colour* published in 1810, reveals Goethe's strengths and weaknesses as a scientist. He was committed to empirical observation, but he disliked the mental and physical apparatus that accompanied science: contrived experimental conditions, doctrinaire theoreti-cal models, and arid mathematical methods, as he saw them. His allergy to the formal scientific method limited his progress but also inspired some of his more interesting ideas.

The initial reaction of scientists to the *Theory of Colour* was negative. Goethe's physics looked like the work of an amateur and was guilty of the same errors as the speculative post-Kantian *Naturphilosophie* of Schelling and others. His ideas about the physiology of color perception did find some reso-nance, but this was slow in developing. Had Goethe only worked in the life sciences, where mathematical methods were not yet widely used, and had he published his work on the life sciences when it was still fresh—the only sub-stantial piece he published before 1817 was the essay on the "Metamorphosis of Plants"—his stock might have been higher among contemporary scientists. As it was, much of his most interesting work, including his general statements about plant and animal morphology, was published only after 1817 and then in the context of autobiographical retrospect (see pp. 977–983). His reticence was not borne of a lack of confidence. He did send the short essay of 1784 on the intermaxillary bone to the great Dutch anatomist Petrus Camper in Gron-ingen, but Camper, who held precisely the view Goethe was opposing, advised against publication, even though he did accept some of Goethe findings. For these reasons—his ill-judged campaign against Newton's physics, which ob-scured the value of his work on the physiology of color; his apparent closeness to *Naturphilosophie*; his failure to publish his ideas on morphology—Goethe's stature as a scientist was not recognized until very late in his life, when some of his ideas had already been formulated by more established scientists. Still, his influence was felt and his contribution recognized. For instance, his friend Carl Gustav Carus took up Goethe's ideas about the morphology of mammal bone structure; Richard Owen adopted Carus's theory, and Charles Darwin then developed the Carus-Owen model. Darwin recognized Goethe's place in the history of evolutionary theory in the preface to the third edition of *The Origin of Species* (1861):

> It is rather a singular instance of the manner in which similar views arise at about the same period, that Goethe in Germany, Dr. [Erasmus] Darwin in England, and Geoffroy Saint Hilaire . . . in France, came to the same conclusion on the origin of species, in the years 1794–5. (p. xiv)

In the 1810s Goethe realized that his ideas risked becoming obsolete, if they were not already so. Hence he decided to publish some of his earlier work with an autobiographical commentary. He also continued to make his own observations and to follow the work of others. He was particularly excited about Luke Howard's classification of cloud formations, a subject on which Goethe had written extensively though unsystematically since the 1780s (pp. 988–993). He was one of the first to take regular measurements of changes in atmospheric pressure (or "elasticity," as he termed it) using a simple teapot-shaped vessel, the Goethe Glass as it is now known.

From 1809 he began to plan a full-length autobiography, and the first parts of *From My Life: Poetry and Truth* appeared in 1811. Between 1813 and 1817, he adapted his Italian journals. The autobiographical turn is evident in his poetry too; some of the later lyrics are highly self-conscious and self-referential, with a remarkable gentleness and lightness of touch (e.g. "Found," pp. 36–37). There is also exceptional vigor. On the threshold of his later work is a poem, "The Diary," which was too obscene and blasphemous to be published in his lifetime. (We print here the suitably outrageous, if overly free version by John Frederick Nims that first appeared in *Playboy* magazine in 1968, pp. 31–36.) In this richly crafted and ironic narrative of a failed adultery, the traveling narrator is prevented from reaching home by a broken carriage—a metaphor for impotence, as it turns out—and spends the night at an inn, where he catches the eye of the waitress. She visits his room, but he is momentarily impotent. Lying ashamed in bed next to the now sleeping girl, he recalls his wedding—the blasphemy is his erection standing in church before Christ on the cross: the healthy pagan phallus confronts the Christian god of pain—and the lusty sex life of his earlier married years. And as he reminisces, so his potency returns, but he leaves the girl to sleep undisturbed and remains (technically) faithful to his wife. The poem makes a playful allusion to Kant's ethics of renunciation, to which it opposes a more naturalistic morality: illness cures itself. The poem is typical in some ways: it ironically blends philosophical ambition with earthiness and lust for life. To the end Goethe remained a son of the Enlightenment, a pagan intellectual (see "The Stork's Profession," p. 40).

In securing his legacy Goethe was concerned to show his readers that his writings were anchored in his life. As well as looking back at his own progression, he surveyed the present state of Germany and the world and extrapolated into the future. The long-planned *Wilhelm Meister* sequel appeared in 1821, with an expanded version following in 1829. Goethe referred to *Wilhelm Meister's Journeyman Years, or the Renunciants* as a novel, though it breaks the conventional bounds of the novel form. Wilhelm embarks on a journey with his young son under two strict conditions: that they will never stay more than three nights under one roof, and that they will not travel with a third companion for long. The journey serves principally as a means to frame a number of shorter elements: stories, collections of aphorisms, and plans for social and educational reform. It is part novel, part framed narrative à la Boccaccio, part literary archive.

The continuation of *Faust* shares similar features and themes: episodic structure, a broad survey of the intellectual and social world of the early nineteenth century, and grand projects for the benefit of human welfare. During the completion of *Faust: Part One*, Goethe made plans for Part Two and composed the scenes in which Faust returns to ancient Greece to meet Helen of Troy. After Part One was finished, he put the material aside, only resuming work in 1825—in the same year as a group of U.S. businessmen announced a plan for constructing a canal through Panama, which Goethe followed with interest. In February 1827 he discussed the canal with Eckermann:

So much . . . is certain, that, if they succeed in cutting such a canal that ships of any burden and size can be navigated through it from the Mexican Gulf to the Pacific Ocean, innumerable benefits would result to the whole human race, civilized and uncivilized. But I should wonder if the United States were to let an opportunity escape of getting such work into their own hands. It may be foreseen that this young state, with its decided predilection to the West, will, in thirty or forty years, have occupied and peopled the large tract of land beyond the Rocky Mountains. It may, furthermore, be foreseen that along the whole coast of the Pacific Ocean, where nature has already formed the most capacious and secure harbours, important commercial towns will gradually arise, for the furtherance of a great intercourse between China and the East Indies and the United States. In such a case, it would not only be desirable, but almost necessary, that a more rapid communication should be maintained between the eastern and western shores of North America, both by merchant-ships and men-of-war, than has hitherto been possible with the tedious, disagreeable, and expensive voyage round Cape Horn. I therefore repeat, that it is absolutely indispensable for the United States to effect a passage from the Mexican Gulf to the Pacific Ocean; and I am certain that they will do it.

Would that I might live to see it!—but I shall not. I should like to see another thing—a junction of the Danube and the Rhine. But this undertaking is so gigantic that I have doubts of its completion, particularly when I consider our German resources. And thirdly, and lastly, I should wish to see England in possession of a canal through the Isthmus of Suez. Would I could live to see these three great works! It would be well worth the trouble to last some fifty years more for the very purpose. (21 February 1827)[1]

The completed *Faust: Part Two*, in five acts, was published several months after his death, a deeply ironic bequest to his fellow Germans. Faust lives to a ripe old age, frustrating Mephistopheles' attempts to satisfy him. In Act IV he is able to win victory for the emperor's army, with Mephistopheles' magical help. In gratitude the emperor grants Faust an area of low-lying coastal swamp, where Faust can establish a new colony free from the inhibiting social and religious legacies of the old regime—Faust's own America. What Faust does not know is that the archbishop, exploiting Faust's ill repute as a magus, has persuaded the emperor to grant the church tithes in perpetuity from Faust's land. The future will after all be shackled to the past. He finally dies expressing his satisfaction at the completed draining of the land, though in another bitter irony the blind old Faust cannot see that Mephistopheles' magical labor force is in fact digging his grave (*Grab*), not the drainage ditches (*Graben*). A struggle ensues over Faust's (vaguely named) "immortal part" (*Unsterbliches*), and Mephistopheles' demons are defeated by a host of amorous seraphs, who carry Faust's remains up to heaven. There the penitent spirit of Gretchen resides with the loving mother of God, though Faust's role—or the role of whatever survives of him, for perhaps only a trace of our mental activity remains in the world, as Spinoza suggested—will be to educate the spirits of children who died in infancy. Not the least of Part Two's surprises is that, again in the spirit of Spinoza, there will be no punishment in the afterlife for Faust, only more work. In an ironic mixture of florid pseudo-Christian imagery and materialist philosophy, the close of the drama self-consciously performs the passing of Goethe's ambiguous legacy into the future.

---

1 *Conversations of Goethe with Eckermann and Soret*, trans. by John Oxenford, 2 vols. (London: Smith, Elder & Co., 1850), vol. I, pp. 364–365.

Chronology of Goethe's Life and Times

Goethe's works are assigned to the date of publication unless noted otherwise.
Unpublished works are assigned to the approximate date of composition.

	GOETHE'S LIFE	GOETHE'S WORKS	CULTURAL AND INTELLECTUAL CONTEXT	HISTORICAL EVENTS
1749	Born 28 August in Frankfurt am Main to Johann Caspar and Catharina Elisabeth (née Textor)		Buffon, *Histoire naturelle* (to 1788)	
1750	Sister Cornelia born		Rousseau, *Discourse on the Arts and Sciences* J. S. Bach dies	Witch trials abolished in Prussia
1751			Publication of the *Encyclopedia* begins (to 1772)	
1752			Franklin demonstrates lightning is electricity	
1753	Grandmother gives Goethe puppet theater for Christmas			
1754			Rousseau, *Discourse on the Origins and Basis of Inequality among Men*	

	GOETHE'S LIFE	GOETHE'S WORKS	CULTURAL AND INTELLECTUAL CONTEXT	HISTORICAL EVENTS
1755	Renovation of Goethe family home		Winckelmann, "Thoughts on the Imitation of Ancient Works in Painting and Sculpture," Lessing, *Miss Sara Sampson*	Lisbon earthquake
1756	Begins to learn Latin and Greek		Mozart born	Seven Years' War (to 1763)
1757			Fontenelle dies Blake born	Austria occupies Berlin Prussia defeats Austria at Battle of Leuthen Karl August of Sachsen-Weimar-Eisenach born
1758			10th edition of Linnaeus's *Systema Naturae* formalizes biological nomenclature	Ernst August II of Sachsen-Weimar-Eisenach dies and his wife Duchess Anna Amalia becomes regent
1759	French army occupies Frankfurt		Schiller born Voltaire, *Candide* Young, *Conjectures on Original Composition*	Prussia defeated at Battle of Kunersdorf
1760			McPherson, *Fragments of Ancient Poetry* ("Ossian")	Russia and Austria briefly occupy Berlin
1761			Rousseau, *Julie, or the New Heloise*	
1762			Wieland's translations of Shakespeare (to 1766) Rousseau, *Emile* and *The Social Contract*	Elizabeth of Russia dies and is succeeded by pro-Prussian Peter III Treaty of St. Petersburg between Russia and Prussia

	GOETHE'S LIFE	GOETHE'S WORKS	CULTURAL AND INTELLECTUAL CONTEXT	HISTORICAL EVENTS
1763	Confirmation Visits recital by Mozart		Winckelmann, *History of the Art of Antiquity*	Prussia regains control of Silesia and occupies parts of Austria Treaty of Hubertusburg confirms Prussian control of Silesia
1764				Coronation of Joseph II as Holy Roman emperor in Frankfurt
1765	Leaves for Leipzig to study law		Spallanzani invents hermetic sealing of food	
1766	Reads Dodd's *Beauties of Shakespeare*		Goldsmith, *The Vicar of Wakefield*	
1767			Lessing, *Minna von Barnhelm* and *Hamburg Dramaturgy* (to 1768) Wieland, *History of Agathon*	
1768	Serious illness and return to Frankfurt		Winckelmann murdered in Trieste Sterne, *Sentimental Journey* Gerstenberg, *Ugolino*	
1769	Interest in Pietism	First collection of poems published anonymously	Wood, *Essay on the Original Genius of Homer* Watt patents steam engine	Napoleon born
1770	In Strasbourg to finish law studies Meets Herder and collects Alsatian popular songs		Hölderlin, Wordsworth, Beethoven born	

	GOETHE'S LIFE	GOETHE'S WORKS	CULTURAL AND INTELLECTUAL CONTEXT	HISTORICAL EVENTS
1773	Cornelia marries			Boston Tea Party
1774	Knebel appointed tutor to Konstantin, younger brother of Duke Karl August	*The Sufferings of Young Werther* Begins *Faust*		Louis XV dies
1775	Engagement to Lili Schönemann (broken off in October) Travels in Switzerland Duke Karl August and Knebel visit Goethe in Frankfurt Moves to Weimar		Lavater, *Physiognomic Fragments* (to 1778)	
1776	Friendship with Charlotte von Stein Interest in geology	Begins *Wilhelm Meister*	Adam Smith, *The Wealth of Nations* Lenz, *The Soldiers* Klinger, *The Twins*	U.S. Declaration of Independence Expulsion of Jesuits from France and Spain
1777	Cornelia dies Travels in the Harz and climbs the Brocken		Kleist born	
1778			Voltaire and Rousseau die	
1779	Travels in Switzerland	*Iphigenia in Tauris* (prose version)	Lessing, *Nathan the Wise*	
1780	Becomes Freemason			Judicial torture abolished in France

	GOETHE'S LIFE	GOETHE'S WORKS	CULTURAL AND INTELLECTUAL CONTEXT	HISTORICAL EVENTS
1782	Becomes president of ducal chamber Ennoblement Moves into house on the Frauenplan Father dies			
1784	Discovers *os intermaxillare* in humans Launches Montgolfier hot air balloon in Weimar Rereads Spinoza		Johnson and Diderot die Herder, *Ideas on the Philosophy of the History of Mankind*	
1785		Essay "On Granite"		Diamond Necklace Affair
1786	Leaves for Rome, via Verona and Venice		Mozart, *The Marriage of Figaro*	Frederick the Great dies Balmat and Paccard ascend Mont Blanc
1787	To Naples and Sicily			
1788	Returns to Weimar Begins living with Christiane Vulpius		Byron born Kant, *Critique of Practical Reason*	Convocation of French States-General U.S. Constitution officially adopted
1789	Son August born	*Torquato Tasso* published Essay *On the Metamorphosis of Plants*	Schiller appointed to chair in Jena Mozart, *Così fan tutte*	French Revolution begins Storming of the Bastille
1790	Travels to Venice	*Venetian Epigrams* (published 1796) *Faust. A Fragment*	Kant, *Critique of Judgement*	Abolition of the nobility and civil constitution of the clergy in France Joseph II dies

	GOETHE'S LIFE	GOETHE'S WORKS	CULTURAL AND INTELLECTUAL CONTEXT	HISTORICAL EVENTS
1793	Present at the siege of Mainz			Execution of Louis XVI September Massacres The Terror
1794	Friendship with Schiller begins	Agrees contract for *Wilhelm Meister* with Unger	Fichte, *Theory of Science*	Execution of Robespierre
1795	Father's library auctioned	*Roman Elegies* *Wilhelm Meister's Apprenticeship* published (to 1796)	Schiller, *On the Aesthetic Education of Man* Keats born	End of the Terror Treaty of Basle
1796			Schiller, *On Naive and Sentimental Poetry*	Napoleon's victories in northern Italy
1797	Travels in Switzerland	*Hermann und Dorothea* "Year of Ballads" Resumes work on *Faust*	Hölderlin, *Hyperion* Schelling, *Philosophy of Nature* Heine, Schubert born	
1798		Napoleon takes *Werther* to Egypt	Schiller, *Wallenstein* trilogy first performed in Weimar Wordsworth and Coleridge, *Lyrical Ballads* Malthus, *An Essay on the Principle of Population*	French troops occupy Rome Napoleon in Egypt Battle of the Nile
1799	Begins correspondence with Zelter		Novalis, *Christendom, or Europe*	Formation of Second Coalition against France Napoleon becomes First Consul

	GOETHE'S LIFE	GOETHE'S WORKS	CULTURAL AND INTELLECTUAL CONTEXT	HISTORICAL EVENTS
1801	Seriously ill with shingles	*Faust: Part One* substantially finished	Schiller, *The Maid of Orleans* Novalis dies	
1802			Dumas, Hugo born Howard, *Essay on the Modification of Clouds*	Piece of Amiens
1803	Mme de Stael and Benjamin Constant in Weimar (to 1804)		Schiller, *The Bride of Messina* Herder dies Klopstock dies	
1804			Schiller, *William Tell* Kant dies	Napoleon crowned emperor
1805		*Winckelmann and his Century*	Schiller dies	Third Coalition against France Battles of Trafalgar and Austerlitz
1806	French troops occupy Weimar Goethe and Christiane Vulpius are married		Arnim and Brentano, *The Boy's Magic Horn*, vol. 1 (dedicated to Goethe)	Treaty of Pressburg and creation of Federation of the Rhine Fourth Coalition against France French victory at Battle of Jena-Auerstedt and capitulation of Prussia Dissolution of Holy Roman Empire
1807	Duchess Anna Amalia, mother of Duke Karl August, dies		Hegel, *Phenomenology of Mind*	Treaties of Tilsit and end of the Fourth Coalition against France
1808	Meets Napoleon at Erfurt and receives Légion d'Honneur Mother dies	*Faust: Part One* published	Friedrich and Dorothea Schlegel convert to Catholicism	

	GOETHE'S LIFE	GOETHE'S WORKS	CULTURAL AND INTELLECTUAL CONTEXT	HISTORICAL EVENTS
1810		*Theory of Colour* "The Diary"		
1811		*Poetry and Truth*, Books I to III (to 1814; Book IV published posthumously 1833)	Kleist dies	
1812	Meets Beethoven in Teplitz		Grimm, *Fairy Tales* Hammer-Purgstall's translation of Hafiz' *Divan*	Napoleon's Grande Armée invades Russia French victory at Battle of Borodino and occupation of Moscow Retreat of Grande Armée from Russia Sixth Coalition against France Victories of Wellington in Peninsular War
1813	Wieland dies	Begins revision of Italian notebooks	Verdi and Wagner born	French victories at Battles of Lützen and Bautzen French defeat at Battle of Leipzig
1814	Travels on the Rhein and Main	Starts poems in the manner of Hafiz		Bonaparte exiled to Elba Congress of Vienna
1815				The Hundred Days Battle of Waterloo
1816	Christiane dies	*Italian Journey* (to 1817)	Clausewitz, *On War* Rossini, *The Barber of Seville*	

	GOETHE'S LIFE	GOETHE'S WORKS	CULTURAL AND INTELLECTUAL CONTEXT	HISTORICAL EVENTS
1818	Birth of first grandson		Mary Shelley, *Frankenstein*	
1819		*West-Eastern Divan*	Schopenhauer, *The World as Will and Imagination* Mary Ann Evans (George Eliot) born	Carlsbad Decrees for suppression of liberal-national student movement
1820	Birth of second grandson		Scott, *Ivanhoe*	
1821		*Wilhelm Meister's Journeyman Years*, 1st edition		Greek uprising against Turkish rule Mexico becomes independent Peru declares independence
1822			Shelley dies	Brazil declares independence
1823	Eckermann moves to Weimar Correspondence with Byron Falls in love with Ulrike von Levetzow and proposes			
1824			Byron dies	
1825	Interest in Panama Canal	Resumes work on *Faust: Part Two*	Manzoni, *The Betrothed*	
1826	Successfully lobbies for copyright protection for his works		Cooper, *The Last of the Mohicans*	
1827			Heine, *Book of Songs*	

	GOETHE'S LIFE	GOETHE'S WORKS	CULTURAL AND INTELLECTUAL CONTEXT	HISTORICAL EVENTS
1829		*Wilhelm Meister's Journeyman Years*, 2nd edition First public performance of *Faust: Part One*, in Braunschweig		
1830	August dies in Rome Suffers stroke	*Chinese-German Days and Seasons* Agrees with Zelter on posthumous publication of their correspondence		July Revolution in Paris
1831		Completes *Faust: Part Two*	Hegel dies Darwin begins voyage of *Beagle*	
1832	Goethe dies on 22 March	*Faust: Part Two* published posthumously		

The Essential Goethe

Selected Poems

WELCOME AND FAREWELL
(1771; 1789)

My heart beat fast, a horse! away!
Quicker than thought I am astride,
Earth now lulled by end of day,
Night hovering on the mountainside.
A robe of mist around him flung,
The oak a towering giant stood,
A hundred eyes of jet had sprung
From darkness in the bushy wood.

Atop a hill of cloud the moon
Shed piteous glimmers through the mist,
Softly the wind took flight, and soon
With horrible wings around me hissed.
Night made a thousand ghouls respire,
Of what I felt, a thousandth part—
My mind, what a consuming fire!
What a glow was in my heart!

You I saw, your look replied,
Your sweet felicity, my own,
My heart was with you, at your side,
I breathed for you, for you alone.
A blush was there, as if your face
A rosy hue of Spring had caught,
For me—ye gods!—this tenderness!
I hoped, and I deserved it not.

Yet soon the morning sun was there,
My heart, ah, shrank as leave I took:
How rapturous your kisses were,

What anguish then was in your look!
I left, you stood with downcast eyes,
In tears you saw me riding off:
Yet, to be loved, what happiness!
What happiness, ye gods, to love!

ROSEBUD IN THE HEATHER
(1771)

Urchin saw a rose—a dear
Rosebud in the heather.
Fresh as dawn and morning-clear;
Ran up quick and stooped to peer,
Took his fill of pleasure,
Rosebud, rosebud, rosebud red,
Rosebud in the heather.

Urchin blurts: "I'll pick you, though,
Rosebud in the heather!"
Rosebud: "Then I'll stick you so
That there's no forgetting, no!
I'll not stand it, ever!"
Rosebud, rosebud, rosebud red,
Rosebud in the heather.

But the wild young fellow's torn
Rosebud from the heather.
Rose, she pricks him with her thorn;
Should she plead, or cry forlorn?
Makes no difference whether.
Rosebud, rosebud, rosebud red,
Rosebud in the heather.

PROMETHEUS
(1773)

Cover your heaven, Zeus,
With cloudy vapors
And like a boy
Beheading thistles

Practice on oaks and mountain peaks—
Still you must leave
My earth intact
And my small hovel, which you did not build,
And this my hearth
Whose glowing heat
You envy me.

I know of nothing more wretched
Under the sun than you gods!
Meagerly you nourish
Your majesty
On dues of sacrifice
And breath of prayer
And would suffer want
But for children and beggars,
Poor hopeful fools.

Once too, a child,
Not knowing where to turn,
I raised bewildered eyes
Up to the sun, as if above there were
An ear to hear my complaint,
A heart like mine
To take pity on the oppressed.

Who helped me
Against the Titans' arrogance?
Who rescued me from death,
From slavery?
Did not my holy and glowing heart,
Unaided, accomplish all?
And did it not, young and good,
Cheated, glow thankfulness
For its safety to him, to the sleeper above?

I pay homage to you? For what?
Have you ever relieved
The burdened man's anguish?
Have you ever assuaged
The frightened man's tears?
Was it not omnipotent Time

That forged me into manhood,
And eternal Fate,
My masters and yours?

Or did you think perhaps
That I should hate this life,
Flee into deserts
Because not all
The blossoms of dream grew ripe?

Here I sit, forming men
In my image,
A race to resemble me:
To suffer, to weep,
To enjoy, to be glad—
And never to heed you,
Like me!

IN COURT
(c. 1774–75)

Who gave it me, I shall not tell,
The child I've got in me;
Call me a whore, if you like, and spit:
I'm an honest woman, see?

He's good and kind, I'll not say who,
My sweetheart that I wed,
A chain of gold on his neck he wears
And a straw hat on his head.

Chuckle and scorn to your heart's content,
I'll take the scorn from you;
I know him well, he knows me well,
God knows about us, too.

Lay off me, folks, you, reverend,
You, officer of the laws!
It is my child, it stays my child,
And it's no concern of yours.

ON THE LAKE
(1775)

And fresh nourishment, new blood
I suck from a world so free;
Nature, how gracious and how good,
Her breast she gives to me.
The ripples buoying up our boat
Keep rhythm to the oars,
And mountains up to heaven float
In cloud to meet our course.

Eyes, my eyes, why abject now?
Golden dreams, are you returning?
Dream, though gold, away with you:
Life is here and loving too.

Over the ripples twinkling
Star on hovering star,
Soft mists drink the circled
Towering world afar;
Dawn wind fans the shaded
Inlet with its wing,
And in the water mirrored
The fruit is ripening.

AUTUMN FEELING
(1775)

More fatly greening climb
The trellis, you, vine leaf
Up to my window!
Gush, denser, berries
Twin, and ripen
Shining fuller, faster!
Last gaze of sun
Broods you, maternal;
Of tender sky the fruiting
Fullness wafts around you;
Cooled you are, by the moon

Magic, a friendly breath,
And from these eyes,
Of ever quickening Love, ah,
Upon you falls a dew, the tumid
Brimming tears.

WANDERER'S NIGHT SONG
(1776)

Thou that from the heavens art,
   Every pain and sorrow stillest,
And the doubly wretched heart
   Doubly with refreshment fillest,
I am weary with contending!
   Why this rapture and unrest?
Peace descending
   Come, ah, come into my breast!

ANOTHER NIGHT SONG
(1780)

O'er all the hill-tops
   Is quiet now,
In all the tree-tops
   Hearest thou
Hardly a breath;
   The birds are asleep in the trees:
   Wait, soon like these
Thou, too, shalt rest.
(Longfellow)

Over mountains yonder,
   A stillness;
Scarce any breath, you wonder,
   Touches
The tops of all the trees.
   No forest birds now sing;
A moment, waiting—
   Then take, you too, your ease.
(CM)

TO CHARLOTTE VON STEIN
(1776)

Why confer on us the piercing vision:
All tomorrow vivid in our gaze?
Not a chance to build on love's illusion?
Not a glimmer of idyllic days?
Why confer on us, O fate, the feeling

Each can plumb the other's very heart?
Always, though in storms of passion reeling,
See precisely what a course we chart?

Look at all those many thousands drudging
(Knowing even their own nature less
Than we know each other), thousands trudging,
In the dark about their own distress;
Drunk on exultation, when they're treated
Suddenly to joy's magenta dawn.
Only we unlucky lovers, cheated
Of all mutual comfort, have forgone
This: to be in love, not understanding;
This: to see the other as he's not;
Off in gaudy dreams go hand-in-handing,
In appalling dreams turn cold and hot.

Happy man, a fleeting dream engages!
Happy man, no premonitions numb!
We however—! All our looks and touches
Reaffirm our fear of days to come.
Tell me, what's our destiny preparing?
Tell me, how we're bound in such a knot?
From an old existence we were sharing?
You're the wife, the sister I forgot?

Knew me then completely, every feature,
How each nerve responded and rang true;
Read me in a single glance—a nature
Others search bewildered for a clue.
To that heated blood, a cool transfusion;
To that crazy runaway, a rein;
In your clasp, what Edens of seclusion
Nursed to health that fellow, heart and brain.
Held him tightly, lightly, as enchanted;
Spirited the round of days away.
Where's a joy like this?—you'd think transplanted
At your feet the flushing lover lay;
Lay and felt his heart, against you, lighten;
Felt your eye approving; *but he's good!*
Felt his murky senses clear and brighten;
On his raging blood, a quietude.

Now, of all that was, about him hovers
Just a haze of memory, hardly there.
Still the ancient truth avails: we're lovers—
Though our new condition's a despair.
Only half a mind for earth. Around us
Twilight thickens on the brightest day.
Yet we're still in luck: the fates that hound us
Couldn't wish our love away.

TO THE MOON
(1777; THIS SECOND VERSION PUBLISHED 1789)

Flooding with a brilliant mist
Valley, bush and tree,
You release me. Oh for once
Heart and soul I'm free!

Easy on the region round
Goes your wider gaze,
Like a friend's indulgent eye
Measuring my days.

Every echo from the past,
Glum or gaudy mood,
Haunts me—weighing bliss and pain
In the solitude.

River, flow and flow away;
Pleasure's dead to me:
Gone the laughing kisses, gone
Lips and loyalty.

All in my possession once!
Such a treasure yet
Any man would pitch in pain
Rather than forget.

Water, rush along the pass,
Never lag at ease;
Rush, and rustle to my song
Changing melodies.

8

How in dark December you
Roll amok in flood;
Curling, in the gala May,
Under branch and bud.

Happy man, that rancor-free
Shows the world his door;
One companion by—and both
In a glow before

Something never guessed by men
Or rejected quite:
Which, in mazes of the breast,
Wanders in the night.

A WINTER JOURNEY IN THE HARZ
(1777)

As the buzzard aloft
On heavy daybreak cloud
With easy pinion rests
Searching for prey,
May my song hover.

For a god has
Duly to each
His path prefixed,
And the fortunate man
Runs fast and joyfully
To his journey's end;
But he whose heart
Misfortune constricted
Struggles in vain
To break from the bonds
Of the brazen thread
Which the shears, so bitter still,
Cut once alone.

Into grisly thickets
The rough beasts run,
And with the sparrows

The rich long since have
Sunk in their swamps.

    Easy it is to follow that car
Which Fortune steers,
Like the leisurely troop that rides
The fine highroads
Behind the array of the Prince.

    But who is it stands aloof?
His path is lost in the brake,
Behind him the shrubs
Close and he's gone,
Grass grows straight again,
The emptiness swallows him.

    O who shall heal his agony then
In whom each balm turned poison,
Who drank hatred of man
From the very fullness of love?
First held now holding in contempt.
In secret he consumes
His own particular good
In selfhood unsated.

    If in your book of songs
Father of love, there sounds
One note his ear can hear,
Refresh with it then his heart!
Open his clouded gaze
To the thousand fountainheads
About him as he thirsts
In the desert!

    You who give joys that are manifold,
To each his overflowing share,
Bless the companions that hunt
On the spoor of the beasts
With young exuberance
Of glad desire to kill,
Tardy avengers of outrage
For so long repelled in vain
By the cudgeling countryman.

But hide the solitary man
In your sheer gold cloud!
Till roses flower again
Surround with winter-green
The moistened hair,
O love, of your poet!

With your lantern glowing
You light his way
Over the fords by night,
On impassable tracks
Through the void countryside;
With daybreak thousand-hued
Into his heart you laugh;
With the mordant storm
You bear him aloft;
Winter streams plunge from the crag
Into his songs,
And his altar of sweetest thanks
Is the snow-hung brow
Of the terrible peak
People in their imaginings crowned
With spirit dances.

You stand with heart unplumbed
Mysteriously revealed
Above the marveling world
And you look from clouds
On the kingdoms and magnificence
Which from your brothers' veins beside you
With streams you water.

SONG OF THE SPIRITS OVER THE WATERS
(1779)

The soul of man,
It is like water:
It comes from heaven,
It mounts to heaven,
And earthward again
Descends
Eternally changing.

If the pure jet
Streams from the high
Vertical rockface,
A powdering spray,
A wave of cloud
Splashes the smooth rock
And gathered lightly
Like a veil it rolls
Murmuring onward
To depths yonder.

If cliffs loom up
To stem its fall,
It foams petulant
Step by step
To the abyss.

Along a level bed
Through the glen it slips,
In the lake unruffled
All the clustering stars
Turn their gaze.

Wind woos
The wave like a lover,
Wind churns from the ground up
Foaming billows.

Soul of man,
How like the water you are!
Fate of man,
How like the wind.

THE FISHERMAN
(END OF 1770S)

The water washed, the water rose;
A fellow fishing sat
And watched his bobbin coolly drift,
His blood was cool as that.
A while he sits, a while he harks
—Like silk the ripples tear,

And up in swirls of foam arose
A girl with dripping hair.

She sang to him, she spoke to him:
"Cajole my minnows so
With lore of men, with lure of men,
To death's unholy glow?
If you could know my silver kin,
What cozy hours they passed,
You'd settle under, clothes and all
—A happy life at last.

"The sun, it likes to bathe and bathe;
The moon—now doesn't she?
And don't they both, to breathe the wave,
Look up more brilliantly?
You're not allured by lakes of sky,
More glorious glossy blue?
Not by your very face transformed
In this eternal dew? "

The water washed, the water rose;
It lapped his naked toe.
As longing for the one he loved
He yearned to sink below.
She spoke to him, she sang to him;
The fellow, done for then,
Half yielded too as half she drew,
Was never seen again.

THE GODLIKE
(EARLY 1780S)

Noble let man be,
Helpful and good;
For that alone
Distinguishes him
From all beings
That we know.

Hail to the unknown,
Loftier beings

Our minds prefigure!
Let man be like them;
His example teach us
To believe those.

For unfeeling,
Numb, is nature;
The sun shines
Upon bad and good,
And to the criminal
As to the best
The moon and the stars lend light.

Wind and rivers,
Thunder and hail
Rush on their way
And as they race
Headlong, take hold
One on the other.

So, too, chance
Gropes through the crowd,
And quickly snatches
The boy's curled innocence,
Quickly also
The guilty baldpate.

Following great, bronzen,
Ageless laws
All of us must
Fulfill the circles
Of our existence.

Yet man alone can
Achieve the impossible:
He distinguishes,
Chooses and judges;
He can give lasting
Life to the moment.

He alone should
Reward the good,
Punish the wicked,

Heal and save,
All erring and wandering
Usefully gather.

And we honor
Them, the immortals,
As though they were men,
Achieving in great ways
What the best in little
Achieves or longs to.

Let noble man
Be helpful and good.
Create unwearied
The useful, the just:
Be to us a pattern
Of those prefigured beings.

LIMITS OF HUMAN NATURE
(1781)

When the primeval,
Holy Father
With temperate hand
From thundering cloud forms
Over Earth scatters
Lightings of blessing,
I kiss the lowest
Hem of his garment,
Childlike awe throbbing
True in my breast.

For with gods
No man should ever
Dare to be measured.
If he uplifts himself
And bestirs
The stars with his cranium,
Nowhere then cleave
His uncertain footsoles,
And with him play
The clouds and the winds.

If he stands firm with
Marrowy bones
On the deep-founded,
Enduring Earth,
Then he aspires not,
Save to the oak tree
Or to the vine
Himself to liken.

What then distinguishes
Gods from men?
That many waves
Before them move,
An eternal stream:
Us the wave gathers,
Us the wave swallows,
And we sink.

A little ring
Confines our life,
And many generations
Link up, enduring
On their existence's
Endless chain.

ERLKÖNIG
(C. 1782)

Who rides by night in the wind so wild?
It is the father, with his child.
The boy is safe in his father's arm.
He holds him tight, he keeps him warm.

My son, what is it, why cover your face?
Father, you see him, there in that place.
The elfin king with his cloak and crown?
It is only the mist rising up, my son.

"Dear little child, will you come with me?
Beautiful games I'll play with thee;
Bright are the flowers we'll find on the shore.
My mother has golden robes fullscore."

Father, O father, and did you not hear
What the elfin king breathed into my ear?
Lie quiet, my child, now never you mind:
Dry leaves it was that click in the wind.

"Come along now, you're a fine little lad.
My daughters will serve you, see you are glad;
My daughters dance all night in a ring,
They'll cradle and dance you and lullaby sing."

Father, now look, in the gloom, do you see
The elfin daughters beckon to me?
My son, my son, I see it and say:
Those old willows, they look so gray.

"I love you, beguiled by your beauty I am,
If you are unwilling I'll force you to come!"
Father, his fingers grip me, O
The elfin king has hurt me so!

Now struck with horror the father rides fast,
His gasping child in his arm to the last,
Home through thick and thin he sped:
Locked in his arm, the child was dead.

ROMAN ELEGIES
(c. 1788–90)

I

Deign to speak to me, stones, you high palaces, deign to address me
    Streets, now say but one word! Genius, will you not stir?
True, all is living yet within your sanctified precincts,
    Timeless Rome; only me all still in silence receives.
O, who will whisper to me, at what small window, revealing
    Her, the dear one, whose glance, searing, will quicken my blood?
Can I not guess on what roads, forever coming and going.
    Only for her sake I'll spend all my invaluable time?
Still I'm seeing the sights, the churches, the ruins, the columns,
    As a serious man ought to and does use his days.
That, however, will pass, and soon no more than one temple,
    Amor's temple alone, claim this initiate's zeal.

17

Rome, you remain a whole world; but without love the whole world would
  Always be less than the world, neither would Rome still be Rome.

IA

Fortune beyond my loveliest daydreams fulfilled is my own now,
  Amor, my clever guide, passed all the palaces by.
Long he has known, and I too had occasion to learn by experience,
  What a richly gilt room hides behind hangings and screens.
You may call him a boy and blind and ill-mannered, but, clever
  Amor, I know you well, never corruptible god!
Us they did not take in, those façades so imposing and pompous,
  Gallant balcony here, dignified courtyard down there.
Quickly we passed them by, and a humble but delicate doorway
  Opened to guided and guide, made them both welcome within.
All he provides for me there, with his help I obtain all I ask for,
  Fresher roses each day strewn on my path by the god.
Isn't it heaven itself?—And what more could the lovely Borghese,
  Nipotina herself offer a lover than that?
Dinners, drives and dances, operas, card games and parties,
  Often merely they steal Amor's most opportune hours.
Airs and finery bore me; when all's said and done, it's the same thing
  Whether the skirt you lift is of brocade or of wool.
Or if the wish of a girl is to pillow her lover in comfort,
  Wouldn't he first have her put all those sharp trinkets away?
All those jewels and pads, and the lace that surrounds her, the whalebone,
  Don't they all have to go, if he's to feel his beloved?
Us it gives much less trouble! Your plain woollen dress in a jiffy,
  Unfastened by me, slips down, lies in its folds on the floor.
Quickly I carry the child in her flimsy wrapping of linen
  As befits a good nurse, teasingly, into her bed.
Bare of silken drapery, mattresses richly embroidered,
  Spacious for two, it stands free in a spacious room.
Then let Jupiter get more joy from his Juno, a mortal
  Anywhere in this world know more contentment than I.
We enjoy the delights of the genuine naked god. Amor,
  And our rock-a-bye bed's rhythmic, melodious creak.

IV

Pious we lovers are, and in silence revere all the spirits,
  Long to propitiate each, god and goddess alike.

And resemble in that you victors of Rome! To the gods of
　　All the world's peoples you gave dwellings, a home far from home,
Whether black and severe out of ancient basalt Egyptians
　　Or all white a Greek shaped it in marble that charms.
Yet no timeless one bears any grudge if by discrimination
　　One amongst them receives incense more precious from us.
Freely, indeed, we confess that still, as in past times, our prayers,
　　Daily service to one, one above all, we devote.
Roguish, lively and serious we celebrate rituals in secret,
　　Knowing that silence behooves all who are pledged to that cult.
Sooner by horrible acts to our heels we should summon and fasten
　　Vengeful Furies, or else dare the harsh judgement of Zeus,
Suffer his rolling wheel or in fetters be clamped to the rock-face,
　　Than from that service of love sever our hearts and our minds.
And the goddess we serve? She is called Opportunity. Know her!
　　Often to you she appears, always in different shapes.
Daughter of Proteus she'd like to think herself, mothered by Thetis,
　　Hers by whose mutable guile many a hero was tricked.
So now her daughter tricks those inexperienced or timid,
　　Teasing some in their sleep, flying past others who wake;
Gladly surrendering only to one who is quick, energetic.
　　Gentle she is to that man, playful and tender and sweet.
Once she appeared to me too, as an olive-complexioned girl, whose
　　Dark and plentiful hair, glistening, covered her brow,
Shorter ringlets curled round a neck that was graceful and slender,
　　Wavy, unbraided hair rose from the top of her head.
And I recognized her; as she hurried I held her: and sweetly
　　She, most willing to learn, soon paid me back each caress.
Oh, how delighted I was!—But enough, for that era is over.
　　Now by you, Roman braids, tightly, all round, I'm entwined.

v

Happy now I can feel the classical climate inspire me,
　　Past and present at last clearly, more vividly speak.
Here I take their advice, perusing the works of the ancients
　　With industrious care, pleasure that grows every day.
But throughout the nights by Amor I'm differently busied,
　　If only half improved, doubly delighted instead.
Also, am I not learning when at the shape of her bosom,
　　Graceful lines, I can glance, guide a light hand down her hips?
Only thus I appreciate marble; reflecting, comparing,

See with an eye that can feel, feel with a hand that can see.
True, the loved one besides may claim a few hours of the daytime,
　　But in night hours as well makes full amends for the loss.
For not always we're kissing, often hold sensible converse;
　　When she succumbs to sleep, pondering, long I lie still.
Often too in her arms I've lain composing a poem,
　　Gently with fingering hand count the hexameter's beat
Out on her back; she breathes, so lovely and calm in her sleeping
　　That the glow from her lips deeply transfuses my heart.
Amor meanwhile refuels the lamp and remembers the times when
　　Them, his triumvirs of verse, likewise he's served and obliged.

XX

Men distinguished by strength, by a frank and courageous nature,
　　All the more, it would seem, need to be deeply discreet!
Secrecy, you that subdue a whole city and rule over peoples.
　　Tutelar goddess to me, leading me safely through life,—
What a reversal now in my fate! When, all facetious, the Muses,
　　Jointly with Amor, the rogue, loosen the lips that were sealed.
Hard enough it's already to cover up royal disgraces!
　　Crown or Phrygian cap, neither now serves to conceal
Midas' long pointed ears. Any servant of his will have noticed,
　　And at once feels oppressed, awed by the secret within.
Deep he'd like to bury it, and be rid of the worrying knowledge.
　　Yet mere earth will not keep secrets like that one intact,
Rushes shoot from the ground and they whisper and sough in the breezes:
　　"Midas, Midas the king, Midas has long pointed ears!"
Harder now it's for me to preserve my more beautiful secret,
　　Given such fullness of heart, easily lips overflow.
To no woman friend I can tell it; for she could reproach me;
　　In no male friend confide: danger could come from that source.
To proclaim my rapture to groves and the echoing hillsides
　　I'm not young enough now, lonely enough, come to that.
So to you; elegiacs, alone let me tell and entrust it.
　　How she delights me by day, fills me with rapture by night.
She, sought after by many men, skilfully shuns all the snares which
　　Brashly the bold ones lay, subtly the shame-faced and sly;
Lithe and clever, she gives them the slip, for she knows all the footpaths
　　Where her lover will wait, listening, confident, keen.
Luna, be late, for she comes! And make sure that our neighbour won't see
　　　　　　　　　　　　　　　　　　　　　　　　　　her;
　　Rustle, leaves, in the shrubs! No one must hear her light step.

20

And, dear elegies, you, may you flourish and blossom, be cradled
 Warm in the lightest of breaths lovingly wafted by air,
Then give away to all Rome, as they did, those garrulous rushes,
 Secrets one fortunate pair treasured and kept to themselves.

NEARNESS OF THE BELOVED
(C. 1795)

I think of you when from the sea the shimmer
 Of sunlight streams;
I think of you when on the brook the dimmer
 Moon casts her beams.

I see your face when on the distant highway
 Dust whirls and flakes.
In deepest night when on the mountain byway
 The traveller quakes.

I hear your voice when, dully roaring, yonder
 Waves rise and spill;
Listening, in silent woods I often wander
 When all is still.

I walk with you, though miles from you divide me;
 Yet you are near!
The sun goes down, soon stars will shine to guide me.
 Would you were here!

THE BRIDE OF CORINTH
(1797)

To Corinth came a solitary stranger,
Whom none yet knew, a young Athenian;
He sought there to obtain a certain favour
From his father's comrade in the town:
Long had it been planned
For his daughter's hand
To be given to his comrade's son.

Might perhaps his welcome there be hindered?
Might the price of it his means exceed?

He is still a pagan, like his kindred;
Baptized the others in the Christian creed.
When new faiths are born,
From the heart are torn,
Sometimes, love and troth like any weed.

All the house was hushed, to rest retiring
Father, daughters—not the mother yet;
Him she welcomed, of his state inquiring,
And to a well-appointed guestroom led.
Wine and food she brought.
Ere of them he thought.
Solicitous, and "Sleep you well," she said.

Yet he felt no hunger and unheeded
Left the wine, and eager for the rest
Which his limbs forspent with travel needed,
Down upon the bed he lay, still dressed;
Drowsing now, when lo,
Gliding forward, slow—
At the door another, wondrous guest.

By his table lamp's unsteady glowing
He sees a girl walk in the room, and stand:
Gentle, modest, veiled in white, a flowing
Snowy robe, a black and gold headband.
As she meets his eyes,
Startled, in surprise,
She has lifted up a snowy hand.

"Is a stranger here, and no-one told me?
Am I then forgotten, just a name?
Ah! Tis thus that in my cell they hold me.
Now I feel quite overcome with shame.
Do not stir," she said,
"Now you are in bed,
I will leave as quickly as I came."

"Do not leave me, lovely one!" and springing
Out of bed he's quickly on his feet.
"Ceres, here, and Bacchus, gifts are bringing,
What you bring is Amor, his delight.
Why are you so pale?

Sweet, now let us hail
The joyous gods, their gifts, with appetite!"

"No, O no, young stranger, come not nigh me.
Joy is not for me, nor festive cheer.
Ah! such bliss may not be tasted by me,
Since my mother, sickened with a fear,
By long illness bowed,
Me to heaven vowed:
Youth and nature I may not come near.

They have left our household, left it lonely,
The jocund gods of old, no more they reign;
One, unseen, in heaven, is worshipped only,
And a saviour crucified and slain.
Sacrifices here—
Neither lamb nor steer,
But man himself in misery and pain."

Weighing all her words, now he must ponder:
Can it be that in this silent spot
He beholds her—what surpassing wonder!—
The beloved bride that he had sought?
"Be mine only now,
Look, our fathers' vow
Heaven's blessing to us both has brought!"

"No, good heart, not me," she cries in anguish;
"Your company is my second sister's place.
When I weep inside my cell and languish,
Think of me, though in her fond embrace.
She who pines for thee
Never shalt thou see:
Soon beneath the earth she'll hide her face."

"No! By this flame I swear between us burning,
Fanned by Hymen, lost thou shalt not be!
Not lost to me or joy, no, but returning
Back to my father's house, come back with me!
Stay, my sweetheart, here,
Taste the bridal cheer,
Spread for us so unexpectedly."

Tokens they exchange, to him she proffers
Her golden necklace now for him to wear,
But she will not touch the cup he offers,
Silver, wrought with skill exceeding rare:
"That is not for me.
All I ask of thee
Is one curly lock of thy own hair."

Dully boomed the ghosting midnight hour;
Only now her eyes take on a shine,
Pallid lips of hers, now they devour,
Gulping it, the bloody-coloured wine,
But of wheaten bread
Offered by the lad
Not a single crumb to take would deign.

Now she gave the cup, and so he drained it,
Impetuous, in haste, he drained it dry;
Love was in his heart, desire pained it,
Till it ached for what she must deny,
Hard as he insists,
She his will resists—
On the bed he flounders with a cry.

She throws herself beside him: "Dearest, still thee!
Ah, how sad I am to see thee so.
But alas, my body would but chill thee,
Thou wouldst find a thing thou mayst not know;
Thou wouldst be afraid,
Finding then the maid
Thou has chosen, cold as ice and snow."

Vehement strong arms the girl emprison
And muscle from the thrill of love acquire:
"Even from the grave wert thou arisen,
I would warm thee well with my desire!"
Breathless kiss on kiss!
Overflowing bliss!
"Dost thou burn and feel my burning fire?"

Closer still they cling and closer, mixing
Tears and cries of love, limbs interlaced,

She sucks his kisses, his with hers transfixing,
Each self aware the other it possessed.
All his passion's flood
Warms her gelid blood—
Yet no heart is beating in her breast.

Meanwhile, down the corridor, the mother
Passes, late, on household tasks intent:
Hears a sound, and listens, then another:
Wonders at the sounds and what they meant.
Who was whispering so?
Voices soft and low.
Rapturous cries and moans of lovers blent.

Ear against the door herself she stations,
Making certain nothing is amiss;
Horrified she hears those protestations
Lovers make, avowals of their bliss:
"The cockerel! Tis light!"
"But tomorrow night
Wilt thou come again?"—and kiss on kiss.

Now she can contain her rage no longer.
Lifts the latch, flings open wide the door:
"Not in my house! Who's this that any stranger
Can slip into his bed, who is this whore?"
Now she's in the room.
By lamplight in the gloom—
God! This girl her daughter was before!

And the youth in terror tried to cover
With her flimsy veil the maiden's head.
Clasped her close; but sliding from her lover,
Back the garment from her face she spread,
As by spirit power
Made longer, straighter, now her
Body slowly rises from the bed.

"Mother! Mother!"—hollow-voiced—"Deprive me
Not of pleasures I this night have known!
From this warm abode why do you drive me?
Do I waken to despair alone?

Are you not content
That in my cerement
To an early grave you forced me down?

Strange is the law that me perforce has brought now
Forth from the dark-heaped chamber where I lay;
The croonings of your priests avail but nought now,
Powerless their blessings were, I say.
Water nor salt in truth
Can cool the pulse of youth:
Love still burns, though buried under clay.

This young man, to him my troth was plighted,
While yet blithely Venus ruled the land,
Mother!—and that promise you have slighted,
Yielding to an outlandish command.
But no god will hear
If a mother swear
To deny to love her daughter's hand.

From my grave betimes I have been driven,
I seek the good I lost, none shall me thwart,
I seek his love to whom my troth was given,
And I have sucked the lifeblood from his heart.
If he dies, I will
Find me others, still
With my fury tear young folk apart.

Fair young man, thy thread of life is broken.
Human skill can bring no help to thee.
There, thou hast my necklace as a token,
And this curl of thine I take with me.
Soon thou must decay,
Dawn will find thee gray,
In Hades only shalt thou brownhaired be.

Mother! Listen to my last entreaty!
Heap the funeral pyre for us once more;
Open then my little tomb, for pity,
And in flame our souls to peace restore.
Up the sparks will go,
When the embers glow,
To the ancient gods aloft we soar."

PARABASIS
(c. 1820)

Years ago the mind with pleasure
Keenly could investigate,
Could experience the measure
Nature lives by to create.
And it is the One Eternal
Multiply self-manifest:
Small the big is, big the small,
All things to their type attest.
Self-insistent, always changing,
Near and far and far and near,
Birth of shapes, their rearranging—
Wonder of wonders, I am here.

THE METAMORPHOSIS OF PLANTS
(1798)

Overwhelming, beloved, you find all this mixture of thousands,
    Riot of flowers let loose over the garden's expanse;
Many names you take in, and always the last to be spoken
    Drives out the one heard before, barbarous both to your ear.
All the shapes are akin and none is quite like the other;
    So to a secret law surely that chorus must point,
To a sacred enigma. Dear friend, how I wish I were able
    All at once to pass on, happy, the word that unlocks!
Growing consider the plant and see how by gradual phases,
    Slowly evolved, it forms, rises to blossom and fruit.
From the seed it develops as soon as the quietly fertile
    Womb of earth sends it out, sweetly released into life,
And to the prompting of light, the holy, for ever in motion,
    Like the burgeoning leaves' tenderest build, hands it on.
Single, dormant the power in the seed was; the germ of an image,
    Closed in itself, lay concealed, prototype curled in the husk,
Leaf and root and bud, although colourless yet, half-amorphous;
    Drily the nucleus so safeguards incipient life,
Then, aspiring, springs up, entrusting itself to mild moisture,
    Speedily raises itself out of encompassing night.
Single, simple, however, remains the first visible structure;
    So that what first appears, even in plants, is the child.

Following, rising at once, with one nodule piled on another,
    Always the second renews only the shape of the first.
Not the same, though, for ever; for manifold—you can observe it—
    Mutably fashioned each leaf after the last one unfolds,
More extended, spikier, split into lances or segments
    Which, intergrown before, lay in the organ below.
Only now it attains the complete intended perfection
    Which, in many a kind, moves you to wonder, admire.
Many-jagged and ribbed, on a lusciously, fully fleshed surface,
    Growth so lavishly fed seems without limit and free.
Forcefully here, however, will Nature step in to contain it,
    Curbing rankness here, gently perfecting the shapes.
Now more slowly the sap she conducts, and constricts the vessels,
    And at once the form yields, with diminished effects.
Calmly the outward thrust of the spreading leaf-rims recedes now,
    While, more firmly defined, swells the thin rib of the stalks.
Leafless, though, and swift the more delicate stem rises up now,
    And, a miracle wrought, catches the onlooker's eye.
In a circular cluster, all counted and yet without number,
    Smaller leaves take their place, next to a similar leaf.
Pushed close up to the hub now, the harbouring calyx develops
    Which to the highest of forms rises in colourful crowns.
Thus in fulness of being does Nature now glory, resplendent,
    Limb to limb having joined, all her gradations displayed.
Time after time you wonder as soon as the stalk-crowning blossom
    Sways on its slender support, gamut of mutable leaves.
Yet the splendour becomes an announcement of further creation.
    Yes, to the hand that's divine colourful leaves will respond.
And it quickly furls, contracts; the most delicate structures
    Twofold venture forth, destined to meet and unite.
Wedded now they stand, those delighted couples, together.
    Round the high altar they form multiple, ordered arrays.
Hymen, hovering, nears, and pungent perfumes, exquisite,
    Fill with fragrance and life all the environing air.
One by one now, though numberless, germs are impelled into swelling,
    Sweetly wrapped in the womb, likewise swelling, of fruit.
Nature here closes her ring of the energies never-exhausted
    Yet a new one at once links to the circle that's closed,
That the chain may extend into the ages for ever,
    And the whole be infused amply with life, like the part.
Look, beloved, once more on the teeming of so many colours,
    Which no longer may now fill with confusion your mind.

Every plant now declares those eternal designs that have shaped it,
    Ever more clearly to you every flower-head can speak.
Yet if here you decipher the holy runes of the goddess,
    Everywhere you can read, even though scripts are diverse:
Let the grub drag along, the butterfly busily scurry,
    Imaging man by himself alter the pre-imposed shape.
Oh, and consider then how in us from the germ of acquaintance
    Stage by stage there grew, dear to us, habit's long grace,
Friendship from deep within us burst out of its wrapping,
    And how Amor at last blessed it with blossom and fruit.
Think how variously Nature, the quietly forming, unfolding,
    Lent to our feelings now this, now that so different mode!
Also rejoice in this day. Because love, our holiest blessing
    Looks for the consummate fruit, marriage of minds, in the end,
One perception of things, that together, concerted in seeing,
    Both to the higher world, truly conjoined, find their way.

EPIRRHEMA
(c. 1819)

You must, when contemplating nature,
Attend to this, in each and every feature:
There's nought outside and nought within,
For she is inside out and outside in.
Thus will you grasp, with no delay,
The holy secret, clear as day.

———————

Joy in true semblance take, in any
Earnest play:
No living thing is One, I say,
But always Many.

PERMANENCE IN CHANGE
(1803)

Early blossoms—could a single
Hour preserve them just as now!
But the warmer west will scatter
Petals showering from the bough.

How enjoy these leaves, that lately
I was grateful to for shade?
Soon the wind and snow are rolling
What the late Novembers fade.

Fruit—you'd reach a hand and have it?
Better have it then with speed.
These you see about to ripen,
Those already gone to seed.
Half a rainy day, and there's your
Pleasant valley not the same,
None could swim that very river
Twice, so quick the changes came.

You yourself! What all around you
Strong as stonework used to lie
—Castles, battlements—you see them
With an ever-changing eye.
Now the lips are dim and withered
Once the kisses set aglow;
Lame the leg, that on the mountain
Left the mountain goat below.

Or that hand, that knew such loving
Ways, outstretching in caress,
—Cunningly adjusted structure—
Now can function less and less.
All are gone; this substitution
Has your name and nothing more.
Like a wave it lifts and passes,
Back to atoms on the shore.

See in each beginning, ending.
Double aspects of the One;
Here, amid stampeding objects,
Be among the first to run,
Thankful to a muse whose favor
Grants you one unchanging thing:
What the heart can hold to ponder;
What the spirit shape to sing.

THE DIARY
(1810)

We've heard and heard, and finally believe:
There's no enigma like the heart of man.
The things we do! No good to twist or weave—
We're human yet, in Rome as Turkestan.
What's my advice? Forget it. Maybe heave
One sigh, and then live with it if you can.
Also, when sins come nudging with that leer,
Count on some Sturdy Virtue to appear.

Once, when I left my love and had to travel
Off on affairs a traveling man transacts,
Collecting facts and figures to unravel
(Thinking of her, *her* figure and its facts),
As always, when the night spread, thick as gravel,
Its load of stars, my mind went starry. Stacks
Of paper (balanced on my solar plexus)
Told of the day, in mostly O's and X's.

Finally I'm rolling homeward, when—you'd know it!—
Cru-ungk! and the axle goes. So one less night
Back in the bed I'm dreaming of—but stow it!
There's work now. Cross your fingers and sit tight.
Two blacksmiths come. I'm grumpy, and I show it.
Shrugging, the one spits left, the other right.
"It'll be done when done," they grunt, and batter
Whang! at the wheel. Sparks flying. Clang and clatter.

Stuck in the sticks! With just an inn; The Star,
It says outside. Looks bearable. I'm glad
To see a girl with lantern there. So far
So good. She lifts it higher and—not bad!—
Beckons me in: nice lounge, a decent bar.
The bedroom's cozy as a travel ad.
Poor sinners! When they're wandering on the loose,
Nothing like pretty girls to jerk the noose.

I take the room, and shuffle papers out.
My diary—got to keep it up to date
The way I do just every night, about.

I like to write; my darling says I'm great.
But now, though, nothing comes. Some writer's gout?
I seem distracted, somehow. Better wait.
That girl again. She lays the table first.
Hands deft and cool. Nice manners. I'm immersed

In studying her skirt, flung out and in.
I ask. She knows the answers. That's my girl!
Can she disjoint a chicken! Flick the skin!
Those arms! And hands with fingertips in pearl!
I feel that certain stirring-up begin
And dizzy with her, crazy for—I hurl
The chair away; impulsively I twist her
Into my arms, close, closer. "Listen, mister,

Cool it," she cuddles murmuring. "My aunt,
Old hatchet face, is listening all the time.
She's down there guessing what I can or can't
Be up to every minute. Next she'll climb
Up with that cane of hers, sniff, snuffle, pant!
But look, don't lock your door. At midnight I'm
More on my own—" Untwisting (it's delicious!)
She hurries out. And hurries back with dishes.

Dishes—and warmer eyes. I'm in a blur.
The heavens open and the angels sing.
She sighs, and every sigh looks good on her:
It makes the heaving breast a pretty thing.
She loves me, I can tell: Such colors stir
Deeper on neck and ear—she crimsoning!
Then sad, "Well, dinner's over, I suppose."
She goes. She doesn't want to, but she goes.

The chimes at midnight on the sleeping town!
My double bed looks wider by the minute.
"Leave half for her. That's friendlier, you clown!"
I say, and squiggle over. To begin it,
We'll leave the candles lit, I plan—when down
The hall a rustle! Slinky silk—she's in it!
My eyes devour that fully blossomed flesh.
She settles by me and our fingers mesh.

32

Then sweet and low: "First tell me once or twice
You love me as a person? Say you do.
As girls around here go, I'm rather nice.
Said *no* to every man, till I saw you.
Why do you think they call me 'Piece of Ice'?
Of ice, indeed! Just feel! I'm melting through.
You did it to me, darling. So be good.
And let's be lovers, do as lovers should.

"I'm starting out, remember. Make it sweet.
If I had more to give, I'd even dare."
She pressed her cooler breasts against my heat
As if she liked it and felt safer there.
Lips linger on her lips; toes reach and meet,
But—something funny happening elsewhere.
What always strutted in the leading role
Now shrank like some beginner. Bless my soul!

The girl seemed happy with a kiss, a word,
Smiling as if she couldn't ask for more.
So pure a gaze—yet every limb concurred.
So sweet a blossom, and not picked before.
Oh, but she looked ecstatic when she stirred!
And then lay back relaxing, to adore.
Me, I lay back a bit and . . . beamed away.
Nagged at my dragging actor, "Do the play!"

The more I brooded on my situation,
The more I seethed with curses, inwardly.
Laughed at myself, God knows without elation.
It got me down. And sleeping, breathing, she
Lay lovelier yet, a gilt-edged invitation.
The candles stood and burned, derisively.
Young people who work hard to earn their bread
Soon as they hit the hay are turned to lead.

She dreamed—I'd swear, an angel—flushed and snug;
Breathed easily, as if the bed were hers.
I'm scrunched up by the wall—there's *that* to hug!
Can't lift a finger. It's like what occurs
To thirsty travelers in the sands when—glug!—
There's water bubbling. But a rattler whirs!

Her lips stir softly, talking to a dream.
I hold my breath: O honeychild! And beam.

Detached—for you could call it that—I say,
Well, it's a new experience. Now you know
Why bridegrooms in a panic start to pray
They won't get spooked and see their chances go.
I'd rather be cut up in saberplay
Than in a bind like this. It wasn't so
When first I saw my real love: from the gloom
Stared at her, brilliant in the brilliant room.

Ah, but my heart leaped then, and every sense,
My whole man's-shape a pulsing of delight.
Lord, how I swept her off in a wild dance
Light in my arms, her weight against me tight.
You'd think I fought myself for her. One glance
Would tell how I grew greater, gathered might
For her sake, mind and body, heart and soul.
That was the day my actor lived his role!

Worship and lovely lust—with both in view
I wooed her all that year, until the spring
(Violins, maestro!), when the world was new
And she outflowered, in June, the floweriest thing,
The date was set. So great our passion grew
That even in church (I blush) with heaven's King
Racked on his cross, before the priest and all,
My impudent hero made his curtain call!

And you, four-posters of the wedding night,
You pillows, that were tossed and rumpled soon,
You blankets, drawn around so our delight
Was ours alone, through morning, afternoon;
You parakeets in cages, rose and white,
Whose twitter music perked our deeper tune—
Could even you, who played your minor part,
Tell which of us was which? Or end from start?

The days of make-believe! The "Let's pretend,
Honey, we're sexy tramps!'" I'd toss her there
Laughing, among the cornstalks, or we'd bend
Reeds by the river, threshing who knows where?

In public places, nearly. What a friend
My sturdy plowboy then! He wouldn't scare!
But now, with all the virgin field to reap,
Look at the lousy helper sound asleep.

Or was. But now he's rousing. He's the one!
You can't ignore him, and you can't command.
He's suddenly himself. And like the sun,
Is soaring full of splendor. Suave and bland.
You mean the long thirst's over with and done?
The desert traveler's at the promised land?
I lean across to kiss my sleeping girl
And—hey!—the glorious banner starts to furl!

What made him tough and proud a moment? She,
His only idol now, as long ago;
The one he took in church exultantly.
From worlds away it comes, that rosy glow.
And, as before it worried him to be
Meager, so now he's vexed at swelling so
With her afar. Soft, soft, he shrinks away
Out of the magic circle, all dismay.

That's that. I'm up and scribbling, "Close to home,
I almost thought I wouldn't make it there.
Honey, I'm yours, in Turkestan or Rome.
I'm writing you in bed, and by a bare
—Well, call it piece of luck or something, hmmmm!
Impotence proved I'm superman. Now where
'S a prettier riddle? Leave it; read the rest.
Dearest, I've told you all. Except the best."

Then *cook-a-doodle-doo!* At once the girl's
Thrown off a bed sheet and thrown on a slip;
She rubs her eyes, shakes out her tousled curls,
Looks blushing at bare feet and bites her lip.
Without a word she's vanishing in swirls
Of underpretties over breast and hip.
She's dear, I murmur—rushing from above
Down to my coach. And on the road for love!

I'll tell you what, we writers like to bumble
Onto a moral somewhere, forehead glowing

Over a Noble Truth. Some readers grumble
Unless they feel improved. My moral's showing:
Look, it's a crazy world. We slip and stumble,
But two things, Love and Duty, keep us going.
I couldn't rightly call them hand in glove.
Duty?—who really needs it? Trust your Love.

DEATH OF A FLY
(1810, FROM 'SIXTEEN PARABLES')

With greed she quaffs and quaffs the traitorous drink,
Unceasing, from the start wholly enticed,
She feels so far so good, and every link
In her delicate little legs is paralyzed—
No longer deft they are, to groom her wings,
No longer dexterous, to preen her head;
Her life expended, thus, in pleasurings,
Her little feet soon have nowhere to tread;
So does she drink and drink, and while she does,
Comes misty death her myriad eyes to close.

FOUND
(1813)

Once in the forest
I strolled content,
To look for nothing
My sole intent.

I saw a flower,
Shaded and shy,
Shining like starlight,
Bright as an eye.

I went to pluck it;
Gently it said:
Must I be broken,
Wilt and be dead?

Then whole I dug it
Out of the loam

And to my garden
Carried it home,

There to replant it
Where no wind blows.
More bright than ever
It blooms and grows.

HEGIRA
(1814)

North and West and South are breaking,
Thrones are bursting, kingdoms shaking:
Flee, then, to the essential East,
Where on patriarch's air you'll feast!
There to love and drink and sing,
Drawing youth from Khizr's spring.

Pure and righteous there I'll trace
To its source the human race,
Prime of nations, when to each
Heavenly truth in earthly speech
Still by God himself was given,
Human brains not racked and riven.

When they honored ancestors,
To strange doctrine closed their doors;
Youthful bounds shall be my pride,
My thought narrow, my faith wide.
And I'll find the token word,
Dear because a spoken word.

Mix with goatherds in dry places,
Seek refreshment in oases
When with caravans I fare,
Coffee, shawls, and musk my ware;
Every road and path explore,
Desert, cities and seashore;

Dangerous track, through rock and scree:
Hafiz, there you'll comfort me
When the guide, enchanted, tells

On the mule's back, your ghazels,
Sings them for the stars to hear,
Robber bands to quail with fear.

Holy Hafiz, you in all
Baths and taverns I'll recall,
When the loved one lifts her veil,
Ambergris her locks exhale.
More: the poet's love song must
Melt the houris, move their lust.

Now, should you begrudge him this,
Even long to spoil such bliss,
Poets' words, I'd have you know,
Round the gate of Eden flow,
Gently knocking without rest,
Everlasting life their quest.

UNBOUNDED
(1814–15)

What makes you great is that you cannot end,
And never to begin you are predestined
Your song revolves as does the starry dome,
Beginning, end for ever more the same;
And what the middle brings will prove to be
What last remains and was initially.

Of poets' joys you are the one true source,
Wave after numberless wave you give to verse.
Lips that of kissing never tire,
Song from the breast that sweetly wells,
A throat that's never quenched, on fire,
An honest heart that freely tells.

And though the whole world were to sink,
Hafiz, with you, with you alone
I will compete! Delight, despair,
Let us, the twins, entirely share!
Like you to love, like you to drink
My life and pride I here declare.

38

Self-fuelled now, my song, ring truer!
For you are older, you are newer.

BLESSED LONGING
(1814)

Tell it only to the wise,
For the crowd at once will jeer:
That which is alive I praise,
That which longs for death by fire.

Cooled by passionate love at night,
Procreated, procreating,
You have known the alien feeling
In the calm of candlelight;

Gloom-embraced will lie no more,
By the flickering shades obscured,
But are seized by new desire,
To a higher union lured.

Then no distance holds you fast;
Winged, enchanted, on you fly,
Light your longing, and at last,
Moth, you meet the flame and die.

Never prompted to that quest:
Die and dare rebirth!
You remain a dreary guest
On our gloomy earth.

HUMILITY
(1815)

The masters' works I look upon,
And I can see what they have done;
When looking upon this or that by me,
What I should have done is what I see.

THE STORK'S PROFESSION
(1820s)

The stork that feeds on frog and perch
Beside our pond, so free,
Why does he nest upon the church
Where he has no right to be?

He clatters about and snaps enough,
Sounds we all detest:
But young and old folks lack the guff
To plague him in his nest.

What squatting rights—all due respects—
Entitle him to it,
Save that he pleasingly elects
On the church's roof to . . . ?

PARABLE
(1830)

Went to open my garden door,
Three friends are standing there, or four—
Told them come in (all politesse),
Bid them welcome at my place;
Folks, here it is, the table's laid
For breakfast, we'll go shares, I said.
They certainly like the garden a lot:
One slinks off to a shady spot,
One gawks at apples high in the trees,
They're nosing around just as they please,
Another reaches for a bunch of grapes—
Aha, says he, *what cultured shapes.*
Take all you want, said I, from the dish
On the round table—and I wish
One and all *guten Appetit.*
Rascals, they preferred to eat
What they could steal. The fourth, I think,
Snuck through the house and out in a wink.
So I stumped off back inside, and broke
My fast alone, without those folk.

𝕰𝕲𝕸𝕺𝕹𝕿

A TRAGEDY

Translated by Michael Hamburger

CHARACTERS

MARGARET OF PARMA, daughter of Charles V
and Regent of the Netherlands
COUNT EGMONT, Prince of Gavre
WILLIAM OF ORANGE
DUKE OF ALBA
FERDINAND, his natural son
MACHIAVELLI, in the Regent's service
RICHARD, Egmont's private secretary
SILVA ⎫
       ⎬ in Alba's service
GOMEZ ⎭
CLARE, Egmont's mistress
HER MOTHER
BRACKENBURG, a burgess
SOEST, grocer ⎫
JETTER, tailor ⎪
            ⎬ citizens of Brussels
CARPENTER ⎪
SOAPBOILER ⎭
BUYCK, soldier under Egmont
RUYSUM, disabled soldier, hard of hearing
VANSEN, a clerk
People, attendants, guards, etc.

The scene is Brussels.
The year is 1568.

ACT I

Crossbow Target Shooting
Soldiers and Citizens with crossbows. Jetter, citizen of Brussels, a tailor, steps
forward and prepares to shoot. Soest, citizen of Brussels, a grocer.

SOEST. Well, go ahead and shoot so there'll be an end to it. You won't beat me, anyway. Three in the black is more than you ever got in all your life. That means I'm champion for the year.

JETTER. Champion, indeed, and king as well. Who would begrudge you the honour? But you'll have to pay for two rounds; you'll have to pay for your skill as every champion does.

Buyck, a Dutchman, soldier serving under Egmont.

BUYCK. Jetter, I'll buy those shots off you, share the prize, pay for the gentlemen's drinks: I've been here so very long and feel indebted to them for so much courtesy. If I miss, the turn shall count as yours.

SOEST. I should really protest, for your bargain makes *me* the loser. But never mind, Buyck, shoot ahead.

BUYCK (*shoots*). Well, here goes—One, two, three, four.

SOEST. What, four in the black? You're the winner, then.

ALL. Three cheers for the king. Hip, hip, hurray, hurray, hurray.

BUYCK. Thank you, gentlemen. But even "Champion" would be too much. Thank you for the honour.

JETTER. You've yourself to thank for it.

Ruysum, a Frisian, disabled soldier, hard of hearing.

RUYSUM. Let me tell you!

SOEST. Tell us what, old man?

RUYSUM. Let me tell you: he shoots like his master, like Egmont.

BUYCK. Compared to him I'm only a poor bungler. You should see him on the musket range; he hits the mark like no one else in the world. I don't mean when he's lucky or in the right mood. No: every time, he's no sooner taken aim than he's got the bull's-eye. It's he who taught me. I'd like to see the fellow who's served with him and not learnt anything from him! But I haven't forgotten, gentlemen. A king looks after his people; so let's have some wine, at the king's expense.

JETTER. It was agreed between us that each of us—

BUYCK. I'm a stranger here, and king, and I pay no attention to your laws and customs.

JETTER. Why, you're worse than the Spaniards; they've had to leave our laws and customs alone, till now, anyway.

RUYSUM. What do you say?

SOEST (*loudly*). He wants to stand all the drinks; he doesn't want us to put our money together and let the king only pay double.

RUYSUM. Let him, then. But no offence. That's his master's way too—to be lavish and never leave money to burn a hole in his pocket.

They bring wine.

ALL. Good health, your Majesty, and a prosperous life!

JETTER, *to* BUYCK. That's right: your Majesty. You deserve the honour.

BUYCK. Well, if it must be, thank you with all my heart.

SOEST. It must be; for no true citizen of the Low Countries will easily drink the health of our Spanish Majesty—not with all his heart.

RUYSUM. Whose health, did you say?

SOEST (*loudly*). Philip the Second, King of Spain.

RUYSUM. Our most gracious King and Lord! May God grant him a long reign.

SOEST. Didn't you prefer his father of blessed memory, Charles the Fifth?

RUYSUM. God have mercy on his soul. He was a great gentleman. He had the whole earth to take care of, but he was a father and brother to us all. And if he met you in the street, he greeted you as one neighbour greets another, and if that gave you a start, he was gracious enough to—Don't misunderstand me. I mean: he went out, rode out just as the fancy took him, with only a few men. There wasn't a dry eye to be seen when he abdicated and made his son governor of these parts. Don't misunderstand me, I say. But Philip's different, you'll admit; more majestic, if you like.

JETTER. No man ever saw him, when he was here, but in royal pomp and ceremony. He doesn't talk much, people say.

SOEST. He's not the man for us of the Low Countries. Our princes must be light-hearted like ourselves, live and let live. We won't be despised or pressed, good-natured fools though we are.

JETTER. The King would be gracious enough, I think, if only he had better advisers.

SOEST. No. Never. He doesn't take to our sort, he has no sympathy for us, he doesn't love us. How, then, can we love him in our turn? Why is every single one of us so fond of Count Egmont? Why would we gladly carry him about on our hands? Because you can see that he wishes us well; because you can read his cheerfulness, the free life he lives, the good opinion he has of us, in his eyes; because he hasn't a single possession that he wouldn't give away to a needy man, even to a man who didn't need it. Let's drink to Count Egmont! Buyck, it's your privilege to propose the first toast. Propose the health of your master!

BUYCK. With the greatest pleasure: Count Egmont.

RUYSUM. Victor at St. Quentin!

BUYCK. To the hero of Gravelingen!

ALL. To his health!

RUYSUM. St. Quentin was my last battle. I could hardly move another inch, hardly drag my heavy musket any further. And yet! I gave the Frenchman one last thing to remember me by, and got something too, though it only grazed my right leg.

BUYCK. But Gravelingen, friends, that was a pretty lively affair. There victory was ours alone. Hadn't those French dogs been burning and laying waste the whole length and breadth of Flanders? But, there's no doubt about it, we gave them what they deserved. Their old, tried soldiers held out for a long time, but we pressed and shot and slashed at them till they pulled faces and their lines began to give way. Then Egmont's horse was shot away from under him, and there was a long uncertain struggle, man to man, horse against horse, troop against troop, on the broad flat sand of the seashore. Then suddenly it came as if down from heaven, from the river mouth—the "bow, bow" of the big cannons firing right into the midst of the French. It was the English, who just happened to be passing on their way from Dunkirk under Admiral Malin. They didn't help us much, it's true; they could only get in with their smallest ships, and not close enough at that; and sometimes they shot at us by mistake. But it did us good, all the same. It broke the Frenchmen's spirit and gave us new courage. So now we made short work of them. Killed the whole lot or drove them into the water. And those fellows drowned as soon as they tasted water. As for us Dutchmen, we went in after them. Amphibians that we are, we didn't feel happy till we were in the water, like frogs, and we just went on fighting the enemy in the river, shot them down as if they were ducks. The few that got away after that—well, the peasant women saw to them: beat them down as they ran with pitchforks and pickaxes. So his French Majesty had no choice but to come to heel and make peace. So it's to us you owe that peace, to our great Egmont!

ALL. To our great Egmont! And again! And again! And yet again!

JETTER. If only he'd been appointed our Regent in Margaret of Parma's place!

SOEST. No, that's going too far. Honour where honour is due. I won't hear Margaret's name abused. Now it's my turn. Long live our gracious lady!

ALL. Long live Margaret!

SOEST. It's true, there's no denying the excellence of the women in the ruling house. Long live the Regent!

JETTER. She's clever and moderate in everything she does. If only she didn't stick to the parsons through thick and thin. It's partly her fault that we have those fourteen new bishoprics in our country. What can they be for? Only to push a lot of strangers into the best positions, where they used to put abbots elected by the chapter. And they want us to believe it's all for religion's sake. That's the root of the trouble. Three bishops were enough for us; honesty and decency were the rule in those days. Now everyone has to pretend that they're really necessary, and so there's no end to the trouble and bickering. And the more you look into the thing, the more murky it seems.

They drink.

SOEST. That was simply the King's will; she can do nothing about it either way.

JETTER. And now they tell us we mustn't sing those new psalms. And yet they're beautifully versified, and their tunes couldn't be more uplifting. We mustn't sing those, but as many profane and scurrilous ditties as we please. Why, do you think? They say those psalms contain heresies and goodness knows what else. And yet I've sung them before now and I couldn't see anything bad in them. It's a new idea.

BUYCK. I shouldn't dream of asking their permission. In our province we sing what we like. That's because Count Egmont is our governor; he doesn't interfere with things of that kind—in Ghent, in Ypres, in the whole of Flanders, whoever wants to, sings them.

Loudly:

Surely there's nothing more innocent than a spiritual song? Isn't that so, Father?

RUYSUM. Indeed. For it's a form of devotion and it purifies the heart.

JETTER. But they say it doesn't do so in the right way—not in *their* way. And it's always dangerous, so one leaves it alone. The servants of the Inquisition creep and snoop about everywhere. Many an honest man has come to grief already. To suppress our freedom of conscience—that was the last straw. If I can't do what I please, they might at least let me think and sing what I please.

SOEST. The Inquisition won't get the better of us. We're not like the Spaniards and will never let anyone tyrannize over our conscience. And the nobility too will have to start resisting it soon.

JETTER. We're in a very awkward position. If those fine people take it into their heads to come rushing into my house, and I'm sitting down, doing my work, and just happen to be humming a French psalm, without a thought in my head, whether virtuous or wicked, but I simply hum it because the tune is there inside me—well, that makes me a heretic, and they put me in jail. Or I'm out for a walk and stop when I see a crowd of people listening to some new preacher—one of those who've come from Germany—that makes me a rebel, no less, and they'll chop off my head as likely as not. Have you ever heard one of them preach?

SOEST. Very fine preachers, if you ask me. The other day I heard one speak to thousands and thousands of people. That was a different kettle of fish—not like ours, always beating about the bush, stuffing Latin tags down the people's throats. That one made no bones about it. He told us straight how they've been leading us by the nose till now, keeping us ignorant, and how we could have more light for the asking. And he proved it all from the Bible.

JETTER. I'm sure there is something in that. I've often said so myself and pondered on those matters. It's been troubling my head for a long time.

BUYCK. I suppose that's why they're so popular.

SOEST. And no wonder. Who wouldn't go to hear something that's good and new?

JETTER. What's the matter, then? Why can't any man be allowed to preach in his own way?

BUYCK. Drink up, gentlemen. All this chatter is making you forget your wine—and William of Orange too.

JETTER. Oh, we mustn't forget him. He's a real tower of strength: you've only to think of him to feel that you can hide behind him, and the devil himself wouldn't be able to get you out. To William of Orange, then!

ALL. To his health!

SOEST. Now, old man, propose your own health too!

RUYSUM. Old soldiers! All soldiers! Long live war!

BUYCK. Well said, old man. All soldiers! Long live war!

JETTER. War, war! Do you know what you're saying? That word comes to you easily enough, and I suppose that's natural, but I can't tell you how wretched it sounds to those of my kind. To hear nothing but drumbeats the whole year round; and hear nothing but one troop marching in here, another there; how they came over a hill and stopped by a windmill, how many were left there, how many in another place, and how they fight, and how one wins, the other loses, though for the life of me I can't understand who's won anything, who's lost. How a town is captured, the citizens murdered, and what becomes of the poor women, the innocent children. Affliction and terror, that's what it means to us, and every moment one thinks: "Look, they're coming! And they'll do the same to us."

SOEST. That's why a citizen too should always be trained to use arms.

JETTER. Yes, whoever has a wife and children learns to defend them. But I'd still rather hear about soldiers than see them.

BUYCK. I should take offence at that remark.

JETTER. It isn't aimed at you, friend. We were all relieved when we'd got rid of the Spanish occupation forces.

SOEST. Yes, indeed. You found those most irksome of all, didn't you?

JETTER. Don't try to make a fool of me.

SOEST. They were sorry to leave your house.

JETTER. Shut your mouth.

SOEST. They'd driven him out of his kitchen, his cellar, his sitting-room—and his bed.

Laughter.

JETTER. You're a fool.

BUYCK. Peace, gentlemen! Do you need a soldier to make peace between you? Well, since you don't want to have anything to do with our sort, you'd better propose a toast to yourselves, a civil toast.

JETTER. That we'll do gladly. Security and quiet!

SOEST. Order and freedom!

BUYCK. Bravo! That suits us too.

> *They clink glasses and cheerfully repeat these words, but in such a way*
> *that each calls out a different word and a kind of canon results.*
> *The old man listens and finally joins in also.*

ALL. Security and quiet! Order and freedom!

The Regent's Palace
Margaret of Parma in hunting attire. Courtiers. Pages. Servants.

REGENT. You will cancel the hunt; I shall not ride today. Tell Machiavelli to come to me.

Exeunt all.

The thought of these terrible happenings gives me no peace. Nothing pleases me, nothing distracts me; always these misgivings, these cares torment me. The King will say that these are the fruits of my kindness, my consideration; and yet my conscience tells me that at every moment I did what was most advisable, that my only purpose was to do the right thing at the right time. Should I, then, have fanned these flames even sooner and made them spread, by exposing them to a tempest of wrath? It was my hope to set limits to their progress and stifle them by driving them back upon themselves. I know that this is the truth and by reminding myself of it I can absolve myself from all self-reproach. But how will my brother receive the news? For there is no denying it: the insolence of the new preachers has been growing daily. They have blasphemed against our most sacred tenets, subverted the dull minds of the common people, and released the spirit of confusion in their midst. Arrant rogues have joined the ranks of the insurgents and caused dreadful atrocities to be committed. Only to think of them makes me shudder, and now I must report them one by one to the Court, one by one and speedily, so that the general rumour will not forestall our account, so that the King will not suspect us of trying to conceal the rest. I can see no means, whether stern or gentle, of opposing this evil. Oh, what are we, then, the great on the crest of humanity's wave? We think that we rule its fury, but it bears us up and down, to and fro.

Enter Machiavelli.

REGENT. Have those letters to the King been drafted?

MACHIAVELLI. They will be ready for your signature in an hour's time.

REGENT. Have you made the report sufficiently detailed?

MACHIAVELLI. Detailed and elaborate, as the King likes them to be. I recount how the iconoclastic fury first broke out at St. Omer. How a raging mob, furnished with staves, axes, hammers, ladders, and ropes, accompanied by a few armed men, began by attacking chapels, churches, and monasteries, driving out the worshippers, breaking open the doors, throwing everything into disorder, tearing down the altars, breaking the statues of saints, destroying every painting, shattering, ripping up, stamping to pieces every consecrated and holy thing they could lay hands upon. How this rabble grew in numbers as it proceeded, how the inhabitants of Ypres opened the gates to them. How they laid waste the cathedral there with incredible speed, how they burnt the bishop's library. How a great mob of common folk, seized with the same frenzy, poured into Menin, Comines, Verwich, Lille, encountered no resistance anywhere, and how, in the twinkling of an eye, the conspiracy declared itself and struck almost throughout the whole of Flanders.

REGENT. Oh, the repetition of it renews my pain. And now there is the added fear that the evil will only grow and grow. Tell me what you think, Machiavelli?

MACHIAVELLI. Forgive me, your Highness, if my thoughts are more like whims; and though you have always been satisfied with my services, you have rarely chosen to take my advice. Often you have said in jest: "You're too farsighted, Machiavelli! You should be a historian: the man who acts should keep his eyes on what is nearest to him." And yet, didn't I predict this whole story? Did I not foresee it all?

REGENT. I too foresee a great deal without having the power to forestall it.

MACHIAVELLI. Briefly, then, and to the point: you will not suppress the new doctrine. Let them have their way but separate them from the orthodox. Give them churches, integrate them in the framework of society, restrict their influence: then you will have silenced the rebels at a single stroke. Every other measure will be in vain, and you will lay waste the country.

REGENT. Have you forgotten with what repugnance my brother condemned the very suggestion that the new doctrine might be tolerated? Don't you know how in every letter he reminds me most emphatically of my duty to maintain the true faith? That he will not hear of a peace and a unity established at the expense of religion? Even in the Provinces does he not keep spies unknown to us, so as to observe who is likely to go over to the new creed? Did he not amaze us by naming more than one person close to us who has become guilty of heresy, though in secret? Does he not command us to practise severity and ruthless justice? And you want me to be merciful? To make proposals to him that call on him to be considerate and tolerant? Should I not lose all his confidence, all his trust?

MACHIAVELLI. Well I know it; the King gives orders, he lets you know his intentions. You are to establish peace and quiet once more by a measure that will only increase the general embitterment, that will inevitably fan the fires of war from every direction. Consider what you are doing. The most powerful merchants have been infected, the nobility, the people, the soldiers. What is the use of adhering to his ideas, when everything around us is changing? If only some benevolent spirit would make it clear to Philip that it is more fitting for a king to rule citizens of two different creeds than to incite one party against the other.

REGENT. I forbid you to speak in that way. I know very well that in politics one can rarely keep faith or troth, but must ban frankness, kindness, and indulgence from one's heart. In worldly affairs that is only too true, but are we to toy with God, as we toy with one another? Are we to be indifferent to our proven doctrine, for which so many have offered up their lives? Should we yield even that to an upstart, uncertain, and self-contradictory fad?

MACHIAVELLI. Please don't think ill of me on that account.

REGENT. I know you to be a loyal servant, and I know that a man can be honest and prudent even though he has missed the nearest, straightest way to his soul's salvation. You are not the only one, Machiavelli, not the only man whom I must both respect and reproach.

MACHIAVELLI. To whom are you alluding?

REGENT. I will confess to you that Egmont aroused my deep and acute displeasure today.

MACHIAVELLI. By what kind of conduct?

REGENT. By his usual conduct, by his nonchalance and recklessness. I received the terrible news just as I was coming out of church in his and many others' company. I could not contain my grief, voiced my complaint and, turning to him, cried out: "Look what is happening in your province! And you put up with it, Count, you of whom the King expected so much?"

MACHIAVELLI. And what did he reply?

REGENT. As if it were nothing, a mere irrelevance, he retorted: "If only the people of the Netherlands were assured that the Constitution is safe, the rest could easily be settled."

MACHIAVELLI. Perhaps he spoke with more truth than prudence or piety. How can confidence be established and preserved when the people of the Netherlands see that we are more concerned with their possessions than with their well-being or the good of their souls? Have the new bishops saved more souls than they've swallowed rich benefices, and are not most of them foreigners? Still all the town governorships are held by Netherlanders: do the Spaniards trouble to conceal their irresistible covetousness for these places? Does not a people prefer to be ruled by its own kind, in its own fashion, rather than by strangers who begin by endeavouring to acquire property in the country at everyone's expense, who apply strange standards, and who rule harshly and without sympathy?

REGENT. You are placing yourself on the opposing side.

MACHIAVELLI. Not in my heart, certainly, and I wish that my head could be wholly on ours.

REGENT. If that is your view, it would be necessary for me to abdicate from the Regency; for Egmont and Orange once lived in high hopes of occupying that place. At that time they were rivals; now they are in league against me and have become friends, inseparable friends.

MACHIAVELLI. A dangerous couple!

REGENT. To be frank, I fear Orange, and I fear for Egmont. Orange is up to no good, his thoughts reach out to the distant future, he is secretive, seems to accept everything, never contradicts, and with the deepest reverence, with the greatest caution, he does what he pleases.

MACHIAVELLI. Quite the contrary of Egmont, who walks about as freely as if the world belonged to him.

REGENT. He wears his head as high as if the hand of Majesty were not suspended over it.

MACHIAVELLI. The people's eyes are all fixed on him, and all their hearts.

REGENT. He has never troubled about appearances—as if there were no one to call him to account. Still he bears the name of Egmont; is glad to hear himself called "Count Egmont," as if loath to forget that his ancestors were the lords of Geldern. Why doesn't he call himself Prince of Gavre, as he is entitled to? Why does he do it? Does he want to re-establish obsolete rights?

MACHIAVELLI. I look upon him as a loyal servant of the King.

REGENT. If he only wanted to, what indispensable services he could render the Government, instead of causing us endless annoyance without any profit to himself, as he's already done! His receptions, banquets, and carousals have done more to unify the nobility than the most dangerous secret conferences. From his toasts the guests have drawn a lasting intoxication, a chronic giddiness. How often his jests and jibes have stirred up the people's minds, and how the populace gaped at his new liveries, at the foolish badges of his servants!

MACHIAVELLI. I'm sure this was not his intention.

REGENT. So much the worse for us all. As I was saying: he harms us and does himself no good. He turns serious things into a joke, and we, so as not to appear idle and careless, must take his jokes seriously. So one worries the other, and what we try to avert is all the more certain to occur. He is more dangerous than the declared head of a conspiracy, and I should be very much surprised if at Court they don't keep a record of all his misdeeds.

There's no denying it: hardly a week passes without his causing me grave discomfort, the very gravest discomfort.

MACHIAVELLI. It seems to me that in all things he acts according to his conscience.

REGENT. His conscience has a flattering mirror; his conduct is often offensive. Often he looks as if he were firmly convinced that he is really our master, though out of kindness he's obliging enough not to make us feel it, to refrain from simply driving us out of the country—with the assumption that we'll go in any case, all in good time.

MACHIAVELLI. I beg of you, don't put such a dangerous construction upon his frankness, his happy disposition, that takes important things lightly. You will only harm him and yourself.

REGENT. I put no construction on anything. I am merely speaking of the inevitable consequences and I know him well. His Netherlandish nobility and the Order of the Golden Fleece strengthen his confidence, his boldness. Both can guard him against the King's sudden, arbitrary displeasure. Just examine the matter precisely and you must agree that he alone is responsible for all the misfortunes that have descended on Flanders. He was the first to tolerate the new teachers, easy-going as he is, and perhaps secretly pleased that they gave us something to reckon with. No, don't interrupt me: I am taking the opportunity to tell you all that is on my mind. And I don't wish to discharge my arrows in vain; I know where he is vulnerable. Yes, Egmont too is vulnerable.

MACHIAVELLI. Have you summoned the Council? Is Orange coming too?

REGENT. I've sent to Antwerp for him. I propose to move the burden of responsibility very close to them; they must join me in seriously resisting the evil or else declare themselves rebels. Lose no time in finishing the letters and bring them to me for signature! Then quickly send off the experienced Vasca to Madrid—he is indefatigable and loyal—so that he shall be the first to convey the news to my brother, so that the rumour will not precede him. I will speak to him myself before he leaves.

MACHIAVELLI. Your commands will be executed both speedily and exactly.

Citizen's House
Clare. Clare's Mother. Brackenburg.

CLARE. Won't you hold the thread for me, Brackenburg?

BRACKENBURG. I beg you to spare me, my dear.

CLARE. What's the matter with you tonight? Why do you refuse me this little attention?

BRACKENBURG. Your thread keeps me so spell-bound that I can't avoid your eyes.

CLARE. Nonsense! Come and hold it!

MOTHER (*knitting in her arm-chair*). Why don't you sing? Brackenburg makes such a good second. You used to be so cheerful, both of you, and I never stopped laughing at your pranks.

BRACKENBURG. We used to be.

CLARE. Let's sing, then.

BRACKENBURG. Whatever you wish.

CLARE. Well, then, sing up; and make it lively. It's a military song and my favourite.

She winds the thread and sings with Brackenburg.

> Strike up! To your drumming!
> And blow the fife loud.
> My sweetheart in armour
> Commands the whole crowd.
> His lance held aloft rules
> Their going and coming.
> Now faster my blood flows
> My heart goes pit-pat.
> O, would I wore doublet
> And breeches and hat!
>
> Then marching I'd follow
> Him out through the gate
> And roam with him fighting
> Through province and state.
> Our enemy's fleeing.
> We shoot them as they run!
> There's nothing like being
> A man with a gun!

As they sing Brackenburg looks at Clare repeatedly; at the end his voice fails him, tears come into his eyes, he drops the thread, and goes to the window. Clare finishes the song by herself, her mother signals to her half-angrily, Clare rises, takes a few steps towards him, turns back irresolutely, and sits down.

MOTHER. What's going on outside, Brackenburg? I hear the sound of marching.

BRACKENBURG. It's the Regent's Life Guards.

CLARE. At this hour? What's the meaning of that?

She gets up and goes to the window with Brackenburg.

That's not the ordinary guard, there are many more of them, nearly the whole regiment. Oh, Brackenburg, do go and find out what's happening. It must be something special. Please go, my dear. Do me this favour!

BRACKENBURG. I'm going. I shall be with you again in a moment.

He holds out his hand to her as he leaves; she clasps it.

MOTHER. There you go again, sending him off!

CLARE. I'm curious; and besides—don't be angry with me—his presence pains me. I never know how to behave towards him. I'm in the wrong where he's concerned, and it grieves me to see him suffer so much because of it. When there's nothing I can do about it.

MOTHER. He's such a loyal fellow.

CLARE. That's why I can't help being kind to him. Often my hand seems to close of its own accord when his hand touches me in that tender, loving way. I reproach myself for deceiving him, for keeping a vain hope alive in his heart. I'm in a terrible quandary. God knows I'm not deceiving him. I don't want him to hope and yet I can't let him despair.

MOTHER. That's not right of you.

CLARE. I used to be fond of him and still wish him well with all my soul. I could have married him, and yet I think I was never in love with him.

MOTHER. But you would have been happy with him if you had.

CLARE. I'd have been well provided for and led a quiet life.

MOTHER. And you've lost all that through your own fault.

CLARE. I'm in a very strange position. When I ask myself how it came about, I know the answer and I don't know it. And then I've only to look at Egmont again to understand everything that's happened—and *more* than what's happened. What a man! All the Provinces idolize him; so how could I help being the happiest creature in the world when he holds me in his arms?

MOTHER. But what will become of us? What of the future?

CLARE. Oh, all I ask is whether he loves me; and would you call that a question?

MOTHER. Distress and anxiety, that's all one gets from one's children. How will it end, I ask you? Worry and grief all the time. No good will come of it. You've made yourself unhappy and made me unhappy.

CLARE (*nonchalantly*). You raised no objection at first.

MOTHER. Unfortunately not. I was too kind, too easy-going. I always am.

CLARE. When Egmont rode past and I went to the window, did you tell me off? Didn't you go to the window too? When he looked up, smiled, nodded, and called to me: did you mind? Didn't you feel that he honoured you by honouring your daughter?

MOTHER. Now you're reproaching me!

CLARE (*moved*). And then when he came more often to our street and it was clear to us that he came this way because of me, weren't you pleased in secret? Did you call me away when I stood behind the panes, waiting for him?

MOTHER. Could I know that it would go so far?

CLARE (*in a halting voice, restraining her tears*). And when he surprised us in the evening, wrapped in his cloak, and we were working by lamplight, who was it that hurried to receive him, since I remained seated, amazed, and glued to the chair?

MOTHER. And had I any reason to fear that this unhappy love would knock my clever little Clare off her feet and so quickly too? Now I have to accept the fact that my daughter——

CLARE (*breaking into tears*). Mother! There's no need to put it like that. Anyone would think you enjoy frightening me.

MOTHER (*weeping*). Yes, go on and cry on top of everything! Make me even more miserable by being sad! Isn't it bad enough that my only daughter is a fallen creature?

CLARE (*rising coldly*). Fallen? Egmont's mistress a fallen creature? There isn't a duchess who wouldn't envy little Clare her place in his heart. Oh, Mother, you've never used such words till now. Be patient with me, dear. . . . Leave other people to think *that* of me, leave the neighbours to whisper what they please. This room, this little house have been heaven to me since Egmont's love first crossed the threshold.

MOTHER. Well, it's true one can't help liking him. He's always so amiable and frank and easy.

CLARE. There's no strain of falsehood in him at all. And yet, Mother, he's the great Egmont. And when he comes to see me, he's all kindness and goodness. Why he even does his best to conceal his rank and his courage, he's so concerned about me. Here he's simply a man, a friend, and my dearest love.

MOTHER. Do you think he will come today?

CLARE. Didn't you notice how often I've been to the window? Didn't you notice how I listen when there's a noise at the door? Though I know that he won't come before nightfall, I still expect him every moment from the instant I get up in the morning. If only I were a boy and could go about with him all the time, to Court and everywhere! If only I could carry his standard for him in battle!

MOTHER. You've always been a sort of tomboy, even when you were a small child, now wild, now pensive. Don't you think you should put on something a little better?

CLARE. Maybe, Mother—if I feel bored. You know, yesterday some of his men passed by, singing songs in his praise. At least his name was part of the songs; I couldn't catch the rest. I could feel my heartbeats right up in my throat. I should have liked to call them back, if I hadn't been afraid of drawing attention to myself.

MOTHER. You be careful! Or your impulsive nature will spoil everything. You'll give yourself away. Just as you did the other day at your cousin's, when you found that woodcut and the inscription and exclaimed with a cry: "Count Egmont!" I turned crimson with shame.

CLARE. How could I not cry out? It was the battle of Gravelingen, and I found the letter C at the top of the picture, so I looked for C in the description.

There I read: "Count Egmont, when his horse was shot dead under him." I felt my blood rise—and later I had to laugh at the woodcut Egmont, who was as tall as the tower of Gravelingen just next to him and the English ships on one side. What a strange idea I used to have of what a battle is like and what Count Egmont himself is like, when I was a girl, when they told stories about him, and of every Count and Duke—and how different they all seem now!

Re-enter Brackenburg.

CLARE. What's happening?

BRACKENBURG. No one is sure. They say that a new riot has broken out in Flanders, that the Regent is afraid it may spread to our parts. The Palace Guard has been strongly reinforced, there are crowds of citizens at the gates, the streets are full of people. . . . I think I should call on my old father.

As if about to leave.

CLARE. Shall we see you tomorrow? I'm just going to dress. We're expecting my cousin, and I look too slovenly for words. Will you help me, Mother? Take that book, Brackenburg, and bring me another of those histories!

MOTHER. Good-bye.

BRACKENBURG (*holding out his hand*). Won't you give me your hand?

CLARE (*refusing the hand*). When you come again.

Exeunt mother and daughter.

BRACKENBURG (*alone*). I had intended to leave at once, and now that she accepts the gesture and lets me go, I can hardly bear it. Oh, what a wretch I am! Not even moved by the fate of my country, the growing unrest. My own kind or the Spaniards, it's all the same to me, who's in power and who's in the right. How very different I was when I was a schoolboy! When they set us a piece called "Brutus's Speech on Liberty, an Exercise in Oratory," it was always Fritz who came first, and the headmaster said: "If only it were more tidy, not such a jumble of enthusiasms." I was all drive and ferment then! Now I drag myself along, hanging on that girl's eyes. Since I can't leave her alone, and she can't love me. Oh, she can't have rejected me entirely— can't have, yes or no, but half her love is no love. I'll not put up with it a moment longer! . . . Could it be true, then, what a friend whispered in my ear the other day? That she secretly receives a man at night, since she always drives me out so respectably before the evening? No, it's not true, it's a lie, a shameful, slanderous lie! Clare is as innocent as I'm unhappy. She's rejected me, cast me out of her heart. And can I go on like that? I'll not put up with it. . . . Already my country is divided against itself—more violently each day—and I simply languish away in the midst of all that turmoil! No, I'll not put up with it. When the bugle sounds, when a shot rings out it pierces me to the marrow. Yet it doesn't provoke me, doesn't challenge me to enter the fray, to save and dare with the rest. . . . Oh, wretched, despicable state. Better to put an end to it once and for all. Already once I threw myself into the water and sank—but my terrified nature was stronger. I felt that I could swim and reluctantly saved myself. . . . If only I could forget the time when she loved me or seemed to love me! . . . Why did that happiness pervade every bone of my body? Why have these hopes deprived me of all pleasure in life by showing me a paradise from afar? And that first kiss, the only one! Here (*resting his head on the table*) at this very place we were alone together—she had always been kind and pleasant to me—then she seemed to soften, she looked at me, all my senses were in a whirl, and I felt her lips on mine. And now? There's only death. Why do I hesitate?

He takes a small bottle out of his pocket.

This time it must not be in vain; not in vain that I stole this poison out of my brother's medicine chest. It shall rid me once and for all of this anguish, this uncertainty, this fever worse than death.

ACT II

Square in Brussels
Jetter and a Carpenter meet.

CARPENTER. Didn't I predict it? Only a week ago, at the Guild meeting, I said there would be serious clashes.

JETTER. Is it true, then, that they've robbed the churches in Flanders?

CARPENTER. Plundered them, ruined them completely, both churches and chapels. Left nothing but the four bare walls. A lot of hooligans, every one of them. And that put a bad face on our good cause. We should rather have pleaded our just cause to the Regent in an orderly and firm manner and insisted on it. If we make speeches now or meet, they accuse us of joining the rebels.

JETTER. Yes. And so everyone thinks: why should I stick out my face—since my neck is all too close to it?

CARPENTER. I feel very uncomfortable, now that this turmoil has taken possession of the mob, the people who have nothing to lose. They make a mere pretext of what we too profess and will plunge our country into misfortune.

Soest joins them.

SOEST. Good morning, gentlemen. What's the news? Is it true that the iconoclasts are on their way here?

CARPENTER. They'd better keep their hands off here.

SOEST. A soldier came into my shop to buy tobacco. I questioned him. The Regent, clever, brave woman though she remains, has lost her head this time. Things must be very bad for her to hide like this behind her Guard. The Palace Guard has been heavily reinforced. It's even rumoured that she intends to flee from the town.

CARPENTER. She mustn't leave. Her presence protects us, and we shall give her more security than her clipped beards. And if she maintains our rights and liberties, we shall carry her aloft.

Soapboiler joins them.

SOAPBOILER. A nasty, filthy roughhouse! There's more and more trouble, and it will come to a bad end. . . . Be careful, now, and keep quiet, so that they won't take you for rebel agents.

SOEST. Look! There are the seven sages from Greece!

SOAPBOILER. I know there are many who secretly support the Calvinists, slander the bishops, and have no respect for the King. But a loyal subject, a true Catholic——

One by one various people join them, listening. Vansen joins them.

VANSEN. Greetings, gentlemen! What's been happening?

CARPENTER. Have nothing to do with that one. He's a scoundrel.

JETTER. Isn't he Dr. Wiet's clerk?

CARPENTER. He's had a good many masters. First he was a clerk and, when one employer after another had kicked him out for his knaveries, he began to botch the briefs of solicitors and barristers, and he's too fond of the brandy bottle.

More and more people gather and stand about in groups.

VANSEN. Why, you've got quite a crowd collected here and, what's more, you're putting your heads together. Quite an interesting occasion.

SOEST. I think so too.

VANSEN. Now, if one or the other of you had the heart, and one or the other had the head as well, we could break the Spanish chains with one blow.

SOEST. Sir, you must not speak like that! We have sworn loyalty to the King.

VANSEN. And the King to us! Don't forget that!

JETTER. Very true! Tell us your views!

SOME OTHERS. Listen to him! He knows what he's talking about.

VANSEN. I had an old employer once, who owned documents and letters about the most ancient decrees, contracts, and laws. He collected the rarest books. In one of them our whole constitution was set out: how we Netherlanders were ruled at first by single princes, all according to traditional rights, privileges, and customs; how our ancestors had every kind of respect for their Prince, as long as he ruled them as he must; and how they sat up as soon as he looked like being too big for his boots. Our deputies were after him at once; for every Province, however small, had its parliament and deputies.

CARPENTER. Shut your mouth! We've known all that for a long time. Every decent citizen knows as much about the constitution as he needs to know.

JETTER. Let him speak; there's always something new to be learnt.

SOEST. He's quite right.

SEVERAL OTHERS. Go on, tell us more. We don't hear that kind of thing every day.

VANSEN. That's what you're like, citizens. You just drift along from day to day and, just as you took over your trades from your parents, you let the government rule you as it pleases. You ask no questions about tradition, about history, about the rights of a Regent; and because you have failed in that, the Spaniards have pulled tight the net right over your heads.

SOEST. Who worries about that? If only a man has enough to eat.

JETTER. Damnation! Why didn't somebody get up in time and tell us these things?

VANSEN. I'm telling you now. The King in Spain, who happens to own all our provinces, has no right, all the same, to rule them any differently from the little princes who once owned them separately. Do you understand that?

JETTER. Explain it to us.

VANSEN. It's as clear as daylight. Should you not be judged according to the laws of your country? How could it be otherwise?

A CITIZEN. True enough!

VANSEN. Hasn't the citizen of Brussels other laws than the citizen of Antwerp? And the citizen of Antwerp than the citizen of Ghent? How could it be otherwise?

OTHER CITIZENS. By God, it's true.

VANSEN. But if you let things go on as they are, they'll soon show you a very different picture. Shame on it! What Charles the Bold, Frederick the Warrior, Charles V could not do, Philip does through a woman!

SOEST. Indeed. The old princes too tried to get away with it.

VANSEN. Naturally. . . . Our ancestors were on their guard. When they had a grudge against one of their masters, they would capture his son and heir, keep him prisoner, and only release him when all their conditions had been met—or something of that kind. Our ancestors were real men! They knew what was good for them. They knew how to get hold of things and keep them. Real men, I say. And that's why our privileges are so clearly outlined, our liberties so securely guarded.

SOAPBOILER. What's that you're saying about our liberties?

THE CROWD. Yes, our liberties, our privileges! Tell us more about our privileges!

VANSEN. We men of Brabant especially, though all Provinces have their advantages, we have the most splendid rights. I've read about them all.

SOEST. Tell us what they are.

JETTER. Let's have them all.

A CITIZEN. I beg you.

VANSEN. Firstly, it is written: The Duke of Brabant shall be a good and loyal master to us.

SOEST. Good, was that the word? Is that what it says?

JETTER. Loyal? Is that so?

VANSEN. That's what I'm telling you. He's bound to us by oath, as we are to him. Secondly: he must not impose on us, make felt, or propose to apply to us any power or expression of his will in whatever manner.

JETTER. Excellent. Must not impose on us.

SOEST. Not make felt.

ANOTHER. And propose to apply. That's the crux of it. Apply to no one, in whatever manner.

VANSEN. Most emphatically.

JETTER. Bring in the book.

A CITIZEN. Yes, we must see it.

OTHERS. The book, the book!

ANOTHER. Let's go to the Regent and show her the book.

ANOTHER. And you, Doctor, shall be our spokesman.

SOAPBOILER. Oh, the poor fools!

OTHERS. Give us another extract from the book.

SOAPBOILER. Another word out of him, and I'll make him swallow his teeth!

THE CROWD. Just let anyone try to do that! Tell us more about the privileges! Haven't we any more privileges?

VANSEN. Quite a number, friends, and very good and wholesome ones they are. It is written there too: The ruler must neither improve nor increase the status of the clergy without the consent of the nobles and the commons. Mark that, my friends! Nor alter the constitution of the Province in any way.

SOEST. Is that so?

VANSEN. I'll show it to you in writing, as set down two, three centuries ago.

CITIZENS. And we put up with the new bishops? The nobles must protect us, we must make trouble at once.

OTHERS. And we allow the Inquisition to terrorize us?

VANSEN. That's your fault.

THE PEOPLE. We still have Egmont! And Orange! They will see to it.

VANSEN. Your brothers in Flanders have begun the good work.

SOAPBOILER. You rat!

He hits him.

OTHERS (*resist and cry out*). Are you a Spaniard too?

ANOTHER. What? Strike that honourable gentleman?

ANOTHER. Strike a man of such erudition?

They fall upon the Soapboiler.

CARPENTER. For heaven's sake, stop it.

Others join in the brawl.

Citizens! Are you out of your senses?

Boys whistle, throw stones, incite dogs to attack. Citizens stand and gape,
new people arrive, others walk about calmly, others again play
all sorts of clownish tricks, shriek, and cheer.

OTHERS. Freedom and privileges! Privileges and freedom!

Enter Egmont with retinue.

EGMONT. Steady, steady now, all of you. What's going on? Silence! Separate them!

CARPENTER. Your lordship, you come like an angel from heaven. Quiet, all of you! Can't you see it's Count Egmont? Pay your respects to Count Egmont!

EGMONT. You here too? What do you think you are doing? Citizen against citizen. Doesn't even the proximity of our royal Regent restrain you from this folly? Disperse, all of you. Go back to your work. It's a bad sign when you start celebrating on working days. What was it all about?

The tumult dies down gradually, they all surround Egmont.

CARPENTER. They're brawling for their privileges.

EGMONT. Which they will recklessly destroy in the end. And who are you? You seem honest people to me.

CARPENTER. That is our endeavour.

EGMONT. Your trades?

CARPENTER. Carpenter, and master of the Guild.

EGMONT. And you?

SOEST. Grocer.

EGMONT. You?

JETTER. Tailor?

EGMONT. I remember, you worked at the liveries of my men. Your name is Jetter.

JETTER. It is gracious of you to recall it.

EGMONT. I don't easily forget anyone I have seen and spoken to. . . . Now do what you can to restore order, all of you, and to maintain it. Your position is awkward enough as it is. Do not provoke the King even more, for it is he who is in power, and will show it too. A decent citizen, who earns an honest and industrious living, will always have as much freedom as he needs.

CARPENTER. Very true, sir. And that's the rub. The pickpockets, the drunkards, the idlers, by your lordship's leave, those are the ones who make trouble out of boredom and root for privileges out of hunger, and tell lies to the inquisitive and credulous, and start brawls for the sake of a tankard of beer that someone will stand them, though many thousands will suffer because of it. That's just what they want. We keep our houses and cupboards too well locked, so they'd like to drive us out with fire-brands.

EGMONT. You can rely on every kind of help. Measures have been taken to resist this evil in the most effective way. Stand fast against the alien doctrine, and never think that privileges can be secured by riots. Stay at home. Do not allow them to create disturbances in the streets. A few sensible people can do much.

Meanwhile the great crowd has dispersed.

CARPENTER. Thank you, Your Excellency, thank you for your good opinion of us. We shall do all we can.

Exit Egmont.

A gracious gentleman! A true Netherlander! Nothing Spanish about him.

JETTER. If only he were our Regent! It would be a pleasure to obey him.

SOEST. The King takes good care to prevent that. He always puts one of his people in that place.

JETTER. Did you notice his dress? It was in the latest fashion, the Spanish cut.

CARPENTER. A handsome gentleman.

JETTER. His neck would be a real feast to the executioner.

SOEST. Are you mad? What's got into your head?

JETTER. Yes, it's silly enough, the things that get into one's head. It's just what I happen to feel. When I see a fine, long neck, I can't help thinking at once: that's a good one for the axe. . . . All these cursed executions! One can't get them out of one's mind. When the young fellows go swimming and I see a bare back, at once I remember dozens that I've seen lashed by the cat-o'-nine-tails. If I meet a really fat paunch I can already see it roast on the stake. At night in my dreams I feel pinches in all my limbs. It's simply that one can't be carefree for one hour. Every sort of pleasure or jollity is soon forgotten; but the horrible apparitions might be branded on my forehead, they never leave me alone.

Egmont's House
Secretary at a table covered with papers; he rises restlessly.

SECRETARY. He still doesn't come, and I've been waiting these two hours pen in hand, papers in front of me; and it's the very day when I want to leave early. My feet itch to be gone; I can hardly bear the delay. "Be there on the stroke of the clock," he commanded before he went out. And now he doesn't come. There's so much to be done, I shan't be finished before midnight. True, he's quite capable of closing an eye. But I should still prefer him to be strict and then let me go at the proper time. One could arrange things in that case. It's two whole hours since he left the Regent; I wonder who it is he's button-holed on the way.

Enter Egmont.

EGMONT. Well, how is it?

SECRETARY. I am ready, and three messengers are waiting.

EGMONT. It seems I was out too long for your liking—to judge by the face you're making.

SECRETARY. I have been waiting for some considerable time to execute your orders. Here are the papers!

EGMONT. Donna Elvira will be angry with me when she hears that I've kept you.

SECRETARY. You are joking.

EGMONT. No, my dear fellow. There's no need to feel ashamed. You have shown the best taste. She's pretty enough, and I'm very glad that you have a lady friend in the Palace. What do the dispatches say?

SECRETARY. All kinds of things, but little that is pleasing.

EGMONT. In that case it's a good thing that we have no lack of pleasantness in our own house and needn't wait for it to come to us from outside. Are there many letters?

SECRETARY. Quite enough, and three messengers are waiting.

EGMONT. Tell me, then! Only what's essential.

SECRETARY. It's all essential.

EGMONT. One thing after another, then, but be quick about it.

SECRETARY. Captain Breda sends a report on the latest occurrences in Ghent and the surrounding district. Things are more quiet there, on the whole.

EGMONT. I suppose he mentions certain isolated cases of insolence and insubordination?

SECRETARY. Yes, there are incidents of that sort.

EGMONT. Well, spare me the particulars.

SECRETARY. They've arrested six more persons who tore down the statue of Our Lady at Verwich. He asks whether they are to be hanged like the others.

EGMONT. I'm tired of hangings. Let them be soundly whipped and released.

SECRETARY. There are two women among them. Are they to be whipped as well?

EGMONT. As for them, he is to let them off with a warning.

SECRETARY. Brink, of Breda's company, wants to marry. The captain hopes you will forbid it. There are so many women hanging around the regiment, he writes, that when we're on the march it looks less like a body of soldiers than a troop of gipsies.

EGMONT. Let it pass in Brink's case. He's a fine young fellow. He begged me most urgently before I left. But after him no one is to receive permission, much as it grieves me to refuse the poor devils their best amusement—and they've troubles enough as it is.

SECRETARY. Two of your men, Seter and Hart, have behaved abominably towards a girl, an innkeeper's daughter. They caught her when she was alone, and the girl had no means of defending herself.

EGMONT. If she's an honest girl, and they used force, they are to be birched for three days in succession, and if they have any possessions, Captain Breda is to confiscate enough of them to make provision for the girl.

SECRETARY. One of the foreign preachers entered Comines in secret, and was apprehended. He swears that he was on his way to France. According to orders he is to be beheaded.

EGMONT. They are to take him to the frontier quietly and assure him that he won't get away with it a second time.

SECRETARY. A dispatch from your Receiver-General. He writes that too little money is coming in, that he can hardly send the required sum within a week, that the disturbances have thrown everything into the greatest disorder.

EGMONT. The money must be sent. Let him find it how and where he can.

SECRETARY. He says he will do his best and will at last take action against Raymond, who has been your debtor for so long, and have him arrested.

EGMONT. But Raymond has promised to repay the money.

SECRETARY. Last time he gave himself a fortnight to do so.

EGMONT. Well, let him have another fortnight; after that they may go ahead and sue him.

SECRETARY. You are right. It's not incapacity, but ill will on his part. He will certainly take notice as soon as he sees that you're in earnest. . . . The Receiver-General goes on to say that he proposes to withhold half a month's pay from the old soldiers, widows, and some others to whom you have granted pensions. That would give him time to make arrangements, and they would have to manage as best they can.

EGMONT. How does he think they will manage? Those people need the money more than I do. He will refrain from witholding the pensions.

SECRETARY. What are your orders then? Where is he to obtain the funds?

EGMONT. That's his business, and I told him so in my previous dispatch.

SECRETARY. That's why he makes these proposals.

EGMONT. They are not good enough. He must think of other measures. He is to make other proposals, acceptable ones, and above all, he must find the money.

SECRETARY. I have left Count Oliva's letter here for you once more. Forgive me for drawing your attention to it again. More than anyone, the old gentleman deserves a full reply. It was your wish to write to him in person. Without doubt, he loves you like a father.

EGMONT. I haven't the time. And of all odious things, writing is the most odious to me. You're so good at imitating my handwriting, write it in my name. I'm expecting Orange. I haven't the time—and I would like his doubts to be answered by something truly comforting.

SECRETARY. Only tell me roughly what you think; I can then draft the reply and submit it to you. It shall be penned in such a way that it could pass for your handwriting in a court of law.

EGMONT. Give me the letter.

After glancing at it:

The dear, honest old man! I wonder were you as cautious as that when you were young? Did you never climb a fortress wall? In battle, did you remain at the back, as prudence demands? The loyal, solicitous old man! He wants me to live and be happy and does not feel that to live for safety's sake is to be dead already. Tell him not to be anxious; I shall act as I must and shall know how to protect myself. Let him use his influence at Court in my favour and be assured of my wholehearted gratitude.

SECRETARY. Is that all? He expects a great deal more.

EGMONT. What more should I say? If you want to be more long-winded, be so by all means. The crux is always the same: they want me to live in a way that is not my way. It's my good fortune to be cheerful, to take life easy, to travel light and fast, and I will not exchange these for the security of a tomb. It happens that I haven't a drop of blood in my veins that accords with the Spanish way of life; nor any desire to adapt my gait to the measured courtly cadence. Do I live only to take thought for my life? Should I forbid myself to enjoy the present moment, so as to be certain of the next? And consume the next moment too with cares and apprehensions?

SECRETARY. I beg you, sir, don't be so hard on the good gentleman. You are kind to everyone else. Only tell me a few agreeable words that will calm your noble friend. You see how careful he is, how delicately he touches you.

EGMONT. And yet he always touches this same string. He has long known how I hate these incessant admonitions. They serve only to unnerve me, never to help. And if I were a sleepwalker, balanced on the knife-edge of a roof top, would it be a friendly act to call out my name to warn me, wake me, and kill me? Let every man go his own way and look after himself.

SECRETARY. It is fitting for you not to be worried. But someone who knows and loves you——

EGMONT (*reading the letter*). There he goes again, repeating the old tales of what we did and said one evening in the easy expansiveness of sociability and wine! And of all the consequences and proofs drawn and dragged from them the whole length and breadth of the kingdom. Very well, we had cap and bells embroidered on the arms of our servants, and later had this badge of folly changed to a sheaf of arrows—an even more dangerous symbol to all those who looked for significance where there was none. There was this folly and that, conceived and born within a single moment of merriment; we were responsible for sending off a most noble band, furnished with beggars' scrips and a self-chosen sobriquet to remind the King of his duty with mock humility; are responsible for—what else? Is a carnival charade to be accounted high treason? Are we to be grudged the small coloured rags which our youthful exuberance, our excited imagination may wrap around the wretched bareness of our lives? If you take life too seriously, what is it worth? If the mornings do not rouse us to new pleasures, if the evenings leave us without the comfort of hope, is it worth while to dress and undress at all? Does the sun shine for me today so that I may ponder on what happened yesterday? So that I may fathom and link that which is not to be fathomed or linked—the destiny of a future day? Spare me these considerations, leave them to scholars and courtiers. Let these reflect and make plans, creep and crawl, arrive where they may, creep their way into what positions they can. If any of this is of any use to you, without turning your epistle into a book, you are welcome to it. The dear old man takes everything too seriously. His letter makes me think of a friend who has long held my hand in his and presses it once more before releasing it.

SECRETARY. Forgive me, but it makes a pedestrian dizzy to watch a traveller rush past him with such speed.

EGMONT. Enough, my dear fellow! Not another word! As though whipped by invisible spirits, the horses of the sun, Time's horses, run away with the light chariot of our destinies; and we have no choice but to grip the reins with resolute courage and, now to the right, now to the left, avert the wheels from a stone here, a precipice there. As for the end of the journey, who knows what it is? When we hardly remember where it began.

SECRETARY. Oh, sir!

EGMONT. I stand in a high and prominent place and must rise still higher. I have hope, courage, and strength. I have not yet attained the crest of my growth and when I *have* attained the highest point, I shall stand there unwavering, without fear. If I must fall, let a thunderbolt, a gale, even a false step hurl me down into the depths; I shall not be alone there but with thousands of good men. I have never disdained to stake my all in war for the slightest gain, like any decent soldier; and do you expect me to turn niggard when the prize is nothing less than the entire worth of a free life?

SECRETARY. Oh, sir! You do not know what you are saying. May God preserve you!

EGMONT. Collect your papers now. Orange is coming. Complete whatever is most urgent, so that the couriers can leave before the gates are shut. Other things can wait. Leave the letter to the Count till tomorrow. Don't fail to visit Elvira and give her my regards. Find out how the Regent is keeping; they say that she's not well, though she conceals it.

Exit secretary. Enter Orange.

EGMONT. Welcome, Orange. You seem somewhat constrained.

ORANGE. What do you say to our conversation with the Regent?

EGMONT. I saw nothing extraordinary in her manner of receiving us. It wasn't the first time I have seen her in that state. I had the impression that she was unwell.

ORANGE. Didn't you observe that she was more reticent? At first, she wanted to be calm and express her approval of our conduct during the new upris-ing of the mob. Later, she hinted that this could easily appear in a false light, then diverted the conversation to her usual topic: that her amiable, benevolent disposition, her friendship for us Netherlanders have never been duly appreciated, that we have taken it too much for granted, that none of her efforts seemed to lead to the desired results, that she might well grow weary in the end and the King resort to very different measures. Did you note all this?

EGMONT. No, not all of it; I was thinking of something different at the time. She is a woman, dear Orange, and women always wish that everyone will meekly creep under their gentle yoke, that every Hercules will doff his lion's skin and join their knitting group; that, because they desire peace, the ferment that seizes a people, the tempest that mighty rivals raise among themselves, can be soothed by a kind word, and that the most hostile ele-ments will lie down together at their feet in gentle concord. That is the case with her also. And since she cannot bring about this state, she has no alternative but to become ill-tempered, to complain of ingratitude and lack of wisdom, to threaten us with terrible consequences and to threaten—that she will leave us!

ORANGE. And don't you believe that this time she will carry out her threat?

EGMONT. Never! How often I've seen her in her travelling clothes! Where could she go? Here she is Governor, Queen. Do you suppose that she relishes the thought of going into insignificant retirement at her brother's court? Or of going to Italy and burdening herself with the old family matters?

ORANGE. People think her incapable of such a decision because they have seen her hesitate and withdraw. And yet she has it in her; new circumstances drive her to the long-delayed resolution. What if she did go? And the King sent someone else?

EGMONT. Well, he would come, and would find plenty of things to occupy him. He would come with great plans, projects, and ideas of how to arrange, control, and hold together all things; and would be struggling with this trifle today, that trifle tomorrow, would come up against this obstruction the day after, spend a month on preparations and schemes, another on being disappointed with undertakings that have failed, half a year on the troubles caused by a single Province. For him too time would pass, his head would grow giddy, and one thing follow another as before, so that he would have cause to thank God if he succeeded in keeping his ship off the rocks instead of navigating great oceans along a charted course.

ORANGE. But what if someone advised the King to make an experiment?

EGMONT. And what might that be?

ORANGE. To see what the torso would do without a head.

EGMONT. What do you mean?

ORANGE. Egmont, for many years now I have been deeply concerned with all our affairs, my head always bent over them as over a chessboard, and I do not regard any move on the other side as insignificant. And just as idle persons enquire with the greatest care into the secrets of nature, so I consider it the duty, the vocation, of a prince to know the views and strategy of all parties. I have cause to fear an eruption. The King has long acted according to certain principles; he sees that these are inadequate; what can be more likely than that he will try other means?

EGMONT. That's not my opinion. When one grows old and has tried so many things and the world still refuses to become a tidy place, surely one puts up with it in the end.

ORANGE. There's one thing he hasn't tried.

EGMONT. Well?

ORANGE. To spare the people and destroy the princes.

EGMONT. An old fear, and widespread. It's not worth worrying about.

ORANGE. Once it was a worry; gradually it became a probability to me; finally, it's become a certainty.

EGMONT. And has the King any subjects more loyal than ourselves?

ORANGE. We serve him in our fashion; and we can admit to each other that we know well how to balance the King's rights against ours.

EGMONT. Who wouldn't? We are his subjects and pay him such tribute as is due to him.

ORANGE. But what if he claimed *more*, and called disloyalty what we call insisting on our rights?

EGMONT. We shall be able to defend ourselves. Let him convoke the Knights of the Golden Fleece; we shall submit to their judgement.

ORANGE. And what if the verdict precedes the trial, the punishment precedes the verdict?

EGMONT. That would be an injustice of which Philip could never be guilty, and an act of folly of which, in my view, both he and his counsellors are incapable——

ORANGE. And what if they did prove to be unjust and foolish?

EGMONT. No, Orange, it's impossible. Who would dare to lay hands on us? ... To arrest us would be a vain and useless act. No, they do not dare to raise the banner of tyranny so high. The gust of wind that would bear this news across the country would fan an enormous blaze. And what would be the point of it? It is not the King alone who has the right to judge and condemn. And would they destroy us in secret, like a band of vulgar assassins? They cannot even think of such a thing. A terrible pact would unite the whole people at once. Undying hatred and eternal separation from the Spanish name would violently declare themselves.

ORANGE. In that case the fire would rage over our graves, and the blood of our enemies would flow as an idle expiatory offering. Let us take thought to prevent it, Egmont.

EGMONT. But how can we?

ORANGE. Alba is on his way.

EGMONT. I don't believe it.

ORANGE. I know it.

EGMONT. The Regent would not hear of it.

ORANGE. Another reason for my conviction. The Regent will yield her place to him. I know his murderous disposition, and he will bring an army with him.

EGMONT. To harass the Provinces once more? The people will grow most unruly.

ORANGE. They will take care of the people's heads.

EGMONT. No, no, I say.

ORANGE. Let us leave, each for his Province. There we shall reinforce ourselves. He will not begin with a show of brute force.

EGMONT. Must we not be there to welcome him when he comes?

ORANGE. We shall procrastinate.

EGMONT. And if he demands our presence at his arrival, in the King's name?

ORANGE. We shall look for evasions.

EGMONT. And if he presses us?

ORANGE. We shall excuse ourselves.

EGMONT. And if he insists on it?

ORANGE. We shall refuse all the more firmly.

EGMONT. And war will have been declared, and we shall be rebels. Orange, don't let your cleverness mislead you; I know that it isn't fear that moves you to retreat. Consider the implications of this step.

ORANGE. I have considered them.

EGMONT. Consider what you will be guilty of, if you are wrong: of the most ruinous war that has ever laid waste a country. Your refusal will be the signal which calls all the provinces to arms at once; it will serve to justify every act of cruelty for which Spain has never lacked anything but a pretext. What we have long kept down with the utmost difficulty, you will rouse up with a single call to the most frightful turmoil. Think of the cities, the nobles, the people; of commerce, agriculture, the trades. And think of the destruction, the slaughter! . . . True, in the field the soldier looks calmly upon his dying comrade; but it is the corpses of citizens, children, young women which will float down the rivers to where you stand. So that you will be filled with horror, no longer knowing whose cause you are defending, since those are perishing for whose freedom you took arms. And how will you feel when you have to tell yourself: it was for my safety that I took them?

ORANGE. We are not individual men, Egmont. If it is fitting for us to sacrifice ourselves for the sake of thousands, it is fitting too to spare ourselves for the sake of thousands.

EGMONT. The man who spares himself must become suspicious of himself.

ORANGE. The man who knows himself can advance or retreat with confidence.

EGMONT. The evil which you fear becomes a certainty by your deed.

ORANGE. It is prudent and bold to meet the inevitable disaster.

EGMONT. In a peril so great the slightest hope should be fostered.

ORANGE. There is no room left for the lightest manoeuvre on our part; the abyss lies right in front of us.

EGMONT. Is the King's favour so narrow a ledge?

ORANGE. Not so narrow, but slippery.

EGMONT. By God! You do him an injustice. I will not suffer anyone to think ill of him. He is Charles's son and incapable of baseness.

ORANGE. Kings are never guilty of baseness.

EGMONT. You should get to know him better.

ORANGE. It is that very knowledge which advises us not to await the outcome of this dangerous test.

EGMONT. No test is dangerous if one has the necessary courage.

ORANGE. You are getting excited, Egmont.

EGMONT. I must see with my own eyes.

ORANGE. Oh, if only you would see with mine for once! My dear friend, because your eyes are open you think that you see. I am going! Wait for Alba's arrival if you must, and God be with you! Perhaps my refusal will save you. Perhaps the dragon will think it has caught nothing if it cannot devour both of us at once. Perhaps it will hesitate, so as to be more sure of success, and perhaps by then you will see the matter in its true light. But be quick then! Quick as lightning! Save yourself. Save yourself, my friend. Farewell. Let nothing escape your watchfulness: the size of his army, how he occupies the city, how much power the Regent retains, how well your friends are prepared. Keep me informed. . . . Egmont—

EGMONT. Well?

ORANGE (taking his hand). Let me persuade you. Come with me!

EGMONT. What, Orange, tears in *your* eyes?

ORANGE. To weep for one who is lost is not unmanly.

EGMONT. You regard me as lost?

ORANGE. You are. Think again! You have only the briefest of respites. Farewell.

Exit.

EGMONT (*alone*). Strange that other people's thoughts have such influence on us! It would never have occurred to me, and this man's apprehensions have infected me . . . Away! It's an alien drop in my blood. Let my sound nature throw it out again! And there's one kind remedy still to bathe away the pensive wrinkles on my brow.

ACT III

The Regent's Palace
Margaret of Parma.

REGENT. I should have guessed it. Oh, if one's days are spent in toil and stress, one always thinks one is doing one's utmost; and the person who looks on from afar and gives orders believes he demands only what is possible. . . . Oh, these Kings! . . . I should never have thought that it could grieve me so. It is so pleasant to rule! . . . And to abdicate? . . . I cannot think how my father could do it; and yet I shall do it also.

Machiavelli appears in the background.

REGENT. Come closer, Machiavelli! I am just thinking about my brother's letter.

MACHIAVELLI. And may I know what it contains?

REGENT. As much tender attention to me as solicitude for his states. He commends the steadfastness, industry, and loyalty with which I have hitherto upheld the rights of His Majesty in these Provinces. He pities me because the unruly people is causing me so much trouble now. He is so entirely convinced of the profundity of my insight, so extraordinarily pleased with the prudence of my conduct, that I must almost say: the letter is too well written for a King, certainly for a brother.

MACHIAVELLI. This is not the first time he has informed you of his well-deserved satisfaction.

REGENT. But the first time it is a mere figure of rhetoric.

MACHIAVELLI. I don't follow you.

REGENT. You will. For after this induction, he expresses the opinion that without a bodyguard, without a small army, I shall always cut a bad figure here. We were wrong, he says, to withdraw our soldiers from the Provinces because the population complained. An occupation force, he believes, which loads down the citizen's neck prevents him by its weight from indulging in high leaps.

MACHIAVELLI. It would have a most unsettling effect on the people's state of mind.

REGENT. The King, however, is of the opinion——Are you listening? He is of the opinion that an efficient general, one who does not listen to reason, would very soon put the people and nobility, citizens and peasantry, in their place; and is therefore sending a powerful force commanded—by the Duke of Alba.

MACHIAVELLI. Alba?

REGENT. That surprises you?

MACHIAVELLI. You say he is sending. I suppose he asks you whether he should send.

REGENT. The King does not ask, he sends.

MACHIAVELLI. In that case you will have an experienced military man in your service.

REGENT. In my service? Speak your mind, Machiavelli!

MACHIAVELLI. I am anxious not to anticipate, madam.

REGENT. And I am anxious to disguise the truth! It is very painful to me, very painful. I wish my brother had said what he thinks instead of sending formal epistles which a Secretary of State has drawn up.

MACHIAVELLI. Should we not try to understand . . .

REGENT. But I know them by heart. They want the place cleaned and swept; and since they do not act themselves, they lend their trust to any man who appears broom in hand. Oh, I can see the King and his Council as clearly as if they were embroidered on this tapestry.

MACHIAVELLI. So vividly?

REGENT. Not a single feature is missing. There are good men among them. Honest Rodrick, who is so experienced and moderate, does not aim too high and yet lets nothing fall too low. Honest Alonzo, hard-working Freneda, solid Las Vagas and a few others who will cooperate when the good party comes into power. But on the other side there sits the hollow-eyed Toledan with the brazen brow and the deep, fiery glance, mumbling between his teeth of female softheartedness, misplaced indulgence, and that women may sit a horse already broken, but make poor equerries themselves, and other such pleasantries to which I once had to listen in the company of the political gentlemen.

MACHIAVELLI. You have chosen a good palette for the portrait.

REGENT. Admit it, Machiavelli, of all the colours and shades with which I could choose to paint no tone is as yellow-brown, as gall-black as the colour of Alba's face or as the colour with which he paints. To him, everyone is a blasphemer, a traitor to the King; for on that score he can have them all racked, burnt, hanged, drawn and quartered. . . . The good I have done here probably looks like nothing from a distance, simply because it is good. So he will seize on every caprice long past, recall every disturbance long ago put down; and the King will have such a vision of mutiny, rebellion, and recklessness that he will think the people here devour one another, when we have long forgotten some fleeting, passing misconduct of a nation still rough. Then he will conceive a deep, heartfelt hatred for these poor people; they will seem repulsive to him, indeed like beasts and monsters; he will look around for fire and sword, imagining that that is how to tame men.

MACHIAVELLI. I think you exaggerate a little and take the whole matter too seriously. After all, you will be Regent still.

REGENT. Oh, I know all about that. He will bring a royal directive. I have grown old enough in affairs of state to know how one displaces a person without depriving him of his rank and title. First he will bring a royal directive, which will be twisted and vague; he will make changes all around him, for he has the power, and if I complain he will use the pretext of a secret directive; if I ask to see it, he will prevaricate; if I insist, he will show me a document that contains something quite different; and if I am still not satisfied, he will do no more than he would if I were speaking. Meanwhile he will have done what I fear and irrevocably averted what I wish.

MACHIAVELLI. I wish I could contradict you.

REGENT. What I have calmed with unspeakable patience, he will stir up again by hardheartedness and cruelty. I shall see my work perish before my very eyes and bear the blame for his acts into the bargain.

MACHIAVELLI. Do not anticipate, Your Highness.

REGENT. Well, I still have enough self-control to be quiet. Let him come, I shall make way for him with good grace before he pushes me out.

MACHIAVELLI. And you will take this grave step with such alacrity?

REGENT. It's more difficult for me than you think. If one is accustomed to rule, if it was given to one in youth to hold the fate of thousands daily in one's hand, one descends from the throne as into a grave. But sooner that than remain like a spectre among the living and with hollow gestures lay claim to a place which another has inherited, possesses, and enjoys.

Clare's House
Clare and Mother.

MOTHER. Never have I seen such love as Brackenburg's; I thought it was only to be found in legends about heroes.

CLARE (*walks up and down the room, humming a song with closed lips*).

Happy alone
Is whom love has in thrall.

MOTHER. He suspects how you stand with Egmont. And I think that if you gave him a little encouragement, if you wanted him to, he would still marry you.

CLARE (*sings*).

Gladdened
And saddened
And troubled in vain,
Longing
And thronging
With wavering pain,
Raised up to heaven,
The deeper to fall,
Happy alone
Is whom love has in thrall.

MOTHER. Oh, leave off the "by-low, lie-low."

CLARE. No, don't say anything against it. It's a powerful song. More than once I've lulled a big child to sleep with it.

MOTHER. You can't think of anything except your love. If only you wouldn't forget everything because of that *one* thing. You should have some respect for Brackenburg, I tell you. He might still make you happy one day.

CLARE. Brackenburg?

MOTHER. Oh yes, there will come a time. . . . You children foresee nothing and will not listen to our experience. Youth and true love, it all comes to an end; and there comes a time when one gives thanks to God for somewhere to lay one's head.

CLARE (*shudders, keeps silent, and then bursts out*). Mother, let the time come then, like death. To think of it in advance is horrible! And what if it does come! If we must—then—then we shall face up to it as best we can. To think of losing Egmont!

In tears.

No, it's impossible, quite impossible.

Enter Egmont in a riding cloak, his hat pressed down onto his face.

EGMONT. Clare!

CLARE (*utters a scream, totters*). Egmont!

She runs to him.

Egmont!

She embraces him and rests her head on his shoulder.

Oh, my dear, good, darling Egmont! So you've come. You're here!

EGMONT. Good evening, Mother.

MOTHER. Welcome to our house, Your Lordship. My little girl nearly pined away because of your long absence; she spent the whole day, as usual, talking and singing about you.

EGMONT. You'll give me some supper, won't you?

MOTHER. You do us too much honour. If only we had something to offer you.

CLARE. Of course we have. Don't worry about it, Mother; I've made all the arrangements already and prepared something. But don't let me down, Mother.

MOTHER. It's paltry enough.

CLARE. Just be patient. And besides, I say to myself: when he's with me, I'm not in the least hungry, so he shouldn't have too big an appetite when I'm with him.

EGMONT. Do you think so?

Clare stamps her foot and turns her back on him in a pique.

EGMONT. What's the matter with you?

CLARE. Oh, you're so chilly today. You haven't offered to kiss me yet. Why do you keep your arms wrapped in your cloak like a new-born baby? It isn't right for a soldier or a lover to keep his arms wrapped up.

EGMONT. At times it is, sweetheart, at times. When the soldier is on his guard and trying to get the better of his enemy by stealth, he pulls himself together, puts his arms around himself, and waits till his plan of action has matured. And a lover . . .

MOTHER. Won't you sit down, make yourself comfortable? I must go to the kitchen. Clare forgets everything when you're here. You will have to make do with what we have to offer.

EGMONT. Your good will is the best spice.

Exit Mother.

CLARE. And what would you call my love?

EGMONT. Anything you like.

CLARE. Compare it to something, if you have the heart.

EGMONT. Well, first of all . . .

He throws off his cloak and stands there splendidly dressed.

CLARE. Goodness!

EGMONT. Now my arms are free.

He hugs her.

CLARE. Stop it! You'll spoil your appearance.

She steps back.

How splendid it is! Now I mustn't touch you.

EGMONT. Are you satisfied? I promised I'd come dressed in Spanish fashion one day.

CLARE. I never asked you again. I thought you didn't want to. . . . Oh, and the Golden Fleece!

EGMONT. Well, there it is for you.

CLARE. And did the Emperor hang it around your neck?

EGMONT. Yes, child. And the chain and the pendant grant the most noble liberties to the man who wears them. There is no one on earth who has the right to judge my actions other than the Grand Master of the Order, together with the assembled company of Knights.

CLARE. Oh, you could let the whole world stand in judgement over you! The velvet is too lovely for words, and the gold thread! And the embroidery! . . . One doesn't know where to begin.

EGMONT. Look your fill.

CLARE. And the Golden Fleece! You told me the story and said it was a symbol of all that is great and precious, only to be earned and won by the most strenuous endeavours. It is very precious—I can compare it to your love. I wear it next to my heart as well—and then . . .

EGMONT. What were you going to say?

CLARE. And then the comparison doesn't apply.

EGMONT. How do you mean?

CLARE. Because I haven't won your love by strenuous endeavours; I haven't earned it.

EGMONT. In love it's different. You have earned it because you don't try to win it, and usually only those people get it who don't chase after it.

CLARE. Did you derive that conclusion from yourself? Did you make this proud observation about yourself? You, whom all the people loves?

EGMONT. If only I'd done something for them! If only I could do something for them. It is their kind will to love me.

CLARE. I suppose you saw the Regent today?

EGMONT. I did.

CLARE. Are you on good terms with her?

EGMONT. It looks that way. We are amiable and helpful to each other.

CLARE. And in your heart?

EGMONT. I wish her well. Each of us has his own aims. But that is neither here nor there. She's an excellent woman, knows her men, and would see deep enough even if she weren't suspicious. I cause her a great deal of trouble because she is always looking for secret motives behind my conduct, and I have none.

CLARE. None at all?

EGMONT. Well, yes. A few little reservations. Every wine leaves a deposit of tartar if it's left long enough in the barrel. But Orange provides better entertainment for her all the same, and sets her new puzzles incessantly. He has made people believe that he always harbours some secret project; and so now she is always looking at his forehead wondering what he's thinking, or at his steps, wondering where he may be directing them.

CLARE. Does she conceal her motives?

EGMONT. She's the Regent. What do you expect?

CLARE. Forgive me. What I meant to ask was: is she deceitful?

EGMONT. No more and no less than anyone who wishes to attain his ends.

CLARE. I could never be at home in the great world. But then she has a masculine mind; she's a different kind of woman from us seamstresses and cooks. She is noble, brave, resolute.

EGMONT. Yes, as long as things are not too topsy-turvy. This time she's not so sure of herself.

CLARE. How so?

EGMONT. She has a little moustache too, on her upper lip, and occasional attacks of gout. A real Amazon.

CLARE. A majestic woman! I should be afraid to enter her presence.

EGMONT. You're not usually so shy. But then it wouldn't be fear, only girlish modesty.

Clare casts down her eyes, takes his hand, and nestles against him.

EGMONT. I understand you, my dear. You can raise your eyes.

CLARE. Let me be silent. Let me hold you. Let me look into your eyes: find everything in them, comfort and hope and joy and grief.

She puts her arms around him and looks at him.

Tell me. Tell me. I don't understand. Are you Egmont? Count Egmont, the great Egmont who raises such an ado, whom the newspapers write about, whom the Provinces adore?

EGMONT. No, my little Clare, I am not.

CLARE. What?

EGMONT. You see—Clare! Let me sit down.

He sits down, she kneels in front of him on a stool, puts her arms on his knees, and looks at him.

That Egmont is an ill-tempered, stiff, cold Egmont, who has to keep up appearances, now make this face, now that; who is tormented, misunderstood, entangled, while other people think he is gay and carefree; loved by a people that does not know its own mind, honoured and carried aloft by a mob for which there is no help; surrounded by friends on whom he must not rely; closely watched by men who desire to harm him in every possible way; toiling and striving, often aimlessly, nearly always unrewarded. . . . Oh, let me say no more about him! How he fares, how he feels! But this one, Clare, this one is calm, candid, happy, beloved and understood by the best of hearts, which he too understands wholly and presses to him with complete love and trust.

He embraces her.

That is *your* Egmont.

CLARE. Then let me die. The world has no joys beyond these!

ACT IV

A Street
Jetter. Carpenter.

JETTER. Hey, there. Hush. Hey, there, neighbour, a word with you!

CARPENTER. Be on your way and keep quiet.

JETTER. Only one word. No news?

CARPENTER. None, except that we've been forbidden to talk of the news.

JETTER. What do you mean?

CARPENTER. Come close to the wall of this house. Keep your eyes and ears open. As soon as he arrived the Duke of Alba issued an order to the effect that if two or three are found talking together in the street they will be declared guilty of high treason without examination or trial.

JETTER. Oh, dreadful!

CARPENTER. The penalty for discussing affairs of state is life imprisonment.

JETTER. All our liberty lost!

CARPENTER. And on pain of death no one is to express disapproval of the government's actions.

JETTER. And our heads likely to be lost as well!

CARPENTER. And great rewards will be promised to induce fathers, mothers, children, relations, friends, servants to reveal what is going on in the home to a special court appointed for that purpose.

JETTER. Let's go home.

CARPENTER. And those who obey are promised that they will suffer no harm in their persons or property.

JETTER. How gracious of them! Didn't I feel aggrieved as soon as the Duke entered our city? Ever since, I've felt as though the sky were covered with black crêpe and hung down so low that one has to bend down to avoid knocking one's head against it.

CARPENTER. And how did you like his soldiers? They're a different kettle of fish to the ones we're used to. Don't you agree?

JETTER. Disgusting! It freezes your marrow to see a body of them march down the street. Straight as posts, their eyes glued on the next man's back, not a single man out of step. And when they're on guard duty and you pass by, you feel as though they could see right into your head, and they look so stiff and grumpy that you seem to see a taskmaster at every corner. They made me feel ill. Our militia, at least, was a gay lot. They took liberties, stood about with legs straddled, wore their hats over one eye, lived, and let live; but those fellows are like machines with a devil inside.

CARPENTER. If one of them calls out "Halt!" and jumps to the alert, do you think one would stop?

JETTER. It would be the death of me at once!

CARPENTER. Let's go home.

JETTER. No good will come of this. Good-bye.

Enter Soest.

SOEST. Friends! Comrades!

CARPENTER. Quiet. Don't detain us.

SOEST. Have you heard?

JETTER. Only too much!

SOEST. The Regent has left.

JETTER. Now God have mercy on us!

CARPENTER. She was our only hope.

SOEST. Suddenly, and in secret. She didn't get on with the Duke; she sent a message to the nobles to say she will return. No one believes it.

CARPENTER. May God forgive the nobles for allowing this new scourge to descend on our backs. They could have prevented it. All our privileges are lost.

JETTER. Not a word about privileges, for God's sake. I can smell the powder of a firing squad. The sun refuses to rise, the mists reek of rotten flesh.

SOEST. Orange is gone too.

CARPENTER. That means we've been left to our fate.

SOEST. Count Egmont is still with us.

JETTER. Thank God for that. May all the saints give him strength, so that he'll do his best; he is the only one who can help us.

Enter Vansen.

VANSEN. Well, fancy that. A few citizens who haven't yet crept away into their dens!

JETTER. Do us a favour: be on your way.

VANSEN. You're not very polite.

CARPENTER. This isn't the time for fine phrases. Are you looking for trouble again? Has your back healed already?

VANSEN. Never ask a soldier about his wounds. If I couldn't take a hiding at times, I shouldn't have got anywhere.

JETTER. Things may become more serious.

VANSEN. It seems that the approaching thunderstorm is making all your limbs feel miserably tired.

CARPENTER. If you don't keep quiet your limbs will soon start moving in a different direction.

VANSEN. Poor little mice, to fall into despair, just because the master of the house has got himself a new cat! Things have changed a bit, that's all; but we shall go about our business just as we did before, never you worry!

CARPENTER. You're a loud-mouthed good-for-nothing.

VANSEN. As for you, brother nitwit, let the Duke do his worst. The old tomcat looks as if he's been eating devils instead of mice, and now he's got indigestion as a result. Just let him get on with it; he has to eat, drink, and sleep like the rest of us. I'm not at all anxious about us, if only we take our time. At the start all goes easily; but later he too will find out that it's more pleasant to live in the larder where the bacon is stored, and to rest at night than to stalk a few mice in the loft, with nothing but fruit all around. Just keep calm. I know what governors are like.

CARPENTER. There's no telling what a fellow like that will blurt out. If I'd ever said anything like it, I shouldn't feel safe for a minute.

VANSEN. Don't you worry, God in heaven doesn't hear anything about worms of your sort, let alone the Regent.

JETTER. Filthy blasphemer!

VANSEN. I know of some people for whom it would be a lot better if they acted the hero less and had a little more discretion instead.

CARPENTER. What do you mean by that?

VANSEN. Hmm! The Count is what I mean.

JETTER. Egmont? What has he got to fear?

VANSEN. I'm a poor devil and could live a whole year on what he loses in one night. And yet he'd do well to give me his income for a whole year if he could have my head for a quarter of an hour.

JETTER. That's what you think. Egmont's got more sense in his hair than you have in your brain.

VANSEN. Say what you like. But he hasn't got more subtlety. It's the great lords who're the first to deceive themselves. He shouldn't be so trusting.

JETTER. Stuff and nonsense. A nobleman like Egmont?

VANSEN. That's just it. Just because he isn't a tailor.

JETTER. Dirty slanderer!

VANSEN. What I wish him is to have your courage just for an hour, so that it could trouble him and make him itch till it drives him out of town.

JETTER. You speak like a fool; he's as safe as a star in the sky.

VANSEN. Have you never seen one shoot off? . . . Gone in a jiffy.

CARPENTER. Who could harm him?

VANSEN. Who could harm him? Why, do you think you could prevent it? Are you going to start a rebellion when they arrest him?

JETTER. Oh!

VANSEN. Would you risk your skin for his sake?

SOEST. Eh!

VANSEN (*imitating them*). Ee, ah, oo! Run through the whole alphabet to express your surprise! That's how it is and how it will be. God have mercy on him.

JETTER. I'm shocked by your impudence. Such a noble, righteous man——
And you talk of danger?

VANSEN. It's the knave who does well for himself everywhere. On the stool of repentance he makes a fool of the judge; on the judgement seat he delights in making a criminal out of the prosecutor. I once had to copy one of those documents, when the Chief of Police received a load of praise and money from Court because he'd made a self-confessed rascal out of some honest soul they wanted out of the way.

CARPENTER. That's another arrant lie! How can they find any evidence, if the man is innocent?

VANSEN. Oh, my poor sparrow-brain! When there's nothing to be read out of the evidence, they read something into it. Honesty makes you rash—it can make you stubborn too. So they start by asking harmless questions, and the accused is proud of his innocence, as they call it, so he blurts out everything which a sensible man would conceal. Then the prosecutor makes new questions out of the answers and carefully notes any little contradiction that may appear. That's where he attaches his rope, and if the poor fool allows himself to be convinced that he's said too much here, too little there, and perhaps withheld some piece of evidence for no reason at all; or if, in the end, he allows them to frighten him—well, in that case, they're well on the way. And I assure you that the beggar women who pick rags out of the rubbish bins are not more thorough than one of those rogue-makers when he's set his heart on patching together a straw-and-rag scarecrow out of every little crooked, twisted, rumpled, hidden, familiar, denied indication and circumstance, if only to be able to hang his victim in effigy. And the poor fellow has cause to be thankful if he lives to see himself hanged.

JETTER. No one can say he hasn't a fluent tongue in his head.

CARPENTER. That kind of talk may work with flies. But wasps laugh at the yarns you spin.

VANSEN. After the spiders have gone. Look, that tall Duke looks just like one of your garden spiders; not one of the fat-bellied ones—they're less dangerous—but one of the long-legged kind with small bodies that don't get fat with eating and spin very fine threads, though all the tougher for that.

JETTER. Egmont is a Knight of the Golden Fleece: who would dare to lay hands on him? He can only be judged by those of his own kind, by the entire Order. It's your foul mouth and your bad conscience that make you talk such gibberish.

VANSEN. What makes you think I don't wish him well? I've nothing against him. He's an excellent gentleman. He let off a couple of my best friends, who would otherwise have been hanged by now, with a sound whipping. Now, off with you! Get along! That's my advice to you now. I can see a new patrol just starting their rounds over there, and they don't look as if they're going to drink our health. We mustn't be in too much of a hurry, but stand and look on for a while. I've a couple of nieces and an old crony who keeps a tavern; if those men aren't tame by the time they've tasted their wares, they must be as tough as wolves.

Culenburg Palace. The Duke of Alba's Residence
Silva and Gomez meet.

SILVA. Have you carried out the Duke's instructions?

GOMEZ. Punctiliously. All the daily patrols have been ordered to appear at the appointed time at the different places I have detailed to them; meanwhile, they will patrol the town as usual to maintain the peace. None knows about any of the others; each patrol thinks that the order concerns only its own men, and the cordon can be closed in a moment when necessary so that every approach to the Palace will be cut off. Do you know the reason for this order?

SILVA. I am accustomed to obey orders without questioning them. And who is easier to obey than the Duke, since the outcome will soon prove that his instructions were judicious?

GOMEZ. Oh yes, of course. And I am not surprised to find that you're growing as uncommunicative and monosyllabic as he is since you have to attend him all the time. It seems strange to me, since I am used to the lighter Italian etiquette. My loyalty and obedience are the same as ever; but I have got into the habit of chattering and arguing. As for you people, you keep silent all the time and never relax. The Duke seems to me like an iron tower without any door to which his staff have the key. The other day I heard him remark at table about some carefree, affable fellow that he was like a bad tavern with a sign advertising brandy to attract idlers, beggars, and thieves.

SILVA. And did he not lead us in silence to this place?

GOMEZ. There's no denying that. Certainly, anyone who witnessed his skill in moving the army here from Italy has seen something worth remembering. How he twined his way, as it were, through friend and foe, through the French, the King's men, and the heretics, through the Swiss and their confederates, maintained the strictest discipline and succeeded in conducting so potentially dangerous a movement with such ease and without giving offence to anyone. We have certainly seen something and learnt something.

SILVA. And here too. Isn't everything peaceful and quiet, as though there had never been any uprising?

GOMEZ. Well, it was quiet in most places when we arrived.

SILVA. The Provinces are a great deal calmer than they were; and if anyone does move now, it's in order to flee. But he will soon put an end to that as well, if I'm not mistaken.

GOMEZ. The King will be pleased with him as never before.

SILVA. And nothing remains more urgent for us than to be sure of *his* pleasure. If the King should come here, the Duke and anyone whom he commends will doubtless be generously rewarded.

GOMEZ. Do you think that the King will come?

SILVA. The many preparations that are being made would suggest that it is very likely.

GOMEZ. They don't convince me.

SILVA. In that case, at least refrain from evincing an opinion on the matter. For if it is not the King's intention to come, what is certain is that we are intended to believe so.

Enter Ferdinand, Alba's natural son.

FERDINAND. Has my father not come out?

SILVA. We are waiting for him.

FERDINAND. The princes will soon be here.

GOMEZ. Are they expected today?

FERDINAND. Orange and Egmont.

GOMEZ (*softly to Silva*). Something has dawned on me.

SILVA. Then keep it to yourself!

Enter the Duke of Alba. As he enters and comes forward, the others step back.

ALBA. Gomez!

GOMEZ (*comes forward*). My Lord!

ALBA. You have instructed and detailed the guards?

GOMEZ. With the utmost precision. The daily patrols——

ALBA. Very well. You will wait in the gallery. Silva will inform you of the exact moment when you will call them in and occupy the approaches to the Palace. You know the rest.

GOMEZ. Yes.

Exit.

ALBA. Silva!

SILVA. Here I am.

ALBA. Everything I have valued in you—courage, determination, promptness in the execution of orders—all these you must show today.

SILVA. I thank you for giving me the opportunity to prove that I am unchanged.

ALBA. As soon as the princes have entered my cabinet, lose no time in arresting Egmont's private secretary. You have made all the necessary arrangements to seize the other persons who have been indicated?

SILVA. Rely on us! Their fate, like a well-calculated eclipse of the sun, will meet them punctually and terribly.

ALBA. You have kept all their movements under observation?

SILVA. Not one has escaped me. Especially not Egmont's. He is the only one whose conduct has not changed since your arrival. Spends the whole day trying out one horse after another, invites guests, is always merry and amusing at table, plays at dice, shoots, and creeps to his sweetheart at night. Whereas the others have made a distinct break in their way of life. They stay at home; the fronts of their houses look like those of men who are ill in bed.

ALBA. Hurry, therefore, before they recover against our will.

SILVA. I shall catch them. At your command we shall overwhelm them with official honours. Panic will seize them. Diplomatically they offer us cautious thanks and feel that it would be wisest to flee; not one of them dares to move one step; they hesitate, cannot get together; and his social sense prevents each one from acting boldly for himself. They would like to avoid all suspicion and yet they become more and more suspect. With the greatest pleasure I foresee the complete success of your stratagem.

ALBA. I take pleasure only in the accomplished act . . . and not easily even in that, for there always remains something to give us cause for thought and anxiety. Fortune, in her obstinate way, may insist on conferring glory on what is base and worthless, and on dishonouring well-considered deeds with a base outcome. Wait here till the princes come, then give Gomez the order to occupy the streets and at once proceed in person to arrest Egmont's secretary and the others that have been indicated to you. When you have done so, come here and report it to my son, so that he may convey the news to me in the cabinet.

SILVA. I hope to have the honour of attending on you tonight.

Alba goes to his son, who has been standing on the gallery.

SILVA. I dare not tell him, but I am losing hope. I fear it will not be as he thinks. I see spirits who, silent and pensive, weigh the destiny of princes and many thousands of men on black scales. Slowly the pointer vacillates, the judges seem deep in thought. At last this scale goes down, that one rises at the breath of obstinate Fortune, and the verdict has been pronounced.

Exit.

ALBA (*stepping forward with Ferdinand*). What was your impression of the city?

FERDINAND. Everything has become very quiet. As though to pass the time of day I rode up and down the streets. Your well-distributed patrols keep their fear so tense that no one dares to breathe a word. The city looks like a field when a thunderstorm flashes in the distance: one doesn't see a bird or an animal that isn't scurrying off to seek shelter.

ALBA. Is that all you saw and encountered?

FERDINAND. Egmont came riding into the market-place with some men. We exchanged greetings; he had an unruly horse, which I was compelled to praise. "Let us lose no time in breaking in horses, we shall need them soon!"

he called out to me. He said we should meet again this very day, as he was coming at your request to confer with you.

ALBA. He will meet you again.

FERDINAND. Of all the noblemen I know here I like him best. It seems that we shall be friends.

ALBA. You are still too impetuous and incautious; you always remind me of your mother's fecklessness which drove her unconditionally into my arms. More than once appearances have led you to enter into dangerous relationships precipitately.

FERDINAND. You will find me flexible.

ALBA. Because of your young blood I forgive these impulsive affections, this heedless gaiety. Only never forget what is the work I was called to accomplish, nor what part in it I wish to entrust to you.

FERDINAND. Admonish me and do not spare me, where you think it necessary.

ALBA (*after a pause*). My son!

FERDINAND. My father!

ALBA. The princes will soon be here. Orange and Egmont are coming. It is not out of mistrust that I now reveal to you what will happen. They will not leave this Palace.

FERDINAND. What is your plan?

ALBA. It has been decided to hold them here. . . . You are astonished! Now, hear what you are to do. As for the reasons, you will know them when it is done; there is no time now to go into them. You are the one with whom I would wish to discuss the greatest, most secret issues. A strong bond unites us. You are dear and close to me. I should like to confide everything to you. It is not the habit of obedience alone that I wish to inculcate in you, but also the capacity to plan, to command, to execute—these too I should like to perpetuate in you. To leave you a great inheritance and the King the most useful of servants; to provide you with the best that I have, so that you need not be ashamed to take your place among your brothers.

FERDINAND. How can I ever repay the debt of this love that you bestow on me alone, while a whole Empire trembles with awe of you?

ALBA. Now listen: this is what I want you to do. As soon as the princes have entered, every point of access to the Palace will be occupied. Gomez will see to this. Silva will hasten to arrest Egmont's secretary and other highly suspicious persons. You will supervise the guards at the gate and in the courts. Above all, put your most reliable men into the rooms adjoining this one, then wait in the gallery till Silva returns to bring me some insignificant paper as a sign that his commission has been executed. Then stay in the antechamber till Orange leaves. Follow him; I shall detain Egmont here, as if there were something else I wished to discuss with him. At the end of the gallery demand Orange's sword, call the guard, quickly put away the dangerous fellow; and I shall seize Egmont here.

FERDINAND. I shall obey you, Father. For the first time with a heavy heart and with anxiety.

ALBA. I forgive you; it's the first great day you have known.

Enter Silva.

SILVA. A messenger from Antwerp. Here is Orange's letter! He is not coming.

ALBA. Is that what the messenger tells you?

SILVA. No, it's my heart that tells me.

ALBA. My evil genius speaks in you.

After reading the letter he waves his hand at both of them, and they withdraw to the gallery. He remains alone in the front.

He is not coming! And he puts off his explanation till the last moment. He dares *not* to come. So this time, contrary to my expectations, the prudent man was prudent enough not to be prudent. Time presses. Only a little turn more of the minute hand and a great work will have been done or missed, irrevocably missed; for it can neither be repeated not kept secret. Long ago I had considered every possibility, even this one, and determined what was to be done in this case. And now that it has to be done I can hardly prevent the *pro* and *contra* from vacillating once more in my mind. . . . Is it wise to catch the others if he escapes me? Should I postpone it and let Egmont go with his men, with so many of them, who now, perhaps only today, are in my power? Thus Fate compels me, who was invincible. How long I pondered it! How well I prepared it! How fine and great was my plan! How close my hope to its aim! And now, at the moment of decision, I am placed between two evils. As into a lottery urn, I plunge my hand into the dark future: what I draw out is still tightly folded, unknown to me, perhaps a winner, perhaps a blank.

He grows alert, as if he can hear something, and steps to the window.

It's he! Egmont! Did your horse carry you in so easily, without sensing the smell of blood or the spirit with drawn sword who received you at the gate? . . . Dismount! . . . Now you have one foot in the grave; and now both feet! Yes, go on and stroke it, pat its neck for serving you so bravely—for the last time—and to me no choice remains. Never could Egmont hand himself over a second time as dazzled as he is now. . . . Listen!

Ferdinand and Silva approach hurriedly.

ALBA. You will do as I commanded; I do not change my mind. I shall detain Egmont as best I can until you, Ferdinand, have brought me news about Silva. Then remain close to me! You, also, Fate deprives of this great merit, to have caught the King's greatest enemy with your own hands.

To Silva.

Make haste!

To Ferdinand.

Go to meet him!

Alba, left alone for a few moments, paces the room in silence. Enter Egmont.

EGMONT. I come to hear the King's will, to discover what service he asks of our loyalty which remains eternally devoted to him.

ALBA. What he desires above all is to know your opinion.

EGMONT. On what matter? Is Orange coming too? I expected to find him here.

ALBA. I much regret his absence at this important hour. The King desires your opinion, your advice, as to how these States can be pacified. Indeed he hopes that you will effectively collaborate in the task of curbing the unrest and establishing complete and lasting order in the Provinces.

EGMONT. You must know better than I that everything is quiet enough already, and indeed was more quiet still before the appearance of the new soldiers filled the people with fear and anxiety.

ALBA. If I am not mistaken, you wish to imply that it would have been most advisable on the King's part never to have placed me in the position of asking your advice.

EGMONT. I beg your pardon. It is not for me to judge whether the King should have sent the army, whether the power of his royal presence alone would not have proved more effective. The army is here; he is not. But we should be very ungrateful, very unmindful, if we did not remember what we owe to the Regent. Let us admit it: by her conduct, as wise as it was brave, she succeeded in quelling the insurgents by force and by esteem, by cunning and persuasion; and, to the astonishment of the whole world, in the space of a few months she recalled a rebellious people to its duty.

ALBA. I don't deny it. The riot has been put down, and everyone seems to have been driven back into the bonds of obedience. But does it not depend on each one's arbitrary whim whether or not he chooses to remain in them? Who will prevent the people from breaking out again? Where is the power that will restrain them? Who guarantees to us that they will continue to prove loyal subjects? Their good will is all the security we have.

EGMONT. And is not the good will of a people the safest and noblest of securities? By God! When can a King feel more secure than when all of them stand by one, and one stands by all? More secure, I mean, from internal and external enemies?

ALBA. Surely we are not going to persuade ourselves that this is the case in these Provinces at present?

EGMONT. Let the King issue a general amnesty, let him set their minds at rest, and we shall soon see loyalty and love return in the train of trust.

ALBA. And let everyone who has profaned the King's majesty, the sanctity of religion, go about scot-free where he pleases? To serve as a walking proof to others that atrocious crimes go unpunished?

EGMONT. But should not a crime of folly, of drunkenness, be excused rather than cruelly punished? Especially where there is well-founded hope, if not certainty, that these evils will not recur? Were kings any less secure, are they not praised by contemporaries and by posterity alike for finding it in them to pardon, pity, or despise an affront to their dignity? Is it not for that very reason that they are likened to God, who is far too great to be affected by every blasphemy?

ALBA. And for that very reason the King must fight for the dignity of God and religion, and we for the King's honour. What the One Above disdains to parry, it is our duty to avenge. Where I am judge, no guilty man shall rejoice in his impunity.

EGMONT. Do you think, then, that you will reach them all? Don't we hear daily that terror is driving them from one place to another, and out of the country? The richest will remove their wealth, themselves, their children, and their friends; the poor will place their hands at their neighbours' service.

ALBA. They will, if we cannot prevent them. That is why the King demands advice and help of all the princes, seriousness of every governor; not only tales about how things are and how they might be if we allowed everything to go on as it is. To look upon a great evil, flatter oneself with hope, put one's trust in time, at the most to deliver one blow, as in a carnival farce so that one can hear the smack and appear to be doing something when one's desire is to do nothing— might not this arouse the suspicion that one is watching the rebellion with pleasure, unwilling to incite it, yet glad to encourage it?

EGMONT (*about to lose his temper, restrains himself and, after a short pause, says calmly*). Not every intention is manifest, and the intentions of many are early misinterpreted. Thus we are told everywhere that the King's intention is not so much to rule the Provinces in accordance with clear and unambiguous laws, to protect the majesty of religion and grant general peace to his people, as to enslave them absolutely, deprive them of their ancient rights, grasp their possessions, curtail the fine privileges of the aristocracy, for whose sake alone the noble man would dedicate body and soul to his service. Religion, they say, is only a splendid screen behind which every dangerous scheme can be more easily hatched. The people are on their knees and worship the holy embroidered emblems, but behind the screen the bird catcher lurks and listens, waiting to ensnare them.

ALBA. Must I hear this from *you*?

EGMONT. These are not my views. Only what is said and rumoured abroad by great and small, foolish and wise alike. The Netherlanders fear a double yoke; and who has pledged to maintain their freedom?

ALBA. Freedom? A fine word, if only one could understand it! What kind of freedom do they want? What is the freedom of the most free? To do what is right! . . . And in this the King will not hinder them. No, no! They do not feel free if they cannot harm themselves and others. Would it not be better to abdicate than to rule such a people? When foreign enemies press us, of whom no citizen is aware because he is concerned with the most immediate things, and the King asks for help, they will quarrel among themselves and make common cause with their enemies. Far better to hedge them in, to treat them like children, so that one can lead them to their own welfare like children. Believe me, a people does not grow up, or grow wise; a people remains perpetually childish.

EGMONT. How rarely a King attains discretion! And should not the many put their trust in the many rather than in one? And not even in one, but in the few that surround the one, the clan that grows old under its master's gaze? I suppose this clan alone has the right to grow wise.

ALBA. Perhaps it has, just because it is not left to its own devices.

EGMONT. And for that reason is reluctant to leave anyone else to his own devices. Do what you please. I've replied to your question and repeat: it will not work. It cannot work. I know my compatriots. They are men worthy to walk on God's earth; each one a world to himself, a little king, steadfast, active, capable, loyal, attached to old customs. It is hard to win their confidence, easy to keep it. Stubborn and steadfast! Pressure they will bear; oppression never.

ALBA (*who meanwhile has turned his head several times*). Would you repeat all that in the presence of the King?

EGMONT. All the worse, if his presence made me afraid! All the better for him, for his people if he inspired me with courage, gave me confidence to say a great deal more!

ALBA. If what you have to say is useful, I can listen to it as well as he can.

EGMONT. I should say to him: the shepherd can easily drive a whole herd of sheep along, the ox draws its plough without resisting. But if you wish to ride a thoroughbred horse, you must learn to read its thoughts, you must demand nothing foolish nor demand it foolishly. That is why the citizens wish to retain their old constitution, to be ruled by their compatriots, for they know how they will be led and can expect these leaders to be both disinterested and concerned with the people's fate.

ALBA. But shouldn't the Regent be empowered to change these old traditions? And could not this be the most precious of his privileges? What is permanent in this world? And should one expect a political institution to be permanent? Must not the circumstances change in time, and, for that very reason, must not an old constitution become the cause of a thousand evils, because it takes no account of the present state of the people? I fear that these old rights are so acceptable because they offer dark recesses in which the cunning and the mighty can hide and hold out at the people's cost, at the expense of the whole.

EGMONT. And these arbitrary changes, these unrestricted interferences on the part of the highest authority, do they not forebode that one desires to do what thousands must not do? He desires to liberate himself alone, so that he may gratify every whim, translate every thought into action. And if we were to put all our trust in him, a good wise King, can he speak for his successors? Can he assure us that none will rule without mercy and consideration? Who then would save us from absolute despotism, when he sends us his servants and minions to rule and dispose as they please, without knowledge of our country or of its needs, meet no resistance, and feel free of all responsibility?

ALBA (*who has looked behind him again*). Nothing is more natural than that a King should seek to rule by his own means and prefer to entrust his orders to those who understand him best, endeavour to understand him, and obey his will unconditionally.

EGMONT. And it is just as natural that the citizen should wish to be ruled by those who were born and bred where he was, who were imbued with the same ideas of right and wrong, whom he can look upon as brothers.

ALBA. And yet the aristocracy can hardly be said to have shared equally with these brothers?

EGMONT. This occurred centuries ago and is now accepted without envy. But if new men were sent to us gratuitously to enrich themselves once more at the nation's expense, if the people knew themselves to be at the mercy of a severe, bold, and unlimited avarice, it would cause a ferment that would not easily subside into itself.

ALBA. You tell me what I ought not to hear; I too am a foreigner.

EGMONT. My telling it to you shows that I don't mean you.

ALBA. Even so I would rather not hear it from you. The King sent me in the hope that I should receive the support of the nobility. The King *wills* his will. The King, after long reflection, has seen what the people requires; things cannot go on, cannot remain as they were. It is the King's intention to restrict them for their own good, if need be to thrust their own welfare upon them, to sacrifice the harmful citizens so that the best may live in peace and enjoy the blessing of wise government. This is his resolve. To convey it to the nobility is my charge; and what I demand in his name is advice as to how it is to be done, not what is to be done, for this he has decided.

EGMONT. Unfortunately your words justify the people's apprehension, the general apprehension. For he has decided what no prince has the right to decide. His will is to weaken, oppress, destroy the strength of his people—their self-confidence, their own conception of themselves—so as to be able to rule them without effort. His will is to corrupt the very core of their individuality; doubtless with the intention to make them happier. His will is to annihilate them so that they will become something, a different some-thing. Oh, if his intention is good, it is being misguided. It is not the King whom this people resists; what it opposes is only the King who is taking the first unfortunate steps in a direction utterly wrong.

ALBA. In your state of mind it seems useless for us to try to come to an un-derstanding. You belittle the King and hold his advisers in contempt if you doubt that all this has already been considered, investigated, and weighed up. It is not my business to go into every *pro* and *contra* once more. Obedi-ence is what I ask of the people—and of you, the foremost and greatest, I ask counsel and action as pledges for this absolute duty.

EGMONT. Demand our heads and have done with it! Whether his neck will bend under this yoke or bow to the axe is all one to a noble soul. It was in vain that I spoke at such length. I have shaken the air, and gained nothing more.

Enter Ferdinand.

FERDINAND. Forgive me for interrupting your conversation. The bearer of this letter requires an urgent reply.

ALBA. Excuse me while I see what it contains.

Steps aside.

FERDINAND, *to* EGMONT. That's a fine horse your men have brought to fetch you.

EGMONT. It's not the worst. I've had it for a while; I'm thinking of parting with it. If you like it, perhaps we can come to terms.

FERDINAND. Good. Let's discuss the matter.

Alba motions to his son, who withdraws to the back.

EGMONT. Good-bye. Dismiss me now, for, by God, I can think of nothing more to say.

ALBA. A happy chance has prevented you from betraying your thoughts farther. Recklessly you opened the very folds of your heart and have accused yourself much more severely than any opponent could have done in his malice.

EGMONT. The rebuke does not touch me; I know myself well enough, and am aware how devoted I am to the King—much more than many who serve their own interests in his service. It is with reluctance that I leave this quarrel without seeing it resolved, and only wish that our service of one master, the welfare of a country, will soon unite us. Perhaps a second conference and the presence of the other princes, who are absent today, will bring about at some happier moment what today seems impossible. With that hope I leave you.

ALBA (*giving a sign to Ferdinand*). Stop, Egmont! Your sword!

> *The middle door opens; one catches a glimpse of the gallery*
> *occupied by guards, who remain immobile.*

EGMONT (*after a brief, astonished silence*). So that was your purpose! It was for that you called me?

> *Clutching his sword, as if to defend himself.*

Did you think I'm defenceless?

ALBA. It is the King's order; you are my prisoner.

> *At the same moment armed men enter from both sides.*

EGMONT (*after a silence*). The King? Oh, Orange, Orange!

> *After a pause, handing over his sword.*

Well, take it, then. It has served me more often to defend the King's cause than to protect this body.

> *Exit through the middle door. The armed men follow him out;*
> *also Alba's son. Alba remains standing.*

ACT V

Street at Dusk
Clare. Brackenburg. Citizens.

BRACKENBURG. Darling. For heaven's sake! What are you doing?

CLARE. Come with me, Brackenburg. You can't know much about people or you wouldn't doubt that we shall free him. For don't they love him dearly? I swear that every one of them is filled with a burning desire to save him, to avert this danger from a precious life and give back freedom to the most free of all. Come on! All that's lacking is a voice to call them together. They haven't forgotten what they owe to him and they know that it's his mighty arm alone that protects them from disaster. On his account and their own they must stake all they have. And what is it we stake? Our lives, at the most, and those are not worth preserving if he dies.

BRACKENBURG. Poor, foolish girl! You don't see the power that fetters us hopelessly!

CLARE. They don't seem unbreakable to me. But let's not waste time on idle words! Here come some of those honest, brave fellows of the old sort. Listen, friends. Listen, neighbours. . . . Tell me, what news of Egmont?

CARPENTER. What does the child want? Tell her to be quiet.

CLARE. Come closer, so that we can talk softly till we're in agreement, and stronger. We haven't a moment to lose. The insolent tyranny that dares to put him in chains is drawing its dagger to murder him. Oh, friends, every minute of the gathering dusk makes me more anxious. I fear this night. Come on! Let's divide into small groups and run through every district, calling the citizens out into the street. Each will take his old weapons. We shall meet again in the marketplace, and our stream will sweep everyone along with it. Our enemies will find themselves surrounded and flooded, and will know that they are defeated. How can a handful of slaves resist us? And he, back in our midst, will turn about, know that he's free, and thank us all one day, thank us who were so deeply in his debt. Perhaps he'll see—no, certainly he'll see—another dawn break in an open sky.

CARPENTER. What's the matter with you, girl?

CLARE. Don't you understand me? I'm speaking of the Count! I'm speaking of Egmont.

JETTER. Don't mention that name. It's deadly.

CLARE. Not that name. What? Not mention his name? Who doesn't mention it at every possible opportunity? Who can escape it anywhere? Often I've read it in these stars, every letter of it. And you ask me not to mention it? What can you mean? Oh, friends, dear good neighbours, you're dreaming, come to your senses. Don't stare at me so blankly and timidly. Nor glance about you in that furtive way! I'm only calling out to you what every one of you wants. Isn't my voice the very voice of your own hearts? Who, in this ominous night, before retiring to a restless bed, would not fall on his knees in earnest prayer imploring Heaven for his safety? Ask one another; let each of you ask himself! And who will not say after me: Egmont's freedom or death!

JETTER. God preserve us! This will end in disaster.

CLARE. Don't go. Stay here instead of cringing from his name, which once you welcomed, happily applauded. When rumour announced him, when the news spread: "Egmont is coming! He is coming back from Ghent!" the inhabitants of those streets through which he must pass thought themselves lucky. And when you heard the clatter of his horses each one threw down his work at once, and over all the careworn faces which you thrust out of the windows there passed a gleam of joy and hope like a ray of sunlight cast by his face. Then you lifted up your children on the threshold and pointed out to them: "Look, that's Count Egmont, the tallest, there! That's Egmont! The one from whom you can expect better times than ever your poor fathers knew!" Don't wait to let your children ask one day: "Where is he gone? Where are the times you promised us?" . . . And here we stand chattering! Wasting idle words, betraying him!

SOEST. You should be ashamed of yourself, Brackenburg. Don't let her go on. Stop her before it's too late.

BRACKENBURG. Clare, my dearest, let's go. What will your mother say? It could be . . .

CLARE. Do you take me for a child, or a madwoman? What could be? You won't drag me away from this terrible certainty with any hope you can invent. You must listen to me and you shall: for I can see you're deeply troubled and can find no guidance in your own hearts. Just let a single glance pierce through the present danger, back to the past, the recent past. Or turn your thoughts to the future! Can you live at all, *will* you live if he perishes? With his last breath our freedom too expires. What was he to you? For whose sake did he deliver himself up to the most pressing danger? Only for you his wounds bled and healed. The great spirit that supported you all languishes in a cell, and treacherous murder lurks in the dark corners. Perhaps he is thinking of you, placing his hopes in you, though accustomed only to give and to fulfil.

CARPENTER. Come along; let's be off.

CLARE. And I have no strength, no muscles like yours; but I have what all of you lack—courage and contempt for danger! If only my breath could infuse you with some of it! If only I could lend you human warmth and vigour by pressing you to my breast! Come with me! I shall walk in your midst! Just as a floating banner, in itself defenceless, leads a band of noble warriors on, so, flaring over all your heads, my spirit hovers, and love and courage will weld this wavering, scattered people into a terrible army.

JETTER. Get her away from here! I feel sorry for her.

Exeunt Citizens.

BRACKENBURG. Clare, my dear. Can't you see where we are?

CLARE. Yes: under the sky that so often seemed to expand more gloriously when noble Egmont walked under it. It's from these windows they looked out, four or five heads, one above the other. In front of these doors they bowed and scraped when he looked down at the lily-livered wretches. Oh, how I loved them then, because they honoured him. Had he been a tyrant, they would have every right to sneak away from him now. But they loved him! Oh, those hands that could raise hats are too feeble to lift a sword. . . . Brackenburg, what about us? Can we reproach them? These arms, that so often held him fast, what are they doing for him? Cunning has always succeeded so well in this world. You know the ins and outs, you know the old Palace. Nothing is impossible. But tell me what to do!

BRACKENBURG. What if we went home?

CLARE. A good idea!

BRACKENBURG. There's one of Alba's patrols on that corner; do listen to the voice of reason. Do you think I'm a coward? Don't you think me capable of dying for you? But we're both out of our senses, I no less than you. Can't you see what's impossible? Try to pull yourself together. You're beside yourself.

CLARE. Beside myself? That's disgusting, Brackenburg. It's you who're beside yourself. When you were loud in your reverence for the hero, called him your friend, your protector, your hope, and cheered him when he appeared—then I stood in my corner of the room, half raised the window, listened, and hid myself, and yet my heart beat faster than the hearts of all your men. And now again it beats faster than all your hearts! You hide yourselves because it's good for you, deny him and don't even feel that you will perish if he dies.

BRACKENBURG. Let's go home.

CLARE. Home?

BRACKENBURG. Only try to think! Look about you. These are the streets where you walked only on Sundays, through which you passed modestly on your way to church, where, with excessive respectability, you were angry with me if I joined you with a friendly word of greeting. Here you stand and talk and act in full view of the public. Only try to think, my dearest. What's the use of it all?

CLARE. Home! Oh yes, I remember. I'm thinking, Brackenburg. Let's go home! Do you know where my home is?

Exeunt.

Prison
Lighted by a lamp, a bunk in the background. Egmont, alone.

EGMONT. Old friend, ever-faithful sleep, do you forsake me too, like my other friends? How willingly once you descended upon my free head and, like a lovely myrtle wreath of love, cooled my temples. In the midst of battle, on the wave of love, lightly breathing I rested in your arms like a burgeoning boy. When gales roared through trees and foliage, branch and crest creaked as they bent, yet deep within the heart's core remained unmoving. What is it that shakes you now? What is it that shivers your steadfast loyal will? I feel it, it is the sound of the murderous axe that nibbles at my root. Still I stand fast and upright, but an inward shudder runs through me. Yes, treacherous power prevails, it is stronger than I. It undermines the high, solid trunk; before the bark has withered, roaring and shattering, the crest will fall.

Why, now, you that so often blew away mighty cares from your head like soap-bubbles, why now can you not drive off the thousand-limbed forebodings that stir within your heart? Since when has Death assumed a fearful appearance for you, who once lived calmly with this changing image as with all the other shapes of the familiar world? But then, it is not he, the swift enemy, whom the healthy man longs to meet in close combat; the prison cell it is, prefiguring the grave, repulsive to the hero and the coward

94

alike. I found it insufferable enough to sit on my padded chair when in solemn council the princes endlessly and repetitively debated what could have been decided in a moment, and when between the gloomy walls of a great hall the beams of the ceiling seemed to throttle me! Then I would hurry out as soon as possible and leap upon my horse's back with a deep breath! Then quickly out where we belong! Out to the fields, where from the earth all Nature's most immediate remedies, vaporous, rise, and through the heavens, wafting all the blessings of the planets, enwrapping us, descend upon our heads; where, like the earthborn giant, strengthened by our mother's touch, we rise to our full height; where we feel wholly human, one with all that's human, human desire pulsing through every vein; where the urge to press forward, to be victorious, to seize, to use one's fists, to possess, to conquer glows in the young huntsman's soul; where the soldier is quick to arrogate to himself his inborn claim to all the world and in his terrible freedom rages like a hailstorm through meadow, field, and forest, wreaking destruction, and knows no bounds that human hands have set. A mere phantasm, this, this dream of remembered bliss that so long was mine. What has treacherous Fortune done with it? Does Fortune now refuse to grant you that quick death you never shunned in the full glare of the sun, to offer you instead a foretaste of the grave in nauseous mustiness? How vilely now it breathes upon me from these stones! Already life congeals; and from my bed, as from the grave, my foot recoils.

O Care, you that begin your murderous work before the event, leave off! Since when has Egmont been alone, utterly alone in this world? It's doubt that makes you helpless now, not Fortune. Has the King's justice, in which you trusted all your life, has the Regent's friendship which—why not admit it now?—was almost love, have these vanished like a shining, fiery mirage of the night? And do they leave you lonely now, plunged into darkness, on a dangerous track? Will not Orange venture out scheming at the head of your assembled friends? Will not a crowd collect and, with growing force, go out to rescue an old friend?

O walls that now enclose me, do not halt the kindly progress of so many spirits. And that courage which once poured out of my eyes into theirs, let it now flow back from their hearts into mine. Oh yes, they stir in their thousands, they are coming, to stand by me now. Their pious wishes wing their way to Heaven and beg for a miracle. And if no angel comes to my aid from above, I see them take up their swords and lances. The gates split in two, the bars burst asunder, the wall comes crashing down with their impact, and gladly Egmont steps out towards the freedom of approaching day. How many familiar faces receive me jubilantly. Oh, Clare, if you were a man, I should surely see you here, the very first to welcome me, and I should owe you what it is hard to owe to a King, freedom.

Clare's House

Clare comes out of her bedroom with a lamp and a glass of water.
She sets down the glass on the table and goes to the window.

CLARE. Brackenburg? Is that you? What was that noise? No one yet? It was no one. I shall put the lamp on the window-sill so that he can see that I'm still awake, that I'm still waiting for him. He promised to bring me news. News? No, horrible certainty. Egmont condemned! What court of law has the right to summon him? And yet they condemn him. Does the King condemn him, or the Duke? And the Regent washes her hands of it. Orange dilly-dallies, and all his friends. . . . Is this the world of whose inconstancy and unreliability I have heard much, but experienced nothing? Is this the world? Who would be so wicked as to be an enemy to him? Could malice be powerful enough to cause the sudden downfall of one so generally loved and esteemed? And yet it *is* so. It is. . . . Oh, Egmont, both from God and men I thought you safe as in my arms! What was I to you? You called me yours, and I was truly yours, wholly devoted and dedicated to you. . . . What am I now? In vain I stretch out my arms towards the noose that grips you. You helpless, and I free! Here is the key to my door. My coming and going depend on my own free will, and yet I am nothing to you. Oh, fetter me to keep me from despair! And cast me down into the deepest dungeon to beat my head against damp walls, to whimper for freedom, dream of how I would help him if I weren't fettered and chained— how I should help him then! But now I'm free, and in that freedom lies the fear of impotence. Fully conscious, yet incapable of moving a finger to help him. Oh, even the smaller part of you, your Clare, is a prisoner as you are and, separated from you, wastes her last strength in a deathly convulsion. . . . I hear someone creeping in—a cough, Brackenburg—yes, he's come. Poor, honest Brackenburg, your fate is always the same. Your sweetheart opens the door to you at night, but oh, for how unhappy, ill-omened a meeting!

Enter Brackenburg.

CLARE. You look so pale and harassed, Brackenburg. What is it?
BRACKENBURG. I've passed through dangers and detours to see you. All the main streets are guarded. I stole my way to you through alleys and dark nooks.
CLARE. Tell me what's happening.
BRACKENBURG (*taking a seat*). Oh, Clare, I feel like weeping. I had no love for him. He was the rich man who lured away the poor man's only sheep to a better pasture. I've never cursed him. God made me loyal and softhearted. But all my life dissolved in pain and flowed out of me, and my daily hope was that I should languish away.

CLARE. Forget it, Brackenburg! Forget yourself. Tell me about him. Is it true? He's been condemned?

BRACKENBURG. He has. I know it beyond doubt.

CLARE. And he's still alive?

BRACKENBURG. Yes, he's still alive.

CLARE. How can you be sure about it? Tyranny murders the glorious man overnight. His blood flows where no one can see him. The people lies drugged in anxious sleep and dreams of rescue, dreams the fulfilment of its impotent wish. Meanwhile, dissatisfied with us, his soul forsakes this world. He's gone! Don't deceive me. Don't deceive yourself.

BRACKENBURG. No, he's alive, I assure you. . . . But the Spaniard is preparing a terrible spectacle for the people whom he wants to tread underfoot violently and forever; he will crush every heart that stirs for freedom.

CLARE. Carry on and calmly pronounce my death sentence also. Already I am walking closer and closer to the fields of the blessed and can feel the comfort wafted over from those regions of everlasting peace. Tell me all.

BRACKENBURG. I could tell by the patrol and gather from stray remarks that something gruesome is being prepared in secret in the market-place. Through byways, through familiar passages, I crept to my cousin's house and looked down on the market-place from a back window. Torches flickered in a wide circle of Spanish soldiers. I strained my eyes, unaccustomed to such sights, and out of the night a black scaffold loomed up at me, spacious and high. I felt faint with horror. A great many men were busy around it, draping black cloth around any of the woodwork that was still white and visible. Last of all they covered the steps as well; I saw them do it. They seemed to be dedicating the site for an abominable sacrifice. A white crucifix, which shone in the night like silver, had been erected high up on one side. I looked on and grew more and more certain of the terrible certainty. Still torches swayed about here and there; gradually they vanished or went out. All at once this monstrous progeny of the night had returned to its mother's womb.

CLARE. Quiet, Brackenburg. Be silent now. Let this veil cover my soul. The spectres are gone, and you, lovely night, lend your cloak to the earth that's in ferment inwardly; no longer Earth will bear her loath-some burden but opens her deep jaws and, grating, swallows down the murderous scaffold. And surely an angel will be sent by that God whom they have blasphemously made a witness to their fury; bolts and fetters will break at the messenger's holy touch, and he will surround our friend with a mild radiance; gently and silently he'll lead him through the night to freedom. And my way too leads through that darkness secretly, and I go to meet him.

BRACKENBURG (*detaining her*). Where, child, where? What are you going to do?

CLARE. Quiet, my dear, so that no one will wake up; so that we shan't wake ourselves. Do you know this little bottle, Brackenburg? I took it away from you for a joke, when you used to threaten suicide in your impatience. . . . And now, my friend——

BRACKENBURG. By all the saints!

CLARE. You won't prevent it. Death is my part. And don't begrudge me this quick, gentle death, which for yourself you held in readiness. Give me your hand! At the very moment when I open the dark door which permits no going back, I could tell you by the pressure of this hand how much I loved you and how much I pitied you. My brother died young, it was you I chose to take his place. Your heart protested, tormented itself and me—more and more hotly you demanded what was not meant for you. Forgive me, and farewell. Let me call you brother; it is a name in which a host of other names are contained. And faithfully treasure my last parting gift—accept this kiss. Death unites all things, Brackenburg, and it unites us too.

BRACKENBURG. Then let me die with you. Share it with me, share it! There is enough of it to put out two lives.

CLARE. No, you shall live, you can live. Help my mother, who but for you would die of poverty. Be to her what I can no longer be; live together and weep for me. Weep for your country and for him who alone could have preserved it. The present generation will not recover from this shame, even the fury of revenge will not blot it out. Poor people, drag out your lives through this age that is no age at all. Today the world comes to a sudden stop; its turning ceases, and my pulse will beat but a few minutes longer. Farewell.

BRACKENBURG. Oh, live with us, as we for you alone! You murder us in you. Oh, live and suffer! Inseparable we shall support you at either side, and always considerate, love shall grant you the utmost comfort, two living arms. Be ours, because I may not say, be mine.

CLARE. Quiet, Brackenburg, you're not aware how you touch me. What is hope to you is despair to me.

BRACKENBURG. Share that hope with the living. Stay on the brink of the abyss; glance down it once and look back at us.

CLARE. I have conquered; don't call me back into the battle.

BRACKENBURG. You're in a daze; wrapped up in night you seek the depth. But even now not every light is out, still many a day will dawn.

CLARE. Woe to you, woe! Cruelly you tear up the curtain before my eyes. Yes, that day will break! In vain pull all the mists about itself and break against its will. Anxiously the citizen will look out of his window, the night leave behind a black stain; he looks, and, horribly, the murderous scaffold grows in daylight. In renewed anguish the profaned image of Christ will raise an imploring eye to the Father above. The sun will not dare to shine, refusing to mark the hour at which he is to die. Wearily the hands of the clock move on their way, one hour after another strikes. Stop! Now it is time! The premonition of morning drives me to my grave.

She goes to the window as if to look out and secretly drinks.

BRACKENBURG. Clare! Clare!

CLARE (*goes to the table and drinks the water*). Here is the rest. I do not ask you to follow. Do what you may, farewell. Put out this lamp quietly and without delay. I am going to lie down. Creep away softly, close the door behind you. Quietly! Don't wake my mother. Go, save yourself! Save yourself! If you don't want to be taken for my murderer.

Exit.

BRACKENBURG. She leaves me, as usual, for the last time. Oh, if a human soul could know its power to rend a loving heart! She leaves me standing here, left by myself, and death and life are equally loathsome to me now. To die alone! Weep, you lovers, there is no harder fate than mine. She shares the poison with me and dismisses me. Sends me away from her! She drags me after her and pushes me back into life. Oh, Egmont, what a praiseworthy lot is yours! She is the first to set out, you'll take the wreath of victory from her hand; bringing all heaven with her she meets you on your way. . . . And shall I follow? To stand aside again? And carry inextinguishable envy into those celestial realms? On earth there is no staying now for me, and hell and heaven offer equal anguish. How welcome the dreadful hand of annihilation would be to this wretch!

Exit Brackenburg. The stage remains unchanged for a while. Then music, signifying the death of Clare, strikes up; the lamp, which Brackenburg forgot to extinguish, flares up a few times more, then goes out. Soon the scene changes to

Prison

Egmont lies sleeping on his berth. There is a rattling of keys, and the door opens. Servants enter with torches, followed by Ferdinand, Alba's son, and Silva, accompanied by armed men. Egmont wakes up with a start.

EGMONT. Who are you, who so roughly shake away sleep from my eyes? What do your defiant, uncertain glances betoken to me? Why this dreadful procession? What lying nightmare have you come to present to my half-awakened spirit?

SILVA. The Duke sends us to announce your sentence to you.

EGMONT. Have you brought the hangman too to execute it?

SILVA. Listen to it, then you will know what awaits you.

EGMONT. This befits you well and befits your shameful undertaking. Hatched out at night and carried out at night. So this insolent deed of injustice may remain hidden. Step forward boldly, you who keep the sword concealed beneath your cloak. Here is my head, the freest that ever tyranny severed from its socket.

SILVA. You are mistaken. What fair judges have resolved they will not conceal from the face of day.

EGMONT. In that case their insolence exceeds all measure and conception.

SILVA (*takes the verdict from one of the attendants, unfolds it, and reads*). "In the name of the King, and by authority of a special power bestowed on us by His Majesty to judge all his subjects, of whatever station, not excluding Knights of the Golden Fleece, after due . . ."

EGMONT. Can the King bestow that power?

SILVA. "After due, lawful, and exact examination of the evidence we declare you, Henry, Count Egmont, Prince of Gavre, guilty of High Treason, and pronounce the sentence: that at the first break of day you be led from your cell to the marketplace and that there, in the full view of the people, as a warning to all traitors, you suffer death by the sword. Signed in Brussels on . . ."

Date and year are read out indistinctly, so that audience do not catch them.

". . . by Ferdinand, Duke of Alba, President of the Court of the Twelve." Now you know your fate; you have little time left to reconcile yourself to it, put your house in order, and take leave of your nearest and dearest.

Exeunt Silva and attendants. Ferdinand remains with two torch bearers. The stage is dimly lit.

EGMONT (*has remained standing, deep in thought, and allowed Silva to leave without looking up. He thinks he is alone and as he raises his eyes he sees Alba's son*). You stay behind? Is it your wish to add to my astonishment, my horror, by your presence? Are you perhaps waiting to bring your father the welcome news of my unmanly despair? Go, then! Tell him. Tell him that he deceives neither me nor the world with his lies. At first they will whisper it behind his back, then tell it to him, the ambitious seeker of fame, aloud and more loudly still; and when one day he descends from this peak, thousands of voices will cry it out at him! Not the welfare of the state, not the dignity of the King, not the peace of the Provinces brought him here. For his own sake he counselled war, so that the warrior might prove himself in war! It was he who created this monstrous confusion, so that he would be needed! And I fall as a victim to his vile hatred, his mean jealousy. Yes, I know it and have the right to say it: the dying man, the mortally wounded, may say it. The conceited man envied me; to destroy me was his dear and long-deliberated plan. Even when we were younger and played at dice together, and piles of gold, one after another, speedily moved from his side to mine, he stood there grimly, pretending indifference but inwardly consumed with anger, more at my gain than at his loss. I still recall the glowering gaze, the significant pallor when, at a public festivity, in front of many thousands of people, we competed in a shooting match. He challenged me, and both nations, Spaniards and Netherlanders, stood there betting and wishing. I beat him; his bullet missed, mine hit the mark. A loud cheer broke from my supporters and resounded in the air. Now his shot hits me. Tell him that I know it, that I know him, that the world despises every sign of victory which a petty mind erects for itself by base wiles. As for you, if it is possible for a son to forsake the ways of his father, practise shame in time, by feeling ashamed for him whom you would like to revere with all your heart.

FERDINAND. I listen to you without interrupting. Your reproaches weigh on me like the blows of a club on a helmet. I feel the impact but I am armed. You strike home but you do not wound me. All I feel is the pain that rends my heart. Woe is me that I should have grown up to look on such a sight, that I was destined to act in such a play!

EGMONT. What am I to make of that lamentation? Why should you be moved or troubled? Is it belated remorse at your part in the shameful conspiracy? You are so young, and your appearance promises well. You were so candid, so friendly towards me. As long as I looked at you, I was reconciled to your father. And just as false, more false than he, you lured me into the snare. You are the hideous one! Whoever trusts *him* does so at his peril; but who would suspect any peril in trusting you? Be off with you. Don't rob me of these last moments! Be off, so that I may collect my thoughts, forget the world, and you before all else! . . .

FERDINAND. What can I say to you? I stand and look at you and yet I do not see you nor feel that I am myself. Shall I excuse myself? Shall I assure you that I did not discover my father's intentions till late, till right at the end; that I acted as a passive, inanimate instrument of his will? What can it matter now what you may think of me? You are lost; and I, wretch that I am, only stand here to convince you of it and to bewail you.

EGMONT. What a strange voice, what unexpected comfort to meet on my way to the grave! You, the son of my first, almost my only enemy, you feel sorry for me, you are not on the side of my murderers? Speak up. Tell me! In what light am I to regard you?

FERDINAND. Cruel father! Oh yes, I recognize you in that command. You knew my feelings, my disposition, which so often you rebuked as the inheritance of a tender mother. To mould me in your image you sent me here. To see this man on the edge of his yawning grave, in the grip of a violent death, you compel me; no matter what becomes of me, no matter that I suffer the deepest anguish. If only I become deaf and blind to every kind of plight. If only I become insensitive!

EGMONT. You astonish me! Control yourself! Stand up and speak like a man!

FERDINAND. Oh, that I were a woman! So that one could say to me: what's moving you? What disturbs you so? Tell me of a greater, a more monstrous evil—make me the witness to a more abominable deed. I shall thank you, I shall say: it was nothing.

EGMONT. You forget yourself. Remember where you are!

FERDINAND. Let this passion rage, let me lament unrestrained! I have no wish to appear firm, when all is collapsing inside me. To think that I must see you here! You of all men! Oh, it's horrible. You don't understand me. And should you understand me? . . . Egmont! Egmont!

EGMONT. Solve me this riddle!

FERDINAND. No riddle.

EGMONT. How can you be so deeply moved by the fate of a stranger?

FERDINAND. No stranger. You're no stranger to me. It was your name that in my first youth shone to me like a star of heaven. How often I listened to tales about you, asked about you! The child's hope is the youth, the youth's hope the man. That is how you strode in front of me, always ahead of me, and always unenvious I saw you in front and followed you, step by step. Then at last I hoped to see you and did see you, and my heart went out to you. You I had chosen for myself, and confirmed my choice when I saw you. Now, only now, I hoped to be with you, to live with you, to grasp you, to—Well, all that has been cut off now, and I see you here.

EGMONT. My friend, if it is of any help to you, accept my assurance that from the first moment I felt drawn to you. And listen to me. Let's exchange a few calm words. Tell me: is it the strict, serious intention of your father to kill me?

FERDINAND. It is.

EGMONT. This sentence, then, is not an idle show devised to frighten me, to punish me by fear and threats, to humiliate me, only to raise me up again by royal grace?

FERDINAND. No, alas, it is not. At first I consoled myself with this remote hope: and already then I felt pained and troubled to see you in this state. Now it is real, definite. No, I shall not control myself. Who will help me, advise me, how to escape the inevitable?

EGMONT. Then listen to me! If you are possessed by such a mighty urge to save me, if you abhor the superior strength of those who keep me fettered, save me then. Every moment is precious. You are the son of the all-powerful and powerful enough yourself. . . . Let us escape! I know the ways; the means cannot be unknown to you. Only these walls, only a few miles divide me from my friends. Loosen these fetters, take me to them, and be one of us. You can be sure the King will thank you one day for rescuing me. At present he is surprised, and perhaps he hasn't been informed of anything. Your father dares and decides; and His Majesty must approve what has been done, even if he is horrified by it. You are thinking? Oh, think out my way to freedom! Speak, and feed the last hope of my living soul!

FERDINAND. No more, I beg you. Every word you speak adds to my despair. There is no way out, no help, no refuge. . . . This torments me, it lacerates my heart. I myself helped to pull the net tight; I know how strongly and tightly it is knitted; I know how the way has been barred to every bold or ingenious resort. I feel that I share your fetters and those of all the others. Should I be lamenting now if I hadn't tried everything? I have lain at his feet, argued and implored. He sent me here to destroy in one moment all the joy and zest that still remained in me.

EGMONT. And there's no escape?

FERDINAND. None.

EGMONT (*stamping his foot*). No escape! Sweet life, dear lovely habit of living and of being active! I must part from you! And so indifferently too! Not in the tumult of battle, in the uproar of arms, in the scattering of a teeming crowd, do you grant me a brief farewell; you take no brusque leave of me, do not shorten the moment of parting. I am to seize your hand, look into your eyes once more, feel your beauty and worth intensely, poignantly as never before, then resolutely tear myself away and say: Good-bye!

FERDINAND. And I am to stand beside you, looking on, unable to hold or hinder you. Oh, what voice would suffice for this complaint? What heart would not break its bonds at this misery!

EGMONT. Calm yourself!

FERDINAND. You can be calm, you can renounce and take this difficult step like a hero, since Necessity holds you by the hand. What can I do? What should I do? You conquer yourself and us; you have come through. As for me, I survive both you and myself. In the banquet's merriment I shall have lost my light, in the tumult of battle my banner. Dreary, confused, and flat the future seems to me.

EGMONT. Young friend, whom by a strange twist of fortune I win and lose at the same time, who feel my death agony, suffer it on my behalf, look at me now; you do not lose me. If my life to you was a mirror in which you liked to contemplate yourself, let my death be the same. Men are not together only when they meet; even the most distant, the departed lives in us. I live for you and have lived long enough for myself. Every day of my life I was glad to be alive, every day of my life I did my duty with quick efficiency, as my conscience demanded. Now life comes to its end, as it could have done sooner, much sooner, even on the sands of Gravelingen. I cease to live; but at least I *have* lived. Now live as I did, my friend, gladly and with zest, and do not shun death!

FERDINAND. You might have preserved yourself for our sake; you should have done. You killed yourself. Often I've heard people talk about you—wise men, both hostile to you and well-disposed, and heard them debate your worth at great length. But in the end they agreed, no one dared to deny, everyone admitted: yes, he treads a dangerous path. How often I wished I could warn you! Did you have no friends, then?

EGMONT. I was warned.

FERDINAND. And, point by point, I found all these accusations set down once more in the present charge—and your replies! Good enough to excuse you; not pertinent enough to exculpate you——

EGMONT. That is as it may be. Men think that they direct their lives and are in control of themselves; yet their inmost selves are irresistibly pulled towards their destinies. Let's not reflect on it; I can easily rid myself of such thoughts—but not of my concern for this country. Yet even this will be taken care of. If my blood can flow for many and buy peace for my people, it flows willingly. I fear it won't be so. But men should cease to fret where they may no longer act. If you can limit or divert your father's nefarious power, do so! Who will be able to do it? . . . Farewell.

FERDINAND. I can't go.

EGMONT. I heartily commend my servants to you. I have good men and women in my service; see that they are not dispersed or made unhappy! What's become of Richard, my secretary?

FERDINAND. He preceded you. They beheaded him as your abettor in High Treason.

EGMONT. Poor soul! . . . One thing more, and then good-bye. My strength is exhausted. Whatever may preoccupy our minds, in the end Nature exacts her dues and that most insistently; and as a child entwined by a snake enjoys refreshing sleep, so the tired man lies down once more on the very threshold of death and deeply rests, as if a long day's journey lay ahead of him. . . . And one thing more—I know a girl; you will not despise her, since she was mine. Now that I have entrusted her to your care, I die at peace. You are a noble-minded man; a woman who finds such a man is safe from harm. Is my old William alive? Is he at liberty?

FERDINAND. The vigorous old man who always rides out with you?

EGMONT. That's the one.

FERDINAND. He's alive and at liberty.

EGMONT. He knows where she lives; let him take you there and pay him to the end of his days for showing you the way to that treasure. Farewell!

FERDINAND. I am not going.

EGMONT (*pushing him to the door*). Farewell!

FERDINAND. Oh, let me stay!

EGMONT. No leave-taking, friend.

He escorts Ferdinand to the door and tears himself away from him there.
Ferdinand, in a daze, hurries away.

EGMONT (*alone*). Malevolent man! You never thought to render me this favour through your son. Through him I have been relieved of my cares and pain, of fear and every anxious feeling. Gently, yet urgently, Nature demands her last tribute. All is resolved; and all concluded. And that which in the previous night kept me awake on my uncertain bed now lulls my senses with unalterable certainty.

He sits down on his berth. Music.

Sweet sleep! Like purest happiness most willingly you come unbidden, unimplored! You loosen every knot of strenuous thought, consuming all the images of joy and pain; unobstructed flows the circle of inner harmonies and swathed in agreeable delirium, we sink and cease to be.

He falls asleep; the music accompanies his sleep. Behind his bed the wall seems to open, a radiant apparition enters. Liberty in heavenly raiment, shining, rests upon a cloud. She has Clare's features and bows down towards the sleeping hero. She expresses a feeling of compassion, she seems to commiserate with him. Soon she calms herself and, with an enlivening gesture, shows him the quiver of arrows, then her staff and helmet. She invites him to be of good cheer and, by indicating to him that his death will win freedom for the Provinces, acclaims him victor and hands him a laurel wreath. As she approaches his head with the wreath, Egmont moves, like one stirring in his sleep, so that he comes to lie with his face turned up to her. She holds the wreath suspended over his head; from the distance one hears the warlike music of drums and fifes. At the first, soft sound of this the apparition vanishes. The music grows louder. Egmont awakes; the prison is dimly lit by the dawn. His first movement is to put his hand to his head: he rises and looks about, keeping his hand on his head.

Gone is the wreath! Beautiful image, the light of day has driven you away! But it was they! Truly it was, combined, the two most treasured comforts of my heart. Divine Liberty, borrowing my beloved's features and shape; the sweet girl dressed in the heavenly raiment of her friend. In one solemn moment they appear united, more solemn than charming. With blood-stained soles she came before me, the billowing folds of her garment stained with blood. My blood it was, and that of many noble men. No, it was not shed in vain. Press on, brave people! The goddess of Victory leads you. And as the sea bursts through the dykes you build, so you shall burst and tumble down the mound of tyranny and, flooding all, wash it away from the dear site it has usurped.

Drumbeats come nearer.

Listen! Listen! How often this sound called me to stride freely towards the field of battle and victory! How blithely the companions trod that dangerous, honourable course! I too go from this cell to meet an honourable death; I die for freedom, for which I lived and fought and for which I now passively offer up myself.

The background is filled with a line of Spanish soldiers, carrying halberds.

Yes, go on and summon them! Close your ranks, you won't frighten me. I am accustomed to stand in front of spears, facing spears, and surrounded on all sides by the threat of death, to feel brave life flow through me with redoubled speed.

Drumbeats.

The enemy encircles you! His swords are flashing! Courage, friends, more courage! Behind you parents, wives, and children wait!

Pointing at the guards.

And these, the ruler's hollow words impel, not their true feelings. Protect your property! And to preserve your dearest ones, willingly, gladly fall as my example shows you.

*Drumbeats. As he walks towards the guards, towards the back exit,
the curtain falls; the music strikes up and concludes in a victorious strain.*

Iphigenia in Tauris

A PLAY IN FIVE ACTS

Translated by David Luke

CHARACTERS

IPHIGENIA, daughter of Agamemnon and Clytemnestra
ORESTES, her brother
PYLADES, his friend
THOAS, king of the Taurians
ARCAS, his attendant

*The scene is a grove in front of the
temple of Diana in Tauris.*

Translator's note: The translation imitates Goethe's five-foot iambic blank verse and is intended to be metrically correct in that sense. A reading with correct scansion is in all cases possible provided (a) that the words are pronounced as in British English (e.g., "détail," not "detail"), and (b) that the (anglicized) classical proper names are pronounced correctly. "Iphigenia," for instance, must be read as five syllables with penultimate stress. I have added the stress-accent in cases where doubt might arise. "Atreus" may be read either as two syllables (1. 340) or as three (1. 360), where the diaeresis (¨) indicates this.

ACT I

IPHIGENIA. Into your shade, you gently stirring treetops,
    Into this ancient sacred leafy grove,
    The goddess's own silent sanctuary,
    I come forth, and come even now with dread
    As if it still were my first time of coming: 5
    For still I feel a stranger in this place.
    So many years ago, divine decree,
    To which I bow, brought me and hid me here;
    But now, as then, I am in alien land.
    For from the friends I love the sea divides me   10
    And day by day I stand upon the shore
    Seeking with all my soul the land of Greece;
    And to my sighs, alas, there comes no answer
    But hollow echoes of the roaring wave.
    How lonely is the man who lives alone   15
    Far from his family! Bitter grief corrupts
    Each present joy before his very lips.
    His yearning thoughts swarm back unceasingly
    Towards his father's house, where first the sun
    Disclosed the heavens to him, where between   20
    Brothers and sisters tender bonds of love
    Were forged for ever as they lived and played.
    I will not wrangle with the gods; and yet,
    How lamentable is the lot of women!
    A man rules in his home, and rules in war,   25
    And in a foreign land he finds recourse;
    Possessions gladden him, victory crowns him,
    He lives assured of honourable death.
    But strict and narrow is a woman's fortune:
    Even to obey a boorish husband is   30
    Duty and solace—how much harsher then
    The fate that drives her into distant exile!
    Such is my case: here noble Thoas holds me
    To sacred office solemnly enslaved.
    And I confess in shame that with a mute   35
    Resentment I have served you, oh my goddess,
    My rescuer! For should not my whole life
    Be dedicated willingly to you?
    And I have always hoped, and I still hope,
    For help from you, holy Diana: you   40
    It was who caught me in your gentle arms,

The banished daughter of the mightiest king.
O maid of Zeus, if he, that king of men,
If by your guidance godlike Agamemnon,
Whose heart shook when you asked him for his daughter,   45
Who to your altar brought what he loved best:
If he with honour from Troy's toppled ramparts
Has now returned and reached his fatherland,
And found his wife, Electra and his son,
Dear treasures all, preserved for him by you—   50
Then give me also to my friends again,
And save me, whom you saved from death, at last
From this life here as well, this second death!

Enter Arcas.

ARCAS. The king has sent me here, and bids me greet
    The priestess of Diana and to hail her.   55
    This is the day on which we thank our goddess
    Of Tauris for new glorious victories.
    I haste ahead of Thoas and his army
    To tell you that he comes, that it draws near.
IPHIGENIA. We are ready to receive them worthily;   60
    Our goddess too will look with gracious eyes
    Upon the welcome offerings of the king.
ARCAS. Oh, in your eyes as well, most honoured lady,
    Our dear and holy priestess, shall I not find
    In your eyes too a look more bright and radiant,   65
    Portending joy to all of us? For still
    Mysterious grief obscures your inmost soul,
    And vainly we have waited for long years
    To hear from you some friendly, heartfelt word.
    As long as I have known you in this place   70
    Your eyes have frozen me with that same look:
    And to this very day, deep in your breast,
    As if with iron chains your heart is locked.
IPHIGENIA. And such reserve befits the exiled orphan.
ARCAS. Do you feel orphaned and in exile here?   75
IPHIGENIA. Can a strange land become our native soil?
ARCAS. And yet your own land has grown strange to you.
IPHIGENIA. That is why my heart bleeds and cannot heal.
    In my first youth, when scarcely bound by love
    Yet to my parents and their other children,   80
    When the new tender shoots, growing together
    Around the older stems, so sweetly strove

Towards the sky, alas! an alien curse
Suddenly struck me, separated me
From those I loved; and by its brazen hand   85
The dearest bonds were severed. It was lost,
Our youth's best happiness, the thriving growth
Of early years. Even when saved, I felt
No more than a mere shadow; and the joy
Of life never took root in me again.   90
ARCAS. If you are so unhappy as you say,
    Then I may say you are ungrateful too.
IPHIGENIA. Have I not always thanked you?
ARCAS.   But was that
    The pure and loving thanks, the benefactor's
    Truest reward, the fleeting glance, the smile   95
    That tells him he has given happiness?
    When you came here so many years ago,
    Brought by a deep mysterious destiny,
    The gods' gift to this temple, Thoas met you
    And showed you his respect and his affection;   100
    And you found refuge, you found welcome on
    Our shore which until then, to any stranger
    Who landed, was a place of fear: they all,
    By ancient custom, perished bloodily
    Here on the sacred altar of Diana.   105
IPHIGENIA. Is life no more than leave to draw one's breath?
    What life is this, that in this holy place
    I pass in sorrow, like some mournful shade
    Lingering by its own grave? How can we say
    We are alive and glad and know ourselves,   110
    When every day, spent in vain reverie,
    Is a mere presage of the dull grey days
    That we shall spend in dreary self-oblivion
    As sad departed ghosts on Lethe's shore?
    What early death is worse than useless life?   115
    And I, a woman, chiefly bear this fate.
ARCAS. Your noble pride, your self-dissatisfaction
    I pardon, though I pity you as well,
    For it has robbed you of the joy of life.
    You say you have done nothing since you came here: 120
    Have you not cured the king's deep melancholy?
    Have you not changed the ancient cruel custom
    That dooms all strangers landing here to death
    Upon Diana's altar, year by year

Gently persuading Thoas to suspend it,   125
Saving so many wretched prisoners' lives
And letting them set sail for home again?
The goddess was not angered when she saw
That ancient bloody sacrifice withheld,
But heard the prayers of her gentle priestess: 130
For now, does not winged victory salute
Our warriors, fly ahead of them indeed,
And do we all not feel a new contentment
Since Thoas, having reigned so long with wisdom
And warlike valour, takes new pleasure now,   135
With you to counsel him, in showing mercy,
Easing the duty of our mute obedience?
Can you call your life useless, when on thousands
The balm of your sweet influence falls like dew,
When you have been an ever-welling spring   140
Of happiness to us, since some god sent you,
And when to strangers you have given safe
Homecoming from our wild and fatal shore?
IPHIGENIA. So little done we soon lose sight of, when
    We look ahead and see so much to do.   145
ARCAS. Do you praise those who underprize themselves?
IPHIGENIA. We censure those who measure their own deeds.
ARCAS. We censure those too proud to know their worth
    No less than those too vain for modesty.
    Oh hear me, and believe the honest word   150
    Of a plain-speaking man and faithful friend:
    When the king speaks to you today, be kind,
    And make it easier for him to speak.
IPHIGENIA. Your well-meant words dismay me; many times
    I have been pressed to answer his proposal.   155
ARCAS. You must consider what is best for you.
    Since the king lost his son, there are not many
    Among his friends and followers he trusts,
    And these no more than he has ever done.
    He looks askance at every noble youth   160
    Who might succeed him, fears that in old age
    He will be alone and helpless, perhaps ousted
    By some bold rising, killed before his time.
    The Scythian thinks little of fine speech,
    And the king least of all. He is accustomed   165
    Only to giving orders and to acting:
    He does not know the art of delicately

Steering a conversation to its point.
You must not make it hard for him with cold
Reserve, with seeming not to understand   170
His meaning. Meet him gracefully half-way.
IPHIGENIA. Must I invite the fate that threatens me?
ARCAS. How can you call his wooing you a threat?
IPHIGENIA. Of all I dread, I dread this most of all.
ARCAS. Surely you will reward his love with trust.   175
IPHIGENIA. If first he will release me from this fear!
ARCAS. Why do you hide your name and race from him?
IPHIGENIA. Because such secrecy befits a priestess.
ARCAS. Nothing should be held secret from the king.
He does not order you to speak, and yet   180
He feels it deeply, his great heart is sad
That you should keep such a defensive silence.
IPHIGENIA. Does he resent it, have I angered him?
ARCAS. I almost think so; he is silent too
But casual words that he lets fall convince me   185
That he has set his heart upon one thing:
To gain possession of you. Do not leave him,
Oh do not leave him now to his own thoughts!
Or in his soul resentment will take root
And grow into some terror for you. Then,   190
Too late, you will remember my advice.
IPHIGENIA. What! are the king's intentions so ignoble?
No man of honourable name, whose heart
Is governed by some reverence for the gods,
Should ever harbour them; and would he dare   195
To drag me from the altar to his bed?
Then I will call on all the heavenly ones
And on my goddess above all, Diana
The resolute! I am her virgin priestess,
And she, herself a virgin, will protect me!   200
ARCAS. You need not be alarmed; he is not a boy,
To be impelled to rash hot-blooded deeds.
I fear a different danger as I watch
Him brood, another harsh decision which
He will stand by inflexibly. For when his   205
Mind is made up, nothing can move him. Therefore
I beg you, trust him, show him gratitude
Even if that is all that you can offer.
IPHIGENIA. Oh, if you know more, tell me what you know!
ARCAS. The king himself will tell you; he is coming.   210

You honour him, and your own heart invites you
To treat him kindly and without reserve.
Kind words from women have great influence
With noble-minded men.

Exit.

IPHIGENIA.   He counsels well;
    And yet how can I follow his advice?   215
    But I will gladly give the king the thanks
    I owe him for his magnanimity;
    And let me hope to please him with kind words,
    Yet speak the truth into his mighty ear.

Enter Thoas.

Now may our goddess bless you royally,   220
Oh king, and grant you victory and fame
And wealth and the well-being of your people
And every pious wish in plenitude!
That you, the careful ruler of so many,
May know a happiness reserved for few.   225
THOAS. The praises of my people would content me,
    But I have won what others now enjoy
    More than myself. How happy is that man,
    A king or humble subject, who can say
    That fortune smiles upon his house and home!   230
    You shared with me my days of deepest grief
    When I had lost my last and dearest son,
    Snatched from my side, killed by my enemies.
    So long as thoughts of vengeance filled my mind
    I could not feel my dwelling's desolation;   235
    But now that I have laid their kingdom waste
    And have avenged him, I return and find
    No satisfaction here with my own people.
    Once I read happiness in all their faces,
    Gladness to serve me; but their service now   240
    Is dulled by anxious care and mute resentment.
    They brood upon the future, and obey me
    Because they must, but think: He has no heir.
    I come now to this temple; many times
    I have come before, to pray for victory   245
    Or to give thanks for it. Today I bring
    A hope long cherished, not unknown to you
    Or unexpected: that you will confer

A blessing on my people and on me
By coming home with me to be my wife.   250
IPHIGENIA. My lord, I am a stranger, and you offer
Too much to me; I stand ashamed before you,
A fugitive who never have sought more
Than peace and shelter here—these you have given.
THOAS. That you still keep your origins a secret   255
From me, as from the least among my subjects,
Would not seem right and just to any people.
My shores mean fear to strangers; so the law
And so necessity command. But you
Enjoy here every hospitable right,   260
You we have welcomed, and you spend your days
As your own mind and your own choice determine.
You, I had hoped, would trust me, as a host
Is trusted by a guest whom he befriends.
IPHIGENIA. I have not named my parents to you, not   265
From lack of trust, but from a kind of shame,
My lord; for if you knew who stands before you,
How cursed and steeped in infamy I am
Whom you have cherished and protected—then
Perhaps, alas, your generous heart would quail   270
With horror and strange dread, and far from bidding
Me share your throne, you would drive me from your kingdom
Before my time, before the gods had yet
Decreed my glad homecoming and the end
Of all my wanderings, you would banish me   275
Perhaps, into the weary wretchedness
Which like an ice-cold alien menace waits
For all the homeless exiles of the world.
THOAS. I do not know the counsel and intent
Of the high gods for you and for your house.   280
But since you have lived here with us, enjoying
The gentle rights of hospitality,
I have not lacked their blessing, and you shall not
Persuade me easily that I have taken
A cursed outlaw under my protection.   285
IPHIGENIA. Your kindness brings you blessing, not your guest.
THOAS. The gods curse good deeds done to evil-doers.
So make an end now of your reticence!
I ask this of you, and will treat you justly.
The goddess has entrusted you to me: 290
You have been sacred to me, as to her,

And henceforth too her will shall be my law.
If there is hope of your returning home,
Then I release you from all obligation;
But if that way is barred to you for ever,   295
Your family scattered or annihilated
By some disastrous fortune, then I shall
Claim you as mine, and have some rights to do so.
Speak freely then! for I shall keep my word.
IPHIGENIA. My tongue has lain in bondage: it is hard   300
    To free it now and to disclose at last
    A secret so long kept, for once confided,
    The words are out, and cannot find their way
    Back to the heart's deep refuge, but must fly
    To do harm or do good, as the gods will.   305
    Hear then: my ancestor was Tantalus.
THOAS. That was a weighty word, so calmly spoken.
    Are you of his race, whom the world remembers
    As one to whom the gods once showed high favour,
    That Tantalus whom Zeus himself invited   310
    To counsel him and sit at table with him,
    Whose conversation, rich in wise experience
    And many an oracular subtlety,
    Was fascinating even to the gods?
IPHIGENIA. This was the man. But the gods should not mix   315
    With humankind as if men were their peers.
    The mortal race is weak, and giddiness
    Must seize it on those unaccustomed heights.
    He was no traitor, he was not ignoble,
    Only too great to serve, and as a friend   320
    Of the great Thunderer, all too human. So
    His fault was human, and their judgement stern;
    And poets sing of him that bold presumption
    And breach of trust hurled him from Jove's right hand
    Down to the shades of ancient Tartarus.   325
    Alas, and his whole house the gods now hated!
THOAS. For his offence, or did they too offend?
IPHIGENIA. His sons and grandsons, violent of heart
    They were, and marrow of the Titans' strength
    They inherited from him; but the high god,   330
    He forged a brazen ring about their brows,
    And he made blind their wild and gloomy eyes
    To patience, moderation and wise counsel.
    All their desires turned into raging lust

And raged all round them, fierce and limitless.   335
Pelops himself, the son of Tantalus,
Self-willed and violent—he won his wife,
Oenomáos's daughter Hippodámia,
By treachery and murder. Then she bore him
Two brothers, Atreus and Thyestes. They,   340
As they grew older, watched with envious eyes
Their father's preference for his first son
Born of another marriage. Hatred joined them,
And secretly they planned and carried out
Together their first deed of fratricide.   345
Pelops, supposing the boy's stepmother
To be his murderess, cried out against her,
Demanding back his son, and Hippodámia
Killed herself—

THOAS.   You are silent? Tell the rest.
Do not regret your trust in me; speak on.   350

IPHIGENIA. Happy the man with ancestors whose deeds
    Are a glad memory, a lofty tale
    And good to tell, who proudly sees himself
    As one more link upon a noble chain.
    For generations of a family   355
    Take time to breed a hero or a monster;
    A lineage of good or evil men
    Brings forth at last one whom the whole world loves
    Or one who horrifies the world. When Pelops
    Died, his two sons, Atreüs and Thyéstes,   360
    Ruled Argos jointly. But this peace was not
    A lasting one. Thyestes before long
    Seduced his brother's wife; he in revenge
    Banished him from the kingdom. But Thyestes,
    Brooding on evil deeds, had long ago   365
    Stolen a son from Atreus; secretly,
    With flattering malice, reared him as his own;
    And now, filling his heart with rage and vengeance,
    Sent him into the city, where he planned
    To kill his father, thinking him his uncle.   370
    The would-be murderer was caught, and Atreus
    Doomed him to cruel death, believing him
    To be his brother's son. In drunken rage
    He watched the tortured boy, and learnt too late
    Who he had been. Then, lusting for such dire   375
    Revenge as never had been known before,

He fell to silent scheming. He pretended
A reconciliation with his brother,
Lured him and his two nephews back to Argos,
Seized the young boys, slaughtered and cooked them both   380
And for the first day's dinner served this foul
And nauseous dish of horror to their father.
Thyestes, glutted now on his own flesh,
Felt a strange sadness, asked: Where are my children?
And thought he heard their voices and their footsteps   385
Already at the door, when Atreüs,
With his teeth bared in dreadful glee, threw down
In front of him their severed heads and feet.
My lord, you turn your face away in horror:
So the bright sun's face turned, its chariot swerved   390
From its eternal path across the sky.
From such a house your priestess is descended;
And her ancestral story has much more
To tell of hideous fates and deeds of madness
Which now the heavy wings of night have hidden,   395
And dreadful mirk obscures their memory.
THOAS. So let your silence hide them. I have heard
  Enough abominations! Tell me by
  What miracle you sprang from that wild race.
IPHIGENIA. Atreus's eldest son was Agamemnon;   400
  He is my father. Yet I will declare
  That since my childhood I have known in him
  The very model of a perfect man.
  I was his first-born child by Clytemnestra;
  Electra was the next. He reigned in peace,   405
  And so the royal house of Tantalus
  Rested from its long turmoil. But my parents
  Lacked one thing for their happiness, a son;
  And scarcely had this wish been granted, scarcely
  Was dear Orestes born and his two sisters   410
  Lovingly tending him, than as he grew
  So a new evil grew to threaten us.
  Your countrymen have heard of the great war
  In which the might of all the lords of Greece
  Is laying siege to Troy, to avenge the abduction   415
  Of the world's loveliest woman. Whether they
  Have yet destroyed the city and completed
  Their vengeance, is not known to me. My father
  Led the Greek army. His ships vainly waited

At Aulis for a favourable wind; 420
Diana, angry with the king, delayed them,
Demanding, through her priest, a sacrifice;
And Calchas named my father's eldest daughter.
They lured me with my mother to the camp,
They dragged me to the altar, and my life 425
Was offered to the goddess—this appeased her!
She did not want my blood, she rescued me,
Hiding me in a cloud. When I regained
My life, my senses, I was in this temple.
I who now stand before you, I am she: 430
Atreus's grandchild, Agamemnon's daughter,
Iphigenia, great Diana's handmaid.

THOAS. The unnamed stranger and the royal princess
Merit my trust and favour equally;
And I repeat the offer I have made: 435
Come, follow me, and share all that is mine.

IPHIGENIA. My lord, how can I dare accept? The goddess
Who saved me, must not she alone dispose
Of me and of my consecrated life?
She sought and found this place of refuge for me 440
And keeps me here, to be perhaps one day
A joy to my old father, who has now
Suffered enough her seeming punishment.
Perhaps my happy homecoming is near;
And should I now, blind to her purposes, 445
Bind myself here against her will? I prayed
Her for some token, if I was to stay.

THOAS. This is her token: that you still are here.
You need not be so anxiously evasive.
Refusal wastes its breath in eloquence: 450
The only word the other hears is 'no'.

IPHIGENIA. I am not using mere misleading words.
I have disclosed my deepest feelings to you.
And you must know yourself how anxiously
I long to see my father and my mother, 455
Electra and Orestes—you must feel
My hope that in our ancient halls one day,
Where often grief still murmurs out my name,
Joy yet may welcome me like one new-born,
And deck our door-posts with the festive garland! 460
Oh, if you sent me home again, you would
Be giving life to me and to us all.

THOAS. Set sail then, and return! Do your heart's bidding,
    Ignore the voice of reason and good counsel,
    Be nothing but a woman, and surrender   465
    To such ungoverned impulse as may seize you
    And drag you restlessly about the world.
    For when the hearts of women are inflamed
    No sacred bond can hold them, flattering
    Seducers can entice them; fathers, husbands,   470
    In constant love have cherished them in vain.
    But if that sudden ardour of the blood
    Is silent in them, then they will be deaf
    To any power of golden-voiced persuasion.
IPHIGENIA. My lord, do not forget your noble promise!   475
    Is this your answer to my confidence?
    You seemed prepared for all that I might say.
THOAS. But not for such unhoped-for words as these.
    Yet I should have expected them; I knew
    That I had come to parley with a woman.   480
IPHIGENIA. My lord, do not speak ill of our poor sex.
    A woman's weapons are not glorious
    Like those of men, yet they are not ignoble.
    Believe me, here I am a better judge
    Than you of what is in your interests.   485
    You do not know yourself or me, and yet
    You think we could find happiness together.
    Full of this confidence, in all good will,
    You urge me to consent to what you wish;
    And here I thank the gods that they have given me   490
    The strength that will not let me undertake
    This marriage-bond which they have not approved.
THOAS. This is no god, but your own heart that speaks.
IPHIGENIA. Their only speech to us is through our hearts.
THOAS. And have I not the right to hear it too?   495
IPHIGENIA. The storm of passion drowns that gentle voice.
THOAS. Only the priestess hears it, I dare say.
IPHIGENIA. A king should hearken to it most of all.
THOAS. Your sacred office and your family's
    Celestial dining-rights no doubt bring you   500
    Nearer to Jove than a mere earthborn savage.
IPHIGENIA. This is how you reward me for the confidence
    You forced from me.
THOAS.   I am no more than human.
    Let us make an end of this. My word still stands:

Be priestess of Diana, as she chose you. 505
But may she pardon me the sin of having,
Against old usage and against my conscience,
Withheld her sacrificial victims from her.
No stranger lands here with impunity:
He is condemned to death by ancient law. 510
You alone bound me with such magic ties
Of kindness—half a gentle daughter's love
And half the sweet affection of a bride,
Or so it seemed—which charmed and held my heart
So fast that I forgot my royal duty. 515
For you had lulled my senses into slumber:
I did not hear my people's murmurings
Of discontent. Now my son's early death
Is blamed more openly on me; the crowd
Demands immediate sacrifice, and I 520
No longer will delay it for your sake.
IPHIGENIA. It was not for my sake I spoke against it.
The gods do not demand blood-offerings;
If men think so, it is their own illusion,
The fantasy of cruel human lusts. 525
Did not Diana save me from the priest?
She wanted me to serve her, not to die.
THOAS. For us it is not fitting to interpret
And bend a sacred custom thus or thus
To suit our needs and fickle reasonings. 530
Do now your duty, as I shall do mine.
Two strangers have been found, hiding in caves
By the sea shore; they have brought danger to
My kingdom, and they are my prisoners.
Your goddess shall reclaim with these first victims 535
The due so long withheld from her. They shall
Be sent to you; you know the ceremony.

Exit.

IPHIGENIA. You have clouds, oh gracious rescuer,
To snatch up innocent victims, to hide them
And on winds to bear them away from their 540
Grim fate's grasp, far over the sea,
Over the wide earth's uttermost reaches,
Carrying them to the place of your choosing.
You are wise, you behold the future,
And the past is still present for you, 545

And your eyes watch over your servants
As your light, the life of the night-time,
Watches serenely over the earth.
Oh let my hands be preserved from bloodshed!
It can bring no rest and no blessing;   550
Even the shade of a fated victim
Haunts his wretched involuntary murderer,
Waits for the evil hour of his terror.
For the immortals love the far-flung
Goodly races of humankind,   555
And they gladly extend man's fleeting
Life for a little, glad to grant him
A longer look at their own eternal
Heavens, sharing their sight with mortals,
Pleasing them with it a little longer.   560

ACT II

Orestes. Pylades.

ORESTES. This is a road that leads us to our death;
And every step we take fills me with peace.
When I prayed to Apollo for a respite
From the avenging demons that pursue me
So horribly, his divine words held out,   565
Or so it seemed, sure hope of help and rescue
Here in the temple where his dearest sister
Rules over Tauris. Now he keeps this promise,
For now my misery is all to end
Here with my life. How easily do I,   570
Whose heart a god's hand seized and crushed, whose mind
Is numbed with pain, how easily renounce
The sun's sweet light! And if it is decreed
That Atreus's descendants shall not fall
In battle, crowned and conquering—if I must   575
Die as my ancestors and father did
Wretchedly, like a beast, bloodily slaughtered,
Then let it be! Better the altar here
Than the dark infamous corner where some next-
Of-kin assassin's nets ensnare their victim.   580
Leave me in peace till then, daughters of hell,
You unleashed hounds who sniff behind my feet,

Hunting the blood that drips from them, this blood
That marks the path for you to follow me!
Leave me, for I shall soon come down to you!   585
The daylight must not look on you or me,
The green and lovely earth must not become
A playground for such spectres! I shall seek
You in the underworld, where all alike
Are bound by fate in dull eternal gloom.   590
Only you, Pylades my friend, the guiltless
Companion of my guilt and of my exile,
I grieve to take with me so prematurely
Into that land of grief! Your life and death
Are all I now have hopes and fears about.   595
PYLADES. Orestes, unlike you I am not ready
    Yet to go down into that shadow-kingdom.
    I am still pondering how in this dark maze
    Of paths that seem to lead us to our doom
    We yet may find some steep way back to life.   600
    I do not think of death; I wait and watch
    For some god-given opportunity
    To make our glad escape from here. For death
    Must come inevitably, whether men
    Fear it or not; and even when the priestess   605
    Raises her hand to cut the fatal lock
    From each of our death-consecrated heads,
    My only thought shall be of how to save us.
    Lift yourself out of this despondency!
    Our danger is increased by your misgivings.   610
    We have Apollo's word: Orestes shall
    Find help and consolation and homecoming
    Here at his sister's shrine. No double sense
    Hides in the words of gods, as sad men think.
ORESTES. When I was still a child, my mother wrapped   615
    This mantle of life's darkness round my head.
    And so I grew, an image of my father,
    And on my mother and her paramour
    My mute gaze rested as a sharp reproach.
    How often when my sister, poor Electra,   620
    Sat silent by the fire in the great hall,
    I would cling to her knees in dumb distress
    And stare at her with my wide childish eyes
    As she wept bitterly. Then she would tell
    Me many things about our noble father.   625

I longed to see him, longed to be with him,
And wished myself at Troy, or his return.
Then the day came when he—
PYLADES.   Oh let hell's goblins
   Gibber at night about that darkest hour!
   Let us remember better times: let them   630
   Nerve us afresh to new heroic deeds.
   The gods have need of many men to serve them,
   Many good men on this wide earth, and they
   Are counting on your service still. They did not
   Destine you to accompany your father   635
   When he went his unwilling way to Hades.
ORESTES. If only I had caught his garment's hem
   And followed him!
PYLADES.   The gods who saved your life
   Were provident for mine, for what would have
   Become of me, if you did not exist?   640
   Since we were children I have only lived
   With you and for you, wishing nothing else.
ORESTES. Do not remind me of those happy days
   When I had taken refuge in your house
   And wisely, lovingly, your noble father   645
   Tended me like a young half-frozen flower;
   And you, an ever livelier companion,
   Like a light many-coloured butterfly
   Round some dark blossom, every day you danced
   And played round me with new abundant life   650
   And joy that overflowed into my soul,
   Till I was borne along with you on tides
   Of eager youth, my troubles all forgotten.
PYLADES. I loved you: that was when my life began.
ORESTES. Say rather, that was when your troubles started.   655
   This is the dreadful secret of my fate:
   That like a plague-infected exile, I
   Bear hidden pain and death about with me,
   That in whatever wholesome place I come to
   I soon see all those faces fresh with health   660
   Wither and wince in slow death-agony.
PYLADES. Orestes! I would be the first to die
   Like that, if there were poison in your breath;
   Yet here I am, still happy and undaunted.
   And happiness and love are wings that lift us   665
   To heroes' deeds.

ORESTES.   To heroes' deeds? Ah yes,
   There was a time when we were planning them!
   Often we would go hunting then together,
   And chase our quarry over hill and dale,
   Hoping one day to equal our great forebears   670
   In strength and valour, and with club and sword
   Hunt the earth clear of monsters and of bandits;
   Then in the evening we would sit and rest
   On the wide sea's shore, lean against each other
   And watch the waves lapping about our feet,   675
   And all the world lay open wide before us.
   Then one of us would start, and seize his sword,
   And our innumerable future deeds
   Would throng like stars around us in the night.

PYLADES. The great achievement that one's soul desires   680
   Is infinite. We should like all our deeds
   To be at once as great as they become
   When long years later, in the mouths of bards,
   Their fame has spread to many lands and peoples.
   How fine the deeds of our forefathers sound   685
   When we are young and in the quiet evening
   Drink in their music as some minstrel plays!
   Yet what we do is what it was to them:
   Mere hard, unfinished labour.
   And thus we chase the things that flee from us   690
   And hardly heed the path that we are treading,
   Or see the footprints of our ancestors,
   The traces of their lives, left there beside us.
   We hurry in pursuit of their mere shadows,
   Glimpsing them far ahead, a godlike vision   695
   That crowns the golden-clouded mountain-tops.
   I can respect no man who ponders how
   Public opinion may one day exalt him.
   But you should thank the gods that in your youth
   They have done such great things through you already.   700

ORESTES. When by their will a man does some glad deed,
   Defending his own family, increasing
   His kingdom, making safe its boundaries,
   Slaying old foes or putting them to flight—
   Then let him thank the gods for granting him   705
   Our life's chief satisfaction. I was chosen
   To be a butcher, singled out to murder
   My mother whom I nonetheless revered,

Infamously avenging infamy.
Thus they decreed my ruin. Oh believe me,   710
The gods have cursed the house of Tantalus
And have ordained for me, his last descendant,
No innocent or honourable death.
PYLADES. The gods do not avenge ancestral crimes
On the descendants: each man, good or evil,   715
Gets his requital when his deed is done.
Blessings, not curses, are inherited.
ORESTES. Did a parental blessing bring us here?
PYLADES. At least we know it was the high gods' will.
ORESTES. It is the high gods' will, then, that destroys us.   720
PYLADES. First do their bidding, then you may have hope.
Brother and sister must be reunited:
When you have brought Diana back to Delphi
And she again is worshipped with Apollo
There by a noble people, they will both   725
Reward this deed with favour; they will save you
From the infernal demons, none of whom
Has even dared enter this sacred grove.
ORESTES. Then I shall have at least a peaceful death.
PYLADES. I think quite otherwise. I have reflected   730
With care on what has been and what will be,
And think I understand the combination.
In the gods' counsels this great deed perhaps
Has long been ripening. Diana wearies
Of this rude shore, this barbarous people, their   735
Bloodthirsty human sacrifices. We
Were chosen for this noble enterprise:
It is our task, and we have been brought here
Already very strangely to its threshold.
ORESTES. How very artfully you interweave   740
The counsels of the gods with your own wishes.
PYLADES. What else is human wisdom but to listen
Attentively for hints of heaven's will?
A noble man who has done some great wrong
May be called by the gods to some hard task,   745
Something that seems impossible to us:
This hero conquers, and his penance serves
The gods and serves the world, which then reveres him.
ORESTES. If I am called upon to live and act,
Then let some god lift from my burdened brow   750
The nauseous swoon that drags me on and on

Along this path smeared with my mother's blood,
Downwards to death! Let him be merciful
And stanch this fountain that for ever wells
Out of her wounds, raining defilement on me!   755
PYLADES. Be calm and wait. You are making matters worse.
Leave to the Furies their own office! Let
Me think, and do not speak. When the time comes
And our joint strength is needed for the deed,
I will call on you, and with considered daring   760
We both shall move to its accomplishment.
ORESTES. I hear Ulysses talking.
PYLADES.   Do not mock me.
We each must choose someone to emulate,
Some hero who will guide us up the steep
Paths to Olympus. And I must confess   765
I do not think that trickery and cunning
Disgraces any man bent on bold deeds.
ORESTES. I prefer one who is both brave and honest.
PYLADES. That is why I did not ask your advice.
I have made a beginning. From our guards   770
I have elicited some facts already.
There is a stranger here, a god-like woman
Who holds in check that old bloodthirsty law;
Incense and prayer and purity of heart
She offers to the gods instead. Men praise   775
Her gentle nature. She was born, they say,
Of the Amazon race, and fled her country,
Escaping from some terrible misfortune.
ORESTES. Her reign of light, it seems, has lost its power
Now that a criminal is here, pursued   780
And hooded by the curse as by vast darkness.
Now pious bloodlust has released old custom
From its new bondage, to destroy us both.
The savagery of the king condemns us;
A woman will not save us from his rage.   785
PYLADES. Be glad it is a woman! for a man,
Even the best, grows used to cruelty
And in the end will even bind himself
By law to what he loathes; hardened by habit
He changes almost out of recognition.   790
But when a woman has made up her mind
She is inflexible, one can rely
More surely on her, both for good and ill.

126

—Hush, she is coming; leave us. I must not
Tell her our names at once, I will only half   795
Confide our story to her. Go, and let
Us meet again before she speaks to you.

Exit Orestes. Enter Iphigenia.

IPHIGENIA. Tell me, oh stranger, from what land you come,
  For you resemble, if I judge aright,
  A Greek and not a Scythian.   800

She removes his chains.

                    This freedom
  Which I restore to you puts you in peril;
  May the gods shield you both from what awaits you.
PYLADES. Oh sweetest voice! Thrice welcome music of
  My mother-tongue here in a foreign land!
  Now the blue mountains of my native shore   805
  Appear before my captive eyes again,
  Bringing new gladness. Oh let this my joy
  Persuade you that I also am a Greek!
  For a brief moment I forgot how much
  I stand in need of you; I had allowed   810
  My mind to feast upon that splendid vision.
  Oh tell me then, unless your lips are sealed
  By some decree of fate, from which of our
  Peoples you claim your godlike origin.
IPHIGENIA. I am the priestess who now speak to you,   815
  Chosen and consecrated by her goddess;
  Let it suffice you to know that. Say now
  Who you are, and what ineluctable
  Misfortune brought you here with your companion.
PYLADES. Easily I can tell you of the fate   820
  That dogs our steps with burdensome persistence;
  I would it were no harder, godlike lady,
  For you to give us some bright glimpse of hope.
  We are from Crete, the sons of great Adrastus;
  I am the youngest, Cephalus, and he   825
  Laódamas, the eldest of the house.
  Between us stood another brother, rude
  And wild, who even in our childish games
  Sowed discord and destroyed all pleasure in them.
  We were content to do our mother's bidding   830
  While our father was absent at the war

With Troy; but when he came back, rich with spoils,
And then soon died, the three of us fell out
About the title and the inheritance.
I took the eldest's part, and it was he   835
Who slew our brother. Still the Fury drives him
Hither and thither for this deed of blood.
But now Apollo's oracle at Delphi
Sends us with words of hope to this wild shore.
Here in his sister's temple, as he told us,   840
Help was at hand, we should be blessed and saved.
We have been captured and brought here and offered
To you in sacrifice. That is our story.

IPHIGENIA. Then did Troy fall? Oh tell me so, dear friend!

PYLADES. Troy is no more. Oh tell me you will save us!   845
Hasten the help a god has promised us;
Have pity on my brother, oh let him
Soon hear you say a kind and gracious word!
And yet I beg you, when you speak to him
Be gentle with him, for so easily   850
He can be seized and shaken to the core
By joy or grief or by his memories—
A fever and a madness will attack him
And his clear generous soul be given over
To all the rage of the avenging Furies.   855

IPHIGENIA. Great as your trouble is, I do implore you
Forget it now, till you have answered me.

PYLADES. The lofty city that for ten long years
Withstood the assembled might of all the Greeks
Now lies in ruins, and will stand no more.   860
But round it many graves of our best warriors
Remind us still of that barbarian place.
Achilles fell, with his beloved friend.

IPHIGENIA. They too, those godlike heroes, in the dust!

PYLADES. Ajax, Télamon's son, and Palamedes—   865
They too were not to see their homes again.

IPHIGENIA. (He does not name my father, does not say
He was among the slain. Yes! he still lives!
I shall see him again. Oh hope, my heart!)

PYLADES. But happy are the thousands who died there   870
Their death in battle, bitter and yet sweet:
For those who did return found, by some god's
Hostility, no triumph waiting for them,

But hideous terrors and a dismal end.
Do these shores lie beyond the voice of man?   875
For as far as it reaches it bears word
Of the appalling crimes that were committed.
Have you not heard what happened in Mycene,
What deed still makes its stricken halls re-echo
With never-ending grief?—Great Agamemnon,   880
On the day he returned, was trapped and murdered,
With the help of Aegisthus, by his wife.—
I see that you revere that royal house:
This unexpected monstrous news has moved
You to distress you try in vain to hide.   885
Are you the daughter of a friend, or were you
A neighbour to the king, born in that city?
Do not conceal it; and forgive me for
Being the first to tell you of these horrors.
IPHIGENIA. How did they carry out the dreadful deed?   890
PYLADES. When the king, on the day of his arrival,
    Stepped from his bath, refreshed and calm, and asked
    His wife to hand his robe to him, the deadly
    Clytemnestra cast round his noble head,
    Over his shoulders, an ensnaring fabric,   895
    Cunningly folded, intricately wrought;
    And as he vainly struggled to break free
    As from a net, the treacherous Aegisthus
    Struck him: and thus this mighty prince went down
    To death and Hades, with his eyes enshrouded.   900
IPHIGENIA. And what was her accomplice's reward?
PYLADES. A kingdom and a bed, both his already.
IPHIGENIA. So wicked lust inspired this shameful crime?
PYLADES. And a deep-seated long desire for vengeance.
IPHIGENIA. And how had Agamemnon wronged the queen?   905
PYLADES. By a dark deed which would, if there could be
    Any excuse for murder, have excused her.
    He had lured her to Aulis, where the Greek
    Ships were delayed at a divinity's
    Behest, by violent adverse winds; and there   910
    He dragged their eldest child, Iphigenia,
    To great Diana's altar, where she fell
    A bloody sacrifice to the Greek cause.
    And this, they say, bred such a deep resentment
    In Clytemnestra's heart, that when Aegisthus   915

Wooed her, she yielded to him, and herself
Ensnared her husband in a fatal net.
IPHIGENIA (*covering her head*). It is enough; I shall return to you.

Exit.

PYLADES. She seems much moved: the royal house's fate
    Concerns her, for whoever she may be   920
    She must have known King Agamemnon well
    And is some member of a noble house,
    Sold to this place. Thus fortune favours us.
    Be calm, my heart! We must be bold and wise,
    And steer towards this rising star of hope.   925

ACT III

Iphigenia. Orestes.

IPHIGENIA. Unhappy prisoner, I loose your bonds
    In token of a still unhappier fate.
    The freedom granted in this sanctuary
    Is like a last bright glimpse of life to one
    Mortally sick: a messenger of death.   930
    And still I cannot, dare not tell myself
    That you are lost. How could I consecrate
    You both to death, murder you with my hand?
    No one, no other hand, may touch your heads
    So long as I am priestess of Diana,   935
    And yet if I refuse to do that duty,
    The duty which the angry king demands,
    He will appoint one of my maidens in
    My place, and all the help I then could give you
    Would be no more than ardent wishes. Oh,   940
    Dear fellow-countryman, even a slave
    Who has approached our hearth and household gods
    Is welcome to us in a foreign land;
    With what blessings and joy must I not then
    Receive you both, who represent to me   945
    The heroes I have learnt from early childhood
    To hold in reverence, who soothe and flatter
    My inmost heart with a sweet hope's renewal!
ORESTES. Is it with wise intent that you conceal

Your name and origin, or may I know 950
   Whom, like a goddess, I have here encountered?
IPHIGENIA. This you shall know. But now, complete the tale
   Which I have only half heard from your brother:
   What dire and unexpected fate awaited
   Those who returned from Troy, and speechlessly, 955
   Upon their very thresholds, struck them down?
   When I came to this shore I was still young,
   Yet I remember how I shyly gazed,
   Half in astonishment and half in fear,
   Upon those heroes, watching them set forth. 960
   It was as if Olympus had been opened
   And all the noble figures of the past
   Sent down to terrify our enemy;
   And Agamemnon splendid above all!
   Oh tell me! so he fell, no sooner home 965
   Than murdered by his wife and by Aegisthus?
ORESTES. It is as you have said.
IPHIGENIA.   Oh poor Mycene!
   How wild a crop of curses they have sown
   Upon you, the accursed Tantalids!
   Like monstrous weeds that shake their heads and scatter 970
   A thousand seeds of evil all around them,
   So they engendered for their children's children
   Next-of-kin-killers, like an endless madness!
   A sudden swoon of fear darkened my hearing
   Of what your brother said: tell me the rest. 975
   How did the last son of that royal race,
   The noble child destined one day to avenge
   His father's death—oh say, how did Orestes
   Escape the hour of blood? Did the same fate
   Ensnare him with the nets of hell, or is 980
   He saved? Is he alive? And is Electra
   Still living?
ORESTES.   They still live.
IPHIGENIA.   Oh golden sun,
   Lend your bright rays, lay them before Jove's throne
   As thanks from me, for I am poor and mute.
ORESTES. If you are bound by friendship, or by some 985
   Bond even closer, to that royal house,
   As by your sweet delight you seem to tell me,
   Oh then check your heart's impulse, hold it fast!

For when we feel such joy, sudden relapse
Into great grief is hard to bear. I see   990
You only know of Agamemnon's death.
IPHIGENIA. Need I know more? Is this not news enough?
ORESTES. You have been told of only half the horror.
IPHIGENIA. Need I fear for Electra and Orestes?
ORESTES. They live; but what of Clytemnestra's fate?   995
IPHIGENIA. No fear nor hope avails against it now.
ORESTES. She is no longer in the land of hope.
IPHIGENIA. Did she shed her own blood in mad remorse?
ORESTES. No, yet she met her death by her own blood.
IPHIGENIA. Tell me more plainly, to resolve my doubt.   1000
    A thousand troubled and uncertain thoughts
    Beat with dark wings of fear about my head.
ORESTES. So the gods have elected me to be
    The bearer of this tale, this deed that I
    So long to bury in the speechless caves   1005
    Of night's mute underworld! Against my will
    I am compelled by your sweet voice; but it
    May ask a gift of pain and still receive it.
    The day their father died, Electra rescued
    And hid Orestes: Strophius, the king's   1010
    Brother-in-law, received him willingly
    And brought his nephew up with his own son
    Pylades, who befriended the newcomer
    With sweetest ties of brotherly affection.
    And as they grew up, so there grew in them   1015
    A burning, deep desire to avenge
    The murder of the king. Unheralded,
    Disguised, they reached Mycene with the grievous
    News of Orestes' death, as they pretended,
    Bringing his ashes; and Queen Clytemnestra   1020
    Received them well. When they were in the palace,
    Electra made herself known to Orestes,
    Rekindling in him the hot fire of vengeance
    Which in the sacred presence of his mother
    Had flickered low. She took him secretly   1025
    To the place where their father was struck down,
    Where on the floor that had been washed so often
    The traces of that blood so foully shed,
    Though old and faint, still ominously lingered.
    With an inflaming passion she described   1030

132

To him each detail of the infamous deed,
Described her slavish miserable life,
The arrogance of the successful traitors,
The danger to them both, brother and sister,
Whose mother now had grown unnatural;   1035
Then thrust on him that ancient dagger which
Had slain so many Tantalids already;
And Clytemnestra fell by her son's hand.
IPHIGENIA. Oh you immortals, who live blessedly
In the pure day above the changing clouds,   1040
Was this why you have kept me all these years
So far from humankind, so near to you,
Why you imposed on me this childlike task
Of nourishing a flame of sacred fire,
And why my soul, as if it were that flame,   1045
Has been drawn upwards everlastingly,
In gentle love, to your bright dwelling-place:
All this, that I might be so late to learn
These horrors of my kin, feel them more deeply?
—Oh tell me of the unfortunate Orestes!   1050
ORESTES. If only I could tell you he is dead!
Like a hot ferment, from his mother's blood
Her slaughtered ghost
Rose up, and summoned the Night's ancient daughters:
'Seize him, the matricide, let him not flee!   1055
Your appointed prey, this murderer, hunt him!'
They heard, they listened, and like hungry eagles
They peered about them with their hollow eyes,
In their black caverns they began to stir;
Out of the hidden corners their companions,   1060
Doubt and Remorse, crept noiselessly to join them.
From the waters of hell foul vapours rose
Before them, circling round their guilty victim,
Befogging him with endless rumination
On what he did and cannot now undo.   1065
Thus these appointed demons, these destroyers
May tread again the gods' sweet fertile earth
From which an ancient curse once banished them.
Their quarry flees, they follow tirelessly,
Each pause portends an onset of new terror.   1070
IPHIGENIA. Alas, poor fugitive! the same pursuit
Afflicts you, and you feel what he must suffer.

ORESTES. What do you mean by that? What same pursuit?
IPHIGENIA. You are like him, haunted by fratricide;
    Your younger brother has already told me.   1075
ORESTES. I cannot bear that you who are so noble
    And great of heart, should be deceived by falsehood.
    Let strangers deal with strangers in this way,
    Weaving their subtle webs of careful fiction
    Around each other's feet; but between us   1080
    Let there be truth!
    I am Orestes, and my guilty head
    Bows itself to the grave and longs for death;
    I welcome it in any form! For you,
    Whoever you may be, and for my friend,   1085
    I desire rescue, but not for myself.
    It seems that you live here against your will.
    Seek some means, then, how you may both escape
    And leave me here. Let my slain corpse be cast
    From the cliff-top, my blood reek to the sea,   1090
    And bring a curse on this barbarian shore!
    Go home together and begin a new
    And better life, in the sweet land of Greece.

He moves away from her.

IPHIGENIA. Grace of fulfilment, sweetest daughter of
    Most mighty Zeus, at last you have descended   1095
    Upon me! How your image towers above me!
    My gaze can scarcely reach up to your hands
    Which are so full of fruit, garlands of flowers,
    The blessings and the treasures of Olympus.
    And as one knows a king by his excess   1100
    In giving, for what must to him seem little
    Is wealth enough for thousands: so we know
    You, oh immortals, by your long withheld
    Gifts that have been wisely and long prepared.
    For you alone know what is good for us,   1105
    You who behold the future's far-flung kingdom,
    Which every evening sky, each cloak of stars
    And clouds conceals from men. Calmly you listen
    As like impatient children we implore you
    For swifter gifts; you do not pluck for us   1110
    The heavens' golden fruit till it is ready;
    But woe to him who snatches what is still

Unripe, and eats the bitterness of death.
Oh let this happiness so long awaited,
Which I scarcely dared think of, let it not   1115
Dissolve and vanish like the dear dream-shadow
Of a lost friend, leaving a threefold grief!
ORESTES (*returning to her*).
    If you are praying to the gods, pray for yourself
    And Pylades, but do not speak my name.
    You will not save the criminal you are   1120
    Befriending, merely share his cursèd fate.
IPHIGENIA. My fate and yours are closely intertwined.
ORESTES. No! let me make my way to death alone
    And unaccompanied. Even if you could cloak
    An evildoer in your priestly veil,   1125
    You could not hide me from the Sleepless Ones;
    Your heavenly presence, lady, though it may
    Turn them aside, it cannot drive them back.
    They dare not set their brazen insolent feet
    Within the precinct of your sacred grove;   1130
    But here and there, from far off, I can hear
    Their hideous laughter. Wolves will wait like this
    Around the tree a wayfarer has climbed
    To save himself. They lie in wait for me
    Out there: and if I leave this wooded shelter   1135
    Then they will rise, shaking their snaky heads
    And stamping up the dust all around me, rise
    And drive their quarry on.
IPHIGENIA.   Hear me, Orestes;
    I have a loving word to say to you.
ORESTES. Keep it to say to one whom the gods love.   1140
IPHIGENIA. The gods are lighting you to a new hope.
ORESTES. From the river of death, through smoke and fog
    I see a pale glint lighting me to hell.
IPHIGENIA. Have you no other sister but Electra?
ORESTES. There was an eldest whom I scarcely knew,   1145
    Whom lucky death, hard though it seemed to us,
    Soon rescued from our house's misery.
    Oh, question me no more; would you become
    Yourself one of the Furies? Gloatingly
    They are blowing the ashes from my soul,   1150
    They will not even let the last dull embers
    Left over from our family's holocaust

Die out in me. Oh must this fire forever,
Fanned to fresh rage deliberately fed
With hell's hot sulphur, burn and scourge my soul? 1155
IPHIGENIA. I will scatter sweet incense in the flame.
Oh let this conflagration in your heart
Be cooled by love's pure breath, its gentle breeze!
Orestes, oh my dear, can you not hear me?
Have the demons of terror that pursue you 1160
Made the blood run so dry in all your veins?
Does some creeping enchantment, like the head
Of the foul Gorgon, turn your limbs to stone?
Oh, if a mother's blood calls from the ground
And cries its hollow summons down to hell, 1165
Shall a pure sister's blessing not have power
To call the gods of healing from Olympus?
ORESTES. It calls! It calls! Do you then seek my ruin?
Are you a vengeance-goddess in disguise?
Who are you, you whose voice so terribly 1170
Can stir my soul into so deep a turmoil?
IPHIGENIA. There in your deepest soul you know the answer.
Orestes, it is I, Iphigenia!
I am alive.
ORESTES.   You!
IPHIGENIA.   Oh my brother!
ORESTES.   Leave me!
Go, I advise you, do not touch my hair! 1175
It scorches like Creüsa's bridal garment,
With unquenchable fire: do not come near me!
Vile as I am, I want to die alone
Like Hercules, enclosed in my own shame.
IPHIGENIA. You are not going to die! Oh, if you only 1180
Could calm yourself, speak one calm word to me!
Resolve my doubts, let me be sure of this
Great happiness that I so long have prayed for.
Like a great turning wheel, delight and grief
Change places in me. You are a man, a stranger, 1185
A tremor holds me back: yet my whole soul
Draws me and drives me to embrace my brother.
ORESTES. Is this some Bacchic temple, has the priestess
Been seized by a disordered sacred frenzy?
IPHIGENIA. Oh hear me, look at me! see how my heart 1190
After so many years, opens to joy:
The joy of greeting what is dearest now

To me in all the world, kissing your head,
Holding you in my arms, which hitherto
Were open only to the empty winds! 1195
Oh let me, let me do so! for the eternal
Fountain that gushes from Parnassus, down
From rock to rock into the golden valley,
Flows no more clearly than this joy that pours
Out of my heart and like a blessed sea 1200
Surrounds me. Oh Orestes, oh my brother!

ORESTES. Sweet nymph, I do not trust you or your flattery.
Diana's servants should be more austere:
She punishes those who profane her temples.
Do not embrace me in this way! Or if 1205
You wish to love and rescue some young man
And offer him a tender happiness,
You should turn your attention to my friend:
He is worthier of it. Go and look for him
Where he is wandering on that rocky path; 1210
Show him the way, and spare me.

IPHIGENIA.   Oh my brother,
Come to yourself! You have found me: recognize me!
Do not mistake your sister's pure delight
For reckless, lawless passion. O blest gods,
Lift the delusion from his staring eyes, 1215
Or this our moment of extremest joy
Will plunge us into threefold wretchedness!
She is here, your long-lost sister! I was saved
From death: the goddess snatched me from the altar
And brought me here, to her own sanctuary. 1220
You are a captive, marked for sacrifice,
And in the priestess you have found your sister.

ORESTES. Unhappy woman! Let the sun then watch
The last abominations of our house!
Is Electra not here? for she must perish 1225
Along with us, she must not now live on
To suffer further grievous blows of fate.
It is well, priestess! Take me to the altar:
For fratricide is a tradition in
Our ancient family, and I thank the gods 1230
They have decreed I should be rooted out
Before I have had children. Take my advice
And do not love the sunlight or the starlight
Too much; come, follow me to the dark kingdom!

As in hell's sulphurous pit a brood of dragons   1235
Fight and destroy their misbegotten kin,
So our hate-frenzied race destroys itself.
Come down with me, still childless and still guiltless!—
You look at me with sorrow? Let me be!
That was the look in Clytemnestra's eyes,   1240
Trying to find the way to her son's heart;
And yet he raised his hand and struck her down:
He killed his mother! Come, offended ghost!
Come, all you Furies, make a circle here
And be spectators of this welcome scene,   1245
This last and foulest act, devised by you!
The knife is sharpened not by hate or vengeance
But by my loving sister, forced to strike
This blow! Oh, do not weep! You are not to blame.
I never loved, not since I was a child,   1250
Anything as I could love you, my sister!
Yes, do not spare me; wield your priestly dagger,
Tear my heart open, and the seething streams
That rage in it will find release at last.

He collapses in exhaustion.

IPHIGENIA. I cannot bear this joy and misery   1255
  Alone. Where are you, Pylades? Dear friend,
  I need your help; where shall I find you now?

She goes in search of him.

ORESTES (*waking from his stupor and raising his head*).
  One more! Oh let me drink from Lethe's water
  One cool refreshing cup, the last of all!
  Soon it will wash away the spasm of life   1260
  Out of my heart, soon my surrendered spirit,
  Bathed in oblivion, silently will flow
  Into the eternal mist and join the shades.
  May they be kind and let their quietness
  Comfort me now, an earthborn wanderer!—   1265
  What is this whispering among the branches?
  What is that sound that murmurs from the dusk?
  How soon they come to see the new arrival!
  What is that company so gladly met,
  Exchanging greetings, like some princely house   1270
  Assembled? Old with young, and men with women,
  They walk in peace; godlike and like each other

138

These wandering figures seem. Ah yes, they are,
They are my ancestors!—See, with Thyestes
Atreus walks, deep in friendly conversation,   1275
And round them the boys play, their little sons.
Is there no enmity between you here?
Has vengeance been extinguished with the sunlight?
Why then, I too am welcome, and I may
Join in your ceremonial procession.   1280
Welcome, my forebears! Orestes greets you:
He is your race's last survivor.
You sowed the harvest and he has reaped it:
He has come down to you laden with curses.
But here is a place where burdens are lighter: 1285
Oh then accept him, accept him as one of you!—
Atreus, I honour you: you too, Thyestes;
We are no longer enemies here.—
Show me my father! In all my life I have
Only once seen him!—Are you my father,   1290
Walking beside my mother in friendship?
Are you hand in hand with Clytemnestra?
Why then, Orestes too can approach her
And say to her: Look at me, I am your son!
Your son and his! You may bid me welcome.   1295
On earth, in our family, friendly greetings
Were passwords signalling certain murder;
And now the descendants of old Tantalus
Are happy at last, on the far side of night!
You bid me welcome, you take me among you!   1300
Oh lead me to him, to the old man, the ancestor!
Where is the old man? I must see him,
My venerable, my beloved forebear,
He who sat with the gods in council.
You seem to hesitate, you turn from me?   1305
How is this? He is suffering, that great hero?
Alas! the powerful gods have bound him,
Their noble victim, with adamantine
Chains for ever, in cruel torment!

Enter Iphigenia and Pylades.

You too! have you both come down here already,   1310
My sister? How wise of you! Where is Electra?
She is still missing: may some kind god
Soon send her with swift sweet arrows to join us!

Poor friend, I am sorry for you! But come,
Come with me! at Pluto's throne let us gather,   1315
We, his new guests, to bring him greeting!
IPHIGENIA. Brother and sister, radiant sun and moon
Who rise into the wide expanse of heaven
To shine on men, and must withhold your light
From the departed: brother and sister, save us!   1320
Oh maiden goddess, more than all that earth
And heaven contain you love your gracious brother,
And turn your gaze in ceaseless speechless longing
On his eternal brightness. Oh Diana,
Let not my only brother, lost and found   1325
Again at last, rave in this gloomy madness!
And if your purpose when you hid me here
Is now accomplished, if you mean to show
Mercy to me through him, to him through me,
Then free him from the bondage of that curse,   1330
That we may use this precious time of rescue.
PYLADES. Do you not know us, and this sacred grove?
This daylight never shone upon the dead!
These are our arms, your sister and your friend
Still hold you fast, and you are still alive!   1335
Hold on to us: we are not empty shadows.
Listen to me, hear what I say! collect
Your senses: every moment now is precious
And our return hangs on a thread, which now,
It seems, some favourable Fate is spinning.   1340
ORESTES (to Iphigenia). Oh, in your arms, now with my heart set free,
Now let me feel pure joy for the first time!
You gods, who visit the storm-swollen clouds,
Consuming them with your all-powerful fire,
Who with grave mercy, as your thunder roars   1345
And your winds howl, pour the long-prayed-for rain
In mighty torrents down upon the earth,
Yet soon dispel our fearful expectation
With blessings, and transform our wondering dread
Into glad looks and words of thankfulness,   1350
As drops of rain refreshing thirsty leaves
Mirror a myriad-fold the newborn sunlight
And the sweet many-coloured rainbow-nymph
Parts the grey lingering veil with gentle hand:
Oh gods, let me too, in my sister's arms,   1355
On my friend's bosom, here hold fast with joy

And gratitude to what you now have granted!
The curse is lifting, my heart tells me so.
The Eumenides return to Tartarus—
I hear their flight, I hear the brazen gates   1360
Clang shut behind them like far deep-down thunder.
The earth breathes out a sweet refreshing fragrance,
Invites me to explore its wide expanse
Seeking great deeds and life and happiness.
PYLADES. Our time is limited, do not delay!   1365
  Let us set sail for home first, then that wind
  May carry our full praises to the gods.
  Come, we must all take counsel and act quickly.

ACT IV

IPHIGENIA (*alone*). When the heavenly gods
  Ordain for an earthborn mortal   1370
  Many bewilderments, many
  Chances and changes, deeply
  Shaking the heart as it passes
  Out of joy into anguish
  And from anguish to joy again: 1375
  Then they prepare for him also,
  Whether close to the city
  Or on a distant shore,
  A friend not easily moved,
  That in his hour of need   1380
  Help, too, may be at hand.
  To our friend Pylades, oh gods, show favour,
  And bless whatever he may undertake!
  For he is the young hero's arm in battle,
  The bright eye of the aged councillor: 1385
  His soul is tranquil, it has treasured up
  A sacred store of unexhausted stillness,
  And from its depths he offers help and counsel
  To those whom fate has driven about the earth.
  He snatched me from my brother's arms, at whom   1390
  I had been gazing, wondering and still gazing:
  I could not grasp such happiness, I could
  Not let him go, I had no feeling for
  The nearness of the danger that surrounds us.
  Now they have gone to carry out their plan,   1395

Down to the coast where our ship lies in hiding
With our companions, waiting for the sign;
And they have given me a cunning tale
To tell the king, they have taught me what to say
When he sends urgent orders bidding me   1400
Perform the sacrifice. Oh, now I see
That I must let them guide me like a child.
I have not learnt to speak with hidden thoughts
Or to persuade by trickery. Alas,
Alas that we should lie! Do lies unburden   1405
Our hearts, like every truthful word we speak?
No, they do not relieve us; full of dread
We forge them secretly, they are like arrows
Which when we shoot them off are intercepted
By some god's hand that turns them from their mark   1410
And strikes the marksman with them. I am swayed
By many fears. Perhaps the Furies will
Attack my brother savagely again
Down by the shore, on that unhallowed ground.
Perhaps he and his friends will be discovered!—   1415
I think I hear armed men approaching!—Here!
The king has sent his messenger to me;
He comes in haste. My heart beats, and my soul
Is troubled, when I see this good man's face,
Knowing I must confront him with a lie.   1420

Enter Arcas.

ARCAS. Priestess, make haste, offer the sacrifice!
   The king waits, and the people are impatient.
IPHIGENIA. I would have heeded you and done my duty
   But for an unexpected obstacle
   Which came between me and its execution.   1425
ARCAS. And what is this that thwarts the king's command?
IPHIGENIA. Chance fortune, which is outside our control.
ARCAS. Then tell me, that I may report it quickly,
   For it is his decree those two shall die.
IPHIGENIA. That has not been decreed yet by the gods. 1430
   Guilt stains the elder of those men, the blood
   Of a close relative which he has spilt.
   He is pursued by the avenging Furies:
   Even in the temple's inner sanctuary
   The frenzy seized upon him, and his presence   1435
   Defiled the holy place. Now, with my maidens,

142

I must make haste to the seashore and cleanse
Diana's holy image in the waves,
Reconsecrating it with secret rites.
No one must interrupt our ceremony.   1440
ARCAS. I shall inform the king at once of this
   New difficulty; you must not begin
   The sacred work until he gives consent.
IPHIGENIA. That is a matter only for the priestess.
ARCAS. So strange a case the king must know as well.   1445
IPHIGENIA. What he may say can make no difference.
ARCAS. It may be courtesy to ask a king.
IPHIGENIA. I should refuse you, therefore do not press me.
ARCAS. Do not refuse what is expedient.
IPHIGENIA. I will consent if you will not delay.   1450
ARCAS. I will go quickly with this news to where
   He lies encamped, and quickly bring his answer.
   Yet still I long to take him one more message
   That would resolve all these perplexities!
   You did not follow my well-meant advice.   1455
IPHIGENIA. I have done what I could, most willingly.
ARCAS. I think you still may change your mind in time.
IPHIGENIA. It is not in our power so to change.
ARCAS. The impossibility is your own reluctance.
IPHIGENIA. Your wishes cannot make it possible.   1460
ARCAS. Are you so calm, with everything at stake?
IPHIGENIA. The gods are great: I have laid it in their hands.
ARCAS. The gods save humankind by human means.
IPHIGENIA. All hangs upon their will: I wait to know it.
ARCAS. I say again, it all hangs upon yours.   1465
   These strangers are condemned to bitter death
   By the king's anger, and by nothing else.
   Our warriors long ago lost appetite
   For the bloodthirsty ritual sacrifices:
   Many of them indeed, when adverse fate   1470
   Drove them to some strange land, learnt for themselves
   How sweet a blessing for poor wanderers,
   Cast on a foreign shore, it is to meet
   Some human face that speaks of friendly welcome.
   You give this blessing: do not take it from us!   1475
   Easily you may end what you began;
   For when a gentle influence from heaven
   Comes down in human form, it soon gains sway
   Over a new, not yet enlightened people

Which full of life and energy and courage,   1480
    Ruled only by its own wild intuitions,
    Endures the heavy burdens of man's life.
IPHIGENIA. Do not harrow my soul, which still in vain
    You seek to move to do as you desire.
ARCAS. While there is still time, I will spare no pains   1485
    Or repetition of my wiser counsel.
IPHIGENIA. The pains are yours, and only pain is mine,
    And both are useless; therefore leave me now.
ARCAS. But it is to your pain that I appeal,
    For it is kindly and gives good advice.   1490
IPHIGENIA. It seizes me, it overpowers my soul,
    But does not conquer my unwillingness.
ARCAS. How can a lofty soul be so unwilling
    To accept the kindness of a noble man?
IPHIGENIA. It is unseemly that the noble giver   1495
    Should ask, not for my thanks, but for myself.
ARCAS. When love is lacking, words can soon be found
    To serve us as a pretext for refusal.
    I shall inform the king of what has happened.
    Again I beg you, ponder in your heart   1500
    How nobly he has always dealt with you
    From your arrival here until this day.

Exit.

IPHIGENIA. Now at this most untimely of all times
    This good man's words stir me and trouble me
    And fill me with confusion and alarm!   1505
    For as the tide rising in rapid flood
    Engulfs the sand-surrounded rocks that lie
    Along the shore, so a great flood of joy
    Engulfed my inmost soul. Here in my arms
    I hold what I had thought impossible.   1510
    Once more a cloud seemed to surround me gently,
    To lift me from the earth, and rock and lull me
    Again into that sleep which the dear goddess
    Laid lovingly and soothingly about
    My brow, when she reached out her arm to rescue   1515
    Me from the altar. Thus my heart embraced
    My brother in extremity of joy.
    I listened only to his friend's advice,
    My whole soul longed for nothing but to save them.
    And as a sailor gladly turns his back   1520

Upon the wild cliffs of some barren island,
So Tauris lay behind me. Now the voice
Of this good faithful man wakes me again,
Reminds me these are human beings too
Whom I abandon here. Now this deceit   1525
Seems doubly hateful. Oh, be calm, my soul!
Why are you full of doubt and hesitation?
You leave your solitude's sure foothold now
And launch into the deep, where the waves toss you,
Where in dismay you look upon the world   1530
And on yourself, and fail to recognize them.

Enter Pylades.

PYLADES. Where is the priestess? I must quickly bring
    The happy news to her that we are saved!
IPHIGENIA. Here, as you see, I anxiously await
    These words of reassurance which you promise.   1535
PYLADES. Your brother—he is healed! We reached the shore,
    The unconsecrated ground, and stepped upon
    The sand, among the rocks, happily talking,
    Forgetting we had left the grove behind us;
    And the bright flame of youth, brighter than ever,   1540
    More glorious than ever, blazed around
    His head and locks, his eyes were wide and glowing
    With courage and with hope, and his free heart
    Was filled with nothing but the joyful thought
    Of saving me, and saving you who saved him.   1545
IPHIGENIA. May the gods bless you, may no voice of sorrow
    Or lamentation ever pass your lips
    Which now have spoken such good words to me!
PYLADES. I bring you more than these, for when good fortune
    Approaches us, it comes with princely escort.   1550
    We have found our companions too: the ship
    Is hidden in a rocky inlet, where
    They have been sitting, sadly waiting for us.
    They saw your brother, and at once they all
    Surrounded us, excited and rejoicing,   1555
    And begged us to set sail without delay.
    Their hands all long to seize and ply the oars
    And all could even hear a gentle murmur
    Of wind from landward stirring its sweet wings.
    Let us make haste then, lead me to the temple,   1560
    Admit me to the sanctuary, where

I reverently will seize and carry off
The object of our quest, Diana's image.
I need no help, my back is strong enough;
How I look forward to this longed-for burden!   1565

As he speaks these last words he moves towards the temple without noticing
that Iphigenia does not follow him: finally he turns round.

You stand there hesitating—tell me—you
Say nothing, and you seem confused! Is our
Good fortune threatened by some new disaster?
Tell me, have you now sent the king that message,
Cunningly phrased, that we agreed upon?   1570
IPHIGENIA. I have done so, dear friend; but you will blame me—
Your coming was a mute reproach already.
Thoas's messenger came here; I spoke
To him the words you put into my mouth.
He seemed astonished, and insisted he   1575
Must first inform the king of these strange rites,
To learn of his decision in the matter;
And now I am awaiting his return.
PYLADES. Alas! the peril now is poised again
Over our heads! Why did you not adopt   1580
A prudent cloak of priestly secrecy?
IPHIGENIA. I have never used my priesthood as a cloak.
PYLADES. And thus your purity of soul destroys
Yourself and us! Why did I not foresee
This difficulty too? I would have taught you   1585
What you should say to counter his insistence.
IPHIGENIA. Blame only me, I feel the fault is mine,
And yet I could not give another answer
To a man seriously demanding of me
Something I knew was right and reasonable.   1590
PYLADES. We are in more dangerous straits; but even so
Let us not give up hope, or over-rashly
And over-hastily betray ourselves.
Wait calmly for the messenger's return,
And then stand fast, no matter what he says.   1595
The ordering of such rites of consecration
Concerns the priestess only, not the king.
And say, if he demands to see the stranger,
The man afflicted and weighed down by madness,
That you forbid it, that you have us both   1600
Well guarded in the temple. Thus gain time,

146

That we may carry off the sacred trophy
And quickly flee from this barbarian people.
Apollo sends us happy auguries:
We have not yet done his divine command, 1605
And yet his promise has been kept already.
Orestes has been healed, has been set free!
Oh favouring winds, carry us with him now
To the god's rocky island habitation,
Then to Mycene: we shall bring it back 1610
To life, we shall rekindle the dead ashes
In the cold hearth, and our ancestral gods
Shall rise again with joy as the bright flames
Surround their dwellings. You shall be the first
To scatter incense there from golden vessels; 1615
You shall bring life and blessing to that house,
Redeem it from the curse, adorn your kin
With the fresh living blossoms of renewal.
IPHIGENIA. I hear you speak, dear friend, and my soul turns
Towards you like a flower to the sun, 1620
Touched by the warmth and radiance of your words
And turning to them for sweet consolation.
How precious is the presence of a friend
And his unfailing voice! In solitude
We lack its heavenly power, and droop and fade, 1625
For thought and resolution ripen slowly
When hidden in the heart, but with a loving
Friend at our side they easily bear fruit.
PYLADES. Farewell! I will now quickly satisfy
The anxious expectation of our comrades; 1630
Then I will hasten back, hide in the bushes
Among the rocks, wait till you give the signal—
What are your thoughts? A sudden and unspoken
Sadness steals over your unclouded brow.
IPHIGENIA. Forgive me! As light clouds across the sun, 1635
So a light cloud of care and apprehension
Has moved across my soul.
PYLADES.   Banish your fears!
For fear is danger's sly confederate;
They are companions, and increase each other.
IPHIGENIA. And yet it is a noble care that warns me 1640
Not to deceive and treacherously rob
This king who has become my second father.
PYLADES. You are escaping from your brother's murderer.

IPHIGENIA. He is the same man as my benefactor.
PYLADES. Necessity annuls your obligation.   1645
IPHIGENIA. No; it is my ingratitude's excuse.
PYLADES. It justifies you before gods and men.
IPHIGENIA. Yet still it does not satisfy my heart.
PYLADES. Such high ideals betoken secret pride.
IPHIGENIA. I do not analyse, I only feel.   1650
PYLADES. Then feel that you are right, respect yourself!
IPHIGENIA. No heart not free from taint can be contented.
PYLADES. You have remained untainted in this temple;
    Life teaches us, and you will learn it too,
    To be less rigorous with ourselves and others.   1655
    Mankind is of such strange complexity,
    So variously made up and interwoven,
    That to remain pure, to avoid confusion
    Within ourselves or in our dealings with
    Our fellow men, is possible to no one.   1660
    Nor are we meant to judge ourselves: a man's
    First duty is to walk and watch his path,
    For he can seldom rightly judge what he
    Has done, and still less judge what he is doing.
IPHIGENIA. I think you almost have persuaded me.   1665
PYLADES. Need I persuade you when you have no choice?
    To save yourself, your brother and a friend
    There is one way only: can you hesitate?
IPHIGENIA. Oh let me hesitate! for you yourself
    Would not with a good conscience do such wrong   1670
    To any man whom you had cause to thank.
PYLADES. If we are killed, a bitterer reproach
    Awaits you; it is then you will despair.
    It seems you have not known the pain of loss
    If to avoid such suffering you will not   1675
    Even permit yourself to speak a falsehood.
IPHIGENIA. Oh, if I only had a man's heart in me
    Which when it harbours some bold resolution
    Closes itself to all dissuading voices!
PYLADES. It is vain to resist; the brazen hand   1680
    Of stern Necessity, its supreme law
    Must overrule us, for the gods themselves
    Obey it. Silently it reigns, the sister
    Of everlasting Fate, and heeds no counsel.
    Bear what it has imposed upon you, do   1685

What it commands. The rest you know. I shall
Return here soon, and from your sacred hands
Receive the welcome symbol of our rescue.

Exit.

IPHIGENIA. I must do as he tells me, for my loved ones
 Are now in desperate danger. But alas!   1690
 My own fate fills me more and more with dread.
 Must I abandon now that silent hope,
 That sweet hope nourished here in solitude?
 Must this curse reign for ever? Is the house
 Of Atreus doomed never to rise again   1695
 Blessed with new promise? Surely in the end
 All things diminish, all life's happiness
 And strength must fade and fail! Why not the curse?
 So it was vainly, saved and hidden here
 Far from my family's fortunes, that I hoped   1700
 One day with a pure hand and a pure heart
 To cleanse it of its heavy stains of guilt!
 No sooner has my brother in my arms
 Been suddenly, miraculously healed
 Of his fierce sickness, and a ship long prayed for   1705
 No sooner puts ashore to take me home
 Than brazen-handed deaf Necessity
 Enjoins on me a double crime: to steal
 The sacred, venerated statue here
 Entrusted to me, and betray the man   1710
 To whom I owe my life and destiny.
 Oh gods, Olympian gods! now at the last
 Let me not feel resentment, let the bitter
 Hatred your ancient enemies the Titans
 Harbour for you, not stir in me as well,   1715
 Seizing my tender heart with vulture's talons!
 Save me, and save your image in my soul!
 That old forgotten song now haunts my ear,
 A song that I was thankful to forget—
 The song of the Three Fates; shuddering they sang it   1720
 When Tantalus was hurled from his golden chair.
 They sorrowed for their noble friend, fierce anger
 Filled them, and their lament was terrible.
 Our nurse sang it to us when we were children,
 Brother and sisters; I recall it well.   1725

Let the gods be feared
By the race of men!
For they are the masters,
In their hands they hold
Everlasting power   1730
To use as they please.

Let him fear them doubly
Whom ever they honour!
On clouds and on cliff-tops
The chairs are in readiness   1735
Round golden tables.

If strife arises
The guests are hurled headlong,
Reviled and dishonoured,
Deep down into darkness,   1740
And bound in the shadows
They vainly lie waiting
For judgment and justice.

But still, everlastingly,
At golden tables,   1745
The gods are feasting.
To them, as they stride
From mountain to mountain,
The breath of the stifled
Titans steams upwards   1750
From bottomless caverns,
Floats upwards like incense,
The lightest of vapours.

Those lords of the heavens
Avert from whole races   1755
Their eyes that have blessed them,
And in the descendant
Are blind to the mute plea
Of once-loved features,
His forefather's face.   1760

Thus the Three Fates sang;
The ancestor hears them,
The old man, exiled
In gloomy caverns,

And thinks of his children   1765
And shakes his head.

ACT V

ARCAS. What are we to suspect, and whom? I must
    Confess I am in some perplexity.
    Are the two prisoners plotting to escape,
    And is the priestess giving them assistance?   1770
    There are increasing rumours that the ship
    Which brought the two men here still lies concealed
    In some inlet or bay along our coast.
    And this man's madness, this reconsecration,
    This whole postponement on a sacred pretext,   1775
    Calls for increased suspicion and precaution.
THOAS. Send the priestess to me at once! Then let
    A thorough search be made of the whole shore
    Between the headland and Diana's grove.
    Its sacred depths must not be violated;   1780
    Ambush the enemy with care, and when
    You find them, show your customary valour.

Exit Arcas.

    Fierce fury rages to and fro inside me:
    First against her, whom I supposed so holy,
    And then against myself, that by forbearance   1785
    And kindness I have taught her to betray me.
    Man soon gets used to slavery, and learns
    Obedience soon enough, if we remove
    His freedom altogether. Why, if she
    Had fallen into the hands of my rough forebears   1790
    And if the sacred wrath had spared her life,
    She would have been content to save herself
    And no one else, she would have gratefully
    Bowed to her fate, and shed the blood of strangers
    Here on the altar, calling it her duty   1795
    Because it was compulsion. Now my kindness
    Tempts her to arrogant audacious wishes.
    I hoped in vain to bind her life to mine;
    Now she is planning her own destiny.
    She won my love by flattery; now that I   1800

Resist her flattery, she tries to get
Her way by cunning, taking my good will
For granted, as an old and stale possession.

Enter Iphigenia.

IPHIGENIA. You wish to see me: what has brought you here?
THOAS. You have postponed the ceremony: why?   1805
IPHIGENIA. I gave a clear account of that to Arcas.
THOAS. I wish to hear it now from you in person.
IPHIGENIA. The goddess offers you time for reflection.
THOAS. A time, it seems, which you too will use well.
IPHIGENIA. If your heart has now hardened into this   1810
  Cruel resolve, then you should not have come here!
  A king who orders an inhuman deed
  Will soon find servants who to gain his favour
  Will share the guilt of it most willingly,
  While in his presence all remains untainted.   1815
  He plans death, sitting on a thundercloud,
  And as his messengers flash fiery ruin
  Down on the heads of wretched men, he hovers
  Serene and unapproachable, a god
  High overhead, who floats on through the storm.   1820
THOAS. This is a wild song from your sacred lips.
IPHIGENIA. I do not speak as priestess, but as the daughter
  Of Agamemnon! You respected me
  Even as a stranger: is a princess now
  Your subject to command? No! I have learnt   1825
  Obedience all my life, first to my parents,
  Then to a goddess, and have felt sweet freedom
  In such submission: but to bow before
  A man's harsh overbearing orders this
  I have not learnt, neither at home nor here.   1830
THOAS. It is an ancient law, not my command.
IPHIGENIA. We are most willing to appeal to laws
  When we can make them weapons of our wishes.
  I know another law, one still more ancient,
  Which tells me to resist you: by that law   1835
  All strangers are considered sacred.
THOAS. It seems those captives have so touched your heart
  And moved you to such fervent sympathy
  That you forget a law of simple prudence:
  Not to provoke the powerful to anger.   1840

IPHIGENIA. Whether I speak or not, I cannot hide
    My feelings from you, for you know them well.
    Must not the hardest heart dissolve in pity
    When it remembers suffering the same fate?
    And my heart above all! I see myself   1845
    In them: I too trembled before an altar
    An early death's solemnities surrounded
    Me as I knelt, the knife was raised already
    To pierce my living bosom, everything
    In me was dizzy, whirling, horror-stricken,   1850
    My eyes darkened, and then—then I was saved.
    Are we not bound, when gods have shown us grace,
    To render grace to wretched fellow-mortals?
    All this you know, and yet you would compel me.
THOAS. Obey your priestly duty, not the king.   1855
IPHIGENIA. Enough! Why lend false colour to an act
    Of force that glories in a woman's weakness?
    I was born no less free than any man.
    If I were Agamemnon's son and you
    Demanded some unseemly thing of him—   1860
    He has a sword as well, and with his arm
    He would defy you and defend his honour.
    My words are all I have, and to pay heed
    To woman's words befits a noble man.
THOAS. I heed them more than any brother's sword.   1865
IPHIGENIA. Armed conflict is uncertain; no wise fighter
    Should underestimate an enemy.
    And nature has not left the weak defenceless
    Against rude force. She taught them to enjoy
    The exercise of subtlety and cunning;   1870
    How to evade, delay and circumvent.
    Such arts are what the violent deserve.
THOAS. Prudence takes due precaution against cunning.
IPHIGENIA. And a pure soul does not resort to it.
THOAS. Make no rash claim that might itself condemn you.   1875
IPHIGENIA. Oh, if you only knew how my soul struggles
    To stand its ground, drive back the first assault
    Of evil fate that seeks to master me!
    Do I then stand defenceless here before you?
    Gentle entreaty, and the upraised branch   1880
    Of supplication, in a woman's hand
    Stronger than weapons—this you have rejected:

How can I now defend my inmost self?
Shall I pray to the goddess for a miracle?
In my soul's depths is there no strength remaining?   1885
THOAS. The fate of the two strangers seems to cause you
    Immoderate concern. Who are these men,
    For whom you make so spirited a plea?
IPHIGENIA. They are—they seem—I think that they are Greeks.
THOAS. Your fellow-countrymen? So your sweet hope   1890
    Of homecoming has been revived by them?
IPHIGENIA (*after a silence*). Can it be true? Are men alone entitled
    To do heroic deeds? Do only they
    Embrace sublime impossibility?
    What is called great? What lifts and thrills the heart   1895
    Of tellers and retellers of a tale?
    What else but bravest enterprises which
    Succeed against all expectation? When
    One man at night steals in like sudden fire
    Among the enemy, and in hot rage   1900
    Attacks them as they sleep and as they wake,
    And then, when they are roused and press him hard,
    Can still escape, riding a captured horse
    And carrying spoils—does he alone earn praise,
    And only he? Or one who scorns safe roads   1905
    And boldly scours the mountains and the forests
    To purge a land of bandits who infest it?
    Is nothing left for us? Must a weak woman
    Renounce her native rights, become a savage
    To savages, and like an Amazon   1910
    Snatch from you men the right to wield the sword
    And avenge wrongs with blood? Now my heart lifts
    And sinks, as it conceives a daring plan:
    I shall incur great censure if it fails,
    This I know well, and grievous suffering—   1915
    But oh you gods, I lay it on your knees!
    If you are truthful, as men say you are,
    Then show it now: stand by me, that through me
    Truth may be glorified!—Hear then, my lord:
    There is a plot intended to deceive you.   1920
    You ask in vain to see the prisoners;
    They have left the temple, gone to seek their friends
    Whose ship is waiting for them off your shore.
    The elder, who was stricken by the sickness
    And now is healed of it—he is my brother   1925

154

Orestes, and the other, Pylades,
His childhood friend. Apollo's oracle
At Delphi sends them here: by his command
They must remove by stealth Diana's image
And bring it to the god, her brother. He   1930
Has promised for this service to release
Orestes from the guilt of matricide
And from the Furies who pursue him. Now
I have delivered both of us, the last
Of Tantalus's house, into your hands.   1935
Destroy us, if you think it right to do so.
THOAS. Do you expect a rude and barbarous Scythian
    To hear the voice of truth and human kindness,
    When Atreüs, the Greek, was deaf to it?
IPHIGENIA. All men can hear it, born in any land,   1940
    If they have hearts through which the stream of life
    Flows pure and unimpeded.—You are silent,
    My lord? What are you brooding on so deeply,
    What fate for me? If death, then kill me first!
    For now I feel the hideous peril, now   1945
    That there is no way left of saving us,
    The peril I have brought upon my friends
    By my own hasty choice. Alas, I shall
    See them in chains before me! How shall I,
    My brother's murderer, take leave of him,   1950
    How look him in the eyes? Never again
    Dare I gaze into his beloved face.
THOAS. So this is the invention these impostors
    Most artfully have woven round the head
    Of one so long secluded, and so eager   1955
    To be deceived by her own wishes.
IPHIGENIA.   No!
    My lord, that is not so! I could have been
    Deceived, but they are true and faithful. If
    You find them otherwise, then let them fall,
    And banish me to some sad rocky island,   1960
    There to repent in exile of my folly.
    But if this man is the beloved brother
    I have been longing for, then let us go!
    Show kindness to the brother and the sister—
    To both as to myself. My father died   1965
    By his wife's crime, she by her son's; he is
    The last hope of the race of Atreüs.

Let me return, and with my heart and hands
Still pure, cleanse the defilement from our house.
You will be keeping faith with me! You swore   1970
That if an opportunity should come
For me to join my family again
You would release me—now I have that chance.
A king does not promise, like lesser men,
To fob the troublesome petitioner off   1975
For the time being, nor because he hopes
The case will not arise: his dignity
Lies in contenting a just expectation.
THOAS. As angry fire struggles against water,
Hissing with rage and fighting to destroy   1980
Its enemy, so anger in my heart
Resists your words.
IPHIGENIA.   Oh then let mercy burn,
And like the quiet sacrificial flame
Shed upon me its sacred light, surrounded
By songs of joy and praise and gratitude.   1985
THOAS. How many times this gentle voice has moved me!
IPHIGENIA. Oh now make peace with me, give me your hand!
THOAS. You ask for too much in so short a time.
IPHIGENIA. Why need we ponder whether to do good?
THOAS. We must, for evil follows good deeds too.   1990
IPHIGENIA. It is by doubt that good is turned to evil.
Do not reflect; give as your heart dictates!

Enter Orestes, armed.

ORESTES (*to his followers off-stage*).
Fight harder still! Only a moment more!
Do not give way! You are outnumbered, but
Hold on, and cover me till I can bring   1995
My sister to the ship!

To Iphigenia, without seeing the king:

We are betrayed:
Come quickly, we have just time to escape!

He notices the king.

THOAS (*reaching for his sword*).
No man appears unpunished before me
With a drawn sword.

IPHIGENIA.   Do not profane with murder
  And violence the dwelling of the goddess.   2000
  Tell your men to stop fighting! Heed the words
  Of the priestess, your sister.
ORESTES.   Who is this,
  Tell me, who threatens us?
IPHIGENIA.   Respect in him
  The king, who has become my second father.
  Forgive me, brother; but my childish heart   2005
  Has placed our fate entirely in his hands.
  I have confessed your plot to him, and saved
  My soul from treachery.
ORESTES.   Is he prepared
  To let us leave in peace and return home?
IPHIGENIA. Your bright sword still forbids me to reply.   2010
ORESTES (*sheathing his sword*).
  Then speak, for as you see, I heed your words.

           Enter Pylades, followed by Arcas. both with drawn swords.

PYLADES. Do not delay! Our men are making one
  Last desperate stand; the enemy is forcing
  Them slowly back towards the shore. But what   2015
  Is this I see, a conference of princes!
  This is the noble person of the king!
ARCAS. Calmly, my lord, for so it well befits you,
  You face your enemies. Their insolence
  Will soon be punished: their supporters yield
  And fall, we are about to seize their ship: 2020
  One word from you and it will be in flames.
THOAS. Go, call a truce on our side! Not a blow
  Is to be struck while we are parleying.

                        Exit Arcas.

ORESTES. Go, I accept the truce; make haste, good friend,
  Collect our stragglers, and await with patience   2025
  The gods' decision on our enterprise.

                       Exit Pylades.

IPHIGENIA. I ask you both, first set my mind at rest
  Before you speak. I fear a bitter quarrel
  If you, king, will not heed the gentle voice
  Of reason, and if you, my brother, will   2030

Not bridle your impetuous youthful spirit.
THOAS. I will restrain my anger, as befits
    The older man. Now answer me: what proof
    Have you that you are Agamemnon's son
    And brother to this woman?
ORESTES.   This good sword   2035
    With which he smote Troy's valiant warriors:
    I took it from his murderer, and prayed
    The gods that they would grant me all the strength
    And courage and good fortune of the king,
    And a more honourable death than his.   2040
    Choose one man from the noblest of your army,
    Your finest warrior, and let me fight him.
    In every land on earth that nurtures heroes
    This boon is not refused to any stranger.
THOAS. It is a privilege which by old custom   2045
    Has always been denied to strangers here.
ORESTES. Then let us make new custom, you and I!
    When kings act nobly, a whole people hallows
    Their great example, deeming it a law.
    And let me fight not only for our freedom   2050
    But, as a stranger, on behalf of strangers.
    If I should fall, then let their fate be sealed
    With mine; but if good fortune grants to me
    The victory, then henceforth let no man
    Visit this shore and not at once encounter   2055
    A friendly greeting, generous assistance,
    And let none leave again uncomforted.
THOAS. You seem a noble youth, and not unworthy
    Of those you claim as ancestors. I have
    No lack of brave and valiant followers   2060
    To fight for me, but I myself, despite
    My years, can still confront an adversary.
    I am prepared to stand my chance with you.
IPHIGENIA. Not so! There is no need, my lord, for this
    Bloody arbitrament! Forbear your swords!   2065
    Consider me and what must be my fate.
    Fights are soon fought, and they make men immortal:
    For songs will praise them even if they fall.
    But does posterity count the endless tears
    Of the forsaken women who survive?   2070
    Poets are silent about them, and keep
    No record of the thousand nights and days

Spent weeping by some gentle soul who mourns
Her lover, lost so soon, and wastes away
In her vain grief that cannot call him back.   2075
I was myself warned by an inner voice
That some pirate might snatch me by deceit
From this safe place of refuge, and betray me
To slavery. I have questioned them with care,
Asked about every detail and demanded   2080
Evidence: now my heart is satisfied.
See, here there is a mark on his right hand,
As of three stars: it could be seen already
On the day he was born, and the priest said
It meant that with this hand he would perform   2085
A grievous deed. And I was twice convinced
When I saw this old scar across his eyebrow.
He got it when he was a child: Electra,
Who was always so hasty and so careless,
Was holding him and let him fall, striking   2090
His head against a stool. And so I know
He is Orestes! Must I give more proofs
And speak of his resemblance to my father,
The joy that welled up in me when I saw him?
THOAS. Yet even if your words could clear my mind   2095
Of doubt, and I could overcome my anger,
Weapons would still have to decide between us;
I cannot see a peaceable solution.
You have yourself admitted that they came
To rob me of Diana's sacred image: 2100
Am I to stand and calmly watch this happen?
Greeks often cast covetous eyes upon
The distant treasures of barbarian peoples,
Their golden fleeces, horses, lovely women.
But force and guile have not secured them always   2105
A safe homecoming with their captured prize.
ORESTES. Oh king, the image of the goddess need not
Divide us now! For now I understand
The error that bemused us, by Apollo's
Decree, when he commanded us to come here.   2110
I prayed to him for counsel and for rescue
From the Furies' pursuit, and he replied:
'If you can bring *the sister,* who against
Her will dwells in the shrine at Tauris, back
To Greece, the curse upon you will be lifted.'   2115

We thought he meant Diana, his own sister,
But he meant you. The bonds that held you fast
Are loosed now, holy lady, and you are
Restored to those you love. I felt your touch
And was free from my sickness; in your arms   2120
It seized me in its claws for the last time
And shook the very marrow of my bones
In a dire paroxysm; then it fled
Like an escaping snake into its den.
Now, thanks to you, I can enjoy the light   2125
Of day again. The goddess's intentions
Are veiled no longer. Like a holy image
To which a city's changeless destiny
By some unknown divine decree is bound,
She took you from us, guardian of our house,   2130
And kept you here apart in sacred stillness
To save your brother and your family.
All hope seemed to have vanished from the earth,
And it is all restored to us by you.
Great king, now let your heart be turned to thoughts   2135
Of peace! Do not prevent what now must be:
Let her reconsecrate our father's house,
Cleanse it of guilt and give me back to it
And place our ancient crown upon my head!
Repay the blessing that she brought to you   2140
And let me now enjoy near kinship's rights.
For force and guile, so highly prized by men,
Must bow in shame before the truthfulness
Of this great soul, and her pure childlike trust
In a man's noble nature be rewarded.   2145
IPHIGENIA. Think of your promise to me, and allow
My brother's honest faithful words to move you!
Look at us both! The opportunity
For such a noble deed does not come often.
Can you refuse? Then quickly give consent!   2150
THOAS. Well, take your leave!
IPHIGENIA.   Not so, my lord! I will
Not part from you unreconciled, without
Your blessing. Do not banish us! Let friendship
And hospitality prevail between us,
Not final separation. As my father   2155
Was dear to me and honoured, so are you,
And you have made a mark upon my soul.

Let even the humblest of your people come
And bring back to my ears the sound, the speech
I have grown used to hearing here among you,   2160
Let me see Taurian costume on the poorest .
Of men—I will receive him like a god,
I will prepare a bed for him myself,
Invite him to sit down at our fireside
And ask no news but of how you are faring!   2165
Oh may the gods reward as they deserve
Your deeds and your great generosity.
Farewell! Oh turn your face to us and speak
One gentle parting word to me in answer!
For then the wind will swell our sails more sweetly   2170
And tears will flow more soothingly from eyes
That take their leave. Farewell: give me your hand
In pledge of our long friendship.
THOAS.   May you both
    Fare well.

𝕿orquato 𝕿asso

A DRAMA

Translated by Michael Hamburger

CHARACTERS

ALFONSO THE SECOND, Duke of Ferrara
LEONORA OF ESTE, the Duke's Sister
LEONORA SANVITALE, Countess of Scandiano
TORQUATO TASSO
ANTONIO MONTECATINO, Chancellor

The setting is Belriguardo, a summer palace.

ACT I

Garden scene decorated with busts of the epic poets.
To the right of the front of the stage, Vergil, to the left Ariosto.

Scene I

Princess. Leonora.

PRINCESS. Smiling you look at me, my Leonora,
    Then at yourself you look and smile again.
    What is it? Do not keep it from a friend.
    Pensive you seem to be, yet cheerful too.
LEONORA. You're right, Princess, it pleases me to see   5
    The two of us here in rustic finery.
    We're like two very happy shepherdesses
    And like those happy ones we spend our time.
    Garlands we wind. And this one, many-coloured
    With flowers grows even thicker in my hand;   10
    You, with a mind more lofty, heart more large
    Chose for yourself the slender, delicate laurel.
PRINCESS. Those boughs that absentmindedly I twined
    At once have found a head most worthy of them:
    Vergil I crown with them in gratitude.   15

She crowns the bust of Vergil.

LEONORA. My full and gaudy garland, then, I'll place
    On Ariosto's high and masterly forehead.

She crowns Ariosto's bust.

He, whose good jests have never wilted, let
    Him have his share at once of this new spring.
PRINCESS. It was obliging of my brother to   20
    Have brought us out so early in the year:
    The time is all our own; for hours we can
    Dream ourselves back to poetry's golden age.
    I love this Belriguardo, for the days,
    Many of them, enjoyed here in my youth;   25
    And this new verdure, the mere sunshine even
    Brings back to me my feelings of those years.
LEONORA. Yes, it's a whole new world surrounds us here!
    The shade alone of these old evergreens

Delights the senses. Then the plashing of   30
These fountains quickens us. The young boughs glitter,
And sway responsive to the morning breeze.
These flowers with friendly, trustful children's eyes
From beds and borders seem to look at us.
Confident, too, the gardener is removing   35
Covers from orange and from lemon trees.
A blue and limpid sky rests over us,
And on the horizon's distant mountain tops
Into soft fragrance the late snow dissolves.

PRINCESS. Still more wholeheartedly I'd welcome Spring,   40
    Did it not take away from me my friend.

LEONORA. Allow me not to darken these bright hours,
    With thinking of my imminent departure.

PRINCESS. Whatever here you leave behind, twice over
    That noble city will restore to you.   45

LEONORA. Duty and love combine to call me back
    To him, my husband, after such long absence.
    I bring him a dear son who this past year
    Has grown so fast in stature and in mind
    And to his fatherly pleasure add my own.   50
    Florence is large and glorious, but the worth
    Of all its heaped-up treasures does not match
    That of our own Ferrara's rarest jewels.
    The people made that city what it is,
    Ferrara owes her greatness to its prince.   55

PRINCESS. But more to those good men and women who
    Met here by chance in fortunate conjunction.

LEONORA. Too easily chance disperses what it gathers.
    A noble man attracts more noble men
    And has the power to hold them, as you do.   60
    Like calls to like; your brother and yourself,
    Magnetic centres, draw into your orbit
    Minds great as you are and your forebears were.
    Here happily the splendid light was kindled
    Of Science and of bold untrammelled thought,   65
    When barbarism's murky twilight still
    Concealed the wider world. From childhood I
    Knew the full resonance of those famous names,
    Ercole and Ippolito of Este.
    My father in his praises linked Ferrara   70
    With Rome and Florence. Often then I longed
    With my own eyes to see it. Now I'm there.

Here Petrarch was hospitably received,
And Ariosto found his paradigms here.
Name anyone whom Italy calls great,   75
Ferrara's princes called that man their guest.
And there's advantage, too, in harbouring
A genius: for the bounty you bestow
He leaves behind him bounty twice as precious.
The ground on which one excellent has walked   80
Is sanctified; his word and deed resound
A century later in a grandchild's ears.
PRINCESS. A grandchild's, true, with feelings keen as yours.
Quite often I have envied you that gift.
LEONORA. Which you enjoy, as few do, quietly   85
And purely. When my overflowing heart
Prompts me to speak at once things keenly felt;
Better you feel it, deeply—and keep silent.
The moment's seeming does not dazzle you,
Wit does not win you over, flattery   90
In vain with affectation woos your ear:
Your mind stays constant and your judgement straight,
Your taste assured, and knowing what is great
As your own self you know, you prize it greatly.
PRINCESS. Who's flattering now, supremely? In the wrapping   95
Of intimate friendship, too, to make it worse!
LEONORA. Friendship is just; and it alone can measure
Your virtue's full circumference and weight.
But though I grant to opportunity,
To fortune, its due share in shaping you,   100
You have that shape, and what you are, remain;
You and your sister all the world esteems
More than all other women of our time.
PRINCESS. That, Leonora, hardly touches me
When I consider what a little thing   105
One is, and, but for others, how much less!
My knowledge of the ancient tongues and what
Was best in ancient times, I owe my mother;
Yet neither daughter ever equalled her
In scholarship, far less in proper judgement,   110
And if comparison nonetheless were made,
Lucretia has a better right to it.
Also, I can assure you, I have never
Counted as rank or property those things
That nature or good fortune lent to me.   115

I'm glad when clever men converse, that I
Can understand them and can catch their meaning.
Whether it be a judgement on some famous
Man of antiquity, and on his deeds;
Whether it be a science they discuss   120
That, spread, developed by experiment
Is useful to our kind, and elevates:
Wherever noble minds direct their talk,
I like to follow, since with ease I follow.
I like to hear those clever men dispute   125
When round the powers that move a human heart
So kindly now, and now so awesomely,
With grace the lips of witty eloquence play;
Or when the princely appetite for fame,
For increase of possession, becomes the stuff   130
For thinkers, and when subtlety of mind,
Finely spun out by one who masters it,
Serves not to trick us, but to enrich our minds.

LEONORA. After such serious conversation, though,
    Our hearing and our inner faculties   135
    Rest sympathetically on that poet's rhymes
    Who with sweet music pours into our souls
    The ultimate and loveliest of feelings.
    Your lofty mind embraces wide domains,
    While I prefer to linger on the island   140
    Of poetry, and walk its laurel groves.

PRINCESS. In that delicious country, I am told,
    More than all other trees the myrtle thrives.
    And though of Muses there are many, yet
    More rarely among the others one seeks out   145
    A friend and playmate, giving preference
    To meeting and acquaintance with the poet
    Who seems to shun us, to escape us even,
    Who seems to look for something we do not know
    And he himself perhaps does not truly know.   150
    Pleasant enough, we think, it would be, then,
    At the right time to meet him, all on fire
    To find in us the treasure that in vain
    The wide world over he has been looking for.

LEONORA. Well, I must bear with it, your little taunt,   155
    It hits the mark, but does not pierce too deeply.
    I honour every man and his achievement,
    And towards Tasso am no more than fair.

His vision hardly dwells on this our earth;
His ear responds to nature's harmony;   160
What history offers, what this life can give him
At once and willingly his heart takes up:
Disparate, scattered things his senses fuse,
And lifeless things his feeling animates.
He will ennoble what to us seems common   165
And what we value, will reduce to nothing.
In his own magic circle that strange man
Moves, has his being, and attracts us others
To move with him and share his marvellous realm;
He seems to approach us, yet stays far from us;   170
He seems to look at us, yet in our place
May well see only ghosts, phantasmal shapes.

PRINCESS. Finely and aptly you've described our poet
   Who hovers on the plane of honeyed dreams.
   And yet it seems to me that real things too   175
   Attract him strongly and can hold him fast.
   Those beautiful lyrics that from time to time
   We find here in the garden, pinned to trees,
   Like golden apples that, fragrant, make for us
   A new Hesperia, don't you think them all   180
   The precious fruits of a quite genuine love?

LEONORA. I too take pleasure in those lovely leaves.
   He can enrich with multiple conceits
   A single image in his many rhymes.
   Now he will raise it up in bright effulgence   185
   To the starred heaven, reverently bows,
   Like angels above clouds, before that image;
   Now he slinks after it through quiet meadows
   And winds into a chaplet every flower.   190
   Should the beloved leave, he sanctifies
   The path her graceful foot has softly trodden.
   Hidden in copses like the nightingale
   Out of his love-sick heart he richly fills
   Both woods and air with plaintive euphony: 195
   His charming lilt, that blessed melancholy
   Lures every ear, and every heart must follow—

PRINCESS. And when he gives a name to his one theme,
   That name, be sure of it, is Leonora.

LEONORA. But that's your name, Princess, as well as mine.   200
   And any other name I'd hold against him.
   I'm pleased that in such ambiguity
   He can conceal his feelings towards you;

And I'm content to think that with that name's
Dear sound I, too, was present in his mind.   205
What is in question here is not a love
That seeks to master and appropriate,
Exclusively possess and jealously
Fend from all others' sight the one beloved.
If in rapt contemplation he adores   210
Your worth and dignity, then let him too
Take pleasure in my easier, lighter nature.
Forgive my saying so: he does not love us,
But carries what he loves from every sphere
Down to a name the two of us bear in common,   215
Imparts to us his feelings; we appear
To love the man, yet, with him, only love
The highest point within our loving's range.

PRINCESS. You're deep into that science, Leonora,
    And are expounding things to me that hardly   220
    Do more than touch the surface of my ears,
    Almost as though my soul rejected them.

LEONORA. What, you? The Platonist? You cannot grasp
    Things that a novice dares to prattle of?
    Surely that means that I'm too much in error;   225
    And yet I know I am not wholly wrong.
    In this rare school love does not prove itself,
    As elsewhere it appears, a pampered child;
    It is the youth who married Psyche once
    And has a seat now where the gods confer,   230
    A voice that's listened to. He does not scamper,
    Roguishly rush from one breast to another;
    He does not cling to beautiful face and body
    At once, with dear delusions, nor atones
    For that quick frenzy with a sick revulsion.   235

PRINCESS. There comes my brother. Let's not give away
    Where once again we've drifted in our talk:
    We'd have to bear his teasing, as we did
    When he made fun of our bucolic dress.

Scene II

Enter Alfonso.

ALFONSO. I have been looking everywhere for Tasso   240
    And cannot find him—even here, with you.

Could you not give me news of him at least?
PRINCESS. Yesterday I saw little of him, nothing today.
ALFONSO. It's an old fault in him that he seeks out
    Solitude rather than society. 245
    I pardon him for fleeing motley crowds,
    Preferring to converse with his own mind
    Freely in private, but I can not approve
    When he avoids the circle of his friends.
LEONORA. Duke, if I'm not mistaken, you will soon 250
    Turn your reproaches into happy praise.
    I saw him from far off today; he carried
    A book and tablet, wrote and walked and wrote.
    A casual hint he gave me yesterday
    Seemed to announce the completion of his work. 225
    His only care now is to polish details
    So that a worthy offering in the end
    He can return for so much grace received.
ALFONSO. He shall be welcome, if he does present it,
    And for a long time free of obligation. 260
    Much as his compositions mean to me,
    Much as in some regards his major work
    Pleases, must please me, so much, too, at last
    Impatience grows in me, and lessens pleasure.
    He cannot finish, never can have done, 265
    But always alters, creeps a little farther,
    Stands still again, and so deceives our hope:
    Put off, the pleasure sours, and irritates—
    What seemed so near, incalculably distant.
PRINCESS. No, I commend the modesty, the care 270
    Of his progression, gradual, pace by pace.
    Only by favour of the Muses will
    So many rhymes cohere and harmonize:
    And this one impulse dominates his spirit,
    To make his poem one harmonious whole. 275
    Not to pile legend upon legend, jumbled,
    To charm and entertain, but leave you then
    With mere loose words that like mirages fade.
    Leave him alone, dear brother, for not time
    Can be the measure of a work well done; 280
    And to assure posterity of pleasure
    Artists' coevals must forget themselves.
ALFONSO. Together, then, dear sister, let us work,
    As often we have done, to joint advantage.

If I'm too zealous, then you moderate! 285
If you're too gentle, I will drive you on.
Then all at once perhaps we'll see him where
So long we've wished to see him, at his goal.
Our country, then, and all the world will wonder
At the great work accomplished and completed. 290
I will accept my part in so much glory,
And he will be inducted into life.
No man of parts can find full nourishment
Within a narrow circle. His native land
And more, the world, must form him. He must learn 295
To bear both praise and censure, forced by that
To know himself and others for what they are,
No longer lulled by flattering solitude.
Enemies will not, friends, though, *should* not spare him;
Then struggle whets the stripling's faculties, 300
He feels himself, and soon will feel a man.
LEONORA. In that way, sir, you will do all for him,
As generously, much you've done already.
A talent in tranquility is formed,
A character in the turbulence of affairs. 305
O may his temperament, like his art, be moulded
By your example! So that no longer he
Shuns human company, and his mistrust
Is not transmuted into fear and loathing!
ALFONSO. No man fears human beings, if he knows them, 310
And if he shuns them he will soon misjudge them.
That is his case, and so by little stages
A free mind is entangled and constrained.
Thus often he is anxious about my favour,
Much more than would be fitting; towards many 315
He harbours a suspicion, who, I'm sure
Are not his enemies. If it should happen
That letters go astray, or that a servant
Leaves him for service in another house,
A paper is mislaid and found by others, 320
At once he sees a scheme in that, a plot,
And malice that will undermine his ways.
PRINCESS. Yes, but, dear brother, let us not forget
That no man can be other than himself.
And if a friend, out with us on a walk 325
Injured a foot, undoubtedly we'd rather
Slow down our pace and gladly, willingly

Give him a helping hand.
ALFONSO.   Far better, though,
  If we could heal him, and immediately,
  With a good doctor's help, attempt a cure,   330
  And then, together with the man restored,
  Be on our way again, a new life's way.
  And yet, my dears, I hope that never I
  Shall bear the blame of a too rough physician.
  I'm doing all I can to implant in him   335
  Security and trust, to palliate.
  Often, in diverse company, I give him
  Sure tokens of my favour. When with complaints
  He comes to me, I have the case examined,
  As I did lately, when he thought his room's   340
  Door had been forced. If nothing is discovered,
  I calmly tell him how I see the matter;
  And since all things need practice, and the man
  Deserves it, then, on Tasso I practice patience:
  And you, I know, will offer me support.   345
  I've brought you here now, to our country seat,
  And leave for town this evening. You'll see
  Antonio here, though for a moment only;
  He comes from Rome to fetch me. There is much
  We must discuss and settle. Resolutions   350
  To be arrived at, letters to be written.
  All this compels me to return to town.
PRINCESS. Will you allow us to accompany you?
ALFONSO. You stay in Belriguardo, and together
  Drive over to Consandoli. Enjoy   355
  These fine days here at leisure, at your ease.
PRINCESS. And you can't stay with us? Can't deal with those
  Affairs out here as easily as in town?
LEONORA. And take Antonio off with you at once
  When there's so much he'd tell us about Rome?   360
ALFONSO. It cannot be, dear innocents; but as soon
  As possible I shall be back with him:
  Then he will tell you stories, and you two
  Shall help me to reward him for so much
  New work, and trouble taken in my service.   365
  And once our consultations are concluded,
  Let the whole bevy come, so that our gardens
  Are merry once again, and even I,
  As it is fitting, meet in these cool walks

Some beauty, when I look for her, care-free.   370
LEONORA. If so, rely on us to turn blind eyes!
ALFONSO. And you can be as sure of my forbearance.
PRINCESS (*her back to the audience*).
    Long I've seen Tasso come this way. How slowly
    He shifts his feet, then suddenly stops a while
    As though he were undecided, in two minds,   375
    And then approaches faster, but to halt
    Once more.
ALFONSO.   Don't jolt him from his dreams when he
    Is deep in verse or musing. Let him wander.
LEONORA. But he has seen us, and is coming here.

Scene III

Enter Tasso.

TASSO (*with a book in parchment covers*).
    Slowly I come, to bring you a new work,   380
    And still I hesitate to hand it to you,
    Knowing too well it has not been completed,
    However finished it may seem to be.
    But if that imperfection made me loath
    To give it to you, now a new care outweighs   385
    The other: my reluctance to appear
    Too apprehensive, thus to seem ungrateful.
    And much as one announces: Here I am!
    Hoping that one's considerate friends are pleased,
    So I can only say to you: Here it is!   390

He hands over the volume.

ALFONSO. With this, your present, Tasso, you surprise me
    And make a festival of this fine day.
    So in my own two hands at last I hold
    This work, and, within limits, call it mine!
    A long time I have wished you would decide   395
    To say at last: Enough! I hand it over.
TASSO. If you are satisfied, the work is done;
    For wholly it belongs to you alone.
    When I considered all the labour spent,
    Or looked at all the letters I had scrawled,   400
    Then I felt free to say, this work is mine.

But if I look more closely and enquire
What lends this poem worth and dignity,
I'm well aware, to you alone I owe them.
If Nature gave me the good gift of verse   405
Out of her generous but random bounty,
Capricious fortune, too, with cruel force
Had cast me out, and left me comfortless;
And if the beauty of this world attracted
Gloriously with its wealth the young boy's gaze.   410
Soon, very soon, my parents' misery,
Quite undeserved, troubled my youthful mind.
If my lips opened, loosening for song,
It was a doleful melody that flowed out,
And with soft music I accompanied   415
My father's anguish and my mother's pain.
You only raised me from a narrow life
To one of beauty and of liberty,
Of every care unburdened my cramped mind
And set me free, so that my soul, unfolding,   420
Could venture forth into courageous rhyme;
And any praise my work may now be granted,
To you I owe it, for to you it's due.
ALFONSO. Twice over you have earned all approbation,
And humbly honour both yourself and us.   425
TASSO. Would I could utter what I feel so strongly,
That what I bring you comes from you alone!
The idle youth—out of himself could he
Draw such a poem? The ingenious conduct
Of rapid war—did he invent that skill?   430
The martial arts that every hero proves
By his own prowess on the appointed day,
The general's strategy and the knight's bold acts,
The conflict between watchfulness and cunning,
All these, brave, clever Prince, did you not pour,   435
Infuse into my faculties, as though
You were my genius, whom for once it pleased
Through a mere mortal's witness to reveal
His high, his unattainably high being?
PRINCESS. Enjoy your laurels now, that give us pleasure!   440
ALFONSO. Be glad of every excellent mind's applause!
LEONORA. Take pleasure in your universal fame!
TASSO. This moment is enough for me. Of you,
Musing, composing, only of you I thought.

To please you three was my consummate wish,   445
My ultimate aim was to delight you three.
If in one's friends one does not see the world
One is not worthy of the world's regard.
Here is my fatherland, here is the circle
In which my spirit finds its resting-place.   450
Here I intently listen, note every hint,
Here taste, experience, knowledge speak to me;
You are my world and my posterity.
A crowd confounds an artist, makes him shy:
Only those like you understand and feel,   455
No one but they shall judge, reward my work.
ALFONSO. If we're your world and your posterity,
    It's not enough for us to idly take.
    The honoured emblem that's reserved for poets,
    That even heroes, who have need of poets,   460
    See without envy placed upon their heads,
    Here I have noticed on your forebear's brow.

Pointing at the bust of Vergil.

Was it blind chance, or did a genius wind
And bring it here? No matter. Not for nothing
We find it here. I can hear Vergil say: 465
Why honour dead men? Why, they had their pleasure
And their reward when they were living men.
And if you reverence, admire our kind,
Then to the living poets give their due.
My marble image has been amply crowned—   470
The bough that's green befits a living head.

*Alfonso signals to his sister. She takes the wreath from Vergil's bust
and approaches Tasso. He steps back.*

LEONORA. You won't accept? Look what a hand it is
    That offers you the bright, unwithering garland!
TASSO. Oh, give me time! For me the question is:
    How am I to live on, after this hour?   475
ALFONSO. Why, in enjoyment of the great possession
    That for a moment only gives you pause.
PRINCESS (*holding the wreath high*).
    You're granting me rare satisfaction, Tasso,
    Conveying what I think, without one word.
TASSO. The happy burden from your precious hands   480
    Kneeling I'll take upon my feeble head.

He kneels down, the Princess crowns him with the wreath.

LEONORA (*applauding*).
　　Long live the poet for the first time crowned!
　　How well the garland fits a modest man!

Tasso rises.

ALFONSO. It is the model only of that crown
　　That shall adorn you on the Capitol.　　　　　　　485
PRINCESS. There louder voices will be raised in greeting;
　　Here low-voiced friendship offers you reward.
TASSO. O take it off my head again, remove it!
　　It singes me, I feel it burn my temples.
　　And like a sun's ray that too hotly were　　　　　490
　　To strike my forehead, it consumes my power
　　To think, numbs and confuses. Feverish heat
　　Stirs up my blood. Forgive me. It's too much.
LEONORA. Not so. This garland will protect the head
　　Of one who in the torrid zone of fame　　　　　　495
　　Now has to journey, and will cool his brow.
TASSO. I am not worthy of the cooling air
　　That only round a hero's brow should waft.
　　O raise it up, you gods, transfigure it
　　Amid the clouds, so that it hovers high　　　　　500
　　And higher, never reached! So that my life
　　Becomes an endless striving towards that goal!
ALFONSO. A man rewarded early, early learns
　　To value the rare blessings of this life;
　　One who enjoys when young, not willingly　　　　505
　　Ever forgoes what once he had possessed;
　　And to possess is to have need of weapons.
TASSO. And one who arms himself must feel a strength
　　Within himself, a strength that never fails him.
　　Ah, but it fails me now! In my good fortune　　　510
　　It is forsaking me, my inborn strength
　　That staunchly faced misfortune, proudly faced
　　Up to injustice. Can it be that joy,
　　The rapture of this moment, has unmanned me,
　　Melting the very marrow in my bones?　　　　　515
　　My knees give way. A second time, Princess,
　　You see me bend before you. I beseech you,
　　Do what I asked of you: Take it away!
　　So that, awakening from a happy dream,
　　I am myself again, invigorated.　　　　　　　520

PRINCESS. If modestly and calmly you can bear
    The talent given to you by the gods,
    Then learn to bear this laurel too. It is
    The best thing that we mortals can bestow.
    The head that's worthy of it, once it's crowned,   525
    Wears it for ever, like an aureole.
TASSO. Well, then, in shame let me depart from here,
    To hide my head in the deep shade of groves,
    As formerly I hid my anguish there.
    Alone there I shall wander, where no eye   530
    Reminds me of good fortune undeserved.
    And should some clear well show me there by chance
    In its pure mirror the image of a man
    Who, strangely garlanded, in light reflected
    From heaven, among the trees, among the rocks,   535
    Pondering, rests, then it will seem I see
    Elysium limned upon that magic surface.
    Quietly I shall think a while, and ask:
    Who could that dead man be? That young man there
    Out of an age long past? So proudly wreathed?   540
    Who'll tell me the man's name? Or what he did?
    I wait a long time, thinking: Oh, if only
    Another now would come, and then another
    To join him here in friendly conversation!
    If I could see the heroes and the poets   545
    Of ancient times conjoined around this well!
    If I could see them gathered here for ever,
    Inseparably bonded, as in life.
    As by its power the magnet holds together
    Iron and iron, in a firm conjunction,   550
    So one urge binds the hero to the poet.
    Homer forgot himself, his whole life was
    Devoted to his thoughts about two men,
    And Alexander in Elysium
    Hurries to seek out Homer and Achilles.   555
    O that my living eyes might look upon
    The greatest spirits, all assembled now!
LEONORA. Wake up! Wake up! Don't leave us with the feeling
    That utterly you scorn all present things.
TASSO. It is the present that exalts me here,   560
    Absent I only seem to be. I'm rapt.
PRINCESS. It pleases me, when you converse with ghosts,
    To hear you speak so humanly to them.

A page goes up to the Duke and delivers a message quietly.

ALFONSO. He has arrived! And just when he was needed.
    Antonio!—Show him here.—Ah, there he comes!   565

Scene IV

Enter Antonio.

ALFONSO. Twice welcome! Both for bringing us yourself
    And for the news you bring us.
PRINCESS.   Welcome here!
ANTONIO. Hardly I dare to tell you how your presence
    Revives my spirits, fills me with new zest.
    Seeing you now, I feel I have regained   570
    All that so long I've lacked. You seem content
    With what I have accomplished on my mission:
    And so for every care I'm compensated,
    For many a day of vexed, impatient waiting,
    Or of deliberate waste. But now we have   575
    What we were out for: the dispute is settled.
LEONORA. I also greet you, though I'm angry with you:
    For you arrive just when I have to leave.
ANTONIO. Ah! Lest too great a happiness should cloy,
    At once you rob me of its better part.   580
TASSO. My greetings too! I also hope to enjoy
    Access to one who knows the ways of the world.
ANTONIO. You'll find me truthful, should you ever wish
    To cast a glance from your world into mine.
ALFONSO. Although in your despatches you informed me   585
    Of what you did and how it went for you,
    Antonio, I have some questions yet
    About the means that settled the affair.
    On terrain so precarious every step
    Must be well calculated, if in the end   590
    It is to bring you to the chosen goal.
    A man who seeks his sovereign's advantage
    In Rome has shouldered a most mighty task;
    For to take all is Rome's way, to give nothing:
    And if you go there to obtain some object,   595
    Nothing you'll get unless you've brought them something,
    And even then you are a lucky man.
ANTONIO. It's not my conduct, sir, nor yet my skill
    By which I could accomplish your desire.

The most astute of diplomats could not fail 600
To meet his master in the Vatican.
I made the best of favourable factors.
Gregory sends his blessing and esteem.
That agèd man, worthiest of those whose heads
Are burdened with a crown, with joy recalls 605
The day when he embraced you. That same man,
Who can distinguish men, both knows and praises
Your excellence. For you he has done much.

ALFONSO. His good opinion of me pleases me
As far as it is honest. But well you know, 610
Seen from the Vatican the nations look
Little enough, all lying at its feet;
How little, then, mere princes, human beings!
Come, out with it! What helped you above all?

ANTONIO. If you insist: the Pontiff's noble mind. 615
He sees the small thing small, the large one large.
In order to rule a world, he willingly
And graciously gives in to all his neighbours.
The little strip of land he grants to you
He values greatly, as he does your friendship. 620
He wants a quiet Italy, around him
Wants to see friends, and wants to keep the peace
Along his borders, insuring that the power
Of Christendom, which firmly he controls,
Will rout the Turks and crush the heretics. 625

PRINCESS. Are the men known whom he especially favours,
Those he admits to his most private councils?

ANTONIO. Heed he gives only to experienced men,
To active men his confidence and favour.
He who had served the State since he was young 630
Now rules it and has influence on those courts
That years ago, as an ambassador,
He saw and knew and more than once directed.
Now to his glance the world lies no less open
Than does the interest of his own State. 635
To watch him now in action is to praise him
And to be glad when time uncovers what
In secret long he had prepared and furthered.
There is no sight more pleasing in this world
Than that of sovereigns who cleverly reign. 640
The sight of realms where proudly all obey,
Where each believes he serves none but himself
Because all's right that law and rule command.

LEONORA. How dearly I should like to see that world
　　From the inside! 645
ALFONSO. 　　　　Surely to play a part!
　　For never Leonora will merely look.
　　It would be pleasant, wouldn't it, dear friend,
　　If in that powerful game from time to time
　　We too could dabble with our delicate hands.
LEONORA. You're trying to provoke me. I won't respond. 650
ALFONSO. I've debts to settle with you, from old days.
LEONORA. All right, today I will remain indebted!
　　Forgive me, and don't interrupt my questions.
(*To Antonio*) Would you describe him as a nepotist?
ANTONIO. Not any less, nor more, than what is fitting. 655
　　A powerful man not generous to those
　　Closely related, will be blamed for that
　　By his own people. Gregory has the knack
　　Of quietly and moderately using
　　His kinsmen, trusty servants of the State, 660
　　So with one act performing two linked duties.
TASSO. The sciences, the arts, do they enjoy
　　The Pope's protection? Does he emulate
　　In that the illustrious rulers of the past?
ANTONIO. Those sciences he honours that are useful, 665
　　That help to govern or to know the peoples;
　　He values arts that are an ornament,
　　Beautify Rome and make its palaces,
　　Its temples marvelled at throughout the world.
　　No idleness he'll tolerate around him. 670
　　To count, a thing must prove itself, must serve.
ALFONSO. And do you think that soon we can conclude
　　This business? That they'll not decide to put
　　More obstacles in our way, before it's over?
ANTONIO. Unless I'm much mistaken, it will need 675
　　Only your signature, a few more letters
　　To settle this contention finally.
ALFONSO. In that case I consider these past days
　　A period of great happiness and gain.
　　I see my realm enlarged, and know its frontiers 680
　　Will be secure. Without one blow of a sword
　　You have achieved it, well and truly earning
　　A citizen's crown. Our ladies here will place it,
　　Wound of new oak leaves on the finest morning,
　　Around your forehead, to reward your service. 685

Meanwhile our Tasso has enriched me too:
For us has conquered, freed Jerusalem
And so has shamed our modern Christendom,
With happy zeal, and rigorous industry
He has attained a high and distant goal.   690
It's for those pains you see him garlanded.
ANTONIO. You solve a puzzle for me. Two crowned heads
    I saw to my amazement, when I came.
TASSO. If my good fortune's evident to your eyes
    I wish that you could also see the shame   695
    Within me, in a single flash of vision.
ANTONIO. Long I have known that in rewarding merit
    Alfonso is immoderate. You experience
    What everyone around him has experienced.
PRINCESS. Once you have seen what Tasso has achieved   700
    You'll find us wholly just and moderate.
    We are the first and quiet witnesses
    Of that applause the world will not deny him
    And years to come will grant him ten times over.
ANTONIO. He's certain of his fame by you alone.   705
    Who'd dare to doubt where you can give him praise?
    But tell me who it was that placed this garland
    On Ariosto's brow?
LEONORA.   This hand of mine.
ANTONIO.
    And you did well. Indeed, it more becomes him
    Than any laurel garland would have done.   710
    As Nature with a green and motley garment
    Covers her richly procreative breast,
    So he draped all that can make human kind
    Worthy of veneration and of love
    In charming fable's many-flowered array.   715
    Contentment, wide experience, understanding,
    Keen intellect, sure taste and a pure feeling
    For what is truly good, all these appear
    To rest as under ever-blossoming trees,
    Austere, yet personal also, in his poems,   720
    Strewn with the snow of lightly carried petals,
    Twined round with roses, marvellously threaded
    With the free magical play of amoretti.
    Beside them superfluity's well-spring purls,
    Revealing to us bright, fantastic fishes.   725
    The air is filled with birds of rarest plumage,

Meadow and copses with exotic herds;
Roguishness listens, half concealed in verdure,
From time to time out of a golden cloud
Wisdom lets fall her lofty apothegms,   730
While Madness on a lute well-tuned will seem
To strum at random, romping to and fro,
And yet in loveliest rhythm keeps its bounds.
Whoever ventures to that great man's side
For his mere boldness well deserves a garland.   735
Excuse me, if I, too, become enthused,
Like one ecstatic cease to be aware
Of time and place, and cannot weigh my words;
For all these poets, all these garlands here,
This weirdly festive dress of our fair ladies   740
Out of myself transports me to strange lands.
PRINCESS. A man so sensible of one achievement
　　Will not misjudge another. Later you
　　Shall gloss for us in Tasso's poetry
　　What we have sensed but only you have grasped.   745
ALFONSO. Antonio, come with me. There are loose ends
　　I'm anxious still to question you about.
　　But after that, until the sun goes down,
　　I'll leave you to the ladies. Come! Excuse us.

　　　　The Duke is followed out by Antonio, the ladies by Tasso.

ACT II

Large Room.

Scene I

TASSO. With faltering steps I follow you, Princess.   750
　　And thoughts that lack all reason and proportion
　　In my poor head are jostling one another.
　　It seems that solitude beckons, lisping at me
　　Alluringly, as though to tell me: Come,
　　I will dissolve those newly stirred up doubts.   755
　　Yet if I glimpse you, if my listening ear
　　Catches a single sentence from your lips
　　A new day dawns for me, and all is light,
　　All my constricting turmoil is allayed.

Freely I will confess to you, that man   760
Who unexpectedly joined us, in a manner
Not gentle roused me from a beautiful dream;
His character, his words so strangely struck me
That more than ever I feel split in two,
Once more confused, in conflict with myself.   765
PRINCESS. It cannot be that one so old a friend,
Who, long abroad, has led an alien life,
On coming home immediately will resume
Old ways, and be himself again at once.
It's not his inmost nature that has changed;   770
Just let us live with him for a few days
And, one by one, the strings will be re-tuned,
Until once more familiar harmony
Between them is established. If he then
Acquaints himself more closely with the work   775
That meanwhile you've completed, rest assured:
He'll place you at the side of that same poet
He made a giant of, to dwarf you, now.
TASSO. Oh, dear Princess, his generous eulogy
Of Ariosto gave me more delight   780
Than injury or offence. It is a comfort
For such as me to hear that poet praised
Who serves us as a mighty paragon.
Deep down in secret we can tell ourselves:
If you attain one fraction of his merit,   785
A fraction of his glory, too, is yours.
No, what much more profoundly stirred my heart,
What still transfuses and pervades my soul
Was something else—the figures of that world
That restless and uncanny, but alive,   790
Around one great uniquely clever man
Calmly revolves and runs the ordered course
That demigod presumes to set for it.
Keenly I listened, and with pleasure heard
The experienced statesman speak of what he knows.   795
But, ah, the more I heard him speak, the more
I shrank in my own sight and grew afraid
That like poor Echo against rocks I'll vanish,
A resonance, a nothing, fade away.
PRINCESS: Yet minutes earlier had so purely felt   800
The hero and the poet's intergrowth,
How they seek out each other, need each other,

183

And never should feel envy, or compete?
The deed deserving song is glorious, true,
But it is also good in worthy song to carry   805
Into a later age the pith of deeds.
Friend, ask no more than from a little State,
That harbours you, to calmly watch the world's
Turbulent, savage ways, as from a shore.
TASSO: Was it not here, though, that I first observed   810
How lavishly a brave man is rewarded?
Callow I came here, as an ignorant boy,
Just when repeated celebration seemed
To make Ferrara both the home and pivot
Of honour. And a heartening sight it was.   815
The spacious piazza where in all its splendour
Skilled bravery was to prove and show itself,
Seated, a circle of a kind the sun
Not very soon once more will shine upon.
Here, in one place, the loveliest women sat   820
And here the men most eminent in our time.
Such noble multitude amazed the eye.
All these, one cried, a single fatherland,
Our narrow, sea-surrounded Italy,
Sent to this place. Together they comprise   825
The foremost court that ever sat in judgement
On merit, virtue, honour, gallantry.
If one by one you test them, none you'll find
With cause to feel ashamed of those beside him.
And then the barriers opened, horses stamped,   830
Helmets and shields began to flash and glitter,
The squires pressed forward, trumpets blared,
And lances clashed, to splinter or to hold,
Struck shield and helmet clanged, for moments only
A cloud of dust whirled up, hid from our sight   835
The victor's triumph and his peer's disgrace.
O let me draw a curtain on the whole
Too dazzling spectacle, and spare myself,
For else too vehemently I shall feel
My own small worth, and spoil this lovely moment.   840
PRINCESS. If that exalted circle, if those deeds
Urged you at that time to your own endeavours,
Then I, dear friend, at the same time could prove
For you a quiet doctrine, mere acceptance.
Those tournaments that you praised, hundreds of tongues   845

Commended to me then and did again
Many years later, I have never seen.
Withdrawn to where a faint last resonance
Of joy could hardly reach me, I endured
Many a pain and many a sad thought.   850
With wings spread wide, before my eyes there hovered
Death's image, and shut out for me the view
Of all that might be happening in the world.
Gradually only it would lift, and let me
See again palely but agreeably,   855
As through a veil, the colours of this life.
Softly they moved again, its living shapes.
For the first time, still with my women's help,
I left my sickroom, ventured out again,
Just when Lucretia, full of happy vigour,   860
Arrived and led you to us by her hand.
Unknown to me and new, you were the first
To enter, to impinge on my new life.
So both for you and me I had high hopes;
And until now those hopes have not deceived us.   865
TASSO. And I who, numbed by all the surge and bustle
That fills a court, half-dazzled by such splendour
And stirred by a diversity of passions,
Through quiet passages of the palace walked
In silence at your sister's side, then entered   870
That room in which, supported by your women,
Soon you appeared. O what a moment
That was for me! Allow me to be frank:
As one enchanted by deluded frenzy
Is promptly, willingly cured when gods are near,   875
So I was cured of every fantasy,
Of all obsession, every devious urge,
Cured by a single glance that met your glance.
If previously my inexperienced senses
Strayed to a thousand objects of desire,   880
Shamed there, at first I hid within myself,
Then slowly learned what is desirable.
So in the wide sands of an ocean shore
In vain one seeks a pearl that lies concealed
Within the stillness of an oyster shell.   885
PRINCESS. It was the beginning of a happy time
And, if the Duke of Urbino had not taken
My sister from us, years would have gone by

185

In tranquil and unclouded happiness.
But now we are too conscious of the lack   890
Of cheerful spirit, of exuberant life
And of that amiable woman's nimble wit.
TASSO. Too well I know it, ever since that day
  On which she left us, no one could restore
  To you such plenitude of zest and joy.   895
  How often it has pained me! And how often
  My grief for you I've voiced to quiet groves!
  Oh, I cried out, is no one but her sister
  Privileged to mean much to one so dear?
  Is there no heart now so deserving that   900
  She can confide in it, no mind or spirit
  Attuned to hers? Are zest and wit extinct?
  And could one woman, however excellent,
  Be all to her? Again, Princess, forgive me!
  Of my own self at times I thought then, wishing   905
  I could be something to you. Oh, not much,
  But something, not in words but by a deed
  Brought home to you, a living testimony
  Of how my heart was pledged to you in secret.
  I found no way, though, and too often I   910
  In awkwardness did things that could but pain you,
  Slighted the man to whom you gave protection,
  Bungling, confused what you desired to solve,
  And always, when I wanted to draw closer,
  Felt I was farther from you than before.   915
PRINCESS. Tasso, I've never yet misjudged your motives,
  Nor your good will, and know how you're intent
  On damaging yourself. Unlike my sister,
  Who can put up with anyone whatever,
  After so many years you've hardly made
  A single friend, or kept one.   920
TASSO.   Blame me, then!
  But tell me afterwards: Where is the man
  Or woman I could dare to talk with freely
  And from the heart, as I can talk with you?
PRINCESS. There is my brother. You should confide in him. 925
TASSO. He is my sovereign! But don't believe
  That liberty's wild urge inflates my heart.
  Human kind is not fashioned to be free,
  And one not vulgar knows no satisfaction
  Greater than service to a prince he honours.   930

And so he is my master, and I feel
The entire import of that laden word.
Now I must learn to keep silent when he speaks,
And act when he commands, however strongly
Both heart and mind may contradict his words. 935
PRINCESS. That, with my brother, never is the case.
And now that our Antonio has returned
You're certain of another clever friend.
TASSO. That was my hope once, now it almost fails me.
How valuable to me, how useful too 940
Would be relations with him, his advice
In countless matters! For I freely grant
That he has every quality that I lack.
But if an entire pantheon was convoked
With rich endowments offered at his cradle, 945
Unhappily the Graces would not come,
And one who lacks the gifts of those so dear ones
Much may possess and much may have to give,
But there's no resting ever on his bosom.
PRINCESS. But there is trusting him, and that is much. 950
You can't ask every virtue of one man.
And this one keeps what he has promised you.
If once he has declared himself your friend
Where your gifts fail you, he'll step in to help.
You must be allies! And I will presume 955
To bring off that good work in a short time.
But don't resist, as usually you do!
Take Leonora, who has long been with us,
She's delicate and graceful, easy, too,
To live with; yet you've always been reluctant 960
To get to know her better, as she wished.
TASSO. I was obedient to you. Otherwise
I should have drawn away from her, not closer.
Amiable though at times she will appear,
I don't know how it is, but only rarely 965
I could be wholly frank with her, and though
To please her friends may be what she intends,
One's conscious of the intention, and put off.
PRINCESS. Tasso, that way, I'm sure, we'll never find
Companionship! That way of yours must lead us 970
To ramble on through solitary copses,
Through silent valleys; more and more our feelings
Grow pampered, spoilt, for ever they'll be striving

Inwardly to restore that golden age
Which outwardly they cannot find, though never   975
That effort has succeeded, or can succeed.
TASSO. A powerful word you've spoken, my Princess.
  The golden age, what has become of it,
  That for which every heart still longs in vain?
  When on a free earth human beings roamed   980
  Like happy herds, to pasture on delight;
  When a most ancient tree on flowery meadow
  Cast shade for shepherds and for shepherdesses,
  A younger shrub entwined with delicate boughs
  Languishing love, as though in league with it;   985
  Where clear and still on sand for ever pure
  Gently the lissom river clasped the nymph;
  Where in the grass a snake, surprised and startled,
  Harmlessly vanished, and the fearless faun,
  Soon punished by a young man bolder, fled;   990
  Where every bird in unrestricted air
  And every beast that rambled hill and valley,
  Said to our kind: What pleases, is allowed.
PRINCESS. My friend, that golden age, I think, is over;
  Only consummate goodness brings it back.   995
  And if I may confess to you what I think:
  That golden age with which the poets like
  To flatter us, that beautiful age no more
  Existed ever than it now exists;
  And if it did, I'm sure it was none other   1000
  Than that which ever again we can make ours.
  Still hearts that are akin can find each other
  To share the enjoyment of our lovely world;
  The only change, my friend, is in the motto,
  A single word: What's fitting, is allowed.   1005
TASSO. If only, called from persons good and noble,
  A general court of justice would decide
  What's truly fitting! When now each one believes
  That what is useful to him befits him too.
  As we can see, to strong or cunning men   1010
  All is permitted, by themselves and others.
PRINCESS. If you're in doubt, and wish to know what's fitting,
  Ask a high-minded woman. She will tell;
  Because it's women whom it most concerns
  That nothing should occur but what is fitting.   1015
  This tender, vulnerable sex a wall

Of seemliness surrounds, and should defend.
Where seemliness reigns, there women also reign.
Where impudence thrives, there women are as nothing.
And if you ask both sexes you will find   1020
Where men seek freedom, women seek good morals.
TASSO. You think us coarse, then, unrestrained, unfeeling?
PRINCESS. Not that! But you are out for distant ends,
And all your striving must be violent.
You dare to work for all eternity,   1025
When on this earth we do not ask for more
Than to possess one near and narrow patch,
And only wish it could be always ours.
We can't be sure of any masculine heart,
However warmly once it yielded to us.   1030
Beauty, which seems the only thing you value
In us, will fade. What's left, when beauty's faded,
Attracts no more, and that means, it is dead.
If there were men who prized a feminine heart
And who could recognize or sense or guess   1035
What a great treasury of love and trust
For a whole lifetime a woman's breast can hold;
Or if the memory of rare, good hours
Would stay alive and vivid in your souls;
Or if your glance, so piercing otherwise,   1040
Could also penetrate the ugly veil
That sickness or old age casts over us;
If the possession that should give you peace
Did not arouse your lust for other conquest:
Then a fine day would truly dawn for us   1045
And we should celebrate our golden age.
TASSO. You tell me things that in my head stir up
Troubles and cares that had been half asleep.
PRINCESS. Tasso, what do you mean? Speak with me freely.
TASSO. Often I've heard, and just the other day   1050
Heard it once more—and if I had not heard it,
Should have assumed—that noble princes seek
Your hand in marriage. What we must expect
We greatly dread, and almost we despair.
That you will leave us seems most natural;   1055
But how we are to bear it, I don't know.
PRINCESS. Oh, for the moment, you need have no fear.
Almost I could say, rest assured for ever.
I like it here, and here I'll gladly stay.

At present there's no match that could attract me; 1060
And if you want to keep me here for ever,
Prove that to me by concord, make for yourselves
A happy life, and so make one for me.
TASSO. Yes, teach me how to do the possible!
To you my every day is dedicated. 1065
When to praise you, to show you gratitude
My heart expands, then, only then, I feel
The purest happiness that men can feel:
What's most divine in you alone I've found.
The deities of this earth so differ from 1070
All other human beings as high destiny
Does from the will and schemes of even those
Most perspicacious. Many things the elect,
While we watch breaker after breaker surge,
Let pass unnoticed, rippling like wavelets only, 1075
Lapping their feet, and never so much as heed
The gale that rushes round us, hurls us down,
Scarcely can hear our cries for help, and leave
Us poor, myopic children to our way,
To fill the air with screaming and with groans. 1080
Often you've shown indulgence to me, goddess,
And like the sun your downward glance has dried
The dew that on my eyelids night had left.
PRINCESS. It is quite proper that we women should
Be well disposed towards you; for your poem 1085
In many ways has glorified our sex.
The timid and the bold, you've always known
How to present them as both dear and noble;
And if Armida seems less amiable,
Soon we're won over by her love and charm. 1090
TASSO. Whatever in my poem may re-echo,
Only to one, to one I owe it all.
No vague and merely mental image hovers
Before me when I write, now brightly close,
Now dim again, withdrawing from my soul. 1095
With my own eyes I've seen the prototype
Of every virtue, every loveliness;
What in that image I have made, will last:
Tancred's heroic love for his Chlorinda,
Ermina's tacit, unacknowledged faith, 1100
Sophronia's greatness and Olinda's plight;
These are not phantoms conjured from delusion,

I know they will endure, because they are.
And what is better fitted to live on
For centuries, effective, though in silence,   1105
Than the kept secret of a noble love,
Humbly confided to the lilt of rhyme?
PRINCESS. And shall I tell you one more rare distinction
That unremarked, your poem gains by stealth?
It draws us on, and on, we listen to it,   1110
We listen and we think we understand,
What we do grasp of it, we cannot censure,
And so we are won over in the end.
TASSO. O what a heaven you open up for me,
Princess! If I'm not blinded by this light,   1115
I see unhoped for, endless happiness
Gloriously pour on me in golden rays.
PRINCESS. Tasso, no more! There may be many things
That we should seize upon with vehemence:
But there are others that by moderation,   1120
By self-denial only we can win.
Virtue, they say, is one of them, and love,
Akin to it, another. Mark that well!

Scene II

TASSO (*alone*). To raise your open eyes now, is that permitted?
Can you presume to look? You are alone!   1125
These pillars, did they overhear her words?
And are there witnesses that make you fear
These dumb ones of your utmost bliss? Now rises
The sun of a new era in your life
Incomparable with the one now ended.   1130
Descending, now the goddess swiftly raises
The mortal to her heights. What a new sphere
Is opened to my vision, what a realm!
How richly has my fervent wish been granted!
I dreamed myself close to consummate bliss   1135
And this awakening transcends all dreams.
One blind from birth imagines light and colours
As best he may; but if a new day dawns
Visible to him, a new sense is his.
Full of new hope and courage, drunk with joy.   1140
Reeling I take this path. You give me much.

191

As earth and heaven from overflowing hands
Pour out their gifts upon us lavishly,
You give, and in return you ask for that
Which only such a gift exacts of me.   1145
Patient I am to be, and moderate,
And so to earn the right to your sweet trust.
What have I ever done that she should choose me?
What shall I do to merit that she did?
She could confide in you; that makes you worthy.   1150
Yes, to your words, Princess, and to your gaze
For ever, wholly, I'll devote my soul.
Ask of me what you will, for I am yours.
Let her despatch me to seek toil and danger
And fame in distant countries, let her hand me   1155
The golden lyre to pluck in quiet groves,
Dedicate me to contemplation and its praise:
I'm hers, and to her shaping I'll submit,
For her my heart has hoarded all its wealth.
O if a god had granted me the means   1160
A thousandfold, still hardly I could express
Fitly a veneration beyond words.
The painter's brush, the poet's tongue and lips,
The sweetest that were ever nourished on
Earliest honey, I should need. In future   1165
No more shall Tasso lose himself amid
Tree trunks or men, despondent, lonely, weak!
He is alone no longer, but with you.
O that the noblest of all feats confronted
Me palpably here, all girt and hedged around   1170
With horrible danger! I rush in, press on,
And readily would risk my life, which now
I have received from her—I should invite
The best of men to join with me in friendship,
To do the impossible with a noble band,   1175
According to her will and her command.
Precipitous fellow, why did your mouth not hide
Your feelings for her till you could lie down
Deserving, more deserving, at her feet?
That was your resolution, your prudent wish.   1180
No matter, though! It's lovelier by far
That such a gift should come unmerited, pure,
Than half to think that possibly one might
Have been allowed to ask for it. Look up!

What lies before you is so large and wide: 1185
And hopeful youth once more is drawing you
Into a future that's unknown and bright.
—Breathe deeply!—Weather of good fortune, now
For once be favourable to this plant!
Heavenward it aspires, a thousand shoots   1190
Burgeon from it, prepare their blossoming.
O may it bear fruit also, and shed joys!
So that a loved hand plucks the golden jewels
Out of its living, richly laden boughs.

Scene III

Tasso. Antonio.

TASSO. Welcome, the man whom for the first time now   1195
    I look upon, as it were! No meeting ever
    More happily was announced to me. So welcome!
    I know you now, and know your full distinction,
    Without reserve can offer my heart and hand,
    Hoping that you for your part will not spurn me.   1200
ANTONIO. You lavish offers of good gifts on me,
    And I appreciate them, as I should:
    So let me hesitate before I take them,
    Not sure as yet that I can make return
    In equal measure. For I think it best   1205
    Not to seem rash, and not to seem ungrateful:
    Let me be prudent, cautious for us both.
TASSO. Who would belittle prudence? Every step
    In life persuades us how it's needed;
    But better still when one's own spirit tells one   1210
    That delicate caution is not needed here.
ANTONIO. In that, each one should question his own mind,
    For it is he who'll pay for the mistake.
TASSO. So be it! I have done my duty now,
    Honoured the word of our Princess, whose wish   1215
    Was for a friendship; placed myself before you.
    Withhold I could not; but, Antonio, neither
    Will I impose myself. So let it be.
    Time and acquaintance may impel you yet
    More warmly to request the gift that now   1220
    So coldly you repel and almost flout.

ANTONIO. The moderate man quite often is called cold
 By those who think themselves more warm than others,
 Because they suffer fits of sudden heat.
TASSO. You censure what I censure and avoid.   1225
 Young though I may be, I can well distinguish
 Permanence from mere vehemence, and prefer it.
ANTONIO. Most wisely said! Be guided by it always.
TASSO. You have the right, Antonio, to advise me.
 And warn me too, because experience stands   1230
 Beside you as an amply proven friend.
 But do believe me, a quiet heart attends
 To every day's, to every hour's grave warning
 And learns in secret those good qualities
 Which your severity thinks it newly teaches.   1235
ANTONIO. Pleasant it may be, to be self-occupied,
 But one does ask oneself: is it useful too?
 Inside himself no person comes to know
 His inmost nature, by his own gauge seeming
 Too small at times, more often far too great.   1240
 Only from men a man's self-knowledge comes,
 Life only teaches each one what he is.
TASSO. I hear you with approval and applause.
ANTONIO. And yet, I'm sure, you will construe my words
 Quite otherwise than I intend their meaning.   1245
TASSO. This way we cannot reach an understanding.
 It's neither clever nor commendable
 Deliberately to misjudge a man,
 Whoever he may be. Her Grace's words
 Were scarcely needed, for it was not hard   1250
 To know you're one who seeks and does what's good.
 Your own well-being does not trouble you,
 You think of others, give support to others
 And on the easily ruffled wave of life
 Your heart stays steadfast. That is how I see you.   1255
 And what should I be if I'd kept aloof?
 Did I not hanker for a little share
 In the locked treasure to which you hold the key?
 I know you'll not regret my access to it,
 You'll be my friend, once you have come to know me: 1260
 And long I've needed such a friend as you.
 Of inexperience I am not ashamed,
 Nor of my youth. Around my head still shimmers
 The future's golden cloud, and hangs at rest.
 Excellent man, admit me to your trust,   1265

Initiate me, who am quick and callow,
Into more thrifty management of life.
ANTONIO. Yet in one moment you demand from me
What, well-considered, only time can grant.
TASSO. Yes, in one moment, love accords us that   1270
Which our long efforts scarcely can attain.
I do not beg it of you, I demand it,
By right, entitled by the name of virtue,
Whose zeal is to unite those who are good.
And shall I now invoke another name?   1275
The Duchess wants it so—Eleonora,
Wishes to lead me to you, you to me.
Let us comply, and expedite her wish!
In fellowship appear before the goddess,
Offer our service to her, and all our souls,   1280
To do what's best together and allied.
Once more! I offer you my hand. Now take it!
Do not step back, do not recoil again,
As you are noble, grant me the great pleasure,
The best that's known to good men, trustingly,   1285
Without reserve, to accede to one who's better.
ANTONIO. With full sails you drive on! And it would seem
You're used to winning battles, everywhere
To find the highroads wide, the gates all open.
Gladly I grant you every dignity   1290
And happiness, yet all too clearly see
That, Tasso, still we stand too far apart.
TASSO. In years perhaps, in worth achieved and proved;
In will and courage I am anyone's match.
ANTONIO. Will does not draw the action after it;   1295
Courage sees ways as shorter than they are.
Crowns are reserved for those who reach their ends,
And often one that's worthy wins no crown.
But there are easy garlands, there are garlands
Of many diverse kinds: some can be snatched   1300
Quite comfortably on a walk, in passing.
TASSO. What to this man a goddess freely grants,
Strictly denies to that one, such possession
Not anyone can attain, try as he may.
ANTONIO. Attribute that to Fortune, no other gods,   1305
And I'll assent, since Fortune's choice is blind.
TASSO. But Justice, too, is blindfold; and she blinks
Or shuts her eyes at all that merely dazzles.
ANTONIO. Let fortunate men extol the goddess Fortune!

Ascribe to her a hundred eyes for merit,   1310
Discrimination, strict exactitude,
Call her Minerva, call her what they will,
Mistake a gracious bounty for reward,
Fortuitous frippery for true ornament!
TASSO. Your meaning's clear, too clear now. That's enough.   1315
Deep into you I look, and for a lifetime
Now know you through and through. If only she
So knew you, my Princess! No longer waste
The arrows of your eyes and of your tongue.
In vain you aim them at the garland placed   1320
Evergreen, never wilting, on my head.
First prove you do not meanly envy it!
Then you may challenge me for it perhaps.
I hold it sacred, and most prized of treasures.
Yet show me the man who can attain that end   1325
To which I have aspired, show me the hero
Whose legends only have come down to me;
Present to me the poet who to Homer,
To Vergil can compare himself; or, what
If saying more still, show me the man   1330
Who thrice deserves that honour, who three times
As much as me was shamed by that fine garland:
Then you will see me on my knees before
The same divinity that endowed me so;
No sooner should I rise than when she pressed   1335
That ornament from my head on to his.
ANTONIO. Till then, it's true, you have a right to it.
TASSO. Probing and weighing up, those I'll not shirk.
But your contempt's gratuitous, undeserved.
The garland that my Prince thought fit for me   1340
And that was wound for me by my Princess
No one shall cast in doubt or grin upon!
ANTONIO. That grandiose tone of yours, your sudden flaring,
Between us two, and here, are most unfitting.
TASSO. What you presume on here, I too may practise.   1345
Or has the truth been banished from this place?
This palace, does it put free minds in dungeons?
Must a good man endure suppression here?
I think that here nobility is in place,
The soul's nobility. May it not enjoy   1350
Proximity to the masters of this world?
It may and must. We've access to the Duke

Only through titles won by ancestors;
Why not through character and mind that nature
Not greatly gave to all, as not to all   1355
It could give lineage of great ancestry.
Smallness alone should feel endangered here,
Envy, that to its shame reveals itself:
Just as no dirty spider's web should cling
To the pure marble of these palace walls.   1360
ANTONIO. You yourself prove my right to scorn, repel you.
    So, the too hasty boy should take by storm
    The confidence and friendship of a man?
    Unseemly as you are, you think yourself good?
TASSO. Sooner the thing that you would call unseemly   1365
    Than that which I should have to call ignoble.
ANTONIO. You're young enough to profit by good breeding
    That still could teach you to improve your ways.
TASSO. Not young enough to bow before base idols,
    And old enough to counter scorn with scorn.   1370
ANTONIO. Where play of lips and play of lyrestrings count,
    You, I dare say, could prove the conquering hero.
TASSO. It would be arrogant to praise my fist,
    For it's done nothing; yet I trust in it.
ANTONIO. Your trust is in forbearance, which too greatly   1375
    Has spoilt you in your fortune's impudent course.
TASSO. Thanks to your taunts, at last, I feel mature.
    You are the last with whom I should have wished
    To try the gambling game of weaponry:
    But you have stoked me up, my inmost marrow   1380
    Is on the boil, the painful lust for vengeance
    Is bubbling over, foaming, in my heart.
    If you're the man you claim to be, then fight me!
ANTONIO. You know as little who, as where you are.
TASSO. No sacred law compels us to bear insult.   1385
    You desecrate, blaspheme against this place,
    Not I who proffered rust, respect and love,
    Most valuable of offerings, to you.
    Your spirit makes impure this paradise,
    Your words defile the purity of this room,   1390
    Not the emotion swelling in my heart
    That rages, loath to bear the slightest taint.
ANTONIO. What lofty spirit in a narrow chest!
TASSO. There's space enough to vent its fullness here!
ANTONIO. The rabble, too, vents passion in mere words.   1395

TASSO. If you're a gentleman, as I am, show it!
ANTONIO. I am, but I am conscious where I am.
TASSO. Come down with me, where weapons can decide.
ANTONIO. As you've no right to challenge, I won't follow.
TASSO. A welcome subterfuge for cowardice.   1400
ANTONIO. A coward threatens only where he's safe.
TASSO. Gladly I can dispense with that protection.
ANTONIO. Forgive yourself! This place will not forgive you.
TASSO. May this good place forgive my long forbearance.

He draws his sword.

Draw or come down, unless for ever more   1405
On top of hatred I am to pile contempt.

Scene IV

Enter Alfonso.

ALFONSO. What quarrel is this I see, and hate to see?
ANTONIO. Your Grace, you find me calm in face of one
    Whom a mad rage has utterly possessed.
TASSO. I beg of you, as of a deity,   1410
    To tame me, then, with one reproachful look.
ALFONSO. Tell me, Antonio, Tasso you explain,
    How could such enmity burst into my house?
    How did it grip you, sweep you from the course
    Of decency, of laws—responsible men   1415
    Caught in a frenzy? It amazes me.
TASSO. The reason must be that you do not know us.
    This man, so famed for prudence and good manners,
    Maliciously and coarsely, like an ill-bred,
    Ignoble ruffian has behaved to me.   1420
    Trustingly I approached him, he repulsed me;
    Constant, I pressed my love upon him still.
    And bitter, ever more so, he would not rest
    Until he'd turned to gall in me the purest
    Drop of my blood. Forgive me! You have found me   1425
    Whipped up to fury here. The guilt is his
    Who by his goading forced me into guilt.
    Deliberately he had fanned the blaze
    That rose in me, to hurt him and hurt me.
ANTONIO. It was the poet's high afflatus, sir!   1430

I was the first to be addressed by you
And asked a question. Now, with your permission,
After this heated orator I will speak.

TASSO. Oh, yes, go on, and tell him, word for word.
And if before this judge you can report   1435
Each syllable, gesture, tone, I dare you to!
Insult yourself all over again, go on,
Bear witness against yourself! I shan't deny
One breath, one pulse-beat, if you tell that tale.

ANTONIO. If you have more to say, then say it now;   1440
If not, keep quiet and don't interrupt me.
Whether this hothead, Prince, or I began
This quarrel? Which of us is to blame for it?
This is a sweeping question, sir, that may
Have to remain unanswered at this juncture.   1445

TASSO. How so? I think it is the foremost question.
Which of us two is in the right or wrong.

ANTONIO. Not quite as an extravagant mind may like
To see the case.

ALFONSO.   Antonio!

ANTONIO.   Gracious Duke,
I take the reprimand. But silence him: 1450
When I have spoken, let him babble on;
You will decide. So now I only say,
I cannot argue with him, and can neither
Accuse him nor defend myself, nor offer
Him satisfaction now, as he demands.   1455
For, as he stands, he's lost his liberty.
A rigorous law hangs over him, so grave
That your own mercy at the most can lighten.
He threatened me, he challenged me in this place;
Hardly he hid the naked blade from you.   1460
And if, your Grace, you had not stepped between us,
I too should stand before you an offender,
Sharing his guilt, with equal cause for shame.

ALFONSO (to Tasso). You acted unacceptably.

TASSO.   Sir, my heart
Acquits me, as I'm sure that your heart will.   1465
Yes, I admit, I threatened and I challenged,
I drew. But how maliciously his tongue
With carefully chosen words had wounded me.
How swiftly his sharp fang into my blood
Discharged its venom, how he'd fed my fever   1470

199

And raised its temperature—you cannot guess.
Coldly and calmly he had needled me,
Driven me to extremes. You do not know him,
You cannot know him now, and never will!
My heart-felt friendship I held out to him—   1475
He hurled the offered present at my feet;
And if my soul then had not flared and blazed,
It would have proved unworthy of your favour,
Your service, ever. If I forgot the law,
And where I was, I beg forgiveness of you.   1480
No spot exists on which I may be base,
No spot on which I'll bear to be debased.
If that heart, wheresoever it may be,
Fails you or fails itself, then punish, banish,
And never again let me set eyes on you.   1485
ANTONIO. How lightly this young man bears heavy loads
And brushes off iniquities like dust!
One would be moved to wonder, were not the magic
Of poetry a commonplace, well-known
How with impossibility it likes   1490
To play its little games. But whether you,
My Prince, and all your servants too can think
This act so trifling, I take leave to doubt.
Majesty spreads its aegis over all
Who, as to high divinity, come to it   1495
And to its pure, unviolated home.
As at an altar's foot, upon its threshold
All passion keeps within its bonds, restrained.
No swordblade flashes there, no threat is voiced,
There even insult does not seek revenge.   1500
The field of honour remains an open space
Wide enough for all grievance and contention:
There will no coward threaten, no man take flight.
These walls of yours your distant forbears founded
Upon security, raised for their dignity   1505
A sanctum whose tranquility they maintained
With heavy penalties, gravely and wisely pondered;
Banishment, dungeon, death requited wrongs.
There rank was not considered, nor did mercy
Hold back the arm of justice or of law,   1510
And even villainous men recoiled in fear.
Now after long and most desirable peace
We see raw fury reeling back into

The sphere of manners. Sir, decide the case
And punish! For what man can walk within   1515
His duty's narrow bounds, unless protected
Both by the law and by his sovereign's power?
ALFONSO. More than you both have said and could have said
Is audible to my impartial mind.
Both of you would have done your duty better   1520
Had I been spared the need of judging you.
For right and wrong here are close relatives.
If, Tasso, you were slighted by Antonio,
In one way or another he must give
You satisfaction, as you will demand.   1525
I should be pleased to arbitrate for you.
Meanwhile, however, Tasso, your offence
Makes you a prisoner. With due allowance
For your sake I shall palliate the law.
Now leave us, Tasso, keep to your own room,   1530
Guarded by you and with yourself alone.
TASSO. Is that your judge's sentence, Duke Alfonso?
ANTONIO. Be grateful for a father's leniency.
TASSO (*to Antonio*).
With you, for now, I've nothing more to discuss.
(*To Alfonso*) My sovereign, your solemn verdict sends   1535
A free man to imprisonment. So be it!
You think it just. Revering your sacred word
I bid my inmost heart be deeply silent.
It's new to me, so new, that almost I
Don't recognize you, me, this place I loved.   1540
But this man I know well.—I will obey,
Although there's much that here I still could say,
Should say, did not my lips refuse their function.
Was it a crime? It seems one, anyway,
And I'm regarded as a criminal.   1545
No matter what my heart says, I'm in prison.
ALFONSO. You're making more of it, Tasso, than I do.
TASSO. However it may be, still I can't grasp it:
Well, I'm no child, and know about such things;
I almost think I ought to understand it.   1550
Clarity comes in flashes, blinks at me,
But a mere moment later it's obscured.
The judgement is all I hear, and I comply.
These are too many wasted words already.
From now on, powerless creature, teach yourself   1555

To follow orders: You forget your station:
The seat of gods seemed on this very earth,
And now the sudden downfall leaves you stunned.
Gladly obey, for it befits a man
Willingly, too, to do the irksome thing.   1560
Here, for a start, take back the sword you gave me
When with the Cardinal I went to France:
No fame I won with it, nor yet disgrace,
Even today. That hopeful gift I now
Discard, with feelings better left unspoken.   1565
ALFONSO. How I'm disposed to you, you do not feel.
TASSO. My part is to obey, not speculate.
And to deny a splendid gift, alas,
I am compelled, my destiny demands it.
A garland does not suit a prisoner: 1570
With my own hands I'll doff the ornament
That seemed my own for all eternity.
Too soon supreme good fortune came to me
And now, as though I'd overreached myself,
Too soon is snatched away.   1575
What none can take away, you take yourself,
And what no god will give a second time.
We human beings are most strangely tried;
We could not bear it, had not nature lent us
That boon, light-hearted equanimity.   1580
With priceless treasures our most pressing need,
A spendthrift, teaches us to calmly play:
Quite readily we open our own hands
To let a treasure slip from them for ever.
A tear commingles with this kiss of mine   1585
And to oblivion dedicates you. This,
The dear sign of our weakness, is permitted.
Who would not weep when the immortal thing
Itself is not impervious to destruction?
Garland, you join the sword which, to my shame,   1590
Did not obtain you. Twined around its hilt,
You rest as on a brave man's coffin, on
The grave of my good fortune and my hopes!
Both I lay down, and willingly, at your feet:
For who, when you are angry, can be armed?   1595
And who, disowned by you, sir, wear adornments?
A prisoner I go, awaiting judgement.

At a signal from Duke, a page picks up the sword and garland and carries them away.

Scene V

ANTONIO. What flights of fancy! With what colours does
    That boy splash out his worth and destiny?
    Confined and inexperienced, youngsters think   1600
    Themselves unique, elect, beyond compare,
    Permit themselves all action, against all.
    Let him feel punished, for that punishment is
    To help the youth, so that the man will thank us.
ALFONSO. He has been punished: only too much, I fear.   1605
ANTONIO. If mercifully you wish to deal with him,
    Then, Prince, restore to him his liberty
    And let the sword decide our quarrel then.
ALFONSO. If that is the consensus, I will do it.
    But tell me, how did you provoke his rage?   1610
ANTONIO. I find it hard to say just how it happened.
    I may have hurt him deeply as a man,
    But as a gentleman did not insult him.
    And from his lips in utmost fury not
    One mannerless word escaped.
ALFONSO.   That's what I thought   1615
    About your quarrel. What you say confirms
    My first impression, my original guess.
    When two men clash, one rightly blames the man
    More adept and more prudent. You should not
    Be angry with him; it would be more proper   1620
    For you to guide him. There is time for that:
    This is no case that forces you to fight.
    While peace obtains, so long it is my wish
    To enjoy it in my house. So my request
    Is, mend that peace. You will not find it hard.   1625
    Lenora Sanvitale could begin
    By soothing him with her more gentle lips;
    Then go to him, restore to him in my name
    His total liberty, and with sincere
    And noble words regain his confidence.   1630
    Do that as soon as possible, Antonio:
    You'll speak to him as a father and a friend.
    Before we leave I wish to see that peace,
    And anything you will to do, you can.
    If need be, we can stay another hour   1635
    And leave the women then to gently finish
    What you began; and when we can return

They will have wiped away the last faint trace
Of this occurrence. It would seem, Antonio,
You mean to keep in practice! Hardly you   1640
Have settled one negotiation, when
You come back here and get yourself another.
I hope that this one will succeed as well.
ANTONIO. I am ashamed, and in your words I see
As in the clearest mirror, my transgression.   1645
It's easy to obey a noble master
Who, in commanding us, persuades us too.

ACT III

Scene I

PRINCESS (*alone*). Why doesn't Leonora come? Each moment
Is more distressing than the last, and racks
My anxious heart. I scarcely know what happened,   1650
Or which of them was guilty of offence.
If only she would come, when I'm as loath
To ask Antonio as to ask my brother
Till I am more composed, before I've heard
How matters stand and what may come of them.   1655

Scene II

Enter Leonora.

PRINCESS. Well, Leonora? What's the news? What's happened?
How is it with our friends? Enlighten me!
LEONORA. I found out nothing that we did not know.
They violently clashed, and Tasso drew,
Your brother separated them. It seems   1660
That it was Tasso who set off the quarrel:
Antonio freely walks about, with access
To Duke Alfonso; as for Tasso, he
Remains confined to his own room, alone.
PRINCESS. Antonio surely must have needled him,   1665
Unkindly, coldly riled that high-strung man.
LEONORA. I think so too. For when he went to Tasso
A cloud already hung around his forehead.

PRINCESS. Oh, how we lose the habit of responding
    To the pure, quiet hints our hearts transmit! 1670
    Within us, very softly, a god speaks,
    Quite audibly, but very softly, tells us
    What course we should pursue, and what avoid.
    To me this morning our Antonio seemed
    Still more abrupt than usual, more withdrawn. 1675
    My intuition warned me when beside him
    Tasso appeared. Just look at the exterior
    Of either man, their faces and their tones,
    Their gait, their way of looking! All contrary,
    Not in a blue moon they could like each other. 1680
    Yet Hope, that hypocrite, persuaded me:
    Both, she asserted, are reasonable men,
    Both are your friends, both noble, well-instructed;
    And what bond's firmer than between the good?
    I urged the youth, wholeheartedly he gave in. 1685
    How warmly, wholly he gave in to me!
    Why did I not prepare Antonio first?
    I hesitated: time was short, too short;
    Something in me held back from rushing in
    To strongly recommend the young man to him; 1690
    On courtesy, convention I relied,
    On wordly usage that so smoothly creeps
    Between two enemies even; did not fear
    That one so tested could relapse into
    The suddenness of quick youth. And now it's happened. 1695
    Disaster seemed unlikely, now it's here.
    Advise me, Leonora. What's to be done?
LEONORA. After what you have said, I need not tell you
    How hard it is to advise. This is no case
    Of like minds tangled in misunderstanding; 1700
    That, words can mend or, if it comes to the worst,
    Weapons can easily and wholly settle.
    These are two men, I've felt it for some time,
    Who are in opposition because nature
    Failed to make one man out of both of them. 1705
    And if they recognized their own advantage
    They would make up for that, unite as friends:
    Then they would stand as one man, and pursue
    Life's course with strength, good fortune and delight.
    That was my hope, like yours; and it was vain. 1710
    This morning's quarrel, however it occurred,

Can be patched up; but that would not insure us
For times to come, not even for tomorrow.
It would be best, I'd say, if Tasso left
Our region for a while; he could set out   1715
For Rome, or Florence, for that matter. There
In a few weeks I'd meet him and as a friend
Work on his mind and feelings, soothingly.
Here meanwhile you could work towards renewed
And closer understanding between you,   1720
Antonio, and your friends; good time perhaps
Will then effect what seems impossible now,
And reconcile, as only time can do.
PRINCESS. I see, dear friend: you plan to have the pleasure
That I'm to do without. You call that fair?   1725
LEONORA. Nothing you'll do without, but what in these
Conditions would not give you any pleasure.
PRINCESS. So calmly then, I am to ban a friend?
LEONORA. Keep one, by mere pretence of banishment.
PRINCESS. My brother will not readily let him go.   1730
LEONORA. When he can see it as we do, he'll yield.
PRINCESS. In a friend's shape to damn oneself is hard.
LEONORA. Yet that way for yourself you save a friend.
PRINCESS. I don't give my consent to this hard measure.
LEONORA. Then be prepared for a much harder blow.   1735
PRINCESS. You torture me, and can't be sure you're helping.
LEONORA. Before much longer we shall see who's wrong.
PRINCESS. If it must be, give up the questioning.
LEONORA. Those who decide can put an end to pain.
PRINCESS. I'm not decided, but you have your way,   1740
If not for long he has to part from us.
And let us take good care of him, Leonora,
So that no disadvantage comes to him.
The Duke will see to it that his allowance
Is duly paid to him while he stays abroad.   1745
Talk with Antonio, who has great influence
With him, my brother, and will not hold the quarrel
Against our friend, far less against ourselves.
LEONORA. A word from you, Princess, would have more weight.
PRINCESS. You know, dear friend, that I can't bring myself,   1750
As my dear sister of Urbino can,
To ask a favour, for myself or friends.
I like to drift along and let things be,
And from my brother gratefully accept

What he feels able, and disposed, to give me.   1755
For that I have reproached myself before now;
Not any more, though: now I have come through.
A woman friend would often scold me, too:
You are disinterested, she would say,
And that is good; but carry it so far   1760
That neither can you truly feel the needs
Of your most intimate friends. I let it pass,
And must put up with it, bear the reproach.
All the more pleased I am that now in practice
I can be useful, and can help our friend.   1765
My mother's legacy is due to me
And gladly I'll contribute to his welfare.
LEONORA. And I, Princess, am also able now
　　To prove my friendship for you by an action.
　　He's a poor housekeeper; where he falls short   1770
　　I shall be deft in helping him to manage.
PRINCESS. Well, take him, then, and if I have to lose him
　　You more than anyone are welcome to him.
　　I see it now, he will be better off.
　　Once more, then, must I call my anguish good,   1775
　　And beneficial? That has been my fate
　　From youth—and now become a habit also.
　　The loss of utmost happiness is halved
　　If never we could count on its possession.
LEONORA. My hope is that, as you deserve to be,   1780
　　You will be happy.
PRINCESS.　　　　　　Leonora! Happy?
　　Who's happy, then? My brother, true, I'd call so,
　　But meaning only that his generous heart
　　With constant equanimity bears its lot;
　　Yet what he merits, he has never had.   1785
　　Or is my sister of Urbino happy?
　　That lovely woman, that large and noble heart.
　　Her younger husband she has borne no children;
　　He honours her, and shows her no resentment,
　　But joy has never dwelt with them in their house.   1790
　　What did our mother's cleverness profit her?
　　Her various knowledge and wide sympathies?
　　Could they protect her from strange heresies?
　　They took us out of her charge: and now she's dead,
　　Leaving her children without the consolation   1795
　　That she died reconciled with her God and faith.

LEONORA. Don't fix your eyes on what all mortals lack;
    Observe those things that to each one remain.
    How much remains for you, Princess!
PRINCESS.   For me?
    Patience, dear Leonora; that I could practise   1800
    Ever since youth. When friends, or when my siblings
    Enjoyed themselves at galas or at play,
    Illness confined me to my lonely room.
    And in the company of many sorrows
    Early I learned to renounce. There was one thing   1805
    That did delight me in my solitude,
    The joy of song. With my own self I held
    Converse, I cradled all my pain and longing
    And every wish in sweet and gentle tones.
    Then often suffering turned to satisfaction.   1810
    Sad feelings even turned to euphony.
    But before long this comfort was denied
    To me by the physician; his strict order
    Silenced my singing; I was to live, to suffer
    Without resort to that consoling joy.   1815
LEONORA. So many friends, though, found their way to you,
    And now you are restored to vigorous health.
PRINCESS. I'm healthy, if that means, I am not ill:
    And I have many a friend whose loyalty
    Gives me much happiness. And I had a friend—   1820
LEONORA. You have him still.
PRINCESS.   And very soon shall lose him.
    The moment when I first set eyes on him
    Meant much to me. For hardly I'd recovered
    From many ailments; pain and sickness had
    Only just left me. Still humbly I looked out   1825
    Into the world, and once again took pleasure
    In every day. My brother and my sisters,
    Breathed in, relieved, sweet hope's most heady balm.
    I dared to peer again into the wide world,
    Look forward also, and from far away   1830
    Kind, kindred spirits came to me. Just then
    It happened that my sister brought that youth,
    Held by the hand, presented him to me,
    And, I confess it, so my heart received him
    That for eternity it holds him there.   1835
LEONORA. Never you must regret it, dear Princess.

To recognize what's noble, is an asset
That never can be snatched away from us.
PRINCESS. Things rare and beautiful are to be feared
    As is a flame that serves our need so well   1840
    As long as on the useful hearth it burns,
    As long as like a torch it flares before you.
    How welcome! Who can do without it there?
    But if unfended it runs loose, devouring,
    How wretched it can make us! But enough!   1845
    I'm garrulous, and even from you should rather
    Conceal how weak I am, how sick at heart.
LEONORA. Heart-sickness is most easily dissolved
    In our complaining and our true confiding.
PRINCESS. If confidences cure, soon I'll be well;   1850
    Purely and wholly I confide in you.
    Ah, my good friend. It's true, I am resolved:
    He is to go. But I can feel already
    The long, protracted anguish of those days
    When I must lack the thing that was my joy.   1855
    The sun no longer raises from my eyelids
    His beautifully dream-transfigured image;
    The hope of seeing him no longer fills
    The scarcely wakened mind with happy longing;
    My first look down into our gardens here   1860
    Seeks him in vain amid the dew of shades.
    How sweetly granted did my wishing feel
    To share with him each evening's tranquil light!
    How all our talking still increased the need
    To know, to understand each other more!   1865
    And daily better our two minds were tuned
    To the pure pitch of richer harmonies.
    Oh, what a dusk descends upon my eyes!
    The sun's effulgence, and their glad response
    To day's high noon, the multifarious world's   1870
    Most radiant presence, drearily and deeply
    Are shrouded in an all-obscuring mist.
    Before, each day to me was a life entire;
    Care was asleep, foreknowledge even silent,
    The current bore us, happily embarked,   1875
    On lightest wavelets, oars and rudder idle:
    Now in a darkened present into me
    By stealthy shifts fears for the future creep.

LEONORA. The future will give back your friends to you,
  Bringing you new good fortune and new joy.   1880
PRINCESS. I like to keep whatever is my own:
  Change entertains, but does us little good.
  Never with youthful cravings greedily
  My fingers combed a strange world's lucky bag,
  To snatch for my poor inexperienced heart   1885
  Haphazardly some plaything that might please.
  To love a thing I had to treasure it:
  I had to love it for its power to make
  My life a life such as I'd never known.
  At first I said: avoid him, keep away!   1890
  I did draw back, yet with each step drew closer,
  So sweetly lured, and so severely punished.
  With him I lose a true and pure possession,
  An evil spirit thrusts into my longing
  Not joy and happiness, but related pains.   1895
LEONORA. If a friend's words can give no consolation,
  The quiet energy of this lovely world
  And happy times will be your hidden healers.
PRINCESS. The world *is* lovely, true. In its wide spaces
  Always so much that's good moves to and fro.   1990
  Why only must it always seem to be
  One single step ahead of us, withdrawing,
  And leading on our timid longings too
  With every step through life, up to our graves!
  So rarely does a man or woman find   1905
  What seemed a proper and predestined right,
  So rarely do we hold within our keeping
  That which a fortunate hand had touched and seized.
  It yielded to us once, then pulls away,
  And we release what greedily we grasped.   1910
  There is a happiness, but we don't know it:
  We know it well, but do not treasure it.

Scene III

LEONORA (*alone*). Oh, how I pity her, so good, so loving!
  What a sad lot for one so excellent!
  Oh. She's the loser—and do you think you'll win?   1915
  Is it so urgent, then, for him to leave?
  Or do you make it so, thus to secure

His undivided heart and all those talents
That with another you have shared till now.
And shared unequally? Can that be honest?   1920
Are you not rich enough? What do you lack?
Husband and son and properties, rank and beauty,
All these you have, and now want him as well
As all those blessings. Do you love him then?
If not, what is it that makes you so unwilling   1925
To do without him? Be honest with yourself:—
What a delight to mirror one's own person
In his great mind! Does not our happiness
Grow in degree and splendour when his song
As on celestial clouds bears us aloft?   1930
That only makes you enviable. Then
You are and have much more than many crave:
Everyone also knows and sees you have it!
Your country speaks your name, looks up to you,
And that's the consummation of all bliss.   1935
Is Laura, then, the only name that should
Be voiced by every gentle tongue and lip?
And did no man but Petrarch have the right
To deify a beauty else unknown?
Where is the man that could compete with him,   1940
My friend? Just as the present world reveres him
So will posterity revere his name.
How splendid, in the brightness of this life
To have him at your side! And so with him
Light-footed skip into futurity!   1945
Then neither time nor age has any power
Over your person, nor insolent reputation
That pulls and pushes approbation's waves.
What's perishable, his great rhymes preserve.
You're beautiful still, still happy, though for years   1950
The round of mere occurrence has borne you on.
You need to have him, and from her take nothing;
For what she feels for that most worthy man
Is of one kind with all her other passions.
They shed, as does the cold moon's tranquil shine,   1955
Sparse light for travellers on nocturnal tracks:
Impart no warmth and pour out no delight
Or joy of living round them. She'll be glad
To feel that he is far away, and safe,
Just as it pleased her once to see him daily.   1960

Besides, together with my friend I will not
Exile myself from her or from this court:
I shall return and bring him back to her.
That's how it shall be!—Here comes our bearish friend:
We'll try him out, see whether we can tame him. 1965

Scene IV

Enter Antonio.

LEONORA. Instead of peace, you bring us war, as though
You'd come here from a camp, a battlefield
Where violence reigns and the clenched fist decides,
And not from Rome, where grave diplomacy
Raises its hands in blessing, and at its feet 1970
Sees a whole world all eager to obey.
ANTONIO. I must put up with the reproach, dear friend,
But the excuse is not far distant from it.
It's dangerous when for too long one has
To demonstrate one's patience and restraint. 1975
An evil spirit lurks beside you then,
From time to time by force exacting from you
A sacrifice. This time, unhappily,
I had to make it at our friends' expense.
LEONORA. You have been working for so long with strangers, 1980
Adapting to their ways and policies;
Now that you're back again among your friends
You wrong them, argue with them as with strangers.
ANTONIO. And that, my dear, is where the danger lies!
With strangers one must pull oneself together, 1985
There one's alert, there one pursues one's end
In their good favour, to make them serve that end;
With friends, though, one relaxes, lets oneself go,
Rests in their love and will permit oneself
A mood, a temper, or indeed a passion 1990
Immoderate in effect, and so one hurts
Those most for whom one's love is tenderest.
LEONORA. In that dispassionate reflection, dear,
You're quite yourself again, I'm glad to see.
ANTONIO. Well, yes, I'm sorry—I don't mind admitting— 1995
That I so utterly lost my grip today.
But you imagine, when an active man

Returns from gruelling work, his brow still hot,
And late at night in the much longed-for shade
Intends to rest, recover, for new efforts,   2000
Only to find that shade is occupied,
And widely, by an idler—will he not
Then feel some human motion in his heart?
LEONORA. If he is truly human, he'll be prepared
And even glad to share that shade with one   2005
Who can make rest more sweet, and work more easy
With conversation and with lovely tones.
The tree, dear friend, that casts the shade is wide,
And no one needs to drive away the other.
ANTONIO. All right, Eleonora; but let's drop   2010
This game of shuttlecocks with metaphor.
In this world there are many things that one
Gladly grants others and will share with others.
There is one treasure, though, you gladly grant
Only to one who highly has deserved it,   2015
And there's another you will never share
With anyone, however great his merit—
And if you need the names of those two treasures:
They are the laurel and a woman's love.
LEONORA. Oh, did that wreath upon our young man's head   2020
Offend his earnest senior? When you yourself
Could not have found for his fine poetry,
For his long labours, a reward more modest.
For work that's supernatural, not of this world,
That hovers in the air, and with mere sounds   2025
And gossamer images play upon our minds,
In a fine image, too, a lovely token
Has its appropriate and sole reward;
And if he hardly touches the earth he walks,
No more can that high honour touch his head.   2030
The gift in question is a fruitless bough
That his admirers' fruitless recognition
Gladly bestows, so that most easily
They can discharge a debt. You'd not begrudge
The martyrs' picture its bright aureole   2035
Around a head that's bald; and rest assured:
The laurel wreath, wherever you may see it,
Tells you much more of suffering than of pleasure.
ANTONIO. Could you be trying, with your lovely mouth,
To teach me scorn for the world's vanity?   2040

LEONORA. Antonio, there's no need for me to teach you
    To set their proper value on all things.
    And yet, it seems, at times the wise man needs,
    As much as other men, that someone show him
    His own possession in the proper light.   2045
    You, being excellent, will make no claim
    To a mere phantom of reward and favour.
    The service that connects you with your prince
    And with your friends by mutual obligation,
    Is real, alive, effective; and so must   2050
    Your recompense be: real, alive, effective.
    Your laurel is your princely sovereign's trust
    Which on your shoulders as a welcome burden
    Lies heaped and lightly carried; as for your fame,
    It is the general, the public trust.   2055
ANTONIO. And not one word about a woman's love?
    You cannot mean that one can do without it.
LEONORA. That's one construction. For you're not without it,
    And much more easily you could do without it
    Than could that other, tender-hearted man.   2060
    For, tell me: could a woman who set out
    To care for you, to occupy herself
    With you in her own fashion, bring that off?
    With you, all things are orderly, secure;
    You can take care of yourself as of all others,   2065
    You have whatever one would give you. He
    Employs us in the very trade that's ours:
    He lacks a thousand little things a woman
    With pleasure undertakes to see to, manage.
    The finest linen, and a coat of silk   2070
    With some embroidery—these he likes to wear.
    He likes to be well dressed, or rather he
    Cannot endure rough cloth that marks the servant
    Anywhere on his body, all clothing must
    Fit him not only well, but beautifully.   2075
    And yet he has no skill to get himself
    Such finery, nor, when acquired, to keep it
    In good condition; always he is short
    Of money, application. Now he leaves
    A garment here, now there; never returns   2080
    From any journey without having lost
    A third of all his things. Then it's a servant
    Who's robbed him. So you see, Antonio, how
    One has to care for him the whole year round.

ANTONIO. And that same care endears him more and more.   2085
    A lucky fellow, to have his very faults
    Credited to him, with a special right
    To play the boy in his maturity
    And brag of that perpetual feebleness!
    You must excuse me, lovely friend, if here   2090
    I show a little bitterness once more.
    You've not said all, have not said what he dares,
    Or that he's cleverer than people think.
    He boasts of two great flames! He ties and loosens
    Now this knot, now the other, and he wins   2095
    Such hearts with *such* an art. Is that to be
    Believed?
LEONORA. All right. Yet even that would prove
    It's only friendship you are speaking of.
    And if we did then barter love for love
    Would that not justly recompense a heart   2100
    That quite forgets itself and, all abandoned
    To beautiful dream, lives for its friends alone?
ANTONIO. Pamper him, then, and spoil him more and more,
    Interpreting as love his selfishness,
    Slight other friends who truly are devoted   2105
    To you with all their souls, by your own choice
    Pay tribute to that proud man, wholly break
    The precious circle of our mutual trust!
LEONORA. We are not quite as partial as you think;
    In many cases we exhort our friend.   2110
    We wish to educate him, so that more
    He will take pleasure in himself and so
    Have more to give to others. We, his friends,
    Know well enough his shortcomings, his defects.
ANTONIO. Yet much you praise in him that should be censured.   2115
    I've known him long, to know him is so easy
    And he's too proud to hide his feelings. Now
    He quite submerges in himself, as though
    The whole world were inside him, and he were
    Utterly self-sufficient in his world,   2120
    All things outside had vanished. He lets them be,
    Drops them or shoves them off, rests in himself—
    Suddenly, as an unseen spark ignites,
    Sets off a mine, be it with joy or sorrow,
    Caprice or anger, he breaks out, explodes;   2125
    Then he wants everything, to have and hold it,
    Then what he thinks or fancies, is to happen;

And in one moment things be brought to pass
That call for years of work and preparation;
And in one moment things undone, removed,   2130
That effort hardly could resolve in years.
If of himself he asks the impossible,
That's licence to demand the same of others.
His mind wants nothing less than to tie up
The ultimate ends of all things; a rare feat   2135
Not one man in a million can achieve,
And he is not that man: but in the end,
Quite unimproved, falls back into himself.
LEONORA. He harms himself, and does no harm to others.
ANTONIO. Ah, but he hurts, offends them grievously.   2140
Can you deny that at the point of passion
That promptly and adroitly seizes him
He dares to slander, to blaspheme against
The sovereign himself, and the Princess?
For moments only, true; but that's enough,   2145
Those moments will recur; he can control
His tongue no more than he can curb his feelings.
LEONORA. I should have thought that if he went away
From here for a short time, that would be good
Both for himself and for each one of us.   2150
ANTONIO. Perhaps, and perhaps not. But just at present
There is no question of it. For I have no wish
To shoulder all the blame for what's occurred;
It could well seem that I was driving him
Away, and I am not. For all I care,   2155
He can stay here, at court; he's welcome to it.
And if he wants us to be reconciled,
And has the sense to follow my advice,
Some sort of modus vivendi could ensue.
LEONORA. Now you yourself hope to affect a mind   2160
That minutes ago, you thought incorrigible.
ANTONIO. We always hope, and in all things it's better
To hope than to despair. For who can gauge
Or calculate what's possible? He means
Much to our Prince. So he must stay with us.   2165
And if in vain we try to shape him, then
He's not the only one we must tolerate.
LEONORA. Quite so impartial, quite so dispassionate
I never thought you. What a fast conversion!
ANTONIO. Well, one advantage must accrue to age—   2170
This, that albeit not immune to error,

At least it can compose itself at once.
It was your aim at first to reconcile
Me to your friend. Now I beg that of you.
Do what you can to make that man himself,   2175
And to restore things soon to an even course.
I shall go to him also, as soon as I hear
From you that he is calm again, and ready,
As soon as you believe my presence will
Not make the trouble worse. Whatever you do,   2180
Do it without delay; for before nightfall
Alfonso leaves for town, and I go with him.
So lose no time. Meanwhile I say farewell.

Scene V

LEONORA (*alone*). This time, dear friend, we are not of one mind:
Your best advantage and my own do not   2185
Go hand in hand. I'll make good use of this
Respite to win our Tasso over. Quick!

ACT IV

Room.

Scene I

TASSO (*alone*). Have you awakened from protracted dream
And has the dear delusion suddenly left you?
The very day of your consummate joy   2190
Did a sleep cage you, to hold and awe your soul
With heavy fetters now? There's no denying,
You dream, awake. Where have those good hours gone
That played around your head with flowery garlands?
The days when with free longing your mind could soar   2195
Through the extended azure of the sky?
And yet, you are alive and touch real flesh,
Can touch real flesh, and doubt that you're alive.
Is it my fault, is it the other's fault
That, faulted, I am here, a guilty man?   2200
Have I committed that for which I suffer?
Was not my whole fault that I did what's right?
I looked at him, moved only by good will,

Moved on too fast by the heart's folly, hope:
That he who wears a human face is human.   2205
With open arms I flung myself at him,
To meet no arm's response, but lock and bolt.
And yet so tactically I had planned
How to receive, confront a person who
From old acquaintance had been suspect to me!   2210
Whatever may have happened to you now,
Hold on, hold fast to this one certainty:
I saw her! She was there, in front of me!
She spoke to me, I heard her. She was there!
Her glances, tone, her words' most precious meaning,   2215
They're mine for ever, not to be stolen from me
By time, by fate, or by ferocious fortune.
And if too quickly then my spirit rose,
And if too fast in my own heart I gave
Air to the flames that now have turned on me,   2220
I cannot rue it, even if all my life's
Predestined course were ended now for ever.
To her I pledged myself, glad to obey
The beckoning hint that drew me to disaster.
Let it be so! At least I have proved worthy   2225
Of the sweet confidence that thrills me yet,
At this hour even that has forced wide open
For me the blackened gates of a long term
Of mourning.—Nothing now can be undone.
The sun of warmest favour suddenly   2230
Goes down for me; the Duke averts his gracious
Eyes from my person, leaving me to stand
Bewildered here, on the dark, narrow track.
Those ugly beasts, ambiguously winged,
The nasty retinue of ancient Night,   2235
Swarm from their lairs and flap around my head.
Where, where shall I direct my footsteps now
To flee this loathsomeness that whirrs all round me,
Avoid a precipice, too, more fearful still?

Scene II

Enter Leonora.

LEONORA. What has been happening? Dear Tasso, did   2240
     Your zeal or your mistrust impel you to it?

218

How did it happen? All of us are staggered
And your great gentleness, your amiable ways,
Your perspicacious eye, the understanding
By which you give to each what is his due,   2245
Your equipoise that suffers what to suffer
Excellent men soon learn, the vain but seldom,
A prudent mastery over tongue and lips—
My dearest friend, I scarcely recognize you.
TASSO. What if I'd lost them all, those qualities!   2250
  If as a beggar suddenly you found
  A friend whom you had thought a wealthy man?
  What of it? True, I am not who I was
  And yet I am as much myself as ever.
  It seems a puzzle, but it isn't one.   2255
  The tranquil moon that gladdens you at night
  And irresistibly draws your eye, your feelings
  With its bright shining, in the day-time drifts
  An insignificant pale wisp of cloud.
  The day's effulgence has outshone my light,   2260
  You know me, but I do not know myself.
LEONORA. What you have said, dear friend, I cannot follow,
  The way you've said it. Please explain yourself.
  Did that curt fellow's insult hurt you so
  That now you wish to utterly disown   2265
  Both your own self and us? Confide in me.
TASSO. I'm not the injured party; as you see,
  It is for injuring that I was punished.
  A sword will easily and quickly cut
  The knot of many words, but I'm in prison.   2270
  You may not know it—don't be startled, though,
  My delicate friend. You find me in a cell.
  A schoolboy, I've been disciplined by the Duke.
  I will not argue with him, and I cannot.
LEONORA. You seem more shaken than you need to be.   2275
TASSO. So feeble, then, you think me, such a child
  That such a case at once could leave me shattered?
  Not the occurrence has left me deeply hurt,
  But what it signifies; that hurts me deeply.
  Still, let them have their way, my enemies   2280
  And enviers! The field's wide open for them.
LEONORA. Oh. You suspect too much, suspect too many
  Who wish you well, as I have ascertained.
  Even Antonio bears no grudge against you,
  As you suppose. The unpleasantness today—   2285

TASSO. I leave aside entirely, only take
    Antonio as he was and will remain.
    I've never liked his starched sagacity,
    His air of stiff, unerring rectitude.
    Instead of probing whether the listener's mind   2290
    On its own track might not be making progress,
    He lectures you on things that you know better,
    Feel more intensely, and never hears a word
    You say to him, so that he must misjudge you.
    To be misjudged, misjudged by one so proud,   2295
    Who thinks he can ignore you with a smile!
    I am not old, nor worldly-wise enough
    To merely bear that, and return the smile.
    Sooner or later the tension had to break,
    We had to break; and if it had been later,   2300
    So much the worse for all. One master only
    I recognize, the master who supports me,
    Whom gladly I obey, but want no other.
    In thought and poetry I will be free;
    The world imposes curbs enough on action.   2305
LEONORA. He speaks of you quite often with respect.
TASSO. No, with restraint, you mean, with cunning forethought.
    And that repels me; for he has the knack
    Of talk so glib, so calculated that
    His praise is worse than censure, and that nothing   2310
    Can cut more deeply, hurt you more, than praise
    Out of his mouth.
LEONORA.   I wish, dear friend, you'd heard
    How in all other instances he spoke
    Of you and of those gifts that more than others
    Nature endowed you with. He truly senses   2315
    All that you are and have, and values both.
TASSO. Believe me, a self-centred heart and mind
    Cannot escape the torturing bonds of envy.
    A man like that may well forgive another
    Status, possessions, honour; for he thinks: 2320
    You have those too, you have them if you wish,
    If you persist, if fortune favours you.
    But that which only nature can bestow,
    No effort, no ambition makes attainable,
    Not gold, not sword, not clever scheming, nor   2325
    Persistence wins, he never can forgive.
    How can he bear it who by force of will

Thinks he can bend the favour of the Muses?
Who when he strings together thoughts he's culled
From many poets, thinks himself a poet? 2330
He'd sooner let me have the Prince's favour,
Much as he'd like to keep it all himself,
Than the mere talent that the heavenly powers
Gave to a miserable orphaned boy.
LEONORA. Would you could see as clearly as I do! 2335
You're wrong about him. He is not like that.
TASSO. If I am wrong about him, let me be wrong!
I think of him as my worst enemy
And should be inconsolable if now
I'd have to think him otherwise. It's foolish 2340
To be consistently fair; that's to destroy
One's own true selfhood. Are our fellow beings
Always so fair to us? Not so. Far from it!
A man within his small identity needs
Twofold awareness that is love and hate. 2345
Doesn't he need the night as much as day?
Sleep just as much as waking? No, henceforth
I must hold on to that man as the object
Of my profoundest loathing. Nothing can
Deprive me of this pleasure, to think worse 2350
And worse of him.
LEONORA.   If that is your intention,
And irreversible, dear friend, it's hard
To see how you can hope to stay at court.
You know how much he means here, and must mean.
TASSO. Yes, lovely friend. I'm very well aware 2355
How even now I am superfluous here.
LEONORA. That you are not, that you can never be!
Rather you know how happy is the Duke,
How happy the Princess, to have you here.
And when her sister of Urbino comes 2360
It's almost for your sake as much as theirs.
All of them think alike and well of you.
Each of them trusts in you without reserve.
TASSO. What kind of trust can that be, Leonora?
Has he once spoken with me seriously 2365
About affairs of State? And if it happened
That even with his sister or with others
He did discuss such matters in my presence,
Some special case, he never once asked me.

Always it only was: Antonio's coming!   2370
Write to Antonio promptly! Ask Antonio!
LEONORA. You owe him thanks, not grumbles. And by leaving
You total, unconditional liberty,
He honours you as greatly as he can.
TASSO. He lets me roam because he thinks me useless.   2375
LEONORA. Because you roam, that's why you are not useless.
Too long you've harboured grievance and misgiving
Like a loved child, and hugged it to your breast.
I've often thought about it, and however
I turn it round, it's clear: on this rich soil   2380
To which good fortune has transplanted you
You do not thrive. Dear Tasso! May I say it?
May I advise you?—You should leave this place!
TASSO. You need not spare your patient, dear physician!
Pass him the medicine, and have no care   2385
Whether it's bitter. Whether he can recover,
That weigh up well, my dear and clever friend!
I see it all myself: it is all over!
I *can* forgive him, it's he who can't forgive.
It's he who's needed here, not me, alas.   2390
He is politic, I, alas, am not.
He works, intrigues against me, and I can't,
I won't take counter-measures. As for my friends,
They let it pass, they see it differently.
They hardly jib at it, and ought to fight it.   2395
You think I ought to leave; I think so too—
Goodbye to you, then! I shall endure that also.
You have already left me—now may I
Summon the strength and courage to leave you.
LEONORA. Oh, from a distance all becomes more clear   2400
That, while it's present, may confuse us only.
Perhaps you'll recognise what love surrounded
You in these parts, and come to appreciate
The loyalty of your true friends, and how
The whole wide world can never take their place.   2405
TASSO. That we shall see! From childhood I have known
The world, and know how easily it leaves us
Helpless and solitary, while like the sun
And moon and other gods, it goes its way.
LEONORA. If you will listen to me, you need never   2410
Repeat that sad experience. If I may
Offer advice, you will set out at first

For Florence, where a woman friend will take
Most tender care of you. And rest assured:
I am that woman friend. I'm travelling there   2415
To meet my husband in the next few days
And nothing would delight him more, or me,
Than if I brought you there, into our midst.
I'll say no more, for you know well enough
What he is like, the Prince who will receive you,   2420
What kind of men that beautiful city harbours
And—need I add?—what charming women too.—
You're silent? Think it over! And decide!
TASSO. A most attractive prospect, what you tell me,
Quite in accordance with my inmost wish;   2425
Only, it is too new: I beg of you,
Let me consider. Soon I shall decide.
LEONORA. I leave you with the best of hopes for you
And for us all, and for this ducal house.
Yes, ponder it, and if you do so wisely   2430
You'll hardly hit upon a better plan.
TASSO. One more thing, dearest friend, before you go:
How does she feel towards me, the Princess?
Has she been angry with me? What did she say?—
She was reproachful, blamed me, then? Speak freely!   2435
LEONORA. Knowing you well, readily she excused you.
TASSO. Am I disgraced? Don't flatter me, don't spare me.
LEONORA. A woman's favour is not so easily lost.
TASSO. Will she dismiss me gladly, when I go?
LEONORA. Certainly, if you go for your own good.   2440
TASSO. Shall I not lose the favour of the Duke?
LEONORA. Rely on him: he is magnanimous.
TASSO. Would she be quite alone, then, the Princess?
You're leaving; and however little I
May mean to her, I do know I meant something.   2445
LEONORA. A far-off friend can be good company,
As long as we're assured that he is happy.
And all is well: I see you well. Content,
With nothing that could trouble your departure.
The Duke's wish was: Antonio will look you up.   2450
He himself blames the bitterness with which
He hurt your feelings. With composure, please,
Receive him, just as he will show composure.
TASSO. In every sense, I shall stand up to him.
LEONORA. And by the grace of Heaven, friend, before   2455

You leave, may I yet open up your eyes:
There's no one in our land who persecutes,
Hates you, oppresses you in secret, mocks you!
You are in error, and as otherwise
You please with fictions; here, unhappily,   2460
You're spinning out a curious web of fictions
To harm and hurt yourself. I'll do my utmost
To tear that web in pieces so that, free,
You can make headway on your life's good course.
I'll leave you, and await a happy message.   2465

Scene III

TASSO (*alone*). I am to recognize that no one hates me.
That no one persecutes me, all the schemes,
The secretive and secret webs are woven,
Spun out within the confines of my head.
Am to confess that I am in the wrong,   2470
That I do wrong to many a person who
Never deserved such treatment! And all that
Just when my total rightness and their guile
Lies there for all to see in broadest sunlight!
I'm to feel deeply with an open heart   2475
The Duke accords me his implicit favour
And all his bounty, too, in generous measure
At the same moment as, with weak indulgence,
He lets my foes throw dust into his eyes
And lets his hands be bound by them, no doubt.   2480

That he's deceived, he has no eyes to see,
That they are cheats, I cannot prove to him;
And only so that he may gull himself,
And they, at leisure too, may calmly gull him,
I'm to keep mum, or, better, go away!   2485

And who advises that? Who, so adroitly,
And with such dear, true urging, pushes me?
Who else than Leonora Sanvitale,
My tender friend! But ah, I know you now!
Why did I ever trust those lips of hers!   2490
She was not honest, though with sweetest words
She showed me her concern, her tenderness—
Least of all then! No, she has always had,

And has a wily heart; with creeping steps,
With calculated ones, she curries favour.   2495

How often, too, I have deceived myself,
And about her! At bottom, though, it was
Vanity only that deceived me. So:
I knew her, but preferred self-flattery.
That's how she is to others, I told myself,   2500
But towards you she's limpidly sincere.
Now I do see it clearly, but too late:
I was in favour, and she nestled up—
So coyly—to the favoured. Now I'm falling
She turns her back on me, as fortune does.   2505

Now as my enemy's implement she comes,
Winds her way in, and lets her smooth tongue hiss,
Small serpent that she is, seductive tones.
How lovable she seemed! More so than ever!
How soothing, from her lips, was every word!   2510
Yet not for long could flattery conceal
The venomous gist: as though on her own forehead
The contrary sense of everything she said
Too clearly was inscribed. I'm soon aware
When someone seeks an opening to my heart   2515
And is not open-hearted. Shall I go?
Be off to Florence, quickly as can be?

And why to Florence? I can see it all.
There the new house of Medici is in power,
Not, true, in open enmity with Ferrara,   2520
Yet quiet envy with its clammy hand
Divides the best, most generous of minds.
If I were granted by those noble princes
Exalted tokens of their favour, as
I surely might expect, the courtier here   2525
Would soon cast doubt upon my loyalty
And gratitude. He'd easily succeed.

Yes, I'll be off, but not as you intend;
I wish to go, but farther than you think.
Why should I stay here? What can keep me here?   2530
Oh, yes, too well I understood each word
That I could draw from Leonora's lips!
Hardly from syllable to syllable I
Could catch it, but I know exactly now

What the Princess is thinking—and must bear it.   2535
"She will dismiss me gladly, when I go,
Because I go for my own good." O that
She felt a passion in her heart that would
Destroy my welfare and myself! Much sooner
I'd suffer Death's cold hand than hers that, colder   2540
And rigid, lets me go:—Well, go I will!—
Now take good care and let no single semblance
Of friendship or of kindness hoodwink you.
If you don't fool yourself, now no one will.

Scene IV

Enter Antonio.

ANTONIO. Tasso, I'm here, to have a word with you,   2545
    If you will listen quietly, and can.
TASSO. To act, as you're aware, I am forbidden;
    So it befits me now to wait and listen.
ANTONIO. I find you more relaxed now, as I wished.
    And long to speak to you without constraint.   2550
    First of all, in the Duke's name, I release you
    From the weak bonds that seemed to fetter you.
TASSO. The absolute will that bound me, sets me free;
    I yield to it, and do not ask for judgement.
ANTONIO. Then for myself I tell you: with my words,   2555
    It seems, more sorely and more deeply I
    Offended you than, moved by many a passion,
    I knew or felt. However, not one word
    That's reprehensible escaped my lips,
    No cause for vengeance as a gentleman—   2560
    And as a man you'll not withhold your pardon.
TASSO. Which hits us harder, jibes or calumny,
    I'll not examine: the former penetrate
    To the deep marrow, the latter scratch the skin.
    Calumny's dart rebounds on him who thinks   2565
    He's struck a wound; opinion and repute
    A sword well-wielded easily allays.
    An injured heart, though, does not soon recover.
ANTONIO. Now it's for me to beg you urgently:
    Do not withdraw, accede to my request,   2570
    It is the Duke's, and he has sent me to you.

TASSO. I know my duty, and give in to it.
    Pardon, as far as possible, is granted.
    The poets tell us of a spear empowered
    To heal the wound that it had once inflicted   2575
    By one benevolent, beneficent touch.
    The human tongue has something of that power;
    I'll not resist it now with petty spite.
ANTONIO. I thank you, and I'd have you test at once,
    Without reserve, both me and my desire   2580
    To be of service to you. Tell me, Tasso,
    Can I be useful to you? Let me prove so!
TASSO. You offer me the very thing I wish.
    You gave me back my liberty; now obtain
    For me the use of that same liberty.   2585
ANTONIO. What can you mean? Make yourself clearer, please.
TASSO. I've finished my long poem, as you know;
    Yet much is needed still for its perfecting.
    Today I gave it to the Duke, and hoped
    At the same time to ask a favour of him.   2590
    I find that many friends of mine at present
    Have met in Rome; though individually
    They've commented in letters on this passage
    Or that—to my great profit in some cases,
    Others not so convincingly—at certain points   2595
    I cannot well amend the text until
    I am more sure that what they write is apt.
    All this can not be done by correspondence:
    Immediate presence soon unties the knots.
    I should have put that to the Duke himself,   2600
    But failed to do so; and now can not presume,
    So by your mediation seek this leave.
ANTONIO. Absence seems inadvisable to me
    Just at the moment when your finished work
    Commends you to the Duke and the Princess.   2605
    A day of favour is like harvest-time:
    One must be busy at it when it's ripe.
    If you absent yourself you'll have no gain,
    But well could lose what you've already gained.
    The present is a powerful deity: 2610
    Learn to respect its influence, and stay here.
TASSO. I have no fears. Alfonso, sir, is noble.
    Always he's proved most generous to me;
    And to his heart alone I wish to owe

My hopes, extort no grace from him by stealth 2615
Or by intrigue; want nothing of him that
He could regret to have accorded me.
ANTONIO. Then don't demand of him that he dismiss
You now, when with reluctance he would do it—
Or, if my fears are grounded, not at all. 2620
TASSO. Gladly he'll do it, if the request is right,
And you are equal to it, if you're willing.
ANTONIO. What reasons, though, am I to give for it?
TASSO. Let every stanza of my poem plead!
My aim was laudable, even if my strength 2625
Fell short of it in places, now and then.
I did not lack endeavour, application.
The carefree progress of many a fine day,
The silent spaces of many a deep night
Religiously were given to that work. 2630
My hope, a humble one, was to come close
To past great masters, and my bold intention
To rouse from a long sleep to noble deeds
My own contemporaries, then perhaps
To share with a devout and Christian army 2635
A new crusade, its dangers and its glory.
And if my song is to arouse the best
It must be worthy also of the best.
What I achieved, I owe to Duke Alfonso;
I wish to owe him its perfection too. 2640
ANTONIO. And that same Duke is here, with others,
To guide you, like those Romans, with advice.
Polish your poem here, this is the place,
And then, to further it, be off to Rome.
TASSO. Alfonso was the first to prompt, inspire me, 2645
But to correct me surely is the last.
Greatly I value your advice and that
Of clever persons gathered at this court.
You shall decide, if my good friends in Rome
Should fail to convince me by their arguments. 2650
But I *must* see them. For Gonzaga has
Convened a kind of court for me at which
I must appear. And I can hardly wait.
Flaminio de Nobili, Angelio
Da Barga, Antoniano, and Speroni! 2655
You'll know those names.—And what great names they are!
With confidence and with anxiety
They fill my mind, so ready to submit.

ANTONIO. You're thinking of yourself, not of the Duke.
    I tell you that he will not let you go;   2660
    And if he does, he will not do it gladly.
    Nor can you wish to ask a favour of him
    He hates to grant. Am I to mediate here
    In an affair of which I can't approve?
TASSO. Do you refuse this first request, when I   2665
    Have put your proffered friendship to the test?
ANTONIO. True friendship's proved in saying no to friends
    At the right time, and often love accords
    A harmful boon, if to the asker's will
    More than his welfare it has given heed.   2670
    It seems to me that at this moment you
    Consider good the thing you dearly crave.
    And in a moment want the thing you crave.
    By vehemence a man at fault makes up
    For lack of truth and of capacity.   2675
    Duty demands that now I do my best
    To curb the haste that drives you to disaster.
TASSO. Oh, it's not new to me, this tyranny
    Of friendship, most unbearable to me
    Of all the tyrannies. It's only that   2680
    You don't think as I do, and then assume
    That you think rightly. Yes, I grant you freely,
    It is my good you seek. But don't demand
    That I must look for it along your path.
ANTONIO. So, in cold blood, against my full and clear   2685
    Conviction, I'm to do the thing that harms you?
TASSO. Let me relieve you of that grave misgiving!
    You'll not deter me with those words of yours.
    You have declared me free, and now this door
    Opens for me new access to the Duke.   2690
    I leave the choice to you: it's you or I.
    The Duke is leaving. There's no time to lose.
    So promptly now decide. If you don't go,
    I'll go myself, regardless of the outcome.
ANTONIO. Give me a little time, at least await   2695
    The Duke's return from urgent work at court.
    Of all days, not today!
TASSO.   This very hour,
    If possible. My feet are burning here,
    On this cold marble floor. Until my horse
    Whirls up the dust along the open road   2700
    My mind won't rest. I beg of you. It must

229

Be obvious to you how unfit I am
Just now to face my sovereign. You can see—
How can I hide it?—that at this same moment
No power on earth can force me to submit.   2705
Only real fetters now can hold me here.
Alfonso is no tyrant, and he freed me.
How gladly I obeyed him in the past!
Today I can't obey. Today, of all days,
Let me go free, so that my mind recovers!   2710
I shall resume my duty before long.

ANTONIO. You shake my certainty. What shall I do?
I note once more that error is infectious.

TASSO. If I am to believe you, if you mean well,
Do what I ask of you, do what you can.   2715
The Duke will give me leave then, I shall lose
Neither his future help nor his good favour.
That I shall owe you, and with gratitude.
But if you bear an ancient grudge against me,
If it's your will to banish me from court,   2720
If it's your will to bend my fate for ever,
And drive me helpless out into the world,
Then stick to your own purpose and resist!

ANTONIO. Since you insist that I must do you harm,
I'll choose the way that you have chosen for me.   2725
The outcome will soon show us who's in error.
You long to leave: I'll tell you in advance:
Almost before you've turned your back on us
Your heart will urge you to return, your stubborn
Self-will impel you onward; what you'll find   2730
In Rome is pain, dejection, mental stress;
And you will miss your chance both here and there.
Not to advise you, though, I speak these words,
But to predict what before long must happen,
And also to invite you in advance   2735
To trust me, if the worst comes to the worst.
Now I will see the Duke, as you demand.

Scene V

TASSO. Yes, go ahead, and go away assured
That you've persuaded me to do your will.
I'm learning to dissimulate, for you   2740

Are a great teacher, I am quick to learn.
So life coerces us to seem, indeed
To be like those whom proudly, boldly once
We could despise. Completely I've seen through
The intricate art of courtly politics.   2745
Antonio wants to drive me from this place
And does not want to seem to be so doing.
He puts on prudence and solicitude
To prove me very awkward, very sick,
Appoints himself my guardian, to reduce me   2750
To a mere child, because he could not make
A slave of me; and so befogs the eyes
Of both our sovereign and our Princess.
I'm to be kept here, he opines, because
Nature did lend to me a fine distinction;   2755
Unhappily, though, it almost spoiled that gift
With weaknesses of character, thrown in,
Unbounded arrogance, exaggerated
Susceptibility, and gloomy moods.
It can't be helped. If destiny has made   2760
A man like that, and once the mould has set,
You have to take the fellow as he is,
Put up with him, support him, and perhaps
Even enjoy in him, on a good day,
His pleasant sides, an unexpected bonus;   2765
Beyond that, as by birth the fellow was,
So you must let him live, and let him die.

Can I still see Alfonso's steadfast mind,
Defying enemies, protecting friends?
Is that the same man I encounter now?   2770
What I see clearly now is my undoing!
It is my fate that only towards me
Everyone changes who for others still
Is faithful, constant; shifted easily,
Within one moment, by a single breath.   2775

Did not the arrival of that man alone
Destroy my whole life's pattern in one hour?
Demolish the whole edifice of my fortune
And happiness, down to its deep foundations?
Oh, must I know it, too, all in one day?   2780
Yes, just as all things surged towards me, so
They ebb away from me; as each and all

Stretched out to clasp me to them, hold me fast,
So they repulse me now and turn from me.
And for what reason? And can that man outweigh   2785
The scale of my own worth and all the love
That in the past so richly I possessed?

Yes, all things flee me now. You too, you too,
Princess, my loved one, you withdraw from me.
In all these dreary hours she has not sent me   2790
One single hint or token of her favour.
Have I deserved such treatment?—My poor heart,
Whose very nature was her adoration!—
Merely to hear her voice was to be thrilled
With an emotion words can not express.   2795
But if I saw her, the bright light of day
Seemed dim to me; her eyes, her mouth so drew me,
So irresistibly, that scarcely could
My knee refrain from bending, and I needed
All my mind's rigour to stay upright there,   2800
Not falling at her feet; and with great effort
Only I could dispel that giddiness.
Here take your stand, my heart; and, my clear mind,
Let nothing cloud you here. Accept: She, too!
Dare I say that? I hardly can believe it;   2805
I do believe it, wishing I need not.
She too! She too! Excuse her utterly
But do not hide it from yourself: She too!

Oh, those two little words I ought to doubt
As long as there's one breath of hope in me,   2810
Those very words incise themselves at the end
On the hard rim of the small tablet crammed
And wholly covered with my written torments.
Now, only now, my enemies are strong
And I for ever robbed of every power.   2815
How can I fight when in the opposing ranks
She stands? Or how with patience can I wait
When *her* hand's not held out to me from afar?
If *her* gaze does not meet imploring eyes?
You dared to think it, dared to speak it even,   2820
And, with no time to fear it, it's come true.
And now before despair with iron claws
Rips all your senses, tearing them apart,
Go on, accuse your bitter destiny,
And say again, again: She too! She too!   2825

ACT V

Scene I

Alfonso. Antonio.

ANTONIO. At your suggestion, for a second time
    I spoke with Tasso, and come straight from him.
    I've argued, pleaded with him, even pressed him;
    But from his purpose still he will not budge
    And he beseeches you to grant him leave   2830
    To go to Rome, for a brief absence only.
ALFONSO. Well, I don't like it. Frankly, I'm displeased,
    And think it better now to tell you so
    Than to conceal and deepen my displeasure.
    He wants to go; all right, I'll not detain him.   2835
    He wants to leave, for Rome; I'll let him leave.
    If only Scipio Gonzaga or
    That cunning Medici does not take him from me!
    What's made the whole of Italy so great
    Is that each neighbour squabbles with the other   2840
    To keep and to employ superior men.
    A prince who does not gather talents round him,
    I think, is like a general without troops:
    And barbarous, whatever else he may be,
    The prince who's deaf to poetry and poets.   2845
    This one I have discovered, I have chosen,
    And as my servant I am proud of him,
    And having done so much for him already,
    I'm loath to lose him for no urgent reason.
ANTONIO. I am embarrassed, for in your eyes I bear   2850
    The blame for those occurrences today;
    And readily I do admit my fault
    That to your grace I still submit for pardon;
    But if you should believe I have not done
    My utmost to conciliate the man,   2855
    You'd leave me quite disconsolate. So please
    Absolve me with one look, so that again
    I can compose myself and trust myself.
ALFONSO. No, as to that, Antonio, rest untroubled,
    By no means do I put the blame on you;   2860
    Only too well I know his stubborn mind,
    Only too well I know my own endeavours,
    How I considered him, how I forgot

Entirely that it was for me to ask
Him to serve me! Although there's much a man   2865
Can master in himself, his mind is one
That neither time nor need can quite subdue.
ANTONIO. If many make allowances for one,
It's right that he in turn should ask himself
Repeatedly what is of use to others.   2870
And if he's nurtured all his faculties,
So hoarded every science for himself
And every kind of knowledge we're permitted
To make our own is he not doubly bound
To curb himself? And does he think of that?   2875
ALFONSO. Whatever happens, peace is not for us!
As soon as we are minded to enjoy,
An enemy comes to try our courage out,
And then, to try our patience, comes a friend.
ANTONIO. A man's first duty, to choose food and drink   2880
For his own use, since nature's not restricted
Him like the beasts, has he proved equal to it?
Doesn't he rather, like a child, give in
To any lure that's flattering to the palate?
Who's ever seen him mix water with his wine?   2885
Strong spices, sweetmeats, the most potent liquors
Higgedly-piggedly he gobbles, swills,
And then complains of heaviness of mind,
His fiery blood, his too ebullient temper,
Scolding both nature and his destiny.   2890
How hotly, foolishly I've seen him argue
Not once, but many times, with his physician;
Laughably almost, if it were right to laugh
At what torments one man and pesters others.
"I feel this ailment," anxiously he insists,   2895
And peevishly: "How dare you vaunt your skill?
Get me a cure!"—All right, says the physician,
Avoid the following.—"I can't do that,"—
Then drink this medicine.—"Oh no, it tastes
Disgusting, it revolts my very nature."—   2900
Drink water, then.—"What, common water? Never!
I'm hydrophobic as a man with rabies."
Then there's no help for you.—"Why not? How so?"—
One ailment still will chase the one before
And if it cannot kill you, will torment   2905
You more and more each day.—"A fine prognosis!

As good as your profession. You know my ailment,
So you should know the remedies, and make them
Inviting too, so that I do not need
To pay with suffering for relief from pain."   2910
You too are smiling, but I'm sure you've heard
Those words repeated out of his own mouth?
ALFONSO. I've often heard them and excused them often.
ANTONIO. There is no doubting it: an immoderate life,
Just as it gives us wild and heavy dreams,   2915
Will make us waking dreamers in the end.
What's false mistrust, suspicion, but a dream?
In every place he thinks himself surrounded
By enemies. No one perceives his talents
Who doesn't envy him, and, envying,   2920
Hates him and persecutes him cruelly.
How often he has vexed you with complaints:
All those forced locks and intercepted letters,
Poison and dagger! Phantoms that beset him!
You've had each case investigated, looked   2925
Into it yourself, and found—less than a glint.
No ruler's aegis makes him feel secure,
No friend's affection comforts or assures him.
Can you give peace or joy to such a man?
Can you expect that man to give *you* pleasure?   2930
ALFONSO. You would be right, Antonio, if I looked
To him for my immediate advantage;
Though you could call it my advantage that
I do not look for usefulness that's direct.
Not everything serves us in the selfsame fashion;   2935
If much you wish to use, then use each thing
In its own way; and you will be well served.
It was the Medicis who taught us that,
It was the Popes who proved it by their actions.
With what forbearance, with what princely patience   2940
And what long-suffering those men supported
Many great talents that seemed not to need
Their bountiful favours, but in truth did need them.
ANTONIO. Undoubtedly, my Prince. Life's drudgery
Alone makes us appreciate life's rewards.   2945
So young, too much already he's attained
To enjoy it modestly and frugally.
Oh, let him earn those honours and those boons
Now offered to him by wide-open hands:

Then like a man he would exert himself   2950
And step by step he would feel satisfied.
A gentleman who's poor fulfils his hopes,
His highest hopes, if an exalted prince
Elects him to companionship of his court
And so with merciful fingers pulls him out   2955
Of deprivation. If he grants him also
Favour and trust, and to his very side
Wishes to raise him above others, be it
In war, affairs of state or conversation,
Then, I should think, a man not arrogant   2960
In quiet gratitude will respect his luck.
And Tasso in addition to all this
Has the young man's best fortune: that already
His country recognizes, hopes for him.
Believe me, sir, his moody discontentment   2965
Rests on the wide, soft cushion of his luck.
He's coming. Give him leave, with grace, and time
In Rome or Naples, anywhere he likes,
To look for what he thinks he misses here
And only here can find, when he returns.   2970
ALFONSO. Does he intend to set out from Ferrara?
ANTONIO. His wish is to remain at Belriguardo.
    A friend is to send on the few things needed
    And indispensable to him abroad.
ALFONSO. Well, I give in. My sister and her friend,   2975
    Too, will be leaving, and on horseback I
    Shall be at home before those two arrive.
    You'll follow soon, when you have seen to him.
    Instruct the castellan accordingly,
    So that our friend can stay here at his leisure,   2980
    That is, until his friends have sent the luggage
    And we have sent the recommending letters
    For Rome that I'll provide. He comes. Farewell!

Scene II

TASSO (*with restraint*). The grace that you have shown me many times
    Today appears to me in its full light.   2985
    You have forgiven what in your own precincts
    Recklessly, reprehensibly I did,
    Have reconciled me with my adversary,

236

And now permit that for a time I take
My leave from you, while your good favour too   2990
Magnanimously you reserve for me.
Now with whole-hearted confidence I depart
And calmly hope that this brief interim
Will cure me of all present stress of mind.
My energies, I hope, will be renewed   2995
And on that course which, bold and cheerful, first
I took, encouraged by your kind attention,
Once more I shall prove worthy of your favour.
ALFONSO. I wish you all good fortune on your travels
And hope that happy, wholly cured, you will   3000
Return to us. In that way you'll make up
Twice over for each day and hour of which
Your absence has deprived us, being happy.
I'll give you letters to my people there,
My friends in Rome, and it's my urgent wish   3005
That trustfully you will approach them all,
Just as yourself, however distant from me,
I shall continue to regard as *mine*.
TASSO. With favours, Prince, you overwhelm a man
Who feels unworthy of them and, for the moment,   3010
Incapable even of returning thanks.
Instead of thanks I offer a request!
My poem is what's dearest to my heart.
There's much I've done, sparing no pain or labour,
But much, too much, remains to be improved.   3015
So in that place where still the spirit of
Great men is hovering, and effectually so,
I wish to go to school again: my song
Would more deserve your approbation then.
I beg of you, return those sheets to me   3020
Which, in your keeping, fill me now with shame.
ALFONSO. You will not take away from me today
What only hours ago, today, you gave me.
Between you and your poem let me step in
As mediator, plead with you: beware   3025
Of hurting with too strict an application
The lovely life of nature in your rhymes,
And do not heed the advice of all and sundry!
The thousandfold thoughts of many diverse persons
Whose ways of life and ways of thinking clash,   3030
The poet skilfully combines, not sharing

237

This one's displeasure, if the other's pleasure
Will be the greater for it. Yet I do not say
That here and there you should not file a little;
And at the same time promise: very soon   3035
You shall receive a copy of your poem.
In *your* hand in *my* hands it will remain,
So that together with my sisters I
May have its full enjoyment. If you then
Emended bring it back, we shall be glad   3040
Of a still heightened pleasure, and as friends
Alone shall cavil at this line or that.
TASSO. Ashamed, I can but beg you once again,
Return that copy, promptly! For my mind
Utterly now is fixed upon that work.   3045
It must become now what it can become.
ALFONSO. I do approve the impulse behind your plea.
Only, dear Tasso, if it could be done,
First, for a time, you should avail yourself
Of the world's freedom, should distract yourself,   3050
And in a cure improve your blood. For then
The harmony of faculties restored,
A new well-being, would accord you what
In turbulent effort now you vainly seek.
TASSO. So it may seem, Your Highness; but I'm well   3055
When all my energies converge in work,
And so it's work again that makes me well.
You've seen yourself that in luxurious leisure
I don't feel well, nor thrive. Of all things, rest
Makes me most restless. Nature has not lent me   3060
A temperament, I'm painfully aware,
That in the yielding element of days
Can blithely drift into time's wider sea.
ALFONSO. All that you do and plan for ever drives you
Deeply into yourself. We are surrounded   3065
By many a chasm dug for us by fate;
But here in our own hearts the deepest lies,
And it is sweet to plunge into that chasm.
Save yourself, *from* yourself, I beg of you!
All that the poet loses, the man will gain.   3070
TASSO. In vain I pit my will against the urge
That flows and ebbs in me, by day, by night.
If I am not to ponder and compose
I have no life to lead, my life's no life.
As soon forbid the silkworm its cocoon,   3075

Though closer to its death it spins itself:
Out of its inmost being it has drawn
That precious web, and never will desist
Till it has locked itself inside its coffin.
Oh, may a kindly god allot us too   3080
That enviable worm's good fate, one day
Swiftly and joyfully to spread its wings
In a new sun-warmed valley!

ALFONSO.   Listen to me!
You give redoubled joy of life to many,
So many; learn, I earnestly beseech you,   3085
To value life, that life which still is yours,
And ten times over richly. Now, goodbye!
The sooner you return to us from Rome,
The more you will be welcome here again.

Scene III

TASSO (*alone*). Stay on this course, my heart, it was the right one!   3090
You found it hard, for never yet you had
The wish or power so to disguise yourself.
You clearly heard: he did not speak *his* mind,
Nor in *his* words. It seemed to me that only
Antonio's voice resounded from *his* lips.   3095
Yes, take good care! You'll hear that voice henceforth
From every side. So you stand fast, stand fast!
Only one moment more is needed now.
A man who learns dissembling late in life
Profits by that because he seems sincere.   3100
It will work out, just let them teach you how!

After a pause.

But you exult too soon, when, there *she* comes!
The dearly loved Princess. Most cruel test!
She's coming closer; bitterness, mistrust
Fade as she nears, dissolving into pain.   3105

Scene IV

Enter Princess.

PRINCESS. You plan to leave us, or rather you intend

To stay in Belriguardo for a while
And then remove yourself from us, dear Tasso?
Not for protracted absence, though, I hope.
It's Rome you're going to?

TASSO.   Yes, that will be   3110
My first objective, and if my friends in Rome,
As I have grounds to hope, receive me kindly,
With care and patience there perhaps I'll give
My poem the last touches it still needs.
There I shall find a number of good men   3115
With claim to mastery of every kind.
And in that foremost city of the world
Does not each square, each building speak to us?
How many thousands of mute teachers beckon
Affably to us in grave majesty!   3120
If there I cannot finish my long poem,
I never shall or can; yet feel already
That no endeavour that is mine will thrive!
Change it I shall—finish, perfect it, never.
I feel, I feel it clearly, that great art   3125
Which nourishes all, which strengthens and refreshes
The healthy mind, to me brings my undoing,
Will drive me into exile. I must be off!
Soon I go on to Naples.

PRINCESS.   Should you risk it?
Still that strict prohibition is in force   3130
Placed upon you together with your father.

TASSO. Your warning's apt, I have considered that.
Disguised I'll travel there, in the poor tunic
Of pilgrim or of shepherd, pauper's garb.
So I shall creep through streets in which the bustle   3135
Of thousands easily conceals the one.
I'll hurry to the shore, where soon I'll find
A boat, and folk both honest and obliging,
Peasants returning from the city market,
Bound for their homes now, people of Sorrento: 3140
For I must hurry over to Sorrento.
There lives my sister, who with me once shared
My parents' painful joy, solicitous love.
On board I shall be silent, and in silence
Shall disembark, and stealthily make my way   3145
Up the familiar path, to ask at a door:
Where does Cornelia live? Direct me there.

Cornelia Sersale? A spinner amiably
Points to the street, describes the house for me.
So I climb on, up through the terraced alleys.   3150
The children run beside me, staring at
My windblown hair, the dark, uncanny stranger.
So at the threshold I arrive. The door
Is open, so I walk straight in, I go . . .
PRINCESS. Tasso, look up, if you can raise your eyes,   3155
And recognize the danger you are in!
I'm sparing you, for else I should be saying:
Is it not base to speak as you have done?
To give no thought to anyone but oneself,
As though by that you did not hurt your friends?   3160
Are you not conscious of my brother's care?
Of the esteem both sisters have for you?
Have you not felt and recognized those feelings?
Has everything been changed so much within
A mere few moments? Tasso, if you must   3165
Go from us, do not leave us anxious, grieved.

Tasso turns away from her.

PRINCESS. How comforting it is to give a friend
Who is about to take a little journey
Some little present, though it be no more
Than a new cloak or weapon on his way.   3170
Now I can give you nothing more, when gruffly
You throw away whatever you possess.
You choose the pilgrim's shell and the black kirtle,
The long, thick staff, and then you wander off
In poverty self-assumed, and so deprive us   3175
Of what with us alone you could enjoy.
TASSO. It's not your wish, then, quite to banish me?
Sweet utterance, a dear and lovely comfort!
Oh, take my part! And give me your protection!—
Let me stay here, at Belriguardo, move me   3180
On to Consandoli, no matter where!
The Prince has many splendid palaces,
And many gardens that the whole year round
Are tended, though you scarcely enter them
Once every year, or spend one hour in them.   3185
Choose the most distant, if you like, and one
You do not visit in the course of years,
One that perhaps lies waste now, not looked after:

Send me to that place! There let me be yours!
How I will tend your trees! In autumn cover   3190
The lemon trees with boards and brick them in,
With canes and rushes keep them safe from harm!
Beautiful plants in flowerbeds shall put down
Their struggling roots; and every avenue,
Each plot, each bower be charming and well trimmed.   3195
And leave to me the palace's maintenance too!
At the right time I'll have the windows open.
So that no dampness shall impair the paintings;
With a plume duster I shall brush the walls
And the fine ornament of stucco friezes,   3200
The plastered floor shall gleam with cleanliness,
No stone, no tile shall shift from its right place,
No blade or tuft of grass sprout from one crack!
PRINCESS. In my own heart I see no help, no hope.
No consolation for yourself—or us.   3205
My vision casts about for some kind god
To succour us, I search for some good potion
Or rare remedial herb that to your senses
Might give some peace and rest, and so to us.
The truest word that human lips can speak,   3210
The best of medicines is powerless now.
I have to let you be, though never my heart
Can leave you.
TASSO.   By the deities, she it is
Who speaks with you, takes pity on you here!
And you could wrong that noble heart of hers?   3215
In her own presence could mean pettiness
Take hold of you and utterly possess you?
No, no, it's you, and now I am myself.
Continue, then, speak on, and from your mouth
Let me receive all comfort! Don't withhold   3220
Advice from me! Tell me, what can I do
To win forgiveness from the Duke, your brother,
To win your own forgiveness, gladly granted,
So that with pleasure once again you may
Count me as one of you, as yours indeed?   3225
PRINCESS. What we demand of you is very little:
And yet it seems too much for you to give.
You're to entrust yourself to us, in friendship.
No thing that you are not we ask of you,
If only you will be yourself, and like it.   3230

You give us pleasure when you yourself are pleased,
Distress us only by your flight from pleasure.
And though you drive us to the end of patience,
It's only that we dearly wish to help you
And, to our sorrow, see there is no help   3235
As long as you refuse the helping hand
Your friend extends with urgency, in vain.
TASSO. It's you entirely, as you were when first,
A holy angel, you appeared to me!
Excuse a mortal's dim and murky vision   3240
If for mere moments he misprized your kind.
He knows you now, again! And his whole soul
Opens to worship only you for ever.
Wholly his heart is filled with tenderness—
It's she, she stands before me. What a feeling!   3245
Is it confusion that attracts me to you?
Is it a madness? Is it that heightened sense
Which grasps the highest and the purest truth?
Yes, it's that feeling which alone can make me
Supremely happy on this earth of ours,   3250
And which alone could leave me so downcast
When I resisted it and strove to drive it
Out of my heart. For to subdue that passion
I did my utmost, fought and fought against
My deepest being, shamelessly destroyed   3255
My own true self, to which so wholly you—
PRINCESS. Tasso, if I'm to listen to you further,
Dampen this ardour, for it frightens me.
TASSO. Does the cup's rim set limits to a wine
That bubbling, rises, foaming, overflows?   3260
Each word you utter adds to my great joy,
With every word your eyes more brightly shine.
I feel transformed, down to the depth of me,
Feel freed of all constriction, every stress,
Free as a god, and it is all your doing!   3265
Ineffable power that rules and masters me
Flows from your lips most truly, now you make
Me yours, yours only. Nothing of my own self
From now on can belong to me alone.
Excess of bliss and light half-blind my eyes,   3270
My senses reel. My feet refuse their stance.
You draw me to you irresistibly,
My heart will brook no barrier, no delay.

For ever you have made me wholly yours.
So take it, too, the gift of all I am!   3275

He falls into her arms and clasps her to him.

PRINCESS (*pushing him away and rushing out*). Away!
LEONORA (*who has been visible for a while in the background, hurrying forward*).
    What's happened here? Oh Tasso, Tasso!

She follows the Princess.

TASSO (*about to follow them*). Oh, God!
ALFONSO.

    (*who has been approaching for some time together with Antonio*).

He's out of his mind. Hold on to him!

Exit.

Scene V

Tasso. Antonio.

ANTONIO. If now, just as you always think yourself
    Surrounded everywhere with enemies,
    An enemy stood by you, how he'd triumph!   3280
    Unhappy man, I scarcely yet can speak.
    When something quite unheard-of has occurred,
    When our own eyes have glimpsed a monstrous act,
    Then for a while our very minds are halted:
    All measure fails then, all comparison.   3285
TASSO (*after a long pause*).
    Oh, yes, fulfil your office—I see it's you!
    Yes, you deserve the princely confidence;
    Go on, fulfil your office, torture me,
    Since now I am condemned, by little stages
    To death! Yes, go on tugging at the arrow   3290
    So that I feel the cruel barb in it
    That rips my flesh!
    You are a precious tool of tyranny;
    You be my warder, you my torturer.
    How well, how perfectly those functions fit you!   3295

With his back to the audience:

    Yes, tyrant, do your work. You could not keep
    Dissembling to the last, so now exult!

244

You've truly chained the slave, have saved him well
For torments most ingeniously devised:
Go on, I loathe you, feel without reserve   3300
The detestation due to every power
That lawlessly, unjustly punishes.

After a pause:

So in the end I am an outlaw here,
A beggar, wholly banished and cast out.
For that, they garlanded me, a votive beast   3305
That must not reach the altar unadorned!
For that, on the last day they lured from me
My one possession, the completed poem,
With their smooth talk, and held it in their keeping.
So now you have it, my sole wealth and asset   3310
That would have been my passport anywhere,
That would have saved me from starvation later.
Now I can see the ceremony's purpose.
It is conspiracy, and you're its head.
So that my song should never be perfected,   3315
So that my fame should never spread from here,
So that my enviers should find it blemished,
So that at last I might be quite forgotten,
For that I was to relish idleness,
For that to spare myself, relax my mind.   3320
Most precious friendship, dear solicitude!
Vile I had thought the plotting, the intrigue
Spun round me ceaselessly, invisibly,
But it has grown more vile than I could think it.

And you, my Siren, who so tenderly,   3325
Celestially enticed me, all at once
I see you as you are. But, oh, too late!

But to deceive ourselves is our delight,
To honour those, the base, who honour us.
We human beings do not know each other;   3330
Galley slaves only know their fellow slaves,
Because they moan in concert, chained together;
Where none has anything to ask, and none
Has anything to lose, they know each other.
Where every manjack claims to be a rogue   3335
And takes his fellow slave to be another.
We only courteously misjudge the others
So that in turn they will misjudge us too.

How long your holy image hid from me
The mere seductress at her little games.   3340
The mask has dropped: I see Armida now
Stripped of all charms—yes, that is who you are.
Prophetically my poem sang of you!

Oh, and that cunning little go-between!
How she's debased now in my clearer sight!   3345
Now I can hear the stealthy footsteps rustle,
I know the circle that her creeping traced.
I know you all now. And let that suffice me.
And if my wretchedness has left me nothing,
Still I can praise it—it has taught me truth.   3350
ANTONIO. I listen to you, Tasso, with amazement,
Well as I know how easily your mind
Leaps from the one extreme to its opposite!
Come to your senses! And control your rage!
Slanderous, blasphemous, you're letting loose   3355
Word after word your anguish may excuse
But never you'll forgive yourself for speaking.
TASSO. Oh, don't reproach me now with gentle lips,
Let me hear apt, sagacious words from you!
Leave me my last dank joy, or first I shall   3360
Come to my senses, then be out of them.
Down to my bones, my bowels, I feel shattered,
And only am alive now to feel that.
Despair with all its fury clutches me
And in the hellish torment that destroys me   3365
Cursing's no more than the least gasp of pain.
I want to go! And if you're honest with me,
Show me the way and let me leave at once!
ANTONIO. In such extremity I will not leave you;
And if you're wholly lacking in composure,   3370
You may be sure, my patience will not fail.
TASSO. So as your prisoner I must submit?
I do so now, and there's an end to it;
I don't resist, and that is best for me—
And then most painfully let me repeat   3375
What bliss it was that my own doing lost me.
They're leaving now—O God, already there
I see the dust that's rising from their coach—
Horsemen precede them. There they make their way,
That place they make for! Didn't I come from there?   3380

They've gone from here, and I've provoked their anger.
O if but *once* more I could kiss his hand!
O if I could but take my leave of them!
Once only say again to them: Forgive me!
Only to hear: Be off, then. You're forgiven.   3385
I do not hear it, though, nor shall again—
I want to go! But let me take my leave,
Just take my leave! O for a moment only
Give me, O give me back the presence lost.
Perhaps I shall recover. No, I am   3390
Outlawed and banished, have outlawed myself,
Never again to hear it, that sweet voice,
Never again to meet it, that sweet gaze,
Never again . . .
ANTONIO. Let a man's voice recall you, Tasso—one   3395
Who stands beside you not without emotion!
You're not as miserable as you think.
Come! Be a man! For once, exert your will!
TASSO. And am I, then, as wretched as I seem?
As feeble as I show myself to you?   3400
Is everything lost? And has my agony,
As though the ground were quaking, quite reduced
The building to a gruesome heap of rubble?
Have I no talent left, a thousandfold
To entertain, distract, sustain my mind?   3405
Has all that energy failed which in my heart
At one time stirred? Have I annulled myself,
A nothing now, mere nothing?
No, all is there, and only I am nothing;
To myself I am lost, and she to me!   3410
ANTONIO. But if you seem to lose yourself entirely,
Compare yourself! Remember who you are!
TASSO. Yes, at the right time you remind me of it!—
Does history now provide not one example?
Does not one excellent man occur to me   3415
Who suffered more than ever I have suffered—
So that from likeness I could wrest composure?
No, it's all gone!—One thing alone remains:
Nature endowed us with the gift of tears,
The agonized outcry when at last a man   3420
Can bear no more—and me above all others—
In pain she left me euphony and speech
To voice the deepest amplitude of my grief:

When in their anguish other men fall silent
A god gave me the power to tell my pain.   3425

Antonio goes up to him and takes him by the hand.

TASSO. You noble man. You can stand firm and still,
 While I seem a mere billow, tempest-lashed.
 But think again and do not overreach
 Your faculties! Nature, more mighty yet,
 That founded that same rock, gave to the wave   3430
 Its proper virtue, too, mobility.
 She sends her gale, the billow rushes on,
 And swells and wavers and then, foaming, breaks.
 In that same wave so splendidly the sun
 Mirrored himself, and all the planets rested   3435
 Upon that bosom, in its tender motion.
 That radiance has gone out, all rest is ended.—
 Such is my peril, I have lost my way
 And lost the shame that keeps the admission mute.
 The rudder's broken, and the vessel cracks   3440
 On every side. The boards beneath me split
 Wide open, leave me with no foothold, none,
 With both my arms I clutch at you, Antonio.
 So in the end will a poor boatman cling
 To the same rock on which he was to founder.   3445

Faust. A Tragedy

Translated by John R. Williams

DEDICATION

Once more I sense uncertain shapes appearing,
Dimly perceived in days of youth long past.
Now in my heart I feel the moment nearing
When I can hold those phantom figures fast.
The haze and mist that swallowed them is clearing,   5
They gather round me, bodied forth at last.
Within me now a youthful passion surges
As from a magic spell their throng emerges.

They bring back scenes of youthful jubilation,
And with them many well-loved shades appear;   10
A half-forgotten distant intimation
Of those in early times I held so dear.
The grief returns, once more the lamentation
Of life's obscure and wayward course I hear
For those capricious fortune cruelly treated,   15
Who all too soon of joy and life were cheated.

They cannot hear the songs within these pages,
Those souls to whom I sang; I sing alone.
That friendly throng was scattered to the ages,
And those first echoes on the wind were blown.   20
My sorrow now the stranger's mind engages,
Whose praise I cannot in my heart condone;
And some by whose applause my gifts were flattered,
If they still live, to the world's ends are scattered.

And now I feel a long-forgotten yearning;   25
That solemn, quiet world calls me once more,
Its spirit music to my lips returning

Like the Aeolian harp's uncertain chord.
I tremble, and my cheeks with tears are burning,
The stern heart softens, melted to its core. 30
What I possess now vanishes before me,
And what was lost alone has substance for me.

PRELUDE ON THE STAGE

DIRECTOR, POET, CLOWN

DIRECTOR. You two have stood beside me now
  For years and shared my troubles all the way.
  I'd like to have your views on how 35
  To make our mark in Germany today.
  I want to entertain the crowd out there—
  They put up with an awful lot, you know.
  The posts and boards are up, so let's prepare
  To give the audience a proper show. 40
  They're all agog and sitting patiently,
  Something spectacular is what they want to see.
  How to please the public— that's the test,
  But nowadays I find I'm in a fix;
  I know they're not accustomed to the best, 45
  But they've all read so much they know the tricks.
  How can we give them something fresh and new
  That's serious, but entertaining too?
  I love to see a crowd of people pour
  Into the theatre like rolling waves, 50
  And painfully like new-born babes
  Squeeze themselves through that narrow door;
  At four o'clock, in broad daylight,
  Breaking their necks to get a seat,
  Pushing and shoving as they fight 55
  Like starving beggars for a piece of meat.
  And who can work this miracle? I say
  The poet can: my friend, do it today!
POET. Don't talk to me about the many-headed,
  My spirit fails me at the very sight. 60
  Preserve me from that motley mob, the dreaded
  Rabble that puts poetry to flight.
  The poet to the silent Muse is wedded,
  In heavenly peace he finds his true delight,

Where love and friendship godlike forge and cherish   65
The blessings of the heart that never perish.

And what our hearts from deep within created
Or what our timid lips had sought to say,
No matter if it's good or bad, is fated
To be forgotten in the present fray,   70
And only when the tide of time's abated
Appears in its true form another day.
What glitters for the moment is but passing;
Posterity will value what is lasting.

CLOWN. I don't want to hear about posterity!   75
And even if I did, what's it to me?
It's here and now they want to have some fun,
That's what they like, what they're entitled to.
That's just the sort of thing a lad like me can do—
It's what I'm best at, when all's said and done.   80
If you can get across to them, then you can cope
With anything the audience throws at you,
And a full house will give you much more scope
To entertain them—and to move them, too.
So don't be shy and write a proper play.   85
Let your imagination weave its magic spell,
Let sense and reason, love and passion have their say—
But let us have a bit of fun as well.

DIRECTOR. But most of all, put in a lot of action!
That's how to get your audience satisfaction—   90
Don't give them an excuse for getting bored.
They like to see things happen on the stage;
Just keep them happy, you'll get your reward—
They'll love you, you'll be all the rage.
A lot of people like a lot of stuff   95
To choose from, and they have to be presented
With a spectacle that has enough
For everyone—then they'll go home contented.
Let's have a play that plays to every taste!
It's easy to concoct a tasty stew.   100
Get busy with your scissors and your paste;
Don't try to get it perfect—if you do,
The public will demolish it for you.

POET. You've no idea what it does to me
To prostitute my talents in this way;   105
You want the sort of rubbish you can see
In any West-End theatre every day.

DIRECTOR. I'm not offended by such taunts as these;
    I want to put a show on that will run,
    And I don't really care much how it's done.   110
    The public isn't difficult to please;
    Just try to keep your audience in mind.
    Some of them come here simply to unwind,
    Some have just stuffed themselves with food;
    And if they've read the papers, then you'll find   115
    They can be in a very nasty mood.
    These people don't want anything too arty,
    They come because they're curious to know
    What's on; the women think they're at a party,
    Parading around—it's all part of the show.   120
    Why are you poets all such dreamers, though?
    Doesn't a full house give you a big thrill?
    Just take a close look at our patrons, and you'll know
    Some don't appreciate us, others never will.
    After the play they'll trot off to some gambling den,   125
    Look forward to a wild night with their floozies.
    You needn't look too far for inspiration, then—
    I don't know why you bother the poor Muses.
    I tell you, give them lots and lots of action
    And rivet their attention, that's the way.   130
    They only want a few hours of distraction—
    You'll never satisfy them anyway.
    Now what's the matter? Are we having a contraction?
POET. Oh, go and find yourself another slave!
    You want the poet to betray his Muse?   135
    The highest birthright nature ever gave
    You'd have him wantonly abuse?
    How does the poet move all people's hearts?
    Command the elements with all his arts?
    It is the harmony that dwells within us   140
    So that the whole world is reflected in us.
    When nature's spindle twists the thread of ages,
    Indifferently she spins the endless strand,
    And when the world's discordant clamour rages
    In dire confusion none can understand—   145
    Who then enlivens that monotony
    And makes it pulse with rhythmic motion?
    Who summons every voice, united in devotion,
    And blends them into glorious harmony?
    Who makes the furious tempest rage and sing,   150

Gives solemn meaning to the sunset glow?
Who scatters all the lovely flowers of spring
At the beloved's feet wherever she may go?
Who weaves the modest laurel leaves that crown
The heads of those whose deeds set them apart? 155
Preserves Olympus and the gods' renown?
Man's power, embodied in the poet's art!
CLOWN. Why don't you use them then, these splendid powers?
Let's see them in this theatre of ours!
Approach your story like a love-affair; 160
You meet, you feel attracted, so you hang around,
And gradually you find you really care.
Of course, you'll find it has its ups and downs;
There's pain and pleasure, if you're truly smitten—
Before you can turn round, you'll have a novel written. 165
That's the kind of play we ought to give—
The whole parade of life that people live!
Plunge in and take it as it is, and you
Can offer something interesting and new.
Some vivid scenes, a measure of illusion, 170
A grain of truth and plenty of confusion,
That's the surest way to mix a brew
To please them all—and teach them something, too.
Our finest youth will flock to see your play,
Expecting some momentous revelation; 175
Their melancholy minds will soak up what you say
And in your words they'll find sweet consolation.
Arouse their feelings for them, and reveal
Their own emotions—that's what will appeal.
They're young enough to move to tears or laughter, 180
Excitement and illusion's what they're after.
You'll never please the older ones, I know—
Impressionable minds will love it, though.
POET. Then give me back the time when I was young,
When all my life before me lay, 185
A constant stream of words and song
Burst from my lips with every passing day,
When clouds of glory hid the world from view,
And budding youth still found it all so new;
When flowers in thousands seemed to fill 190
The fields for me to gather them at will.
Though I had nothing, what I had was this:
The urge for truth, delight in make-believe.

Give me those passions back, let me retrieve
The keenest pangs of adolescent bliss,   195
Extremes of love and hate, of joy and pain—
Give me back my youth again!
CLOWN. Such youthful energy, my friend, you'll find
      Is needed in the frantic heat of war,
      Or when some pretty girl might feel inclined   200
      To take you in her arms and ask for more;
      Or in the race before your weary eyes
      You see the finish and the winner's prize,
      Or when the whirling dance is at an end
      You spend the night carousing with a friend.   205
      But if you've confidence enough to play
      A graceful tune and let us hear your voice,
      Or let your pleasant fancy stray
      Towards a destination of your choice—
      That is a task for the maturer man,   210
      And we respect you for it all the more.
      They say age makes us childish—but it can
      Make truer children of us than before.
DIRECTOR. You've bandied words enough, now let me see
      Some action from you both for once.   215
      We could have spent the time more usefully
      While you two were exchanging compliments.
      What's all this talk of inspiration in the end?
      You can't just sit and hope it might descend.
      If you're a poet, as you claim to be,   220
      Get on with it and write some poetry.
      You know exactly what we have to do—
      To give them something with a kick in it,
      So hurry up and make a decent brew.
      Don't leave it till tomorrow, stick at it—   225
      Today will pass you by before you know.
      You've got to grab your chance, or else it's gone,
      It doesn't come round twice, so don't be slow,
      And once you've taken it, don't let it go;
      That's the only way to get things done.   230

      On German stages, everybody knows,
      They like to try out anything that goes;
      And so today let's have some splendid scenery
      And plenty of spectacular machinery.
      We'll have the sun and moon—use all the lights—   235

And lots of stars, as many as you want,
Fire, water, rocky mountain heights,
And birds and animals—just be extravagant.
This narrow stage is wide enough to gird about
The whole of God's creation. Very well: 240
Go carefully but quickly—measure out
The way from heaven through the world to hell.

PROLOGUE IN HEAVEN

The LORD, *the Heavenly Host, then* MEPHISTOPHELES.
The three Archangels step forward.

RAPHAEL. With choirs of kindred spheres competing,
    The sun intones its ancient sound,
    And runs its thunderous course, completing   245
    Its preordained diurnal round.
    This vision none has comprehended,
    Though angels quicken at the sight;
    These high and wondrous works are splendid
    As when the world first shone with light.   250
GABRIEL. The earth in majesty rotating
    Spins on itself as swift as light,
    Celestial radiance alternating
    With dread impenetrable night.
    In rocky depths the foaming ocean   255
    Surges with elemental force,
    Swept on by the eternal motion
    That speeds the worlds upon their course.
MICHAEL. And mighty tempests rage unceasing
    From sea to land, from land to sea,   260
    A furious clash of power, releasing
    A chain of vast causality.
    Before the crash of rolling thunder
    The flashing bolts blaze out the way;
    But we, thy angels, watch with wonder   265
    The peaceful progress of thy day.
ALL THREE. Thy vision none has comprehended,
    Though angels quicken at the sight;
    Thy mighty works, O Lord, are splendid
    As when the world first shone with light.   270
MEPHISTO. Since, Lord, you deign to visit us once more

To find out how we manage our affairs,
And since you've often welcomed me before,
I've come to join your household staff upstairs.
I'm not much good at lofty words, I fear,   275
It doesn't worry me if they all sneer.
Pathos from me would make you laugh—although
I know you gave up laughing long ago.
I can't sing hymns about the universe,
I only see how people go from bad to worse.   280
He hasn't changed, your little god on earth—
He's still peculiar as the day you gave him birth.
He'd live a better life, at least,
If you'd not given him a glimpse of heaven's light.
He calls it reason—which gives him the right   285
To be more bestial than any beast.
Saving your gracious presence, Sire, I'd say
He's like a silly grasshopper in the hay.
He chirps and sings and flitters to and fro,
And chirps the same old song and jumps about;   290
If only he were satisfied with that—but no,
In every pile of filth he dips his snout.
THE LORD. Why are you telling me all this again?
    Do you always come here to complain?
    Could there be something good on earth that you've forgotten? 295
MEPHISTO. No, Lord! I'm pleased to say it's still completely rotten.
    I feel quite sorry for their miserable plight;
    When it's as bad as that, tormenting them's not right.
THE LORD. Do you know Faust?
MEPHISTO.   The Doctor?
THE LORD.   Yes—my servant.
MEPHISTO. He serves you in a very curious way indeed.   300
    It isn't earthly nourishment he seems to need;
    His fevered mind is in a constant ferment.
    Half-conscious of his folly, in his pride
    On all the joys of earth he wants to feed,
    And pluck from heaven the very brightest star.   305
    He searches high and low, and yet however far
    He roams, his restless heart returns dissatisfied.
THE LORD. Though in confusion still he seeks his way,
    Yet I will lead him to the light one day.
    For in the budding sapling the gardener can see   310
    The promise of the fruit upon the full-grown tree.
MEPHISTO. What would you wager? Will you challenge me

To win him from you? Give me your permission
To lead him down my path to his perdition?
THE LORD. While he's on earth, while he is still alive,   315
   Then you may tempt him—that is my condition.
   For man will err as long as he can strive.
MEPHISTO. I take up your kind offer, Sire, most gratefully;
   The dead are of no interest to me.
   I like them fresh and full of life, well fed.   320
   A corpse is very boring; I'm like a cat, you see—
   It's no fun once the mouse is dead.
THE LORD. Well then, it shall be left to you.
   Entice this spirit from its primal source,
   And drag him down, if you are able to,   325
   Upon your own infernal course;
   With shame you will confess to me one day,
   A good man, though his instincts be obscure,
   Is still quite conscious of the proper way.
MEPHISTO. So be it! And it won't take long, I'm sure.   330
   I have no doubts about my wager, none—
   And I will come before you when it's done,
   Triumphant with the glory that I've won.
   He shall eat dust, and on his belly I will make
   Him go, like my old aunt, the celebrated snake.   335
THE LORD. I give you freedom to appear at will;
   For you and for your kind I feel no hate.
   Of all the spirits of denial and of ill,
   Such rogues as you I can well tolerate.
   For man's activity can slacken all too fast,   340
   He falls too soon into a slothful ease;
   The Devil's a companion who will tease
   And spur him on, and work creatively at last.
   But you, true sons of God, attend your duty:
   Rejoice in rich creation's living beauty!   345
   The vital process that eternally informs
   All things, embrace you with the bonds that love has wrought;
   To what appears in evanescent forms
   Give substance with the lasting power of thought.

Heaven closes, the Archangels disperse

MEPHISTO. I like to drop in on him if I can,   350
   Just to keep things between us on the level.
   It's really decent of the Grand Old Man
   To be so civil to the very Devil.

THE FIRST PART OF THE TRAGEDY

Night. In a high-vaulted narrow Gothic room
FAUST *sits restlessly at his desk.*

FAUST. Medicine, and Law, and Philosophy—
   You've worked your way through every school,   355
   Even, God help you, Theology,
   And sweated at it like a fool.
   Why labour at it any more?
   You're no wiser now than you were before.
   You're Master of Arts, and Doctor too,   360
   And for ten years all you've been able to do
   Is lead your students a fearful dance
   Through a maze of error and ignorance.
   And all this misery goes to show
   There's nothing we can ever know.   365
   Oh yes, you're brighter than all those relics,
   Professors and Doctors, scribblers and clerics;
   No doubts or scruples to trouble you,
   Defying hell, and the Devil too.
   But there's no joy in self-delusion;   370
   Your search for truth ends in confusion.
   Don't imagine your teaching will ever raise
   The minds of men or change their ways.
   And as for worldly wealth, you've none—
   What honour or glory have you won?   375
   A dog could stand this life no more.
   And so I've turned to magic lore;
   The spirit message of this art
   Some secret knowledge might impart.
   No longer shall I sweat to teach   380
   What always lay beyond my reach;
   I'll know what makes the world revolve,
   Its inner mysteries resolve,
   No more in empty words I'll deal—
   Creation's wellsprings I'll reveal!   385

   Sweet moonlight, shining full and clear
   Why do you light my torture here?
   How often have you seen me toil,
   Burning last drops of midnight oil.
   On books and papers as I read,   390
   My friend, your mournful light you shed.

If only I could flee this den
And walk the mountain-tops again,
Through moonlit meadows make my way,
In mountain caves with spirits play—   395
Released from learning's musty cell,
Your healing dew would make me well!

But no, you're stuck inside this lair,
In this accursed dungeon, where
The very light of heaven can pass   400
But dimly through the painted glass.
Immured behind a pile of books,
Motheaten, dusty, in the reek
Of papers stuffed in all these nooks—
This is the wisdom that you seek.   405
These jars and cases row on row,
Retorts and tubes and taps and gauges,
The useless junk of bygone ages—
This is the only world you know!

And still you wonder why this pain   410
Constricts your heart and hems it in,
Why agonies you can't explain
Sap all life's energies within?
When God created us, he founded
His living nature for our home;   415
But you sit in this gloom, surrounded
By mildewed skull and arid bone.

Escape into a wider sphere!
This book of secrets will provide
The magic writings of the Seer;   420
Let Nostradamus be your guide.
If nature helps us, we can seek
The paths the stars in heaven go;
Through her we have the power to know
How spirits unto spirits speak.   425
Your dusty learning can't expound
The magic symbols written here.
The spirits hover close around:
Now answer me, if you can hear!

He opens the book and sees the Sign of the Macrocosm

Ah, what ecstatic joy at this great sight   430
I feel at once through all my senses flowing!

259

What vital happiness, what sheer delight
Through veins and nerves with youthful passion glowing.
Was it a god that wrote these signs for me?
The raging in my soul is stilled,   435
My empty heart with joy is filled,
And through some urgent mystery
All nature's forces are revealed.
Am I a god? My mind's so clear!
With mystic vision now I see concealed   440
In these pure symbols nature's rich activity.
At last I grasp the wisdom of the Seer:
'The spirit world is with us still,
Your mind is closed, your heart is dead.
Up, worldly scholar, drink your fill—   445
At heaven's gate the dawn is red!'

He studies the Sign

How all into a wholeness weaves,
Each in the other moves and lives!
The powers of heaven ascending and descending,
And to each other golden vessels sending,   450
With fragrant blessings winging,
From heaven to earth their bounty bringing—
In harmony the universe is ringing!
Ah, what a vision! But a vision, and no more.
I do not feel the pulse of nature, nor   455
Feed at her breasts. The springs of life that nursed
All things, for which creation yearns,
To which the flagging spirit turns,
They flow, they suckle still, but I must thirst!

Disconsolately he turns the pages and sees the Sign of the Earth Spirit

I see more inspiration in this sign!   460
Earth Spirit, we are of a kind.
I feel new energies, my mind
Now glows as if from new-fermented wine.
Now I can dare to face the world again,
To share in all its joy and all its pain.   465
Into the eye of storms I'll set my sail,
And in the grinding shipwreck I'll not quail.
Clouds gather overhead,
The moon conceals its light!
The lamp burns low!   470

Mist swirls around! Red flashes flicker
About my head. A chill shiver
Blows down from the vault above
And grips me!
I feel your presence round me,   475
Great Spirit, you have found me—
Reveal yourself!
It tears my heart, my senses reel
And burn with passions new. I feel
My heart goes out to you, I have no fear;   480
If it should cost my life, you must appear!

He seizes the book and with mysterious words invokes the Sign of the Earth Spirit.
A red flame flickers, the Spirit appears in the flame.

SPIRIT. Who calls me?
FFAUST. [*turning away*] A dreadful shape I see!
SPIRIT. Your potent spells have brought me here;
    You sought to draw me from my sphere,
    And now—
FAUST.   You are too terrible for me!   485
SPIRIT. With sighs you begged me to appear,
    My voice you would hear and my face you would see;
    Your mighty pleas have summoned me.
    I'm here! But now—what piteous fear
    Has seized you, superman? The soul that cried for me, where   490
    Is it now? The heart that in itself could bear
    A whole created world, and in its swollen pride
    Puffed up, with us, the spirits, would have vied?
    Where are you, Faust, whose voice reached to my sphere,
    Who summoned all your powers to draw me here?   495
    This is you? who scarcely felt my breath,
    And quake as if you go to meet your death,
    A frightened worm that twists and writhes!
FAUST. Creature of flame, to you I'll not give in;
    I, Faust, I am your equal, am your kin!   500
SPIRIT. In all life's storms and surging tides
    I ebb and flow
    From birth to grave,
    Weave to and fro,
    An endless wave   505
    Through all life's glowing
    Fabric flowing.
    On time's humming loom, as I toil at the treads,

For God's living garment I fashion the threads.
FAUST. Industrious spirit, to the world's furthest end   510
    You rove; how close you seem to me!
SPIRIT. You match the spirit that you comprehend,
    Not me!   [*vanishes*
FAUST. [*shattered*] Not you?
    Who then?   515
    I, made in God's image,
    No match for you?

A knock at the door

Oh death! It's my assistant at the door.
To turn my highest bliss into despair,
Dissolve these teeming visions into air,   520
It only needs that plodding bore.

WAGNER *in nightgown and nightcap, holding a lamp.*
FAUST *reluctantly turns to him.*

WAGNER. Forgive me, but I heard your voice—
    It sounded like a tragedy in Greek.
    That is an art that I would learn by choice.
    These days one has to know just how to speak   525
    One's lines; an actor, people often say, could teach
    A parson in the art of how to preach.
FAUST. Why, surely—if the parson's only acting,
    And many times I daresay that's the case.
WAGNER. But all this study I find so distracting;   530
    One scarcely sees the world beyond this place,
    And only from afar—so how can all our arts
    Of eloquent persuasion guide men's hearts?
FAUST. If you don't feel, your words will not inspire;
    Unless from deep within you speak sincere,   535
    And with a charismatic fire
    Compel the hearts of all who hear.
    Oh, you can sit there glueing bits together
    Or mixing cold leftovers in a stew,
    Blowing at the ashes, wondering whether   540
    There's any fire left to warm your brew.
    Yes—fools and children you'll impress—
    If that is really what you want to do;
    But you will never know another's heart, unless
    You are prepared to give yours too.   545
WAGNER. A good delivery can help the speaker, though;
    I feel there's still so much I ought to know.

262

FAUST. Speak honestly, speak from the heart!
 Your foolish tricks are all in vain!
 Good sense and reason—they don't need the art   550
 Of eloquence to make their meaning plain.
 If with sincerity you speak,
 Why, then for words you need not seek.
 The dazzling rhetoric a speaker spins,
 The frills and flourishes with which he weaves   555
 His spell, are all as barren as the frosty winds
 That play among the arid autumn leaves.
WAGNER. Ah God, but art is long,
 And short our life's duration!
 In all my critical deliberation   560
 I often fear the way I chose was wrong.
 How hard it is to get the method right
 To follow learning to its very source;
 Before we're half-way through our course
 We'll surely die and never reach the light.   565
FAUST. The manuscripts, are they the sacred springs
 From which one drink will slake your thirst for ever?
 You'll find no profit in these things
 Unless your own heart flows with fresh endeavour.
WAGNER. Forgive me, but it's such delight   570
 To bring the spirit of the past to light,
 To study all the thoughts of history's wisest men—
 And marvel at the progress we have made since then.
FAUST. Oh yes, we've reached the stars! And yet
 The past, my friend, by which you set   575
 Such store, is a book with seven seals to us.
 It is a mirror that reveals to us
 Only the minds of those who seek
 This spirit of the past of which you speak.
 Believe me, all you'll find is bunk,   580
 A lumber-room stuffed full of junk,
 At best a blood-and-thunder play
 From which most audiences would run away;
 A catalogue of pompous commonplaces,
 A puppet-play that's full of empty phrases.   585
WAGNER. Yes—but the world! The human heart and mind!
 We all seek knowledge, surely, in this sphere?
FAUST. Why, yes, however knowledge is defined.
 But who will dare to speak the truth out clear?
 The few who anything of truth have learned,   590
 And foolishly did not keep truth concealed,

Their thoughts and visions to the common herd revealed,
Since time began we've crucified and burned.
But please, my friend, it's deep into the night,
And I must sleep now—if I can.   595
WAGNER. I'd gladly stay much longer, for it's such delight
Exchanging thoughts with such a learned man.
But then tomorrow, as it's Easter Day,
I'll put more questions to you if I may.
I've studied very hard, and yet, although   600
I know a lot, there's so much more to know.   [exit
FAUST. [alone] How is it that his mind can take such pleasure,
Forever dabbling in these shallow terms.
He digs so avidly for hidden treasure,
And then rejoices when he digs up worms.   605
Why is it that this tiresome nuisance can
Dispel the throng of spirits gathered round me?
And yet for once I'm glad the wretched man
Came in and broke the magic spell that bound me.
His interruption saved me from despair   610
That threatened to destroy my shattered mind.
The mighty vision I confronted there
Showed me the pygmy stature of mankind.

And I myself, made in God's image, thought
That I had glimpsed eternal truth's reflection,   615
Exulting in the radiance of heaven, sought
To shed all earthly imperfection;
I, higher than Cherubim, imagined I was free
To surge through nature's very veins, I vied
With gods in their creative power, and tried   620
To share their joy—I pay now for my pride!
That voice of thunder has annihilated me.

Your peer, great Spirit, I can never be.
Although my powers could summon you, I fear
I had no power to hold your presence here.   625
That moment was sublime beyond compare,
I felt myself so small and yet so great;
But cruelly you drove me back to share
Humanity's obscure uncertain fate.

Who now will counsel me or warn me? Who?   630
Should I obey that urge that drives me on?
Not just our sorrows, everything we do
Confines the course our lives would freely run.

Against our spirit's loftiest conception
Some foreign element continually conspires;   635
The good to which the soul on earth aspires,
The better part of it is vain deception.
The glorious feelings that life gave us, all emotion
Is numbed and coarsened in the world's commotion.

Once our imagination boldly sought   640
To reach eternity; but now a tiny scope
Is all it needs. The swirling tide of time has brought
An end to all our joy and all our hope.
Deep in our hearts is lodged the worm of care,
It works its secret pain and worry there.   645
In ever-changing guises it appears,
Gnaws at our peace of mind and turns our joys to tears,
As house and home, as child and wife,
As fire or flood, as poison or as knife;
We tremble at the things that never harmed us yet,   650
And what we never lost we bitterly regret.

I am not like the gods! Too well I know
That I am like the snake that eats the dust,
That must for ever on its belly go
And by the feet of those who pass be crushed.   655

These drawers, these cluttered shelves that line the wall
Confining me inside this dismal cell,
This useless and motheaten bric-à-brac, and all
This junk surrounding me—is this not dust as well?
Shall I discover what I seek in here?   660
And should I read a thousand books to find
How men have agonized in vain, or hear
Of one or two whom fate has been kind?
You empty skull, I see you grinning down;
Perhaps your brain, like mine, sought in confusion   665
The light of day, but in the gloomy twilight found
Your joyful urge for truth had ended in delusion.
Those instruments that hang there mocking me,
That cobwebbed tangle, clamps and pulleys, cogs and wheels—
With these I thought I could unlock the seals   670
That guard the door to nature's mystery.
But it was barred; the veil that shrouds from sight
All nature's secrets cannot be dispelled,
And what from your inquiring mind she has withheld

These screws and levers will not bring to light. 675
This rusty apparatus I've retained
Only because it's from my father's time;
The lamp that gutters on my desk has stained
This ancient parchment black with soot and grime.
Far better to have squandered what I had than stay 680
And struggle with the useless junk of yesterday!
What we inherit from our fathers should
Be ours to have and hold, to use it as we would,
Or else it is a millstone that we carry with us;
We can use only what the here and now will give us. 685

Why do my eyes turn to that place again?
Is it that phial that attracts me so?
Why do I sense a sudden lightening, as when
The darkness of the woods is bathed in moonlight's glow?

I take you down with reverent devotion, 690
And welcome you, most precious, rarest potion!
In you I honour human skill and art;
Quintessence of all kindly opiates, austere
Tincture of subtlest poisons, play your part—
Do one last service for your master here! 695
I see you, and all pain is stilled at last;
I hold you, and my restless striving ceases.
The surging of my mind is ebbing fast,
Borne on fresh tides to ocean's furthest reaches.
Here at my feet the shining waters stretch away, 700
And to a new shore beckons now a bright new day!

A chariot of fire descends on buoyant wings
And finds me ready! Soon I shall be free
To soar aloft to realms of higher things,
To other spheres of pure activity. 705
You who were as a worm, do you deserve such bliss,
Such radiant life, such godlike joy as this?
Yes, turn your back on earth, and resolutely go
Into a sunlight such as here you'll never know!
Now you must dare to fling those portals wide, 710
The gates through which none willingly would go;
Now is the time to act, and by your action show
That man is fit to stand at the immortals' side,
And not to quail before that gloomy cavern, where
Imagination damns itself to torment and despair; 715
Press on towards that passage from which none returns,

Around whose narrow mouth all hell-fire burns.
To make that awful journey freely I decide,
Although oblivion await me on the other side.

Come down, you glass of purest crystal bright!   720
Out of your ancient case I bring you to the light.
For all these years you lay forgotten here;
You sparkled at our fathers' banquets long ago,
And brought those solemn gatherings good cheer
When as a loving-cup from hand to hand you'd go.   725
It was the drinker's duty to convey in rhymes
The richly wrought engravings round the bowl,
Then in one draught to drain the cup—how you recall
For me those far-off youthful times!
Today I shall not pass you to a fellow-guest,   730
Nor try my wit against the figures round your rim;
This darker juice that fills you to the brim
Inebriates more swiftly than the rest.
I made it well, and choose it for this final test:
With all my heart I bring, as day is dawning,   735
My festive greeting to this solemn morning!

He sets the cup to his mouth. The sound of bells and a choir are heard.

CHOIR OF ANGELS. Christ is arisen!
   Joy he has brought for us
   Sin he has fought for us
   Salvation sought for us   740
   In his dark prison.
FAUST. What distant voices, what exalted singing
   Now from my eager lips have snatched this cup away?
   Are those deep-throated bells already ringing
   The first glad message of the Easter Day?   745
   You early choirs, you sing as once the angels sang
   When from the dark night of the tomb there rang
   Assurance of a covenant renewed that day.

CHOIR OF WOMEN. With fragrant lotion
   Gently his limbs we dressed,   750
   With true devotion
   Laid our dear Lord to rest,
   Clean linen round him
   Binding with loving care.
   Alas, we found him   755
   No longer there.

267

CHOIR OF ANGELS. Christ is arisen!
   Saviour who loves us best
   Ever thy name be blessed
   Who for us stood the test   760
   In thy dark prison.
FAUST. You gentle, potent choirs of heaven, why do you seek
   To visit me within this dusty cell?
   I hear your message, but my faith is weak;
   Go, on more tender minds to cast your spell   765
   And work the miracles that faith loves well.
   I do not dare to reach towards those spheres,
   Your gracious gospel calls to me in vain;
   And yet these sounds bring memories of early years
   That call me back to life on earth again.   770
   Then, in the solemn stillness of the sabbath day
   I felt the loving kiss of heaven descend on me;
   The pealing bells rang out the sacred mystery,
   And with a fervent joy I knelt to pray.
   I did not understand the joyful urge   775
   That drove me out to wood and field and lane,
   Or why I wept a thousand tears to feel the surge
   Of life as if a world was born in me again.
   Those songs would promise carefree childish play,
   And herald the unfettered joys of spring;   780
   The memories of childhood innocence they bring
   From that last solemn step turn me away.
   Sweet choirs of heaven, your hymns were not in vain;
   My tears run free, I am restored to earth again!

CHOIR OF DISCIPLES. Though in the tomb he lay,   785
   All was not ended;
   Our loving Lord today
   Heavenward ascended.
   Now through his second birth
   Glad transformation nears,   790
   But we remain on earth
   Still in this vale of tears.
   We who were not reborn
   Languish here comfortless;
   We who were left to mourn   795
   Envy his bliss!

CHOIR OF ANGELS. Christ is arisen
   Out of corruption's woe.
   Now from your prison

Joyfully go,   800
Praises declaring
Loving and caring
Brotherhood sharing
His gospel bearing
Heaven's joys preparing.   805
For you the Lord is near,
See, he is here!

OUTSIDE THE CITY GATE

All kinds of people walking out

SOME APPRENTICE TRADESMEN. Why are you going out that way?
OTHERS. We're going to the hunting lodge today.
1ST GROUP. We're going to walk as far as the mill.   810
APPRENT. The watergate's a better bet.
2 APPRENT. The path's no good, it's far too wet.
2ND GROUP. Are you coming with us?
3 APPRENT.   I don't think I will.
4 APPRENT. Let's go up to Bergdorf, there's better beer
    And prettier girls than you get down here.   815
    They have good fights up there as well.
5 APPRENT. If I were you, I'd just go steady—
    You've had two hidings there already;
    I'd avoid the place like hell.
SERVANT GIRL. Oh come on! Let's go back to town.   820
2ND SERVANT GIRL. I'm sure he's waiting by that tree.
1ST GIRL. And anyway, it's not much fun for me,
    It's you he always hangs around.
    He'll only ever dance with you—
    There's nothing much for me to do.   825
2ND GIRL. Oh, he won't be the only one up there,
    He said he'd bring that boy with curly hair.
STUDENT. My God, just watch those girls go by!
    Come on, let's give them both a try.
    I like a pint and a damn good smoke, but still   830
    There's nothing like a housemaid dressed to kill.
A MIDDLE-CLASS GIRL. What is it with the boys around these parts?
    There's lots of nice girls, they could take their pick—
    But they go chasing after those two tarts.
    It really is enough to make you sick!   835
2 STUDENT. [*to the first*] Hey, not so fast! Look at the other two,

269

They're really smart. I've seen that one before—
Yes, she's the pretty one that lives next door.
I fancy her—the other one's just right for you.
They're in no hurry, leave it all to me;   840
They'll let us go along with them, you'll see.
I STUDENT. Oh no, it's boring when you have to be polite.
Come on, don't let those two birds out of sight.
They're much more fun; believe me, if you want to score,
These working girls know what their hands are for.   845
A CITIZEN. No, I don't like our present Burgomaster,
Since he got in, he's just been a disaster.
Whatever good has he done for the town?
Things go from bad to worse, and every day
There's something else for which we have to pay.   850
He gives his orders—we just have to knuckle down.

A BEGGAR. [*sings*] Fair ladies and fine gentlemen
With rosy cheeks and pretty dress,
I beg you, spare a thought for them
That suffer hunger and distress.   855
You're lucky if you have the choice
To help the poor, a Christian deed;
On Easter Day, when all rejoice,
Give charity to those in need!
2 CITIZEN. What I like best when I'm on holiday   860
Is talk about a bloody foreign war,
In Turkey or some country far away—
The din of battle and the cannon's roar!
You sit at the window with a glass of beer,
And on the river watch the ships go by,   865
Then in the evening go home with a grateful sigh
And thank the Lord that things are peaceful here.
3 CITIZEN. Yes, neighbour, that's the way I see it.
Just let them fight among themselves, I say,
And make a mess of things—so be it—   870
As long as we can go on in the same old way.
AN OLD WOMAN. [*to the middle-class girls*] Well now, young ladies! All dressed
up today?
Why not, to make the young lads gawk at you!
But not so hoity-toity now, that's not the way;
Just come to me, I'll make your dreams come true.   875
1ST MIDDLE-CLASS GIRL. Agatha, come on! I don't like to be seen
Talking to witches like her in the street.

But still, she showed me just last Hallowe'en
The boy I'd marry; he was really sweet.
THE OTHER. She showed me mine once in her crystal ball,   880
With all his cheeky friends—a soldier, I could swear.
But it's no good, I've looked around them all,
I just can't find him anywhere.

SOLDIERS. Castles with mighty
Ramparts and towers,   885
Girls proud and flighty
Force overpowers
And makes them ours!
Bold enterprises
Win the best prizes.   890
We stick together,
We're always willing,
Whether it's pleasure,
Whether it's killing.
A girl or a castle,   895
Tough ones or tender,
After a tussle
They all surrender.
No one is bolder,
We take the prize—   900
And then the soldier
Says his goodbyes.

FAUST *and* WAGNER

FAUST. The ice has melted, the streams and rivers,
Released from the frozen hills, now bring
To the valleys the hopeful promise of spring.   905
Old winter, defeated, retreats and shivers
High in the desolate mountain snows,
And from his bitter exile blows
His icy blasts in feeble showers
That turn the green fields hoary white.   910
The sun will put his frost to flight,
And soon will paint the meadows bright.
All round us new life stirs and grows;
But now in the fields instead of flowers
A motley throng of people flows.   915
Here from this rise we can look down
And see them pouring in full spate

Through the dark and narrow gate
Out of the confines of the town.
They celebrate with one accord   920
The resurrection of the Lord,
For they themselves are now reborn;
Away from the workshops and counting-tables,
From narrow hovel and dismal room,
Out of the shadow of roofs and gables,   925
Out of the churches' pious gloom,
Out from the squash of the streets they swarm,
All streaming out into the light,
Into the open countryside—
How eagerly they take their flight!   930
See, on the river far and wide
The painted boats go sailing past,
And packed with revellers they glide
Until they're lost to sight at last.
You see the tiny figures crawl   935
Along the mountain tracks up there,
And hear the noisy village fair.
This is a paradise for all;
They all proclaim on every side
What joy it is to be alive!   940
WAGNER. Doctor, although it makes me very proud
To keep you company and hear your learned talk,
Alone I would not care to come and walk
With this uncouth and vulgar crowd.
Their shouting, fiddling, bowling and the rest,   945
It grates upon my ears, I have to say.
They rant and shriek as if they were possessed,
And take their pleasures in this raucous way.

PEASANTS *under the linden tree, dancing and singing*

The shepherd in his Sunday best
In coloured coat and ribbons dressed,   950
I'm really smart, he says, oh!
Around the linden tree the boys
And girls were dancing—what a noise!
Diddle dee! Diddle dee!
And fiddle-me diddle-me dee!   955
That's how the fiddler plays, oh.

He joined the dance and in a while
He sees a girl, and with a smile

He digs her in the stays, oh.
The lively lass she turns about   960
And says, stop that, you stupid lout!
Diddle dee! Diddle dee!
And fiddle-me diddle-me dee!
Just watch your cheeky ways, oh.

Then round and round the couple flew,   965
They danced and danced the whole night through—
Her skirts fly as she sways, oh!
They danced until they both got warm,
And lay together at the dawn.
Diddle dee! Diddle dee!   970
And fiddle-me diddle-me dee!
On her thigh his hand he lays, oh.

Now, don't be so familiar, you!
I'm not so sure you love me true.
The girl it is that pays, oh.   975
But he coaxed her on, and very soon
From the linden tree you heard this tune:
Diddle dee! Diddle dee!
And fiddle-me diddle-me dee!
All shout and the fiddler plays, oh.   980

OLD PEASANT. Doctor, we be very proud
  That such a learned man today
  Should come and join our merry crowd.
  We welcome you, and bid you stay,
  And beg you, Sir, to be the first   985
  To sample this, our finest cup.
  We hope that as you drink it up
  It will do more than quench your thirst;
  May it as many drops contain
  As years on earth to you remain.   990

FAUST. I thank you for your welcome here;
  I drink, and wish you all good cheer.

The people gather round

OLD PEASANT. Indeed, it is a fitting thing
  That you should be with us on this glad day,
  For you have helped relieve our suffering   995
  In former times on many a bad day.
  There's several of us be here still
  Your father treated with devoted care

273

When fever raged, and with his healing skill
Saved them from death, and saved us from despair.   1000
And you yourself were then a young man, you
Would visit the plague-houses without fear,
Among the dead and dying all night through
You toiled, and lived to work among us here.
Through all those many trials you endured,   1005
And many of us with God's help you cured.
ALL. Good health to a true and trusted friend,
    May he be with us to the end!
FAUST. Give thanks to God in heaven above,
    Who helps and heals us with his love.   1010

He walks on with WAGNER

WAGNER. What pleasure it must give you, Sir, to find
    Such honour and respect among the crowd!
    How happy is the man who is allowed
    To use his talents in the service of mankind.
    The father shows you to his son,   1015
    They rush to see you, every one.
    The music stops, the dance is done,
    They crowd around you everywhere you go
    And doff their caps with reverence—why,
    You'd almost think they'll kneel as though   1020
    The Sacred Host were being carried by.
FAUST. We'll walk a few steps further to that stone,
    And then we'll sit and rest awhile up there.
    Here deep in thought I've often sat alone
    In agony of mind, with fasting and with prayer.   1025
    So rich in hope and strong in faith I thought
    To force God's will, and heaven I besought
    With pleas and tears and pious abstinence
    To put an end to that vile pestilence.
    How hollow in my ears their plaudits ring!   1030
    If you could read my inmost thoughts, you'd learn
    How little son or father did to earn
    The praises that these simple people sing.
    My father was a decent man who strove
    To fathom holy nature's secret lore;   1035
    His honest but eccentric efforts drove
    Him to a science occult and obscure.
    In the dark workshop of his trade
    With his initiates he hid away,

274

And from some ancient formulae   1040
Repellent and arcane concoctions made.
There in a warm solution he would wed
The lily to the lion, white to red,
Then both were forced with open flame
Through narrow bridal chambers time and time again.   1045
And if the glowing colours then revealed
The young queen in the phial deep inside,
That was the medicine—but the patients died,
And no one thought to wonder who was healed.
And so with hellish brews and deadly skills   1050
Among these valleys and these hills
We did more mischief than the plague could ever do.
I gave the poison to a thousand men who died;
Now to my shame I have to listen to
The praises of the murderers sung far and wide.   1055

WAGNER. How can you be disturbed by such a thought?
It's quite enough for any honest man
To practise scrupulously as he can
The skills and disciplines he has been taught.
As young men we respect our fathers' guidance,   1060
And from their teachings willingly we learn;
If then as grown men we extend their science,
Our sons will surely further it in turn.

FAUST. How fortunate are those who can still hope
To rise above this sea of error all around!   1065
For what we need to know is quite beyond our scope,
And useless all the knowledge we have found.
But with such dismal thoughts let us be done,
And marvel at the bounty that this evening yields!
See how the glory of the setting sun   1070
Touches the huts among the lush green fields.
It dips and sinks, completes its daily round,
And brings new life to lands still plunged in night.
If only I had wings to lift me from the ground,
To soar and track it on its onward flight!   1075
In everlasting sunset I would greet
The quiet world spread out beneath my feet,
The valleys hushed, the mountain summits glowing,
The silver streams to golden rivers flowing.
For nothing then could check my godlike flight,   1080
No rocky peaks or chasms interrupt my gaze,
And soon the ocean with its balmy bays

Reveals itself to the unfettered sight.
Again the fiery disk begins to sink,
And with fresh energies I hurry on to drink   1085
And quench my thirst in its eternal light,
The day before me, and behind me night,
The heavens above me, under me the waves!
A glorious vision, even as it fades.
The sullen body's burden always brings   1090
To earth the impulse of our spirit's wings.
Yet every creature's by its nature led
To strive and climb beyond its earthly ties;
The lark pours out its shrilling descant overhead,
Lost in the azure spaces of the skies;   1095
On spreading wings the soaring eagle seeks
The solitude of fir-clad mountain peaks;
Towards its distant home the wandering crane
Flies onward over forest, lake and plain.
WAGNER. I've often felt a certain restlessness,   1100
But not an urge like that, I must confess.
You soon get tired of woods and fields and suchlike things,
And I would never envy birds their wings.
For I prefer more intellectual delights;
From book to book, from page to page I go—   1105
It helps me pass the bitter winter nights.
For as I read, I feel a warming glow;
And if I find a manuscript of any worth—
Why, then it's like a very heaven on earth.
FAUST. You only know that single urge; far better so—   1110
That other impulse you should never seek to know.
Two souls are locked in conflict in my heart,
They fight to separate and pull apart.
The one clings stubbornly to worldly things,
And craves the pleasures of our carnal appetites,   1115
The other has an inborn urge to spread its wings,
Shake off the dust of earth and soar to loftier heights.
If there are hovering spirits that hold sway
In the sublunary regions of the sky,
Oh, come down from the golden clouds and let me fly   1120
With you to new adventures far away!
Or if I had a magic cloak at my command
To lift and take me to some distant land,
I'd not exchange it for a cloth of gold,
For a king's ransom, or for wealth untold!   1125

276

WAGNER. Do not invoke that too familiar swarm
 Of demons that infest the atmosphere,
 And bring from every quarter and in every form
 The countless ills and perils that we fear!
 From the cold north the spirit hordes descend   1130
 With cutting teeth and arrow-pointed tongues;
 And from the east a barren drought they send
 That shreds and feeds upon our gasping lungs;
 From southern deserts comes the heat that overpowers
 And sears us with its torrid glow;   1135
 The west brings us relief with drenching showers
 That drown us and the crops just as they grow.
 They listen well, on mischief always bent,
 Obey our call, beguile us to believe
 They speak with angels' tongues, as if from heaven sent 1140
 To serve us here—but only to deceive.
 But come, let's leave; the world is grey and still,
 The mist is gathering and the air is chill.
 At such times I appreciate my cosy room.
 You look amazed, why do you stop and stare?   1145
 Can you see something out there in the gloom?
FAUST. You see that black dog running through the stubble there?
WAGNER. That's nothing odd; I noticed it a while ago.
FAUST. Look carefully! What kind of creature can it be?
WAGNER. It's just a poodle running to and fro   1150
 And picking up its master's scent, it seems to me.
FAUST. It's running circles round us; there, look back—
 It's getting closer to us all the time.
 I seem to see a streak of red, a line
 Of fire marking out its track.   1155
WAGNER. It's just a stray black poodle that has found us;
 I daresay it's an optical illusion, have no care.
FAUST. It seems to me it's weaving magic lines around us,
 To draw us into some infernal snare.
WAGNER. It doesn't know us, so it feels unsure,   1160
 Because it was its master it was looking for.
FAUST. The circle's getting smaller now, it's coming near!
WAGNER. You see—a dog! There is no witchcraft here.
 It growls and cowers, wags its tail, lies flat
 Upon its belly—every dog does that.   1165
FAUST. Perhaps you're right; then let it come with us.
WAGNER. It's just a silly dog that wants some fun with us.
 It stands and waits there every time we stop,

You speak to it, it begs and does its tricks.
  It'll bring back anything you drop,   1170
  Jump in the river just to fetch some sticks.
FAUST. I see no evil spirit in it, sure enough;
  It's just a dog that's trained to do its stuff.
WAGNER. There is no reason why a learned man
  Should not approve a well-trained poodle, too;   1175
  The students teach him everything they can,
  Just as the students learn so much from you.
                    [*they go in through the city gate*

FAUST'S STUDY

FAUST *enters with the poodle*

FAUST. The fields and pastures now lie still,
  And night its canopy has spread;
  The solemn darkness seems to fill   1180
  Our better soul with holy dread.
  Our wilder impulses are stilled,
  And all our hasty actions, when
  The peaceful heart with love is filled
  For God and for our fellow men.   1185

Be quiet, poodle! Stop running everywhere!
  Why are you snuffling around the door?
  Sit by the stove, Sir, over there—
  I'll put my best cushion on the floor.
  This running and jumping and sniffing about   1190
  Was all very well out there on the hill;
  You're welcome here, but I'll turn you out
  If you can't settle down and just lie still.

When the friendly lamp burns bright
  Confined within this narrow cell,   1195
  The heart that knows itself aright
  Can find enlightenment as well.
  Then hope once more within us swells,
  And reason speaks again, it seems;
  We long to seek the deepest wells   1200
  Of life, and drink from living streams.

Poodle, stop growling! These animal cries
  Disturb the calm and reverent mood
  That fills my mind in this solitude.

We know that men only mock and despise   1205
What they don't understand or never knew;
In the minds of most there is no place
For goodness, beauty, love or grace—
Do such things make dogs uneasy, too?

But though my spirit wills it, still I cannot find   1210
That true contentment and serenity of mind.
Why must we thirst and search in vain, and why
Must every source of hope run dry?
How often have I sought such consolation,
How often have my efforts been in vain!   1215
And so we look beyond this world again
And seek the witness of God's revelation,
The truth that with majestic beauty shines
In the Evangelist's most solemn lines.
A reverent impulse now inspires me   1220
To take the ancient text, and with sincerity
Translate the Holy Gospel of St John
Into my own beloved native tongue.

He opens a large volume and begins to write

I read: In the beginning was the Word. But here
Already I must hesitate. The mere   1225
Word for me has no such resonance;
I must translate it in a different sense.
Now, if the spirit guides me right, I ought
To say: In the beginning there was Thought.
Consider well; the deeper truth escapes   1230
The hasty pen. For is it thought that shapes
And drives creation at its very source?
Far better: In the beginning was the Force!
Yet something tells me even as I write
That this is not the meaning that I need.   1235
The spirit helps me, now I see the light,
I have it: In the beginning was the Deed!

If I'm to share this room with you,
Poodle, stop growling
And stop your howling!   1240
I won't have such a hullabaloo,
So stop your fuss,
Or one of us
Will leave the house, and quickly, too.
You don't have to stay here, you know—   1245

279

The door is open, you can go.
But what's this apparition that I see?
Is it real or is it fantasy?
It can't be natural, there's magic in it—
The poodle's getting bigger by the minute!   1250
It's heaving and swelling violently—
That's not a dog in front of me!
It's like a hippopotamus in size,
With fearsome teeth and glowing eyes.
What kind of spirit have I let in here?   1255
But I know how to make your sort appear:
Solomon's Key has just the spell
To exorcise this brood of hell.

SPIRITS. [*in the passage outside*]
There's somebody trapped in there!
Stay out, don't follow him, beware!   1260
It's the old hell-hound, like a fox
Caught in a box!
Listen to me:
Fly high and low,
Weave to and fro,   1265
And he'll soon be free.
Help him, don't let him
Just sit there, they'll get him!
He's helped us before,
Done us favours galore.   1270

FAUST. First I'll need the fourfold spell
To summon up this beast of hell:

Salamanders aglow,
Undines so fair,
Sylphs of the air,   1275
Kobolds below!
You represent
Each element,
Through your powers
The gift is ours;   1280
Spirits will fall
Under our thrall.
Vanish in the fiery glow,
Salamander!
With the rippling waters flow,   1285
Undine!
Like a glorious meteor blaze,

Sylph!
Show your helpful homely ways,
Incubus! Incubus!   1290
Be done, and show yourself to us!

None of the four
Dwells in the beast,
It leers and lies there just as before—
I haven't hurt it in the least.   1295
But I can weave
A stronger spell.

My friend, I believe
You're a minion of hell.
This sign can quell   1300
The hordes that dwell
In the pit beneath.

Ah! Now it's bristling and showing its teeth.

Vile creature, it seems
You know what it means: 1305
The uncreated one,
Undesignated one,
Through all heavens glorified,
Infamously crucified.

Now behind the stove it goes,   1310
And like an elephant it grows.
It fills the room, it swirls and flows,
Like mist it seems to disappear.
It rises to the roof again—
Now, at your master's call, come here!   1315
You see, my threats were not in vain—
I'll singe your fur with holy flame!
Do not invite
The threefold glowing light,
Do not invite   1320
The most commanding spell of all!

    MEPHISTOPHELES *steps out from behind the stove as the mist clears,*
dressed as a travelling scholar

MEPHISTO. Why all the fuss? I'm here, Sir, at your call.
FAUST. So that was what the poodle had in it—
    A travelling scholar! Well, I like your style.

MEPHISTO. Congratulations to you; I admit   1325
    You had me rather worried for a while.
FAUST. What is your name?
MEPHISTO.   The question seems absurd
    For someone who despises the mere word,
    Who treats appearances as vain illusion
    And seeks the truth in such remote seclusion.   1330
FAUST. But with you gentlemen the name
    And nature's usually the same,
    And we can often recognize
    The Liar, the Destroyer, or the Lord of Flies.
    Who are you, then?
MEPHISTO.   A part of that same power that would   1335
    Forever work for evil, yet forever creates good.
FAUST. And does this puzzle have some explanation?
MEPHISTO. I am the spirit of perpetual negation.
    And that is only right; for all
    That's made is fit to be destroyed.   1340
    Far better if it were an empty void!
    So—everything that you would call
    Destruction, sin, and all that's meant
    By evil, is my proper element.
FAUST. You call yourself a part? You seem entire to me.   1345
MEPHISTO. I'm telling you the simple truth. You see,
    While man, that poor deluded soul,
    Imagines he's a perfect whole,
    I am part of that part that at the first was one,
    Part of the darkness from which light has sprung,   1350
    Proud light, that now competes with Mother Night
    For room and status, and disputes her ancient right.
    But it will not succeed, because it clings
    To stubborn matter, to corporeal things.
    It blazons forth their beauty to the eye,   1355
    But matter hinders its triumphant course;
    It cannot last for ever, and perforce
    When matter perishes, then light must die.
FAUST. Ah, now I see what you're about; you fail
    To bring wholesale destruction to the universe,   1360
    And so you work your mischief on a smaller scale.
MEPHISTO. Indeed; but frankly, things just go from bad to worse.
    This awkward world, this object, this obstruction,
    Resists all my best efforts at destruction.
    Whatever harm I do to it, it seems   1365

Quite unaffected by my nihilistic schemes.
Flood, fire or earthquake, storm—whatever I can send
To ravage land or sea, they calm down in the end.
And that accursed brood of man and beast—
That rabble I can't cope with in the least.   1370
I've buried millions in my time, but then
They breed and multiply—I have to start again!
So it goes on, it drives you to despair;
In water, in the earth and in the air,
A dry, a moist, a cold or warm environment,   1375
A thousand germinating seeds are sown.
If fire were not my native element,
There would be nothing left to call my own.
FAUST. I see; against the ever-living power
That tends and nurtures all creation,   1380
You rage in vain with all the sour
Malice of your cold negation.
Strange son of chaos! No, you ought
To change your strategy and start again.
MEPHISTO. Indeed, I'll give the matter careful thought,   1385
And we'll go into it more fully then.
But now, with your permission, may I go?
FAUST. I don't see why you need my leave.
We've got to know each other—so
Feel free to visit when you please.   1390
There's the door, and there's the window—you
Could surely get out through the chimney, too?
MEPHISTO. Well—yes, there is a snag, I have to say;
There's just one little obstacle in the way.
That magic sign drawn on the floor—   1395
FAUST. Is it the pentagram that keeps you in?
So tell me then, you son of hell and sin,
However did you get in through the door?
How could a demon let himself be fooled?
MEPHISTO. Take a close look; it's not perfectly ruled.   1400
That corner pointing out into the street—
As you can see, the two lines don't quite meet.
FAUST. Now that's a very fortunate mistake!
I've caught the Devil, and he can't escape—
And quite by accident, it would appear.   1405
MEPHISTO. The poodle didn't notice when he came in here;
But now the situation's changed, and so
The Devil could get in, but he can't go.

FAUST. You could leave by the window, I'd have thought.
MEPHISTO. Demons and spirits have their code; we may   1410
    Come in just as we please, but then we're caught;
    We have to leave the house by the same way.
FAUST. So hell has its own laws and regulations too?
    That's very good! So tell me—I dare say
    It's possible to make a pact with you?   1415
MEPHISTO. Indeed; if you negotiate with us,
    You'll find the offer tempting—and we never cheat.
    But these things can't be rushed, so we'll discuss
    The matter in more detail the next time we meet.
    For now, I would respectfully require   1420
    Your kind permission to retire.
FAUST. Come, stay a little longer; you can tell me
    Something about the bargains you might sell me.
MEPHISTO. Please let me go—I'll soon be back again,
    And you can ask me all about it then.   1425
FAUST. I didn't trick you into coming here, you know—
    You got yourself into this snare.
    It isn't often that you get the Devil where
    You want him—so you don't just let him go.
MEPHISTO. If that is what you wish, I will remain   1430
    And keep you company a while.
    On one condition, though—that I can entertain
    You with my talents in the proper style.
FAUST. Why, yes, of course, you must feel free;
    I hope you've something pleasant, though, to offer me.   1435
MEPHISTO. My friend, in just one hour tonight
    You'll have more sensual pleasure and delight
    Than in a year of everyday monotony.
    What these airy spirits sing you,
    And the visions that they bring you   1440
    Are no empty magic dream.
    Sweetest perfumes will beguile you,
    All your senses ravish while you
    Feast on fruits you've never seen.
    You're here—you don't have to rehearse your part;   1445
    Now, spirits of the air, show us your art!

SPIRITS. Let the dark ceiling
    Over us vanish!
    Blue sky revealing,
    Sweetly appealing   1450
    Comforting light!

If the concealing
Clouds we could banish,
Stars would be gleaming,
Milder suns beaming   1455
Through the dark night.
Spirit perfection,
Heaven's reflection,
Gracefully swinging,
Overhead winging.   1460
Yearning affection
After them sighing;
Ribbons are flying,
Draperies streaming,
Scattered like flowers   1465
Garland the bowers.
See lovers dreaming,
Pledging together
Love that's for ever.
Green leaves surround them,   1470
Tendrils wind round them,
Heavy grapes cluster,
Ripe for the treading,
Vats overflowing.
Now the wine gushes,   1475
Foaming in fountains
Through the rocks' lustre
Trickling, it rushes
Down from the mountains
Streaming and pouring,   1480
Into lakes spreading,
Round the hills flowing,
Emerald glowing.
Birds above soaring
Sunwards are streaming,   1485
Effortless motion
Blissfully winging
Where in the gleaming
Waters of ocean
Islands are dreaming,   1490
Where we hear singing
Joyfully ringing,
Soft pipes are playing,
Dancers are straying

Through the fields gliding,   1495
Stepping and swaying.
Some we see striding
Over the mountains,
Others are playing
In the cool fountains,   1500
Others are soaring,
All are adoring,
Stars high above us
Cherish and love us,
Bless us with grace.   1505
MEPHISTO. Well done, my gentle spirits of the air!
He's sleeping like a babe without a care.
For this recital I am in your debt.
You're not the man to hold the Devil yet!
Now plunge him in an ocean of delight,   1510
Entrance him with deluded fantasy.
But here I need a rodent's teeth to bite
The magic charm around this door for me.
They'll not take long to answer to my call—
I can already hear one rustling in the wall.   1515

The master of all rats and mice,
Of flies and frogs and bugs and lice,
Commands you to come forth and gnaw
That symbol chalked upon the floor.
There, where I mark it with a drop   1520
Of oil; ah, yes, he's coming, hippety-hop!
Now, get to work! The point that's holding me
Is on the edge, right at the top. Now then,
Another bite, and I'll be free.
So, Faust, dream on until we meet again!   1525
FAUST. [*waking*] Have I been cheated then once more,
And has my throng of spirits vanished into air?
Did I only dream the Devil was there,
And was it just a poodle that I saw?

FAUST'S STUDY

FAUST *and* MEPHISTOPHELES

FAUST. Who's there? Come in! Now who the devil's pestering me?   1530
MEPHISTO. It's me.

FAUST.   Come in!

MEPHISTO.   Just one more time, to make it three.

FAUST. Well, come in then!

MEPHISTO.   And here I am, you see.

    I hope we shall get on together, you and I;
    I've come to cheer you up—that's why
    I'm dressed up like an aristocrat   1535
    In a fine red coat with golden stitches,
    A stiff silk cape on top of that,
    A long sharp rapier in my breeches,
    And a cockerel's feather in my hat.
    Take my advice—if I were you,   1540
    I'd get an outfit like this too;
    Then you'd be well equipped to see
    Just how exciting life can be.

FAUST. In any costume I would still despair
    Of life, its misery and care.   1545
    I am too old to kindle youthful fire,
    And yet too young to be beyond desire.
    What has this world to offer me, what sort of choice?
    You must forgo, renounce, abstain—
    That is the tedious refrain   1550
    That echoes in our ears, that dismal song.
    Hour after hour we hear its croaking voice,
    It mocks and follows us our whole life long.
    Each morning when I wake, I wake with dread,
    With bitter tears I greet the day that brings   1555
    No promise and no hope of better things,
    No wish fulfilled, not one, for hope is dead;
    The day whose leering grimace only stifles
    The faintest inkling of delight or joy.
    The warmest promptings of the heart it can destroy 1560
    With all its stubborn and capricious trifles.
    And even when night falls, and on my bed
    Fearful and uneasy I must lie, I find
    No welcome rest to comfort me—instead
    Wild dreams will come to haunt my anxious mind. 1565
    The God who dwells within me and who fires
    My inner self, my passionate desires,
    The God who governs all my thoughts and deeds,
    Is powerless to satisfy my outer needs.
    This weary life, this burden I detest;   1570
    I long for death to come and bring me rest.

MEPHISTO. Death is not always such a welcome guest.
FAUST. How happy is the blood-stained hero who
    Meets death in furious battle face to face,
    The man who's wildly danced the whole night through,   1575
    And finds death in a woman's passionate embrace.
    That night I saw the Spirit in the flame,
    If only I had fallen lifeless at its feet!
MEPHISTO. And yet on Easter morning, all the same
    A certain potion didn't taste so sweet.   1580
FAUST. You have some talent as a spy, I see.
MEPHISTO. I don't know everything; but much is known to me.
FAUST. That night I heard familiar voices call
    To save me from my terrible confusion,
    And childhood memories, a sweet illusion   1585
    Of happiness long past held me in thrall.
    But now I curse that power whose spell
    Deludes our souls with its enticing wiles,
    And with its false alluring tricks beguiles
    Us in this dreary cavern where we dwell.   1590
    I curse the self-conceit and pride,
    The high opinions of the mind!
    I curse appearances that blind
    Our senses to the truth they hide!
    I curse the dreams of vain obsession,   1595
    Of reputation, fame or merit,
    I curse our pride in all possession,
    Of wife or child, and all that we inherit.
    A curse on Mammon's glittering treasures
    That spur ambition on to reckless things,   1600
    And on the sybaritic pleasures,
    The luxury that his indulgence brings!
    I curse the honeyed nectar of the grape,
    The grace of love for which all creatures thirst,
    A curse on hope, a curse on faith—   1605
    Above all, patience be accursed!

CHORUS OF INVISIBLE SPIRITS. Alas! Alas!
    You have destroyed
    This lovely world!
    A demigod has smashed it,   1610
    His fist has dashed it
    To pieces and hurled
    Them into the void!
    Ours is the duty

To gather the fragments and mourn   1615
The lost beauty.
Great son of earth,
Give it new birth;
Let it be born
More splendid still   1620
Within your heart again.
And with fresh will
And vision then
New life begin;
New songs we'll sing   1625
To ring it in!
MEPHISTO. My little creatures
Are wise little teachers.
They promise you action,
Delight and distraction;   1630
Leave this seclusion,
That withers body and mind;
Out in the world you'll find
Life in rich profusion!

Stop toying with this misery in your scholar's den,   1635
It's like a vulture gnawing at your heart.
Even in the worst company you'll find a part
To play among your fellow men.
But that's not what I have in mind,
Simply to mingle with the crowd;   1640
I'm not so very grand, but if I were allowed
To keep you company, you'd find
That I could help you on your way.
I would be glad to travel by your side,
Attend to everything you say,   1645
Be your companion, be your guide,
Supply you with whatever you might crave—
In short, I'd be your servant, nay, your slave.
FAUST. And what would you want from me in return?
MEPHISTO. There's time enough for that, I should have thought.   1650
FAUST. Oh no! The Devil's not the altruistic sort.
You have to treat such offers with suspicion;
He'll scarcely do you a good turn
Unless he's going to get a fat commission.
So tell me straight, then: what is your condition?   1655
MEPHISTO. I undertake to serve you here most faithfully,
Fulfil your every wish in every way,

Provided you will do the same for me
When we meet over there one day.

FAUST. It doesn't worry me, your 'over there';   1660
If you can manage to destroy
This world, the next can have its turn for all I care.
This world's the source of all my joy,
This sun shines on my anguish and despair,
And if I have to leave it all behind one day,   1665
So be it—let it happen, come what may.
I am not curious in the least to know
That in a future life there will be hate or love,
Whether it's in the regions up above,
Or in the other places down below.   1670

MEPHISTO. Then take a chance—what are you waiting for?
Sign up with me, and you can feast your eyes
On everything my talents can devise.
I'll show you things no one has seen before.

FAUST. Poor devil, what have you to offer me but lies?   1675
The highest aspirations of the human mind,
Such things mean nothing to your kind.
Oh, yes—I'm sure you've food that never satisfies,
Or liquid gold that instantly will melt and run
Like quicksilver between my fingers,   1680
A game that no one's ever won,
A girl who even while she lingers
In my arms, makes eyes at someone new;
Or meteoric fame, and honour too,
That blazes once before it fades away.   1685
Show me the fruit that rots before it's ripe,
And trees that put out new leaves every day!

MEPHISTO. Of course I can provide you with that type
Of thing—you only have to say.
But they soon pall, and then, my friend,   1690
We look for something that will give more lasting pleasure.

FAUST. If I should ever choose a life of sloth or leisure,
Then let that moment be my end!
Or if you can beguile or flatter me
Into a state of self-contented ease,   1695
Delude me with delight or luxury—
That day shall be my last. These
Are my terms.

MEPHISTO.   It's done!

FAUST.   So let it be:
If I should bid the passing moment stay, or try

To hold its fleeting beauty, then you may 1700
Cast me in chains and carry me away,
For in that instant I will gladly die.
Then you can sound my death-knell, for you will
Have done your service and be free.
Then let the hands upon the clock stand still, 1705
For that will be the end of time for me!

MEPHISTO. Consider well; we don't forget these things, you see.

FAUST. That is a right you are entitled to.
This is no frivolous adventure that I crave;
If I succumb to lethargy, I'll be a slave— 1710
Whether to another, or to you.

MEPHISTO. I'll serve you dutifully when you dine
At the graduation feast tonight.
There's just one thing; if you would sign
A document for me—I like to do things right. 1715

FAUST. Why, how pedantic! Have you never heard
That you can take a man's word as his bond?
It's not enough to stake my fate here and beyond
Upon the honour of my spoken word?
Life rushes past us on its headlong course— 1720
Why should a promise have such binding force?
But in our hearts we all cling to that whim,
From such illusions we are never free;
An honest man will not regret his own integrity,
Nor all the sacrifices that are asked of him. 1725
But such a document, drawn up with stamps and seals—
That is a daunting spectre, for the word congeals
And freezes as it's written by the pen;
Vellum and wax are all that matter then.
Well, evil spirit, what is it to be? 1730
Bronze, marble, parchment, paper—what you will.
Do I use a chisel, stylus or a quill?
The choice is yours, it's all the same to me.

MEPHISTO. What an extraordinary display!
Don't let your rhetoric carry you away. 1735
Any scrap of paper here will do, I think;
We'll use a drop of blood instead of ink.

FAUST. If you think it will be of any use,
I'm willing to join in your comic act.

MEPHISTO. Blood is a very special kind of juice. 1740

FAUST. You needn't fear that I will break this pact;
I undertake to strive with all my heart
And all my energy to play my part.

I was too swollen with conceit and pride;
The mighty Spirit has rejected me,   1745
And now I see my place is at your side.
All nature's secrets are concealed from me,
The thread of thought is broken, for
Henceforth all knowledge I abhor.
To satisfy my seething passions I'll explore   1750
The very depths of sensuality;
Reveal your wonders and your miracles to me
Behind impenetrable veils of mystery!
We'll plunge into the headlong rush of time,
Into the whirling turmoil of each day.   1755
Let pain or joy, the monstrous, the sublime,
Success or failure, triumph or vexation
Follow each other as they may;
Such restless striving is our true vocation.
MEPHISTO. There are no limits, no restrictions in your way;   1760
    Dip into everything and sample every dish,
    Grasp every opportunity without delay,
    Do as you please, take what you wish—
    Just help yourself, and don't be coy.
FAUST. Listen: it's not on happiness I'm bent.   1765
    I want a frenzied round of agonizing joy,
    Of loving hate, of stimulating discontent.
    Learning and knowledge now I leave behind;
    I shall not flinch from suffering or despair,
    And in my inner self I wish to share   1770
    The whole experience of humankind,
    To seek its heights, its depths, to know
    Within my heart its joys and all its woe,
    Identify myself with other men and blend
    My life with theirs, and like them perish in the end!   1775
MEPHISTO. Believe me, many thousand years I've had to chew
    That rancid stuff; that's long enough to know
    That from the cradle to the grave not even you
    Could ever manage to digest such sour dough.
    You have the Devil's word that such totality,   1780
    Such wholeness is for God alone, for he
    Dwells in a realm of everlasting light,
    While we were banished to the darkness down below—
    And all you ever see is day and night.
FAUST. But that is what I want!
MEPHISTO.   Bravo!   1785

There's just one problem, I'd have thought,
For art is long, and life is short.
You haven't got all that much time, and so
I think you'd better go and hire a poet,
Who'd let his wild imagination go—   1790
And he could soon provide, before you know it,
Every noble quality to your liking:
Bold as a lion,
Swift as a stallion,
Passionate as an Italian,   1795
Tough as a Viking.
He would teach you how to reconcile
High-minded generosity with subtle guile,
Or if you want to fall in love, he'd fashion
A scheme for you to satisfy your youthful passion.   1800
I'd like to meet a gentleman like that;
I'd call him 'Mr Universe' and raise my hat.
FAUST. What am I then, if it's not possible to earn
    The crown of human life for which I yearn
    With all my senses and with all my heart?   1805
MEPHISTO. You are—just what you have been from the start.
    Wear a full-bottomed wig and play the sage,
    Put on high heels and strut about the stage—
    You're still the same, whichever way you act the part.
FAUST. In vain it seems to me that I have strained   1810
    To grasp the riches of the human mind, for when
    I pause to reckon what I might have gained,
    I feel no new vitality within my breast,
    I am no further in my futile quest—
    The infinite is still beyond my ken.   1815
MEPHISTO. My dear Sir, that's a very common view
    Of things—but come now, we must try
    To find a more imaginative plan for you,
    Before life's pleasures pass you by.
    Why, damnit man, your hands, your feet, your name,   1820
    Your head, your arse, are yours alone;
    But all the other things we use and own—
    Are they not ours just the same?
    Look, it's like this: suppose I can
    Afford six horses, then it's just as though   1825
    Their strength were mine. I could put on a proper show—
    I'd be what you might call a six-horse-power man.
    So cheer up! Let your brooding be,

And come out into the wide world with me.
A man who speculates like that, you know,   1830
Is like a beast grazing on barren ground;
Some evil spirit leads it round and round,
While all about it lush green pastures grow.
FAUST. Where do we start?
MEPHISTO.   We just leave, here and now.
What kind of prison is this anyhow?   1835
What sort of life is this for you,
Boring yourself—and all your students too?
Just let your paunchy colleagues do it,
It's time to leave this treadmill, so go to it!
In any case, you mustn't talk too loud   1840
About the best things that you know—it's not allowed.
You've got a student here already at the door.
FAUST. I cannot possibly see him today.
MEPHISTO. Come, the poor lad's been there an hour or more,
He'll be so disappointed. Don't send him away;   1845
Give me your cap and gown, I'll see him for a while—
This sort of fancy dress is just my style.

                              [*he dresses in Faust's costume*

I'll use my wits and tell him something wise.
A quarter of an hour is all I need; meanwhile
Go and prepare yourself for our great enterprise!   1850
                                        [*Faust leaves*

MEPHISTOPHELES *in Faust's long gown.*

Reason and knowledge, the highest powers of humankind,
You have rejected, to oblivion consigned.
Now let the Prince of Lies confuse you,
With magic spells and fantasies delude you—
And I will have you then once and for all.   1855
For fate has given him a mind
So restless, so impetuous, so unconfined
That his impatient spirit, like a waterfall,
Pours headlong over all the pleasures life can give.
I'll plunge him into such distraction, he will live   1860
A life so futile, so banal and trite,
He'll flap and flutter like a bird stuck tight.
He is insatiable, and so I'll tantalize
Him, dangle food and drink before his greedy eyes.
In vain he'll beg relief on bended knee,   1865
And even if he hadn't pledged himself to me,
He'd still be damned for all eternity!

294

STUDENT. I've recently arrived at College
 In my earnest quest for knowledge;
 On you, Sir, with respect I call—   1870
 You are acclaimed by one and all.
MEPHISTO. Well, your politeness pleases me;
 A man like other men you see.
 You've had a good look round the place?
STUDENT. Please take me on, if you've the space!   1875
 I'm young and eager, keen to please,
 And I've enough to pay my fees.
 My mother was sad to see me go,
 But there's so much that I want to know.
MEPHISTO. Why, then you've come to the right door.   1880
STUDENT. But to be frank, I'm not quite sure.
 These rooms and walls, so gaunt and tall,
 I just don't like it here at all.
 They hem you in, and you can see
 No green leaves, not a single tree.   1885
 The lecture halls are all so grim
 I get confused, my mind goes dim.
MEPHISTO. You'll soon get used to it, you know.
 A baby's often very slow
 To suckle at its mother's breast,   1890
 But in the end it feeds with zest.
 Just so at Wisdom's breasts you will
 Quite soon be glad to drink your fill.
STUDENT. I'll feed from her with joy; but will you say
 Just what I have to do to find my way?   1895
MEPHISTO. Well, first of all, it seems to me
 You need to choose a Faculty.
STUDENT. I'd like to study every sphere
 Of nature and learning while I'm here,
 And find out all there is to know   1900
 Of the heavens above and the earth below.
MEPHISTO. Well, yes, you've got the right idea;
 But you must be careful how you go.
STUDENT. I'll do my best, I promise you—
 Although of course I have to say   1905
 I'd like some fun and freedom too,
 Whenever there's a holiday.
MEPHISTO. Use your time well, for time so quickly passes.
 A little discipline will help you with your classes;

And so, young friend, my pedagogic   1910
Judgement is, you start with Logic.
For there your mind is trained aright;
It's clamped in Spanish boots so tight
That henceforth with a clearer head
The wary path of thought you'll tread,   1915
And not like Jack o' Lantern go
Hopping and flickering to and fro.
For here with rigour you'll be taught
That things you'd never given a thought,
Like eating, drinking and running free,   1920
Must be done in order: one, two, three!
The mind, however, needs more room;
It's like a master-weaver's loom.
A thousand warps move as he treads,
The shuttle flies, and to and fro   1925
The fibres into patterns flow—
One stamp combines a thousand threads.
Send for a philosopher, and he
Will prove to you that it must be:
The first is thus, the second so,   1930
Ergo: the third and fourth we know.
If first and second were not here,
Then third and fourth would disappear.
The students love it, I believe—
But none of them have learned to weave.   1935
To know what nature is about,
First you must drive the spirit out;
And when you've pulled it all apart,
What's missing is the vital spark.
'Nature's knack!' the chemists cheer—   1940
But that just means they've no idea.
STUDENT. I'm not quite sure I follow you.
MEPHISTO. Don't fret, my boy, you'll still get through
    When you've learned the tricks and when you're able
    To simplify things and give them a label.   1945
STUDENT. I'm afraid I've simply lost the thread;
    It's like a mill-wheel grinding in my head.
MEPHISTO. And after Logic, what should you do?
    Ah! Metaphysics is the thing for you;
    You'll learn without the slightest trouble   1950
    Stuff that would make your brain-cells bubble.
    For notions that won't fit inside your head,
    You'll find a splendid word instead.

But this first term, whatever you read,
A strict routine is what you need.   1955
Five hours a day—it's not a lot,
Be in the classroom on the dot;
Prepare the texts at home with care,
And study all the details there—
You'll know without even having to look   1960
He's reading straight out of the book.
But write it all down, concentrating
As if it were the Holy Ghost dictating!
STUDENT. I'm sure that's very good advice,
And you won't have to tell me twice;   1965
If you've got it down in black and white,
You can take it home to read at night.
MEPHISTO. But now you must choose a Faculty!
STUDENT. I don't think Law is quite the thing for me.
MEPHISTO. I can't say that I blame you, for the Law,   1970
Believe me, is a monumental bore.
Those dreary statutes, rights and cases,
Like a congenital disease are handed on
Through generations from the father to the son.
They spread like germs to other places,   1975
Turn sense to nonsense, bad to worse;
If you inherit them, your heritage is a curse.
The human rights that you were born with, though—
Those are the rights that you will never know.
STUDENT. All that you say confirms my previous view.   1980
How fortunate I am to be advised by you!
I rather think Theology's the course for me.
MEPHISTO. I'm not too sure that that's the way
You ought to choose, for in that discipline, you see,
It is so easy to be led astray.   1985
The subtle poison it contains is so refined,
The antidote is difficult to find.
It's best if you have only ever heard
One teacher, and then take him at his word.
In other words, words are the things to hold to,   1990
And if you swallow everything he's told you,
Then you will never doubt that what he says is true.
STUDENT. But surely words must have some meaning too!
MEPHISTO. Perhaps—don't let that worry you a bit;
For even if the meaning's problematic,   1995
Then you can always find a word for it.
With words you can be so dogmatic,

With words you can be systematic.
You can believe in words, with words all can be proved;
Not one iota from a word may be removed.   2000
STUDENT. Forgive me if I pester, you're so kind.
    But I would much appreciate your view
    Of whether Medicine is the thing to do,
    For it's a course I also have in mind.
    Three years can very soon be past,   2005
    And one must learn it all so fast.
    They say the course is very tough;
    With your advice I'd cope, I know.
MEPHISTO. [*aside*] I'm tired of all this academic stuff;
    Now let the Devil have a go.   2010
    [*aloud*] It's not too hard to learn a Doctor's skill;
    You study till there's nothing left to know,
    And in the end you let things go
    According to God's will.
    But all that science doesn't get you very far;   2015
    We all learn willy-nilly what we can—
    But if you learn to seize your chance, you are
    The up-and-coming man.
    You're well-built, a good-looking chap,
    You've got a saucy manner, too;   2020
    Self-confidence, that's the secret, that
    Will give your patients confidence in you.
    The women are the ones to make for;
    They're always ready to complain
    About a little pain—   2025
    I'm sure you know the remedy they ache for.
    And if they think you understand,
    You'll have them eating from your hand.
    There's nothing like a Doctor's title for
    Persuading them they really can respect you,   2030
    And in your first examination you'll explore
    Places that others would take years to get to.
    You take her hand to check the pulse is steady,
    Look deep into her eyes, and then be ready
    To slip your arm around her slender waist,   2035
    Just to make sure she's not too tightly laced.
STUDENT. That sounds much better! That makes sense to me.
MEPHISTO. Listen, my friend: the golden tree
    Of life is green, all theory is grey.
STUDENT. I never dreamed I'd learn so much today!   2040

298

I'd like to come along another day
To hear more of your wisdom, if I may.
MEPHISTO. What I can do, it shall be gladly done.
STUDENT. Just one thing more; and I'll be gone.
    I've got my album here; please could you say   2045
Some words to help me on my way.
MEPHISTO. Of course.   *[he writes and hands back the book*
STUDENT. [*reading*] Eritis sicut Deus scientes bonum et malum.

    He shuts the book reverently and takes his leave.

MEPHISTO. 'You'll be like God'; my aunt, the serpent, was quite right.
    Just heed her words, and one day you'll get such a fright!   2050
FAUST. [*enters*] Now where do we go?
MEPHISTO.   Wherever you like; just come with me.
    We'll see the small world first, and then the wider scene.
    Pleasure and profit await you, sights you've never seen—
    For my beginner's course there's no tuition fee!
FAUST. With this long beard I shall stick out a mile,   2055
    I haven't got the confidence or style.
    This crazy scheme of yours won't work at all,
    I never was at ease with other men;
    In company I always feel so small
    And so inadequate—you'll have to think again.   2060
MEPHISTO. My dear friend, that will come in time;
    Self-confidence is all you need, and you'll be fine.
FAUST. And how do we travel, how do we get away?
    You've got a coach and horses out there, I daresay.
MEPHISTO. We simply spread our cloaks, and they will bear   2065
    Us up as we sail gently through the air.
    Just one thing, though—we mustn't carry too much weight,
    That makes it difficult to navigate.
    Some flame for hot air, which I shall provide,
    Will give us lift-off. Spread your arms out wide;   2070
    We've shed our ballast, and the sky is clear—
    Congratulations on your new career!

AUERBACH'S CELLAR IN LEIPZIG

Drinkers carousing

FROSCH. Come on, drink up, let's have a ball!
    What's the matter with you all?

I've never seen such po-faced gits—   2075
   You'd get on anybody's tits.
BRANDER. Well, you're not much fun, anyway—
   No laughs or filthy jokes today.
FROSCH. [*tips a glass of wine over his head*]
   You asked for it!
BRANDER.   You bloody swine!
FROSCH. Well, it was your idea, not mine!   2080
SIEBEL. Whoever quarrels gets thrown out!
   Let's have a sing-song, drink and shout!
   Holla la la la!
ALTMAYER.   God, what an awful din!
   Give me some cotton wool, or pack it in.
SIEBEL. When the deep bass voices start to sing,   2085
   The echoes make the vaulting ring.
FROSCH. Yes—if you make any trouble, you're out on the street!
   Ah! Tra la! Tra la la!
ALTMAYER. Ah! Tra la la!
FROSCH.   We're all in tune, now watch the beat.

   [*sings*] To the Holy Roman Empire—but whatever,   2090
   I ask you, holds the dear old thing together?
BRANDER. Urgh! What a rotten song! That's political blether!
   You should thank God every night, and every morning, too,
   That the Holy Roman Empire's nothing to do with you!
   I pity the poor sod who's got to be   2095
   Emperor or Chancellor, that's not the job for me.
   Still, someone's got to be the boss round here;
   We'll have a drinking contest, wine or beer—
   The last one standing who can hold a glass
   Will be the Pope, and we'll all kiss his arse.   2100

FROSCH. [*sings*] Oh nightingale, fly to my love,
   A thousand kisses for my turtle dove.
SIEBEL. Not for mine there ain't, don't give me all that crap!
FROSCH. A thousand kisses—just you shut your trap!

   [*sings*] Open up! The coast is clear.   2105
   Open up! Your lover's here.
   Slide the bolt when morning's near.
SIEBEL. Yes, go on, tell us all about her, sing her praises!
   One day the laugh will be on you.
   She led me on, the bitch—you'll get the treatment too.   2110
   I'd give her a hobgoblin, she can go to blazes
   Or meet him at the crossroads—he'd know what to do.

A randy goat who's been up on the Brocken could
Give her a galloping for all I care.
A normal decent bloke is much too good   2115
For her, the little tart. It's just not fair.
I'll smash her window with a brick before
I send her any kisses, that's for sure.
BRANDER. [*banging on the table*] Now then! Now then! Just let it be!
I know a thing or two, you'll all agree.   2120
Some people here appear, unless I'm wrong,
To be in love, and so it falls to me
To serenade these lovers with a song.
So here's a new one I've just written for us—
And you can all join in and sing the chorus.   2125

[*he sings*] In a cellar once there was a rat
Who lived off lard and butter.
She grew and grew, she got as fat
As Doctor Martin Luther.
The cook put poison down the drain,   2130
And soon she felt an awful pain—
As if love's dart had stuck her!
CHORUS. [*exuberantly*]
As if love's dart had stuck her!
BRANDER. She twitched as if she'd had a fit
And drank from every puddle,   2135
She chewed and scratched and gnawed and bit,
Her wits were in a muddle.
She jumped till she could jump no more,
And very soon lay at death's door—
As if love's dart had stuck her!   2140
CHORUS. As if love's dart had stuck her!
BRANDER. In panic then at break of day
She ran into the kitchen,
And by the fireside she lay
In agony a-twitchin'.   2145
The cook just laughed and said 'Oh my,
That rat is surely going to die—
As if love's dart had stuck her.'
CHORUS. As if love's dart had stuck her!
SIEBEL. Whatever are you laughing at?   2150
Well, I don't think it's very nice
To go and poison that poor rat.
BRANDER. I take it you're quite fond of rats and mice?
ALTMAYER. Poor Siebel here, he's getting bald and fat,

And love has made him suffer terribly.   2155
He's gone all soft, and so that rat
Reminds him of himself, you see.

FAUST and MEPHISTOPHELES

MEPHISTO. It's most important you should be
    In entertaining company,
    And see the common folk at play;   2160
    For this lot, every day's a holiday.
    They're pretty witless, but they have their fun;
    They drink a lot, and like small cats they run
    In circles chasing their own tails—and then
    Next day they have a hangover again.   2165
    As long as their credit with the landlord's good,
    They're quite a happy little brotherhood.
BRANDER. These two are on a journey of some kind—
    There's something odd about the way they're dressed.
    I'll bet they've just arrived in town today.   2170
FROSCH. You're right, they've come to Leipzig, it's the best!
    They call it Little Paris, 'cause we're so refined.
SIEBEL. They're strangers—but what sort of folk are they?
FROSCH. Leave it to me! We'll have a drop to drink,
    And I'll soon worm it out of them, you'll see—   2175
    Easy as pulling milk-teeth, I should think.
    They look like aristocrats to me,
    They've got that surly stuck-up sort of look.
BRANDER. Get on! They're cheapjacks from the fair!
ALTMAYER.   Maybe.
FROSCH. Just watch me, I'll soon have them on the hook!   2180
MEPHISTO. [to Faust] These people never know the Devil's in the place,
    Even when they're looking at him face to face.
FAUST. Good evening, gentlemen!
SIEBEL.   The same to you.
    [aside, looking askance at MEPHISTOPHELES]
    That fellow's got a limp—look at his shoe.
MEPHISTO. We'll join you at your table, if we may.   2185
    If we can't get a decent drink, at least we can
    Enjoy your conversation, anyway.
ALTMAYER. You seem to be a very choosy man.
FROSCH. When you left Rippach, was it late at night?
    You'll have had supper with old Hans there, right?   2190
MEPHISTO. No, we didn't call on him today,
    But when we saw him last, he had a lot to say

About his cousins who live over here,
And told us we should wish them all good cheer.

[he bows to Frosch

ALTMAYER. [*aside*] So much for you—he knows the joke!
SIEBEL.   He's pretty fly!   2195
FROSCH. Just wait a bit, I'll have him by and by.
MEPHISTO. I thought I heard—correct me if I'm wrong—
    Some well-trained voices raised in song.
    It must be fine to hear the echoes ring
    Around this splendid vaulting when you sing.   2200
FROSCH. I suppose you think you're quite a virtuoso?
MEPHISTO. Oh no! I love it, but my voice is only so-so.
ALTMAYER. Give us a song!
MEPHISTO.   I'll give you three or four.
SIEBEL. But let's have one we haven't heard before!
MEPHISTO. We've just come from abroad, we haven't been back long—   2205
    From Spain, the lovely land of wine and song.

    [*sings*] Once upon a time there was a king,
    Who had a great big flea—
FROSCH. Did you hear what he said? A great big flea!
    I wouldn't ask a flea to live with me!   2210

MEPHISTO. [*sings*] Once upon a time there was a king,
    Who had a great big flea.
    He loved him more than anything,
    More than a son did he.
    He said to his tailor, listen to me—   2215
    Get busy with tucks and stitches;
    Just measure him up and make my flea
    A pair of silken breeches!
BRANDER. You'd better tell the tailor, too—
    Just measure him good and proper,   2220
    'cause if there's any creases, you
    Will surely get the chopper!

MEPHISTO. So soon that flea was kitted out,
    In finest velvet dressed,
    With silks and ribbons fitted out,   2225
    And medals on his chest.
    They gave him a knighthood, called him Sir—
    He really was a swell;
    And all of his relations were
    Created peers as well.   2230

The court was in a dreadful stew,
They weren't allowed to fight 'em;
The Queen and all her ladies, too—
The fleas knew where to bite 'em!
They itched and scratched, but not a man   2235
Could harm the little blighters.
But we can catch 'em if we can,
And squash 'em when they bite us!

CHORUS. [*exuberantly*]
But we can catch 'em if we can,
And squash 'em when they bite us!   2240
FROSCH. Bravo! Bravo! Very fine!
SIEBEL. That's how to deal with fleas, it never fails!
BRANDER. You squash 'em in between your fingernails!
ALTMAYER. Here's to freedom! Here's to wine!
MEPHISTO. I'd gladly drink a toast to freedom—but I fear   2245
I just can't drink the wine you get round here.
SIEBEL. Don't let us hear that kind of talk again!
MEPHISTO. Well, if I didn't think the landlord would complain,
I'd offer our respected guests a choice selection
Of some of the best wines in our collection.   2250
SIEBEL. Don't worry about that, I'll see to him.
FROSCH. If you provide us with a drop of the right stuff,
We'll be quite happy; but you must give us enough.
I like a glass that's full right to the brim,
And then I can appreciate it properly.   2255
ALTMAYER. [*aside*] These guys are Rhinelanders, if you ask me.
MEPHISTO. Fetch me a gimlet!
BRANDER.   Now what's all this for?
I suppose you left your barrels just outside the door?
ALTMAYER. The landlord's tools are in a basket over there.

MEPHISTOPHELES *takes the gimlet*

MEPHISTO. [*to Frosch*] Well, what can I offer you then, Sir? 2260
FROSCH. What do you mean? What wines have you got? Where?
MEPHISTO. It's up to you—just say which you prefer.
ALTMAYER. [*to Frosch*] Licking your lips already then, you greedy swine?
FROSCH. Well, my choice would be something from the Rhine.
The fatherland produces the best wine.   2265

MEPHISTOPHELES *bores a hole in the table where* FROSCH *is sitting*

MEPHISTO. We need some stoppers—get some wax here, quick!
ALTMAYER. Oh God, it's just another conjuring trick.

MEPHISTO. [*to Brander*] And you?

BRANDER.   Champagne, if it's not too much trouble—
And nice and fizzy, 'cause I like to see it bubble!

> MEPHISTOPHELES *bores a hole. Someone has meanwhile made*
> *the wax stoppers and plugs the holes.*

BRANDER. You must admit sometimes, I know it's sad,   2270
But foreign stuff is really not that bad.
Us Germans just can't stand the Frogs, but then
We like to drink their wine now and again.

SIEBEL. [*as Mephistopheles approaches him*]
I must say, I don't like my wine too dry.
Have you got something nice and sweet to try?   2275

MEPHISTO. [*bores a hole*] I've just the thing for you—a good Tokay!

ALTMAYER. Now gentlemen, be honest, look me in the eye;
Don't play your tricks on us, we're not so dumb.

MEPHISTO. Play tricks on such distinguished guests? Oh, come!
I wouldn't dream of taking such a liberty.   2280
But tell me, quick, what can I offer you?
I'm sure you'd like a taste of something, too.

ALTMAYER. Oh, anything is good enough for me.

MEPHISTO. [*with mysterious gestures*]
Luscious fruit the grapevine bears,
Curly horns the billy-goat wears;   2285
Juice comes from the wooden vine—
A wooden table can give us wine.
Just believe, and you will see
Nature's deepest mystery!
Now draw the plugs and let it pour!   2290

> *They draw the plugs, and the chosen wine flows into each glass.*

ALL. Fountains of wine! There's wine galore!

MEPHISTO. Be careful! Not a drop must fall upon the floor!

> *They drink again and again*

ALL. [*sing*] We're all as pissed as cannibals,
And happy as pigs in clover!

MEPHISTO. Man is born free—and how he loves his liberty!   2295

FAUST. I want to go, there's nothing here for me.

MEPHISTO. Just watch a while, and you will see
A demonstration of man's bestiality.

SIEBEL. [*drinks clumsily, the wine spills on the floor and turns
to flame*] Help! I'm on fire! Help! These are flames from hell!

MEPHISTO. [*addressing the flame*]
    Down, friendly element! Obey my spell.   2300
    [*to the drinkers*] That was just a little taste of purgatory.
SIEBEL. What's going on here? Nobody does that to me!
    You don't know how unfriendly I can be.
FROSCH. Don't try that one on us again!
ALTMAYER. We need to get this bloke outside, and quick.   2305
SIEBEL. You have the cheek to walk in here, and then
    You try to scare us with that stupid trick!
MEPHISTO. Quiet, you old wine-tub!
SIEBEL.   You beanpole!
    He's trying to insult us now as well!
    Just wait, we'll kick you right back down to hell.   2310
ALTMAYER. [*pulls one of the plugs out of the table; a flame shoots up at him*]
    Help! I'm burning!
SIEBEL.   Sorcery! Don't let him
    Scarper, he's an outlaw, he's fair game. Let's get him!

They draw their knives and advance on MEPHISTOPHELES

MEPHISTO. [*with a solemn gesture*]
    Confuse the eye, deceive the ear,
    Make a different scene appear.
    Be there and here!   2315

They stand amazed and look at each other

ALTMAYER. Where am I? What a lovely place!
FROSCH. Vineyards! I'm seeing things!
SIEBEL.   Grapes right in front of your face!
BRANDER. Underneath the leaves here I can see
    A luscious bunch of grapes, and all for me!

He takes hold of Siebel's nose. The others do the same
to each other and raise their knives.

MEPHISTO. [*as above*] Illusion, let them be! I hope that shows   2320
    The lot of you you don't mess with the Devil!

He disappears with FAUST; *the drinkers let each other go.*

SIEBEL. What is it?
ALTMAYER.   Eh?
FROSCH.   Is that your nose?
BRANDER. [*to Siebel*] And I've got yours! This isn't on the level.
ALTMAYER. I felt a shock, and then I seemed to freeze.
    Get me a chair, I feel weak in the knees.   2325

FROSCH. But what the hell was going on just then?
SIEBEL. Where is he? If I see that bloke again
He won't perform his tricks here any more.
ALTMAYER. I saw him ride out of the door
Astride a barrel—well, that's what I thought I saw. 2330
I just can't move my feet, they feel like lead.
[turning to the table]
D'you think there's any more wine left in there?
SIEBEL. It was a trick. We've all been fooled. Let's go to bed.
FROSCH. But I did drink some wine, I swear.
BRANDER. And what about those grapes we saw? 2335
ALTMAYER. And people say they don't believe in magic any more!

A WITCH'S KITCHEN

*A low hearth with a large cauldron on the fire. In the steam rising
from it various shapes can be seen. A female monkey sits by the
cauldron and skims it, taking care not to let it boil over. The male
monkey sits and warms himself by the fire with his young ones. The walls
and ceiling are decorated with the weird paraphernalia of witchcraft.*

FAUST *and* MEPHISTOPHELES

FAUST. These magic spells and tricks of yours repel me!
You think I'll find recuperation, then,
Here in this bedlam, in this witch's den?
You think an ancient crone can tell me 2340
How I'm going to shed some thirty years,
Or brew some potion that will make me young again?
But you have nothing else to offer, it appears,
And you have only raised my hopes in vain.
Is there no natural remedy, has no great mind 2345
Devised an elixir to meet my need?
MEPHISTO. My friend, this ranting isn't very clever.
There is a natural way to make you young, indeed—
But that's another story altogether,
From a mysterious book of a quite different kind. 2350
FAUST. Well, tell me then.
MEPHISTO. The other way is cheap,
It needs no medicine and no magic. You just go
Out into the fields, you dig and hoe,
And plough and harrow, sow and reap;
You keep yourself and all your thoughts confined 2355

Within the limits of your small domain,
Take nourishment of the most frugal kind,
Live as a beast among your beasts, and don't disdain
To fertilize the land you work with your own dung.
That's the best way, believe me—you will find   2360
You'll live for eighty years, and still be young!
FAUST. I'm just not used to it, I couldn't stand
    A narrow life like that, it's not for me—
    And I could never work upon the land.
MEPHISTO. Then you must take the witch's remedy!   2365
FAUST. But does it have to be this ancient crone?
    Why can't you brew a potion of your own?
MEPHISTO. You don't think I've got that much time to spare!
    I've rather more important things to do, indeed.
    It's not just skill and knowledge that you need,   2370
    But time and patience, and a lot of care.
    The spirit must ferment for many years until
    The mixture is mature and powerful enough,
    And then it's ready to distil.
    The witches can do all that tedious stuff—   2375
    The Devil hasn't got the knack, although
    The Devil taught them everything they know.

                                        [*he sees the animals*

    Look, what a charming family!
    This is the servant, that's the maid, I see.
    [*to the animals*] And your dear mistress, where is she?   2380
ANIMALS. Can't see you,
    Gone to a do
    Up the chimney-flue!
MEPHISTO. Out gallivanting! How long will she be?
ANIMALS. As long as it takes to warm a paw.   2385
MEPHISTO. [*to Faust*] How do you like this pretty pair?
FAUST. The most repulsive animals I ever saw!
MEPHISTO. Oh come, my friend, that's hardly fair;
    I like their lively repartee.
    [*to the animals*] So tell me, little imps from hell,   2390
    What have you got in that foul brew?
ANIMALS. We're cooking watery beggars' stew.
MEPHISTO. You'll have a lot of customers—I hope they like the smell.

MALE MONKEY. [*approaches Mephistopheles ingratiatingly*]
    Let's throw the dice,
    It would be nice   2395
    To have a pot

308

Of gold, and then
I'd have a lot
Of sense again.
MEPHISTO. How happy would this little monkey be   2400
  To have a winning ticket on the lottery!

> *Meanwhile the young monkeys roll a large ball around.*

THE MALE MONKEY. The world's so small,
  It's like a ball,
  Up and down
  It rolls around.   2405
  It gleams like brass,
  It's brittle as glass.
  It shines like tin,
  It's hollow within.
  I live, but you,   2410
  My son, beware
  The danger there;
  You must die too.
  It's made of clay,
  It'll break one day.   2415
MEPHISTO. And what's this sieve?
THE MALE MONKEY. [*takes down the sieve*]
  If you're a thief, it'll give
  You away.

> *He runs to the female monkey and makes her look through it.*

  Look through the sieve!
  It's my belief he's a thief,   2420
  But his name you mustn't say.
MEPHISTO. [*approaching the fire*] And what's in this pan?
THE TWO ANIMALS. That's a pot,
  You silly clot!
  He can't tell a pot from a pan!   2425
MEPHISTO. You cheeky pair!
THE MALE MONKEY. Here, take this fan
  And sit in the chair!

> *He makes* MEPHISTOPHELES *sit down.* FAUST *has meanwhile been standing
> in front of a mirror, moving towards it and stepping away again.*

FAUST. What is this heavenly vision that I see
  Reflected in the magic glass in front of me?   2430
  Oh Love, lend me your wings to spread them wide
  And fly me swiftly to her side!

Alas, when I approach her, when I dare
To reach out to that lovely vision there,
The image blurs and fades into the air!   2435
How is it possible, can any woman be
So beautiful, her shape so heavenly?
Shall I find anything on earth so fair?
In this recumbent body do I see
The very essence of all paradisal bliss?   2440
MEPHISTO. Of course—if God toils for six days without a break
And then congratulates himself, you'd think he'd make
A sight worth looking at like this.
Well, go ahead and feast your eyes. I can provide
A sweetheart for you just like her,   2445
And you shall have her—or, if you prefer,
You might be glad to take her as your bride!

> FAUST *continues to gaze into the mirror.*
> MEPHISTOPHELES *lounges in his chair and plays with the fan.*

MEPHISTO. I sit here like a monarch on his throne;
I've got my sceptre, but no crown to call my own.

> THE ANIMALS *have meanwhile been up to all sorts of strange antics.*
> *They bring* MEPHISTOPHELES *a crown with loud screeches.*

Oh Sir, if you could,   2450
Please mend the crown
With sweat and blood.

> *They fumble and drop the crown. It breaks in two,*
> *and they dance round with the pieces.*

You clumsy clown!
We chatter and curse
And speak in verse.   2455
FAUST. [*looking at the mirror*]
I'm driven to distraction at this sight!
MEPHISTO. [*pointing to the animals*]
I must admit, my own head feels unsteady, too.

ANIMALS. If we get it right
Why, then we might
Think just like you!   2460
FAUST. [*as above*] My heart's on fire, I just can't stay
In here. Come on, let's get away!
MEPHISTO. [*as above*] You've got to hand it to the little beast—
He's quite a poet, and his verses rhyme, at least.

The cauldron, which the She-Monkey has neglected, starts to boil over;
a great flame shoots up the chimney. THE WITCH *comes tumbling*
down through the flames, screaming horribly.

WITCH. Ow! Ow! Ow! Ow!   2465
    A curse on you, you bloody sow!
    You let the cauldron boil, you've burnt me now!
    You stupid cow!   [*she sees Faust and Mephistopheles*

    So who are you?
    And you as well?   2470
    Where did you two
    Get in here, how?
    I'll shrivel you
    With fire from hell!

She thrusts the ladle into the cauldron and sprays flame at FAUST,
MEPHISTOPHELES *and the animals. The animals whimper.*

MEPHISTO. [*takes the other end of the fan and lashes out at the pots and glasses*]
    Take that, and that!   2475
    I'll spill your brew
    And smash your glasses flat!
    You carrion, you old bat,
    I'll call the tune for you
    To whistle to.   2480
    [THE WITCH *retreats in fury and terror*]
    You skeleton, you gargoyle, can't you recognize
    Your lord and master right before your eyes?
    Why should I stop, why not smash you to bits as well,
    Thrash you and your demon monkeys back to hell?
    Doesn't the red doublet call for more respect?   2485
    And can't you see my face, you loathsome dame?
    You see this cockerel's feather? Do you expect
    Me to announce myself by name?
WITCH. Oh Sir, forgive my rude reception, pray,
    I didn't see your cloven hoof at all—   2490
    And your two ravens, where are they?
MEPHISTO. Well, this time we'll forget our little brawl.
    It's been some time now since I went away.
    We haven't seen each other for a while,
    And these days fashions change from year to year—   2495
    Even the Devil has to change his style.
    Your northern Gothic Devil's out of date, I fear,
    I just can't wear a tail or horns round here.

But I can't go without my foot, I wish I could—
It doesn't do my reputation any good.   2500
And so for years, as many young men do,
I've worn a fashionably built-up shoe.
WITCH. [*dancing*] I'm all of a dither, I could throw a fit—
Squire Satan here! That's really made my day.
MEPHISTO. That name's not to be mentioned, by the way.   2505
WITCH. Why? What the devil's wrong with it?
MEPHISTO. It only comes in fairy stories nowadays.
But even so, humanity's no better off—
The Evil One has gone, they've kept their evil ways.
Just call me Baron, that will do for me—   2510
I move in the best circles now, I'm quite a toff;
I think you know my noble pedigree,
I've got a coat of arms as well—this is my crest!

[*he makes an obscene gesture*

WITCH. [*laughs immoderately*]
Ha Ha! Ha Ha! Yes, that's what you do best!
You're still the same rogue that you always were.   2515
MEPHISTO. [*to Faust*] Just take a note of this, my friend, and you
Will know the way to deal with crones like her.
WITCH. Now tell me, gentlemen, what can I do?
MEPHISTO. We want a glassful of your special brew—
But one that's been a long time on the shelf.   2520
Its strength increases with the years, I know.
WITCH. Of course! Here's one I brewed up long ago,
I often take a drop of it myself.
It doesn't smell at all bad, I assure you—
I'd be delighted to mix up a cupful for you.   2525
[*aside to Mephistopheles*]
But if he's not prepared, this stuff could fuck him up;
A single drop could kill him on the spot.
MEPHISTO. Well, he's a friend of mine, I need to buck him up,
So let him have the very best you've got.
Now draw your circle, say your magic spell,   2530
Give him a proper dose and make him well!

THE WITCH *with weird gestures draws a circle and puts strange objects in it.*
Meanwhile the glasses start ringing and the cauldron makes a musical sound.
Finally she brings a large book, makes the monkeys stand in the circle,
and uses one of them as a lectern. The others hold torches.
She beckons FAUST *to her.*

FAUST. [*to Mephistopheles*] Oh no, what is this rabid stuff?
These signs and gestures are absurd!

I hate this crazy ritual, I've heard
   It all before, I know it well enough.   2535
MEPHISTO. Don't take it all so seriously! You know
   It's not for real, it's just for show.
   She needs some mumbo-jumbo, as all doctors do,
   To make her potion work—it's nothing new.

He pushes FAUST *into the circle.* THE WITCH *begins to recite*
solemnly from the book.

WITCH. So hear me, then!   2540
   From one make ten,
   And let two be,
   The same with three—
   You're rich, you see!
   The four is nix,   2545
   From five and six
   The witch can mix
   A seven and eight,
   That's got it straight!
   From nine make one,   2550
   And ten is none.
   That's the witches' one-times-one!
FAUST. The old woman's raving now, she's had a fit.
MEPHISTO. There's plenty more of it to go,
   The whole damn book is full of it.   2555
   I've wasted time on it myself, so I should know.
   I've always found that you can fox
   A wise man or a fool with paradox.
   It's an old trick, but it works all the same,
   And every age has tried time and again   2560
   To spread not truth, but error and obscurity,
   By making three of one and one of three.
   And so the fools can preach and teach quite undisturbed—
   Who wants to argue with them? Let them wander on;
   Most men believe that when they hear a simple word,   2565
   There must be some great meaning there to ponder on.

WITCH. [*still reading*] The mystery
   Of alchemy
   From all the world is hidden.
   But if it's sought   2570
   Without a thought,
   Then it will come unbidden!
FAUST. What is this nonsense that she's spouting for us?

313

She's giving me a headache with her blether.
It's like a hundred thousand idiots in chorus   2575
All gibbering and chattering together.
MEPHISTO. Enough, most excellent of Sibyls, stop!
Just bring your potion over here, and please
Be sure to fill the bowl right to the top.
The stuff won't hurt him, let him drink his fill,   2580
For he's a man with several degrees—
He's drunk a lot before and not been ill.

> THE WITCH *with much ceremonial pours the liquid into a bowl;*
> *as* FAUST *sets it to his lips, a gentle flame rises from it.*

MEPHISTO. Down with it, quickly! Come on, drink the brew,
And that will make your heart feel young again.
If you rub shoulders with the Devil, then   2585
A little bit of fire shouldn't worry you.

> THE WITCH *breaks the circle.* FAUST *steps out of it.*

MEPHISTO. You must keep moving now, so off we go!
WITCH. I hope my little mouthful puts you right!
MEPHISTO. [*to the Witch*] I owe you one for this; just let me know—
I'll see you at the next Walpurgis Night.   2590
WITCH. Here's a song for you; you sing it twice a day—
It heightens the effect enormously, they say.
MEPHISTO. [*to Faust*] Come on now, quickly, you must move about;
You've got to sweat the potion out
So it works through your system all the way.   2595
Then you'll be able to appreciate your leisure,
And all the more intensely feel the pleasure
When Cupid stirs you up and lights your fire.
FAUST. Let me look in that mirror just once more!
That lovely woman's all that I desire.   2600
MEPHISTO. No, leave that phantom, and I promise you'll enjoy
A real woman as you never have before.
[*aside*] A drop of that stuff in your guts, my boy,
And every woman looks like Helen of Troy.

A STREET

FAUST. MARGARETA *walks by.*

FAUST. Fair lady, you are all alone;   2605
May I take your arm and see you home?

MARGARETA. I'm not a lady, nor am I fair,
    And I can find my own way there.

                       [*she pulls herself away and goes*

FAUST. That girl is just so lovely, she
    Has really captivated me.   2610
    Demure and virtuous, you can tell—
    But with an impish look as well.
    And such red lips and cheeks so bright,
    How could you ever forget that sight!
    The bashful look she had just now,   2615
    It touched my heart, I can't say how.
    She sent me packing, and quite right—
    But that's what gave me such delight!

MEPHISTOPHELES *enters*

FAUST. I've got to have that girl, d'you hear?
MEPHISTO. Which one?
FAUST.   The one that just went by.   2620
MEPHISTO. But she came straight from church! I fear
    The priest just gave her the all clear.
    I listened to them on the sly;
    She's just too innocent, I guess—
    She had nothing whatever to confess.   2625
    I can't touch her, she's far too pure.
FAUST. But she's over fourteen, that's for sure.
MEPHISTO. My, what a lecher we've become!
    He thinks he can pick them one by one.
    His head's so turned by his conceit   2630
    He thinks they'll all fall at his feet.
    It's not as simple as all that.
FAUST. Yes, you can preach and you can scoff,
    But spare me all that moral chat,
    And just you listen carefully: 2635
    If you can't get that girl for me,
    And by tonight, I tell you, we
    Are finished, and the deal is off.
MEPHISTO. Be reasonable, you randy beast.
    I'll need a good two weeks at least   2640
    To sniff around and see what's what.
FAUST. I don't need you to show the way;
    I wouldn't take more than a day
    To bed a little girl like that.
MEPHISTO. You're getting a bit French, my friend!   2645
    Why are you so impatient, though?

You mustn't rush these things, you know—
You'll get your pleasure in the end.
Take time to talk her round to it,
Impress her, flatter her a bit.   2650
Soften her up with little advances—
That's how Italians get their chances.
FAUST. I can do without all that.
MEPHISTO. But seriously, I tell you flat,
You can't just have that girl today;   2655
You've got to plan, prepare the way.
You'll never get in there by force—
We'll think of a more subtle course.
FAUST. Get me something of hers to keep,
Show me where she lies asleep,   2660
Get me a scarf that's touched her breast,
A garter, anything she's possessed!
MEPHISTO. Well, I'll do everything I can
To help you on your lovesick way.
We'll not waste time; I have a plan   2665
To take you to her room today.
FAUST. And shall I see her? Have her?
MEPHISTO.   No.
Tonight she's at a neighbour's, so
For a few minutes you can go
And breathe the atmosphere at leisure,   2670
And dream about your future pleasure.
FAUST. Can we go now?
MEPHISTO.   No, I'll say when.
FAUST. Get me a present for her, then.   [*exit*
MEPHISTO. A present, already? Good! That's what I like to see!
I know a place where there might be   2675
Some buried treasure to be found.
I'll go and take a look around.   [*exit*

EVENING

A small, tidy room

MARGARETA. [*plaiting and tying up her hair*]
I wonder who that man could be
Who stopped today and spoke to me.
A handsome gentleman he was,   2680
A nobleman, I'm sure, because

316

He had a certain air, I knew—
And he was very forward, too.   [*exit*

Enter MEPHISTOPHELES *and* FAUST

MEPHISTO. You can come in now, the coast is clear.
FAUST. [*after a pause*] Just leave me for a moment here.   2685
MEPHISTO. [*prying around*]
   Tidier than most girls are, it would appear.   [*exit*
FAUST. [*gazing around him*] The gentle light of evening falls
   Into this sanctuary. Within these walls
   Love's pangs clutch at your heart, but you
   Must still your cravings with hope's meagre dew.   2690
   This peaceful homestead seems to breathe
   A sense of order and content.
   Such poverty is wealth indeed,
   And there is bliss in such imprisonment!

He throws himself into the leather chair by the bed.

   How many generations has this seat   2695
   Borne through all the years of joy and care!
   Her forebears sat upon this very chair,
   A throng of children playing at their feet.
   Perhaps my love, when Christmastime was near,
   With pious thanks and childish cheeks so sweet   2700
   Would kiss the feeble hand that rested here.
   Dear child, I sense your presence all around me,
   Integrity and order everywhere.
   The traces of your daily tasks surround me;
   The table that you set with loving care,   2705
   The sand you scattered on the flagstones there.
   One touch of your dear hand, and in a trice
   This humble dwelling is a paradise.
   And here! [*he raises the curtain round the bed*]
      Ah, what a shiver of delight!
   Here I could sit for hours and dwell   2710
   On dreaming nature's magic spell
   That fashioned that angelic sight.
   As she lay here, the glowing surge
   Of life pulsed in her gentle breast,
   And here a pure creative urge   2715
   God's image on the child impressed.

   And you! What brought you to her door?
   What do you want? Why is your heart so sore?

317

What feelings hold you in their sway?
Ah Faust, poor fool, I fear you've lost your way.   2720

Is there some magic spell around me?
I lusted for her, and I find
A dream of love comes to confound me.
Are we the playthings of a breath of wind?

And what if she should come while you are here?   2725
You'd answer for your recklessness, and all
Your bold bravado would just disappear—
Abject and sighing at her feet you'd fall.
MEPHISTO. Quickly! She just came through the gate.
FAUST. I'll never come back here again. Let's go!   2730
MEPHISTO. Here is a box of jewels—just feel its weight;
    I got it from—well, from a place I know.
    Put it in this cupboard here; I swear
    She'll fall into a faint, your little dove.
    The finery I put in there   2735
    Was meant to win another woman's love—
    But then, they're all just kids at heart.
FAUST. I don't know if I should.
MEPHISTO.   Oh please, don't start!
    D'you want to keep it for yourself? Then,
    Lecherous Sir, I beg of you,   2740
    Think what you really want to do,
    And please don't waste my time again.
    I hope you're not a miser, too!
    I rack my brains and toil away—
    [*he puts the casket in the cupboard and locks it up again*]
    Now, come with me!   2745
    So you can have your wicked way
    With that sweet child, and all I see
    Is the sort of miserable expression
    You wear before you give a lesson,
    As if physics and metaphysics too   2750
    Were standing there in front of you.
    Come on!   [*exeunt*

MARGARETA *with a lamp*

It feels so close and stuffy here,   [*she opens the window*
And yet outside it's not so warm.
I don't know why, I feel so queer—   2755
I wish my mother were at home.

318

You silly girl, you're shivering—
You really are a timid thing!
[*she sings as she undresses*]

There was a king in Thule, he
Was faithful to the grave.   2760
To him his dying lady
A golden goblet gave.

He would drink from no other,
It was his dearest prize;
Remembering his lover   2765
The tears would fill his eyes.

And on his death-bed lying,
To his beloved son
He left his lands, but dying
He gave the cup to none.   2770

And many a faithful vassal
And knight sat by his knee
In his ancestral castle
Beside the northern sea.

One last time he drank up then,   2775
His cheeks with wine aglow,
And hurled the sacred cup then
Into the waves below.

He watched it falling, sinking
Beneath the ocean deep;   2780
Then he had done with drinking—
His eyes were closed in sleep.

    She opens the cupboard to put her clothes away, and sees the casket.

Whoever put that casket there?
I locked the cupboard up, I swear.
That's very strange! What can it be?   2785
Perhaps it was left as surety,
And mother lent some money for it.
And here's a ribbon with a key—
Well, really, I can't just ignore it.
But what is this? Ah, glory be!   2790
I've never seen such jewels before.
All this expensive finery
Was made for some great lady, that's for sure.

319

I wonder how they'd look on me?
But who can it belong to, though? 2795

She tries on some jewels and stands in front of the mirror.

I'd love to have these earrings—oh,
What a different girl you are!
But youth and beauty, what's it worth?
It's not your fortune on this earth;
It doesn't get you very far. 2800
They flatter you and call you pretty,
But it's gold they crave,
For gold they slave—
And poverty they pity!

AN AVENUE

FAUST *pacing up and down, deep in thought,*
then MEPHISTOPHELES

MEPHISTO. By all frustrated love! By all hell's fires, and worse! 2805
    I wish I knew more dreadful things by which to curse!
FAUST. What is it now? What's biting you today?
    I never saw a face as black as yours.
MEPHISTO. I'd go to the Devil right away—
    That is, if I weren't one myself, of course. 2810
FAUST. Has something happened to disturb your mind?
    This snarling and spitting suits you well, I find.
MEPHISTO. That box of jewels I got for Margaret—
    A bloody priest has snaffled it!
    Her mother found the jewels last night— 2815
    They gave her quite a nasty fright;
    That woman smells brimstone a mile away,
    She's forever kneeling down to pray.
    She only needs to sniff a chair
    To tell the Devil's been sitting there. 2820
    As for our jewels, well, that's clear—
    She knows there's something fishy here.
    'Gretchen', she says, 'ill-gotten gold
    Corrupts the heart, ensnares the soul.
    The Blessed Virgin must have this hoard, 2825

And manna from heaven be our reward.'
Poor little Gretchen nearly weeps—
She thought her gift horse was for keeps,
And whoever put it in her drawer
Can't be all that bad, for sure.   2830
Her mother summons up the priest;
He'd hardly heard her out, the beast,
When he began his peroration:
'A Christian act! For there's no question
That victory lies in abnegation.   2835
The Church has an excellent digestion;
It's gobbled up countries by the score,
But still has room for a little more.
Only the Holy Church, dear ladies,
Can properly digest the Devil's wages.'   2840
FAUST. That's the way it is, it's true—
    But Jews and kings can do it too.
MEPHISTO. He raked those rings and bangles in
    As if they were just bits of tin;
    He packed them up and took them away   2845
    As if this happened every day.
    'Heaven will surely reward you,' he sighed—
    And they, of course, were greatly edified.
FAUST. And Gretchen?
MEPHISTO.   She's unhappy, too;
    Doesn't know what she ought to do.   2850
    Thinks of her jewels night and day—
    But even more, who put them in her way.
FAUST. The darling girl! It's such a shame.
    Well, go and get more of the same;
    The first ones weren't much, anyway.   2855
MEPHISTO. Oh yes, to you it's just child's play!
FAUST. Now listen, do exactly what I say:
    Get to know her neighbour, act the pimp—
    I never knew the Devil was such a wimp.
    And get more jewels—do it now, today!   2860
MEPHISTO. Your slightest wish is my command, my lord.

                                                          [exit Faust

    That lovesick fool's completely lost his wits;
    Just in case his girlfriend might get bored,
    He'd blow the sun, the moon and all the stars to bits.

                                                             [exit

THE NEIGHBOUR'S HOUSE

MARTHA. [*alone*] May God forgive my husband, he   2865
    Has not done the right thing by me.
    He took off one day on his own,
    He left me flat, and all alone.
    I didn't nag, and never took the huff;
    God knows, I loved him well enough. [*weeping*]   2870
    And if he's dead, I'm in a sorry state—
    I haven't even got a death certificate!
MARGARETA. [*enters*] Oh, Martha!
MARTHA.   Gretchen, what's the matter, pet?
MARGARETA. Oh Martha, I'm in such a sweat;
    There's another box of jewels for me!   2875
    A lovely box, it's made of ebony,
    Such precious things in it, I swear
    They're even finer that the others were.
MARTHA. Don't show them to your mother, then,
    Or else she'll give them to the priest again.   2880
MARGARETA. Look at this necklace! And this ring!
MARTHA. [*dressing her in some jewels*]
    Oh Gretchen, you're a lucky thing!
MARGARETA. I can't wear them in public, that's forbidden,
    Or to church—I'll have to keep them hidden.
MARTHA. Just you come over to my place   2885
    Whenever you like, and put your jewels on,
    See yourself in the mirror and do up your face—
    We'll have our little bit of fun.
    Then maybe at a wedding or a party
    You gradually start to dress a bit more smartly—   2890
    A gold chain first, then pearl drops in your ear;
    We'll tell your mother that they weren't too dear.
MARGARETA. Who could have brought two jewel boxes, though?
    There's something not quite right, I know.

A knock at the door

MARGARETA. Oh God! Is that my mother at the door?   2895
MARTHA. [*peering through the curtain*]
    Come in! It's a man I've never seen before.
MEPHISTO. [*enters*] May I come in? Oh, please excuse me, Miss.
    It's very rude of me to walk straight in like this.

He bows respectfully to MARGARETA

It's Mrs Martha Schwerdlein that I called to see.

MARTHA. How can I help you, Sir? For I am she.   2900

MEPHISTO. [*aside to Martha*] Ah yes, of course, I could have guessed.
But you're entertaining a distinguished guest;
Forgive me, I'll retire right away,
And come again—around noon, shall we say?

MARTHA. [*aloud*] Now, child, there's a compliment for you—   2905
This gentleman thinks you're a lady, too!

MARGARETA. You're quite mistaken, Sir, I fear;
I'm just a girl who lives round here,
And all this finery's not my own.

MEPHISTO. Ah, but it's not the jewels alone;   2910
It's in your bearing, in your gracious smile—
How fortunate that I can stay awhile.

MARTHA. What is your business, may I ask?

MEPHISTO. I only wish I had a happier task.
I hope the messenger won't get the blame;   2915
Your husband's dead, but greets you all the same.

MARTHA. He's dead? The poor man's gone, you say?
My husband's dead! Oh, what a dreadful day!

MARGARETA. Oh Martha dear, please don't despair.

MEPHISTO. Would you like to hear the tragic story?   2920

MARGARETA. I'll never fall in love, I do declare;
I'd die of grief if my love died before me.

MEPHISTO. But joy and grief are never far apart.

MARTHA. Please tell me of my husband's sad demise.

MEPHISTO. Of course, dear lady. Now, where shall I start?   2925
In Padua at St Anthony's he lies,
And in that cool and pleasant spot
He rests for ever in a consecrated plot.

MARTHA. And have you nothing else for me?

MEPHISTO. Oh yes—a serious and solemn plea   2930
To say three hundred Masses for his soul.
But otherwise I fear, dear lady, that is all.

MARTHA. What! Not a single keepsake, not a ring?
What every poor apprentice carries in his kit,
A token of affection, some small thing   2935
He'd rather starve or beg than part with it?

MEPHISTO. Madam, I have to say with great regret,
It wasn't trifling sums that got him into debt.
He saw the error of his ways, it's true—
But then, he blamed it all on bad luck, too.   2940

MARGARETA. I find it sad that fate is so unkind.

I'll pray for him, say lots of Masses for the Dead.
MEPHISTO. You are a lovely child, it must be said.
    Have thoughts of marriage never crossed your mind?
MARGARETA. Oh no, Sir, I can't think of such a thing.   2945
MEPHISTO. If not a husband, what of a lover's charms?
    It is the highest gift that heaven can bring
    To hold such a sweet creature in one's arms.
MARGARETA. That's not the custom in these parts, for shame!
MEPHISTO. Custom or not, it happens all the same.   2950
MARTHA. But tell me about my husband!
MEPHISTO.   Ah yes, I was at his side.
    It was as a good Christian, repenting, that he died.
    Confessed his sins as he lay there upon some filthy straw—
    But then, he had so many he could scarcely keep the score.
    'Alas!' he cried aloud, 'it is a wicked thing I've done,   2955
    To quit my trade, my home, and leave my poor wife all alone!
    It tortures me to think of it, and now before I die
    I pray that she'll forgive my sin.'
MARTHA. The dear man! I've forgiven him.
MEPHISTO. 'But then, God knows,' he told me, 'she was more to blame
    than I.'   2960
MARTHA. The liar! What, he lied when he was at death's door?
MEPHISTO. He was delirious at the end, I'm sure;
    I've seen it happen many times before.
    'I never had a minute's rest,' he said,
    'With her and all her children to be fed,   2965
    And always wanting more—
    I never had the peace to eat my share.'
MARTHA. Had he forgotten all the love and care,
    The way I slaved for him by day and night?
MEPHISTO. Oh no, dear lady, he remembered that all right.   2970
    He told me: 'As we left Valletta Bay,
    I prayed most fervently for wife and children too,
    And heaven heard me, for that very day
    We took a Turkish vessel, who
    Had some of the Great Sultan's wealth on board.   2975
    And as I wasn't backward in the fight,
    When it was over, as was only right,
    I got my proper share of the reward.'
MARTHA. Oh, fancy! Did he bury it, d' you think?
MEPHISTO. Gone with the wind, on women and on drink.   2980
    When he was in Naples feeling lonely,
    A pretty lady took him as a friend,

And she was kind and loving to him, only—
Love left its mark on him right to the end.
MARTHA. The wretch! With children and a wife to feed,   2985
He left us here in poverty and need.
Oh, what a shameless life he led!
MEPHISTO. Well yes, you see—that's why he's dead.
If I were you, if you'll take my advice,
I'd mourn him for a year or so,   2990
And then look round for someone really nice.
MARTHA. I'll never find another like him, though,
I'm sure of that, however hard I try.
He was a scamp, but still I liked him fine.
He never could stay put, I don't know why,   2995
And chasing other women too, and all that wine,
And gambling everything he earned.
MEPHISTO. Well, many couples get on well like that.
If he'd been easy-going, if he'd turned
A blind eye to whatever you were at—   3000
Why, I myself, on that condition
Might be prepared to make a proposition.
MARTHA. Ah, you will have your little joke with me!
MEPHISTO. [aside] It's time to go; this tough old bird
Would take the very Devil at his word.   3005
[to Gretchen] And you, Miss—all alone and fancy-free?
MARGARETA. Sir, what do you mean?
MEPHISTO. [aside]   Sweet innocence of youth!
[aloud] Goodbye then, ladies.
MARGARETA.   Good night!
MARTHA.   No, wait! I need some proof!
I need a death certificate to show
How, when and where my loved one passed away.   3010
I want to put it in the paper, too, you know—
One must do these things properly, I always say.
MEPHISTO. Madam, of course; two witnesses will do
To prove in law that what they say is true.
I have a good friend living near—   3015
He'll tell the magistrate just what you want to hear.
I'll bring him here tonight.
MARTHA.   Oh, do!
MEPHISTO. And this young lady, will she be here too?
He's a fine lad, well-travelled, very charming;
The ladies find his manners quite disarming.   3020
MARGARETA. Oh, I would only blush if we should meet.

MEPHISTO. You needn't blush before a king, my sweet.
MARTHA. Until this evening in the garden, then.
 We shall expect you—shall we say, at ten?

[they all leave

A STREET

FAUST. MEPHISTOPHELES

FAUST. Well, what's the news? Did you get anywhere? 3025
MEPHISTO. Ah, bravo! All on fire—that's what I like to see!
 Soon Gretchen will be yours, I guarantee.
 At Martha's place, this evening—she'll be there.
 That woman's born to be a go-between,
 By far the finest pimp I've ever seen. 3030
FAUST. All the better!
MEPHISTO. There's a small price to pay.
FAUST. Well, one good turn deserves another—so?
MEPHISTO. We have to swear a solemn oath and say
 What's left of her dear husband here below
 Now rests in Padua—at least till Judgement Day. 3035
FAUST. Oh, brilliant! Now we've got to go to Italy.
MEPHISTO. *Sancta simplicitas!* Of course we don't—
 Just swear, and leave the rest to me.
FAUST. You want me to commit perjury? I won't!
MEPHISTO. Oh, what a Holy Joe! Is that your problem, then? 3040
 You mean you've never told a lie before?
 Was it the truth you told your students, when
 You spoke of God, the world, the hearts and minds of men,
 And heaven knows what else that lay beyond your ken,
 When you defined your terms with such authority, 3045
 With brazen confidence and great superiority?
 And if the truth were told, you lied with every breath;
 If you were honest, you'd admit you knew no more
 Of all these matters than of Schwerdlein's death.
FAUST. The Devil always deals in sophistry and lies. 3050
MEPHISTO. Oh yes, with you of course it's otherwise.
 Tomorrow, I suppose, in all sincerity,
 With all the tricks of the seducer's art
 You'll try to capture little Gretchen's heart?
FAUST. And I shall mean it, too.
MEPHISTO. That's as may be. 3055

You'll swear undying love and true emotion,
Assure her of your passionate devotion—
Will that stand up to closer scrutiny?
FAUST. Indeed it will, for that is truly what I feel.
  If I can't find the phrases to confess   3060
  This fevered love that makes my senses reel,
  And search in vain for ways that would express
  This passion burning deep inside me,
  And if I grasp at lofty words to guide me,
  And swear that love's for ever, that it never dies—   3065
  Is that a tawdry pack of Devil's lies?
MEPHISTO. I beg to differ.
FAUST.   You always do, of course,
  So hold your tongue and bottle up your spite.
  You talk and never stop to listen, so perforce
  You're always right.   3070
  I'm tired of all this talk, I'll spare my voice—
  And you are right, because I have no choice.

A GARDEN

MARGARETA *on* FAUST'S *arm,* MARTHA *strolling to and fro
with* MEPHISTOPHELES

MARGARETA. I feel, Sir, that you only speak to me
  So kindly and so condescendingly
  Because a travelled man like you   3075
  Believes it is the proper thing to do.
  My conversation's dull, it is so shaming—
  I can't think why you find it entertaining.
FAUST. One look, one word from you diverts me more
  Than all the wisdom that the world could store.   3080
                               [*he kisses her hand*
MARGARETA. Oh no, how could you? You embarrass me.
  My hands are rough, and unattractive, too;
  It's all the housework that I have to do—
  My mother's so particular, you see.   [*they walk on*
MARTHA. And you, Sir, always travelling, I dare say?   3085
MEPHISTO. Indeed, we visit many different places.
  But then business and duty summon us away,
  And it is sad to leave such friendly faces.
MARTHA. Ah yes, for younger men it can be fun

To roam the world alone and see its ways;   3090
But soon one's years of travelling are done,
And as a lonely bachelor to end one's days—
Why, that's a dismal thought for anyone.

MEPHISTO. A distant prospect that I dread to contemplate.

MARTHA. Then make your plans before it is too late.   3095
                                                        [*they walk on*

MARGARETA. But out of sight, I'll soon be out of mind.
    You're very gracious and polite to me,
    But you have many friends of your own kind
    Far cleverer than I could ever be.

FAUST. Oh dearest! Cleverness isn't all, you know;   3100
    It's often vain and superficial—

MARGARETA.   Oh?

FAUST. While innocence and sweet simplicity
    Are rarely valued as they ought to be.
    Humility and modesty—they
    Are the highest gifts that loving nature gave us, when—   3105

MARGARETA. If you can think of me just now and then.
    I shall have time enough when you're away.

FAUST. And are you often on your own?

MARGARETA. Oh yes, our household's very small, but even so
    It doesn't run itself alone.   3110
    We have no maid, I have to knit and sew
    And cook and clean, all day I'm on my feet;
    My mother wants it all so very neat
    And tidy, too.
    She doesn't really need to scrimp and save at all,   3115
    We have far more than many others do.
    My father left us well provided for—
    A little house, a plot outside the city wall.
    But still, it's very quiet here, it must be said;
    My brother is a soldier in the war,   3120
    My little sister's dead.
    She gave me so much trouble while she lived, and yet
    I'd do it all again for her, the little pet.
    I loved her so.

FAUST.   An angel, if she was like you.

MARGARETA. I brought her up, she loved me dearly too.   3125
    The little thing was born after my father died;
    We feared the worst, my mother was so ill.
    We nursed her, I was always at her side,
    And slowly she recovered, by God's will.

But then she couldn't even think 3130
Of feeding the poor creature at her breast,
And so I had to do my best
And gave it water mixed with milk to drink.
She grew up in my arms, smiled up at me,
And squirmed and wriggled when I held her on my knee. 3135
FAUST. Those must have been such happy times for you!
MARGARETA. Yes, but we often had our troubles, too.
Her cradle always stood beside my bed;
She only had to stir once in the night,
I'd wake up, and she wanted to be fed. 3140
I'd take her into bed with me and hold her tight,
And if she wouldn't settle, out of bed I'd creep,
Walk up and down and rock her back to sleep.
Then in the mornings I would have to sweep
And wash and cook, and go to market, too; 3145
All day and every day I had enough to do.
It's hard work, and there's not much time for fun;
But then, we eat and sleep the better when it's done.

[they walk on

MARTHA. It's hard for women who are all alone;
You bachelors seem quite happy on your own. 3150
MEPHISTO. But it might only take someone like you
To make me see a different point of view.
MARTHA. On all your travels, Sir, you mean to say
You never lost your heart along the way?
MEPHISTO. Proverbially, of course, we're told 3155
A good wife and a home are worth their weight in gold.
MARTHA. But have you met no one for whom you really care?
MEPHISTO. I've always found a civil welcome everywhere.
MARTHA. I mean, have you been seriously committed?
MEPHISTO. To trifle with a woman's heart is not permitted. 3160
MARTHA. Oh, you don't understand!
MEPHISTO.   You mustn't mind;
I understand—that you are very good and kind.

[they walk on

FAUST. My angel, so you knew me at first sight
The moment that I came in here tonight?
MARGARETA. You must have noticed how I hardly dared to look. 3165
FAUST. And you don't mind the liberty I took?
You weren't disturbed by what I had to say
When you came out of church the other day?
MARGARETA. I was put out, I thought it rather rash.

I thought: there's something forward, something brash   3170
About me that this gentleman's detected,
To talk to me like that. It was so unexpected
To be approached so boldly in the street
Like any common girl, it seemed so indiscreet.
I was confused, I must admit, but still   3175
I couldn't bring myself to wish you ill.
And I was angry with myself, because I knew
That I could not feel angry towards you.
FAUST. My sweet love!
MARGARETA.   Wait a moment.
[*she picks a daisy and plucks off the petals one by one*]
FAUST.   What is this?
MARGARETA. You'll laugh at me, it's just a game.
FAUST.   But what?   3180
[*she plucks and murmurs*]
What are you whispering?
MARGARETA. [*half aside*] He loves me—loves me not—
FAUST. You sweet and lovely vision of heaven's bliss!
MARGARETA. [*continues*] Loves me—not—loves me—not—
[*plucking the last petal, joyously*]
He loves me!
FAUST.   Yes, my dear child. Let the flowers spell
The judgement of the gods, for it is this: 3185
He loves you! Loves you more than he can tell!
[*he takes her hands in his*]
MARGARETA. I'm shivering!
FAUST. Oh no, don't tremble! Let this look,
Let one touch of my hands convey
What words cannot express.   3190
Just trust your feelings, don't resist
This ecstasy that has to be for ever!
Ever! To end it would be to despair.
No, it must never, never end!

MARGARETA *presses his hands, tears herself away and runs off.*
He stands for a moment in thought, then follows her.

MARTHA. [*enters*] It's getting dark.
MEPHISTO.   Ah yes, and we must go.   3195
MARTHA. I'd ask you to stay longer, both of you,
But it's a spiteful neighbourhood, you know.
You'd think these folk had nothing else to do
But watch their neighbours like a hawk—
And how they talk!   3200

330

You can't turn round before the whole street knows.
And our young couple?
MEPHISTO.   Fluttered off up there
Like wanton butterflies!
MARTHA.   He seems quite fond of her.
MEPHISTO. And she of him. And that's the way it goes.

A SUMMERHOUSE

MARGARETA *runs in breathless, hides behind the door,*
holds a finger to her lips and peers through a crack in the door.

MARGARETA. He's coming!
FAUST. [*enters*]   Where are you? Don't be such   3205
A tease! [*he kisses her*]
MARGARETA. [*puts her arms round him and returns the kiss*]
Oh dearest man, I do love you so much!

MEPHISTOPHELES *knocks*

FAUST. [*stamps his foot*] Who's there?
MEPHISTO.   A friend.
FAUST.   A beast!
MEPHISTO.   It's time to go, you two.
MARTHA. [*enters*] Yes, Sir, it's late.
FAUST.   May I not come with you?
MARGARETA. What would my mother say! Goodbye!
FAUST.   I'll have to leave you, then.
Goodbye, my love.
MARTHA.   Good night!
MARGARETA.   Until we meet again!   3210
                              [*Faust and Mephistopheles leave*
MARGARETA. Dear God, I'm sure I never heard
A man so clever, so well-bred,
And I can only nod my head
And scarcely say a single word.
It makes me blush, I just can't see   3215
What he finds in a simple girl like me.   [*exit*

FOREST AND CAVERN

FAUST. [*alone*] You gave me, sublime Spirit, gave me all
I asked of you; and it was not in vain

You turned your face upon me in the fire.
You gave me glorious nature as my kingdom,   3220
The power to feel it and delight in it.
No cold encounter, no mere spectacle
You granted me, for nature's very heart
Is like the bosom of a friend revealed.
Creation's ordered scale of life you've shown me;   3225
I learn to know my brother creatures here
In quiet woods, in streams and in the air.
And when the forest shudders in the storm,
The mighty fir-tree falls, and falling tears
Its neighbours with it, crushing all around,   3230
Its thundering echoes booming from the hills—
Then I find refuge in this cavern, where
I see into myself, and in my heart
Deep mysteries and wonders are unveiled.
And when the pure moon rises overhead   3235
Within its soothing beams the silver forms,
The hovering spirits of the past emerge
From mountain crags and mossy woods to ease
The austere pleasure of my contemplation.

But now I see that we can never know   3240
Perfection here on earth. For with this bliss
That brings me ever closer to the gods,
You gave that cold and insolent companion
From whom I can no longer free myself,
Who makes me feel my shame and my disgrace,   3245
And turns your gifts to dross with every breath.
He fans the flames that burn within my heart,
And fires my longing for that lovely form.
I satisfy desire with pleasure, then
In pleasure languish for desire again.   3250
MEPHISTO. [*enters*] This outdoor life is really not for you—
Haven't you grown tired of it yet?
It's all right for a while, but then you get
The urge to go and sample something new.
FAUST. I wish you could find something else to do   3255
Than spoil my day by pestering me here.
MEPHISTO. Why, you can rest all day, and all night too,
As far as I'm concerned; you make yourself quite clear.
I wouldn't miss your company at all,
You're so uncivil, so erratic and ill-bred.   3260

It's no fun being at your beck and call—
I can find better things to do instead.
I can't tell what you want just from your attitude.
FAUST. That's rich! You even want my gratitude
    For ruining what peace I might have had?   3265
MEPHISTO. Poor mortal fool! What kind of life would you have led
    Without my help? You should be glad
    I've cured your whimsical imagination
    Of all that harebrained speculation.
    And if I hadn't intervened, you know,   3270
    You would have left this planet long ago.
    Whatever makes you come here like an owl to brood
    Among these crags and caverns all this time?
    You're like a toad that sucks its food
    From soggy moss and rocks that drip with slime.   3275
    I can't imagine that you're having fun—
    You're still a professor, when all's said and done.
FAUST. Can you not understand what new vitality
    This barren solitude inspires in me?
    Of course, if you had any inkling, you   3280
    Would use your devil's tricks to cheat me of it, too.
MEPHISTO. Oh yes! It must be heavenly to sit the whole night through
    Out on the mountainside among the dew
    Embracing earth and heaven with ecstatic bliss,
    Imagining a god must feel like this,   3285
    Whose spirit penetrates the marrow of the earth,
    Rehearsing in yourself creation's very birth.
    You feel no limits to your grand ambition,
    Love's heady rapture holds you in its sway;
    All earthly crudities just melt away,   3290
    Till finally your lofty intuition
    [*with a gesture*] Ends in—well, I hardly like to say.
FAUST. You are disgusting! Shame on you!
MEPHISTO.   And shame
    On your hypocrisy! You prudes are all the same;
    Chaste ears must never hear us speak about   3295
    What no chaste heart can ever do without.
    In any case, I've really no objection
    If now and then you need a little introspection.
    But you won't stand it long, my friend,
    And you will realise you must   3300
    Escape from it, or you will end
    In madness, horror and disgust.

Enough of that! Your sweetheart sits at home,
She feels shut in, bereft and all alone.
She thinks about you all the day,   3305
And loves you more than she can say.
Your passion overwhelmed her at the start,
Just like a mountain torrent fed by melting snow;
It poured into her unresisting heart—
But now your stream is running very slow.   3310
It would become Monsieur much better, though,
Instead of lording it out in the wild
To go and comfort that poor child,
And give her something to reward her love.
Beside the window in her room she stands,   3315
Watching the clouds as they go by above,
And time hangs very heavy on her hands.
'I wish I were a bird with little wings'
All day and half the night she sings.
Sometimes she's happy, other times she's glad,   3320
Sometimes she can only sit and weep;
Then she'll calm down and go to sleep—
But it's always, always love that makes her sad.
FAUST. You snake! You serpent! You are vile!
MEPHISTO. [*aside*] Yes—and you'll feel my fangs in just a while.   3325
FAUST. You monster, get out of my sight!
    Don't mention her, and let that lovely woman be.
    Don't tempt me with the thought of the delight
    That her sweet body might have given me.
MEPHISTO. What do you want? She thinks you've done a flit—   3330
    And that's at least half true, you must admit.
FAUST. I'm always close to her, no matter where
    I go, and she will be with me forever.
    I envy the very body of the Lord whenever
    She puts it to her lips in prayer.   3335
MEPHISTO. Ah yes! And the two young twins like roes that feed
    Among the lilies—those I envy you indeed.
FAUST. Get out, you pimp!
MEPHISTO.   Come, spare me your derision.
    For God himself approved that laudable vocation;
    When he created girls and lads, he made provision   3340
    To give them opportunity for procreation.
    Get on, let's have less of this gloom!
    You're going to see your girl tonight,
    And not to meet your doom!

FAUST. Though at her breast I might feel heaven's bliss,   3345
   And in her arms the warming passion of her kiss,
   I would still feel the pity of her plight.
   I am accursed, a homeless refugee,
   An aimless outcast driven relentlessly
   Like a cascading torrent over rock and precipice,   3350
   Raging and seething into the abyss.
   And in a peaceful meadow by that stream
   She lived her simple life, her daily round
   And all the childish thoughts that she could dream
   In that small world were safely hedged around.   3355
   And I, whom God has cursed,
   Was not content to thunder
   In a foaming rage and burst
   The tumbling rocks asunder.
   I had to undermine that girl's tranquillity—   3360
   That was the sacrifice that hell required of me.
   What must be done, let it be quickly done,
   Now, Devil, help me end this agony;
   My fearful destiny and hers are one,
   And she is doomed to share my fate with me.   3365
MEPHISTO. Oh, what a boiling stew we're in again!
   Go in and comfort her, my friend.
   A fool like you just needs to lose the plot, and then
   He thinks the world is coming to an end.
   You're quite a devil now—but mind   3370
   You keep your nerve; for there
   Is nothing more deplorable, I find,
   Than a devil who's been driven to despair.

GRETCHEN'S ROOM

GRETCHEN *at the spinning wheel, alone*

My peace is gone,
My heart is sore,   3375
It's gone for ever
And evermore.

Whenever he
Is far away,
The world for me   3380
Is cold and grey.

And my poor head
Is quite bemused,
My scattered wits
Are all confused.   3385

My peace is gone,
My heart is sore,
It's gone for ever
And evermore.

It's him I look for   3390
On the street,
It's only him
I go to meet.

And in his walk,
Such dignity.   3395
His gracious talk
Bewitches me.

And when he smiles
At me, what bliss,
To feel his hand—   3400
And ah, his kiss!

My peace is gone,
My heart is sore,
It's gone for ever
And evermore.   3405

Here in my heart
I long for him,
And if I could
Belong to him,

I'd hold him and kiss him   3410
All the day,
Though in his kisses
I'd melt away!

MARTHA'S GARDEN

MARGARETA, FAUST

MARGARETA. Tell me something, Heinrich.
FAUST.   Gladly, if I can.

MARGARETA. What is your faith? I feel I ought to know.　　　　3415
　　You're such a good and kindly man;
　　You seem to have no true religion, though.
FAUST. Oh, do not ask! You know I love you well, indeed
　　For those I love I'd hazard life and limb,
　　And never seek to hurt their feelings or their creed.　　　　3420
MARGARETA. But that's not right, you must believe in Him!
FAUST. Must we?
MARGARETA.　　　I wish I could persuade you to
　　Respect the Holy Sacraments as I do.
FAUST. I do respect them.
MARGARETA.　　　　　　Yes—but is your faith sincere?
　　You don't go to confession or to Mass, I fear.　　　　3425
　　Do you believe in God?
FAUST.　　　　　　　　My love, who can
　　Say such a thing?
　　Go ask the cleverest priest, the wisest man—
　　Their answers only mock our questioning,
　　And mock us too.
MARGARETA.　　　　You have no faith, I see.　　　　3430
FAUST. Sweet child, you misinterpret me.
　　For who can name,
　　Who can proclaim
　　Belief in Him?
　　Who can reveal　　　　3435
　　He does not feel
　　Belief in Him?
　　All-embracing
　　And all-preserving,
　　Does He not hold　　　　3440
　　And keep us all?
　　Is not the vault of heaven above us,
　　The earth's foundation here below?
　　Do not eternal stars smile down
　　Upon us as they climb the skies?　　　　3445
　　And when I look into your eyes, do you
　　Not feel how all things
　　Flood your heart and mind all through,
　　And weave their everlasting spell
　　Unseen, yet visible beside you?　　　　3450
　　Just let it fill your heart, and when
　　You feel the highest bliss, why, then
　　You call it what you will:

Joy! Heart! Love! God!
I have no name for it;   3455
Feeling is all,
A name's mere sound, a haze that veils
The radiance of heaven from view.
MARGARETA. I daresay that's all very true;
The priest says more or less the same thing, too—   3460
He doesn't put it quite the same way, though.
FAUST. You'll hear it everywhere you go,
As far as heaven's light can reach,
All hearts, all languages will teach
That message; why should I not speak in mine?   3465
MARGARETA. Yes, put like that it all sounds very fine,
But still it doesn't seem quite right; you see,
It's not what I think of as Christianity.
FAUST. Dear child!
MARGARETA.   It's always troubled me
To see you in that person's company.   3470
FAUST. But why?
MARGARETA.   That man you call your friend
Is deeply hateful to me, and I can't pretend
To like him, for in all my life
I never saw a face so grim;
His look goes through me like a knife.   3475
FAUST. My sweet, you mustn't be afraid of him.
MARGARETA. His presence chills the very blood in me.
I always think the best of folk, but he—
Although I long to be with you, I swear,
It makes me shudder when I see him there.   3480
I've thought he was a villain all along—
May God forgive me if I do him wrong.
FAUST. He's odd—no more than many others, though.
MARGARETA. How you can live with him, I just don't know.
He only has to come in here   3485
With such a mocking look, a sneer
About his lips, and you can tell
He cares for nothing, wishes no one well.
It's written on his face, it's plain to see
That he could never love his fellow men.   3490
I feel so safe when you are holding me,
So free, so loving and so warm, but then
I freeze and shiver when I feel his presence.
FAUST. You angel! Ah, what knowing innocence!

338

MARGARETA. It overwhelms me more than I can say. 3495
  I even think, whenever he is here,
  My very love for you might ebb away,
  And I could never pray when he is near.
  That is what really tears my heart in two—
  But Heinrich, you must feel his menace too. 3500
FAUST. You have a loathing for him, that is clear.
MARGARETA. And I must go now.
FAUST.   Ah, my dear,
  If only we could have one hour tonight
  To lie together, hold each other tight.
MARGARETA. If I were on my own, for sure, 3505
  I'd willingly unlock my door.
  My mother sleeps so lightly, though;
  I'd die upon the spot, I know,
  If she should come and find us there.
FAUST. My angel, we can easily prepare 3510
  For that; you only have to take
  This bottle, put three drops into her drink tonight,
  And she'll sleep undisturbed until daylight.
MARGARETA. What would I not do, Heinrich, for your sake?
  You're sure it won't be dangerous for her? 3515
FAUST. My love, would I suggest it if it were?
MARGARETA. Oh dearest man, my love for you is such,
  I would do anything you asked me to.
  For your sake I've already done so much,
  There's little more for me to give to you.   [*exit* 3520
MEPHISTO. [*enters*] The little monkey!
FAUST.   Eavesdropping again, I see.
MEPHISTO. I have been listening most attentively.
  Was that the catechism I heard you reciting?
  I trust Herr Doktor found it to his liking.
  These girls are keen on simple faith and piety, 3525
  They think: if he's had a religious education,
  He's much more likely to resist temptation.
FAUST. You monster, you have never known
  How an angelic child like this,
  Whose faith is pure and whole, 3530
  Whose faith alone
  Sustains her hope of heaven's bliss,
  Could fear the one she loves might lose his soul.
MEPHISTO. What supersublimated sensuality!
  A little girl has got you on a string. 3535

FAUST. You misbegotten spawn of hell-fire and depravity!
MEPHISTO. She's good at reading faces too, the cheeky thing!
    She feels a bit uneasy when I'm there;
    She looks at me, and seems to see
    A touch of genius, a certain flair—   3540
    She might even suspect some devilry in me.
    Well, and tonight?
FAUST.   That's no concern of yours.
MEPHISTO. I like to have my fun—it's all in a good cause.

AT THE WELL

GRETCHEN *and* LIESCHEN *carrying pitchers*

LIESCHEN. And what about Barbara? Haven't you heard?
GRETCHEN. No, not a word; I don't get out as much as you.   3545
LIESCHEN. Sibyl told me today—it's true!
    At last she's got what she deserved,
    Miss Hoity-Toity!
GRETCHEN.   What?
LIESCHEN.   It stinks!
    She's feeding two when she eats and drinks.
GRETCHEN. Oh, no!   3550
LIESCHEN. Oh yes, she came a cropper in the end.
    That man she always went about with,
    The one she boasted she was 'walking out with',
    Going to fairs and dances with her 'friend'—
    She always had to be the first in line.   3555
    He treated her to cakes and wine,
    She thought she was so very fine.
    And all those presents he gave her, too—
    I'd be ashamed to take them, so would you.
    And all those cuddles in the wood!   3560
    Well, now her flower's gone for good.
GRETCHEN. Oh, the poor girl!
LIESCHEN.   Now don't be soft!
    While you and I were spinning in the loft
    Because we weren't allowed out after dark—
    She was with her lover in the park.   3565
    Behind the house and in the alleyway,
    For hours they were together, every day.
    Next time she goes to church she'll have to do
    Her public penance in the sinners' pew!

GRETCHEN. But he will marry her, for sure.   3570
LIESCHEN. He's not so daft as that. And he's a likely lad
   Who'll want the chance to look around for more.
   And anyway, he's gone.
GRETCHEN.   Oh, that's too bad!
LIESCHEN. And if she does catch him, she'll still be had.
   The boys will snatch her wreath, and at the door   3575
   Instead of flowers we'll throw bits of straw.   [*exit*
GRETCHEN. [*walking home*] If some poor girl got into trouble, you
   Would always scoff and gossip like that too.
   And you were always quick to lay the blame
   And wag your tongue at someone else's shame!   3580
   And though their sin was black as black could be,
   It never could be black enough for me.
   I crossed myself and felt so proud—
   And now my own sin cries aloud!
   But what I did, dear God in heaven above,   3585
   It was so good—and it was all for love.

A SHRINE

*In a niche in the city wall a sacred image of the Mater Dolorosa with
vases of flowers in front of it.* GRETCHEN *puts fresh flowers into the vases.*

Our Lady, thou
So rich in sorrows, bow
Thy face upon my anguish now!

Thy heart transfixed,   3590
Thy gaze is fixed
Towards thy son upon the Cross.

The Father beseeching,
Thy sighs are reaching
To heaven to assuage thy loss.   3595

Who can feel
And who reveal
Such pain, such bitter woe?
Why my heart with fear is shaking,
Why it's yearning, why it's quaking,   3600
Only you can truly know!

Wherever I may be,
I feel such misery

Within my bosom aching.
When I am on my own   3605
I weep, I weep alone,
My fearful heart is breaking.

The early sun was shining
When I rose from my bed.
In grief and sorrow pining,   3610
What bitter tears I shed!

The boxes in front of my window
Were watered with the dew
Of my tears as early this morning
I picked these flowers for you.   3615

Help! Keep me safe from death and blame!
Our Lady, thou
So rich in sorrows, bow
Thy gracious face upon my shame!

NIGHT

The street in front of Gretchen's house.
VALENTIN, *a soldier, Gretchen's brother.*

VALENTIN. When I was drinking with the rest,   3620
   They used to argue who was best
   Of all the girls they ever knew,
   The way that soldiers always do.
   And then they used to fill their glasses
   And drink a toast to all the lasses.   3625
   I'd sit there with a quiet smile,
   And let them brag on for a while;
   I'd stroke my beard and hide my thoughts,
   And when they'd finished, I'd fill my jar
   And tell them: Well, it takes all sorts.   3630
   But of all the lasses near and far,
   Not one could hold a candle to
   My sister Gretchen—ain't that true?
   He's right, they'd shout, let's drink a toast
   To little Gretchen, she's the one,   3635
   She's the girl we all like most.
   And all the boasters sat there dumb.

But now! It drives you to despair,
It makes you want to tear your hair;
The neighbours talk, the gossips sneer,   3640
And every lout thinks he can jeer.
All I can do is look away,
Dreading every word they say.
And even if I knocked them flying,
I couldn't tell them they were lying.   3645

What's that? Who's lurking over there?
It must be him—the other one as well.
If I get hold of him, I swear
I'll send him and his friend straight down to hell.

FAUST, MEPHISTOPHELES

FAUST. Through that church window softly gleams   3650
　The warm reflection of the sanctuary light;
　But here outside its ever fainter beams
　Are smothered in the darkness of the night.
　That darkness, too, encompasses my heart.
MEPHISTO. And I feel like a tom-cat in the dark,   3655
　Up on the roof-tops by the fire-escapes,
　Padding along the walls and roaming free,
　A bit of thieving, getting into scrapes,
　Screwing around—that's just the life for me!
　In all my limbs I feel these ghostly twitches—   3660
　Walpurgis Eve is just two nights away.
　Now that's worth staying up for any day—
　I just can't wait to get among those witches.
FAUST. Perhaps by then you might have raised the treasure
　That I see glowing dimly over there?   3665
MEPHISTO. I promise, very soon you'll have the pleasure
　Of dipping into it—you'll get your share.
　I took a peep at it not long ago;
　It's full of silver coins, a fine collection.
FAUST. No jewels? Not a single ring to show   3670
　That lovely girl a token of affection?
MEPHISTO. Ah yes, indeed, I might have seen
　Some jewellery—a string of pearls, it could have been.
FAUST. I'm glad to hear it; when I go to see
　My love, I like to take a gift with me.   3675
MEPHISTO. I don't see why you should be too upset
　If you don't have to pay for what you get.

343

But now, the stars are shining overhead—
I'll treat you to a little serenade,
A cautionary song about a lovesick maid.   3680
It's sure to turn her pretty little head.
[*he sings to a guitar*]

Oh, Katie dear
What brings you here
To your lover's door
Before the day is dawning?   3685
Be careful, or
You'll be betrayed,
Let in a maid—
A maid no more by morning.

Sweet maid, begone,   3690
For when it's done
He'll up and run—
With you he will not linger.
Sweet maid, beware,
Don't go in there   3695
Unless you wear
A ring upon your finger.

VALENTIN. [*comes forward*] You damned ratcatcher! Curse you, who
    D'you think you're serenading to?
    I'll send your instrument to hell,   3700
    And then I'll send the singer there as well!

MEPHISTO. My poor guitar is ruined! What a shame!

VALENTIN. And now you're going to get more of the same!

MEPHISTO. [*to Faust*] Come on now, Doctor, don't hold back!
    Keep close to me, out with your snicker-snack!   3705
    I'll parry, all you have to do
    Is watch your chance and run him through.

VALENTIN. Right, parry that!

MEPHISTO.   Why, certainly.

VALENTIN. And that!

MEPHISTO.   Of course!

VALENTIN.   Is this the Devil fighting me?
    What's going on? My hand's gone numb!   3710

MEPHISTO. [*to Faust*] Now thrust!

VALENTIN. [*falls*]   Ah God!

MEPHISTO.   That's settled him! Now come,
    We've got to get away from here before
    They start to raise a mighty hue and cry.

I'm on good terms with the police, but even I
Can't get away with murder, that's against the law. 3715
MARTHA. [*at her window*] Help! Help! Outside!
GRETCHEN. [*at her window*]   Quick, fetch a light!
MARTHA. [*as above*] They're shouting in the street, there's been a fight!
PEOPLE. There's someone lying here. He's dead!
MARTHA. [*coming outside*] Where are the killers? Have they cut and run?
GRETCHEN. [*coming outside*] Who's this?
PEOPLE.   It is your mother's son. 3720
GRETCHEN. Almighty God, what have I brought upon my head?
VALENTIN. I'm dying! That's soon said,
   And even sooner done.
   You women, stop your wailing, and instead
   Hear what I have to say before I'm gone. 3725
   [*they all gather round him*]
   Gretchen, listen. You are young, and still
   Unable to distinguish good from ill.
   You've got yourself into a pretty mess. Before
   I die, I want to say, just between you and me,
   That you are nothing but a whore— 3730
   So go ahead and do it properly.
GRETCHEN. Brother! Dear God, what can you mean?
VALENTIN. Just leave God out of it. What's been
   Has been, what's done is done;
   But you'll go on as you've begun. 3735
   First you take a secret lover,
   And soon you think you'd like another.
   And when you've had a dozen or so,
   Then the whole town will want a go.

   When you give birth to sin and shame, 3740
   You never call it by its proper name;
   You cover it with the veil of night,
   And keep it hidden out of sight.
   You want to stifle it, but then
   It can't be hidden, and it grows, 3745
   And in the light of day it shows
   Itself in all its ugliness again.
   And the more hideous your disgrace,
   The more it seeks to show its face.

   Indeed, I can foresee the day 3750
   When decent folk will turn away
   From you, you slut, and they will shun

You like the plague, yes, every one.
Your blood will freeze within you when
They look at you, your heart will quail.   3755
You won't wear any jewels then,
Nor stand and pray at the altar-rail!
At dances you won't show your face,
You'll not wear finery or lace—
You'll crouch in a corner in misery   3760
With cripples and beggars for company.
God may forgive you yet, but I
Give you my curse before I die!
MARTHA. Commend your soul to God in death!
    Would you blaspheme with your last breath?   3765
VALENTIN. If only I could lift my sword,
    You scrawny pimp, you shameful bawd,
    Then surely I could hope to win
    Forgiveness for my every sin.
GRETCHEN. Dear brother, ah, what misery!   3770
VALENTIN. I tell you, let your weeping be!
    You are dishonoured, and your fall
    Was the unkindest cut of all.
    I go to God, and to my grave,
    An honest soldier, true and brave.   3775
                                     [he dies

CATHEDRAL

Mass, organ and choir. GRETCHEN *among a crowd of people.*
An evil spirit behind GRETCHEN.

EVIL SPIRIT. How different, Gretchen, you felt
    When you, still all innocent,
    Came here to the altar
    Thumbing the well-worn pages,
    Lisping your prayers,   3780
    Half childish play,
    Half pious worship!
    Gretchen!
    What's on your mind?
    And in your heart,   3785
    What misdeed?
    Are you praying for your mother's soul, which

Through your doing now spends long, long years in purgatory?
Whose blood is on your doorstep?
And there below your heart,   3790
Can you not feel it quickening,
That fearful presence, boding ill
For both of you?
GRETCHEN. No! No!
If only I could rid myself   3795
Of these oppressive thoughts
That swarm around me!
CHOIR.
Dies irae, dies illa
Solvet saeclum in favilla.   [*organ music*
EVIL SPIRIT. Dread fear grips you!   3800
The trumpet sounds!
The graves gape!
And your heart,
From the ashes
Where it slept   3805
Awakes to hell-fire
And quakes!
GRETCHEN. I must get out!
The organ seems
To stifle me,   3810
The chanting voices
Melt my heart within me.
CHOIR.
Judex ergo cum sedebit,
Quidquid latet adparebit,
Nil inultum remanebit.   3815
GRETCHEN. I'm suffocating!
The pillars
Press in on me,
The vaults above
Are crushing me! I need air!   3820
EVIL SPIRIT. You try to hide! Sin and shame
Cannot be hidden.
Air? Light?
Woe on you!
CHOIR.
Quid sum miser tunc dicturus?   3825
Quem patronum rogaturus?
Cum vix justus sit securus.

EVIL SPIRIT. The blessed
  Turn their faces from you.
  The pure   3830
  Shudder to reach out their hands to you.
  Woe!
CHOIR.
  Quid sum miser tunc dicturus?
GRETCHEN. Neighbour! Your salts!

                                                   [she falls in a swoon

WALPURGIS NIGHT

The Harz Mountains, near Schierke and Elend.
FAUST *and* MEPHISTOPHELES

MEPHISTO. A broomstick's what you really need—   3835
  Or a randy goat would make an even better steed.
  We'll never get there at this speed.
FAUST. I'll trust my own two legs to carry me,
  And this good stick to help me, that will be
  Quite adequate. And what's the hurry, anyway?   3840
  I find it very pleasant just to stray
  Along the winding valley, then
  To climb the rocky cliffs again,
  And see the never-ending torrents flow
  Foaming and dashing to the chasm far below.   3845
  The birches and the firs can feel the breath of spring—
  Why shouldn't our legs feel its bracing thrill?
MEPHISTO. To be quite honest, I can't feel a thing.
  For me it's deepest winter still;
  I like the frost and snow, the icy chill.   3850
  The waning moon is rising overhead,
  And casts a dismal glow of sullen red.
  It sheds no light, and we could break
  A leg with every step we take.
  These Jack o' Lanterns are a much more cheerful sight,   3855
  I'll go and ask one if he'd like to guide us.
  Hullo, my friend! Can we not share your light?
  We'd be most grateful if you'd walk beside us
  And help us to negotiate this slope.
WILL O' THE WISP. Why, I'd be honoured, Sir! I only hope   3860
  I can restrain my natural frivolity;
  We go in zig-zags as a rule, you see.

MEPHISTO. You imitate the human race, it would appear.
    Now, in the Devil's name, don't gad about—
    Go straight, or else I'll blow your lantern out!   3865
WILL O' THE WISP. I see you are the master around here.
    I'll do my best, Sir, not to go astray;
    But don't forget the Brocken is bewitched tonight,
    And if a Jack o' Lantern shows the way,
    You mustn't be surprised if things don't go quite right.   3870
    FAUST, MEPHISTOPHELES, WILL O' THE WISP. [*chanting alternately*]

Wonderland of magic dreams
We have entered now, it seems.
Lead us well and show your paces,
So that we can safely go
Through these vast and barren places.   3875

See the fir-trees, row on row,
Speeding past us in the gloom.
Cliffs above us rear and loom,
Rocks like giants' noses soaring,
Hear them blowing, hear them snoring!   3880

Through the rocks and meadows pouring
Streams and torrents dash along.
In the rushing waters' song
Do we hear a sweet lament
For the days in heaven spent,   3885
Days of love and hope now gone?
From the past the ancient tales
Echo through the woods and vales.

Tuwhit! Tuwhoo! Here close by wails
The screech-owl, peewit and the jay;   3890
All have stayed awake today.
Long-legged newts with shiny tails
And bloated bellies crawl about.
Twisted roots come winding out
From the rocks and sandy soil,   3895
Slithering like snakes to seize
Stumbling walkers as they go.
From the gnarled and knotted trees
Living tentacles uncoil,
Twisting, writhing to and fro.   3900
Fieldmice in their thousands pour
Through the moss, across the moor;

Fireflies swarming in the dark
Dance and flicker, flash and spark—
But they do not light our way.   3905

Now we can no longer say—
Are we moving? Standing here?
Everything around us races,
Trees and rocks with grinning faces,
Lights that float and sway and veer,   3910
Blaze and flicker far and near.
MEPHISTO. Grab my coat-tails, Doctor, follow me!
Stand up here and take a look around;
Inside the mountain over there you'll see
Mammon's palace glowing underground.   3915
FAUST. How eerily that faint and spectral glow
Glimmers among the chasms far below!
Even the very deepest gorges seem
To catch the last reflection of that gleam.
Great swathes of smoke and vapour billow round,   3920
A fiery shaft lights up the clouds, and then
It flows, a slender thread, beneath the ground.
And now it gushes like a spring again,
And branches in a hundred veins that stream
Along the valley to that narrow corner, where   3925
It merges into one again, and there
Becomes a single precious seam.
Now sparks are flying ever higher,
Like golden sand flung in the air,
And higher still, look, over there—   3930
The mountainside is all on fire.
MEPHISTO. Yes, Mammon's palace is a splendid sight,
He does his best to give us all a treat.
You're lucky to be here—and soon you'll meet
Some of our wilder guests tonight.   3935
FAUST. The storm is howling now, and I can feel
It tugging at my back, it makes me reel.
MEPHISTO. Just cling on to the rock's old ribs like this,
Or else you'll be swept into the abyss.
The fog is dense, and dark the night,   3940
Listen how the forests whine!
Startled owls are put to flight,
Pillars split in evergreen
Palaces of fir and pine.

Grating branches scrape and scream, 3945
Mighty trunks are cracking and groaning,
Heaving roots are creaking and moaning!
With a fearful crash they all
Topple others as they fall,
They choke the gorges, and the gale 3950
Whistles through them with its dismal wail.
Can you hear the voices everywhere,
Far and near, high in the air?
Yes, the whole mountainside is ringing
With the witches' furious singing. 3955

WITCHES. [*in chorus*]
Witches to the Brocken streaming,
The stubble is yellow, the shoots are greening.
To the summit swarms the witches' chorus,
Up there Old Nick is waiting for us.
Hurry to get there before they start! 3960
The billy-goats stink and the witches fart.
A VOICE. Here comes Baubo, the ancient crone,
Riding a sow, and all alone.

CHORUS. All honour then where honour's due;
Old Mother Baubo, be our guide. 3965
A sturdy pig with you astride—
Lead on, and we'll all follow you!
A VOICE. Which way did you come?
A VOICE. By Ilsenstein!
I looked in at the owl's nest as I flew by—
She glared at me with her beady eye. 3970
A VOICE. Damn you, don't ride so fast, or go to hell!
A VOICE. The creature went for me as well—
Just take a look at these scratches of mine!

WITCHES. [*in chorus*]
The way is broad, the way is long,
Along it pours a giddy throng. 3975
The broomstick scrapes, the pitchfork pokes,
The mother bursts and the baby chokes.

WARLOCKS. [*half-chorus*]
We creep along like weary snails—
The women are faster than the males.
If it's the Devil you're looking for, 3980
They'll beat you by a mile or more.

THE OTHER HALF-CHORUS.
> We needn't hurry; what's the fuss?
> Women need more time than us.
> They think the men are far too slow—
> But we can do it in one go.   3985

A VOICE. [*above*] You down by the lake, come up from below!

VOICES. [*from below*] We'd like to come with you, for sure;
> We wash till we're pure as driven snow,
> But we'll be barren for evermore.

BOTH CHORUSES. The starlight fades, the wind has died,   3990
> The dismal moon creeps out of sight.
> A thousand sparks blaze in the night
> As the witches to the Brocken ride.

VOICE. [*from a rocky chasm*]
> Stop! Wait for me! Oh, won't you stop?

VOICE. [*from above*] Whose voice is that from far below?   3995

VOICE. [*from below*] Let me come with you, please! Although
> I've climbed three hundred years or so,
> And still I haven't reached the top,
> I'd rather be with folk I know.

BOTH CHORUSES. A good stout broomstick carries you,   4000
> A pitchfork or a goat will do;
> If you can't get up there today,
> You'll never make it anyway.

HALF-WITCH. [*below*] I trot along all on my own,
> And try to keep up with the crowd.   4005
> I can't get any peace at home—
> But then, up here it's just as loud.

WITCHES. [*in chorus*]
> The witch-grease gives us all a thrill,
> For a boat we use a rusty pail,
> And any old rag will make a sail.   4010
> If you don't fly now, you never will.

BOTH CHORUSES. Around the summit we shall ride,
> And settle on the ground beneath.
> A swarm of witches far and wide
> Will cover all the blasted heath.   4015
> [*they land on the ground*]

MEPHISTO. They're pushing and shoving and sliding and clattering,
> Jostling and squirming and hissing and chattering,
> They flicker and fizzle and stink like bitches—

352

They're in their element, these witches!
Hold on to me, or you'll get lost. Hold tight, I say!   4020
Where are you?
FAUST. [*in the distance*] Here!
MEPHISTO.   What, so far away?
I'll have to show them who's the boss round here.
Stand back! Squire Voland's here! Good folk, make way!
Now, Doctor, take my hand! We must break free
From all this milling crowd—I fear   4025
It's too much, even for the likes of me.
Look, by those bushes over there I see
A cosy glow that looks much more inviting.
Come on, you never know, it could be quite exciting.
FAUST. You spirit of perversity! All right,   4030
Lead on—but it's not very clever, I must say,
To come here to the Brocken on Walpurgis Night,
When all we do is go our own sweet way.
MEPHISTO. Look, what a cheerful blaze! And we're
Part of a jolly club in here.   4035
Just a small circle, but good company.
FAUST. Up there is where I'd rather be!
The crowd streams upwards to the summit, where
The Evil One is sitting in a fiery glow.
What mysteries would be revealed up there!   4040
MEPHISTO. New mysteries would be created, though.
Just let the world outside go by, and we
Will take it easy over here.
For folk have always had a tendency
To form small worlds within the wider sphere.   4045
See those young naked witches over there, how sweet;
The older ones, I'm glad to say, are more discreet.
Now make an effort to be friendly, just for me;
They'll give you a nice time—and it's all free.
Is that an orchestra that I can hear?   4050
We'll have to put up with the awful noise, I fear.
Just come with me, we can't avoid the din;
Come on, I'll go ahead and introduce you—
I might find someone else who will seduce you.
And take a look at this great room we're in,   4055
It's huge, it stretches nearly out of sight.
A hundred cheerful fires are burning bright,
They're dancing, talking, flirting, drinking, eating—
I tell you, this place takes a lot of beating.

FAUST. What role have you assumed for this surprise—   4060
    A conjuror, or the Devil in disguise?
MEPHISTO. I often travel incognito, that is true,
    But I wear my decorations at a proper do.
    I haven't got the Order of the Garter—though
    My cloven hoof commands respect up here, you know.   4065
    You see this snail here slowly crawling by?
    It's only got those feelers in its face,
    But it can sense something, perhaps it knows my limp—
    I can't disguise myself here even if I try.
    Come on, let's have a good look round the place;   4070
    You can be the punter, and I'll play the pimp.
    [*to a group sitting round a dying fire*]
    Now, gentlemen! What, sitting all alone?
    I am surprised at you! Why do you shun
    These youthful revels? Why not join the fun?
    If you wanted solitude, you should have stayed at home.   4075
GENERAL. You cannot put your trust in any nation!
    Whatever you've done for them in your day,
    The people are just like the women—they
    Will always want the younger generation.
MINISTER. They just don't do things properly these days.   4080
    When I think of the old traditional ways,
    There was a time when we had their respect.
    It was our Golden Age—in retrospect.
SOCIAL CLIMBER. We took our chances when they came along,
    And did some shady business in the past;   4085
    But somehow nowadays it's all gone wrong,
    Just when we thought we'd made the grade at last.
AUTHOR. They don't read anything I'd call
    Good literature or decent prose today.
    Young people now, they think they know it all—   4090
    They're just not interested in what you say.
MEPHISTO. [*suddenly looking very old*]
    To hear them talk, you'd think Doomsday was nigh!
    Indeed, I even feel my barrel's running dry.
    This is the last time I shall come up here;
    The world is coming to an end, I fear.   4095
PEDLAR-WITCH. Wait, gentlemen! Don't pass me by,
    You'll miss your chance, so come and buy!
    Take a good look—knick-knacks galore,
    There's everything you need, and more.
    There's nowhere in the world you'll find   4100

Such a well-stocked shop as mine.
There's nothing here that hasn't done
A serious injury to someone,
No dagger here that hasn't run with blood,
No cup that hasn't sent a deadly flood   4105
Of poison scorching through some healthy veins. You'll find
No trinket that has not seduced a sweet young maid,
No sword that has not treacherously betrayed
A friend, or stabbed a rival from behind.

MEPHISTO. Oh Grandma, you're just too set in your ways!   4110
That stuff's old hat. Believe me, you
Should try to offer people something new—
It's novelty they look for nowadays.

FAUST. How I keep my wits about me, I don't know;
This really is a most amazing show!   4115

MEPHISTO. They're making for the summit in a swirling throng,
You can't resist, you just get swept along.

FAUST. Who is that woman I see over there?

MEPHISTO. Take a good look; it's Lilith.

FAUST.   Who?

MEPHISTO. Adam's first wife. You see her lovely hair?   4120
That is her chief attraction—but take care!
If any young man falls for her, he should beware—
He'll be an old man by the time she's through.

FAUST. That young witch, and the old one, sitting there together—
I saw them dancing just now hell-for-leather!   4125

MEPHISTO. We're going to get no peace tonight, I know.
They're playing a new dance, come on, let's have a go!

FAUST. [*dancing with the young witch*]
A lovely dream once came to me;
I thought I saw an apple-tree.
I climbed it, and a gorgeous pair   4130
Of apples I found hanging there.

PRETTY YOUNG WITCH.
You men like apples, I believe,
Since Adam had a bite from Eve.
I'm overjoyed, and very proud
My garden is so well-endowed.   4135

MEPHISTO. [*dancing with the old witch*]
I had a wild dream some time back;
I saw a tree with a great big crack.

It had a gaping hole inside—
I like a hole that's nice and wide.

OLD WITCH. You and your cloven hoof, Sir Knight,   4140
  Are very welcome here tonight.
  A hole like that needs a big stopper,
  So you can plug it good and proper!
SPOOKYBUM. What impudence! Accursed crew!
  Haven't I proved that ghosts like you   4145
  Can't walk around like normal folk—
  And now you're dancing, too. This is beyond a joke!
PRETTY WITCH. [*dancing*] What does he want up here with us?
FAUST. [*dancing*] Oh, he gets everywhere, and always makes a fuss.
  He likes to watch while other people dance;   4150
  He analyses every step you take,
  And criticizes every small mistake.
  He gets annoyed whenever we advance—
  If we dance round in circles, then he will
  Admit it's better than just standing still.   4155
  Going around in circles is what he does best;
  He still expects our thanks though, the old pest.
SPOOKYBUM. Are you still there? But this is an outrage!
  Away with you! We live in an enlightened age.
  This devil's rabble just ignores the rules. We've proved   4160
  They don't exist, yet Tegel's haunted still.
  I've done my best to clear them out, but will
  They go? It's scandalous! They simply can't be moved!
PRETTY WITCH. So stop annoying us and pack it in!
SPOOKYBUM. I tell you spirits to your face,   4165
  This spiritual tyranny is a disgrace;
  It upsets all my spiritual discipline.
  [*they carry on dancing*]
  I see I shan't get anywhere today;
  I'm going on a journey, and before I'm through
  I'll have worked out the proper way   4170
  To deal with devils—and with poets, too.
MEPHISTO. He'll go away and sit down in a puddle,
  That's how he gets his wits out of a muddle.
  And when the leeches have all feasted on his bum,
  The ghosts have vanished—but his brain's gone numb.   4175
  [*to Faust, who has left the dance*]
  Why did you let that pretty girl escape just then?
  She sang so nicely as you jigged about.

FAUST. She'd scarcely started singing to me, when
    She opened up her mouth, and a red mouse jumped out.
MEPHISTO. Ah well, you can't be too particular today.   4180
    You're lucky that the mouse was red, not grey.
    Lovers shouldn't notice these things, anyway.
FAUST. And then I saw—
MEPHISTO.   What?
FAUST.   Look, Mephisto, can you see
    That lovely child, so pale and lonely over there?
    She shuffles awkwardly along; it seems to me   4185
    She's wearing chains around her feet. I swear
    She looks like Gretchen. Can it be
    That she and I will meet again up here?
MEPHISTO. No, stay away from her! Keep clear!
    She's just a magic phantom, an illusion. Those   4190
    Who fall under her spell are terrified;
    Her lifeless stare will freeze your blood with fear
    And make your rigid limbs seem petrified.
    You've heard of the Medusa, I suppose?
FAUST. Indeed, her gaze is lifeless, cold and dead;   4195
    No loving hand has closed those eyes that cannot see.
    Yet that is the sweet body Gretchen gave to me,
    That is the breast on which I laid my head.
MEPHISTO. You unsuspecting fool, that is her sorcery!
    For everyone she can take on a lover's shape.   4200
FAUST. What anguish! And what ecstasy!
    This vision holds me fast, I can't escape.
    How strange! Around that lovely neck I see,
    No thicker than a blade, a single red
    And slender line drawn like a scarlet thread.   4205
MEPHISTO. Of course! That's nothing new to me.
    She puts her head under her arm as well;
    You fall for every magic spell!
    Perseus chopped it off for her, believe me.
    Come on, let's take a walk up there,   4210
    You'll find as much fun here as any fair.
    And look, unless my eyes deceive me,
    They've even got a theatre set up for us.
    What's all this then?
LICKSPITTLE.   We're just about to start.
    It's a new play, the seventh, and the last.   4215
    We have to give them seven, or they make such a fuss.
    A dilettante wrote it, and the cast

Are dilettantes too—they all expect a part.
Excuse me now, I've got to raise the curtain—
I mustn't dilly-dally, that's for certain!   4220
MEPHISTO. Amateur theatricals on Walpurgis Night! Well yes—
The Brocken's where you all belong, I guess.

A WALPURGIS NIGHT'S DREAM, OR OBERON AND TITANIA'S GOLDEN WEDDING

Intermezzo

STAGE MANAGER. We're Mieding's trusty band of men,
And we're on holiday.
Ancient hill and misty glen—   4225
That's the scene today!
HERALD. Fifty summers have gone past
Since their wedding year.
Now their quarrel's done at last,
Golden days are here!   4230
OBERON. Elves and spirits all unseen
Show yourselves and see
Your Fairy King and Fairy Queen
Rejoined in harmony.
PUCK. Puck has come to join the throng   4235
With his merry laughter.
He dances right, he dances wrong—
And hundreds follow after.
ARIEL. Ariel's songs will fill the air
With pure ethereal sound;   4240
Monstrous shapes and creatures fair
Gather all around.
OBERON. Couples all should take this test
If they're brokenhearted;
Learn from us that you'll love best   4245
When you have been parted.
TITANIA. A wife who never shuts her mouth,
A husband who's a boor,
Send him north and send her south—
That's the only cure.   4250
ORCHESTRA TUTTI. [*fortissimo*]
Snout of fly and nose of gnat,
All sorts and conditions,

Croaking frog and squeaking bat—
    These are our musicians.
SOLO. Look, here comes the bagpipe now!   4255
    All blown up and groaning,
    Making an infernal row—
    His nose does all the droning.
FLEDGLING SPIRIT. Paunch of toad and spiders' toes,
    Stick some wings upon it;   4260
    It's not a creature, but who knows—
    It might just make a sonnet.
WEE COUPLE. Through scented honeydew we fly,
    We hop and skip around;
    We'd dearly love to soar on high,   4265
    But just can't leave the ground.
INQUISITIVE TRAVELLER. Ah! A satirical revue!
    And do my eyes deceive me?
    Lord Oberon is up here too—
    Whoever will believe me?   4270
ORTHODOX THEOLOGIAN. He's got no claws, no tail, but still
    There's no doubt in my mind;
    Just like the gods of Greece, he's still
    A devil of some kind.
NORTHERN ARTIST. My talents hitherto, I know,   4275
    Were scant and immature;
    But soon it will be time to go
    On my Italian tour.
PURIST. This is a most distressing sight,
    They're slovenly as pigs!   4280
    Of all the witches here tonight,
    Just two wear powdered wigs.
YOUNG WITCH. Your powder and your petticoat
    Are for the old and paunchy;
    I ride stark naked on my goat,   4285
    And show 'em something raunchy!
MATRON. We're too experienced, too mature
    To bandy words with you.
    Your youthful bloom will fade for sure—
    We hope you wither, too.   4290
CONDUCTOR. Snout of fly and nose of gnat,
    Keep off that naked floozy!
    Croaking frog and squeaking bat,
    Your tempo's gone all woozy!
WEATHER-VANE. [*looking one way*]

You meet nice people at this do,   4295
  There's pretty girls a-plenty;
There's lots of nice young men here, too—
  And not one over twenty.
WEATHER-VANE. [*looking the other way*]
  Why can't an earthquake or hell-fire
Consume them all like Sodom?   4300
  And if it won't, then I'll retire
To hell myself. God rot 'em!
SATIRES. Little insects bite and sting
  With their sharpened claws;
Satan's our papa, we bring   4305
  Honour to his cause.
HENNINGS. Satirists! God, what a crew,
  So silly and malicious.
They claim to be good-hearted, too,
  But mostly they're just vicious.   4310
MASTER OF THE MUSES.
  These witches, though—it seems to me
That they could have their uses;
  If they were on my staff, they'd be
Less trouble than the Muses.
SOMETIME SPIRIT OF THE AGE.
  I'll take you on if you can write,   4315
There's talent here in masses;
  You'd think the Brocken was tonight
A real German Parnassus.
INQUISITIVE TRAVELLER.
  Who's that man who stalks about
So rigid and austere?   4320
  He snoops around—he's sniffing out
The Jesuits up here.
A CRANE. The pure and pious have the right
  To fish in muddy waters;
That's why you see me here tonight   4325
  Among the Devil's daughters.
A CHILD OF THE WORLD. The pious will choose any site
  To practise their affairs;
All kinds of sects come here tonight
  To meet and say their prayers.   4330
DANCER. Like bitterns booming by the shore,
  I hear a distant drumming.
Another choir? Oh, what a bore—

Philosophers are coming!

DANCE-MASTER. See how they hop and skip and prance!　　4335
  Each thinks he's got it right.
  The clumsy cripples try to dance—
  And don't they look a fright!

MERRY FIDDLER. They hate each others' guts, you know—
  Each one would kill his fellow;　　4340
  Like Orpheus with his lyre, though,
  The bagpipes keep them mellow.

DOGMATIST. I won't be shouted down, d'you hear?
  Let carping critics doubt us;
  But devils must exist, it's clear—　　4345
  We see them all about us.

IDEALIST. It's all a product of my brain,
  But still, it does amaze me;
  If this is me, then it's quite plain
  I must be going crazy.　　4350

REALIST. This nonsense undermines my sense
  Of all reality;
  I can't believe the evidence
  Of what's in front of me.

SUPERNATURALIST. I'm overjoyed! I much prefer　　4355
  To think all this is true.
  If there are devils, I infer
  There are good spirits, too.

SCEPTIC. They dig for gold and poke about,
  But truth is just a fiction;　　4360
  It's D for devil and D for doubt—
  That sums up my conviction.

CONDUCTOR. Croaking frog and squeaking bat,
  Oh, damn these amateurs!
  Snout of fly and nose of gnat,　　4365
  Just try to keep in time, Sirs!

OPPORTUNISTS. We call ourselves the Sans-Souci,
  We don't care how we're fed;
  We can't stand on our feet, so we
  Walk on our heads instead.　　4370

THE HELPLESS. We used to fawn and mop and mow,
  And snap up many a rare treat;
  But now we're destitute, and so
  We run around in bare feet.

WILL O' THE WISPS. In the fetid swamps and meres　　4375
  We originated;

Now we're dashing cavaliers,
 Lionised and fêted.
A SHOOTING STAR. Once I blazed across the sky,   4380
 Leaving trails of flame;
 I fell to earth, and here I lie—
 Who'll help me up again?
THE HEAVIES. Stand back and give us room, or you
 Will surely all be flattened;
 Spirits can be clumsy, too,   4385
 Provided they're well-fattened.
PUCK. Don't stamp about so heavily
 Like elephants run wild!
 Come, don't be clumsier than me,
 Stout Puck, the sturdy child.   4390
ARIEL. Some have nature's wings, and some
 The spirit lifts on high;
 To the hill of roses come,
 Follow where I fly!
ORCHESTRA. [*pianissimo*] On drifting cloud and mist the day 4395
 Spreads its early gleam;
 Whispering leaves and rushes sway—
 All's vanished like a dream.

GLOOMY DAY. A FIELD

FAUST. MEPHISTOPHELES

FAUST. In misery and despair! Pitifully wandering the country all this time, and now imprisoned! That sweet, hapless creature shut up in a dungeon like a criminal, exposed to appalling suffering! For so long, so long! And you kept this from me, you treacherous, despicable demon! Yes, stand there rolling your malevolent devil's eyes at me! Stand there and defy me with your insufferable company. In prison! In irredeemable misery! At the mercy of evil spirits and the pitiless judgement of humanity! And meanwhile you lull me with vulgar distractions, you conceal her growing misery from me and let her perish helplessly!

MEPHISTO. She's not the first.

FAUST. You hound! You vile monster! Oh infinite Spirit! Change him, change this snake back into his dog's shape, when he would delight in trotting ahead of me in the night, rolling at the feet of harmless wayfarers and leaping onto their shoulders as they fell. Turn him back into his favourite shape, so that he crawls before me on his belly in the sand, and I can crush the depraved creature under my feet! Not the first! Oh, misery! Misery such as no human soul can grasp, or understand how more than one creature has been plunged into such wretchedness, that the writhing death-agony of the first was not enough to atone for the guilt of all the others in the sight of ever-forgiving God! The suffering of this one creature sears me to the heart, and you grin calmly at the fate of thousands.

MEPHISTO. Now we've reached our wits' end, the point where you humans lose your head. Why do you seek our company, if you can't handle it? You want to fly, but you have no head for heights. Did we force ourselves on you—or was it the other way round?

FAUST. Don't bare your ravening fangs at me! It revolts me! Great, glorious Spirit, you deigned to appear to me, you know my heart and soul, why did you fetter me to this infamous companion, who feeds on mischief and delights in destruction?

MEPHISTO. Have you finished?

FAUST. Save her! Or woe betide you! The most atrocious curse on you through all the ages!

MEPHISTO. I cannot undo the bonds or draw back the bolts of retribution. Save her? Who was it that dragged her to her ruin? I or you?

FAUST. [looks wildly about him]

MEPHISTO. Are you reaching for thunderbolts? It's just as well they were not given to you miserable mortals. That is the way a tyrant seeks to relieve his fury, by crushing any innocent person who gets in his way.

FAUST. Take me to her! She must be freed!

MEPHISTO. And what about the risks you run? Don't you realize that you're still wanted for murder in that town? Avenging spirits still haunt the grave of the man you killed, waiting for the murderer to return.

FAUST. I have to hear that from you! You monster, may the deaths and murders of the whole world come on your head! Take me to her, I say, and rescue her!

MEPHISTO. I'll take you there, and let me tell you what I can do. I don't have power over everything in heaven and earth, you know. I will drug the gaoler, you take the keys and release her by human hand. I will keep a lookout. The magic horses will be ready, and I will get you away. That I can do.

FAUST. Away then!

NIGHT. OPEN COUNTRY

FAUST, MEPHISTOPHELES *storming past on black horses*

FAUST. What's going on around the gibbet there?

MEPHISTO. I don't know what they're stewing and brewing.   4400

FAUST. They're swaying about and stooping and bowing.
MEPHISTO. A witches' coven.
FAUST. They're sprinkling and blessing.
MEPHISTO. Ride on! Ride on!

A DUNGEON

FAUST *with a bunch of keys and a lamp, in front of a small iron door.*

A long-forgotten shudder seizes me,   4405
I feel the very depth of human misery.
Within these dripping walls she is confined,
Her only crime a love that was too blind.
Are you reluctant to go in and free her?
Or is it that you are afraid to see her?   4410
Come! If you falter, death is close behind.
[*he grasps the lock, from within a voice is heard singing*]

My mother, the whore, she's
Murdered me!
My father, the villain, he's
Eaten me!   4415
My little sister found
The bones that lay around.
In a cool place she laid them down.
I turned into a little bird that day.
Fly away! Fly away!   4420
FAUST. [*unlocks the door*]
She cannot know her lover's at the door
And hears the rattling chains, the rustling straw.
                                                       [*he goes in*
MARGARETA. [*hiding her face in the straw*]
No! No! They're coming! Bitter death is near!
FAUST. [*softly*] I've come to set you free! Hush, I am here!
MARGARETA. [*throws herself at his feet*]
If you have human feelings, pity me.   4425
FAUST. Hush! You will wake your gaolers. Hush, speak quietly!
[*he takes hold of the chains to unlock them*]
MARGARETA. [*on her knees*] Who gave you, executioner, the right
To come so early to my cell
And fetch me in the middle of the night?
Have pity, let me live a little spell.   4430
The dawn will not be long—can you not wait?

[she stands up

I am so young, so young, but I
Am not, alas, too young to die.
Once I was beautiful, that was my fate;
My friend was with me, but he would not stay. 4435
My wreath is torn, my flowers blown away.
Don't lay such violent hands on me!
What have I done to you? Oh, let me be,
And spare my life, I beg you—for
I've never seen you in my life before. 4440
FAUST. How can I bear this anguish any more?
MARGARETA. You have the power over me, I know;
But let me feed my child before I go.
I held it in my arms all night;
They took it from me out of spite, 4445
And said I'd killed it, that was wrong
And wicked of them. Now they sing a song
About me, but it isn't true—
It's just a fairy tale that ends like that, you see.
Why do they put the blame on me? 4450
FAUST. [*throws himself at her feet*]
Your love lies at your feet, imploring you
To come with him and end this misery!
MARGARETA. [*kneels down with him*]
Oh, let us kneel and offer up a prayer!
The saints will guard us. Underneath the stair,
Below the threshold there, 4455
Hell seethes beneath the floor!
The Evil One is near,
His angry roar
Brings dread and fear!
FAUST. [*shouts*] Gretchen! Gretchen! 4460
MARGARETA. [*listens attentively*]
That was my lover's voice! He's here!
[*she jumps to her feet. The chains fall from her*]
Where is he? Was he calling me?
No one can hold me now, for I am free!
To my love I'll fly,
In his arms I'll lie! 4465
'Gretchen,' he called, I heard him speaking.
Through all the devilish taunting and shrieking,
Through all the howling and clatter of hell
I heard that sweet voice I remember so well.

365

FAUST. I'm here!

MARGARETA.   You're here! Say it once more. You're here!   4470
   [*she takes hold of him*]
   He's here! Now where is all my pain,
   Where are my fetters now, my prison and my fear?
   He's here! I've found my love again!
   I'm free!—
   I see again the little street where I   4475
   First saw you passing by,
   The pretty garden, and the gate
   Where I and Martha used to wait.

FAUST. [*urging her away*] Come with me! Come!

MARGARETA.   Don't go away!
   I want to be with you so much, please stay!   4480
                          [*she caresses him*

FAUST. Hurry!
   If you don't hurry, we shall miss
   Our chance, and have a heavy price to pay.

MARGARETA. What? Can you not kiss me any more?
   We were not parted long, for sure;   4485
   Have you forgotten how to kiss?
   I feel so fearful in your arms. Why should that be?
   Once, when you spoke, or when you looked at me,
   I felt all heaven's rapture, heaven's bliss;
   You stifled me with kisses, it was not like this.   4490
   Oh, kiss me, do—
   Or I'll kiss you!   [*she embraces him*
   Oh no, your lips are cold
   And dead.
   Where has love fled?   4495
   Oh tell me, say—
   Who stole my love away?   [*she turns away from him*

FAUST. Dearest, take heart and follow me!
   I will save up a thousand kisses for you,
   But follow me this minute, I implore you!   4500

MARGARETA. [*turning towards him*]
   And is it really you? How can this be?

FAUST. It is! Come with me, now!

MARGARETA.   You have unlocked the chain,
   And now you want to take me in your arms again.
   How is it that you don't recoil from me?
   Do you know who it is, my friend, you have set free?   4505

FAUST. Come with me! It will soon be dawn!

MARGARETA. I killed my mother in the early hours,
    I drowned my child when it was scarcely born.
    That child was ours,
    Your child, and mine. It's you! I can't believe it yet.   4510
    Give me your hand! This is no dream—
    It is your own dear hand! But what is this? It's wet!
    There's blood upon it, too.
    Oh, wash it clean!
    Dear God, what have you done?   4515
    Oh, put your sword away,
    I beg of you!
FAUST. The past is past, it's done and gone.
    Your grief will be the death of me.
MARGARETA. No! You must stay,   4520
    For you must tend the graves, you see.
    I'll show you how it is to be—
    Tomorrow you must start.
    The best plot shall be for my mother,
    Beside her then will be my brother.   4525
    Put me a little way apart,
    But not too far.
    My child, and no one else, shall rest
    With me, just here, at my right breast.
    To lie with you, my love, was such sweet bliss,   4530
    There never was such happiness as this!
    But now it is as if you would
    Be gone from me, as if you shrink away;
    I have to force myself on you and make you stay,
    And yet it's you, it is your face, so kind and good.   4535
FAUST. If that is what you feel, then come with me!
MARGARETA. Out there? Oh, no!
FAUST. You will be free!
MARGARETA. Yes! If the grave is out there, then I would
    Be free. If death is waiting, then I'd gladly go   4540
    To my eternal rest—not one step further, though!
    I would come with you, Heinrich, if I could.
FAUST. You can! You must! The door is open, see!
MARGARETA. I cannot come with you; what use is it to flee?
    There is no hope out there, they lie in wait for me.   4545
    A beggar's life is such a wretched fate—
    Far more when you're pursued by guilt and hate.
    To go from door to door, from town to town—
    And in the end, I know, they'll hunt me down.

FAUST. I'll stay with you. 4550

MARGARETA. No, you cannot stay—
    Save your poor child, it's not too late,
    Quick, quick! Away!
    Up the stream and through the gate,
    Over the bridge 4555
    And into the wood,
    Left at the fence,
    There, in the pond,
    Quick! Take hold of it!
    It's struggling, you see— 4560
    It's wriggling still!
    Save it! Save it!

FAUST. Be calm! Listen to me!
    One step, and you're free! You'll be mine!

MARGARETA. If only we were past that hill! 4565
    My mother's sitting there on a stone—
    An icy shiver runs up my spine!
    My mother's sitting there all alone,
    Her head's too heavy, it's lolling about,
    She cannot wave or nod, she can't call out. 4570
    She slept so we could be happy, you and I;
    She slept so long, she'll never wake again.
    Those were such happy times. We were together then.

FAUST. If all my pleading fails, then I must try
    To take you up and carry you away with me. 4575

MARGARETA. I'll not put up with force! No, let me be,
    How could you be so brutal? Let me go!
    I always did your bidding, for I loved you so.

FAUST. My love! My love! It is already light!

MARGARETA. Day! Yes, it's day! My last day—my last dawn. 4580
    It was to be my wedding day—
    Tell no one that you were with me tonight.
    Alas, my wreath is torn
    And thrown away.
    We'll meet again, I know— 4585
    We shan't be dancing, though.
    The people press around,
    But make no sound.
    They fill the streets and pack
    Into the market square. 4590
    The bell tolls, and the staff breaks with a crack.
    They seize me, tie me, drag me to the chair.

The sword sweeps. Every neck can feel
The sharpness of that biting steel.
The world is silent as the tomb.   4595
FAUST. I wish I never had been born!
MEPHISTO. [*appears outside*]
    Come! Or you will surely meet your doom.
    Morning is here! It is the dawn!
    Stop all this useless talk and come away,
    My horses shake and stamp, they will not stay!   4600
MARGARETA. What is that rising from the ground below?
    It's him! It's him! Tell him to go!
    What is he doing in this holy place?
    He wants me!
FAUST.   No, you shall live!
MARGARETA.   Lord, hear my cry!
    Thy judgement be upon me. Give me Thy grace.   4605
MEPHISTO. [*to Faust*] Come! Come, or I'll leave you both to die.
MARGARETA. Father, I am yours. Do not reject me now!
    You angels, all you hosts of heaven, I pray,
    Surround me and protect me now!
    You horrify me, Heinrich, more than I can say.   4610
MEPHISTO. She is condemned!
A VOICE. [*from above*]   Redeemed!
MEPHISTO. [*to Faust*]   Here, to me! Away!
                              [*he disappears with Faust*
VOICE. [*from within, dying away*] Heinrich! Heinrich!

Wilhelm Meister's Apprenticeship

BOOK ONE

Chapter One

The play lasted for a very long time. Old Barbara went to the window several times to see if the coaches had already started leaving the theater. She was waiting for Mariane, her pretty mistress who was that night delighting the audience as a young officer in the epilogue—waiting for her with more impatience than usual, when she merely had a simple supper ready. For this time a surprise package had come in the mail from a wealthy young merchant named Norberg, to show that even when he was away, he was still thinking of his beloved. A trusty servant, companion, adviser, go-between and housekeeper, Barbara had every right to open the package. And this evening she could not resist, for the favors of this generous lover meant even more to her than they did to Mariane. To her great delight she found in the package not only fine muslin and elegant ribbons for Mariane, but for herself a length of cotton material, scarves and a roll of coins. She thought of the absent Norberg with great affection and gratitude, and eagerly resolved to praise him to Mariane, to remind her of what she owed him, and of his hopes and expectations that she would be faithful to him.

The muslin, brightened by the color of the half-unrolled ribbons, lay like a Christmas present on the table, and the light of the candles added a special luster to the gift. Everything was in place as she heard Mariane's footsteps on the stairs and she hastened to meet her. But how surprised she was when this female officer disregarded her affectionate greeting, and, pushing past her, rushed into the room, dropped the sword and plumed hat with unusual haste, walked restlessly up and down and never noticed the festive candles.

"What is it, my dear?" asked the old woman, puzzled. "For heaven's sake, girl, what's wrong? Look at these presents. Who could they be from but your loving friend? Norberg has sent you a length of muslin for a nightgown. He'll soon be here, and seems more eager and generous than usual."

Barbara was about to show Mariane the gifts that she too had received from him when Mariane, turning away from the gifts, cried out: "No! No! I don't want to hear any more about all this. I did what you wanted, so be it! When Norberg comes back, I'll be his again, I'll be yours—do with me what you will. But until then, I want to be myself. If you had a thousand tongues, you couldn't change my mind. I am going to give all of myself to the one who loves me and whom I love. Don't make such faces! I am going to love him with everything I have as if it could last forever."

The old woman had counterarguments enough. But when the exchange began to get violent and bitter, Mariane jumped up and grabbed her. The old woman only laughed uproariously and said, "If I am to be sure of my life, I have to see to it that you are soon in a long dress again. Go and change! I hope that you will apologize, as a girl, for the harm you did me as a flighty officer: off with that coat and with everything underneath it. It's an uncomfortable costume, and dangerous for you, I see. The epaulettes have gone to your head."

Barbara tried to hold her but Mariane broke free. "Not so fast!" she said, "I'm expecting a visitor tonight."

"That's not good," the old woman replied. "Surely not that young, lovesick, unfledged merchant's son?" "Exactly! Him!" said Mariane.

"Magnanimity seems now to be your ruling passion," the old woman scornfully replied. "You exert yourself for those who are either immature or poor. It must be nice to be adored as an unselfish benefactress."

"Make fun of me if you like! I love him! I love him! Oh, how happy I am to say this, for the first time in my life. This is the passion I have acted on the stage and yet never really known. I will throw myself at him, embrace him as if I would hold him forever. I shall show him all my love and enjoy all of his!"

"Calm down! Calm down," said the old woman quietly. "I must interrupt your joy with the news that Norberg will be here in two weeks. Here is his letter, which came with the presents."

"The dawn may take my lover away, but I won't think about that now. Fourteen days! That's an eternity! Just think what can happen, what can change, in two weeks."

Wilhelm entered the room. How eagerly she rushed towards him! And how passionately he embraced that red uniform and the white satin vest. Who would dare to describe, who has the right to describe, the bliss of two lovers. The old womanservant went off muttering, and we, too, leave the happy couple to themselves.

Chapter Two

When Wilhelm greeted his mother the next morning, she told him that his father was very angry and would soon forbid those regular visits to the theater. "I, too, like to go to the theater sometimes," she continued, "but I am often annoyed at the way our domestic peace and quiet are disturbed by your wild addiction to this pleasure. Your father is always saying, 'What's the use of this? Why waste one's time in the theater?'"

"I've often heard him say that," said Wilhelm, "and I may have answered him too rudely; but for goodness' sake, Mother, why is everything useless that doesn't bring in money or enlarge our property? Didn't we have enough room in the old house? Was it necessary to build a new one? Doesn't my father spend a sizable amount of his profits every year in decorating these rooms? All these silk wallpapers and this English furniture, do we need all that? Couldn't we do with less? These striped walls, with their endless rows of flowers, their scrolls and baskets and figures, seem so unpleasant, like a stage curtain in our own house. It's different in a real theater where you know that the curtain will go up and reveal all sorts of things to entertain, enlighten and elevate us."

"Don't overdo it!" said his mother. "Your father likes to have his own fun of an evening. Moreover, he believes that it only distracts you, and in the end I'll be blamed when he gets cross. How often have I been reproached for giving you that wretched puppet theater for Christmas twelve years ago. It gave you that taste for the theater!"

"Don't blame the puppet theater, don't regret that token of your love and care for me. Those were my first happy moments in the new and empty house. I can still remember it, that moment of wonder: after we had received our usual presents, we were told to sit down in front of a door to an adjacent room, which then opened, not just to let us in or out, but for some unexpected festive event, with a great gate closed by a mystic curtain. We watched this from a distance and then, as we were dying to know what was twinkling and rattling behind the half-transparent curtain, we were told to draw up our chairs and to wait.

"So, we all sat quietly until a whistle blew, the curtain rolled up and revealed, in bright red, a view into a temple. Samuel, the High Priest, appeared with Jonathan, and their curious exchange of voices sounded very dignified. Then Saul came on the scene, annoyed by the pompous and heavily armored warrior who had challenged him and his followers to battle. I was glad when the dwarf-like son of Jesse leaped forward with his shepherd's crook, bag and slingshot and said, 'Almighty King and Master! Let no man's heart fail because of him. If Your Majesty will permit me, I will go and fight this mighty giant.' That was the end of the first act, and the audience was eager to see what would happen next. Everyone wished the music would stop. Then the curtain rose again. David was consecrating the giant's flesh to the birds of the air and the beasts of the field. The Philistine vented his scorn, stamped both feet, then fell down like a log and put the matter to a glorious end. And then the maidens sang: 'Saul hath slain his thousands, and David his ten thousands!' The head of the giant was carried in before the tiny victor and he won the hand of the king's daughter. But I, for all my delight, was annoyed by the fact that this lucky prince was fashioned like a dwarf, for 'little David' and 'big Goliath' had really been presented true to life. But Mother, where are those puppets now? I promised to show them to a friend who was amused by what I told him recently of these childhood games."

"I am not surprised that you remember these things so vividly, you were so interested in them from the beginning! I remember how you sneaked the text away from me and then learned the whole play by heart. I noticed that one evening, when you made a David and Goliath out of wax, let them talk to each other, gave the giant a whack, stuck his shapeless head onto a big pin and put it in little David's hand. Your mother was so delighted at your good memory and the fine speeches, that she decided to give you the whole company of wooden puppets on the spot. Little did I know what trouble that would give me."

"Don't grieve over that," Wilhelm replied. "Those playthings have given us both so many pleasant hours." He then asked for the keys for the room where the puppets were kept, rushed off, found the puppets and for a moment was transported back to the time when he thought they were real, live creatures, when he thought he could bring them alive by his own lively voice and the movements of his own hands. He took them up to his room and guarded them carefully.

Chapter Three

If, as is often said, first love is the best that any heart can experience early or late, our hero must be considered thrice blest for being able to enjoy these supreme moments in full measure. Few of us are so favored, for in our early years our feelings often take us through a hard school and, after a few paltry indulgences, we must forgo our highest wishes and learn forever to do without what we once dreamed of as utter bliss.

It was on the wings of imagination that Wilhelm's desire for this charming girl soared. He won her affection after a short acquaintance and soon found himself in possession of someone he both loved and worshipped. She had first appeared in the flattering light of a theatrical performance, and his own passion for the stage was closely connected with his first love for a woman. Being young, he could fully enjoy the offered pleasures which were sustained and intensified by the poetry of her world. And her own ambiguous situation, her fear that he might discover all too soon what her position was—this gave her a pleasing semblance of modesty and anxiety, which only enhanced his fondness for her. As she loved him so dearly, her uneasiness only increased her tenderness. In his arms she was the most adorable creature.

When he awoke from the first frenzy of joy, and thought about his life and his circumstances, everything seemed different—his duties more compelling, his pastimes more absorbing, his knowledge clearer, his talents much stronger, his purposes more definite. It was therefore easy for him to avoid his father's reproaches, to pacify his mother, and to enjoy Mariane's love undisturbed. He performed his daily tasks promptly, stopped going to the theater regularly and made sure to be pleasant at supper; but when everyone had gone to bed, he put on his cloak, crept quietly into the garden and hurried straight to his beloved, his heart beating fast like that of a young lover in a play.

"What did you bring?" asked Mariane one evening when he arrived with a parcel, which Barbara, hoping for a nice present, scrutinized closely. "You'll never guess," said Wilhelm.

Mariane was amazed (and Barbara dismayed) when what he unwrapped turned out to be a jumbled pile of miniature puppets. Mariane laughed as he untangled the wires and proudly displayed each figure. Barbara slunk off, displeased.

Not much is needed to amuse two lovers; they had a wonderful evening. The little band of puppets was paraded, every figure carefully examined and laughed over. Mariane did not like King Saul in his black velvet gown and gold crown: she thought him much too stiff and pedantic. She preferred Jonathan's smooth chin, his yellow and red costume and his turban; she moved him nicely by the wires and made him bow and declare his love. But she wouldn't pay any attention to the prophet Samuel, although Wilhelm proudly pointed to his breastplate and told her that the taffeta of his gown was from one of his grandmother's old dresses. David was too small for her, and Goliath too big. It was Jonathan she loved. Him she treated with particular delicacy, and in the end transferred her cherishing embraces from the puppet to Wilhelm. And so, once again, a little game became the preliminary for hours of bliss.

They were interrupted in their sweet dreams of love by a noise in the street. Mariane called to the old woman, who was busy as usual altering Mariane's costumes for the next play. Barbara reported that some merrymakers were just leaving the tavern nearby where they had been treating themselves to fresh oysters (which had just come in) and champagne.

"A pity we didn't think of that earlier," said Mariane. "We could have done ourselves a bit of good, too."

"It's not too late," Wilhelm replied, and gave Barbara a gold coin. "Go and get what we want; and you can have some with us."

The old woman hurried off, and in no time a well arranged collation was set out before the lovers. Barbara had to join them. They ate, drank—and were merry.

On such occasions there is never any lack of entertainment. Mariane took out her Jonathan, and the old woman steered the conversation to Wilhelm's favorite subject: "You once told us," she said, "about the first performance of your puppet theater one Christmas Eve. It was very amusing, and you were interrupted just when your ballet was about to begin. But now we have met with the distinguished cast that produced such splendid effects."

"Yes," said Mariane, "do tell us more, and what your feelings were at the time."

"It is always pleasant, my dear, to remember old times and our past, but harmless, mistakes. Especially when this occurs as we feel we have achieved a high point from which we can now look about and reflect on the path that brought us to this lofty view. It is pleasant and satisfying to remember the obstacles that we sadly thought were insurmountable, and then compare what we, as mature persons, have now developed into, with what we were then, in our immaturity. I cannot tell you how happy I am now that I can talk to you about the past—now that I gaze out towards the joyous landscape that we shall travel hand in hand."

"Well—how was that ballet?" interrupted the old woman. "I fear that it didn't turn out as well as it should have."

"Oh, yes, it did," said Wilhelm. "It was just fine! Those marvelous leaps of the Moors, the shepherds and the dwarves—little men and women—have remained something like a dim memory through all my later life. The curtain came down, the door closed and we all went off to bed, dizzy and drunk with delight—but I couldn't sleep. I wanted to know more, and was still so eager to ask questions that I didn't want the nursemaid who put us to bed to leave.

"Next morning that magic structure had vanished, the mystic curtain was gone and you could once again move without hindrance from one room to the next. All the enchantment had disappeared and left no trace. My sisters and brothers ran about with their toys, but I crept around silent and alone. It seemed impossible that there should be just two doorposts where the night before there had been such wonders. No one, not even if he were looking for a lost love, could have been more unhappy than I seemed to be."

His glance at Mariane, filled with joy, convinced her that he had no fear of ever being in such an unhappy state.

Chapter Four

"My only wish," Wilhelm continued, "was to see a second performance. I talked to my mother, and when the moment seemed right, she tried to persuade my father; but all her efforts were fruitless. He insisted that if a pleasure was to have any value, it must be infrequent, and that young and old don't appreciate the good things that come their way every day.

"We would have had to wait a long time, perhaps till the following Christmas, if the maker and secret director of the theater had not himself wanted to repeat the performance and in an epilogue introduced a clown he had just made.

"A young soldier from the artillery, who had all sorts of talents and especially great mechanical skill, had helped my father considerably in the building of our house and been handsomely rewarded for this; but he wanted to show his special gratitude to the family at Christmastime, and made us a present of this fully equipped theater which he had put together and painted in his free time. He was the one who, with the help of a servant, had animated the puppets and recited the various parts in different tones of voice. It was not hard for him to persuade my father, who gladly granted to a friend the favor he as a matter of principle had refused his own children. So, the theater was set up again, some children invited from the neighborhood, and the play was repeated.

"The first time I had the joy of surprise and astonishment; at the second performance I was intensely curious and observant. This time I wanted to find out exactly how everything was done. I had decided on that first evening that it couldn't be the puppets themselves that were speaking, I had even suspected that they could not move by themselves. But why it was all so agreeable, and why the puppets themselves seemed to speak and move, and where the lights were, and the people who operated all this—these mysteries disturbed me so much that I wanted to be both among the enchanted and the enchanters, somehow secretly to have a hand in it, and at the same time, as a spectator, be able to enjoy the pleasure of the illusion.

"The play came to an end, and preparations were being made for the epilogue. The audience stood up and chatted. I made my way to the door and from the clatter that was going on inside, realized that they were clearing up. I lifted the lower curtain, and looked through the framework. My mother noticed me and pulled me back; but I had already seen how my friends and foes, Saul and Goliath, and whoever all the others were, were being put away in a drawer. This was fresh nourishment for my half-satisfied curiosity. To my great astonishment I saw the lieutenant busy in this sanctuary. And as a result the clown in the epilogue, despite his heel-clattering, had no appeal for me. I was lost in thought, and after this discovery seemed both calmer and more restless than before. Having discovered something, I felt that I didn't really know anything, and I was right: for what I lacked was a sense of the enterprise as a whole, and that after all is the most important thing."

Chapter Five

"Children in well-established and well-organized homes feel rather like rats and mice: They seek out cracks and crannies to find their way to forbidden dainties. The furtive and intense fear with which they indulge in this search is one of the joys of childhood.

"I noticed more quickly than any of my sisters or brothers when a key was left in a lock. Much as I respected those closed doors, when I had to walk past them week after week or month after month, I would peek in unobserved when my mother opened that sanctuary to get something out, and I was quick to use the brief moments which the negligent housekeeper sometimes provided.

"As could be expected it was the pantry door that drew my sharpest attention. Few joys of anticipation matched those when my mother called me in to help her carry something and, whether by her kindness or my cunning, I managed to pick up some dried prunes. Those piles of wonderful things filled my imagination with a sense of abundance, and the marvelous smell of all the spices had such a mouth-watering effect on me that I never failed to breathe in deeply when I was nearby. One Sunday morning this special key was left in the keyhole as my mother was caught unawares by the bells ringing for the church service and the rest of the house was wrapped in sabbath stillness. As soon as I noticed it, I crept gingerly along the wall, moved quietly to the door, opened it, and with one stride was in the midst of so many long-desired delights. I rapidly scrutinized all the chests, sacks, boxes, cases and jars and, wondering what to take, I finally picked up some of my beloved prunes, some dried apples and some preserved pomegranate skin, and was about to slip out with my loot when I noticed some boxes with wires and hooks hanging out of the lids, which had not been properly closed. I had an idea what these might be, fell upon them and discovered to my delight that here packed away was the whole world of my joys and my heroes. I tried to pick up the ones on top to look at them, and then those underneath, but soon I had tangled up all the wires and got very upset and frightened, especially since I heard the cook moving in the adjoining kitchen. I stuffed everything back as quickly as I could and closed the drawer, taking with me only a handwritten little book, the play of David and Goliath, which had been lying on top, and with my booty escaped to the attic.

"From this time on I spent every hour that I could have by myself in reading over and over 'my' play, learning it by heart, and imagining how wonderful it would be if with my own fingers I could bring the figures to life. I felt myself becoming David and Goliath. I absorbed the play by studying it wherever I could find a corner—in the attic, the stable or the garden—I took each part and memorized it thoroughly, except that I caught myself taking the parts of the main characters and imagining the others trotting along like attendants. The grandiose speeches of David, in which he challenged the boastful Goliath, filled my mind day and night; I muttered them to myself, but no one paid attention except my father who sometimes noticed one of my exclamations and secretly praised the good memory of his son, who seemed to have retained so much after so little listening. As a result I became bolder and one evening recited almost the whole play to my mother, making actors out of lumps of wax. She seemed surprised and wanted an explanation—and I confessed.

"Fortunately all this occurred just when the lieutenant had proposed to initiate me into the secrets of the performance. My mother told him about my unexpected talent, and the lieutenant managed to get permission to use some rooms on the top floor of the house, which were usually empty: one for the spectators and one for the actors, with the doorway between as proscenium. My father allowed his friend to do all this, pretended not to be aware of it, as he was convinced that one ought not to let children see how much one loves them, or else they will ever ask for more. One should appear stern while they are enjoying themselves, and sometimes spoil their pleasures so that they do not become too easily satisfied—and impertinent."

Chapter Six

"The lieutenant set up the theater and looked after everything else. I had noticed him several times during the week coming into the house at an unusual hour, and suspected what was going on. My eagerness increased amazingly, as I knew I couldn't take part in what was being prepared until the following Saturday. But at last the longed-for day arrived, and at five o'clock the lieutenant took me upstairs. Trembling with joy I entered the room and saw the puppets hanging on both sides of the stage, in the order they were to appear. I studied them carefully, and then climbed on the step which set me above the stage, so that I seemed suspended above this miniature world. With a sense of awe, I looked down between the boards, because I remembered how splendid it had all seemed from the outside, and realized that I was now being initiated into the inner mysteries. We made a trial run and everything worked beautifully.

"The next day, in a performance before a group of children we had invited, we managed well, except that in the heat of the moment I dropped my Jonathan and had to reach down with my hand to pick him up—an accident which destroyed the illusion, provoked much laughter, and upset me greatly. My father seemed pleased by this slip-up, for very wisely he kept his pride in my skill to himself and, when the play was over, rather concentrated on the mistakes, and said that it would have been nice if only this or that hadn't gone wrong.

"I was deeply hurt and was miserable all evening, but by next morning had slept off my irritation and was now happy at the thought that, apart from one mishap, I had done very well. The applauding spectators had all agreed that though the lieutenant used coarse and refined tones of voice to good effect, his speech had on the whole been too artificial and stiff, whereas the new helper spoke his David and Jonathan to perfection. My mother praised especially the straightforward way in which I had summoned Goliath to battle and later presented the modest victor to the King.

"To my great joy, the theater remained set up and when spring arrived and we could do without a fire, I spent all my free time in my room playing with the puppets. Often enough I invited my brothers and sisters as well as friends; and if they didn't want to come, I played alone, my imagination brooding over that little world, which soon began to take on a different shape.

"After I had several times performed that first play for which theater and actors had been set up, I began to lose interest in it. But among my grandfather's books I found the collection of plays by Professor Gottsched called 'The German Stage,' and texts of several operas in German and Italian, in which I immersed myself, and, having counted up the characters at the beginning of the text, proceeded to perform the play. As a result King Saul in his black velvet robe now had to stand for some tyrant, or for Darius, or Cato. Usually it was not the whole play but only the fifth act, where the stabbing to death took place, that was performed.

"It was quite natural that the operas with their constant changes of scene and ever new adventures should appeal to me most. For they had everything— storms at sea, gods descending in clouds and, what I especially liked, thunder and lightning. Using cardboard, paper and paint, I provided an excellent night sky: The lightning was fearsome, though the thunder didn't always work. But that didn't matter much. There were also more opportunities to make use of my David and Goliath in the operas than in regular plays. I became more and more attached to that little room where so much pleasure had come my way; and I must admit that the smell of the larder, which still clung to the puppets, added considerably to my delight.

"The scenery for my theater was now pretty well complete, for I had always had a knack for using compasses, cutting up cardboard and making sketches. Now I was all the more disappointed that the limited number of available puppets should prevent me from performing more demanding plays.

"When I saw my sisters dressing and undressing their dolls, I had the idea of getting exchangeable clothes for my heroes. The costumes were taken off in small sections, and I recombined them as well as I could. I saved some money, bought ribbons and finery, begged bits of taffeta, and little by little assembled a whole collection of stage costumes, not forgetting hooped skirts for the ladies.

"I now had enough costumes for even the longest play and, one would have thought that other plays would surely follow. But what often happens with children happened to me. They think up grand schemes and make elaborate preparations, perhaps even a trial run, but ultimately nothing materializes. I made the same mistake. My greatest pleasure was in inventing and imagining. A play interested me only because of a particular scene, for which I immediately had new costumes made. As a result the original costumes got into a state of complete disorder, some had disappeared, so that we could not do even the first of our full-length plays again. I was living entirely in my imagination, trying out this or that, always planning, building a thousand castles in the air, but not realizing that I had destroyed the very foundations of this small world."

During this long recital, Mariane had been at pains to conceal her sleepiness by mustering all her affection toward Wilhelm. Amusing as the whole business might seem in one sense, she found it all too simple, and Wilhelm's commentary too ponderous. She would tenderly place her foot on his, and gave what appeared to be signs of attentiveness and approval. She drank from his glass, and Wilhelm was persuaded that not a word of his narration had been lost.

After a while he said: "Now it is your turn, Mariane, to tell me about the first joys of your childhood. We have been much too busy with the present to be concerned about the past. Tell me, how were you brought up and what early impressions do you remember?"

These questions might have been embarrassing for Mariane, if the old woman had not come to her aid. "Do you really believe," she said sensibly, "that we took so much notice of what happened to us earlier in life, that we have such pleasant things to tell as you have, and even if we did, that we could describe them so cleverly?"

"As if that were necessary!" Wilhelm exclaimed. "I love this tender, sweet, good, lovely girl so much that I would regret every moment of my life that I spent without her. Let me at least share, in my imagination, in your past life. Tell me all about it and I will tell you about mine. Let's use our imagination as much as possible, and try to recover those past times that were lost to our love."

"If you insist, we can certainly satisfy you on that score," said old Barbara. "But you tell us first how your love of the theater grew, how you rehearsed so that you are now quite a good performer. Surely there must have been some amusing incidents. It's not worth going to bed now; I have another bottle in reserve, and who knows when we shall be together again like this, so relaxed and content."

Mariane looked at her with a melancholy glance, but Wilhelm did not notice it and continued with his story.

Chapter Seven

"The distractions of youth began to take their toll of the solitary pleasures, especially when the circle of my friends grew larger. I was huntsman, foot-soldier, cavalryman, as our games demanded; but I always had a slight edge over the others, because I could provide the necessary properties for these occasions: The swords were mostly from my workshop, it was I who decorated and gilded the sleds, and some curious instinct made me transform our whole militia into Romans. We made helmets and topped them with paper plumes; we made shields, even suits of armor, and many a needle was broken by those of our servants who knew how to sew or make clothes. Some of my young comrades were now well armed, the rest were gradually, though not quite so elaborately, equipped, and soon we were a respectable army. We marched into courtyards and gardens, knocking against each other's shields and heads; there were occasional fights, but these were settled easily enough.

"These games, which much appealed to my friends, very soon ceased to please me. The sight of all those armed figures only intensified visions of knights and knighthood which, since I had taken to reading old romances, had recently been filling my mind.

"A translation of Tasso's *Jerusalem Delivered* that I happened to find gave my rambling thoughts a definite direction. I could, of course, not read the whole poem, but there were passages in it that I soon knew by heart and whose images haunted me. Especially Clorinda, in all that she did, fascinated me. Her almost masculine femininity, the serenefulness of her being had a stronger effect on my developing mind than the artificial charms of Armida, however much I was captivated by her 'Bower of Bliss.'

"Time and again in the evening I walked on the balcony between the gables, looking out over the landscape that was illuminated by the last quivering gleam of the setting sun on the horizon, the first stars coming out. As darkness descended from every depth and corner and crickets chirped through the solemn stillness, I recited to myself the sad story of that final combat between Tancred and Clorinda.

"Although I was quite properly on the side of the Christians, my whole heart stood by the heathen Clorinda as she was about to set fire to the tower of the besiegers. And when at night Tancred came upon the supposed warrior, the combat began under cover of darkness and they fought so fiercely, I could never, without tears coming to my eyes, utter the words:

> But now the measure of Clorinda's days is full
> The hour draws near, the hour when she must die.

My tears flowed freely as the unhappy lover plunged his sword into her breast, loosened her helmet, recognized who it was, and trembling, fetched water to baptize her. And how my heart overflowed when Tancred's sword struck the tree in the enchanted wood, blood spurted out and a voice resounded in his ears, telling him that he had wounded Clorinda again, that he was destined unwittingly to harm everything he ever loved!

"My imagination was so enthralled by this story, and everything that I had read in the poem began to form some kind of whole in my mind that I longed somehow to perform it on the stage. I wanted to play both Tancred and Rinaldo, and found two suits of armor that I had made which were quite suitable for these characters. One, made of dark-grey paper with scales, would do for the sober Tancred, the other, gold and silver, for the dazzling Rinaldo. Excited by the whole idea, I told my friends the entire story; they were thrilled, but wondered how all this could be performed, and by them.

"I easily dispelled their hesitation. I decided to take over a few rooms in the neighboring house of one of my friends, without considering that the old lady would on no account let us have them. And I had no clear notion of how to set up a stage, except that it must rest on beams, and we would use folding screens for scenery and a big sheet for the backdrop. But where the materials and tools to make all this were to come from, I had absolutely no idea.

"We found a good way to produce a forest by persuading a fellow who had been a servant in one of the households and was now a forester, to find us some young birches and spruces, which, as a matter of fact, arrived sooner than we had expected. Now the problem was how to put on the play before the trees withered. We sorely needed advice, for we had no room, no stage, no curtain—only the folding screens.

In this predicament we once again approached the lieutenant, giving him an elaborate account of all the splendor that was in the offing. Though he scarcely understood what we were really about, he did help us by pushing together in the little room all the tables we could find, setting up the side walls on these and making a backdrop of green curtains; the trees were placed in a row.

"Evening came, the candles were lit, children and maidservants settled in their places, the company of warriors were all decked out in their costumes and the play was about to begin. Suddenly it dawned on us for the first time that we didn't know what we were going to say. My imagination was so excited by the whole enterprise that I had completely forgotten that everyone should know what and when he had to speak. The others, so thrilled to be performing, hadn't thought about it either. They imagined that all they had to do was to present themselves as heroes and that it would be easy to act and speak like the characters in the world I had told them about. Now they all stood in astonishment, wondering what was to happen next, and having from the beginning thought of myself as Tancred, I came on alone and began to recite some of Tancred's words from the poem. But since the passage soon turned into a narration where I was referred to in the third person, and Godfrey was mentioned without actually appearing on the stage, I had to withdraw, much to the amusement of the spectators—a mishap which grieved me greatly. The whole show turned out to be a failure.

"The audience sat there waiting to see something; and as anyway we were all in our costumes, I pulled myself together and decided to play David and Goliath instead. My fellow actors had seen this at the puppet theater many times, some had even assisted me. We divided up the parts, everyone promised to do his best, and a funny little fellow painted a black beard on his chin so that he could come on as a clown if there was any unforeseen hitch in the performance. I did not like to do this, for I thought it would detract from the solemnity of the play. But I swore that once I was out of this fix, I would never again put on a play without a great deal more thought."

Chapter Eight

Mariane, overcome by sleep, had put her head on her lover's shoulder. He held her tight while he continued his narration; Barbara finished off in a leisurely fashion what remained of the wine.

"The embarrassment of having tried to perform a nonexistent play was soon forgotten. My passionate determination to turn any novel that I read, any story that I heard from my teachers, into a play was not to be diminished by even the most unsuitable subject matter. I was convinced that any story that appealed to me would be still more effective on the stage, where I could actually see it happening before my eyes. When we were taught world history at school, I reflected in great detail on the particular way in which a personage was stabbed or poisoned; my imagination leapt over exposition and development, and hurried to the much more interesting fifth act. And so I actually started to compose a few plays from the ending and working back to the beginning. At the same time, both on my own impulse and at the instigation of like-minded friends, I read my way through a whole stack of plays—whatever happened to come to hand. I was at that happy age when one delights in all sorts of things, when plenty and variety satisfy. My judgment was warped in still another way: My preference was for plays in which I thought I would myself have particular success, and I read few plays where I did not feel this would be the case. My lively imagination, by which I could put myself into any part, misled me into thinking that I could successfully act them all. As I distributed the parts, I gave myself roles for which I was not at all suited and, if possible, gave myself more than one.

"When children play, they can make something out of anything: A stick becomes a gun, a piece of wood a sword, any old bundle a doll, and any corner a hut. This is how our little theater came about. Totally unaware of our limited abilities, we embarked on anything and everything; we never realized that we sometimes confused one character with another, and assumed that everyone would take us for what we claimed to be. The results were so ordinary and uninteresting that I don't have even one amusing piece of silliness to report. First we performed the few plays that had only male characters. After that some of us dressed up as women, using what costumes we had. And finally we persuaded our sisters to join in. A few of our families thought that what we were doing was useful enough, and invited some friends. And our lieutenant did not leave us in the lurch. He showed us how to enter and exit, how to declaim, how to use gestures. But he got little thanks for his pains, for we were sure that we knew more about acting than he did.

"We started with tragedies, because we had heard—and believed it—that it is easier to write and perform a tragedy than to excel in comedy. We really felt in our element when we tried our hand at tragedy, representing high social station and nobility of character by a certain stiffness and affectation. We thought we really amounted to something. But we weren't completely happy until we could rant, stamp our feet, and in rage and desperation, throw ourselves on the ground.

"It was not long before natural instincts began to stir in boys and girls, and the company divided up into little love affairs—plays within plays. In the wings, the couples held hands tenderly, idealizing each other in their beribboned finery, while the disappointed rivals, eaten up with envy and spite, embarked on all sorts of mischief.

"Yet, all this playacting, though it lacked both understanding and direction, was not without its usefulness. We trained our memory, exercised our bodies, achieved greater ease in speaking and greater refinement in behavior than children at that age usually acquire. Certainly, now, for me that time was a turning point, because as a result my whole being was directed towards the theater and from then on I knew no greater pleasure than reading, writing and performing plays.

"At school, lessons with my teachers continued, and since it had been decided that I should go in for commerce, I was assigned to work in a neighbor's firm. But at the same time, my whole being rebelled violently against what I could only consider a base occupation. I wanted to devote myself entirely to the stage, there to find my happiness and satisfaction.

"I remember writing a poem, which must still be somewhere among my papers, in which the Muse of Tragedy and another female figure representing Commerce were struggling for possession of my worthy self. The whole idea is, of course, trivial and I don't remember whether the verse was any good, but you should have seen it, if only to get an idea of the fear and horror, the love and passion that I put into it. How timid was my portrayal of the old housewife with her keys and distaff, spectacles on her nose, always busy and bustling, quarrelsome and domestic, petty and pompous! How pitiful my account of those who had to submit to her and perform their menial duties in the sweat of their brow.

"And how different the other figure! What a vision for an oppressed spirit! Noble of stature, she was in every ounce of her being and behavior the true daughter of freedom. Her sense of herself gave her dignity and pride. Her garments suited her perfectly, the wide folds of her dress moved like echoes of the graceful movements of a divine creature. What a contrast between the two! You can well imagine which way my inclination turned. And my muse had all the accoutrements—crowns and daggers, chains and masks—that our literary predecessors had given their muses. The altercation between these two females was heated, their speeches, in the usual black-and-white of a fourteen-year-old, suitably contrasted. The old woman talked like one who had to pick up and save every pin, and the other as though she were distributing kingdoms. The warnings and threats of the old woman were treated with scorn; I turned my back on the riches she promised me, and, naked and disinherited, I gave myself to the muse who lent me her golden veil to cover my nakedness.

"If only I could have imagined," Wilhelm exclaimed as he pressed Mariane close to him, "that another and more lovely goddess would confirm me in my resolve and accompany me on my path—my poem would have turned out much better and achieved a far more interesting ending! But life in your arms is no poem—it is reality. Let us savor the sweet joy in full consciousness."

His voice was so loud and his grasp so tight that Mariane suddenly woke up. She tried to conceal her embarrassment by caressing him, for she had not heard one single word of the last part of his narration; it is to be hoped that in the future our hero will find more attentive listeners for his favorite stories.

Chapter Nine

And so Wilhelm spent his nights in the intimate pleasures of love and his days in anticipation of further hours of bliss. Earlier, when he had set his desire and hopes on winning Mariane, he had begun to feel a different person. Now that he was joined to her, the satisfaction of his desires became a pleasant habitual occupation. His heart strove to ennoble the object of his affections, and his mind to lift them both on to a higher plane. He was always thinking of her when for a short time she was not with him. She had been important to him before—now she was indispensable, because he was bound to her by every fiber of his being, and his mind felt, in all its unclouded innocence, that she was half—more than half—of himself. He was grateful, and absolutely devoted, to her.

Mariane, too, was able to deceive herself for a while, because she shared his feeling of intense joy, despite the cold reproaches that sometimes passed over her heart and from which she was never entirely free even in his embraces and the exhilaration of his love. When she was alone and had descended from the heights to which his passion had transported her back into a true sense of her position, she was indeed to be pitied. Her natural frivolity sustained her as long as she lived thoughtlessly, not realizing or even knowing the situation she was really in, she would take this or that incident as just part of a total picture, and cheerfully alternate between pleasure and displeasure, humiliation and pride, deprivation and momentary abundance, accepting necessity and habituation as a justifiable law of living, and shaking off any feeling of unpleasantness from one moment to the next. But now, when for moments this poor girl felt herself transported to a better world and looked down from all this sunshine and joy to the drab emptiness of her ordinary life, aware of the wretchedness of not being able to inspire love and respect as well as arousing desire, and therefore no better off than she was before, she found nothing in herself to help her rise above this state of mind, for her mind was empty and her heart had no resistance. The sadder she felt, the more she clung to her passion for her beloved, which grew stronger from day to day, as the danger of losing him loomed ever larger.

But Wilhelm soared happily in loftier regions. For him, too, a new world had opened up, a world with vistas of endless delight. The full measure of his initial joy was succeeded by a clear realization of what had obscurely moved him before: "She is yours! She has given herself to you who loved, sought and adored her—given herself in faith and trust to you, and not to someone who is ungrateful." He talked to himself, no matter where he was. His heart was full to the brim and he recited to himself the loftiest of sentiments in the most grandiloquent phrases. Fate, he decided, was extending its helping hand to him, through Mariane, to draw him out of that stifling, draggle-tailed middle-class existence he had so long desired to escape. It seemed to him the easiest thing in the world to leave his family and his father's house. He was young and inexperienced in the ways of the world, eager to seek happiness and contentment anywhere, and elated by love. That his future lay in the theater had now become quite clear to him, and the high goal that he envisioned for himself seemed nearer to realization as he aspired to the hand of Mariane. In self-satisfied modesty he saw in himself the great actor, the founder of a future National Theater that he heard various people pining for. Everything that had been dormant in the recesses of his heart suddenly came alive. From all these thoughts and aspirations he painted, with colors from the palette of love, a picture against a misty background; the fact that the figures in the picture were not easily distinguishable made the general effect all the more pleasing.

Chapter Ten

He now sat at home, rummaging amongst his papers and preparing for his departure. What smacked of earlier intentions was put aside, for he did not want to take anything with him on his journey into the wide world that might arouse unpleasant memories. Only works embodying good taste, poets and critics, were admitted as trusty friends to the company of the Elect. Up to now he had not spent much time on critics, and so he looked through his books in search of enlightenment but found that the theoretical works were still mostly uncut. He had acquired many such works in the full conviction that they would be essential to him; yet, with the best will in the world, he had never succeeded in getting further than halfway into any of them. But he had zealously read model texts, and tried his hand at writing in those styles he had become familiar with.

Werner came in, and seeing his friend busied with his manuscripts, said: "Are you poring over those things again? I bet you don't intend to finish any of them. You'll just look through them again and again—and then start something new."

"It is not the business of a pupil to finish a thing. He should try his hand at everything."

"But surely he should finish them as best he can."

"But you can also consider it promising if a young man does not continue with something that he feels is clumsily done, and refuses to spend more time and effort on something that can never have any value."

"I know that you were never concerned with bringing something to completion; you were always tired of it before it was half done. When you were directing our puppet theater, new costumes always had to be made for our little company and new sets constructed. First one tragedy was to be performed, then another, and the most you ever put on was the fifth act where everything got confusing and people stabbed each other."

"Since you are talking about those days, tell me: Who was responsible for taking apart the costumes we had fitted to our puppets, and setting up a large and useless wardrobe? Wasn't it you who was always trying to sell us some new ribbon or other, and you who encouraged this hobby of mine to your own advantage?"

Werner laughed, and said: "I still remember with delight how I profited from your theatrical forays, like suppliers from the wars. While you were preparing to deliver Jerusalem, I made a handsome profit, much as the Venetians did on a similar occasion. I think there is nothing in life more sensible than making profit out of the follies of others."

"I would think it a nobler pleasure to cure people of their follies."

"That might be a fruitless undertaking, judging from the people I know. It takes some effort to be smart and become rich, and that usually happens at the cost of others."

"I have just found that poem I wrote called 'The Youth at the Crossroads,'" said Wilhelm, pulling out a copybook. "That *was* finished, such as it was."

"Throw it out! Burn it!" said Werner. "As a piece of artistic invention it was not remarkable. It irritated me at the time and displeased your father. The verses were pretty enough but the whole presentation was absolutely wrong. I well remember your personification of commerce as a miserable, shrivelled-up old witch. You must have filched that portrait from some old junk shop. At the time you had no idea what the world of business is really like. The mind of a true businessman is more wide-ranging than that of all other men—has to be so. What an overview we gain by the orderly fashion in which we conduct business. It permits us to survey the whole without being confused by the parts. What tremendous advantages accrue to the businessman by double bookkeeping. This is one of the finest inventions of the human mind, and every serious manager should introduce it into his business."

"Forgive me," said Wilhelm with a smile, "but you are treating form as though it were substance, and in all your adding up and balancing of accounts you usually ignore the true sum total of life."

"Unfortunately, my friend, you don't seem to understand that in this case form and substance are identical, in that the one cannot exist without the other. Order and clarity increase the desire to save and to acquire. A man who doesn't keep good accounts, who doesn't reckon up what he owes, easily finds himself in a foggy state, whereas a good manager knows no greater pleasure than watching his fortunes mounting daily. A setback may be an unpleasant surprise for him, but it does not scare him; he can balance this out with the gains he has made elsewhere. I am convinced, my friend, that if you could only acquire some lively interest in our affairs, you would convince yourself that many faculties of the mind are freely involved in such matters."

"Maybe the journey I am about to undertake will make me change my opinions!"

"Surely it will. Believe me, all you need is to see for yourself some big enterprise, and you will feel yourself one of us. And when you come back you will be glad to join those who know how, by speculating and the transmission of goods, to acquire part of the money and prosperity that must always circulate in the world. Just look at the natural and artificial products of every country and see how, now the one, now the other, have become necessities. What a pleasant exercise of careful ingenuity it is to find out what is most wanted at a given moment and is therefore bound to be in short supply and difficult to get. You can quickly and easily provide everyone with what is needed by building up stocks in advance, and reaping the advantages of wide circulation. That, it seems to me, should appeal greatly to anyone who has a head on his shoulders."

Wilhelm seemed not to disapprove, and so Werner went on: "First visit a few big trading centers, a few seaports, and you will certainly be fascinated. When you see how many people are occupied, and how many things come in and go out, you will surely enjoy seeing them pass through your own hands. You will see the smallest commodity in relation to trade in general, and as a result you will not consider anything insignificant because everything increases the circulation from which your life too receives its nourishment."

Werner, who had sharpened his own mind by his contact with Wilhelm, had come to think of his trade and business activities in terms of spiritual elevation, and always believed that he did so with greater justification than his otherwise sensible and respected friend who placed such high value, indeed the whole weight of his soul, on what seemed to Werner the most unreal thing in the world. He sometimes thought that such false enthusiasm could not fail to be overcome and this good fellow be brought back on to the right path. And so, with such hopes, he continued: "The mighty of this world have seized the earth and live in luxury and splendor. Every small corner of this earth is already taken possession of, every property firmly established. Official positions do not bring in much in remuneration. What other regular occupation, what more reasonable means of aggrandizement is there than trade? The princes of this world control the rivers, roads and harbors and make good profits from what goes through them or past them. Why shouldn't we also relish the opportunity of extracting by our labors custom duties on those articles made indispensable by the requirements and caprices of men and women? And I can assure you that if you would but engage your poetic imagination, you could establish *my* Goddess as the undoubted victor over yours. She bears the olive branch rather than the sword, has no daggers and chains, but she does distribute crowns to her favorites, which, it can be said without demeaning that other woman in your poem, are of pure gold from mountain streams and gleaming with pearls fetched from the depths of the ocean by her always industrious helpers."

Wilhelm was somewhat peeved by this outburst, but concealed his irritation, for he remembered that Werner used to listen to his speeches without losing his composure. He was also reasonable enough to be pleased when people spoke so warmly about their occupations—but they should not demean his own, which he had espoused with such fervor.

"And since you take such an interest in human affairs," Werner exclaimed, "what a spectacle it will be for you to see what joy accompanies bold enterprises for those who take part in them! What could be more pleasing than the sight of a ship returning from a successful journey, a trawler returning early with a good catch! Everyone is excited—relatives, friends, associates, even complete strangers—when the shipbound sailor leaps joyfully on land even before his boat touches it, feeling free once more and ready to entrust to solid land what he has extracted from the treacherous water. Profit is not just a matter of figures, my friend—Fortune is the sovereign goddess of all living things, and, to experience her favors fully, one must *live* and see people who exert their powers and enjoy their senses."

Chapter Eleven

It is high time that we become better acquainted with the fathers of these two friends. They were two very different temperaments but of one mind in that they regarded commerce as the noblest of all occupations and were attentive to every advantage to be gained by speculation. Wilhelm's father had, on the death of his own father, sold a valuable collection of paintings, drawings, etchings and antiques, had remodelled and refurnished his house from the ground up, all in the newest taste. He used what remained of his capital in various profitable ways, investing a considerable part of it in the business of Werner's father, who was respected for his initiative and for his speculative ventures, which usually turned out to his advantage. What he desired above all else was to impart to his son Wilhelm the qualities that he himself lacked, and to leave to his children those possessions which he particularly valued. He had indeed a certain penchant for sumptuousness, for what was impressive and yet had real lasting value. Everything had to be solid and massive in his house—plentiful provisions, heavy silver, costly china—but there were few guests, for every party turned into a celebration which, owing to cost and inconvenience, could not be repeated very often. His household was characterized by calm and monotony, and any change or innovation was always in those things which gave no one any pleasure.

Old Werner led a totally different life in his dark and gloomy house. Once he had finished his day's work at his decrepit old desk in his poky office, all he wanted to do was to eat well and, if possible, drink even better. He did not like to enjoy good things by himself, and so he wanted, beside his close family, to have all his friends, even strangers who had any sort of connection with his business, at his table. The chairs were very old but every day he invited someone to sit on them. The guests were so much attracted by the good quality of the food that they never noticed that it was served in very ordinary dishes. His cellar did not contain much wine, but when a bottle was finished it was usually replaced by a better one.

This is how they lived, these two fathers who often consulted each other on business matters, and this very day they had decided to send Wilhelm on a commercial journey.

"Let him see the world," said old Meister, "and at the same time do business for us in various places. There is nothing better one can do for a young man than introduce him early to his future career. Your son profited so much from his expedition and conducted his affairs so well, that I am curious to see how my son makes out, but I fear he will need more money than yours did." He had a high opinion of his son's ability, and so, in saying this, had hoped that the other would contradict him and emphasize Wilhelm's excellent qualities. But he was mistaken, for old Werner, who in practical matters trusted no one that he had not himself tested, calmly added: "One should try everything. We could send him on the same route and give him instructions to follow. There are debts to be collected, old acquaintanceships to be renewed and new ones to be made. He could also help to advance the venture I talked to you about recently, for we can do little unless we gather exact information on the spot."

"Let him get ready then, and leave as soon as possible," said Wilhelm's father. "But where shall we get a suitable horse for him?"

"We won't have to look far for that. There is a shopkeeper in H . . . who still owes us money, a good fellow who has offered me a horse in lieu of payment. My son has seen it; it seems to be perfectly acceptable."

"Well, let him go and get it. If he takes the postchaise he can be back in good time the day after tomorrow, and in the meantime we can get his bag ready and the letters he is to deliver, so that he could leave early next week."

They called Wilhelm and told him of their decision. He was absolutely delighted that the means to achieve his purpose were being provided for him without his having to find them for himself. He was so passionately convinced that he was doing the right thing in escaping from the burden of his present form of life by embarking on a new and nobler course that he did not have the least pangs of conscience or anxiety: indeed, he felt that this deception was somehow sanctioned by Heaven. He was sure that his parents and relations would eventually approve the step he was about to take. He perceived in this concatenation of circumstances the guiding hand of Fate.

How time dragged till nightfall, when he would be able to see his beloved again! He sat in his room, thinking over his travel plans, like a crafty thief or magician in prison, easing his feet out of the shackles that bind him in order to persuade himself that liberation is not only possible, but nearer than his imperceptive goalers imagine. But at last the longed-for hour arrived, he left the house and, shaking off all sense of oppression, he walked through the quiet streets, raising his hands to Heaven on the open square, disembarrassed, discarding everything, imagining himself in Mariane's arms, then alongside her in the bright lights of the theater, transported in a welter of hopes and anticipations, until the voice of the night watchman sounding the hours reminded him that he was still on this earth.

She met him on the stairs, and how beautiful, how lovely, she was. She was wearing her new white negligé, and he thought she had never looked so charming. For the first time she wore the gift of her absent lover in the arms of her present one, showering him passionately with natural affection and studied caresses, and—need we ask whether he was blissfully happy? He told her what had happened, and gave her a general idea of his plans and desires. He would look for somewhere to live and then send for her; he hoped she would not refuse him her hand in marriage. The poor girl said nothing, suppressing her tears and clasping him to her breast. He interpreted her silence favorably, though he would have liked an answer, especially since he had recently asked her in all modesty, and in the gentlest terms, whether he was not about to become a father, to which she had only replied with a sigh, and a kiss.

Chapter Twelve

Next morning Mariane awoke once more in a sad state. She felt very much alone, did not want to begin the day, stayed in bed, and wept. The old woman sat by her and tried to talk to her and console her, but she did not succeed in healing this wounded heart so quickly. The moment was fast approaching which the poor girl had been dreading as if it were to be her last. Can one imagine a more anxious state than that she was in? The man she really loved was leaving, an unwelcome admirer was due to arrive any moment and it would be a real calamity if, which was perfectly possible, they were to encounter each other.

"Don't get upset, my dear, don't spoil your pretty eyes by weeping," said Barbara. "Is it such a misfortune to have two lovers? Even if you only love the one, you can always be grateful to the other who, by the way he looks after you, deserves to be called a friend."

But Mariane tearfully replied: "My dear Wilhelm sensed somehow that we would part; a dream told him what I had so carefully tried to conceal from him. He was sleeping so peacefully beside me, when suddenly I heard him murmuring barely audibly. I was frightened, and woke him up. How tenderly, how lovingly, how passionately he embraced me. 'Oh Mariane!' he said, 'What a frightful situation you rescued me from! How can I thank you for freeing me from such hell? I was dreaming that I was far away from you in some strange part of the country, but your image hovered before me and I saw you standing on a beautiful hilltop in the sunlight. How charming you looked! But it didn't last long: your image floated down from the hill, down and down, and I stretched out my arms to you, yet couldn't reach you. You were slipping towards a big lake at the foot of the hill, more of a swamp than a lake, when suddenly some man took your hand. He seemed to be wanting to lead you back up, but in fact led you off to the side, trying to drag you towards him. I called out, since I myself couldn't reach you, to warn you. When I tried to move, the ground held me fast, and when I could move, the water blocked me and even my cries were stifled in my anxious breast.'—That's what the poor fellow told me as he was recovering from his fright on my breast, happy at finding such a terrifying dream dispelled by blissful reality."

The old woman did her best in her own sober prose to bring Mariane from her flights of poetry down to everyday reality, using the tricks of birdcatchers, who imitate on a tin whistle the song of those they wish to catch in their nets. So she praised Wilhelm—his figure, his eyes, his affection—and the unfortunate Mariane listened with approval, then got up, dressed and seemed calmer. "I don't want to worry or offend you, or rob you of your happiness, my child," the old woman said, ingratiatingly. "Don't you understand what I have in mind? Don't you know that I have always been more concerned for you than for myself? Just tell me what you want to do, and we'll see how to bring it about."

"How can I do anything?" Mariane replied. "I am miserable, and shall be miserable for the rest of my life. I love him, he loves me, and yet I see that I must part from him and don't know how I can survive this. Norberg will come. We owe our whole existence to him. We cannot do without him. Wilhelm's means are very limited. He cannot do anything for me."

"Yes indeed, he is unfortunately one of those lovers who have nothing to give but their heart and are therefore the most demanding."

"Don't make fun of him! Unfortunately he intends to leave home, go on the stage, and offer me his hand."

"We already have four empty hands between us, you and me."

"I have no choice," Mariane went on. "So why don't *you* decide? Push me this way or that, but let me tell you one thing: I most likely carry a pledge within me that should bind us even closer together. Think of that, and decide: whom should I leave and whom should I follow?"

The old woman fell silent, then said: "Why do young people always think in terms of irreconcilable opposites? What could be more natural than to combine pleasure and profit? Why not love the one, and let the other pay? It's only a question of our being smart enough to keep them apart."

"Do as you like," said Mariane. "I can't think anymore. But I'll do what you want."

"The Director's stubborn insistence on maintaining the good morals of his actors can be used to our advantage. Both your lovers are accustomed to go to work secretly and cautiously. I'll arrange time and place, but you play the part I assign you. Who knows what circumstances might not assist us. If only Norberg would come now when Wilhelm is away! And who is to prevent you from thinking of the one when you are in the arms of the other? I hope you have a son. He shall have a rich father."

Such thoughts did not encourage Mariane for long, for she could not reconcile her feelings or her conviction with her present situation, the misery of which she longed to forget, but a thousand small matters reminded her of it at every turn.

Chapter Thirteen

In the meantime Wilhelm had completed his short journey and delivered his letter of recommendation to the wife of the business associate to whom he had been sent, for the husband was not at home. She was not able to give much of an answer to his questions, because she was much perturbed and the whole house was in a state of confusion.

However, she did not take long to inform him confidentially of something that could not be kept secret, namely that her stepdaughter had gone off with an actor, a creature who had recently left a small theatrical company, stayed for a while in this place, and given French lessons. The girl's father, beside himself with distress and irritation, had run to the authorities to have the fugitives pursued. The wife expressed her anger at the girl and her scorn of the lover with such vigor that nothing remained to be said in favor of either of them, and she vociferously bewailed the scandal that had befallen the family;

she put Wilhelm in considerable embarrassment at finding his future, secret plans reviled and rejected by this sibyl, as if by some prophetic voice. But he was even more deeply affected by the deep sorrow and the half-uttered words of the father when he returned, and told his wife about his expedition to the authorities. He was unable to conceal his distraction and bewilderment; he read the letter and had the horse fetched for Wilhelm.

Wilhelm fully intended to mount his horse and leave this house where, under the circumstances, he could not possibly feel at ease, but the good man would not let the son of someone to whom he was so indebted leave without showing him due hospitality, and put him up for the night.

So our friend partook of a sad supper, spent a restless night, and left hurriedly next morning, to escape these people who by their tales and utterances had unwittingly so tormented him.

He was riding slowly and pensively down the street, when he saw a group of armed men crossing a field. From their long, baggy coats, wide lapels, shapeless hats and clumsy firearms, and their stolid gait and relaxed posture, he recognized them as a detachment of the local militia. They halted beneath an old oak tree, put down their flintlocks and settled comfortably on the grass to smoke a pipe. Wilhelm joined them and got into conversation with a young man who rode up on a horse. And so he had once again to hear the familiar story of the two fugitives, but this time laced with comments that were not especially favorable either to the young people or the parents. He also learned that the militiamen had come to take the young people, who had been stopped and apprehended in the neighboring town, into safe custody. Soon they saw a wagon drawing up, which was guarded in a fashion more ridiculous than terrifying. An unofficial looking town clerk rode ahead and exchanged compliments at the town limits with an actuary on the other side (the same young man that Wilhelm had been talking to), punctiliously and accompanied by fantastic gestures such as a magician and a spirit, the one inside and the other outside the magic circle, might well use during some ominous nocturnal operations.

Meanwhile all eyes were fixed on the farm-wagon; and the poor fugitives, who were sitting together on bundles of straw and gazing at each other lovingly and almost unaware of the bystanders, were observed with sympathy. It so happened that they had had to be transported in this unsuitable way from the last village, because the old coach in which the girl had been placed had broken down. As a result she asked to be with her friend, who, because they believed him guilty of a capital crime, had been made to walk beside the coach, in heavy chains. The sight of this loving pair was made even more appealing by these chains, especially since the young man handled them gracefully as he repeatedly kissed his beloved's hands.

"We are very unhappy," she cried out, "but not so guilty as we may seem. This is how cruel people reward true love, and parents utterly neglectful of their children's happiness tear them away from the joy that is theirs after so much sadness."

The bystanders expressed their sympathy in various ways while the authorities went through their ceremonial actions. The wagon moved on, and Wilhelm, very concerned about the fate of the lovers, hurried ahead on a footpath to make the acquaintance of the magistrate before the others arrived. But just before he reached the courthouse where everyone was busily preparing for the arrival of the fugitives, the actuary caught up with him and gave him a detailed account of all that had happened, and expansively praised his horse which he had got from some Jew the day before—which prevented any further conversation.

The unfortunate couple had been set down in the adjoining garden at the side of the building, and then led quietly into the courthouse. Wilhelm expressed to the actuary his appreciation of this consideration, though the actuary had simply wanted to play a trick on the people assembled in front of the courthouse by depriving them of the pleasing spectacle of a humiliated townswoman.

The magistrate was not especially fond of such unusual cases as this, because he usually made some mistake or other and, for all his good will, earned a harsh reproof from the government. He walked stolidly toward the courtroom where the actuary, Wilhelm and some of the respected citizens joined him.

The girl was the first to be led into the room. She showed respect as she came in, and a true sense of what she was. The way she was dressed and the nature of her behavior showed that she was indeed a self-respecting girl, and she began, without being asked, to talk about her situation in a seemly manner.

The actuary told her to be silent and held his pen over his opened sheaf of paper. The magistrate settled himself, looked at the actuary, cleared his throat, and then asked the girl what her name was, and how old she was.

"Well, sir," she replied, "it seems very odd that you ask for my name and my age, since you know very well who I am and that I am of the same age as your eldest son. I will gladly tell you without beating about the bush what you wish to know from me, and what you are required to find out.

"Since my father's second marriage I have not been at all well treated at home. I could have made several attractive matches if my stepmother had not ruined everything by worrying about my dowry. And when I became acquainted with young Melina, I fell in love with him, and since we foresaw the obstacles that would be placed in our way, we decided to seek together the happiness in the world at large that seemed not likely to be granted to us at home. I have taken nothing with me that was not my own. We did not run off like thieves and robbers. And my friend has not deserved to be dragged around in chains and fetters. Our prince is just; he will not approve of such harshness. If we are guilty, we are not guilty in a way to justify such treatment."

The old magistrate became doubly—and trebly—embarrassed at this. The prince's reprimands were already buzzing in his head, and the girl's fluent speech had completely wrecked his ideas on how to write up the case. His distress grew even worse when she repeatedly refused to say anything more and steadfastly insisted on what she had already maintained.

"I am not a criminal," she said. "Yet, I was in shame brought here on bundles of straw. But there is a higher justice that will restore our honor."

The actuary had in the meantime been writing down what she said and whispered to the magistrate that he should just continue. A formal protocol could easily be drawn up later. The old man was encouraged by this and began to enquire in plain terms and conventional dry phrases about the sweet secrets of love.

Wilhelm turned red at this, and the charming criminal herself blushed with shame. She maintained silence until her embarrassment finally gave her courage to speak. "Be assured," she declared, "that I would not flinch at telling the truth, even if it meant discrediting myself, but in this case, when the truth does me honor, why should I hesitate and refuse to speak? Yes indeed, from the moment that I was convinced of his affection and loyalty, I thought of him as my husband. I gladly gave him everything that love demands and a heart that is sure of itself cannot deny. Do with me what you will. If I hesitated for a moment to confess all this, the reason was simply that I feared some evil consequences for my beloved."

Having heard her confession, Wilhelm formed a high opinion of the girl's character, whereas the officials treated her as a brazen hussy, and the good burghers in the courtroom were thankful that nothing like this had happened in their families—or at least was not public knowledge.

Wilhelm pictured his Mariane being thus brought to judgment, put even finer words in her mouth, and let her appear even more heartfelt in her sincerity and nobler in her confession. He was seized by the most passionate desire to help these two young lovers, and not concealing this, he quietly urged the magistrate to bring matters to a speedy conclusion, for everything was as clear as daylight and needed no further investigation. This helped, in the sense that the girl was told to step down; but the young man was ordered to come in, once they had removed his chains at the door. He seemed more concerned about his fate than she. His answers were more composed, and although in some ways he seemed less heroic than the girl, he made a good impression by the precision and orderliness of his statements. After his examination, which coincided in every point with hers except that, to spare the girl, he resolutely denied what she had already admitted, she was brought in again, and there followed a scene which entirely won them Wilhelm's affection. For what usually happens only in plays and novels, was now played out before his very eyes in this wretched courtroom—generosity of each toward the other, the strength of love in misfortune.

"Is it then true," he said to himself, "that bashful affection, which shuns the light of day and only displays itself in extreme seclusion and deep secrecy, when it is dragged out into the open by hostile circumstance, reveals itself to be stronger, bolder, more courageous than the most raging, grandiloquent of passions?"

Much to his relief the whole affair was settled very quickly. The young people were placed in minimum confinement, and if it had been possible he would have returned the girl to her parents that very evening. For he decided to act as a mediator and help to bring about a happy and respectable union of these two young people. So he asked permission of the magistrate to talk with Melina alone, which was granted him without further ado.

Chapter Fourteen

Their conversation soon became quite friendly and lively. For when Wilhelm told the downcast youth about his acquaintance with the girl's parents, when he had offered to act as intermediary and expressed the fondest hopes, the mournful and troubled spirit of the prisoner revived, he felt he was free again, reconciled with his parents-in-law—and the conversation moved on to considerations of what they should live on and where.

"But that should not be a problem for you," said Wilhelm, "for you both seem by nature well equipped to achieve success in the profession you have chosen. A good figure, a melodious voice, a heart full of feeling—what more do actors need? If I could help you with some introductions, I would be very happy to do so."

"I thank you from the bottom of my heart," said Melina, "but I could hardly make use of them, because I shall most likely not return to the theater."

"That would be a great mistake," said Wilhelm, after a pause to recover from his surprise, for he had assumed that, once freed with his young wife, the actor would resume his work in the theater. This seemed to him as natural and necessary as water to a frog. He had not doubted this for a moment, and so was astonished to find that he was mistaken.

"No, I do not intend to return to acting," said the young man. "I would rather find some occupation like other townsfolk have, whatever it may be—if only I can find it." "I cannot say I approve of such a strange decision," said Wilhelm. "For it is never a good idea to change the life one has chosen, except for a really good reason. Also I cannot think of any profession that is as attractive and offers such agreeable prospects as that of an actor." "That shows that you have never been one yourself," said Melina; to which Wilhelm replied: "But sir—rarely is a man satisfied with the conditions in which he finds himself! He is always wishing he had those of his neighbor, and the neighbor is equally eager to change his." "But there is a difference between bad and worse," said Melina. "It is experience, not impatience, that makes me decide as I have. Is there any livelihood in the whole world more meager, insecure and tedious? One might just as well be a beggar in the street. What one has to put up with from the jealousy of colleagues, the favoritism of managers, and the fickleness of the public! You have to be really thick-skinned, like a bear on a chain, beaten with a stick in the company of dogs and apes, to dance to the bagpipes before children and riff-raff."

Wilhelm was having all sorts of thoughts that he did not dare voice to this worthy fellow. What he did say had a certain detachment about it, whereas Melina talked more and more volubly and openly. "Shouldn't every theater manager beseech the town council to allow more money to circulate for four weeks during the annual trade fair? I have often felt sorry for our manager, for he is quite a good fellow, even though at times he has given me cause for dissatisfaction. A good actor profits him, but the bad ones he can't get rid of, and if he tries to make his takes more or less keep pace with his expenses, that's too much for the public, the theater is empty and, so as not to fold entirely, we have to play at a loss. No, sir, if, as you say, you want to take our part, then I beg you to talk seriously to her parents and get them to provide for us here and find me some small job as a copyist or tax collector. Then I shall feel happy."

After some further exchange between them Wilhelm went off, with the promise that he would go to her parents early next day and see what he could do. Once he was alone, he vented his feelings in a series of exclamatory out-bursts: "O, unhappy Melina, the misery that oppresses you, lies not in your profession but in yourself! What man in the whole world would not find his situation intolerable if he chooses a craft, an art, indeed any form of life, without experiencing an inner calling? Whoever is born with a talent, or to a talent, must surely find in that the most pleasing of occupations! Everything on this earth has its difficult sides! Only some inner drive—pleasure—love— can help us overcome obstacles, prepare a path, and lift us out of the narrow circle in which others tread out their anguished, miserable existences! The stage is for you, Melina, just a set of boards, and your roles are nothing more than school assignments! You view the spectators as they see themselves—part of the daily grind! It would be just the same for you if you were sitting over ledgers at a desk, recording interest payments and worming our arrears from people. You never feel that sense of a conglomerate, inflammable whole that can only be created, comprehended and executed by the mind. You have never felt that there is a brighter spark in man which, if it receives no nourishment, if it is not allowed to ignite, becomes covered ever more deeply by the ashes of daily needs and indifference, and yet is never entirely extinguished—or only very late. You don't feel any strength within you to ignite it, no riches in your heart to give it sustenance. You are driven by hunger, inconveniences upset you, and you are quite unaware that such adversaries lurk in every human soul, no matter what it is engaged in, and that only by joyfulness of spirit and evenness of purpose can they be vanquished. You do well to long for the limitations of some vulgar occupation, for how could you fulfil the obligations of one that demands courage and spirit! Transfer your sentiments to any soldier, any statesman, any priest, and he too would complain with equal justification about the miseries of his station. Have there not been men, so deprived of any feeling for life, that they considered all human life worthless, a pitiable existence of dust? If the examples of active men were always present to your mind, if your bosom were inflamed by a desire to participate, if your whole being were enveloped in some feeling that came from your inmost self, if the sounds of your voice, the words of your mouth were pleasing to listen to, if you felt that strength of self, you would surely look for places and opportunities where you might feel your own strength in other people."

With such fine words and thoughts our hero undressed and went to bed with a feeling of inmost satisfaction. In his mind a whole romance began to develop around what he would do next day in the place of this unworthy fellow. Pleasant fantasies led him to sleep and delivered him up to dreams which received him with open arms and surrounded him with images of heaven.

Next morning he awoke and began thinking of the business at hand. He returned to the house of the girl's parents, who received him with some surprise. In a few simple words he told them what he had to propose, and encountered both more and less opposition than he had expected. For what had happened, had happened; and although people with firm and strict opinions usually tend to voice vigorous disapproval of what has already irrevocably taken place, and thereby increase their misfortune, the fact that it *has* already happened works on them irresistibly and what had seemed unthinkable has become part of their everyday experience. It was therefore soon settled that Melina should marry their daughter, but that, because of her behavior, she should receive no dowry, and leave the inheritance she had from an aunt in her father's hands for a few years, receiving only a modest interest from it. This second point—the matter of financial provision for her—encountered considerable difficulties. For they did not wish to set eyes on their errant child, nor materially advance this union of a vagrant with a member of a highly respectable family (which even counted a Superintendent among its members), and as for an official position for the husband—there was little prospect of that. Both parents were vigorously opposed to it, and though Wilhelm spoke strongly in favor of the idea (because he agreed that this man, of whom he had no high opinion, was not worthy to return to the delights of the stage), he could not, despite all his arguments, move them in his direction. If he had only known their true motives he would not even have tried to persuade them. The father wanted to keep his daughter at home, and hated the young man because his own wife had cast a favorable eye on him, and that meant that she would never have welcomed a rival in her stepdaughter. And so Melina was obliged to leave in a few days with his young bride (who wanted more than he to see the world and be seen by it) in order to find a position in some other theatrical company.

Chapter Fifteen

Happy youth, happy those first gropings for love, when we converse readily with ourselves, delighting in echoes of our own conversation and satisfied when our invisible partner merely repeats the last syllables of what we have just uttered!

Wilhelm was in this state during the first days of his love for Mariane—and even more so later, when he began to shower her with all the wealth of his feelings and to regard himself as a beggar living from what she gave him in return. And as a landscape is always, or indeed only, pleasing when the sun shines upon it, so everything that surrounded her, everything she touched, was beautified and glorified by her presence.

He would often stand in the wings, once he had been allowed this privilege by the manager, and although the illusion disappeared from this perspective, the far greater magic of love began to operate. He would stand for hours alongside the grubby cart on which the lights were fixed, breathing in the smell of tallow, and looking to see his beloved who, when she finally came on stage, would gaze at him lovingly and transport him into a realm of bliss amidst the skeletal framework of slats and crossbeams. The stuffed lambkins, glittering cloth waterfalls, cardboard rosebushes and thatched cottages with only one side to them aroused in him pleasing poetic images of a distant pastoral world. Even the dancers, so ugly at close quarters, did not displease him, for they were on one and the same stage with his dearly beloved. The love needed to bring life to rosebushes, myrtle groves and moonlight can certainly also endow woodchips and paper snippers with a degree of real live existence. Such seasoning is so potent that it can give flavor to the blandest or most distasteful concoction.

Some such seasoning was needed to make the usual state of Mariane's dressing room, and even sometimes her own appearance, palatable to him. For he had been brought up in a superior middle-class household, where cleanliness and order were the very air he breathed; and since he had inherited something of his father's love of finery, he had, even as a boy, arranged his room like a small kingdom. The curtains of his bed were gathered in folds and fastened with tassels, the way one imagines thrones to be. He had put a rug in the middle of the room, and a coverlet, of finer quality, on his table, with his books and other objects arranged on it, so meticulously that a Dutch painter could have made a still life from them. A white cap would be fastened on his head like a turban, and he turned up the sleeves of his dressing gown in oriental fashion, asserting that the long sleeves got in his way when he was writing. Of an evening, when he was alone and without fear of being disturbed, he would girdle himself with a silk sash, and sometimes stick a dagger in, which he had got from some old junk room, and, thus accoutred, rehearse the tragic roles that he had assigned to himself. He even knelt on the carpet to say his prayers.

How fortunate, he used to think, were actors in former days, when—so he imagined—they had magnificent costumes, suits of armor and weapons and always presented a model of noble behavior, their minds reflecting the noblest and best in attitudes, sentiments, and emotions. He pictured the domestic life of such an actor as a sequence of worthy actions and occupations of which his appearances in the theater were the climax—like silver, long treated in the refiner's fire and then finally emerging, free of all base elements, in all its resplendent brilliance.

How startled he was when, emerging from such a haze of beautiful fancies, he first looked at the chairs and tables in his beloved idol's dressing room! The remains of some momentary false adornment lay scattered around in complete disorder, like the glittering coat of a descaled fish. The instruments of human hygiene, such as combs, soap and washcloths, were there for anyone to see. Music, shoes, dirty laundry, artificial flowers, little boxes, hairpins, makeup jars, ribbons, books and straw hats lay in unabashed proximity to each other, covered with a uniform layer of powder and dust. But since Wilhelm, when he was in her presence, noticed little but her and even everything associated with her, everything she touched, was necessarily dear to him, he discovered a certain charm in this household of disorder such as he had never experienced in the splendor of his own room. When he removed her corset to get to the piano, or put her petticoats on the bed so that he could have a place to sit, or when she did not put away certain objects that she would normally have concealed from others out of a sense of decorum but had no scruples at leaving around when he was there, he felt that he was drawing closer to her all the time and invisible bonds were strengthening their union.

It was not so easy for him to relate to his idealized concept of their calling the behavior of the other actors that he sometimes met when he called on her the first few times. Busy at idling, they never seemed to be concerned about their profession and calling. He never heard them discussing the poetic merit of a play or criticizing it (rightly or wrongly). All they talked about was: "How much will it make? Will it be a hit? How long will it run? How many performances will we give? . . ." and such like. Then they usually went on to attack the manager: that he was too stingy with salaries, and unjust to one or the other of them; that the public seldom applauded the right man, that the German theater was getting better every day, that the actors were more and more appreciated for their merits and should be more respected. There was a lot of talk about coffeehouses and wine restaurants, and what had happened there, how much one of them was in debt, how much his salary had been docked, the inadequacy of their weekly wages, and the intrigues of one group against the other. Finally there was some consideration given to the importance of having an attentive audience; and the influence of the theater on the cultural level of the nation, indeed of the world, was not overlooked.

All these matters, which had caused Wilhelm much uneasiness, returned vividly to his mind as his horse carried him slowly toward home and he reflected on the various events he had witnessed. He had observed at first hand the disturbance that the flight of one girl had created in a good middle-class family and indeed a whole town. He recalled those scenes on the road and in the courthouse, the opinions expressed by Melina, and all that had resulted filled his mind, always eager to press on, with such uneasiness that he spurred on his horse and hurried toward the town.

But in so doing he ran into new unpleasantness. For Werner, his friend and presumptive brother-in-law, was waiting to have a serious and unexpected talk with him.

Werner was one of those who, having settled into a particular mode of existence, are usually taken to be cold, because they never flare up quickly or visibly. His relationship with Wilhelm was one of continual conflict, which, however, brought them ever closer together, for despite their different attitudes, each of them profited from the other. Werner gave himself credit for being able to restrain in some degree Wilhelm's lively, but occasionally over-enthusiastic, spirit, and Wilhelm, for his part, had a sense of real triumph when in the heat of his emotion he was able to carry his sober-minded friend with him. The one tried himself out on the other, they saw each other almost every day, and one could have said that their desire to discover each other through their conversations was only increased by the impossibility of making themselves mutually understood. Basically, however, they were both good men, and both working towards one and the same goal, separately and together, and yet never able to understand why the one could not reduce the other to his way of thinking.

Werner had been aware for some time that Wilhelm's visits were becoming less frequent, that he was curt and inattentive when he got on to his favorite topics, and that he no longer plunged so intensely into the active elaboration of unusual ideas; it seemed to Werner that Wilhelm, in his own mind, was seeking peace and contentment in the presence of his friend. Werner, cautious and careful by disposition, assumed at first that the fault was his, until some town gossip gave him the clue, and certain indiscretions of Wilhelm's confirmed his suspicions. He started to investigate and soon found out that some time ago Wilhelm had been visiting an actress, had spoken with her at the theater and even taken her home. He would have been desolate if he had known about the nocturnal meetings, for he heard that Mariane was a seductive girl who was probably after his friend's money, and in addition to that, was kept by a worthless lover.

Having satisfied himself as far as possible of the truth of his suspicions, he decided to make an assault on Wilhelm, and was fully prepared for this, when Wilhelm returned in a bad humor from his journey.

On that very evening Werner told him all he knew, quite calmly at first but then with all the intense earnestness of a well-meaning friend, leaving nothing imprecise and making him taste to the full all the bitterness that calm people in their vindictive virtuousness lavish on passionate lovers. But as might be expected, he achieved little. Wilhelm responded with irritation but quite firmly: "You don't know the girl. Appearances may be against her, but I am as sure of her loyalty and virtue as I am of my own love."

Werner, however, persisted in his accusations and offered to provide evidence and witnesses. But Wilhelm rejected all this and left his friend in a disturbed and vexed frame of mind, like someone having a defective but firmly rooted tooth grasped by a clumsy dentist, who vainly tries to dislodge it.

Wilhelm was ill at ease to find his shining image of Mariane becoming tarnished and almost distorted by the vagaries of his journey and Werner's unkind words. So he decided on the best means of restoring it to its pristine clarity and beauty—and hastened that very night to go and see her by the usual route. She greeted him cheerfully and eagerly. She had earlier in the day seen him ride by, and so was waiting for him at night. One can well imagine that all his doubts were soon dispelled, for her tenderness restored his confidence in her, and he told her how other people, including his friend Werner, had been maligning her.

Many a lively conversation led them back to the beginning of their relationship, the memory of which always remains a favorite subject for lovers. The first steps into the maze of love are always so delightful, our first prospects so bewitching that we always like to recall them. And each of the two claims precedence over the other, each claims to have been the first in his or her unselfish affection, and each would rather be proved wrong than the opposite.

Wilhelm told Mariane once again what she had heard so often, namely that she had soon distracted his attention from the play so that he was entirely taken up with her, and had been captivated by her figure, her acting, her voice, and finally only went to the plays that she was performing in, and even crept onto the stage and stood alongside her without her noticing. And he remembered that blissfully happy evening when he had the occasion to do her some small service and thereby start a conversation. Mariane for her part would not agree that it was so long before she noticed him. She had often seen him out walking, she said, and could describe the clothes he was wearing that day, for even at that time she had liked him better than all the rest, and she had wanted to make his acquaintance.

How pleased Wilhelm was to believe all this, pleased to be persuaded that she had come to him as he to her, both led by some irresistible force to each other—that she had purposely come up beside him in the wings, so that she might look at him from close by and get to know him, and that finally, since his shyness and reserve seemed impossible to overcome, she herself had given him the opening by almost forcing him to bring her a glass of lemonade.

Time passed quickly in this lovers' competition, for they followed through every moment in the course of their short romance, and Wilhelm left her with his mind completely at peace, and the firm determination to put his plan into action immediately.

Chapter Sixteen

Wilhelm's parents had got together everything that he would need for his journey, but there were still a few items lacking, and that delayed his departure for several days. He used the time to write a letter to Mariane in order to bring out into the open the matter that she had always avoided discussing. This is how the letter ran:

"Wrapped in the beloved cloak of night, which usually covers me in your arms, I sit and think and write to you. And what I think and what I do is all for you. O Mariane, I am the happiest of men, and feel like a bridegroom who senses a whole new world opening up for him and through him when he stands on the festive carpet and is transported during the sacred ceremony in lusting thoughts towards those dark curtains of mystery behind which the joys of love enticingly rustle. I have steeled myself to not seeing you for a few days. This was not so difficult because I am hoping to make up for this loss by being with you always, by being all yours. Must I tell you once more what I desire? I feel that I must; for it seems that so far you have not understood me.

"How often have I, with a few words of loving trust, fearing to lose what I have by saying more, ventured to question your feelings about a lasting union between us. You must have understood me, for in your heart the same wish must have grown, you heard me in every kiss, in the nestling peace of all our happy evenings together. I have gotten to know your modesty, and this has but increased my love for you. Whereas any other girl would have used every artifice and by spreading excessive sunshine to bring to fruition a decision in her lover's heart, elicited a declaration that would harden into a promise, you have always withdrawn, closed the half-bared breast of your beloved and tried by seeming indifference to conceal your approval. But I understand—and what a miserable creature I would be if I did not recognize in these signs the purity of your unselfish love, your concern for your dear friend! Trust me and do not be anxious! We belong together and neither of us will forgo anything when we live for each other.

"Take my hand, take it solemnly as a further sign of my love. We have tasted all the joys of love but new blessings are in store for us once we decide on a lasting relationship. Don't ask how, and don't worry. Fate takes care of love, and all the more so, since love is its own reward.

"In my mind I have long left my parents' home, in order to be in spirit with you on the stage. O, my beloved, was ever a man so fortunate in combining his desires as I? My eyes are closed in sleep, for your love and your happiness keep appearing before me, the dawn of a new life.

"I can hardly stop myself from rushing to you and wresting from you your approval, and then off next morning early into the wide world to work towards the goal I have in mind. But I must control myself, I should not rush foolhardily and impatiently, for I have thought out a plan of action and must pursue it circumspectly.

"I am acquainted with a theater manager named Serlo, and will go straight to him. About a year ago he urged his people to develop my enthusiasm for the theater and wished they had something of the same. He will certainly be glad to see me. I would not like to join your company, for various reasons. And Serlo's company is playing at such a distance from here that I can initially conceal this step. I'll find somewhere decent to stay, look around at what the audiences are like, get to know the actors—and then send for you to join me there.

"You see, Mariane, how I can conquer my desire in order to get you for sure. For not to see you a long time, knowing you are somewhere or other out there in the world, that I do not dare to think about! But then when I think of your love—that will sustain me, if you meet my request and, before we part, give me your hand before the priest, I will go in peace. It will only be a formality for us, but a lovely one, to have the blessing of Heaven as well as that of the earth. It can be done quite quietly and secretly here in the neighborhood, I have enough money to start with. We can divide it up, there will be sufficient for us both. And when that is used up, Heaven will provide.

"You see, my dear, I am not at all worried. What started so joyfully, must end happily, I have never had any doubts that one can make one's way in the world, so long as one is serious. And I am determined enough to find ample support for two, even for more. 'The world is ungrateful,' people say, but I have never found it so, if one knows what to do for the world, and how my whole soul is aglow with the thought of at last being on the stage and telling men's hearts what they have long been yearning to hear. Convinced as I am of the glory of the stage, I have many times been distressed watching wretched actors imagining that they could speak noble words to our eager hearts, whereas what they produce is worse than a squeaky falsetto, and a coarse clumsiness that is beneath contempt.

"The theater has often found itself in conflict with the church, but this should not be so. How desirable it would be if both would glorify God and Nature through the mouths of noble human beings. These are not dreams, Mariane! I have felt your heart and know that you are in love. Likewise I believe in my brilliant idea, and say—better perhaps not say, but hope—that someday we will appear together, a pair of noble spirits, opening up the hearts of men, touching their souls, and offering them heavenly delights. I believe this because the joys of being with you were always heavenly delights, because we were lifted beyond ourselves, and felt above ourselves.

"I can't finish. I have already said too much, and yet do not know if I told you all that you should know. For no words are adequate to express the movement of the wheel that turns within my heart.

"Yet keep this letter, my dear. I have read it again and feel I should start once more at the beginning. But it does contain everything that you should know, to prepare you for my joyful return to your loving breast. I feel like a prisoner in his cell, listening as he files off his shackles. I bid my blissfully sleeping parents goodnight!—Farewell, my beloved, farewell. I will stop now. My eyes have already closed two or three times. For it is very late at night."

Chapter Seventeen

The day would not end when Wilhelm, his letter nicely folded in his pocket, longed to be with Mariane. Although it was hardly dark, he made his way to her lodging, with the idea of announcing his return at nightfall and leaving the letter in her hands before he absented himself for a while, intending to return at night to get her answer, receive her approval or, if need be, force it from her by the passion of his caresses. He flew into her arms and could hardly control himself as he clasped her to him. The intensity of his feelings was such that he did not at first notice that she failed to respond as warmly as usual. But she could not conceal her anxiety for long, claiming she was not feeling well, had a headache and did not welcome his coming back that night. He did not suspect anything, and did not press her, but felt this was not the right moment to give her the letter. So he kept it in his pocket, and since several words and gestures of hers politely indicated to him that she wished him to leave, he grabbed one of her scarves in the heat of his unsatisfied emotion, stuck it in his pocket, unwillingly tore himself away from her lips and left her. He walked slowly home, but could not stay there for more than a short while. He changed his clothes and went out again to get some fresh air.

He walked around the streets, and then a stranger approached him and asked him the way to a certain inn. Wilhelm offered to take him there. The stranger asked the name of the street, and those of the owners of several large houses that they passed, enquired after certain local police regulations, and by the time they reached the door of the inn the two men found themselves involved in a very interesting conversation. The stranger persuaded his guide to step inside and have a glass of punch with him. He told Wilhelm his name and place of birth, and the nature of the business that had brought him here, urging Wilhelm to be equally communicative. So Wilhelm began by telling him his name and where he lived.

"Aren't you a grandson of old Meister who had such a fine art collection?" the stranger asked. "Yes, I am," said Wilhelm. "But my grandfather died when I was ten, and I was very grieved to see those lovely things sold." "But your father got a great sum of money for them." "How do you know that?" "Oh, I saw those treasures when they were still in your house. Your grandfather was not just a collector, he knew a great deal about art. He had been in Italy in earlier and happier times, and brought back with him treasures such as could now not be bought at any price. He possessed marvelous paintings by the best artists, and you could hardly believe your eyes when you looked through his collection of drawings. He had various priceless fragments of sculpture and an instructive array of bronzes. His coins were collected with regard to art as well as history, his precious stones, few though they were, were of the highest quality. And everything was well arranged, even though the rooms in the old house were not designed symmetrically."

"Then you can imagine what a loss we children felt when all these things were taken down and packed," said Wilhelm. "Those were the first sad days of my life. I remember how empty the rooms seemed, as we watched one thing after the other disappear, things that we had enjoyed since childhood, things which had seemed to us as permanent as the house itself or the town we lived in."

"If I am not mistaken," said the stranger, "your father invested the proceeds in a neighbor's business and formed a sort of company with him?"

"Right! And their business has worked out very well. In those twelve years they have substantially increased their capital and both are all the more concerned now with increasing it even further. And old Werner has a son who is much better suited to this sort of thing than I am."

"I am sorry that this town should have lost such a treasure as your grandfather's collection. I saw it shortly before it was sold, and I can honestly say that I was the instigator of the sale. A rich nobleman and great connoisseur, who, however, did not trust his own judgment in so large a deal, sent me here so that I might give him my advice. I examined the collection for six whole days, and on the seventh I advised my friend to pay the asking price without questioning it. I remember you then as a bright boy, always at my side, telling me what the paintings were about and making quite good comments on the collection."

"I remember such a person being there, but I wouldn't have recognized you."

"Well, it was quite a while ago and we all change to some degree. I seem to remember that you had a favorite picture from which you were unwilling to let me move on."

"Yes, indeed. It was the picture of a sick prince consumed by passion for his father's bride."

"It wasn't exactly the best painting in the collection: the composition was not good, the colors were nothing special, and the execution was mannered."

"I didn't understand that, and still don't understand it: The subject is what appeals to me in a painting, not the artistry."

"Your grandfather seemed to think otherwise, for the major part of his collection consisted of excellent things in which one always admired the merits of the painter without reference to the subject. And that particular picture was hanging in an anteroom to show that he did not value it highly."

"That was where we children were allowed to play," said Wilhelm, "and where that particular picture made such an indelible impression on me which not even your criticism (which, on the whole, I have great respect for) could obliterate if we were standing before it now. How distressed I was—and still am—that a young man should have to keep bottled up in himself those sweet feelings, the best that Nature gives him, and must hide those fires which should warm him and others, so that his soul is consumed with pain and suffering! And how I pity an unhappy woman being joined to someone other than the one her heart felt worthy of her true, pure love!"

"Such emotion is certainly far removed from the way an art lover looks at the work of great artists. But if the paintings had remained in your home, you would probably have developed more understanding for the works themselves, instead of always putting yourself and your feelings into them."

"I always regretted the sale of the pictures and missed them often even when I was older. But when I consider that it was necessary, so to speak, in order that I myself could develop a passion, and talent, of my own which will affect my life more than all those dead pictures ever did, then I accept the fact and respect it as a stroke of fate which opened up the best in me, as it does in others."

"I am sorry to hear the word 'fate' used once again by a young man at a time in his life when passionate inclinations are all too often interpreted as the workings of higher forces," said the stranger.

"But don't you believe in fate, some power which rules over us and guides everything to our advantage?" Wilhelm asked.

"It is not a matter of believing, or trying to make sense out of what is otherwise incomprehensible, but simply of deciding which way of looking at things suits us best. The texture of this world is made up of necessity and chance. Human reason holds the balance between them, treating necessity as the basis of existence, but manipulating and directing chance, and using it. Only if our reason is unshakeable, does man deserve to be called a god of the earth. Woe to him who, from youth on, is prone to find arbitrariness in necessity and ascribes a certain reasonableness to chance and accepts this religiously. For that amounts to denying one's rational self and giving free play to one's feelings. We think we are god-fearing people if we saunter through life without much thought, we let ourselves be carried along by happy chance, and then finally declare that our wavering existence was a life governed by divine guidance."

"But have you never experienced a situation where some small circumstance made you take a certain path on which a favorable opportunity soon presented itself to you, and a whole series of unexpected occurrences brought you to a goal you had yourself hardly envisioned? Shouldn't that encourage you to trust in fate and its guidance?"

"With such opinions no girl would keep her virtue and no man his money, for there are enough opportunities to lose them both. But I can be really happy only with a person who knows what is useful to him and others, and works at controlling his own arbitrariness. Everyone holds his fortune in his own hands, like a sculptor the raw material he will fashion into a figure. But it's the same with that type of artistic activity as with all others. Only the ability to do it, only the capability, is inborn in us, it must be learned and attentively cultivated."

They went on discussing this and many other things, and finally parted, without seeming to have convinced each other, but they agreed on a place to meet again next day.

Wilhelm walked up and down the streets. He heard clarinets, horns and bassoons and was delighted at their sound. Some travelling musicians were giving a pleasant serenade. He spoke with them and paid them to follow him to where Mariane lived. He positioned the singers under the tall trees before the house, lay down on a bench some distance away and abandoned himself entirely to the soaring sounds that floated around him in the soothing night. Stretched out beneath the beauty of the stars he felt that his whole existence was one golden dream. "She can hear these melodies," he said to himself. "She will know in her heart whose thoughts and sounds of love are resounding through the night. Even at a distance we are bound together by such music with all its delicate sounds. For two loving hearts are like a pair of magnetic compasses: when the one moves, the other moves with it, for only one thing is at work, one force permeates them both. When I am in her arms, how can I possibly imagine being separated from her? And yet I will be far from her, seeking a sanctuary for our love, and she will therefore always be with me.

"How often has it happened that, being away from her, or lost in thoughts of her, I touched a book or some garment, and thought it was her hand I felt, so absorbed was I in her presence, and remembered those precious moments which shunned the light of day as if it were some icy interloper, those moments to enjoy which gods would gladly abandon their state of bliss. But how can one talk of remembering—as if one could ever relive that frenzied intoxication which enslaves with heavenly bonds all our senses—and her figure. . . ." He lost himself in thoughts of her, thoughts that soon changed to desire, embraced a tree, cooled his cheek on the bark, and breathed out his excitement into the night air that was all too ready to receive it. He tried to find the scarf that he had taken from her room, but he had left it in his other suit. His lips were burning and his limbs quivering with desire.

The music stopped, and he felt as if he had fallen down from the heights scaled by his soaring emotions. His restlessness increased, now that his feelings were no longer being nourished and tempered by the sweetness of the music. He sat down on the steps of her house and became somewhat calmer. He kissed the ring on the brass knocker, kissed the threshold of the door she went in and out of, warming it at the fire in his heart. Then he sat still for a while, thinking of her up there behind the curtains, sleeping in her white nightgown with the red ribbon round her head, and imagined himself so close to her as to make her dream of him. His thoughts were as lovely as twilight spirits, sometimes peaceful and sometimes eager. Love's quivering hand passed over every string in his soul. He felt as if the music of the spheres had halted to listen to the melodies of his heart.

If he had had the key on him which usually let him into her house, he would not have hesitated to enter the temple of love. But since he had not, he slowly and dreamily sauntered along beneath the trees, in the direction of his own home but always turning back, until finally he reached the corner and, looking once more, thought he saw Mariane's door open and a dark figure emerge. He was too far away to see clearly, but by the time he collected himself and looked, the shadow was lost in the night, though he thought he could perceive it far off against a white wall. He stood and blinked, and before he could pull himself together and hurry after it, the figure had disappeared. Where should he look? What street had swallowed up that person, if it was a person?

His eyes and his emotions were confused like those of a man unable to find his way again when he has just been blinded by the sudden illumination of an area nearby. And like a ghost at midnight that scares the wits out of us, and when we regain our composure seems the product of our own anxiety and leaves us with doubts whether in fact we ever saw it, a great uneasiness came over Wilhelm as he stood leaning against the corner of a wall, unaware that day was breaking and the cocks were crowing. Tradesmen began to go about their morning rounds, and that drove him home.

By the time he got back he had more or less found reasons to dismiss the surprising phantom from his mind; but all the beauty of the night, which now seemed equally unreal, was gone as well. And so to assuage his heart and put a seal on his returning faith in his beloved, he took out her scarf from the pocket of the suit he had been wearing earlier. As he raised it to his lips a piece of paper fell out. He picked it up, and read: "Well, my little rogue and loved one, what was the matter with you yesterday? I'll come tonight. I can well understand that you will be sorry to leave here. But be patient, I'll follow you to the fair. And listen, don't wear that black, green and brown jacket. It makes you look like the Witch of Endor. Didn't I send you that white negligé, so that

I could hold a white lamb in my arms? Always send me your messages by the old harridan, for she's the devil's own messenger."

BOOK TWO

Chapter One

Anyone whom we observe striving with all his powers to attain some goal, can be assured of our sympathy, whether we approve of the goal or not. But once the matter is decided, we turn our attention elsewhere, for when something is completed or resolved our concern with it diminishes, especially if we have, from the start, foreseen an unsatisfactory outcome. So we will not treat our readers to a detailed account of the woes and sorrows of our unfortunate friend when he saw his hopes and desires so unexpectedly shattered, but rather jump over a few years and join him again where we shall hope to find him more pleasurably occupied. But before that we must fill in with what is necessary for our story to make sense.

Plague and high fever take a firmer and quicker hold on healthy and vigorous persons than on others, and Wilhelm had been so unexpectedly struck down by misfortune that his whole being was instantaneously disorganized. When a firework catches light unexpectedly and all those carefully shaped and filled rockets, which were intended to eject balls of colored fire in predetermined succession, suddenly start hissing and crackling, ominously and without any pretense of order, this was not unlike the tumult of disorder into which all his hopes and joys, all his dreams and realities collapsed. In such moments of utter desolation the friend who hastens to help, stands petrified, and the person affected is fortunate if his sensitivities are numbed.

Days of repeated, and constantly revived, pain followed, days when nature was working beneficially in Wilhelm. For during this time he had not yet lost his beloved entirely, and his sorrow was a series of insistently renewed attempts to hold on to the happiness that had left him, recapture it in his imagination and prolong for a little while those joys that had gone forever. A body is not entirely dead while the process of decay is still underway and its various powers are working themselves off by systematically destroying those members that they normally activate. Only when everything has worn away everything else and reduced the whole to indifferent dust, only then are we invaded by that wretched sense of emptiness that we call death, a state that can only be quickened by the breath of eternal life.

There was so much to disrupt, to destroy, to kill off in this young, loving spirit, that the healing powers of youth merely stoked the fires of sorrow. What had happened, had struck at the roots of his whole existence. Werner, of necessity the only person that Wilhelm could confide in, did all he could to pour fire and flame onto this hateful passion, the dragon in his entrails. The occasion was so apposite, the evidence was so everpresent, that he made use of everything he had heard in the way of rumors and stories. He did this so systematically and with such vehemence and savagery that he did not leave his friend one consoling moment of illusion, one escape hatch from his despair. And so nature, determined not to lose a favorite son, afflicted him with sickness, so that he had, in his own way, time to breathe.

A raging fever, and what followed—medication, overexcitement and lassitude, ministrations from the family, affection from his acquaintances that showed itself only now that he really needed it—these were distractions in changed circumstances and meager occupations for his mind. When he felt better—that is to say when all his energies were exhausted—he gazed in horror down into the empty abyss of torment and misery that opened up before him, barren like the burnt-out hollow crater of a volcano.

He now began to reproach himself bitterly when, having lost so much, he could enjoy a moment of calm, painless reflection. He despised his very heart, and longed again for the refreshment of tears and misery. To restore this he would persistently recall every moment, every scene of his past happiness. He recreated them in the brightest colors, thought himself back into them, and when he had worked himself up to the point where the sunshine of past days was beginning to warm his body and spirit, he would look back at the ghastly abyss, feast his eyes on the dizzying depths, and then hurl himself into them and exact from nature all the torments of bitter pain. And so he tore himself to pieces in repeated accesses of savagery, for youth, so rich in hidden powers, never knows what it is robbing itself of when it joins trumped-up sorrows to the pain of a real loss, as if this were necessary to impart real significance to the pain of what has been foregone. Also, he was so convinced that this would be the only loss, the first and the last, that he would ever experience, that he despised any consolation that might suggest such sorrow as his could not last forever.

Chapter Two

Accustomed as he was to torment himself in this way, he began also to pour savage criticism onto what, apart from his love, had been his greatest hope and joy—his abilities as a poet and an actor. His own compositions now seemed to him mere sterile imitations of conventional models, with no life of their own—school exercises, totally devoid of any trace of reality, truth or inspiration. His poems were rhythmically monotonous, held together by wretched rhymes, with commonplace thoughts and feelings ponderously expressed. There was no longer any pleasure or expectation of recovery for him from this quarter. Nor was there from his acting talent. He reproached himself for not having understood earlier that vanity was at the bottom of that, and nothing more. He reconsidered his figure, his movements, his gestures and declamation, and decided that they had no particular merit or distinction, were nothing above the ordinary. This merely increased his silent desperation. Hard as it is to abandon one's love of a woman, it is equally painful to desert the company of the muses because one feels unworthy of their company, and to forego those delightful rounds of applause at one's person, one's demeanor and one's voice.

And so our friend resigned himself fully to active participation in the world of business. To the astonishment of Werner and to the great delight of his father, no one was more industrious than Wilhelm in the countinghouse, on the exchange, in the office or the warehouse. He dealt with correspondence and bills and everything else assigned to him with the greatest efficiency. Not indeed with that joyful eagerness which is its own reward when one executes in an orderly fashion what one is born to do, but with a certain quiet sense of duty, based on solid foundations and sustained by conviction, self-rewarding on the whole. But sometimes he was unable to suppress a sigh even when his best qualities were being engaged.

Wilhelm went on living in this way for quite a time, industrious and convinced that the hard school of fate was working to his advantage. He was glad to see that he had been warned in time, though rather unpleasantly, and that others would not later have to pay heavily for the errors of his youthful self-satisfaction. For usually a man resists, as long as he can, having to admit that he is a fool at heart, that he has made a big mistake. Men are unwilling to admit a truth that may drive them to despair.

Determined as he was to give up his dearest aspirations, it took some time for him to be convinced of his misfortune. But finally he had so completely eradicated, and with convincing arguments, every hope of love, of poetic creativity and acting in himself, that he found the necessary courage to wipe out every trace of his former folly, everything that might possibly remind him of it. One chilly evening he lit a fire and got out a box of keepsakes, in which there were all sorts of things he had received or snatched from Mariane in certain memorable moments. There were dried flowers to remind him of the time when they were fresh in her hair, little notes inviting him to hours of bliss, ribbons from her lovely bosom where he had rested his heart. Did not these souvenirs serve to renew every feeling he had thought dead, revive every passion that he thought he had mastered, now that he was separated from her? For we never notice how sad and unpleasant a gloomy day is, until a ray of sunshine suddenly breaks through and presents the brightening gleam of a joyful hour.

He was not unmoved as he watched these treasures go up in smoke that he had preserved for so long. Once or twice he hesitated, and he still had a string of beads and a flowered scarf left when he decided to stoke the fire with the poetic efforts of his youth. Up to now he had carefully preserved everything that had flowed from his pen since his mind began to develop. His writings were tied up in bundles which he had packed in the trunk he had hoped to take with him on his journey. How different was his frame of mind now as he opened them from when he had bundled them together.

When we open a letter that we once wrote and sealed on a particular occasion but which never reached the friend it was sent to, and was returned to us, we have a strange feeling as we break the seal, our own seal, and converse with our different self as with a third person. Just such a feeling it was that gripped our hero as he opened the first packet and threw the various sheets into the fire, which burned up brightly. At this moment Werner came into the room, was surprised at the blazing fire and asked Wilhelm what he was up to.

"I'm giving you a proof," said Wilhelm, "that I'm serious about abandoning an occupation I wasn't born to," and with these words he threw the second package into the flames. Werner tried to prevent him, but he was too late.

"I don't see why you should go to such extremes," he said. "Why should these pieces of work, imperfect though they may be, be completely destroyed?"

"Because a poem should either be perfect or not exist at all. Anyone without the ability to produce the very best, should not engage in artistic activity and should resist any temptation to do so. Of course there is a vague longing in all of us to imitate what we see, but that does not prove that one has the power to achieve what one aims at. Look how boys who have seen acrobats performing, walk up and down trying to balance on planks and beams till some other pastime attracts them. Haven't you seen that amongst our own friends? When we hear a virtuoso performer, there are always some of us who start learning the instrument. And how many falter on the way! Happy is he who realizes early enough that desire is no indication of ability!"

Werner didn't agree. The conversation became heated, and Wilhelm found himself using against his friend the same passionate arguments that he had been tormenting himself with. Werner insisted that it was ridiculous to abandon a talent he had exercised with pleasure and some skill, simply because he would never achieve perfection through it. There were always those dull hours that could be filled up in this way, and something would gradually emerge that would give pleasure to us and to others.

Our hero, whose opinion was quite different, cut in and exclaimed vehemently: "How wrong you are, my friend, in thinking that a work, the first concept of which must fill one's whole soul, can possibly be produced in odd spots of snatched time. Oh no, a poet must live *entirely* for himself and in his beloved subjects! Endowed by heaven with a fund of inner riches, he must labor to increase this by living, happy and undisturbed, with his own treasure. No man can acquire such happiness by the mere amassing of riches. Just look at how men rush after fortune and pleasure, driven on restlessly by money, effort and desire, but to what end? To the same state that the poet has received by nature: to enjoyment of the world, the sense of being a part of a community, harmonious coexistence with many different things that often seem irreconcilable with each other.

"What troubles most people is that they are unable to reconcile their ideas with reality, pleasure evades them, wishes are fulfilled too late, and what they do achieve does not give them the pleasure they had expected in anticipation. Fate has placed the poet above all this—like a god. He sees the whirlpool of passions, the fruitless activity of families and nations, the serious problems born of misunderstandings, fraught with dangerous consequences, that a single word could often dispel. He experiences in himself all the joys and sorrows of human existence. And whereas men of the world either consume their time in melancholy brooding over losses, or embrace their fate with unbridled joy, the poet with his receptive and fluid mind moves like the sun from night to day, tuning his harp with gentle transitions from joy to pain. The flower of wisdom grows naturally out of the soil of his heart, and whereas others, when they dream in waking life, are frightened by the images that arise from their senses, the poet lives out the dream of life in constant wakefulness, and integrates even the most extraordinary occurrence into both past and future. The poet is teacher, prophet, friend of gods and men. How can you expect him to lower himself to some miserable trade or occupation? Built like a bird to soar above the earth, nest in high trees, nourish himself from buds and fruits, moving easily from branch to branch—how can he at the same time be an ox pulling a plough, a hound trained to follow a scent, or a watchdog on a chain in a farmyard, barking to ward off intruders?"

Werner listened to all this, as one can well imagine, with some astonishment, and then said: "If only men were made like birds and, instead of laboring away, could spend their days in a state of blissful pleasure! If only, when winter comes, they could escape to faraway climes, and avoid all dearth and cold!"

"That is indeed how poets lived when true value was better recognized, and so they should always live," Wilhelm declared. "Inwardly they are so well provided for, that they need little sustenance from outside. The gift that they have of presenting to men glorious feelings and wondrous images in sweet words and melodies that clothe every object, has always captivated the world and secured them a rich inheritance. They were listened to at the courts of kings, the tables of the rich, and the doors of lovers, while eyes and minds were closed to all else, just as the song of the nightingale strongly affects us from out of the dark thickets through which we wander, and we stand still and listen, enraptured and grateful. They found a world that was always open to them, and their seemingly humble station increased the respect that was paid to them. Heroes listened to their songs and conquerors revered them, because, without the poet's songs, their mighty presence would vanish like the wind. Lovers wished to experience their desires and joys as strongly and harmoniously as the poet described them. Even rich men could not see the value of their treasured possessions as clearly as when these were transfigured and enriched by the poet's sense of values. Who but the poet, one might say, fashioned gods, lifted us up to them, and brought them down to us?"

"My dear Wilhelm, I have often regretted your strenuous attempts to banish from your mind what you feel so strongly," said Werner after some thought. "If I am not mistaken, you might better try to achieve some reconciliation with yourself, instead of working yourself up into a state of irritation at the magnitude of your loss. Why deprive yourself of all other pleasures because of the loss of the joys of innocence?"

"Don't think me ridiculous," Wilhelm replied, "when I tell you that I am still pursued by the images of those joys, however much I try to banish them from my thoughts, and all those former desires are still firmly implanted in my heart—even more so than before. For what else is left for me in my misery? If anyone had ever told me that the arms of my spirit, with which I reached out into infinity and hoped to grasp great things, would so soon be broken, I would have been utterly despondent. And now that judgment has been passed on me and I have lost her who, instead of a god, was to lead me towards the fulfilment of all my desires, what is left for me but resignation to pain and bitterness? I must admit, Werner, that, in all my secret plans, she was the foundation block on which my rope ladder was secured. Hopefully courting dangers this adventurous spirit of mine floated in the air, but the foundation broke and it fell to the ground, shattered at the base of its aspirations. There is no hope or consolation for me anymore! I will not keep any of these wretched papers." With these words he jumped up, grabbed a few more bundles, tore them open and threw them in the fire. Werner tried to stop him, but in vain. "Let me be!" said Wilhelm, "what's the use of these wretched scribbling—they are not a stage toward anything, nor encouragement for anything anymore— are they to remain to torment me till the end of my days, a mockery instead of arousing sympathy or wonder? What a wretched state I am in, what a miserable fate is mine! Now I understand at last the laments of those poets, who achieved wisdom through suffering. I used to think I was indestructible, invulnerable, but now I see that an early but deep wound will never, never heal. I feel that I will take it with me into the grave. The pain will not leave me all my life. It will finally kill me. And the memory of her, worthless as she was, will stay with me always, live and die with me.—But, my friend, if I am to speak truthfully, she was not entirely worthless. Her profession, her experiences have absolved her a thousand times in my mind. I was too cruel. You yourself savagely imbued me with your own coldness and harshness. You fettered my distracted feelings, prevented me from doing for her and me what I owed to us both. Who knows what state she is in now, all because of me—what despair and helplessness I have abandoned her to—all this is gradually beginning to weigh on my conscience! Isn't it possible, perhaps, that she could have given me some explanation? Isn't that possible? Misunderstandings can create such confusion, circumstances can so often pardon mistakes! I picture her so often, sitting alone in the quiet, resting her head on her elbows, and saying: 'So this is the troth he swore, the love he promised me! How could he so cruelly destroy the beautiful life we were sharing!'" Wilhelm burst into a flood of tears, sank his head onto the table, and covered the remaining papers with his tears.

Werner stood beside him in acute embarrassment. He had not expected such a wild outburst of passion. Several times he tried to interrupt and change the course of the conversation, but always without success. He was quite unable to halt the flow. But his long-lasting friendship with Wilhelm took control of the situation, and as Wilhelm poured out his misery, he showed his deep and sincere concern by maintaining silence. And so they spent that evening: Wilhelm still immersed in sorrowful reflection, and Werner alarmed by this new outbreak of a passion that he thought he had long since curbed in his friend by what he thought was good advice and active encouragement.

Chapter Three

After such setbacks Wilhelm usually devoted himself all the more vigorously to business affairs, and this was indeed the best way for him to flee the labyrinth that was once again opening up enticingly before him. His easy manner with strangers and his ability to conduct correspondence in almost all languages gave his father and his associates increased hope, and compensated for the break in their plans due to the sickness of which they did not know the cause. So they decided once again to dispatch him on a business trip, and we catch up with him riding along on his horse, his clothes in a saddlebag— stimulated by the good fresh air and by the thought of going somewhere. He was proceeding in the direction of a mountainous area where he had some business to attend to.

He passed through valleys and hills with a feeling of extreme pleasure, seeing for the first time in his life overhanging cliffs, deep ravines, raging streams and tree-clad slopes, though such landscapes had haunted his dreams from his earliest days. In fact, he felt young again. All the pain he had suffered was washed away from his thoughts, and he began joyfully to recite passages from certain poems, especially from the *Pastor Fido* of Guarini, which crowded in on his mind in these isolated spots. He even recalled certain passages from his own poems and declaimed these with particular satisfaction. He was filling the world around him with figures from the past, and every step forward was accompanied by a sense of important actions he was destined to perform, and noteworthy events that would occur.

Several persons, coming up from behind him, greeted him and then hurried on ahead up the steep footpaths through the mountains, interrupting the silent course of his meditation without, however, his paying much attention to them. But finally a talkative fellow told him the reason why all these people were going this way. "At Hochdorf," the man said, "there is to be a play tonight and people from all around are going to see it." "Are you telling me," said Wilhelm, "that the art of the theater has penetrated these dense woods and built a temple, and that I am on my way to celebrate there?" "You will be even more surprised when you learn who the actors are. There is a large factory in the neighborhood, which employs many people. The owner, living as he does apart from all human society, knows no better way of occupying his workers in winter, than encouraging them to perform plays, for he will not countenance card playing and other coarse amusements. So this is how they spend their long evenings; and today being the old man's birthday, they are putting on a special performance."

So Wilhelm went to Hochdorf, where he had planned to spend the night anyway. He dismounted at the factory whose owner was on his list of creditors. When he gave his name, the old man expressed his delight at seeing him: "So you, sir," he said, "are the son of that worthy man to whom I owe so much thanks, and still some money. Your father has been very patient with me, and I would really be an utter rascal if I did not pay up promptly and gladly. You have arrived at just the right time to see that I mean what I say." He called in his wife, who was just as pleased to see Wilhelm as he was, said how like his father he was and regretted that, because of the many visitors, she could not put him up for the night. The business matter was soon settled, and Wilhelm put the small roll of gold in his pocket, hoping that all his other transactions would be so easily completed.

The hour was approaching when the play was due to begin. They were still waiting for the head forester, who eventually arrived, accompanied by several hunters, and was greeted with the greatest respect. The assembled company was then led into the barn alongside the garden, which was to serve as the theater. The whole place had been made pleasant and cheerful, though without any particular signs of good taste. One of the painters at the factory, who had worked for a time at the court theater, had produced some sort of forest, street and interior to serve as backdrops. The text of the play had been borrowed from a travelling company of actors and adapted to the needs of the present performers. And such as it was, it was entertaining enough. The plot, in which two lovers try to steal a girl from her guardian and then from each other, produced all sorts of interesting situations. This was the first play that Wilhelm had seen for a long time, and he engaged in various reflections as a result. It was full of action but lacking in real character portrayal. It amused and delighted, like all primitive forms of drama. For simple people are satisfied by seeing plenty of action, whereas a more cultured spectator will have his feelings engaged as well, and only a truly cultured person wants to reflect on a play. Wilhelm would gladly have helped the actors a bit here and there, for little would have been needed to improve the performance considerably.

He was disturbed in his silent musings by the tobacco smoke, which got thicker and thicker. The forester lit his pipe soon after the play started, and gradually several others took the same liberty. The big dogs were also a troublesome nuisance. They had indeed been left outside, but they soon found their way through a back door into the theater, ran onto the stage and into the actors, then jumped over the pit to their master who was sitting in the front row.

As an epilogue they offered a tribute. A portrait of the old man in his wedding clothes had been placed on an altar and decked out with flowers. All the actors paid homage to it in appropriate postures of respect. The youngest child, dressed in white, stepped up and delivered a speech in verse, by which the whole family and the forester, who was thinking of his own children, were moved to tears. And so the play ended, and Wilhelm could not refrain from stepping onto the stage to look at the actresses at closer range, praising their performance, and giving them advice for the future.

He attended to his other business obligations, in various mountain places, but not all of them were absolved so easily or pleasantly as here in Hochdorf. Some of the creditors asked for further time, some were plain rude, and some even denied that they owed any money. According to the instructions that had been given him, Wilhelm was required to start proceedings against some of them—which meant finding a lawyer, briefing him, appearing in court, and engaging in various other tiresome duties. It was just as aggravating when people tried to show him their respect. He found few who could give him information, few with whom he could hope to enter into a useful business relationship. In addition there were unfortunately several rainy days, and journeying on horseback in this sort of country became extremely arduous. He was therefore relieved when he came into flat country again, and found a pleasant little country town at the foot of a hill, on a beautiful fertile plain beside a gentle river, all bathed in sunshine. He had no business to transact in this particular place, but decided to stay there for a few days to give himself some rest, and some respite for his horse, which had suffered from the bad roads.

Chapter Four

Wilhelm stopped off at the inn on the marketplace. Inside things were very lively indeed and everyone seemed to be having a good time. A company of acrobats, jugglers and tightrope dancers had just moved in with their families, and there was even a strong man amongst them. They were preparing for a public performance, and occupied themselves in the meantime with all sorts of pranks. They argued with the landlord, then quarrelled amongst themselves. The subjects of their disputes were certainly not worth quarrelling about, and the way they expressed their satisfaction was absolutely insufferable. So

Wilhelm hesitated whether to stay there or not, as he stood by the entrance watching the workmen assembling a platform on the square.

A young girl came up selling roses and other flowers from a basket, he bought a nice bouquet, tied it up to his satisfaction, and was contemplating his handiwork with pleasure, when the window of another inn on the other side of the square was opened and an attractive woman appeared in it. He could see, despite the distance, that her face had a pleasant gaiety. Her blond hair fell loosely around her neck, and she seemed to turn and look at him. Shortly afterward a boy wearing a barber's apron and a white jacket came out and greeted him with the message that "the lady at the window ventured to ask if he would give her some of his beautiful flowers."—"She may have them all," said Wilhelm, giving the boy the whole bunch, and with it his compliments to the lovely lady, who responded to his message with a friendly greeting and then retired from the window.

Reflecting on this pleasant episode, he was going upstairs to his room when a young creature jumped out at him and immediately attracted his attention. The child was neatly dressed in a short silk bodice with slashed Spanish sleeves and puffed-out long slim trousers. Its long black hair was curled and wound in locks and braids on its head. He looked at the figure with amazement, uncertain whether it was a boy or a girl. But he finally decided in favor of the latter and stopped her as she was rushing past, wished her goodday, and asked to whom she belonged, although he could easily see that she must be a member of the group of acrobats and dancers. With a dark and penetrating sidelong glance she broke loose and rushed into the kitchen, without saying a word.

Further up the stairs there was a broad landing on which two men were practicing fencing, trying out their skill on each other. One of them obviously belonged to the troupe, the other had a somewhat less savage appearance. Wilhelm watched them and had cause to admire them both, and when the wilder one, who was husky and had a black beard, left the scene, the other one offered Wilhelm his rapier, with a gesture of great courtesy. "If you are prepared to take on a pupil," said Wilhelm, "I would be glad to try a few passes with you." They fenced together, and although the other was far superior to Wilhelm, he was polite enough to say that it was all a matter of practice, and Wilhelm had shown he had been taught by a good, solid, German fencing master.

Their conversation was interrupted by the hubbub created by the troupe leaving the inn in order to inform the townsfolk of the forthcoming spectacle and thereby arouse their interest in the performance. First came a drummer, and behind him the manager on horseback, and then, mounted on an equally skinny nag, a female dancer, holding a child decked out in ribbons and finery. The rest of the troupe came on foot, some of them carrying children in fantastic positions comfortably on their shoulders, and amongst these Wilhelm noticed again the dark, somber-looking young girl. A clown was running around in the gathering crowd, handing out playbills as he kissed a girl or smacked a little boy, all the time making jokes, which were so easy to grasp that every-body felt drawn towards him and eager to get to know him better. The play-bills underscored the many different skills of the performers, especially those of a Monsieur Narcisse and Mademoiselle Landrinette, who, as principals, were wise enough to absent themselves from the procession, in order to give themselves a higher status and arouse more curiosity.

During the parade the lovely woman in the neighboring inn reappeared at the window, and Wilhelm lost no time in enquiring about her from his fenc-ing partner, whom we shall call Laertes. He offered to take Wilhelm over to meet her. "She and I," said Laertes with a smile, "are the remains of a company of actors which was disbanded here recently. We liked the place so much that we decided to stay here for a while and use up our little remaining cash, while a friend has gone off to find a place for himself and us."

Laertes accompanied his new acquaintance to the door of Philine's room, where he left him for a moment while he went to buy candy in a nearby store. "You will certainly be grateful to me," he said on his return, "for providing you with this delightful acquaintance." The girl came out to meet them, wearing a pair of light slippers with high heels. She had thrown a black mantilla over her white negligé which, because it was not quite clean, gave her a domes-tic, relaxed appearance; and her short skirt revealed a pair of the tiniest feet imaginable.

"I am glad to see you," she called out to Wilhelm, "and thank you so much for the lovely flowers." She led him into the room with one hand while she pressed the flowers to her bosom with the other. When they had sat down and were engaged in some casual conversation to which she managed to give a charming twist, Laertes shook into her lap some burnt almonds which she immediately began to nibble. "Just look what a baby this young fellow is," she said: "He will try to persuade you that I am a passionate sweet eater, but actually he's the one who can't exist without eating something sweet." "Well," said Laertes in reply, "let us agree that in this as in so much else we like to keep each other company. For example, today is such a nice day. I would suggest that we ride out and have lunch at the mill." "Good idea," said Philine. "We must provide our new friend with a change of scene."

Laertes ran off (he never walked) and Wilhelm wanted to go back for a moment to his room to fix his hair, which was still a bit untidy from the jour-ney. "You can do that here," said Philine, calling her young servant boy, and persuaded Wilhelm very sweetly to take off his coat, put on her smock and let the boy fix his hair right there in her presence. "One can't waste time," she said, "for one never knows how long one will be together."

The boy did not do his job very well, more because of his surly indifference than because he lacked the necessary skill. He kept pulling Wilhelm's hair and it seemed he would never be finished. Philine reproved him several times for his ill-mannered behavior, and finally lost her patience, shoved him aside and threw him out. She then took things into her own hands and curled Wilhelm's hair very efficiently and elegantly. She didn't hurry over this, kept changing her mind on what she was doing, and couldn't avoid her knees touching his, and her bouquet and bosom getting so close to his lips that he was more than once tempted to give her a kiss.

When Wilhelm had removed some powder from his forehead with a knife that she had for this purpose, she said: "Keep that in remembrance of me." It was a pretty little knife with a handle of inlaid steel on which were engraved the words: "Remember me." Wilhelm put it in his pocket, thanked her, and asked her permission to give her something in exchange.

Now they were all ready. Laertes had found a coach, and off they went on a very pleasant excursion. Philine threw something or other out of the window to every beggar, with a few kind and cheerful words. They came to the mill and had just ordered something to eat, when musicians started playing in front of the building. They were miners, singing pleasant songs in loud, shrill voices to the accompaniment of a zither and triangle. They were soon surrounded by people who came up to listen, and guests applauded them from the windows of the mill. Noticing this extra attention the musicians spread out in preparation, so it seemed, for something really special. After a short pause, a miner stepped forward with a hoe, and made digging motions whilst the others played a solemn melody. After this, up came a farmer from the crowd and made threatening gestures at the miner, indicating that he should remove himself from here. The spectators were puzzled by this, and only when the "farmer" opened his mouth to reprove the other man for digging in his field, did they realize that he was a miner dressed as a peasant. The first man calmly told the other that he had every right to start digging here, and began to explain the basic elements of mining. The farmer, who didn't understand the strange terminology, asked all sorts of stupid questions at which the spectators, feeling superior, burst into laughter. The miner tried to explain to the farmer the advantages he would gain, once he had dug up the treasures that lay beneath the earth; and the farmer's threatening attitude became gradually modified, and they parted as good friends. But the miner had won the argument.

"This little dialogue," said Wilhelm as they sat at table, "shows quite clearly how useful the theater could be for all classes of society, and what profit the state could derive from displaying on the stage the best side of human occupations, vocations and undertakings, those aspects that the state must itself respect and support. Nowadays all we seem to see is the ridiculous side of things; the writer of comedies has become a sort of malicious monitor of human follies, always on the lookout for some new one to register on his list, and jubilant when he finds one. Wouldn't it be a satisfying and worthy occupation for any statesman to survey the influence of the various classes of society on each other, and thereby give support to a writer with a real sense of humor? I am convinced that in this way many useful as well as entertaining plays could be produced."

"So far as I have been able to observe in my own travels," said Laertes, "there is more discouragement than the opposite, more refusals, denials and rejection than permission, encouragement and rewards. Everything is allowed to go on until it becomes harmful; and then it is angrily and violently terminated."

"Let's stop talking about the state and statesmen," said Philine. "They always suggest full-bottomed wigs to me, and it doesn't matter who is wearing a wig, I have a twitchy feeling in my fingers and long to pull them off the venerable gentlemen, and dance around in the room laughing at their bald pates."

She cut off the conversation with some lively songs, which she performed very prettily, and pressed for a speedy return to the town, so that they should not miss the evening performance by the acrobats and tightrope dancers. Comical almost to the point of eccentricity, she continued to show her generosity to the wayside beggars on the return journey, and, since she and both the men had run out of money, she threw her hat out of the window to a young girl, and her scarf to an old woman.

Philine invited her two companions to her quarters, saying that there would be a better view of the performance from her windows than from the other inn.

When they arrived, they found the platform already set up and carpets hung up to make a colorful background for the show. The springboards were already in place, the slack rope fastened to the posts, and the tightrope pulled over the blocks. The square was filled mostly with the common people, and the windows with persons of quality. The clown began to put the audience in a good mood and capture their attention with some silly tricks, and these, as always, were greeted with laughter. Then several children, executing the weirdest contortions with their bodies, aroused both horror and amazement; and Wilhelm was filled with deep pity when he saw amongst them the same child that had so interested him earlier, striving to achieve these abnormal postures. But then came the merry acrobats who delighted everybody by twisting and turning in the air, first alone, then one after another, and finally all together. At this there was vigorous clapping and shouts of joy from all the spectators.

And then all eyes were fixed on something quite different. One after another the children stepped onto the tightrope. First came those who were still learning the art, so that the performance would be prolonged and the difficulties of this particular skill amply demonstrated. Then came the men and women who showed only a moderate amount of skill—but not yet Monsieur Narcisse or Mademoiselle Landrinette. Finally these two appeared from behind the red curtains of a sort of tent, and fulfilled every expectation of the eager spectators by their attractive figures and elegant costumes. He was a lively young man of medium height with black eyes and a heavy pigtail; she was equally attractive and looked just as strong. They followed each other on the tightrope, executing steps and leaps with the greatest ease and maintaining unusual postures. Her lightness, his boldness, and the precision with which both of them carried out their artistic feats, increased the enthusiasm of the spectators at every new twist or turn. The easy grace with which they conducted themselves, as compared with the apparent strain and effort of the others, gave them such an air of superiority, that they might well have been the lord and master of the entire troupe; indeed everyone thought they deserved such an important position.

The enthusiasm of the people at the windows was just as great as that of the people down on the square, for the ladies had their eyes fixed on Narcisse and the gentlemen on Landrinette. The people on the square yelled with delight; the more refined watchers at the windows expressed their approval by clapping their hands, but they did not laugh at the clown, as those down below did. Only a few of those on the square slunk away when members of the troupe came through the crowd with pewter plates to collect money.

"It seems to me that they did very well," said Wilhelm to Philine, who was with him at the window. "I admire their ability to make even quite small feats have a really telling effect by bringing them on in succession, each at the appropriate moment; and also how they managed to combine the clumsiness of the children and the virtuosity of their star performers into a total effect which held our attention and pleasantly diverted us."

The people on the square had gradually dispersed, leaving it empty, and meanwhile Philine and Laertes were arguing about the relative quality of the figures and skills of Narcisse and Landrinette, and teasing each other. Wilhelm saw the strange girl standing alongside children playing on the street, and drew this to the attention of Philine, who called and beckoned to the child with her usual vivacity. But since the child seemed unwilling to come to her, she went to fetch it herself, singing as she clattered down the stairs on her high-heeled slippers.

"Here's our mystery," she said, drawing the child into the room. But the girl standing in the doorway, as if eager to slip away, placed her right hand on her chest and her left on her temple, and made a deep bow. "Don't be afraid, little one," said Wilhelm, walking up to her. She looked at him with an expression of uncertainty, and stepped forward a few paces. "What is your name?" he asked. "They call me Mignon." "How old are you?" "Nobody has counted." "Who was your father?" "The big devil is dead."

"Well, that's all very odd!" said Philine. They asked her a few more questions, which she answered in broken German and a strange, formal manner, bowing deeply each time and placing her hands as before on her chest and temple.

Wilhelm could not take his eyes off her; her whole appearance and the mystery that surrounded her completely absorbed his mind and feelings. He thought she was probably twelve or thirteen years old. She was well built, but her limbs suggested further development to come, which possibly had been arrested. Her features were not regular, but striking: her forehead seemed to veil some secret, her nose was unusually beautiful, her mouth, though too tight-lipped for her age and inclined to twitch at times on one side, had a certain winsome charm about it. The grease paint almost obscured her dark complexion. Wilhelm was so absorbed in contemplating her, that he lapsed into silence and became completely oblivious of the others. But Philine roused him out of his daze by offering the child some of the candy she had left over, and then gave the girl a sign that she should leave, which she did, with her usual bow, and in a flash ran out of the door.

The time came for the other three to separate for the evening, but before doing so they agreed to embark next day on another excursion. They decided to go out again for lunch, but this time to a different place, a nearby hunting lodge. Wilhelm spent much of the evening praising Philine to Laertes, to which the latter reacted lightheartedly and curtly.

The next morning, after an hour's fencing practice, they went to Philine's inn, having earlier seen the rented coach. But Wilhelm was surprised to find that the coach had left and Philine was nowhere to be found. They were told that she had driven off with two strangers who had arrived that very morning. He had been looking forward to a pleasant time in her company and could not conceal his irritation. Laertes, on the other hand, just laughed, and said: "That's what I like about her! That's exactly how she is! But let's go straight to the hunting lodge, and let's not give up our excursion on her account, wherever she may have taken herself off to."

On the way Wilhelm expressed his disapproval of such fickle behavior, but Laertes replied that he did not think it was fickle to remain true to character. "When Philine agrees to something, or gives someone a promise, she does so on the unspoken condition that it will suit her when the time comes. She likes to make gifts, but one must always be prepared to give them back."

"What a strange character!" said Wilhelm. "Not strange at all," Laertes replied, "and in no wise hypocritical. I love her for it, and am her friend, because she represents in all its true colors the sex that I have such good reason to hate. She is the real Eve, the progenitrix of the whole female race. They're all like her, though they won't admit it."

The conversation continued in this vein, with Laertes venting his wrath against the whole female sex but without giving any reasons. Wilhelm was depressed by what Laertes had been saying, because it reminded him all too vividly of his own experience with Mariane. They entered a forest, and what should they find but Philine sitting alone at a stone table beside a spring shaded by a group of fine old trees. She greeted them with a cheerful song and when Laertes asked what had happened to her companions, she said: "I led them a real dance, and fooled them. That's just what they deserved. On the way here I tested their generosity, and when I found out they were skinflints

I decided to punish them. When we arrived, they asked the waiter what there was to eat, and with usual glibness of tongue he recited a list of everything they had, and other things too. I saw their embarrassment: they looked at each other, dithered a bit, and then asked the prices. 'Why should you concern yourselves with all that?' I said. 'It's the business of the lady to decide on the menu. Let me take care of it.' So I ordered the craziest lunch, some of which had to be brought from elsewhere in the neighborhood. The waiter, after some grimacing on my part, had become my ally in all this and gave me good solid help, and we scared them both so much at the thought of the sumptuous banquet we had ordered, that they decided to take a walk in the woods, and I doubt whether they will come back! I laughed and laughed for full fifteen minutes, and I shall go on laughing whenever I recall the expression on their faces." Laertes regaled them at table with similar stories, and they all entertained each other with tales of misunderstandings and hoodwinkings of one kind and another.

A young man whom they knew from the town came walking through the woods with a book in his hand, sat down beside them and praised the beauty of the place. He directed their attention to the rustling spring, the movement of the branches, the light effects and the song of the birds. At this Philine sang a song about a cuckoo, which seemed to displease the newcomer, and he soon left.

"I don't want to hear another word about Nature and all its beauties," said Philine, once he had gone. "There is nothing more insufferable than having one's pleasure analyzed while one is enjoying it. When the weather's fine, you go for a walk; when the music starts, you dance. But who wants to *think* about the fine weather or the music? It's the dancers that interest us, not the music; and to look into a pair of beautiful dark eyes doesn't do a pair of blue eyes any harm. Compared with that, what's the use of rustling springs and old worm-eaten lime trees?" As she said this, she was gazing into Wilhelm's eyes, and her glance could not but penetrate to the gates of his heart. "You're quite right," he said, with some embarrassment. "People are what's most interesting, and perhaps that's all we should be interested in. For everything else around us is either the atmosphere in which we live, or instruments that we use for ourselves. The more we occupy ourselves with our environment, the more we think about it or partake of it, the less alive is our sense of our own value and of belonging to a community of fellow men. People who attach great importance to gardens, buildings, clothes, jewels or possessions of any kind, are not very sociable and not very agreeable. They lose sight of other people, and few of them succeed in entertaining them and amusing them. Don't we see that in the theater? A good actor can make us forget a wretched decor, but a fine theater simply makes us more aware of the poverty of the acting."

When they had finished eating, Philine ensconced herself in the tall, shady grass. Her two companions had to bring her flowers in quantity. She made a single wreath out of these and set it on her head, which made her look un-believably charming. There were enough flowers left for her to make another wreath, which she did while the two men sat down beside her. When after much joking and innuendo she had it finished, she lowered it delicately onto Wilhelm's head, and kept rearranging it till she had it just right. "Am I then to go empty-handed?" asked Laertes. "Not at all," replied Philine. "You shall have no cause for complaint"; and with that she took the wreath off her own head and put it on his. "If we were rivals in love, we could have a fierce argument as to whom you are favoring more," said Laertes. "In that case," she replied, "you would be silly fools." She leaned over him, offering her mouth to be kissed and turned immediately to put her arm around Wilhelm and plant a passionate kiss on his lips. "Which tasted better?" she said, teasingly. "Marvelous!" said Laertes. "It seems that something like that could never taste of wormwood." "As little as any present enjoyed without envy or pride. But now," she said, "I would like to dance for an hour or so, and then we should go back to our acrobats."

They went into the house, and there they found music. Philine, who was a good dancer, cheered them both up. Wilhelm was not clumsy, but he lacked experience in dancing; so Philine and Laertes decided to give him a few lessons.

By now it was getting late, and when they arrived back, the rope dancers had already begun the show. There were still many spectators on the market-square, but a good number of them had gone over to the door of the inn where Wilhelm was staying, because, as our three friends noticed when they got out of the coach, there was some kind of trouble there. Wilhelm rushed over and pushed his way through the crowd to see what was happening, and, to his horror, saw the manager of the troupe dragging the mysterious child by the hair out of the building and beating her frail body mercilessly with the handle of a whip.

Wilhelm tore over to the man and seized him by the chest. "Let go of that child!" he cried, yelling like a maniac, "or one of us will be dead!" With that, inflamed with anger, he grabbed the man by the throat so fiercely that the fellow thought he was going to choke, let go of the girl, and tried to defend himself. Some of the bystanders, equally concerned about the child but un-willing to start a fight, now grabbed his arms, took away the whip, threatened him and poured abuse on him. The man himself, his only weapon now being his mouth, began to threaten and curse abominably, and said that this useless, lazy creature wouldn't do what she was supposed to, refusing to perform the egg dance that he had promised the public. He was going to kill her, and no one would stop him. He then tried to break loose to find the child who was hiding in the crowd. But Wilhelm held him back and said: "You shall not see or touch that child until you explain to the magistrate where you stole her from. I will go to any length; you will not escape me." These words, which Wilhelm uttered in the heat of his anger, trusting some deep dark feeling (or inspiration, if you like) but without much thought or intention, brought the infuriated fellow to his senses. "What should I do with such a creature?" he said: "She's utterly useless to me. Just pay me what her clothes cost and then you can keep her. But let's settle the matter this very evening." With this he rushed off to continue the show and appease the spectators with a few worthwhile artistic feats.

When things had quietened down, Wilhelm looked around for the child, but couldn't find her anywhere. Some people said they had seen her in the attic, some on the roofs of neighboring houses. But after searching everywhere they decided to wait and see if she would turn up again of her own accord.

Meanwhile Narcisse had come back and Wilhelm questioned him about the child and where it came from. He did not know anything about this, for he had only recently joined the troupe. Instead, he went on to tell Wilhelm volubly and very amusingly about his own experiences. When Wilhelm congratulated him on his success with the public, he seemed quite indifferent. "We are used to being laughed at and being admired, but all this approval doesn't improve our lot. The manager pays us, and has to make his profit." He then was about to take his leave and hurry away, when Wilhelm asked him where he was off to in such a hurry. The young man smiled, and admitted that his figure and his talents aroused elsewhere more solid approval than he got from the public. Several women had sent messages that they were eager to know him better, and he was afraid that, with all the visits that he had to pay, he would hardly get through by midnight. He went on to enumerate very frankly all his assignations, and would have given names and street numbers if Wilhelm had not disdained such indiscretion and politely dismissed him.

While this was going on, Laertes had been entertaining Landrinette and assuring her that she was fully deserving of being a woman and remaining one.

The negotiations with the manager began, and the child was transferred to Wilhelm's keeping for the sum of thirty thalers. The black-bearded, intemperate Italian gave up all his rights to her, but would say nothing about her origins, except that he had acquired her on the death of his brother who, because of his extraordinary performing skills, had been known as the Big Devil.

Most of the next morning was spent in trying to find the child. Every corner of the house, every inch of the neighborhood was searched—but with no results. She had disappeared; and it was feared that she might have drowned herself, or done herself harm in some other way.

Even the charms of Philine could not distract Wilhelm from his anxiety. He spent a mournful day, just brooding. Even the performance that night, when acrobats and dancers exerted all their powers to make the very best impression, did not cheer or divert his heavy mind.

The number of spectators was so greatly increased by those from neighboring villages that the applause snowballed in intensity. The leaps over swords and through the paper bottom of a cask created a great sensation. The strong man, to everyone's horror and amazement, stretched himself out across the space between two chairs and then lifted an anvil onto his arched stomach and had two husky smiths forge a horseshoe on it. To end the show, there was the so-called Hercules Tower, never before seen in these parts, in which a row of men stood on the shoulders of another row, and on top of them women and youths, so that a living pyramid was built, with a child standing on its head at the top as the pinnacle and weather vane. Narcisse and Landrinette were carried in sedan chairs on the shoulders of the others, through the best streets of the town, which was greeted by the populace with shouts of delight. They were showered with ribbons, flowers and silks, and everyone pressed forward to get a closer look at them, happy to see them and to be honored by a glance from them.

"What actor, writer, or indeed what human being would not feel he had reached the summit of his desires when, by some noble word or deed, he produced such a universal impression? What a rich experience it would be to disseminate worthy human feelings so quickly—like electricity—through the ranks of the common people, such as these people did by the display of their bodily skill—to impart a sense of common humanity to the masses, inflame and disturb them with a display of all our pleasures and misfortunes, wisdom and follies, stupidity and idiocy, and release their sullen minds into a state of active, vigorous, unimpeded freedom!" Thus spoke Wilhelm, but since neither Philine nor Laertes seemed inclined to continue such a discourse, he was obliged to articulate to himself these favorite reflections of his, as he walked through the streets far into the night, and indulge once more in his passionate desire to incorporate into drama all that was great, noble and good. And he could do so now in the full vigor and freedom of his unfettered imagination.

Chapter Five

The next day, as soon as the tightrope artists had departed with a great deal of noise, Mignon appeared and stepped up to Wilhelm and Laertes who had resumed their fencing practice. "Where have you been hiding?" Wilhelm asked her gently. "We were very worried about you." The child looked at him, but said nothing. "Now you are ours," said Laertes. "We have bought you." "How much did you pay?" she asked curtly. "A hundred ducats," said Laertes. "And when you pay us back, you may go free." "That's a lot, isn't it?" the child asked. "Yes indeed, so just see that you behave well." "I'll be your servant," she replied.

From that moment on, she watched carefully to see what services the waiter had performed for the two friends, and would not let him enter the room anymore. She wanted to do everything herself and performed her various services, though slowly and sometimes awkwardly, but correctly and very attentively.

She would often take a vessel of water and wash her face so vigorously and thoroughly that she almost rubbed her cheeks raw. Laertes teased her about this, but found out that she was trying to get rid of the paint on her cheeks and thought that the red patches she had caused by her vigorous rubbing, were particularly stubborn paint. They explained this to her, and once she stopped what she had been doing, a fine brown complexion, brightened by only a hint of red, was revealed.

Attracted more than he cared to admit to himself both by the wanton charms of Philine and the mystery surrounding the child, Wilhelm spent several days in this strange company. He justified this by diligent practice in fencing and dancing, since he might not so easily have an opportunity to indulge in these two occupations.

One day, to his surprise and delight, he saw Melina and his wife arriving. Once they had greeted him, they enquired about the actors, and were dismayed to learn that the director had long since left, and the actors, except for very few, had also gone off to various other places. Since getting married—in which, as we have seen, Wilhelm had been helpful—the young couple had been looking in various places for a job, but so far without success. They had been advised to try here: several people they met on the way reported that they had seen good theater. Philine took a dislike to Madame Melina, and the lively Laertes to her husband. They would gladly have gotten rid of the newcomers immediately, and Wilhelm was not able to change their unfavorable opinion despite his repeated assertions that they were really quite decent people.

This addition to the company disturbed in several ways the happy-go-lucky existence of the adventurous spirits of Philine, Laertes and Wilhelm. They found a room in the inn where Philine was staying, and Melina began immediately to haggle and complain, demanding better quarters, more copious meals and faster service for less money. In a very short time he had the innkeeper and the waiters scowling; and whereas the others, intent on enjoying life, accepted what was served and paid promptly in order not to think about what they had been eating, Melina criticized every meal and then went over it again afterwards, so that Philine had no hesitation in declaring that he chewed over everything.

Madame Melina was even more distasteful to the vivacious Philine, for although she was not uneducated she was totally lacking in mind and soul. She recited quite well, but was always reciting, and just words, emphasizing particular passages but without expressing the spirit of the whole. She was by no means unpleasant to people—especially not to men, and those she associated with usually felt that she had a fine mind. For she knew how to adopt the feelings of others. She would feel her way into the respect of a friend by agreeing with his ideas until she was out of her depth, and then wax ecstatic at what was new to her. She knew when to talk and when to keep quiet, and although she was not malicious, she knew how to find someone's weak spot.

Chapter Six

Melina spent his time discovering what was still left of the properties which had belonged to the troupe. The scenery and costumes had been left as securities with some local merchants, and a lawyer had the authority of the previous director to sell these, under certain conditions, if anybody turned up who wanted them. Melina wanted to see what there was, and took Wilhelm along. Although he would not admit it, Wilhelm felt a certain attraction towards these things when they entered the rooms where they were stored. Although the scenery was all spotty and in bad shape, and the costumes—turkish, saracen, grotesque, and cowls for wizards, jews or priests—were no longer very convincing, he could not resist the feeling that it was amidst such junk as this that he had spent the happiest moments of his life. If Melina could have gazed into his heart, he would have urged him even more strongly to provide a sum of money to redeem these scattered remnants and put them together again into a living whole. "How happy I would be if I had two hundred thalers to secure these basic theatrical materials," exclaimed Melina; "I could soon get a play together that would provide for us in this town." Wilhelm said nothing. The precious things were locked up again. And they left, both of them deep in thought.

From now on Melina talked of nothing else but plans and proposals for setting up a theater and making a profit. He tried to interest Philine and Laertes in this, and it was suggested to Wilhelm that he should advance some money and act as security. But this matter only made Wilhelm realize that he should not have spent so long in this town. He excused himself, saying that he really must think about continuing on his journey.

But the person and character of Mignon attracted him more and more. There was something strange about everything she did. She never walked up or down stairs, she always ran. She climbed upon to banisters, and before one knew it, there she was on top of a closet, sitting quite still. Wilhelm also noticed that she had a different greeting for everybody. For some time now she had been greeting him with arms folded on her breast. Some days she would be completely silent; on others she would answer certain questions, but always strangely so that it was difficult to decide whether it was a joke or her German mixed with French and Italian was intentional or simply the result of an imperfect knowledge of German. She was tireless in Wilhelm's service, getting up at sunrise but retiring early to rest on the bare floor of one of the rooms. Nothing could persuade her to sleep in a bed or on a straw mattress. He often found her washing herself. Her clothes were clean though heavily patched. Wilhelm was also told that early every morning she went to mass, and once he followed her and saw her kneeling in a corner of the church, piously saying her rosary. She did not see him, and he went home full of thoughts about this strange creature and unable to make up his mind about her.

When Melina pressed him further for money to buy the theater properties, Wilhelm became even more determined to move on. He decided that very day to write to his family, who had had no news of him for quite a while, and even began a letter to Werner. He had got quite far in the account of his various adventures—often straying from the truth without noticing it—when he discovered on the other side of the sheet some lines he had been copying for Madame Melina from his own notebook. So he tore up the sheet in a fit of displeasure, and put off writing his letters to the next post day.

Chapter Seven

One day they were all together as usual, when Philine, who was observing every horse and scrutinizing every carriage that passed, suddenly shouted: "Look! There's our dear old pedant! I wonder whom he has with him in the carriage!" She called to him, waving from her window, and the carriage stopped. A pitiful old fellow who, with his shabby, greyish-brown coat and soiled linen, looked like a musty old schoolman, got out of the carriage and respectfully took off his hat to Philine, revealing a badly powdered and very stiff wig. Philine blew him a multitude of kisses. For though there were always men she loved and whose love she enjoyed, she took almost equal delight, and that as often as possible, in teasing those she was not in love with at the moment.

The noise with which Philine greeted her old acquaintance and the confusion which that created, was such that they neglected to look at the other persons with him. These were an oldish man with two women. Wilhelm had the feeling that he had met them somewhere before, and it soon turned out that this was indeed the case. Several years previously he had seen all three of them take part in a theatrical performance in his hometown. The two daughters had changed a lot in the meantime, but not their father. He usually played those good-natured, garrulous old men that German drama is full of and whom you can often encounter in everyday life. Since it seems to be a part of our national character to do good without ostentation, we seldom reflect on the fact that it is also possible to do what is right with some degree of graciousness and style, and as a result we tend all too easily to be cross-grained in order to emphasize by contrast the sweetness of our virtues. It was these roles that this actor played so well. He played them so often, indeed so exclusively, that he began to take on the same character in real life.

Wilhelm, once he had recognized him, became very perturbed, for he remembered having often seen him playing alongside his beloved Mariane. He could still hear him scolding and the gentle voice with which she had to counter his brusqueness in so many plays.

The first question addressed to these newcomers was an eager inquiry whether there was any hope of finding employment elsewhere, but they said that they had approached various theater troupes only to be told that there were no vacancies. Some of these companies were even concerned that the threat of approaching war might cause them to disband. The old man and his two daughters had just given up a favorable engagement because they were bored and wanted a change, and had hired a carriage together with the "schoolmaster," or "pedant" as Philine always called him, whom they had met on the road, in order to come to this particular town. But the opportunity they had hoped to find here was obviously not forthcoming.

While all the others were discussing their affairs, Wilhelm was deep in thought. He would have liked to talk to the old man privately. He wanted to hear about Mariane, but was also afraid of what he might learn; and so he was in a state of extreme uneasiness.

The two young women were very pleasant to him but even this did not rouse him from his brooding, until one particular exchange of words claimed his full attention. Friedrich, the blond boy who had been performing various services for Philine, suddenly refused to lay the table and get the meal. "I agreed to serve you," he said to Philine with some heat, "but not to wait on all sorts of other people." At this, there was a violent argument. Philine insisted that he must do his job, but he stubbornly refused. So she told him he could leave, and go wherever he pleased. "Do you think I can't leave you, if I want to?" he said, with an air of defiance. He packed up his things and hurriedly left the house. "Go and get us what we want, Mignon!" said Philine. "Tell the waiter, and help him serve!"

At this point Mignon came up to Wilhelm and asked, in her usual laconic fashion: "Shall I? May I?" "Yes, my child," said Wilhelm. "Do what Mademoiselle requests." So she took care of everything and waited very attentively on the guests at table. After dinner Wilhelm found the opportunity to take a walk alone with the old man, and after various questions about how life had been treating him, he succeeded in turning the conversation on to the troupe he had been part of, and finally ventured to ask after Mariane.

"Don't mention that despicable creature!" the old man exclaimed. "I have vowed never to think of her again." Wilhelm was shocked, and even more discomfited by the way the old man went on to upbraid her for her frivolity and wantonness. He would gladly have terminated the conversation, but he had to suffer through the garrulous effusions of this strange man.

"I am ashamed that I was so fond of her. But if you had known her well, you would have pardoned me for that. She was so nice, so natural and good, so pleasing in her manner, so thoroughly agreeable. I would never have imagined that insolence and ingratitude were so deeply ingrained in her character."

Wilhelm had by now become resigned to hearing nothing but the very worst, when he suddenly noticed with astonishment that the old man's tone was changing. He became more gentle, and finally the words stuck in his throat, and he took out a handkerchief to dry his tears. "What is the matter?"

said Wilhelm. "What makes you suddenly feel so differently? Do tell me. I am more concerned about this girl than you know. But do tell me everything."

"I have little more to say," the old man replied, lapsing back into that earlier tone of petulant severity. "I will never forgive her for what she made me suffer. She always had a certain trust in me. I loved her like a daughter and, while my wife was still living, I had decided to take her into my family in order to get her out of the clutches of the old man from whose protection I saw no possible benefits for her. But my wife died, and the whole plan came to nothing.

"Towards the end of our stay in your home town, I noticed a certain sadness about her. That would be about three years ago. I asked her about this, but she evaded my questions. Then we got ready to leave. She rode with me in the same coach and I noticed something which she herself soon confirmed: namely, that she was pregnant. She was terribly afraid that the manager would dismiss her. And indeed he soon did, cancelling her contract (which was only for six weeks anyway), and totally unconcerned about the appearances she was engaged for. He paid out what he owed her, and left her in a wretched inn in a small town.

"To Hell with all such lewd whores," said the old man, full of anger, "and especially this one. For she has ruined so much of my life. Why should I spend my time telling you how attentive I was to her needs, even when she was away from us. I would rather throw my money into a pond and spend my time training mangy dogs than ever again devote my attentions to such a creature. For what happened? At first I got some letters of thanks, with news of various places where she had stayed; but in the end not a word, not even thanks for the money I sent her for her confinement. Dissemblance and wantonness combine in women to provide them with a comfortable life and honest fellows like me with hours of sorrow!"

Chapter Eight

Imagine Wilhelm's state of mind as he returned home from this conversation! All the old wounds had been torn open, and the feeling that she had not been quite unworthy of his love came over him again. For her whole loveable nature had come through the old man's account of his attentions to her and what he had said, albeit grudgingly, in her praise. Even his most violent denunciations of her had contained nothing to discredit her in Wilhelm's eyes, because he himself felt that he shared responsibility for her misdeeds, and her ultimate silence seemed to him not something to reproach her with, but something that filled him with anxious thoughts of what she must have been through. First the confinement, then as a mother, having to wander around the world, without anyone to assist her, wandering about with a child that was probably his—all this distressed him greatly.

Mignon had waited up for him, with a light to guide him up the stairs. When she had put down the candle, she asked his permission to give a performance for his benefit that evening. He would rather have said no, for he did not know what this might turn out to be. But he could not refuse this good-hearted creature anything. She came back into the room after a little while, carrying under one arm a carpet which she spread out on the floor. Wilhelm let her continue. She brought four lighted candles and put one at each corner of the carpet. When she next fetched a basket of eggs, her intentions became clearer. With the measured steps of an artist she paced back and forth on the carpet, distributing the eggs in definite groups. Then she called in a servant who played the violin. He stood with his instrument in one corner. She blindfolded herself, gave a sign for the music to begin, and started to move like a wound-up mechanism, beating the time of the melody with the clap of her castanets.

Nimbly and lightly she executed the dance with rapid precision, stepping so briskly and firmly between and beside the eggs that at any moment one thought she would crush one of them or dislodge it by the swiftness of her twistings and turnings. But she never touched an egg despite the variety of her steps, now short, now long, including some leaps. She finally wound her way through the rows in a half-kneeling position. She pursued her course relentlessly like clockwork and the strange music gave a new twist to the movement of the rousing dance every time it started up again. Wilhelm was absolutely transported by this strange spectacle; forgetting all his cares, he followed every step of the beloved creature, amazed to see how completely her character was manifested in the dance. Severe, sharp, dry and violent—all this she certainly was; and in her quieter movements there was solemnity rather than grace. He suddenly realized what he had been feeling about her all this time. He wanted to take this abandoned creature to his bosom as his own child, caress her and by a father's love awaken to her the joys of life.

The dance came to an end. With her feet she rolled the eggs into a pile, not overlooking or breaking one of them. Then she stood beside the pile of eggs, took off her blindfold, and terminated the performance with a bow. Wilhelm thanked her for so pleasantly and unexpectedly executing for him alone the dance that he had so much wanted to see. He stroked her cheeks and said how sorry he was that she had been treated so harshly. He promised her a new suit of clothes, whereupon she exclaimed: "In your color." He agreed to this, though he was not quite sure what she meant. She gathered up the eggs and the carpet, asked if he had any further orders, and leapt out of the room.

Wilhelm learnt from the musician that she had spent much time and effort singing the tune of the dance to him, which was a fandango, until he could play it himself; and that she had offered him money for his pains, which he had refused.

Chapter Nine

Wilhelm spent a restless night, partly wide awake and partly harried by disturbing dreams in which he saw Mariane at one moment in all her beauty, then in pitiful shape, first with the child in her arms and then without it. Dawn was just breaking, when in came Mignon with a tailor. She brought with her some grey cloth and blue taffeta, saying, in her own peculiar way, that she wanted a new jacket and sailor pants, such as she had seen on boys in the town, with blue ribbons and lapels.

Wilhelm had not worn any bright colors since losing Mariane, and had accustomed himself to grey, as the color of shades, except that he had somewhat livened up this somber garb by a light blue lining or a little collar of the same hue. Mignon, eager to wear his colors, put pressure on the tailor, who promised to deliver the suit in a short while.

That day, the dancing and fencing lessons with Laertes did not turn out too well; they were interrupted by Melina, who expatiated on the fact that they now had assembled a little company of actors that could put on plenty of plays. He renewed his request that Wilhelm should put down some money to get things started, but Wilhelm still hesitated.

Philine and the two girls came in laughing and shouting. They had worked out a plan for another outing, always eager to have a change of place and new things to look at. What they desired most, was to eat in a different place every day. This time it seemed to be a river trip. The Pedant had already found a boat to take them down the winding course of the river, and urged on by Philine, the whole company fell in with the idea and were soon on board.

"So—what shall we do now?" said Philine when they had all found somewhere to sit. "The simplest thing would be to extemporize a play," said Laertes. "Let everyone pick a role that suits his character, and we'll see how it turns out."

"Excellent idea!" said Wilhelm. "If people don't dissemble at all but simply act according to their own impulses, harmony and contentment will not be theirs for long; and never, if they dissemble all the time. It will not be a bad idea if we assume a personality at the beginning and then show as much as we wish of the real self hidden beneath the mask."

"Yes," said Laertes. "That's why women are so agreeable, for at first they never show their true colors."

"That's because they're not as vain as men," said Madame Melina. "Men always think they are quite attractive enough as nature made them."

All this time they were moving past delightful hills and woods, gardens and vineyards, and the young women showed their enthusiasm over the landscape. Especially Madame Melina, who began ceremoniously to recite a pretty poem in the descriptive mode on a similar scene. But she was interrupted by Philine, who now proposed a rule that no one be allowed to talk about inanimate objects. She returned to the idea of extemporizing a play, supporting it vigorously. The blustering old man should be a pensioned officer, Laertes a travelling fencing master, the Pedant a Jew, and she herself a Tyrolean girl. The others could be what they wanted. They should pretend they were meeting each other for the first time on a boat going to some market town. She herself began to play her part with the Jew, and general merriment broke out.

After a while the skipper asked them whether he might take on another passenger, for a man was standing on the shore, waving. "Just what we need," said Philine. "What we need is a stowaway." An attractive man stepped on board, and from his clothing and dignified appearance he looked as though he might be a clergyman. He greeted the assembled company, which thanked him and then told him about the little amusement they were planning. He took on the role of a country parson, and to their amazement played it extremely well, admonishing at one moment and telling yarns at the next, revealing certain weaknesses but always maintaining an air of respectfulness.

Anyone who failed to act in accordance with his or her role had to pay a forfeit. Philine gathered these conscientiously and threatened particularly to shower the clergyman with kisses when the forfeits had to be redeemed. But he always remained true to character. Melina, on the other hand, was stripped of buttons, buckles and anything else that was detachable. He had chosen to represent a travelling Englishman, but could not really get into the part.

The time passed very pleasantly, with everybody exerting their wits and imagination, embroidering their parts with all sorts of quips and sallies. They arrived at the place where they intended to spend the day, and Wilhelm, taking a walk with the clergyman (let's call him such because of his appearance and the role he was playing), found himself involved in a most interesting conversation.

"I think this kind of exercise amongst actors, especially when in the company of friends or acquaintances, is extremely useful," said the stranger. "It is the very best way to take people out of themselves and, by way of a detour, return them to themselves. It should be introduced in all theatrical companies. They should practice in this way, and the public would surely profit greatly if every month or so an unwritten play were performed, though the actors would have to prepare for this by several rehearsals."

"But an extemporized play should not be made up on the spur of the moment," Wilhelm objected. "The general plan, action and division of scenes should have been decided on, and the actors left to work out the presentation."

"Yes, indeed," said the stranger. "And once the actors were in the swing, the presentation should benefit by this procedure. Not so much the verbal presentation, for the words must be the product of the author's considered reflection, but the gestures, facial expressions, cries and the like, all that belongs to miming and what is partially articulated—an art which seems to be disappearing from our stage. There are certainly still actors in Germany whose bodies show what they are thinking and feeling, who can work up to a speech by silences, hesitations, slight and delicate movements, and can fill out pauses between speeches with appropriate gestures, connecting these pauses with the rest into a coherent whole. This use of mime to complement an actor's natural talent and to make him equal to the playwright's use of words, is however not so widespread as it should be for the benefit of those who come to the theater."

"But," said Wilhelm, "shouldn't natural talent be all that an actor, like any other artist, or indeed any human being, needs to enable him to reach the high goal he has set himself?"

"That should certainly be, and continue to be, the alpha and omega, beginning and end; but in between he will be deficient if he does not somehow cultivate what he has, and what he is to be, and that quite early on. It could be that those considered geniuses are worse off than those with ordinary abilities, for a genius can more easily than ordinary men be distorted and go astray."

"And yet," said Wilhelm, "will not a genius be able to save himself, to heal the wounds that he has inflicted on himself?"

"Not at all," said the stranger. "Or if so, then not very effectively. Nobody should ever believe that one's first youthful impressions can be counteracted. If a person is brought up in great freedom, surrounded by fine and beautiful objects, exposed to the company of good people, taught by excellent teachers to understand what he must first know in order to appreciate everything else, if he has learned what he will never need to unlearn, if his first actions are so guided that he will later be able to accomplish good things more easily and readily, without having to disaccustom himself from past tendencies, then he will live a happier, better life than someone who expended his youthful energies in resistance and error. So much is talked and written about education; and yet I see very few people who understand what that simple, noble, all-embracing concept means, and who can translate it into action."

"That may well be true," said Wilhelm. "We are all so limited in our thinking, that all we want is to make the other person exactly like ourselves. Happy are those who are educated by Fate, each in his own way."

"Fate is a distinguished but costly tutor," the other replied with a smile. "I would rather entrust myself to the reason of a human tutor. Fate, for whose wisdom I have indeed the greatest respect, may well have in Chance a very clumsy means through which to operate. For Chance rarely seems to bring about exactly what Fate has decided."

"That seems to me a very strange way of thinking," Wilhelm replied.

"Nonsense!" said the stranger. "Almost everything that happens in the world, will confirm what I am saying. Doesn't many a train of events begin by displaying some lofty purpose and then end in sheer stupidity?"

"Surely, you're joking," said Wilhelm.

But the stranger continued: "And isn't the same true of the course of individual experience? Let's suppose that Fate has destined someone to become a good actor (and why shouldn't Fate provide us with good actors?), but unfortunately chance has it that as a child this young man became so addicted to the absurdities of the puppet theater that he finds stupidity not only tolerable but even interesting, and cannot regard these childish impressions, which never fade and continue to attract, from the proper perspective."

"What got you on to the puppet theater?" asked Wilhelm in a state of some alarm.

"It was just an arbitrary example. If you don't like it, we can take another. Suppose Fate has destined a man to be a great painter and chance has it that he spends his early years in dirty cottages, stables and barns: do you believe that he would ever rise to purity, nobility and freedom of soul? The more vigorously he took hold of all that was impure in his youth and tried to ennoble it, the more this would take its toll of him in later life. For while he was trying to eradicate these impurities, the hold that they exercised over him would become ever stronger. If a man has spent his early years in base company, he may later wish for better associates and yet yearn for those earlier companions, whose influence on him will always be colored by the recollection of the youthful pleasures which can rarely be regained."

The rest of the company had dispersed while this conversation was going on. Philine in particular had taken herself off right at the start. The two men took a side path and rejoined the others. Philine produced the forfeits which were redeemed in various ways, and while this was going on, the stranger delighted the company, and particularly the ladies, with the most amusing stories and his unabashed participation in the proceedings. And so the hours passed most pleasantly in joking, singing, kissing and other sorts of light-hearted amusements.

Chapter Ten

When they were about to start back, they looked around for the clergyman, but he had disappeared and was nowhere to be found. "That's not very nice of the man, who seemed otherwise to have such good manners, to leave people who have welcomed him so warmly, without even so much as saying good-bye," said Madame Melina. "I, for my part," said Laertes, "have been wondering all the time where I had seen that strange man before; and I meant to ask him, when we said goodbye." "I've had the same feeling," said Wilhelm, "and I certainly would not have let him go off without his telling us more about who and what he was. I must be very mistaken if I haven't spoken to him somewhere before." "And yet you could actually be wrong," said Philine. "This man gives one the impression of being someone familiar because he looks like a real person, not just anyone." "What does that mean?" said Laertes, "don't we also look like real persons?" "I know what I'm talking about." Philine replied, "and if you don't understand what I mean, then let it be. I'm not going to explain."

Two coaches drove up. Laertes was complimented for his thoughtfulness in ordering them. Philine took a seat next to Madame Melina, opposite Wilhelm, and the others fitted in where they could. Wilhelm's horse had been brought along too, so Laertes rode it back to town.

Once Philine had sat down, she started singing pretty little songs and switched the conversation to subjects which she insisted would make good plays. By this skillful maneuver she soon had our friend in the best of moods, and from his vast store of imaginative material he put together a whole play with acts, scenes, characters, and twists and turns of plot. It was decided to include some arias and songs and the words for these were composed. Philine, who was joining in everything, used some well-known melodies and sang them without further ado. She was having one of her best, her very best, days. She cheered up our friend by constant teasing, and he felt better than he had for a long time.

Since that cruel discovery which had torn him away from Mariane, Wilhelm had remained true to his vow to avoid the traps of all female embraces, to shun the fickle sex and keep his sorrow as well as his yearning and desire locked up in his own bosom. The conscientiousness with which he stuck to this resolve provided him with secret nourishment, but since his heart could not remain entirely unaffected, some kind of loving communication became a pressing need for him. So he went about once more in a youthful daze, joyfully watching every attractive object, and tolerant in his judgment of every pleasing person that met his eyes. It is easy to understand how dangerous such a frolicsome creature as Philine was bound to be for a man in his state of mind.

When they returned home, they found Wilhelm's room all set up for a reading, a table in the middle for the punch bowl.

At that time the latest thing in the theater was plays that were attracting great attention and approval from the public about medieval German knights. The old Blusterer had brought one of these, and it was decided that this should be the subject of the reading. They all took their seats, and Wilhelm began to read. The knights in armor with their ancient fortresses, the honesty, loyalty, righteousness and especially the solid independence of the characters—all these were received with great acclaim. The reader gave of his very best, and the assembled company were transported by what they heard. Between the second and third acts the punch arrived in a huge bowl, and since there was a great deal of toasting and drinking in the play, what could be more natural than that the audience each time joined the heroes in clinking their glasses and singing the praises of the most favored personages in the play.

Everyone was enflamed by national fervor. Being Germans they were delighted to indulge poetically in a piece that expressed their own national character and played on their native soil. The vaults and cellars, ruined castles, moss, hollow trees, and especially the nocturnal gypsy scenes and secret tribunals had a stunning effect. Every one of the actors began to see himself in a helmet and cuirass, and the actresses envisioned themselves in big stiff collars proclaiming their Germanness to the public. Each of them decided immediately to assume a name from the play or from German history, and Madame Melina, who was pregnant, swore that if she bore a son, his name should be Adelbert, or if it were a daughter, she should be christened Mechthilde.

The applause grew louder and louder as the fifth act got underway, and toward the end, when the hero finally escaped his oppressor and the tyrant was punished, spirits were running so high that they all declared that they had never spent a better evening. Melina, excited by drink, was the most vociferous, and when the second punch bowl was emptied and midnight was approaching, Laertes swore full heartily that the lips of no other human being were worthy of drinking from these glasses, and with this assertion, threw his glass over his shoulder through the window on to the street. The others followed suit and despite the protestations of the innkeeper, who came running up, the punch bowl itself was broken into a thousand pieces so that, after such a festival, it should never be desecrated by base liquor. Philine, apparently not so intoxicated as the others (the two girls were stretched out in dubious positions on the sofa) took a malicious pleasure in instigating the others to make even more noise. Madame Melina recited a few sublime verses, and her husband, rather unpleasant while in his cups, began to criticize the poor preparation of the punch—he had quite different ideas on how to give a party. When Laertes told him to be quiet, he became more and more obnoxious and noisy, and finally Laertes threw the remains of the punch bowl at his head, which merely increased the general tumult and hubbub.

Meanwhile the night watch had arrived and insisted on being let into the house. Wilhelm, who had drunk little but was excited by his reading, had his work cut out, by words and money, and with some assistance from the innkeeper, to quieten people down and get the rest of the group home, despite the miserable state they were in. When he himself got back, he fell into his bed without bothering to undress, overcome by sleepiness and in a thoroughly bad mood. Next morning when he opened his eyes and gloomily surveyed the mess and destruction of the previous evening, he felt thoroughly depressed at the sad results which a stimulating, spirited and well-intentioned work of literature had produced.

Chapter Eleven

After short reflection Wilhelm summoned the innkeeper and had the cost of the party and the damage put on his account. At the same time he was annoyed to learn that his horse had been so badly treated by Laertes, when he rode it home the previous day, that it was probably, as they say, "ill-shod," and the smith thought that there was little hope of making it serviceable again. On the other hand a greeting from Philine, who waved to him from her window, restored his spirits, and he went immediately to the nearest store to buy her a present to compensate for the powder knife she had given him. We must admit that he did not limit himself to equal compensation. For not only did he buy her a pair of delicate earrings, but also a hat, a scarf and various other things like those she had that first day thrown out of the carriage.

Madame Melina, who came to see him just when he was delivering these presents, found an occasion before dinner to speak to him seriously about his feelings for the girl, and he was utterly astonished at being, as he thought, so unjustly reproached. He declared most emphatically that it had never entered his head to start something with Philine, of whose mode of living he was well aware. He excused himself, as well as he could, for his friendly behavior to her, but this did not satisfy Madame Melina. On the contrary, she became increasingly ill-tempered when she noticed (as indeed she had to) that the flattery with which she herself had gained some degree of attention from Wilhelm, was insufficient to ward off the attacks of this younger, livelier creature who was more pleasantly endowed with nature's gifts.

At table they found Melina in a bad frame of mind, and Wilhelm was beginning to charge him with various pettinesses, when the host entered and announced that a harper was in the house. "You will certainly take pleasure in his playing and his songs: no one who hears him can fail to admire him and give him some reward."

"Let's not bother with him," replied Melina. "I'm not in the mood to listen to a droning musician and there are plenty of singers amongst us who are eager to earn a little." He accompanied these words with a malicious sidelong glance at Philine. She got the point, and decided to annoy Melina by favoring the musician. So she turned to Wilhelm and said: "Why can't we listen to the man? Are we to do nothing to escape this miserable boredom?" Melina was about to answer and a vigorous quarrel would probably have ensued if Wilhelm had not welcomed the man as he entered the room, and beckoned him towards them.

The strange appearance of the harper so astonished the company that he had already taken his seat before anyone had the heart to ask him anything or make some appropriate remark. His bald head was wreathed by a few grey hairs, and his large blue eyes peered gently from beneath heavy white eyebrows. He had a finely shaped nose, and a long white beard which, however, left his kindly mouth uncovered. His slender body was clothed from head to foot in a dark brown garment. He began to let his fingers glide gently over the strings of the harp, and the pleasing sounds he produced, immediately delighted the group.

"You sing, too, my dear old man, don't you?" said Philine.

"Give us something to please heart and mind," said Wilhelm. "An instrument should be just an accompaniment for the voice. Melodies, runs and passages without words and meaning seem to me like butterflies or colorful birds that swirl around before our eyes as we try to catch them and hold them. Whereas singing is like an airy spirit leading us heavenward and inducing our better self to follow."

The old man first looked at Wilhelm, then cast his eyes upward, plucked the strings a few times, and began to sing. The ballad paid tribute to the art of song and praised the work of singers, urging all to respect and honor them. He presented the song with such vigor and sincerity, that he seemed to have composed it at that moment specially for this occasion. Wilhelm could hardly resist throwing his arms around him, but the fear of being laughed at kept him in his seat; the others were already muttering silly remarks and arguing whether the old man was a priest or a Jew.

When they asked him who had written the song, he gave an evasive answer. He did, however, assure them that he knew a large number of songs which he hoped might please them. Most of the company were in a cheerful mood, and even Melina was receptive in his own way. So while they were all gossiping and joking with each other, the harper intoned a splendid song in praise of the pleasures of being together. He sang of harmony and grace in limpid, mellifluous phrases; but, suddenly, the music became harsh, discordant and troubled when he expressed his disapproval of acrimonious indifference, short-sighted enmities and the dangers of strife—shackles of the mind that everyone listening was all too ready to cast off as the melody of his song soared upwards into praise of all peacemakers and of men's joys at rediscovering each other.

When he had finished, Wilhelm exclaimed: "Whoever you may be, you have come into our midst bestowing blessings and new life on us, like a protective spirit. Please accept in return my thanks and respect. Be assured of our admiration; and be sure to tell us if you need anything."

The old man fell silent, letting his fingers glide gently over the strings of the harp, then plucked them firmly, and sang this song:

> "What do I hear outside the gate,
> Resounding on the drawbridge?
> Bring your song into the hall
> That we may hear it better!"
> Thus spake the king, the page-boy ran,
> The boy returned, the king cried out:
> "Bring the old man within here!"

> "My greetings to you, noble lords,
> My greetings, beauteous ladies!
> The sky is studded full with stars,
> And who can name them rightly?

444

Inside this splendid noble hall
Close up, o eyes; this is no time
To gape and feast on wonders."

The singer pressed his eyelids close
And rich full tones he struck.
The knights looked proud and sternly on
The ladies bowed attentive heads.
The king took pleasure in the song,
And wishing to reward the bard,
A golden chain had straightway brought.

"O give me not that golden chain,
Bestow it on your warriors
Before whose bold and fierce visage
The enemy lances splinter.
Or give it to your chancellor,
That he may add its golden weight
To all his other burdens.

"My song soars freely like the bird's
That sounds from out the branches.
And music coming from the throat
Rewards itself right richly.
If I may but one gift entreat,
Then bring me now of your best wine
A draught in purest goblet."

The wine was brought; he drank it up,
The drink of sweet refreshment.
Thrice blessed he declared a house
Where gifts like this were trifles.
"And if you flourish, think of me,
And render unto God like thanks
As I for what you gave me."

When the singer, having finished, grasped a glass of wine that had been poured for him and drank it down with a grateful glance at his benefactors, general delight spread throughout the company. They applauded and expressed the wish that the wine would be good for his health and strengthen his aged limbs. He sang a few more ballads and the mood of all those present became even livelier.

"Do you know the tune to 'The Shepherd Dressed Himself for the Dance,' old man?" asked Philine. "Yes, I do," he said. "If you would sing and act it, I will be glad to do my part."

Philine stood up and was ready. The old man began playing the melody and Philine sang the song—which we cannot repeat for our readers because they might well think it in bad taste, or even indecent.

Meanwhile they were all getting merrier and merrier, drinking more and more wine, and beginning to make a lot of noise. Since the bad effect of such behavior was still all too vividly present in our friend's mind, he tried to break up the proceedings, giving the old man a handsome recompense for his labors. The others contributed something as well, and let him go and rest, looking forward to that same evening and the pleasure of another demonstration of his skill.

After the Harper had left, Wilhelm said to Philine: "Your favorite song didn't seem to me to have either poetic or moral distinction. But if you were ever to perform something that was decent, with the same freshness, originality and charm, you would certainly be applauded."

"Yes," said Philine. "It must be quite pleasant to warm oneself on ice."

"Moreover," said Wilhelm, "this fellow puts many an actor to shame. Did you notice how perfect his dramatic expression was in those romances? There was more live presence in his singing than in our stiff stage personages. Many plays are performed as if they were simply being narrated, whereas music that tells stories really touches us."

"You are unfair," Laertes objected. "I don't pretend to be a great actor or a great singer. But this I do know: when music accompanies bodily movements, enlivening and at the same time controlling them, and the manner of delivery and the expression needed are indicated to me by the musical composer, then I am a totally different person from when I have to create these for myself, as I have to in spoken drama, inventing my own tempo, my own manner of speaking, and always liable to be disturbed in this by my fellow actors."

"For my part," said Melina, "I must say that in one respect this fellow has put us all to shame, and in a most important respect. The strength of his talent is shown by the use he puts it to. Whereas people like us may be uncertain where the next meal is coming from, he persuades us to share our meal with him. He knows how to extract from us the money that we might well use to improve our lot—and all that for one little song. It seems such a nice thing, to squander the money that could have been used to give us and others a stable livelihood."

This remark was not exactly a pleasant turn. Wilhelm, who was the real target of the reproach, answered with some heat, and Melina, who was by no means the subtlest of persons, was reduced to repeating his objections in harsh and direct terms. "Two whole weeks have gone by," he said, "since we looked at those props and costumes. We could have bought them for a modest amount. You gave me reason to hope that you would advance the necessary sum, but I cannot see that you have given the matter any further thought, let alone come to a decision. If you had taken action, we would already be in business. You said you intended to leave on a journey, but you haven't done so; and you don't seem to have been sparing of your money lately. At least there

are certain persons who are apparently all too ready to provide you with opportunities of getting rid of it faster."

This reproach, which was not totally unjustified, hit home. Wilhelm made
some rejoinder, with some passion, even vehemence, and took the occasion to
leave, just as the company was about to break up, explaining in no uncertain
terms that he did not wish to stay longer with such unfriendly and ungrateful people. He hurried away in a bad humor, and took himself off to a stone
bench in front of the inn, not noticing that, partly for pleasure and partly
from irritation, he had drunk more than usual.

Chapter Twelve

After a short while, as he sat there racked by disturbing thoughts, and staring
straight in front of him, Philine came sauntering through the door singing,
and sat down beside him, or rather on him, for she edged up so close, laid her
head on his shoulders, played with his curly hair, stroked him and talked in
the sweetest manner. She urged him to stay, not to leave her alone with the
others who bored her to death; she simply could not continue to exist under
the same roof with Melina and had therefore moved over to the inn where
Wilhelm was staying.

He tried in vain to get rid of her, and make her understand that he could
and would not stay here any longer. She continued her entreaties and unexpectedly put her arm around his neck and kissed him fervently.

"Are you crazy, Philine?" he said, trying to break loose. "Making a public
street a witness to caresses that I have in no wise deserved! Let me go. I cannot
and I will not remain here."

"I will keep hold of you and kiss you here in public until you give me your
word that you will do what I want. I'm just dying with laughter," she went on.
"After these intimacies people will think we've been married just four weeks,
and husbands who observe this tender scene will praise me to their wives as a
model of childlike, unabashed affection."

At that moment some people passed by, and she caressed him so tenderly
that he was obliged, in order to avoid a scandal, to play the role of the patient
husband. Philine made faces at these people behind their backs and behaved
so outrageously that he finally had to agree to stay on for today, tomorrow,
and the next day.

"You're a regular stick-in-the-mud!" she said, letting go of him, "And I am a
silly fool to waste such affection on you." She got up and sulkily walked away;
then turned back laughing, and said: "But I suppose that's because I'm so crazy
about you. I'm just going to fetch my knitting, so that I have something to
do. Stay here, and let me find the stone man sitting on the same stone bench
when I return."

Actually she was this time being quite unjust to him; for much as he tried to keep away from her, he would probably not have failed to respond to her caresses, if he had been alone with her in some leafy arbor. She for her part went into the house, darting a roguish glance at him as she left. He felt no particular compulsion to follow her; indeed her recent behavior had again been quite distasteful to him. And yet he got up from the bench, without really knowing why, and went after her.

He had just reached the door of the inn, when up came Melina, spoke to him in modest terms and apologized for those rather harsh words he had uttered during their recent dispute. "Don't think ill of me," he went on to say, "if in the state I'm in, I seem rather worried; but my concern for a wife, and perhaps soon for a child as well, prevents me from going on quietly from day to day, displaying pleasant emotions, as you are still able to do. Think it over, and if it is at all possible, do let me acquire those props. I won't be your debtor for long. And I will be eternally grateful to you."

Wilhelm, unwilling at that moment to be held up on the threshold when some irresistible attraction was impelling him towards Philine, spoke to him in a state of surprised distractedness and hasty generosity, saying: "If I can make you contented and happy, then I will not hesitate any longer. Go and arrange everything as seems fit. I am prepared to pay the money tonight or tomorrow morning." A handshake confirmed his promise, and he was delighted to see Melina hurry away down the street. But unfortunately he was prevented for a second time from entering the house, and this time in a more unpleasant manner.

A young man with a bundle on his back came rushing down the street towards Wilhelm who immediately recognized him as Friedrich. "I'm back!" he said, merrily rolling his big blue eyes and looking up at all the windows. "Where's Mademoiselle? Devil take me if I can live a day longer without seeing her!" The innkeeper, coming up, told him she was upstairs, and he leapt up the steps, leaving Wilhelm rooted to the spot. He would gladly have pulled the boy back by his hair, but fierce jealously cramped the flow of his spirits and of his thinking, and once he had recovered from this paralysis he felt more uneasy and more uncomfortable than ever before.

He went to his room, and there found Mignon occupied in writing. The child had for some time been applying herself diligently to writing down everything that she knew by heart, and giving it to her friend and master to correct. She was tireless at what she was doing, and did it quite well except that the letters were uneven and the lines not straight. In this too her body seemed to be at variance with her mind. Wilhelm, who, when he was at peace with himself, took great pleasure in the child's attentiveness, paid on this occasion little attention to what she showed him. She felt this and was especially distressed because she thought that this time she had done her work quite well.

Wilhelm was so restless that he walked up and down the corridors and back to the door of the house. A horseman came riding up, good-looking and sprightly, though quite mature in years. The innkeeper rushed up and greeted him as an old friend, saying: "Well, Mr. Stablemaster, are we once more to have the pleasure of your company?" "I'm just stopping here to feed my horses, then I really must ride to the estate to see that things are in order. Time is pressing, because the count is arriving tomorrow with his wife and they will be staying for a while in order to receive the Prince of *** and entertain him as best they can. The prince will probably set up headquarters in this neighborhood." "What a pity that you can't stay with us," said the innkeeper, "for we have interesting people in the house." A groom came and took the stablemaster's horse, while he was conversing with the innkeeper in the doorway and casting sidelong glances at Wilhelm.

When Wilhelm noticed that they were talking about him, he left and walked up and down the nearby streets.

Chapter Thirteen

Wilhelm was so restless and ill-tempered that he decided to look up the Harper in the hope that his music might dispel the evil spirits. He inquired where he lived and was directed to a shabby inn in a remote part of the town, and then up a flight of stairs to an attic room from which came the sweet sounds of the harp. The somber, deeply moving music was accompanied by anguished melancholy singing. Wilhelm crept up to the door. The old man was rhapsodizing, repeating stanzas, half singing, half reciting, and then, after a short while, Wilhelm heard something like this:

> Who never with hot tears ate his bread,
> Who never through the nighttime hours
> Sat weeping in sorrow on his bed,
> He does not know you, Heavenly Powers.
>
> You lead us into life, ordain
> That wretches pile up guilt from birth,
> And then you yield them up to pain;
> For all guilt is atoned on earth.

This mournful, heartfelt lament affected the listener deeply. It seemed to him as if the old man was at times prevented by tears from continuing to sing, and the strings of the harp resounded until the voice came in again, softly and with broken sounds. Wilhelm stood by the door, deeply moved, his own constricted heart opened up by the immense grief of the stranger. He was overcome by such fellow feeling that he did not, could not, restrain the tears brought to his eyes by the old man's bitter lamentation. The sorrows oppressing his heart all came out into the open. He abandoned himself completely to them, pushed open the door, and stood facing the old man who was sitting on his wretched bed, the only piece of furniture in the miserable room.

"Oh what feelings you have aroused in me, good old man!" he cried. "You have released everything that was hidden in my heart. But don't let me disturb you. Go on—and while you are soothing your own pains, you will make a friend happy." The old man was about to stand up and say something, but Wilhelm kept him from doing this. He had noticed at noon that the Harper did not speak readily. Instead Wilhelm sat down beside him on the straw sack that was his bed.

The old man dried his tears and asked with a friendly smile: "Why did you come? I was intending to see you this evening." "It's quieter here," Wilhelm replied. "Sing me whatever you have a mind to, whatever you're in a mood for—and just pretend I'm not here. It seems to me that today nothing can go wrong for you. I think you are very fortunate to be able to occupy yourself so pleasantly in your solitude, and, since you are a stranger everywhere, to find your dearest friend in your own heart."

The old man looked down at the strings of his harp, his fingers gliding softly over them, and then started to sing:

> He who turns to solitude
> Is soon, alas! alone.
> Life comes to each, love comes to each,
> And leaves him to his pain.
> Oh leave me to my torment here,
> And if I dwell in solitude
> I'll never be alone.
>
> A lover softly creeps and listens
> Whether she is alone.
> And so come creeping, day and night,
> My sorrow and my pain
> To me in all my solitude,
> And in my solitary grave
> At last leave me alone.

We could expend a great number of words and still not be able to convey the charm of the extraordinary conversation which our friend had with the curious stranger. The old man responded, as though agreeing with everything the young man said, by producing music that evoked all sorts of similar feelings and opened up the full range of the imagination.

Anyone who has been present at an assembly of pious people seeking a degree of purer, richer, more spiritual edification than is to be found within the church, will have some idea of the nature of this encounter. He will recall how the leader will adapt to what he is saying the verse of some hymn which directs the mind to where he himself is tending in his homily. Then someone in the group will break in with a different tune, a verse from another hymn. Then a third person will add something from still another hymn, with the result that the community of ideas in these various hymns is evoked, and each individual passage by reason of these associations takes on a new light, as if it had just been composed. A new synthesis is evolved out of familiar ideas and hymns and verses for this particular audience, in the enjoyment of which they are edified, quickened and fortified. In a similar way the old man wove together for his guest well known and unknown songs and snatches, and thereby set moving a complex of recent or more remote feelings, waking and slumbering, pleasant and painful emotions, from which only good could be expected for our friend in his present state.

Chapter Fourteen

On his way back Wilhelm did indeed begin to reflect more deeply on his present situation, and by the time he reached home, he had resolved to extricate himself from it. The innkeeper told him in confidence that Philine had made a new conquest in the person of the duke's stablemaster, and, having attended to his duties at the estate, this man had returned very quickly and up in her room was enjoying a good dinner with Philine.

At this very moment Melina arrived with a notary, and both went to Wilhelm's room, where Wilhelm somewhat reluctantly fulfilled his promise to Melina. He gave him a draft in the amount of three hundred thalers, which Melina immediately handed to the notary, receiving in exchange a document confirming the sale of all the theatrical effects which would early next day be handed over to Melina.

Just after the others had left, Wilhelm heard a terrible cry from somewhere in the house. It was a young person's voice, angry and threatening, and constantly interrupted by weeping and moaning. Then down the stairs it came, past his room, out on to the square. Curiosity impelled him to go downstairs and look: he found Friedrich in a state of frenzy. The boy was weeping, stamping, grinding his teeth, clenching his fists, and almost beside himself with anger and dismay. Mignon stood looking at him with amazement, and the innkeeper offered some sort of an explanation.

He said that on his return the boy had been cheerful and content, since Philine treated him well, and had gone around singing and dancing until the time when the stablemaster made her acquaintance. Since then—half boy and half man that he was—he had shown outbursts of temper by slamming doors and running up and down stairs. Philine had ordered him to wait at the table that evening, and at this he became even more sulky and defiant, so that finally instead of putting a dish of stew on the table he threw it between Mademoiselle and her guest, who were sitting quite close to each other. Whereupon the man gave him a couple of mighty clouts and threw him out. The innkeeper himself had been obliged to clean up the two; their clothes were in a sorry state.

When the boy saw the results of his revenge he burst out laughing while tears continued to roll down his cheeks. For a time he was intensely happy, but when he remembered the insult he had suffered from someone bigger than himself, he started howling again and threatening.

Pensively and somewhat disconcertedly Wilhelm observed this whole scene. What he saw was an exaggerated display of his own self, for he too had been consumed by fierce jealousy, and if his sense of propriety had not prevented him, he too would have indulged his wildest fancies, gleefully and maliciously harmed his beloved, and challenged his rival. He would gladly have obliterated everybody who seemed to be there just to exasperate him.

Laertes joined them, having also heard what had happened. He was rogue enough to encourage Friedrich when the angry boy asserted that the stablemaster would have to fight a duel with him, for he, Friedrich, had never taken insults. And if the fellow refused, he would take his revenge in some other way. Laertes was really in his element. He solemnly went upstairs and challenged the stablemaster in the boy's name. "That's amusing," said the man, "I hadn't expected such entertainment this evening." They went downstairs, Philine following them. "My boy," said the stablemaster to Friedrich, "you're a fine fellow and I won't refuse to fight with you. But since our ages and skills are so unequal that the whole affair will be somewhat bizarre, I propose rapiers instead of other weapons. Let's mark the buttons with chalk and whoever scores the most hits on the other's jacket shall be declared the winner and be treated to the best wine in town."

Laertes decided to accept this proposal, and Friedrich abode by his master's decision. The rapiers were brought. Philine sat down with her knitting, watching the two combatants with complete composure.

The stablemaster, who was a very good fencer, was obliging enough to spare his opponent by letting him achieve several chalk marks on his jacket, whereupon they embraced and the wine was brought in. The man wanted to know about Friedrich's home and his life, and Friedrich for his part spun a tale he had often told, which we will reserve for some other occasion.

The duel was for Wilhelm an additional externalization of his own feelings. He couldn't deny that he himself would have liked to direct a rapier, or still better, a sword, at the stablemaster, although he soon observed that the man was a far better fencer than he was. But he did not deign to cast on Philine a single glance, avoided anything that might betray his feelings, and once he had drunk several times to the health of the combatants, he hurried up to his room. There he was overcome by a host of unpleasant thoughts.

He recalled the time when his spirit was uplifted by an eager surge of boundless activity, full of hope and promise, a striving that knew no limits, swimming in the enjoyment of everything. But now, as he realized, he had fallen into a state of continual floundering, sipping at life instead of drinking deeply as before. He could not perceive clearly that there was an irresistible yearning which nature had imposed on him as a law of his being, and that this was being stimulated, but only half satisfied, and ultimately frustrated by circumstance.

It was therefore not surprising, whenever he considered his condition and his desire to work himself out of it, that he became completely confused. It was not right that, because of his friendship with Laertes, his attraction to Philine and his concern for Mignon, he should stay longer than was reasonable with these people in a place where he could foster his prime desire, fulfil it, so to speak, on the side, and still go on dreaming as before, without really setting himself a definite goal. He had thought to have enough strength to break loose from this situation, and leave. But now just a few moments ago he had entered on a business deal with Melina and had come to know the mysterious harper whose secret he was so anxious to discover. But, after much thinking, he decided that not even this should stop him from leaving—or at least he thought he had so decided. "I must leave," he cried out. "I want to leave." In a state of great agitation he threw himself into a chair. Mignon came into the room and asked if she might fix his hair for him. She came in very quietly; his curtness to her earlier that day had hurt her deeply.

There is nothing more moving than when a secretly nourished love and silently strengthened devotion suddenly finds itself face to face with the object that has hitherto been unworthy of its affection, but now at least realizes it. The bud that had been tightly closed for so long was ready to open, and Wilhelm's heart was ready to receive it.

She stood before him and saw his unrest.—"Master!" she said, "If you are unhappy, what shall become of Mignon?" "Dear creature," he said, grasping her hands, "you too are part of my sorrow. I must leave this place."—She looked into his eyes, which were dimmed with tears, and then threw herself on her knees before him. He held her hands; she laid her head on his knees and stayed quite still. He stroked her hair like a friend. She did not move. Suddenly he felt her twitching, a movement which began quite gently and then increased, spreading through all her limbs. "What is it, Mignon?" he cried. "What is the matter with you?" She raised her head, looked at him, then put her hand to her heart as if to stop some pain. He lifted her up and she fell onto his lap. He pressed her to him and kissed her. She did not respond, neither with her hands nor with any other movement. She kept clutching her heart and suddenly let out a cry which was accompanied by convulsive movements of her body. She jumped up, and then immediately fell down in front of him, as if every limb of her body were broken. It was a terrifying sight. "My child," he said, lifting her up and gripping her with his arms, "what is it?"—But the convulsions persisted, spreading from the heart into her dangling limbs. She was just hanging in his arms. He clasped her to his heart and covered her with tears. Suddenly she seemed taut again, like someone experiencing great bodily pain. All her limbs became alive again, and with renewed strength she threw herself around his neck, like a lock that springs shut, while a deep cleft opened up inside her and a flood of tears poured from her closed eyes on to his breast. He held her close. She wept tears such as no tongue can describe. Her long hair hung loosely around her as she wept, and her whole being seemed to be dissolving into a steady flood of tears. Her rigid limbs unfroze, her whole inner self poured itself out, and in the confusion of the moment Wilhelm feared that she might melt away in his arms so that nothing of her would remain. He grasped her more and more firmly to himself. "My child!" he cried, "My child! You are mine. Let that console you. You are mine! I will keep you. I will never leave you!"—Her tears continued. Finally she raised her head, and a gentle serenity lit up her face.—"My father!" she cried. "You will never leave me! You will be my father!—I am your child!"

From outside the door came the soft sounds of the harp. The old man was singing his most heartfelt songs, as an evening offering to his friend who, holding his child ever closer in his arms, experienced a feeling of the most perfect, indescribable bliss.

BOOK THREE

Chapter One

Know you the land where lemon blossoms blow,
And through dark leaves the golden oranges glow,
A gentle breeze wafts from an azure sky,
The myrtle's still, the laurel tree grows high—
You know it, yes? Oh there, oh there
With you, O my beloved, would I fare.

Know you the house? Roof pillars over it,
The chambers shining and the hall bright-lit,
The marble figures gaze at me in rue:
"You poor poor child, what have they done to you?"
You know it, yes? Oh there, oh there,
With you, O my protector, would I fare.

Know you the mountain and its cloudy trails?
The mule picks out its path through misty veils,
The dragon's ancient brood haunts caverns here,
The cliff drops straight, the stream above falls sheer.
You know it, yes? Oh there, oh there
Our path goes on! There, Father, let us fare!

When Wilhelm looked around for Mignon the next morning he could not find her; but he heard that she had gone out early with Melina, who had left to fetch the costumes and other props.

Some hours later he recognized music outside his door, and assumed at first that this was the Harper; but he then heard the sound of a zither and the voice that began to sing was Mignon's. He opened the door for Mignon who came in and sang the song we have just communicated. The melody and the expression pleased Wilhelm greatly, though he could not make out all the words. So he asked her to repeat it, and explain it; then he wrote it down and translated it into German. He found, however, that he could not even approximate the originality of the phrases, and the childlike innocence of the style was lost when the broken language was smoothed over and the disconnectedness removed. The charm of the melody was also quite unique.

She intoned each verse with a certain solemn grandeur, as if she were drawing attention to something unusual and imparting something of importance. When she reached the third line, the melody became more somber; the words "You know it, yes?" were given weightiness and mystery, the "Oh there, oh there!" was suffused with longing, and she modified the phrase "Let us fare!" each time it was repeated, so that one time it was entreating and urging, the next time pressing and full of promise.

When she had finished the song a second time she paused, looked straight at Wilhelm, and asked: "Do you know that land?" "It must be Italy," Wilhelm replied. "Where did you get the song?" "Italy!" said Mignon in a meaningful tone; "if you go to Italy, take me with you. I'm freezing here." "Have you ever been there?" asked Wilhelm; but the child kept silent and not one word more could be elicited from her.

Melina, who came in, saw the zither and was delighted that it had been put into such good shape. It had been part of the props. Mignon had asked for it that morning, the Harper had restrung it, and the child showed a talent that they had not known about.

Melina had already taken possession of the whole wardrobe. Some members of the town council promised to get him a permit to put on performances. He was overjoyed and his face shone when he returned. He seemed a different person: gentle, polite to everyone, even obliging and considerate. He hoped he would be lucky as he was now able to give work to his friends who had been idle for quite a while and at a loss what to do. He could give them a fixed engagement for a time, though he regretted that at first he could not pay those excellent actors that fate had brought his way in a manner consonant with their ability and talents; he first had to settle his debt to their generous friend Wilhelm.

"I cannot tell you what a display of friendship this is on your part that enables me to become the director of a theater. For when I first met you, I was in a very strange position. You will recall that at our first meeting I expressed my strong antipathy to the theater, but when I got married, I had to look around for an engagement, out of love for my wife who hoped thereby to find satisfaction and appreciation. I couldn't find anything, at least nothing lasting, but I did have the good fortune to meet several officials who sometimes could use someone who knew how to wield a pen, understood French and was experienced in bookkeeping. And so for a while things went quite well for me. I was fairly well paid, bought various things and my standard of living was quite respectable. But the commissions I had from my employers began to peter out, there was no hope of permanent support, and my wife was so desperately anxious to go onto the stage—unfortunately at a time when, because of her pregnancy, she could not expect to make the best impression on the public. But now I hope that the company which, thanks to your help, I am to direct, will be a good start for me and mine, and to you I will owe my future fortune, whatever it may turn out to be."

Wilhelm listened to these words with satisfaction, and all the actors were fairly content with what their new director had said, were secretly delighted at having secured an engagement so soon, and inclined to make do for the start with a small wage. Most of them considered what they were so unexpectedly being offered as a supplement they could not have counted on. Melina used this situation to talk to each of them individually, and to use every argument to persuade them that it was in their interests to sign their contracts without delay. As a result they gave little thought to this new arrangement, feeling sufficiently safeguarded by being able to terminate it any time at six weeks' notice.

The conditions of the agreement were then spelled out in proper form, and Melina was already thinking about what plays should be put on first in order to capture the public's interest. At this very moment a messenger came for the stablemaster, announcing the impending arrival of the count and countess and that he had been told to bring out the horses that he had in his charge.

Soon a heavily loaded carriage drew up in front of the inn. Two servants jumped down from the box of the coach, and Philine, true to character, was the first to be at hand in the doorway. "Who is that?" asked the countess as she went into the inn. "An actress, and at your Grace's service," the roguish girl replied, putting on a sober face, curtseying modestly, and kissing the lady's skirt. The count saw several people standing around, who also claimed to be actors and inquired how large the company was, where they had last performed, and who their director was. "If they are French," he said to his wife, "we might delight the prince with an unexpected pleasure by providing his favorite form of entertainment in our own house."

"Even if these people are unfortunately only Germans," said the countess, "we still might seriously think of letting them perform at the castle while the prince is there. They must have acquired some skill. The best way of entertaining a large number of people is to have some theater, and the baron will coach them."

With these words they went up the stairs and Melina introduced himself as the director. "Call your people together and present them to me," said the count, "so that I can see what they're like. I also want to see a list of the plays they would be ready to do."

Melina made a deep bow, hurried out of the room and came back with the actors. They pushed and shoved each other in all directions, some presenting themselves poorly as they hoped to please, and others no better because they adopted a silly manner. Philine showed great respect to the countess, who was extremely gracious and friendly, and the count took a good look at the others. He asked all of them what their specialties were, and told Melina that he should insist on maintaining set roles, an opinion that Melina accepted with the greatest respect.

The count then told each of them what he or she should particularly work at, what needed improvement in figure and posture, instructing them in what Germans always lack and thereby revealing such unusual knowledge of these matters, that they all stood there in deep humility before such a distinguished connoisseur and lofty patron, hardly daring to breathe in his presence.

"Who's that fellow over there in the corner?" the count asked, staring at someone who had not yet been presented to him, and a thin man in a shabby coat with patches on the elbows and a wretched wig on this humble fellow's head came over to him. This was the man, familiar to us from the previous Book as Philine's favorite, who usually played pedants, teachers and poets, and took on those roles where someone has to be beaten or doused with water. He had acquired a rather unctuous, nervous, ridiculous manner of bowing, and his halting speech, so well suited to the roles he played, always made the spectators laugh, so that he was still considered a useful member of the troupe, and was always ready to take on an assignment and to please. He came up to the count, bowed in his own special way, and answered all his questions about the gestures that he employed in his roles. The count observed him with pleasure and attention, and then, after some reflection, he said to his wife: "Just look at that man, my dear. I guarantee he's a good actor, or could become one." The fellow was so overjoyed at this that he made the stupidest bow and the count just burst out laughing, and said: "This man is excellent. I bet he could play anything he has a mind to, and it's a shame that he hasn't been given better parts."

It was rather irritating for the others that the Pedant should be singled out, but Melina did not take it to heart. He agreed wholeheartedly with the count, and added in a tone of the greatest respect: "Yes, indeed. All he and some of the others have lacked, is the encouragement of someone as knowledgeable as your Excellency."

"Is this the whole company?" the count asked. "A few of them aren't here just now," Melina shrewdly replied, "but we could soon get some others from nearby to make up the complement, if we had the necessary funds." Meanwhile Philine was saying to the countess: "There's quite a handsome young man upstairs who would do well as *jeune premier*." "Why can't we see him?" the countess asked. "I'll go fetch him," said Philine and hurried out of the door.

She found Wilhelm still occupied with Mignon, but she persuaded him to go downstairs with her. He followed her somewhat unwillingly, but with some curiosity, for having heard mention of persons of high station, he was anxious to become acquainted with them. He walked into the room and his eyes immediately encountered those of the countess directed at him. Philine took him to the lady whilst the count was busy with the others. Wilhelm bowed to the countess and answered with some confusion the questions this charming lady addressed to him. Her beauty, her youthful grace, her elegance and refinement of manner made the most pleasing impression on him, all the more so because a certain shyness—even embarrassment—was in her words and gestures. He was also introduced to the count, who paid little attention to him, and instead walked up to the window with his wife and seemed to be asking her about something. It was apparent that her opinion was entirely in agreement with his. She seemed to be urging him eagerly to follow his own inclinations.

He came back to the group and said: "I can't stay here any longer at the moment, but I will send a friend of mine to you, and if you make reasonable conditions and work really hard, I am disposed to let you play at the castle." They all expressed their delight at this, especially Philine, who ardently kissed the hands of the countess. "Now listen, little one," the lady said, patting the cheeks of the flighty girl, "Listen, my child. You come back to me, and I will keep my promise. But you must be better dressed." Philine apologized for having so little to spend on her wardrobe, and the countess immediately ordered one of her ladies-in-waiting to bring up an English hat and a silk scarf, which could easily be taken out from the luggage. The countess began to dress up Philine, who continued behaving delightfully with a hypocritical expression of innocence on her face.

The count escorted his wife down the stairs. She greeted the whole company in passing, turning again to Wilhelm, and finally saying, in the most gracious manner: "We'll see each other again soon."

These favorable prospects brought new life to the whole company. Everyone began to talk about his or her hopes and wishes, the ideas each had in his head, the roles they would play and the applause they would receive. Melina began to think of how he could quickly make some money by a few performances to the townsfolk, which would at the same time get the actors in trim. Others went into the kitchen to order a better meal than they had been used to.

Chapter Two

A few days later the baron arrived and was received by Melina with some trepidation. The count had described him as a connoisseur, and it was to be feared that he would soon discover the deficiencies of the little company and realize that this was not an organized troupe, because they could hardly get together an adequate cast for any play. But both the director and the other members were relieved to discover in the baron a man with great affection for the native theater, a man for whom every actor and any company was a source of welcome pleasure. He greeted them all ceremoniously, and expressed his delight at having the good fortune to come so unexpectedly into contact with German theater and being able to introduce the national muses into the castle of his relatives. Thereupon he drew from out of his pocket a notebook from which Melina hoped to learn the terms of their engagement; but it turned out to be something quite different. For the baron asked them to listen carefully to a play he had himself composed and wished them to perform. They gathered round, delighted at the prospect of winning the favor of such an important person at such little cost, although, noticing the length of the manuscript, they feared they were in for quite a long sitting. Which indeed it turned out to be. The play was in five acts and was one of those which seem never to end.

The hero was a noble, virtuous, generous but unappreciated and persecuted man, who finally won out over his adversaries, dispensing the finest poetic justice, but not pardoning them immediately.

During the reading of the play all of the actors had ample opportunity to think about themselves and move from inadequacy into a state of jubilant self-satisfaction and radiant future prospects. Those who did not find in it a suitable role for themselves, decided that it was a bad play, and its author untalented; others, noticing a passage which would earn them acclaim, to the great satisfaction of the author, followed the reading with appreciation.

The business end of things was soon settled. Melina succeeded in negotiating with the baron a contract that was favorable to him, and did not reveal its terms to the other actors.

He spoke to the baron in passing about Wilhelm, saying that he was well suited to be a writer of plays and had no mean acting talent. The baron treated Wilhelm immediately as a colleague, and Wilhelm recited for him some brief pieces that, with a few other relics, had by chance survived from the conflagration that had consumed most of his manuscripts. The baron praised the plays and Wilhelm's delivery, taking for granted that Wilhelm would come to the castle with the others, and promising them all, as he left, the best reception, comfortable accommodation, good food, appreciation and rewards; and Melina guaranteed them a fixed amount of pocket money.

It is easy to imagine the good mood that prevailed amongst the actors after this visit. Instead of an anxious, lowly existence, they saw themselves about to enter on a life of honor and comfort. They amused themselves by calculating all this in advance, and dismissed as improper the idea of keeping any money in their pockets.

Wilhelm considered whether he should go with them to the castle or not, and decided that there were several good reasons to do so. Melina hoped by this advantageous engagement to repay part of what he had borrowed, and

Wilhelm, always eager to meet people, did not wish to forego the opportunity of getting to know the "world" from which he hoped to derive insights on life, on himself and on art. Also he did not dare admit how much he wished to become better acquainted with the beautiful countess. He tried to persuade himself of the great advantages that would accrue to him by closer contact with the world of sophistication and wealth. He thought about the count and countess and the baron, the confidence, grace, and ease of their manner, and, once he was alone, he broke out into words of rapture: "Thrice happy and praiseworthy are those whose high birth elevates them above the lower classes of humanity. They never—not even occasionally—need to labor under conditions which afflict so many good people with constant anxiety their whole life long. From their higher position, their view must be clear-sighted, and every step they take in life light-footed. By their birth they are, so to speak, in a ship that, in the journey we all must undertake, can profit from favorable winds and can wait till unfavorable ones have passed, whereas we others swim, struggling for our lives, without much help from favorable winds, and perishing in rapidly exhausted energy. What comfort and ease an inherited income provides! How well a business flourishes if it is based on fixed capital, so that every faulty transaction need not result in inactivity! Who can judge the value or lack of value of earthly goods better than someone who has been able to enjoy these from early years! Who can apply his mind earlier to what is necessary, useful and true than he who becomes aware of errors at an age when he still has sufficient energy to begin a new life."

Thus did our friend ascribe good fortune to those who dwell high up; but also to those who approach such lofty realms, and find sustenance there. He praised his guiding spirit for leading him upward on this path.

Meanwhile Melina, having racked his brains to distribute type roles to the various members of the company (as the count wanted and he himself believed desirable), and specifying to each of them what their particular contribution would be, was very satisfied to discover, when he had finally worked this out, that every member of the little company was prepared to take on this or that role. Laertes usually took the part of lovers and Philine that of the maids. The two young girls divided the innocent and the sentimental sweethearts between them, and the old Blusterer played himself and that was best of all. Melina thought he could play the part of the gentleman; his wife, to her great chagrin, had to take on the young women's parts, even that of the affectionate mothers. And because there were not many pedants or poets ridiculed in modern plays the count's favorite had to play presidents and ministers because these were usually represented as wicked and in the fifth act came to a bad end. As chamberlain or such like Melina gladly suffered the insults that trusty German gentlemen were subjected to in many popular plays of the time, because in such scenes he could dress up and affect the airs of a courtier, which he believed he had at his command.

Before long, more actors began to arrive from different parts of the country, and were taken on without much testing and without any special conditions. Several times Melina tried in vain to persuade Wilhelm to play the *jeune premier.* Wilhelm took great interest in all the preparations, although the new director did not give him much credit for his trouble. Melina believed that, with his honorific position he had assumed greater powers of insight. One of his favorite occupations was to make cuts to reduce all plays to a suitable length, without any other considerations. He was encouraged in this by the fact that the public was well satisfied, and those with taste declared that the theater at the court was nothing like as well established as theirs.

Chapter Three

The time finally came to move to the count's castle. Coaches and carriages were awaited to transport the whole company. Various arguments ensued as to who should ride with whom and where everybody should sit. The order and arrangement was eventually worked out with some difficulty but little effect. Fewer vehicles than had been expected came at the appointed hour, and everyone had to make do. The baron, following on horseback, said the reason was that at the castle everything was in a state of confusion, not merely because the prince was to arrive several days early, but also because unexpected visitors had already arrived. They were getting short of space, so the actors could not be so well housed as they had been promised, the baron was sorry about that.

They distributed themselves as best they could in the carriages, and since the weather was passable and the castle was not a great distance away, the sprightlier ones preferred to walk rather than wait for the coaches to come back to fetch them. The caravan left with shouts of joy and for the first time not worrying how the innkeeper was to be paid. The count's castle hovered before their minds like a fairy palace, they were the happiest and luckiest people on earth, and everyone associated this day in his thoughts with what he conceived to be fortune, honor and well-being.

Even unexpected heavy rain did not divert their minds from such pleasant thoughts; but when it kept up and got steadily worse, many of them did feel a certain discomfort. Night began to fall and nothing was more welcome than the sight of the count's residence, with lights on every floor, gleaming towards them from a hill, so that they could count the windows. As they came nearer they could see that even the side-tracts were brightly illuminated. Each of them wondered which would be his quarters, and most of them would have been quite satisfied with a small room under the roof or on the side.

They drove through the village past an inn. Wilhelm called a halt so that he could alight, but was told that there was absolutely no room at all there. The count had taken over the whole inn because those unexpected guests had arrived, and at every door the name of the guest occupying it, was written in chalk. And so our friend was obliged, against his will, to drive with the others into the castle courtyard.

They saw cooks busy around the kitchen fires in one of the side-buildings, and this cheered them up considerably. Servants bearing lighted candles came running up to the staircase of the main building, and our travelers' spirits bubbled over in anticipation. But how amazed were they when this reception dissolved into a torrent of abuse! The servants yelled at the coachmen for coming in on this side; they should turn around and go to the old part of the castle—there was no room here for guests! This unfriendly and unexpected reception was accompanied by jeering remarks; they laughed to see the newcomers exposed once again to the rain because of this mistake. It was still pouring, there were no stars in the sky, and the whole company was now dragged down a bumpy road between two walls into the old castle, which had stood unoccupied since the count's father had built the new one. The carriages came to a halt in the courtyard or in the long arched gateway, and the drivers from the village unharnessed the horses and rode home.

Since no one came forward to welcome them, they all got out, called for assistance, then went to look for it, but without any results. Everything remained dark and silent. The wind blew through the open gate, and the old turrets and courts, hardly visible in the darkness, made a gruesome effect. Everybody was freezing and shuddering, the women trembling, the children crying. Their impatience was mounting with every moment, for this sudden change of fortune had caught them quite unawares and completely robbed them of their composure.

They continued to wait for someone to open the doors for them, mistaking the sound of the rain and the wind for the steps of an approaching steward, and there they stayed for quite a long time, losing their tempers but doing nothing about their situation. It never occurred to any of them to go over to the new castle and ask for help from some sympathetic soul. They could not understand where their friend the baron was and were in an exceedingly troublesome state.

At last some people did arrive, and were recognized by their voices as those who had followed the carriages on foot. They reported that the baron had fallen from his horse and seriously hurt his foot. They too had gone first to the new castle and been angrily told to come here.

The whole company was completely perplexed; discussed what to do and came to no decision. At last a light approached from a distance, and they gave a sign of relief; but their hopes of deliverance were sooon dashed when they saw that this was the count's stablemaster with a groom holding a lantern to light his path. The stablemaster inquired eagerly after Mademoiselle Philine; she detached herself from the others, and he offered to escort her to the new castle, where a place was reserved for her with the countess's ladies-in-waiting.

Without a moment's hesitation she accepted his offer, grasped his arm and, leaving her trunk in the care of the others, was about to rush off with him, when their path was barred and the stablemaster bombarded with questions and requests, so that, in order to escape with his beloved, he had to promise them everything and assured them that the castle would soon be opened up and they themselves well lodged. They watched his lantern disappear from sight, and waited a long time for another light and new hope to appear; but nothing came. Then finally, after much waiting, grumbling and cursing, they saw it coming, and were again consoled and hopeful.

An old servant opened the door of the old building, and they all rushed inside. Each attended to his own possessions, unloading them and bringing them into the house. Most of the things, like the owners themselves, were soaked through. There was only one light, so things went very slowly, with a good deal of shoving, stumbling and falling down. They asked for more lights, they asked for a fire. The uncommunicative servant was obliged to leave his lantern for them, went away, and did not come back.

Then they began to search through the house. The doors of all the rooms were standing open. There were massive stoves, tapestry wallcoverings and in-laid floors as reminders of past splendor, but no ordinary household furniture, no tables, no chairs, no mirrors, just a few huge empty bedsteads, stripped of necessities as well as decoration. So they used their wet boxes and knapsacks as seats; some of our tired wanderers even stretched out on the floor. Wilhelm seated himself on some steps, with Mignon's head on his knees. She was rest-less, and when he asked her what was wrong, she said, "I'm hungry!" He found that he had nothing to give her, and the rest of the company had already used up their provisions; so he had to leave the poor creature hungry. He had been uninvolved in what was going on and meditative, vexed and angry that he had not stuck to his own intention and stayed at the inn, even if he had to sleep on the attic floor.

The others all behaved in accordance with their character. Some of them brought down a pile of old wood, lugged it into one of the huge fireplaces in the room, and set it alight with shouts of glee. But unfortunately their hope of drying and warming themselves was to be frustrated by the fact that this particular fireplace was purely ornamental and the chimney had been bricked up, so that the smoke came pouring back into the rooms, while the wood was so dry that it crackled into flames and shot out into the room, fanned by the draught through the broken windowpanes and darting hither and thither, so that it was feared that the whole castle might catch on fire. They separated the burning wood, stamped on it, doused it, and that made even more smoke. The whole situation became unbearable and everyone was by now quite desperate.

Wilhelm had retreated from the smoke into a distant room. Mignon followed him, bringing with her a well-dressed servant carrying a brightly burning pair of candles who turned to Wilhelm and said, handing him a fine

WILHELM MEISTER'S APPRENTICESHIP

porcelain dish of fruit and sweetmeats: "The young lady over there sends you these with the request that you join the company." He then added somewhat frivolously: "She asked me to tell you that everything is fine with her, and that she would like to share her satisfaction with her friends." Nothing could have surprised Wilhelm more than this message: since the episode on the stone bench he had treated Philine with open scorn, quite determined never to have anything more to do with her. He was just about to return the gift when he caught an imploring expression on Mignon's face; so he sent back his thanks on Mignon's behalf, but for himself he politely declined the invitation. He asked the servingman to pay some attention to the needs of the others, and inquired after the baron. He was told that the baron was confined to his bed, and, so far as he knew, had given orders to someone else to look after the needs of the actors who were so miserably housed.

The man went away, leaving Wilhelm one of his candles which, for lack of a chandelier, he had to fix on one of the windowsills, so that at least all four walls of the room were illuminated as he pursued his various thoughts. But it still took a long time before arrangements were made so that the guests could go to their rest. More candles were brought in, though without snuffers, then some chairs, then, one hour later, blankets, then pillows (all wet), and it was long past midnight when finally mattresses and sacks of straw were brought in, which, if these had been provided first, would have been most welcome.

Meanwhile some food and drink was delivered, which was consumed with few objections, although it looked like an untidy mess of leftovers instead of an indication of the respect usually paid to guests.

Chapter Four

The ill manners and impertinence of some in the company added to the restlessness and discomfort of that night. They teased one another, woke each other up, and played all sorts of tricks between them. The next morning everyone complained about their "good friend" the baron for having misled them and giving them such a false picture of the orderliness and comfort which was to be theirs. But to their amazement and consolation the count himself came to see them quite early, accompanied by several servants, and inquired after their circumstances. He was very angry when he learned how badly they had been treated. The baron, limping, blamed the steward for not carrying out his orders and gave him what he thought was a real dressing down.

The count immediately gave orders that while he was still there, everything should be done to ensure the greatest possible comfort for his guests. Up came several officers who straightway made the acquaintance of the actresses, and the count had the whole company introduced to him, calling each by his or her name and leavening the interviews with some jocular remarks, so that

464

everybody was simply delighted with such a gracious lord. Wilhelm was the last to be presented, with Mignon clutching him. He apologized as best he could for being so bold, but the count seemed to accept his being there as a foregone conclusion.

There was one man standing near the count, whom they thought was an officer, though he was not wearing a uniform. He was engaged in conversation with Wilhelm, and seemed somehow superior to the others. He had big blue eyes gleaming from beneath a high forehead, and blond hair loosely combed back. His medium height gave him a sturdy, firm and rather stolid appearance. His questions were pointed, and he seemed to have considerable understanding of what he inquired about.

Wilhelm asked the baron about this man, but the baron had little good to say about him. He was referred to as the major, was really the prince's favorite, attended to his most private business and was considered his right arm. There was even reason to believe that he was the prince's natural son. He had been with embassies in France, England and Italy, and was treated everywhere as a person of distinction, which made him conceited. He professed to know German literature through and through, and indulged in constant shallow mockery of it. The baron for his part had given up all contact with him, and thought that Wilhelm would do well to maintain a certain distance, for ultimately he did harm to everybody. He was known as Jarno, but no one knew what to make of such a name. Wilhelm had nothing to say, for, although the man had something cold and repellent about him, he felt a certain attraction toward him.

The actors now all had their separate quarters in the castle, and Melina gave strict orders that they should behave properly, the women keep to themselves, and everybody apply themselves to their roles and concentrate their thoughts on art. He posted rules and regulations, each consisting of several points, on all the doors. Fines were fixed and had to be deposited in a communal box.

Little attention was paid to these strictures. Young officers strolled in and out, joking with the actresses in what was certainly not the most refined manner, played tricks on the actors, and created havoc with Melina's attempts at policing his company before these had had time to establish themselves. People raced through the rooms, disguising themselves and hiding from each other. Melina, who had at first shown some seriousness, was soon driven to distraction by all this mischief, and when the count summoned him to see the place where the stage was to be set up, everything became worse. The young gentlemen, egged on by some of the actors, began to engage in stupid pranks which got coarser and coarser, so that it seemed as if the whole castle had been occupied by a frenzied troop of soldiers. The noise and confusion continued until mealtime.

The count had taken Melina into a large hall which was still part of the old building but connected to the new castle by a gallery. In this room a small stage could very well be set up, and the knowledgeable lord of the house explained how he wanted everything arranged.

Work was begun at great speed. The frame of the theater was set up and decorated, and the sets put together from what they had in their baggage that was usable; what they still needed was assembled with the help of some resourceful members of the count's entourage. Wilhelm took part in all this, making sure the perspectives were right, measuring distances, and generally concerned that nothing should look clumsy. The count, who often looked in, was very satisfied, explained how they should do some particular thing—rather than the way they were doing it—and showed remarkable artistic sense.

Then the rehearsals began in earnest. They would have had plenty of time and space, if they had not been constantly interrupted by the many strangers. More and more such guests kept arriving daily, and every one of them wanted to take a look at the company of actors.

Chapter Five

For some days the baron had been holding out to Wilhelm the hope of being personally presented to the countess. "I have told this excellent lady so much about your intelligent and very moving plays," he said, "that she is very eager to talk with you and hear you read one or the other of them. So be prepared, at the first signal from her, to come right over, for she will certainly be sending for you when she next has a morning that is not taken up with other things." Wilhelm should read the epilogue first, in order to make a particularly favorable impression. The lady had said how much she regretted that Wilhelm had come at such a busy time and that he had been obliged to make do with the rest of the troupe in the old part of the castle with such poor lodging.

Wilhelm took great pains choosing the play with which he should make his debut in the world of the great. "Up till now," he said to himself, "you have labored away quietly for yourself, and the approval you have received was only from a few personal friends. For a time you were in a state of complete despair as to whether you had any talent at all; and you are still deeply concerned whether you are on the right path and whether you have as much talent for the theater as you have liking for it. What you are about to attempt, in a private room where no theatrical illusion is possible and before experienced listeners, is a much riskier enterprise than it would be elsewhere, and yet I would not willingly forego the pleasure of regaining contact with previous joys and expanding my hopes for the future."

He read through several of his plays with close attention, making corrections here and there, then read them aloud in order to get the right tone and expression, and slipped into his pocket the one he had worked at most and hoped to gain most respect for, when one morning he was summoned in to the presence of the countess.

The baron had assured him that she would be there with one other lady who was one of her best friends. As he entered the room the Baroness von C** came towards him, expressed her pleasure at meeting him and presented him to the countess, who was just having her hair done and received him with friendly words and glances. Unfortunately, however, he saw Philine kneeling beside the countess's chair and engaged in all sorts of nonsense. "This dear child," said the baroness, "has been singing us a variety of songs. Do finish the one you have just started," she said to Philine, "so that we don't miss any of it."

Wilhelm listened very patiently to Philine's ditty, wishing the while that the hairdresser would leave before he began his reading. He was offered a cup of chocolate, and the baroness herself brought him a biscuit, but he took no pleasure in this, being too eager to recite to the lovely countess something that might interest her, and earn him her good graces. Philine was also very much in his way, for as a listener she had often been a nuisance. Anxiously he watched the hands of the hairdresser, hoping that his creation would any moment be completed.

Meanwhile the count had come into the room to inform them of the guests who would be arriving that day, and how the day should be divided up. He also mentioned various domestic matters that were liable to come up. After he had left, several of the officers sent a message asking the countess's permission to pay their respects at this time, because they would have to ride off before she went to table. Her valet de chambre having by now finished doing her hair, she asked the officers to come in.

Meanwhile the baroness was doing all she could to keep our friend entertained, and giving him her whole attention, to which he responded respectfully, albeit somewhat distractedly. Every now and again he would finger the manuscript in his pocket, hoping for the blessed moment to arrive, and almost losing his patience when a peddler was admitted to the room, who infuriatingly proceeded to open up all his boxes, chests and cases one after the other, displaying all his merchandise with the importunateness common in those of his trade.

More and more people came into the room. The baroness looked at Wilhelm and then to the countess. He noticed this, without appreciating the reason. This became clear to him only when he arrived back in his room after a fruitless hour of nervous waiting, and found a beautiful English wallet, which the baroness had managed to slip into his pocket. Soon after this the little moorish servant of the countess brought him a handsomely embroidered vest, without clearly indicating where it came from.

Chapter Six

The rest of that day was spoilt for Wilhelm by mixed feelings of irritation and gratitude, until the evening brought him a new task when Melina informed him that the count had spoken about a prologue to extol the prince on the day of his arrival. In it the qualities of this great hero and friend of humanity were to be personified. His various virtues should appear side by side praising him and proclaiming the honor of this noble personage; finally, his bust should be crowned with wreaths of laurel and flowers, and his decorated initials should shine forth from beneath a coronet. The count had entrusted Melina with providing the necessary verses as well as everything else that would be needed, and Melina hoped that Wilhelm would help him in what ought to be something that came quite easily to him.

"What!" said Wilhelm petulantly, "Are we to have nothing but portraits, illuminated initials and allegorical figures to honor a prince who, to my mind, deserves quite a different demonstration of acclaim. How can an intelligent man be flattered by seeing himself displayed in effigy and his name glittering on oiled paper! My fear is that, with our restricted range of costumes, the allegory might give rise to inappropriate jokes. If you want to do this or have it done for you, I have no objections; but I must ask you to leave me out of it."

Melina apologized, saying that the count had only given rough instructions, and it was entirely left to them to arrange the whole affair as they thought fit. "I will be very glad," said Wilhelm after hearing this, "to contribute to the pleasure of our noble lord, and my muse has never had so pleasing an assignment as to speak out, even hesitantly, in praise of such a worthy prince. I will think the matter over, and perhaps I may succeed in getting our little company to put on something that will make an impression."

From this moment on Wilhelm seriously pondered the task that was facing him. And before he went to sleep that night, he had it all fairly well sketched out. The next morning he got up early, completed the plan, worked out the individual scenes and even set down on paper some of the more imposing passages and the verses for the songs.

Wilhelm hastened to see the baron in order to ask him about certain details and lay before him his plan. The baron was well pleased, but somewhat perplexed, for, the evening before, he had heard the count talking about quite a different play which he had said was to be turned into verse.

"I do not believe it is the count's intention to have the play exactly as he described it to Melina," said Wilhelm. "Unless I am mistaken, all he was trying to do was to give us a hint as to the right type of thing. A connoisseur and man of taste indicates to an artist what he wants, but leaves it up to him how it should be produced."

"You're quite wrong," said the baron. "The count will insist that the play be performed exactly as he indicated. Your work does indeed have a remote resemblance to what he had in mind, and if we are to succeed in deflecting him from his first intentions, then we shall need the help of the ladies. The baroness in particular is superb at such operations; but the question will be whether your plan appeals to her sufficiently for her to espouse it. If it does, then everything will be all right."

"We need the assistance of the ladies anyway," said Wilhelm, "for our performers and costumes will hardly suffice for this performance. I am reckoning on the assistance of several pretty young children I have seen running about the house, who seem to belong to the valet and the steward."

He asked the baron to make the ladies acquainted with his plan. The baron returned soon afterwards with the news that the ladies would like that evening to talk to Wilhelm in private. They would pretend to be indisposed and retire to their chamber when the gentlemen sat down to cards, which would be a more serious affair than usual because of the arrival of a general. Wilhelm would be conducted there by way of a secret staircase, and then be in the best position to given account of his project. The element of furtiveness made the whole occasion into a doubly attractive prospect, especially for the baroness who was as excited as a child at the thought of this clandestine meeting arranged without the approval of the count.

Toward evening Wilhelm was fetched at the appointed time and cautiously led up to the ladies' apartment. The manner in which the baroness received him in the small anteroom reminded him of former happy occasions. She conducted him to the countess's room, and there then began a whole series of questions. He put forward his plan with so much enthusiasm and vigor that the ladies were immediately taken by it. And our readers will surely allow us to acquaint them with it.

The play was to begin with a pastoral scene in which children performed a dance representing a game of changing places. This should be followed by an exchange of pleasantries and culminate in a round dance to a merry song. Then the Harper and Mignon would come on, and the countryfolk gather round them, attracted by their strange appearance. The old man would sing songs about peace, repose and happiness and then Mignon would perform the egg dance. This atmosphere of innocent joy should be disrupted by the sounds of martial music, and the whole company set upon by a troop of soldiers, with the men trying to defend themselves but being captured, and the women fleeing and being brought back. Just when everything seems to be collapsing into disorder, a certain person appears—the author had not finally decided who this should be—and announces that the leader of the army is approaching, and order is restored. The character of this heroic leader would now be described in all its finest features, safety from every attack will be assured, and arrogance and violence put an end to. Then should follow a general celebration in honor of the magnanimous captain of the army.

The ladies were well satisfied with all this, but maintained that there must be something allegorical in the play to be acceptable to the count. The baron proposed that the leader of the attacking soldiers should be presented as the spirit of discord and violence, and that Minerva should restrain him with shackles toward the end, announce the arrival of the hero, and proclaim his praises. The baroness assumed the responsibility for persuading the count that

the plan he had suggested would be adhered to with only a few minor alterations; but she insisted that the bust, initials and coronet must appear at the
end of the play, or else the whole performance would have lost its raison d'être.

Wilhelm, who had already sketched the fine words that he would place in
Minerva's mouth in praise of his hero, objected for a while to what the baroness was insisting on, but finally gave way, because he felt pleasantly compelled
to do so. The beautiful eyes of the countess and her charming manner would
quite easily have persuaded him to abandon his most cherished ideas, the
unity of the composition together with every contributing detail that he so
much desired, and to act against all his poetic convictions. He faced a real
struggle with his middle-class state of mind when, during the casting, the
ladies insisted that he himself should play one of the roles.

Laertes was given the role of the mighty god of war. Wilhelm should play
the leader of the countryfolk, who had some very nice and impassioned lines
to speak. He objected at first, but finally had to give in, having no excuse after
the baroness had explained to him that theater at this castle was really only a
social affair in which she too would be happy to participate, if they could find
a proper way to include her. The ladies then dismissed him with many signs
of their friendly feelings toward him. The baroness assured him that he was a
most exceptional person, and accompanied him back to the staircase, wishing
him goodnight with a clasp of the hands.

Chapter Seven

Wilhelm was fired up by the sincere interest shown by the ladies and his own
description of the action of the play; the whole structure now became clear to
him, and he spent most of the night and next morning carefully composing
dialogue and songs. He was almost finished, when he received a summons to
go to the new part of the castle where the count, having just finished breakfast,
wished to speak to him. He entered the hall, and once again it was the baroness who came to meet him, and, under the pretext of wishing him a good
morning, whispered in his ear: "Don't tell him anything about the play, except
in answer to his questions."

"I am told," said the count, "that you are busily working at my prologue in
honor of the prince. I approve of the idea of bringing in Minerva, but I have
been wondering how she should be costumed so as not to arouse offense. I
have therefore asked that all the books in my library which include a picture
of her should be brought here." And at that very moment in came several servingmen with huge baskets containing books of all shapes and sizes.

Montfaucon's *Antiquity Illustrated*, catalogues of Roman sculptures, gems
and coins, together with all kinds of treatises on mythology were consulted
and the representations of Minerva compared with each other. But even that

did not satisfy the count, whose excellent memory recalled all sorts of Minervas from title pages, vignettes and other places. And so one tome after another had to be fetched from the library, and the count was soon surrounded by piles and piles of books. Finally, when he could not think of any more Minervas, he exclaimed with a laugh: "I bet there isn't a single Minerva left in my library, and this must be the very first time that a collection of books completely lacks a true representation of their presiding goddess."

Everyone was amused at this, and Jarno laughed the hardest, for it was he who had been urging the count to have more and more books brought in.

"Well," said the count, turning to Wilhelm, "is it really important which goddess? Minerva or Pallas? The goddess of war, or the goddess of the arts?"

"Wouldn't it be best, your Excellency, not to be specific on that point?" Wilhelm suggested. "Why not present her in the double character which she had in mythology? She announces the arrival of a fighter, but only to bring peace to the populace. She praises a hero for his humaneness. She forcibly restrains force and thereby restores peace and quiet."

The baroness, afraid that Wilhelm might give himself away, cut this short by pushing forward the countess's tailor, who simply had to give his opinion on how a Roman garment could best be created. This man, experienced in providing costumes for masquerades, knew the easiest way to make things, and since Madame Melina, despite her advanced pregnancy, was to play the role of Minerva, he was instructed to measure her. The countess had to decide, much to the chagrin of her maids, which of her dresses was to be cut up for the purpose.

The baroness slyly drew Wilhelm aside and told him that she had taken care of everything else. She sent him the director of the count's orchestra, so that he could start composing the necessary music or find suitable melodies from the stock of music in the castle. Everything was proceeding satisfactorily, the count made no further inquiries about the play, being mainly occupied with the transparent decoration at the end, which was to be a real surprise. His own inventiveness combined with the producer's skill did indeed achieve a very pleasing effect. On his journeys the count had seen big festivities of this kind, and had collected innumerable engravings and drawings. He really knew what was needed, and he had good taste.

Meanwhile, Wilhelm had finished the text of the play, gave everyone his part, took on his own, and the music director, who was equally knowledgeable about dance, arranged the ballet; everything was going along splendidly.

But then there occurred an unexpected obstacle, which threatened to make a big gap in all his well-laid plans. He had reckoned that Mignon's egg dance would make the strongest impression, and was therefore absolutely stupefied when with her usual curtness she refused to dance at all, saying she was now his and would never again appear on the stage. He tried every possible argument to persuade her, and did not give in until the poor child began to weep bitterly, fell at his feet, and cried: "Oh, Father, you stay away from it too!" He did not respond to this. Instead he began thinking of some other means of making the scene interesting.

Philine, who was to be one of the country maidens and sing the solo in the round dance, with the chorus taking up what she sang, was overjoyed at this prospect. She had everything she desired: her own room, constant proximity to the countess whom she entertained with her foolery and was daily rewarded for this, a costume for the play made specially for her, and, since she was the sort of person who delights in imitating others, she soon observed from being with the ladies as much decorum as she could comfortably assume, and in a very short time developed good manners and real savoir vivre. The attentions of the stablemaster increased rather than diminished, and since the officers were also constantly currying her favors, she found herself with an excess of riches, and decided for once to play the prude, using all her wits to affect an air of sophisticated superiority. This cool refinement enabled her to discover within a very few days all the weak spots in the company at the castle, and, if she had really wanted to, she could have made her fortune by this means. But in this too she only used her advantage to amuse herself, to give herself a pleasant day, and to be impertinent when she saw it was safe to be so.

When the actors had all memorized their parts, a full rehearsal was set. The count wanted to be present and his wife began to be nervous about his reactions. The baroness summoned Wilhelm privately, and the nearer the time for the rehearsal approached, the more embarrassed they all became, for absolutely nothing of the count's original idea remained in the play. Jarno, who happened just then to come in, was let in on the secret, and was delighted. He felt inclined to offer his services to the two ladies. "It would be unfortunate if you could not by your own efforts extricate yourself from this situation," he said to the countess. "But I will be lying in wait for any eventuality." The baroness then told him that she had talked to the count about the whole play, but only in bits and pieces and those not in any particular order so that he would be prepared for the details. But he still thought that the plan of the whole would conform with his original idea. "I will sit next to him this evening at the rehearsal," she said, "and try to distract him. I have also suggested to the decorator that he do the decorations at the end really well, but make sure that some little thing is not quite right."

"I know a court where we could use such active and intelligent people as you," said Jarno. "And if for some reason your skills are not producing the desired results, then just give me a sign and I will get the count out of the rehearsal and not let him back again until Minerva has made her appearance; the illuminations can be depended on to carry the day. For several days now I have had something to tell him concerning his cousin, which, for one reason or another, I have kept putting off. That will be a distraction for him, though certainly not the pleasantest."

Various business matters prevented the count from being there at the start of the rehearsal. Then he was entertained by the baroness. Jarno's help was never needed. For since the count found plenty to put right, to improve and to insist on, he totally forgot everything else, and since Madame Melina spoke her lines exactly as he would have wanted them, and the final tableau turned out well, he seemed completely satisfied. It was only when the prologue was over and they went on to the play itself, that he began to notice things and to wonder whether this play was really what he had thought up. At this point Jarno did come out of his ambush position, and the evening passed with the news of the prince's arrival being confirmed, and various people riding out to see the vanguard of the prince's entourage encamped in the neighborhood. The whole house was full of noise and commotion, and our actors, who had not always been looked after properly by the surly servingmen, were obliged to spend the time waiting and practicing in the old part of the castle without anyone paying any particular attention to them.

Chapter Eight

The prince finally arrived. The generals, staff officers and the rest of his attendants who arrived with them, and all those who visited them or came on business—all these turned the castle into a regular beehive. Everyone was pushing and shoving to catch a glimpse of the illustrious prince, everyone admired his affable condescension, everyone was astonished to find that this great hero, this noble commander, was the smoothest of courtiers.

The household staff had been ordered by the count to be at their posts when the prince arrived, but none of the actors was to be visible because the count wanted to surprise the prince with the festivities that were being prepared. The prince, when he was escorted that evening into the handsomely lit great hall decorated with wall coverings from the previous century, seemed in no wise to be expecting a theatrical presentation, let alone a prologue in his honor. Everything went off splendidly, and when the performance was over all the actors had to appear before the prince, who graciously asked a question of every one of them, or had something pleasant to say to them. Wilhelm, as the author, had to step forward separately, and he too received his share of appreciation.

Nobody had anything much to say about the prologue, and in a few days it was as if there had been no performance at all, except that Jarno occasionally talked to Wilhelm about it, and praised it, showing real understanding. But he added: "It is a pity that you play for empty nuts with empty nuts." Wilhelm pondered this expression for several days, not knowing how to interpret it or what he should make of it.

Every evening the troupe performed and exerted every effort to capture the audience's attention. Applause, barely deserved, encouraged them to think that it was on their account that the guests came pouring in here, just in order to be present at the performances, which were the center of attraction for all the guests at the castle. Wilhelm, however, realized to his regret that this was not the case. For although the prince sat through the first performances and followed them conscientiously from start to finish, he soon seemed to find good reasons to absent himself. The very people who from their conversation had seemed to Wilhelm to be the most intelligent, above all Jarno, only spent fleeting moments in the room where the stage was set up, and preferred to sit in the anteroom playing cards or talking about business.

He was disappointed that, despite persistent effort, he had failed to receive the amount of approval he thought he had earned. He assisted Melina in selecting the plays and copying the parts, he was always at hand during the frequent rehearsals and when anything else needed attention. Melina, secretly conscious of his own inadequacy, eventually accepted his help. Wilhelm meticulously memorized his parts and performed with feeling and vigor and as much style as his self-education allowed him.

The continued interest of the baron in their undertaking removed any doubts that the rest of the actors might have had, for he assured them that they were very successful and would be even more so especially if they were to perform one of his own plays. But he was sorry to say that the prince's taste was exclusively for French drama, and that some of his acquaintances, foremost among them Jarno, had a passionate preference for those monstrous productions of the English stage.

The artistry of our actors may not have been adequately observed and respected; but as for their persons they were certainly not greeted with indifference by the spectators, both male and female. We have already reported that the actresses had from the start attracted the attention of the young officers. As time went on things went even better for them, and they made some important conquests. But let us not go into that, noting only that Wilhelm was becoming more interesting every day to the countess, and an unavowed affection for her was beginning to blossom in him. When he was on stage she could not take her eyes off him, and he soon seemed to be acting and speaking only for her. It was an indescribable delight for them just to look at each other, and they abandoned themselves to this harmless pleasure without nourishing stronger desires or worrying about what might happen. They exchanged glances despite what separated them as to birth and station, just like two outposts of opposing armies, facing each other across a river, and engaging in lighthearted talk without any thought of war—both entirely trusting their own feelings.

The baroness for her part had sought out Laertes, whose lusty vigor appealed to her, and he, despite his avowed hatred of women, was not averse to a passing adventure; this time he would have been really captivated against his will by the vivaciousness and attractions of the baroness, if the baron had not had occasion to do him a good, or perhaps bad, service by making him better acquainted with her sentiments. For one day when Laertes was singing her praises as the best of all women, the baron jokingly observed: "I see where matters stand. Our friend has secured another one for her stables." This unfortunate choice of metaphor, referring all too clearly to the blandishments of Circe, made Laertes extremely angry, and he was annoyed to hear the baron go on to say pitilessly: "Every newcomer believes he is the first to deserve such attentions, but he is utterly mistaken, for we have all, at one time or another, been led up the garden like this. Man, youth or boy—no matter who it is—every one of us has devoted himself to her for a time and striven to gain her favors."

Nothing is more dispiriting to a happy man who, entering the gardens of a sorceress, finds himself surrounded by the joys of an artificial spring, but, while listening for the song of the nightingale, finds his ears invaded by the grunts of some transformed predecessor.

Laertes was heartily ashamed after this disclosure that he had once more been led astray by his vanity to think well of a woman. So he avoided her from now on, consorting instead with the stablemaster, with whom he fenced vigorously and went hunting, but treating the whole matter as insignificant when he was rehearsing or performing on stage.

Sometimes of a morning the count and countess would summon members of the troupe, and on these occasions all had reason to envy Philine's undeserved good fortune. While he was dressing, the count often had his favorite actor, the Pedant, at hand, sometimes for hours on end. The fellow was gradually decked out from head to toe, equipped even with a watch and snuffbox. Sometimes after dinner the entire company were bidden to appear before the lord and lady; they considered this a singular honor, not realizing that at the same time a whole pack of dogs were brought in by huntsmen and servants, and the horses being readied in the courtyard.

Wilhelm had been advised to praise Racine, the prince's favorite dramatist, when an appropriate opportunity presented itself, and thereby put himself in the prince's good graces. He found such an occasion one afternoon, when he had been summoned to appear with the others, and the prince asked him whether he too had studied the great French dramatists. Wilhelm said that he had. He did not notice that the prince had already turned to speak to someone else, without waiting for his answer. Almost interposing himself, he claimed the prince's attention by declaring that he had indeed a very high opinion of French drama and had read its masterpieces with great appreciation; and he had been delighted to hear that the prince paid great respect to the talents of a man like Racine: "I can well imagine," he went on to say, "that persons of noble station will appreciate an author who portrays so excellently and correctly the circumstances of high social rank. Corneille, if I may put it thus, portrays great people, but Racine portrays persons of quality. As I read his plays I can always picture a poet residing at a brilliant court, with a great king before his eyes, surrounded by all that is best, who can penetrate to the secrets of men which are concealed behind richly woven hangings. Whenever I study his *Britannicus* or his *Bérénice*, I have the sense of being at court myself, of being privy to things great and small in these dwellings of the gods of this earth, and through the eyes of a sensitive Frenchman I perceive kings adored by whole nations, courtiers envied by multitudes, all in their natural shape with all their defects and sorrows. The report that Racine died of grief because Louis XIV showed his dissatisfaction by no longer looking at him—that to me is the key to all his works. It was impossible for such a talented writer, whose whole life, and his death, depended on the eyes of a king, not to write plays worthy of the admiration of a king—and of a prince."

Jarno had joined them and listened with amazement to what Wilhelm said. The prince, who never answered but signified approval only by an appropriate glance, turned away. Wilhelm, still unaware that it was not seemly in such circumstances to prolong a conversation and try to exhaust a topic completely, would gladly have gone on talking and proved to the prince that he had read the prince's favorite poet with profit and emotional involvement.

Taking him aside, Jarno asked him: "Have you never seen a play by Shakespeare?" "No," Wilhelm replied, "for since his plays have become better known in Germany, I have not been close to the theater; and I don't know whether I should be pleased that mere chance has reawakened in me a passion which in my youth occupied me intensely. But I must say that what I have heard about his plays has not made me eager to know more about such strange monstrosities which transcend all probability and overstep all propriety."

"I would nevertheless advise you take a look at them," said Jarno. "It can't do anyone any harm to observe with one's own eyes something that is strange. I will lend you a few samples, and you could not employ your time better than by disassociating yourself from everything else and, in the solitude of your own room, peering into the kaleidoscope of this unknown world. It is a sinful waste of time for you to spend it in dressing up these apes as humans and in teaching these dogs to dance. But one thing I would insist on in advance: don't take offense at the form of what you read. As for the rest—that I can leave to your own true judgment."

The horses were standing ready outside the door, and Jarno swung himself into the saddle to entertain himself by hunting with some of the other courtiers. Wilhelm followed him sadly with his eyes. He would have liked to talk about many things with this man who, though not in a very friendly fashion, had nevertheless given him new ideas, ideas that he needed to think about.

When a man approaches the point at which his powers, capabilities and concepts are about to develop decisively, he often finds himself in a state of uncertainty, which some good friend could easily help him overcome. He is like a traveler who falls into the water close to the shelter that he seeks. If someone comes to his aid right away and drags him on to dry land, then he only has to put up with getting wet, whereas if he has to get himself out of the water onto the other bank, he still has to take a big, tiresome detour to reach his destination.

Wilhelm was beginning to feel that things work out differently in the world from what he had imagined. He was now observing at close range the life, full of importance and significance, of those in high station, the great of this world, and he was surprised at the easiness of manner which he had acquired thereby. An army on the march, with a princely hero at its head, surrounded by so many active soldiers and so many eager admirers—all this gave wings to his imagination. It was in this state of mind that he received the books that Jarno had promised him. And in a very short while, he was seized, as one would expect, by the torrent of a great genius which swept toward a limitless ocean in which he completely lost and forgot his own self.

Chapter Nine

The baron's relationship with the actors had gone through various modifications since their arrival at the castle. At first it had been one of mutual satisfaction. For since the baron, for the first time in his life, had one of his own plays, which up to then had only been social entertainment for amateurs, in the hands of real actors, with the prospect of a reasonably good performance, he was in the best of moods and full of generosity, purchasing little gifts for the actresses from various peddlers who appeared and many a bottle of champagne for the actors. They in return took great pains over his works, and Wilhelm spared no effort in memorizing every detail of the lofty speeches of the illustrious hero the portrayal of whom was entrusted to him.

But gradually certain disagreement arose: the baron's preference for certain of the actors became more noticeable every day, and that naturally displeased the other members of the company. His praise was reserved exclusively for his favorites, and this aroused jealousy and discord in the troupe. Melina, who never knew what to do in such cases of dissension, found himself in a very unpleasant situation. Those who received praise were not particularly grateful for it, and those who did not indicated their displeasure in all sorts of ways and made things uncomfortable for their erstwhile respected benefactor. Their malicious attitude toward him was encouraged by a certain poem, of unknown authorship, which circulated in the castle. There had always been gossip about the baron's relations with the actors, with all sorts of tales told and certain events improved in the telling to make them amusing and more interesting. All this had been done in a relatively subtle way. But now the assertion was made that professional envy had broken out between him and some of the actors who fancied themselves as writers; and this was the basis for the poem we spoke of, which ran as follows:

O Baron, how I envy you
Your high place in society.
Poor wretch I am, and would that I
Were near to thrones, and had such land,
Proud castle as your father has,
With hunting and with shooting.

O Baron, how you envy me,
Poor wretched me; for so it seems,
That Mother Nature cared for me
And wished me well from childhood on
With easy heart and easy head,
I'm poor, but not in brains or wit.

So I would think it best if we,
Dear Baron, leave things as they are.
You stay your father's own true son
And I'll remain my mother's child.
Let's live without distrust and hate,
And neither grudge the other's title,
You on Parnassus seek no place
And I none with their lordships.

Opinions on this poem, which was circulating in several not very legible copies, were sharply divided, but no one could hazard a guess as to who had written it. When people began to take a malicious delight in it, Wilhelm declared himself very much against this.

"We Germans," he exclaimed, "have fully deserved that our muses are still suffering from the disdain in which they have languished for so long, if we are not able to respect men of station who occupy themselves in one way or another with our literature. There is no contradiction between birth, station and wealth on the one hand, and genius and taste on the other. Foreign countries have taught us that, for amongst their best minds are many who belong to the aristocracy. So far it has been a miracle if anyone of our German nobility has devoted himself to learning, and few famous names owe their fame to their interest in art and learning, whereas others have emerged from obscurity and appeared as unknown stars on the horizon. But this will not always be so, and unless I am much mistaken, the uppermost class of our nation is in the process of employing its advantageous condition to gain in future the laurel wreath of the muses. Nothing is more distasteful to me than to hear not only members of the middle classes making fun of aristocrats who set store by the muses, but also those persons of quality, who with ill-considered frivolity and despicable malice watch others of their own station being scared away from a path that would bring honor and gratification to everyone."

This last utterance seemed to be directed at the count, for Wilhelm had heard that he thought the poem was really good. The count was of course accustomed to joke in his own particular style with the baron, and so he had welcomed this opportunity to tease him in various ways. Everyone had his own conjectures regarding the authorship of the poem, and the count, not willing to be proven less perspicacious, lighted on an idea that he swore must be the truth, namely that the author of the poem was his own Pedant, who was a really fine fellow and in whom he had long observed some signs of poetic genius. So to provide himself with good entertainment he sent for the man one morning and made him read the poem aloud in the presence of the countess, the baroness and Jarno, which the Pedant did in his own special way; he earned praise, applause, and a present for his efforts. He cleverly evaded answering the count's questions whether he had poems that he had written earlier. And so the Pedant gained the reputation of being a poet and a wit, but, in the opinion of those who were well disposed toward the baron, of a lampooner and a bad character. The count applauded him more and more, no matter how he played his roles, so that the poor fellow became quite puffed up, in fact almost crazy, and even thought of taking a room in the castle, like Philine.

If he had done this immediately, a most unfortunate accident might have been avoided. Late one night, when he was going to the old part of the castle and fumbling about in a narrow dark passage, he was set upon by several persons who held him fast while others rained blows on him and beat him up so badly that he could hardly drag himself to his feet. But he managed to creep upstairs to his companions who, although pretending to be outraged, felt some inward pleasure at the occurrence and had to laugh at seeing him so thoroughly pummelled, his new brown coat covered with white dust as if he had had a fight with some millers.

The count, as soon as he got news of this, was absolutely furious. He treated the incident as a serious offense, an incursion on his jurisdiction, and instituted through his marshal a thoroughgoing inquiry. The spattered coat was to be the major evidence. Everybody in the castle having anything to do with powder or flour was drawn into the investigation. But all in vain.

The baron swore on his honor that although the kind of joke to which he had been subjected was not at all to his liking, and the count's own behavior had not been of the kindest, he had got over all that, and had in no wise been implicated in the misfortune that had befallen the poet or lampooner, whatever he should be called.

The activities of the guests and the general commotion in the castle led to the whole incident being quickly forgotten, and the count's unfortunate favorite had to pay dearly for his brief pleasure of wearing borrowed plumes.

The troupe performed every evening and was on the whole well looked after, but the better things went, the more demands they made, soon claiming that food, drink, service and accommodation were inadequate. They urged their protector, the baron, to see that they were better provided for and finally given the pleasures and comforts that he had promised them. Their complaints became more and more insistent, and the baron's efforts to satisfy them, ever more fruitless.

Wilhelm was less and less visible except at rehearsals and performances. Shut up in one of the back rooms, which only Mignon and the Harper were allowed to enter, he lived and moved in the world of Shakespeare, entirely oblivious of all that was going on outside.

There are said to be certain sorcerers who by magic can entice a host of different spirits into their chamber. The conjurations are so powerful that the whole room is filled and the spirits, jostled up to the tiny magic circle that the wizard has drawn, swirl around it and float above his head, constantly changing and increasing in number. Every corner is crammed full, every shelf occupied, eggs keep expanding, and gigantic shapes shrink to toadstools. But unfortunately the necromancer has forgotten the magic word to make this flood of spirits subside. As Wilhelm sat there reading, hosts of feelings and urges arose within him of which he had previously no conception or intimation. Nothing deflected him from this state of total absorption, and he was most impatient when someone came to tell him what was going on outside.

Hence he hardly paid any attention when he heard that some public punishment was about to take place in the castle yard and a boy be whipped, who was under suspicion of breaking into the castle at night. Since he was wearing a wigmaker's coat, he might well have been one of the baron's assailants. The boy categorically denied this and could not therefore be formally punished, but the intention was to accuse him of vagrancy and send him packing, because he had been wandering around the neighborhood for several days, spending the nights in mills, and had finally placed a ladder against a garden wall and climbed over.

Wilhelm did not think there was anything remarkable about this, but then Mignon came rushing in and told him the boy was Friedrich who, since his dispute with the stablemaster, had been lost from sight, both for the actors and us readers.

Wilhelm, who took an interest in this boy, hurried down to the courtyard where preparations for the occasion were already underway. For the count loved ceremony, even in small matters like this. The boy was brought in, but Wilhelm intervened on his behalf, asking for a delay because he knew the boy and had various things concerning him to report. He had some difficulty in making his point, but was finally given permission to speak privately with the delinquent. Friedrich assured him that he was in no wise implicated in the maltreatment of an actor. He had been strolling around the castle and had crept in at night to visit Philine, for he had spied out the location of her bedroom and would certainly have got to it if he had not been apprehended.

Wilhelm, not anxious to reveal this relationship (which might affect the good reputation of the company), rushed off to see the stablemaster, and asked him, in view of his acquaintance with the person involved and those at the castle, to act as an intermediary and get the boy released. With Wilhelm's help the whimsical fellow thought up quite a tale: the boy had once belonged to the troupe, then run away, then wanted to join it again, and so had decided to visit some of his previous associates at night, in order to win their good graces. Everyone said that he had always behaved well, the ladies too gave their opinion, and he was set free.

Wilhelm took charge of him, and so Friedrich became the third member of the strange family that for some time Wilhelm had considered his own. The Harper and Mignon were pleased to see Friedrich again, and all three of them were now determined to be attentive to the needs of their friend and protector, and to provide him with what pleasure they could.

Chapter Ten

As each day passed, Philine discovered more and more how to ingratiate herself with the ladies. When they were alone together she would move the conversation on to the subject of the men who had been around, and Wilhelm was not the last to be talked about. She was bright enough to be aware that he had made a great impression on the countess's feelings; and so she told her what she knew (and didn't know) about him, carefully avoiding anything that might be to his disadvantage, and praising his nobility of character, his generosity, and especially his moral behavior toward women. All other questions that were addressed to her she answered prudently, and when the baroness noticed the countess's increasing emotional attachment, she was delighted at the discovery. For her own relationships with various men, and most recently with Jarno, were not unknown to the countess, whose pure soul could not possibly observe such frivolity without disapproval and gentle reproach.

The baroness and Philine, therefore, had, each in her own way, a special interest in bringing Wilhelm and the countess closer together. Philine hoped in addition to regain his favor and to operate to her own advantage when such opportunity should arise.

One day, when the count had gone off hunting with the rest of the company and the men were not expected back till the following morning, the baroness thought up an amusement of the sort she particularly favored. She liked to dress up and was always appearing, in order to surprise everybody, as a peasant girl, or a page boy, or a huntsman. She acquired thereby a sort of faery reputation, flitting hither and thither and emerging where she was least expected. She was simply delighted when she was able to wait at table, or mingle with the guests without being recognized, only to reveal her identity in some humorous fashion.

That evening she summoned Wilhelm to her room, and since she had something else to do first, Philine was told to prepare him for what was to come. He arrived, and was surprised to find the flighty girl there instead of the noble ladies. She received him with an air of decorous ease, which she had worked at perfecting, and thereby made him likewise adopt a stance of politeness. First she referred jocularly and in general terms to the good fortune that attended him and that, as she well observed, had brought him here at this very moment. Then she reproached him gently for his behavior toward her, which had so tormented her. She blamed herself for this as she had deserved his attentions; she vividly described what she called her former condition, and added that she would despise herself if she were unable to change and make herself worthy of his friendship.

Wilhelm was astounded by this speech. He had too little experience of the world to know that irreparably frivolous persons are often those who demean themselves most, admit their faults most openly, and deplore them, although they do not possess the slightest ability to abandon the course which their strong natures have impelled them to take hitherto. He therefore could not be unkind to the winsome sinner, engaged in conversation with her and learnt the plan for an unusual masquerade which was intended to be a surprise for the beautiful countess.

He had some misgivings, which he voiced to Philine. Yet when the baroness came in, she left him no time to express further doubts, but carried him off, and said the hour had come. It was already dark. She led him into the count's dressing room and made him take off his coat; Wilhelm slipped into the count's silk dressing gown, and she put the count's red-ribboned nightcap on his head. She then took him into the count's sitting room, told him to settle himself in the big armchair with a book, lit the reading lamp in front of him, and instructed him on what kind of role he was to play.

The countess, she said, would be told that the count had returned unexpectedly and was in a bad mood. She would then come in, walk up and down, seat herself on the arm of the chair and say a few words. He should continue playing the role of the husband as long and as well as he possibly could; and if at last he had to reveal his identity he should be courteous and gallant.

Wilhelm felt very uncomfortable in this strange disguise. The whole idea had astonished him, and its execution was proceeding before he had time to think about it. The baroness had already left him before he realized how dangerous the position in which he had put himself really was. He could not deny that the countess's beauty, youth and grace had made a considerable impression on him, but he was by nature in no sense inclined to empty shows of gallantry; yet his principles did not induce him to undertake anything more serious. So he was in a state of some perturbation—afraid of displeasing the countess and yet equally concerned not to please her too much.

His imagination recalled all those occasions when female charms had affected him. Mariane in her white négligé was there, begging him to remember her. Philine's amiability, her lovely hair and her ingratiating behavior had worked on him once again when he saw her just now. But all this receded into the distance when he thought of the noble, radiant countess, whose arm he should feel on his neck in a few moments and whose innocent caresses he was called upon to return.

He could however never have guessed the strange manner in which he would be relieved of his discomfort. How astonished and frightened he was when he heard the door open behind him, and a quick look in the mirror showed him quite clearly that it was the count entering with a candle in his hand! His hesitation what to do now, whether to remain seated or get up, run away, confess, prevaricate or ask for forgiveness, all that lasted only a few moments. For the count, who had stood motionless in the doorway, turned back, gently closing the door behind him. At that very moment the baroness rushed in through a side door, extinguished the lamp, dragged Wilhelm out of the chair and pulled him into the dressing room, where he discarded the count's dressing gown, putting it back in its usual place. She then hung Wilhelm's coat over her arm, and hurried away with him through various rooms, passageways and box rooms until they reached her own room. There she told him, once she had recovered, that she had gone to the countess to spin the yarn that the count had arrived earlier than expected. "But I know that already," the countess had said. "What can have happened? I've just seen him riding through the side gate." So the baroness in fright had rushed to the count's room to fetch Wilhelm.

"Unfortunately you came too late!" said Wilhelm. "The count had just come into the room, and he saw me sitting there."

"Did he recognize you?"

"I don't know. He saw me in the mirror, as I did him, and before I knew whether it was a ghost or he himself, he went out again and closed the door behind him."

The baroness became even more disconcerted when a servant called her and said the count was with his wife. She went there, crestfallen, and found the count sitting quietly brooding; when he spoke he was gentler and kinder than usual. She did not know what to make of this. They talked about what had happened on the hunt and why he had come back earlier. The conversation soon petered out. The count fell silent, and the baroness was particularly struck by the fact that he inquired after Wilhelm and expressed the wish that he should be asked to come and read to them.

Wilhelm, who meanwhile in the baroness's room had dressed and recovered himself somewhat, obeyed the summons with some trepidation. The count handed him a book from which with a certain uneasiness he read them an adventure story. His voice had something unsteady about it, something quivering that, thank goodness, was appropriate to the content of the story. From time to time the count signalled his approval, and when he finally let him go, he praised the expressiveness with which Wilhelm had been reading.

Chapter Eleven

Wilhelm had read but a few of the plays of Shakespeare, when he found that he had to stop because they affected him so deeply. His mind was in a state of ferment. He sought out an opportunity to speak with Jarno and told him that he could not thank him enough for providing him with such an experience.

"I foresaw that you would not be insensitive to the great merits of this most extraordinary and marvelous of writers," said Jarno. "Yes indeed," said Wilhelm, "I cannot remember a book, a person, or an event that has affected me as deeply as these wonderful plays that you so kindly brought to my attention. They seem to be the work of some spirit from heaven that comes down to men and gently makes them more acquainted with themselves. They are not fictions! One seems to be standing before the huge open folios of Fate in which the storm winds of life in all their turbulence are raging, blowing the pages back and forth. I am so astonished by the forcefulness and tenderness, the violence and the control of it all, that I am completely beside myself and long for the time when I will be able to continue reading." "Bravo!" said Jarno, clasping our friend's hand, "that's just what I wanted; and the results that I hoped for will not be long in coming."

"I wish," said Wilhelm, "that I could describe to you all that is going on in my mind. Presentiments that I have had from youth on, without being aware of them, about human beings and their destinies, all these I have found confirmed and enlarged in Shakespeare's plays. He seems to reveal all the mysteries without our being able to point to the magic word that unlocked the secret. His personages seem to be ordinary men and women, and yet they are not. Mysterious composite creatures of nature act out their lives before us in his plays, like clocks with faces and movements of crystal, showing the passage of time in accordance with their regulated progression; at the same time one can perceive the springs and wheels that make them go. The few glances that I have cast into Shakespeare's world have impelled me more than anything else to take more resolute steps into the real world, to plunge into the flood of destinies that hangs over the world and someday, if fortune favors me, to cull several drafts from the great ocean of living nature and distribute these from the stage to the thirsting public of my native land."

"I am pleased at the state of mind you are in," said Jarno, clapping his hand on the impassioned youth's shoulder. "Don't give up your intention of embarking on an active life, and be quick to take full advantage of the good years that are given you. If I can assist you in any way, I will gladly do so with all my heart. I have never asked you how you came to be in this company of actors, to which you were neither born nor trained. What I would hope is that you will want to get yourself out of this situation; and I see that you do. I know nothing of your origins or your domestic circumstances, but you can entrust me with as much as you are willing for me to know. This much I would say to you now: that this present war can bring about rapid changes of fortune, and if you are prepared to put your talents and abilities at our service, and do not shy away from hard work, perhaps danger if needs be, then I would have an opportunity to put you in a position which you will not regret having occupied for a time." Wilhelm, extremely grateful for this, now felt in the mood to tell his friend and benefactor his whole life story.

While they were talking, they strayed into the middle of the park and came to the road that ran right through it. Jarno stood still for a moment, then said: "Think over my proposal, make your decision, give me your answer in a few days, and have confidence in me. I assure you that I have found it totally incomprehensible that you should have joined forces with such people as these. I have been distressed, indeed disgusted, that, in order to have some experience of life, you should have given your heart to an itinerant ballad singer and a silly androgynous creature."

He was about to continue, when an officer came riding up in haste, followed by a groom leading another horse. Jarno gave him a warm welcome. The officer dismounted and the two of them embraced each other, then started a conversation while Wilhelm, dismayed at Jarno's last words, stood to the side, deep in thought. Jarno looked through some papers the officer had brought him, and this man went up to Wilhelm, extended his hand to him and said with emphasis: "I find you in worthy company. Take your friend's advice, and fulfil the desires of someone unknown to you who nevertheless is deeply concerned about you." As he said this, he embraced Wilhelm, pressing him warmly to his breast. Then Jarno came up and said to the stranger: "The best thing would be for me to accompany you. You can get the necessary orders and ride off before nightfall." They both got on their horses and left our astonished friend to his own reflections.

Those last words of Jarno's were still ringing in his ears. He could not bear to have these two human beings who had so innocently gained his affection, debased by a man whom he respected so highly. The strange embrace of the officer whom he did not know, affected him little, merely arousing his curiosity and stirring his imagination for a brief moment; but Jarno's words had struck deeply, he felt wounded by them, and recoiling he reproached himself for having temporarily ignored and forgotten that icy harshness of Jarno that was apparent in his every glance and motion. "No, no!" he shouted, "you insensitive man-of-the-world, you only imagine that you can be someone's friend. Nothing you have to offer me can outweigh the affection which binds me to these two unfortunate creatures. What luck that I should have found out in good time what to expect from you."

Mignon came to meet him and he clasped her in his arms, saying: "Nothing shall part us, good little creature! The seeming wisdom of the world shall not persuade me to leave you, or to forget what I owe to you."

The girl, whose passionate embraces he usually warded off, was delighted by this unexpected outburst of affection, and clung so close to him that he had difficulty in loosening her hold.

From that time on he was more attentive to Jarno's actions, not all of which seemed laudable to him, and some he utterly disapproved of. He had, for instance, a strong suspicion that the poem about the baron, which had had such dire consequences for the Pedant, was Jarno's work. Since Jarno had laughed in Wilhelm's presence about the whole incident, our friend concluded that this was the sign of a thoroughly corrupt sensibility; for what could be more cruel than to make fun of an innocent man one had caused suffering to, instead of making amends or somehow repairing the damage. Wilhelm would gladly have done this himself, for, by a strange coincidence, he had tracked down the perpetrators of the nocturnal attack.

Up till now he had been kept unaware of the fact that several of the young officers had been spending whole nights in jollification with some of the actors and actresses in a lower room in the old part of the castle. One morning, having got up early as usual, he happened to enter this room and found the young gentlemen engaged in an unusual form of toilet. They had crumbled chalk into a dish of water, and were brushing the paste on to their vests and trousers, without taking them off, in order to clean them up as quickly as possible. Astonished at such activities our friend remembered the white powder and the stains on the Pedant's coat, and his suspicions increased when he learned that several of the baron's relations were amongst the company.

In order to check out his suspicions further he made sure the young gentlemen were supplied with breakfast. They were very lively and told some amusing stories. One of them in particular, who had been a recruiting officer for a time, was full of praise for his captain's guile and skill in outwitting all kinds of persons and persuading them to enlist. He described in detail how young persons from good families who had been carefully educated, were fooled by promises of excellent treatment, and he laughed heartily at those simpletons who were at the beginning so delighted at earning praise and privileges from some highly regarded, gallant, shrewd and openhanded officer.

Wilhelm blessed his guiding spirit for so unexpectedly showing him the abyss which he had approached so unwittingly! He now saw Jarno simply as a recruiting officer; the embrace of the unknown officer was easily explained. He detested the sentiments of these two men and from that moment on, avoided everyone wearing a uniform; and he would have been delighted by the news he received that the army was moving on, were it not for his fear that this would separate him, maybe forever, from the lovely countess.

Chapter Twelve

The baroness had spent several anxious days, tormented by worries and unsatisfied curiosity. For the count's behavior since that adventurous episode was a complete mystery to her. His whole manner had changed; there was no more of his usual joking. He made no such demands on his friends and servants as previously. There was no longer that characteristic pedantry and officiousness about him; he was quiet, wrapped up in himself, and yet serene—altogether a different person. For the readings that he sometimes instigated he selected serious, often religious books, and the baroness was in a constant state of anxiety that behind this seemingly placid exterior there lurked some secret grudge, some tacit intention to avenge the outrage he had so accidentally discovered. She therefore decided to confide in Jarno, which was easy for her because her relationship with him was of the kind which does not normally involve concealing things from each other. Jarno had recently become her lover, but they were clever enough to keep the world unaware of their inclinations and their pleasures. The countess was the only one to see this new romantic attachment, and the baroness's determination to get the countess involved in something similar was most probably caused by her eagerness to avoid the reproaches that she often had to endure from that noble soul.

When the baroness told the whole story to Jarno, he burst out laughing and said: "The old fellow must surely think that he saw himself, and that this apparition foretells misfortune, perhaps even death, for him. And so he has become tame like all half-men when they think of that dissolution which no one has escaped or can ever escape. But let us quietly work on him so that he will no longer be a burden to his wife and his guests."

So they began, as soon as it was appropriate, to talk in the count's presence about presentiments, apparitions and the like. Jarno played the skeptic, and the baroness took the same line; they pushed this so far that the count took Jarno aside and reproved him for his free thinking, using his own experience to try to convince him of the possibility and reality of such phenomena. Jarno acted as though he were astonished, first expressing his doubts, but finally pretending to be convinced; and then had a good laugh with his friend in the peace of the night at this feeble man-of-the-world, suddenly cured of his incivility by a bogyman but still admired for the equanimity with which he awaited impending disaster, perhaps even death.

"He won't however be prepared for the most natural result of that apparition," exclaimed the baroness with the high spirits to which she always returned once some worrisome thought had been dispelled. Jarno was richly

487

rewarded with her favors, and the two of them began plotting how to make the count even more tractable and to work on the countess's feelings for Wilhelm and intensify them.

With this purpose in mind, they told the countess the whole story. She was displeased at first, but then began to think more and more in her quiet moments about the scenario that was being organized for her, fleshing it out in detail.

The preparations undertaken on all sides soon made it clear that the army would indeed move on further and the prince change the location of his head-quarters. It was even reported that the count would leave his estate and return to town. Our actors could therefore cast their own horoscope; but only Melina acted in accordance with it, the others sought to snatch every possible enjoyment from the moment.

Meanwhile Wilhelm was occupied with a very special task. The countess had asked for a copy of his plays, and he regarded such a request from so charming a lady as the highest possible reward.

Any young author who has not yet seen himself in print, will devote the utmost care to producing a clean and well-written copy of his works. For that is, so to speak, the golden age of authorship. One feels transported back to an era when the printing press had not yet deluged the world with so many useless writings, and only works of real quality were copied and preserved by the noblest of individuals; as a result, it is all too easy for one to arrive at the false conclusion that a carefully copied manuscript is a great work of art, worthy of being owned and displayed by a connoisseur and patron.

A banquet was arranged in honor of the prince, who was soon to depart. Many ladies from the neighborhood had been invited, and the countess had dressed in good time for the occasion. She was wearing a more sumptuous gown than usual, her hair and headdress were more elaborate, and she was wearing all her jewels. The baroness too had done her utmost to be dressed in splendor and with taste.

Philine, when she noticed that time was hanging heavy on the ladies as they waited for the guests to arrive, suggested they should send for Wilhelm, who was anxious to deliver his manuscript and read them some parts of it. He came, and was astonished to see how much the graceful appearance of the countess was enhanced by all this finery. At the bidding of the ladies he read aloud to them, but so inattentively and poorly that, if his listeners had not been so indulgent, they would quickly have sent him away.

As soon as he saw the countess, it seemed as if an electric spark had flashed before his eyes, and he hardly knew how to find breath for his recitation. That beautiful woman had always been a pleasure to look at, but now he thought he had never seen anything so perfect, and his mind was invaded by a multitude of reflections, the sum total of which was roughly this: "How foolish of so many poets and sensitive persons to inveigh against finery and splendor and to demand instead that women of all classes should dress in simple, natural clothes. They rail against finery without considering that it is not the poor old finery we dislike when we see an ugly, or not very pretty person decked out in such odd splendor. But I would ask all men of taste whether they would really prefer to have any of these pleats removed, these ribbons and lace, these puffed sleeves, these curls, these glistening gems. Wouldn't they be afraid of spoiling the pleasing effect that emerges so readily and naturally to meet their gaze? Of course they would! For if Minerva rose fully armed from the head of Jupiter, this goddess seems to have emerged light-footed from some flower in all her finery."

He kept looking at her as he was reading, as if to retain this impression forever, and made several mistakes; but he was not put out by this, though he would usually have been in despair if a wrong word had marred his reading.

A curious noise, as if announcing the arrival of the guests, brought the performance to a close. The baroness left, and the countess, before closing her dressing table, took a box of rings and put several of them on her fingers. "We will soon be parting," she said, fixing her eyes on the box. "Take this to remind you of a good friend who wishes nothing more than that all may go well for you." She then took out a ring with a coat of arms woven of hair and studded with gems, all covered with crystal. She handed this to Wilhelm, who was at a loss what to say or do, so transfixed was he to the spot. The countess closed up her dressing table and seated herself on the sofa.

"And am I to go empty-handed?" said Philine, kneeling before the right hand of the countess. "Just look at that man who has plenty to say at the wrong time but now can't even stammer out his meager thanks. Come along, sir! At least act as though you are grateful, or if no words occur to you, then at least follow my example." She took the countess's right hand and kissed it warmly. Wilhelm fell on his knees, seized her left hand, and pressed it to his lips. The countess seemed embarrassed, but not displeased.

"Oh dear!" said Philine. "I have seen so much finery in my time but never a lady so worthy of wearing it. What bracelets! And what a hand! What a necklace! And what a bosom!"

"Be quiet, you flatterer," said the countess.

"Is that a picture of the count?" asked Philine, pointing to a splendid medallion on a fine chain that the countess was wearing at her side.

"Yes, it was painted at the time of our wedding," the countess replied.

"Was he so young at the time?" asked Philine. "I know you have only been married for a few years."

"His youthful appearance was the work of the artist," the countess replied.

"He is a handsome man," said Philine. "But," she went on, putting her hand on the countess's heart, "did no other image ever creep into this secret compartment?"

"You are very impertinent, Philine!" she exclaimed. "I have spoilt you. Don't ever let me hear anything of that kind again!"

"When you are angry, you make me unhappy," said Philine as she jumped up and ran out of the room.

Wilhelm continued to hold the lovely hand of the countess. His eyes were fixed on the clasp of the bracelet, and, to his great astonishment, he saw that his initials were there in diamonds.

"Do I really have some of your hair in this precious ring?" he timidly asked.

"Yes, indeed," she said in an undertone. Then she regained her composure, and, grasping his hand, she said: "Do get up! Farewell!"

But he, pointing to the clasp, said: "Here by some strange chance, are my initials!"

"How so?" said the countess. "They are those of a lady who is a good friend of mine."

"They are my initials," he said. "Do not forget me. Your image remains graven in my heart. Farewell; now let me leave!"

He kissed her hand and was about to stand up. But as in dreams we are surprised by strange things bringing forth even stranger things, it suddenly happened, without knowing how, he found himself grasping the countess in his arms, her lips touching his, and their blissful exchange of passionate kisses was like the sparkling draft from the freshly filled goblet of a first love.

Her head was resting on his shoulder, and she was totally unconcerned about her disarranged curls and ribbons. She had put her arm around him. He embraced her eagerly and time and time again pressed her to his bosom. If only such a moment could last forever! If only harsh fate had not broken up these few precious moments! Wilhelm was frightened and stunned when this happy dream was shattered by a scream from the countess, who suddenly withdrew her hand and clutched her heart.

Stupefied he stood there. She covered her eyes with her other hand and, after a moment's pause, cried: "Now leave! Leave quickly!"

He still stood there.

"Leave me," she cried, taking her hand away from her eyes; and looking at him with an indescribable expression in her eyes, she added, in a voice full of love: "Leave me, if you love me!"

Wilhelm left her room and was back in his own before he knew where he was.

Unhappy creatures! What strange warning of chance, or fate, had driven them apart?

BOOK FOUR

Chapter One

His head propped on his arm, Laertes was gazing pensively out of the window into the open fields. Philine came creeping through the great hall, leaned on her friend and mocked at his serious expression. "Don't laugh!" he said to her. "It is horrible how quickly time passes, how everything changes and comes to an end! Just look—a little while ago there was a whole encampment out there, splendid to look at, the tents full of life and merriment, the whole area carefully patrolled. And now, suddenly, it is all gone. The only sign that remains will soon be the trampled straw and the holes where they cooked. Then it will all be ploughed up, and the presence of so many thousands of valiant men in these parts will be nothing more than a ghostly remembrance in the minds of a few old people."

Philine began to sing and dragged her friend into the great hall to dance. "Since we can't pursue time that is passed," she said, "let us at least celebrate it joyfully and gracefully while it is passing us by."

They had danced only a few steps when Madame Melina came through the hall. Philine was wicked enough to invite her to join the dance, reminding her of her misshapen appearance because of the pregnancy. "If only," said Philine behind her back, "I did not have to see more expectant mothers!" "Well, she is at least expecting something," Laertes replied. "But it doesn't suit her," said Philine. "Haven't you noticed that wobbling pleat in the front of her shortened skirt which always parades in front of her when she moves? She doesn't have either the sense or the ability to take herself in hand and to conceal her state."

"Never mind," said Laertes. "Time will take care of that."

"But it would be nicer," said Philine, "if children could be shaken off trees."

In came the baron with some kind words from the count and countess, who had left very early, and brought them some presents. He then went to see Wilhelm, who was occupied with Mignon in the adjoining room. The child was friendly and helpful. She had inquired about his parents, his siblings and his other relations, thereby reminding him of his obligation to give them some news.

The baron delivered parting greetings from the count and countess, and assured him of the count's great satisfaction with him, his acting, his poetic productions and his efforts on behalf of their little theater. As a tangible sign of this appreciation he pulled out a purse, through the fine mesh of which the glitter of new gold coins attracted the eye. Wilhelm stepped back, and refused to accept it. But the baron went on to say: "Just consider this gift as a recompense for the time you have expended and a recognition of your hard work, rather than as a reward for your talent. If such talent earns us reputation and the affection of others, it is only reasonable that we should by our efforts and application also acquire the means to supply our ordinary needs, for none of us is all spirit. If we were in a town where anything could be bought, this sum might have been used to buy a watch, a ring, or some such thing. But I am putting a magic wand into your hands for you to conjure up something precious that is to your liking, something you can use, and retain in remembrance of us. Do respect this purse. The ladies knitted it themselves, with the idea that the receptacle should endow the contents with the most pleasing form."

"Forgive my embarrassment and hesitation at accepting this present," said Wilhelm. "But it seems to annihilate the little I did and restrict the free play of such happy memories. Money is a fine way of settling something. I would not wish this house to settle with me in this fashion."

"That is not the case," the baron replied. "But since you are so sensitive, you will surely not demand that the count should remain entirely in your debt; he is a man who sets great store on being attentive and just. It has not escaped him that you have exerted every effort and devoted all your time to the fulfilment of his intentions; he also knows that in order to speed up certain necessary arrangements you spent some of your own money. How can I face him again if I cannot assure him that his recognition has given you pleasure?"

"If I were just to think of myself and could follow my own inclinations," Wilhelm responded, "I would, despite all your reasoning, steadfastly refuse to accept this handsome gift. But I cannot deny that, although it makes me uneasy, it comes at a time when it will relieve me of some embarrassment I have felt toward my family. For I must give them an account of how I have been spending my time and money, and I have not managed either well. Now, thanks to the generosity of his Excellency the count, I will be able to have the consolation of telling my parents about the good fortune that my strange detour has led me into. So I will let the sense of a higher obligation overcome my squeamishness and those slight pangs of conscience which warn us in such eventualities as this. And in order to be able to look my father straight in the eyes, I lower mine shamefacedly before yours."

"It is really odd," the baron replied, "what strange compunction one has in accepting money from friends and benefactors when one would be grateful and delighted at any other gift from them. Human nature has many such peculiar tendencies to create scruples and systematically nourish them."

"Isn't it the same with all matters of honor?" asked Wilhelm.

"True," said the baron, "and also with prejudices. We hesitate to weed them out, lest we should at the same time tear out healthy plants. But I am always happy when some people realize what they can and should disregard. I am pleasantly reminded of the anecdote of an intelligent poet who wrote several plays for a court theater which were greatly appreciated by the monarch. 'I must give him a suitable reward,' the generous prince declared. 'See if there is any particular jewel that would give him pleasure, or a sum of money, if he will accept it.' The poet jokingly responded to the courtier who brought the message: 'I am deeply grateful for such a gracious thought, and since the Emperor takes money from us every day, I do not see why I should be ashamed of taking money from him.'"

No sooner had the baron left the room, when Wilhelm eagerly counted the sum which had so unexpectedly and, as he thought, undeservedly, come to him. For the first time he seemed to have a sense of the value and worth of money (such as we usually acquire only later) as the gleaming pieces came rolling out of the delicately wrought purse. He made a tally and discovered that, mindful of the fact that Melina had promised to repay the advance forthwith, he had as much, or even more, than on the day he bought Philine that first bouquet. With secret satisfaction he thought of his talent, and with a certain pride he reflected on the good fortune that had directed and stayed with him. Confidently he now took up his pen to write to his family to relieve them of all anxiety by depicting his recent behavior in the best of lights. He avoided giving a factual account. Instead he merely hinted, in significant and mystical terms, at what it was that might have happened to him. The favorable state of his finances, the gains that his talents had brought him, the favor of persons of high station, the affections of women, his wide circle of acquaintances, the development of his bodily and mental powers, and his hopes for the future, all this built such a fantastic castle in the air, that not even a fata morgana could have produced a stranger combination.

Such was his mood of exaltation that, when he had finished his letter, he engaged in an extensive monologue, recapitulating the contents of the letter and picturing for himself an active and distinguished future. The example of so many noble warriors had excited him, Shakespeare's plays had opened up a whole new world, and from the lips of the beauteous countess he had drawn a fire that he found it hard to describe. This surely could not, should not, remain without some effect on him.

The stablemaster came in and asked if they were finished packing. "Unfortunately," said Melina, "nobody has thought about that yet." So now they had to get going quickly. The count had promised to provide transportation during the next few days for the whole company: the horses were all ready and could not be done without for long. Wilhelm asked where his trunk was, and discovered that Madame Melina had already taken it for herself; he asked where his money was, only to learn that Melina had carefully packed it at the very bottom of the trunk. Philine told him she still had space in hers, took possession of Wilhelm's clothes, and told Mignon to get everything else. Wilhelm, though somewhat unwilling, let this be done for him.

When everything was packed up and ready, Melina said: "It irritates me that we have to travel like circus folk and mountebanks. I wish that Mignon would put on women's clothes and the Harper have his beard cut." Mignon clung to Wilhelm and said passionately: "I am a boy, I don't want to be a girl." The old man remained silent, and Philine used the occasion to make some funny remarks about the quirks of their patron, the count. "If the Harper does cut his beard," she said, "he should sew it on to a ribbon and keep it, so that he could put it on if he were to meet the count somewhere; that beard was the sole reason for the count's generosity toward him." When they pressed her for an explanation of this strange remark, she told them the following: the count believed that it was a great aid to illusion if an actor continued to play his role and sustain his fictive character into real life, which was why he had so favored the Pedant, and thought it was very sensible of the Harper to wear his false beard not only on the stage but also during the day. He was pleased to see that the disguise looked so natural.

While all the others were making fun of the count's mistake and his strange opinions, the Harper drew Wilhelm aside, took leave of him, and implored him, with tears in his eyes, to let him go at once. Wilhelm assured him that he would protect him against anyone, that no one should be allowed to harm a hair of his head, let alone cut any of it off without his consent.

The old man was very moved by this, and there was a strange fiery glow in his eyes. "That is not what is driving me away," he cried. "I have long reproached myself for remaining with you. I must never stay anywhere, for misfortune pursues me and will harm those who associate with me. You have everything to fear if you do not let me go; but don't ask me why. I do not belong to myself. I cannot stay."

"To whom do you belong? Who can wield such power over you?"

"Sir, let me keep my horrible secret to myself. Give me leave to go! The vengeance that pursues me is not that of any earthly judge. I am caught up in inexorable fate. I cannot remain here, for I dare not."

"I will certainly not abandon you in this state of mind," said Wilhelm.

"It would be high treason against you, my benefactor, if I were to linger here. I feel safe with you, but you are in danger. You don't know whom you are harboring. I am guilty, and even more unhappy than guilty. My very presence dispels happiness, and when I appear every good deed is robbed of its force. I should always be in flight, never at rest, so that my evil genius may not catch up with me; for it is always after me and does not make its presence felt until I lay down my head to rest. I cannot better express my thanks to you than by leaving you."

"What a strange man you are! You can no more shake my trust in you than you can deprive me of the hope of seeing you happy. I do not want to pry into the mysteries of your superstitiousness, but if you believe that your life is entangled in strange associations and premonitions, then I would say to you, for your consolation and enlivement: Associate yourself with my own good fortune, and let us see whose genius is the stronger, your dark spirit or my bright one."

Wilhelm took the opportunity to offer him more words of consolation; for he had believed for some time now that his strange companion was someone who had, through chance or fate, incurred some great guilt and was continually oppressed by the memory of it. Just a few days previously, Wilhelm had heard him singing, and noted these peculiar lines:

> For him the light of morning sun
> With flames the clear horizon paints,
> And round his guilty head there breaks
> The beauteous image of the whole wide world.

Whatever else the old man chose to say, Wilhelm always had a stronger counterargument. He knew how to give everything a positive turn, he knew how to speak honestly, sincerely and sympathetically, and as a result the old man seemed to brighten up again and abandon his melancholy thoughts.

Chapter Two

Melina hoped to find quarters for his company in some small but prosperous town. They had reached the place where the count's horses had brought them, and were looking around for carriages and horses to convey them further. Melina had taken charge of the transportation arrangements, and proved to be as niggardly as ever. Wilhelm, on the other hand, the lovely ducats from the countess still in his pocket, thought he had every right to spend them in a pleasant way, forgetting all too readily that he had proudly included them in the sum which he had so volubly told the baron he was sending to his parents.

His good friend Shakespeare, whom he very much liked to consider his godfather (after all, he too was named William) had acquainted him with a certain Prince Hal who had spent some time with base and dissolute companions and, despite his noble character, taken great pleasure in the rough, unseemly and foolish behavior of his earthy associates. He welcomed this as an ideal against which to measure his present state; this made it much easier for him to indulge in a self-deception that had an almost irresistible appeal.

He began to think about his clothes. A vest which could have a short cloak thrown over it, was a most appropriate garb for a traveler. Long knitted trousers and laced-up boots seemed to be just right for someone on foot. He acquired a splendid silk sash which he put on under the pretext of keeping his body warm, but he freed his neck from the restrictions of a tie, and had some pieces of muslin fastened to his shirt which became rather wide and gave the effect of an old-fashioned collar. The silk scarf, his one memento of Mariane, was loosely attached to the inside of his muslin ruff. A round hat with a brightly colored ribbon and a big feather completed the disguise.

The women assured him that the costume suited him perfectly. Philine seemed quite enchanted by it, and asked for some of his beautiful hair which he had lopped off to come closer to his Shakespearian ideal. She did this in a most agreeable way, and Wilhelm felt that, by acceding to her request, he was justified in behaving like Prince Hal. So he began to take delight in performing some merry pranks and encouraging the others to do likewise. They fenced and danced, thought up all sorts of pastimes, and washed down their high spirits with copious drafts of a tolerable wine they had discovered. In the midst of all this disorderly activity, Philine set her sights on our prim and proper hero. Let us hope that his guardian angel may look out for him.

One excellent form of entertainment which gave the company special pleasure, was the extemporization of a play in which they imitated and ridiculed
their former patrons and benefactors. Some of them had well noted the characteristics of public politeness in persons of such high station, and their imitations were received with great acclaim by the rest of the group; when Philine
produced from her secret archive some declarations of love that had been addressed to her, there was a general outburst of malicious laughter.

Wilhelm reproved them for their lack of gratitude. But they countered
this by saying that they had worked hard for what they had received, and that
the treatment of such worthy people as they believed themselves to be, had
not been of the best. They complained about how little respect had been paid
them, and how they had been put down. The mockery, teasing and mimicry
started up again with everyone getting more bitter and more unjust.

Wilhelm reacted to this by replying: "I wish what you are saying were not
so clearly the reflection of your own envy and egotism, and that you could
judge the life of those people from the proper perspective. Being placed by
birth and inheritance in a high position in society, is a matter of some consequence. If one's existence has been made easy by inherited wealth and one
has been surrounded from one's youth by what I might call the appurtenances
of humanity—and that in plenty—such a person is accustomed to consider
these possessions as the ne plus ultra and is not so able to perceive the value
of what nature has given to less fortunate beings. The behavior of persons of
high station towards those of lesser station—but also amongst themselves—is
determined by external signs of distinction: they will acknowledge anyone's
title, rank, clothes and retinue but not so readily his natural merits."

The company strongly seconded his words. They thought it was horrible
that a person of merit should be obliged to stand back, and that there was no
sign of any spontaneous, sincere relationships in the world of the great. This
last point they discussed in considerable detail.

"Don't blame them for that," said Wilhelm. "Rather be sorry for them.
They rarely have a sense of the joys that are the reward of those inborn riches
which we consider most important. We who are poor in material possessions
are rich in the pleasures of friendship—and only we. We are not able to enrich
our loved ones by gracious favors, or advance them by privileged attention, or
shower them with gifts. We have nothing but ourselves to give. We must give
all of ourselves, and, if such a gift is to have value, we must assure our friends
of its lasting nature. What a joy it is, and what happiness to provide for both
the giver and the receiver! Devotion and loyalty impart a happy and lasting
permanence to what might otherwise be merely passing. These are the richest
possessions we have."

While he was saying all this, Mignon had crept up and put her slender arms
around him, leaning her head against his breast. He placed his hand on her
head, and went on to say: "How easy it is for a noble personage to win men's

496

hearts and minds! A pleasant, relaxed, and only moderately humane behavior achieves miracles, and once a mind is captured, he has plenty of ways to maintain his hold over it. But for us, this is more difficult and not so easy to come by, which means that it is natural for us to put greater value on what we acquire and achieve. How touching is the devotion of some servants to their masters! How splendidly Shakespeare portrayed that! In such cases, loyalty and devotion are the expression of a noble soul striving to equal someone of higher station. By attachment and love, a servant becomes the equal of his master who is otherwise justified in considering him a paid slave. These virtues are only for those of lower station; they are germane to them, and become them well. If one can easily purchase one's freedom, one is easily tempted to cease recognizing what one owes to others. I believe it would be true to say that a person of station can *have* friends, but not *be* a friend."

Mignon pressed closer and closer to him.

"All right," said someone of the company. "We don't need their friendship, and we never asked for it. But they should have shown more understanding for the arts that they claimed to support. When we were playing at our best, no one listened. They were always taking sides; that's what really decided things. An actor, who was favored, always got the applause, and others did not receive the approbation they deserved, because they were not in someone's good graces. It was absurd how often mere stupidity and absurdity captured their attention and applause.

"When I think about all their malice and irony, I believe it's much the same with art as with love. How can a man of the world, with his manifold activities, preserve that concentration which the artist must have if he is to produce a perfect work of art, and which those must have who become involved in it in the way the artist himself would wish and hope for. Believe me, my friends, talents are like virtues; one must love them for their own sake, or give them up entirely. They are recognized and rewarded only if one exercises them in private, like some dread secret."

"Meanwhile, until some perceptive person discovers us, we can die of starvation," a man in the corner cried out.

"But not immediately," said Wilhelm. "So long as one can live and move, one always finds some nourishment, though it may not be of the best. But what have you got to complain about? Weren't we, just when things looked worst for us, unexpectedly taken care of and well provided for? And now, while we're still in good shape, why don't we think of some way of continuing to practice our skills and improve ourselves? We are doing all sorts of other things and, like schoolchildren, pushing everything aside that might remind us of the work we have to do."

"I agree," said Philine. "This is totally irresponsible. Let's choose a play and perform it on the spot. Everyone must do his very best, as if we were performing before a huge audience."

It did not take them long to decide on the play. It was one of those that were very popular in Germany at the time but are now quite forgotten. Some of the actors whistled an overture and each thought about his role in the play. They began, and continued to act out the play right through to the end and with great attention. Everything turned out surprisingly well. They applauded each other, and had an excellent time.

When they were finished, they were all uncommonly satisfied, their time had been well spent, and each of them was especially pleased with his own performance. Wilhelm was expansive in his praise and their own conversation was lively and cheerful.

"You should see," said Wilhelm, "how much we will improve by such exercises and not restricting ourselves to mere memorizing, rehearsing and mechanical repetition. Musicians are to be commended for practicing in groups, for thereby they acquire not only pleasure but also greater precision, attuning their instruments to each other, preserving the right tempo, and modulating the dynamics. No one thinks of gaining praise by too loud an accompaniment to another's solo; everyone tries to play in the composer's spirit, and to perform well what the composer has given him to play, be it much or little. Should we not work just as precisely and intelligently, after all, we are concerned with an art much more subtle than music: we are called on to represent pleasingly and with taste the most ordinary as well as extraordinary utterances of human beings? Can there be anything more abominable than being sloppy at rehearsals and relying on a lucky break in the performance? We should take great pains to concentrate our efforts on pleasing each other, and value the approval of the public only if we have already applauded ourselves for what we are doing. Why is the conductor of an orchestra more certain of himself than the director of a play? Because in an orchestra anyone who makes a mistake is so audible that he must needs be ashamed, but I have rarely encountered an actor whose mistakes, whether forgivable or unforgivable, so offend him that he acknowledges them and is ashamed of them! I only wish the theater were as narrow as a tightrope so that no one without the necessary skill would venture onto it; nowadays everyone thinks he can readily strut on the boards."

This speech was well received, for everyone was convinced that he was not its target, since he had just done as well as the others. They agreed to work together as a group, on this particular journey as well as in the future. Since this was a matter of the right mood and free choice, they resolved that no director should interfere in what must be their own decision. They considered it a foregone conclusion that a republican administration would be the most suitable for good people like themselves, and insisted that the office of director should rotate amongst them. The director should be elected by the whole company, and he should be assisted by a kind of small senate. They were so taken with this idea, that they wanted to put it into practice immediately.

"I have nothing against such an experiment on this journey," said Melina, "and I will gladly give up my directorship until we are again settled in some place." He hoped thereby to save money, and have the republic and its interim director take over some of the expenses. They deliberated how best to organize this new form of government.

"It's a migratory empire," said Laertes, "at least we won't have any border disputes."

They got down to business right away, and elected Wilhelm as their first director. The senate was established, the women had seats and votes, and laws were proposed, rejected and approved. Time passed by without their noticing it while they were engaged in this sport, and because it passed so pleasantly, they thought they had achieved something really useful which through this new form of government opened up new vistas for the national stage.

Chapter Three

Since the company was now in such a good mood, Wilhelm hoped to be able to talk to them about the poetic merits of the plays. "It is not enough," he said when they met again next day, "for an actor to look casually at a play, to judge it merely from first impressions and express approval or disapproval without due study. That may be appropriate for the spectator who merely wants to be moved or entertained but is not really concerned with passing judgment. An actor, on the other hand, must be able to account for his praise or disapproval of a play. And how is he to do that if he does not penetrate to the author's mind and intentions? I have observed in myself these last days the mistake of judging a play from one particular role without considering it in relationship to the others. I felt this so vividly that I would like to tell you about this particular example, if you would lend me willing ears.

"You are acquainted with Shakespeare's marvelous *Hamlet* from a reading of it that gave you such pleasure at the count's castle. We made the decision to perform it and, without knowing what I was doing, I agreed to play the part of the prince. I thought I was studying the role properly, and began by memorizing the most powerful passages—the soliloquies and those scenes which give free play to strength of soul, to elevation of spirit, and intensity, where Hamlet's troubled mind expresses itself with strong emotion. I also believed that I was really getting into the spirit of the part by somehow myself assuming the weight of his profound melancholy and, beneath this burden, following my model through the strange labyrinth of so many different moods and peculiar experiences. I learnt the part and tried it out, feeling that I was becoming more and more identified with my hero.

"But the further I progressed in this, the more difficult it became for me to perceive the structure of the whole, and finally I found it almost impossible to acquire an overview. So I went right through the play from beginning to end without skipping, and found that several things didn't fit together in my mind. At times the characters seemed to contradict each other, at times their speeches, and I well-nigh despaired of finding the right tone in which to act out the role as a whole with all its different nuances and deviations. I battled my way through this thicket for a long time without seeing a way out, until I finally found one particular path by which I thought I could reach my goal.

"I searched for any clues of Hamlet's character previous to the death of his father. I observed what this interesting young man had been like without reference to that sad event and its terrible consequences, and considered what he might have become without them.

"This sensitive, noble scion, this flower of kingship, grew up under the immediate influences of majesty; concepts of right and of princely dignity, the sense of what is good and what is seemly, developed in him simultaneously with an awareness of being born into high station. He was a prince, he was born a prince, and he was desirous of ruling so that good men should be unimpeded in the exercise of goodness. Winsome in appearance, courteous by nature, pleasing by temperament, he was fashioned to be a model for youth and a delight for everybody.

"Without being strikingly passionate, his love for Ophelia represented a gentle premonition of tender needs. His ardor for knightly activities was not entirely of his own making, for this desire had been sharpened and increased by the praise expended on another person. He had a clear sense of honesty in others and treasured the peace accorded to a sincere heart by the affection of a friend. To some extent he had learnt to respect and cherish what is good and beautiful in art and learning. He disliked anything that had no substance or taste, and when he developed real hatred it was only so that he could express his contempt for shifty, deceitful courtiers and have his mocking sport with them. He was by temperament detached, straightforward in behavior, and neither comfortable with idleness nor too desirous for activity. At court he continued his academic sauntering. His moods were more joyous than his heart, he was a good companion, forbearing, unassuming, and concerned. He could forgive and forget an insult, but he would never accept anyone who overstepped the bounds of what is good, right and proper.

"When we shall have read the play again, you will be able to judge if I am on the right track. At least I shall hope to be able to support my opinions by passages in the text."

His presentation received hearty approval; they all thought they could now understand how the actions of Hamlet might be explained. They were delighted to feel that they had really entered the mind of the author. Each of them decided to study some play or other in this way, and discover the author's meaning.

Chapter Four

They only stayed a few days in this place; nevertheless various members of the company became involved in adventures that were far from unpleasant. In particular Laertes, who was attracted by a lady with an estate in the neighborhood, but treated her so coldly and rudely that he had to suffer many a taunt from Philine. She took the occasion to tell Wilhelm about the unfortunate love affair that had turned this poor young man into an enemy of the whole female sex. "Who can blame him," she said, "for hating a sex which treated him so badly and made him imbibe in one concentrated draft all the evils that men have to fear from women? Just imagine: within the space of one day he was lover, fiancé, husband, cuckold, patient and widower! I don't know how he could have fared worse."

Laertes ran from the room, half laughing and half irritated. Then Philine began in her most endearing way to tell how, as a young man of eighteen, Laertes had just joined a company of actors when he met a beautiful girl of fourteen. She was about to leave with her father, who had had some disagreement with the director. Laertes instantly fell head over heels in love with her and used every persuasion to induce her father to stay. Finally he promised to marry the girl. After a few pleasant hours of courtship he was married, spent one happy night as a husband, but while he was at a rehearsal next day, was cuckolded in accordance with his station. Having rushed home much too early in an access of loving desire, he found to his dismay a previous lover in his place, set about him in a fit of uncontrolled rage, challenged both the lover and the girl's father, and received in the process a considerable wound. Father and daughter took themselves off during the night, and Laertes remained behind, doubly wounded. For his misfortune brought him into the hands of the worst surgeon in the world, and the poor chap emerged with black teeth and dripping eyes. He is to be pitied, for he is really the best fellow on earth. What grieves me most, is that the poor fool now hates all women: and how can you live if you hate women?"

Melina interrupted them to report that everything was ready to go, and that they could leave next morning. He produced a plan of how they should arrange themselves for the journey.

"If a good friend takes me on his lap," said Philine, "I am quite satisfied with our miserably cramped position and indifferent to everything else."

"I don't care," said Laertes who had come back and joined them.

"I find it tiresome," said Wilhelm and hurried off to secure, with his own money, another fairly comfortable carriage which Melina had refused to provide. A different seating arrangement was worked out, everybody was feeling happy at being able to travel in comfort, when the ominous news arrived that a gang of partisan soldiers had been spotted on the route they were about to take, and no good was to be expected from them.

In the town great attention was paid to this news, even though it was hazy and uncertain. Given the positions of the opposing armies, it seemed impossible that an enemy detachment could have crept through or that friendly troops stayed back so far. But the townsfolk vividly described the dangers attending the actors, and urged them to take another route. Most of the company became uneasy and fearful, and in accordance with their new republican constitution all of them were then assembled to discuss this extraordinary turn of events. They were almost unanimously of the opinion that they should avoid a calamity either by remaining where they were, or by taking another route. But Wilhelm, who did not share their fears, insisted that it would be disgraceful to abandon a plan they had arrived at after much consideration, simply because of a mere rumor. He urged them to take courage, and his reasoning was manly and convincing.

"This is still only a rumor," he said, "common enough in wartime. Sensible people say that this eventuality is highly unlikely and perhaps impossible. Should we therefore allow ourselves to be swayed in such an important matter by such vague talk? The route the count proposed is the one that our papers are made out for. It is the shortest route, and the best road. It leads us to the town where you have friends and acquaintances and can expect to be treated well. The detour would get us there too; but it will take us a long way out of our course and on sideroads in heaven knows what condition! How can we hope, at this late season, to find our way back on to the direct route—and just think of the time and money we will have wasted in the meantime!" He said a lot more, and pointed out so many advantages, that their fears were diminished and their courage increased. He was able to tell them so much about the discipline of the regular troops, and paint such a lamentable picture of the marauders and accrued rabble, even presenting the danger so amusingly and attractively that their spirits were all fired up.

Laertes was from the start on Wilhelm's side, and swore that he would not flinch or yield. The old Blusterer expressed similar sentiments in his own way, Philine laughed at the whole crew, and when Madame Melina, showing her usual spirit despite her advanced pregnancy, declared that the whole thing was heroic, her husband, hoping to save a packet by taking the shorter route, expressed no objections, and the proposal was heartily approved.

They then began to make preparations to defend themselves, should that prove to be necessary. They bought large bowie knives and slung them across their shoulders. Wilhelm supplemented these by two pistols which he stuck in his belt, and Laertes brought a good musket. So they set out in a state of high exaltation.

On the second day the drivers, who were well acquainted with the district, proposed that they should stop at midday on a wooded hilltop because the village was quite a way off and on such fine days this was what most people did. The weather was indeed beautiful, and everyone soon agreed to this. Wilhelm went ahead on foot through the hills, and everyone he encountered was amazed by his strange appearance. He surged ahead through the forest, happy and contented, with Laertes, whistling, behind him; only the women stayed in the carriages. Mignon ran alongside, proud of her bowie knife, which no one could refuse her when, after all, the whole company was arming itself. Around her hat she had put the beads which Wilhelm still kept as a memento of Mariane. The blond Friedrich carried Laertes's musket. The Harper displayed an expression of perfect peace. His long garment was hitched up into his belt so that he could walk more freely, and he was supporting himself on a knobby staff, his instrument having been left behind in the carriage.

With some difficulty they finally reached the top of the hill, recognized the place from the beautiful stand of beech trees that surrounded and shaded it. A large and inviting forest glade sloped down from it gently and made this a pleasant place to rest. A running brook would quench their thirst, and off to the other side they had a marvelous view across ravines and ridges of trees into a distance full of hope and expectancy. Villages and mills could be seen in the valleys, towns in the plain, and more hills in the far distance. This made the prospect all the more promising because those hills constituted only a minor obstacle in their path.

The first persons who arrived took possession of the area, lay down in the shade, started to build a fire, and waited for the others who came up one after the other and, with one voice, admired the lovely weather, this beautiful spot, and the splendid surroundings.

Chapter Five

Although they had spent many happy hours together indoors, they were all much more alive and alert when their minds were refreshed by the wide-open sky and the beauty of the landscape. Here they felt closer to each other and would have liked to spend their whole lives in such a delightful place. They envied the hunters, the charcoal burners and the woodsmen—all by their occupations tied to such agreeable locations. Most of all they envied the blissful indolence of gypsies reveling in the manifold delights of nature. Indeed they were happy in the feeling that they had a certain kinship with such odd creatures.

By now the women were starting to boil potatoes, and to unpack and start cooking the food they had brought with them. Pots were put around the fire, and the whole company arranged itself beneath the trees and bushes. Their curious garments and their various weapons gave them an exotic appearance. The horses were led off to one side and fed, and if only the coaches could somehow have been concealed from view, our little group would have made a deceptively romantic impression.

Wilhelm was in a state of unusual delight, seeing himself as the leader of a nomadic tribe, and, with this in mind, talking to each and every one and building up this illusion of the moment into a thing of color and poetry. Feelings rose: they ate and drank, and joyfully declared again and again that they had never in their life experienced such a delightful time.

As the enjoyment increased, a desire for activity grew. Wilhelm and Laertes took up their rapiers and this time began to practice with a theatrical end in view. They wanted to perform the duel in which Hamlet and his opponent come to such a tragic end. Both of them were convinced that, in this important scene, one shouldn't just lunge back and forth clumsily, as happens in most theaters; they were hoping to provide a model of how one could make this scene into a spectacle that any knowledgeable fencer would respect. Everyone gathered round. They both fought with vigor and intelligence, and the interest of the spectators increased at every bout.

Suddenly a shot landed in a nearby bush, and before long there was another. The group dispersed in fright. Soon they noticed armed men advancing toward the place near the loaded coaches where the horses were being fed.

The women burst into a cry of alarm, and our two heroes threw down their foils, seized their pistols and rushed at the attackers, demanding an explanation of what was going on, and accompanying this by violent threats. When these were answered laconically by several musket shots, Wilhelm fired his pistol at a curlyhead who had climbed up on the carriage and was cutting the ropes around the luggage. It was a good shot and the fellow fell off immediately. Laertes had been similarly successful, and the two men, encouraged by this, were taking to their sidearms when part of the attacking force descended on them with curses and bellowings, fired a few shots, and came at them with glittering sabres. Our two heroes fought valiantly, and called on the others to prepare for a general defense. But soon after this Wilhelm lost all sight and consciousness of what was happening. Stunned by a shot that hit him between his chest and his left arm, and by a sabre-thrust that split his hat and almost penetrated his skull, he fell down and later had to learn the unfortunate end of this encounter from someone else.

When he came to, he found himself in the strangest position. The first thing he dimly perceived, was Philine's face bent over his. He felt weak, and when he tried to get up, he found he was lying in Philine's lap, and sank back again. She was sitting on the grass, gently nestling the head of the prostrate youth, giving him in her arms as soft a bed as she could. Mignon was kneeling at his feet, fondling them and weeping over them, her hair tousled and soaked in blood.

When Wilhelm saw the blood on his own clothes he feebly asked where he was and what had happened to him and the others. Philine urged him not to exert himself: all the others were safe, she said, only he and Laertes were wounded. She did not want to say any more, and implored him to keep still because his wounds had been bandaged in great haste and not very well. He stretched out his hand to Mignon and inquired why there was blood on her hair: he feared that she too had been wounded.

To put his mind at rest, Philine told him that this good-hearted creature, on seeing her friend wounded, could not think of any other way, in the heat of the moment, to staunch the blood than by stopping the wound with her hair, though she soon realized the futility of this, and gave up. After that they bound up his wounds with sponges and moss; Philine had contributed her scarf.

Wilhelm noticed that she was leaning with her back against her trunk which appeared to be locked and quite undamaged. He asked whether the others had been as lucky in preserving their possessions. With a shrug of her shoulders, she pointed to the adjoining meadow, which was littered with broken boxes, smashed trunks, slashed knapsacks and every kind of small utensil. No one was to be seen. The strange little group was all alone.

Wilhelm soon found out more of what he wanted to know. The other men, who certainly could have offered some resistance, were soon so overwhelmed by fright, that they were easily overcome. Some of them had fled, others just looked in horror at what was happening. The drivers of the carriages, who, because of their horses, fought the most vigorously of all were nevertheless overpowered and tied up, and in a very short while everything was ransacked and the loot taken away. Our terrified travelers, once they no longer feared for their lives, began to lament their losses, and hastened as quickly as possible to the neighboring village, taking Laertes with them, who was only slightly wounded, as well as the slender remains of their possessions. The Harper had left his damaged instrument leaning against a tree, and gone with them to find a surgeon to care for his benefactor, who had been left there for dead.

Chapter Six

Our three unfortunate adventurers remained for a while in this strange situation, for no one came to their aid. Evening came and night was threatening to close in on them at any moment. Philine's calm began to change into agitation; Mignon kept running up and down, her impatience increasing with every moment. Finally their hopes were fulfilled and people were heard approaching. But they were assailed by new fears; they quite distinctly heard horses coming up the path they had arrived by, and were afraid that some new party of uninvited guests was about to return to the battlefield for extra pickings. But they were pleasantly surprised when out of the bushes came a lady mounted on a white horse, accompanied by an oldish man and several young gentlemen, with servants and attendants, and a troupe of hussars to follow.

Philine stared at this sight, and was about to call out to the lovely Amazon for help, when the lady herself turned her eyes in astonishment toward this strange group of three people, and rode up to them. She showed great concern for the wounded man, whose position in the lap of this light-hearted samaritan, seemed to her extremely peculiar.

"Is he your husband?" she asked Philine. "No, just a good friend," Philine replied in a tone of voice that was extremely distasteful to Wilhelm. His eyes were fixed on the gentle, distinguished, calm and compassionate features of the newcomer: he thought he had never seen anything more beautiful or noble. Her figure was concealed beneath a man's loose overcoat which she seemed to have borrowed from one of the attendants as a protection against the cool night air.

The horsemen had meantime also drawn nearer. Some of them dismounted, and so did the lady who inquired most compassionately about the circumstances of the accident, and more particularly about the wounds of the prostrate youth. She then turned quickly around, and went off to the side, back to the carriages that had slowly come up the hill and now arrived at the battleground.

She stood by the door of one of the coaches, talking for a while with those who had just reached the top; a rather thick-set man stepped out and was led by her to our wounded warrior. From the box that he held in his hand and a leather case with instruments that he was carrying, it was clear that he was a surgeon. His manner was brusque rather than ingratiating, but his hand was skilled and his assistance welcome. He examined Wilhelm carefully and declared that none of his wounds was serious, that he would dress them, and then they could take him to the next village.

The lady's anxiety seemed to be increasing. "Just look," she said, having walked up and down a few times, and fetched the old man again, "Look what they have done to him, and this all on our account!" Wilhelm listened to what she said, but without understanding it. She kept pacing up and down, as though she were unable to tear herself away from the sight of the wounded man, and yet afraid of offending against decorum by staying while they began to undress him. The surgeon had just cut open Wilhelm's left sleeve when the old man came up to her and, in a serious tone of voice, insisted that they continue their journey. Wilhelm had his eyes fixed on hers and was so taken with their expression that he hardly felt what was being done to him.

Philine rose to kiss the lady's hand. As the two of them stood side by side, Wilhelm thought he had never seen such a difference. Philine had never appeared to him in so unfavorable a light. She should not even approach such a noble creature—so it seemed to him—let alone touch her. The lady asked Philine various things, but in a low tone of voice. Then she turned to the old gentleman, who was still standing by unmoved, and said: "Dear Uncle, may I be generous on your account?" With that she took off the greatcoat, with the clear intention of covering the wounded and undressed man.

Wilhelm, captivated till then by the healing power of her glance, was now, once the greatcoat was off, amazed at the beauty of her figure. She came up and gently put the coat over him. When he opened his mouth to murmur some words of thanks, the vivid impression of her presence had the strangest effect on his impaired senses. Her head seemed to be surrounded by shafts of light and there was a glow spreading across her whole appearance. The surgeon was at that moment treating him rather less gently, he was about to extract the bullet that was still lodged in the wound. So the saint disappeared from his fainting sight: he lost all consciousness, and when he came to again, the horsemen and carriages, the beauteous lady and her attendants had all vanished into thin air.

Chapter Seven

When Wilhelm's wounds had been attended to and his clothes put back on, the surgeon left just as the Harper returned with several of the countryfolk. They made a stretcher out of twigs and branches, carefully laid the wounded man on it, and carried him slowly down the hill under the direction of a cavalier on horseback whom the lady had left behind to be with them. The Harper, pensive and silent, carried his damaged instrument, others dragged down Philine's trunk, she herself sauntering after them with a bundle in her hands, Mignon running ahead or into the bushes, gazing back longingly at her sick protector.

He lay quiet on his bier, wrapped in the warm overcoat. Electric warmth seemed to be penetrating his body from the fine wool, and he felt transported into a state of extreme comfort. The beautiful owner of that garment had made a strong impression on him. He could still see the coat slipping from her shoulders, her noble form surrounded by shafts of light; and his spirit rushed through forests and crags in pursuit.

It was not until nightfall that the little procession reached the village and stopped in front of the inn where the rest of the company were staying, desperately lamenting their irreplaceable losses. The only parlor in the hostelry was jammed with people, some were lying on the straw, some spread over the benches, some squeezed behind the stove, and Madame Melina in a neighboring room awaiting her delivery, which had been brought on rather earlier than expected because of that frightening occurrence. As a result she was being assisted by the hostess of the inn, an inexperienced young woman from whom not much good was to be expected.

When the new arrivals demanded to be let in, there was general complaining. They said that it was solely on Wilhelm's advice and under his direction that they had chosen to take this dangerous route and exposed themselves to this misfortune, the consequences of which were entirely his fault. They prevented his being let in and told him to find accommodation elsewhere. Philine they treated still more shabbily; and even the Harper and Mignon had to suffer their part. But the cavalier assigned by the fine lady to look after these three unfortunate creatures soon lost all patience, cursed and swore at the whole lot of them, and ordered them to close up and make room for the new arrivals. At this they began to be more accommodating. He made a place for Wilhelm on one of the tables which he pushed into a corner. Philine had her trunk put down beside him, and firmly sat down on it. Everybody squeezed up as much as they could; and the cavalier went off to see if he could not find better quarters for the "married couple."

Anger and reproaches broke out again as soon as he left. Everyone reckoned up, and exaggerated, his losses. They objected to the foolhardiness which had cost them so dearly, and did not conceal their gleeful satisfaction at our friend's being wounded. They vented their scorn on Philine, claiming that the way she had prevented any damage being done to her trunk was absolutely criminal. From various gibes and personal remarks it was clear that, during the looting, she had worked her way into the good graces of the leader of the band of marauders and persuaded him by her craftiness or the bestowal of some favors, to let her have her trunk back. For a while she seemed to have been missing. She did not reply to these allegations, but sat clicking the heavy locks of her trunk to assure her enemies that it was still there and to make them even more furious at her good fortune.

Chapter Eight

Wilhelm, though weak from loss of so much blood and calm and peaceful since the appearance of his angel of mercy, could not fail to be irritated by the harsh and unjust words that these disgruntled people kept repeating while he maintained silence. Eventually, however, he felt strong enough to rise and reproach them for the ill-mannered way in which they were causing anxiety to their friend and leader. He lifted his bandaged head, and supporting himself by leaning against the wall, he said:

"I can forgive your insulting me, when you should be sorry for me, and opposing and rejecting me the first time that I might expect your assistance—I can forgive that as the painful result of the losses you have suffered. Up till now I have felt sufficiently rewarded for the service I have done you and the kindness I have shown you, by your friendly behavior toward me. Don't mislead me, don't force me to go back in my mind and add up all I have done for you, for any such reckoning could only cause me pain. Chance led me to you, circumstance and inclination have kept me with you. I have shared your work and shared your pleasures. What little knowledge I had, was placed at your service. If you now cast bitter reproaches on me as being responsible for the misfortune that has befallen us, you are forgetting that it was not one of us who first proposed we should take this route, and that you all discussed this and gave your approval, as I myself did. If our journey had turned out well, you would all have been proud at having proposed that we take this route in preference to any other, and remembered our discussion, and the vote we took. But now you put the whole blame, the entire responsibility, on me, and this I cannot accept because my conscience is clear and you were as much involved as I was. If you have anything to say, then speak out, and I will defend myself. If you have nothing to accuse me of, hold your peace, and stop tormenting me just when I need all the rest I can get."

The reaction of the girls to this was to start crying again and describing their losses in detail. Melina was quite beside himself, for he had suffered the heaviest losses—more than we can imagine. He was storming about and stumbling in the narrow room, hitting his head against the wall, cursing and swearing in a most unseemly manner, and when, just then, the hostess came out with the news that his wife had given birth to a stillborn child, he lapsed into outbursts of violence, and everyone howled, yelled, growled, and contributed to the general uproar.

Wilhelm was consumed by sincere pity at their situation, but also by disgust at their pettiness; his mind was fully alert even though his body was still weak. "I almost despise you," he said, "pitiful as your situation may be. For no misfortune can justify heaping reproaches so unjustly on an innocent man. If I did have a part in the mistake we made, I too am paying for it. Here I lie, wounded, and if you all have had losses, I have lost the most. The costumes and sets that were looted, belonged to me; you, Melina, have still not paid me, but I release you forthwith from this obligation."

"What's the point of giving away what no one will ever see again?" said Melina. "Your money was in my wife's trunk, and it is your fault that you lost it. But if only that were all!" Then he began again to stamp and swear and shout. Everybody remembered the lovely clothes they had acquired from the count, the buckles, the snuff boxes, the watches and hats that Melina had wheedled out of the valet de chambre. Everyone remembered his own particular small articles of value, and they all looked in irritation at Philine's trunk, indicating to Wilhelm that he had not done so badly to associate with this beauty and through her good fortune save his own possessions.

"Do you really believe that I shall keep anything for myself, while you are in need?" Wilhelm cried. "Is this the first time that I have given you a fair share of what I had? Open the trunk, and let what is mine be used for general needs." "The trunk is *mine*," said Philine, "and I will not open it up until I decide I want to. The few gladrags which I've kept for you, won't bring in much even if you sell them to the most honest of Jews. Think of yourself, what it might cost to get you well again, and what might happen to you in some other part of the country."

"Philine," said Wilhelm, "you will not deprive me of anything that belongs to me, and such as it is, it will get us out of our first difficulties. But there are many ways of helping one's friends, and not all of them depend on the glitter of money. Everything in and of me shall be spent on these unfortunate people who will certainly regret their present behavior, once they come to their senses. Yes," he said, "I know what you all need, and I will do my best to help you. Give me once more your confidence, calm yourselves for the present, and accept what I can promise you. Who will take this from me in the name of all of you?"

He stretched out his hand, and said: "I promise not to desert or abandon you until every one of you has had his losses doubly or three times repaid, and until you have totally forgotten the state you are now in (no matter whose fault it is) and have exchanged it for a better one."

He kept his hand extended, but no one grasped it. "I repeat my promise," he said, falling back on his pillows. Everyone remained silent. They were ashamed but not consoled. And Philine sat on her trunk cracking nuts that she had found in her pocket.

Chapter Nine

The cavalier came back with some others, ready to make preparations to move the wounded man. The village pastor had been persuaded to take in the "married couple." Philine's trunk was carried out and she, quite naturally but in a seemly manner, followed after it. Mignon ran ahead, and when they reached the parsonage, Wilhelm was put into a good-sized double bed that had long been used for guests or persons of distinction. It was only then that they noticed that the wound had broken open. There had been a good deal of bleeding and a new bandage was needed. Wilhelm became feverish. Philine nursed him dutifully and when she was overcome by fatigue, her place was taken by the Harper. Mignon was determined to stay awake, but had fallen asleep in a corner.

In the morning, when Wilhelm had somewhat recovered, he learnt from the gentleman that the lady who had come to their assistance the preceding day, had recently left her estate in order to escape the turmoil of war and withdrawn to a quieter part till peace should return. He told Wilhelm that the elderly gentleman was her uncle, that they had gone first to a certain town, and that they had instructed him to take good care of Wilhelm and his companions.

At that moment the surgeon came in and cut short Wilhelm's expression of gratitude to the gentleman. He described the wounds in detail and assured Wilhelm that they would soon heal, if he would keep absolutely quiet and be patient.

When the cavalier had gone, Philine told Wilhelm he had left in her charge a purse with twenty gold pieces, had given the parson a sweetening in return for the accommodation and left money with him to pay for the surgeon's services. She herself was generally taken to be Wilhelm's wife, would always act as such in his presence, and would not allow anyone else to nurse him.

"Philine," said Wilhelm, "I am already indebted to you for what you have done in all the misfortune that has befallen us, but I would not wish to increase my obligations toward you. I am ill at ease when you are with me, for I do not know how to repay what you are doing for me. Give me back those things of mine that you rescued for me in your trunk, join up with the rest of the company, and look for some other place to stay. Accept my thanks and, as a small recognition, my gold watch. But leave me. Your presence disturbs me more than you know."

She laughed in his face when he stopped talking. "What a fool you are!" she said. "You'll never be sensible. I know better what's good for you. I'm going to stay right here. I won't move from the spot. I've never expected thanks from men, and not from you either. And if I love you, what's that to you?"

She did stay, and soon ingratiated herself with the pastor and his family; she was bright and cheerful, always giving little presents, knowing exactly what to say to everyone—and doing exactly what she pleased. Wilhelm did not feel too bad. The surgeon, not very knowledgeable but not unskillful, let nature take its course, and the patient was soon on his way to recovery. He was eager to be fully restored so that he could continue with what he had planned, and fulfill his ambitions.

Time and time again he recalled the incident which had left such an indelible impression on his mind. He saw the lovely Amazon riding out of the bushes, saw her come towards him, get off her horse, walk up and down, and occupy herself with his needs. He saw the coat falling from her shoulders, her face and figure disappearing in a blaze of light. All his youthful visions returned to his mind and associated themselves with this image. He now thought he had seen the heroic Clorinda with his own eyes; and he also remembered the sick prince with the beautiful loving princess approaching his bed. "Do not images of our future destiny appear before our unclouded eyes in the dreams of our youth as premonitions?" he kept saying to himself, "Is it not possible that Fate sows the seeds of what is later to befall us, a foretaste of the fruits we are later to enjoy?"

His sickbed allowed him ample time to relive the scene. A thousand times he recalled the sweet sound of her voice; and how he envied Philine at having been able to kiss her hand! At times the whole incident seemed a dream, and he would have considered it a fantasy if the coat were not still there to assure him of the reality of the apparition. The care he took of this garment he combined with a passionate desire to wear it; and whenever he got up from his bed, he hung it over his shoulder, fearing all day long that he might get a spot on it, or in some way damage it.

Chapter Ten

Laertes came to visit his friend. He had not witnessed that turbulent scene in the inn, he had been in an upstairs room. He was quite dispassionate about his losses, resorting to his usual reaction of: What does it matter? He recounted the ridiculous behavior of the other members of the company, chiding Madame Melina in particular and saying that the only reason she lamented the loss of her daughter, was that now she would not be able to christen her with the ancient teutonic name Mechtilde. As for her husband, it had become clear that he had plenty of money and did not need the advance which he had wheedled out of Wilhelm. He was intending to leave by the next postchaise, and would be asking Wilhelm for a letter of recommendation to his friend Serlo, the director of the theater, whose company he hoped to join, now that his own venture had collapsed.

Mignon had for several days been very quiet, and when asked why, she finally admitted that she had sprained her right arm. "That's the result of your foolhardiness," said Philine, and then related how the child had drawn her knife in the middle of the fight, and when she saw her friend in danger, had slashed at the assailants. Eventually she had been grabbed by the arm and hurled to the ground. They scolded her for not telling them sooner that she was hurt, but they had noticed that she was afraid of the surgeon who all this time had taken her for a boy. They tried to relieve the pain by putting her arm in a sling. But her discomfort increased, because she now had to leave the better part of nursing and caring for Wilhelm to Philine, and that engaging sinner was becoming daily more attentive, and more active.

One morning when Wilhelm awoke, he found himself in curious proximity to Philine. In the restlessness of his sleep he had moved way back in the big, wide bed and Philine was stretched out across the front of it. It seemed that she had been sitting reading, and had fallen asleep. A book had slipped from her hand, and her head was resting against his chest, her blond hair billowing loosely across it. The disorder created by sleep had increased her charms more than art or intention could have done, and a smiling, childlike peace was spread over her face. He looked at her for a while, reproaching himself, so it seemed, for the pleasure this gave him; and we cannot say whether he blessed or blamed the situation that imposed such immobility and moderation upon him. He had been looking at her closely for some time when she began to move. He closed his eyes quietly, but couldn't resist blinking. He peered at her as she tidied herself up and went off to inquire about breakfast.

All the actors had by now come to see Wilhelm, asking for recommendations and travel expenses with various degrees of rudeness and importunateness, all to Philine's disapproval. In vain did she inform Wilhelm that the gentleman had left the other actors quite a sum, and that Wilhelm was being cheated. They even got into a fierce argument about this, with Wilhelm insisting once again that she should go along with them and try her luck with Serlo.

Her even temper deserted her for a brief span, but then she recovered herself, and said: "If only I had my blond friend with me! Then I wouldn't have to bother about the whole lot of you!" She was referring to Friedrich, who had been missing since the encounter with the marauding soldiers and had not shown his face since.

The next morning Mignon brought the news to Wilhelm's bed that Philine had left during the night, having neatly arranged in the next room everything that belonged to him. He felt her absence: he had lost in her a faithful nurse and a lively companion, and he was no longer used to being alone. But Mignon was soon to fill the gap.

Since the time that frivolous beauty had begun to bestow on Wilhelm her friendly ministrations, the little girl had withdrawn more and more and kept quietly to herself. But now that the coast was clear again, she came forth with all her love and attentiveness, anxious to serve and eager to entertain.

Chapter Eleven

Wilhelm was making good progress toward recovery, and hoped in a few days to be able to proceed on his journey. He did not want to continue drifting through life without a plan; his path into the future was now to be measured with purposeful steps. The first thing he wanted to do, was to seek out that gracious lady who had come to his assistance, and thank her; then hasten to his friend the theater director and do what he could for the unfortunate actors, and at the same time call on those businessmen whose addresses he had been given, to carry out his instructions. He hoped that the same good fortune would attend him as previously, and that he would have an opportunity to compensate himself by some favorable speculation or other for his losses and repair his finances.

The desire to see again the lady who had rescued him grew stronger every day, and in order to decide on his route he sought advice from the pastor, who had excellent topographical and statistical knowledge and owned quite a collection of books and maps. Together they looked for the place where the lady's family had settled during the war and tried to get more information about her; but they couldn't find the place on any map or in any gazeteer, and the genealogical handbooks had nothing to say about the family.

Wilhelm became uneasy at this, and when he expressed his concern, the Harper said that he had cause to believe that the cavalier, for some reason or other, had concealed the lady's true name. Feeling that he was after all somewhere near her, and eager to have news of her, Wilhelm dispatched the Harper to see what he could find out. But his hopes were soon dashed. For despite all his inquiries, the Harper could not find any trace of her. In those days people moved about easily; no one had paid any particular attention to a group of travelers, and the Harper was obliged to return, in order not to be taken for a Jewish spy because of his beard; but had no good news to report to his master. He gave a precise account of how he had tried to carry out his mission, being eager that no suspicion of negligence should be attached to him. He did all he could to alleviate Wilhelm's concern, reminding himself of everything that the cavalier had told him, and advancing various theories, until finally one particular matter came to light which enabled Wilhelm to understand some of her words which had puzzled him.

The robber band had not been lying in wait for the actors but for her, on whom they might well expect to find a considerable amount of money and jewels. They must have had prior knowledge of her movements. It was not known whether the attack was the work of volunteer soldiers, or of marauders or robbers. Be that as it may, it was fortunate for the rich entourage of the lady that what these men came upon first were these poor creatures who were suffering the fate that was intended for the others. This was what the lady had been referring to by her words, "all on our account," which Wilhelm well remembered. Delighted as he was that Fate in its foresight had designated him to be sacrificed for the sake of this peerless woman, he was close to despair at having, at least for the moment, lost all hope of ever seeing her again.

The commotion within him was aggravated by the curious fact that he had discovered a striking resemblance between the countess and his *belle inconnue.* They were as alike as two sisters, neither older than the other, but, seemingly, twins.

The memory of the delightful countess was one of extreme sweetness: he took constant pleasure in recalling her image. But now the person of the noble Amazon had interposed itself, and the two images became one, so that he was quite unable to keep hold of the one and let go of the other. And then their handwriting—how similar that was! He had kept a charming poem that the countess had written in her own hand, and in the overcoat he had found a slip of paper with a tender message of inquiry about the "uncle." Wilhelm was convinced that his rescuer had written this, sent it from one room to another in some inn on the way, and that the uncle had put it in his pocket. He compared the handwriting, and whereas the elegant pen strokes of the countess had especially pleased him beforehand, the similar but freer writing of the Unknown One now seemed inexpressibly fluid and harmonious. Her little note said next to nothing, but its very appearance, like previously that of the lady herself, seemed to set his spirits soaring.

He lapsed into a state of dreamy longing; and the passionate expressiveness of the free duet that Mignon and the Harper were singing, was like an echo of what he himself was feeling:

> Only they know my pain
>> Who know my yearning!
> Parted and lone again,
>> All joy unlearning,
> I scan all heaven's demesne
>> For any turning.
> Ah, but my love and swain—
>> Far he's sojourning.
> Hot is my spinning brain,
>> My insides burning.
> Only they know my pain
>> Who know my yearning!

Chapter Twelve

The gentle enticements of his kindly tutelary spirit did not move Wilhelm in any particular direction; they merely increased his former uneasiness. There was a certain warmth coursing secretly through his veins, definite and indefinite images floated before his mind and aroused desires that had no limit. He might wish for a horse, or wings, but although he felt he could not stay as he was, he was constantly trying to decide what he really wanted.

The thread of his destiny had become strangely entangled and he longed for the knots to be untied or cut. Many times, hearing a horse trot by or a carriage rumble on its way, he rushed to look out of the window, in the hope that it might be someone coming to visit him and, by pure chance, bringing him news that was certain, and happy. He regaled himself with thoughts of how Werner might surprise him by coming to these parts; or Mariane might turn up. He became excited every time he heard a post horn. Melina should be sending him news of how things were going with him, and above all the cavalier might return with an invitation to visit his idolized beauty.

Unfortunately none of this happened, and he was thrown back on his own company. As he thought over the past, one thing became ever more distasteful and intolerable, the more he pondered and reflected on it. This was his disastrous leadership in battle, the very remembrance of which filled him with dismay. For although, on the evening of that fateful day, he had made a pretty good show of talking himself out of any responsibility, he could not persuade himself that this was justified. He even had moments of depression in which he blamed himself for everything that had happened.

Self-love makes us exaggerate our faults as much as our virtues. He had inspired confidence in himself and manipulated the will of others; and he had forged ahead, driven by boldness and inexperience. But these were not sufficient to cope with the dangers that had befallen them. Openly and in the depths of his heart he blamed himself time and time again, and since he had promised not to desert the company he had so misled until he repaid with interest what they had lost, he now had a further indiscretion to reproach himself with, namely that of assuming responsibility for redressing the harm that had been done to all of them. There were times when he rebuked himself for giving such a promise in the excitement and pressure of the moment; at others he felt that his kindly extended helping hand, which no one was ready to accept, was a mere formal gesture compared with the vow he had made in his heart. He tried to think of ways to be useful and generous, and decided there was every reason for him to speed up his journey to Serlo. So he packed his things and, without being fully recovered or consulting either the pastor or the surgeon, hurried off in the company of Mignon and the Harper, eager to escape the inactivity that fate had imposed on him for so long.

Chapter Thirteen

Serlo received him with open arms, and said: "Is it really you? Are you still what you were? You don't seem to have changed much. Have you retained your passionate love for the noblest of all the arts? I am so glad you have come, and the mistrust I felt in your recent letters has completely vanished." Wilhelm was puzzled, and asked for an explanation. "You didn't treat me like an old friend when you wrote, but rather as an important person to whom one can, in good conscience, recommend people who are completely useless. Our whole future depends on the opinion of the public, and I'm afraid that Mr. Melina and his associates are hardly the sort of people we can integrate into our troupe."

Wilhelm was about to say something in their favor, but Serlo launched into such a harsh description of them, that Wilhelm was glad when a woman entered the room, whom Serlo introduced as his sister Aurelie. She received him very graciously, and their conversation was so pleasant that he did not really notice a certain sadness in her intelligent face which made it all the more interesting.

This was the first time for a long while that Wilhelm had really felt in his element. Whereas all he usually had were submissive listeners, he now found himself in the enviable position of talking to artists and connoisseurs who not only understood him perfectly but responded intelligently to what he said. With what speed they went through all the latest plays! What surety of judgment they displayed! How well they could estimate and appreciate how the public would react! How quickly they could explain things to each other!

Wilhelm's admiration for Shakespeare necessarily brought their conversation round to this author, and Wilhelm expressed his expectation that Shakespeare's marvelous plays would have a tremendous effect on the German public. He soon got on to *Hamlet*, which had so much occupied him of late.

Serlo assured him that he would have put on the play long ago if that had been possible, and he himself would have liked to play the part of Polonius. He added with a smile: "And we can find Ophelias, once we have the prince!" Wilhelm did not notice that Aurelie seemed displeased by her brother's jocular remark; instead he lapsed into his usual expansiveness, instructing them on how he would require the part of Hamlet to be played. He laid before them in detail the conclusions which we have seen him arrive at, and did all he could to make his opinions acceptable, despite the doubts that Serlo expressed regarding his hypothesis. "All right," said Serlo, "we'll grant you all that. But what else does it explain?"

"A great deal; in fact, everything," said Wilhelm. "Just imagine a prince as I have described him, whose father dies unexpectedly. Ambition and desire to rule are not his driving passions. He had acquiesced in the fact of being the son of a king, but now for the first time he is obliged to be more aware of the gulf that separates commoner from king. His right to the crown was not hereditary, but his father's long life had strengthened the claims of an only son and his hopes of assuming the crown. But now he sees himself, despite virtual promises, excluded, perhaps for ever, by his uncle, and feels so deprived of grace and possessions, so alienated amidst all that from the time of his youth he had considered his own. This is how his mind first takes on a melancholy cast. He feels that he is no more than all the other nobles—indeed not as much. He considers himself their servant, he is neither polite, nor condescending but feels degraded and destitute.

"His earlier state now seems to him like a vanished dream. In vain does his uncle try to cheer him up and make him take a different view of his situation; his feeling of insignificance never leaves him.

"The second blow that he suffers, is even more wounding and humbling— his mother's marriage. When his father died, this faithful, loving son still had a mother; and he hoped to honor with her the memory of the great man who had departed this life. But now he loses his mother as well, and in a fashion worse than if she had been snatched from him by death. The image of reliability, which every loving child likes to attach to his parents, is suddenly gone: no help from the dead, no support from the living. She is a women, and: 'Frailty, thy name is woman.'

"He now feels really dejected and isolated. No worldly joys can replace what he has lost. As he is not melancholy or pensive by nature, grief and contemplation are now a heavy burden. That's how he appears when we first see him. I do not believe I have read anything into the play that is not there, or overstressed any element in it."

Serlo looked at his sister, and said: "Was I wrong in the way I described our friend? He has just made a good beginning, and he will have much more to tell us about, and persuade us of." Wilhelm swore that his intentions were not to persuade, but to convince; and he asked for a few more moments of their time.

"Just to think clearly about this young man, this son of a prince," Wilhelm went on to say. "Visualize his position, and observe him when he learns that his father's spirit is abroad. Stand by him when, in that terrible night, the venerable ghost appears before his eyes. He is overcome by intense horror, speaks to the spirit, sees it beckon him, follows, and hears—the terrible accusation of his uncle continues to ring in his ears, with its challenge to seek revenge, and that repeated urgent cry: 'Remember me!'

"And when the ghost has vanished, what do we see standing before us? A young hero thirsting for revenge? A prince by birth, happy to be charged with unseating the usurper of his throne? Not at all! Amazement and sadness descend on this lonely spirit; he becomes bitter at the smiling villains, swears not to forget his departed father, and ends with a heavy sigh: 'The time is out of joint; O cursed spite! That ever I was born to set it right!'

"In these words, so I believe, lies the key to Hamlet's whole behavior; and it is clear to me what Shakespeare set out to portray: a heavy deed placed on a soul which is not adequate to cope with it. And it is in this sense that I find the whole play constructed. An oak tree planted in a precious pot which should only have held delicate flowers. The roots spread out, the vessel is shattered.

"A fine, pure, noble and highly moral person, but devoid of that emotional strength that characterizes a hero, goes to pieces beneath a burden that it can neither support nor cast off. Every obligation is sacred to him, but this one is too heavy. The impossible is demanded of him—not the impossible in any absolute sense, but what is impossible for him. How he twists and turns, trembles, advances and retreats, always being reminded, always reminding himself, and finally almost losing sight of his goal, yet without ever regaining happiness!"

Chapter Fourteen

Several persons came in and the conversation was interrupted. They were musicians accustomed to meet once every week at Serlo's for an informal concert. He liked music very much and said that an actor could never achieve a true conception of his art, or the right feeling for it, without a love of music. "You act much more easily and appropriately when your movements are accompanied and controlled by music; and every actor should, as it were, compose his part in his mind, although it's in prose, so that he doesn't drool it out monotonously to his own tune, but modulates its tempo and rhythm."

Aurelie appeared to be taking little interest in what was happening, and eventually led our friend into an adjoining room, where she walked up to the window, gazed at the starry sky, and said, "You still owe us more of your thoughts about *Hamlet*. I don't want to be precipitate, and would like my brother to hear what you have to say, but do tell me what you think about Ophelia."

"There is not much to say about her," said Wilhelm. "Her character is presented in a few strokes of the master's hand. Her whole being is pervaded by ripe, sweet sensuality. Her affection for the prince, whose hand she might justly feel she can claim, rises from the very wellsprings of her being, her heart abandons itself so completely to her desire that both her father and her brother are fearful for her and warn her openly. Her decorum, like the posy on her bosom, cannot conceal the perturbation of her heart—in fact it betrays it. Her imagination is infected, her tender modesty nevertheless breathes desire and love, and if the obliging goddess of fortune should shake the tree, the fruit would fall."

"But when she sees herself rejected, repulsed and reviled," said Aurelie, "when the best turns to the worst in her lover's madness, and he hands her not the sweet goblet of love but the bitter cup of sorrow . . ."

"Then her heart breaks," said Wilhelm. "The whole frame of her existence falls out of joint, her father's death bursts in upon her, and the whole structure of her lovely being collapses."

Wilhelm had not noticed the intensity of expression with which Aurelie was speaking. His attention had been entirely concentrated on the perfect structure of the work of art, and he had no idea of the totally different way Aurelie was reacting to the character, or that some deep grief of her own was being awakened by this shadow play.

Her head was still resting on her arms, and her eyes, filled with tears, were still gazing upward. Finally she could no longer suppress her hidden anguish, and seizing his hands she said to him as he stood there in astonishment: "Forgive, o forgive my troubled heart! The company of others restricts and oppresses me. I have to try to hide my feelings from my unfeeling brother. But your presence has released me from all these restraints. I've only just met you, but you're someone in whom I can confide." Words almost failed her, and she sank on to his shoulder. "Don't think the worse of me," she said, sobbing, "for opening up to you so quickly, for appearing so weak. Be my friend, remain my friend—I deserve it!" He spoke to her compassionately, but without effect. Her tears continued to flow, and stifled her words.

At that moment Serlo came into the room, a most unwelcome interruption, and, totally unexpected, with Philine, whom he held by the hand. "Here's your friend," he said to her. "He will be glad to see you."

"Well!" said Wilhelm in astonishment. "How is it that I find you here?" Philine walked up to him, calmly and unassumingly, bade him welcome, and praised Serlo's kindness in taking her into his excellent troupe, not because of merit but simply in the expectation that she would develop. She acted in a friendly manner toward Wilhelm, though with a certain distance.

But this pretense only lasted while the other two were in the room. For when Aurelie left to hide her agitation and Serlo was called away, Philine first looked to the doors to see that both of them were well and truly gone, then jumped around like a mad thing, sat on the ground and almost choked with tittering laughter. Then she leapt up, said nice things to Wilhelm, and seemed exceedingly pleased at having gone ahead to reconnoitre the terrain and build her own nest.

"There's plenty going on here," she said. "Just what I like. Aurelie has had an unhappy love affair with a nobleman, who must be a splendid fellow. I would like to see him some day. If I am not mistaken, he has left her a little memento; there is a three-year-old boy running around here, pretty as the sun. Papa must have been extremely nice. Usually I can't stand children, but this one appeals to me. I've reckoned it out. Her husband dies, then this new admirer, then the age of the child—everything fits.

"Her friend has gone his own way, and hasn't seen her for a whole year: She is beside herself and utterly inconsolable. Silly fool!—As for her brother, he has a dancer in the company that he makes up to, a little actress that he is intimate with, and several women that he courts in the town; and now I too am on the list. Poor fool!—As for the rest, I'll tell you about them tomorrow. But now a word about your dear friend Philine: the silly fool is in love with you!" She swore that this was true and was a real lark. She implored him to fall in love with Aurelie. "Then there'll be a real chase. She runs after her faithless lover, you after her, I after you, and the brother after me. If that isn't enough to keep us amused for six months, I am ready to die after the first episode in the fourfold complications of this romance." She begged him not to spoil her game, and show her as much respect as she would seek to earn by her public behavior.

Chapter Fifteen

The next morning Wilhelm decided to call on Madame Melina, but found she was not at home. He inquired after the other members of the company and learnt that Philine had invited them all to breakfast. He went there out of curiosity and found them all quite consoled and in very good spirits. The clever little creature had gathered them together, regaled them with chocolate, and given them to understand that all avenues were not closed: she hoped by her influence to convince the director of the advantages of having such proficient people in his company. They listened attentively, drank one cup of chocolate after another, decided that this girl was not all that bad and that they would speak well of her in the future.

"Do you really think," said Wilhelm when he was alone with Philine, "that Serlo will keep our comrades?" "Not at all," replied Philine. "As for me I don't particularly want him to. The sooner they leave, the better. Laertes is the only I would wish to keep; the others we can get rid of gradually."

She made it clear to her friend that she was convinced he should no longer bury his talents but go on the stage under Serlo's direction. She was full of praise for the organization, the taste and intelligence that were in evidence here, and spoke so flatteringly to Wilhelm about his talents that his heart and imagination were as near to accepting this proposal as his mind and his reason withdrew from it. He did not admit to himself nor to Philine where his inclinations were leading him, and spent a restless day, unable to decide whether to go to his father's business associate and collect the letters that were probably waiting there for him. He realized how uneasy his family must have become by now, but shied away from receiving a detailed account of their concern and reproaches; he was looking forward to an evening of unsullied pleasure at the performance of a new play.

Serlo had refused to let him go to the rehearsal. "You must," he said, "get to know us at our very best before we allow you to see us in the planning stage."

Wilhelm was extremely satisfied with the performance which he attended next evening. It was the first time he had witnessed theater of such quality. One could see that all the actors had excellent talents, conducive dispositions and a clear and serious view of their art, and yet they were all different; they supported each other, inspired each other, and were exact and precise in every facet of their acting. One soon realized that Serlo was the soul of the enterprise and that he distinguished himself in it. The moment he stepped onto the stage and opened his mouth he revealed an admirably controlled mood, moderation in his actions, and a true sense of what was fitting, together with an exceptional mimetic talent. His inward composure radiated outward to the spectators, and the intelligent way in which he conveyed every nuance of the role delighted the audience because he was able to conceal the technique he had acquired by persistent practicing.

His sister Aurelie was just as good as he, and received even greater applause because she knew how to move hearts as well as to amuse and lighten them.

After Wilhelm had spent some days in this pleasant fashion, Aurelie one day asked to see him. He hastened to her room and found her lying on a couch. She seemed to be suffering from a headache, and could not hide the fact that she was in a state of feverish unrest. Her eyes brightened when she saw him. "Please forgive me!" she called out. "The confidence you have inspired in me, has made me weak. Up till now I have been able to occupy myself, when I was alone, with my sorrows. They provided me with strength and consolation. But now, I don't know how, you have loosened the bonds of my silence, and you will now unwittingly be a party to the battle I am fighting with myself."

Wilhelm responded with kindness and courtesy, assuring her that her person and her sorrow were constantly before his mind, and urging her to confide in him so that he might be able to become her friend.

While he was speaking, he noticed the little boy sitting on the floor and playing with all sorts of toys. He was, as Philine had said, probably about three years of age, and Wilhelm now well understood why the flippant girl, whose manner of expression was rarely so elevated, had compared him with the sun. For the loveliest golden curls hung over his big brown eyes and his round face, his gleaming white forehead arched over delicate dark eyebrows, and his cheeks glowed with health. "Sit down beside me," Aurelie said to Wilhelm. "I can see you are surprised as you observe this happy child. It's true that it gives me great joy to hold it in my arms, and I take good care of it. But I can measure my sorrows by this child, for they rarely let me appreciate the value of such a gift.

"Let me tell you about myself and my life, for I am very anxious that you should not misjudge me. I thought I would have a few peaceful moments, which is why I sent for you. Now you're here—and I've lost my thread.

"Just one more abandoned creature on this earth! you will say to yourself. You are a man and will think: Look how the fool reacts to a necessary evil, more certain to befall a woman than death itself, namely a man's infidelity! If my fate were ordinary, I would gladly bear ordinary sorrow. But my fate is so very extraordinary. Why can't I show it to you in a mirror, or have someone tell you about it! If it were just a matter of being seduced, surprised and then abandoned, there would be some consolation in despair. But my situation is far worse: I duped myself, deceived myself against my will—that is what I can never forgive myself for."

"But someone with sentiments as noble as yours cannot be completely unhappy," her friend replied.

"And do you know to what I owe these feelings?" asked Aurelie. "The worst possible education that a girl was ever ruined by, the worst example, one that misled my senses and my inclinations.

"After the untimely death of my mother I spent the best years of my growing up in the house of an aunt who made it a rule to disregard all principles of honesty. She abandoned herself blindly to every emotion, no matter whether she controlled its object or was enslaved by it, so long as she could forget herself in the whirl of enjoyment. What sort of view of the male sex could we innocent children form for ourselves from this? How obtuse, insistent, brazen and clumsy were all those whom she attracted to herself; how satiated, arrogant, empty-headed and ridiculous they became once they had satisfied their desires. I watched this woman degraded by base company for years on end.

What encounters she had to put up with, what spirit she showed in accepting her fate, what shameful enslavements she had to learn to live with!

"That was my introduction to the male sex, my friend; and how utterly I despised them when quite decent men seemed, in their relations with our sex, to abandon every good feeling that nature otherwise might have made them capable of.

"Unfortunately I also on these occasions formed some negative opinions of my own sex. As a girl of sixteen I was more sensible than I am now, when I can hardly understand myself. Why are we so sensible when we are young, and why do we become ever more foolish!"

The boy was making a noise. Aurelie became impatient and rang the bell. An old woman came in to take him away. "Have you still got a toothache?" Aurelie said to the woman whose face was all bandaged up. "It's almost unbearable," said the woman in a hollow voice as she picked up the child, who seemed to go willingly, and took him away.

Aurelie began to weep bitterly when the child had gone. "I can't do anything but weep and moan," she said, "and I'm ashamed to behave like a baby before you. My concentration is gone and I can't go on talking to you." She broke off, and lapsed into silence. Her friend, since he had nothing of a general nature that he wanted to say and nothing particular that he could say, pressed her hand and sat looking at her. Not knowing what else to do he finally picked up a book from the table in front of him. It was the works of Shakespeare, opened up to *Hamlet*.

Serlo, who had just come into the room to inquire after his sister, looked at the book in Wilhelm's hand, and said: "So there you are again, you and your *Hamlet*! Good! Many doubts have occurred to me which would seem to reduce considerably the great admiration that you choose to have for it. Haven't the English themselves admitted that the main interest ceases with the third act, and the last two just barely hold the whole thing together? Isn't it true that, toward the end, the play doesn't move along at all?"

"It is quite possible," said Wilhelm, "that some members of the nation which has produced so many masterpieces should be misled by prejudices or limitations into making such false judgments. But that shouldn't stop us from looking at it with our own eyes, and being just. I am unwilling to criticize the plan of the play; in fact, I believe no greater plan could have been conceived. Indeed it isn't conceived at all, the play just is as it is."

"How can you explain that?" asked Serlo.

"I don't intend to explain anything," Wilhelm replied, "I just want to give you my thoughts."

Aurelie raised her head from the pillow, rested it on her hands and gazed at our friend who, absolutely convinced that he was right, continued: "It pleases and flatters us to see a hero who acts of his own accord, loves and hates according to the dictates of his heart, completing what he sets out to do by removing all obstacles that impede his progress toward some lofty goal. Historians and poets like to persuade us that such pride of purpose may be the lot of mankind. But in this case we are differently informed: the hero has no plan, but the play has. A villain is not punished according to some rigid concept of revenge narrowly applied: a monstrous deed is performed, extends its evil consequences, and drags innocent people into its orbit. The evildoer seems to be avoiding the fate that is in store for him, but then plunges into it where he thought he had found a safe way out. For cruel deeds bring evil to the innocent just as good deeds bring advantages to those who do not deserve them, often without the originator being punished or rewarded. How marvelously this is presented in the play before us! Purgatory sends a spirit to demand revenge, but in vain. Circumstances combine to hasten this, but in vain! Neither humans nor subterranean powers can achieve what is reserved for Fate alone. The time of reckoning arrives; and the good perish with the bad. A whole family is mowed down, and a new one emerges."

They looked at each other for a while, and then Serlo said: "You don't much compliment providence by thus elevating the poet. You seem to be assigning to the glory of the poet what others attribute to providence, namely a purpose and plan that he never thought of."

Chapter Sixteen

"Let me now ask you a question," said Aurelie. "I have once more looked over Ophelia's part, and am satisfied that I can play it under certain conditions. But tell me this: Shouldn't the poet have given her in her madness different songs to sing? Couldn't he have chosen parts of some sad ballads? What is such suggestive and indecent nonsense doing in the mouth of this pure young girl?"

"My dear friend," said Wilhelm, "I wouldn't change them one iota. There is deep meaning in what seems to be so strange and inappropriate about these songs. We know from the very beginning of the play what her mind is full of. The dear child lives quietly for herself, but she is hardly able to conceal her desires and wishes. Lustful tones resound throughout her mind and, like an imprudent nurse, she may well have tried more than once to sing her senses to sleep with ballads that merely keep them more awake. And when she has lost all control over herself and when her heart is on her tongue, this tongue betrays her and, in the innocence of her madness, she indulges herself before the king and queen by recalling those loose songs that she so much liked: the girl who was won, the girl who crept to her lover, and so forth. . . ."

He had not yet finished what he was saying, when he witnessed a curious scene which he was quite unable to account for.

Serlo had been pacing up and down, without any apparent purpose. But suddenly he went to Aurelie's dressing table, snatched up something that was lying there, and rushed toward the door with it. Aurelie had not really noticed what he was doing, but suddenly she threw herself in his path, violently grabbed hold of him, and succeeded in wresting from him the object he had picked up. They fought and struggled fiercely with each other, twisting and turning. He was laughing, she was furious, and when Wilhelm rushed up to tear them apart and quieten them down he saw Aurelie jump off to the side with a naked dagger in her hand while Serlo impetuously threw the sheath to the ground. Wilhelm drew back astonished, seeking in silent amazement for the possible cause of so strange a struggle about so unusual an object.

"You shall be the arbitrator between us," said Serlo. "What on earth is she doing with such a sharp weapon? Let her show it to you. This dagger is not suitable for any actress; it's as sharply pointed as a needle or a knife. Why this nonsense? She is such a violent person that some day or other she will do herself harm again. I have an intense hatred of such eccentricities: any serious thought of this kind is crazy, and to have such a dangerous plaything is ridiculous."

"I've got it back again," said Aurelie, lifting the shining blade. "In the future will take better care of my trusty friend. Forgive me," she said, kissing the dagger, "for having been so careless."

Serlo now seemed to be becoming really angry. "Think what you will, brother," she went on; "how can you know whether I have not been granted a precious talisman to provide me in this form with help and advice in the worst of times? Must everything be harmful that looks dangerous?"

"Such crazy talk will drive me out of my mind!" said Serlo as he left the room in barely suppressed anger. Aurelie carefully returned the dagger to its sheath and put it into her pocket. "Let's continue the conversation which my unfortunate brother interrupted," she said, as Wilhelm started to ask her about their strange altercation.

"I have to agree that your interpretation of Ophelia is right," she said. "I wouldn't wish to misinterpret the poet's intentions, but I pity her more than I sympathize with her. Now let me tell you something which you have given me occasion to think about in the short time we have known each other. I admire your profound insights into literature, especially dramatic literature. You are able to penetrate to the very depths of what was in the poet's mind and to appreciate the subtlest nuances in its presentation. Without having ever seen things in reality you can recognize the truthfulness of their image. It seems as if some presentiment of the whole world lies within you, and this is brought to life and developed by your contact with poetry. For truly," she went on, "nothing comes into you from the outside world. I have rarely met anyone who knew so little of the people with whom he lives—indeed fundamentally misjudges them. Let me say this: when I hear you explaining

Shakespeare, it seems as if you have just come from a council of the gods and heard them discussing how to make humans; but when you are associating with real people, you seem like some first child of creation growing up to gape at lions and monkeys, sheep and elephants in strange astonishment and good-natured devotion, treating them affably as your equals, simply because they live and move."

"My own maturity has often troubled me," said Wilhelm, "and I would be grateful to you, if you could help me gain a clearer understanding of the world around me. Earlier in my youth I turned my eyes inward rather than outward, and it is therefore quite natural that I have arrived at some general knowledge of the human race without in the least understanding particular human beings."

"That's true," said Aurelie. "At first I thought you were just playing a game with us when you said such positive things about the persons you sent my brother, and I compared your account of them with what they actually are."

This remark of Aurelie's, true as it might have been, and willing as Wilhelm was to admit his failings, had something about it that was oppressive, even offensive. Wilhelm said nothing. He collected his thoughts, trying to conceal his irritation and to ask himself whether her reproach was justified.

"You need not be embarrassed," said Aurelie. "One can always attain clarity of mind, but no one can give us fullness of heart. If your destiny is to be an artist, you cannot continue for much longer in a state of such imperception and ingenuousness. These are the outer coverings that protect a budding growth, and it is unfortunate if the tender plant is forced too soon. It is however a good thing if we do not always know the people for whom we work.

"I too was once in that blissful state, when I went on the stage with the highest opinion of myself and my nation. There was nothing that in my imagination the Germans didn't possess and nothing that they could not develop into. I spoke to my nation from my slightly elevated platform, edged by lights whose brightness and smoke obscured my view of what was in front of me. How glad I was at the sound of the applause that floated up from the crowd, how grateful for this tribute of acclaim from so many different hands. I went on like this for a long time, lulling myself, through the good relationship I had with a public that responded to everything I offered them, into a sense of complete harmony with the noblest and best of my nation, for I thought that this was what I saw before me.

"But unfortunately it was not just the personality and skill of the actress that appealed to the spectators; they also made claims on the lively young girl. I was given to understand in no uncertain terms that it was my duty to share with them privately the emotions I had aroused in them from the stage. Unfortunately, that was not what I wanted. All I desired was to raise their minds; I had no concern with what they called their hearts, and, no matter what type, age or class they belonged to, they all became burdensome to me and I was irritated at not being able to shut myself up in my room like any honest girl, and spare myself all this trouble.

"The men behaved in a manner familiar to me from my aunt's house, and they would have aroused the same loathing in me if I had not been amused by their idiosyncrasies and stupidities. Since I could hardly avoid seeing them either on the stage itself or in public places, or at home, I decided to be always on the lookout, and my brother gave me valuable assistance in this. And when you consider that slippery shop assistants, conceited merchants' sons, smooth men-of-the-world, brave soldiers and hasty princes, all came into my ken and tried to start a romance with me (each in his own way), you will surely forgive me for believing that I had become fairly well acquainted with my own nation. I saw them all get excited—the fantastically dolled-up students, the professors uneasy in their pride of humility, the tottering and self-satisfied prelates, the stiff and attentive officials, the coarse country squires, the ingratiating courtiers, the young priests off course, the nimble or actively speculating businessmen—but, my heavens, there were very few of them who could arouse the slightest interest in me. On the contrary: it was extremely distasteful to me to cash in on the approval of these fools and endure such wearisome boredom, though in general I was pleased by any approval I received.

"But when I expected some intelligent compliment on my acting, or hoped they would praise an author whom I respected, they would make one silly remark after another and mention some insipid play they would like to see me perform in. When I listened around in company to see if a particularly fine, ingenious or witty point had made its mark and would resurface at an appropriate moment, I rarely found any trace of this. A mistake—if an actor had said the wrong word or used a provincial pronunciation—that was what they fixed on as something so important that they couldn't get off the topic. Finally I no longer knew where I should turn; they seemed to think they were too bright to be entertained, and entertaining me by petting and pawing me. So I began to despise them all intensely, feeling as though the whole nation was purposely prostituting itself by the representatives it sent me. They seemed for the most part so clumsy, ill educated, badly informed, so lacking in graciousness of personality and taste. I often said to myself that a German can't even buckle a shoe without having learned how to do so from foreigners!

"You can see how blind and unjust my hypochondria made me, and it grew steadily worse. I might well have killed myself, but I chose another extreme: I married, or rather I got myself married. My brother, having taken over the direction of the theater, wanted very much to have an assistant. His choice fell on a young man, who was not unattractive, one who lacked everything my brother possessed—genius, vitality, intelligence and impulsiveness—but had everything that my brother lacked—concern for order, industriousness, organizational talent and the ability to manage money.

"This man became my husband, without my really knowing how; we lived together without my knowing why. Suffice it to say that things went well. Thanks to my brother's activities he took in a lot of money; and thanks to my husband's abilities we managed well. I didn't think any more about the world or my nation. I had nothing in common with the world, and I had lost any idea of the nation. When I appeared on stage, I did so in order to live, opening my mouth simply because I was required not to remain silent, having come there in order to speak.

"So that I should do this fairly well I had resigned myself to my brother's wishes. His concern was for applause, and money; for, let me tell you, he likes to be praised and he spends a lot. I no longer acted according to my feelings and convictions, but in the way he instructed me, and when I earned his thanks, I was satisfied. He was guided by the foibles of his public; money came in, he could live according to his desires, and we had good times with him.

"But I began to lapse into a mechanical kind of routine. I spent my days without much joy or interest, my marriage was childless, and lasted only a short while. My husband fell ill, his strength visibly diminished, and my concern for him broke up my state of indifference. During this time I made an acquaintance with whom a new life began for me, a new and shorter life, for it will soon be at an end."

She stopped, and after an interval of quiet continued: "My talkativeness has suddenly dried up, and I don't dare go on. Let me rest for a while. You must not go away until you have had a full account of my misery. Call Mignon and find out what she wants."

The girl had several times come into the room while Aurelie was talking. But since they had lowered their voices every time she appeared, she had settled herself outside in the hall, quietly waiting. When she was asked to come in again, she brought a book, which, from its binding and shape, they could see was an atlas. At the pastor's house she had for the first time seen maps, had put a lot of questions about these to him, and had informed herself as best she could. Her eagerness to learn had apparently been greatly increased by this new sort of information. She had implored Wilhelm to buy the book for her. She had deposited with the salesman her big silver buckles, and, since it was too late to do so today, she wanted to redeem them next morning. It was agreed that she should; whereupon she began to recite what she had learnt and in her own special way asked the strangest questions. Once again it became apparent that, for all her energy, her comprehension was slow and laborious. So too was her handwriting, though she took great pains over it. She still spoke a broken German; and only when she opened her mouth to sing, or played the zither, did she reveal the one organ she had to express her innermost self.

Since we are talking about Mignon, we must also mention the embarrassment that she had been causing our friend for some time. Whenever she came or went, bade him good morning or good night, she clasped him so firmly in her arms and kissed him so passionately, that the violence of her developing nature filled him with alarm. The twitching intensity of her movements increased daily, and her whole being seemed to suggest a suppressed state of unrest. She could not be anywhere without twisting string, crumpling cloth or chewing pieces of wood or paper. All these activities seemed only to deflect great inner commotion. The only thing that appeared to give her peace or serenity, was being with the boy Felix, and she played with him in the most delightful manner.

Aurelie, after a respite, determined to finish her account of what lay so heavily on her mind, became impatient at Mignon's importunity and indicated to her that she should leave. Since nothing else seemed to work, they had to send her away, very much against her will.

"It's now or never," said Aurelie, "if I am to finish telling you my story. If my tender beloved, my unjust friend, were but a few miles from here, I would say to you: get on your horse and try somehow to make his acquaintance, and when you returned, you would certainly have forgiven me and would pity me in your heart. But all I can do is tell you in words how lovable he was, and how very much I loved him.

"I came to know him just at that critical time when I was deeply concerned about my husband's life. My friend had just returned from America where he, in the company of several Frenchmen, had served with great distinction under the colors of the United States. When I met him, he behaved toward me with composure and civility, openness and generosity: he talked to me about myself, my situation, and my acting, like an old acquaintance, so full of understanding that for the first time I could enjoy seeing myself clearly in the mind of someone else. His judgments were apt without being negative, and just without being unsympathetic. There was nothing harsh about him, and when his tone became playful, it was never offensive. He seemed to be used to success with women, and that made me cautious; but he was never flattering or importunate, and so I was never worried.

"He did not cultivate many acquaintances in town. Most of his time was spent riding out to visit his many friends in the surrounding district and dealing with his business affairs. When he returned he would stop off at my house. He showed deep concern for my husband who was steadily failing and found a good doctor to alleviate his suffering. Since he had shown such interest in everything that concerned me, he allowed me in turn to share in his own experiences. He told me about his eagerness to be a soldier, about the campaign he had fought in, and about his family. He also spoke about his present occupations. In short, he had no secrets from me. He opened up his innermost self, letting me peer into the most hidden recesses of his soul, and revealing his capabilities and his passions. It was the first time in my life that I had enjoyed a relationship that appealed to my emotions as well as my mind. I was attracted by him, and enthralled before I could think about myself.

"I lost my husband almost in the same manner as I had found him; and the whole burden of the business affairs connected with the theater now fell upon me. My brother, incomparable on stage, was never much good at managing things. I had to take care of all that, and in addition studied my roles even more intently than before. I played them as I had in the past, but now with new strength and new life because of him, and for him, but not always with complete success if I knew he was in the audience. But there were times when, having seen me act, he surprised and delighted me by his unexpected approval.

"I am certainly a strange creature. No matter what part I was playing, I was really only concerned in praising him and honoring him by the lines I spoke; that was the state of my feelings, whatever the words might be. If I knew he was in the audience, I did not dare to speak out with full intensity; it was as though I did not wish to express my love and admiration for him to his face. If, however, he was not in the theater I had free range, and did my very best with a certain composure and extreme satisfaction. Applause began to please me once more, and if the public was pleased, I felt like saying to them down there: You owe that to him!

"Indeed my attitude to the public, and to the whole nation, had gone through a miraculous change. Suddenly my countrymen appeared to me once more in a very favorable light, and I was astonished at my former blindness.

"'How nonsensical it was for you to revile a nation just for being a nation,' I would say to myself time after time. 'How can individuals be so interesting? The question is whether in a mass of people there is a sufficient distribution of disposition, power and ability which, when developed by favorable circumstances, can be directed by outstanding people toward some common goal.' I was now pleased not to find much striking originality amongst my compatriots, I was glad to see that they did not scorn to take direction from elsewhere, I was glad to have found a leader.

"Lothario—let me call my friend by the name he liked best—had always presented the Germans to me in terms of their valor, and demonstrated to me that there was no more trusty nation in the world, so long as they were properly led; and I was ashamed at not having recognized this prime quality of my nation. He knew about their history, and he was acquainted with the most meritorious men of his age. Young as he was, he had an eye for the promise that was developing in the youth of his nation, and for the quiet achievements in so many fields of active older men. He gave me an overview of what Germany is and can become, and I was ashamed at having judged it from the motley throng in theater dressing rooms. He made it my duty to be truthful, intelligent and inspiring in my own sphere of activity, and I felt inspired every time I walked on to the stage. Mediocre passages turned to gold in my mouth, and if a poet had been there to assist me in what I was doing, I would have produced the most marvelous effects.

"That is how the young widow lived for months on end. Lothario couldn't do without me, and I was miserable when he wasn't there. He showed me letters from his relations, especially from his splendid sister. He took an interest in every detail of our circumstances. A closer and more perfect union could not be imagined. The word love was never mentioned. He went and came, came and went—and now, my friend, it is high time that you went."

Chapter Seventeen

Wilhelm could not put off any longer calling on his business friends. He went with some trepidation, for he knew he would find letters there from his family. He feared the reproaches they were bound to contain, for probably the firm had already been informed of the trouble he had caused. After all those chivalric adventures of his, he was not happy about appearing as a callow youth in their eyes, and so he decided to behave resolutely, and thereby conceal his uneasiness.

But to his great surprise and relief, everything went off fairly smoothly. In the bustle of these busy offices there had been little time for them to consult his letters, and only passing reference was made to his having stayed away so long. When he opened the letters from his father and from Werner, he found them all quite moderate in tone and content. His father, hoping for a detailed account such as on his departure he had urged his son to provide him with, even giving him a systematic plan of how to set it out, seemed in the beginning quite unperturbed by his silence, though he did complain about the mystifying nature of that first and only letter sent from the count's castle. Werner merely joked in his usual fashion, gave some amusing town gossip, and asked for news of friends and acquaintances whom Wilhelm would now be meeting in the city. Extremely glad to be relieved at such little cost, Wilhelm immediately sent back some lively letters, and promised his father a detailed journal with all the geographical, statistical and mercantile observations that he had asked for. He had seen a lot on his journey and hoped to put together an extensive report. He did not notice that he was in almost the same situation as when he had set up the lights and summoned the audience for a play that was not memorized, indeed not even written. When he therefore started to apply himself to his composition, he came to realize that he could talk about his feelings and thoughts, his experiences of heart and mind, but not about external things which, as he now noticed, had not in any way attracted his attention.

He was helped by the knowledge of his friend Laertes. These two young men, for all their differences, had become close friends, and Laertes, with all his faults, was really an interesting person in his own peculiar way. Blessed as he was with radiant vitality, he could have grown old without worrying about his condition. But now misfortunes and sickness had robbed him of the unclouded delights of youth, though at the same time they had given him some insight into the mutability and fragmentation of life. From this had come his inclination toward moody, rhapsodic utterances in which he expressed his immediate reactions. He did not like to be alone, frequented coffeehouses and inns, and when he was at home, his preferred reading, indeed his only reading, was travel books. He could now indulge in this, for he had located a big lending library and his mind was soon buzzing with information about half the globe.

It was therefore easy for him to encourage his friend when Wilhelm told him about his complete lack of facts for the solemnly promised narration. "Let's make an incomparable work of art out of it," said Laertes. "Hasn't Germany been driven through, walked through, crept through, fled through from one end to the other? Hasn't every German traveler been reimbursed by the public for his smaller or larger expenses? Just tell me the route you took before you came to us; I'll know all the rest. I'll find you sources and information for what you are composing, and we will see to it that we get the right distances and the right size of populations, even if those have not been measured or counted. We can find out the revenues of the various districts from calendars and charts, for these are well known to be the most reliable sources. On this information we can base our political speculations—not forgetting some incidental observations on government. We'll describe a few of the princes as being true fathers of the fatherland, so that we will be more easily believed when we cast some blame on others and if we don't actually pass through the towns where some famous people live, we will at least run across them in inns where they will confide arrant nonsense to us. Let's not forget to include a delightful love affair with a simple country girl, and we'll have a work to delight not only fathers and mothers, but one that every bookseller will be glad to stock."

They went to work and both of them had a great deal of fun at it. In the evenings Wilhelm went to the theater and derived the greatest satisfaction from consorting with Serlo and Aurelie. And every day he was expanding the range of his ideas which had for so long been limited to a very narrow sphere.

Chapter Eighteen

It was with the greatest interest that Wilhelm learnt about the career of Serlo, even though piecemeal; for this strange man was not given to confiding in others, nor to coherent exposition. One could well say that he was born and raised in the theater. Even before he could talk he moved the hearts of the audience by his very presence on the stage, for authors of that time were well aware of the effectiveness of natural demonstrations of innocence, and when he first said "Father" and "Mother" in plays that everyone loved, he earned vigorous applause long before he had any idea what all the clapping was about. He descended in a flying machine as Cupid more than once, emerged from an egg as harlequin, and performed at an early age the sweetest tricks as a little chimney sweep.

Unfortunately, however, he had to pay heavily in between for the applause he received on his brilliant evenings. His father, convinced that a child's concentration was best aroused and maintained by beatings, thrashed him at regular intervals while he was learning a new part—not because he was lacking in skill, but rather that his achievement should be the more secure and lasting. In those days parents used to rain blows on children who stood around gawking when a marker was being erected, and old folks still remember the time and place where this happened. The boy grew up showing unusual mental and physical ability and great flexibility of acting powers, both in actions and gestures. While still a boy he could imitate persons so well that people believed they were seeing these very persons, despite the fact that they were quite different from the boy in figure, age and character, and different from each other. In addition he knew how to make his way in the world, and as soon as he was fairly sure of his own powers, he thought it perfectly natural to run away from his father who, as the boy's intelligence developed and his skill increased, thought it necessary to advance these still further by even harsher treatment.

The waggish boy was blissfully happy out there in the world because his merry pranks went down well everywhere. His lucky star led him first on Shrove Tuesday to a monastery, where the reverend father in charge of processionals, who had organized sacred performances for the delight of the Christian community, had just died. Here, suddenly, was a guardian angel to help them out! He took over the role of Gabriel in the Annunciation, and made a favorable impression on the pretty girl playing the Virgin Mary, who gracefully received his polite announcement with a display of humility and inner pride. He then acted in succession all the most important roles in the mystery plays, and formed quite a high opinion of himself when ultimately he was mocked, beaten and nailed to the cross as the Savior of the World.

On this last occasion some of the soldiers played their parts too realistically; and so, to take his revenge in the seemliest possible manner, he dressed them up in the sumptuous garments of kings and emperors at the Last Judgment, and then, at the very moment when they, delighted with what they represented, were about to enter Heaven ahead of all the others, he suddenly appeared before them in the shape of a devil, beating them vigorously with a pitchfork, to the extreme edification of all the spectators and beggars in the audience, and thrusting them mercilessly back into the pit where they were most uncivilly greeted by emerging fire.

He was astute enough to foresee that these crowned heads would take offense at his bold actions and not respect his high office as prosecutor-executioner;

and so, before the Millennium arrived, he crept away quietly, and went to a nearby town where he was received with open arms by a group of people known at that time as the "Children of Joy." These lively people, intelligent and perceptive, well understood that the sum of our existence divided by reason never comes out exactly and that there is always a wondrous remainder. They set out at certain fixed times to get rid of this troublesome and, if it spreads through the whole mass, dangerous remainder, by indulging, one day a week, wholeheartedly in foolishness, and on that day punishing in allegorical presentations the follies they had observed in themselves and others during the other days of the week. If this way of doing things was cruder than some kind of coherent education in which the moral part of man accustoms itself daily to observing, warning and punishing, it was certainly more amusing and more reliable. For without their denying some pet folly, they treated it simply for what it was and nothing more, instead of its becoming through self-delusion a tyrant in the household and secretly enslaving man's reason, which thought it had long ago dispelled it. The fool's mask circulated within the group, and everyone was permitted to deck it out, on his own appointed day, according to the nature of his own, or another's, attributes. At carnival time they exercised the greatest freedom, and competed with the efforts of the clergy in attracting and entertaining the people. The solemn allegorical processions of virtues and vices, arts and sciences, continents and seasons presented in visible form a number of abstract concepts, and gave the people ideas of far-off things, and so these entertainments were not without their uses, whereas the ecclesiastical mummery merely intensified absurd superstitions.

Young Serlo was once again in his element. He was not endowed with real powers of invention, but he did possess extreme skill in making good use of what was available and arranging it so that it became plausible. His ideas, his powers of imitation, that biting wit which he was able to direct, at least one day a week, even against his benefactors, made him a valuable, even indispensable, member of the company.

There was, however, a restlessness in him that drove him out of this advantageous position into other parts of his native land, where he once more had to go through a different school. He went not only to Catholic areas but also to Protestant ones that avoided displaying images, where the good and the beautiful were worshipped with equal sincerity but less inventiveness. His masks were no longer of any use; he had to concentrate on appealing directly to heart and mind. In the short time that he spent with theatrical troupes, some small, some large, he took note of the special characteristics of all the plays and their actors. The monotony prevailing at that time on the German stage, the alexandrines with their ludicrous sound and rhythm, the dialogue that was either stilted or flat, the trivial and tedious moralizing—all this he observed; and soon noticed what really moved people and appealed to them.

He retained in his memory not just individual roles but whole plays that were playable, together with the particular tone an actor had used in performing his part and winning applause for it. On one of his journeys, when he was completely out of money, he lit on the idea of performing whole plays by himself, especially at manor houses or in villages, to cover his board and lodging. He would easily set up his "theater" in any inn, room or garden. With an impish display of seriousness and seeming enthusiasm he would capture the imagination of the spectators and deceive their senses by making before their very eyes a castle out of an old cupboard and a fan into a dagger. His youthful enthusiasm took the place of real deep feeling, his violence gave the appearance of strength, his flattery of tenderness. Those already accustomed to attending the theater were reminded of everything they had already seen and heard, and those who were not were given a foretaste of something marvelous that they wished to know more about. When something was successful in one place, he made sure to repeat it in another, and he experienced malicious glee when he could fool everybody right away, and in the same fashion as before.

His mind was so vigorous, open and uninhibited that he soon improved his performances by frequent repetition of individual parts and whole plays. He acquired the ability of reciting and acting in a manner closer to the spirit of the piece than that of the other actors he had taken as his models. He was gradually able to act in a way that appeared natural, but was, in fact, highly contrived. He seemed transported, but was carefully watching for effect, and his greatest pride was in gradually awakening the emotions of the spectators. This frantic activity soon necessitated a certain degree of moderation, and, partly by design and partly from instinct, he learnt to be economical with gestures and tone of voice, which is something that few actors seem to have any understanding of.

As a result he knew how to deal with rough, unfriendly people and win their favor. Since he was always satisfied with whatever board and lodging there was, gratefully accepted every gift, and even sometimes declined money if he thought he had already received enough, he was sent on to others with letters of recommendation, and for quite a while moved from one manor to another, giving a great deal of pleasure, enjoying himself in the process, and having various charming adventures.

He was, however, so cold-hearted that he could not really love anybody, and so clear-sighted that he did not respect anyone. All he saw were external characterizing signs and these he added to his actor's catalogue. He was, however, extremely offended in his self-assurance if he did not please everybody and win their applause. He had so sharpened his mind and attention toward how best to win such approval that he became ingratiating not only when he was on the stage but also in ordinary life. His temperament, talent and lifestyle combined to make him develop into a superb actor. For by what seemed an unusual, but in fact was a quite natural interplay of effect and reaction, by a combination of natural insight and studied technique, he lifted his powers of recitation and declamation, as well as his use of gestures, onto such a high plane that they took on a truthfulness and unconstrained openness that contrasted with the secretiveness, artificiality and anxious dissimulation of his life.

Perhaps we will say more about his life and adventures in some other place. For the present we simply observe that in later years, when he was already an established person with a respected name and a very good though not secure situation, he played the sophist in his conversation, which took on a subtly ironic and mocking tone and thereby prevented all serious communication. He displayed this especially in talking to Wilhelm whenever the latter chose to embark on a general theoretical discourse, as was so often the case. Nevertheless they enjoyed each other's company, and their different attitudes made for lively discussion. Wilhelm always wanted to deduce everything from the ideas he had already formed and to consider art in a general context. He wanted to establish definite, precise rules of what was good, right, beautiful and deserving of acclaim—in short, he treated everything with utmost seriousness. Serlo, on the other hand, took everything lightly: He never answered a question directly, but by some joke or anecdote would provide the most charming and agreeable explanation, which instructed and enlivened the company.

Chapter Nineteen

While Wilhelm was spending many a pleasant hour in this way, Melina and the others were in a much more disagreeable situation. At times they seemed to Wilhelm like a group of evil spirits whose very presence, not to speak of their sour faces and bitter reproaches, was utterly distasteful to him. Serlo had not even given them temporary positions, let alone hopes of a fixed engagement, despite the fact that he had become steadily more acquainted with their abilities. When the actors met socially at his house he would have them read; sometimes he read himself. He chose plays that were about to be performed, plays which had not been put on for a long time, usually only parts of these. After a first such run-through, he came back to sections which he had something to say about, and had these repeated, so that the actors' understanding was enhanced and the likelihood of making the right point increased. Lesser but meticulous minds can do more to put others at ease than confused and unpolished geniuses; and so Serlo, by the clear understanding that he imperceptibly imparted to them, could turn mediocre talent into remarkable ability. One thing that helped greatly was that he had them read poems aloud, arousing in them a sense of the pleasure that well accented verse rhythms can produce, instead of, as usually happens in such gatherings, just having them read the sort of prose that came naturally to them.

By this means he had familiarized himself with all the actors who had recently arrived, made an assessment of what they were and what they might become, and secretly resolved to use what talents they had to his advantage, in view of a revolution that was threatening among the regular members of his company. He let matters rest for the moment, shrugged off all mediation by Wilhelm, deciding to bide his time, and, to Wilhelm's great surprise, made the proposal that he himself should become a member of the company. If he agreed to that, said Serlo, then he would also engage the others.

"So these people can't be quite so useless as you said they were," Wilhelm replied. "And if they are now to be taken on, their talents will be just as good without mine, I would think."

In strict confidence Serlo revealed to him the situation that he was in. His male lead was threatening to demand a higher salary as soon as his contract was due to be renewed. But Serlo was not inclined to agree to this, especially because this man's popularity with the public was declining. On the other hand, if he were to let him go, all his closer associates would leave with him, and a number of good, but also some mediocre actors, would be lost to the troupe. Then he explained to Wilhelm what he would gain in compensation from him and Laertes and the old Blusterer, and even Madame Melina. He even promised to get great success for the Pedant by giving him Jews, ministers and various villains to play.

Wilhelm hesitated for a moment, uneasy at the proposal. But feeling that he had to say something, he took a deep breath and replied: "Your kind words concern only the good that you see and hope for in us; how about the weaknesses, which have surely not escaped your keen judgment?"

"Those we will soon turn into strengths by hard work, careful thought and much practice. Your people may be artless or bunglers in their acting, but there is not one of them who does not show some degree of promise. As far as I can observe, there are no blockheads amongst them, and those are the only people impossible to train, no matter whether it is conceit, stupidity or hypochondria that makes them so clumsy and inflexible."

Serlo briefly outlined the conditions he was prepared to offer, asking Wilhelm for a quick decision and leaving him in some uncertainty.

While working on the fictitious travelogue which he together with Laertes had undertaken to write, partly for fun and partly because it was such a marvelous idea, he had become more observant than previously of conditions and everyday life in the real world. He now understood for the first time his father's purpose in so strongly urging him to keep a journal. More vividly than ever before he realized how valuable and satisfying it was to mediate between commercial interests and human needs, and help to extend vigorous activity in the farthermost mountain and forest regions of the country. When Laertes dragged him around this busy commercial town in which he found himself, he gained a clearer sense of one big center from which everything flowed and to which everything returned. This was the first time he had experienced real pleasure in the contemplation of such activity. In this state of mind he received Serlo's proposal; and all his desires and hopes, his belief that he had inborn talent for the theater, all his sense of obligation towards his helpless actor companions became alive again.

"Well," he said to himself, "here you are having to choose again between those two women who haunted your thoughts when you were young. The one does not look so paltry now, and the other not so splendid as she did. An inner voice impels you to follow one or the other, and there are valid external reasons for choosing either. But you can't decide. What you would prefer, would be for something from outside to tip the scales in one direction. And yet, if you are honest, you must admit that the urge towards a life of business proceeds entirely from external factors, whereas your inner desires are directed toward the development and perfection of your predisposition, both bodily and mental, toward what is good and beautiful. Must you not respect the power of Fate for having, without any cooperation on your part, brought you to the goal of all you wish? Are not all your previous thoughts and intentions being realized thanks to chance, without your doing anything about it? How very strange! The desires and hopes that a man cherishes in his heart would seem to be what he knows best; and yet, when they suddenly appear before him and are, as it were, pressing in upon him, he retreats from them, not recognizing them for what they are. All my dreams prior to that fateful night which separated me from Mariane, are now standing here before me, offering themselves to me. I came here in flight and yet have been led hither by some kindly hand. My intention was to seek refuge with Serlo; now he seeks me out and offers me conditions such as I could never have hoped for as a beginner. Was it simply my love for Mariane that made me so enthralled by the theater? Or was it love of art that made me so captivated by her? Was it the thought of future prospects, with the stage as the place to realize them, that attracted a restless, disorganized youth who wanted to live apart from the humdrum circumstances of middle-class life? Or was it something much purer, and nobler? What could possibly make you change your former opinions? Haven't you really followed your chosen path without being aware of doing so? Isn't the thing now to take the final step, since there are no other considerations involved; you can keep your solemn promise and relieve yourself honorably of your heavy responsibility toward the others."

Feelings and imaginings swept in on him in lively succession. He would be able to keep Mignon, he would not have to send the Harper away—these things weighed heavily with him. He was not yet quite decided, when he went to pay one of his customary visits to Aurelie.

Chapter Twenty

He found her lying on her sofa, and she seemed calm. "Do you think you will be able to go on stage tomorrow?" he asked. "Oh yes," she said with conviction. "You should know that nothing ever stops me from doing that. If only I could find some way of dissuading the spectators from giving me their applause. They mean well, but someday they will be the death of me. Just the day before yesterday I thought my heart would break. I used to be able to be satisfied with myself. If I had studied my part and was well prepared, I was pleased by the indications ringing out from all quarters that I had succeeded. But now I don't say what I want to say or how I want to say it. I get carried away, become confused, but my acting creates an even stronger impression. The applause is louder, and I think: if only you people knew what it is that delights you! My confused, impetuous, imprecise accents move you deeply, arouse your admiration, but you don't understand that these are the anguished cries of an unhappy woman, on whom you have bestowed your favor.

"I spent this morning learning my part, going over it, and trying it out. Now I am tired and worn out, and tomorrow it will begin all over again. Tomorrow evening is the performance. I drag myself around, bored at the prospect of getting out of bed and unwilling to go back to it. All I do is move in one continuous circle. Meager consolations sometimes occur, but the next moment I reject and revile them. I won't give in, won't give in to necessity—but why should what is destroying me, be necessary? Couldn't it be otherwise? I have to pay dearly for being a German, for Germans are temperamentally inclined to treat everything seriously, and being treated seriously by everything."

"My dear friend," Wilhelm interjected, "why don't you stop sharpening the dagger that you are constantly wounding yourself with? Have you no other thoughts? Are your youth, your figure, your health, your talents of no significance to you? If you have lost something of value through no fault of your own, is that any reason to jettison everything else? Is that really necessary?"

She was silent for a while, and then burst out: "I know it's a waste of time—love is a waste of time. What could I not have done, should have done! Now everything has turned to nothing! I am a miserable creature who's in love— nothing else! Have pity on me, for Heaven's sake, I am a poor wretched creature."

She collapsed into herself, and then after a short pause, violently cried out: "You are accustomed to everything coming your way without any effort. You cannot understand. No man can possibly appreciate a women who respects herself. By all the holy angels, by all the sacred images of bliss that a pure and generous heart may create for itself, I swear there is nothing more divine than a woman who gives herself to a man she loves! When we are worthy of the name of woman, we are cold, proud, superior, clever, clear-sighted;—but all these qualities we lay at your feet when we love, in the hope of gaining love in return. How consciously and willingly I threw away my whole existence! And now I am ready to despair,—I intend to despair! Not one drop of blood in me shall remain unpunished, not one fiber of my being stay untormented! Go on! Smile at me, laugh at my theatrical display of passion!"

Our friend was far from anything approaching laughter. The terrifying, half-natural and half-forced state of this woman tormented him too much for that. He shared the tortures that wracked her unhappy self; his mind was distraught, his feelings in a state of feverish excitement.

She stood up and paced up and down the room. "I keep recounting all the reasons why I should not love him," she said. "I know he isn't worth it. I turn my mind to something else, this way or that, wherever it chooses to go. I take up some new part in a play, even though it is not one that I am going to perform. I go over the old parts that I know so thoroughly, go over them again and again, every detail of them, rehearsing and rehearsing—o my friend, my trusted friend, what a terrible effort it is to separate oneself forcibly from oneself! My mind suffers, my brain is too tense; and so in order to avoid going mad, I return to the feeling that I love him.—Yes, I do love him, I do love him," she cried amidst constant tears, "I love him, and so—I want to die."

Wilhelm seized her by the hand and implored her not to get so worked up. "How strange it is," he said, "that we are denied not only what is impossible but so much that might be possible. You were not destined to find a faithful heart that would have given you every happiness. I was fated to have my whole salvation depend on an unfortunate girl whom I bent to the ground like a reed because of the strength of my devotion—I may even have broken her entirely."

He had already told Aurelie about his relationship with Mariane and could therefore speak of it again now. She stared fixedly into his eyes, and then asked him: "Can you truthfully say that you have never deceived a woman, never tried to elicit her favors by frivolous courtesies, wanton protestations and enticing oaths?"

"I can indeed," said Wilhelm, "and without boasting, for my life has been very simple and I have seldom been tempted to try any such thing. And what a warning it is for me, to see someone as lovely and noble as you reduced to such a pitiful condition! Let me, in your presence, swear a vow, one close to my heart, a vow whose shape and form has been decided on by the emotion that you have aroused in me and will be sanctified by this present moment: I swear to withstand all fleeting attractions and to preserve the serious ones close to my heart, for no woman to whom I will not devote my whole life shall ever hear from my lips a confession of love."

She looked at him with a fierce expression of indifference, and when he put out his hand moved away. "It's all of no consequence," she said. "A few woman's tears more or less, won't make the ocean any bigger. And yet," she continued, "if just one woman out of the thousands is saved, that is at least something— just one honest man discovered, that would be something to accept. Do you realize what you are promising?" "I do," said Wilhelm with a smile, and held out his hand. "I'll accept that," she said, and made a motion with her right hand so that he thought she was about to grasp his; but she plunged it into her pocket and in a flash pulled out the dagger and swept over his hand with its point. He withdrew his hand quickly but blood was already dripping from it.

"You men must be given a sharp cut if you are to take notice!" she cried in wild excitement, soon followed by an access of hasty busyness. She took her handkerchief and bound his hand to stop the bleeding. "Forgive a woman who is half crazy," she said, "but don't regret the loss of these few drops of blood. I am reconciled; I am myself again. On my knees I will beg your forgiveness; let me have the consolation of healing you."

She rushed to a closet, took out some linen and various implements, staunched the blood and looked carefully at the wound. It was in the ball of the hand just below the thumb and cut across the lifeline toward the little finger. She bandaged it quickly, pondering the matter seriously. He asked her several times: "How could you wound your friend?" "Quiet," she said, putting a finger to her lips, "be quiet!"

BOOK FIVE

Chapter One

Along with the two wounds that had not yet fully healed, Wilhelm had now acquired a third, which made him considerably uncomfortable. Aurelie would not allow him the services of a surgeon; instead, she bandaged him herself with all sorts of strange speeches, maxims and ceremonies, which made him extremely embarrassed. Not just he, but indeed everybody around her suffered from Aurelie's restlessness and peculiar behavior, and no one more than little Felix. The lively child became very impatient under such pressure, and more and more ill-behaved when she scolded or corrected him.

He began to take pleasure in certain things that are usually considered signs of ill-breeding, habits that she was in no wise prepared to condone. For example, he always preferred to drink out of the bottle rather than from a glass, and it seemed as if food from the dish tasted better than from his plate. Such impropriety was by no means ignored, and if he left the door open or slammed it shut, if when told to do something he remained rooted to the spot or rushed wildly out of the room, he was treated to a sharp lecture, yet without any noticeable effect. His attachment to Aurelie seemed to lessen from day to day, there was nothing affectionate in his tone of voice when he called her "Mother," and instead clung passionately to his old nurse, who did indeed let him do all he wanted.

But the nurse had been so sick for a while that she had been moved out of the house into quieter quarters, and Felix would have been left entirely on his own if Mignon had not become a loving companion and protective spirit to him as well as to others. Both children entertained each other in the most delightful way; she taught him little songs, and to the amazement of everyone he could recite them, for he had a good memory. She also tried to explain maps to him, for she was still much occupied with these; but she did not go about this in the best way. She was really only interested in whether various countries were cold or warm. She gave a vivid description of the poles and the terrible ice there, and how the warmth increased the further one got away from them. If someone was embarking on a journey, her only question was whether he was going north or south, and then she tried to trace his route on her little maps. When Wilhelm was speaking about his own journeys, she was especially attentive, and became quite sad when the conversation moved to another topic. Though she could never be persuaded to take a part in a play, and never went to a performance, she would learn odes and ballads by heart, and astonished everyone when, often quite unexpectedly and as if on the spur of the moment, she recited some such poem in her own serious and solemn way.

Serlo, always on the lookout for signs of a budding talent, tried to encourage her. What appealed to him most was the delightful variety of her singing which at times was full of life and gaiety; and because of this he came also to appreciate the Harper.

Although Serlo had no particular talent for music and did not play an instrument, he well knew the great value of this art, and did all he could to experience as often as possible a pleasure that he considered superior to any other. Every week he would have a concert, and now he had a marvelous little group of musicians, with Mignon, the Harper, and Laertes, who performed reasonably well on the violin.

Serlo used to say that we are so much inclined to busy ourselves with trivialities; our minds and senses are so easily made indifferent to the effects of beauty and perfection, that we should try to strengthen our faculty of appreciating these things. No one should entirely forego such pleasures, and it is only the fact of being unaccustomed to enjoying good things that makes so many people take pleasure in what is stupid and tasteless. One should, Serlo would say, listen to a little song, read a good poem, or look at a fine painting every single day, and if possible say something sensible about it. Given such sentiments—which were part of his nature—there was bound to be plenty of opportunity for agreeable entertainment by Serlo's associates.

In the midst of this pleasant state of affairs, a letter with a black seal was one day delivered to Wilhelm. Werner's seal indicated sad news, and Wilhelm was distressed at a brief notice of his father's death. He had died quite suddenly after a short illness, and had left his domestic affairs in very good order.

This unexpected news affected Wilhelm deeply. He was overcome by a profound sense of how insensitive and neglectful we are toward our friends and acquaintances while they are still with us, and only when our happy relationship with them is terminated, at least for a time, do we regret what we have failed to do. His distress at the untimely departure of this good man was mitigated only by the feeling that his father had been little loved, and the conviction that he had gained little pleasure from life.

Wilhelm's thoughts soon turned to his own circumstances, and here he felt extremely uneasy. No occasion is more dangerous for a man than when external circumstances produce a serious change in his situation without his thoughts or feelings being prepared for this. The result is change without change, and the tension is heightened all the more as we remain unaware of our being unprepared for the new situation.

Wilhelm suddenly found himself a free man, without as yet having achieved harmony within himself. His sentiments were noble, his intentions sincere, and his envisaged goal by no means contemptible. All this he could confidently assert; but he had often realized that he lacked experience, placed too much trust in the experience of others and attached too much value to what other people derived from their own convictions. Hence he was increasingly at a loss. He tried to acquire what he lacked by noting and assembling everything he heard or read that seemed to him worth considering. He wrote down ideas and opinions of his own and of others—sometimes even whole conversations—that interested him; but unfortunately he preserved much that was false alongside what was good, dwelt too long on one particular idea or one single maxim, and, as a result, abandoned his own natural way of thinking and acting by following the lead of others. Aurelie's bitterness and Laertes's cold contempt for humanity affected his judgment deeply. But no one was more dangerous to him than Jarno, a man whose keen intelligence delivered sharp, severe judgments on particular matters, but was wrong in giving these judgments an air of general applicability; judgments of the intellect are only relevant to a particular instance and false when extended to another.

Thus Wilhelm, in striving to achieve unity within himself, was in fact steadily depriving himself of the possibility of any such regenerative achievement; in this state of confusion his feelings were given free play, and thereby plunged him into even greater confusion about what he now had to do.

Serlo exploited the news of Wilhelm's father's death to his own advantage. Every day he had more cause to think about a different organization of the company. He must either renew the old contracts, which he did not much want to, because several members of the troupe who thought they were indispensable, were in fact becoming quite insufferable; but, on the other hand, he preferred to give the whole operation a new turn.

Without bringing pressure on Wilhelm, Serlo worked on Aurelie and Philine; and all the others who were longing for a fixed engagement did not give Wilhelm a moment's peace. So there he was, standing at the crossroads, and not knowing what to do. Curiously enough, it was a letter from Werner which, though arguing in the opposite direction, eventually brought him to a decision. We will leave out the beginning of the letter, but give the contents with little change.

Chapter Two

". . . That's how it was; and it is probably right that in every eventuality a man should continue with his job and keep up the good work. The dear old man had only just departed this life when everything in the office took on a tone that was very different from his. Friends, relatives and acquaintances stormed in, but especially those who have something to gain from such occasions. There was fetching and carrying, counting, writing and reckoning; some brought cakes and wine, others just ate and drank; nobody seemed busier than the women selecting what they should wear as mourning.

"You will therefore forgive me, my friend, if I myself used the occasion to my own advantage by being as helpful and useful as I could to your sister, and, when the time was proper, I gave her to understand that it was now our business to accelerate the sealing of a union which both our fathers had delayed up to now out of an excessive sense of what was proper form.

"You must not think that what was in our minds was to take possession of that huge empty house. We are much too modest and sensible for that; so let me tell you what we intend to do. After we are married, your sister will move over into our house, and bring your mother with her.

"'How will that be possible,' you will say, 'for you will scarcely have room in that little place.' That's the art of the thing, my friend. Skillful arrangement makes everything possible, and you wouldn't believe how much room you can find when you don't need much. We will sell the big house, for which we already have a good offer. The money that we realize from the sale, we will invest at one hundred percent.

"I hope you are in agreement with this, and my fond expectation is that you will not wish to inherit any of the unproductive pastimes of your father and your grandfather. Your grandfather's major delight was in collecting a number of insignificant works of art which no one, that I can well say, enjoyed as much as he did; and your father lived in a household of expensive luxury that he never allowed anyone else to enjoy with him. We intend to do things differently, and I am hoping for your approval.

"It is true that in our whole house my only place is at my desk and I cannot yet see where we can some day put a cradle. But there is plenty of room outside the house: coffeehouses and clubs for the husband, walks and drives for the wife, and pleasant country excursions for us both. It is a very great advantage that our round table will be fully occupied, and my father will not be able to see friends who would only make frivolous remarks, when he has gone to such trouble to be a good host.

"Above all: There shall be nothing superfluous in our house! Not too much furniture, not too many utensils—no coach and no horses. Just money, which we will spend sensibly in doing what we want to. No extensive wardrobe, just what is newest and best; the husband can wear his coat till it is threadbare and the wife peddle her dress, when both have become somewhat out of fashion. There is nothing I dislike more than an accumulation of old possessions. If someone wants to give me a valuable ring on the condition that I wear it every day, I would not accept it. For what conceivable joy is there in dead capital? So here is my joyous credo: conduct your business, acquire money, enjoy yourself with your family, and don't bother about anybody else unless you can use them to your advantage.

"Perhaps you will say: 'Where do I figure in your neat little plan? Where am I to live if you sell my father's house and there is no room in yours?'

"That, brother, is indeed the crucial point, and I will help you on that score once I have expressed appreciation of your excellent report on how you have been spending your time.

"Tell me, how did you in so short a time manage to acquire such knowledge of so many useful and interesting things? I am aware of your many abilities, but I would not have believed that you were so attentive and zealous. Your travelogue has shown us how much you have profited from your journey. Your description of the iron and copper works is exemplary and reveals your comprehension of the subject. I went there once myself, but my account looks like shoddy work when compared with yours. Your whole account of linen production is extremely instructive, and your remark concerning competitiveness is very apposite. In some places you have made mistakes in addition, but those are easily excusable.

"What gave your father and myself most pleasure were your profound insights into the management and, above all, improvement of agricultural estates. We hope to be able to purchase a big estate, now in sequestration, which is situated in a very fertile area. We shall use the money from the sale of your father's house, transferring part and leaving the rest untouched. We are reckoning on your going there to supervise the improvements. In a few years the value of the land will increase by at least a third; we can sell it and look for a bigger buy, improve that, do another trade—and you are the man for that. Meanwhile we at home will not be idle with our correspondence, and will soon all be in an enviable position.

"Farewell for now! Enjoy your life while you continue your journey, and take yourself off to wherever seems pleasant and useful. We shall not need you for the first six months, so you can now look around in the world. The best education for a smart fellow like yourself in always through travel. Goodbye, I am happy to become more closely associated with you through marriage and to be united with you by the spirit of work."

Well written and full of good business sense as it was, this letter nevertheless displeased Wilhelm in several ways. Its praise of his fictitious statistical, technological and agricultural knowledge was a silent reproach to him; and the ideal of a burgher existence that his brother-in-law depicted, did not attract him in the least. On the contrary, he felt strongly drawn in exactly the opposite direction. He convinced himself that only in the theater would he be able to achieve the education he desired for himself, and he seemed all the more strengthened in this resolve by Werner's vigorous, though unwitting, opposition. He ran through all his arguments in favor of his intentions, confirmed in his belief that he had good reason to present them in a favorable light to a man as perceptive as Werner. He composed a reply, which we shall also communicate to our readers.

Chapter Three

"Your letter was so well written and so intelligently thought out, that there is nothing to be added. But you will forgive me if I say that one may have quite different opinions (and act accordingly), and yet also be in the right. Your way of thinking and your ideal of how to live aim at unlimited possessions and easy, light-hearted enjoyment; but I need hardly tell you that nothing of that kind holds any attraction for me.

"First, I must confess to you that my travelogue was put together from various books with the help of a friend, out of a sense of the need to give my father pleasure, and though I know about the things contained in it, and others as well, I do not understand them, and I have no desire to occupy myself with them. What help is it to me to make good iron if my soul is full of slag? What use is it to me to bring order into the management of an estate if there is disorder within myself?

"Let me put it quite succinctly: even as a youth I had the vague desire and intention to develop myself fully, myself as I am. I still have the same intention, but the means to fulfill it are now somewhat clearer. I have seen more of the world than you think, and made better use of it than you can imagine. Please devote some attention to what I am going to say, even though it may not correspond to your own notions.

"If I were a nobleman, our disagreement would soon be settled; but since I belong to the middle classes, I must stake out my own path, and I hope you will understand what I am doing. I don't know how it is in other countries, but it seems to me that in Germany general education of the self is possible only for the nobility. The middle class can acquire merit and, if driven to extremes, develop the mind; but in so doing it loses its personality, however it presents itself. A nobleman who consorts with distinguished persons is obliged to behave in a distinguished manner, which, since all doors are open to it, becomes a manner that is free and unconstrained, so that, whether at court or in the army, his currency is his person and the figure he cuts. As a result, he has good reason to regard the way he appears as a matter of importance, and to show that he does. A certain formal grace in ordinary affairs, coupled with a certain relaxed elegance in serious and important matters, becomes him well.

He is a public person, and the more cultivated his movements, the richer his voice, and the more controlled and measured his whole personality, the more accomplished he becomes; if he always remains the same, whether talking to the highborn or the lowly, to friends or relations, no fault will be found in him and no one would wish him otherwise. He can be cold, but intelligent; dissembling, but prudent. If he is in control of himself at every moment of his life, no one has any further demands to make of him and everything else about him—ability, talent, wealth—seem only adjuncts or appendages.

"But then imagine a burgher who thinks he might make some claim to these qualities. He is bound to fail, and he will be all the more unhappy for having, as part of his nature, the ability and urge toward such a different way of life.

"Since a nobleman has no restrictions in his everyday life and may possibly be made into a king or the like, he has to appear before his fellowmen with an unspoken awareness of what he is. He can always move to the fore, whereas the burgher does best to respect quietly the limits imposed on him. The burgher should not ask: 'Who am I?' but 'What do I have? What insights, what knowledge, what ability, what capital?' The nobleman tells us everything through the person he presents, but the burgher does not, and should not. A nobleman can and must be someone who represents by his appearance, whereas the burgher simply is, and when he tries to put on an appearance, the effect is ludicrous or in bad taste. The nobleman should act and achieve, the burgher must labor and create, developing some of his capabilities in order to be useful, but without it ever being assumed that there is or ever can be a harmonious interplay of qualities in him, because in order to make himself useful in one direction, he has to disregard everything else.

"The differences are not due to any pretentiousness on the part of the aristocracy or the submissiveness of the bourgeoisie, but to the whole organization of society. Whether this will ever change, or what will change, does not really concern me. Given the present state of things, what I have to do is think about myself, maintain what I know to be the basic need of myself, and achieve its fulfillment.

"I have an irresistible desire to attain the harmonious development of my personality such as was denied me by my birth. Since I left home I have made successful efforts to improve my physical powers, and I have overcome much of my former diffidence in presenting myself as I really am. I have, for example, improved my voice and my speech and can truly say that in society I make a favorable impression. But every day my desire to be a public person becomes more and more irrepressible, with the result that I am always trying to please and be effective in wider circles. Add to that my fondness for poetry and everything connected with it, the need to develop my mind and my taste, so that, in the pleasures I cannot do without, I may gradually come to see good only in what is good, and beauty only in the truly beautiful. You can see that as far as I am concerned, all this is to be found only in the theater; only there can I really move and develop as I would wish to. On the stage a cultured human being can appear in the full splendor of his person, just as in the upper classes of society. There, mind and body keep step in all one does, and there I will be able simultaneously to *be* and to *appear* better than anywhere else. Should I seek other secondary ways of occupying myself, there will be enough routine chores to exercise my patience.

"Don't argue with me about this; for, before you have a chance to write, I will already have taken the decisive step. Because of prevailing prejudices I will change my name; anyhow I would be embarrassed to be known by the name of Meister, which implies mastery. Fare you well. Our finances are in such good hands that I do not need to bother about them; when I need money I will ask you for it. It won't be much, for I hope to support myself by my art."

Having sent off the letter, Wilhelm immediately did what he said he would, and, to the astonishment of Serlo and all the others, suddenly declared that he would become an actor and was ready to sign a contract so long as its conditions were reasonable. They soon agreed, for Serlo had talked about this earlier in terms that Wilhelm and the others found quite easy to accept. The whole pathetic company, with whom we have occupied ourselves for so long, were finally taken on, without anyone except Laertes expressing any gratitude to Wilhelm. They had made their demands without confiding in him, and likewise accepted their fulfillment without thanking him. Most of them preferred to credit their engagement to the influence of Philine, and it was to her that they expressed their thanks. The contracts were drawn up and signed, and by a strange connection of ideas there arose before Wilhelm's mind at the very moment that he was signing his fictitious name, the image of that place in the woods where he lay wounded in Philine's lap. The lovely Amazon came riding up on her white horse from out of the bushes, moved forward, and dismounted. Her generous concern made her pace to and fro, until finally she stood still in front of him. Her coat slipped from her shoulders, her face, indeed her whole body, shone, and then she disappeared. He wrote down his assumed name quite mechanically, without knowing what he was doing, and only after he had signed the contract did he notice that Mignon was standing beside him, holding his arm and gently trying to draw his hand away.

Chapter Four

One condition that Wilhelm made on joining the company was accepted by Serlo only with a certain proviso. Wilhelm had insisted that they should perform *Hamlet* in its entirety, and Serlo agreed to this interesting but extraordinary proposal only to the extent that it was feasible. They had been arguing about this for some time, the question being what was feasible and what was not, but so far they had not been able to agree on what could be cut without destroying the play.

Wilhelm was still at that happy stage in life when it seems inconceivable that there could be any blemish on a girl one loves or an author that one admires. Our feelings are so absolute and so all of a piece that we assert a similar perfection and harmony in the objects. Serlo, on the other hand, liked to analyze, maybe too much; his sharp intelligence tended to see a work of art as a more or less imperfect whole. He thought that there was no need to be so circumspect with plays as one found them; even Shakespeare, and especially *Hamlet*, would have to suffer somewhat.

Wilhelm was not prepared to listen to him talk in terms of wheat and chaff. "It's not a question of a mixture of wheat and chaff," he declared, "this is a tree with branches, twigs, leaves, buds, blossoms and fruit. Everything is related to everything else." Serlo replied that one shouldn't try to serve up a whole tree, but apples of gold in baskets of silver. They exhausted themselves in metaphor, and their opinions differed increasingly.

Wilhelm became nearly distraught when one day, after a long argument, Serlo suggested that the simplest way to settle things was to take a pen and strike out those things in the play that just would not get across, combine several characters into one, and, if Wilhelm did not himself have sufficient knowledge or courage to do this, he should leave it to him, Serlo, and the whole matter would soon be settled.

"That is not what we agreed on," said Wilhelm. "How can you be so reckless when you have such good taste?"

"My friend," said Serlo, "you will soon get that way yourself. I know all too well how despicable such a procedure is, and that it is perhaps something that has not happened in the best theaters. But our German theater is in such a sorry state. Our authors make such mutilations necessary, and the public accepts them. How many plays do we have that do not exceed our resources in personnel, scenery and theatrical machinery, that are too long, have too much dialogue or make demands exceeding the physical power of our actors? And yet we must go on playing, time after time, always offering something new. Shouldn't we use what we have to our advantage, since we achieve just as much by plays that are cut than by ones that aren't? It is the public that makes us do this, for there are few Germans and perhaps few spectators in any nation nowadays that have any sense of an aesthetic whole. They only praise or blame pieces, their pleasure is piecemeal, and whom does that please more than our actors, for theater remains just patchwork, a collection of bits and pieces."

"Not *remains*," said Wilhelm, "though that's what it *is*. But must everything remain as it is? Don't try to convince me that you are right. No power in the world would persuade me to abide by a contract signed in such gross error."

Serlo switched to a lighter touch and urged Wilhelm to think over their many conversations about *Hamlet* and work out by himself what would be a satisfactory version.

After spending a few days by himself, Wilhelm came back with an air of satisfaction. "I must be making a great mistake," he said, "if I don't think I've found a way of dealing with this whole matter. I even believe that Shakespeare himself would have done likewise if his mind had not been so fixed on the central idea and distracted by the novellas he was working from."

"Let me hear what you have to say," said Serlo, seating himself on the sofa somewhat pompously. "I will listen quietly and criticize sharply."

Wilhelm said: "I am not afraid of that. Just listen. After careful examination and reflection I can distinguish two aspects of the composition of the play. Very important is, first, the *internal* relationship between the personages and the events, the powerful effects that emerge from the characters and actions of the main personages—these are all excellently presented and the sequence in which they occur could not be bettered. No production of the play can destroy this, or in any way falsify it. This is what everyone demands to be shown and nobody would dare to interfere with something that makes such a deep impression on the minds of the observers. Almost all of this, I have been told, has been preserved on the German stage. But I believe a mistake has been made with regard to the second aspect of the play, namely the *external* circumstances affecting the characters, how they come to move from one place to another, how they are fortuitously brought into contact with each other; these have, in my opinion, been given insufficient importance, only referred to in passing, or even omitted. These threads are certainly rather loose and thin, but they do run through the whole play and tie up what would otherwise fall apart, and does indeed fall apart when they are left out, as if just leaving the ends were sufficient.

"To my mind these external circumstances include the troubles in Norway, the war with young Fortinbras, the ambassadorial mission to the old uncle, the settlement of the dispute, young Fortinbras's march into Poland, and his return at the end of the play. Likewise Horatio's return from Wittenberg, Hamlet's desire to go there, Laertes's visit to France and his subsequent return, the dispatching of Hamlet to England, his capture by pirates, and the death of the two courtiers because of the treacherous letter. All these things are circumstances and events which would give breadth to a romance, but they seriously disturb the unity of a play in which the hero himself has no plan, and are therefore defects."

"That's how I like to hear you talk!" said Serlo.

"Don't interrupt me," said Wilhelm. "You won't approve of everything I have to say. These faults are like temporary props for a structure and should not be removed unless they are replaced by some stronger support. My proposal would be not to tamper with the big situation at the beginning and, as far as possible, to leave it as it is both as regards its overall structure and the incidentals; and instead to replace all those desultory and distracting separate external motifs by one single motivation."

"And what would that be?" asked Serlo, rising from his comfortable position.

"I would make proper use of something that is already contained in the play," Wilhelm replied, "namely the troubles in Norway. Here is my proposal for you to consider.

"After the death of Hamlet senior, the recently conquered Norwegians become restless. The governor there sends his son Horatio, an old school friend of Hamlet's and superior in courage and shrewdness to all the others, to Denmark, to press for the readying of the fleet, which is not proceeding space because of the easy living of the new king. Horatio knew the previous king, having fought under him in his last battles, and had always enjoyed his favor: the first scene with the Ghost will gain by this means. The new king then gives an audience to Horatio, and sends Laertes to Norway with the news that the fleet will soon be landing there, while Horatio is charged with speeding up its preparation. Hamlet's mother, however, will not agree to her son going to sea with Horatio, as Hamlet himself would have wished."

"Thank God for that!" exclaimed Serlo. "So then we can get rid of Wittenberg and the university, which were always a thorn in my flesh. I think your ideas are quite good, for, apart from the two offstage elements of Norway and the fleet, the audience does not need to supply anything in its thoughts. They can see all the rest, for that is going on before their eyes, and their imagination does not have to be chasing all over the place."

"You can easily see how I would link up all the rest. When Hamlet tells Horatio about his stepfather's crime, Horatio advises him to go with him to Norway, gain control of the army and return with it in force. When Hamlet becomes too dangerous for both the king and the queen, they have no easier means of getting rid of him than sending him to join the fleet and instructing Rosencrantz and Guildenstern to keep an eye on him; and when Laertes returns in the meantime, they send him after Hamlet, for Laertes is in a murderous temper. The fleet is delayed by unfavorable winds; Hamlet returns. His wandering through the churchyard could perhaps be better motivated. But his encounter with Laertes at the grave of Ophelia is a great moment and absolutely indispensable. The king can then decide that it would be better to rid himself of Hamlet at once. The celebration to mark his departure and his apparent reconciliation with Laertes is carried out with great ceremony, including chivalrous combats in which Hamlet and Laertes fence with each other. I cannot do without the four corpses at the end; no one should be left alive. And, since the people now have to elect a new king, Hamlet, as he dies, gives his vote to Horatio."

"Now you sit right down and work the whole thing out," said Serlo, "for your ideas have my complete approval, and let's not allow our satisfaction to dissipate."

Chapter Five

Wilhelm had been working for a long time on a translation of *Hamlet*. In doing so he had used the talented version by Wieland, which had been his first introduction to Shakespeare. Where he found something missing, he put it back, and so he had in his possession a complete text of the play when he talked with Serlo about an acting version, and had achieved relative agreement with him. He now set to work taking things out and putting things in, separating and combining, changing things and then putting them back as they were; for, pleased as he was with his own ideas, he felt that when he put them into practice, the original suffered in the process.

When he had finished, he read it aloud to Serlo and the others. They were extremely pleased with all he had done, and Serlo in particular expressed his approval on several points.

"You were quite right," he said, amongst other things, "in feeling that the external circumstances surrounding the action should be conveyed more simply than this great writer has presented them. Everything that happens off-stage and is therefore invisible to the spectators, should be the background against which the characters move and act. The one big vista entailing the fleet and Norway will add to the effectiveness of the play; if you leave that out, it becomes just a domestic tragedy and the whole stupendous idea that a regal household is destroyed by internal crimes and ineptness would not present itself in its full majesty. If, on the other hand, this background were to be portrayed as one of shifting complexity and confusion, this would detract from the effectiveness of the characters."

Wilhelm then proceeded to defend Shakespeare once more, pointing out that he was writing for an island people, for Englishmen with sea voyages and ships as their background, who are accustomed to seeing with their own eyes the coast of France and pirates, so that what would be confusing and distracting for us, was everyday experience for them.

Serlo had to admit this, but they both agreed that a simpler and more telling background was better suited for a performance on a German stage and the imaginations of German spectators.

The roles had already been assigned. Serlo took on Polonius, Aurelie was to play Ophelia, Laertes his namesake, and a young man, recently arrived and rather squat but nevertheless lively, was given the role of Horatio. They were in some doubt about who should play the king and who the Ghost. The only person available for either of these roles was the old Blusterer. Serlo suggested the Pedant for the king, but Wilhelm protested vigorously. They could not arrive at a decision on this matter. Wilhelm had also left intact the two characters of Rosencrantz and Guildenstern. "Why didn't you combine them into one?" Serlo asked. "That would be an easy saving."

"Heaven preserve me from shortcuts like that, which would work against both sense and effect!" Wilhelm replied. "What these two men are and what they do, cannot be embodied in one and the same person. It is in such details that Shakespeare reveals his greatness. The creepiness, the bowing and scraping, the approving, flattering and insinuating, their adroitness and strutting, wholeness and emptiness, their utter roguery, their ineptness—how could all this be portrayed by one person? There should be at least a dozen of them, if that were feasible. For they are not just something in society, they are society, and Shakespeare was very modest and wise to give us only two such representatives. Also I need them as a pair, so that in my version they will contrast with the one, good, honest Horatio."

"I understand what you mean," said Serlo, "and we can help ourselves out. We'll give one of them to Elmire" (that was the name of the Blusterer's oldest daughter). "It won't hurt so long as she looks good, and I will preen and train the doll so that she is a delight."

Philine was delighted that she was to be the duchess in the play within the play. "I'll make it seem so natural to marry a second husband quickly when one has loved the first so much. I shall hope to receive a huge burst of applause, and every man will wish he could be my third."

Aurelie made a sour face at these remarks; her dislike of Philine was increasing daily.

"It is really a pity that we have no ballet," said Serlo. "Otherwise you could perform a *pas de deux* with each of your husbands, and the old man could fall asleep in keeping with the rhythm and your feet and legs would look just fine on that cute little stage in the background."

"What do you know about my legs?" she said cheekily. "And as for my feet," she added, reaching quickly beneath the table for her slippers and placing them in front of Serlo. "These are my stilts and I defy you to find prettier ones."

"I was quite serious," he said; then, looking at the delicate footwear: "You're right. It would be hard to find anything prettier."

They had been made in Paris, and Philine had received them as a present from the countess, a lady whose beautiful feet were famous.

"What charming things!" said Serlo. "My heart leaps within me when I contemplate them."

"What words of rapture!" said Philine.

"Nothing transcends a pair of slippers of such delicate, beauteous workmanship," he exclaimed; "but their sound is even more charming than their appearance." He picked them up and let one after the other fall several times onto the table.

"What are you doing? Just give them back to me!" she cried.

"May I say," he added with simulated modesty and roguish seriousness, "that we bachelors, who are mostly alone at night and have fears like other men, pine for companionship in the dark and seek it in hostelries and other strange and unsuitable places; we find it very consoling if some goodhearted girl provides us with the support of her company. It's night, we are in bed, and hear a rustling. We are startled, the door opens, and we hear a sweet little piping voice, something creeps in, the curtains swish, click! clack! the slippers fall to the ground, and whoosh! we're no longer alone. Oh that sweet, unique sound of slippers falling on the floor. The smaller they are, the finer they sound. You may talk about nightingales, murmuring brooks, rustling winds, organs and pipes, I'll stick with my click! clack!—that is the best tune to dance to, over and over again."

Philine took the slippers out of his hands and said: "Just look how I have bent them! They're much too wide for me now." Then she played with them, rubbing one sole against the other. "How warm they get!" she said, putting one of the soles flat against her cheek, then she went on rubbing and handed it to Serlo. He was gracious enough to test the warmth, and "Click! Clack!" she said, giving him such a sharp blow with the heel that he withdrew his hand with a yelp. "I'll teach you to think otherwise about my slippers," said Philine with a laugh.

"And I will teach you not to treat old people like children!" he shouted as he jumped up, grabbed her and stole many a kiss, which she pretended to bestow under pressure. In the struggle her long hair came loose, wound itself around everybody, the chair fell to the ground, and Aurelie, disgusted by such goings-on, stood up in anger.

Chapter Six

Although several parts had been left out in this new version of *Hamlet*, there were still enough for the troupe to have difficulty in assigning them all.

"If things go on like this," said Serlo, "our prompter will have to leave his box, become one of us, and take over a part."

"I've often admired the work he does," said Wilhelm.

"Yes, I don't believe we could have a better person to prod our memory. None of the spectators will ever hear him, but on the stage we hear every word he says. He has developed a special kind of voice, and as a sort of guiding spirit whispers in our ears when we're in trouble. He knows instinctively which part of his role an actor will remember correctly, and he senses well in advance when memory will let him down. In some cases when I hardly had the time to read through the part, he spoke each word ahead for me, and I was able to get through it without mishap; but he does have certain peculiarities, which makes him of little use to others. For example, he becomes so passionately involved in the plays that he will give highly personal, emotional renderings of moving passages that should just be declaimed. This unfortunate habit has more than once put me off course."

"He has another odd habit which once let me down in a particularly tricky passage," said Aurelie.

"But how is that possible when he is so attentive?" Wilhelm asked.

"He is so moved by some passages," said Aurelie, "that he weeps bitter tears and for a time completely loses control of himself. And these are not what are normally considered moving passages, but rather, if I may say so, those beautiful passages in which an author's power of feeling becomes evident, which give most of us intense pleasure but cause others to look away."

"But if he has such a tender heart, why doesn't he become an actor?"

"Because his hoarse voice and stiff movements would not do well on the stage, and his melancholy manners make him unsociable," Serlo replied. "What trouble I have had trying to make him get along with me! But without success. He reads excellently. I have never heard anyone read better. And he really can respect the thin dividing line between declamation and emotionally charged recitation."

"That's it," said Wilhelm. "That's what we need. What a stroke of luck! We now have the actor who can recite the passage about the rugged Pyrrhus."

"Only someone as enthusiastic as you can bend everything to his ends," said Serlo.

"I would certainly have been very unhappy if that particular passage had been omitted; it would have crippled the play."

"I can't see why," said Aurelie.

"I hope you will agree with me when you have heard what I have to say," Wilhelm replied. "Shakespeare introduces this group of actors with a double purpose. First: The man who declaims the speech about the death of Priam with so much emotion, deeply moves Prince Hamlet. He pricks the conscience of the vacillating youth, and so this scene becomes the prelude to the play within the play, which makes such a deep impression on the king. Hamlet is put to shame by an actor who becomes so caught up in the sorrow of a fictitious personage, and conceives the idea of 'catching the conscience' of his stepfather the king by this means. What a marvelous monologue that is which concludes the second act! What joy it is to recite:

> O! what a rogue and peasant slave am I:
> Is it not monstrous that this player here,
> But in a fiction, in a dream of passion,
> Could force his soul so to his own conceit
> That from her working all his visage wann'd,
> Tears in his eyes, distraction in's aspect,
> A broken voice, and his whole function suiting
> With forms to his conceit? and all for nothing!
> For Hecuba!
> What's Hecuba to him, or he to Hecuba,
> That he should weep for her?"

"If only we can persuade our man to go on stage," said Aurelie.

"We will have to get him used to the idea gradually," Serlo suggested. "Let him read the speech at rehearsals, and let's say we're waiting for an actor to play the part. Then we'll see whether we can work on him."

Having agreed on this they went on to talk about the Ghost. Wilhelm could not bring himself to give the living king's part to the Pedant and the Ghost to the Blusterer, and thought that they should wait a while; there were several other actors coming their way and perhaps the right person might be found.

One can therefore well imagine how astonished Wilhelm was that same evening to find a letter addressed to him under his stage name, written in strange characters, sealed, and lying on his table, which said: "We know full well, o wondrous youth, that you are in a serious predicament. You can hardly find enough living persons for your *Hamlet*, let alone ghosts. Your zeal deserves to be rewarded by a miracle: We cannot perform miracles, but something miraculous shall happen. If you have confidence in us, the Ghost will appear at the appointed hour. Take courage, and be not afraid. A reply is not necessary, we will be informed of your decision."

He hurried back to Serlo with this curious message. Serlo read it several times, reflected, and then said that he thought this was a matter of importance, and they ought to consider whether they should take the risk. They talked back and forth. Aurelie was very quiet and smiled from time to time; and when some days later they returned to the subject, she made it quite clear that she thought this was one of Serlo's jokes. She urged Wilhelm not to worry and to wait patiently for the Ghost to appear.

Serlo was in the best of humor, for the actors who were leaving did all they could to perform well, so that they would be sorely missed, and he expected good takings from the public that would be anxious to see the new actors.

His association with Wilhelm also affected him. He began to talk more about art, for he was after all a German, and Germans like to be able to justify what they are doing. Wilhelm made a record of many of these conversations, and we will impart these to those of our readers who may be interested in dramaturgical questions, but sometime later, so as not constantly to interrupt the flow of the narrative.

Serlo was in an especially good mood one evening when talking about the role of Polonius and how he conceived it. "I promise you," he said, "this time to come up with a really worthy figure. I will convey his calm assurance, his insaneness and his thoughtfulness, agreeableness as well as tactlessness, free-spirited and yet eavesdropping, a rogue at heart who pretends to be truthful, each of these facets in its place. I will present a graybeard who is honest, long-suffering and timeserving, someone who is half a villain but also the perfect courtier; and for this I will make use of the few indications the author has given us. I will talk like a book when I am prepared, and like a fool when I am in a good mood. I will be insipid enough to parrot what others say, and yet refined enough not to show that I know when they are making a fool of me. I have rarely played a part with such anticipation and malicious enjoyment."

"If only I had as much to anticipate from my role," said Aurelie. "I have neither the youthfulness nor the gentleness to think myself into this character. But one thing I unfortunately do know: The feelings that turned Ophelia's head will always be with me."

"Let's not bother too much about all this," said Wilhelm. "For I can say that, despite my intense study of the play, my desire to act Hamlet has led me astray. The more I worked myself into the part, the more I have become aware that my physical appearance has absolutely none of the characteristics Shakespeare gave to Hamlet. And when I realize that everything in the role fits together into one piece, I have doubts whether I can do even a moderately good performance."

"You are reacting very conscientiously to your new profession," Serlo replied. "An actor fits himself as best he can to the role, and the role will necessarily have to adapt itself to him. But tell me, how did Shakespeare conceive Hamlet's physical appearance? Is it so different from yours?"

"First of all, he is blond," said Wilhelm.

"That seems to me far-fetched," said Aurelie. "Where did you get that idea?"

"As a Dane, a Norseman, he is bound to be blond, and have blue eyes."

"Do you think Shakespeare thought about such things as that?"

"I don't find it expressly stated, but I think it is undeniable if one considers certain passages in the play. The fencing is hard for him, sweat runs off his face, and the queen says: 'He's fat and scant of breath.' How can you imagine him, except as blond and portly? For people who are dark-haired are rarely like that when they are young. And do not his fits of melancholy, the tenderness of his grief, his acts of indecisiveness, better suit someone like that than a slim youth with curly brown hair from whom one would expect more alacrity and determination?"

"You are spoiling my whole image of him," said Aurelie. "Get rid of that fat Hamlet! Don't show us a portly prince. Give us instead some substitute to please us and engage our sympathies. We are not as much concerned with the author's intentions as we are with our own pleasure, and we therefore expect to be attracted by someone like ourselves."

Chapter Seven

One evening the company debated whether drama or novel should be ranked higher. Serlo asserted that this was a futile and ill-conceived argument, since each could be excellent in its own way, so long as it kept within the bounds of its genre.

"I am not quite clear about that," said Wilhelm.

"Who is?" said Serlo. "And yet it would be worth while going into the matter more closely."

They all talked back and forth, and the final result of their conversation was roughly this:

In the novel as well as in the drama we observe human nature and action. The difference between the two genres lies not merely in their external form—people talk in the one and are usually talked about in the other. Unfortunately many dramas are only novels in dialogue, and it should be perfectly possible to write drama in letters.

In the novel it is predominantly sentiments and events that are to be presented; in drama, characters and deeds. The novel must move slowly and the sentiments of the main personage must, in some way or another, hold up the progression of the whole toward its resolution. But drama must move quickly and the character of the main personage must press toward the end, not himself holding up this progression, but being held up in it. The hero of a novel must be passive, or at least not active to a high degree; from the hero of a play we demand effective action and deeds. Grandison, Clarissa, Pamela, the Vicar of Wakefield, even Tom Jones are, if not passive, yet "retarding" personages, and all events are to a certain extent fashioned after their sentiments. In drama, the hero fashions nothing according to himself, everything resists him, and he either clears obstacles or pushes them aside, or he succumbs to them.

They agreed that in the novel Chance might well be given free play, but that it must always be guided and controlled by the sentiments of the personages; whereas Fate, which, without any action by human beings on their part, drives them through circumstances unrelated to themselves toward an unforeseen catastrophe, can have its function only in drama. Chance may indeed produce pathetic, but never tragic situations; whereas Fate must always be terrible and becomes tragic in the highest sense if it brings guilty and innocent deeds that are not connected with each other into some dire connection.

These reflections led them back again to the peculiarities of *Hamlet* as a play. The hero, it was said, really only has sentiments, and it is only external events that work upon him, so that this play has something of the breadth of a novel. But since Fate determines its plan, since it begins with a terrible deed and the hero is driven ever further toward another terrible deed, it is tragic in the highest sense of the term and cannot but end tragically.

The next thing to do was to have a reading rehearsal. Wilhelm envisaged this as a sort of celebration. He had collated the parts in advance, so that there should be no objections raised about them. All the actors were fully acquainted with the play, and all he did before they began was to impress on them how important a reading rehearsal is. It is demanded of every musician that he should be able to play more or less at sight, and therefore every actor, indeed any well-bred person, should practice sightreading, extract the character of a drama, poem or story, and be able to reproduce this with some facility. Memorizing is of no use at all unless an actor has first thought his way into the spirit and intentions of the author; the letter is nothing without the spirit.

Serlo asserted that he would supervise all rehearsals, including the dress rehearsal, once they had agreed on the importance of having the reading rehearsal. "For," he said, "there is nothing more amusing than actors talking about studying. It is like freemasons talking about work."

The rehearsal went well, and the time was well spent, for it created a solid basis for the profit and repute they were to earn.

"You did well, my friend, to talk so seriously to our colleagues," said Serlo once they were alone together, "but I am afraid they will hardly come up to your expectations."

"Why not?" Wilhelm enquired.

"My experience has been that it is easy enough to set people's imaginations working, but, much as they like to be told tales, their minds are rarely productive. This is especially so with actors. An actor is quite content to take on a striking and worthy role, but rarely does more than put himself self-satisfiedly in the hero's place, without any concern as to whether other people will accept that. But having a vivid comprehension of what the author of the play had in mind, and knowing how much of one's own personality one must efface in order to do justice to the role, sensing that one is oneself quite different, and yet having the power to convince the audience that one is what one portrays, having the ability by the compelling truth of the presentation to turn planks into temples and cardboard into forests—that is given to few. The mind's power to create illusion in the spectators, fictitious truth producing solid effects by aiming solely at illusion, who amongst them can understand that?

"Let us therefore not insist too much on spirit and feeling. The safest way to proceed will be to explain quietly to our friends the meaning of the text and open up their minds. Those who have the right talent will quickly find their way into the sort of portrayal that is both intelligent and moving; and those who do not, will at least not act and speak all that badly. There is, according to my observation, nothing more presumptuous in actors (and indeed in everybody else) than claiming to understand the spirit without having a clear understanding of the letter."

Chapter Eight

Wilhelm arrived early for the first full rehearsal, and found himself alone on stage. He was surprised by what he saw and was beset with strange memories.

There were sets for a forest and a village that were just like those in the theater of his home town on the day that Mariane had declared her love for him at a rehearsal and agreed to spend that first blissful night with him. The cottages on the stage were all alike, just as they are in the country; the morning sun shone actually through a half-open window on to a rather rickety stage bench near the door, but unfortunately not, as previously, on Mariane's bosom. He sat down, thought about this strange concatenation of circumstances, and even felt that he might see her again soon. But what he was looking at was only the set for an epilogue such as was at that time customarily given on German stages.

His thoughts were interrupted by the arrival of the other actors, together with two men who seemed interested in the theater and its equipment. These two greeted Wilhelm warmly. One of them was a sort of hanger-on of Madame Melina's, the other was a real devotee of the drama; any good company would be happy to have both as friends. It was hard to say whether they had more love of the theater or knowledge of it. They loved it too much to understand it properly, and they understood enough to approve of what was good and disapprove of what was not. They were not unmoved by what was mediocre, but their pleasure, both in anticipation and in retrospect, at what was really good, seemed to surpass their powers of expression. They delighted in the mechanics, were transported by what appealed to their mind, and their passion for the theater was so strong that even a piecemeal rehearsal would create some degree of illusion in them. The faults always receded into the distance, and the good things touched them deeply. They were the kind of admirers every artist wants. They liked to stroll from the wings down to the auditorium, and back again, they loved to linger in the dressing rooms. Their favorite occupation was to offer comments on the posture, costume, reciting and declamation of the actors, their liveliest conversation concerned the effects produced, and their efforts were constantly directed towards making sure that the actors were attractive, active and to the point, giving them their assistance and affection, and, though shunning extravagance, providing them with various little pleasures. They had secured the exclusive right of being present at every rehearsal and performance. They did not agree with Wilhelm on every point regarding the performance of *Hamlet*. Occasionally he yielded to their opinions, though on the whole he tended to stick to his own. All these conversations contributed to the development of his own taste. He let both men see how much he respected them, and they for their part were of the opinion that this united effort was the harbinger of a new era in the German theater.

The presence of these two men at the rehearsals was extremely useful. Above all they were able to persuade the actors that in a rehearsal positioning and movements should be coordinated with speaking just as in a finished performance, so that the combination would become completely automatic. Especially as regards the hands: there should be no ordinary, trivial actions during the rehearsal of a tragedy such as taking a pinch of snuff. If an actor does that, there is the risk that in the performance he might miss his snuffbox. They were also against actors rehearsing in high boots when the role called for shoes. And nothing distressed them more at rehearsals than actresses who put their hands in the pleats of their skirts.

Another good thing that emerged from the advice of these two men was that the actors learned how to drill and march. "Since nowadays there are so many military roles," they said, "there is nothing more pathetic than seeing men totally without training waddling about the stage in captain's and major's uniforms." Wilhelm and Laertes were the first to take instruction from a drill sergeant while at the same time vigorously continuing their fencing practice.

So these two friends of the theater spent a great deal of effort improving a company that had been brought together by such happy chance. They insured the future satisfaction of the public by talking to the actors about this their most passionate concern. It was difficult to overestimate the value of their efforts, because they concentrated particularly on what was of most importance, namely that it was the duty of the actors to speak loud and clear. On this they encountered more opposition than they had at first expected. Most of the actors wanted to be heard much as they usually spoke, not to speak so that they could be heard. Some blamed the building, others said one shouldn't shout if one was to speak naturally, intimately or tenderly.

Our two friends, patient beyond words, tried to clear up this misapprehension and to overcome such stubborn notions. They tried every argument and every form of flattery, and finally succeeded in their purpose by pointing to Wilhelm as a good example. He asked them to sit during rehearsals at the far end of the building, and to let him know when they could not hear what he was saying by knocking on the bench with a key. He articulated well, spoke in measured tones, raising his voice by stages, but never shouting even in the most violent passages. At each subsequent rehearsal there was less knocking of keys; gradually all the other actors accepted the procedure, and everyone now hoped that the play would be audible in all parts of the house.

One can see how human beings like to reach their ends only by their own means, how much trouble it takes to make them understand what is self-evident, and how difficult it is to implant in someone who has real ambitions the first conditions that will make his efforts likely to succeed.

Chapter Nine

Work proceeded on sets and costumes, and various other things. Wilhelm had some fancies about certain scenes and passages, and Serlo gave in to these, partly because of the contract and partly from being convinced by what he said, but also because he hoped, by obliging him in this respect, to win him over, and then, in the future, to influence him more and more toward his own ends and purposes.

For instance: Wilhelm wanted the king and the queen to be seated on their thrones in the first big scene with the courtiers off to the side and Hamlet placed unobtrusively amongst them. "Hamlet," he said, "must keep quiet, his black garments will sufficiently mark him out. He should conceal himself rather than be readily visible. Only when the audience is over and the king speaks to him as a son, should he step forward and the scene take its appointed course."

A major problem was presented by the two portraits, which Hamlet refers to so passionately in the scene with his mother. "I want them both to be life-size and placed on the back wall on either side of the main entrance, with that of the old king in full armor like the Ghost and on the side where it enters. He should be portrayed with his right hand raised in a gesture of command, slightly turned to one side and almost looking over his shoulder, so that he looks exactly like the Ghost when it goes out of the door. That will be very effective when Hamlet is looking at the Ghost and the queen at the portrait. The stepfather should be presented in full regalia but not make such an imposing impression as Hamlet's father."

There were various other points which we will perhaps have occasion to refer to later.

"Are you adamant about Hamlet dying at the end?" Serlo asked.

"How can I keep him alive," said Wilhelm, "when the whole play has crushed him to death? We've already talked about that at length."

"But the public will want him to remain alive."

"I will gladly grant you anything else, but that cannot be. We also wish that a fine man suffering from a mortal illness should live longer. His family weeps and beseeches the doctor, but he cannot save him; natural necessity cannot be withstood, but no more can a recognized artistic necessity. It would be making a false concession to the mob to arouse feelings that they desire rather than what they should have."

"The one who provides the money should have his choice of the goods."

"Yes, to a certain extent; but a large public deserves to be respected, and not treated like children from whom you take money. If, by showing them what is good, we develop in them a feeling or taste for what is good, they will be all the more willing to pay their money because they will have nothing to reproach themselves for. They can be flattered like a child you wish to improve and help toward greater intelligence, not like a rich grandee to perpetuate his failings from which one profits."

They also settled various matters related to the question of what should be changed and what could be left as it is. We will not go into that any further now, but perhaps we will sometime communicate this new version of *Hamlet* to those of our readers who may be interested.

Chapter Ten

The dress rehearsal was over. It had lasted an unconscionably long time. Serlo and Wilhelm found that there was still much to be concerned about; for, despite the length of time they had spent on preparation, there were certain matters that had been put off till the last moment. For example: The portraits of the two kings were not finished, and the scene between Hamlet and his mother, which they expected would have a terrific effect, was as a result still very thin because neither the Ghost nor its portrait were part of it. Serlo joked about this and said: "We would really be in a sorry situation if the Ghost were not to appear, the watch were to fence with thin air, and the prompter were to supply the Ghost's speech!"

"Let's not scare away our supernatural friend by our doubts," Wilhelm replied. "He will turn up at the right time, that's for sure, and surprise us as much as the spectators." "Yes," said Serlo. "But I'll be glad when tomorrow's over and the play has been performed. It has caused us much more trouble than I thought it would."

"No one will be more pleased than I," said Philine, "when the performance is over, even though I am not worried about my part. But having to listen over and over again to people talking about one and the same thing, whereas all they are really concerned about is a performance which, like hundreds of others, will soon be forgotten—that really tries my patience. For Heaven's sake, don't make so much fuss! When guests have finished a meal they always have some criticism of what they have been eating, and if one listens to them when they are back home, they talk as if they wonder how they managed to stick it out."

"Let's make good use of that comparison, my dear," said Wilhelm. "Just think how much must be contributed by nature and art, by marketing, salesmen and experts to produce a banquet, how long the stag must spend in the forest, the fish in the river or the sea, before it is ready to grace our table, all that to be achieved by the housewife and cook in the kitchen! Just think with what little thought we gulp down the efforts of some distant winegrower, shipper or merchant with our dessert, as if these were to be taken for granted. Do you really think that, on that account, all these people should not exert themselves in production and preparation, and our host should not assemble everything with the utmost care, just because the pleasure provided is not a lasting one? No pleasure is temporary, for it leaves a lasting effect; and our own work and effort conveys some sense of a hidden energy to the audience, and one never knows what effect that may have."

"I don't care about all that. But what I have noticed," said Philine, "is that men always contradict themselves. Despite all your conscientious efforts not to truncate this great author, you have left out the best remark in the play." "The best?" said Wilhelm. "Yes, the best, and one that Hamlet uses to his advantage." "And what might that be?" asked Serlo. "If you had a periwig on, I would snatch it off you," Philine replied; "something needs to be done to clear your head."

The two men thought hard, and conversation stopped. It was already late, so they got up to leave, but while they still stood there pondering, Philine sang a little song with a tune that was very engaging:

> Do not sing in tones depressing
> Of the loneliness of night;
> No, O fair one, it's a blessing
> Made for purposes of delight.
>
> Just as man is given a wife to
> Be his better half—agreed—
> So is night the half of life too,
> And the nicer half indeed.
>
> How can day bring glad elation
> Since it interrupts our joy?
> It's just good for dissipation,
> Worthless else for man or boy.
>
> But when night comes to eclipse the
> Gentle lamplight's dusky glow,
> And from lips to nearby lips the
> Mirth and love well up and flow—
>
> When a wanton lad who's eager,
> Full of fire, the hasty sort,
> Often for a gift that's meager
> Tarries for a bit of sport—
>
> When the nightingale is singing
> Songs of love to lovers' ears,
> It's the sadder echoes ringing
> That a wretched captive hears—
>
> With a heart that beats the time then
> You await the bell's reprise
> Which with twelve slow bongs will chime then,
> Pledging safety, rest and ease!
>
> So, as through long days you hurry,
> Mark this maxim to employ:
> Every day is dark with worry,
> And the night is bright with joy.

When she had finished she made a little bow, and Serlo shouted a loud bravo. She ran out of the room and rushed away laughing. They heard her clattering down the stairs with her heels, still singing.

Serlo went into the adjoining room, but Aurelie remained with Wilhelm who was waiting to bid her goodnight.

"How repulsive she is, repulsive to every one of my feelings," said Aurelie. "Even down to the smallest details. I can't bear those brown eyebrows with her blond hair, which my brother finds so attractive, and that scab on her forehead has something so loathsome, so vulgar about it that I always want to step back ten paces. She told me the other day—she thought it was funny—that, when she was a child, her father had thrown a plate at her head from which she still had this mark. She is certainly marked on her eyes and forehead, so much so that one should avoid her."

Wilhelm did not respond, and so Aurelie went on to express even more of her distaste: "It is almost impossible for me to say anything kind or polite to her, for I hate her so much, even though she is so endearing. I wish I were rid of her. You too, my friend, have a certain affection for this creature, a way of acting toward her that wounds my very heart, an attention that borders on respect which, by God, she does not deserve!"

"I am grateful to her for what she is," said Wilhelm. "Her manners leave much to be desired, but I must do justice to her character."

"Character!" Aurelie exclaimed. "Do you think such a creature has character? Oh, you men, that's just like you. And this is the sort of women you deserve!"

"If you harbor any suspicions on this score regarding me, I assure you that I can account for every minute I have spent with her."

"Well, well," said Aurelie. "It's getting late, so let's not quarrel. One and all, all and one! Good night, my friend; good night, my fine bird of paradise!"

Wilhelm asked her how he came to earn this honorific title.

"Some other time," said Aurelie. "Some other time. It is said they have no feet, only soar in the air, and nourish themselves from the ether. But that's only a fairy tale, just a poetic fiction. Good night, and pleasant dreams—if you are lucky."

She went to her room and he was left alone. Then he hurried off to his own room.

He paced up and down restlessly. The jocular but deliberate tone of Aurelie's words had offended him: He felt she was being profoundly unjust toward him. He could not act ungraciously or hostilely toward Philine. She had done him no wrong. And he felt so far from being in any way attracted to her, that he could proudly and steadfastly maintain that he had stood the test.

He was just about to undress and go to bed when, pulling back the curtains, he noticed to his great surprise a pair of women's slippers at the foot of the bed, one upright, the other turned over. He soon recognized them as Philine's. He also thought he observed that the bed curtains were displaced; it seemed they were moving. He stood and gazed with unaccustomed eyes, catching his breath in some emotion and irritation, then said sharply:

"Get up, Philine! What's the meaning of this?" he shouted. "Where's your common sense! What sort of behavior is this! Are we to be the talk of the household tomorrow?"

But nothing stirred.

"I'm not joking," he said. "This foolishness is not to my taste."

Still no sound, still no movement!

Finally, determined and angry, he stepped up to the bed and tore the curtains aside. "Now get up," he said, "or I'll leave you here on your own."

But to his great astonishment he found his bed empty, the pillows and covers blissfully undisturbed. He looked around, but could not find a trace of the little minx. Nothing behind the bed, nothing behind the stove, nothing behind the closets. He searched and searched. Indeed a malicious observer might have thought that he was hoping to find something.

He could not sleep. He put the slippers on his table, walked around, stopping several times by the table, and if some imp of a spirit had been watching him, he would surely have reported that Wilhelm occupied himself for a good part of the night with the pretty little stilts, looking at them and fondling them, and it was nearly daybreak before he fell fully clothed into his bed and slept amidst a host of the strangest fantasies.

And he was still sleeping when Serlo came in, shouting: "Where on earth are you? Still in bed? How could you! I've been looking everywhere in the theater for you. There is still a lot to do."

Chapter Eleven

The morning and afternoon passed quickly, and the house was already full when Wilhelm hurried to dress. This time he did not don his costume with the same leisureliness as he had the first time; he was now anxious to be ready on time. When he joined the ladies in the greenroom, they all agreed that nothing was right: the plumes on his hat were off to one side, the clasp didn't fit, and they all began to take them apart, sew them together again, and put everything in order. The overture started with Philine's objecting to something about his ruff and Aurelie's about his cloak. "Let me be, dear girls," he said, "this untidiness will make me a real Hamlet." But the women would not let him be, and went on improving his appearance. The overture came to an end, and the play started. Wilhelm looked at himself in a mirror, pulled his hat further down over his face, and touched up his makeup.

At that moment someone came rushing in, crying: "The Ghost! The Ghost!"

Wilhelm had not had the time to remember his prime concern, whether the Ghost would arrive or not. Now all his fears were removed, and a most remarkable guest appearance was to be anticipated. The stage manager came to ask about various things, so that for the moment Wilhelm did not have time to look around for the Ghost. He had to hurry to take his place by the throne, where the king and queen, surrounded by all the courtiers, were established in all their glory. All he had time to hear were the last words of Horatio, who described the appearance of the Ghost, but with some confusion, as if he had forgotten his lines.

The drop curtain was raised, and Wilhelm saw that the theater was full. When Horatio had concluded his speech and been given his orders by the king (in accordance with the addition that Wilhelm had made to the play), he came up to Hamlet and, as if he were presenting arms before his prince, said: "There's a very devil behind that armor! He scared us all to death!"

In the meantime two men could be seen standing in the wings, tall, and dressed in white capes with hoods. Wilhelm had been so distracted, uneasy and nervous that he felt he had bungled the first monologue, though the audience applauded wildly when he left the stage, and now he was about to enter the gruesome winter night of the drama in a state of trepidation. He pulled himself together and delivered the timely speech about the drunken swinishness of the Danes with such fitting distaste that, like the spectators, he forgot about the Ghost, and was therefore quite terrified when Horatio said: "Look, my lord, it comes!" He turned around sharply, and the tall noble figure with its soft silent tread in the seeming heavy armor made such a strong effect on him that he stood there petrified and could only murmur the words: "Angels and ministers of grace defend us!" He stared at the figure, took a few deep breaths, and delivered his address to the Ghost in such a distraught, broken and compulsive manner that the greatest of artists could not have done better.

His translation of this passage was a great help to him, for he had kept very close to the original, conveying the surprise and fright, the horror that was seizing hold of Hamlet's mind as he said:

> Be thou a spirit of health or goblin damn'd,
> Bring with thee airs from heaven or blasts from hell,
> Be thy intents wicked or charitable.
> Thou com'st in such a questionable shape
> That I will speak to thee: I'll call thee Hamlet,
> King, father; royal Dane, O! answer me.

One could feel a strong reaction in the public. The Ghost beckoned, and to the sound of tumultuous applause the prince followed.

The scene changed, and when they reached the distant place the Ghost suddenly stopped and turned, so that Hamlet found himself too close to him. Wilhelm peered eagerly into the shut visor but all he could see were deepset eyes and a well-shaped nose. He stood before him, timid and observing; but when the first sounds emerged from beneath the helmet, uttered in a pleasing but somewhat rough voice, out came the words: "I am thy father's spirit," Wilhelm stepped back shuddering, and the whole audience shuddered. The voice seemed familiar to everyone, and Wilhelm thought it sounded like that of his own father. These mysterious feelings and memories, his eagerness to discover the stranger's identity without offending him, coupled with his own clumsiness in getting too close to him on the stage—all this tore Wilhelm in different directions. He changed position so often during the long narration of the Ghost, he seemed so uncertain of himself and ill at ease, so attentive but at the same time so distracted that his performance aroused the admiration of all and the Ghost heightened their terror. The Ghost spoke in a tone of vexation rather than of sorrow, but it was an anger of the mind, slow and inestimable. It was the malaise of a great soul that is deprived of all finiteness and consigned to infinite suffering. At last there came the moment when the Ghost descended, but he departed in a strange way, for a thin grey veil surrounded him and dragged him down, like a mist rising from the depths.

Then Hamlet's companions returned and swore upon his sword. The old mole worked in the earth so fast that, wherever they moved to, he was always beneath them, crying: "Swear!" They were constantly changing position as if the ground were burning their feet. The effect was heightened by little flames appearing wherever they stood. All this left a deep impression on the public.

The play continued without any mishap. Everything turned out as it should, the public showed its approval, and the actors' spirits rose from scene to scene.

Chapter Twelve

The curtain fell, and loud applause resounded from every corner of the house. The four noble corpses jumped up and embraced each other joyfully. Polonius and Ophelia came out of their graves and heard with keenest pleasure the vigorous applause that greeted Horatio when he stepped forward to tell the audience about the future program. But they would not let him announce any other play; they demanded that this one should be repeated.

"Well, we won the day!" said Serlo, "but let's not have any more intelligent talk tonight! First impressions are the most important. No actor should be blamed for being rather cautious or headstrong on a first night."

The cashier came up with a heavy till. "We've begun very well," he said, "and first opinions will work to our advantage. But where is the supper you promised? We have every right to feast tonight." They had agreed to remain in their costumes and have their own private celebration. Wilhelm had undertaken to find the place, and Madame Melina the food.

A room that was normally used for painting sets had been cleaned up and decked out with small bits of scenery to suggest a garden and a colonnade. As they entered they were dazzled by the bright light of lots of candles shining ceremoniously through plentiful clouds of sweet smelling incense on a richly laid table. There were shouts of joy at the décor and everyone took his seat. It seemed as if a band of regal spirits had assembled. Wilhelm sat between Aurelie and Madame Melina, Serlo between Philine and Elmire; everybody was delighted with the seating, and with themselves.

The two connoisseurs were also present and added to the delight of the company. They had, several times during the performance, stepped on stage and could not say often enough how satisfied they and the public had been. They went into details, praising each individual performance, the merits of this or that actor, the excellence of this or that section. The prompter, who was sitting quietly at the far end of the table, received great praise for his rugged Pyrrhus. The duel between Hamlet and Laertes could not have been better, Ophelia's lament had been inexpressibly sweet and noble, Polonius's acting so good that there was nothing to be said about it. Everyone who was present felt himself praised in and by the others.

Even the absent Ghost received his praise and admiration. He had spoken the part with the appropriate voice and in impressive fashion, they were truly amazed that he seemed to be well informed about what had been happening in the company. He had looked exactly like the portrait, as if he had sat for it himself; and the two men could not adequately express their admiration for the awesome effect produced when he first appeared close to his portrait and then walked right past it. So striking was the combination of truth and illusion that they had been quite convinced that the Queen had not seen the apparition. Madame Melina was praised for staring up at the portrait while Hamlet pointed down at the Ghost.

Everyone wondered how the Ghost could have got into the theater, and learned from the stage manager that the back door, which was usually blocked by sets, had been left free that evening because for the play they needed the feeling of a Gothic hall; and through this door two tall figures in white capes and hoods had come, each indistinguishable from the other, and both had left after the third act, probably through the same door.

What Serlo particularly liked about the Ghost was that he did not dither and moan like a workman about his sorry state, and then exhort his son in words suited to a great hero. Wilhelm remembered that particular speech and agreed to put it back into the stage copy.

They were all enjoying the party so much that they had not noticed that the Harper and the children were not present. But soon they turned up, bizarrely decked out, Felix with a triangle, Mignon with a tambourine, and the Harper with his heavy instrument hanging from his shoulders, holding it in front of him as he played it. They trooped round the table singing all sorts of songs. They were given something to eat, and received what the others thought was a service, by being given as much of the sweet wine as they could drink, for everybody had not stinted themselves in wine, whole baskets of which, and excellent wine at that, had been contributed by the two connoisseurs. The children jumped and danced, and Mignon was particularly uninhibited, more than she had ever been before. She played the tambourine as delicately and then as loudly as possible, sometimes lightly skimming her fingers over the skin, at other times beating on it with the back of her hand or her knuckles, even alternating between striking her knees or her head with the instrument, sometimes just making the bells ring, so that all sorts of sounds were enticed from this simplest of instruments. After the children had made quite a din, they fell into an unoccupied armchair across from where Wilhelm was seated.

"Keep away from that chair!" Serlo shouted. "It's probably reserved for the Ghost, and if he comes, you'll be in a bad way."

"I'm not afraid of him," said Mignon. "If he comes, we'll get up. He's my uncle; he won't hurt me." Nobody understood what she meant, except those who knew that she had called the man she thought was her father "the big devil." They all looked at each other, suspecting more strongly than ever that Serlo knew something about the apparition. They went on talking and drinking, and every now and again the girls would look anxiously in the direction of the door.

Sitting in the armchair like puppets hanging out of a box, the children started a little game of their own, with Mignon making a rasping noise as puppets do. They banged their heads together as if these were made of wood. Mignon was almost frenetically excited and, amusing as this had been in the beginning, it became such that it had to be curbed. But admonishing her seemed to have little effect, for she now began hysterically to rush around the table, tambourine in hand, hair flying, head thrown back and her body flung into the air like one of those maenads whose wild and well-nigh impossible postures still delight us on ancient monuments.

Encouraged by the talents and hubbub of the children, everyone tried to contribute something to the general entertainment. The women sang several canons, Laertes did an impersonation of a nightingale, and the Pedant treated them to a pianissimo concerto on the Jew's harp. All sorts of games were started, hands clasped and grasped beneath the table, sometimes with a definite indication of hope and affection. Madame Melina, so it seemed, did not attempt to conceal her strong liking for Wilhelm. It was already well into the night when Aurelie, who seemed to be the only person still in control of herself, rose and urged the others to break it up.

As everyone was leaving, Serlo gave a firework display, imitating the noise of rockets, squibs and firewheels; he did this with his mouth so skillfully that the illusion was complete if one closed one's eyes. After that everybody got up, the gentlemen gave their arms to the ladies and escorted them home. Wilhelm and Aurelie were the last to leave. On the stairs he was met by the stage manager, who said: "This is the veil in which the Ghost disappeared. It was caught in the trapdoor, and we have just discovered it." "A wondrous relic, indeed!" said Wilhelm, taking it from him. At that very moment he seemed to be grasped by his left arm, and at the same time felt a sharp pain. Mignon had been hiding, and seizing hold of him, she bit him in the arm, rushed past him on the stairs and disappeared.

When our friends emerged into the fresh air, they almost all felt that they had indulged themselves a little too much that evening, and they separated, without bidding each other good night.

Wilhelm threw off his clothes as soon as he got to his room, put out the light and dropped into bed. He fell asleep in no time, but was aroused by a noise which seemed to come from behind the stove. The image of the king in arms came before his heated imagination, and he sat up in order to address the spirit, only to find himself drawn back by a pair of tender arms, his mouth smothered by passionate kisses, and against his chest the breast of another that he did not dare to push aside.

Chapter Thirteen

Next day Wilhelm arose with an uncomfortable feeling, and found his bed empty. His head was still fuzzy from the not yet dispelled intoxication of the evening before, and the memory of the unknown nocturnal visit made him uneasy. His first guess was that it had been Philine, and yet the charming body he had clasped in his arms did not seem like hers. He had fallen asleep amidst eager caresses alongside his mysterious, silent visitor, but now there was no trace of who it was. He jumped up, dressed, and noticed that his door, which he usually kept locked, was ajar; he simply could not remember whether he had closed it the previous evening.

But the most mysterious thing of all was that he found the Ghost's veil lying on his bed. He had probably himself flung it down when he brought it home with him. It was of grey crepe, and there was a border with some words embroidered in black letters. He opened it out, and this is what he read: *For the first and last time, young man, flee!* He was astonished, not knowing what to make of this.

At that very moment Mignon entered, bringing him his breakfast. Wilhelm was surprised by the child's appearance, indeed he was frightened by it. She seemed to have grown taller during the night. She strode up to him with a certain dignity, and looked into his eyes with such a serious expression that he had to turn away. She did not touch him as she usually did—clasping his hand, kissing him on the mouth or cheek or arm or shoulder—but quickly left the room once she had put his things in order.

The time arrived for the reading rehearsal. The whole company assembled, all of them out of sorts because of the jollifications of the previous evening. Wilhelm controlled himself to the best of his ability, so that he should not be the first to offend against the principles which he had advocated so firmly. The extent of his experience assisted him in this; for technique and experience fill up those gaps in any art which temperament and mood so often create.

Actually it might be true to say that one should never begin anything that is intended to last—situation, profession, or lifestyle—by a celebration. Celebrations belong at the end, when something is successfully completed; initial ceremonies exhaust those desires and powers that should encourage aspiration and sustain us in the difficulties of achievement. Marriage is of all such occasions for a celebration the most unsuitable, none should be more marked by silence, humility and hope.

The day crept on and none had ever seemed so ordinary to Wilhelm. Instead of the usual entertainment in the evening, people began to yawn; the interest in *Hamlet* was flagging, and no one found it at all appropriate to repeat it the next day. Wilhelm showed the Ghost's veil, from which it was concluded that the Ghost would not return. Serlo in particular was of this opinion. He seemed well acquainted with the advice of this strange character, but the words: "Flee, young man, flee!" defied explanation. How could Serlo agree with someone who seemed to want to deprive him of the best actor in his company?

It now became necessary to give the part of the Ghost to the Blusterer and the King to the Pedant. They both declared they knew the roles, and no wonder, for the number of rehearsals and the detailed discussions they had had of the play, meant that they were all so well acquainted with it that they could easily switch roles. Some parts were given a quick run-through, and when the actors went their separate ways at quite a late hour, Philine whispered to Wilhelm: "I must have my slippers back. Don't bolt the door." By the time he was back in his room, he was in a state of confusion because of what she had said, feeling more and more certain that his visitor of the previous night had been Philine. We too must share this opinion, because we are not able to reveal the reasons which had made him doubt this and had aroused other suspicions. He walked restlessly to and fro in his room. And he did not bolt the door.

Suddenly Mignon rushed into the room, grabbed him and cried: "Master! Save the building! It's on fire!" Wilhelm jumped through the doorway and was met by a dense cloud of smoke pouring down from the stairs. From the street below the alarm was being sounded, and from above the Harper came rushing down the stairs breathless with his instrument in his hand. Aurelie came running from her room and deposited Felix in Wilhelm's arms. "Save the child!" she cried; "We'll look after the rest."

Wilhelm, who did not think the danger was all that great, decided he would first try to find the source of the fire and extinguish it before it could spread. He handed the child to the Harper and told him to hurry down the stone steps that led into a cellar and out into the garden, and to stay outside with the children. He also asked Aurelie to get their possessions out of the house by this route. He tried to go upstairs through the smoke, but there was no point in exposing himself to danger. For the flames seemed to be spreading from the neighboring house and had already engulfed the attic and one staircase; some who came to the rescue were, like him, overcome by smoke and flames. Nevertheless he urged them on and called for water, imploring them to retreat no more than step by step from the flames, and promising to remain with them. But at this moment Mignon rushed up crying: "Master! Save your Felix! The old man has gone mad! He's killing him!" Without a moment's hesitation Wilhelm tore down the stairs with Mignon close at his heels.

At the bottom of the staircase, just where it led into the cellar, he stopped in horror. Great bundles of straw and brushwood were stored there, and were now burning fiercely. Felix was lying on the ground and crying. The old man stood leaning against the wall, his head bowed. "What are you doing, you wretched man?" exclaimed Wilhelm. The old man said nothing. Mignon picked up Felix and dragged him with difficulty into the garden, while Wilhelm tried to separate the burning wood and smother the fire but only managed to increase the power and heat of the flames. Finally he too had to retreat to the garden, his eyelashes and hair singed as he dragged the old man through the flames, who followed him reluctantly, his beard scorched in the process.

Wilhelm hastened to join the children in the garden. He found them sitting on the steps of a pavilion, Mignon doing her best to calm down the child. Wilhelm took him on his lap, questioned him, stroked him, but could not get any coherent information out of either of the children.

By now the fire had taken hold of several houses and was lighting up the whole neighborhood. Wilhelm inspected the child by the red light of the flames, but could find no wound; there was no blood and there were no bruises. He felt the child all over, but there was no indication of pain. Gradually he settled down to a certain delight at the flames and the orderly progression in which the beams and rafters burned and provided such splendid illumination.

Wilhelm did not think about the clothes and what he might have lost. He thought only of these two human beings, so dear to him, who had escaped such danger. He pressed the little one with unaccustomed intensity to his breast, and would have embraced Mignon with equal affection and joy, had she not gently resisted, taking his hand and holding it firmly.

"Master," she said (she had never called him that before this evening, having addressed him first as "Sir" and then as "Father"), "Master! We have escaped great danger. Your Felix was near to death."

Much questioning finally elicited from her that when they reached the cellar, the Harper had taken the candle from her and set fire to the straw. He then put down Felix, laid his hands with strange gestures on the child's head and pulled out a knife, as if he were going to sacrifice him. She had rushed up and pulled the knife from his hand, screamed, and somebody from the house, who was bringing some things into the garden, came to her assistance, but must in the confusion have gone away again and left the old man with the child.

By now two or three buildings were burning fiercely. Nobody had been able to escape into the garden because of the fire in the adjoining cellar. Wilhelm was more concerned about his friends than his possessions. He did not dare to leave the children and feared still greater misfortune.

He spent several hours in trepidation. Felix was fast asleep in his lap, Mignon lay beside him, firmly clasping his hand. At last they had succeeded in containing the fire. The burnt-out buildings collapsed, daylight came, the children began to shiver, and he himself, lightly clad as he was, found the morning dew quite intolerable. He took the children up to the ruins of the buildings where there was still a pleasant amount of warmth from the ashes and smoldering wood.

The new day brought his friends and acquaintances together again. Everyone was safe; no one had lost much.

Wilhelm's trunk turned up, and around ten o'clock Serlo pressed for a rehearsal of *Hamlet*, or at least of those scenes where the casting had been changed. Then he had some altercation with the police. The clergy were demanding that after such a judgment from God the theater should remain closed, and Serlo was declaring that a performance of this interesting play was just what was needed to brighten up frightened minds—as well as being some sort of compensation for what he had lost during the night. Serlo had his way, and the theater was packed. The actors played their parts with extraordinary vigor and even more freedom and passion than the first time. The spectators, their feelings heightened by nocturnal terrors and their minds, after the boredom of a distracting and ill-spent day more than ever prepared for interesting entertainment showed more receptivity for the extraordinary nature of the play than the previous audience. They were mostly drawn there by what they had heard about the play, and so could not compare this performance with the earlier one. The Blusterer played the Ghost in the same spirit as the unknown stranger, the Pedant had carefully noted the performance by his predecessor, and his pitiful appearance worked very much to his advantage when, despite the purple and ermine, Hamlet truthfully called him a king of shreds and patches.

No one had ever inherited a throne in a stranger fashion. And although the others, especially Philine, made fun of his newly acquired dignity, he reminded them that so knowledgeable a man as the count had prophesied this for him, and much more, when he first set eyes on him. But Philine told him to be more modest and swore that she would put powder on his sleeves to remind him of the misfortune that had befallen him at the castle. He should wear his crown with humility.

Chapter Fourteen

They quickly looked around for new quarters and as a result the company became very scattered. Wilhelm had grown fond of the pavilion in the garden where he had spent the night; he soon got the keys and established himself there. Since, however, Aurelie was very cramped in her new quarters, he had to keep Felix with him, and Mignon would not leave the boy. The children had a nice room on the upper floor and he settled down in the lower part. They slept soundly, but he did not close an eye.

While the moon rose and illuminated the pleasant garden, the sad ruins from which smoke was still rising stood nearby. The air was mild and the night unusually beautiful. Philine had stroked his elbow as she left the theater and whispered something which he had not understood. He was confused and irritated, not knowing what to expect or do. She had been avoiding him for several days, and this was the first sign of recognition she had given him. Unfortunately the door he was to leave unlocked had been burnt, and the slippers with it. How she was to come into the garden, assuming that that was her intention, he did not know. He did not want to see her, though he would have liked to have it out with her.

What troubled him much more was the fate of the Harper, who had disappeared. Wilhelm was afraid that he might be found dead beneath the rubble. He had said nothing to anybody about his suspicion that the Harper had set the fire. For it was from the burning attic that he had first emerged, and his desperate state in the cellar adjoining the garden would seem to have been the result of some such unfortunate action. But during the police investigation it became apparent that the most likely source of the fire was to be found not in their building, but two houses away, and that the flames had spread along the adjoining roofs.

Wilhelm was pondering all this while seated in an arbor, when he heard someone approaching on a nearby walk. From the mournful strains he heard he recognized the Harper. The song, which he understood full well, was about the consolations of someone who feels he is near to madness. Unfortunately Wilhelm could only remember the last verse:

> Let me linger by the gate
> Unobtrusive, silently,
> Pious hand will give me food,
> I move on to other doors.

Every one will show delight
Just to see my face out there,
Down their cheeks a tear will fall,
Why they weep, I do not know.

At this point he reached the garden gate from which a path led to the main highway. Since he found it locked, he tried to climb over the fence, but Wilhelm held him back and talked to him in a kindly fashion. The old man asked him to open the gate because he wanted to, indeed had to escape. Wilhelm explained to him that he could get out of the garden but not leave the town without arousing suspicion. But to no purpose! The old man persisted, Wilhelm would not give way and dragged him almost forcibly into the pavilion, shut himself up with him, and had an extraordinary conversation with him, which, so as not to torment our readers with scattered thoughts and anxious feelings, we will rather say nothing about.

Chapter Fifteen

Wilhelm was really perplexed as to what to do about the unfortunate old man, who was showing definite signs of losing his mind. His reflections were interrupted by Laertes who, accustomed as always to be here, there, and everywhere, had met a man in a coffeehouse who had been suffering from acute attacks of melancholy. This man had been placed in the care of a country pastor, who made a special business of treating such people. The pastor had once again been successful. He was in town, and the family of the man, now restored to health, were expressing their profound respect and thanks to him.

Wilhelm went immediately in search of the pastor, told him about the case, and came to an agreement with him that on some pretext or other the Harper should be entrusted to his charge. Parting from the Harper was extremely painful for Wilhelm, and it was only the hope of seeing him restored to health that made him agree to such a step, so accustomed had he become to see the old man around and listen to his music that was so expressive of his mind and his feelings. The harp had perished in the fire, but a new one was found for him.

Also destroyed in the fire was Mignon's meager wardrobe, and when new things were to be bought for her, Aurelie proposed that she should now at last be dressed as a girl. "No, no!" said Mignon, and insisted on wearing something like her old outfit. So a new one of the same sort was provided for her.

There was not much time for reflection, for the performances were to start soon. Wilhelm often listened to the spectators, but rarely did he hear anything approaching what he would, in fact, have liked to hear, and more often things that depressed or annoyed him. One young man, for instance, described in glowing terms the splendid evening he had had at the first performance of

Hamlet. But he went on to say, to Wilhelm's annoyance, that he had kept his hat on throughout the whole performance in order to irritate those behind him. He remembered this heroic deed with the utmost delight. Someone else said that Wilhelm had played the part of Laertes very well, but one couldn't be as satisfied with the actor who had played Hamlet. This confusion was quite natural, for Wilhelm and Laertes were somewhat alike, though it was a remote resemblance. Still another warmly praised his acting in the scene with his mother, regretting only that in this highly emotional sequence a white ribbon had popped out of his vest and spoilt the illusion entirely.

Several changes had to be made within the company. Since the evening after the fire Philine had made no sign of wishing to approach Wilhelm. She had taken quarters quite a way off—on purpose, so it would seem—spent most of her time with Elmire and only rarely came to see Serlo, which was indeed gratifying to Aurelie. Serlo, who had always been well disposed towards Philine, visited her sometimes, especially when he hoped to find Elmire with her, and one evening he took Wilhelm along. They were both amazed to find Philine in the inner room, in the arms of a young officer in a red uniform and white undergarments, whose face they could not see because it was turned away from them. Philine came to greet them, closing the door of the other room, and said, "You have caught me unawares, while I am having the most extraordinary adventure!"

"Not so extraordinary," said Serlo. "Let's have a look at your handsome and enviable young friend. You've whetted our curiosity so much already that we couldn't bear to be jealous."

"I must let you keep your suspicions for a while," said Philine jokingly. "But I can assure you that it's only a girl friend of mine who is staying for a few days with me incognito. You shall hear all about her later and you may well find her extremely interesting so that I shall have to exercise all my modesty and indulgence, for I fear you may forget your old friend for the new."

Wilhelm stood transfixed to the spot, for the red uniform had immediately reminded him of his beloved Mariane—the same figure, the same blond hair, though this officer seemed somewhat taller.

"For Heaven's sake," he cried, "do let us know more about your friend, let us see this dressed-up girl. We are now part of the secret, and we promise not to reveal it, but do let us see her!" "O how infatuated he is," said Philine. "Take it easy. Be patient. Not today!" "Then at least tell us her name!" said Wilhelm. "That would be keeping a fine secret!" Philine objected. "Well then at least her first name." "See if you can guess it," said Philine. "You can have three tries, but only three. Otherwise I would have to wait while you went through the whole church calendar." "All right," said Wilhelm. "How about Cecilie?" "Not Cecilie." "Henriette?" "Not a bit of it. Go easy. Your curiosity should take its time." Wilhelm hesitated. He trembled, wanting to speak but unable to do so. "How about Mariane?" he stammered out. "Bravo!" said Philine, twisting on her heel as usual, "You've got it." Wilhelm couldn't say another word, and Serlo, not noticing his perturbation, went on urging Philine to open the door.

They were both extremely surprised when Wilhelm hastily interrupted their jocular banter, threw himself at Philine's feet and passionately implored her to let him see the girl, saying: "She is mine, my Mariane, the one I have longed for every day of my life, the one who still exceeds all other women for me. Do at least go to her and tell her I am here, I, the one whose first love, whose youthful joys were fixed on her, and who now wishes to justify himself for having abandoned her so cruelly, to forgive her for all she may have done to him, and make no further claim on her, if only he may see her just this one more time, see that she is still alive and happy!"

Philine shook her head and said: "My dear friend, do lower your voice! Let's not deceive ourselves. If this is really your friend, then we must be considerate, for she will not be expecting to see you here. She has come here for quite different reasons, and you must know that there are certain moments when one would rather see a ghost than one's old lover. I'll ask her, I will prepare her, and we will together consider what would be best to do. I'll send you a message tomorrow telling you at what time you should come, or whether you should come at all. You must do exactly what I say, for I swear that no one shall see this lovely creature against my will or hers. I will keep my doors better locked, and don't try to use an axe to visit me!"

Wilhelm implored her and Serlo tried to persuade her; but all to no avail. They had to give way, and left.

One can well imagine what a restless night Wilhelm spent, and how slowly the daytime hours passed while he was waiting to hear from Philine. Unfortunately, he had to appear on stage that evening; he had never suffered such torment in his life. As soon as the performance was over, he rushed to Philine's quarters, without waiting for an invitation. He found her door locked. The people in the house said she had left early that morning with a young officer, saying she would be back in a few days, but they didn't believe that because she had paid what she owed and taken her things with her.

Wilhelm was beside himself at this news. He went straight to Laertes, suggesting they should follow her and, whatever the cost, find out definitely who her companion was. Laertes reproached his friend for his impulsiveness and credulity. "I bet," he said, "it is Friedrich. He comes from a good family, he's madly in love with the girl, and he has probably extracted enough cash from his relatives to be able to live with her again for a while."

These assertions did not convince Wilhelm, but they did make him pause. Laertes insisted that the whole yarn Philine had spun them was highly improbable, that the figure and hair could just as well be Friedrich's, that the two of them would already have twelve hours' start and not be easy to overtake, and, most important of all, Serlo could not dispense with either Wilhelm or Laertes for the performances.

Wilhelm was finally persuaded by these considerations to abandon any attempt at pursuing them himself. That same night Laertes found a trusty fellow to do it for them. He was a stolid man who had acted as courier and guide for several persons of quality but was at the time without employment. He was given money, informed of the whole matter, and given instructions to find the fugitives and catch up with them, never letting them out of his sight, and informing Wilhelm and Laertes when he discovered them. He mounted his horse that very same hour, and rode after the dubious pair, leaving Wilhelm somewhat more at ease.

Chapter Sixteen

Philine's departure did not create much of a sensation either in the theater or amongst the public. She had never been very serious about anything, was thoroughly hated by all the women, and the men preferred to see her off stage than on, so that her considerable talents as an actress passed unnoticed. The other members of the company worked even harder after she had left, especially Madame Melina, whose zeal and attention were remarkable. She took note of Wilhelm's principles, following him in theory and example, and acquired a certain something that made her more interesting. She achieved a correct style of acting, was able to reproduce the natural tone of conversation to perfection and even that of feeling to a certain degree. She learned how to adapt herself to Serlo's moods, worked at her singing to give him pleasure, and soon acquired sufficient skill in this for her to display her talents socially.

The company was enlarged by some newly engaged actors. Both Wilhelm and Serlo were influential in different ways, Wilhelm concentrating on the general meaning and tone of a play and Serlo conscientiously working away at all the details. The actors were fired by admirable enthusiasm and the public took an active interest in them.

"We're on the right path," said Serlo one day, "and if we stick to it, the public will get there too. It is quite easy to bedazzle people by presenting things in an outlandish and inappropriate fashion: but if one gives them an interesting production that is appropriate and sensible, then they will eagerly accept that. What our German theater lacks most is a sense of necessary limitations and restriction, everything is too higgledy-piggledy, too varied for us to have any standards of judgment—a fact that does not seem to bother either actors or spectators. My opinion is that it was not a good idea to extend the stage into a sort of endless panorama of nature; and now it is difficult for any director or actors to restrict themselves until acceptable limits have been established by public taste. Every valid society must exist within accepted boundaries; so too any theater, if it is to be good. Certain mannerisms and turns of phrase

579

should be eradicated, certain subjects and certain forms of behavior should be excluded from the stage. One does not grow poorer by restricting one's household."

They partly agreed and partly disagreed about that. For Wilhelm and most of the others favored the English style of theater, whereas Serlo and some others preferred the French.

They agreed to work through the most celebrated examples of both styles of drama when they had a free hour (which, as with all actors, was unfortunately quite often), and select what was best and most worthy to serve as a model. They did make a start with some French plays, but Aurelie left the room every time the readings started. At first they thought she might be sick; and then one day Wilhelm, having observed this, asked her about it.

"I will never take part in such readings. How can I listen and exercise judgment when my heart is torn to shreds? I hate the French language from the bottom of my soul."

"How can one hate a language which has provided us with most of our culture and to which we must still be indebted if we are to give our substance any shape and form!"

"My judgment is not based on prejudice!" Aurelie declared. "It is rather an unfortunate impression, a distasteful memory of my faithless friend, which has deprived me of all affection for that beautiful, cultivated language. How I hate it now! During the time of our friendship he always wrote to me in German, and what sincere, true, strong German! But when he wanted to be rid of me, he began to write in French, whereas previously he had done that only as a joke. I recognized the significance of this. For what he was ashamed to say in his mother tongue, he could now set down in good conscience. It is an excellent language for reservations, half-truths and lies—a language that is *perfide*. Thank goodness that there is no German word I can think of to express the full meaning of *perfide*. Our poor word *treulos* is an innocent babe in comparison. *Perfide* is 'faithless,' mixed in with pleasure, arrogance and malice. What an enviable state of culture it is when so many nuances can be expressed in one single word! French is indeed the language of the civilized world and worthy of becoming the universal language so that people can all cheat and deceive each other. My friend's letters in French were always good to read. One could pretend, if one wanted to, that they sounded warm or even passionate; but on closer look they were nothing but phrases, cursed phrases! He robbed me of all pleasure in the language and its literature, even in those fine and precious works by noble poets in that tongue. I now shudder every time I hear a French word!"

She would go on like this for hours on end, venting her displeasure and totally disrupting everything. Sometimes Serlo would cut into these expressions of moodiness by some bitter remark; but usually the evening's conversation was wrecked.

Unfortunately, it is generally the case that something that is assembled by a variety of persons and circumstances rarely maintains its cohesion for long. Whether this be a theatrical company or an empire, a circle of friends or an army, a moment is usually reached when it is at its zenith, its best, its greatest unity, well-being and effectiveness. Then personalities change, new individuals arrive on the scene, and the persons no longer suit the circumstances and the circumstances the persons. Everything becomes different, and what had been unified begins to fall apart. One could well say that Serlo's troupe had for some time possessed a quality unmatched by any other German company. Most of the actors had their appointed place in it, with enough to do, and satisfaction at doing it. Their personal circumstances were tolerable, and every one of them seemed an artist of promise, for they had entered on their profession with enthusiasm and vigor. But it soon became clear that some of them were machines only able to achieve what could be done without feeling, and then those emotions began to make themselves felt, which usually tend to interfere with any well-organized undertaking and disrupt what sensible and thoughtful persons have striven to maintain.

Philine's departure was not quite so insignificant as had at first been thought. She had been very adept at keeping Serlo entertained, and had appealed, in varying degrees, to all the others. She had dealt very patiently with Aurelie's outbursts of violence, and her main concern had been to flatter Wilhelm. She had therefore been a sort of liaison between all of them, and her loss soon made itself felt.

Serlo could not exist without some little love affair. Elmire, who had grown up quickly and, one could almost say, become quite beautiful, had been attracting his attentions for some time, and Philine was smart enough to encourage what she saw to be a budding relationship. "One must," she would say, "at times take to matchmaking; there is nothing else left when we grow old." As a result Serlo and Elmire were already sufficiently acquainted for them to join forces when Philine departed, and their little romance had an even greater appeal for them because they had every reason to keep it secret from her father, who would not have been at all amused by such irregularity. Elmire's sister was in the know, and so Serlo had to be attentive to both girls. One of their worst faults was a passion for sweetmeats, which one could almost call gluttonous. In this respect they were considered to be quite unlike Philine, who now began to take on in retrospect a new air of graciousness because she had seemed to live on air, eat very little and sip only the bubbles from champagne, and that with the utmost delicacy.

But Serlo, in order to please his beloved, had to combine breakfast with lunch and then supper with dinner. He also had a plan that he was anxious to carry out. Having noticed a certain affection growing between Wilhelm and Aurelie, he was eager that this should develop into something serious. What he had in mind was to transfer all the more routine aspects of managing the theater to Wilhelm and so acquire a reliable and active assistant such as his previous brother-in-law had been. He had tacitly been transferring a good deal of this to Wilhelm and, with Aurelie looking after the finances, he was resuming the lifestyle he preferred. But there was one thing that deeply concerned both him and his sister.

The public has an odd way of reacting to persons of acknowledged merit by becoming less and less interested in them and favoring instead much lesser, but newly arrived, talents, making excessive demands on the former and delighting in everything about the latter.

Serlo and Aurelie had plenty of occasions to reflect on this matter. The new members of the company, especially those who were young and handsome, received all the attention and applause, whereas Serlo and Aurelie, despite all their efforts, left the stage without the welcome sound of clapping. There were certainly legitimate reasons for this. Aurelie's pride was very evident and her scorn for the public was well known, and Serlo favored individuals, but his sharp remarks about the ensemble were common knowledge and constantly bandied about. The new actors were either from other parts of the country and unfamiliar, or young, pleasant and needing help, so they easily gained their supporters.

Very soon there developed a certain amount of friction and dissatisfaction amongst the members of the company. For when it was observed that Wilhelm was taking over the duties of a producer, most of the actors became increasingly uncooperative as he tried to bring more order and precision into what they were doing and insisted that the mechanics of the production should proceed smoothly and with regularity.

In a short time the whole operation, which for a time had been running almost perfectly, became as undistinguished as that of any company of strolling players. Unfortunately it was just when Wilhelm, by unrelenting effort, had succeeded in mastering what the job demanded and had trained himself to meet these demands, that he came to the melancholy conclusion that this occupation did not merit the expenditure of time and effort that it required. The work was burdensome and the recompense inadequate. He would rather have done something which, when it was over, would have allowed him some peace of mind such as this work did not permit him. For once all the mechanical difficulties had been overcome, his thoughts and feelings were still totally occupied with reaching the goal which the mechanics were designed to achieve. He had to put up with Aurelie's complaints about her brother's extravagance, had to disregard Serlo's hints encouraging him in the direction of marrying Aurelie, and had to conceal his distress at what troubled him most, for the messenger he had sent after the dubious "officer" had not returned. Nothing had been heard from him, and our friend was afraid that he might have lost his Mariane for a second time.

Just at that time the theater had to be closed for a few weeks because of a period of state mourning. So Wilhelm used this opportunity to visit the pastor in whose care he had left the Harper. He discovered that the place where this man was living was peaceful and pleasant, and the first thing he saw on his arrival was the old man giving lessons on his instrument to a young boy. The Harper was delighted to see Wilhelm again, stood up and shook his hand, and said: "You see, I am still of some use in this world. Please allow me to go on with what I am doing, for my time is carefully organized."

The pastor received Wilhelm warmly and told him that the old man was doing quite well and there was hope of a complete recovery. Their conversation quite naturally turned to methods of curing madness.

"Apart from the physical aspect, which often creates insuperable difficulties and requires the advice of a thoughtful doctor, I find the treatment quite simple," said the pastor. "Basically it is the same as one uses to prevent healthy people from going mad. One has to encourage them to occupy themselves, accustom them to the idea of order, give them the sense of having a common form of life and destiny with many others, and show them that unusual talent, extreme good fortune and excessive misfortune are merely minor deviations from what is normal. Then no madness will ensue, or if it is already there, it will gradually disappear. I have organized the old man's day so that he gives lessons on the harp, and helps in the garden. As a result he is much brighter in spirits. He wants to taste the cabbage he has planted, and he wants to give careful instruction to my son so that he will be able to play the old man's harp, for he wants the boy to have it when he dies. As a pastor I have not said much to him about his strange fears, but an active life brings with it so much occupation that he will soon feel that his doubts can only be overcome by activity. I don't want to rush things, but if I can get rid of his beard and his cowl, I will have achieved a lot; for nothing brings us closer to madness than distinguishing ourselves from others, and nothing maintains common sense more than living in a normal way with many people. Unfortunately there is much in our educational system and everyday life that preconditions us and our children to madness."

Wilhelm stayed for a few days with this intelligent man and heard lots of interesting stories, not just about mad folk, but also about some considered bright or even wise, whose oddities bordered on madness.

The conversation became even more interesting when the doctor made one of his frequent visits to his friend in order to assist and support him in his humane efforts. He was an oldish man who, despite his delicate health, had spent many years in the exercise of such noble duties. He was a great lover of the country, and could hardly exist anywhere but in the open air. On the other hand he was very sociable and for several years now had cultivated friendship with all the country pastors in the neighborhood. He tried to encourage everyone who had some useful occupation, and to suggest ways of spending one's time to those who had not. Since he was in constant contact with nobles, magistrates and judges, he had over the past twenty years quietly contributed to the advancement of agriculture and actively promoted crops, animals and human beings, helping to bring about what one may truly call enlightened attitudes. "There is really only one misfortune that can happen to us," he would say, "and that is when some fixed idea takes hold of us which does not affect our active life and may detract from it. I have such a case at the moment. The persons concerned are a rich married couple of high station, but so far all my efforts have been fruitless, and I believe this case belongs in your territory, my dear pastor. If I tell you about it I am sure this young man will keep it to himself.

"One day when a nobleman was absent from his residence, someone had the not very laudable idea of dressing up a young man in the nobleman's clothes. His wife was to be deceived by this, and although this was presented to me as having been intended as a joke, I am very much afraid that there was the intention of leading the worthy lady astray. The husband returns unexpectedly, goes to his room, thinks he sees himself, and thereupon falls into a state of melancholy, convinced that he is soon to die. He consorts with persons who cajole him with religious ideas, and I don't see how he is to be prevented from joining the Moravians with his wife, and depriving his relatives (he has no children) of the greater part of his fortune."

"With his wife?" said Wilhelm, much alarmed by what he had just heard.

"Yes," said the doctor who simply interpreted Wilhelm's outburst as an expression of human sympathy, "and unfortunately this lady is burdened with an even greater sorrow which makes separation from the world by no means distasteful to her. When the young man was taking his leave of her, she was incautious enough not to conceal a growing affection for him. He boldly clasped her in his arms and pressed hard against her breast a diamond medallion of her husband that she was wearing. She felt a sharp pain, which gradually went away, leaving at first a small red patch, but then no trace. As a man I am convinced she has nothing to reproach herself with; as a doctor I am sure that the pressure on her breast will have no bad effects, but she is convinced that there is a lump there and when by feeling the place I try to dispel this illusion, she says that only then does the pain go away, for she has firmly persuaded herself that this will end in cancer, and with it all her youth and loveliness."

"Heaven help me!" said Wilhelm, striking his brow and rushing out of the house. He had never been in such a state of alarm.

The doctor and the pastor, surprised by this strange reaction, had to devote their full attention to him that evening when he returned and poured out reproaches on himself in an account of what had happened. Both men showed great concern for him, especially when he described his general situation in the darkest of colors.

The next day the doctor agreed to accompany Wilhelm back to town and do what he could for Aurelie, whom our friend had left in a disturbing condition. They found her worse than they had expected. She had a kind of intermittent fever; nothing much could be done about that because she herself induced and encouraged the attacks. Wilhelm's companion was not presented to her as a doctor. He behaved pleasantly and cautiously. There was talk about the condition of her body and the state of her mind, and the newcomer recounted various stories of people who, despite a certain sickliness, lived to a great age; although nothing is more detrimental to the health of such people than intentional revival of passionate feelings. He also admitted that he had found it most beneficial for sickly people, whose health could not be completely restored, to cultivate religious sentiments. He said this quite discreetly, as if he were referring to past experiences of his, but he promised to bring his new friends a manuscript which they would find interesting to read. It had come from a lady now dead, who had been a friend of his and earned his great respect. "This manuscript," he said, "is something that I value greatly, and I am entrusting the original to you. The title, which I have myself supplied, is: *Confessions of a Beautiful Soul.*"

The physician gave Wilhelm the best advice he could regarding diet and medication for the unhappy and wrought-up Aurelie. He promised to write, and if at all possible, to come and see her again.

During Wilhelm's absence, a change had begun to occur, which he could not have expected. Since he took over control of the routine side of the operation he had spent quite liberally, having his eye on the production in hand and getting what best suited in the way of costumes, sets and properties. He also told actors how indispensable they were, since there was no better way of getting the best out of them. Wilhelm felt justified in this because Serlo never claimed to indulge in precise reckoning and was satisfied with hearing his theater praised, and pleased when Aurelie, who managed all the accounts, told him they had no outstanding debts, and provided him with enough money to cover his expenses incurred extravagantly on behalf of his new loves and on himself.

Melina, who was in charge of the costumes, had been observing all this, and, with Wilhelm away and Aurelie increasingly sick, he coldly and maliciously suggested to Serlo that they should take in more and spend less, and either put some money aside or go on living it up even more than before. Serlo listened attentively as Melina came forward with a plan.

"I wouldn't like to suggest," he said, "that there is any one of the actors who is being paid too much. They are all worthy people and would be welcome anywhere. But for what they bring in, they are paid too much. My proposal would be that we should go in for opera; and as for straight plays, you could take on any of these yourself, all by yourself. Don't you feel nowadays that your talents are not properly recognized? Your colleagues are not first rate, they are just good, and so justice is not given to your talents which are truly outstanding. So why don't you feature yourself, as has been done before, surround yourself with mediocre or even bad actors for meager wages, work on the public through stage effects, as only you know how, and use all the rest to perform operas. You will see how with the same effort and expenditure you will create more satisfaction and take in infinitely more money."

Serlo was so flattered by all this, that no objections he might have offered would have carried any weight. He hastened to assure Melina that, with his love of music, he had long wanted to do something of this kind; but he realized that public taste would be sidetracked even more, and this hybrid of a theater—half play and half opera—would simply eradicate what little taste there was left amongst the public for a major work of art.

Melina referred rather crudely to Wilhelm's "pedantic" ideals, his presumptuous claims of educating the public, instead of being educated by them; and both he and Serlo vehemently asserted that all they wanted was to make money, get rich and enjoy life, and to rid themselves of anyone who stood in the way of such plans. Melina regretted that Aurelie's feeble health did not augur a long life, but rather the opposite. Serlo seemed to regret that Wilhelm wasn't a singer, and thus indicated that he did not consider him indispensable. Melina came up with a whole list of savings that could be made, and Serlo saw in him a threefold replacement for his late brother-in-law. They both thought they should keep quiet about this conversation, and as a result felt more closely bound to each other. They took every occasion to discuss in secret everything that turned up, disapprove of everything that Aurelie and Wilhelm did, and in their thoughts promote their new plan.

But although they kept silent about the project, not betraying anything by word of mouth, they were not diplomatic enough to conceal by their behavior what was in their minds. Melina frequently opposed Wilhelm on matters that lay within Wilhelm's jurisdiction, and Serlo, who had never been indulgent toward his sister, became more and more bitter as her sickness increased and she deserved every consideration because of the passionate vicissitudes of her moods.

At this time they were preparing a performance of Lessing's *Emilia Galotti*. It was very well cast and they could all display the full range of their talents within the restricted compass of this tragedy. Serlo was just right as the sinister Marinelli. Odoardo, Emilia's father, was well played, Madame Melina played the mother with considerable insight, and Elmire carried off the role of Emilia to her great advantage. Laertes played Emilia's short-lived fiancé Appiani with great style, and Wilhelm had spent several months studying the part of the Prince. He often reflected on a certain matter and discussed it with Serlo and Aurelie, namely: What is the difference between noble and aristocratic behavior, and to what extent the one is, or is not, part of the other.

Serlo, who played Marinelli straight, as courtier, without any caricature, had various good things to say on this subject. "Aristocratic behavior is difficult to imitate," he said, "because it is fundamentally negative and presupposes a long period of continuous experience. Such behavior should not present a display of dignity, for that would be liable to appear as formality and pride;

it should rather avoid all that is undignified or vulgar. One should never forget oneself, always consider oneself as well as others, never allow oneself any lapses, do neither too much nor too little for others, appear not to be affected or disturbed by anything, never be hurried, always be in control of oneself and externally maintain an equilibrium however tormented one may be inside. A noble man can relax for a moment, a nobleman never. The nobleman is like a well-dressed man: he will never lean up against anything and everyone will avoid brushing against him. He is marked off from others, but cannot stand alone. For as in every form of art what is most difficult has to be achieved effortlessly: the nobleman, despite his distinct status, has to appear in combination with others, never stiff, always pliant—always as the first but never putting himself forward. To appear aristocratic one really has to be an aristocrat. And perhaps that is why, on the average, women can more often give themselves this appearance than men, and why amongst men it is courtiers and soldiers who achieve it most readily."

After this Wilhelm despaired of ever playing the Prince, but Serlo gave him encouragement, making some subtle observations about details and giving him a costume that would turn him into a really fine prince, at least in the eyes of the public.

Serlo promised to comment on Wilhelm's presentation of the part when the performance of the play was over. But an unpleasant argument between him and Aurelie prevented any critical assessment. Aurelie had played the part of the Countess Orsina, the Prince's cast-off mistress, in a way such as one is hardly likely ever to see again. She knew the part very well and had played it rather coolly in the rehearsals; but in the performance she opened up all the floodgates of her personal sorrow, and the result was a performance such as no poet could have imagined in the first heat of his invention. Tumultuous applause rewarded her anguished efforts, but after the performance she lay half lifeless in a chair.

Serlo, having already expressed his disapproval of what he called her exaggerated acting and the way she had bared her soul before the public (which was more or less acquainted with her unfortunate story), had ground his teeth and stamped his feet, as he often did when he was angry. "Just let her be," he said, when he found the others grouped around her in the chair. "One of these days she will appear stark naked on the stage, and then they will really applaud."

"Ungrateful wretch!" she cried. "I'll soon be carried naked to where there is no applause anymore!" With this she jumped up and rushed to the door. Her maid had forgotten to bring her coat, the sedan chair was not waiting for her, it had been raining and a bitter wind was blowing through the streets. She was overheated, but they could not stop her from deliberately walking slowly and eagerly drinking in the cool fresh air. But by the time she reached home she was so hoarse that she could hardly speak, and she did not tell anyone that she was completely stiff from the neck down. Soon afterwards a sort of paralysis of the tongue set in and she began to mix up her words. She was put to bed; some things improved, but others did not. She was running a high fever and her condition became dangerous.

Next morning she was peaceful for a time, and sent for Wilhelm. She handed him a letter. "This," she said, "has long been waiting for the appropriate moment, which has now come. I feel that my life is approaching its end. Promise me that you will deliver this letter personally, and add a few words of your own to avenge my sorrows on this faithless man. He is not without feeling; my death shall at least cause him a few painful moments."

Wilhelm took the letter and consoled her, trying to remove the expectation of death from her mind. "No, no!" she said. "Don't deprive me of my only hope. I've been waiting for it for a long time and will embrace it gladly."

Soon after this the manuscript arrived from the doctor. She asked Wilhelm to read to her from it, and the effect that it had on her can best be judged by the reader from his own perusal of it in the next book. The poor woman's violence and pity suddenly all calmed down. She took back the letter she had handed to Wilhelm, and wrote another one, apparently in a much quieter frame of mind. And she instructed Wilhelm to console her friend for any grief that he might feel at her death, and to assure him that she had forgiven him and wished him every happiness.

From this time on she was very quiet and her mind seemed to be totally occupied with certain thoughts aroused in her by Wilhelm's reading of the manuscript. The decline of her strength was not all that visible, and Wilhelm was therefore shocked one morning when he came to visit her to find her dead.

He had respected her so much and had spent so much time with her that he felt her loss very acutely. She was the only person who was really well disposed toward him, for in these past days he had become only too conscious of Serlo's indifference. He therefore decided to deliver Aurelie's message immediately, and requested leave for a period of time. His absence was welcomed by Melina, who had been engaged in extensive correspondence to secure a male and a female singer, who were to provide attractive intermissions and prepare the public for the forthcoming productions of operas. The loss of Aurelie and the absence of Wilhelm would be compensated for in this way, and Wilhelm himself expressed his approval of such a scheme because it would permit him an extended absence.

He now conceived his mission as one of unusual importance. Aurelie's death had affected him deeply, and since he was losing her so early, he was bound to feel anger towards the man who had shortened her life and made her existence such a painful one.

Despite the last gentle words of the dying woman, he was determined to issue a severe judgment on the faithless friend when he delivered the letter. Since he could not leave this to the mood of the moment, he thought up a speech which became more and more emotional as he elaborated it. Once he was satisfied that his disquisition was well composed, he committed it to memory, and set out on his journey. Mignon was with him as he packed, and she asked whether he was going south or north? When he told her it would be the latter, she said: "Then I will wait for you here." She asked him for Mariane's string of beads, which he could not deny the dear creature; she already had the scarf. But she put the Ghost's veil in his knapsack, although he told her he had no use for it.

Melina took over the management, and his wife promised to keep a motherly eye on the two children, whom Wilhelm was not happy to leave behind. Felix was cheerful as he left, and when asked what he wanted Wilhelm to bring him, he said: "Bring me a father." Mignon took Wilhelm's hand, stood on tiptoe, and gave him a big, trusting kiss, but without any tenderness, saying: "Master, don't forget us, and come back soon."

And so, with many a thought and many a feeling, we leave our friend as he sets out on his journey and record at this point in our story a poem which Mignon had recited several times with great feeling and which we have neglected to offer before because of the pressure of telling about so many unusual incidents.

> Bid me not speak, let me be silent,
> My secret I am bound to keep,
> My inmost heart to thee I'd open,
> But fate decrees I may not so.
>
> There comes a time when sun's advancing
> Dispels the dark and brings the light;
> The stony cliff unfolds its bosom
> And hidden streams bestows on earth.
>
> All men find peace in friend's embrace
> Each breast unloads its pain in words.
> My lips by solemn oath are closed,
> Only a god may unseal them new.

BOOK SIX

Confessions of a Beautiful Soul

Up to my eighth year I was a healthy child; but I have as little memory of those years as I have of my birth. Then, when I had just turned eight, I had a hemorrhage, and from that moment on I was all feeling and memory. Every little detail of what happened then is as present to me now as if it had occurred only yesterday.

During the nine months of convalescence which I bore patiently, the foundations of my present way of thinking were laid—or so it seems to me now. For during that time my mind received various impulses that helped in the shaping of a specific character.

I suffered and I loved—that was the rhythm of my heart. During my sharp spells of coughing and debilitating fever I kept very quiet, like a snail withdrawn into its shell; but as soon as I could breathe again I wanted to feel something pleasant, and since all other pleasures were denied me I entertained myself through eyes and ears. I was brought dolls and picture books, and anyone who came and sat on my bed had to tell me a story.

From my mother I liked to hear biblical stories, and my father entertained me with objects of nature. He had quite a nice collection, and would show me one drawer after another, explaining everything carefully. All sorts of dried plants and insects, anatomical specimens, human skin, bones and mummified objects found their way on to my bed, and birds and animals that he had shot were shown me before they were taken to the kitchen. And so that the Prince of this World should not go neglected in this company, my aunt told me love tales and fairy stories. I absorbed everything, and it all took root. I had moments when I intimately communed with the Invisible Being, and I can still remember some verses which I dictated to my mother at that time.

I often recounted to my father what I had learnt from him. I never took medication without asking where the ingredients came from, what they were called, and what they looked like. Nor had my aunt's stories fallen on barren soil. I imagined myself dressed in beautiful clothes and meeting the most charming princes who could not rest till they found out who this unknown beauty was. Then there was a similar adventure with a delightful little angel, in white garments and with golden wings, who was much drawn to me; and this I kept developing in my mind till I almost reached the point that he actually appeared.

After a year I was more or less recovered, but nothing wild remained with me from my childhood. I couldn't play with dolls any longer, I wanted objects that would return my love. Dogs, cats and the many kinds of birds that my father fed—all these delighted me; but I would have given anything to possess a creature that had played a very important part in one of my aunt's stories. This was a lamb that a peasant girl had found in the forest and succoured, but there was a prince spellbound in that little animal, and he finally emerged as a handsome youth and rewarded his benefactress with his hand in marriage. I would so much have liked to have such a lamb!

But there was none to be found, and since everything around me was taking its natural course, I almost had to abandon all hope of having something so precious for my own. Meanwhile I consoled myself by reading accounts of miraculous adventures. Amongst these I liked best the one called the *Christian German Hercules*, the pious love story which was completely to my liking. For whenever anything happened to his Valiska—and terrible things did happen—the hero would pray before he rushed to her assistance, and the text of the prayers was included in the book, which pleased me greatly. My inclination toward the Invisible, which I had always felt in some obscure way, became strengthened by this reading. For God was to become my closest friend—that was certain.

While I was growing older, I read all sorts of things and not in any particular order. But I do remember that the book I then liked best was the *Roman Octavia*. The persecution of those early Christians, put here into a novel, totally captivated my attention.

But then my mother began to complain about my incessant reading; and to humor her my father would take the books away from me one day—and give them back to me the next. She was smart enough to realize that nothing was to be achieved in this direction, but she did succeed in insisting that I should pay equal attention to the Bible. I did not need to be compelled to do that, for I read the sacred books with the liveliest of interest. My mother was much concerned that no seductive books should come into my hands, and I myself would immediately have rejected anything of the baser sort. For my princes and princesses were all very virtuous, and I knew more about the natural history of the human race than I let appear, for I had learnt it mostly from the Bible. Puzzling passages I associated with particular words and objects that I encountered, and got to the truth in my thirst for knowledge and ability to put things together. If I had heard about witches, I would have had to become acquainted with witchcraft too.

I have to thank my mother, and my own curiosity, for learning to cook as well as reading books. There was always something worth looking at in the kitchen, and cutting up a chicken or a suckling pig was a real occasion for me. I would bring my father the innards, and he would talk to me about them as if I were a young student. He often took pleasure in calling me his errant son.

I passed the age of twelve, learnt French, dancing and drawing, and had the usual religious instruction. During the latter, many feelings and thoughts were aroused, but none that affected my state of mind. I was glad to hear God talked about, and I was proud to be able to talk about Him better than most of my peers. I eagerly read a number of books at this time that would enable me to blabber about religion, but it never occurred to me to ask myself what my situation was, whether my soul was a mirror that would reflect the bright sun of eternity. I had taken that for granted.

French I learnt with great enthusiasm. My teacher was a fine man. He was neither a superficial empiricist nor a dry grammarian; he was acquainted with various branches of knowledge, and had seen much of the world. He satisfied my desire for knowledge with many things besides language instruction. I loved him so dearly that I always awaited his arrival with heartthrobs. I did not have much difficulty with drawing and would have made more progress in that area, if my teacher had had more brains and more knowledge. But all he had were his hands and practice in using them.

Dancing was at first what I enjoyed least. My body was too fragile, and I only learnt to dance with the help of my sister. But pleasure in this activity increased greatly when our dancing master had the idea of arranging a ball for all his pupils.

Amongst the various boys and girls there were two who stood out from the others, two of the Chamberlain's sons, one the same age as myself, the other two years older, but both of them so handsome that their appearance surpassed what was generally considered to be beauty in children. Once I had seen them, I was quite unaware of anyone else in the group. From that moment on I paid more attention to my dancing and wished to dance as well as possible. How did it happen that these two boys singled me out, I wondered. Anyway, within an hour we were the best of friends and before the little celebration had come to an end, we had decided where we would meet again. What a joy that was for me! And I was simply delighted when next morning I received a bouquet from each of them with a polite little note inquiring how I was. Never again have I felt as I felt then. Pleasantries were exchanged, messages went back and forth, rendezvous were arranged at church or on walks, they invited me and my sister at the same time, and we were sufficiently cautious in disguising all this, so that our parents never learnt any more than we thought was advisable.

So now I had acquired two admirers at once. I could not decide between them, for I liked them both and we were all good friends. Suddenly the elder one fell seriously ill, and since I had often been very sick myself, I knew what to send him in the way of kind words and tasty morsels. His parents were so grateful for my attentions that they granted their dear son's wishes and invited me and my sisters to visit him as soon as he was up and about. The affectionate way he received me was not like that of a child, and from that day on my preference was for him. He warned me to keep this concealed from his brother, but his emotion could not remain hidden, and the younger brother's jealousy made this into a full-scale romance. He played one trick after another on us, delighted in spoiling our pleasures, and increased the passion that he was determined to destroy.

So now I had found the little lamb I yearned for, and this passion of mine affected me like all other sickness: it made me withdraw from the busy throng, and silent. I felt alone and deeply affected, and the thought of God came back into my mind. He was my intimate companion, and I prayed and prayed for my ailing friend, shedding many a tear.

Childish as this whole train of events was, it nevertheless contributed greatly to the development of my emotional life. In our French lessons we were required by our teacher to write, not the usual translations, but letters of our own composition. I delivered my own love story using the names of Phyllis and Damon. The old man soon saw through this and, to encourage frankness on my part, he praised my effort highly. As a result I became even bolder, opened up my heart, and kept faithfully to every detail of the truth. I cannot remember at what point it was that he had occasion to remark: "How charming, how natural this is! But your dear Phyllis should take care, for this could soon become quite serious."

I was disturbed by the fact that he did not consider it serious already and, somewhat piqued by this, I asked him what he meant by "serious." He answered without any hesitation, explaining himself so clearly that I could hardly conceal my alarm. But then my irritation returned and since I disliked the idea of his harboring such thoughts, I summoned up my courage, defended my heroine and said, with flaming cheeks: "But, sir, Phyllis is an honest girl!"

Then he was malicious enough to tease me about my heroine and, since we were speaking in French, played on the various meanings of the word *honnête* to expatiate on the "honesty" of Phyllis. I felt how absurd it all was, and was completely bewildered. Not wishing to make me fearful, he terminated the conversation for the moment, but returned to it on other occasions. The plays and stories that I read and translated for him gave him ample opportunity to demonstrate that so-called virtue is a feeble protection against the claims of passion. I did not disagree anymore, but maintained my inner irritation, and found his various remarks troublesome.

I gradually lost all contact with my dear Damon, thanks to the chicanery of his brother. Soon after this, both these promising youths died. I grieved: but they were soon forgotten.

Phyllis grew up fast, quite restored to health and ready to make her way in the world. The crown prince married and took over the reins of government on his father's death. Town and court entered on a flurry of activity, and my curiosity found much to occupy itself with. There were plays and balls, and everything else associated with these, and although our parents restricted us as much as possible, we had to appear at court, where I was presented. Foreigners poured in, every house saw important people, several noblemen arrived with letters of recommendation to my family and still more were introduced to us. My uncle's house became a meeting place for people from all nations.

My worthy mentor continued to warn me, gently and yet pointedly, and in my heart I disliked him for this. I was in no wise convinced of the truth of his allegations, and perhaps I was right at the time, and he was wrong to think women so weak in every situation, but he spoke so persuasively that there was one occasion when I thought he might be right; this was when I said to him that since the danger was so great and the human heart so weak I would ask God to protect me.

This straightforward answer seemed to please him and he praised my intentions. But I had not meant this seriously, these were just empty words, for my feelings toward the Invisible One were well-nigh completely extinguished. The busy crowd of people surrounding me had so distracted me and borne me along, that these had become the emptiest years of my life. For days on end I had nothing to talk about, nothing salutary to think about, nothing to do but go along with the crowd. Even my beloved books remained untouched. The people I associated with had no inkling of serious study: they were German courtiers, and that class of people had at the time no trace of culture.

One would think that such a life had brought me to the edge of ruin. I lived in a continual whirl of gaiety, never had a reflective moment, never prayed, never thought about God or myself. But I consider it providential that none of the many rich, handsome, well-dressed men appealed to me. They had a certain lewdness that they did not trouble to conceal, and that scared me away. They laced their talk with ambiguities that offended me, and I maintained cold aloofness toward them. Their rudeness was sometimes quite beyond belief, and I did not mince my words on that score. My teacher had also told me in confidence that most of these disreputable customers constituted a danger not only to a girl's virtue but also to her health. So I cringed at the thought of them and became really concerned if one of them somehow got too close to me. I avoided cups and glasses, and even chairs they had been sitting on. As a result I became completely isolated, both morally and physically, and all the nice things they said to me I proudly took for incense that was scattered out of a sense of guilt.

Among the strangers was one young man who stood out: we jocularly called him Narcissus. He had acquired a good reputation in the diplomatic service, and hoped, with the various changes taking place at court, to get a good position there. He soon became acquainted with my father, and both his knowledge and his behavior gave him the entrée into the close circle of the most distinguished men. My father said much in his praise, and his handsome figure would have made even more of an impression if his whole manner had not shown a certain degree of self-satisfaction. I saw him, thought well of him, but we did not speak to each other.

He appeared at a big ball, and we danced a minuet together; but even that did not lead to a closer acquaintance. Then came more vigorous dances which, for the sake of my father, who was concerned about my health, I always avoided. I retired to a neighboring room and joined some older women at the card tables whom I was friendly with. Narcissus, having danced for a while, came into the room where I was; when he had recovered from a nosebleed that had afflicted him while dancing, he began to talk to me about various things. Within a short while the conversation became so interesting, though without any trace of tenderness, that we lost all desire to resume dancing. For this we were teased by the others, but that did not trouble us. Next evening we continued our conversation—and preserved our health.

This is how our acquaintance came about. Narcissus called on me and my sisters, and now I began to realize how much I knew, what I thought and felt, and what I could express in conversation. My new friend, having always moved in the best circles, had not only a complete mastery of historical and political events, but also extensive acquaintance with literary matters, and every new publication, especially those in France, was known to him. He brought or sent me many agreeable and useful books, but this had to be kept even quieter than an illicit love affair. Learned women had been ridiculed, and even educated women were unwillingly tolerated, probably because it was considered impolite to put so many ignorant men to shame. Even my father, though he welcomed this new opportunity for me to improve my mind, insisted that this literary exchange should remain a secret.

Our relations with each other continued like this for almost a year, and I cannot say that Narcissus ever expressed any love or affection for me. He remained courteous and obliging, but showed no strong emotion; in actual fact it seemed to be the charms of my youngest sister, who at that time was extraordinarily beautiful, that appealed to him most. He bestowed on her all sorts of pleasant names from various foreign languages, several of which he spoke very well, delighting in introducing their individual idiom into his own German speech. She did not respond particularly to his pleasantries, for she was cut from a different cloth. She was impulsive and he was touchy, so they rarely agreed on details. But he won the good graces of my mother and my aunts, and so gradually became a member of the family.

I do not know how long we would have continued in this fashion, were it not for a strange episode that changed our whole relationship. I was invited with my sisters to a certain house where I did not enjoy going. The company was too mixed and some of the people there were, if not coarse, at least extremely vulgar. On this occasion Narcissus was invited too, so for his sake I was prepared to go, because I knew there would be someone there to whom I could talk as I would wish. We had a lot to put up with already at table, for some of the men had been drinking heavily; and afterwards we had to play a game of forfeits. There was a lot of noisy activity. Narcissus had to pay a forfeit, and he was told to whisper something pleasant in everybody's ear. He stayed too long with the lady next to me, who was the wife of a captain. Suddenly the captain boxed his ears so soundly that the powder from his wig flew into my eyes, for I was sitting right next to him. Once I had wiped my eyes and recovered somewhat from my fright, I saw the two men with naked swords. Narcissus was bleeding, and the other man, inflamed with wine, anger and jealousy, could hardly be restrained by the rest of the company. I took Narcissus's arm and led him through the door and up into another room, and since I did not think he was safe from his crazy opponent, I bolted the door.

Neither of us thought that the wound was serious. All we saw was a slight cut on the hand. But then a stream of blood began to pour down his back, and we saw that he had a large wound in the head. Now I was really frightened. I rushed on to the landing to get help, but there was nobody there because everybody was still downstairs trying to tame the raging man. Finally up came a daughter of the house, in such gay spirits that I was really alarmed by her excessive mirth over what she considered an infernal hubbub and ridiculous performance. I urged her to send for a doctor, and she, in her own wild way, jumped downstairs to fetch one herself.

I returned to my wounded man, bound up his hand with my handkerchief and his head with a towel that was hanging on the door. He was still bleeding profusely; he was pale and seemed about to faint. There was no one nearby to help me, so, quite spontaneously, I put my arm around him and tried to cheer him up by coaxing and stroking. This seemed to restore his spirits; he retained consciousness but was deathly pale.

Finally our busy hostess arrived and was shocked to find my friend in this condition in my arms and both of us spattered with blood. For nobody had imagined that Narcissus was wounded; they all thought I had managed to get him out unharmed.

Suddenly wine, sweet-smelling waters and restoratives in abundance appeared from nowhere, a doctor turned up, I could well have left. But Narcissus held me firmly by the hand, I would have stayed there even if I had not been held fast. While he was being bandaged I continued to moisten his lips with wine, paying little attention to the fact that the whole company was now assembled around us. The doctor finished what he was doing, and the wounded man took a silent but grateful leave of me, and was carried to his house.

Our hostess then took me into her bedroom. She had to undress me completely, and I cannot fail to admit that when I first happened to see myself in the mirror while they were washing his blood off me, I thought I could consider myself beautiful, even without my clothes. I could not put any of these back on, and since everyone else was smaller or bigger than I, I arrived back at my parents' house much to their astonishment in an odd assortment of garments. They were much angered by the fright I had had, the wounding of our friend, the stupidity of the captain, in fact by the whole affair. My father was almost prepared to avenge his friend on the spot and challenge the captain. He chastized those present for not immediately taking action against such a murderous onslaught, for it was all too clear that the captain, after striking Narcissus, had drawn his sword and wounded him from behind; the cut on the hand had only happened when Narcissus tried to draw his own sword. I was extremely upset and affected by all this: but how can I express myself? The emotion that had been lurking in the depths of my heart, had suddenly burst forth like a flame ignited by air. And if joy and pleasure are conducive to the arousing and secret nourishing of love, it is sudden fright that most readily causes love to declare itself decisively. My parents gave their young daughter medication, and put her to bed. And, early next day, my father went immediately to see his wounded friend, who lay quite ill with a high fever.

My father told me very little of what they said to each other, and tried to set my mind at rest regarding the possible consequences of the incident. There was talk as to whether an apology should be considered sufficient, whether the matter should be taken to court, or what else should be done. I knew my father too well for me to believe that he would consider the whole thing settled without a duel. But I kept quiet, for I had long since learnt from my father that women should not interfere in such matters. Furthermore, it did not appear that anything had occurred between the two friends that affected me. But then my father told me about a conversation he had had with my mother. Narcissus, he told me, had been greatly moved by the assistance I had given him, had embraced my father, declared he would be eternally in my debt and desired no joy in life if he could not share it with me. He had requested permission to regard him as a father. Mama repeated all this faithfully to me, adding the salutary reminder that one should not attach too much importance to what is said in the first heat of the moment. "Indeed no," I replied with affected coolness, and heaven knows what or how much I was feeling when I said that.

Narcissus was ill for two months, could not write because of the injury to his hand, but showed by various obliging signs of attentiveness that he was mindful of me. This unusual degree of courtesy became linked in my mind with what I had learnt from my mother, and my head was continually beset by fancies. The whole town was discussing what had happened. People talked to me about it in a particular tone of voice, and drew conclusions that concerned me greatly, much as I tried to dispel them. What had previously been normal flirtation, now became serious affection, and the more I tried to conceal my unsettled state of mind from others, the more intense it became. The thought of losing him terrified me, and the prospect of a closer relationship made me tremble. The thought of marriage inevitably has something frightening about it for a moderately discerning young girl.

These violent perturbations made me think once more about myself. The many images of a distracting life, which had been pursuing me day and night, were suddenly dispelled. My soul came to life again, but the communion with the Invisible Friend, so long interrupted, was not so easily restored. We remained somewhat distant from each other for a while; there was something there, but nothing comparable to what had been.

A duel took place in which the captain was seriously wounded, but I knew nothing about it until it was already over. Public opinion was all on the side of my beloved, who finally reappeared on the scene. With bandaged head and hand he was brought to our house. How my heart leapt at his visit! The whole family was present, and there was a general polite exchange of thanks on both sides, but he did find the opportunity to give me a few secret signs of his affection, which only increased my agitation. When he was completely recovered he came to see us throughout the whole winter, on the same footing as before, and for all his signs of affection, nothing was openly said.

I continued to maintain myself in this fashion. There was no person I could confide in and from God I was too estranged. I had completely forgotten Him during those four wild years, and although I began to think of Him again now and then, my acquaintance had cooled off. It was only ceremonial visits that

I now paid Him, and since I always wore fine clothes when I appeared before Him and gladly displayed my virtue, honesty, and the advantages I believed I had over others, He seemed to disregard me in all my finery.

A courtier would have been very disturbed if his prince, from whom he expected good fortune, had behaved like this toward him. But I was not discouraged by this, for I had all I needed—good health and comfortable circumstances. If God were pleased that I thought of Him, that was good; but if He were not, I still considered I had done my duty toward Him.

At that time I did not think about myself in this way, but this is a true picture of what my soul was like. Yet circumstances were to contribute to a change and purification of my feelings.

Spring came and Narcissus began to visit me unannounced when I was home alone. He came now as a lover, and asked me if I would give him my heart and, when he had secured an honorable and well-paid position, in due course my hand in marriage. He had already been given a post in our social circle, but since people were somewhat fearful of his ambitious nature, he was at first more kept back than speedily advanced in station; and since he had money of his own he was accorded only a meager emolument.

Strong as my inclinations toward him were, I knew that he was not the sort of man that one could deal quite openly with. I therefore constrained myself and referred him to my father, whose approval he seemed to have no doubts about, while wishing to be assured of mine without further delay. Eventually I did say yes, but insisted on the approval of my parents as a necessary precondition. He then made a formal approach to both of them, they expressed their agreement, and he was given their approval on the understanding that, as was soon to be expected, he should be advanced in position. My sisters and aunts were informed of this and sworn to secrecy.

So now my beloved had become my fiancé, and the difference between the two was very obvious. If only the lovers of all well-intentioned girls could be turned into prospective bridegrooms, our sex would be well served, even if no marriage resulted from such relationships. The love between two persons is not thereby diminished; it becomes more reasonable. Countless petty sillinesses, all the flirtatiousness and moodiness suddenly disappear. If our betrothed tells us we look better in our mob cap than in our best headdress, then any sensible girl amongst us will no longer care about how she does her hair, for it is perfectly natural that he should think like a solid citizen and prefer a housewife to a society doll. And that applies to everything.

And if such a girl is fortunate enough for her man to be intelligent and knowledgeable, she will learn more than all the universities or all her travels abroad could teach her. She will not only absorb all the culture he gives her, but take pains to advance herself by this means. Love makes possible much that is impossible, and ultimately there emerges that submissiveness which is so proper and necessary to the female sex. A fiancé does not lord it like a husband: he asks and his beloved tries to sense what he wishes and to fulfill his desires before he expresses them. Experience taught me what I would not have missed for anything. I was happy, as happy as one can be in this world—that is to say, for a short while.

A whole summer passed in these tranquil joys. Narcissus never gave me the slightest cause for complaint. My fondness for him increased, my whole being was bound up with him; he knew this, and delighted in it. But in the meantime something of apparently little consequence developed, which gradually imperilled our relationship.

Narcissus acted toward me like a fiancé but never dared to of ask me what was as yet forbidden us. Yet our opinions differed sharply on the limits of what was virtuous and moral. I wanted to tread warily and would not allow any liberties that the world should not know of. He, used as he was to snacking, found this diet rather severe. This led to constant disagreements; he appreciated my standpoint but tried to undermine it.

I remembered what my old language teacher had said to me about things getting "serious," and the arguments I had used at that time to counter his allegations.

In the meantime I had become somewhat better acquainted with God. He had given me such a beloved bridegroom, and I knew how to thank Him for that. My earthly love absorbed my whole mind and activated it to a point that my relationship with God did not conflict with it. It was quite natural that I should express my anxiety to Him, but I did not realize that what made me so anxious was something that I ardently desired. I thought I was endowed with great strength of mind and did not, for example, pray to be delivered from temptation, for in my thoughts I had moved far beyond temptation. In this tawdry garb of self-righteousness I made bold to appear before my God. He did not reject me; my slightest approach to Him left a pleasant impression in my mind, and this impression encouraged me to seek Him out more frequently.

Except for Narcissus everything else in the world was dead to me, nothing else had any attraction. Even my passion for dressing up took on the sole purpose of pleasing him, and if I knew he would not be there to see me, I did not devote much time or trouble to this. I liked to dance, but when he wasn't there, I felt that I couldn't abide all this moving about. Once at a brilliant soirée where he was not to be present, I could not find anything new to wear, or adapt what I had to what was fashionable. I was quite indifferent to both; or rather, both were equally tiresome to me. My evening seemed to me well spent in playing some card game with elderly persons—something I normally had no desire whatsoever to do—and if it so happened that some old friend of mine teased me about this, I would smile for the first time in the whole evening. The same thing happened on walks and other social diversions:

> Him alone have I selected,
> Born was I for him alone,
> Nothing but his favor craving . . .

WILHELM MEISTER'S APPRENTICESHIP

I was therefore often lonely in society, and complete isolation would have pleased me best. But my busy mind could neither sleep nor dream: I went on thinking and feeling and gradually achieved a facility for expressing my thoughts and sentiments to God. Then different feelings began to arise within me though they did not conflict with the others. For my love for Narcissus was quite in accord with the plan of the whole of creation, and never conflicted with my basic duties. There was no opposition here despite the immense differences. Narcissus was the only person whose image hovered before my mind and claimed all my love; the other feeling was not connected with any image and was inexpressibly pleasant. I don't have it anymore and cannot give it to myself again.

My beloved, who knew all my other secrets, knew nothing about this. I soon noticed that he thought differently. He would often bring me books that attacked with light or heavy artillery what one could call communion with the Invisible. I read these books, because he had brought them to me, and finally could not recall a single word of them.

We also disagreed about studies and the acquisition of knowledge. His attitude was that of men in general. He made fun of learned women and yet kept trying to educate me all the time. He talked to me about everything except jurisprudence and, while constantly bringing me books of various kinds, repeatedly expressed the dubious precept that a woman should keep her learning more secret than a Calvinist his religion in a Catholic country. Although I found it natural not to present myself to the world as more intelligent and better informed than previously, he was at times the first not to be able to resist showing his vanity by praising the qualities of my mind.

One well-known man of the world, highly regarded for his influence, talents and intelligence, who was receiving great acclaim at our court, singled out Narcissus and associated with him continually. They argued about the virtuousness of women. Narcissus imparted to me the general drift of their conversation. I did not hesitate to add my comments, and my friend asked me to set these down in writing. I could write French fairly fluently, having laid a good foundation for this with my old teacher. My correspondence with my friend had been in French, and at that time one could acquire refinement and culture only by reading French books. My little essay pleased the count, and I also had to give him some short poems that I had recently written. Narcissus seemed quite unconstrained in his desire to benefit his beloved, and the whole episode ended to his delight with the count sending him an elegant rhymed epistle in French just as he was about to leave us, which referred back to their friendly arguments and praised Narcissus for being about to acquire, after so many doubts and errors, a true sense of what virtue is, and that in the arms of a charming and virtuous wife.

The poem was shown first to me, and then to all and sundry, and everyone had his own opinions about it. There were various episodes of this kind, and as a result every newcomer whom Narcissus thought well of, was introduced into our household.

Another count and his family spent some time in our town because of the excellent doctor that we had there. Narcissus was treated like a son by this family, and he took me along to see them. The conversation between these distinguished persons was a real delight for heart and mind, and even the usual social diversions did not seem here so empty as elsewhere. Everyone knew how we stood in relation to each other. They treated us as circumstances demanded, and never broached the essential. I mention this particular family because my acquaintance with them was to have a considerable influence on the further course of my life.

We had now been betrothed for almost a year, and our springtime was past. Summer arrived, and everything became hotter and more serious.

Through several unexpected deaths, certain positions at court had become open for which Narcissus was eligible and qualified. The moment was approaching when my whole future destiny was to be decided. While Narcissus and his friends at court were doing all they possibly could to remove whatever disadvantageous impressions he might have created, so that they might help him to secure the desired position, I myself addressed my suit to the Invisible Friend. I was received in such friendly fashion that I took pleasure in returning to Him. I expressed quite openly my desire that Narcissus should obtain the position, but my entreaties were not insistent, nor did I demand that this should come about because of my own prayers.

The position was filled by a very inferior competitor. I was appalled at the news, rushed to my room, and closed the door firmly. My first bitter reaction was to burst into tears; my next thought was that this could not have happened just by chance, and so I decided to accept it in the belief that this apparent misfortune would rebound to my advantage. And then my tenderest feelings came to the fore, dispelling the clouds of my grief. I felt that, with the help I had, anything could be endured. And I went to dinner in a tranquil frame of mind, much to the amazement of the other members of the household.

Narcissus did not have my strength of mind, and I had to console him. He had to suffer unpleasantness even from his own family and this disturbed him, but our relationship was based so much on trust that he confided in me about everything. His negotiations to find a position elsewhere were equally unsuccessful; I suffered on his account and my own, but took everything to the place where my concerns had been so well received. My experiences in this quarter were so soothing that I returned there ever more often, always seeking the consolation that I had found before. But I did not find it always. I felt like someone wishing to warm himself in the sun when the shadow obstructs him. What was causing this? I asked myself, seeking the reason and coming to the conclusion that it all depended on the state of my own soul: if it were not entirely directed straight toward God, I remained unwarmed, felt no reciprocity, could not make out His answer. Then came the second question: What was obstructing my relationship? Here there was a whole realm of possibilities and I spent almost the whole second year of my friendship with Narcissus involved in this investigation. I could have concluded this earlier, for I soon found the answer; but I was not willing to admit it and tried in various ways to avoid doing so.

What I soon discovered was that foolish pastimes and trivial occupations were obstructing the directness of my soul's approach to God. The why and wherefore was now quite clear to me; but how was I to exist in a world where everything was folly and emptiness? Gladly would I have let the matter rest, and lived without thinking about it, like other people whom I saw prospering. But I could not do that. My inmost self constantly opposed it. If I thought of changing my situation by withdrawing from society, I found this impossible to do. I was now confined within a narrow circle, unable to give up certain relationships, and disaster after disaster poured increasingly in upon me. I would often go to bed weeping, and get up next morning after a sleepless night with nothing changed. I needed strong support and this was not to be vouchsafed me by God when I was running around in a fool's cap.

I then began to think about all my activities. First I considered dancing and card playing. Nothing had ever been thought, said, or written for or against these which I did not consult, ponder, discuss, elaborate on, or reject, tormenting myself in the process. If I were to give up such pastimes I would be sure to offend Narcissus, because he was mortally afraid of our being ridiculed for appearing so anxiously moralistic in the eyes of society. Since I did not engage in these things, which I considered foolish, dangerously foolish, out of a sense of pleasure to me, but simply in order to please him, all this became terribly difficult for me.

It would be hard for me to describe without tiresome repetition and undue wordiness the efforts I made to pursue these activities which diverted me but disturbed my inner peace, without closing my heart to the influence of the Invisible Being, and how painful it was to realize that the conflict was not to be resolved in this way. For as soon as I donned the robe of folly, this did not remain a mask but enveloped my whole being.

May I interrupt my narration at this point and offer some observations on what was going on inside me? What could have affected my taste and my whole temperament at the age of twenty-two, nay, even earlier, so that I felt no pleasure in things which provide most people of my age with harmless entertainment? Why weren't they harmless to me? My answer had to be that these things were not harmless to me because I was not, like others of my age, unaware of my own soul. Indeed I knew from experiences which had come to me unsought, that there are higher emotions which guarantee us a pleasure not to be gained in idle entertainments, and that these higher pleasures provide a source of strength when misfortune overtakes us.

But the social pleasures and diversions of youth must have had a strong attraction for me, because I had not been able to engage in them as if I were not involved. But now I could, if I so desired, show great indifference to many things which were then bewildering to me and threatened to assume mastery over me. There was no middle course; I had to give up either these pleasant pastimes or the enlivening feelings within me.

But the conflict in my soul was soon settled without my being conscious of this happening. Despite the fact that I still had a certain hankering after the pleasures of the senses, they no longer provided me with satisfaction. Much as one may enjoy drinking wine, the pleasure dissipates when one finds oneself in a fully stocked wine cellar where the bad air is almost suffocating. Good clean air is better than wine—that I felt quite strongly—and it would not have taken much reflection on my part to see that what is good is preferable to what is attractive, had I not been held back by the fear of losing Narcissus's good graces. But when finally, after much debate and constant consideration, I took a sharp look at the nature of the bond that held me to him, I became aware that it was not all that strong and could easily be broken. I realized that it was a glass cover enclosing me in an airless space, and if only I could summon up enough strength to shatter it, then I would be free.

No sooner thought, than done. I removed my mask and began to act always according to the dictates of my heart. My fondness for Narcissus remained, but the thermometer that had been standing in hot water was now in the open air, unable to rise any higher than the temperature outside. Unfortunately, it sank considerably. Narcissus began to withdraw and act like a stranger. He had every right to do so, but my thermometer went down when he was no longer near. My family noticed the change, was surprised, and questioned me about it. I declared with almost manly defiance that I had made enough sacrifices, that I was prepared to suffer every adversity together with him until the end of my days, but demanded complete freedom to determine my actions according to my own convictions. I would never stubbornly insist on what I thought was right without listening to the opinions of others, but I myself must decide on my own happiness and I would not accept pressure from elsewhere. The reasoning of the greatest physician in the world would never persuade me to eat or drink something that was normally considered healthy and was enjoyed by many, if I myself knew it would be harmful to me, such as coffee, for instance, and I would never consider any action that bewildered me as morally suited to me.

Since I had been quietly working toward this conclusion for a long time, arguments about it were welcome rather than irritating to me. I aired my feelings and sensed the importance of the decision I had made. I did not yield an inch, and those to whom I did not owe a childlike respect were sharply dealt with. I soon won over my own family. My mother had entertained similar sentiments ever since she was a young girl, but they had never fully matured, for she had never been pressured by necessity, never had to pluck up courage to defend her convictions. She was pleased to see her latent desires fulfilled in me. My younger sister seemed to take my part; my other sister remained quiet and attentive. My aunt was the one who raised most objections. The reasons she gave seemed to her incontrovertible, and they were so because they were ordinary reasons. I was finally forced to tell her that she had no voice in this matter, and she, for her part, only rarely indicated that she still thought she was right. She was the only one, I should add, who really considered the matter closely, and quite dispassionately. I am not doing her an injustice by saying that she had no soul and very limited opinions.

My father reacted in accordance with his character. He expressed himself in few words, but did speak to me quite often about the matter. His reasoning was sensible and as such, irrefutable; and it was only my strong sense of being in the right that gave me the power to argue against him. But soon there came a change in the scenario: I had to appeal to his heart. Oppressed by his intelligence, I lapsed into emotional outbursts. I gave free rein to my tongue and my tears. I revealed to him the strength of my love for Narcissus, the compulsion I had been obliged to exercise over myself these past two years, and the certainty I now felt that I was doing right by being prepared to suffer the loss of my beloved and the likelihood of happiness, ever, if needs be, to sacrifice wealth and possessions for the sake of what I knew to be right; that I would rather leave my country, my parents and my friends and earn my bread elsewhere, than abandon my convictions. My father concealed his emotion, said nothing for a while, and then openly declared his agreement.

From that time on, Narcissus ceased to come to our house, and my father to attend the weekly gatherings where Narcissus would be present. The whole affair created quite a stir at court and in the town. People spoke about it in the way that such things are usually discussed when the public feels heavily involved, because it had been pampered into thinking it can exert some influence on the decision-making of weak minds. I was sufficiently acquainted with the world to know that one is often reproved for doing something by the very same persons who persuaded one to do it, and, quite apart from that, my state of mind was such that all these fleeting expressions of opinion were of no significance.

On the other hand, I did not deny myself the indulgence of my affection for Narcissus. He had become invisible to me, and my feelings had not changed toward him. I loved him dearly—in a new way, and somehow more firmly than before. If only he would not disturb my convictions, I would be his; but without this condition I would have refused to share a kingdom with him. For several months I kept these feelings and thoughts to myself, and then, when I felt sufficiently calm and composed, I wrote him a polite, but not affectionate letter asking why he no longer came to see me.

Since I knew that as a person he was not given to expressing his opinion on minor matters, but instead did what he thought was right without saying anything about it, I now presented my proposal as a matter of immediate importance. I got back a long letter which seemed to me rather tasteless, couched in a wordy style and empty phrases, saying that without a better position he could not offer me his hand, that I knew better than anybody how difficult things had been for him, that he believed a protracted and fruitless engagement might harm my reputation, and that I should permit him to maintain his present distance. As soon as he were in the position to make me happy, the promise he had given me would be sanctified.

I answered him immediately, saying that since our relationship was now public knowledge it might well be too late to patch up my reputation, of which my conscience and my innocence were the strongest safeguards. I relieved him of his obligation toward me without further hesitation, expressing the wish that he would thereby find happiness for himself. Within the hour I received a brief reply saying basically the same as his previous letter, namely that once he had secured a position, he would ask me if I were willing to share his joy with him.

This seemed to me saying as good as nothing. I told my relations and friends that the whole affair was over and done with, and indeed it really was. For when nine months later he did receive a most desirable advancement, he asked again for my hand in marriage, but this time with the condition that, as the wife of a man who would have to establish a suitable household, I should change my way of thinking. I thanked him politely, and tore my heart and mind away from the whole affair, with the same eagerness as one leaves a theater after the final curtain has been lowered. Shortly afterwards he found himself a rich and socially respected wife (which was now quite easy for him), and since I knew he would now be happy in the way he desired, I felt completely at ease.

I should not fail to mention that several times, both before and after he obtained his appointment, I received offers of marriage, all of which I declined without further consideration, though my father and mother wished I had been more accommodating.

After my stormy March and April, fine May weather seemed to be bestowed on me. I enjoyed good health and an indescribable peace of mind. Wherever I turned my thoughts, I knew I had gained by my loss. Young as I was, and full of feeling, I found God's creation much more beautiful than when I had to have parties and card playing to while away my hours in His lovely garden. No longer ashamed of my piety, I did not need to conceal my love of art and study. I drew, painted and read, and found enough people to encourage me in this. In place of the society I had withdrawn from, or rather that had withdrawn from me, I gathered a small circle around me that provided much richer entertainment. I did have a leaning toward social life, and I cannot deny that when I had abandoned my former friends, I had shuddered at the thought of loneliness. But now I was sufficiently, perhaps even too well, compensated for my loss. My acquaintance grew not only with persons nearby, who shared my sentiments, but also with several from farther places. My story had become common knowledge, and there were many persons curious to meet a girl who valued God more than her betrothed. In Germany at that time a particular religious trend was noticeable. Several ducal and princely houses became concerned about the salvation of their souls. There were also members of the lesser nobility who shared the same concern, and it was even widespread amongst the other social classes.

The family of the count whom I mentioned earlier began to cultivate closer relations with me. Its size had increased by the addition of relatives coming to live in our town. These admirable people sought out my company, and I theirs. The family circle was a large one and in that household I became acquainted with many princes, dukes and lords of the Empire. My sentiments were no longer a secret to anybody, and whether they were respected or just tolerated, I attained my goal and was not assailed for this.

There was another way in which I was brought back into society. A stepbrother of my father's, who had visited us only very occasionally, came and spent a considerable time with us. He had given up a respected and influential position at another court because things had not gone as he wished. He was a man of keen intelligence and sober character, and therefore very like my father; but my father had a certain gentleness, which made it easier for him than for my uncle to yield on certain matters, and, when something was against his convictions, not doing it himself but being prepared to let it happen, keeping his disapproval to himself or venting it only in the intimate circle of the family. My uncle was much younger, and his self-assurance was bolstered by his external circumstances. His mother had been very rich, and in addition he now had expectations of a sizeable inheritance from her close and distant relatives. He needed no financial support from anywhere, whereas my father had to eke out his modest means by what he earned from his position.

Domestic misfortunes had made my uncle even sterner. He had suffered the early loss of a loving wife and a promising son, and from that time on he seemed to want to keep aloof from everything that did not depend on his own will.

Occasionally one heard it said in our family, with some satisfaction, that he would probably not marry again, and so we children could consider ourselves heirs to his large fortune. I paid little attention to this, but the behavior of my siblings was affected by it. He was strong-willed but never contradicted anyone, preferring to listen attentively to the opinions of others and trying to support them by arguments and examples of his own. If you did not know him you might think he shared your opinions, for he had such outstanding intelligence that he could transport himself with ease into the minds and thinking of everyone else. This did not happen so readily in my case, for I had feelings of which he had no comprehension. Although he was considerate, sympathetic and understanding in speaking to me about my sentiments, it was abundantly clear that he had no conception of the true reasons for my actions.

Secretive as he normally was, the purpose of his unaccustomed visit was eventually revealed. He had selected my youngest sister as the one he had decided on to get married and be given happiness in the fashion he desired. It is true that with her physical and intellectual gifts, especially when supplemented by a sizeable fortune, she could claim the very best of suitors. His feelings about me were demonstrated by his securing for me the position of a canoness, from which I soon began to receive emoluments.

My sister was not particularly pleased with his efforts on her behalf, and not as grateful as I was. She confided in me a matter of the heart that she had so far very wisely concealed, for she was afraid of what in fact did actually happen, namely that I would advise her in the strongest possible terms against a union with a man who should not have been attractive to her. I did my utmost, and was successful in persuading her. My uncle's intentions were too serious and too plain, and the prospect for my sister, worldly-minded as she was, too attractive, for her not to muster sufficient strength to reject an involvement that her own mind disapproved of. She began to cease evading the gentle hints of our uncle, and a basis was soon established for him to pursue his intentions. She became a lady-in-waiting at a neighboring court, where he was able to entrust her to the surveillance and nurture of a friend of his who, as chief governess, stood in excellent repute. I went with her to her new habitation. We were both well satisfied with the reception we received, and I was often obliged to smile at my new social role as a young, pious canoness.

Previously I would have been perplexed by this situation, maybe to the point of losing my head; but now I remained quite calm. I spent several hours having my hair dressed and decking myself out, with no other thought than that this was the fancy dress I was required to put on. I talked to everybody in the crowded halls without being affected by the cast of mind or appearance of any person that I met. When I returned home, the only sense I had was that of dragging my tired feet behind me. My mind profited from mingling with the many people that I encountered, amongst them several women who were models of all the virtues and of proper, dignified behavior, especially the governess to whom my sister had the good fortune to be entrusted for her education.

But on my return home I became aware of certain unpleasant physical results from my stay at court. Despite my extreme abstemiousness and strict diet I was no longer in complete control of my time and my powers. Meals, exercise, getting up and going to bed, dressing and going out for rides—none of this had been dependent on my own will and inclination as it was back home. One cannot stand still in the midst of the social whirl without being impolite, and so I did everything that was required of me, and willingly, because I considered it part of my duties and knew it would not last long, but also because I felt in better health than ever before. Nevertheless the unaccustomed restlessness of my life must have taken a heavier toll on me than I had realized. For no sooner had I arrived home and given my parents a satisfying account of my doings than I suffered a hemorrhage which, although not serious and of short duration, left me noticeably weaker for a long time.

I now had to recite a new lesson to myself, and did so gladly. There was nothing binding me to the world of society, and I was convinced that I would never find there what was right for me. And so I entered on a state of peace and calm, and in renouncing one sort of life, I was sustained in life.

I had to suffer new afflictions when my mother was stricken with a serious illness, which lasted five full years till nature took its course. During that time there was much to test me. Often, when her anxiety became too acute for her to manage, she would call us at night to come and stand round her bed so that she might be at least distracted, if not made better, by our presence. Even more difficult, in fact almost impossible to bear, was the pressure on me when my father too began to feel wretched. He had suffered from violent headaches since the time of his youth; while frequent, they did not last more than thirty-six hours. But now they were continuous, and when they got really severe, my heart was torn with pity for him. In these troublesome times I was more aware than ever of my own physical frailty, which hindered me in the fulfillment of my most sacred, my tenderest duties, or made them extremely burdensome to me.

I was now able to examine myself to see whether the path I had chosen was one of truth or of fancy, whether I had only been imitating others, whether the object of my faith was a reality or not; to my great consolation I always found that it was. My heart was directed straight to God, I had sought and found communion with the "beloved ones," and this it was that lightened my burden. Like a traveller in search of shade, my soul sped to this place of refuge when all else oppressed me from without, and I never returned unsolaced.

In recent times many champions of religion, more from zeal than from true religious feeling, it would seem, have urged their brethren in the spirit to publicize instances of prayer being answered, probably in order to have chapter and verse with which to outwit their opponents by proof and argument. How little they know what true feeling is, how few real experiences they themselves will have had!

I can vouch that I never returned empty-handed when I went to God in distress and anxiety. That is claiming a lot, but I cannot, I dare not try to be more explicit. Important as all these experiences were for me at the crucial moments, any attempt to try to list them individually would be flat and make them sound insignificant, maybe improbable. I was merely happy that so many different occasions had proved that I was not without God in this life, just as every breath I drew proved I was alive. God was near to me, I was constantly in His presence. That is what I can declare as the ultimate truth, and can do so without resorting to the language of theological systems.

How I wished that I could have lived without recourse to such systems. But who can so early reach a state of complete blissful absorption in his own self without reference to external forms and systems? I was seriously concerned about my eternal salvation, and humbly placed my trust in the experience and repute of others. I applied myself thoroughly to the system of achieving conversion advocated by the pietist theologians at Halle, but I could not adapt myself to it at all.

According to the stages of this system, a change of heart must begin with a deep sense of alarm at one's sinfulness. In this state of extremity the heart must recognize the punishment one has deserved, and have a foretaste of hell which will sour the sweetness of sin. Then one should experience a noticeable assurance of grace, but this will not often come readily in the process but must be sought after.

None of this was in any way applicable to me. For when I sought out God in all sincerity, He was always to be found and never reproached me with my past actions. I did see afterwards where I had acted unworthily, and I knew in what ways I was still unworthy, but the recognition of my failings did not cause me any alarm. Not for a moment was I overcome by the fear of hell, indeed the whole idea of evil spirits and a place of punishment and torment after death was entirely alien to my thinking. The people I knew whose hearts were closed to love and trust in the Invisible One, who lived without God, seemed to me extremely unhappy already, so that hell and external punishment would, I thought, constitute a lesser rather than a severer punishment. When I thought about those people whose hearts were full of hatred and closed to all that was good, loading evil onto themselves and others, closing their eyes by day in order to assert that there is no light from the sun, then they seemed to me wretched and miserable beyond degree. What sort of hell could one think of to make their situation worse?

For ten full years this was my mental attitude. It sustained me through many trials, including my beloved mother's suffering and death. I was honest enough not to conceal my serenity of spirit during these afflictions when I was talking to persons conventionally trained in piety. I had to suffer many a friendly reproof from them to the effect that it was high time I seriously understood the importance of laying a firm religious foundation in times of good health.

But there was no lack of seriousness in me. I allowed myself to be momentarily convinced by what they said, and would willingly enough have felt sad and terrified. But to my astonishment I found that I could not. When I thought about God, I was happy and content. Even during my dear mother's painful last days on earth, I was not afraid of death. But in these momentous hours I learned much more than my uncalled-for instructors believed, and different things.

As time went on I became skeptical about the opinions of some well-known people, but I kept these feelings to myself. There was one particular woman friend, in whom I had confided too much, who was always trying to meddle in my affairs. I was obliged to break loose from her too, and finally told her firmly that she should not expend such efforts on me, for I did not need her advice: I knew my God and He alone should be my guide. She was very offended and I believe she has never quite forgiven me.

My decision to extricate myself in spiritual matters from the influence and advice of my friends resulted in my acquiring the courage to pursue my own course in external relationships. But without the help of my faithful Invisible Guide things would not have turned out so well for me, and I still marvel at the wise and propitious guidance that I received. Nobody really knew what I was about—not even I myself.

The thing, that evil thing that has never been explained, which separates us from the Being we owe our life to, the eternal Being by whom all that we call Life is sustained, the thing that is called Sin—this I did not yet know.

In my communion with the Invisible Friend I had the feeling of deep pleasure at the involvement of all my powers. The longing to enjoy this continuously was so intense that I would gladly forgo anything that impeded it; and here experience was my best teacher. But I was like a sick person without medication who resorts to dieting. It helped me somewhat, but not enough.

I could not remain all the time in isolation, although I found that was the best means of avoiding my natural tendency towards dispersing my thoughts. But when I returned to the hurly-burly, this affected me more strongly. My greatest advantage was that more than anything I loved to be quiet, and so ultimately I always withdrew to my solitude. In a kind of twilight state I recognized that I was weak and miserable, and tried to spare rather than expose myself.

For seven long years I persisted in this careful diet. I did not see anything wrong in myself, and I thought my state was enviable. Had it not been for some unusual circumstances I would have remained at this stage, and I departed from it in the strangest manner. Against the advice of all my friends I entered on a new human relationship. Their arguments made me hesitate at first, so I addressed myself to my Invisible Friend without delay, and since He expressed approval, I continued on my path without further concern.

A man of intelligence, feeling and talents had bought a house in the neighborhood. He and his family were amongst those newcomers whose acquaintance I had made. We were very much alike in customs, habits and domestic arrangements, and soon became close friends.

Philo, as I shall call him, was a man in middle life, who was extremely helpful to my father, whose powers were beginning to fail, in certain business matters. He soon became a close friend of the family, and since, as he said, he saw in me someone who had neither the extravagance and vanity of high society nor the bloodless timidity of the conventiclers, we two became intimate friends. He was both agreeable and useful to me.

Although I did not have the slightest inclination to engage in worldly affairs or have any influence in them, I did like to hear people talk about them and discover what was going on around me. I sought dispassionate, clear information: feeling, affection and intensity I reserved for my God, my family and my friends. I may say that my family and friends were jealous of my attachment to Philo, and they were right in more than one respect to warn me about it. I suffered much in the stillness of my heart, for I could not dismiss their objections as entirely empty or selfish. I had long been accustomed to give less weight to my own opinions, but this time I could not stifle my convictions. I beseeched my God to warn, hinder, or guide me in this matter too, and since my heart did not gainsay me afterwards, I felt relieved, and continued along my chosen path.

There was a vague general resemblance between Philo and Narcissus, but Philo's religious education had given his emotional life greater unity and strength. He had less vanity and more character. Narcissus had been shrewd, meticulous, persistent and tireless in worldly matters; Philo was clear, sharp, quick and incredibly expeditious. From him I learned all about the private circumstances of those distinguished persons I knew by sight, and I enjoyed surveying the busy throng from my lookout. Philo did not withhold anything from me, and gradually told me all about his own public and private relationships. I was afraid on his behalf, because I foresaw certain situations and complications developing, and bad things came sooner than I had anticipated. For there were certain matters that he had always avoided telling me about, but he finally revealed sufficient of these to make me assume the worst. The effect of this on me was devastating, for I encountered experiences which were quite new to me. With infinite sadness of heart I saw in Philo some sort of counterpart to the hero of Wieland's novel *Agathon*, who had to repay the cost of his education in the sacred grove of Delphi with heavy overdue interest—and this second Agathon was the man I was so closely associated with! I was filled with ardent concern for him, I suffered with him, and we both found ourselves in a very strange state of mind.

Having occupied myself for a long time with the state of his soul, I turned my attention to my own. The thought that I was no better than he came over me and descended like a cloud which darkened my mind. I didn't just think this, I felt it, felt that I was no better than he, and felt it so strongly that I would not wish to have any such feeling again. The transition was not sudden. For more than a year I had been feeling that if some invisible hand had not prevented me, I could have become the foulest of evildoers, for I sensed the tendency in my heart. What a discovery this was!

Up to then I had not experienced the reality of sinfulness in the least, but now the possibility of sin had become terrifyingly clear and conceivable to me.

I was not yet acquainted with evil, but I feared it; I felt that I could be guilty, but I could not reproach myself. Convinced as I was that a disposition such as I now recognized mine to be, would not make for a union with the Supreme Being after death such as I hoped for, I did not have any fears of incurring such separation at present. Despite the evil that I discovered in myself, I loved Him, hated my own feelings, wished to hate them even more intensely, my only desire being to be freed of this sickness and this whole disposition toward sickness. I was sure that the Great Physician would not refuse me help in this.

The only question was: How was this defect to be overcome? By virtuous actions? This I did not even contemplate, for during the past ten years my exercise of virtue had been far more than outward actions, and yet the horrors I now recognized had been deeply ingrained in my soul all the while. Couldn't they have broken loose as they did when David saw Bathsheba? Was David not also a friend of God, and was I not deeply convinced that God was my friend?

Was this perhaps an inescapable weakness in all mankind? Are we to accept the fact that we sometimes sense the sovereign power of inclination and, with the best will in the world, can do nothing more than deplore what we have done and then fall into the same situation on a similar occasion?

I found no solace in treatises on morals. Neither the severity of their efforts to make us subdue our instincts, nor their accommodating attempts to make virtues out of instincts, were in any way satisfying to me. The basic ideas that my communion with the Invisible Friend had instilled in me, had a much more decisive importance for me.

Once when I was studying the songs written by David after that ugly catastrophe, I was struck by his assertion that the evil within him was already in the material from which he was made; but he wished to be freed from sin and prayed earnestly for purity of heart.

But how was I to attain this? The answer, I knew, was given me in symbolic form in the Bible, where it was written that the blood of Christ shall wash away all sin. I now perceived for the first time that I had not really understood these words I had so often repeated, and such questions as: What does that mean? or, How is that to take place? tormented me day and night. Finally I seemed to catch the glimmer of an answer: What I was seeking was to be found in the mystery of the Incarnation through which the Word, in which we and all things are made, becomes flesh. It was revealed to me in darkling distance that our ultimate maker once descended to the depths in which we travail, penetrating and absorbing them, passed through every stage of our human condition from conception and birth to the grave, and, emerging from this strange detour, rose once again to those clear bright heights where we too must dwell in order to gain happiness.

Why must we always resort to images of external conditions in order to speak of such innermost things? What are heights and depths, darkness and light to Him? Only we have an above and below, a day and night. And He became like us so that we might be part of Him.

But how are we to share in such immeasurable beneficence? By Faith, the scripture tells us. But what is Faith? Merely accepting the report of an event as truth, how can that help me, I asked myself. I need to experience its effects and results. It must require an unusual state of mind for human beings, to be able to make such Faith part of themselves.

"Grant me such Faith, oh almighty God!" was the prayer of my heavy heart. I leaned over the little table at which I was sitting, hiding my tear-stained face in my hands. I was in the state that we must be in if God is to hear our prayer; and how rarely are we in that state!

How can I find the proper words to describe what I felt at that moment? A strong impulse lifted my soul to the cross on which Jesus died. I cannot call it other than an impulse, like that which carries one toward an absent friend, someone one loves dearly, making a connection that is more intense, more real than one would have imagined. My soul drew nigh to the incarnate, the crucified One, and at that moment I knew what Faith was.

This is Faith! I cried, and leapt up half in fright. I examined myself in order to make quite sure what I did feel, what I did perceive, and I was soon persuaded that my spirit had acquired the facility to rise aloft—a faculty that was quite new to it.

Words fail us when we have such feelings. I could clearly distinguish what I felt from any fancies of the mind—there were no imaginings, no images, and yet what I felt had the certainty of being attached to something definite, just as one's imagination conjures up the features of a distant loved one.

When my first rapture had abated, I recognized that what I was experiencing was something I had felt before, but never with such intensity. I had never been able to prolong such a state of mind for myself. I do believe that every human being has had some such feelings at one time or another; for it is undoubtedly this sort of experience that teaches us all that there is a God. From time to time I had been content to feel such an access of strength, and would probably have remained satisfied with this, had it not been for the misfortunes which had constantly and unexpectedly been my lot and the consequent diminution of my powers and abilities. But now, since that one great moment, I had taken on wings. I could now rise above all that had threatened me before, like a bird effortlessly soaring with joyful song above a raging torrent, beside which a dog remains standing, barking anxiously.

My joy was beyond description and although I revealed none of this to anybody, my family noticed a new radiance about me, without knowing the cause. If only I had maintained silence and striven to preserve in my soul the purity of the mood! If only I had not allowed myself to be misled by circumstances into revealing my secret, I could have spared myself a huge detour.

During the past ten years of my Christian experience I had not myself possessed the strength I needed, and so I had done what other serious-minded persons in my condition had, namely supported myself by filling my imagination with images related to God, which is definitely useful, for by this means the evil effects of injurious images are prevented. Our soul grasps at one or the other of these spiritual images and by so doing it soars upward like a young bird flitting from branch to branch. So long as one has nothing better, this exercise is not to be discounted.

We are provided with images and impressions directing us toward God by the activities of the church, by bells, organs and hymns, and especially by the homilies of preachers. My desire to profit from all this was so intense that neither bad weather nor poor health would prevent me from going to church, and church bells of a Sunday were the only thing that would make me impatient when I was lying on my bed of sickness. I listened with great attention to our chief Court Preacher, who was an excellent man. His colleagues were also of value to me, and I knew how to pick out the golden apples of the divine Word from the ordinary fruit in such earthly vessels. I supplemented these public religious exercises with all sorts of private "devotional practices," as they are called, but all this did was to feed my imaginative powers and refine the activity of my senses. I had grown so accustomed to this course of action, and set such a high value on it, that I did not have the sense of anything higher. My soul had feelers, but no eyes; it felt, but didn't see. If only it would acquire eyes so that it could really see!

I still continued to go and listen eagerly to the sermons. But what an experience I had! I no longer found what I had previously valued. These preachers were gnawing away at shells, whereas I was enjoying the kernels. I soon grew tired of them, but I was too spoilt to limit myself to what I had discovered for myself. I had to have images for my feelings, impressions from outside, and I believed this to be a truly spiritual need.

Philo's parents had connections with the pietistic community at Herrnhut, and in his own library there were many writings by its founder, Count Zinzendorf. On several different occasions he spoke to me in clear and reasonable terms about these works, and urged me to look at some of them, if only in order to acquaint myself with a particular psychological phenomenon. I myself considered Count Zinzendorf as a thorough heretic; so I did not look at the Moravian hymnal either, which Philo had pressed upon me. But one day, lacking all other external stimulation, I chanced to pick it up, and, to my astonishment, found hymns in it which, in their own very different and strange form, seemed to point in the direction of my own feelings. There was no rigid, commonplace, school terminology in them. I became convinced that these people felt what I felt, and I took great pleasure in committing this or that verse to memory and sustaining myself for several days by this means.

Almost three months had passed since that moment when I had been granted insight into the truth. So finally I reached the decision to tell my friend Philo everything and ask him to let me have those books from his library which I was now extremely curious to see. I did this, despite the fact that there was something in my heart that strongly urged me not to.

I told Philo my whole story in every detail. Since he was one of the main characters in it, and since my account contained a homily that was a call for him to repent, he was deeply affected by it. He burst into tears; and I was happy at the thought that a complete change of heart was taking place in him too.

He provided me with all the works I asked for, and I soon had more than ample food for my imagination. I made great progress in the Zinzendorf way of thinking and speaking. Let it not be thought that I do not continue to respect Count Zinzendorf's way of doing things. One must have just regard for what he does. He is no empty enthusiast: he speaks about great truths mostly in bold, imaginative flights, and those who have disparaged him, do not recognize or appreciate his qualities.

I became extremely attached to him; and if I had been my own master I would certainly have left my home and friends, and gone to join him. We would undoubtedly have understood each other well, but we would not have found it easy to get along with each other for a length of time.

Thanks be to my presiding genius, which kept me confined at that time to my domestic sphere! It was quite a big trip for me to go into the garden. The care of my ailing old father gave me plenty to do, and I spent my leisure hours in cultivating the noblest flights of my imagination. The only person I saw was Philo, whom my father loved dearly; but his frankness toward me had been somewhat curtailed by what I had recently said to him. The effect of my words had not been deep: he tried several times to adapt himself to my terms, but without success, and so avoided all further discussion of this subject, which was not difficult for him because, with his broad range of knowledge, he could always introduce new topics into the conversation.

So I became a Herrnhut sister of my own accord, and had to conceal this change of mind and inclination from the Court Preacher whom I had good reason to respect and had as my confessor, and his many excellent qualities were not diminished in my eyes by his strong opposition to the Herrnhut community. Unfortunately, this fine man would suffer great distress on my account and that of many others!

Several years previous to this he had elsewhere become acquainted with a certain pious, honest gentlemen, with whom he still maintained an active correspondence, for this man was an earnest seeker after God. As his spiritual mentor he was therefore deeply distressed when this nobleman embraced the Herrnhut persuasion and dwelt for a long time in their community. He was equally pleased when this same man fell out with the brethren and came to live in his own vicinity, placing himself once again completely, so it appeared, under his guidance.

The newcomer was displayed in triumph to the most beloved lambs of the pastor's flock, though he was not brought to our house, because my father was no longer seeing anybody. He was well approved of: The outward polish of the courtier combined with the inner sincerity of one of the brethren, and, in addition to that, many fine natural qualities that soon made him into a major saint for all those who came to know him, much to his spiritual patron's delight. Unfortunately his quarrel with the Herrnhut community was only superficial in nature and concerned with external circumstances; in spirit he still belonged to them completely. He believed in the basic validity of the cause, but also did not reject the frills and flounces that Count Zinzendorf had added. He was by now quite accustomed to their ways of thinking and speaking, and although he endeavored to conceal this fact from his old friend, he necessarily came out with their hymns, litanies and metaphorical language when he saw he was in the company of like-minded persons, and thereby gained their approval. I myself knew nothing about all this, drifted along in my own way, and it was quite a while before he and I met each other.

One day I went to visit a woman friend who was sick, and when I got there I found several of my acquaintances deep in a conversation, which was broken off at my arrival. I pretended not to notice this, but did observe to my great astonishment several pictures of persons and events connected with Herrnhut hanging in fine frames on the wall. I quickly grasped what must have happened since I had last been in this house, and celebrated the change by reciting some appropriate verses. My friends were naturally amazed by this. We opened our hearts to each other and from that moment on were of one mind and intimate associates.

I now took opportunities to go out as often as I could, but unfortunately this was only possible once every three or four weeks. I became acquainted with the nobleman apostle and gradually with the whole clandestine community. I attended their meetings whenever I could and, because of my social sense, I took great pleasure in hearing testimony from others, and myself testifying to others about the things I had up till then worked out for myself and within myself.

I was not so completely absorbed by all this as not to notice how few of them understood the real meaning of delicate words and phrases, and even then were no more helped than they had been by the old symbolic language of church ritual. But I continued to use these words and expressions, not allowing myself to be led astray into thinking I was called upon to judge their hearts and minds, for, in my own case, many a harmless religious exercise had prepared me for higher things. I made my particular contribution by insisting, when my turn came to speak, on that meaning which is more concealed than expressed in words that deal with delicate and intimate matters; and, for the rest, tacitly agreeing that everyone should be allowed to express himself in his own way.

These quiet times of secret sociability were followed by a stormy period of open disagreements and hostilities, which produced factions at court and in the town and led to a real uproar. Our Court Preacher, that fierce opponent of the Herrnhut community, had come to the humiliating discovery that his best and most devoted parishioners were all siding with the brethren. He was deeply offended, and, having expressed himself quite intemperately in the first moment of shock, he could not later retract, even if he had wished to. There were violent debates, in which, thank goodness, my name was not mentioned, since I was only an occasional participant in what he considered their horrible meetings, and because our zealot of a leader could not dispense with the support of my father and my friend Philo in his dealings with the townspeople. I maintained my neutrality in silent satisfaction, for to engage in discussion of such feelings and topics, even with well-meaning persons, had become distasteful to me when they could not grasp the essentials and only occupied themselves with superficial matters; and to argue about these things with adversaries when one could hardly make one's own friends understand, seemed to me useless and even disadvantageous. For I soon noticed that kind and noble persons, unable to keep their minds free of aversion and hatred, soon lapsed into injustice and, while striving to preserve some external set of forms, almost destroyed what was best in their own inner convictions.

However wrong this worthy man may have been in such matters and however much people tried to incite me to take sides against him, I could not deny him my heartfelt respect. I knew him well and I could easily adapt myself to his way of seeing things. I never knew a person completely without faults, but these are more conspicuous in superior persons. We earnestly desire that those who are especially privileged should not have to pay tribute or tithes. I respected him for the excellent man that he was, and hoped that the influence of my silent neutrality might help bring about peace, or at least an armistice. I do not know what effect I might have had on him; for God dealt with the matter quickly by taking him unto Himself. Over his bier all those wept who had but recently exchanged words with him. His righteousness, his God-fearing nature, was never doubted by anyone.

I too had to put away childish things at this time, for these took on a different aspect for me during this period of troublesome conflict. My uncle had quietly continued with his plans for my sister's future. He presented her with a young man of wealth and station as her future bridegroom, and produced a dowry as rich as could be expected from him. My father gladly signified his agreement, and my sister was free and quite ready and willing to assume the married station. The wedding was arranged to take place at my uncle's castle, family and friends were invited, and we all arrived in high spirits.

This was the first time in my life that entering a house aroused my admiration. I had often heard people speak of my uncle's taste, his Italian architect, his fine collections and library; but I had measured this against what I already knew, and had a very mixed image in my mind of what it would be like. How astonished I was at the impression of gravity and harmoniousness that came to me as I entered the house, and this increased with every new room that I walked into. Splendor and magnificence had usually led me away from myself, but here I felt led back into myself. The grandeur and dignity of the arrangements for all the festive celebrations aroused in me a sense of calm and composure, and it was just as incomprehensible to me that one man could have thought all this out and arranged for it to be done, as that many different persons could have combined their efforts to achieve such a unified, grand result. And with all this, our host and his helpers seemed quite at ease, totally without stiffness or empty ceremoniousness.

The marriage ceremony began quite unexpectedly in a heart-warming way, excellent vocal music came to us as a surprise, and the priest gave to the ceremony the solemn feeling of truth. I was standing next to Philo, and instead of wishing me happiness, he said with a deep sigh: "When I saw your sister extend her hand, it was as though I had been showered with boiling water." "How so?" I asked. "I always have that feeling at weddings," he said. I laughed, but have had good occasion to remember his words since.

The joyous state of the company, which included many young people, seemed even more striking because of the distinguished quality of everything that surrounded them. The household utensils, table linen, dishes and centerpieces were as fine as everything else. I had already thought that the architects seemed to belong to the same school as those who arranged the decorations, but now it seemed as if those responsible for setting the tables had been instructed by the architect too.

Since we were to be together for several days, our thoughtful and considerate host had provided various sorts of entertainment. I did not have the unpleasant experience I have often had in a large, mixed company, when people are left to themselves and tend to turn to the most trivial of pastimes so that neither the best nor the worst of them shall feel deprived of entertainment. My uncle arranged things quite differently. He had appointed two or three masters of ceremonies, if I may call them such. One of these was in charge of amusements for the young people—dances, excursions, and various pastimes which he thought up and himself directed; and since young people like to be outdoors and are not afraid of fresh air, the garden and the conservatory were turned over to them, with all the adjoining galleries and pavilions which, although only made of clapboard and canvas, suggested in these magnificent surroundings real stone and marble. How rare it is that the person who invites his guests to a festivity feels such a real obligation to take care of their needs and comfort! Hunting expeditions, card parties, short strolls, and occasions for intimate conversations were provided for the older guests, and those accustomed to go to bed earliest were given lodgings farthest removed from all the noise.

All these excellent arrangements made the space in which we were living seem like a world of its own, and yet, if one examined it closely, the castle was not all that big, and it would have been hardly possible to accommodate so many people, and attend to all their different individual needs, without a precise knowledge of its layout and a mind such as that of our host.

Equally pleasing as the appearance of a well-built person is the experience of a well-organized household that reveals the presence of an understanding and intelligent host. Just to come into a clean house is a pleasure in itself, even though it be lacking in taste and overornate, for it does at least show the presence of one aspect of a cultured owner. But how much more satisfying it is to feel the presence of high culture, even though this be only culture of the senses. This was visible to a high degree in my uncle's home. I had heard and read a great deal about art. Philo was himself a great connoisseur of paintings and had a fine collection of his own. I myself had done a good deal of sketching; but on the one hand I was far too much occupied with my own feelings and expressing what I had to, and on the other hand everything I saw seemed to disperse my concentration. Now for the first time, external things brought me back to myself, and I learnt the difference between the natural beauty of the song of the nightingale and a four-part alleluia from human throats. I did not conceal my joy at this discovery from my uncle who, when everything else had been taken care of, spent much time conversing with me. He spoke very modestly about his possessions and achievements, but with great conviction about the principles that had governed his collections and their arrangement, and I could easily see that he was sparing my feelings by subordinating all the good that he was lord and master of to what I considered to be right and best.

"If we can imagine," he said to me one day, "that the Creator of the world should take on the form of His creature and inhabit the world for a time in this guise, then this human creation must seem perfect indeed if the Creator Himself could ally Himself so closely with it. In the concept of humanity there cannot be a contradiction with the idea of godhead, and if we often feel remoteness and difference from the godhead, then it is our urgent responsibility not to dwell on our weaknesses and faults like the devil's advocate but to seek out our finest qualities by which we can legitimately confirm our godlikeness."

At this I smiled, and replied: "Don't embarrass me so by your kind attempts to speak my language. What you have to tell me, is so important for me that I would prefer to hear it in your very own language, and then I will translate what I cannot quite accept of it, into mine."

"I will go on," he said, "in my own language without changing my tone. Man's greatest achievement is to be able to control circumstances as much as possible, and allow himself to be controlled by them as little as possible. The whole world is spread out before us like a stone quarry before a builder, and no one deserves to be called a builder unless he can transform these raw materials into something corresponding to the image in his mind, with the utmost economy, purposefulness and sureness. Everything outside us is just material, and I can well say the same about everything about us: but within us there lies the formative power which creates what is to be, and never lets us rest until we have accomplished this in one way or another in or outside ourselves. You, my dear niece, have perhaps chosen the best way; you have striven to unite your moral self, your profoundly loving nature, within itself and with the Supreme Being, and we others are not to be blamed either if we strive to know the full extent of our sensual being and actively promote its unification."

Through such conversations we became ever more closely acquainted with each other and I succeeded in making him speak to me without adapting to my way of thinking, just as he would with himself. "Don't believe I am flattering you," he said, "if I praise your manner of thinking and acting. I respect a person who knows quite clearly what he wants and steadfastly proceeds in that direction, with a true sense of direction and purpose. Whether the purpose is noble or not, and deserves praise or blame—that is only a subsequent consideration. Believe me, my dear, the greater part of misfortune, and what is considered evil in the world, comes about because people fail to recognize their true goals, or, if they do, to work steadily toward them. They are like those who have the sense that a tower should be built, but whose materials and efforts only suffice for a cottage. If you, my friend, whose highest aspiration was to come to terms with your moral nature, had adapted yourself to your family, a fiancé, or perhaps a husband, instead of making the great and bold sacrifices that you have, you would have been in continual conflict with yourself and never known a single moment of peace."

"You have used the word 'sacrifices,'" I said, "and I have often thought that we do sacrifice lesser things to higher aspirations, as if to a god, even though those lesser things are dear to our heart; as when a cherished lamb is brought to the altar lovingly and willingly for the sake of a beloved father's health."

"Whether it be reason or feeling that makes us abandon one thing for another, or choose this over that, it is my belief that steadfastness and persistence are the qualities most to be respected in any human being. One can't have the goods and the money one pays for them at the same time, and a man who craves for the goods without the heart to pay for them, is in just as bad a state as one who regrets a purchase when he has already made it. But I am far from censuring such persons: they are not really responsible, but rather the complicated conditions of their existence that make it difficult for them to control themselves. For instance, you will find fewer bad innkeepers in the country than in towns, and fewer in small towns than in large ones. Why is that? Man is born into a limited situation, he can comprehend aspirations that are simple, readily accessible and precise, and he accustoms himself to using means that are close at hand; but as soon as he branches out from his restricted sphere, he knows neither what he would like to do nor what he is obliged to do, and it is a matter of complete indifference whether he is confused by a multitude of objectives or disconcerted by their loftiness and importance. Either way he will be unhappy at having to strive after something that he cannot combine with ordinary regular activity.

"Nothing can be achieved in the world," he continued, "without serious-mindedness, and there is little of this to be found amongst those we deem cultured. They approach work and business affairs, art, and pleasures with a sort of self-defensiveness. They live their lives in the way one reads a pile of newspapers, just to be finished, and I well remember a young Englishman in Rome who once said at a party that he had polished off six churches and two galleries that day. People want to learn a lot, and know a lot, especially regarding those things which are not really important to them, and they don't notice that hunger is not stilled by snatching at air. When I get to know somebody, I always ask at once what is he occupying himself with, and how and in what order. And my interest in him will always depend on the answers he gives."

"Perhaps, uncle, you are rather too strict and deprive yourself of acquaintances that you could be useful to and really help."

"Is one to be blamed for losing interest in them, seeing that one has labored for so long with them and for them, and all in vain? How one suffers in one's youth from those who think they are inviting us to a pleasant excursion by promising us the company of Sisyphus or the Danaids! Thank goodness I have been able to keep free of such persons, and if one of them should chance to stray into my purview, I usher him out as politely as possible. For from such people one hears the bitterest complaints about the confusion of worldly events, the shallowness of learning, the frivolity of artists, the hollowness of poets, and the like. They never understand that neither they nor all those like them would ever read a book written according to their demands, that they are ignorant of what real poetry is, and that even a fine work of art will only earn their approval if it has already been accredited with excellence by someone else. But let's stop talking about all this. Now is not the time to complain or censure."

He directed my attention to the various paintings hanging on the wall. My eyes fixed on those which looked pleasant or had a notable subject. He let this happen for a while, and then said: "Now pay some attention to the spirit that produced these works. Noble souls like to see God's hand in His creation; but why shouldn't we give some consideration to the hands of His imitators?" He then drew my attention to some pictures that had not struck me particularly, and tried to make me understand that only study of the history of art can give us a proper sense of the value and distinction of a work of art. One must first appreciate the burdensome aspects of technical labor that gifted artists have perfected over the centuries, in order for one to comprehend how it is possible for a creative genius to move freely and joyfully on a plane so high that it makes us dizzy.

With this in mind he brought together a number of pictures, and when he explained them to me, I could not avoid seeing in them images and symbols of moral perfection. When I told him this, he said: "You are absolutely right, and one should not pursue the cultivation of one's moral life in isolation and seclusion. We are more likely to find that a person intent on moral advancement will have every cause to cultivate his senses as well as his mind, so as not to run the risk of losing his foothold on those moral heights, slipping into the seductive allurements of uncontrolled fancy and debasing his nobler nature by indulging in idle frivolities, if not worse."

I never suspected that this was aimed at me, but I did feel affected when I thought back to certain rather insipid things in those hymns which had contributed to my edification. I also realized that the images which had attached themselves to my spiritual concepts would hardly have found favor in my uncle's eyes.

Philo had been spending a good deal of time in the library and now he took me there. Together we admired the selection and number of books it contained. They had been assembled, in every sense of the word; for they consisted almost entirely of works that would help us toward true enlightenment and the achievement of proper perspective, either by providing us with the right materials or by giving us a sense of the unity of our mental powers.

I had read a great deal in the course of my life, and in some areas there was hardly a book that was not known to me. It was therefore particularly pleasant for me now to think in terms of a whole and observe where I had gaps, whereas previously I had always thought in terms of the confusion caused by limitation and the vast extent of what there was to learn.

We made the acquaintance of an unassuming, but very interesting man. He was a physician and a naturalist, and seemed to belong more to the presiding deities of the house than to its actual, present inhabitants. He showed us the collection of specimens which, like the books in the library, were arranged in glass cases along the walls of the rooms, enlarging rather than narrowing the space between them. This reminded me of the joys of my youth, and I showed my father several things that he had brought to the sickbed of his child before she had any real sense of the world around her. This doctor did not conceal the fact, either then or in our later discussions, that it was his interest in religious sentiments that made him seek me out. But he never failed to praise my uncle's tolerance and respect for everything that demonstrated and advanced the unity and worth of human nature, demanding this from everybody else, and consistently opposing and condemning every kind of mere self-satisfaction and exclusive narrowness.

My uncle was extremely happy at my sister's marriage, and he spoke to me several times about what he intended to do for her and her children. He had splendid estates, which he managed himself and hoped to bequeath to his nephews in excellent condition. He seemed to have special thoughts regarding the small estate where we were at the moment: "This I will only give to the person who knows, appreciates and can enjoy what it contains, who understands the responsibility of those who are rich and belong to the nobility, especially in Germany, to establish something that shall serve as a model."

Very soon the majority of the guests had departed, and we ourselves were getting ready to leave. To conclude the celebrations, my uncle most considerately provided us once again with an entertainment of the highest quality. We had openly expressed our delight at the unaccompanied choral music at my sister's wedding, and we had urged him to let us hear this again. But he had not seemed to take any notice. We were therefore extremely surprised when he said one evening: "The dance music has gone, our young, flighty friends have deserted us, even the married couple looks more serious than it did a few days ago. And so, since the time to leave has come, and we may never see each other again, or at least as we are now, this calls for a festive atmosphere that I cannot better induce than by having that music repeated which you asked for earlier."

He then had four- and eight-part motets performed by the same choir, now increased in size and profiting from further practice, and this, I may well say, gave us all a foretaste of heaven. So far I had only been acquainted with hymn-singing, in which pious souls, often with hoarse throats, believe they are birds of the forest singing praises to God, because of the pleasant feeling it gives them, or with the vanity of concert music that provokes admiration for the talents of the performer, but rarely provides even passing pleasure. But now I heard music issuing from the richest depths of noble, human hearts, through practiced organs and in perfect harmony, speaking to the very best in us and making us fully aware of our godlikeness. The motets were sacred, with texts in Latin; they were like jewels in the golden ring of this cultured, secular society. By them I was spiritually uplifted and made happy, without laying any claim to so-called spiritual enlightenment.

On our departure we were all given handsome presents. I received the cross of my order, more artistically and delicately wrought and more richly enamelled than is usual. It was suspended from a large diamond, by which it was fastened to the ribbon, and this stone he considered one of the finest from his collection of gems.

My sister left with her husband for his estates, and we all went back to our homes, returning, as regards external circumstances, to what seemed a very ordinary life. We had returned to earth from a fairy palace and had to accommodate ourselves to this, each of us adjusting in his own way.

The unusual experiences that I had undergone in the new environment of my uncle's house left me with pleasing impressions, but these did not continue to be so vivid in my mind, although he did all he could to sustain and revive them by sending me from time to time some of his finest and most agreeable works of art, and then exchanging these for others when I had had sufficient time to enjoy them.

I was too accustomed to occupying myself with the affairs of my own heart and soul and talking about these with like-minded persons to pay much attention to a work of art without soon withdrawing again into myself. It was my custom to view a painting or an engraving as letters in a book. Good printing gives pleasure: but who reads a book for the quality of the printing? A pictorial presentation had to say something to me—teach me, move me, improve me; and no matter how much my uncle had to say about works of art in his letters, I continued to react as I always had.

Not only my own nature but also external events, changes in my family, distracted me from such consideration, even sometimes from my own self, for I had to tolerate and perform duties which exceeded my feeble physical powers.

My unmarried sister had always been my right hand. She was healthy, strong and infinitely kind, and it was she who had taken over the responsibility of running the household while I was occupied with the care of our aged father. But she was struck with a catarrh that turned into pneumonia; and in three weeks she was dead. Her death afflicted me so deeply that even today I hardly dare to think about it.

I was sick in bed myself before she was laid in her grave. The old trouble in my chest seemed to be flaring up again, I was racked by coughing and so hoarse that I could hardly speak.

My married sister had a miscarriage because of fear and anxiety. My poor old father was afraid of losing at one and the same time his children and all hopes of grandchildren. His justified tears increased my sorrow, and I prayed to God for the restoration of some degree of health in myself, asking merely that my life should be prolonged until after my father's death. I recovered, and was as well as I could ever be, assuming once more my obligations and fulfilling them as best I could.

My sister became pregnant again. Various concerns, which in such cases are usually borne by mothers, were loaded on me. She was not entirely happy in her marital life, but this was not something my father should be made aware of. I myself had to be the judge of such matters. Things were made easier by the confidence which my brother-in-law always placed in me. Both he and my sister were good people, but instead of being considerate of each other, they were always arguing; and in their desire to live in complete harmony with each other they never achieved unity in anything. I was now learning to deal seriously with worldly matters, and practice what I had been singing hymns about.

My sister gave birth to a son, and my father's indisposition did not prevent him from traveling to see her. When he saw the child, he was overcome with joy and satisfaction, and at the christening he seemed to me inspired, quite different from his usual self, almost like a spirit with two faces, one of which looked forward joyfully to the region he would soon be entering, while the other contemplated, full of hope, this new earthly life awakened in the boy who was descended from him. All the way home he never ceased talking to me about the child and its healthy appearance, and he expressed his eagerness that the qualities of this new citizen of the world should be well nurtured and developed. He continued to speculate on this after we arrived home, and it was not until a few days later that we noticed he had a kind of fever, which came on after meals in the form of an enervating temperature, though without any chills. But he would not lie down, and every morning he would leave the house to attend punctiliously to his business affairs, until finally some more lasting and more serious symptoms prevented him from this. I will never forget the orderliness and tranquility with which he attended to the affairs of the household and the arrangements for his own burial, as if it were the affair of someone else.

With a composure of mind unusual in him, which almost approached joy, he said to me one day: "Where has that fear of death gone which I used to feel so strongly? Why should I fear to die? God is merciful, the grave holds no terrors for me, I shall have eternal life." One of the most pleasant occupations in my solitary life is to recall the circumstances of his dying, and nobody will argue me out of the sense I had then of the workings of some higher force.

My father's death changed my whole mode of living. From a life of strictest obedience and extreme restrictions I passed into one of greatest freedom, which I enjoyed like food I had long had to do without. Whereas I had usually not been able to spend more than a couple of hours each day away from the house, there was now hardly a day that I remained in my own room. The friends with whom I had only been able to snatch fleeting visits, now wanted to see me all the time, and I them. I was often invited to meals, walks and excursions, and never declined. But once I had run the gamut I came to see that the greatest value of freedom is not to do everything one wants to when this is favored by circumstances but rather to be able to achieve what is good and right by the most direct way, without let or hindrance. And I was old enough by now to arrive at this conviction myself without instruction from others.

What I could not deny myself, however, was to continue to strengthen as quickly as possible my contacts with the members of the Herrnhut community, and I eagerly participated in one of their very next functions. But here too I did not find what I had hoped for. I was honest enough to tell them this, and they tried to persuade me that their little group was nothing compared to a regularly organized community. I was prepared to accept that; but my belief was that the true spirit should be able to emerge from a small group just as well as from a large assembly.

One of their bishops, a pupil of Count Zinzendorf himself, devoted much attention to me. He spoke perfect English, and because I knew some too, he decided this was an indication that we belonged together. But I didn't think so at all, for his whole manner was very distasteful to me. He was a knife grinder from Moravia, and his whole way of thinking was that of an artisan. I got on much better with a certain Mr. von L . . . , who had been a major in the French army; though I could not display the same subservience as he showed towards his superiors— indeed it felt as though someone had slapped me when I saw his wife and other respected ladies kissing the bishop's hand. Meanwhile a journey to Holland was agreed upon, which, however, never came about—and that certainly turned out to my advantage.

My sister gave birth to a daughter, and now it was the turn of us women to be pleased, and think about how the little girl could be brought up as we had been. My brother-in-law, on the other hand, was very disappointed when, in the following year, another daughter arrived, for, with his vast estates, he wanted to have boys around to help him manage them.

Because of my feeble health I kept myself to myself, and achieved a certain equilibrium in my life of calm repose. I had no fear of death, I even wished to die, but at quiet moments I felt that God was granting me time to examine my soul and bring myself ever closer to Him. In my many sleepless nights I had a feeling which I find hard to describe. It was as if my soul were thinking without my body, looking on the body as something apart from itself, like some garment or other. My soul vividly recalled past times and events and sensed what was to come. These times were all gone by, and what was to come would also pass; the body will be rent like a garment, but I, the well-known I, I am.

I was persuaded by a noble friend who became ever more closely acquainted with me, not to yield too much to the consolation afforded by this lofty thought. This was the physician whom I had met at my uncle's house. He had informed himself about the state of my mind and body, and he explained to me that such feelings, if nurtured without reference to external things, will drain us dry and undermine our existence. "Man's first task," he said, "is to be active, and one should use those intervals when one is obliged to rest, to acquire a clear knowledge of external things, for that will assist us in all our further activity."

Since he was aware of my tendency to consider my body as a thing apart, and because he knew that my constitution, its failings and the medical means of treating these were fairly well known to me, so much so that I had almost become a doctor myself in attending to my own ills and those of others, he directed my attention away from the human body and various salves to the other objects of creation around me, so that I wandered around as if in paradise and, if I may continue the metaphor, only after this was I allowed to sense from afar the presence of the creator walking of an evening in the cool of the garden. With gladness I now perceived God in Nature as clearly as I felt Him in my heart; and I gave thanks that He should have deigned to give me life by the breath of His mouth.

My sister and all the rest of us were hoping for the birth of another boy, which my brother-in-law dearly desired. But, sad to say, he did not live to see it happen. This fine man died from the results of an unfortunate fall from his horse, and my sister, after having given birth to a lovely boy, followed him soon afterwards. It pained me to look at the four children she left behind. So many healthy people had died before me, sick as I was; and was I not destined to see some of these promising fruits wither and die? I was sufficiently acquainted with the world to know how many dangers there are for a child—especially one belonging to the upper classes of society—when it is growing up, and it seemed to me that these perils had increased since the time of my youth. I felt that, with my infirmity, I was not in a position to do much for these children, if indeed anything. I was therefore very glad when our uncle decided to devote his whole attention to the upbringing of these dear little creatures. This, of course, was quite natural for someone of his frame of mind, and the children deserved it in every way, for they were comely and, despite their differences from each other, they all gave promise of becoming kind and intelligent human beings.

Once my physician friend had made me aware of family resemblances in children and relatives, I began to take special pleasure in following this up. My father had carefully preserved the portraits of his ancestors, and had himself and his children painted by reasonably good artists, along with my mother and her relatives. We knew therefore the characteristics of the whole family, and, having pondered and compared these, we looked for similar traits of mind and body in the children. My sister's eldest son seemed to resemble his paternal grandfather, of whom there was a good portrait as a young man in my uncle's collection. This grandfather had liked to present himself as a fine officer, and the boy preferred nothing more than handling a gun when he came to see me. My father had bequeathed us a fine assortment of guns, and the little boy would not rest until I had given him a brace of pistols and a hunting piece, and he had figured out for himself how to manipulate a flintlock. He was not at all clumsy or hasty in his movements, but rather gentle and thoughtful.

The eldest daughter claimed the greater part of my affection, probably because she looked like me and, of all the four, it was she who clung to me most. But I must say that the more I observed her growing up, the more she put me to shame. I could not fail to be amazed at her; I might almost say that I developed respect for her. One could not imagine a more noble presence, a more peaceful disposition, a greater evenness of attention to every kind of goal or object. Never for a moment was she idle, and everything she turned her hands to became a worthy object. Nothing troubled her so long as she could do what was demanded of her by circumstances, and she could be quite content when she did not find anything that needed doing at the moment. This ability to remain active without feeling the need for some particular occupation, was something that I never again encountered. Her behavior toward the needy and suffering was always exemplary. I must confess that I myself had never had the ability to make an occupation out of works of charity. I was not parsimonious in my gifts to the poor, and often gave more than I should have in my circumstances, but in a way I was buying myself off, and if someone were to receive my full care and attention, this would have to be someone of my own flesh and blood. But with my niece it was just the opposite, and I admired her for this. I never saw her giving money to a pauper;

what she received from me for this purpose, she would use to fulfill practical needs. She was never more attractive in my eyes than when she rummaged around in my clothes and linens, always finding something I was no longer wearing or using, then cutting it up and making a garment for some ragged urchin. This was her greatest delight.

Her sister soon revealed quite a different disposition. She had inherited many of her mother's qualities, showed promise quite early on of becoming very charming and attractive, and she seems to be fulfilling that expectation still, being very much concerned about her appearance and knowing how to dress and carry herself in a striking way. I can still remember the delight she showed as a little girl at looking at herself in a mirror when I put around her neck the lovely pearls my mother had bequeathed me, which she happened to find in my room.

As I observed these various characteristics in the children, I took pleasure in the thought that, after my death, my possessions would be divided amongst them and preserved by them. I could envision my father's guns passing through the fields on my nephew's back, and game hanging out of his hunting bag. I could see all my garments on the backs of little girls as they left church after their Easter confirmation, and my finest clothes on some modest burgher girl on her wedding day. For my niece Natalie took especial delight in decking out children and poor honest girls, though she herself showed no sign of love for, or need for attachment to, any visible or invisible being such as I had felt so strongly in my youth. When I thought that the youngest of the girls would be wearing my jewels and pearls at court, I was quite content to see my possessions, like my body, returned to the elements.

The children grew apace and to my delight they have become healthy, handsome human beings. I have borne with patience the fact that my uncle has kept them apart from me, and I do not see them very often when they are nearby or in town. A wonderful man, whom people take for a French abbé (though no one knows really where he comes from), has been entrusted with the supervision of all four children, who are being educated and provided for in different places. At first I could not perceive any plan or purpose in this education. But then the doctor informed me that the Abbé had convinced my uncle that, in order to promote a child's education, one must first find out where its desires and inclinations lie, and then enable it to satisfy those desires and further those inclinations as quickly as possible. If someone has chosen a wrong path, he can correct this before it is too late, and once he has found what suits him, stick to this firmly and develop more vigorously. I hope this strange experiment will succeed. Perhaps it may, with such good material.

But one thing I cannot condone about these educators, that they deprive children of anything that might lead to their communing with themselves and with their Invisible, and only true Friend. And I am often irritated with my uncle that for this reason he thinks I would be detrimental to the children. Nobody is really tolerant in practice, for however much someone may assure us that he is leaving a person to his own desires and inclinations, in effect he does all he can to exclude them from activities not acceptable to himself.

The manner in which these children are being kept away from me, is all the more distressing as my conviction increases of the reality of my faith. Why shouldn't this have a supernatural origin and a real, natural goal, seeing that it proves to be so effective in practice? Only through our practical activity do we become fully aware of our own individual existence; and why shouldn't we by this means demonstrate also to ourselves that there is a Being who gives us this power to do good?

Since I am always moving forward and never backward, since my actions are always drawing nearer and nearer to the idea of perfection which I have worked out for myself, and I find it easier every day to do what I think is right, despite my bodily infirmity that restricts me so much—is this accountable solely to human nature, whose corruption I have become so profoundly aware of? Not for me, at least.

I cannot recall having followed any commandment that loomed before me as a law imposed from without: I was always led and guided by impulse, freely following my own persuasion, and experiencing neither restriction nor regrets. Thanks be to God that I am fully aware to whom I owe my happiness, and can accept my good fortune in humility. For I will never be tempted to pride myself on my own ability and powers, having so clearly recognized the monster that grows and feeds in every human breast, if some higher power does not preserve us.

BOOK SEVEN

Chapter One

The spring had arrived in all its glory. An early thunderstorm, which had been threatening to break all day, rolled down the mountains, the rain moved into the valley, the sun burst forth again in splendor and a marvelous rainbow appeared against the dark grey background. Wilhelm rode up toward it and gazed at it with a feeling of sadness. "Why is it," he said, "that the brightest colors in life always appear against a dark background? Must raindrops, or tears, fall if we are to experience true joy? A bright day is no different from a gray one if we observe it unmoved. And what is it that moves us but the silent hope that the native desires of our hearts may not remain without objects to focus on? We are moved by the account of good deeds, the contemplation of harmonious objects, and as a result we feel that we are not completely adrift in this world, but are drawing nearer to some sort of destination toward which all that is deepest and best in us has long been impatiently tending."

Meanwhile a traveler had caught up with him, walking briskly up to his horse; and, after a few innocuous remarks, said to Wilhelm: "If I am not mistaken, I have met you somewhere before."

"I think so too," said Wilhelm. "Didn't we take part in an amusing river trip together?"

"That's right!" said the other.

Wilhelm looked at him more closely, and, after a few moments of silence, said: "I don't know how it is that you have changed. At the time I thought you were a Lutheran pastor, but now you look more like a Catholic priest."

"This time, at any rate, you are not mistaken," said the man, taking off his hat and revealing the tonsure. "But where has your theatrical company gone to? Did you stay with them for a long while?"

"Longer than I should have. Unfortunately, when I think back on the time I spent with them, I seem to be peering into an unending void. Nothing about it means anything to me anymore."

"You're wrong about that. Everything that happens to us leaves its traces, everything contributes imperceptibly to our development. But it is dangerous to try to draw up a balance sheet, for in doing so we become either proud and carefree, or depressed and discouraged, and the one is as bad as the other in its results. The safest thing remains to concentrate on what lies immediately ahead; and that, for the moment," he added with a smile, "is to make sure we find quarters for the night."

Wilhelm asked him how far it was to Lothario's estate, and he said it was just over the hill. "Then perhaps I'll see you there," he said. "I still have a few errands to do in the neighborhood. So goodbye for now!" With these words he hastened up a steep path, which seemed the shortest way over the hill.

"He's certainly right," said Wilhelm as he rode along. "One should think of the first thing one has to do, and for me nothing is more pressing than to deliver the sad message I am charged with. Let's just see if I can still remember my speech to put this cruel man to shame!"

He began to recite to himself his work of art. He could recall every word of it, and the more his memory was activated, the more his boldness and passion increased. Aurelie's sufferings and death were still very much in his mind.

"Spirit of my beloved friend!" he cried. "Draw nigh and give me a sign, if you can, that you are pacified and reconciled!"

With such words and thoughts he reached the top of the hill and observed on the other side a strange looking building which he immediately decided must be Lothario's residence. Originally it had been an irregular building with turrets and gables; but even more irregular were the later additions, some close by and others at a distance, connected with the main building by galleries and covered walks. All external symmetry and architectural distinction seemed to have been sacrificed to considerations of domestic comfort. There was no sign of ramparts or moats, nor of formal gardens or broad allées. An orchard and kitchen garden ran right up to the buildings, and there were other small domestic gardens set in between. A cheerful looking village was to be seen nearby; all gardens and fields seemed to be in very good condition.

Wilhelm rode on, immersed in his own impassioned reflections and hence not thinking much about what he saw around him, stabled his horse at an inn, and proceeded without further ado to the castle.

An old retainer received him at the door and informed him very politely that he would hardly be able to see the master of the household that day, because he had lots of letters to write and had already sent away several tradesmen. Wilhelm pressed him further and finally the old man gave in, and reported Wilhelm's arrival to his master. He came back and conducted Wilhelm into a large, ancient hall, asking him to be patient for a while because it might be some time before his master would be able to see him. Wilhelm walked restlessly up and down, casting a few glances at the lords and ladies whose pictures were hanging on the walls. He repeated to himself the beginning of his speech, and it seemed to him more appropriate than ever in the presence of all these people in armor and high-standing collars. Whenever he heard a noise he took up position so as to be ready to receive his adversary with suitable dignity, hand him the letter and then assail him with a whole battery of reproaches.

After several false alarms he was beginning to get cross and dispirited, when in through a side door came a good-looking man in topboots and an unostentatious surtout. "What good news do you bring me?" he said in a kindly tone of voice to Wilhelm. "I'm sorry to have kept you waiting so long."

As he said this he was folding a letter that he held in his hand. Wilhelm, somewhat nonplussed, handed him Aurelie's communication, saying: "I bring you the last words of a lady friend of yours which will not leave you unmoved."

Lothario took the letter and went back to his room where, as Wilhelm could see through the open door, he first addressed and sealed a few more letters, then opened Aurelie's and read it. He apparently read it through several times, and Wilhelm, though he felt that the pathos of his speech hardly suited the unpretentiousness of his reception, nevertheless got ready to deliver his oration and was walking up to the dividing door when in from a door in the wall came the priest.

"I have just received the strangest message," said Lothario to the Abbé, and then, turning to Wilhelm, he said: "Excuse me if I am at the moment not in the mood to talk further with you. Do stay the night here with us! And would you please, Abbé, look after our guest and see that he has all he needs." With this he bowed to Wilhelm, and the priest took Wilhelm by the hand, who readily followed him.

Silently they walked along strange looking passageways and finally arrived in a very pleasant room. The priest ushered him in, and left without further explanation. Soon after this a bright young boy appeared, announced that he was to wait on Wilhelm, and brought him his supper; and while he was serving this he told him a good deal about the arrangements of the household, how one took breakfast and the other meals, the division between work and recreation, and much else that redounded to the praise of Lothario.

Pleasant as the boy was, Wilhelm was anxious to get rid of him. He wanted to be alone, for he felt stifled and oppressed by his present situation; he reproached himself for having carried out his intentions so inefficiently and only delivering half his message. One moment he was determined to communicate the rest on the very next day, but then he realized that Lothario had aroused quite unexpected feelings in him. The house in which he found himself was so very strange, that he could not adapt himself to these conditions. He decided to undress, opened his rucksack and, taking out his nightclothes, found the Ghost's veil, which Mignon had packed along with the other things. The sight of this aggravated the melancholy of the mood he was in. "Flee, young man, flee!" He repeated the words to himself, then thought: "What are these mysterious words supposed to mean? What should I flee? Where to? It would have been better if the Ghost had said: 'Return to yourself!'" He looked at the engravings on the wall, finding them mostly not worthy of his attention; but one of them depicted a shipwreck with a father and two beautiful daughters awaiting death from the encroaching waves. One of the daughters bore a certain resemblance to the Amazon. Wilhelm was overwhelmed by a sense of pity, he felt an irrepressible need to open up his heart, tears burst from his eyes, and he could not contain himself until sleep overcame him.

Strange dream visions overcame him toward morning. He found himself in a garden where he had often been as a child, and joyfully recognized the familiar hedgerows, walks, and flowerbeds. Mariane came up to him, he spoke tenderly to her, without any reference to the past disturbance of their relationship. Then his father appeared, in his housecoat, and, with more than customary friendliness, asked his son to bring up two garden chairs, took Mariane's hand and led her to an arbor. Wilhelm went to the conservatory to fetch the chairs, but found it empty. He did, however, see Aurelie standing at a nearby window. He went up to speak to her, but her back was turned, and although he went and stood next to her, he could not see her face. He looked out of the window, and, in another garden, he saw a group of people, some of whom he immediately recognized: Madame Melina was sitting beneath a tree, toying with a rose that she held in her hand, Laertes stood beside her counting out money from one hand into the other. Mignon and Felix were lying in the grass, she stretched out on her back, he lying face downward. Philine came up and clapped her hands above the children's heads. Mignon did not move, but Felix jumped up and ran away from Philine. At first he was laughing as he ran and Philine chased him, but suddenly he cried out in fear as the Harper pursued him with long, slow strides. He ran straight up to a pond, Wilhelm rushed after him, but too late to reach him before he had fallen into the water. Wilhelm stood rooted to the spot. Then he saw the beauteous Amazon on the other side of the pond. She stretched out her right hand toward the child and went to the bank. The child moved through the water in the direction of her extended finger, and followed her as she went, until she reached and pulled him out of the pond. Meanwhile, Wilhelm had drawn nearer, the child was burning all over, and drops of fire were falling off him. Wilhelm became more and more alarmed, but the Amazon quickly took a white veil from off her head and covered the child. The fire was soon quenched, and when she lifted up the veil, two boys jumped up and played mischievously with each other while Wilhelm and the Amazon walked hand in hand through the garden. He could see his father strolling with Mariane way off, in an allée with tall trees which seemed to encircle the whole garden. He directed his path in their direction, was walking right across the garden with his lovely companion, when suddenly the blond Friedrich stood in their path and blocked their progress, with raucous laughter and all sorts of foolery. Despite this, they insisted on continuing on their path, so he hurried away toward the other, more distant couple. But his father and Mariane seemed to be running away from him, he ran faster and faster after them, and they seemed to Wilhelm to be soaring through the trees in flight. Impulse and desire impelled him to go to their assistance, but the Amazon's hand held him back—and how gladly he let himself be held! And so, with this mixed feeling, he woke up and found his room brightly lit by the morning sun.

Chapter Two

The boy summoned Wilhelm to breakfast. The Abbé was already there, and said he had heard that Lothario had gone out for a ride. The Abbé himself was pensive and not very talkative, but he did ask after the circumstances of Aurelie's death, and listened with interest and compassion to Wilhelm's account. "Alas!" he said, "for someone who is deeply concerned about how infinitely complicated the operations of nature and art must be to produce a cultured human being, and himself has done all he can to educate his fellow-men, it is enough to make one despair, when one sees how wantonly a person can destroy herself, or be destroyed with or without being responsible. When I reflect on that, then life seems to me such a casual gift that I would approve of anyone who does not value it too highly."

He had just finished speaking, when the door burst open and a young woman came rushing in, pushing aside the old manservant who had tried to stop her. She tore up to the Abbé and, grasping him by the arm, was hardly able to speak for weeping and sobbing, but did manage to blurt out: "Where is he?

Where have you put him? This is outrageous treachery! Admit it! I know what you're up to! But I'm determined to get him, and I want to know where he is."

"Calm yourself, my child," said the Abbé, with affected composure. "Go to your room. You shall be told everything in due course. But you must be in a position to listen when I do tell you." He offered her his hand, intending to escort her out of the room. "I won't go to my room," she cried. "I hate these walls within which you have kept me a prisoner so long. But I've found out everything. The colonel has challenged him to a duel and he has ridden out to meet him, and perhaps at this very moment . . . Several times I thought I could hear the sound of shooting. Harness the horses, and ride out with me, or I'll fill the whole house and the whole village with my cries." Weeping bitterly, she rushed up to the window. The Abbé restrained her and tried to calm her.

A carriage was heard arriving. She opened the window and cried: "He's dead! They're bringing him back." "He's getting out of the carriage," said the Abbé. "He's alive, you see." "He's wounded," she replied anxiously, "otherwise he would have come on horseback. They're bringing him in. He is gravely wounded!" She ran out of the door and down the steps, the Abbé rushing after her and Wilhelm following behind. He saw the lovely girl greet the arrival of her lover.

Lothario, leaning on a companion whom Wilhelm recognized as his old acquaintance Jarno, spoke kindly and lovingly to the disconsolate girl; then, supporting himself on her, he walked slowly up the steps, greeted Wilhelm, and was then led to his room.

Soon after this Jarno came out and walked up to Wilhelm. "It seems," he said, "that you are predestined to encounter actors and theater everywhere you go. We are in the midst of a drama that is not precisely amusing."

"I am glad," replied Wilhelm, "to see you again in these peculiar circumstances. I am puzzled and frightened, and your presence will bring me calm and composure. Tell me, is there any danger? Is the baron seriously wounded?" "I don't think so," Jarno replied.

After a short while a young surgeon came out of the room. "Well, what do you think?" Jarno asked him. "It is very serious," he said, replacing his instruments in a leather case. Wilhelm noticed a ribbon hanging out of the case, which seemed familiar to him. Bright contrasting colors, a strange pattern of gold and silver in curious shapes, this distinguished the ribbon from all others he had ever seen. Wilhelm was convinced that these instruments were those of the old surgeon who had tended his wounds in the forest, and the hope of finally discovering some trace of the Amazon brought new life to his whole being.

"Where did you get that case?" he cried. "Who owned it before you? Please tell me." "I bought it at an auction," the man said. "What does it matter to whom it belonged?" He moved away as he spoke, and Jarno said: "If only that young fellow would speak the truth!" "Then he didn't buy the case at an auction?" said Wilhelm. "Right!" said Jarno. "That's as far from the truth as Lothario's being in danger."

Wilhelm was still immersed in a host of thoughts, when Jarno asked him how things had been going with him. He told him in general terms, and when he got to Aurelie's death and the message he was bearing, Jarno exclaimed: "But that is very strange!"

The Abbé emerged from the room, signalled to Jarno to take his place, and then said to Wilhelm: "The baron requests that you stay here for a few days more to enrich the company and enliven him in his present circumstances. If you need to send any message to your relatives, your letter will be immediately dispatched, and so that you may understand the strange occurrence which you have been witness to, I have to tell you something that is not really a secret. The baron has had a little adventure with a lady, which has attracted more attention than it should have, because she was too eager to relish the triumph of having snatched him from a rival. Unfortunately, after some time he did not find her as amusing as he had, and he avoided her, but she with her passionate temperament was not able to reconcile herself to what had happened. There was a violent and public disagreement at a ball, she considered herself gravely insulted and wanted revenge, but no knight was there to defend her, until her husband, from whom she had long been separated, heard about the affair, took her part, challenged the baron to a duel, and has wounded him today. But the colonel, as I have heard, fared even worse."

From this time on our hero was treated like a member of the family.

Chapter Three

The invalid was read to several times, and Wilhelm was happy to do him this small service. The young woman, whose name was Lydie, would not leave his bedside, her care of the wounded man engaging all her attention. Lothario seemed distracted too and asked not to be read to any longer.

"Today," he said, "I feel so strongly how stupidly people let time pass. There are so many things I have been intending to do, so many plans I have thought about, and yet one procrastinates, even regarding one's very best intentions! I have read the proposals for the changes I wish to introduce on my estates, and I can truly say that I am glad that the bullet did not take a more dangerous route."

Lydie looked at him affectionately, even with tears in her eyes, as if she wanted to know whether she and his friends could not assist in increasing his pleasure in living. But Jarno answered: "Changes such as you have in mind are best first considered from every angle before one makes a decision."

"Lengthy consideration usually indicates that one has not clearly visualized the point at issue, and hasty actions that one does not even know what it is," said Lothario. "It is quite apparent to me that, in many matters concerning the management of my estates, I cannot do without the services of my farmhands, and also that I must rigidly insist on certain rights; but it is also clear to me that certain dispositions, though advantageous to me, are not absolutely essential, and some of them could be changed for the benefit of my workers. One doesn't always lose by giving up something. Am I making better use of my estates than my father? Will I be able to increase my revenues? And should I alone derive all the extra profit from this? Should I not grant advantages to those who work with me and for me, from the greater knowledge that our progressive era has provided us with?"

"That's how we human beings are!" said Jarno, "and I do not reproach myself for observing the same characteristic in myself. We want to acquire all we can, in order to be able to dispose of it as we wish, and money that we do not expend ourselves, always seems ill spent."

"Yes, indeed," replied Lothario. "We could do without much of our capital, if we did not so arbitrarily dispose of the interest."

"There is one thing I have to remind you of," said Jarno, "and that is why I would advise you not to proceed with the alterations right now. These would result in temporary losses. You still have debts, and repaying these will restrict you. I would therefore advise you to postpone your plans until you are completely in the clear."

"And meanwhile leave it to a bullet or a rooftile to destroy the results of my life and activity for ever? My dear fellow, that is one of the major mistakes of all educated persons: they refer everything to an idea, very rarely to a specific object. Why did I run up debts? Why did I break with my uncle and leave my siblings to look after themselves, except to follow an idea? In America I thought I could achieve something, I felt I was needed overseas, and could be useful there—if action was not accompanied by danger, it seemed to me unimportant, not worth doing. But now I see things differently: What is nearest at hand, seems to me now most important and most desirable."

"I well remember the letter you sent me from overseas," said Jarno. "You wrote: 'I will return, and in my own house, my own orchard, in the midst of my own people, I will say: *Here, or nowhere, is America!*'"

"Yes, my friend, and I still say the same," Lothario responded. "But at the same time I reproach myself for not being as active here as I was over there. To achieve some sort of steady existence, all we need is reasonableness, and we become the embodiment of reasonableness and nothing else, when we do not perceive the abnormal demands that every normal day exacts from us, or even if we do, we make a thousand excuses not to meet these demands. Reasonableness is fine for one's self, but not of much value for the community."

"Let's not discredit reasonableness too much, for we should recognize that when something extraordinary occurs, it is usually foolish."

"Yes, but that is because men do extraordinary things without respecting orderliness. Take, for instance, my brother-in-law, who has given all the money he could realize to the Herrnhut brethren, in the belief of thereby furthering his salvation. By disposing of just a small part of his income, he could have made many people happy and secured for himself and them a heaven on earth. Our sacrifices rarely represent a personal impulse, for by renouncing what is ours and giving it to others, we are acting out of despair, not from conscious determination: all we are doing is relieving ourselves of the weight of our possessions. I must confess that, during these last few days, I have constantly had the count in my mind, and I have firmly decided to do out of conviction what he is doing from fear and delusion. I shall not wait until I am well again. The papers are here, all we need is fair copies. Let the magistrate help you. Our guest will help you too. You know as well as I do what the issue is; and I will lie here, recovering or dying, and proclaim: *Here, or nowhere, is Herrnhut!*"

When Lydie heard her friend mention dying, she flung herself down beside his bed, hung over him, and wept bitterly. The surgeon came back; Jarno gave Wilhelm the papers, and persuaded Lydie to leave.

"For Heaven's sake," said Wilhelm when he and Jarno were alone in the hall, "what is all this about the count? What count is it who is joining Herrnhut?"

"The one you know full well," Jarno replied. "You yourself are the ghost that drove him into the arms of religion. You are the villain who reduced his nice wife to a state where she finds it tolerable to follow her husband."

"Is she then Lothario's sister?" Wilhelm asked.

"Yes, she is."

"And does Lothario know . . . ?"

"Everything."

"Let me get out of here!" Wilhelm cried; "how can I possibly face him? What can he possibly say?"

"That no one should cast stones and no one should compose long speeches to put others to shame, unless he delivers them before a mirror."

"You know that too?"

"And a good deal more," said Jarno with a smile. "But this time I won't let go of you so easily, and you need have no more fear of my trying to make you enlist. I'm not a soldier anymore, and even when I was, I should not have aroused such suspicions in you. Since I last saw you, a lot has changed. After the death of my friend and benefactor, the prince, I withdrew from society and all worldly relationships. I took pleasure in furthering what was reasonable, and did not keep silent when I thought something was absurd. As a result I gained the reputation of having a restless mind and a malicious tongue. There is nothing more feared by the general mass of human beings than shrewdness; they should fear stupidity, if only they knew how fearful that is. But shrewdness is uncomfortable and to be avoided, whereas stupidity is simply destructive, and one can wait out its results. But let that pass. I have what it takes, and I'll tell you more about what I am planning. You shall participate in this, if you wish. But tell me, how have things been with you? I can see; indeed I can sense that you too have changed. How is it now with that old fancy of yours of achieving something good and beautiful in the company of gypsies?"

"I've suffered enough for that!" Wilhelm exclaimed. "Don't remind me where I came from and where I am tending. People talk a lot about the theater, but unless one has been on the stage oneself, one cannot conceive what it is like. How ignorant actors are of themselves, how utterly thoughtless they are in the conduct of their work, how exorbitant their demands are—no one has any idea. Every one of them wants to be first and foremost and exclude all the others. None of them understands that by this means he and the others cannot hope to achieve much. They all think they are absolutely unique, but in fact they are totally unable to do anything that is not mere routine, though they are always restless and clamoring for something new. They work strenuously against each other, and yet a modicum of self-interest and self-love would suffice to bring them together again. One cannot speak of any mutual behavior toward each other, for constant mistrust is kept up by hidden malice and slanderous talk. Those who don't live a loose life, live foolishly. They all make claim to the utmost respect and are sensitive to the slightest blame. The one knew better than the other what was right: why then did he do the opposite? They are always lacking something, have no confidence in anyone or anything, and it seems as though what they most retreat from is reasonableness and good taste, and what they most strive after is the unlimited exercise of their own arbitrary desires."

Wilhelm paused before continuing his oration, and Jarno broke in with riotous laughter. "Those poor actors," he cried, throwing himself on to a chair, and still laughing, "those poor, dear actors! Don't you realize," he went on, once he had recovered, "don't you realize that you have been describing the whole world, not just the theater? I could provide you with characters and actions from all classes of society for your savage brushstrokes. Forgive me, but I must continue to laugh at your belief that these fine qualities are limited to the stage."

Wilhelm composed himself, for Jarno's uncontrolled, ill-timed laughter had quite disconcerted him. "You can't conceal your dislike of the human race if you assert that these faults are to be found everywhere." "And you," Jarno countered, "show your ignorance of the world if you place such heavy responsibility for them on the theater. I would gladly excuse an actor for any fault that arose from self-deception and a desire to please, for if he does not appear as something to himself and others, he is nothing at all. His job is to provide appearances, and he must needs set high store on instantaneous approval, for he gets none other. He must try to delude and dazzle, for that's what he's there for."

"Please allow me now to smile," Wilhelm replied. "I would never have thought that you could be so reasonable and considerate."

"In all seriousness, that is my opinion," said Jarno. "I can readily forgive an actor all the human failings, but not humans for an actor's failings. But don't let me start intoning my lamentations about that: my objections would be much more vehement than yours."

At this point the surgeon came out of Lothario's room and, on being asked how he was, he said: "Pretty well. I hope to have him fully recovered soon." He then rushed out without Wilhelm being able to ask him once more and this time more eagerly about the bag in which he carried his instruments. The desire to find out more about the Amazon gave Wilhelm more confidence in talking to Jarno, to whom he explained what he wanted to know and asked for his assistance. "You already know so much," he said to Jarno, "couldn't you find that out for me?"

Jarno thought for a moment and then said: "Be patient and don't trouble yourself any more. We'll get on her trail. But for the moment it is Lothario's situation that concerns me. His condition is serious—I gather that from the politeness and encouragement of the surgeon. I would like to get Lydie out of the way, for she is not doing any good, but I don't know how to set about that. Our old physician is coming tonight, I hope. Then we can discuss what next to do."

Chapter Four

The old physician arrived. He was the good little doctor we already know, the one who delivered to us that interesting manuscript. He came primarily to examine Lothario, and he seemed not at all satisfied with his condition. He had a long talk with Jarno, but neither of them made any reference to this when they appeared at dinner.

Wilhelm welcomed him most cordially and inquired after the Harper. "We still have some hope," said the doctor, "of effecting a recovery for that poor, unhappy creature." "That man was a sorrowful addition to your strange and restricted existence," said Jarno. "What happened to him later? Do tell me."

After Jarno's curiosity had been satisfied, the doctor continued: "I have never witnessed a mind in such a peculiar state. For many years now he has not taken the slightest interest in anything outside of himself, even to the point of not noticing much at all. Completely shut up in himself, all he looked at was his own hollow and empty self, which was a bottomless pit for him. How touching it was when he spoke of his sorry state! 'I see nothing before me, and nothing behind me,' he would say, 'nothing but the endless night of loneliness in which I find myself. I have no feeling left, except that of my guilt, but even that is only a distant, shapeless ghost that lurks behind my back. There is no height or depth, no forwards or backwards, nothing to describe this continual sameness. Sometimes I cry out: "forever, forever!" in the face of this terrifying indifference, and that strange, meaningless word is a beacon of light in the darkness of my condition. No gleam of any godhead comes to me in this continual blackness, my tears are shed all for myself and because of myself. There is nothing more horrifying to me than friendship and love: for these evoke in me the wish that the phantoms surrounding me might be real. But even these two specters from the abyss have only risen to torment me and rob me finally of my own precious consciousness of my monstrous existence.'

"You should hear how he unburdens his heart like this in his moments of confidentiality," the doctor continued. "Several times I have been deeply moved in listening to him. When something happens that compels him for a moment to realize that time has passed, he seems astonished at this, but then rejects whatever change has occurred as simply one more phantom. One evening he sang a song about his grey hair; and we all sat there and wept."

"Oh, do get the song for me!" Wilhelm cried.

"But," said Jarno, "have you not been able to find out something about what he calls his 'crime,' the reasons for his strange garb, his behavior during the fire and his frenzied rage at the child?"

"We have only been able to make surmises about his life story: direct questioning would be against our principles. Since we have observed that he had a Catholic upbringing, we thought we might gain some relief for him by suggesting he go to confession. But every time we try to get him to go to a priest, he avoids this in the strangest manner. Since, however, I do not wish to leave your request for more information about him completely unanswered, I will tell you what we surmise. He spent his early years in the priesthood, which is why he still wears his long gown and will not shave his beard. The joys of love were foreign to him for most of his life, but later it may be that some episode with a woman closely related to him, and possibly her death at the birth of some unfortunate creature, completely destroyed his mind.

"His strongest delusion is that he brings misfortune wherever he goes and that he will die at the hands of an innocent boy. At first he was afraid of Mignon, until he found out that she was a girl; then he became terrified of Felix, and since, despite all his misery, he passionately loves life, his dislike of the boy seems to have come from this delusion."

"What hope, then, do you have of his recovery?" Wilhelm asked.

"Things are developing slowly, but not backwards," the doctor replied. "He continues in his specific occupations, and we have accustomed him to reading newspapers, which he now looks forward to with great eagerness."

"I would be curious to see his songs," said Jarno.

"I will bring you some of them," said the doctor. "The pastor's eldest son, who always makes transcripts of his father's sermons, has written down several verses and put them together into songs without the old man noticing."

The next morning Jarno came to see Wilhelm and said: "You must do us a favor. Lydie must be removed from here for a while. Her violent and, I may say, inconvenient passion is impeding the baron's recovery. His wound is such that he needs peace and quiet, even though, with his good health, it is not dangerous. You have observed how Lydie torments him with her vigorous ministrations, uncontrollable anxiety and unceasing tears and—well, the doctor expressly demands that she leave the house for a while," he added with a smile. "We have pretended that a certain woman, with whom she is very friendly, is staying in the neighborhood, wants to see her, and is expecting her visit any day. Lydie has been persuaded to go to the magistrate, who lives only two hours' drive from here. He is informed of the situation and will express his regrets that Miss Therese has just left. He will probably pretend that one might still be able to catch up with her, and Lydie will hurry off and, if luck is with us, she will be directed on from one place to another. When she finally insists on returning here, she should not be thwarted. Darkness will aid our purposes, and the coachman is a smart fellow with whom one can come to an agreement. What you have to do, is seat yourself beside her in the carriage, entertain her, and manage the whole adventure."

"You are giving me a strange and highly dubious assignment," Wilhelm replied. "Frustrated true love is a troublesome thing. And should I be the instrument to prolong its anguish? Never in my whole life have I deceived anyone in this way. For my view has always been that to engage in deceit, even for good or useful purposes, can lead us too far."

"But how can we educate children except by this means?" said Jarno.

"That may be all right with children," said Wilhelm, "if we love them dearly and watch over them carefully. But with people of our own age, especially when they do not always appeal so loudly for forbearance, it may often turn out to be dangerous. But," he continued after a moment's reflection, "don't conclude from this that I decline this obligation. The respect that I have for your intelligence, my affection for your friend and my desire to hasten his recovery by whatever means, will encourage me to forget myself. It is not enough to risk one's life for a friend; one must, if needs be, disclaim one's convictions for his sake. We are obliged to abandon our deepest feelings and desires on his account. I will accept this commission, though I foresee the anguish I will have to suffer from Lydie's tears and desperation."

"On the other hand," said Jarno, "you will experience no small recompense by getting to know Therese, a woman with few like her. She would put a hundred men to shame, and I would call her a real Amazon, whereas others who go around like her in ambiguous clothing are nothing but dainty hermaphrodites."

Wilhelm was struck by this remark. He now hoped to find his Amazon in Therese, especially since Jarno, from whom he tried to find out more, broke off what he was saying, and hurried away.

This new, impending expectation of seeing once more the person he so much loved and adored, aroused within him the strangest perturbations. He now interpreted the assignment given him as an express indication of providential guidance, and the fact that he was perfidiously about to separate a poor girl from the object of her devoted, impassioned love became just a fleeting consideration, like the shadow of a bird passing over the brightness of the earth.

The carriage stood ready. Lydie hesitated for a moment before getting into it, and said to the old retainer: "Give my greetings once more to your master, and tell him I will be back before evening." There were tears in her eyes as she once again looked back while they were leaving. Then she composed herself, and turning to Wilhelm, she said: "You will find Therese a very interesting person. I am surprised that she is here in this area, for you must know that she and the baron were deeply in love with each other. Despite the distance, Lothario used to go to see her frequently. I was with her at the time, and it seemed that they could not live without each other. Then things suddenly went wrong, without anyone knowing why. Lothario had got to know me, and I cannot deny that I was really jealous of Therese, did not conceal my affection for him, and did not discourage him when he seemed suddenly to prefer me to her. She behaved toward me in a manner that I could not have wished better, despite the fact that it seemed almost as if I was robbing her of a worthy lover. This love of mine has cost me so many tears and so much suffering! At first we met only occasionally and furtively in some neutral place, but I could not put up with that sort of life for long: I was only happy, only truly happy, when I was with him. When I was separated from him, my eyes filled with tears and my pulse raced. Once he was absent for several days, and I was frantic, started out after him, and surprised him here. He received me affectionately, and if that wretched business had not intervened, I would have had a glorious life. But what I've suffered since he has been in danger, I cannot describe; and even at this very moment I am thoroughly reproachful of myself for having left him for just a day."

Wilhelm was about to ask her more about Therese when they arrived at the magistrate's house. The magistrate came out and expressed deep regret that Therese had already left. He offered the travelers some breakfast, and added that they should be able to catch up with her carriage in the next village. It was decided therefore to go straight on, and the coachman did not waste any time. But they passed through several villages without seeing a sign of her. Lydie then insisted they should turn back. But the coachman went on, as though he had not understood. Finally she demanded, this time with great firmness, that they must go back. Wilhelm called to the coachman, giving him the sign they had agreed on. He replied: "We don't need to take the same road back, I know a shortcut which will be much more convenient." He then drove off to the side through a forest over long tracts of meadowland. At length, since no familiar place came into view, he confessed that he had unfortunately lost his way, but said he would soon know where he was, once they reached the next village. Night began to fall, and the coachman managed things well by constantly asking directions but never waiting for the answers. So they rode the whole night long, and Lydie never closed an eyelid. She kept seeing familiar things in the moonlight, but they immediately disappeared. In the morning things seemed more familiar, and all the more unexpectedly so. The carriage stopped before a small, nicely built house. A woman came out and opened the carriage door. Lydie stared at her, looked around, stared at the woman again, then fell senseless in Wilhelm's arms.

Chapter Five

Wilhelm was shown into an upstairs room. The house was new, quite small, and extremely tidy and clean. It was Therese who had welcomed him and Lydie as they got out of the carriage, but she turned out not to be his Amazon: she was a totally different person. She was well built, though not tall, moved about very briskly, and her bright, blue eyes seemed to take in everything that was happening.

She came into Wilhelm's room and asked if there was anything he needed. "Forgive me for putting you in a room that still smells of paint," she said, "but my little house is only just finished, and you are inaugurating this room, which is intended for my guests. If only there were a more agreeable reason for your being here! Poor Lydie will not give us a very easy time, and in addition I must crave your indulgence because my cook has just left my service at this very inconvenient time, and one of my menservants has crushed his hand. This means that I shall have to do everything myself, but so long as you all accept this, it should be all right. There is no greater plague than servants. They never want to do what they are employed for, not even for themselves." She said a good deal more about other matters. She seemed altogether to enjoy talking. Wilhelm asked after Lydie, and whether he could see her and make his excuses.

"That won't have any effect on her at the moment," said Therese. "Time will make the excuses, and bring her consolation. Words are of little value in such cases. Lydie does not wish to see you. 'Don't let him come anywhere near me,' she was saying when I left her. 'I almost despair of humanity—such an honest face, such openness and sincerity of behavior but secretly so full of guile!' Lothario is totally exculpated: he said in a letter that it was his friends who persuaded him, forced him, to do this. And Lydie counts you amongst these 'friends,' and condemns you with the rest."

"She does me far too great an honor by placing the blame on me," said Wilhelm. "I cannot yet claim to enjoy the friendship of that excellent man: at the moment I am just an innocent tool. I don't approve of what I did, but still I was able to do it. We were all concerned about the health, even whether he would remain alive, of this man whom I respect more highly than anyone I have ever met. What a man he is, and what persons he has gathered around him! Believe me: In this company I have, for the first time, had a real conversation, and for the first time in my life I find my own words returned to me, enriched from the mouth of another—richer, fuller and endowed with greater import. What I had dimly sensed, suddenly became clear to me, and I learned how to see what I had thought. Unfortunately this pleasurable state was interrupted by concern and moodiness, and finally cut short by this disagreeable assignment. I took it upon myself in complete seriousness, for I thought it was my duty, even against my own feelings, to discharge my obligation to this admirable group of people."

Therese had been observing her guest in a sympathetic manner as he spoke. "Oh, how sweet it is," she declared, "to hear one's own convictions voiced by another. We only really become ourselves when someone else thoroughly agrees with us. I have exactly the same feeling about Lothario as you do. People do not always do him justice, but all those who are closely acquainted with him, are infatuated with him; and even in my case, where painful feelings are associated with his memory, I cannot resist thinking about him every day of my life." A deep sigh and a becoming tear accompanied her words. "Don't think I am so easily moved to softness!" she said. "It's only my eye that sheds the tear. There is a little wart on the lower lid, it has been treated, but the eye is somewhat weakened by this, and tears appear at the slightest provocation. This is where the wart was. You can't see any trace of it now."

Indeed he could not; but he did look straight into her eye which was clear as crystal. He felt he was looking into the very depths of her soul.

"Well," she said, "we've both found the password for a relationship. Let's deepen it as soon as possible. The history of every human being lies in his character. Let me tell you my life story; and please grant me the same favor, so that we may remain in contact with each other even when we are apart. The world is so empty if we think of it just as a collection of mountains, rivers and cities; but to find someone somewhere who sees eye to eye with us, someone with whom we can continue to commune in silence, makes the whole world into a populated garden."

She tore herself away, promising to fetch him soon for a walk. Her presence had affected Wilhelm very favorably, and he longed to know more about her relationship with Lothario. Eventually he received a summons from her, and she came out of her room to meet him.

They went down the steep, narrow steps, and then she said: "These steps could be wider and bigger if I had listened to your generous friend's proposal, but to remain worthy of him I had to preserve that part of myself which he so valued in me. Where is the steward?" she asked, when she had reached the bottom of the steps. "You must not think I am so rich that I need a steward. I can myself well look after the few fields that my little estate contains. The steward belongs to my new neighbor who has bought a fine estate, which I know inside out. The dear old man is afflicted with gout, and all his helpers are new to this area. So I am happy to help them get things organized."

They took a walk through fields, pastures and orchards. Therese instructed the steward on everything, explaining every detail, and Wilhelm had good cause to marvel at her knowledge, precision, and ability to suggest ways of dealing with every problem that came up. She never wasted time in getting to the essential point, and each problem was soon settled. "Give your master my best wishes," she said, as the man was leaving. "I will come and see him as soon as I can, and I hope he will soon be fully recovered." When the steward had left, she turned to Wilhelm with a smile, and said: "As a matter of fact, I could get rich quickly, if I so desired; for my dear neighbor would not be disinclined to marry me."

"An old man with gout?" said Wilhelm. "I cannot imagine how you at your age could embrace such a counsel of despair?" "I am not tempted in that direction!" Therese replied. "One is rich if one knows how to manage what one has. Being wealthy is a burdensome affair, if one does not understand what it entails."

Wilhelm expressed his amazement at her managerial abilities. "Definite inclination, early opportunities, external impetus and continuous occupation in useful pursuits make all sorts of things possible in this world of ours," said Therese, " and once you have learnt what instigated me in these matters, you will not be so surprised at this seemingly unusual talent of mine."

When they returned to the house, she let him into her garden, which was so tiny that he could hardly turn around in it, so narrow were the walks and so thickly planted the beds. He had to smile when they walked back through the courtyard, for there was the firewood all neatly cut, split and stacked crosswise, as if it were part of the building. All the receptacles were clean and in place, the little house was painted red and white and amusing to look at. Everything that handiwork could produce, all with good proportions but made to serve the purpose, to last and to delight, seemed to be assembled here. His dinner was brought to his room, and he had ample time to collect his impressions. He was especially struck by the fact that here, once again, he had met a very interesting person who was closely associated with Lothario. "It is understandable," he said to himself, "that a man of the quality of Lothario should attract such admirable women! Manly dignity has far-reaching effects! It's a pity, however, that there are those who get short shrift in the process. Go ahead, say what it is that you are afraid of: should you one day discover your Amazon, that being above all beings, she will, despite all your hopes and dreams, probably turn out, to your shame and humiliation, to be—his bride."

Chapter Six

Wilhelm had been spending a restless afternoon, and was somewhat bored, when, toward evening, his door was opened and in came a comely young huntsman who saluted and said: "Well, shall we go for a walk?" Wilhelm instantly recognized Therese by her lovely eyes.

"Excuse this costume, which, unfortunately, is at the moment only a costume. But since I intend to tell you about the days when I preferred to see myself in this garb, I want to recall that time as visibly as I possibly can. Come along! Let's go to the place where we used to rest from all our hunting and walks, and that will add to the picture."

They walked off, and, as they went, Therese said: "It's not right that you should just let me talk. You know enough about me already, but I know nothing about you. Tell me something about yourself, while I am gathering strength to tell you about my life and my situation." "Unfortunately," said Wilhelm, "I have nothing to relate except one mistake after another, one false step after the other, and I cannot think of anybody I would rather not tell about the constant confusion I was and still am in, than you. Your appearance, your whole nature, and everything around you, show that you have reason to be satisfied with the life you have led, its clear and steady progress, with no time wasted, and no regrets to labor over."

Therese smiled, and said: "We must wait and see if you still think the same when you have heard my story." They walked on, and after some general remarks had passed between them, she asked him: "Are you unattached?" "I believe so," said Wilhelm, "but I wish I wasn't." "Fine!" she said. "That suggests a complicated romance, and shows me that you do have something to relate."

During this exchange they climbed up to the top of the hill and sat down beneath a large oak tree that cast its shade all around. "Here beneath this German tree," said Therese, "I will tell you the tale of a German maiden. Listen carefully.

"My father was a wealthy nobleman of this province, a clear-sighted, industrious, upright man, loving father, reliable friend, and generous host, whose only fault in my eyes was that he was too easy on his wife, who did not properly appreciate him. I regret having to say that about my own mother. Her personality was the very opposite of his. She was impulsive, erratic, with no concern for her household nor love for me, her only child. She was extravagant, but beautiful, witty, full of all sorts of talents, the delight of the circle she gathered around herself. Her circle was certainly never large, or did not remain so for long, and it consisted mainly of men, for no woman felt comfortable in her presence, and she could not tolerate merit in any others of her sex. I resembled my father in appearance and personality. Just as a duckling soon finds water, so my element from my earliest years was the kitchen, the store room, barns and attics. Even during my years of play, my natural instinct and my sole concern were to preserve order and cleanliness in the house. My father was delighted at this and gradually provided my childish desires with appropriate opportunities for fulfillment. But my mother did not love me, and never concealed this fact for a moment.

"I grew up, my activities increased, and with them my father's love for me. When we were alone together, when we walked across the fields or when I helped him check his accounts, I could feel how happy he was. When I looked into his eyes, it was as though I was peering into my own self. For it was in the eyes that I resembled him most. But his spirits flagged and his expression changed when he was with my mother. He made gentle excuses for me when she attacked me savagely and unjustly. He took my part, not in order to protect me, but because my good qualities merited that I be excused. He never opposed any of her wishes. She developed a great passion for acting, a theater was built, and there was no lack of men of all shapes and ages, to appear on stage alongside her, but few women. Lydie, a nice girl who had been educated with me and from early on had shown every prospect of becoming quite charming, took over the supporting female roles, an old chambermaid played aunts and mothers, whereas the female leads, both heroic and pastoral, were always reserved for my mother. I cannot tell you how ridiculous it seemed to me that people I knew very well dressed up and stood on the stage, demanding to be taken for something other than what they really were. What I saw, was always just my mother, Lydie, and this or that baron or secretary, whether they presented themselves as princes, counts, or peasants, and I did not understand how they could presume I would believe they were sick or well, in love or not, miserly or generous, when I usually knew they were the very opposite. So I was not often to be found amongst the spectators. I trimmed the lights, in order to have something to do, got their suppers, and next morning while they were still asleep, I would create some order in their costumes, which they had usually flung down all over the place the previous evening.

"My mother seemed to approve of what I did, but I never gained her love. In fact she despised me, and I remember very well that more than once she said bitterly: 'If mothers could be as unsure as fathers, one would never take this scullion for my daughter.' I will not deny that her behavior gradually set me apart from her completely, her actions seemed like those of a stranger to me, and since I was accustomed to watch servants like a hawk (for, between you and me, that is the basis of all good housekeeping), I became struck by the relationships between my mother and the members of her entourage. It was easy to observe that she did not look on all these men with the same eyes. I watched more carefully, and soon noticed that Lydie was her confidante and was becoming steadily more acquainted with emotions she had been imagining to herself since her early years. I knew about all my mother's rendezvous, but I kept quiet, not telling my father anything that might distress him. Finally I had to, for there were certain things she could not engage in without bribing the servants, who began to defy me, ignoring my father's instructions and my own commands. The complete disorder that ensued as a result was unbearable to me, and I complained to my father, telling him everything.

"He listened to me quietly, and finally said, smiling: 'My dear child, I know all about that. Keep calm, and be patient; it is only for your sake that I put up with this.'

"But I wasn't calm, and I wasn't patient. I reproved my father in my own heart, for I did not think he needed to put up with so much, for whatever reason. I insisted on maintaining order, and was determined to bring matters to a climax.

"My mother had wealth in her own right, but she spent more than she should, and that, as I could see, led to altercations between my parents. Nothing happened to change matters until my mother's emotions led to a certain development.

"Her first lover became ostentatiously unfaithful—and our house, the neighborhood, and all the circumstances of her life became distasteful to her. She wanted to move to another estate, but then that would be too isolated for her. So she wanted to go to town, but there she would not cut a sufficient figure. I don't know what passed between her and my father. All I know is that he finally agreed, under conditions which I never ascertained, that she should take the trip to the south of France that she desired.

"He and I were now free and lived in seventh heaven. I really believe that my father suffered no loss by the considerable sum that he paid out to be rid of her presence. All the servants we no longer needed were dismissed, and fortune smiled on the order we established. We enjoyed several good years, with everything going according to our wishes. But unfortunately this happy state of affairs did not last long. My father quite unexpectedly suffered a stroke, which paralyzed his right side and deprived him of the power of clear speech. You had to guess at what he was asking for, for he never produced the word he had in his mind. I suffered many anxious moments when he insisted on being alone with me, and, after having sharply dismissed with a gesture all the others, was not able to produce the word he wanted. He would grow extremely impatient, and his condition caused me great unhappiness. I was quite sure that he was trying to communicate something of special concern to me, and I greatly desired to know what it was. Normally I could tell everything from his eyes, but now his eyes no longer spoke to me. One thing was clear: he did not want or require anything except to tell me something which, alas, I never found out. A second stroke followed, and he became totally inactive and incapacitated. And very soon he was dead.

"I don't know how I got the idea that somewhere he had deposited money that, on his death, he wanted to come to me rather than to my mother. I searched for it while he was still alive, but without success. Then after his death everything was sealed. I wrote to my mother and offered to remain at the house to be in charge of things, but she rejected this and I had to leave. A reciprocal will came to light according to which she acquired ownership and use of everything, and I at least for the term of her life, remained her dependent. It was now that I believed I could understand the hints my father was giving me. I regretted that he had been such a weak character and so unjust to me after his death. Some of my friends even said that it would have almost been better if he had disinherited me, and urged me to contest the will, but I could not bring myself to do that. I revered my father's memory too much and put my trust in fate, and in myself.

"There was a lady in the neighborhood who owned large estates, with whom I had always been on good terms. She was pleased to take me into her household, and I was soon to become the head of it. She lived a regular life, and liked to have order in everything, and I gave her valiant help in her battles with stewards and retainers. I am not miserly, nor am I spiteful, but we women are more seriously concerned than any man to see that nothing is wasted. All fraudulent action arouses our displeasure; we want people to have only what they deserve.

"I was now once again in my element, lamenting in my quieter moments the loss of my father. My patroness was satisfied with me, and there was only one small thing that disrupted the peace of my existence. Lydie came back; my mother had been cruel enough to reject the poor girl now that she was thoroughly corrupted. She had learnt from my mother to consider passion as a way of life, and had accustomed herself never to display moderation in anything. When she unexpectedly reappeared, my benefactress took her in too. Lydie was eager to assist me, but she was of no use at anything.

"About this time my lady's relatives, and future heirs, would frequently come to the house and occupy themselves by arranging hunts. Lothario was sometimes among them, and I decided in no time that he was far superior to the rest, though he did not pay any particular attention to me. He was polite to everybody, but it soon became clear that it was Lydie he was attracted to. I always had plenty to do and was therefore socially rarely much in evidence. Lively conversation has always been the spice of life for me, but I must confess that in Lothario's presence I said less than usual. I had enjoyed talking with my father about everything that came up. If you don't talk about things, you don't really think about them adequately. There was no one I enjoyed listening to more than Lothario, when he was telling about his journeys and his military campaigns. The whole world lay as open and clear before him as the small sphere of my own activity. What I heard from him was not outlandish adventures, exaggerated half-truths of a traveler with limited perceptions always putting himself ahead of the country he was describing. He didn't tell us about places, he took us there. I have rarely experienced such unadulterated pleasure.

"One evening I had the inexpressible satisfaction of hearing him talk about women. The topic came up quite naturally. Several ladies from the surrounding area were visiting us and were saying all the usual things about the education of women. Our sex was treated unfairly, they were saying: Men want to restrict all higher culture to themselves, we are not allowed to study, we are only to be playthings or housekeepers. Lothario said little to all this, but when the company had diminished in size, he did speak his mind openly. 'It is strange,' he said, 'that a man is thought ill of for wishing to place a woman in the highest position she is capable of occupying; and what is that but governing a household? Whereas the man labors away at external matters, acquiring possessions and protecting them, even maybe participating in the government of a state, he is always dependent on circumstances, and, I may say, controls nothing that he thinks he is controlling. He always has to be politic when he wants to be reasonable, covert when he wants to be open, deceitful when he wants to be honest, and for the sake of some goal that he never attains, he must every moment abandon that highest of all goals: harmony within himself. But the sensible housewife really governs, rules over all that is in the home and makes possible every kind of satisfying activity for the whole family. What is the greatest joy of mankind but pursuing what we perceive to be good and right, really mastering the means to our ends? And where should these ends be if not inside the home? Where should we expect to encounter the constantly recurring, indispensable needs, except where we get up in the morning and lay ourselves to rest at night, where kitchen and wine cellar and storerooms are always there for us and our families? And what a round of regular activity is required to maintain this constantly recurring order of things in undisturbed, never failing sequence! How few men are able to reappear like a star, regularly presiding over the day as well as the night, making household implements, sowing and reaping, preserving and expending, and treading the circle with calm, love and efficiency! Once a woman has assumed this internal governance, she makes thereby the man she loves into the sole master. Her attentiveness acquires all skills, and her activity uses them all. She is dependent on nobody and assures for her husband true independence—domestic independence, inner independence. What he owns, he now sees secured; what he acquires, he sees well used, and then he can turn his mind to bigger things, and if fortune favors him, be to the state what his wife is so admirably at home.'

"He followed this up with a description of the wife he desired. I blushed, for what he described was myself, just as I was. I secretly revelled in my triumph, and all the more so because everything indicated that it was not me he was referring to, for he did not really know me. I cannot remember a more pleasing experience in my whole life than to see a man I respected giving preference to my character over my appearance. I felt rewarded, and encouraged.

"When the others had left, the lady who had become my friend said with a smile: 'What a pity that men do so much thinking and talking about things they never put into practice, otherwise an excellent match for my dear Therese would have been just discovered.' I laughed at her statement, adding that men's minds look around for housekeepers, but their hearts and their imagination long for other qualities; and we housekeepers can't compete with charming young girls. I said this so that Lydie should hear it; for she made no secret of the big impression that Lothario had made on her, and he for his part seemed to pay more and more attention to her every time he visited us. She was poor, not a person of quality, and could not contemplate marriage to him; but she could not withstand the delights of being charming and being charmed. I had never been in love, and was not then, but although it pleased me greatly to see how my character was rated by a man I so highly respected, I cannot deny that I was not entirely satisfied. I wanted him to get to know me and take a personal interest in me. I had no thought of what this might lead to.

"The greatest service I could perform for my benefactress was to bring some order into the beautiful woodlands on her estates. These valuable tracts of land, which were increasing steadily in value owing to various circumstances and the passage of time, were being treated without any imagination, plan or order, and there was no end of stealing and trickery. Whole hillsides were bare, and only the oldest stands of trees had equal size of growth. I went through every such area with an experienced forester, had measurements made, trees cut down, others started, and soon everything was progressing favorably. So as not to be encumbered, whether on foot or on horseback, I had men's clothes made for me. I moved around a lot, and everyone was scared of me.

"I heard that the company of young people, including Lothario, were organizing another hunt, and for the first time in my life I decided to appear in my true colors, or perhaps I had better say, as I wanted to appear in Lothario's eyes. I put on my men's clothes, slung my gun over my back, and went out accompanied by our own huntsman, to await the others at the edge of the estate. They arrived, but Lothario did not recognize me right away. One of my lady's nephews introduced me to him as an accomplished forester, joked about my youthfulness, and continued the game, praising me all the while, until Lothario finally recognized me. This nephew backed me up in all this, as though we had planned it ahead. He described at length and with gratitude all that I was doing for his aunt's estates, and consequently also for him.

"Lothario listened attentively, then inquired about all sorts of things connected with the estates and the neighborhood, and I was glad to be able to display my knowledge. I passed my examination with flying colors, then asked his opinion about various improvements, which he approved, mentioning similar cases, and strengthened my arguments by giving them an appropriate context. My satisfaction steadily increased. But fortunately I only wanted to be understood, not to be loved, for when we returned to the house I noticed more clearly than ever that his attentions to Lydie indicated a growing affection. I had achieved my aim, but I was not at ease. From that day on he displayed real respect and close confidence in me, began to talk to me when others were present, asked me for my opinion and seemed to trust my views on household matters as though I knew everything. His interest encouraged me greatly, and even when the talk was about agricultural or financial matters, he drew me into the conversation, and when he was not present I did all I could to acquire more knowledge of the area, even of the whole district. This was not difficult for me, because it represented on a bigger scale what I already knew in a smaller sphere.

"He began to visit us more frequently from then on. The conversation turned on a variety of subjects, but ultimately it always came down to questions of economics in the broader sense, and there was much talk of the vast results that can be achieved by efficient use of time, money and ability, even by means that may seem quite small in themselves.

"I did not resist the affection that was drawing me toward him, and unfortunately I soon became aware how strong, how sincere and pure my love for him was, when I observed ever more clearly that his repeated visits were in order to see Lydie, not me. At least that was her passionate conviction. She confided in me, and that was consoling to some extent. What she interpreted in her own favor, seemed to me of little significance. There was no sign of any intention of a lasting union, but I could easily see the emotional girl's craving to belong to him at any price.

"That's how matters stood when my lady surprised me one day with an unexpected communication. 'Lothario,' she said, 'offers you his hand in marriage; he wants to have you at his side for his whole life.' She then described at length my qualities, and told me something that I was very glad to hear: that Lothario was quite sure he had found in me the person he was looking for.

"I had now achieved my greatest joy: a man wanted me, whom I greatly respected, and at his side, and in his company I could envision the free and full expansion of my natural inclinations and practiced talents for the benefit of many people: my whole existence seemed at once to be extended into infinity. I gave my consent. He came and talked to me, gave me his hand, looked in my eyes, embraced me, and pressed a kiss on my lips—the first, and the last, he ever gave me. He confided to me his whole situation, told me what his American campaign had cost him, the debts he had incurred on his estates, the friction this had caused with his great-uncle, and the latter's way of caring for him, namely to find a rich wife for him, since an intelligent man needs someone to take over the domestic side of his affairs. Lothario hoped through his sister to persuade the old man to agree to his union with me. He outlined his financial resources, his plans and prospects and solicited my cooperation. But until his uncle gave his agreement, everything should remain secret.

"Just after he left, Lydie asked me whether he had said anything about her. I said that he hadn't, and bored her with an account of some economic matters. She was restless, ill-humored, and Lothario's behavior when he returned, did nothing to improve her state of mind.

"But I see that the sun is going down, my friend. That's fortunate for you, for otherwise you would have had to listen to my whole story, which I enjoy recounting to myself, in every detail. So let me speed things up! We are now reaching a period that it is not good to dwell on.

"Lothario introduced me to his wonderful sister who, in turn, introduced me to his uncle. I won the old man over, he agreed to what we wanted, and I returned to my lady with the joyful news. The whole matter was no longer a secret in the household. Lydie found out about it, and couldn't believe what she heard. When finally she could doubt it no longer, she immediately disappeared from sight, and nobody knew where she had taken herself off to.

"The wedding day was approaching. I had asked him several times for a picture and reminded him of his promise one day when he was about to leave. 'You have forgotten to give me the frame you wanted to have it mounted in,' he said. He was referring to the fact that I had received from a woman friend a gift that I greatly prized. The outer glass covering had a monogram fastened by strands of her hair, and inside there was a piece of ivory on which her portrait was to have been painted—but to my great sorrow she died. Lothario's affection brought me joy while her loss was giving me pain, and so I wanted to fill the gap left in her gift to me by the portrait of my friend.

"I went quickly to my room, fetched my jewel case, and opened it in his presence. Inside he saw a medallion with a woman's picture on it. He took it into his hands, examined it carefully, and quickly asked: 'Who is this a picture of?' 'My mother,' I replied. 'I could have sworn that this was a certain Mme. de Saint Alban whom I met several years ago in Switzerland,' he said. 'That's who it is,' I replied with a smile. 'So you met your mother-in-law without knowing it. Saint Alban is the romantic name that my mother uses when she's travelling: she's still using it, in France.' 'I am the most unfortunate of men!' he cried, putting the medallion back in the jewel case. He covered his eyes, left the room immediately, and threw himself into the saddle. I called after him from the terrace. He looked around, waved, then rushed away—and I have never seen him since."

The sun went down, and Therese gazed straight at the evening glow, her eyes brimming with tears. Silently she laid her hand on that of her new friend.

He kissed it lovingly, she dried her tears, and stood up. "Let's go back," she said, "and pay some attention to the others."

Their conversation as they walked back was not animated. They arrived at the garden gate and saw Lydie sitting on a bench. She got up, but avoided them, and went back into the house. She was holding a paper in her hands, and there were two little girls with her. "I see," said Therese, "that she still keeps with her what is her only consolation—Lothario's letter, in which he assures her that, as soon as he is better, she shall return to him, but for the time being she should stay quietly with me. She hangs on his words and consoles herself with them, but she has a poor opinion of his friends."

The two children came up, welcomed Therese, and gave her an account of all that had happened while she was out. "Here you see another branch of my activity," she said. "I have entered into an arrangement with Lothario's sister. Together we are educating a group of children—I take care of the vigorous, eager, domestic types and she takes charge of those who reveal quieter and more refined talents. For it is reasonable to provide in every way possible for the happiness of menfolk and the smooth running of the household. When you have met my good friend, his sister, your life will be different: her beauty and her goodness make her the object of everyone's adoration." Wilhelm did not venture to tell her that unfortunately he had already met the countess and his fleeting acquaintance with her would always remain painful for him. He was very glad that Therese did not continue this particular conversation, her household duties requiring her immediate attention. When she had left, he was overcome by a sense of distress at this last piece of news regarding the countess: that she was obliged to substitute for her own happiness the hope of providing happiness for others. He admired Therese for not feeling any need to change her way of life despite the unexpected sad change in her expectations. "How happy those are," he said to himself, "who do not have to reject the whole of their past life in order to accommodate themselves to fate!"

Therese came to his room, and asked to be forgiven for disturbing him. "Here in that wall cabinet is my whole library," she said. "It consists of books that I don't throw away, rather than those I wish to keep. When Lydie wants a religious book, she'll be able to find something of the kind. People who are worldly most of the time, get the idea they must be religious when they're in trouble. Things that are good and moral are like medicine they force down when they feel bad, and any priest or moral teacher is regarded as a physician one dispenses with as soon as possible. I must however confess that morality for me is a kind of diet, but only becomes a diet if practiced as a rule of life the whole year through."

She rummaged amongst the books and found a few so-called devotional works. "Recourse to such books is something that Lydie learnt from my mother," said Therese. "My mother lived on novels and plays so long as her lover remained faithful. But when he left, these other books came into their own. I simply cannot understand how anyone could believe that God speaks to us through books. If the world itself does not reveal to someone its relationship to him, if his heart does not tell him what his duties are, he is unlikely to learn that from books which provide us with little more than names for our mistakes."

She left Wilhelm to himself, and he spent the evening examining this little collection of books. It did seem to have been quite arbitrarily assembled.

Therese remained just the same for the few days that Wilhelm stayed with her. She told him in great detail, and at various intervals, about the results of what she had already related. Dates and places were all vividly present in her mind, and we will summarize that part which our readers need to know.

Unfortunately, the reason for Lothario's rapid departure soon became all too obvious. He had encountered Therese's mother during her journey, and succumbed to her charms, which she readily bestowed. This unfortunate interlude now prevented him from joining a woman, who seemed destined by nature to be his. Therese continued in her clearly defined sphere of activity and duties. As for Lydie, it became known that she was secretly dwelling in the neighborhood, happy that the marriage, for some unknown reason, had not taken place. She tried to draw closer to Lothario, and it seemed that he, more out of desperation than desire, more from surprise than due reflection, more from boredom than intention, responded to her wishes.

Therese was not upset by this. She made no further claims on him and, even if he had become her husband, she might have had strength enough to put up with his relationship with Lydie, so long as it did not disturb her domestic order. At least she often expressed the opinion that a woman who kept her household duties in good order could tolerate any flight of fancy on her husband's part, and still be certain that he would come back to her.

Therese's mother soon reduced her capital to a state of shambles, for which the daughter had to suffer, since nothing much remained for her. The old lady who had so befriended Therese, died and left her this small freehold estate and a sizeable amount of capital. Therese adapted herself immediately to her restricted circumstances. Lothario offered her a better piece of property and Jarno was the go-between. But this Therese declined, saying: "I want to show Lothario in something small, that I was worthy of sharing with him something that was bigger. But if some circumstance or other should put me in a situation of embarrassment for myself or others, I claim the right to address myself without further ado to my dear friend."

Nothing remains less concealed or less exploited than purposeful activity. As soon as she had established herself on her small estate, the neighbors came to make her acquaintance and seek her advice, and the new owner of the adjoining estates made it quite clear to her that it was entirely up to her whether she would accept his hand in marriage and become heir to the greater part of his fortune, or not. She had already mentioned this to Wilhelm and joked about marriage and mismarriage.

"There is nothing people enjoy talking about more than when a marriage takes place which they consider a mismarriage, or *mésalliance*. And yet 'mismarriages' are commoner than marriages, for most unions turn out soon enough to be misfits. Mixture of social classes through marriage only merits the name of 'mismarriage' when the one party cannot share in the established, accustomed and therefore necessitated existence of the other party. Different strata of society have different lifestyles that they cannot share or exchange with each other, and that is why marriages of this kind are better not concluded. But exceptions, and very happy exceptions, are possible. For instance the marriage of a young girl to an old man is always a misfit, but I've known such a marriage to turn out quite well. For me there could only be one kind of mismarriage—if I had to spend my time in shows and ceremonies. I would much rather marry an honest farmer's son from the neighborhood."

Wilhelm thought it was now time for him to return to Lothario's residence, and he asked Therese to create an opportunity for him to take his leave of Lydie. The hot-tempered girl was persuaded to see him and he was able to say a few kind words to her, to which she replied: "I have overcome my earlier distress. Lothario will always remain dear to me, but I regret that he is surrounded by friends whose real natures are now known to me. The Abbé is quite capable of leaving a person in a state of distress, or plunging him into it, on account of some mood that comes over him. The doctor always wants to clear things up. Jarno has no soul, and you, my friend, have at least no character! Continue what you are doing, allow yourself to be used as a tool by these three men, and they will certainly give you plenty of assignments. I realize that for a long time my presence has been distasteful to them. I have never discovered their secret, but I know that they have one. Why all these locked rooms? These mysterious corridors? Why can't anyone get to the big tower? Why did they confine me to my own room? I must confess that it was jealousy that first made me discover this; I feared that some favored rival was hidden away somewhere. I don't believe that any longer. I am convinced that Lothario loves me and means well, but I am equally convinced that he is misled by his pretentious, false friends. If you want to do him a service, if you are to be forgiven for the trouble you have caused me, then get him out of the hands of these men. But what can I hope for! Give him this letter, and repeat what it says: that I will always love him and rely on him. Oh!" she cried, standing up and sobbing on Therese's neck, "he is surrounded by my enemies, they will try to persuade him that I have made no sacrifices for him. The best of men like to hear they deserve every sacrifice without having to show their gratitude."

Wilhelm's leave-taking from Therese was a happier one. She expressed the desire to see him again soon. "You know all about me!" she said. "You let me do all the talking. Next time it will be your duty to respond equally confidentially."

While he was on his way back, he had ample time to reflect on this new, radiant personality. What confidences she had bestowed on him! He thought how happy Mignon and Felix would be in her care, and then he thought about himself and what a delight it would be to dwell in the presence of such a clear-minded human being. As he drew near to Lothario's castle, he was struck by the tower with the numerous corridors and side buildings. And he decided to ask the Abbé or Jarno about them.

Chapter Seven

When Wilhelm entered the castle he found that Lothario was well on the way to recovery. Neither the doctor nor the Abbé was there, but Jarno was. Lothario was soon well enough to ride, alone or with his friends. His talk was both serious and pleasant, his conversation with others instructive and stimulating. There were often signs of a quite delicate sensitivity, though he did what he could to conceal this; and if it showed itself against his will, he seemed almost to disapprove.

One evening he was very quiet at dinner, though he looked quite cheerful. "You must have had some adventure or other today, but apparently a pleasant one," said Jarno. "What a sound judge you are of people!" Lothario replied. "Yes indeed, I have had the most delightful adventure. Perhaps I would not have thought it so charming at any other time, but today it caught me in a very receptive mood. Toward evening I was riding through the various villages on the other side of the water, a route I had often taken in earlier years. My bodily sickness must have mellowed me more than I thought; I felt soft but, as my strength revived, I felt born anew. Every object around me appeared in the same light as they had in former years, so pleasant, so delightful, so charming—such as they had not seemed to me for a long time. I realized this was a form of weakness, but accepted it willingly, and rode gently on, understanding exactly how some people get to like illnesses that induce pleasant feelings. You know perhaps the reason why I used to take this particular path in the past?"

"If I remember correctly," said Jarno, "it was some little love affair involving a farmer's daughter."

"One might call it a big love affair," Lothario said in reply, "for we were both very much in love with each other, seriously in love and for quite a long time. Chance would have it that today everything combined to bring back to me those first days of our love. Boys were once again shaking june bugs out of trees, and the ash trees were no further in leaf than they were the first day that I saw them. It was a long time since I last saw Margarete, for she married and moved far away, though I had happened to hear that she had come with her children a few weeks earlier to stay with her father."

"So this particular route of yours was not accidentally chosen?" said Jarno.

"I cannot deny that I did hope to encounter her," said Lothario. "When I was drawing near to the house I saw her father sitting outside the door, with a child, about a year old, standing by his side; and as I came closer, a woman appeared briefly at an upstairs window. And when I got to the gate, I heard someone rushing down the steps. I thought this was certainly she, and flattered myself that she had recognized me and was running to meet me. But I was quite disconcerted when she rushed out of the door, picked up the child whom the horses were coming up to, and carried it back into the house. This gave me an unpleasant feeling, and my vanity was only slightly appeased when I noticed that her neck and one ear were reddened as she hurried away.

"I remained standing where I was, spoke to her father, and peered up at all the windows in search of some sign of her. But found none, and since I did not want to ask after her, I rode on. My irritation was somewhat tempered by the strange observation that, although I had scarcely been able to see her face, she seemed totally unchanged; and ten years is a long time! She seemed as young as ever: just as slim and just as quick on her feet, her neck almost lovelier than before, her cheek just as capable of that loving blush as ever—and yet the mother of six children, perhaps more. This vision was so appropriate to the world of magic surrounding me, that, feeling totally rejuvenated, I rode on further and did not turn back until the sun was going down over the next patch of woodland. And though the evening dew reminded me of my doctor's instructions and I knew it would be advisable for me now to go straight home, I did not, but instead went back by way of the farmhouse. I noticed that a woman was walking to and fro in the garden, which is surrounded by a low hedge. I rode up to the hedge on the outside path, and soon found myself near the person I was seeking.

"Although the evening sun was in my eyes, I could see that she was working near the hedge, which only partly obscured her. I believed this was my old love. As I came up to her, I stood still, not without some heartthrobs. Tall branches of wild roses, swayed by a gentle breeze, were concealing her somewhat. I spoke to her, and asked how she was. She answered me, rather softly : 'Quite well.' Then I noticed that there was a child behind the hedgerow picking flowers and I took the occasion to ask her where the other children were. 'This is not my child,' she said. 'That would be too early!' and at that moment it so happened that I caught sight of her face through the branches, and did not know what I should say to what I saw. For it was, and was not, my loved one. She was almost younger, almost lovelier than when I had known her ten years ago. 'Aren't you the farmer's daughter?' I asked, in some confusion. 'No,' she said. 'I'm her cousin.' 'But you are so extraordinarily alike.' 'That's what everyone says who knew her ten years ago,' said the girl.

"I proceeded to ask her about various other things. Although I had soon realized my mistake, I was quite pleased with it and could not tear myself away from the living image of former happiness that stood before me. The child had gone off in the direction of the pond looking for flowers. She took leave of me and ran after the child.

"Meanwhile I had discovered that my former beloved was indeed in her father's house, and as I rode back I was busy guessing whether it was she or her cousin who had protected the child from the horses. I went over the whole train of events in my mind and would find it hard to think of anything that could have delighted me more. But I do feel that I am still not well; so let's ask the doctor to relieve us all from further indulgence in this mood."

When love stories are being narrated, what usually happens is that one leads to the other, just like ghost stories. So our little group of people found much to retail in the way of recollection of times past. Lothario had most to relate. Jarno's stories all had their own individual stamp. And we know what Wilhelm had to contribute. He was afraid that someone would remind him of his experience with the countess; but nobody thought about that.

"It is true," said Lothario, "that there is no pleasanter sensation than when one's heart, after a period of non-involvement, opens up in love to some new object; but I would gladly have done without that for the whole rest of my life, if fate had permitted me to join myself to Therese. Youth doesn't last forever, and childhood shouldn't either. What can be more desirable for a man who knows the world and what he has to do in it and hope from it, than to find a wife to work alongside him, taking care of everything that he cannot, operating in a broad sphere whereas he must follow a strait course? What a blessed life I dreamt of with her: not the blessings of ecstatic bliss, but the joys of a secure earthly life: order in joy, courage in misfortune, concern for every little detail, and a soul able to cope with larger matters and, in due course, dismiss them. I saw in her those qualities we admire when history shows us women far superior to any men: a clear perception of circumstances, ability to deal with all eventualities, that confidence in dealing with detail which works to the advantage of the whole without their thinking about it. You will surely forgive me," he said, turning to Wilhelm with a smile, "for being seduced away from Aurelie by Therese. With Therese I could hope for lifelong happiness, whereas with Aurelie I could not hope for one happy hour."

"I cannot deny that I came here with great bitterness," said Wilhelm, "and had made up my mind to upbraid you for your behavior toward Aurelie."

"I certainly deserve blame for that," said Lothario. "I should not have confused friendship with love. I should not have allowed affection to invade the respect she deserved, affection that she could neither arouse in me nor receive from me in return. She was not lovable when she loved, and that is the worst misfortune that can befall a woman."

"That may be," said Wilhelm in reply. "But we cannot always avoid the reproach that our actions and sentiments have been diverted in some strange way from their natural course. There are responsibilities we must never lose sight of. May she rest in peace; and let us, without blaming her or ourselves, scatter blossoms of pity upon her grave. But let me ask you this: faced with the grave of this unhappy mother, why do you not take charge of the child, a boy that everyone would delight in but you seem entirely to neglect? How can you, with all your good-heartedness and delicate feelings, completely deny those of a father? You have not said one word the whole time about the precious child whose grace and charm beggar description?"

"Whom are you referring to? I don't understand," said Lothario.

"Why, your son, of course: Aurelie's son, that lovely child who only lacks the care of a loving father to make him happy."

"You're making a big mistake," said Lothario. "Aurelie never had a son. At least, not by me. I know nothing about a child. If I did, I would of course have taken charge of it. As for the present situation: I will consider this little creature as a bequest from her, and gladly take charge of its education. Did she ever give any indication that the child belonged to her or to me?"

"I do not recall any express statement to that effect," said Wilhelm. "But it was generally assumed to be so, and I myself never doubted it for a moment."

"I can offer some clarification," said Jarno, breaking into their conversation. "An old woman, whom you must have seen often, brought the child to Aurelie, who was delighted to take it over, hoping that its presence would mitigate her sufferings. And it did indeed provide her with many happy moments."

Wilhelm was greatly disturbed by this report. He had a clear mental picture of the good-hearted Mignon standing beside the handsome Felix, and this made him wish to remove them both from their present environment.

"Let's deal with that right away," said Lothario. "We'll place the strange girl in the charge of Therese, where she couldn't be in better hands. And, as for the boy, I would suggest that you, Wilhelm, should take care of him. For what women leave unfinished in our education, children complete by our association with them."

"I think," said Jarno, "that you should abandon your association with the theater, for you have no talent for it."

Wilhelm was thunderstruck. He had to compose himself, for Jarno's harsh words had deeply offended his self-esteem. "If you can convince me of that," he said with a forced smile, "you will be doing me a great service, though it is always sad to be shaken out of a pleasant dream."

"Let's not discuss that any further at the moment," Jarno replied. "I would urge you to go and fetch the children. The rest will take care of itself."

"I am prepared to do that," said Wilhelm. "I am uneasy, both eager to find out more about the boy and anxious to see the girl again who has attached herself to me so peculiarly."

It was agreed that he should leave as soon as possible. He was ready to go the next day, his horse was saddled, but he first wanted to take his leave of Lothario. When dinner time came around, they all seated themselves at table, but without their host. He arrived rather late, but did not join them. "I bet you have been testing out your tender feelings again today, and have not withstood the urge to see your former beloved once more." "Correct!" said Lothario. "Tell us how it went. I'm very curious," said Jarno.

"I won't deny that this whole adventure was unduly obsessing my mind, and so I decided to ride out there once more and really see the person whose rejuvenated appearance had caused me such a pleasant illusion. I dismounted at some distance from the house, had the horses led off to the side so as not to disturb the children playing by the gate. I went into the house, and it so happened that she came walking toward me, for it was she, and I recognized her despite the fact that she had greatly changed. She was heavier, and seemed to be taller. Her grace of manner shone through a certain setness, and her gaiety had been transformed into a quiet reflectiveness. Her head, which she had formerly held aloft so freely and easily, hung a little, and there were slight wrinkles in her forehead.

"She lowered her eyes when she saw me, but there was no blushing to indicate that her feelings were engaged. I gave her my hand; she gave me hers. I asked after her husband: he wasn't at home. I inquired after the children: she stepped up to the door and called them in. They gathered around her. There is no more charming sight than that of a mother with a child in her arms, and none more dignified than that of one surrounded by a group of children. I asked what their names were—just in order to have something to say. She invited me to step inside and wait for their father. I did this, was led into the parlor, where I found that almost everything was still as it had been, and, strange to say, her attractive cousin, her living image, was sitting on the same stool behind the distaff where I had so often seen my loved one, and looking exactly like her. A little girl, the living image of her mother, had followed us, and I found myself presently situated between past and future, strangely like being in an orange grove where in one small area blossoms and fruits are ranged side by side. Her cousin left the room to get some refreshments. I pressed the hand of the woman I had once loved so dearly, and said: 'It is a great joy for me to see you again.' 'You are very kind to say that,' she replied. 'I can assure you that I too am extremely pleased to see you. Many has been the time that I have wished to see you once more during my life, sometimes at moments that I thought might be my last.' She said this in a firm voice, without pathos, quite naturally, in the tone that had always delighted me. Her cousin came back, then her husband arrived—and I will leave you to imagine my feelings as I stayed, and when I left."

Chapter Eight

On his way to the town Wilhelm thought about all the fine women he knew or had heard about, their strange lives, so deprived of happiness, painfully present to his mind. "Oh, poor Mariane," he cried, "what more do I have to learn about you? And you, glorious Amazon, noble guiding spirit, to whom I am so greatly indebted, whom I am always trying to find again and never can, in what sad circumstances shall I find you when we meet again!"

None of his acquaintances were at home. So he ran to the theater, expecting to find them rehearsing. Everything was quiet, the whole house seemed empty, but he saw that one shutter was open. When he walked on to the stage he found Aurelie's old servant-woman stitching together some pieces of canvas for a new piece of scenery, and the only light coming in was what was needed for her to see what she was doing. Felix and Mignon were sitting on the floor beside her, holding a book. Mignon was reading aloud and Felix repeating the words after her as if he already knew his letters and could really read.

Both children jumped up to welcome him. He embraced them fondly and then led them back to where the old woman was. "Are you the one who brought this child to Aurelie?" he asked her in a solemn tone of voice. The old woman looked up from her work and turned her face toward him. He looked at her in the light, shuddered, and stepped back a few paces: it was old Barbara. "Where is Mariane?" he cried. "Far away," said the old woman. "And Felix . . . ?" "Is the son of that unhappy girl who loved too ardently. May you never realize the pain you have caused us! May the treasure that I hand over to you make you as happy as he has made us unhappy!"

She stood up with the intention of leaving. But Wilhelm held her fast. "I'm not trying to run away from you," she said. "Just let me fetch a document that will give you both pleasure and pain." She left, and Wilhelm gazed at the boy in timorous joy, for he could not yet acknowledge the child as his own. "He is yours," said Mignon, "he is yours," and she pressed the child against his knees.

The old woman returned, and handed him a letter. "Here are Mariane's last words," she said. "She is dead, then?" he cried. "Yes, dead!" said Barbara. "I wish I could spare you all my reproaches."

Surprised and bewildered, Wilhelm broke open the letter. He had only read the first words of it when bitter sorrow overcame him. He dropped the letter, fell down on a mossy bank, and lay there for some time. Mignon busied herself with him, Felix picked up the letter and tugged her until she responded by kneeling down beside him and reading it aloud to him. Felix repeated the words after her, and Wilhelm was therefore obliged to hear them twice over. "If this letter should ever reach you, then have pity on the unhappy girl who loved you. Your love has killed her. This boy, whose birth I shall outlive but a few days, is yours. I die faithful to you, however much appearances may speak against me. In losing you, I lost all that bound me to life. I die content, because they assure me that the child is healthy and will live. Listen to what Barbara has to say, forgive her, farewell, and do not forget me!"

What a painful and yet, thank goodness, unclear and mysterious letter, the contents of which he only really understood as the children, stumbling and stammering, read it aloud and repeated it.

"There you have it!" said the old woman, not waiting until he had recovered himself. "Give your thanks to Heaven that, after the loss of such a good young woman, you are left with such a marvelous child. When you learn how true she was to you, right up to the end, how unhappy she was, and what sacrifices she made for your sake, you will be utterly distressed."

"Let me drink to the dregs the cup of sorrow and joy!" he exclaimed. "Convince me, indeed persuade me by what you have to say, that she was a good girl who deserved my respect as well as my love; then leave me to my sorrow at her irreplaceable loss."

"Now is not the time," she replied. "I have work to do, and I don't want anyone to find us together. Let it remain a secret that Felix is yours, otherwise I will have to put up with too many reproaches from the company for my previous pretenses. Mignon won't give us away: she is a good girl and keeps her mouth shut."

"I've known it for a long time, but I haven't said anything," Mignon answered. "How is that possible?" the old woman said. "How did you find it out?" Wilhelm asked. "The Ghost told me." "How? When?" "In the cellar when the old man drew the knife. I heard someone say: 'Go and get his father.' Then I knew it was you." "But who said this to you?" "I don't know. In my heart, in my head, I was so terrified, I was trembling, I prayed, then I heard it, and I understood."

Wilhelm pressed her to his heart, told her to look after Felix, and left. Only then did he notice that she had become much thinner and paler since he went away. The first of his acquaintances that he ran across was Madame Melina, who welcomed him warmly. "I hope," she said, "that you will find everything as you would wish it." "I doubt that," said Wilhelm, "and I'm not expecting to. Why don't you admit that all the arrangements have been made to dispense with my services?" "But why did you go away?" she said. "It's never too early to realize that no one is indispensable in this world," said Wilhelm. "How important we think we are! We imagine that we are the only real driving force in our sphere of activity and that when we are no longer there, everything will come to a standstill and wither away. But the space, at first hardly noticed, is filled up quite quickly, and even becomes the seed-ground of more pleasant, if not better things."

"And no allowance is made for the sorrow of our friends?" she asked in return.

"Our friends," Wilhelm replied, "will do well to reconcile themselves immediately to the change and say to themselves: Wherever you are, wherever you settle, be active and gracious, and let your life be untroubled."

On further inquiry Wilhelm discovered that what he had expected, had indeed happened: opera had been introduced, and was captivating the public. His former roles had now been divided up between Laertes and Horatio, both of whom were receiving much greater acclaim than he himself had ever done.

At that moment in came Laertes, and Madame Melina exclaimed: "Just look at this fortunate young man who will soon be a capitalist and heaven knows what else!" Wilhelm embraced him and felt the fine texture of his coat. The rest of his clothing was simple, but all of the highest quality. "Explain the mystery!" Wilhelm said to him. "It is high time you knew that my restlessness is at last paying off," said Laertes. "The head of a big business house is profiting from my unsettledness, as well as from my knowledge and acquaintanceships, and allows me a good cut for myself. I would give a great deal if I could also negotiate trust from the women, for there is a pretty niece in the office and I can see that, if I so desired, I could soon become a made man."

"You probably don't know," said Madame Melina, "that there's been a wedding here. Serlo is married to the lovely Elmire, her father having refused to approve of the continuation of their private intimacy."

They told him about many things that had occurred in his absence, from which he perceived that he had long since become estranged from the general tone and spirit of the company.

He waited anxiously for Barbara, who had announced that she would come to see him at the strange hour of dead of night, when everyone was asleep, as if she were a young girl creeping to her lover. While he was waiting, he read through Mariane's letter time and time again, read the word "faithful" from her beloved hand with inexpressible delight, and then, with horror, the announcement of her impending death, which she seemed not to fear.

It was past midnight when there was a noise at the half-open door and Barbara came in with a basket. "I am here," she said, "to give you an account of all our sufferings, but I expect that you will remain quite unmoved. Your eagerness to see me is simply in order to satisfy your curiosity and I expect that you will envelop yourself in your own cold selfish interests, as you always did while our hearts were breaking. But look here! This is how I brought out the champagne on that happy evening, put three glasses on the table, and you began to beguile us and make us drowsy with happy childhood tales, whereas tonight I will enlighten you and keep you alert with sad truths."

Wilhelm did not know what to say when the old woman removed the cork and filled three glasses. "Drink up," she said, quickly emptying her own glass, "drink up before the mood passes. I will let this third glass lose its sparkling bubbles, in memory of that unhappy girl. How red her lips were when she spoke of you then, and how pale and rigid they have become for evermore!"

"You old witch, you monstrous fury!" Wilhelm cried, jumping up and banging his fist on the table. "What sort of evil spirit can it be that possesses and impels you? Who do you think I am, if you imagine that even the simplest account of Mariane's sorrow and death would not distress me greatly, and why do you need to have recourse to such devilish tricks to increase my torment? If your incessant tippling won't refrain from indulging itself at a funeral feast, then go ahead, and drink as you talk! I have always loathed you, and I cannot contemplate the idea of Mariane's being innocent, when I look at her companion."

"Take it easy, sir," she said in reply. "You won't rattle me. You still owe us a great debt, and one doesn't allow oneself to be insulted by debtors. But you're right: just the simplest account will be punishment enough for you. Listen then to Mariane's struggles, and her victory in the battle to remain yours."

"Mine?" said Wilhelm. "What sort of fairy tale is this to be?"

"Don't interrupt me, just listen to what I have to say. Then believe what you will—it makes no difference any longer. On that last evening with us did you not find a note and take it away with you?"

"I did not find it at the time, but afterwards. It was tucked in the scarf, which I grabbed in the heat of my emotions and put in my pocket."

"What did the note contain?"

"The expectations of a discontented lover to be better received the following night than he had the previous one. And I saw with my own eyes that his hopes were fulfilled, for it was daybreak when he came creeping out of your house."

"You may well have seen him then, but only now shall you learn how sadly Mariane spent that night and how vexed I was. I will be quite honest and not deny or gloss over the fact that I did encourage Mariane to give herself to this man named Norberg. She followed my advice, but, I can truly say, with distaste. He was rich, appeared to be in love with her, and I hoped he would remain constant. Soon after this he had to go on a journey, and it was then that Mariane came to know you. What I had to put up with as a result of that! The things I had to prevent, or to tolerate! 'Oh!' she would cry, 'if only you had spared my youth and my innocence for four more weeks, then I would have found a worthy object for my love. I would have been worthy of him, and love would have given me with a clear conscience what I have now sold against my will.' She abandoned herself entirely to her affection, and I dare not ask if you for your part were happy. I had unlimited power over her mind, for I was acquainted with every means of satisfying her smallest desires; but I had no power over her heart, for she never approved anything I did for her or tried to persuade her to do, if it was against the dictates of her heart. She only yielded to inescapable need, and need soon become oppressive to her. In her early youth she had been provided with everything, but her family lost its fortune through a series of complicated circumstances. The poor girl had grown accustomed to various needs, and some good principles had been implanted into her young mind, which made her uneasy but did not help much. She had absolutely no adroitness in worldly affairs, she was innocent in the true sense of the word, she had no idea that one could buy something without paying for it. What she feared most was being in debt, she would always rather give than take, and it was this sort of situation that forced her to give herself in order to clear up a number of minor debts."

"And couldn't you have saved her from that?" Wilhelm exclaimed angrily.

"Of course," the old woman replied, "with hunger and want, sorrow and privation, but I was never prepared for that."

"You hideous, despicable procuress! So you sacrificed this unhappy creature for the sake of your own swilling and gluttony?"

"You would do better to control yourself and stop using such insulting expressions," said the old woman. "If you want to curse and swear, why not go into one of your fine houses—you will find mothers there who are anxiously concerned to find the most loathsome men for their lovely, radiant daughters, so long as they are very rich. And you will see the poor young creatures trembling at the fate in store for them, and utterly distressed, until some more experienced woman friend points out to them that by marrying they will acquire the right to dispose of their hearts and persons as they wish."

"Hold your tongue!" Wilhelm shouted at her. "Do you really think one crime can be excused by another? Get on with your story without further asides!"

"Then listen, and stop reproaching me! Mariane became yours against my will. I have nothing to blame myself for in the whole adventure. Norberg came back and rushed to see Mariane. She received him coldly and petulantly and did not even allow him one kiss. I needed all my skill to excuse her behavior. I told him that a father-confessor had pricked her conscience, and that when conscience speaks, one must respect it. I finally got him to leave and promised to do my best for him. He was rich and coarse, but he was basically good-natured, and loved Mariane intensely. He promised me to be patient, and I worked all the harder to see he was not too much tested. I had a hard time with Mariane: I persuaded her—in fact I forced her finally, by threat of leaving her, to write to her lover and invite him for that night. Then you came and accidentally picked up his reply in her scarf. Your unexpected arrival wrecked my plans. No sooner had you left than all her torment returned. She swore she would not be unfaithful to you. She was so full of passion, so completely beside herself, that she aroused my heartfelt pity. I finally promised her that

I would pacify Norberg that night and try to get him to leave on some pretext or other. I urged her to go to bed, but she seemed not to trust me. She remained fully dressed, but finally fell asleep in her clothes, overwrought and drained by tears as she was.

"Norberg came. I tried to ward him off, presenting to him in darkest colors her anguish of conscience and remorse. He asked only to see her, and I went into her room to prepare her for this. But he followed me in and we both approached her bed at the same moment. She awoke, jumped up angrily and tore herself away from us, imploring, beseeching, threatening and finally declaring she would not give way. She was unwise enough to let drop a few hints as to where her real affections lay, which poor Norberg interpreted in a spiritual sense. At length he left her, and she locked herself in. I kept him for a long time, talking to him about the condition she was in, telling him she was pregnant and should therefore be treated with consideration. He was so proud at the thought of becoming a father, so looking forward to having a son, that he agreed to everything she demanded of him, promising to go away for a while rather than cause her anxiety and harm. With such thoughts in his mind he crept off in the early morning, and you, sir, standing sentry as you were, would have needed only to look into your rival's heart, which you thought was so privileged and happy, for your own assurance, though his appearing at that moment had persuaded you to despair."

"Are you telling the truth?" Wilhelm asked. "Truth, such as I hope will cause you once more to despair," she replied.

"You would certainly be driven to despair if I could describe to you in true colors the morning that followed. How happy she was when she woke up! Her voice was so cheerful when she called me in, she thanked me eagerly, pressing me affectionately to her bosom. 'Now,' she said, looking at herself smilingly in the mirror, 'now I can be pleased with myself and my appearance, now that I belong to myself and my beloved friend once again. How sweet it is to have overcome! What a glorious feeling it is to follow one's own heart! How thankful I am to you for taking my part and using your shrewdness and wits to my advantage! Help me to attain my greatest happiness.'

"I went along with what she was saying, not wishing to upset her. I encouraged her in her expectations, and she caressed me fondly. When she left the window for a moment I had to stand guard, for sometime you were bound to walk past and we were anxious at least to see you. And so the whole day passed, and we were restless. We were sure you would come that night at the usual hour. I was watching on the stairway, time hung heavy on me, and so I went back up to her room. To my surprise I found her in her officer's costume, looking charming and radiant. 'Don't I deserve to appear in men's clothing today? Haven't I been bold? I want my lover to see me as he did that first evening, and I will hug him as warmly and with even more abandon than I did then. For now I am much more his than I was when I had not yet broken loose in a noble decision. But,' she added somewhat pensively, 'I have not yet completely won out. I must still take the great risk of telling him everything about my situation, in order to be worthy and certain of him—then it will be up to him whether he keeps me or rejects me. This is a scene which I am arranging for us both; and if he finds himself able in his heart to reject me, then I will once more belong only to myself, find consolation in that punishment, and bear whatever fate has in store for me.'

"It was with such feelings and hopes, sir, that the lovely girl waited for you; but you never came. How shall I describe that state of waiting and hoping? I can still see her, speaking in such passionate, loving terms of the man whose cruelty she was still to experience!"

"Dear, old Barbara," Wilhelm cried, jumping up and grabbing her by the hand. "That's enough pretense and preparation. Your calm sober tone has given you away. Mariane is still alive, living somewhere in the neighborhood. Give her back to me. It was not by chance that you chose this late, lonely hour to visit me, and prepared me by recounting that excellent tale. Where have you hidden her? I'll believe everything you say, I give you my word on that, when you show me where she is and restore her to my arms. I saw her shadow passing over us. Let me now clasp her firmly in my arms. Then I will kneel before her, asking for forgiveness, congratulating her on her success in her battle with herself and you—and then I will bring my Felix to her. Tell me: Where have you hidden her? Don't leave me any longer in this state of uncertainty! You've achieved your purpose. Now, where is she? Let's use this light to find out, to see her lovely face once more!"

He dragged the old woman up from the chair; she looked blankly into his face, tears streamed from her eyes and she was seized by a sudden access of grief. "What unfortunate confusion is it that gives you any such hope? I have indeed hidden her—beneath the earth, and neither the open light of the sun nor the intimate gleam of a candle will ever shine upon her sweet face. Take little Felix to her grave, and tell him that there lies his mother whom his father unjustly condemned. Her loving heart no longer throbs impatiently to see you. She is not waiting in some nearby room for me to finish my story. The dark chamber has received her where no bridegroom may follow, from where no one can walk toward his beloved."

She threw herself down beside a chair and wept bitterly. For the first time Wilhelm was completely convinced that Mariane was dead, and he was overcome with grief. Barbara rose to her feet, declared that she had nothing more to say to him, and threw a wallet on to the table. "These letters," she said, "will make you ashamed that you were so cruel. Read them through with dry eyes, if you can." She crept quietly away, and Wilhelm did not have the heart that night to open the wallet, which was the same one as he had given Mariane, for he knew that in it she had carefully kept all the messages he sent her. Next morning he felt able to take this upon himself, he opened the seal, and little pencilled notes in his own hand fell out, reminding him of every occasion from the first day of their relationship to that last ghastly moment of parting. In bitter distress he read through a whole series of notes she had written to him which, he could see from their content, had been returned by Werner.

"None of my letters has got through to you, none of my pleas and appeals has reached you. Was it you yourself who gave those cruel orders? Am I really never to see you again? I will try once more; I implore you to come! I shall not insist on keeping you here, but if only I could press you one more time to my heart."

"When I was sitting beside you, holding your hands, gazing up into your eyes, and from the depths of my heart would say, lovingly and trustingly: 'you dear, good man,' you used to like to hear that, and I had to say it over and over again. So now I say once more: 'dear, dear, good man,' be as good as you were, come, and don't let me perish in misery."

"You think I'm to blame, and I am, but not in the way you think. Come, so that I may have the consolation of your knowing all about me, no matter what may happen to me afterwards."

"It is not for my sake alone, but also for yours that I am asking you to come to me. I can feel your unbearable suffering in fleeing me. Please come, so that our parting may be less cruel! Never perhaps was I more worthy of you than when you thrust me into utter misery!"

"I implore you by all that is sacred, by everything that can move a human heart, to consider that a soul is at stake, a life, two lives, one of which must always remain dear to you. Your mistrustful nature will not believe this, but I will maintain it even in the hour of my death: the child that I carry is yours. Since I fell in love with you, nobody else has even clasped my hands. If only your love and your goodness had been the companions of my youth!"

"You will not listen to me? Then I must keep silent, but these letters will not disappear. Perhaps they will speak to you when my lips are covered by a shroud, and the sound of your regrets shall no longer reach my ear. My only comfort throughout the whole sad course of my life shall be to know that I was not guilty, though I cannot call myself innocent."

Wilhelm could not read any further. He gave way entirely to grief, but was even more oppressed when Laertes came in and he tried to conceal his feelings from him. Laertes pulled out a purse full of ducats, counted them and firmly declared there was nothing more splendid than being about to be rich, for then nothing can disturb or impede us. Wilhelm remembered his dream, and smiled; but at the same time he recalled with a shock that in that same dream Mariane had left him and followed his dead father, and that both of them had floated over the garden like spirits.

Laertes distracted him from his reverie by taking him to a coffeehouse, where he found himself surrounded by several persons who had enjoyed seeing him on the stage, and were glad to see him again; but they regretted that, as they had heard, he was intending to give up acting. They spoke so perceptively and positively about him and his acting, the quality of his talent, and their hopes for him—so much so that Wilhelm finally exclaimed: "If only you had shown such appreciation several months ago! How I would have valued that! How encouraging that would have been! I would then never have so totally turned away from the theater in my mind, and no longer despaired of my public."

"You should never have felt like that about your audience," said an elderly man in the group. "The public is large, and keen understanding and sincere appreciation are not as rare as you think. But no artist should demand unlimited approbation of what he does; for unlimited approval is not worth much, though you gentlemen of the stage do not care for limited approval. I know full well that, in life as in art, we must seek our own opinion before doing or producing something, and only after we have done or produced it, should we pay attention to the opinions of others; and, once one has had some experience in this, one will know how to deduce a total judgment from a variety of opinions, for those persons whose opinion could spare us this labor, usually keep silent."

"But they shouldn't," said Wilhelm. "I have often heard that persons who themselves express no opinion on even good plays, complain when no opinions are expressed."

"Well, let's be vocal today, anyhow," said one young man. "You must dine with us, and then we will be able to catch up on what we should have said to you, and sometimes to dear Aurelie."

Wilhelm declined the invitation and went to visit Madame Melina. He wanted to talk to her about the children, since he was intending to take them away from her.

The secret that Barbara had entrusted to him he was not well able to keep to himself. Every time he looked at Felix he gave himself away. "Oh, my child, my dear child," he cried, picking him up and pressing him to his chest. "What did you bring me, father?" the child asked. Mignon looked at both of them, as if to warn them not to give themselves away. "What's all this about?" said Madame Melina. The children were taken aside, and Wilhelm, feeling he did not have to maintain secrecy on what the old woman had told him, revealed the whole story to Madame Melina. She looked at him with a smile. "O, men are such credulous creatures! It's easy to sell them a bill of goods if their thoughts were tending in that direction anyway; and there are times when they blindly assert the value of what they previously had termed a passing infatuation." But she could not suppress a sigh, and if Wilhelm had not been completely blind, he would have noticed that her behavior revealed a fondness for him that she had never entirely overcome.

He then spoke to her about the children, telling her that he was intending himself to keep Felix, but send Mignon to the country. Although Madame Melina was unwilling to be parted from both children at once, she thought his proposal was a good one, indeed a necessary one. Felix was becoming rather wild, and Mignon seemed to need fresh air and a different environment, for the poor child was sickly, and was not getting any better.

"Make no mistake about it," said Madame Melina. "I was not being frivolous when I expressed some doubts whether the boy is really yours. That old woman is not all that much to be trusted; and yet someone who can use untruth to her advantage, can also speak the truth if that seems useful to her. She pretended to Aurelie that Felix was the son of Lothario, and we women have this peculiarity that we love the children of our lovers, even if we do not know, or profoundly hate, their mothers." Felix came running into the room, and she clasped him to her breast with affection unusual in her.

Wilhelm went straight home and asked Barbara to come to see him, which she agreed to do but not before dusk. He received her angrily, and said: "There is nothing more disgraceful than depending on lies and idle fictions. You've already done enough harm with such things, and now, when what you have said may determine my whole life's happiness, I'm full of doubts and don't dare to embrace this child, whose undisturbed possession could make me blissfully happy. The very sight of you fills me with hatred and contempt."

"If I'm to be honest, I must say that your behavior seems to me insufferable," she replied to this outburst. "And even if this were not your own son, it is such a beautiful, such a delightful child, that anyone would buy it for any price, just to have it around. Doesn't he deserve your taking charge of him? Don't I deserve for all the pain and trouble I have taken on this child's account, don't I deserve some little support for the rest of my life? Oh you fine gentlemen, you who have everything, you do well to talk about truth and honesty; but there would be much to say on how a poor creature whose meager needs were never answered, who in all her troubles was entirely without friends, help or advice and had to make her way amidst selfish people and finally succumb—there would be much to say about that, if you would only listen. Have you read Mariane's letters? She wrote them at the time of her greatest unhappiness. In vain did I try to reach you and give you those letters, but your brutal brother-in-law had so hedged you around that all my guile and skill did not suffice, and when at length he threatened me and Mariane with imprisonment, I had to abandon all hope. Doesn't everything in those letters confirm what I have told you? Doesn't Norberg's own letter remove all your doubts?"

"What letter from Norberg?" Wilhelm asked.

"Didn't you find it in the wallet?" she replied.

"I haven't yet read all it contains."

"Then hand me the wallet! Here, this is the document I mean. It was Norberg's unfortunate letter that caused the confusion, but this other one will clear things up, if indeed there is anything to clear up." She took a sheet of paper out of the wallet, Wilhelm recognized the hateful hand, pulled himself together, and read these words: "Tell me, girl, how can you treat me like this? I would not have believed that a goddess could change me into a sighing swain. Instead of greeting me with open arms, you draw back as though in distaste. Is it right that I should spend the night sitting on a trunk with old Barbara in her room, with my beloved girl behind two closed doors? That is absolutely absurd. I promised to allow you some time for reflection and not to rush you, but I am maddened by every hour we lose. Haven't I done all I could to give you all the presents I could think of? If you still doubt my love, what else would you like to have? Just tell me, and you shall have it. I wish that priest who put such stuff in your head would go deaf and blind! Why did you have to land one like him; there are plenty of others more indulgent toward young people. All I can say is that things must change. I shall expect an answer these next few days, for I have to go away again soon, and if you are not kind and friendly again, then I will not come to see you anymore. . . ."

The letter went on at length in this fashion, always returning to the same point (to Wilhelm's painful satisfaction), and thereby vouching for the truth of Barbara's account. Another letter proved quite clearly that Mariane had not yielded, and several others sadly revealed to Wilhelm the whole story of this unfortunate girl right up to the time of her death.

Barbara had succeeded in calming the vulgar fellow down by degrees. She told him when Mariane died, leaving him to believe that Felix was his son. He sent her money from time to time, but she kept this for herself, having talked Aurelie into taking over the responsibility for Felix's upbringing. Unfortunately this secret source of funds soon dried up. Norberg had gone through most of his fortune in riotous living, and constant love affairs hardened his heart against the child he imagined to be his firstborn son.

Probable as this all sounded, and admirably as it all fitted together, Wilhelm could still not confidently give way to joy; he seemed to be afraid of a gift bestowed on him by some evil fate.

The old woman sensed his state of mind and said: "Only time will heal your uncertainty. Regard the child as not your own, pay careful attention to it, observe his talents, personality and abilities, and if you don't gradually come to see yourself in him, then you must have bad eyesight. For I can assure you that if I were a man, nobody would plant a child on me, but it is fortunate for us women that in such matters men are not as clear-sighted as we are."

After this Wilhelm came to an agreement with Barbara that he should take Felix with him and she would take Mignon to Therese. He would give Barbara a small allowance to spend however she wished.

He then summoned Mignon, to prepare her for the change. "Master!" she said. "Keep me with you, it will do me both good and ill." He explained to her that she was now fully grown and something should be done for her further education. "I am educated enough to love and to sorrow," she replied. He said she should pay attention to her health, that she needed constant care and the services of a competent doctor. "Why should they care for me, when there are so many to care for," she answered.

Having tried very hard to persuade her that he could not take her with him, he told her that he would take her to the house of friends, where he would often come to see her. But she seemed not to have heard anything he said. "You don't want me with you?" she asked. "Then perhaps it would be better to send me to the old Harper. The poor old man is so much alone." Wilhelm tried to assure her that the Harper was well taken care of. "I long for him every hour of the day," she said. "I did not notice that you were so attached to him while he was still living with us," said Wilhelm. "I was afraid of him when he was awake, I could not bear to look into his eyes," she said, "but when he was asleep, I would sit by his bedside, warding off the flies, and could never see enough of him. He gave me support in moments of terror. No one will ever know how much I owe him. If I had only known the way, I would have run to him before now."

Wilhelm gave her an account of the situation, and told her she was such a reasonable child, that this time too she should follow his wishes. "Reason is cruel," she said, "the heart is better. I will go wherever you wish, but let me have your Felix."

After much talk to and fro she stuck to her position, and so Wilhelm had to resign himself ultimately to entrusting both children to Barbara, who would take them to Therese. This was all the easier for him, because he was still afraid of acknowledging the handsome Felix as his son. He picked him up and carried him around. Felix liked to be lifted up to a mirror, and Wilhelm, without admitting it, searched out resemblances to himself. When these seemed apparent he would press the child to his bosom, but then, suddenly frightened by the thought that he might be deceiving himself, he would set the child down and let it run off. "Oh," he would cry, "if I were to claim this precious creature as my own and then it was taken away from me, I would be the unhappiest man on earth!"

The children left, and Wilhelm now decided to take his formal departure from the theater, feeling that he was already divorced from it, and only needed to make the break final. Mariane was no more, his two guardian spirits had left, and he followed them eagerly in his thoughts. The handsome boy was constantly in his mind's eyes, a vague vision of beauty, and he pictured him walking hand in hand with Therese through the fields and woods, growing up in the open air and alongside this open-minded, serene companion. Therese herself seemed to him even more estimable when he thought of Felix in her company. He thought about her, with a smile, when he was in the audience at the theater, for like her he found that these performances hardly created any illusion for him.

Serlo and Melina were very polite as soon as they found out that he made no further claims to his previous position. Some members of the public wanted to see him appear again on stage, and, of the actors, no one more than Madame Melina.

It was with some feeling that he took his leave of her, saying: "If only people would not venture promises for the future! One is unable to keep the smallest of them, let alone realize those ambitions which are substantial. How ashamed I am when I remember what I promised you all on that unfortunate night when we were huddled together—despoiled, sick, injured and wounded—in that wretched inn. Misfortune had bolstered up my courage, and what value I placed on my own good intentions! But nothing has come of all that, absolutely nothing! I leave as your debtor, and I am lucky that no one respects my promise for more than it was worth, and no one has ever pressed me to make it good."

"Don't be unjust toward yourself," Madame Melina replied. "If no one else recognizes what you have done for us, I at least will acknowledge it. Our whole situation would have been totally different if we had not had you with us. Our intentions, like our desires, look quite different when they are accomplished and fulfilled, and we think we have not done or achieved anything."

"You will not calm my conscience by your friendly interpretation," Wilhelm replied. "And I will always think of myself as your debtor."

"It is quite possible that you are that, but not in the way that you think," she said. "We think it scandalous not to fulfill a promise given by word of mouth. But, my friend, a good person always makes too many promises, just by being himself! The confidence that he inspires, the affection he awakens, the hopes he arouses, are limitless; he will always remain a debtor, without being aware of that. Farewell. Our external conditions have turned out well under your guidance, but with you leaving, a gap will open up in my heart that will not be so easily filled."

Before he left, Wilhelm wrote a long letter to Werner. They had exchanged a few letters, but because they could never agree on anything, they had stopped writing to each other. Now that Wilhelm was about to do what the other had so ardently advocated, contact was possible again. He was in a position to say: I am leaving the theater and I am associating myself with men whose company is bound to lead me into a life of firm, honest activity. He inquired after his money and was surprised at himself for not having done so earlier. He did not know that people much concerned with their own inner life are apt to neglect external circumstances. This was the state in which he found himself: he seemed, for the first time now, to be aware that he needed external means to promote effective activity. He ventured forth in quite a different frame of mind than on his first journey. The prospects before him were appealing, and he hoped to achieve happiness along the way.

Chapter Nine

When Wilhelm arrived back at Lothario's estate, he found that much had changed. Jarno greeted him with the news that Lothario's uncle had died, and Lothario had gone to take possession of the estates willed to him. "You've come just at the right time," he said, "to help me and the Abbé. Lothario has entrusted us with important business regarding the purchase of estates in the neighborhood, a matter that has been brewing for quite a time—and now we have the requisite funds and credit. The only matter of concern is that another business house, not in this area, has designs on these estates also. But we have finally decided to go partners with them, otherwise each of us would have driven up the price unreasonably and unnecessarily. We seem to be dealing with a shrewd businessman. So we are working out calculations and proposals, and we must consider from a farming point of view how best to divide up the land so that each receives a good piece of property." The documents were produced, and the fields, pasturelands and buildings were carefully surveyed; but Wilhelm expressed the desire that Therese should also be consulted. They spent several days on all this, and Wilhelm had little time at first to tell his friends about his adventures—nor to inform them of his doubtful paternity which, though important to him, was treated lightly and received indifferently by them.

He had noticed that when the others were engaged in private conversation, at table or on walks, they would sometimes stop short and change the subject, thereby revealing that they had secrets amongst themselves. He remembered what Lydie had said, and gave it ever more credence because the whole side of the castle in front of him remained always inaccessible. Up till now he had sought in vain to find a passage and entry to certain galleries and above all to the ancient tower.

One evening Jarno said to him: "We can now justly consider you as one of us, and therefore it would be unreasonable not to introduce you further into our mysteries. When a man makes his first entry into the world, it is good that he have a high opinion of himself, believes he can acquire many excellent qualities, and therefore endeavors to do everything; but when his development has reached a certain stage, it is advantageous for him to lose himself in a larger whole, learn to live for others, and forget himself in dutiful activity for others. Only then will he come to know himself, for activity makes us compare ourselves with others. You will soon come to know the small world that exists right here, and how well known you are in it. Be dressed and ready tomorrow morning before sunrise."

Jarno came at the appointed hour and conducted him through familiar and unfamiliar rooms in the castle, then through several galleries, until finally they arrived before a huge old door strengthened with iron bands. Jarno knocked and the door opened just wide enough for a man to slip through.

Jarno pushed him through, but did not follow behind. Wilhelm found him-self in a narrow dark space, everything was darkness around him and when he tried to take a step forward he stumbled. A voice, not entirely unfamiliar, called out to him: "Enter!" He then realized that the walls were covered with tapestries through which shone a dim light. "Enter!" it said once more. He lifted the tapestry and went in.

The hall in which he now found himself seemed at one time to have been a chapel. Instead of an altar there stood, at the top of some steps, a large table covered with a green cloth, and over it a drawn curtain which seemed to cover some painting or other. Off to the sides were some finely wrought cupboards, with wire grilles as in libraries, behind which were, instead of books, a large number of scrolls side by side. There was nobody else in the room. The light of the rising sun shone through the stained-glass windows directly into his face, and welcomed him.

"Be seated!" said a voice which appeared to come from the altar. Wilhelm sat down on a small armchair standing against the partition by the entrance. There was no other seat in the room, so he had to make do with this one, de-spite the fact that the morning sun was blinding him. But the chair was good and steady, so he could shield his eyes with his hand.

Then there was a slight sound and the curtain above the altar opened show-ing an empty dark space inside a frame. A man in ordinary clothes stepped forward and greeted him, saying: "Don't you recognize me? Don't you, amongst all the other things you would like to know, wish to find out where your grandfather's collection of works of art now is? Don't you remember the painting that especially appealed to you? Where do you think the sick prince is languishing at the moment?" Wilhelm had no difficulty in recognizing the stranger who on that momentous night had talked with him in the hostelry. "And perhaps this time," the man continued, "we could come to some agree-ment on fate and character."

Wilhelm was about to say something in reply, when the curtains quickly closed. "How strange!" he said to himself. "Can there be some pattern in chance events? Is what we call 'fate,' really only chance? Where can my grand-father's collection be; and why am I reminded of it in this solemn hour?"

He had no time for further reflection, because the curtain opened again, and there before his eyes stood a man whom he immediately recognized as the country priest of the boat trip with his jolly companions. He looked like the Abbé, but did not seem to be him. The man spoke with dignity and with a certain radiance on his face. This is what he said: "The duty of a teacher is not to preserve man from error, but to guide him in error, in fact to let him drink it in, in full draughts. That is the wisdom of teachers. For the man who only sips at error, can make do with it for quite a time, delighting in it as a rare pleasure. But a man who drinks it to the dregs, must recognize the error of his ways, unless he is mad." The curtain closed again, and this time Wilhelm did have time to reflect. "What error can the man be referring to," he asked himself, "except that which has dogged me all my life: seeking cultivation where none was to be found, imaging I could acquire a talent to which I had no propensity."

The curtain opened more quickly this time and an officer stepped out, saying in passing: "Learn to become acquainted with persons one can trust!" The curtain closed; and Wilhelm needed little time to recognize this officer as the one who had embraced him in the park of the count's castle, the man who was responsible for his thinking that Jarno was a recruiting officer. How he got here and who he was, were a complete mystery to Wilhelm. "If so many people have been taking an interest in you, knew what your life was and what was to be done about it, why didn't they guide you more firmly, more seriously?" he said to himself. "Why did they encourage your pastimes instead of deflecting you from them?"

"Do not remonstrate with us!" a voice declared. "You are saved, and on the way to your goal. You will not regret any of your follies, and not wish to repeat any of them. No man could have a happier fate." The curtain opened again, and there stood the old King of Denmark in full armor. "I am your father's ghost," said the figure in the frame, "and I depart in peace, for all I wished for you has been fulfilled more than I myself could imagine. Steep slopes can only be scaled by bypaths; on the plains, straight paths lead from one place to another. Farewell, and remember me when you partake of what I have prepared for you." Wilhelm was dumbfounded: he thought he heard his father's voice, and yet not; so confused was he by present reality and past memories.

He had not been musing long when in came the Abbé and stationed himself behind the green table. "Step forward!" he said to his astonished friend. Wilhelm stepped forward and mounted the steps. On the cloth covering the table lay a small scroll. "These are your Articles," said the Abbé. "Cherish them well, their content is important." Wilhelm took the scroll, opened it and read:

CERTIFICATE OF APPRENTICESHIP

Art is long, life is short, judgment difficult, opportunities fleeting. Action is easy, thinking is hard: acting after thinking, uncomfortable. Every beginning is joyous, every threshold a point of expectation. The boy stares in wonder, impressions condition him, he learns in playing, seriousness takes him by surprise. Imitation is natural to us all, but what to imitate is not easily ascertained. Rarely is the best discerned, still more rarely appreciated. Height attracts us, not the steps upwards; with the mountaintop in our eyes we linger lovingly on the plain. Only a part of art can be taught, an artist needs the whole. Those who know only half of it, are always confused and talk a lot; those who have the whole, act and talk little, or long afterwards. The former have no secrets and no strength, their teaching is like freshly baked bread, tasty and satisfying for one day; but flour cannot be sown and the fruits of the grain should not be ground. Words are good, but they are not the best. The best is not made clear by words. The spirit in which we act, is what is highest. Action can only be grasped by spirit and portrayed by spirit. No one knows what he is doing when he acts rightly, but we are always conscious of what is wrong. He who works only with signs, is a pedant, a hypocrite or a botcher. There are many such, and they get on well together. Their gossiping impedes the student, and their persistent mediocrity alarms those who are best. The teaching of a real artist opens up sense; for where words are lacking, action speaks. A true pupil learns how to unravel the unknown from the known, and thereby develops toward mastery.

"That's enough!" said the Abbé. "Save the rest for some other time. Now look around in these cupboards."

Wilhelm walked up to them and looked at the names on the scrolls. To his amazement he found there Lothario's apprenticeship, Jarno's apprenticeship, and his own, in amongst many others with names unknown to him.

"May I hope some time to take a look at these scrolls?"

"Nothing is closed to you in this room anymore."

"May I ask one question?"

"Of course you may! And you can expect a decisive answer if it concerns a matter that is close to your heart and should be so."

"Very well, then! You strange wise men, whose sight can pierce so many mysteries, tell me if you will: is Felix really my son?"

"Praise be to you for asking that question!" exclaimed the Abbé, clapping his hands with joy. "Felix is your son! I swear it by all our most sacred mysteries. Felix is your son, and in spirit his deceased mother was not unworthy of you. Take unto yourself this lovely child from our hands, turn around, and dare to be happy."

Wilhelm heard a noise behind him, turned round, and saw the face of a child peering mischievously through the tapestries covering the entrance: it was Felix. The boy hid himself laughingly, once he was seen. "Come out!" said the Abbé. He came, his father rushed toward him, folded him in his arms and pressed him to his heart. "Yes, oh yes," said Wilhelm, "you are indeed mine! What a gift this is from Heaven that I have to thank my friends for! Where have you come from at this moment, my child?"

"Don't ask," said the Abbé. "Hail to you, young man. Your apprenticeship is completed, Nature has given you your freedom."

BOOK EIGHT

Chapter One

Felix ran out into the garden, and Wilhelm followed him in a state of ex-hilaration. It was the most beautiful morning, everything around him looked lovelier than ever, he was sublimely happy. Felix was a newcomer in this world of freedom and beauty, and his father was not much better acquainted with the things that the boy repeatedly and tirelessly asked about. They finally went up to the gardener, who could tell him names and uses of various plants. Wilhelm was observing nature through a new organ, and the child's curiosity and desire to learn made him aware how feeble his interest had been in the things outside himself and how little he knew, how few things he was familiar with. On this day, the happiest of his entire life, his own education seemed also to be beginning anew: he felt the need to inform himself, while being required to inform another.

Jarno and the Abbé had not reappeared, but in the evening they came with a visitor. Wilhelm was so astonished he could not believe his eyes. Werner hesitated a moment before recognizing him. They embraced each other affec-tionately, and neither could conceal the fact that he found the other changed. Werner thought that his friend was taller, stronger, more upright, more cul-tivated in manner and more pleasant in behavior. "I miss something of your earlier spontaneity, however," he added. "That will come back once we have re-covered from our initial amazement at seeing each other again," said Wilhelm.

The impression that Werner made on him was by no means so favor-able. The good fellow seemed to have regressed rather than advanced. He was much thinner, his pointed face seemed sharper and his nose longer, he was bald, his voice was loud and strident and his flat chest, dropping shoulders and pallid cheeks showed quite clearly that this was a sickly creature with a mania for work.

Wilhelm did not go out of his way to comment on this change, but Werner gave full vent to his delight in his friend. "My goodness!" he exclaimed, "you may have spent your time poorly and, as I suspect, made little profit, but you have become a man of parts who will, in fact is bound to, make his own for-tune. Don't squander or dissipate it this time; with your figure you should be able to get yourself a rich heiress." "You haven't changed a bit," said Wilhelm with a smile. "You've just seen your friend again after a long interval, and you are already treating him as a commodity, a source of speculation, from which profit may be gained."

Jarno and the Abbé seemed in no way surprised by this recognition scene, and left the two friends to expatiate at will on both past and present. Werner looked at Wilhelm from all sides, twisting and turning him to the point of making him embarrassed. "I've never seen anything like this," said Werner, "and yet I know I am not deceiving myself. Your eyes are more deep set, your forehead is broader, your nose is more delicate and your mouth is much more pleasant. Look at how you stand! How well everything fits together! Indolence makes one prosper, whereas I, poor wretch," he said, looking at himself in the mirror, "if I had not spent my time earning a mint of money, there wouldn't be anything to say for me."

Werner had never received Wilhelm's last letter. It was his firm with which Lothario intended to accomplish the joint purchase of the estates; and this was the occasion of Werner's visit. He had no idea that he would find Wilhelm there. The magistrate came, the papers were produced, and Werner found the conditions reasonable. "If you, as it seems, are well disposed towards this young man," he said, "see to it that our part of this is not reduced. It depends on my friend whether he wants to acquire the estate and expend part of his funds on it." Jarno and the Abbé assured him that they did not need to be reminded of that. They quickly settled their business and then Werner wanted to play a game of cards, in which the Abbé and Jarno joined him, for he was by now accustomed to spending every evening in this way.

When dinner was over and the two friends were alone together, they spent their time in eager questionings and discussion, each informing the other what he wished him to know. Wilhelm was full of praise for his present situation and his good fortune at being received into the company of such excellent persons. Werner, however, shook his head and said: "One should only believe what one sees with one's own eyes. Some of my most obliging friends have told me that you are consorting with a loose-living young nobleman, provide him with actresses, help him squander his money, and are responsible for his being on such bad terms with all his relatives." "I would be very distressed, both on my own account and on that of those good people, if actors were so misjudged," Wilhelm replied. "But my theatrical career has accustomed me to all kinds of slanderous defamation. How is it possible for people to judge our actions, when all they see is bits and pieces, a small part of something that contains both good and bad, and in its appearances is neither one nor the other. Put actors and actresses before them on an elevated platform, light the lamps, the whole thing is over and done with in an hour or so, and nobody really knows what to make of it."

He then asked about the family, his old friends, and his home town. Werner told him very quickly all that had changed, what was still there, and what was happening. "The women in the house are happy and content, for there is no lack of money. They spend half their time preening themselves, and the other half displaying themselves. They devote a reasonable amount of time to household affairs. My children are growing into sensible boys. I can already envision them sitting and writing, doing accounts, running errands, bargaining and selling things off. I want them all to have their own business as soon as possible. As for our capital, you will be delightfully surprised. As soon as we have settled about these estates, you must come back with me, for it seems as if you, by exercising some degree of reason, could take an active part in our affairs. Your new friends are to be complimented for putting you on the right path. I'm a silly fool to find out only now how fond I am of you, and I'm unable to take my eyes off you when you look so fine and well. Your appearance is quite different from the picture you once sent your sister, which caused quite a furor in the house. Mother and daughter thought the young man was charming, with his open-neck shirt, chest half bared, big ruff, loose hanging hair, round hat, short vest and baggy trousers—but I thought that outfit was pretty close to a clown's. But now you look like a man, except that I urge you to have your hair done in a pigtail, else you will be taken, with that loose hairstyle, for a Jew, and have to pay tolls."

Felix had come into the room while they were talking, and since no one was taking any notice of him, he had sat down on the sofa and fallen asleep. "Who's that brat?" Werner asked. For the moment Wilhelm did not have the courage to tell him the truth, nor the inclination to relate the whole story to someone who was by nature disinclined to believe him.

They then went off to inspect the estates and conclude their business. Wilhelm kept Felix close by him and, for his sake, took great pleasure in the property they were looking at. The child's eagerness for cherries and berries that would soon be ripe, reminded him of his own youth and his father's dutiful way of preparing, creating and preserving pleasures. He examined the plantings and buildings with great attention, actively considering how to restore and rebuild. He surveyed the world around him, but not like a bird of passage; a building was for him no longer a rapidly assembled shelter that would wither away before one left. Everything he planned was now to mature for the boy, and everything he built was to last for several generations. His apprenticeship was therefore completed in one sense, for along with the feeling of a father he had acquired the virtues of a solid citizen. His joy knew no bounds. "All moralizing is unnecessarily strict," he exclaimed. "Nature turns us, in her own pleasant way, into what we should be. Strange indeed are those demands of middle-class society that confuse and mislead us, finally demanding more from us than Nature herself. I deplore all attempts at developing us which obliterate the most effective means of education by forcing us towards the endpoint instead of giving us a sense of satisfaction along the way."

Much as he had seen in his life already, he now understood human nature through the eyes of the child. The theater, like the world as a whole, had appeared to him like a throw of dice, each of which counted for more on one face and less on the other, and only added up to a whole when they were counted together. But here in the child was, so to speak, one single die, on whose various faces the worth and worthlessness of human nature were clearly marked.

The child's demand for distinctions grew daily: once he had learnt that things have names, he wanted to hear them all. He believed his father must know everything, pestered him constantly with questions, and gave him cause to inquire after objects that he had never paid much attention to. A native impulse to find out the origin and end of everything soon became apparent. When he inquired where wind came from and where flames went to, his father became all too aware of his own limitations. He wondered how far human curiosity can extend and how much he could hope to satisfy it. The child's anger when it saw a living creature maltreated, pleased his father, who saw in it the sign of superior character. Felix set about the kitchenmaid when she was cutting up pigeons. However, this admirable disposition of his was counteracted by his merciless destruction of frogs and butterflies, and Wilhelm was reminded that there are many people who appear quite righteous when their passions are not aroused or when they are observing the actions of others.

The pleasant feeling that the boy was having a really good influence on his life was dispelled in a trice when he realized that the boy was educating him more than he the boy. He had nothing to object to in the boy, he was not capable of giving him a direction that he was not taking of his own accord, and even those bad habits that Aurelie had worked so hard to eradicate seemed to return after her death. He would still not close the door behind him, he still would not finish what was on his plate, and he was never more delighted than when people observed that he ate from the platter rather than his plate, left his glass standing, and drank out of the bottle. He was also quite charming when he sat in the corner with a book, and said, very earnestly: "I must study this learned stuff!" even though he couldn't as yet (and wouldn't) distinguish the letters of the alphabet.

When Wilhelm thought of how little he had done for the child and how little he was able to do for him, he was overcome by a sense of uneasiness, and this well-nigh outweighed his happiness. "Are we born so selfish," he said to himself, "that we are unable to care for someone other than ourselves? Here you are at the same point with this boy as you were with Mignon. You took charge of the poor child, her companionship delighted you, and yet you have cruelly neglected her. What have you done to give her the development she longed for? Nothing! You left her to her own devices, and to all the mischance she was necessarily exposed to in an uncultivated society. And now with this boy, who attracted you even before he was so precious to you—has your heart ever impelled you to do the slightest thing for him? It is high time that you stopped wasting your time and that of others: pull yourself together and just think what you have to do for yourself and for those dear creatures that nature and affection bind so closely to you."

Actually, this soliloquy was just a prelude to his recognition of all that he had been thinking, worrying about, looking for, and finally decided on. He could no longer put off admitting to himself that, after repeated outbursts of sorrow at the loss of Mariane, he must now find a mother for the boy, and he could not find a better one than Therese. He now knew this excellent woman completely, and a wife and companion like her seemed the only possible person to whom he could safely entrust himself and his loved ones. Her noble affection for Lothario did not cause him any qualms, for the two of them were separated forever by a strange train of events. Therese thought of herself as free, and had spoken of marriage with a certain indifference, though also as something that was self-evident.

Having reasoned with himself for some time, he finally decided to tell her as much as he knew about himself. She should get to know him as well as he knew her, and he began to work over his own life story; but it seemed so totally lacking in events of any significance, and anything he would have to report was so little to his advantage that more than once he was tempted to give up the whole idea. Finally he decided to ask Jarno for the scroll of his apprenticeship from the tower, and Jarno said this was just the right time. So Wilhelm got possession of it.

It is a terrifying feeling for any worthy person to find himself in a situation where he is about to be informed about himself. All transitions are crises, and is not crisis a form of sickness? How unwilling we are, after we have been sick, to look at ourselves in a mirror! One feels better, but sees only the evidence of one's illness. Wilhelm was by now sufficiently prepared for the occasion, circumstances had given him the lead, his friends had not been sparing in their opinions, and although he unrolled the parchment with a certain hastiness, he found that he calmed down the more he read in it. The account of his life was related in every detail and with great incisiveness. His attention was not distracted by the report of individual events or momentary emotions, sympathetic comments enlightened him without embarrassing him, and he saw a picture of himself, not like a second self in a mirror, but a different self, one outside of him, as in a painting. One never approves of everything in a portrait, but one is always glad that a thoughtful mind has seen us thus and a superior talent enjoyed portraying us in such a way that a picture survives of what we were, and will survive longer than we will.

As the manuscript recalled every detail of Wilhelm's life, he began to compose in his mind his story for Therese, feeling almost ashamed at having nothing to match her own fine qualities, nothing that testified to any active purpose in his life. Detailed as the survey was in his thoughts, when he came to write it down in a letter, this turned out quite short: he asked for her friendship, if possible for her love, offered her his hand in marriage, and asked for a speedy reply.

After some inner doubt whether to seek the advice of his friends, especially Jarno and the Abbé, on this important matter, he decided not to. His mind

was too firmly made up; the whole matter was too important for him to submit to the judgment of the best or most reasonable person in the world, and
he was judicious enough to see that his letter went out with the very next post.
Perhaps it was the feeling that, as emerged quite clearly from the scroll, there
had been so many occasions in his life when he thought he was acting freely
and unobserved, only to discover that he had indeed been observed, even
directed; perhaps it was this that made him now unburden his heart freely, at
least to Therese's heart, and let his fate depend on her decision alone. And so
he had no qualms of conscience about circumventing his guardians and over-
seers on this important issue.

Chapter Two

He had just dispatched his letter when Lothario returned. Everyone expressed
satisfaction that the important business in hand would soon be concluded,
and Wilhelm awaited with eager anticipation for many different threads to
be severed or joined and his future prospects be decided. Lothario greeted
everyone most cordially. He was by now fully recovered, cheerful, and looking like a man who knows what he has to do, which nothing will prevent him
from doing.

Wilhelm was not able to return his greeting with equal cordiality. "This," he
had to admit to himself, "is the friend, the lover, the bridegroom of Therese,
whom you intend forcibly to replace. Do you really think you can ever erase
or banish the impression he has made on her?" If the letter had not already
been on its way, he would probably never have dared to send it. But fortunately the die was cast, perhaps Therese had already decided, and perhaps only
the distance between them was delaying a happy resolution. It would soon be
decided whether there was to be gain or loss. He tried to find solace in such
thoughts, but his heart was filled with feverish agitation. He had difficulty in
giving much thought to the important business transactions on which to a
certain extent his future prosperity depended. In such emotional moments as
this, nothing else has much importance for any man, neither what is outside
him nor what belongs to him.

It was fortunate for him that Lothario dealt with the matter nobly and
Werner speedily. Werner, in his eagerness to acquire the splendid property,
showed great delight at this gain to himself or rather to his friend Wilhelm,
whereas Lothario for his part seemed to have quite other thoughts. "I cannot
be pleased at acquiring such property unless it be honestly gained," he said. "Is
that not the case here?" asked Werner. "Not exactly," Lothario replied. "Didn't
we give them ready money for it?" "That we did," said Lothario, "and perhaps
you will consider what I must remind you of as being unnecessarily scrupulous. I do not consider any acquisition of property an honest deal unless the

State is accorded that part which is due to it." "What do you mean?" said Werner. "Would you prefer that our freely bought lands were subject to taxation?" "Yes, I would," said Lothario, "up to a certain point. Our land will only be secure if it is treated like everybody else's. What reason should a farmer have in these times to consider his land as a less firmly established possession than that of a nobleman, except that the latter is not encumbered but encumbers him?"

"And what about the return on our capital investment?" said Werner.

"That will not be adversely affected if the State, in return for reasonable and regular tax payments, continues to allow us the feudal hocus-pocus by which we have complete right of disposal over our property, are not obliged to maintain it in such large units, and can divide it up more equally among our children, so that all of them may indulge in free vigorous activity instead of being restricted by hereditary privileges to justify which we have to invoke the spirits of our ancestors. And how much happier would men and women be, if they could have the free opportunity of advancing some worthy young woman or promising young man to a better position in life, without any further considerations. The State would acquire more and better citizens, and not be so often lacking in heads and hands."

"I can assure you," said Werner, "that in all my life I have never thought about the State, and only paid my dues and taxes because that was customary."

"Well," said Lothario, "I hope to be able to make a good patriot out of you. A good father is one who at mealtimes serves his children first; and a good citizen is one who pays what he owes the State before dealing with everything else."

These general reflections facilitated rather than delayed the completion of their business transaction, and when things were pretty well in order, Lothario said to Wilhelm: "I must now send you to a place where you are more urgently needed than here. My sister requests that you come to her as soon as possible. Poor Mignon seems to be wasting away and they think your coming may perhaps check her decline. My sister has sent me this letter from which you will see how important your coming would be to her." Lothario handed him the letter and Wilhelm, who had been listening to him in a state of great perturbation, recognized the countess's handwriting in the hastily written lines, and did not know what answer to give.

"Take Felix with you," Lothario added, "so that the two children may cheer each other up. My sister's carriage, in which my servants came back, is still ready. I'll give you horses to take you halfway; then you can take the posthorses. Goodbye; give my greetings to my sister, and tell her I will be coming to see her soon, and she should be prepared for a number of guests. My great-uncle's friend, the Marchese Cipriani, is on his way here. He was hoping to find the old man still alive so that they could entertain each other with recollections of past experiences and their mutual love of art. The Marchese is much younger than my uncle, to whom he owed the greater part of his education. We must do all we can to try to fill the gap for the Marchese, and that is best done by assembling a fairly large group of people."

Lothario then went to his room, accompanied by the Abbé, Jarno having already left. Wilhelm rushed off to his own room, with no one to confide in, no one to dissuade him from embarking on what he anticipated with such trepidation. The young servant boy came and urged him to start packing, because they wanted to load up the horses that night, so as to be able to start out at dawn. Wilhelm did not know what to do, and finally said to himself: "Just see to it that you get away from this house; then you can decide what to do as you go along. You could stop at the halfway point and send a message back, putting in writing what you did not dare to say, and then just let things take their course." Despite having reached this decision, he spent a sleepless night; but the sight of Felix peacefully asleep encouraged him. "Oh!" he cried. "Who knows what tests still lie in store for me; who knows how much my past mistakes will return to torment me, and my good, sensible plans for the future miscarry! But the treasure I have here, may this never be taken from me, by inexorable, or beseechable, Fate! If this very best part of me were ever to be destroyed, this heart be torn from my heart, then farewell reason and sense, farewell care and caution, farewell every impulse of preservation! Be gone, all that sets us off from the animals! And if I am not permitted to put an end to all my misery, may early madness obliterate my consciousness before death's dark night dissolves it forever!"

He grasped the boy in his arms, kissed him, pressed him to his breast, and covered him with copious tears. The boy woke up. His bright eyes and friendly glance affected his father deeply. "What a scene it will be," he cried, "when I present you to the lovely countess, and she presses you to her bosom, that bosom which your father so deeply wounded! Must I not fear that she will thrust you from herself with a cry, when your touch reawakens her real, or imaginary, pain!"

The coachman did not allow him time for further reflection or choice, constraining him to get into the carriage before daybreak. Wilhelm saw to it that Felix was well wrapped up, for the morning was cold, though bright. The child saw the sun rise for the first time in his life. His astonishment at the first fiery glow, the increasing brightness of the light—his whole joy, and the strange remarks that accompanied this, were a delight to the father, who gazed into the child's heart, a calm, clear lake over which the sun rose and hovered.

The coachman unharnessed the horses in a small town, and rode back. Wilhelm secured a room in the inn, then asked himself whether he should go on, or stay there. Undecided, he took out the letter again, which he had not yet dared to reread, and saw that it contained the following words: "Send your young friend to me very soon. Mignon's condition has taken a turn for the worse these last two days. Sad as the occasion is, I would very much like to meet him."

Wilhelm had not paid attention to those final words when he first looked at the letter. He was frightened by them, and now firmly determined not to go. "Why is it," he cried, "that Lothario, who knows the whole story, did not tell her who I am? She can't be calmly expecting someone she already knows and would rather not see again; she is expecting a stranger—and who should walk in but me! I can see her recoiling, see her blushing. No; I cannot possibly face such a scene!" The horses had just been readied, but Wilhelm was determined to unload and stay where he was. His mind was in a state of complete turmoil. Hearing a girl coming upstairs to tell him all was prepared, he quickly tried to think up a reason that made it necessary to delay his departure. His eyes glanced through the note in his hand. "Heavens! what is this?" he cried. "This is not the countess's handwriting; it is the Amazon's!"

The girl came into the room, urging him to go down, and taking Felix with her. "How is this possible?" he said. "Can this be true? What am I to do? Stay and wait for an explanation, or get there quickly and plunge into whatever ensues? You are on your way to join her; why do you hesitate? This evening you will see her; why voluntarily shut yourself up in here? It is her hand, of course it is; her hand summons you, her carriage is ready to go and take you to her. The mystery is now solved: Lothario has two sisters. He knows about my relationship to one of them, but he does not know how much I owe the other. And she doesn't know that the wounded traveler, who owes his recovery, if not his very life, to her, has been received with such unmerited generosity in the house of her brother."

Felix, rocking to and fro down there in the carriage, called up to him: "Father, come down here and look at these beautiful clouds with their lovely colors!"—"I'm coming," said Wilhelm, racing down the stairway. "And let me tell you that the heavenly phenomena you so much admire, are nothing compared to what awaits me!"

While he was seated in the carriage, he went over everything in his mind. "So this Natalie is the friend of Therese! What a discovery, what hopes, what prospects! How strange that my fear of hearing about the one sister had completely obscured the fact that the other existed!" He looked at Felix, full of joy, hoping that he and the boy would be well received.

Evening drew on, the sun went down, the road was not of the best, and so the coachman drove slowly. Felix fell asleep, and new cares and doubts rose in Wilhelm's mind. "What crazy ideas these are that are occupying your mind," he said to himself. "A dubious resemblance of handwriting removes all your doubts and gives rise to the wildest fancy." He took out the letter again, and in the fading light again thought he recognized the countess's hand. His eyes persisted this time in not finding what his heart had been telling him. "So these horses are dragging you toward the most frightful scene! Who knows whether they will not bring you back here in a few hours! And suppose you find her there alone! Suppose her husband is there, or the baroness? Will she be much changed? Shall I be able to remain upright before her gaze?"

Only a vague hope of seeing the Amazon pierced the gloom of these melancholy reflections from time to time. Night had fallen, the carriage rumbled into a courtyard, and halted. A servingman with a wax candle came out through a splendid portal and down a flight of broad steps to the carriage. "We've been expecting you for quite a while," he said, opening the carriage door. Wilhelm stepped out, holding the sleeping Felix in his arms, and the servant called to another man standing in the doorway with a light, saying, "Take this gentlemen straight to the baroness."

In a flash Wilhelm thought to himself: "What luck! The baroness is here, whether by chance or by design. I shall see her first. Perhaps the countess is already sleeping. Kindly protective spirits, grant that this moment of extreme embarrassment may pass without mishap!"

He went into the house, and found himself in the most solemn and, for him, sacred place he had ever seen. A low-hanging lantern gave light to the stairway opposite him, which was wide and rose gradually until it divided into two arms at a landing. There were marble statues and busts standing on pedestals and in niches. Some of them seemed familiar to him. Youthful impressions never fade away entirely. He recognized a muse which had belonged to his grandfather, not by its shape or quality, but because one arm had been restored along with various sections of the drapery. He felt as though he were in a fantasy world. The child began to weigh heavy on him, so he paused and knelt down on the steps, as if to get a better hold of him, but really just to relax a minute. He had difficulty in getting up again. The servant with the light offered to take the child from him, but he did not want to let go of it. They then went into an anteroom where, to his utter amazement, he saw the picture of the sick prince hanging on the wall. He had no time for more than a fleeting glance at it, because the servingman ushered them through a series of rooms into a small chamber where, beneath a lampshade and partly obscured, a woman sat reading. "If only it were she!" he said to himself in this decisive moment. He put down the child who seemed to be waking up, and was about to move toward the woman, when, as the child sank back into sleep, she stood up and came toward him. It was the Amazon! He could not control himself, fell on his knees, and cried: "It is she!" He clasped her hand and kissed it with rapturous delight. The child lay between them both on the carpet, fast asleep.

They lifted him on to the sofa, Natalie sat down beside him and asked Wilhelm to take a seat on a nearby chair. She offered him some refreshment, which he declined, being far too busy making sure that this was really she, looking closer at her features shaded by the lamp and finally deciding for sure that it was. She spoke to him in general terms about Mignon's illness, telling him that the girl was becoming more and more the prey of strong emotions, and, highly sensitive as always, concealed the fact that she often suffered from violent cramps around the heart, but so dangerously severe that sometimes this prime organ of life stopped beating suddenly when she was unexpectedly excited, and there seemed to be no sign of life in the dear child's body. Once this frightening convulsion had passed, the strength of her nature returned in strong pulse beats which now frightened the child by the intensity of what before had been completely lacking.

Wilhelm remembered one such scene, and Natalie referred him to the doctor, who would explain things further and give the reason why they had summoned the child's friend and protector just now. "You will notice a peculiar change in her; she now wears only women's clothes, which formerly she utterly despised."

"How did you get her to do that?" Wilhelm asked.

"One might say it was pure chance. Let me tell you what happened. You perhaps know that I always have a group of young girls around me with the purpose of encouraging in them, by letting them grow up in close proximity to me, a sense of what is good and right. From me they never hear anything that is not true, but I cannot prevent them—nor would I wish to—from acquiring from others errors and prejudices current in the world at large. If they ask me about these, I try my best to show the difference between such undesirable ideas and what, for me, are correct attitudes, so that these errors, though never useful, may at least not become harmful to them. Recently my girls had been hearing from some peasant children about angels, and about Santa Claus and the Christ Child, who come every now and then to reward good children and punish the naughty ones. The girls suspected that these were real persons dressed up; I encouraged them in this belief and, without offering any explanation, decided to organize such a spectacle on the first appropriate occasion. It so happened that two of them, twin sisters and always well behaved, had a birthday coming; I promised them that an angel would bring the presents they had so well deserved. They looked forward to this with great excitement. I chose Mignon to play the part of the angel, and on the appointed day, she was clothed in a long, thin white garment with a girdle of gold around her chest and a golden crown in her hair. I first thought I would omit the wings, but the women who dressed her insisted on a pair of big golden wings with which she could demonstrate her skill. And so this miraculous vision appeared, a lily in one hand and a little basket in the other, right in the midst of the girls, and surprised me as well. "Here comes the angel!" I said. All the children made as if to withdraw, but then finally shouted: "It's Mignon!" though still not venturing any closer to the wondrous sight.

"'Here are your presents,' she said, handing them the basket. They gathered around her, gazed, touched her, and then one of them asked: 'Are you an angel?' 'I wish I were,' Mignon replied. 'Why are you holding a lily?' 'My heart should be open and pure as a lily, then I would be happy.' 'What are the wings for? Let me see!' 'They stand for lovelier wings which are not yet opened.'

"She continued to give these remarkable answers to their simple questions. When their curiosity was satisfied and the first impressions of her appearance began to fade, they wanted to undress her. But she would not allow this. She took up her zither, climbed up on this high desk, and sang with unbelievable grace and appeal this song:

> So let me seem till I become:
> Take not this garment white from me!
> I hasten from the joys of earth
> Down to that house so fast and firm.
>
> There will I rest in peace a while,
> Till opens wide my freshened glance.
> Then I will cast my dress aside.
> Leaving both wreath and girdle there.
>
> For all those glorious heavenly forms,
> They do not ask for man or wife,
> No garments long or draperies fine
> Surround the body now transformed.
>
> I lived indeed untouched by care.
> And yet I felt deep sorrow there,
> Sorrow has made me old too soon,
> Now make me young for ever more!

"I decided immediately," Natalie went on, "to let her keep the dress, and had others made that were similar. These she is now wearing, and in them, it seems to me, her whole being appears quite different."

Since it was already late, Natalie bade Wilhelm leave, which he did in a state of some anxiety. "Is she married, or not?" he wondered. When he heard a noise he feared that a door might open and a husband come in. The servant who conducted him to his room, left him before he had summoned up the courage to ask about Natalie's circumstances. His uncertainty kept him awake for a time, which he spent comparing the image of the Amazon with his new friend. The two would not coalesce: the former had been fashioned, as it were, by him, the latter seemed almost to be refashioning him.

Chapter Three

The next morning, while everything was still peaceful and quiet, he walked around looking at the house. The building had clean lines and was the finest and noblest he had ever seen. "Good art," he said to himself, "is like good society: it obliges us, in the most pleasing way, to recognize form and limitations like those which govern our being." His grandfather's statues and busts gave him unusual pleasure. He returned eagerly to the picture of the sick prince, still finding it as moving and affecting as ever. The servant opened the doors to several other rooms: there was a library, a collection of natural history specimens, and another of stones and metals. He felt quite strange, standing in front of all these objects. Felix had by now woken up and was following him around. Wilhelm was concerned to know when and how he would receive a reply from Therese. He felt some trepidation at seeing Mignon—also, in a way, at seeing Natalie. How different his present mood was from when he sent the letter to Therese, joyfully entrusting his whole self to such a noble being!

Natalie asked him to come to breakfast. He went into a room where several neatly dressed girls, all apparently less than ten years old, were laying the table while an older person was bringing various beverages.

Wilhelm's attention was drawn to a picture that hung over the sofa. He took it for a portrait of Natalie, but not a very satisfying one. At this point she entered the room, and the resemblance seemed to disappear entirely. However, he noticed that she was wearing the cross of some order, just like the woman in the picture.

"I've been looking at that portrait," he said, "and am amazed that the artist could be so true and so false at the same time. It is a good general likeness of you, a very good one really, but it does not capture either your features or your character."

"What is still more amazing," Natalie replied, "is that it is such a good likeness, for it is not a picture of me, but of an aunt who, even as an old lady, resembled me as a child. It was painted when she was about the age I am now, and most people, when they first see it, think it is a picture of me. I wish you had known this splendid person, for I am indebted to her for so much. Her delicate health, along with perhaps too much concern about herself, and in addition an extreme moral and religious reserve, prevented her from becoming for the world what, in other circumstances, she might well have been. She was a light that shone on just a few friends—and especially brightly on me."

"Can it be possible," said Wilhelm after a moment's reflection on how strangely so many different circumstances seemed to be combining in this moment, "can it be possible, that the noble, beautiful soul whose private confessions I was privileged to read, was your aunt?"

"You have read what she wrote?" asked Natalie.

"Yes, I have!" said Wilhelm. "I did so with sympathetic understanding and it has had a great effect on the course of my life. What emerged for me most clearly was, I would say, the purity of her life and of everything that surrounded her, her independent spirit and her inability to make anything part of herself which did not conform to her noble loving nature."

"You are more liberal and more just toward her fine character than many others who have read her manuscript. Every cultured person knows how hard one has to struggle with a certain degree of coarseness in oneself and others, how costly self-cultivation is, and how often one thinks solely of oneself and forgets what one owes to others. Every good human being reproaches himself occasionally for not having acted gently enough; and yet if such a fine person becomes too gentle, too considerate, too cultivated, if you will, the world shows no tolerance, and no consideration for what such a person is. Persons like her are outside us what ideals are inside us, models not to be imitated, but to be striven after. People laugh at the cleanliness of Dutch women, but would my friend Therese be what she is, if she did not have some such ideal of cleanliness in her mind when she is engaged in domestic activities?"

"So you, Natalie, are the friend of Therese to whom she is so devoted, the precious relative who, as a young girl and since, has always been so affectionate, sympathetic, and helpful! A person like you could only come from such a family, and now that I know your heritage and the whole circle you belong to, I feel immense vistas opening up before me!"

"Indeed," said Natalie, "you could not have been better informed about us all than from my aunt's account. One must admit that her affection for me presumed too much good in me as a child, but when one talks about children, it is one's hopes for them rather than what they actually are which one has in mind."

Wilhelm was now informed about Lothario's origins and early youth. He could picture the charming countess as the child with her aunt's pearls around her neck. And he had been so near these pearls when her delicate, loving lips had pressed themselves on his. He tried to dispel these memories with other thoughts. He ran through all the people he had become acquainted with from the manuscript. "So here I am," he declared, "in the house of that remarkable uncle; yet, it isn't a house, it's a temple, and you are its noble priestess, indeed, its presiding genius. I shall remember all my life the impression I had yesterday evening when I came in here, and there in front of me were those old treasures from my youth—there once more. I remembered the sorrowing statues in Mignon's song; but these objects have no need to sorrow for me, they looked at me in solemn seriousness, linking my earliest memories to this present moment. Here I have rediscovered the family treasures, the joys of my grandfather, set between so many other noble works of art. And I, whom nature made the favorite child of that good old man, I, unworthy as I am, find myself in such worthy company, such a wealth of relationships!"

The young girls had left the room one by one, in order to get on with their various jobs. Now that he was alone with Natalie, Wilhelm had to offer some explanation of what he had just been saying. The discovery that a notable part of these works of art had belonged to his grandfather, put him in a cheerful, sociable mood. The manuscript had made him acquainted with this house, and he now found himself reunited with his own inheritance. He wanted to see Mignon, but Natalie asked him to be patient and wait until the doctor, who had been summoned away to somewhere in the neighborhood, should return. It will come as no surprise that this was the same busy little man whom we already know, the same we met in the *Confessions of a Beautiful Soul*.

"Well, here I am in the midst of your family," said Wilhelm, "and so I suppose that the Abbé who is mentioned in your aunt's narrative, is that strange, mysterious man whom I rediscovered after a train of peculiar circumstances in your brother's house? Perhaps you would give me some more information about him?"

To this Natalie replied: "There would be a great deal to say about him. What I am best informed about, is his influence on our education. He was convinced, at least for a time, that all education should build on inclination. What his present opinion is, I do not know. He used to say that the most important thing is to be active, but one cannot engage in any activity without the necessary predisposition or the instinct impelling us in that direction. 'It is agreed,' he would say, 'that poets are born, not made; and this claim is made for all the arts. But if one considers the matter more closely, we are only born with minimal ability, and there is no such thing as indeterminate ability. It is only our piecemeal, vague education that makes us uncertain of ourselves; it arouses desires rather than active impulses, and instead of helping to develop predispositions, it directs our activity toward objects, which are often out of line with the minds that are so taken up with them. A child or young person who goes astray on his chosen path is, in my opinion, preferable to many of those who pursue uncongenial paths. When the former do find the right path, either by themselves or under direction, it will be the path suited to their nature, and they will never depart from it; but the latter will constantly be in danger of casting off an alien yoke and abandoning themselves to complete freedom of action.'"

"It is strange that this extraordinary man has taken an interest in me too," said Wilhelm, "and if he has not precisely guided me according to his fashion, he has at least encouraged me for a time in my mistakes. How he will in future account for the fact that, in company with several others, he has almost made a fool of me, is something that I can only wait patiently to discover."

"I can't complain about this peculiarity of his, if indeed it is a peculiarity," said Natalie. "For, of all my siblings, I am the one who has least suffered from it. I cannot imagine that my brother Lothario could have been better educated. Perhaps my dear sister, the countess, might have been treated differently— they could have tried to give more seriousness and strength to her character. And what is to become of my brother Friedrich, I haven't the least idea. I'm afraid that he may well be the victim of these pedagogical experiments."

"So you have a second brother?" said Wilhelm.

"Yes I do," she replied, "and he is the merriest, most lighthearted creature. Since he has never been prevented from wandering about the world, I do not know what will come from his frivolous, carefree nature. I haven't seen him for a long while. My only consolation is that the Abbé and all my brother's friends always know where he is and what he is doing."

Wilhelm was about to inquire further of Natalie about these paradoxes, and try to obtain more information about the secret society, when at that very moment the doctor came into the room and, having greeted them briefly, began to talk about the condition of Mignon. Natalie took Felix by the hand, saying that she would bring him to Mignon and prepare her for Wilhelm's coming.

The doctor, now that he and Wilhelm were alone, began as follows: "What I have to tell you, is stranger than you could possibly expect. Natalie has given us an opportunity to speak openly about matters that I have learnt only from her but which cannot be discussed freely in her presence. What we are concerned with is the strange personality of that dear child Mignon. It consists almost entirely of a deep sort of yearning: the longing to see her motherland again, and a longing, my friend, for you—these, I may say, are the only earthly things about her, and both of them have an element of infinite distance about them, both goals being inaccessible to her unusual nature. She may have come originally from near Milan. She was taken from her parents when she was very young by a company of acrobats. No further details could be ascertained from her, partly because she was too young at the time to remember exact names and locations, and partly because she made a vow never again to reveal her home and origins to a living soul. For she did give an exact account of her home to the persons who found her wandering about, begging them earnestly to take her back there, but they dragged her away with them and joked at night, when they thought she was asleep, about the good catch they had made, resolving that she should never be allowed to find her way back. The poor creature was overcome by utter despair, in the midst of which the Mother of God appeared to her and promised to take care of her. So she swore a sacred oath that she would never again trust anyone, never tell anyone her story, and live and die in the expectation of direct divine sustenance. What I have been telling you, was not something she conveyed in so many words to Natalie, but what Natalie has pieced together from occasional remarks, from songs and childish indiscretions which revealed what they intended to keep secret."

Wilhelm could now account for many a song, many an utterance of the poor girl. He beseeched his friend not to withhold from him anything else that he had gathered from the songs and confessions of this extraordinary child.

"Well then," said the doctor, "be prepared for a strange revelation concerning an event in which you had an important part, though you may not remember, and which, I fear, became decisive for the life and death of this dear creature."

"I am very eager to hear about it," said Wilhelm.

"Do you remember the night after the performance of *Hamlet* when you had a mysterious female visitor?"

"Of course I do," said Wilhelm with some embarrassment, "but I wasn't expecting to be reminded of that at this particular moment."

"Do you know who it was?"

"You scare me! Surely not Mignon? Who was it then? Tell me!"

"I do not know myself."

"Not Mignon, then?"

"Certainly not! But: Mignon was on the point of coming to you secretly, when with horror she observed from a corner that a rival had anticipated her."

"A rival!" exclaimed Wilhelm. "Do go on. You are completely bewildering me."

"Be thankful," said the doctor, "that you shall quickly learn what we found out. Natalie and I, though only indirectly involved, were greatly distressed by the troubled state of the girl whom we desired to help, until we obtained some clearer insight. From some frivolous remarks of Philine and the other girls, as well as from a certain song, Mignon conceived the idea of how delightful it would be to spend a night with her beloved, without any further thought than fond, peaceful nestling. Her affection for you, my friend, was so strong; she had already recovered from many a sorrow in your arms, and now she wanted to enjoy her happiness to the full. Her first impulse was to ask you quietly, but inner anxiety made her desist from that. It was the hilarity of the evening and the mood induced by frequent drafts of wine that finally gave her the courage to creep up to your room that night. She went ahead in order to conceal herself in your room, which was not locked, and had just ascended the staircase when she heard a noise. She took cover, and saw a woman in white enter your room. Then you yourself arrived and she heard you bolt the door.

"Mignon was deeply distressed. Violent jealousy combined with the unrecognized urgency of latent desire to take its toll of her only half-developed nature. Her heart, which up till then had been beating with expectation and yearning, suddenly stopped. It was like a dead weight, she could not breathe, she didn't know what to do. Then she heard the sound of the old man's harp, rushed to his room, and spent the night at his feet, in terrible convulsions."

The doctor paused for a moment, but since Wilhelm remained silent, he went on: "Natalie assures me that nothing scared her so much in her whole life as when the child told her all this. In fact, she reproached herself for eliciting by her questions these confidences and so cruelly reviving the memory of all that the dear child had suffered. Natalie told me that when the girl reached this point in her story, she suddenly fell down at her feet, clasped her breast and complained that the pain of that terrible night had come back again. She rolled about on the ground, and Natalie had to concentrate all her efforts on deciding, and using, the best means she knew of dealing with such a state of mind and body."

"You put me in a very painful position by making me feel my injustice toward the poor creature, just at the moment when I am to see her again," said Wilhelm. "If I am to see her again, why do you take away from me the courage to meet her freely and openly? And how can my being here help her if she is in that state of mind? Are you convinced, as a doctor, that the twofold yearning you have described has so undermined her nature that she is in danger of dying? If that is the case, why should I aggravate her misery by my presence and perhaps bring on her death?"

"My dear friend!" the doctor replied, "even if we cannot help, we have an obligation to appease. And I know several notable instances where the physical presence of what one loves can relieve the imagination of its destructive tendencies and transform longing into calm contemplation. Everything should be undertaken with moderation and purpose. For it is also possible that such encounters may revive flagging emotions. Go and see her, be kind to her, and let's see what happens."

Natalie came back into the room and asked Wilhelm to accompany her to Mignon. "She seems to be quite happy with Felix, and I hope she will also be pleased to see you," she said. Wilhelm followed her with some trepidation: He was deeply disturbed by what he had heard and was afraid of a highly emotional scene. But when he arrived, he found exactly the opposite.

Mignon, in a long white dress, her thick brown hair partly hanging loose and partly arranged, was seated with Felix on her lap, pressing him to her breast. She looked like a departed spirit, and the boy like life itself: it seemed as though heaven and earth were here conjoined. She smiled and, stretching out her hand to Wilhelm, said: "Thank you for bringing back the child. You stole it from me, I don't know how. And since then I could not live. As long as my heart has any needs on earth, this child shall fill them."

The tranquillity with which Mignon greeted Wilhelm was a source of great satisfaction to the rest of the company. The doctor insisted that Wilhelm should go and see her often, and that they should all try to restore her physical and mental equilibrium. He himself departed, but promised to return soon.

Wilhelm was now able to observe Natalie in her own environment. One could not imagine anything better, he thought, than living in her proximity. Her presence had a most salutary influence not only on the young girls but on women of various ages, some of whom lived in her house and others came to visit her from nearby.

One day Wilhelm said to her: "The course of your life seems always to have been very even. For the description your aunt gave of you as a child still seems to be apposite. One feels that you never lost your path; you were never obliged to take a step backward."

"For that I am indebted to my uncle and to the Abbé," said Natalie, "for they had such a clear sense of my personal inclinations. I remember that the strongest impression of my youth was that of human need everywhere; and I had an irresistible urge to do something about this. A child that could not yet stand on its feet or an old man who could no longer do so, a rich family's longing to have children or a poor family's inability to support theirs, one man's search for a trade and another's to develop some talent—all such situations were what I seemed by nature predisposed to discover. I saw things that nobody directed my attention to; I saw them because I seemed born to do so. The delights of inanimate nature, so meaningful to others, left me unmoved, and art appealed to me even less. My greatest delight was, and still is, to be presented with some deficiency, some need in others, and be able to think of some way of repairing or alleviating it.

"If I saw someone poor and in rags, I thought of the unnecessary garments hanging in the closets of my friends. If I saw children languishing for lack of care and attention, I remembered this or that woman consumed by boredom in the midst of wealth and comfort. If I saw a crowd of people crammed into a tiny room, I thought how they might be better housed in the vast halls of many a fine residence. This way of seeing things came quite naturally to me; I never had to think twice about it, and I sometimes did the oddest things as a child, embarrassing people on more than one occasion by the strangest requests. Another peculiarity of mine was that I rarely thought of money, and then only later as the means to satisfy needs; my generosity consisted in the giving of natural objects, and I know I was often laughed at for this. The Abbé was the only one who seemed to understand me, and he assisted me by making me better acquainted with myself, my desires and inclinations, and by teaching me the most effective way of fulfilling these."

"Did you, in the instruction of your women charges, carry out the principles of these extraordinary men?" asked Wilhelm. "Do you allow each human being to develop by itself? Do you let them search and lose their way, make mistakes, and either happily reach their goal or lose themselves miserably in the process?"

"No, I do not," said Natalie. "To treat people thus would be quite contrary to my convictions. If someone does not provide help when it is needed, he will, to my mind, never be of any help; if he does not come up with advice immediately, he will never provide any. It seems to me of the utmost importance to enunciate certain principles and inculcate these into children— principles that will give their lives some stability. I would almost be inclined to say that it is better to err because of principles than to do so from arbitrariness of nature, and my observation of human beings tells me that there is always some gap in their natures which can only be filled by a principle expressly communicated to them."

"Your procedure, then, is radically different from that followed by our friends?" said Wilhelm.

"Yes it is!" Natalie replied. "But you should respect their tolerance in letting me go my own way, just because it is my own."

We will postpone a more detailed account of how Natalie operated with the children under her supervision.

Mignon constantly asked to join the company, which was gladly permitted because she was gradually becoming accustomed to Wilhelm again, opening up her heart to him and generally seeming to be recovering her good spirits and her love of life. She liked to put her arm in his as they walked, for she easily got tired. "Well," she would say, "Mignon can't jump and climb anymore, but she still feels the urge to walk over the tops of mountains, from one house to another, from one tree to the next. How I envy the birds, especially when they are building their nests nicely and quietly."

Mignon frequently took occasion to ask Wilhelm to go with her into the garden. If he was busy or somehow not to be found, Felix had to take his place, and if the girl seemed at times quite detached from the earth, there were others when she clung to father and son, fearing more than anything that she might be separated from them.

Natalie seemed puzzled and concerned. "We have tried," she said, "to open up her poor dear heart by bringing you here; but whether we did right, I do not know." She stopped, and seemed to be waiting for Wilhelm to say something. It occurred to him that, as things were at present, Mignon would be greatly upset if he married Therese, but he was uncertain whether he should mention what he had in mind to Natalie. He did not suspect that she knew about it already.

He also could not listen with an open mind when she spoke about her sister, praising her good qualities and lamenting her situation. And he was quite ill at ease when she announced the impending arrival of the countess. "Her husband," she said, "has now only one thought in his head; he is determined to take over the position of the late Count Zinzendorf in the community, and support and develop that great undertaking by his insight and activity. He is coming here with his wife to take a sort of leave from us. He will then visit the various places where the community has established its settlements. It seems that his intentions are generally approved of; and it could be that he will venture on a journey to America with my poor sister, so as to emulate his predecessor. Since he seems almost convinced that he lacks little to acquire sainthood, he may be inspired as well by the desire to be a shining martyr."

Chapter Four

They had often talked about Therese, or mentioned her in passing, and time and time again Wilhelm was about to tell Natalie that he had offered his heart and his hand to that excellent woman. But he was restrained from doing so by a certain feeling, which he could not account for. He hesitated so long that Natalie, with that radiant, serene, and gentle smile so characteristic of her, finally said to him: "So it is I who must eventually break the silence and force my way into your confidence. Why, my friend, do you keep secret from me a matter that is so important to you, and also affects me closely? You have offered your hand to my friend Therese. I am not willfully interfering in your affairs, here is my justification—here is the letter she has written to you and sends you through me."

"A letter from Therese!" he cried.

"Yes! And your fate is decided. You are a happy man. Allow me to congratulate both you and my friend."

Wilhelm lapsed into silence, staring in front of him. Natalie looked at him, noticing that he had turned pale. "Your happiness is so extreme," she said, "that it has taken the form of fright and robbed you of speech. My pleasure is not less because it still permits me to speak. I hope you will be grateful when I tell you that my influence on Therese's decision was not inconsiderable. She asked for my advice, and strangely enough you were here at the time. I was easily able to dispel the few doubts she still had as messengers went quickly back and forth between us. Here is her decision! Here's the solution! And now you shall read all her letters and look freely and directly into her noble heart."

Wilhelm opened the letter, which she handed to him unsealed, and read these kindly words:

"I am yours—just as I am, and as you know me. And I shall call you mine—just as you are, and as I know you. Whatever is changed by marriage in us and our relationship, we will accept with good will, intelligence and happy hearts. Since it is not passion, but mutual inclination and trust that brings us together, we run a lesser risk than thousands of others. You will surely forgive me if I sometimes still think about my former friend; and I, for my part, will clasp your son to my bosom as a mother. If you would like to share my little house with me right now, you shall be lord and master, and that will give time for the purchase of the estate to be concluded. I do not want any changes to be made in the estate without me, so that I may show that I deserve the trust you are placing in me. May things fare well with you, my dear, dear friend! Beloved bridegroom, honored spouse! Therese clasps you to her heart in hope and joy. My friend Natalie will tell you more—indeed everything."

Wilhelm, for whom this letter revived his whole image of Therese, had by now completely recovered himself. As he read, various thoughts were coursing through his mind. With some alarm he became aware of definite signs of a growing affection for Natalie within him; he reproved himself, terming all such thoughts pure madness, recalled Therese in all her perfection, read the letter again, brightened up—or rather recovered sufficiently to appear bright. Natalie then showed him the other letters from which we will select some passages.

Therese, having described Wilhelm in her own fashion, had gone on to say: "This is how I see the man who is offering me his hand. How he sees himself, will become clear to you when you read the frank account he has given me of himself. I am convinced I will be happy with him."

"As far as social status is concerned, you know what my opinions have always been. Some persons suffer acutely from disparity in external conditions and cannot adjust to this. I never try to convince anybody, but I act according to my own convictions. I never try to set an example, though I do myself act

WILHELM MEISTER'S APPRENTICESHIP

according to an example. It is only disparities in inner conditions that trouble me, vessels unsuited to what they are to contain, external show without inner satisfaction, riches combined with miserliness, nobility with vulgarity, youth with pedantry, neediness with ceremoniousness. Such combinations are enough to destroy me completely, no matter what the world calls them or how it values them."

"When I say that I have hopes we will suit each other, my belief is based primarily on his similarity to you, dear Natalie, whom I treasure and respect so greatly. Like you he has that noble seeking and striving for betterment which enables us to do good where we think we perceive the possibility. I have often blamed you in my mind for treating this or that person differently and reacting to this or that situation differently from how I would have; and yet the outcome usually showed you were right. 'If we just take people as they are,' you once said, 'we make them worse; but if we treat them not as they are but as they should be, we help them to become what they can become.' I can't think or act like that—this I know all too well. Insight, order, discipline, commands—that is my way. I remember Jarno once saying to me: 'Therese trains her pupils, whereas Natalie cultivates hers.' He even went so far as to deny me completely the three primary virtues of faith, love, and hope. 'Instead of faith' he said, 'she has insight; instead of love, persistence; instead of hope, confidence.' Before I met you, I believed there was nothing of greater value than clarity and common sense, but knowing you has convinced me, given me new life, overcome my previous belief, and now I yield the palm to your finer, loftier spirit. I respect my friend Wilhelm in the same terms. His life has been continuous searching and failure to find. But his searching has not been just idle seeking; it is sustained by the well-intentioned but curious belief that he will receive from without what can only come from within. And so, my dear, this time my belief in the importance of clarity has been beneficial to me, for I know my future husband better than he does, and respect him all the more for that. I see him, but I do not oversee him, and all my powers of insight do not suffice to estimate what he is capable of achieving. When I think about him, his image is always merging with yours; and I do not know how I have deserved the association with two such remarkable people. But I will try to deserve this by doing my duty in fulfilling what is expected and anticipated from me."

"Whether I ever think about Lothario? A great deal, and every day of my life. He is never absent from my mind. How sorry I am that, related to me by an error of his youth, this excellent man should also be so closely related to you. For someone like yourself would be more worthy of him than I. I could and would gladly let him be yours. Let us be everything to him that we possibly can, until he finds a suitable wife, and even then let us remain together as close friends."

"Now, what will our friends have to say?" Natalie began. "Your brother knows nothing about it?" Wilhelm asked. "No more than your family does," she replied. "This time the whole thing was a matter between us women. I don't know what ideas Lydie has put into Therese's head, for she seems to mistrust both the Abbé and Jarno. Lydie has made her somehow mistrust certain secret plans and arrangements of theirs, which I know about in a general way but have never involved myself with, and so, at this decisive point in her life, Therese sought no other opinion than mine. She had agreed with my brother that when either of them got married, they would simply announce this without seeking each other's advice beforehand."

Natalie thereupon wrote to her brother, inviting Wilhelm to add a few words, as Therese had asked her to do. They were just about to seal the letter when Jarno unexpectedly arrived. He was received very warmly, seemed extremely cheerful and jocular, and finally said: "I have actually come here today to bring you the strangest piece of news, though a very pleasant one. It concerns our friend Therese. You have often blamed us, Natalie, for busying ourselves with so many different things; but now you will see how useful it is to have spies everywhere. Guess what has happened—and let's see how sagacious you are!"

He said this in a very self-satisfied way, and his malicious expression as he looked at both Wilhelm and Natalie led them to believe that their secret was discovered. Natalie smiled and said: "We are much more skillful than you think, for we have put the solution to the riddle on paper before you told us what the riddle was."

She then handed him the letter to Lothario, pleased by this means to be able to counter the surprise and embarrassment he had prepared for them. Jarno received the letter with some amazement, skimmed it through, was astonished, let it fall from his hands, and looked at them both wide-eyed, with an expression of stupefaction, indeed of horror, such as one was not used to with him. He did not say one word.

Wilhelm and Natalie were distinctly puzzled. Jarno paced back and forth in the room. "What am I to say?" he exclaimed. "Shall I tell them? It can't remain a secret, and some confusion is unavoidable. All right: a secret in exchange for a secret! Surprise for surprise! Therese is not her mother's daughter! The obstacle is removed. I have come here to ask you to prepare her for union with Lothario."

Jarno observed the consternation of both of them. Their faces dropped. "This is one of those cases that is difficult to tolerate socially," he said. "Whatever we may all think, we would best pursue our thoughts in private. I at least will ask for an hour's respite." He hurried off into the garden. Wilhelm followed him instinctively, but at a distance.

After about an hour they met again. Wilhelm was the first to speak, and said: "While I was living an easy, one might say frivolous life, friendship, love, affection and trust came to me with open arms, pressed themselves upon me; but now, when things are serious, fate seems to be taking a different course with me. My decision to offer Therese my hand in marriage was perhaps the first that came to me entirely from within myself. I made my decision after careful consideration, my mind was completely made up, and my fondest hopes were fulfilled by her acceptance. But now the strangest turn of fate casts down my outstretched hand, Therese extends hers from afar, as in a dream, and my whole image of bliss is gone forever. Farewell then, beauteous image, and with you all those happy scenes I had associated with you!"

He stopped for a moment, stared in front of him, and Jarno was about to speak. "Let me just say something else," Wilhelm added, "for at this moment my whole destiny is being decided. I remember now the first impression I had of Lothario, an impression that is still firmly planted in my mind. That man deserves every sort of friendship and affection, and no friendship is conceivable without readiness to sacrifice. For his sake it was easy for me to fool an unhappy girl; therefore it should also be possible for me to renounce the worthiest of brides for his sake. Go to him and tell him the whole extraordinary story; and tell him what I am prepared to do."

Jarno answered: "In such instances as this, I think the ultimate solution is not to act too hastily. Let's do nothing without Lothario's approval. I will go to him, but you stay here quietly and wait either for my return or a letter from him."

He rode off, leaving Wilhelm and Natalie in a melancholy mood. They now had time to look at the situation from various angles and make some observations to each other. First of all, it struck them as strange that they had heard this extraordinary news from Jarno, but had not inquired about the circumstances surrounding it. Wilhelm even began to have some doubts about it; and the next day their astonishment and bewilderment were raised to a peak when a messenger arrived from Therese with this peculiar letter to Natalie: "Strange as it may seem, I must follow up on my last letter immediately and ask you to send Wilhelm to me as quickly as possible. He shall be my husband, no matter what plans others are making to steal him away from me. Give him the enclosed letter! And in private, no matter who else is at your house."

The letter to Wilhelm ran as follows: "What can you be thinking of your Therese pressing suddenly and passionately for an immediate union, whereas it was initiated in such cool consideration? Let nothing stop you from coming here instantly on receiving this letter. Come, my dear, dear friend, my thrice beloved, for they are trying to rob me of having you, or at least making that difficult."

"What is to be done?" exclaimed Wilhelm after reading the letter.

"Never," said Natalie after some thought, "have my heart and my mind maintained such silence. I don't know what to do, or what to advise you to do."

"Could it be possible," exclaimed Wilhelm somewhat angrily, "that Lothario himself knows nothing about this, or if he does, that he and we are the victims of some secret machinations? Did Jarno, when he read our letter, make the whole thing up on the spur of the moment? Would he have told us something else if we had not been so precipitate? What do they want? What are they up to? What plan is Therese referring to? It can't be denied that Lothario is surrounded by secret activities and alliances. I myself have experienced such activities, and learnt that these persons are trying to influence and control the actions, the whole lives of others. I do not understand what the ultimate goal of these clandestine operations is, but this latest attempt to separate me from Therese is clear enough. On the one hand I am regaled with the good fortune awaiting Lothario, though perhaps that is only a pretense; on the other hand I find my beloved, my honored bride urgently calling me to come to her. What shall I do? What shall I leave undone?"

"Just have a little patience," said Natalie, "just take a little time for reflection. In this strange concatenation of circumstances there is one thing I am certain about: We should not act hastily, when what is at stake is irrecoverable. Our defense against idle fictions and secret machinations is to be sensible and maintain patience, for everything will soon be cleared up, and we shall know whether there is any truth in all this or not. If my brother really has hopes now of being united with Therese, it would be cruel to deprive him of that happiness in the very moment it seems so inviting. Let us therefore wait and see whether he knows anything about it, whether he really believes it, and has hopes."

A letter arrived from Lothario which fortunately added further justification to her advice. "I am not sending Jarno back to you," he wrote. "A few words from me will mean more to you than all those of an intermediary. I am quite sure that Therese is not her mother's daughter, and I cannot abandon hope of winning her until she herself is also convinced and can make a considered choice between me and our friend. Don't, I beg you, let him leave you; a brother's happiness, his whole life, is in the balance. I promise you that this state of uncertainty will not continue much longer."

"You see how things stand," said Natalie gently to Wilhelm. "Give me your word that you will not leave the house."

"I will not leave this house against your will," he said, extending his hand to her. "I thank God and my good angel that this time I am being guided, and by you."

Natalie wrote to Therese telling her all that had happened, assuring her she would not let Wilhelm leave, and enclosing Lothario's letter.

Therese replied: "I am quite surprised that Lothario is convinced. He would not pretend that he was, to his sister, not to this extent anyway. I am very upset, and it is best if I say nothing further, but come to you as soon as I have provided for poor Lydie, who is being cruelly treated. I fear we are all being deceived, and in such a manner that we shall never straighten things out. If Wilhelm thought as I do, he would slip away from you and throw himself on the bosom of his Therese, whom no one would then deprive him of; but I am afraid I shall lose him, and yet not regain Lothario. They are snatching Lydie away from Lothario by giving him the distant hope of winning me. I won't say any more; the confusion will get worse. Time alone will decide whether good relationships are becoming so twisted, so undermined, even destroyed, that once everything is cleared up, it will be too late to repair them. If my friend Wilhelm does not break loose, I will come in a few days to see him at your house and keep him there. You will be surprised at such passion taking hold of your Therese; but it is not passion, it is the conviction that, since Lothario could not be mine, this new friend will make my life happy. Tell him this on behalf of the little boy who sat beneath the oaktree with him and cherished his affection! Tell him in the name of Therese, who received his proposal with such honest delight! My first dream—living together with Lothario—is now far removed from my mind; my dream of a life with my new friend is, however, everpresent in it. Have they so little respect for me that they believe it is so easy to exchange one for the other again, on the spur of the moment?"

"I trust you not to run away," said Natalie to Wilhelm, handing him Therese's letter. "Do realize that my whole happiness lies in your hands. My life is so intensely bound up with that of my brother, that when he suffers pain, so do I, and the joys he experiences are what gives me happiness. I can truly say that only through him have I learnt that the heart can be moved and uplifted, that there is joy and love in the world, and feeling which brings contentment beyond all need . . ."

She paused; and Wilhelm took her hand and said: "Do go on! This is the time for confiding in each other. We have never needed more urgently to know each other better."

"Yes, my friend," she said with a smile of indescribably gentle and calm dignity. "And perhaps it will not be the wrong time to tell you that what we read in books about love, and what the world shows us of what it calls love, has always seemed to me idle fancy."

"You have never been in love?" Wilhelm asked.

"Never—or always!" she replied.

Chapter Five

They had been walking to and fro in the garden as they talked. Natalie had picked various strangely shaped flowers quite unfamiliar to Wilhelm, and he asked her for their names.

"You will never guess for whom I am picking these. My little bouquet is for my uncle, whom we are going to visit. The sun is shining so brightly on the Hall of the Past, that I would like to take you there. And I never go without taking some of the flowers my uncle particularly liked. He was a strange man with strong inclinations of his own. He had a decided affection for certain plants and animals, people and places, even stones, and this was often not easy to account for. 'If I had not resisted myself from youth on,' he would say, 'if I had not striven to extend my mind outward from myself into wider vistas, I would have become a very constricted and thoroughly insufferable person. For nothing is more unbearable than isolation and idiosyncrasy in someone who could be expected to indulge in some unselfish, useful activity.' Yet he had to admit also that life would lose its savor if he did not sometimes consider himself and passionately indulge in what he could not always approve of or make excuses for. 'It is not my fault,' he used to say, 'if I have not completely been able to harmonize my mind with my instincts.' He would make fun of me, and say: 'Natalie can truly be said to be in a state of bliss on this earth, for her nature never demands anything but what the world desires and needs.'"

They had now arrived. She conducted him through a wide corridor up to a portal guarded by two granite sphinxes. The portal itself was narrower at the top than at the bottom, after the Egyptian fashion, and its solid iron doors led one to expect a somber, perhaps gruesome, interior. It was therefore a pleasant surprise to find this gloomy anticipation replaced by a world of brightness and light, when one entered a hall in which art and life dispelled all thoughts of death and the grave. Arches were inset in the walls and in them stood large sarcophagi. In the pillars between them there were niches with funeral urns and caskets. The remaining surface of the walls and the vault were divided up into regular spaces, and bright, imposing figures painted on backgrounds of various sizes, surrounded by a whole variety of bright borders, garlands and other decorative motifs. The architectural elements were fashioned from fine yellow marble, which shaded over into reddishness, blue stripes of an ingenious chemical composition reproduced the effect of lapis lazuli, and, pleasing the eye by the contrast, gave coherence and unity to the whole. All this splendor and decoration was achieved by purely architectural means, and everyone who entered felt uplifted by the design of the whole, showing what man is and what he can be.

Across from the entrance, on a magnificent sarcophagus, stood the marble effigy of a distinguished man, his head resting against a pillow. He was holding a scroll in front of him which he appeared to be reading attentively. The scroll was so placed that one could read the words written upon it. These were: *Remember to live.*

Natalie removed some withered flowers from her uncle's tomb (for his it was) and replaced them by those she had brought with her. The effigy was full-length, and Wilhelm thought he recognized the features of the old man he had once seen in the forest. "We used to spend many hours here together," said Natalie, "while the hall was being constructed. In his last years he brought several skilled artists here, and his favorite occupation was to plan and decide on the drawings and cartoons for these paintings."

Wilhelm was overjoyed at everything he saw around him. "What life there is in this Hall of the Past!" he cried. "One could just as well call it the Hall of the Present, and of the Future. This is how everything was, and this is how everything will be. Nothing perishes except him who observes and enjoys. The picture of this mother clasping her child will survive many generations of happy mothers. Some father in a future century will delight in this bearded man casting aside all seriousness and joking with his son. Bashful brides will sit like that for all time, silently asking to be consoled and persuaded; impatient like this one, all bridegrooms will stand, listening to find out when they may enter."

Wilhelm's eyes wandered from one picture to another. In a splendid sequence of vivid representations, ranging from the first childish impulses to employ all one's limbs in play, to the calm, grave detachment of wise old age, showing that there is no inclination or faculty innate in man that he does not need or use. From that first delicate awakening of self with which the maiden delays drawing water while she gazes admiringly at her own reflection, to the grand festivities at which kings and nations call on the gods to sanction their alliances—everything was there in all its power and significance. A whole world, heaven itself, surrounded the observer in this place, and aside from the thoughts and feelings aroused by these images, something else seemed to be there that took hold of the whole man. Wilhelm felt it without being able to account for it. "What is it," he cried, "that, apart from all meaning, aside from the sympathetic interest that all human events and fortunes evoke in us, what is it that affects me so strongly and at the same time so pleasantly? It speaks to me from the whole without my comprehending the whole, and from each of the parts without my being able to relate these especially to myself! What is the magic that for me pervades these surfaces, lines, height and breadth, masses and colors? What is it that makes these shapes, even though only decoration, so appealing? That one could remain here, reflect on all one sees, be happy, and yet feel and think things quite different from what one sees with one's eyes."

If we could only describe how admirably everything was arranged, how everything appeared as it should, by combination or contrast, uniformity or variety of color, and thereby produced a perfect as well as clear effect—if we could do that, we would be transporting the reader to a place he would never wish to leave.

Four large marble candelabras stood in the corners of the Hall, and four smaller ones in the center were ranged around a sarcophagus of exquisite workmanship which, from its size, would seem to have contained the body of a young person of medium height. Natalie stood for a while beside this monument and, placing her hand upon it, said: "My dear uncle had a special love for this classical work. He often said that it is not only the first fruits that wither—and can be preserved up there in those smaller spaces—but fruits that hang on the bough, full of promise for many a day until a hidden worm causes their premature ripening and decay. I fear," she continued, "that he was thinking of the dear girl who is step by step withdrawing from our care and seems to have a yearning for this peaceful resting place."

As they were about to leave, Natalie said: "I must draw your attention to one other thing. Do you see these semicircular openings up there on both sides? Those are for the choirs of singers, so that they may remain unseen, and these metal ornaments below the cornice are for hanging tapestries on, which, according to my uncle's disposition, are to be hung at all funerals. He could not have lived without music, especially vocal music, but he had the peculiarity of never wishing to see the singers. He would say: 'We have been spoilt too much by theaters, where music only serves the eye, accompanying movements, not feelings. In oratorios and concerts the physical presence of the singer is disturbing. Music is only for the ear. A lovely voice is the most universal thing one can think of, and if the limited individual producing it is visible, this disturbs the effect of universality. When I am talking to someone, I need to see him, for he is an individual whose character and figure determine the value of what he says; but when someone is singing, he should be invisible, his appearance should not prejudice me in his favor or distract me. With singing it is a case of one organ addressing another, not one mind speaking to another, not a manifold world to a single pair of eyes, not heaven to a single man.' He also wanted players in an orchestra concealed as much as possible, because one is only distracted and disturbed by the laborings and necessary strange gestures of musicians. He therefore listened to music with his eyes closed, so as to concentrate entirely on the pleasure of the ear."

They were about to leave the Hall when they heard the children running hurriedly toward them and Felix shouting: "No, me! Me!"

Mignon came hurtling through the door, panting for breath and unable to get a word out, while Felix followed some distance behind, saying: "Mother Therese is here!" The children apparently had raced to see who could bring the news first. Mignon lay in Natalie's arms, her heart beating wildly.

"You naughty child!" said Natalie. "Haven't you been forbidden all violent movement? Look how your heart is beating!"

"Let it break!" said Mignon with a deep sigh. "It has been beating long enough!"

They had hardly recovered from their confusion and alarm when Therese entered. She rushed up to Natalie, embraced her, and then the child. She turned to Wilhelm, looked at him with her clear eyes, and said: "Well, my friend, what's the situation? I hope you haven't let yourself be deluded." He took one step toward her, she moved toward him and fell into his arms. "Oh, my Therese!" he cried. "My friend! My beloved! My husband! Yours for evermore!" she replied amidst passionate kisses.

Felix tugged her coat and said: "Mother Therese! I'm here too!" Natalie stood gazing in front of her, when all of a sudden Mignon shot up, clasped

707

her heart with her left hand, flung out her right arm, and fell with a cry at Natalie's feet, as if dead.

Everyone was greatly alarmed. There was no sign of any movement in heart or pulse. Wilhelm took her into his arms and quickly lifted her up, her body hanging lifeless over his shoulders. The doctor came but gave little hope, though he and the young surgeon whom we already know did all they could—but in vain. The poor dear creature could not be brought back to life.

Natalie motioned to Therese, who took Wilhelm by the hand and led him out of the room. He was speechless, and did not have the courage to look her in the eyes. He sat beside her on the same sofa where he had first seen Natalie. In quick succession he thought about the fates of several people—or rather he did not think at all, he simply let his mind be invaded by what he could not repel. There are moments in our lives when events, like winged shuttles, flit backwards and forwards before our eyes, weaving continuously at a tapestry which we have more or less designed and spun for ourselves. "Dear friend! Beloved Wilhelm!" said Therese, breaking the silence and taking his hand, "let us keep a firm hold on this particular moment, as we will often have to do at other times. Events like these need two people to tolerate them. Do realize that you are not alone, please feel that; show that you love me by sharing your sorrow with me!" She embraced him, pressing him gently to her breast; he clasped her in his arms, and pressed her against him. "That poor child," he said, "in her moments of sadness would look for refuge and protection in my uncertain bosom. May your certainty strengthen me in this terrible hour." They remained in each other's arms. He could feel her heart beating, but his mind was empty and desolate. Only the forms of Mignon and Natalie hovered like shadows before his imagination.

Natalie entered the room. "Give us your blessing!" said Therese. "Let us be united in your presence at this sad moment." Wilhelm's face was buried in Therese's breast; he was fortunate enough to be able to weep. He did not hear Natalie come, did not see her; but at the sound of her voice his tears redoubled. "What God has joined together, I will not put asunder," said Natalie with a smile. "But I cannot unite you, nor can I approve of the fact that sorrow and affection should erase all memory of my brother from your hearts." Wilhelm broke loose from Therese's arms. "Where are you going?" both women asked. "Let me see the child that I have killed," he cried. "Misfortune seen with our own eyes is a lesser evil than when our imagination forces it upon our minds. Let us go and see the departed angel. Her radiance will tell us that all is well with her." Since they could not restrain him, so deeply was he affected, they both followed him, but the good doctor, accompanied by the surgeon, dissuaded them from approaching the dead girl, and said: "Stay away from this mournful sight and let me use my art to give some permanence to the remains of this unusual person. I will start immediately to employ the delicate art of embalming, and also preserve an appearance of life in this beloved creature.

Since I foresaw that she was dying, I have made all preparations, and my assistant and I will see that we succeed. Grant me but a few days and don't ask to see her until we have brought her into the Hall of the Past."

The young surgeon again had with him the instrument case they had noticed earlier. "Where did he get that case from?" Wilhelm asked the doctor. "I am very familiar with it," said Natalie, "he got it from his father who bound your wounds that day in the forest."

"So I was not mistaken," Wilhelm said. "I recognized the ribbon immediately. Give it to me! That ribbon first put me on the track of my benefactress. Inanimate objects like this outlast so much joy and sorrow! It was present at so much suffering, and yet its threads still hold. It was there at the last hours of many persons, but its colors have never faded. It was there at one of the most precious moments of my life, when I lay wounded on the ground and you came to my aid, while that poor child with blood on her hair was tenderly caring for my life, that girl whose own untimely death we now are mourning."

They did not have much time to acquaint Therese with the probable cause of the child's unexpected death; for visitors were announced, who turned out to be Lothario, Jarno and the Abbé. Natalie went up to her brother while the others stood in silence. Therese smiled and said to Lothario: "You hardly expected to see me here, and it is hardly suitable for us to seek each other out at this particular moment. But I am glad to see you after so long an absence."

Lothario grasped her by the hand and said: "If we must suffer and forebear, then let us do so in a spirit of love and goodwill. I do not demand any influence on your decision, and my confidence in your heart and mind and your good sense, is as strong as ever; so I gladly entrust to you my fate and that of my friend."

The conversation then turned to more general and less important matters. They divided up into pairs. Natalie walked with Lothario, Therese with the Abbé, and Wilhelm stayed in the house with Jarno.

The arrival of the three friends at that moment when Wilhelm was weighed down with sorrow, in no wise distracted him; it irritated him and made his mood worse. He was ill-tempered and suspicious, and made no attempt to conceal this when Jarno asked him to account for his sullen silence. "What more do we need?" said Wilhelm. "Lothario arrives with his supporters, and it would be a miracle if the mysterious forces of the Tower, always so busy at something, did not work on us to achieve heaven knows what strange purpose. Those holy men, so far as I can make out, seem always to have the laudable intention of breaking up alliances and bringing together again what has been separated. What sort of pattern will eventually emerge from this, that will always remain a mystery to our unholy eyes."

"You're ill-tempered and bitter," said Jarno. "That's all well and good. But when you get angry, that will be still better."

709

"That can be easily managed," Wilhelm replied, "for I am very much afraid that delight is being taken in driving my native and my assumed patience to extremes."

"In that case I would like, while we are waiting to see how our adventures turn out, to tell you something about this Tower that you seem so much to distrust."

"It's up to you," Wilhelm replied, "if you feel like risking it when I am so distracted. My mind is occupied with so many things that I do not know whether I will be able to give the attention I should to your worthy adventures."

"I will not be dissuaded by your pleasantry from informing you about this matter. You take me for a shrewd fellow, but I will also show you that I am honest—and what's more, I have been instructed to give you this information." "I could wish," Wilhelm replied, "that you let your feelings speak with the intention of enlightening me. But since I cannot listen to you without mistrust, why should I listen to you at all?" "If all I have to do is to spin yarns for you, then you will surely have time to attend to those," said Jarno. "Perhaps you will be more inclined to do so, if I first tell you that everything you saw in the tower was the relics of a youthful enterprise that most initiates first took very seriously but will probably now just smile at."

"So they are just playing games with those portentous words and signs?" Wilhelm exclaimed. "We are ceremoniously conducted to a place that inspires awe, we witness miraculous apparitions, are given scrolls containing mysterious, grandiose aphorisms which we barely understand, are told we have been apprentices and are now free—and are none the wiser." "Do you still have the document?" asked Jarno. "There's much that is good in it. Those general maxims have real solid foundation, though they may seem obscure, perhaps even meaningless, to someone without experience of his own. Would you please give me the so-called Certificate of Apprenticeship, if you have it at hand?" "Indeed I do," Wilhelm replied. "One should carry an amulet like that always on one's chest." "Well," said Jarno with a smile, "maybe someday its contents will enter your heart and your head."

Jarno skimmed through the first half of the manual. "These remarks refer to the cultivation of our artistic sense—other persons will talk to you about that; the second part deals with life, and here I feel more at home."

He then began to read certain passages, interspersing them with remarks, comments and stories. "Young people have an unusually strong hankering after mysteries, ceremonies and grandiloquence: this is often the sign of a certain depth of character. For at that time a person wants to feel, albeit dimly and indefinitely, that his whole being is affected and involved. A young man who is full of presentiments believes that he can account for much and discover even more in mysteries, and that he must work by means of mysteries. The Abbé encouraged a group of young people in this way of thinking, partly because it corresponded to his own principles, partly out of inclination and habit, for he had previously been connected with people who worked in this mysterious way. But I was the least able to conform to this; I was older than the others, had seen things clearly from early on, and valued clarity more than anything else. My sole interest was to know the world as it was, and I infected the best of the others with this passionate concern. As a result I almost deflected our whole pedagogic efforts on to a wrong track, for we began to see only the faults and limitations of others and consider ourselves as perfect. The Abbé came to our assistance, instructing us that we should not observe others except in order to show interest in their cultivation of themselves, and that we are only really able to observe or eavesdrop on ourselves when we are engaged in activity. He advised us to return to earlier forms of social life. As a result there was a certain adherence to laws in our meetings and a perceptible mysticism in our whole organization, which thereby, so to speak, transformed itself from craft into art. That's why we evolved the appellations of Apprentice, Assistant, and Master. We wanted to make our own observations, and establish our own archive of knowledge. That is how the various confessions arose, written sometimes by ourselves and sometimes by others, from which the records of apprenticeship were subsequently put together. Not all are equally concerned with their self-cultivation—many want merely panaceas for contentment, or recipes for wealth and happiness. Those who did not want to be set on their feet, were obstructed or deflected by mystifications and all sorts of hocus-pocus. We assigned freedom of action only to those who felt deeply and saw clearly what they were born to, and had enough experience of their own to pursue their chosen course with ease and gladness."

"Well then," said Wilhelm, "you were much too precipitate with me, for since that moment of liberation I know less than ever what I can do, or what I desire, or should do." "It is not our fault that we got ourselves into this muddle," said Jarno. "Let us hope that good fortune will get us out of it. Meanwhile let me say this: A person who has great potentiality for development will in due course acquire knowledge of himself and the world. Few people have the understanding and simultaneously the ability to act. Understanding extends, but also immobilizes; action mobilizes, but also restricts."

"Do desist from giving me any more of these wondrous observations," Wilhelm interjected. "Such verbiage has confused me quite enough." "Very well then, let me go on with my story," said Jarno, half rolling up the scroll and only glancing at it occasionally. "I myself have been very little use to the Society or mankind. I am a very bad teacher, for I find it unbearable to observe someone making clumsy attempts to do something. When someone is off the track, my inclination is always to alert him, even if it were a sleepwalker in danger of breaking his neck. I always had trouble on this score with the Abbé, who claimed that error can only be cured through erring. We often disagreed about you: he was very favorably disposed toward you, and it means a great deal to earn his approval. Whenever I encountered you, I always told you the honest truth." "You certainly didn't treat me with any indulgence," said Wilhelm, "and you always remained true to your principles, so far as I can see." "What indulgence is needed," Jarno replied, "when it is simply a case of a young man with many a talent, embarking on the wrong course?" "Pardon me!" said Wilhelm, "you were severe enough to tell me that I had no talent for acting. But I must confess that, although I have given that up entirely, I cannot agree that I had absolutely no gift for it." "My view is quite definitely that a man who always plays himself is not an actor," said Jarno. "No one deserves to be called an actor who cannot transform his personality and appearance into that of many other persons. You, for example, played Hamlet quite well and a few other roles, where your character, your physical appearance and your mood of the moment assisted you. That would be good enough for an amateur and someone without higher aspirations. But," said Jarno, with a quick look at the scroll, "one should be wary of any talent that one cannot hope to bring to perfection. However much one may achieve, one finally must regret the expenditure of time and energy on such dabbling when one is brought face to face with the achievements of a master."

"Don't start reading again!" said Wilhelm. "I would urge you just to go on talking: tell me more, give me more information! Am I then right in thinking that it was the Abbé who helped me in *Hamlet* by providing the Ghost?"

"Yes, because he was sure that was the only way to cure you, if you were curable."

"And that is why he left the veil with me, and urged me to flee?"

"Yes; he hoped that the performance of *Hamlet* would be sufficient to satisfy your desire, and that you would never go on stage again. But I thought the opposite, and I was right. We argued about this that same evening after the performance."

"So you saw me act?"

"Yes, indeed I did."

"Then who was it who played the Ghost?"

"That I cannot say. Either the Abbé or his twin brother—probably the latter, for he is a shade taller."

"So you too have secrets amongst yourselves?"

"Friends can—and must—keep secrets from each other, for they are not secrets to each other."

"The very recollection of that confusion is enough to confuse me," said Wilhelm. "Do tell me some more about the man I am so indebted to and have so much to reproach for."

"What makes him so respected by us," said Jarno, "and what gives him supremacy over all of us, is the clear untrammeled perception Nature has given him into all human faculties, and how each is to be best developed. Most persons, even the best of us, are somehow limited. Each one of us values certain qualities in himself and the same in others, and it is only these qualities that we favor and wish to develop. But the Abbé takes an entirely different view; he is interested in everything, takes pleasure in acknowledging and furthering everything. I must now look at the scroll again," he went on, quoting: 'All men make up mankind and all forces together make up the world. These are often in conflict with each other, and while trying to destroy each other they are held together and reproduced by Nature. From the faintest active urge of the animal to the most highly developed activity of the mind, from the stammering delight of the child to the superlative expression of bards and orators, from the first scuffles of boys to those vast undertakings by which whole countries are defended or conquered, from the most meager desire and most fleeting attraction to the most violent passions and deepest involvements, from the clearest sense of physical presence to the dimmest intimations and hopes of distant spiritual promise—all this, and much else besides, lies in the human spirit, waiting to be developed, and not just in one of us, but in all of us. Every aptitude is significant and should be developed. One man cultivates the beautiful and another what is useful, but only the combination of both constitutes the true man. Usefulness cultivates itself, for it is cultivated by the general mass of people, and no one can do without it; but beauty must be expressly cultivated, for few people embody it and many need it.'"

"Stop!" said Wilhelm, "I've read all that already."

"Just a few more lines!" Jarno responded. "Here is the Abbé speaking again: 'One force controls another, but none can create another. In every predisposition, and only there, lies the power to perfect itself. Very few people who want to teach and affect others, understand that.'"

"I don't understand it either," said Wilhelm.

"You will often have the opportunity to hear the Abbé on this subject, so let us perceive quite clearly what we are and how we can develop ourselves, and be just toward others, for we only deserve respect if we respect others."

"Heavens! No more maxims, please! I feel they are inadequate balm for a wounded heart like mine. Tell me rather, with your customary cruel clarity, what you expect from me, and how you intend to victimize me."

"You'll be apologizing to us later for all your suspicions, I can assure you. Your job is to test and to choose; ours to assist you. No one is ever happy until his unlimited striving has set itself a limitation. Don't be guided by me; go to the Abbé. Don't think of yourself, but of those around you. Learn to appreciate Lothario's fine qualities, see how his farsightedness and his activities are indissolubly bound up with each other; he is always moving forward, always expanding and taking others with him. He always has a world around him, no matter where he may be, and his very presence invigorates and instigates. On the other hand, look at our dear doctor with his totally different disposition. Where Lothario always works in wide perspectives for the whole, the doctor directs his clear-sighted attention on the most immediate concerns, providing the means for activity rather than stimulating activity itself. His work is like good housekeeping, his influence consists in gentle encouragement of each in his own particular sphere, his knowledge is a continual process of collecting and transmitting, receiving and bestowing on a small scale. It may well be that Lothario could destroy in one day what the doctor has built over a period of years, but it may also be true that Lothario can impart to others in a single moment the power to restore a hundredfold what has been destroyed."

"It is a sad business," said Wilhelm, "to have to think about the excellent qualities of others at a moment when one is so divided within oneself. Such reflections are appropriate when one is calm, but not when one is tormented by passion and uncertainty."

"Calm rational reflection is never harmful," said Jarno, "and by accustoming ourselves to think about the virtues of others, our own good qualities will imperceptibly find their place, and every wrong line of action that our fancy inclines us toward will be gladly abandoned. Free your mind if you can from all suspicion and fear. Here comes the Abbé. Be polite to him until you have had time to find out how much you have to thank him for. Just look at the old rogue walking between Natalie and Therese! I bet he's up to something. He likes to try his hand at playing the role of Fate, and sometimes he cannot resist indulging in the pastime of arranging marriages."

Wilhelm's petulant, wrought-up mood had not been alleviated by Jarno's fine, sensible words, and he found it extremely indelicate of his friend to mention such a subject at this particular moment. So he said, smiling but with some bitterness: "I would think one should leave the pastime of arranging marriages to those who are in love with each other."

Chapter Six

Since the others had now joined them, our two friends found it necessary to break off their conversation. A courier was announced with a letter to be delivered directly into Lothario's hands. He looked sturdy and reliable, and was dressed in a livery that was sumptuous and in very good taste. Wilhelm had the feeling that he had met this man somewhere before, and he was not mistaken, for it was the same man that he had dispatched after Philine and the presumed Mariane, and who had never returned. He was about to speak to him when Lothario, having read the letter, asked him sternly and somewhat angrily who his master was.

"That is a question I am totally unable to answer," said the courier somewhat bashfully, "I hope the letter will tell you, for I was given no verbal instructions."

"Be that as it may," Lothario replied with a smile. "Since your master has the face to write to me so impudently, we will be glad to see him."

"He won't keep you waiting long," said the courier, as he bowed and retired.

"Just listen to this crazy, absurd communication," said Lothario. "He writes as follows: 'Since good humor is always the most welcome guest, and since I am always accompanied by this wherever I go, I am convinced that the visit I intend to pay your Graces will not be ill received. I hope to arrive with the whole noble family of Absolute Contentment, and then in due course depart, etcetera. Signed: Count Snail's Pace.'"

"That's a new family to me," said the Abbé.

"Maybe he has been temporarily elevated to the rank of Count," said Jarno.

"The mystery is easily solved," said Natalie. "I bet this is our brother Friedrich who has been threatening us with a visit ever since our uncle's death."

"Bull's eye! o wise and beauteous sister," said a voice from a nearby bush, and out came an attractive, lively young man. Wilhelm could not suppress a cry. "Why!" he said, "Is our blond little rogue here too?" Friedrich became attentive, looked hard at Wilhelm, and then said: "My goodness, I would have been less surprised to find in my uncle's garden the famous pyramids that stand so solidly in Egypt, or the tomb of King Mausolus which I am assured no longer exists, than you, my old friend and manifold benefactor. I am very glad to see you again!"

Once he had greeted and embraced everybody, he rushed back to Wilhelm, and said to the others: "Take good care of this hero, this chieftain, this dramatic philosopher! At our first meeting I really hackled him fiercely, yet he saved me from many a blow after that. He is as noble as Scipio, generous as Alexander, at times also in love but always without hating his rivals. Not only does he never heap coals on his enemies' heads, which is said to be a disservice, but he even sends trusty servants after those friends who have run off with his girl, to see that she doesn't come to any harm."

He went on and on in this fashion, with no one able to stop him; and since none of them could answer him in the same vein, he was the only one talking. "Don't be amazed," he said, "at my learning in sacred and profane matters. You will soon find out how I achieved it." They wanted to know how things were with him and where he had come from; but he was so full of moral tags and rusty anecdotes that he was unable to give them any precise information.

"His brand of merriment makes me uncomfortable," said Natalie quietly to Therese. "I bet he is not so happy as he pretends to be."

Since Friedrich's tomfoolery, apart from a few jokes parried by Jarno, did not elicit any response from the company, he said: "Well, it seems the only thing for me to do is to be serious in this most serious company, and since all my sins weigh heavily upon me in such sober circumstances, I must resign myself to making a general confession, but you, noble ladies and gentlemen, shall hear nothing of it. Only my worthy friend here, who is already familiar with some of my doings, shall be treated to this, for he has more cause than anybody to want to know. Aren't you curious," he said to Wilhelm, "to find out the how and the where, the who, the when and the why? And how the conjugation of the verb 'to love' went, and what all the derivatives of that delightful verb were?"

He took Wilhelm's arm and led him away, hugging and kissing him the while.

When Friedrich arrived in Wilhelm's room, the first thing he saw was a powder knife lying in the window, with the inscription: "Remember me!" "You take good care of your things," he said. "That is Philine's, and she gave it to you on the day I roughed you up so badly. I hope it made you think about that girl a lot; I can assure you that she has not forgotten you. If I had not long since removed any trace of jealousy from my heart, I would still view you with envy."

"Don't talk to me about that creature," Wilhelm replied. "I will not deny that for a long time I could not get rid of the impression her agreeableness made on me—but that was all there was to it."

"Shame on you!" said Friedrich. "Who can ever disavow that he loved someone? And you loved her as completely as one could possibly wish. Not a day passed without your giving her some present or other—and when a German gives presents, then he is certainly in love. There was nothing left for me to do but snatch her away from you, and the little red officer finally succeeded."

"How so? Were you the officer we saw at Philine's she went off with?"

"Yes, indeed—the one you took for Mariane. How we laughed at that mistake!"

"How cruel it was to leave me in such a state of uncertainty," said Wilhelm.

"And as for the courier you sent after us—we simply took him into our service! He's a fine fellow and never left us. And I still love the girl as madly as ever. She has so bewitched me that I find myself almost in a mythological situation, expecting every day to be transformed into something or other."

"But do tell me," said Wilhelm, "where have you got your learning from? I am astonished at your habit of referring constantly to ancient tales and fables."

"I became learned—indeed, very learned—in the most amusing way. Philine is living with me, we have rented an old castle, and there we sit like a couple of hobgoblins, having a most amusing time. We have a large, but also very choice, library which includes a huge old folio bible, a world history from the beginnings, two volumes of European history, a collection of anecdotes culled from the best Greek and Roman authors, the works of the celebrated poet Andreas Gryphius, and other titles of lesser importance. Sometimes when we had our fling and felt bored, we had the urge to read something, and before we knew it, were more bored than ever. Then Philine lit on the splendid idea of piling all the books on to the table and opening them up. We sat across from each other and read to each other, always bits and pieces, from one book and then from another. This was the greatest fun! We really thought we were in high society where it is deemed improper to stick to one topic for too long or go into it too deeply; and we felt we were in lively company where no one lets anyone else speak. We entertained ourselves day after day in this fashion, and thereby became so learned that we were astonished at each other. We soon found there was nothing under the sun that our knowledge could not account for. We varied our means of instructing ourselves, sometimes reading against an hourglass that would run out in a few minutes, then be reversed by Philine as she began to read from another book, and when the sand reached the bottom glass, I would begin my piece. And so we studied away in true academic fashion, except that our lessons were shorter and our studies more varied."

"I can understand such a crazy way of doing things when two such merry people as you are sitting side by side; but that you could stay so long together, I find not so easy to understand."

"There's a good and a bad side to that," said Friedrich. "Philine can't let herself be seen, doesn't even want to look at herself, for she is pregnant. You can't imagine anything more shapeless and ridiculous than she is. Shortly before I left she happened to catch sight of herself in a mirror. 'Oh, my god!' she said, turning her face away, 'the living image of Madame Melina! How hideous, how vulgar one looks!'"

"I must confess," said Wilhelm, laughing, "that it is pretty funny to think of you two as father and mother."

"It's a crazy trick that I should finally have to accept being the father. She says I am, and the timing seems to be right. But at first I was somewhat uncertain because of that visit she paid you after the performance of *Hamlet*."

"What visit?" said Wilhelm.

"You surely haven't forgotten it? If you don't know already, I can tell you that the delightfully palpable ghost that night was Philine. This was hard for me to accept as a dowry, but if one can't accept something like that, one shouldn't love at all. Fatherhood rests only on conviction; I am convinced, therefore I am the father. So you see: I can use logic in the right circumstances. And if the child doesn't die laughing as soon as it is born, then it will be a pleasant citizen of the world, if not a useful one."

While these two were conversing with such gaiety about light-hearted matters, the rest of the company had embarked on a serious conversation. As soon as Friedrich and Wilhelm had gone off together, the Abbé led the others into the conservatory and, once they were seated, he delivered the following oration.

"We have made the general assertion that Therese is not the daughter of her mother, and it is now necessary for us all to be informed of the specifics. Here is the story, and I will document and corroborate it in every way possible.

"During the first years of their marriage Madame *** had a very good relationship with her husband, but the children they were hoping for, were all born dead, and on the third such occasion the doctors almost expected the mother to die and told her that the next time this would certainly happen. The two of them therefore had to reach certain decisions, but did not wish to dissolve the marriage because, from a domestic point of view, they were very happy. Mme. *** sought some kind of compensation for childlessness in the cultivation of her mind, in social activities, and vain pleasures. She was joyfully indulgent toward her husband when he developed an interest in a woman who took over the whole running of the household—a woman of beauty and good solid character. She soon came to approve this arrangement, according to which the good woman entrusted herself to Therese's father, continued the supervision of the household, and showed even more devotion than before to the lady of the house, and readiness to serve her.

"Some time later the woman announced that she was pregnant, and the couple arrived at the same idea, though for different reasons. The husband wanted to claim the child of his mistress as his own legitimate offspring, and his wife, annoyed that her doctor had been indiscreet enough to broadcast her situation, thought that she could regain her social status by accepting a substitute child, and by such an agreement maintain her control over her house, which she feared she might otherwise lose. She was more reticent than her husband, but realized what he wanted and knew how, without accommodating herself to his point of view, to make some explanation easier. She made her conditions, obtained almost everything she demanded, and that is how the terms of the will were established, which made very little provision for the child. The old doctor had died in the meantime, and so they turned to a young, intelligent physician who was well rewarded and extremely flattered to have the opportunity of revealing his deceased colleague's lack of skill and patience, and of putting things right. The natural mother agreed to all this, the deception was successfully accomplished, Therese came into the world, and was entrusted to a stepmother because her real mother fell victim to the deception by getting up from childbed too soon, died, and left the poor man disconsolate.

"Madame *** had, however, achieved her purpose. In the eyes of the world she now had a delightful child whom she displayed everywhere with excessive pride, and she had got rid of a rival whose relationship with her husband she regarded jealously and whose influence in the future she secretly feared. She showered the child with affection, and, in moments of intimacy, found ways to win her husband over by expressing great sympathy at his loss, so that he abandoned himself to her completely, placed the fortunes of himself and his child entirely in her hands, and only shortly before his death, and then only through his grown daughter, did he once again become master in his own household. This, my dear Therese, was probably the secret that your ailing father was trying to tell you; this is what I wanted to tell you about in detail while our young friend, your future bridegroom by a strange concatenation of circumstances, was not with us. Here are papers which prove the truth of what I have been telling you. You will see how long I have been on the track of all this and that I have only recently become certain about it. I did not dare suggest to my friend earlier that the achievement of a happy union with Therese was possible, for if this had turned out to be wrong a second time, he would have been utterly despondent. Now you will understand Lydie's suspicions; for I must confess that I never encouraged his affection for that girl, once I contemplated again the possibility of his marrying Therese."

Nobody expressed any reaction to what he had told them. The women returned the papers after a few days, without any further mention of the matter.

There was plenty in the neighborhood to keep the assembled company diverted, and the country was so delightful that they made frequent excursions alone or in groups, either by foot, on horseback or in carriages. On one such occasion Jarno explained to Wilhelm his proposal, showing him the relevant documents, but not pressing for a decision on Wilhelm's part.

Wilhelm's reaction was as follows: "Given the strange situation in which I find myself, I can only repeat what I said earlier with all sincerity in Natalie's presence. Lothario and his friends can legitimately demand every kind of renunciation from me, and so I hereby abandon all claim to Therese's hand. Please secure me the formal permission to leave. I can assure you, my friend, that my decision requires no further reflection. I have felt these last days that Therese is having difficulty in preserving that appearance of delight with which she first greeted me. Her affection is estranged from me; or perhaps I have never had it."

"Such situations resolve themselves better over the course of time, gradually, and in silence, rather than by a lot of talking, which only produces ferment and embarrassment," said Jarno.

"I would have thought," Wilhelm replied, "that just such a situation as this should be resolvable by an act of clear, quiet decision. I have so often been reproached with dilatoriness and indecision; why then, when I am firmly decided, should I be expected to indulge in a failing I have so often been charged with, this time to my own disadvantage? Does the world take such trouble to educate us, merely to show us that it cannot educate itself? Just allow me the satisfaction of ridding myself of a fruitless relationship which I entered into with the best intentions in the world—and that right soon."

Despite his request, several days passed without his hearing any more about the matter or noticing any change in the attitudes of his friends, for all the conversation tended to be general and unconcerned.

Chapter Seven

Natalie, Jarno and Wilhelm were sitting together, when Natalie said: "You have something on your mind, Jarno. I've been noticing that for quite a while."

"Yes I have," he replied. "There is an important venture we have been planning for a long time, and it seems to me that now is the time for it to get started. You," he said to Natalie, "already know about it in general terms, and I must tell our young friend about it, because it will depend on him whether he wishes to take part. You will not be seeing me here much longer, for I am about to embark for America."

"America?" said Wilhelm, with a smile. "I would not have expected such a wild idea from you, still less that you would choose me to accompany you."

"Once you know our whole plan," said Jarno, "you will not consider it a wild idea and might well be taken with it. Let me explain. One does not have to know much about the present state of the world to realize that great changes are impending and property is no longer safe anywhere."

"I have no clear sense of that," said Wilhelm, "and have only recently concerned myself about my possessions. Perhaps I would have done better to neglect them still longer, for concern about their preservation seems to make people gloomy."

"Let me finish what I have to say," said Jarno. "Concern befits age, whereas youth can well do without it for a while. Balanced activity can unfortunately only be achieved by counterbalancing. At the present moment it is highly inadvisable to have all one's property and all one's money in one place, but on the other hand it is difficult to manage them if they are in different places. We have therefore worked out a new plan: from our ancient Tower a Society shall emerge, which will extend into every corner of the globe, and people from all over the world will be allowed to join it. We will cooperate in safeguarding our means of existence, in case some political revolution should displace one of our members from the land he owns. I am now going to America in order to take advantage of the good connections that Lothario made when he was over there. The Abbé will be going to Russia, and you shall have the choice, if you wish to join us, of either staying with Lothario in Germany or coming with me. I would imagine that you would choose the latter, for a long journey can be very advantageous for a young man."

Wilhelm collected himself and replied: "Your proposal is certainly worth consideration, for my motto in the immediate future will be: The farther away, the better. I hope you will give me more details about your plan. It may be due to my insufficient knowledge of the world, but it seems to me that there are insuperable difficulties in establishing such an organization."

"Most of which will be overcome," said Jarno, "because so far there are a few of us honest, intelligent, determined persons, with a broad enough vision to establish such a Society."

Friedrich, who had been listening but said nothing till now, exclaimed: "If you will put in a good word for me, I will go with you."

Jarno shook his head at this.

"Why not?" said Friedrich. "What do you object to in me? A new colony will need young colonists: those I will bring you, and amusing ones at that, I can assure you. And then there is a fine young girl I know, who has no place over here any longer: I mean that sweet, charming Lydie. Where shall the poor girl go with all her sorrow and pain, except into the depths of the sea unless some worthy fellow takes charge of her. I would have thought," he said, turning to Wilhelm, "that since you are good at consoling abandoned women, you would decide to let everyone take his girl along, and then we could all follow this old gentleman."

This made Wilhelm angry. He answered, with seeming composure: "I don't even know whether Lydie is free, and since I do not seem to be very lucky in wooing, I would not want to try that."

"Friedrich," said Natalie, "when you yourself act so frivolously, you imagine that others share your point of view. Our friend here deserves a woman's heart that belongs only to him and is not beset by extraneous memories. Only with someone as sensible and pure in heart as Therese would such a risk have been advisable."

"What do you mean by 'risk?'" said Friedrich. "Love is always a risk, whether under the trees or before the altar, in embraces or wedding rings, when crickets are chirping or drums and trumpets playing, everything is a risk, everything is decided by chance."

"I have always thought," said Natalie, "that our principles are merely supplements to our existence. We are all too ready to give our faults the semblance of valid principles. Look out for the path that pretty girl, who at the moment attracts and claims you so strongly, will lead you."

"She herself is on a very good path," said Friedrich, "the path to sanctity. It is a detour, for sure, but all the more amusing and secure. Mary Magdalene went the same way—and who knows how many others. When the talk is of love, my dear sister, you really shouldn't intervene. I don't believe you will marry until some bride or other is missing, and you, with your customary generosity, will provide yourself as a supplement to someone's existence. So let's conclude our business with this seller of souls, and agree on who is to join the travelling party."

"You're too late with your proposal," said Jarno. "Lydie is already provided for."

"How so?" asked Friedrich.

"I have offered her my hand in marriage," Jarno replied.

"Old man," said Friedrich, "you are embarking on something which, as a substantive, invites various adjectives, and as a subject all sorts of predicates."

"I must honestly confess," said Natalie, "that it seems to me a dangerous venture to take over a girl at the moment when she is desperate because of love for another."

"I have taken the risk," said Jarno. "She will be mine under one condition. There is nothing in the world more precious than a heart capable of love and passion. Whether it has loved, or still loves—that's not what matters. The loved bestowed on another is for me almost more appealing than that with which I may be loved. What I perceive is the power and strength of a loving heart, and my self-love will not cloud this perception."

"Have you spoken to Lydie recently?" she asked.

Jarno nodded with a smile. Natalie shook her head and, getting up, said: "I no longer know what to make of you all. But I can tell you that I myself will not be led astray by you."

She was about to leave when the Abbé came in with a letter in his hand, and said to her: "Don't leave! I have here a proposal that I would like your opinion on. The Marchese, your late uncle's friend, whom we have been expecting for some time now, will be here in a few days. He writes that he is not so much at ease in the German language as he thought, and he needs a companion who is at home in that language and in several others. Since he wishes to establish scholarly rather than political connections, an interpreter of this kind is essential to him. I cannot think of anyone more suited for this than our young friend here. He knows his own language and is informed about many things, and it will be a great advantage for him to get to know Germany in such good company and under such favorable conditions. He who does not know his own country has no yardstick with which to measure others. What do you say, my friends? What do you say, Natalie?"

Nobody could think of any reason to object to this proposal. Jarno did not seem to see in it an obstacle to his plan of going to America; he was not intending to depart immediately. Natalie was silent. Friedrich recited various tags about the usefulness of travel.

Wilhelm was so enraged at this new proposal that he could hardly contain himself. He saw in it an arrangement to get rid of him as quickly as possible, an all too obvious stratagem and, what was worse, one that was announced publicly without any consideration for him. The suspicions that Lydie had aroused in him, together with all that he himself had experienced, came alive in his mind, and the unpretentious way that Jarno had explained things to him now seemed to him false and contrived.

But he controlled himself sufficiently to say: "Your proposal certainly deserves consideration."

"A speedy decision might be necessary," said the Abbé.

"I am not ready for that," Wilhelm replied. "Let us wait until the man arrives. Then we can see whether we are suited to each other. But one condition must be agreed on in advance, that I take Felix with me and that he shall accompany us everywhere."

"That condition will hardly be acceptable," said the Abbé.

"I don't see why I should allow conditions to be dictated to me by anybody, nor why, if I am to see my native land, I need an Italian to accompany me."

"Because a young man, " said the Abbé with impressive solemnity, "always has cause to seek the company of other people."

Wilhelm, realizing full well that he was unable to control himself much longer and that his temper was restrained only by the fact that Natalie was present, replied somewhat hastily: "Allow me a little time to think this over; I believe it will not take me long to decide whether I really need to seek further company, or whether my heart and mind will not irresistibly impel me to liberate myself from so many bonds that threaten to produce a state of wretched, lasting imprisonment."

That he said with deep feeling. A glance at Natalie assuaged him somewhat, her person and all it meant for him affecting him more strongly than ever in this moment of anguish.

"You might as well admit it," he said to himself when he was alone again. "You are in love with her; once again you are experiencing what it means to love someone with your whole being. It was like this when I loved Mariane, and things went so terribly wrong. I was in love with Philine, but could not respect her. I respected Aurelie, but could not love her. I revered Therese, and my paternal feelings led me to feel affection for her. But now when all those emotions which should make one feel happy fill my heart—I am being forced to leave! Oh, why must the irresistible desire to possess her associate itself with what I am now experiencing, and why without the certainty of possession, do these feelings, these convictions destroy all else that makes me happy? Will I ever again be able to enjoy the sun and world, the company of others, or any other pleasures? Will I not always say to myself: 'But Natalie is not here!' And yet, unfortunately, she will always be there. If I close my eyes, she will appear before me; if I open them, she will dominate everything like the effect produced by a blinding image in the eye. Was not the fleeting vision of the Amazon always present in my imagination, though I had only seen her, but did not know her? And now that you do know her and have been close to her, now she has shown such interest in you—now all her qualities are as clearly impressed on your mind as her image was formerly on your senses. It is always troublesome to seek, but more troublesome to find and have to do without. What else should I ask for from the world? Why should I look around any longer? What country, what town contains a treasure equal to this? Why should I travel all over the place just to discover something of lesser value? Is life nothing but a racecourse, where one must turn round immediately once one has reached the outmost limit? Are goodness and excellence a firmly established, immovable goal which one must hastily retreat from just when one believes one has reached it, whereas those who only strive for earthly possessions can acquire them in various places, even at markets or fairs?"

"Come, dear boy," he said to his son who had just run up to join him, "may you be and remain everything for me. You were given to me in place of your dear mother, you shall replace that second mother I had intended for you; now you have a larger gap to fill. Your beauty and charm, your thirst for knowledge and your developing abilities shall totally occupy my heart and mind."

The boy was busy playing with a new toy. His father tried to make it work. But while he was doing this, the child lost interest. "You're just like the rest of us," said Wilhelm. "Come, son! Come, brother-man, let's saunter about in the world, without any particular goal, as well as we can!"

His decision to leave, taking the child with him, and to distract himself by seeing what the world had to offer, was now firmly established. He wrote to Werner, asking him for money and letters of credit, and sent this by Friedrich's courier, instructing him most specifically to return soon. However much he was irritated with all his other friends, nothing clouded his relationship with Natalie. He confided to her what he intended to do, and she accepted it as self-evident that he could, indeed had to, do that; and although her apparent indifference to his decision caused him pain, her kindness and her very presence did much to comfort him. She advised him to visit various cities, where he could get to know some of her friends, both men and women. The courier returned, bringing what Wilhelm had asked for, despite the fact that Werner did not approve of this new venture at all. "I had hoped you were becoming sensible at last," he wrote, "but that seems to have been put off for a while. Where will you all be drifting to? And where will the woman be whose help in domestic affairs you gave me reason to think you had hopes of? None of the others will be around, so the whole burden of the business arrangements will have to be borne by me and the magistrate! Thank goodness he's as good a lawyer as I am a businessman, and we are both accustomed to shouldering responsibilities. Goodbye for the present. Your aberrations are forgivable, for without them we would not have gotten along so well in this part of the world."

As far as external conditions were concerned, Wilhelm could have left immediately, but his mind was preoccupied with two obstacles to this. First: They had refused to allow him to see Mignon's corpse, except at the funeral exequies, which the Abbé was determined to hold, though the preparations were not yet completed. Secondly, the doctor had been called away by a strange letter from the pastor, which had some reference to the Harper, and Wilhelm wanted to find out more about his situation.

In these circumstances neither his mind nor his body could be at rest, by night or by day. When everyone else was sleeping, he was pacing up and down in the house. The presence of those old familiar paintings partly attracted and partly repelled him. He could neither accept nor reject what surrounded him, everything reminded him of something else, he could see the whole chain of his life, but at the moment it lay in pieces which would not join together again. These works of art, the ones his father had sold, seemed to him a symbol of the fact that he too was partly excluded from calm, solid possession of what was desirable, and partly deprived of this by his own fault or that of others. He became so lost in these lugubrious reflections that he sometimes seemed to himself like a ghost, and even when he was feeling and touching objects outside himself, he could hardly resist the sense of not knowing whether he was alive or not.

It was only the stab of pain that he sometimes felt at so wantonly and yet so necessarily having to abandon what he had found and refound, only his tears that gave him once more the sense that he was indeed still alive. In vain did he remind himself of the fortunate state he was in. "Everything is worthless," he said to himself, "if that one single thing is lacking which makes everything else worthwhile."

The Abbé announced the arrival of the Marchese. "It seems," he said to Wilhelm, "that you are determined to go off alone with your son, but do at least make the acquaintance of this man, for wherever you may encounter him on your travels, he could be useful to you." The Marchese appeared, a man not far advanced in years, one of those handsome, agreeable Lombard types. He had made the acquaintance of the uncle, who was much older than he, when he was a young man in the army, and then through business transactions. Later they had traveled together through a great part of Italy, and the works of art that the Marchese rediscovered here, had been largely acquired while he was present, and on various happy occasions which he vividly remembered.

The Italians have a deeper sense of the value of art than other nations. Anyone who does anything wants to be an artist, a master or professor, and acknowledges through this craze for titles that acquiring things by inheritance is not enough, nor is achieving skills by practice. Italians concede that one should be able to think about what one does, establish principles and elucidate for oneself and others the reasons why this or that should be done.

The guest was touched to rediscover these beautiful objects without their owner, and delighted to find the spirit of his friend pervading his admirable descendants. They looked at the various works, and experienced great comfort at being able to relate to each other. The Marchese and the Abbé led the conversation; Natalie, feeling once again in the presence of her uncle, found it easy to agree with their thoughts and opinions. Wilhelm had to translate everything into theatrical terminology, if he was to understand what they said. It was hard to restrain Friedrich's joking. Jarno was rarely present.

In consideration of the fact that fine works of art are rare in modern times, the Marchese said: "It is not easy to contemplate what part circumstances have to play in an artist's activity, and the endless demands an outstanding genius, a person of remarkable talent, has to make on himself, and the immense effort he must expend on his training and development. If external conditions do little for him, if he concludes that the world is easily satisfied and only desires a pleasing and comforting illusion, it would be surprising if convenience and self-satisfaction did not commit him to mediocrity, and it would be strange if he did not prefer to acquire money and praise by producing fashionable wares than by pursuing a course that will more or less result in impoverishment and martyrdom. Therefore the artists of our age are always offering instead of giving. They always aim at attracting rather than satisfying. Everything is suggested, with no solid foundation and no proper execution. One only needs to spend a short while quietly in a gallery, observing what works of art appeal to the multitude, which of them are praised and which are ignored, to lose all joy in the present age and have little hope for the future."

"Yes," said the Abbé, "and as a result the artist and the lovers of art have a mutual influence on each other. The lover of art looks for some general indefinite pleasure: the work of art is to appeal to him just like a natural object. People tend to believe that the faculty of appreciating art develops as naturally as the tongue or the palate, and they judge a work of art as they do food. They do not understand that a different type of culture is required to attain a true appreciation of art. What I find most difficult is the separation a man must achieve within and for himself if he is ever to attain self-cultivation. That is why we encounter so many one-sided cultures, each of which presumes to speak for all."

"I am not quite clear what you mean," said Jarno, who had just joined the others.

"It is difficult," said the Abbé, "to speak briefly and definitively about this matter. All I would say is this: When a person sets himself a goal of manifold activity or experience, he must be capable of developing manifold organs in himself which are, in a manner of speaking, independent of each other. Anyone who aims at acting or experiencing with his total self, or tries to embrace everything outside himself into one total experience, will spend his time in constantly unfulfilled striving. How difficult it is to do what may seem so natural, to consider a fine statue or a superb painting in and for itself, music as music, acting as acting, a building for its own proportions and permanence! Nowadays most people treat finished works of art as if they were soft clay. The finished marble shall modify its shape according to their inclinations, their opinions and whims, the firmly established building expand or contract; a painting shall offer instruction, a play be morally uplifting, everything become something else. But because most people are themselves without form, since they cannot give a shape to their own self, their personality, they labor away at depriving objects of their form, so that everything shall become the same loose and flabby substance as themselves. They reduce everything to what they term 'effects,' to the notion that everything is relative; and so the only things that are not relative are nonsense and bad taste which, in the end, predominate as absolutes."

"I understand what you are saying," Jarno replied. "Or rather, I can see that what you are saying conforms to the principles you always firmly advocate. But I cannot be so hard on those poor devils, those human beings you speak of. It is true that many of them are reminded of their own wretched deficiencies when they are in the presence of great works of art and of nature, that they take their conscience and morality with them to the opera, do not discard their loves and hates before a noble colonnade, and their comprehension necessarily diminishes the grandeur and splendor of what comes to them from outside, so that they may be able to relate it somehow to their own paltry selves."

Chapter Eight

In the evening the Abbé summoned everyone to the funeral rites for Mignon. The whole company repaired to the Hall of the Past, and found it strangely decorated and illuminated. The walls were almost entirely draped with tapestries of azure blue, so that only the base and the frieze remained uncovered. Huge wax candles were burning in the four big candelabras at the corners of the room, and others of appropriate size in the four smaller ones surrounding the sarcophagus in the center. Four boys were standing beside the bier, dressed in silver and blue, fanning with sheaves of ostrich feathers a figure that lay on top of the sarcophagus. The assembled company all took their seats, and two invisible choruses intoned in gentle strains: "Whom do you bring to those at rest?" The four boys answered, with love in their voices: "A weary comrade we bring unto you; here let it stay and rest till joyful comrades in heaven shall wake it once more."

CHORUS. Child so young for this our realm, welcome, be welcome in sorrow! Nor boy, nor girl shall follow thee! Old age alone shall wend its way, eagerly, calmly, here to this silent hall, but thou, dear child, shalt rest here too, rest in solemn company.

BOYS. Sadly we brought her here, here shall she stay. We too will stay, weep and mourn, shed our tears above her corpse.

CHORUS. See now the mighty wings, see the light unspotted robe, the golden circle gleaming in her hair; see the beauty and grace of her repose.

BOYS. They lift her not, those mighty wings. Her garments float no more in easy play. Her head we crowned with roses, sweet and friendly was her gaze.

CHORUS. Lift the eyes of the spirit! May in you dwell the power that transports what in life is finest, loveliest, up aloft, beyond the stars.

BOYS. Down here she is lost to us now. In gardens she wanders no more, flowers she gathers no more. Let us weep and leave her here, let us weep and stay with her.

CHORUS. Children, return to life! Your tears shall be dried in freshness of air circling water's edge. Flee the night! Daylight and joy and continuance—those are the lot of the living.

BOYS. We rise and turn to life again. The day shall give us labor and joy, till evening brings us rest, and night refreshing sleep.

CHORUS. Hasten back to life anew! And beauty clothed in raiment pure shall bring you love, the sight of heaven, and the crown of immortality.

The boys moved away, and the Abbé rose from his seat and stepped behind the sarcophagus. "The man who prepared this silent dwelling-place," he said, "left instructions that each new arrival should be received with due ceremony. The designer and builder of this hallowed place came first; now we have brought here a young stranger, so that this one room encloses two very different victims of the solemn, arbitrary and inexorable goddess of death. Fixed laws govern our entry into life and the number of our days, our maturing in countenance of the light, but there is no law that prescribes the length of our life. The feeblest lifethread may stretch into unexpected length, and the strongest may be forcibly severed by Fate, which seems to delight in inconsistency. The child that we bury here, we know little about. We know not from where it came, nor who its parents were; and we can only guess at the length of its life. Its firmly locked heart gave us no inkling of what was going on inside it; nothing was clear or apparent about her except her love for the man who rescued her from the clutches of a barbarian. This tender affection and her intense gratitude seemed to be the flame that consumed the oil of her life. The doctor's skill could not preserve the beauty of her life, nor could friendship and care prolong it. But if art could not give permanence to her spirit, it could employ every skill to preserve her body and save it from decay. Balsam has been introduced into all her veins and, instead of blood, this colors those cheeks that faded so early. Draw near, my friends, and observe the wonders of art, the sum of solicitude!"

He lifted the veil, and there lay the child in its angel costume, as if sleeping, in the most pleasing position. They all stepped up, and marveled at this semblance of life. Only Wilhelm remained seated. He could not bring himself to do otherwise, he could not think about what he was feeling, for every thought seemed to shatter what he felt.

The Abbé had spoken in French, for the benefit of the Marchese, who stepped up with the others and looked attentively at the figure before him. The Abbé went on to say: "This good heart that was so closed to us, was always open to its God, in whom it had sacred trust. Humility, even a tendency toward self-debasement, seemed to be natural to her. She adhered fervently to the Catholic religion, in which she had been born and raised. She often expressed the desire to be interred in consecrated ground, and we have, according to the custom of her church, consecrated this marble coffin and the small amount of earth it contains, which is concealed in her pillow. In her last moments she fervently kissed the image of the Crucified One, which was delicately traced in hundreds of dots on her little arms." As he said this, the Abbé lifted the sleeve from her right arm, and there on her white skin they saw a bluish crucifix, together with various letters and signs.

The Marchese observed this very closely. "Oh God!" he cried, standing up straight and extending his arms to Heaven, "oh, you poor child, my unhappy niece—it is here that I find you at last! What painful joy it is to find you again, when we had so long abandoned all hope of doing so, to find your dear, sweet body that we thought was snatched by the fish of the lake, to find you again—dead, but preserved! I have witnessed your burial, glorified by its surroundings and even more by the good friends who accompanied you on your road to this place of rest. And when I am able to speak again," he said with a broken voice, "I will thank them all."

Tears prevented him from saying more. Pressing a spring, the Abbé lowered the corpse into the depths of the marble sarcophagus. Four young men, dressed like the boys, came from behind the hangings, placed the heavy, beautifully decorated lid on to the sarcophagus, and began to sing:

THE YOUTHS. The treasure now is well preserved, the beauteous image of the past. Unconsumed, in marble it rests; in your hearts it lives and works. Guide your steps back into life once more! With you take this solemn zeal, for zeal is sacred, it alone transforms life into eternity.

The invisible chorus joined in these final words, but no one heard their fortifying message, so absorbed were they all in the strange revelations and their own feelings. The Abbé and Natalie walked out with the Marchese; Therese and Lothario followed with Wilhelm. Only when the singing had completely died away, were they once more overcome with sorrow, reflection, consideration and curiosity, and longed to be back in the peace of what they had just left.

Chapter Nine

The Marchese avoided saying anything further openly, but he did have some long private conversations with the Abbé. When they were all together, he often asked for music, a request willingly granted because everyone was pleased to be relieved of the necessity of making conversation. Time passed, and he was making preparations to leave. One day he said to Wilhelm: "I do not wish to disturb the remains of that dear child. Let her stay where she loved and suffered. But her friends must promise to visit me in her homeland, in the place where she was born and raised. They must see the columns and statues she remembered in her song, the coves where she gathered pebbles. You, young man, will not decline the thanks of a family that is so indebted to you. I am leaving tomorrow. I have confided the whole story to the Abbé and he will communicate it to you. As an outsider he will be able to relate it more coherently than I could under the stress of my sorrow, for which he has already forgiven me. If you still wish to accompany me on my travels through Germany, as the Abbé has suggested, I would be delighted. And do bring your boy along with you; and if he should cause some occasional inconvenience, we will remember the care and consideration you gave my poor niece."

That same evening they were surprised by the arrival of the countess. Wilhelm was trembling in every limb when she came into the room, and she, though not unprepared, kept close to her sister who showed her to a seat. How simple was now her dress, how changed her appearance! Wilhelm could hardly bear to look at her. She greeted him, and a few general remarks sufficiently revealed her thoughts and feelings. The Marchese had retired early, but the rest of the company had no desire to disperse. The Abbé produced a manuscript, saying he had committed to paper the strange story he had been entrusted with, and that pen and ink had not been spared in recording the details of such a remarkable sequence of events. The countess was informed of what they were referring to, and the Abbé began to read what the Marchese had told him:

"Much as I have seen of the world, I must consider my own father as one of the oddest men I ever knew. He was of noble, upright character, his ideas were broad and, one could well say, big; he was strict toward himself, in all his plans there was unflinching purposefulness, in all his actions, steadiness and consistency. Productive as it was, on the one hand, to consort and do business with him, he himself had difficulty in being at ease in the world, because he demanded from the state, his neighbors, his children and his servants conformity to the same laws that he imposed on himself. His most modest demands became aggrandized by his strictness, and he was never entirely satisfied, because nothing turned out as he had wanted it to. I have seen him when he was building a palace, planning a garden, or acquiring a fine new estate, inwardly resentful at the conviction that fate had condemned him to self-denial and toleration. He maintained great dignity in his behavior: when he joked, it was to show his superior intelligence, he could not bear criticism and I only once saw him lose his temper, which was when he heard someone refer to one of his undertakings as ridiculous. It was in this spirit that he treated his children and handled his wealth. My elder brother was brought up to become the lord of huge estates, I was to enter the church, and my younger brother the army. I was vigorous, fiery, active, quick and good at all bodily activities. My younger brother was more inclined to a life of reflective repose, and devoted to study, to music and to poetry. It was only after a great struggle, when my father became ultimately convinced of the impossibility of his intentions for our future, that he agreed, though even then unwillingly, that my younger brother and I should switch professions; but although he saw that this was what we wanted, he was never resigned to it and foretold that no good would come of it. The older he became, the more cut off he felt from all society, till finally he lived almost entirely alone. Only one old friend, who had served in the German army, lost his wife during a campaign, and had a daughter about ten years old, provided my father with companionship. This man acquired a pleasant property in the neighborhood, visited my father regularly at certain times each week, often bringing his daughter with him. He never opposed my father, who came to consider him finally as the only company he could put up with. After my father's death we noticed that this man had been well provided for by my father—in fact he had not wasted his time. He enlarged his property holdings and his daughter had expectations of a fine dowry. She grew up to be an exceptionally beautiful girl, and my elder brother often teased me by saying I should seek her hand.

"Meanwhile, my brother Augustin was spending his time at the monastery in the most peculiar way: he gave himself over to indulgence in ecstasies of both spiritual and physical nature, which at times transported him into a seventh heaven, but at others plunged him into depths of weakness and a void of misery. While my father was still living, any change for my brother was unthinkable; even so, what could we have wished to propose? After my father's death, Augustin came to see us frequently. His condition, which we had pitied at first, became more tolerable, for he himself had become more reasonable. But the more his reason promised him health and contentment by following the course of nature, the more urgently did he implore us to liberate him from his vows. And he told us that his intentions were directed toward Sperata, the girl in our neighborhood.

"My elder brother had suffered too much from my father's severity to remain unmoved by the condition of his youngest brother. We both spoke with the family confessor, a fine old man, and revealed to him our brother's intentions, urging him to initiate and facilitate the matter. He expressed hesitation such as was unusual for him, but when our brother pressed us further and we advocated the matter more ardently to the confessor, he had to reveal to us a very strange story.

"What he told us was that Sperata was our sister, the child of both our father and mother. Affection and heat of the senses had come over my father once more in those later years when conjugal rights usually have abated. There had been much amusement recently over a similar case in the neighborhood, so my father, in order not to incur ridicule, decided to conceal this late, legitimate fruit of his love with the same care that other people conceal accidental products of their early affections. Our mother's delivery took place secretly, the child was taken into the country, and my father's old friend, who apart from the confessor was the only other person who knew the secret, pretended the child was his own daughter. The confessor had agreed not to reveal the secret except in dire emergency. My father's friend died, the young girl was placed in the care of an old woman. We knew that love of singing and music had led to my brother visiting her, and when he repeatedly demanded that we should release him from his former bonds in order to forge a new one, it became necessary to tell him as soon as possible of the danger with which he was beset.

"He looked at us with wild, scornful eyes. 'Spare me such outlandish tales,' he said, 'they are only for children and credulous ninnies. You will never tear

Sperata away from me. She is mine. Dismiss this terrifying phantom with which you vainly try to scare me. Sperata is not my sister, she is my wife!'—He then ecstatically described how this heavenly girl had led him out of his state of unnatural isolation into what is truly life, how their minds had joined like two throats in harmony, and how he even came to bless his former pain and aberration for depriving him of the company of woman so that he could now devote himself entirely to this lovely girl. We were horrified at this discovery, pitied him, but did not know what to do. He assured us quite definitely that she was carrying a child by him. Our confessor did everything his duty required, but that only made matters worse. My brother vehemently opposed all he said about the demands of nature, of religion, morality and social order; nothing was sacred to him save his relationship to Sperata, no names more worthy than those of father and wife. 'Such designations,' he said, 'are natural, all else is fancy or opinion. Haven't there been great nations that have sanctioned marriage with one's sister? Don't talk about your gods, you only refer to them when you want to fool us, lead us away from nature, distort our noblest instincts into crimes by infamous coercion, committing your victims to utter distraction of mind and disgraceful misuse of their bodies, burying them alive. I should know, for I have suffered more than anybody, falling from the highest pitch of rapture and ecstasy, down into the terrible waste of insensibility, emptiness, destruction and despair, from the loftiest sense of the existence of supernatural beings into the depths of disbelief, disbelief in oneself. I had drunk the terrible dregs of the cup whose lip had been so enticing, and every part of my being was poisoned. And now, when benevolent Nature has healed me by its greatest gift—the gift of love—now that I feel once again, at the bosom of this lovely girl, that I exist, that she exists, that we are one, that from our living union a third person will come and smile at us—now you loose the fires of hell and purgatory, which can only singe morbid imaginations, and hurl them at the unassailable certainty of the experience of true, living, pure love! Come and meet us beneath those cypresses that extend gravely into the sky, visit us in those groves where lemons and pomegranates surround us, and the tender myrtle unfolds its delicate blossoms—and then try to frighten us with your dismal, gray, man-made entrapments!'

"He persisted for a long time in not believing what we had told him, and even when we assured him of its truth, and the confessor confirmed this, he would not be deflected. On the contrary, he cried out: 'Don't listen to the echoes of your cloisters, don't consult your musty parchments, your crotchety and quirky regulations: ask Nature and your hearts. Nature will tell you what you have to tremble at: she will solemnly point to what she has irrevocably laid her lasting curse upon. Consider the lilies: Do not husband and wife grow on one and the same stem? Does not the blossom they bear unite them? And is not the lily the image of innocence? Is not its sibling union fruitful? Nature clearly indicates what it abhors: a creature that should not exist, cannot exist, develops wrongly, or is soon destroyed. The marks of her curse, the signs of her severity are: barrenness, stunted growth, premature decay. She metes out her punishments right away. Look around you: You will not see anything that is forbidden, anything that bears her curse. In the silence of the cloister and the bustle of the world, thousands of actions are honored and sanctified which bear Nature's curse. She regards with sadness both easy leisureliness and over-strained activity, free choice and abundance as well as compulsion and neediness; she advocates moderation. Her terms are valid, her workings gentle. He who has suffered as I have, has the right to be free. Sperata is mine; only death shall take her from me. How am I to keep her? How am I to be happy? That is for you to worry about. I'm going to her now, and never will I be parted from her.'

"He was about to board the ship to join her, but we dissuaded him, urging him not to do what might have the direst results. He should remember, we said, that he was not living in the free world of his own thoughts and ideas but in a state whose laws and customs had the inviolability of natural law. We had to promise the confessor that we would not let our brother out of our sight, and certainly not out of our castle. Augustin left us, promising to return in a few days. What we expected, occurred: His mind was strong, but his heart was weak, his earlier religious feelings revived, and he was overcome by terrible doubts. He spent two fearful days and nights, the confessor tried to help him, but in vain. His reason, when left to itself, absolved him of all blame, but his feelings, his religion, all customary concepts, declared him a criminal.

"One morning we found his room empty. There was a letter on the table telling us that, since we were restraining him by force, he was justified in seeking his freedom; he was going to Sperata, hoping to flee with her, and was prepared for all eventualities, should we try to separate them.

"We were much afraid, but our confessor constrained us to remain calm. Our poor brother had been closely watched, and the boatmen, instead of ferrying him across the water, returned him to his monastery. Tired from two days of wakefulness he fell asleep as soon as the boat began to rock in the moonlight, and did not waken until he was in the hands of his spiritual brothers. He did not recover until he heard the monastery gate closing behind him.

"Painfully affected by our brother's fate, we heaped reproaches on the confessor. But this worthy man soon persuaded us with medical arguments that our sympathy for the poor sick fellow was mortally dangerous. He said he was not acting on his own account but under orders from the bishop and the consistory. The intention was to avoid all public unpleasantness and cover up this sad case with the veil of secret ecclesiastical discipline. Sperata should be spared; she should never discover that her lover was her brother. She was referred to a priest to whom she had previously confided her physical condition. Her pregnancy and delivery were kept secret. She was happy to be the mother of the little creature. Like most of our young girls she could neither read nor write; and therefore she told the priest what he should say to her lover. The priest thought he owed a nursing mother some pious deception; so he brought her news of our brother without ever seeing him, told her in his name to be at peace, take good care of herself and the child, and leave the future to God.

"Sperata was by nature inclined to be religious. Her condition and her loneliness only increased this tendency, and the priest encouraged it so as to prepare her for a lasting separation. As soon as the child was weaned, and she had regained sufficient bodily strength, the priest began to present to her in terrifying colors her offense in giving herself to a priest, which he termed a sin against nature, a form of incest. For he had the strange idea of making her repentance like to that she would have felt if she had known the true nature of her transgression. By this means he brought great grief and misery into her mind, stressing the importance of the church and its high authority, depicting the terrible effects on the salvation of souls if clemency were exercised in such cases and the guilty rewarded by approving such a union. He indicated to her the saving grace of temporal atonement and the consequent attainment of the crown of glory. And in the end, like a poor sinner, she gladly sacrificed herself, imploring them to separate her forever from our brother. Since they had now achieved this much, they allowed her the freedom, though under supervision, to stay in her own dwelling or in the cloister.

"The child grew and soon revealed strange characteristics. It began very early to run and develop great skill in bodily movements, it would sing very pleasingly, and soon learned by its own efforts to play the zither. But it could not express itself in words, and the obstacle seemed to be in its mind rather than in its speech organs. The poor mother had a sad relationship with the child, the priest having so confused her that, without being mad, she found herself in the strangest state of mind. Her crime became ever more fearful and impious to her, and the reference to incest had impressed itself so strongly on her, that she was overcome by repulsion, as if she had known the true nature of their relationship. The confessor often wondered about the image he had used, which had broken the girl's heart. It was pitiful to see how a mother's love, delighting in the living presence of the child, fought with the ghastly thought that the child should not be there at all. The conflict between these two feelings became intensified, but repulsion soon won out over love.

"Quite early on they took the child away from her and gave it to some good people living down by the lake, and with this greater freedom it developed a special delight in climbing. The child made her way up the highest hills, clambered along the sides of ships, and imitated the feats of ropedancers who sometimes came to these parts—all this quite naturally.

"In order to be able to move more freely in all this bodily exercise, she wore boys' clothing, and although her foster parents thought this improper and undesirable, we tried to be as indulgent as we could. Her strange walks and climbs often led her far afield: she would get lost, stay away, but then reappear. When she returned, she would usually seat herself between the columns of the portal of a nearby villa. Nobody searched for her anymore, she was always to be found there, resting on the steps, running into the great hall, peering at the statues and then, unless she was detained by someone, running home.

"But our trust was deceived and our indulgence paid its price, for one day she did not return, her hat was found floating on the water not far from the place where a mountain torrent gushed into the lake. It was assumed that she had fallen whilst clambering over the rocks. Extensive searches were made, but the body was never found.

"Through the thoughtless gossip of some of her companions, Sperata soon learned of the death of her child. She seemed calm and serene and gave it to be understood that she was clearly pleased that God had taken the poor little creature unto Himself and thereby spared it from experiencing or creating even greater misfortune.

"In this connection all sorts of wild tales began to be bruited about regarding our lakes. For example: Every year a lake must have an innocent child, it will not tolerate a dead body and will sooner or later cast it up on the bank, even the very last bone will come up from the bottom. A story was told of one disconsolate mother whose child had drowned in the lake and who implored God and all the saints to allow her at least to bury the bones. The next storm cast up the skull, the next the rump, and when everything was together she carried all the bones in a cloth to the church. But then a miracle happened! As she was entering the building, the package got heavier and heavier, and finally, when she laid it on the steps of the altar, the child began to cry and to everyone's astonishment broke out of the cloth. Only one bone of the little finger of its right hand was still missing, which the mother sought and found, and this was preserved as a memorial amongst other relics in the church.

"These tales had a great effect on poor Sperata. Her imagination awakened and intensified the desire of her heart. She assumed that the child had atoned for itself and its parents, that the curse and punishment which had previously lain upon it were now entirely removed, and that what she had to do now was to find the bones and take them to Rome; then the child would appear before the people, in its fresh white skin, on the steps of the high altar of St. Peter's. It would once again look upon its father and mother, and the Pope, convinced of the approval of God and the saints, would forgive the parents their sins, to the loud acclaim of the assembled throng, absolve them and join them in marriage.

"Her eyes and attention were now always directed toward the lake and its shores. When at night the waves rolled in the moonlight, she would believe that every one of them was casting forth her child, and someone ought surely to run down there and pick it up on the bank.

"During the daytime she tirelessly visited those places where the stony shore ran into shallow parts of the lake, gathering into a little basket all the bones she could find. Nobody dared tell her these were animal bones. She buried the large ones, but kept the smaller ones. She continued relentlessly in her search. The priest who, impelled by an irresistible urge of duty, had brought about her condition, began to devote himself to her in every way he could. Influenced by him, people in the neighborhood began to consider her as someone in a state of religious rapture, not as someone out of her mind. They would stand with folded hands when she passed by; the children would even kiss her hand.

"Her old friend and foster mother was absolved by the confessor of her sin in bringing the two together, on the condition that she stay always with the poor unhappy creature, an obligation which she patiently and faithfully fulfilled until the very end.

"Meantime we had not lost touch with our brother. Neither the doctors nor the monastery authorities would let us visit him; but to convince us that he was well enough in his way, they allowed us, as often as we wished, to observe him in the garden or the cloister, even through a window in the ceiling of his room.

"After many terrible and peculiar periods, which I will not pause to describe, he entered on a strange state of mental repose and bodily restlessness. He hardly ever sat down except when playing his harp, which he often accompanied with song. Most of the time, however, he was restless, though easily guided and glad to follow, for all the violence and passion of his nature seemed now to focus on one thing—the fear of death. One could get him to do anything by threatening him with mortal illness or death.

"Apart from his habit of continually walking about in the monastery and asserting, in no uncertain terms, that it would be still better to be traversing hills and valleys, he spoke about an apparition that was constantly tormenting him. What he said was that every time he woke up, no matter at what hour of the night, he would see a handsome boy standing at the foot of his bed, threatening him with an open knife. They put him in another room, but he said the boy was there waiting for him. His walking back and forth became more and more restless, and people remembered afterwards that at that time he could be frequently seen at the window, looking out over the lake.

"Meantime our poor sister seemed to be steadily more and more worn down by her single preoccupation and her limited activity. So our doctor proposed that the bones of a child's skeleton should gradually be intermingled with those she already had, to increase her hopes. The idea seemed somehow dubious, but what might possibly be achieved, was that, when everything was put together, she might at least be persuaded to cease her endless searching and look forward to a journey to Rome.

"And so it was: her companion secretly exchanged what she had acquired with what Sperata herself had gathered, and a great joy spread over the poor woman's face when the parts gradually fitted together and she was told which were still lacking. She had fastened every part where it belonged with ribbon and thread, and had filled in the gaps with silk and embroidery as is done to honor the remains of saints.

"Everything was by now assembled, except for a few extremities. One morning, when she was still asleep, the doctor came to inquire how she was, and her old companion took the pieces out of the casket in the bedroom in order to show him what she had been busying herself with. Soon after this they heard her getting out of bed, lifting up the cloth, and, finding the box empty, falling on her knees. They came into the room and heard her fervent joyful prayer. 'It is true!' she cried. 'It wasn't a dream, it is true! Rejoice, my friends! I have seen the dear, lovely creature alive again. It rose up, threw off the veil, its radiance filling the room, its beauty transfigured, its feet unable to touch the ground, even had they wished to. It was lifted up lightly into the air and could not even touch me with its hand. Then it called to me, showing me the path I had to follow. I will follow my child, and soon. I feel this, and my heart is easy, so easy. My sorrow is departed; and the sight of my risen child has given me a foretaste of heavenly bliss.'

"From this time on, her whole soul was filled with joyful prospects. She no longer paid attention to earthly things, took little food, and her spirit gradually freed itself from the weight of the body. One day they found her unusually pale and without feeling, she never again opened her eyes, she was what is called dead.

"The report of her vision soon spread amongst the people, and the reverence she had aroused while she was still alive, gave way when she died to the conviction that she was to be considered blessed, maybe even holy.

"When she was carried to her grave, people thronged around to touch her hand or at least her garment. In the experience of passionate exaltation many sick people no longer felt the torments that had afflicted them; they thought they were cured and acknowledged this, praising God and his new saint. The priests were obliged to place her body in a chapel, and the people demanded to worship there. Large numbers came: miners (who always tend toward strong religious feeling) flocked from their valleys; reverence, adoration and miracles increased from day to day. Episcopal ordinances to restrict, and finally discredit, this new form of religious worship, could not be implemented: any attempt to curb it was vigorously opposed by the populace, who began to take active steps against any disbelievers. Did not the saintly Borromeo appear in these parts among our forefathers? Did not his mother experience the joy of his canonization? Does not that great statue on the rock of Arona portray in visible form his spiritual greatness? Do not his own descendants still live amongst us? Has not God agreed to renew his miracles amongst a people of believers like ourselves?

"When, after several days, the body showed no signs of corruption, was whiter than ever, and almost transparent, the people's faith increased and there were several cures, which no attentive observer could explain or dismiss as false. The whole district was in a state of excitement, and even those who did not come to see, heard about nothing else for a long time.

"The monastery where my brother was was filled with reports of these marvels, like the rest of the district, but no one took pains to conceal these things from my brother, since he paid so little attention to anything and his relationship with Sperata was not known to anyone there. But this time he seemed to listen very carefully to what he heard, and engineered his escape so craftily that no one could understand how he managed it. It was later ascertained that he got himself ferried across the lake with a group of pilgrims, and implored the boatmen, who did not notice anything odd about him, to take extreme care that the boat should not capsize. Late at night he came to the chapel where his beloved was resting after her suffering. There were only a few worshippers kneeling in the corners, and her old companion was seated by her head. He went up to the woman, greeted her and asked how her lady was. 'You can see for yourself,' she said, with some embarrassment. He looked at the corpse, but only from the side. After some hesitation he took Sperata's hand but, horrified at its coldness, let it drop immediately, looked around distractedly, and said to the old woman: 'I cannot stay with her now. I still have a long way to go. But I will come back soon. Tell her that, when she wakes.'

"And so he left. We were only told about this later, tried to find where he had gone to, but with no result. How he managed to make his way over mountains and valleys, we do not know. He finally left traces in the canton of Grisons in Switzerland, but it was too late for us to follow them up. After that he disappeared completely; we believed that he was somewhere in Germany, but the war completely obliterated any signs of his whereabouts."

Chapter Ten

The Abbé finished reading. They had all wept as they listened. The countess was still wiping her eyes; finally she stood up and left the room with Natalie. The others were silent. Then the Abbé said: "The question now arises whether we should let the Marchese leave without telling him what we know, but he does not. For how can there be the slightest doubt that Augustin and our Harper are one and the same person? We ought to consider what we should do, both for the sake of that poor unfortunate man and for the family. My advice would be to do nothing hastily, to wait and see what news the doctor will bring us."

Everyone agreed; so the Abbé continued: "There is another question that can perhaps be dealt with more quickly. The Marchese is deeply moved by the kindness his niece has enjoyed from us, and particularly from our young friend. I have told the Marchese all about it, and he has warmly expressed his gratitude. 'That young man,' he said, 'declined to accompany me on my travels before he knew the bond that exists between us. But now I am no longer a stranger for him, one whose moods and temperament he might well feel uncertain about: I am his associate, his close relative as it were, and since the main obstacle to his joining me was his son, may this child now become a finer, firmer bond to knit us together. In addition to what I owe him, his companionship on the journey would be extremely useful to me. Let him return with me, my elder brother will receive him gladly, and let him not despise the inheritance of his foster child, for, according to a private agreement between my father and a friend of his, the money he set aside for his daughter reverts to us, and we will certainly not deny the benefactor of our niece what he has so amply deserved.'"

Therese took Wilhelm by the hand, and said: "We are experiencing once again one of those happy occasions when unselfishness and generosity earn the best interest. Follow this strange call, and while making yourself doubly valuable to the Marchese, hasten toward that beautiful country that has more than once engaged your heart and your imagination."

"I consign myself entirely to my friends and their direction," said Wilhelm, "for it is useless trying to act according to one's own will in this world. What I most wanted to keep, I have to let go, and an undeserved benefit imposes itself upon me."

He pressed Therese's hand and withdrew his. "I leave it entirely to you, what you decide about me," he said to the Abbé. "So long as I do not have to separate myself from Felix, I am ready to go anywhere or undertake anything that is appropriate."

Having heard this, the Abbé unfolded his plan: the Marchese should take his leave, Wilhelm should wait for the doctor's report, and then, when they had considered what should be done about the Harper, Wilhelm should follow with Felix after the Marchese. The Abbé suggested to the Marchese that their friend's preparations for his journey should not prevent him from examining the monuments of the town. The Marchese departed, but not without repeated assurances of his gratitude, which the various presents he left— jewels, gems, fabrics—amply attested.

Wilhelm was now all ready to leave, but everyone was concerned that no news came from the doctor. They feared that some misfortune might have befallen the poor old Harper just when there were good expectations of an improvement in his condition. They dispatched the courier; but the doctor arrived that same evening accompanied by a man of impressively grave appearance, whom nobody recognized. Neither of them said anything at first, then the stranger walked up to Wilhelm, stretched out his hand, and said: "Don't you recognize your old friend?" His voice was that of the Harper, but his appearance was totally different. He was dressed like a normal traveler, clean and tidy, the beard was gone, his hair was cared for, and what made him quite unrecognizable was that there were no signs of age in his features. Wilhelm eagerly and joyfully embraced him, and introduced him to the others. His behavior was completely rational, but he was quite unprepared for how well they knew him. "I must ask you," he said calmly, "to be patient with someone who may look grown-up but, after a long period of suffering, has reemerged into the world as an inexperienced child. I owe it to this fine man here that I can once more appear in the company of others."

They welcomed him into their midst, and the doctor immediately suggested a walk, in order to break off the conversation and turn it into more neutral channels.

Once he was alone with the others, the doctor gave this account of what had happened: "It was the strangest chance that enabled us to effect his cure. For a long time we had been treating him morally and physically as we thought fit, things were going pretty well, but his fear of death was still intense, and he would not give up his beard or his long cloak. Otherwise, he was taking more interest in the things of this world, and his songs as well as his mental reactions seemed to indicate that he was drawing closer to life again. You will remember that strange letter from the pastor, which caused me to rush away last time. I went home and found the man completely changed: he had voluntarily had his beard removed and his hair dressed in a normal fashion, he asked for ordinary clothes, and seemed suddenly to have become a different person. We were curious to find out what had caused this, but did not dare to ask him about it.

"Then by pure chance we discovered a strange chain of events. A glass of liquid opium was missing from the pastor's medicine cabinet, and it was thought necessary to conduct a thorough search. Everyone was eager to absolve himself from suspicion, and there were some violent altercations amongst the persons in the house, until one day the Harper admitted that he had it. He was asked whether he had taken any of it, and said no. But he continued: 'I owe the return of my wits to this. You have the power to take it away from me, but if you do, you will see me lapse back into my former condition. It was the sense that it would be desirable to see one's earthly suffering terminated by death that first put me on the way to recovery. Soon after this the idea occurred to me of terminating it myself, and it was for this reason that I took the flask of opium. The possibility of ending my suffering gave me the strength to bear my suffering, and now that I have this talisman, I have forced my way from the presence of death back into life again. Do not be concerned that I shall make use of it,' he said. 'Satisfy yourselves, as persons with knowledge of the human heart, that you have made me attached to life by allowing me the means of detaching myself from it.' After mature consideration we decided not to press him any further, and he now carries on his person, in a secure glass bottle, this poison, the strangest of antidotes."

They informed the doctor of everything they had discovered, and it was decided not to reveal any of this to Augustin. The Abbé undertook never to let him out of his sight, and to guide him further along the path to recovery.

Meanwhile it was decided that Wilhelm should undertake his tour of Germany with the Marchese, and if it seemed possible to revive in Augustin the desire to see his native land of Italy, this would be communicated to his relatives and Wilhelm could return him to them.

Wilhelm had by now made all preparations for his journey, and if at first it seemed strange that Augustin was glad to hear that his old friend and benefactor was setting out again, the Abbé soon discovered the reason for this unexpected reaction. Augustin had never overcome his fear of Felix, and was therefore glad to see the boy depart as soon as possible.

By now so many guests had arrived that there was no longer any room in the castle and the adjoining buildings, especially since arrangements had not been made in advance for their accommodation. They breakfasted and dined together, and would have liked to persuade themselves that they were living in a delightful state of harmony, were it not for the fact that in their minds they were quietly veering away from each other. Therese had gone riding several times with Lothario, even more frequently on her own, and had made the acquaintance of all the landowners, male and female, in the neighborhood. This was her particular concept of domesticity, and she may well have been right in believing that one should be on the very best footing with neighbors and cultivate mutually helpful relationships. There seemed to be no talk of a marriage between her and Lothario. Natalie and the countess had a great deal to say to each other, the Abbé was always watching out for the Harper, Jarno having frequent conferences with the doctor, Friedrich clinging to Wilhelm, and Felix turning up wherever he could have a good time. They tended to walk in pairs when the company dispersed, and when they had to come together again, they took refuge in music so that they could be together and also alone with themselves.

An unexpected addition to the company was the count, who came to fetch his wife and, apparently, take formal leave of his worldly relations. Jarno ran to meet his carriage, and when the count asked who the company consisted of, Jarno said, in one of those fits of crazy humor that always came over him when he saw the count: "You will find the whole nobility here: Marcheses, Marquises, Mylords and Barons. All we lacked was a Count." They walked upstairs, and Wilhelm was the first person to meet them in the anteroom. "Mylord!" said the count to him in French, after inspecting him for a moment, "I am delighted to be able to renew our acquaintance so unexpectedly, for I must be gravely mistaken if I did not meet you in the prince's entourage when he was in my castle." "I did have the good fortune, Your Grace, to wait on you at that time," said Wilhelm, "but you show me too high a regard in considering me an Englishman, and, in addition, one of high rank. For I am a German and . . ." "A real good fellow," said Jarno, breaking in immediately. The count smiled at Wilhelm, and was about to say something, when the rest of the company came in and greeted him cordially. Excuses were made for not giving him suitable accommodation at once, but a promise was made to remedy this situation as soon as possible.

"Well, well!" he said, laughing. "I see the quartering arrangements have been left to chance, whereas foresight and planning can achieve marvels! But don't move a single thing, otherwise I can see there will be absolute bedlam. Everybody will be uncomfortable, and that shouldn't happen to anybody on my account, not even for one hour. You were witness," he said to Jarno, "and you too, Mister," turning to Wilhelm, "to the large number of people I comfortably housed that time in my castle. Give me a list of the guests and their servants, show me where everyone is housed at present, and I will rearrange things so that, with the least expenditure of effort, everyone gets comfortable quarters and there is still room left for the guest who turns up unexpectedly."

Jarno acted straight away as though he were adjutant to the count, brought him all the necessary information and had the greatest fun, according to his fashion, in leading the old gentleman astray. The latter, however, soon achieved a tremendous triumph. The whole rearrangement was completed, he had the names put over all the doors, and nobody could deny that the goal had been achieved with a minimum of reorganization and fuss. In addition to this, Jarno had so arranged things that persons with a particular interest in each other at the moment were accommodated in adjoining rooms.

When this was all settled, the count said to Jarno: "Help me to get clear about that young man you call Meister, who is said to be a German." Jarno said nothing for the moment, because he was well aware that the count was one of those people who, when they ask to be informed, really want to inform you themselves. Anyhow, the count, without waiting for an answer, went on to say: "It was you who introduced him to me then and commended him to me in the prince's name. If his mother was German, then I would vouch for it that his father was an Englishman, and of high station. The amount of English blood flowing in German veins during the last thirty years is considerable. I won't press the point further; everyone has family secrets. But I can't be hoodwinked in such matters." He then went on to recount various episodes involving Wilhelm at that time in his castle, to which Jarno said nothing, although the count was quite wrong and several times confused Wilhelm with a young Englishman in the prince's retinue. The old gentleman had once had an excellent memory, and was always proud at being able to recall the most insignificant details of his youth. But now he confidently imposed the stamp of truth on the wildest combinations of fancy that his imagination created out of failing memory. He had become very gentle and agreeable, and his presence had a salutary effect on the company. He requested that they should read something useful together, and even arranged little entertaining pastimes with great care, though not participating in them himself. And when people expressed their amazement at his condescension, he would say that it was incumbent on anyone who withdraws from the world in major matters, to consort with the world on minor matters.

More than once Wilhelm had an anxious moment during these entertainments, and frivolous Friedrich irritated him by hinting at an interest in Natalie on Wilhelm's part. How did he arrive at that idea? What gave him the justification for thinking this? And, since he and Wilhelm were much together, would not the company conclude that Wilhelm had slipped him an incautious and unfortunate confidence?

One day when they were amusing themselves and merrier than usual, Augustin appeared at the door, tore it open, and rushed in. His whole appearance was frightening—his face deathly pale, his eyes wild, his attempts to speak, fruitless. They were all alarmed: Lothario and Jarno, suspecting a recurrence of his madness, grabbed him and held him fast. First he stuttered indistinctly, but then shouted loud and clear: "Don't stay here holding me! Hurry up! Help! Save the child! Felix is poisoned!"

They let go of him, and he rushed out of the door with the whole company following in horror. The doctor was called. Augustin directed his steps to the room of the Abbé, where they found the child, frightened and ill at ease when they called to him as they drew nearer, asking him what he had done.

"Father!" said Felix, "I did not drink out of the bottle, I drank from the glass. I was so thirsty."

Augustin wrung his hands and said: "He is lost!" He pushed his way through the others and ran away.

On the table they found a glass of almond milk and beside it a half-empty carafe. The doctor arrived, heard what they had been told, and then observed to his horror the bottle that had contained the opium lying empty on the table. He gave him some vinegar to drink, and used all his skill to help the child.

Natalie had Felix carried to her room, where she anxiously took care of him. The Abbé had run off to find Augustin and elicit more information from him. The unhappy father had done the same, but without success, and when he returned he found consternation on everyone's face. The doctor had examined the drink in the glass and found that it contained a strong admixture of opium. The child was lying on a sofa and seemed very ill. He asked his father not to make him drink any more for it hurt him. Lothario sent people to discover where Augustin had gone, then himself went in search of him. Natalie sat by the child, who crept on to her lap, asking her to protect him and give him a piece of sugar because the vinegar was much too sour. The doctor agreed to this, saying that the child, who was in a very troubled state, should be allowed to rest for a while. All that should be done, had been done; as for the rest, he himself would do everything that was humanly possible. The count came in—somewhat unwillingly, so it would seem—looking grave and ceremonious. He laid his hands on the child, turned his eyes to Heaven, and remained for some minutes in this posture. Wilhelm, who had been stretched out disconsolate in a chair, jumped up, looked despairingly at Natalie, and left the room. The count left soon afterwards.

"I do not understand," the doctor said after a while, "why there are no signs of a dangerous condition in the child. Even if he only took one gulp, he must have absorbed a massive dose of opium, but his pulse shows no acceleration, except that caused by my medication and the state of fright we have put him in."

Jarno then brought the news that Augustin had been found in the attic lying in a pool of blood. There was a razor beside him, so he had probably cut his throat. The doctor rushed off and met the persons bringing down the body. It was placed on a bed and carefully examined. The cut had penetrated the windpipe, and he had fallen unconscious after a severe hemorrhage. But it soon became clear that there were still signs of life, and hope. The doctor placed the body in the proper position, dealt with the laceration, and put a bandage over the place. The night passed uneasily and sleeplessly for everyone. The child would not be separated from Natalie. Wilhelm sat in front of her on a stool, with the child's feet on his lap and its head and chest on hers. So between them they shared the pleasing burden and the pain of anxiety, and remained in this uncomfortable position until daybreak. Natalie had stretched out her hand which Wilhelm was clasping, neither of them said a word, they both looked at the child, and then at each other. Lothario and Jarno were sitting at the other end of the room, engaged in a very important conversation, which we would have gladly communicated to our readers if we were not so preoccupied with the rapid course of events. The boy slept peacefully, and woke quite happy in the early morning, jumped up, and asked for something to eat.

As soon as Augustin was somewhat recovered, they tried to get some more information out of him. What they did find out, was only extracted with difficulty and piece by piece. For instance: when as a result of the count's unfortunate rearrangements Augustin found himself in the same room as the Abbé, he discovered the manuscript with his life story, read it with horror, and became convinced that he could not live any longer. He then took his usual refuge in opium, poured some of it into a glass of almond milk, but recoiled at the moment he lifted it to his lips. He then left it standing while he went into the garden to look at the world once more. When he returned, he found the child about to refill the glass from which it had been drinking.

They urged the poor unhappy man to compose himself, but he grasped Wilhelm's hand frantically. "Oh!" he cried, "why did I not leave you long ago! I knew perfectly well that I would kill the child, and he me." "But the boy is alive," said Wilhelm. The doctor, who had been listening carefully to what Augustin said, asked him if all the drink had contained poison. "No," he said, "only the glass." "Then it was a lucky chance," said the doctor, "that the boy drank only from the bottle. Some good angel guided his hand so that he did not clutch the death that awaited him." "No, no!" cried Wilhelm, covering his eyes with his hands. "What a dreadful thing to say! The boy specifically said that he did not drink from the bottle, only out of the glass. He only seems not to be ill; he will wither away!"—And with these words he hurried out of the room. But the doctor went up to the child, stroked its head, and said: "Tell me, Felix; didn't you drink from the bottle, and not from the glass?" The little boy began to cry. The doctor spoke quietly to Natalie, telling her how matters stood. She then in turn tried to get the truth out of the child, but in vain. He cried bitterly, and continued to cry until he fell asleep.

Wilhelm watched over him, and the night passed peacefully. The next morning Augustin was found dead in his bed. He had deceived the watchful eyes of those attending him by feigning sleep, then quietly taken off the bandage, and bled to death. Natalie went for a walk with the child who was as cheerful as in his happiest days. "You are so kind," he said to her. "You never get angry, you never beat me. So I will tell you: I did drink out of the bottle. My mother Aurelie always slapped my fingers when I reached for the carafe. My father looked so fierce, I thought he was going to hit me."

Natalie flew with winged steps to the castle. Wilhelm came to meet her, still full of anxiety. "Happy father!" she cried, lifting up the child and placing it in his arms, "Here you have your son back! He did drink out of the bottle; his bad habit saved him."

The count was told the fortunate outcome, but he received the news with a smile and that modest, quiet sense of not being surprised, which enables us to tolerate the mistakes of well-meaning persons. Jarno, attentive to everything, could not understand such lofty self-satisfaction, till after much searching he found out that the count was convinced the child really had taken poison but had been miraculously preserved by the count's prayers and his laying-on of hands. The count now decided it was time for him to leave, his packing was as usual done in a trice, and on their departure the countess took Wilhelm's hand with one hand while still holding Natalie's in the other, pressed all four together, turned away quickly and leapt into the carriage.

This large number of terrible and strange events following one upon the other, brought about such a change in everyone's life, such continual disorder and confusion, that a kind of feverish agitation came over the whole household. Times for sleeping and waking, eating, drinking and social gatherings were delayed or reversed. Apart from Therese, everyone was thrown off course. The men tried to regain their normal good spirits by drinking intoxicating liquors, and while they acquired thereby a certain artificial enlivenment, they lost that spontaneity that alone can produce true good spirits and actions.

Wilhelm was disturbed, and disorganized by strong emotions. His whole being became totally bereft, through all these terrible unexpected happenings, of any power to withstand the passion that had taken such a strong hold over his heart. Felix had been restored to him, and yet everything seemed to be wrong. The letters with final arrangements were there from Werner, and all he needed for his journey was the courage to leave. Everything was pressing him to start out. He could well imagine that Lothario and Therese were simply waiting for him to leave, in order to get married. Jarno was unusually quiet; one might even say he had lost some of his usual brightness. Fortunately the doctor helped Wilhelm out of his quandary, by declaring that he was sick and giving him medicine.

The company came together every evening and Friedrich, that uninhibited fellow who usually drank more wine than he should have, monopolized the conversation, making them laugh in his usual way with hosts of quotations and waggish allusions, but often disconcerting them by his habit of saying exactly what he thought.

He seemed not to believe in Wilhelm's "sickness." One evening, when everyone was present, he said: "What's the name of the sickness afflicting our friend, Doctor? Which of those three thousand names would you select to cloak your ignorance? There is no lack of similar cases. There is one," he added ominously, "in Egyptian, or Babylonian, history."

They all looked at each other, and smiled.

"What was the king's name?" he said, pausing for a moment. "If you don't prompt me, I'll know where I can find out." He opened the doors and pointed to the large painting in the anteroom. "What's the name of that old goatee with the crown, pining away at the foot of the bed of his sick son? What's the name of the beauty who enters with poison and antidote simultaneously in her demure, roguish eyes? Who is that botcher of a doctor who suddenly sees the light and for the first time in his life can prescribe a sensible remedy, give medication which is a complete cure and is as tasty as it is effective?"

He went on swaggering in this tone. Everyone present did their best to control themselves and concealed their embarrassment behind forced smiles. A light flush came over Natalie's cheeks and betrayed the feelings she was harboring. Fortunately for her she was walking with Jarno, and when she reached the door, she skillfully managed to slip out, paced to and fro a few times in the anteroom and then went to her own room.

The others were all very quiet. But then Friedrich began to dance, and sing:

> Ah what wonders you shall see!
> What's done, is done,
> What's said, is said.
> Before day breaks,
> Wonders shall you see.

Therese had followed Natalie, and Friedrich led the doctor up to the painting, delivered a ridiculous encomium on medicine, and crept away.

Lothario had been standing motionless in a bay window, looking out into the garden. Wilhelm was in a sorry state. Being at last alone with his friend, he nevertheless remained silent, quickly surveying his life up to that point and finally shuddering at his present situation. Suddenly he jumped up and said: "If I am responsible for what is happening to you and me, then rebuke me! My suffering is now aggravated by your withdrawing your friendship, leaving me without this consolation to go out into the wide world I should long have been part of. If, however, you regard me as a victim of the cruel enmeshment of chance, from which I was unable to disentangle myself, do give me the assurance that your friendship and love will accompany me on a journey I can no longer postpone. The time will come when I can tell you what has been going on within me these last days. Perhaps I do deserve a rebuke for not unbosoming myself to you earlier, for not revealing my whole self. If I had, you would have stood by me and helped me out. Time and time again my eyes have been opened to what I am, but always too late and always to no purpose. How I deserved that dressing down by Jarno! I thought I had understood it well enough to embark on a new life! Could I? Should I? There is no sense in blaming either fate, or ourselves. We are all miserable creatures, destined for misery; and is it not a matter of complete indifference whether it is our own fault or the workings of some higher force, or chance, virtue or vice, wisdom or madness, that plunges us into destruction? Farewell! I will not stay a moment longer in a house where unwittingly I have so grievously abused such gracious hospitality. Your brother's indiscretion is unpardonable, it drives me to the utmost desperation."

"Well," said Lothario, taking him by the hand, "just suppose that your marrying my sister was the secret condition for Therese's agreeing to give me her hand? This was the compensation that noble girl designed for you: she swore that both pairs should go to the altar on the same day. 'His mind chose me,' she said, 'but his heart demands Natalie, and my mind will go to the assistance of his heart.' We agreed to observe you and Natalie, we confided in the Abbé and had to promise him not to take any steps to further your union but rather let things run their own course. This we have done. Nature did the job, and my crazy brother only shook down the ripe fruit. Since we encountered each other in such an extraordinary way, let us not live ordinary lives, let us work together in a worthy enterprise. It is beyond belief what a cultivated man can achieve for himself and others, if, without trying to lord it over others, he has the temperament to be the guardian of many, helping them to find the right occasion to do what they would all like to do, and guiding them toward the goals they have clearly in mind without knowing how to reach them. Let us then join together in a common purpose—that is not mere enthusiasm, but an idea which can quite well be put into practice, and is indeed often implemented, though not always consciously. My sister Natalie is a living example of this. The ideal of human activity which Nature has prescribed for her beautiful soul will always remain unattainable. She deserves this name more than many others—more even, if I may say so, than our noble aunt, who, when our good doctor assembled that manuscript, was the most beautiful personality we knew. But since then Natalie has developed, and everybody must rejoice at such a person."

He was going to continue, but Friedrich came running into the room, shouting: "What sort of garland have I earned? How will you reward me? Bind together myrtle, laurel, ivy, oak leaves—the freshest you can find. There are so many merits in me for you to crown. Natalie is yours! And I'm the sorcerer who raised the treasure!"

"He's crazy," said Wilhelm. "I'm leaving."

"Have you authority to speak?" Lothario asked Friedrich, keeping a firm hold on Wilhelm.

"Yes, on my own behalf, and by the grace of God, if you will; I was the intermediary, and now I'm the emissary. I listened at the door; she revealed it all to the Abbé."

"How disgraceful!" said Lothario. "Who told you to eavesdrop?"

"Who told her to shut herself in?" replied Friedrich. "I heard it all very clearly. Natalie was in quite a state. During that night when the child seemed so ill and was lying half on her bosom, with you sitting glumly there in front of her and sharing the precious burden, she made a vow that if the child should die, she would acknowledge her love and offer you her hand in marriage. Now the child is alive, why should she change her intentions? A promise once made should be kept under all conditions. Here comes the parson to surprise us with the news!"

The Abbé entered. "We know everything," said Friedrich. "Make it short. Your appearance is just a formality, we don't need you gentlemen anymore!"

"He eavesdropped," said Lothario.

"How improper!" exclaimed the Abbé.

"Hurry up!" said Friedrich. "How are the ceremonies to be? Pretty thin; you can count them on five fingers." And turning to Wilhelm, he said: "You have to start on your journey: the Marchese's invitation is very timely! Once you are on the other side of the Alps, everybody will be here, thanking you for all the wonderful things you will be doing, which will provide them with free entertainment. It's as if you were giving an open party to which persons of every station in life can come!"

"You have certainly had great success with the public in providing popular entertainment," the Abbé replied. "It seems as if I shall never get to speak today."

"If everything doesn't turn out as I say," said Friedrich, "then suggest something better. Come here and look at them—and let's be happy!"

Lothario put his arm around his friend. He led him up to his sister, who came toward them with Therese. Nobody said a word.

"Don't delay!" said Friedrich. "You can be ready to leave in a couple of days. Did you ever imagine, my friend," he said, turning to Wilhelm, "when we first met and I asked you for that lovely bouquet, that you would ever receive such a flower as this from me?"

"Don't remind me of those days at this happiest of all moments," Wilhelm replied.

"But you should no more be ashamed of those days than you should be of your parentage. Those times were good times: and I must laugh when I look at you now. You seem to me like Saul, the son of Kish, who went in search of his father's asses, and found a kingdom."

"I don't know about kingdoms," said Wilhelm, "but I do know that I have found a treasure I never deserved. And I would not exchange it for anything in the world."

Italian Journey

PART ONE

I, too in Arcadia

From Carlsbad to the Brenner

REGENSBURG, SEPTEMBER 3, 1786

I stole out of Carlsbad at three in the morning, for otherwise I would never have gotten away. Since my friends had been kind enough to celebrate my birthday on the twenty-eighth of August, no doubt they had earned a right to keep me there, but I could delay no longer. All alone, with no more luggage than a portmanteau and a satchel, I leapt into a mail coach and reached Zwoda at seven-thirty on a fine, still, misty morning. The higher clouds were like strips of wool, the lower ones heavy. I took this for a good sign that I might hope, after such a bad summer, to enjoy a good autumn. At twelve I was in Eger, in hot sunshine; and now I remembered that this town was on the same latitude as my native city. I was happy to eat my midday meal on the fiftieth parallel again, under clear skies.

In Bavaria one immediately comes upon the Waldsassen monastery—the choice possession of clerical gentlemen, who were clever sooner than other people. It lies in a basin more like a dish than a kettle, in a lovely, grassy hollow surrounded by gentle, fertile hills. Other properties owned by the monastery are spread far and wide in the area. The soil is decomposed shale. The quartz present in this species of rock neither decomposes nor weathers away, and it makes the ground friable and thoroughly fertile. The land rises as far as Tirschenreuth. The streams, heading for the Eger and the Elbe, flow toward me. To the south of Tirschenreuth the land slopes downward, and the streams run into the Danube. The smallest stream, once I have determined its direction of flow and the system it belongs to, quickly gives me a grasp of any region. Thus, even in areas one cannot survey, one forms a mental picture of the correlated hills and valleys. At the town mentioned there begins an excellent highway of granitic sand: it is the most perfect one imaginable, for the decomposed granite, which consists of gravel and clay, provides both a firm basis and a fine cohesive material, so that the road is as smooth as a threshing floor. But in consequence the region it runs through only looks worse: it too is of granitic sand, flat and marshy. Therefore the fine road is all the more desirable. Since the land also slopes downhill, one travels at an incredible speed that is quite a contrast to the snail's pace in Bohemia. The enclosed sheet lists the various stations along the way. Suffice it to say, the next morning I was in Regensburg and thus had covered these twenty-four and a half miles in thirty-nine hours. At daybreak I found myself between Schwandorf and Regenstauf, where I noticed an improvement in the farmland. It was no longer detritus from the hills but mixed alluvial soil. In primeval times, all the valleys which at present empty their waters into the Regen river were affected by the ebb and flow from the Danube valley, and thus arose those natural polders which support agriculture. This observation holds true in the vicinity of all rivers large and small, and with this guideline the spectator can readily explain any cultivable soil.

Regensburg is beautifully situated. The region naturally attracted a town, and the clerical gentlemen carefully considered their own advantage too. All the fields around the town belong to them, and in the town there is one church and one institute standing next to the other. The Danube reminds me of my old Main. The river and bridge look better at Frankfurt, but here Stadtamhof, which lies opposite, has a nice appearance. I went straight to the Jesuit college, where the students were putting on their annual theatrical spectacle, and I saw the end of the opera and the start of the tragedy. They performed no worse than any other inexperienced amateurs and were beautifully, indeed almost too gorgeously costumed. This public show convinced me anew of the Jesuits' astuteness. They scorned nothing that could be in some way effective, and they knew how to treat it with loving attention. This is not shrewdness in any abstract sense, for their delight in the thing, their empathetic and personal pleasure, which results from making use of life, is obvious. This great religious society not only has members who are organ builders, carvers, and gilders, but certainly also some with the inclination and ability to attend to the theater. Just as they distinguish their churches with a pleasing magnificence, so these judicious men make use of worldly sensuality with their decorous theater.

Today I am writing at the forty-ninth parallel, which shows great promise. The morning was cool, and here too people are complaining about the cold, damp summer; but the day turned out to be splendid and mild. The balmy air that comes with a great river is something quite unique. The fruit is not remarkable. I have eaten some good pears, but I long for grapes and figs.

I am fascinated by the activities and ways of the Jesuits. Their churches, towers, and buildings have a grandeur and completeness that fill everyone with secret awe. The decorations made of gold, silver, metal, and polished stones are massed together in such splendor and abundance that beggars of all classes must be dazzled by them. Here and there, as a sop and magnet to the common people, something tasteless is included. This is the genius of Catholic public worship in general; but I have never seen it applied with as much intelligence, skill, and consistency as by the Jesuits. Everything is designed, not, as with other religious orders, to preserve an old, worn-out form of worship, but to revive it with pomp and splendor to suit the spirit of the times.

A strange type of rock is processed here which looks like a kind of new red sandstone but must be considered older, primary, indeed porphyritic. It has a greenish admixture of quartz, is porous, and shows large spots of a sort of breccia. One bit was temptingly instructive and appetizing but could not be separated from the stone; and I have sworn not to load myself down with rocks on this trip.

MUNICH, SEPTEMBER 6.

On September fifth at twelve-thirty PM I left Regensburg. Near Abach and extending almost as far as Saal is a beautiful area in which the Danube surges against limestone rocks. This limestone is dense like that near Osteroda in the Harz, but porous nevertheless. At six o'clock in the morning I was in Munich and spent twelve hours seeing the sights, but shall comment on just a few of them. In the picture gallery I felt like a stranger; I must first accustom my eyes to paintings again. The collection is excellent. I was greatly delighted with the Rubens sketches from the Luxembourg gallery.

Also here is that elegant toy, a model of Trajan's column. Gilded figures against a background of lapis lazuli. It is certainly a fine piece of work and pleasant to look at.

In the hall of classical sculpture I could soon tell that my eyes were not trained to appreciate such objects and so did not want to stay and waste time. Many pieces did not appeal to me at all, though I could not have said why. A Drusus attracted my attention, two statues of Antoninus pleased me, as did a few other things. On the whole they were not placed to advantage, despite being meant as decoration; and the room, or rather the vaulted basement, would have profited from being kept neater and cleaner. In the natural history section I found beautiful specimens from the Tyrol which were already familiar to me in small samples which, indeed, I own.

A woman selling figs approached me, and, being my first ones, they tasted delicious. But in general the fruit is not especially good, considering that this is the forty-eighth parallel. People here complain bitterly about the cold and dampness. A fog scarcely distinguishable from rain greeted me this morning outside of Munich. All day the wind blew in very coldly from the Tyrolean mountains. When I looked in that direction from up in a tower I found the mountains shrouded and the whole sky overcast. Now the setting sun is still shining on the old tower that faces my window. Excuse me for paying so much attention to wind and weather: the traveler by land depends on both almost as much as the seafarer, and it would be a pity if my autumn abroad should prove to be as little favored as the summer at home.

Now I am going straight to Innsbruck. How much I am neglecting on all sides in order to carry out my *one* intention, which I have waited almost too long to do!

MITTENWALD, SEPTEMBER 7, EVENING.

It seems that my guardian angel is saying Amen to my Credo, and I thank him for having brought me here on such a fine day. The last postilion, shouting happily, said that it was the finest one of the whole summer. I am silently nurturing my wishful belief that the good weather will continue, but my friends must forgive me for talking again about air and clouds.

When I rode away from Munich at five o'clock the sky had cleared. Huge cloud masses clung motionless to the Tyrolean mountains. Nor did the strips in the lower regions move. The road goes along the heights, below which one sees the Isar flowing past drifts of piled-up gravel. Here one can understand the effects of currents in the primeval sea. In many a granite boulder I found siblings and relatives of the pieces in my collection, which were a gift from Knebel.

The mists from the river and the meadows persisted for a while, but at last they too were dissipated. Between the gravel hills I have mentioned, which must be imagined as several hours' journey long and wide, was the finest, most fertile soil, as in the Regen river valley. Now the way leads back to the Isar, where one sees a profile of the slope of the gravel hills, a good hundred and fifty feet high. I arrived in Wolfrathshausen and reached the forty-eighth parallel. The sun burned fiercely. No one expects the good weather to continue, there is wailing about the evils of the current year and lamenting that our great God is not tending to His business.

Now a new world opened up to me. I was approaching the mountains, which rose up before me gradually.

Benediktbeuern is choicely located, and the first sight of it surprises. In a fertile plain there is a long, broad white building with a broad, high, rocky ridge behind it. Now the road ascends to Lake Kochel; then higher up into the mountains to Lake Walchen. Here I greeted the first snow-capped peaks, and when I expressed my amazement at already being so close to snowy mountains, I heard that it had thundered and lightninged yesterday in the region and snowed in the mountains. In these phenomena hope was seen for better weather, and the first snow was presumed to mean a change in the atmosphere. The rocky cliffs surrounding me are all limestone of the oldest type, which does not yet contain fossils. Enormous uninterrupted ranges of these limestone mountains reach from Dalmatia to the St. Gotthard and beyond. Hacquet has toured a great section of this chain. It rests on a fundament rich in quartz and clay.

I got to Lake Walchen at four-thirty. About an hour's journey from the place I met with a pretty adventure: a harp player was walking ahead of me with his daughter, a girl of eleven years, and he asked me to take the child into my carriage. He went on with the instrument, I put the girl on the seat beside me, and she carefully placed a large new case at her feet. A polite, accomplished little creature, already quite well traveled. She and her mother had made a pilgrimage on foot to Maria Einsiedeln, and the two had been about to start on a longer journey to Santiago de Compostella when the mother departed this life without fulfilling her vow. The girl said that nothing was too much when it was a question of honoring the Mother of God. She herself had seen a whole house burnt down to the ground after a great conflagration, yet over the door, behind a glass, was a picture of the Virgin, quite undamaged, which was obviously a miracle. She had made all her trips on foot, had just played for the elector in Munich, and as a matter of fact had performed before twenty-one princely personages. She entertained me very well. Lovely big brown eyes, a stubborn forehead which sometimes puckered a little. She was pleasant and natural when she spoke, and especially when she laughed loudly, like a child. On the other hand, when she was silent she seemed to want to intimate something and curled her upper lip disagreeably. I discussed many things with her, she was at home everywhere, and very observant of things. Thus she asked me once what kind of a tree that was? It was a fine big maple, the first I had seen on the whole trip. Naturally she had noticed it at once, and when several others appeared one by one, was glad that she too could identify this tree. She said she was going to the fair at Bolzano, where I was also presumably heading. If we met there I was to buy her a present, which I promised to do. There she would also wear the new bonnet she had had made for herself in Munich from her earnings. She wanted to give me a look at it in advance. So she opened her case, and I was required to share her joy in the richly embroidered and much-beribboned head adornment.

We also took mutual pleasure in another happy prospect. Namely, she assured me the weather would be good. They had a barometer with them, that is to say, the harp. When the treble rose in pitch, that meant good weather, and it had done so today. I gladly accepted the omen, and we parted in the best of humor, hoping for an early reunion.

ON THE BRENNER, SEPTEMBER 8, EVENING.

Here I was practically compelled to stop for a rest, in a quiet place that was everything I could have wished for. The day was of a kind that can be enjoyed in retrospect for years. At six o'clock I left Mittenwald, a brisk wind cleared the sky completely. The cold was of a degree permissible only in February. Now, however, the gleam of the rising sun over the dark foregrounds covered with fir trees, the gray limestone rocks between them, and in the background the highest snowy peaks—those were exquisite, constantly changing pictures.

At Scharnitz one enters the Tyrol. The border is closed off by a rampart which seals the valley and adjoins the hills. It looks good; on one side the rock is fortified, on the other it rises up vertically. After Seefeld the road gets more and more interesting, and whereas from Benediktbeuern on it ascended from height to height and all the waters flowed into the Isar basin, now we look over a ridge into the Inn valley, and Inzingen lies before us. The sun was high and hot, I had to lighten my clothing, which I often change because of the day's changeable atmosphere.

At Zirl one rides down into the Inn valley. The locality is indescribably beautiful, and the sunny vapor made it look quite magnificent. The postilion hurried more than I wanted him to; he had not yet been to mass, and wished to hear it all the more devoutly in Innsbruck, today being the Virgin's Nativity. Now we kept on rattling down the Inn, past St. Martin's Wall, an enormous, steeply descending limestone face. It would have been at best a foolhardy undertaking, but I was confident that even without angels fluttering about I could reach the place where Emperor Maximilian is said to have lost his way while climbing.

Innsbruck is splendidly situated in a broad, fertile valley among high cliffs and mountains. At first I wanted to stay there, but I had no rest. For a short time I was amused by the innkeeper's son, my Söller in the flesh. Thus I meet my characters one by one. Everything is decorated in celebration of the Nativity of the Virgin. Crowds of people, looking healthy and prosperous, made the pilgrimage to Wilten, a shrine a quarter of an hour's walk from town in the direction of the mountains. At two o'clock, when my rolling carriage parted the cheerful, colorful throng, everybody was happily on the move.

Above Innsbruck the landscape grows more and more beautiful, no words can describe it. On very smooth roads one goes up a gorge that sends its water to the Inn, a gorge that offers the eye innumerable changes of scenery. While the road comes close to very sheer cliffs, indeed is cut into them, on the opposite side the land slopes gently and can support the finest agriculture. Villages, houses, cottages, huts, all painted white, stand among fields and hedges on the high, broad, sloping surface. Soon everything changes: the land is usable only for meadow, until that too disappears in a steep declivity.

I have gained much to support my view of the creation of the world, but nothing altogether new and unexpected. I have also mused a great deal about the model I have talked about for such a long time, by means of which I would like to make intelligible some ideas revolving in my mind that I cannot readily demonstrate in nature.

Now it grew darker and darker, details merged, the masses became larger and more imposing, but at last, when everything was just moving before me like a mysterious, murky picture, I suddenly saw the high, snowy peaks again, illumined by the moon. Now I wait for the morning to brighten this rocky gorge that hems me in, here on the boundary between south and north.

I shall add some remarks about the atmospheric conditions, which are favoring me, perhaps in gratitude for the many reflections I devote to them. In level country good and bad weather is received fully developed, but in the mountains one is present at its origin. This has happened to me so often on trips, walks, and out hunting, when I have spent days and nights in mountain forests, among rocky cliffs; and so a fanciful thought arose in me, which I do not pretend was anything else but which I cannot rid myself of, as indeed fanciful thoughts are the hardest to get rid of. I see it everywhere, as if it were a fact, and so I shall express it, since in any case I often find myself testing the patience of my friends.

Whether we contemplate the mountains from nearby or afar, now seeing their peaks agleam in the sunshine, now shrouded in fog, encircled by rushing clouds, whipped by pelting rain, or covered with snow, we ascribe it all to the atmosphere, since our eyes plainly see and grasp its movements and changes. On the other hand, the mountains stand there before our external senses, motionless, in their customary form. We consider them to be dead because they are rigid; we think them inactive because they are in repose. For some time, however, I have not been able to desist from ascribing the changes seen in the atmosphere in great part to an inner, quiet, secret action of the mountains. Namely, I believe that the mass of the earth generally, and, as a result, also especially its projecting foundations, do not exercise any constant, unchanging power of attraction, but that this power of attraction expresses itself in a certain pulsation, so that it is alternately increased and diminished through inner, necessary, perhaps also outer, incidental causes. All other attempts to demonstrate this oscillation may be too limited and crude, but the atmosphere is delicate and vast enough to instruct us about those quiet operations. If that power of attraction is diminished in the least, this action is indicated to us by the decreased heaviness, the diminished elasticity of the air. The atmosphere can no longer bear the moisture allocated to it chemically and mechanically, clouds descend, rains pour down, and streams of rain water flow toward the flat land. However, if the mountains increase their gravity, then the elasticity of the air is immediately restored, and two important phenomena occur. Once the mountains have assembled enormous cloud masses around themselves, they hold these firmly and rigidly overhead like second peaks, until, moved by the inner struggle of electrical energies, they descend as storm, fog, and rain; then the elastic air, which is now again capable of absorbing, vaporizing, and processing more water, affects the residue. I quite distinctly saw such a cloud being consumed; it was hanging around the steepest peak, the setting sun shone on it. Slowly, slowly its ends detached themselves, some tufts were drawn away and wafted upwards; they disappeared, as did gradually the whole mass, and it was quite literally unspun before my eyes by an invisible hand, like a distaff.

If my friends have smiled about this ambulant weather observer and his bizarre theories, some other reflections of mine will perhaps make them laugh. For I must confess, since my journey was in the nature of a flight from all the inclement weather I experienced on the fifty-first parallel, that I had hoped to enter a true Goshen on the forty-eighth. But I was deceiving myself, as I should have known earlier; for it is not the latitude alone that makes climate and atmosphere, but also the mountain ranges, especially those that cut across the regions from east to west. Great changes are always occurring in these, and the lands lying to the north suffer the most from them. Thus the weather this summer in the whole north seems to have been determined by the great Alpine chain on which I am writing this. During the last months it has rained constantly here, and southwest and southeast winds have driven the rain straight northwards. In Italy the weather is said to have been beautiful, indeed *too* dry.

Now a few words about the plant realm, which is not independent, but is conditioned in the most varied way by climate, altitude, and moisture. In this sphere too I have found no special change, but nevertheless some gain. Apples and pears are common already in the valley outside of Innsbruck, but peaches and grapes are imported from Italy, or rather the southern Tyrol. Around Innsbruck much Indian corn and buckwheat are grown, which they call "Blende." On the way up to the Brenner I saw the first larch trees, at Schönberg the first stone pine. Would the girl harpist, I wonder, also have asked questions here?

With respect to plants I still feel very much a novice. As far as Munich I believed I was really seeing only the usual ones. To be sure, my hasty night-and-day trip was not conducive to any very fine observations. Now, although I have my Linnaeus with me and have impressed its terminology on my mind, where shall I find the time and leisure for analysis, which in any case, if I know myself rightly, can never become my strong point? Therefore I direct my eye at general characteristics, and when I saw my first gentian at Lake Walchen, it struck me that heretofore also I had always found new plants first by the water.

What attracted my attention still more was the influence that the high altitude seemed to have on the plants. Not only did I find new plants there but also alteration in the growth of the old ones; if in the lower region the branches and stems were thicker and stronger, the buds closer to each other and the leaves broad, then higher in the mountains the branches and stems were more delicate, the buds separated by greater intervals from node to node, and the leaves shaped more lanceolately. I noticed this both in a willow and a gentian and became convinced that it was not, as one might think, a question of different species of these plants. Also at Lake Walchen I noticed longer and slimmer rushes than in the lowland.

The limestone Alps, which I had been traversing up to now, have a gray color and beautiful, curious, irregular forms, although the rock is divided into seams and strata. But because arched layers also occur, and the rock in general is unevenly weathered, the faces and peaks look strange. This species of rock reaches far up the Brenner. In the vicinity of the upper lake I found a change in it. Attached to a dark-green and dark-gray micaceous slate, heavily mixed with quartz, was a dense white limestone that was micaceous at the separation line and outcropped in large but infinitely fissured masses. On top of it I found micaceous slate again, which seemed more fragile to me than the first type. Farther up a special kind of gneiss manifests itself, or rather a type of granite which is being transformed into gneiss, as in the Ellbogen area. Up here, opposite the house, the rock is micaceous slate. The waters coming out of the mountain carry along this rock and gray limestone.

The granite mountain mass, on which everything is based, cannot be far distant. The map shows that we are on the side of the actual great Brenner, out of which the waters pour all around.

I have perceived the following with regard to the appearance of the people. This nation is honest and straightforward. Their figures show little variation, brown, wide-open eyes, and, among the women, finely drawn black eyebrows; among the men, however, thick blond eyebrows. The latter wear green hats that give them a cheerful look amongst these gray rocks. They trim the hats with ribbons or broad sashes of fringed taffeta that are pinned together quite neatly. Each man also has a flower or a feather on his hat. On the other hand the women disfigure themselves with very wide caps of tufted white cotton that look like shapeless masculine nightcaps. These give them a very odd look, whereas when in foreign parts they will wear the green men's hats, which become them very nicely.

I have had occasion to see how the common people value peacock feathers, and how any colorful feather at all is honored. Anyone planning to travel through these mountains should pack some along with him. Such a feather offered at the right place would serve as the most welcome gratuity.

While separating, gathering, fastening, and arranging these pages in such a manner that they may not only soon provide my friends with a cursory review of my adventures to this point but also relieve my mind of what I have experienced and thought, I am on the other hand viewing with a shudder some packets about which, without further ado, I must confess: they are indeed my companions! Will they not exert a great influence on the coming days?

I had taken all my works along with me to Carlsbad, intending finally to compile the edition to be published by Göschen. For a long time I had possessed beautiful copies of the unprinted writings, prepared by the skillful hand of Secretary Vogel. That worthy man had also come along this time to lend me his dexterous assistance. Consequently, with Herder's most faithful cooperation I was enabled to send off the first four volumes to the publisher, and was going to do the same with the last four. In part these consisted of works only in outline, nay, of fragments, for my bad habit of beginning many things, losing interest, and then letting them lie had gradually worsened with the years, because of other occupations and distractions.

Since I had all these things with me I was glad to heed the request of that discerning circle of friends in Carlsbad and read everything aloud to them that was as yet unknown, whereupon they complained bitterly because I had not completed those works and thus entertained them longer.

My birthday celebration consisted chiefly in my receiving several poems written in the name of works I had begun but neglected, in which each of them complained in its own way about my procedure. Especially noteworthy among them was a poem in the name of the "birds," in which a deputation of these cheerful creatures, having been sent to "True Friend," implored him finally to establish and equip the realm promised to them. No less understanding and graceful were the statements about my other fragments, so that suddenly all of them came to life for me again, and I gladly told my friends about my projects and complete plans. This gave rise to urgent demands and wishes and made it easy for Herder to persuade me to take these papers along with me again, and above all to devote some well-deserved attention to *Iphigenia*. The play in its present form is more a sketch than a finished work; it is written in poetic prose that sometimes goes astray into iambic meter and indeed also resembles other meters. This of course detracts a great deal from the effect, unless one is a very good reader and can mask the defects by means of certain techniques. He put this to me very earnestly, believing, since I had concealed my larger travel plans from him as from everyone else, that it was merely a question of another tramp through the mountains. Because he was always scornful of mineralogy and geology he said that I should, instead of hitting barren rocks, apply my tools to this work. I obeyed these many wellmeant importunities; however, until now it has not been possible to turn my attention in that direction. Now I am separating *Iphigenia* from the packet and taking it along as my companion into the beautiful warm country. The day is so long, my reflections are undisturbed, and the splendid sights in the world around me by no means inhibit the poetic sense. Rather, along with movement and open air, they evoke it all the more quickly.

From the Brenner to Verona

TRENT, SEPTEMBER II, 1786, MORNING.

After having been awake and in constant movement for fully fifty hours, I arrived here yesterday evening at eight o'clock, soon retired, and now am again able to continue my narrative. In the late afternoon of the ninth, when I had concluded the first section of my journal, I still tried to sketch the hostel, the posthouse on the Brenner, and its environs, but I did not succeed. I could not grasp its character and went back inside half peevishly. The innkeeper asked me if I did not want to leave, inasmuch as there would be moonlight and the road was in the best condition; and did I know that he needed the horses tomorrow morning for bringing in the hay and would like them home again by that time? So his advice was self-serving, but I accepted it anyway because it coincided with my inner desire. The sun reappeared, the air was tolerable, I packed up, and drove away at seven o'clock. The atmosphere kept the clouds in check and the evening was beautiful.

The postilion fell asleep and the horses trotted downhill very fast, off and away on the familiar road; when they came to a level spot they went a great deal more slowly. The driver woke up and urged them on, and thus, between high rocks, I very swiftly got down the rushing Adige river. The moon rose and illumined enormous objects. Several mills across the foaming stream, among very old fir trees, were perfect Everdingens.

When I arrived in Sterzing at nine o'clock, it was made clear to me that I was not to linger there. In Mittenwald at twelve o'clock sharp I found everyone fast asleep, except the postilion, and so it went until Brixen, where again I was practically abducted, so that I arrived in Kollmann at dawn. The postilions drove at breakneck speed, but, sorry as I was to travel through these splendid regions at night and so dreadfully fast, as though flying, I rejoiced inwardly that a favorable wind was blowing in back of me, driving me to my longed-for goal. At daybreak I caught sight of the first vine-clad hills. A woman selling pears and peaches approached me, and then it was off to Teutschen, where I arrived at seven o'clock and was at once sent further. Now in the full sunshine, after having traveled northwards again for a while, I finally beheld the valley in which Bolzano lies. Girt by steep mountains which are cultivated up to a considerable height, it is open toward the south, but blocked to the north by the Tyrolean mountains. A mild, gentle air filled the region. Here the Adige turns south again. The hills at the foot of the mountains are planted with grapevines. The stocks are drawn over long, low arbors, from the tops of which the blue grapes hang down very prettily and ripen from the warmth of the ground. Even on the valley floor, where usually only meadows are found, grapes are grown in arbors, in such close-standing rows that the Indian corn between them develops higher and higher stalks. I have often seen them as much as ten feet high. The fibrous male blossom has not yet been cut off, as will happen when the fertilization period has been over for a while.

I arrived at Bolzano in cheerful sunshine. Seeing so many merchant-faces gathered in one spot pleased me. Their expression very clearly bespeaks a purposeful, comfortable existence. On the square were sitting female fruit vendors with flat, round baskets over four feet in diameter, in which peaches lay side by side, so as not to press each other. The pears likewise. Here I was reminded of what I had seen written on the window of the inn in Regensburg:

Comme les pêches et les melons
Sont pour la bouche d'un baron,
Ainsi les verges et les bâtons
Sont pour les fous, dit Salomon.

It is obvious that this was written by a northern baron, and of course in these parts he would alter his views.

The Bolzano fair occasions active marketing of silk; woolen cloths are also brought here, and whatever leather the mountainous regions can produce. But many merchants come chiefly to collect debts, take orders, and extend new credit. I was very much minded to describe all the products assembled in one place, but the desire, the restlessness, which drives me onward leaves me no peace, and I at once hurry away again. But I am consoled by the thought that in our statistical era all this is no doubt already printed, and one can learn about it from books at one's convenience. At present I am only concerned with sense impressions, which no book, no picture, can give. The fact is that I am taking an interest in the world again, am trying my powers of observation, and testing the extent of my knowledge and scientific training. Is my eye clear, pure, and bright, how much can I grasp in passing, can the creases be eradicated that have formed and fixed themselves in my heart? These last few days, during which I have had to be my own servant and always be watchful and alert, have already given quite a new elasticity to my spirit; I have to worry about exchange rates, change money, pay, make notes, and write, instead of, as usual, just thinking, wanting, meditating, ordering, and giving dictation.

From Bolzano to Trent the road goes along for nine miles through an increasingly fertile valley. Everything that tries so hard to grow in the higher mountains certainly has more life and strength here, the sun is hot, and I believe in a God again.

A poor woman shouted at me please to take her child into my carriage because the hot ground was burning its feet. I did this charitable deed in honor of the great heavenly light. The child was dressed up and adorned in a strange fashion, but I could not get a word out of it in any language.

The Adige now flows more gently and leaves broad deposits of gravel in many places. On the land near the river everything is planted and intertwined so closely up the hillsides that it seems one thing will surely strangle the other—vineyards, maize, mulberry trees, apples, pears, quinces, and nuts. Dwarf elder cascades gaily over the walls. Ivy grows up the rocks on strong trunks and spreads widely; lizards slip through the gaps and all the people walking to and fro remind one of the most charming artistic images. The tied-up braids of the women, the men's bare chests and light jackets, the fine oxen they drive home from the market, the laden little donkeys, all of it constitutes a living, moving

Heinrich Roos. And now when evening comes and, in the mild air, only a few clouds rest against the mountains, standing rather than drifting in the sky, and right after sunset the shrill chirping of the cicadas makes itself heard, then I feel at home at last, and not as though I were in hiding or exile. I pretend that I was born and raised here, and have now returned from a trip to Greenland, catching whales. I even welcome the dust of the fatherland that sometimes whirls around my carriage, not having experienced it for so long a time. The chiming of the cicadas, like big and little bells, is delightful, penetrating but not unpleasant. It creates a merry sound when mischievous boys whistle in competition with a field of such singers; I fancy that they really intensify each other. The evening too is perfectly mild, like the day.

If someone living in the south, who was a native of the south, were to hear my raptures over this, he would consider me very childish. Alas, what I am describing here has long been known to me, as long as I have suffered beneath an evil sky, and now I am happy to feel, just as an exception to the rule, a joy which should be ours as a perpetual natural necessity.

TRENT, SEPTEMBER 10, EVENING.

I have walked around in the town, which is very old but has well-constructed new houses in some streets. In the church there hangs a picture of the assembled council listening to a sermon of the Jesuit general. I wonder what he has made them believe! The red marble pilasters on the facade mark the church from the very outside as belonging to these fathers; a heavy curtain covers the doorway to keep out the dust. I lifted it up and entered a small anterior church; the church itself is closed off by an iron grating, but in such a way that one can see everything. All was quiet and deserted, for services are no longer held in it. The front door stood open only because all churches are supposed to be open at vesper time.

While I stood there and reflected on the design, which I found similar to the other churches of these fathers, an old man entered and immediately doffed his little black cap. His shabby old black coat indicated that he was an impoverished cleric; he knelt down before the grating and, after a short prayer, stood up again. Turning around, he said softly to himself: "Now that they have driven out the Jesuits, they should also have paid them what the church cost. I certainly know what it cost, and the seminary, many thousands." Meanwhile he had gone out and the curtain had fallen behind him, which I lifted, keeping silent. He had stopped on the upper step and was saying: "The emperor did not do it, the pope did it." With his face turned to the street and unaware of my presence, he continued: "First the Spaniards, then we, then the French. Abel's blood cries out against his brother Cain!" And thus he went down the steps and up the street, still talking to himself. Probably he is someone the Jesuits supported who lost his reason over the tremendous fall of the order. Now he comes daily to look in this empty receptacle for its former inhabitants and after a short prayer curses their enemies.

A young man whom I asked about the curiosities of the town showed me a house called the Devil's House, which the otherwise all too eager Destroyer is said to have built in a single night with quickly procured stones. The good man failed to notice its really curious feature, namely, that this is the only house in good taste that I saw in Trent, certainly erected by a good Italian at an earlier time.

I traveled off at five in the evening; the same spectacle as yesterday evening, and the cicadas, which begin to shrill right at sunset. For at least a mile one rides between walls, over which grapevines can be seen; other walls are not high enough to prevent passersby from picking the grapes, and stones, thorns, and so forth have been used in an attempt to make them higher. Many proprietors spray the first rows with lime, which makes the grapes unpalatable but does not injure the wine at all because fermentation eliminates everything again.

SEPTEMBER 11, EVENING.

Here I am now in Roveredo, which is the language border; north of it there is still alternation between German and Italian. Now for the first time I had a typical Italian postilion, the innkeeper speaks no German, and I must try out my linguistic skills. How happy I am that from now on the beloved language will be alive, the language of everyday use.

TORBOLE, SEPTEMBER 12, AFTER DINNER.

How I wish my friends were here for a moment to enjoy the view I have before me!

I could have been in Verona this evening, but there was one more magnificent work of nature off to my side, a choice spectacle I did not want to miss, Lake Garda; and I was splendidly rewarded for making the detour. After five I rode away from Roveredo and up a side valley that pours its waters into the Adige. Having ascended it, one sees an enormous rocky barrier rising in the background, which must be crossed in order to get down to the lake. Here the most beautiful limestone rocks came into view, good for artistic studies. When one comes down there is a little town at the northern end of the lake, a small harbor or, rather, landing place, called Torbole. Fig trees in great numbers had already accompanied me on the way up, and as I descended into the rocky amphitheater I found my first olive trees, full of olives. Here for the first time I came upon what Countess Lanthieri had promised me I would: little white figs as ordinary fruit.

A door leads down to the courtyard from the room I am sitting in; I have moved my table in front of it and sketched the view with a few strokes. Almost the whole length of the lake can be surveyed, only at the end, to the left, does it elude our eyes. The shore, framed on both sides by hills and mountains, gleams with innumerable little settlements.

After midnight the wind blows from north to south, so whoever wants to go down the lake must travel at this time; for already a few hours before sunrise the air current turns and goes northward. Now in the afternoon it is blowing toward me, cooling the hot sun quite delightfully. At the same time my Volkmann informs me that the lake was formerly called Benacus and quotes a verse from Virgil mentioning it:

Fluctibus et fremitu resonans Benace marino.

This is the first Latin verse whose content has come to life before me, and which is as true at this moment, when the wind is growing ever stronger and the lake is casting higher waves against the landing place, as many centuries ago. Many things have changed, but the wind still churns the lake, and the sight is still ennobled by a line of Virgil.

Written at the latitude of forty-five degrees and fifty minutes.

In the cool of the evening I went for a walk, and now I truly find myself in a new land, in a completely foreign environment. The people lead a careless life of ease: firstly, the doors have no locks, but the innkeeper assured me that I need not worry even if my bags contained nothing but diamonds; secondly, the windows are fitted with transparent oiled paper instead of glass panes; thirdly, a most necessary amenity is lacking, so that one comes rather close to a state of nature here. When I inquired of the porter about a certain facility, he pointed down to the courtyard, saying, "Qui abasso può servirsi!" I asked, "Dove?"— "Da per tutto, dove vuol!" he answered amicably. Indeed I see the greatest negligence, but plenty of life and activity. The neighbor women carry on a lively conversation, a hubbub, all day long, and yet at the same time they are all doing something, working at something. I have not yet seen an idle woman.

The innkeeper announced to me with Italian pomposity that he considered himself fortunate to be able to serve me the choicest trout. They are caught near Torbole, where the brook comes down from the mountains and the fish are seeking a way up it. The emperor's share of this catch amounts to ten thousand gulden. They are not actual trout but big fish sometimes weighing fifty pounds, with bodies all speckled, up to the head; the taste is between trout and salmon, tender and excellent.

However, my real delight is in the fruit, in figs, also pears, which must surely be choice in a place where even lemons grow.

SEPTEMBER 13, EVENING.

This morning at three o'clock I set out from Torbole in a boat with two oarsmen. At first the wind was favorable, and they could use the sails. The morning was splendid—cloudy, to be sure, but tranquil with dawn. We went past Limone, whose mountainside gardens, arranged in terraces and planted with lemon trees, have a rich and well-kept appearance. The whole garden consists of rows of square white pillars, placed at certain intervals, which ascend the mountain in steps. Strong poles are laid over these pillars so that the trees planted in between may be covered in winter. Contemplation and inspection of these pleasant objects was favored by our slow journey, and so we were just past Malcesine when the wind shifted completely, taking its usual daytime direction and blowing toward the north. Rowing was of little help against this superior force, and so we had to land in the harbor of Malcesine. It is the first Venetian town on the east side of the lake. When traveling by water one cannot say, I shall be here or there today. I want to use this stop to the best advantage, and especially for drawing the castle situated at the water's edge, a beautiful object. I made a sketch of it today as we were passing.

SEPTEMBER 14.

The headwind that drove me into the harbor of Malcesine yesterday also caused me to have a dangerous adventure, which I got through with good humor and, in retrospect, find amusing. As planned, I went in the early morning to the old castle, which, having no gates or guards or keepers, is accessible to everyone. In its courtyard I sat down opposite the old tower built on and into the rocks; I thought I had found a very convenient little spot for drawing: next to a locked door at the top of three or four steps, and in the doorjamb an ornate little stone seat of the kind that can also still be seen in old buildings in our country.

I had not sat there long when various people entered the courtyard, looked at me, and walked back and forth. The crowd grew larger and finally stood still, surrounding me. I could plainly see that my sketching had created a stir, but I did not let this disturb me and calmly continued. At last a man not of the best appearance pushed close and asked what I was doing there. I answered that I was drawing the old tower as a souvenir of Malcesine. Thereupon he said that this was not allowed and I should stop it. Since he spoke in the vulgar Venetian dialect and in fact I scarcely understood him, I answered that I did not understand. At this, with true Italian composure, he seized my sheet, tore it up, but let it lie on the cardboard. Hereupon I detected a note of dissatisfaction among the people standing around, and one elderly woman in particular said that this was not right, the *podestà* should be called, for he knew how to judge such matters. I stood on my steps, my back against the door, and surveyed the constantly growing audience. The inquisitive, unswerving looks, the good-natured expression on most of the faces, and whatever else may characterize a mass of foreign folk, made the most comical impression on me. I imagined I had the chorus of birds in front of me that I, as True Friend, had often made fools of on the stage at Ettersburg. This put me into the most cheerful mood, so that when the *podestà* arrived with his clerk I greeted him without reticence and modestly answered his question as to why I was drawing their fortress by saying that I did not recognize this pile of masonry as a fortress. I pointed out to him and the people the decay of these towers and walls, the lack of gates, and, in short, the indefensibility of the whole thing, and I assured him that I had nothing else in mind except to see and draw a ruin.

His answer was, if it was a ruin, then what did I find remarkable about it? I answered, trying to gain time and favor, in great detail that they well knew how many travelers came to Italy only for the sake of its ruins, that Rome, the capital of the world, laid waste by the barbarians, was full of ruins which have been drawn many hundreds of times, and that not everything from antiquity was as well preserved as the amphitheater in Verona, which I also hoped to see soon.

The *podestà*, who was standing in front of me, but on a lower level, was a tall, somewhat gaunt man of about thirty years. The blunt features of his stupid face were in complete harmony with the slow and dreary way he brought forth his questions. The clerk, smaller and nimbler, also seemed a little confused by such an unusual new case. I said more things of the same kind, they seemed willing to hear me and, turning to some kindly female faces, I thought I perceived agreement and approval.

However, when I mentioned the amphitheater at Verona, which is known locally by the name "Arena," the clerk, who had meanwhile collected his thoughts, said that might be true, for that was a world-famous Roman building. But the only remarkable thing about the towers here was that they marked the boundary between the Venetian realm and the Austrian empire, and therefore ought not to be spied on. I explained at length that I did not agree, that not only Greek and Roman antiquities deserved attention, but also those of the Middle Ages. Of course these people should not be blamed for not being able to discover as much picturesque beauty as I could in this building they had known from childhood on. Fortunately, the morning sun was shedding the most beautiful light on the towers, rocks, and walls, and I began to describe this picture to them enthusiastically. However, because my listeners had their backs to these lauded objects and did not want to stop facing me altogether, they abruptly turned their heads around like those birds called wrynecks to see with their eyes what I was praising to their ears. Indeed the *podestà* himself turned to the picture being described, though with a little more dignity. The scene looked so ridiculous to me that my good spirits rose higher, and I spared them no details, least of all the ivy, which had already had centuries of time to adorn the rock and masonry very richly.

The clerk answered that this was all very well, but Emperor Joseph was a restless ruler who surely still had evil designs on the Republic of Venice, and I might well be his subject, delegated to spy out the borders.

"Far from belonging to the emperor," I exclaimed, "I can boast as well as you to be the citizen of a republic. To be sure, it cannot be compared in might and size to the illustrious Venetian state, but it also rules itself and is second to no city in Germany in commercial activity, wealth, and the wisdom of its officials. That is to say, I am a citizen of Frankfurt-on-Main, a city whose name and reputation must have reached your ears."

"From Frankfurt-on-Main!" shouted a pretty young woman. "There, Mr. *Podestà*, you can see right away what kind of a person this foreigner is, and I consider him a good man. Send for Gregorio, who was in service there for a long time, and he will be able to decide best in this affair."

Already there were more numerous benevolent faces around me, the first disagreeable one had disappeared, and when Gregorio arrived, the case turned completely in my favor. He was a man perhaps in his fifties, a brown Italian face of the familiar type. He spoke and behaved like someone to whom a foreign thing is not foreign, told me at once that he had been in domestic service to the Bolongaros and would like to hear something from me about this family and the town he remembered with pleasure. Fortunately he had been there during my younger years, and I had the dual advantage of being able to tell him exactly the state of things at his time and what had changed since then. I told him about all the Italian families, none of which were strangers to me; he was very pleased to hear many details, for example that Mr. Allesina had celebrated his golden wedding anniversary in 1774, that a medal had been struck for the occasion which I owned myself; he remembered quite well that this business magnate's wife had been born a Brentano. I also had to tell him about the children and grandchildren of these families, how they had grown, been provided for, had married, and produced grandchildren.

While I gave him the most exact information concerning almost everything he asked about, cheerfulness and seriousness alternated on the man's features. He was happy and touched, the people grew increasingly cheerful and could not get enough of hearing our conversation, a part of which, of course, he first had to translate into their dialect.

Finally he said, "Mr. *Podestà*, I am convinced that this is an honest, accomplished man, well brought up, who is traveling in order to educate himself. Let us send him on his way in a friendly manner, so that he will speak well of us to his countrymen and encourage them to visit Malcesine, whose lovely location certainly merits the admiration of foreigners." I reinforced these friendly words with praise of the region, the locality, and the inhabitants, not forgetting to praise the justice officers as wise and prudent men.

All this was declared good, and I received permission to inspect the town and its environs with Master Gregorio as I pleased. Now the innkeeper with whom I was staying joined us, already looking forward to the foreign visitors who would be flocking also to him when the good qualities of Malcesine were properly brought to light. He looked at my articles of clothing with lively curiosity, but particularly envied me those little pistols that can be stuck into one's pockets so conveniently. He said those people were lucky who were permitted to carry such fine arms, which were forbidden here under the severest penalties. I interrupted my friendly importuner several times in order to express gratitude to my deliverer. "Do not thank me," answered the worthy man, "you owe me nothing. If the *podestà* understood his trade and the clerk were not the most self-seeking of men, you would not have gotten away like that. The former was more embarrassed than you were and the latter would not have received a farthing for your arrest, the reports, or the transference to Verona. He thought this over quickly and you were already freed before our conversation was at an end."

Toward evening the good man took me out into his vineyard, which was very well located lower down the lake. His fifteen-year-old son accompanied us and had to climb the trees to pick me the best fruit, while his father selected the ripest grapes.

Between these two unworldly, kindly people, and quite alone in the infinite solitude of this corner of the world, I felt very keenly, reflecting on the day's adventures, what a strange creature man is: what he could enjoy with security and comfort in good company, he often makes uncomfortable and dangerous for himself, simply out of a whim to assimilate the world and its contents in his own special way.

Toward midnight my innkeeper, carrying the little basket of fruit that Gregorio had presented to me, accompanied me to my barque, and so, with a favorable wind, I left the shore which had threatened to become Laestrygonian for me.

Now, concerning my lake trip! It ended happily after the magnificence of the watery expanse and the adjacent Brescian shore had refreshed me to the very heart. There, where the west side of the mountains ceases to be steep and the landscape slopes more gently towards the lake, lie Gargnano, Bogliaco, Cecina, Toscolano, Maderno, Verdom, Salo in a row stretching out for approximately an hour and a half's journey, all of them rather elongated also. Words cannot express the charm of this thickly populated region. At ten o'clock in the morning I landed at Bardolino, loaded my bags onto one mule and myself onto another. Now the way led over a ridge which divides the valley of the Adige from the lake basin. The primeval waters seem to have worked against each other here in vast currents from both sides and to have raised this colossal dam of pebbles. Fertile soil was washed over it in calmer epochs; but the farmer is nevertheless constantly plagued by deposits that keep coming to the surface. Every possible attempt is made to get rid of them, they are piled up in rows and layers, and by that means very thick quasi-walls are formed along the road. At this altitude, on account of insufficient moisture, the mulberry trees look sad. There are no springs at all. Occasionally one finds pools of collected rainwater, at which the mules, and their drivers too, for that matter, quench their thirst. Below, at the river's edge, bucket wheels are set up to water at will the plantations situated at the lower levels.

But there are no words to describe the magnificence of the new region which one now surveys while descending. It is a garden that extends for miles both in length and breadth, lying there quite flat and extremely well kept at the foot of high mountains and jagged rocks. And so on the 10th of September, just before one o'clock, I arrived in Verona. Here I am first of all writing this, in order to conclude and stitch together the second installment of my journal. Then towards evening I hope to see the amphitheater in a happy frame of mind.

I report the following about the atmospheric conditions of the last few days. The night of the ninth to tenth was by turns bright and overcast; the moon always had a halo around it. In the morning not long before five o'clock the whole sky became covered with gray but not heavy clouds, which disappeared as daylight progressed. The lower I descended, the more beautiful the weather became. While in Bolzano the great mountain mass remained northerly, the air showed quite a different quality; namely, at the various hollows in the landscape, which were very pleasingly differentiated by a somewhat lighter or darker blue, one could see that the atmosphere was full of equally distributed vapors, which it could bear, and which therefore were neither precipitated as dew or rain, nor gathered into clouds. As I descended further I distinctly noticed that all the vapors rising from the Bolzano valley and all the cloud strips from the more southerly mountains were drifting toward the higher northerly regions, not concealing them but enveloping them in a kind of haze. In the farthest distance, over the mountains, I could detect a so-called "blister," an incomplete rainbow. To the south of Bolzano they have had the finest weather all summer, only a little "water" from time to time (they call gentle rain "acqua"), and then sunshine again right away. Yesterday too a few drops fell from time to time, while the sun kept shining. It has been a long time since they have had such a good year; everything is prospering; they have sent *us* the bad weather.

I shall mention the mountains and minerals only briefly, because Ferber's trip to Italy and Hacquet's through the Alps give us enough information about this stretch of the road. A quarter hour away from the Brenner is a marble quarry, which I rode past in the twilight. It may, and must, lie atop micaceous slate, like the one on the other side. I found this slate near Kollmann when daylight came; farther down, porphyries manifested themselves. The rocks were so magnificent, and heaps of them along the highway so conveniently broken to pieces, that from them one could have immediately formed and packed up little collections like Voigt's. I can also take along a piece of each sort without inconvenience, provided that I accustom my eyes and desires to smaller proportions. Not far below Kollmann I found a porphyry which splits into regular slabs, and a similar one between Branzoll and Neumarkt, in which the slabs further divide into prisms. Ferber considered these to be volcanic products, but that was fourteen years ago, when, in people's minds, the whole world was on fire. Hacquet already ridicules that idea.

Concerning the humans, I can only say a little, and little of a pleasant nature. At daybreak, as I was riding down from the Brenner, I noticed a definite change in their appearance and was especially displeased by the brownish pallor of the women. Their expressions indicated poverty, the children looked just as pitiful, the men a little better, the basic features, however, quite regular and good. I believe the cause of their morbid condition is to be found in their copious use of Indian corn and buckwheat. The former, which they call yellow "Blende," and the latter, called black "Blende," are ground up, the flour cooked in water to a thick paste, and eaten like that. The Germans on the northern side pick the dough apart and fry it in butter. The Italian Tyrolean, on the other hand, eats it as it is, sometimes grating cheese on it, and no meat during the entire year. That must necessarily clog and stop up the first digestive passages, especially in women and children, and their cachetic color indicates such corruption. They also eat fruit and green beans, which they boil and mix with garlic and oil. I asked whether there were not also some rich peasants.—"Yes, indeed!"—"Do they not treat themselves well? Do they not eat better?"—"No, that is what they have always been used to."—"What do they do with their money? How else do they spend it?"—"Oh, as you know, they have their lords, who relieve them of it again."—That was the sum of a conversation with the daughter of my innkeeper in Bolzano.

I also heard from her that the winegrowers, who appear to be the most well-to-do, are the worst off, because they are in the clutches of the urban merchants, who advance them their living expenses in bad years, and then in good ones appropriate the wine for a pittance. But that is the same everywhere.

What confirms my opinion about nutrition is the fact that the women in the towns always look better. Pretty, plump, girlish faces, the body a little too short for its stoutness and the size of the heads, occasionally some quite friendly, obliging faces, however. We know the men because of the Tyrolean journeymen. At home they do not look as ruddy as the women, probably because the latter have more physical work, more activity, while the men are sedentary shopkeepers and tradesmen. At Lake Garda I found the people very brown, and without the slightest reddish glow on their cheeks, but not unhealthy either, instead quite fresh and comfortable-looking. This is probably caused by the intense sunshine to which they are exposed at the foot of their cliffs.

Verona to Venice

VERONA, SEPTEMBER 16.

So the amphitheater is the first significant monument of ancient times that I have seen, and so well preserved! On entering it, but still more while walking around its rim, I felt strange because I was seeing something great and yet actually seeing nothing. Of course it should not be seen empty, but brimful of people, as has been arranged in recent times in honor of Joseph II and Pius VI. The emperor, who surely was used to facing masses of humanity, is said to have been astonished by this. But only in the earliest times was the effect complete, when the populace was more of a populace than it is now. For in truth such an amphitheater is perfectly suited for impressing the populace with itself, for entertaining the populace with itself.

When anything worth looking at takes place on level ground and everyone gathers to see it, the individuals in back try in every possible way to raise themselves above the ones in front; people climb on benches, roll up barrels, drive up in carriages, pile up boards, occupy an adjacent hill, and quickly a crater is formed.

If the spectacle occurs on the same spot quite often, light scaffoldings are built for those who can pay, and the remaining masses help themselves as best they can. It is the business of the architect to satisfy this universal need. He prepares a crater like this by means of art, making it as simple as possible, so that the populace itself will be the decoration. Once having seen itself, it could only be amazed; for whereas it was otherwise accustomed only to see itself running about in confusion, to find itself as a milling crowd without order or particular discipline, now the many-headed, many-minded, fickle, errant beast sees itself united into a noble body, induced into oneness, bound and consolidated into a mass, as if it were one form, enlivened by one spirit. The simplicity of the oval is agreeably perceptible to every eye, and each head serves as a measure of the vastness of the whole. Seeing it empty now, I have no criterion, I do not know whether it is large or small.

The Veronese deserve praise for the way they have maintained this structure. It is built of a reddish marble that is attacked by the elements, for which reason the eroded steps are constantly being restored, in rotation, and they all seem almost new. An inscription commemorates one Hieronymus Maurigenus and the incredible industry he expended on this monument. Only one piece of the outer wall remains, and I doubt that it was ever completely finished. The lower vaults, which abut on the great square, called "il Brà," are rented out to craftsmen, and it is surely a cheerful sight to see these cavities full of life again.

VERONA, SEPTEMBER 16.

The most beautiful but always closed gate is called "Porta stuppa" or "del Palio." As a gate, and considering the great distance at which it is visible, it is not well conceived; for the merit of the structure can only be recognized close up.

They offer various reasons for its being closed. Yet my conjecture is this: the artist obviously intended this gate to effect a relocation of the Corso, for it does not fit at all with the present street. The left side has nothing but hovels, and the line at right angles to the middle of the gate leads to a convent, which would certainly have had to be torn down. No doubt this was perceived, also the rich and aristocratic probably did not wish to settle in this remote quarter. Perhaps the artist died, and so the gate was closed, putting a sudden end to the matter.

VERONA, SEPTEMBER 16.

The portal of the theater building looks quite respectable with its six large Ionic columns. But over the door, in a painted niche supported by two Corinthian columns, the life-size bust of Marchese Maffei in a great wig seems by contrast insignificant. It has an honorable position, but in order to maintain itself against the size and excellence of the columns the bust should have been colossal. Now it stands meanly on a little console, out of harmony with the whole.

The gallery encircling the forecourt is also insignificant, and its fluted Doric dwarfs cut a pitiful figure next to the smooth Ionic giants. But let us excuse that in view of the lovely display set up under the columned porticos. Here a collection of antiquities has been installed that were excavated mostly in and around Verona. Some are even said to have been found in the amphitheater. There are Etrurian and Greek objects, Roman ones down into the inferior period, and also modern things. The bas-reliefs are fixed into the walls and provided with the numbers given them by Maffei when he described them in his work *Verona illustrata*. Altars, column fragments, and similar remains; a quite excellent white marble tripod on which genii busy themselves with attributes of the gods. Raphael imitated and transfigured such subjects in the spandrels of the Farnese palace.

The breeze wafting hither from the graves of the ancients comes laden with fragrance, as if over a mound of roses. The gravestones are heartfelt and touching and always depict life. There is a man who, with his wife beside him, looks out of a niche as though from a window. There stand a father and mother, their son between them, looking at each other with inexpressible naturalness. Here a pair join hands. Here a father, resting on his sofa, is apparently being entertained by his family. I was deeply touched by the absolute immediacy of these stones. They are of a later period of art, but simple, natural, and universally appealing. Here there is no man kneeling in his armor, awaiting a happy resurrection. The artist, with more or less skill, has just presented the simple daily life of people, thus continuing their existence and making it permanent. They do not fold their hands, do not gaze into heaven; on the contrary they are down on the earth, as they were and as they are. They stand together, take an interest in one another, love each other, and that, despite a certain lack of professional skill, is most charmingly expressed in these stones. A very richly decorated marble pillar also gave me some new ideas.

Laudable as this exhibit is, it is nevertheless obvious that the noble spirit of preservation which established it no longer lives on in it. The valuable tripod will soon be ruined because it stands free and is exposed toward the west to the atmosphere. This treasure could easily be preserved with a wooden sheath.

The unfinished palace of the Proveditore, if it had been completed, would have made a fine piece of architecture. Otherwise the *nobili* still do a great deal of building, but each one, unfortunately, builds on the site where his older dwelling stood, therefore often in narrow lanes. Thus the splendid facade of a seminary is now being put up in a little lane in the farthest suburb.

When I was walking with a casual companion past the great, somber gate of a remarkable building, he asked me amiably if I would not care to enter the courtyard for a moment. It was the Palace of Justice, and owing to the height of the building the courtyard looked exactly like a huge well. "Here," he said, "all the criminals and suspects are kept in custody." I looked around and saw that all the stories contained open corridors, provided with iron railings, that went past numerous doors. When the prisoner stepped out of his cell to be led to trial, he stood in the open air but was also exposed to general view; and because there were probably several hearing rooms, the chains would clatter first over this, then over that, corridor through all the stories. It was a detestable sight, and I do not deny that the good humor with which I had dispatched my birds would have had some difficulty maintaining itself here.

I walked along the rim of the amphitheatrical crater at sunset, enjoying a most beautiful view over the town and its environs. I was quite alone, while down below crowds of people were walking on the broad paving stones of the Brà. Men of all classes and women of the middle class promenade. From this bird's-eye perspective the latter look just like mummies in their black outer garments.

The *zendale* and *vesta*, which form the main wardrobe of this class, are after all perfectly suitable dress for a people which, although not very careful about cleanliness, still likes to appear in public constantly. The *vesta* is a black taffeta skirt worn over other skirts. If the woman has a clean white one under it, she deftly lifts the black skirt up on one side. The latter is belted in such a way that it marks the waistline and covers the ends of the bodice, which can be of any color. The *zendale* is a large bonnet with long side pieces. The bonnet itself is made to stand up high over the head by means of a wire frame, but the side pieces are tied around the body like a sash, with the ends hanging down behind.

VERONA, SEPTEMBER 16.

Today, after leaving the "Arena," I came upon a modern public spectacle a few thousand paces away. Four noble Veronese were playing ball with four men from Vicenza. Ordinarily they did this among themselves all year long at about two hours before nightfall; this time, on account of the foreign opponents, an incredible throng of people attended. There may well have been four or five thousand spectators. I saw no women from any class.

Above, while speaking of the needs of the crowd in such a situation, I have already described the type of natural, incidental amphitheater that I saw here, with people positioned one over the other. Even from a distance I heard lively clapping of hands; every significant stroke was accompanied by this. The game proceeds as follows: Two gently sloping wooden ramps are set up at an appropriate distance from each other. The player who hits out the ball stands at the top of the ramp, his right hand armed with a broad, spiked wooden ring. As another man on his team throws him the ball, he runs down to meet it, and in this way increases the power of the stroke with which he hits it. The opponents try to hit it back, and this alternates until at last it remains lying on the court. While this is going on, the most beautiful poses are seen, which are worthy of being copied in marble. Since the players are all well-developed, robust young men in short, close-fitting white garments, the teams are distinguishable only by a colored emblem. The posture assumed by the hitter when he runs down the ramp and lifts his arm to strike the ball is especially beautiful; it is much like that of the *Borghese Warrior.*

It seemed odd to me that they perform this exercise next to an old city wall where the spectators do not have the slightest comfort. Why do they not do it in the amphitheater, which would be the very place for it!

VERONA, SEPTEMBER 17.

I shall just touch briefly on the pictures I have seen and add a few observations. I was making this remarkable journey not to deceive myself but to become acquainted with myself through objects, and so I tell myself quite honestly that I understand little of the art and craft of painters. My attention, my contemplation, can only be directed to the practical part, that is, to the subject and its general treatment.

San Giorgio is a gallery of good paintings, all altarpieces, perhaps not of equal worth yet certainly noteworthy. But the unfortunate artists, what they had to paint! and for whom! A shower of manna, some thirty feet long and twenty high! the miracle of the five loaves as a companion piece! What was there to paint? Hungry people who pounce on the little kernels, countless others to whom bread is being presented. The artists tried desperately to lend significance to such paltry matters. And yet genius, stimulated by coercion, produced beautiful things. One artist, who had to depict St. Ursula with the eleven thousand virgins, handled the problem very intelligently. The saint stands in the foreground as if she had victoriously taken possession of the land. She is very noble, virginal in an Amazon-like way, lacking in charm; her companions, on the other hand, are seen disembarking from the ship and advancing in procession in the distance, which makes everything diminutive. Titian's *Assumption of the Virgin*, in the cathedral, is very blackened, but it is a laudable idea that the goddess-to-be is not looking heavenwards but down at her friends.

In the Gherardini gallery I found very beautiful works by Orbetto and acquainted myself at once with this meritorious artist. At a distance one learns about only the greatest artists, and then often merely their names. However, when one comes nearer to this star-studded sky and even those of the second and third magnitude begin sparkling, each one also emerging as a part of the whole constellation, then the world grows wide and art becomes rich. Here I must praise the conception of one picture. Only two half-figures. Samson has just fallen asleep in Delilah's lap, and she is quietly reaching over him for the scissors, which lie on a table beside a lamp. The idea has been carried out very well. In the Canossa palace my attention was drawn to a Danae.

The Bevilacqua palace contains the choicest things. A so-called *Paradise* by Tintoretto, which is actually the coronation of the Virgin as Queen of Heaven in the presence of all the patriarchs, prophets, apostles, saints, angels, etc., an opportunity for displaying the whole range of that most happy genius. Lightness of brushwork, spirit, variety of expression—to admire and enjoy all this one should own the picture personally and gaze at it for a lifetime. The work goes into infinite detail, even the last angels' heads that disappear into the glory still have character. The largest figures may be a foot in height, Mary and Christ, who is placing the crown on her, about four inches. The Eve is the most beautiful little woman in the picture, however, and, traditionally, still a little lustful.

A few portraits by Paul Veronese have only increased my esteem for this artist. The collection of antiquities is magnificent, a recumbent son of Niobe is superb, the busts mostly very interesting regardless of the restored noses, an Augustus with the civil crown, a Caligula, and others.

It is my nature to be willing and happy to revere what is great and beautiful; and to develop this tendency with the help of such magnificent objects day after day, hour after hour, is the most blissful of all sensations.

In a land where people enjoy the day, but especially delight in the evening, nightfall is most significant. Then work ceases, then the promenader returns, the father wants to see his daughter back at home again, the day is at an end; but we Cimmerians scarcely know what day is. In our eternal fog and gloom it is immaterial to us whether it is day or night; for how much time do we really have to stroll and divert ourselves beneath an open sky? When night falls here the day, which consisted of evening and morning, is definitely past, twenty-four hours have been lived, a new account begins, the bells ring, the rosary is said, the maid enters one's room with a burning lamp and says: "Felicissima notte!" This cycle changes with every season, and the person who lives a lively life here cannot become confused because every joy of his existence is related not to the hour, but to the time of day. If a German clock were forced on this people they would become confused, for their clock is most intimately connected with their nature. One or one and a half hours before nightfall the nobility begins to drive out, it goes to the Brà, down the long, wide street leading to the Porta Nuova, out of the gate, away from town, and when the bell tolls night, everyone turns around. Some of them drive to the churches to pray the "Ave Maria della sera," some stop on the Brà, the cavaliers step up to the coaches, converse with the ladies, and that lasts a while; I have never waited to the end, the pedestrians stay until late in the night. Today just enough rain fell to settle the dust, it was really a lively, cheerful sight.

In order to adapt myself to an important point of local custom, I have invented a device to help me more easily assimilate their way of telling time. The following diagram can give an idea of it. The inner circle signifies our twenty-four hours, from midnight to midnight, divided into two times twelve, as we count and our clocks show. The middle circle indicates how the bells chime here in the present season, namely, also up to twelve twice in twenty-four hours, only in such a way that it strikes one when with us it would strike eight, and so on until fully twelve. In the morning at eight o'clock according to our clock hand, it strikes one again, and so on. Finally, the outermost circle shows how in daily life one counts to twenty-four. For example, at night I hear seven strike and know that midnight is at five, so I subtract this number from that and therefore have two o'clock past midnight. If in the daytime I hear seven strike and also know that noon is at five o'clock, I proceed in the same fashion and get two o'clock in the afternoon. However, if I want to tell the hours according to the local manner I must know that noon is seventeen o'clock, then add two more and say nineteen o'clock, The first time one hears and reflects on this, it seems extremely complicated and hard to put into practice; but quite soon one becomes accustomed to it and finds this an entertaining occupation. The people also delight in this endless back-and-forth reckoning, like children with difficulties that can easily be overcome. Besides, they always have their fingers in the air, figure everything in their heads, and like to work with numbers. Furthermore the matter is all the easier for the native because he really is not concerned about noon and midnight and, unlike the foreigner in his country, does not compare two clock hands with each other. They count the evening hours only as they strike, in the daytime they add the number to the varying noonday number, which is known to them. The rest is explained by the annotations attached to the figure.

VERONA, SEPTEMBER 17.

The populace here moves around in very lively confusion, and things look especially busy in the streets where shops and craftsmen's stalls are closely crowded together. The shop or workroom does not have a door, as might be

THE NIGHT INCREASES A HALF HOUR WITH EVERY HALF MONTH.

MONTH	DAY	BECOMES NIGHT BY OUR CLOCK HAND	IS MIDNIGHT THEN AT
August	1	8½	3½
	15	8	4
Sept.	1	7½	4½
	15	7	5
Oct.	1	6½	5½
	15	6	6
Nov.	1	5½	6½
	15	5	7
FROM THEN ON THE TIME STANDS STILL AND IS		NIGHT	MIDNIGHT
December January		5	7

THE DAY INCREASES A HALF HOUR WITH EVERY HALF MONTH.

MONTH	DAY	BECOMES NIGHT BY OUR CLOCK HAND	IS MIDNIGHT THEN AT
Feb.	1	5½	6½
	15	6	6
March	1	6½	5½
	15	7	5
April	1	7½	4½
	15	8	4
May	1	8½	3½
	15	9	3
FROM THEN ON THE TIME STANDS STILL AND IS		NIGHT	MIDNIGHT
June July		9	3

expected; no, the whole width of the house is open, one can peer all the way inside at everything that is happening. The tailors sew, the cobblers pull and pound, all of them halfway out into the street; indeed the workplaces make up a part of it. In the evening, when lights are burning, it all looks very much alive.

The squares are very full on market days, vast amounts of vegetables and fruit, garlic and onions to one's heart's content. Moreover they shout, joke, and sing all day long, and never stop swaggering and scuffling, exulting and laughing. The mild air, the low cost of food, makes their life easy. Everyone who possibly can be is outside beneath the open sky.

At night the singing and clamor begin in earnest. In all the streets one hears the little song about Marlborough, then a dulcimer or a violin. They practice all the birdcalls on their pipes, the strangest tones ring out everywhere. The mild climate also gives the poor an exuberant joy in life, so that even this shadow populace seems deserving of respect.

The lack of cleanliness and comfort in the houses, which we find so striking, also stems from this: they are always outside, and are so carefree they think of nothing. The common people take life as it comes, the middle-class man also lives from one day to the next, the rich and aristocratic person secludes himself in his residence, which is also not as comfortable as it would be in the north. Their parties are held in public assembly rooms. Forecourts and colonnades are all befouled with ordure, for nature takes its course here. The populace is always edging forward. The rich man can be rich, build palaces, the *nobile* may rule, but when he installs a colonnade or a forecourt, the populace uses this for its needs, of which the most pressing one is to rid itself as quickly as possible of what it has consumed as copiously as possible. Anyone unwilling to tolerate this must not play the great lord, that is, he must not act as though a part of his residence belonged to the public, but simply close his doors; and that is all right too. The people absolutely refuse to give up their claim on public buildings, and this is what foreigners complain about all over Italy.

Today, while going through town on various streets, I observed the costume and manners especially of the middle class, which seems to be very numerous and busy. They all swing their arms when they walk. Persons of a higher class swing only one arm, because they wear a sword on certain occasions and are used to holding the left arm still.

Although the populace attends to its affairs and needs very light-heartedly, it nevertheless has a sharp eye for anything foreign. Thus in the first days I noticed everyone looking at my boots, which are too expensive an article of clothing here to be worn even in winter. Now that I am wearing shoes and stockings, no one looks at me anymore. But this morning, when they were all running around in confusion with flowers, vegetables, garlic, and so much other market produce, I found it remarkable that nobody failed to notice the cypress branch I held in my hand. A few green pine cones hung from it, and besides I was holding some blooming branches of caper. Everybody, child or adult, looked at my fingers and seemed to be having strange thoughts.

I brought these branches from the Giusti garden, which is excellently situated and has enormous cypresses, all of which stand straight up in the air, like German broom. Probably the trimmed and tapered yews of northern horticulture are imitations of this magnificent natural product. A tree whose branches from bottom to top, the oldest as well as the youngest, all strive toward heaven, which lasts its good three hundred years, is surely worthy of veneration. Judging from the time when this garden was laid out, these trees have already reached that great age.

VICENZA, SEPTEMBER 19.

The road here from Verona is very pleasant, one travels northeastwards past the mountains, with the foothills, which consist of sand, limestone, clay, and marl, always on the left; on these hills are situated towns, castles, houses. The straight, wide, well-maintained road goes through fertile fields; one looks into deep rows of trees on which grapevines are drawn up high and then descend as if they were airy branches. Here one can form an idea of what festoons are! The grapes are ripe and burden the tendrils, which hang down long and sway. The road is filled with people of every kind and trade, I was especially delighted by the wagons with low, dish-like wheels, which, drawn by four oxen, transport back and forth the great vats in which the grapes are brought from the gardens and pressed. When these were empty the drivers stood in them; it looked much like a Bacchic triumphal procession. The soil between the rows of vines is used for all kinds of grain, especially Indian corn and millet.

Toward Vicenza little hills rise up from the north and south, they are said to be volcanic, and end the plain. Vicenza lies at their feet and, as it were, in a bosom that they form.

VICENZA, SEPTEMBER 19.

I arrived here a few hours ago, have already walked about the town and seen the Olympian theater and the buildings of Palladio. A very pretty little book with engravings and an expert text has been published for the convenience of foreigners. Only when these works are actually seen can one recognize their great merit; for they must fill the eye with their true size and concreteness and satisfy the spirit with the beautiful harmony of their dimensions, not only in abstract outlines but with all their projecting and receding parts seen in perspective. And so I say of Palladio: he was intrinsically and through and through a great man. The greatest difficulty confronting him, like all modern architects, was the proper use of the columnar orders in civil architecture; for to combine columns and walls is, after all, a contradiction. But how he has

780

managed that! How he impresses with the presence of his works and makes us forget that he is only being persuasive. There is really something godlike about his designs, like the power of a great poet to take truth and lies and out of them frame a third entity, whose borrowed existence enchants us.

The Olympian theater is a theater of the ancients on a small scale and inexpressibly beautiful, but compared to ours it seems to me like a rich, aristocratic, handsome child compared to a clever man of the world, who is neither so aristocratic, rich, nor handsome, but knows better what he can achieve with the means at his disposal.

When, here on the spot, I contemplate the magnificent buildings erected by that man and see how they have been disfigured by people's narrow, base needs, how these designs were mostly beyond the abilities of the builders, how poorly these choice monuments to a lofty human spirit harmonize with the life of the rest of mankind, then it occurs to me that this after all is the way of the world. For one gets little thanks from people when one tries to exalt their inner urges, to give them a lofty concept of themselves, to make them feel the magnificence of a true, noble existence. But when one deceives the birds, tells them fairy tales, leads them along from day to day, debases them, then one is their man; and that is why the modern era delights in so many tasteless things. I do not say this to disparage these friends of mine, I am only saying that this is how they are, and one must not be surprised if everything is as it is.

It is impossible to describe how Palladio's basilica looks next to an old castle-like building bespeckled with dissimilar windows, which the great architect certainly imagined as being absent, tower and all, and in a curious way I have to steady myself; for here too, unfortunately, I find the very things I am fleeing side by side with those I am seeking.

SEPTEMBER 20.

Yesterday was the opera, it lasted until after midnight and I longed to retire. *The Three Sultans* and *The Abduction from the Seraglio* have furnished many scraps, out of which this play was patched together with little intelligence. The music was easy to listen to, but is probably by an amateur, without a single striking new thought. On the other hand the ballets were delightful. The leading couple danced an allemande that was as graceful as could be.

The theater is new, charming, beautiful, modestly sumptuous, everything uniform, as is appropriate for a provincial town; every box has a tapestry of the same color draped over it, the box of the *capitano grande* being distinguished only by a somewhat longer overhang.

The leading female singer, very much favored by the whole populace, receives tumultuous applause when she appears, and the birds grow wild with joy when she does something well, as she often does. She is an unaffected creature, pretty figure, lovely voice, a pleasant face, and a quite decorous manner.

Her arms could be a little more graceful. However, I shall not be coming again; I feel that I shall never make a good bird.

SEPTEMBER 21.

Today I visited Doctor Turra; for some five years he concentrated passionately on botany, assembled a herbarium of Italian flora, and, under the previous bishop, established a botanical garden. But that is all past. Natural history was displaced by medical practice, the herbarium is food for worms, the bishop is dead, and the botanical garden has been replanted, as is proper, with cabbages and garlic.

Doctor Turra is a really fine, good man. He told me his story with candor, purity of heart, and modesty, and in general spoke very precisely and pleasantly. But he was not inclined to open his cabinets, which probably were not in any presentable condition. Our conversation soon faltered and stopped.

SEPTEMBER 21, EVENING.

I went to the old architect Scamozzi, who edited the work on Palladio's buildings and is a worthy, dedicated artist. Pleased with my interest, he gave me some guidance. Among Palladio's buildings there is one I have always been especially partial to, it is said to have been his own residence; but, close up, there is much more to it than is shown in the picture. I would like to have a drawing of it, illuminated with the colors given it by its age and material. But one must not imagine that the master erected a palace for himself. It is the most modest house in the world, having only two windows, which are separated by a broad space meant to contain a third window. A painting of it including the neighboring houses, to show how it is inserted between them, would also be pleasant to look at. Canaletto should have painted that.

Today I visited the palatial house called the Rotonda, which is located on a pleasant height about a half hour from the town. It is a square building which encloses a round salon lighted from above. One climbs up broad steps on all four sides and each time arrives at a vestibule formed of six Corinthian columns. Perhaps there has never been more extravagant architecture. The space occupied by the steps and vestibules is much greater than that of the house itself; for each individual side would make a suitable view of a temple. Inside it can be called habitable, but not comfortable. The salon is very beautifully proportioned, the other rooms also; but they would hardly meet the needs of an aristocratic family for a summer sojourn. On the other hand one can see it from all sides in the whole area, rising up most magnificently. There is great variety in the way its central mass together with the projecting columns moves before the spectator's eye as he walks around it. The owner has completely achieved his goal, which was to leave behind a large entailed estate and at the same time a tangible memorial to his wealth. And just as the building can be seen in its splendor from all points in the area, so too the view away from it is most pleasant. One sees the Bachiglione flowing, carrying ships down from Verona to the Brenta. At the same time one surveys the extensive possessions that Marchese Capra wanted to preserve intact within his family. The inscriptions on the four gable sides, which together make a whole, surely deserve to be recorded:

Marcus Capra Gabrielis filius
qui aedes has
arctissimo primogeniturae gradui subjecit
una cum omnibus
censibus agris vallibus et collibus
citra viam magnam
memoriae perpetuae mandans haec
dum sustinet ac abstinet.

The conclusion in particular is rather strange: a man who had so much wealth and willpower at his disposal still feels that he must endure and abstain. That can be learned with less expense.

SEPTEMBER 22.

This evening I was at an assembly held by the Academy of Olympians. A mere pastime, but a good one, it provides the people with a little intellectual spice and liveliness. A great hall next to Palladio's theater, well lighted, the *Capitano* and some nobility present, indeed altogether an audience of cultivated persons, many clerics, in all about five hundred.

The question proposed by the president for today's session was whether invention or imitation has been of greater benefit to the fine arts. To be sure, the notion was a happy one, for if the alternatives contained in the question are separated they can be discussed from this side and that for a hundred years. The academic gentlemen took full advantage of this opportunity and said various things in prose and verse, many of them good.

Moreover, the audience is very lively. The listeners shouted "bravo," clapped, and laughed. If only we could stand before our nation and personally entertain it! We offer our best efforts in black and white; each reader sits owl-like in a corner and picks at it as best he can.

As can be imagined, Palladio was cited here again at every possible juncture, whether the subject was invention or imitation. At the conclusion, where a most humorous tone is always required, someone had the happy notion of saying that since everyone else had preempted Palladio, he would praise Franceschini, the great silk manufacturer. He then proceeded to show what benefits had accrued to this man, and through him to the city of Vicenza, by the imitation of Lyonnaise and Florentine materials, from which it would follow that imitation is far superior to invention. And he said this in such a humorous way that it caused universal laughter. In general the proponents of imitation won greater approval, for they said nothing but what the multitude thinks and is capable of thinking. At one point the audience, with loud hand-clapping, gave its hearty approval to a very crude sophism, whereas it had not reacted to many good, indeed excellent statements in favor of invention. I am very glad also to have experienced this, and then it is most refreshing to see that Palladio, after so long a time, is still revered by his fellow citizens as a lodestar and paragon.

SEPTEMBER 22.

This morning I was in Thiene, which lies northward toward the mountains, where a new building is being erected according to an old design, surely a commendable idea. Thus it is that everything from the good period is honored here, and people are wise enough to build something new on the basis of an inherited plan. The palace is quite admirably situated in a great plain, with the limestone Alps in the background and no mountains in between. The visitor is greeted by waters flowing toward him on both sides of the perfectly straight highway that leads to the building, and these irrigate the broad rice fields through which he rides.

Although as yet I have seen only two Italian cities and spoken with few people, I already know my Italians well. Like courtiers, they consider themselves the foremost people in the world, and they can imagine this smugly and with impunity because of certain undeniable advantages they have. The Italians seem to me a very good nation; I need only look at the children and common folk, as I now see and can see them, since I am always among them and mix with them. And what faces and figures they have!

I must especially praise the Vicentians, because they grant me the privileges of being in a large city and do not stare at me, no matter what I do; however, when I address them they are pleasant and communicative, and the women delight me particularly. I do not mean to criticize the Veronese women, they have good facial structure and strong profiles; but mostly they are pale, and the *zendale* makes this worse, because one expects to see something charming under that beautiful headgear. Here, however, I find quite pretty creatures, especially a brunette type, which particularly interests me. There is also a blonde type, which is not as much to my taste.

PADUA, SEPTEMBER 26, EVENING.

I rode over here today in four hours in a little single-seat chaise called a *sediola*, packed with all my belongings. Usually the trip is made comfortably in three and a half hours; however, since I wanted to enjoy this delightful day under the open sky, I was glad that the *vetturino* was laggard in his duty. The route is straight southeastwards through the most fertile plain, between hedges and trees, without any other view, until finally on the right the beautiful mountains stretching from the east to the south are seen. The opulence of the plants and fruits hanging over walls and hedges and down from the trees is indescribable. Pumpkins weigh down the roofs, and the oddest cucumbers hang from laths and trellises.

I could survey the splendid location of the city very clearly from the observatory. To the north the Tyrolean mountains, snow-covered, half hidden by clouds, and joined in the northwest by the Vicentian mountains; finally, to the west and closer in, the mountains of Este, whose shapes and hollows can be seen distinctly. To the southwest a green sea of vegetation without a trace of elevation, tree on tree, bush on bush, plantation on plantation, innumerable white houses, villas, and churches peeping out of the greenery. On the horizon I saw the tower of St. Mark's in Venice and other lesser towers quite distinctly.

PADUA, SEPTEMBER 27.

At last I have acquired the works of Palladio, to be sure not the original edition with woodcuts, which I saw in Vicenza, but an exact copy, indeed a facsimile with copperplates put out by an excellent man, Smith, the former English consul in Venice. It must be granted to the English that they have known for a long time how to appreciate what is good and have a grandiose manner of displaying it.

In connection with this purchase I entered a bookstore, which in Italy has quite a characteristic appearance. All the books stand around unbound, and good company is found there all day long. Those secular clergymen, nobles, and artists who are to any degree connected with literature walk to and fro here. A person may request a book, look something up, read, and converse, as he pleases. Thus I found some half-dozen men standing together, all of whom looked around at me when I inquired about Palladio's works. While the owner of the store was searching for the book, they praised it and gave me information about the original and the copy, for they were very well acquainted with the work itself and the merits of its author. Since they took me for an architect, they praised me for proceeding to this master's studies in preference to all others. They said that he provided more material for practical use and application than Vitruvius himself did, for he had thoroughly studied the ancients and antiquity and tried to adapt it to our requirements. I conversed for a long time with these friendly men, learned some more things about the city's noteworthy sights, and took my leave.

Since whole churches have been built for the saints, surely a place can be found in them for monuments to men of reason. The bust of Cardinal Bembo stands between Ionic columns, a handsome face, drawn back into itself by force, if I may put it thus, and a mighty beard; the inscription reads:

Petri Bembi Card, imaginem Hier. Guerinus Ismeni
f. in publico ponendam curavit ut cujus ingenii
monumenta aeterna sint ejus corporis quoque
memoria ne a posteritate desideretur.

The university building alarmed me by all its solemnity. I was glad I did not have to study there. An academic situation as crowded as that is inconceivable, even to someone who, as a student at German universities, has experienced discomfort on lecture hall benches. The anatomical theater especially is a model of how students can be squeezed together. The listeners are layered above one another in a high, sharply tapering funnel. They look almost straight down at the narrow space where the table stands, on which no light falls, so that the teacher must demonstrate by lamplight. In contrast, the botanical garden is pleasant and bright. Many plants can stay outdoors even in the winter, if they are set next to the walls or not far from them. In October the whole place is covered over, and then it is heated for a few months. It is agreeable and instructive to wander amidst vegetation that is foreign to us. We eventually think no more at all about plants we are accustomed to, like other long familiar objects; and what is observation without thought? Here in this newly encountered diversity that idea of mine keeps gaining strength, namely, that perhaps all plant forms can be derived from one plant. Only in this way would it be possible truly to determine genera and species, which, it seems to me, has heretofore been done very arbitrarily. My botanical philosophy remains stuck on this point, and I do not yet see how to proceed. The depth and breadth of the problem seem equally great to me.

The large square, called the Prato della Valle, is a very wide space, and in June the main market is held there. The wooden booths in the middle of it do not look very attractive, but the inhabitants assure me that a *fiera* of stone, like the one in Verona, will soon be seen here. Indeed some basis for this hope is to be found in the surroundings of the square, which provide a very beautiful and significant sight.

An enormous oval is set around with statues representing all the famous men who have taught and studied here. Every native and foreigner is permitted to erect a statue of a specified size to any countryman or relative, as soon as there is proof of that person's merit and of his academic sojourn in Padua.

The oval is surrounded by a moat. On the four bridges crossing it stand popes and doges of colossal size; the rest are smaller and were placed by guilds, private persons, and foreigners. The king of Sweden had Gustavus Adolphus put up here because it is said that he once heard a lecture in Padua. Archduke Leopold revived the memory of Petrarch and Galileo. The statues are made in a worthy modern style, few are excessively manneristic, some very natural, all of them in the costume of their rank and time. The inscriptions are also laudable. None of them are tasteless or trivial.

This would have been a happy idea at any university, and is particularly so at this one, because it is very comforting to see a completely vanished past evoked again. This can become quite a handsome square if the wooden *fiera* is replaced by one of stone, as is said to be the plan.

In the meetinghouse of a brotherhood dedicated to St. Anthony are some rather old pictures which bring the old German masters to mind, alongside them also some by Titian. The latter already show the great step forward that was not taken by anyone north of the Alps. Directly after that I saw some of the newest pictures. When these artists could no longer attain high seriousness, they very successfully turned to humorousness. The beheading of John by Piazzetta is a very worthy picture of this kind, if one accepts the master's manner. John kneels, holding out his folded hands, his right knee against a stone. A hireling soldier, who holds him bound from the back, bends around his side and looks into his face, as if amazed by the composure with which this man submits himself. Up above stands another soldier, who is to execute the stroke, but he does not have the sword and only makes the gesture with his hands, as though practicing in advance. A third man, below, draws the sword out of its sheath. The concept is felicitous, though not great, the composition striking and very effective.

In the church of the Anchorites I saw pictures by Mantegna, one of the older painters, who astonishes me. What a sharp, sure immediacy is displayed in these pictures! It was from this altogether genuine quality of immediacy—by no means specious, with no false effects that speak only to the imagination, but a robust, pure, bright, detailed, scrupulous, circumscribed immediacy, which at the same time had something stern, diligent, laborious about it— that the subsequent artists proceeded, as I noticed in Titian's pictures. And now the liveliness of their genius, the energy of their nature, illuminated by the spirit of these predecessors and invigorated by their strength, could climb higher and ever higher, rise from the earth and bring forth heavenly but true forms. It was thus that art developed after the barbarous times.

The audience room of the city hall, rightly named "Salone," with the augmentative suffix, is a self-contained structure so enormous that it cannot be imagined or even, shortly afterwards, clearly remembered. Three hundred feet long, one hundred feet wide, and one hundred feet high beneath the vaulted roof that covers its whole length. These people are so accustomed to living in the open air that the builders found a marketplace to roof over for them. And there is no question that the huge arched-over space produces a peculiar sensation. It is an enclosed infinity, more analogous to man than the starry sky is. The latter draws us out of ourselves, the former very gently presses us back into ourselves.

For this reason I also like to linger in the church of St. Justine. It is four hundred eighty-five feet long, correspondingly high and wide, a vast but simple building. This evening I sat down in a corner and did some quiet meditating. I felt quite alone, for if any person in the world was thinking of me at that moment, he would certainly never have looked for me there.

Now it is time to pack up again, for tomorrow morning my way goes by water on the Brenta. It rained today, now it has cleared up again, and I trust that my first view of the lagoons and the sovereign city wed to the sea will be in beautiful daylight. And from her bosom I shall send greetings to my friends.

Venice

So it was written on my page in the Book of Fate that in 1786, on the twenty-eighth of September, at five o'clock in the evening by our reckoning, I should for the first time lay eyes on Venice, sailing out of the Brenta into the lagoons, and soon thereafter enter and visit this wonderful island city, this beaver republic. And so, God be thanked, Venice too is no longer a mere word to me, a hollow name which has often made me uneasy, me, the mortal enemy of verbal sounds.

When the first gondola approached the ship (this is done so that passengers who are in a hurry may be taken to Venice more swiftly), I remembered an early childhood toy I had not thought about for perhaps twenty years. My father owned a pretty model gondola that he had brought back; he prized it highly, and I felt very honored when I was actually allowed to play with it. The first prows of shiny iron plate, the black gondola cabins, all of that greeted me like an old acquaintance, and I reveled in a pleasant, long-forgotten childhood impression.

I am well lodged in the "Queen of England," not far from St. Mark's square, and that is the best feature of the inn; my windows open on a narrow canal between tall houses, directly below me a single-arched bridge, and opposite me a busy, narrow lane. Thus I live and thus I shall remain for a while until my packet for Germany is ready and until I have seen my fill of the sights of this city. I have often sighed longingly for solitude, and now I can really enjoy it; for nowhere does an individual feel more alone than in a bustling crowd, through which he presses, unknown to all. Perhaps there is only one person in Venice that knows me, and we shall not soon meet.

VENICE, SEPTEMBER 28, 1786.

Just a few words about my trip from Padua: The voyage on the Brenta, on a public ship in mannerly company (for the Italians are on their guard with each other) is seemly and pleasant. The banks are adorned with gardens and summer houses, little settlements come down to the water, and for a while the busy highway runs alongside it. Since one descends the river by means of locks, there is often a little delay, which one can use for looking around on shore and enjoying the fruit that is abundantly offered. Then one embarks again and moves through a colorful world of fertility and life.

In addition to so many alternating images and forms there was another apparition which, even though coming from Germany, was really quite appropriate here, that is to say, two pilgrims, the first I have seen close up. They have the right to be transported free of charge on this public conveyance; but because the rest of the company shuns their vicinity they do not sit in the covered space, but in the stern with the helmsman. Being a rare phenomenon nowadays, they were stared at and received little respect because formerly much riffraff wandered about under this guise. When I heard they were Germans and knew no other language I joined them and learned that they came from the Paderborn territory. Both were men over fifty, of swarthy but good-natured physiognomy. They had first of all visited the grave of the three sainted kings at Cologne, then had traveled through Germany, and now were on their way together to Rome. Then they intended to return to upper Italy, whereupon one of them would walk back to Westphalia while the other would first pay his respects to St. James at Compostela.

Their clothing was the customary kind but they had tucked it up and so looked better than the "pilgrims" in long taffeta robes we usually see at our balls. The great collar, the round hat, the staff, and the shell serving as the humblest drinking vessel, everything had its significance, its immediate usefulness; the metal case contained their passports. But the most remarkable things were their little morocco wallets holding various small instruments that were probably suitable for filling whatever simple need might arise. They had taken these out, having discovered something on their clothes that needed patching.

The helmsman, much pleased to have found an interpreter, had me ask them several questions; from this I learned something about their views, but more about their journey. They complained bitterly about their coreligionists, including monks and secular priests. Piety, they said, must be a very rare thing, because theirs was not credited anywhere, and in Catholic lands they were treated almost entirely like vagrants, even though they displayed their prescribed clerical itinerary and their episcopal passports. On the other hand, they related with feeling how well the Protestants had received them. They spoke of one particular country parson in Swabia and especially of his wife, who had been able to persuade her somewhat reluctant husband to let her provide them with abundant refreshment, which they had been in great need of. Indeed on their departure she had given them a thaler, which had stood them in good stead when they reentered Catholic territory. Hereupon one of them said with all the solemnity of which he was capable. "We also include this woman in our daily prayer and ask God to open her eyes as He opened her heart to us, and to accept her, even though late, into the bosom of the only true Church. And so we certainly hope to meet her some day in Paradise."

Seated on the little stairs leading to the deck, I explained as much as was necessary and useful of all this to the helmsman and a few other persons who had come out of the cabin to crowd into this narrow space. Some meager refreshments were extended to the pilgrims; for the Italian does not like to give. Hereupon they drew out little consecrated slips of paper showing a picture of the three sainted kings along with Latin prayers in their honor. The good men asked me to give these to the little group with an explanation of their great value. I was quite successful in this, for when the two men seemed very much at a loss, Venice being so big, as to how they would find the monastery designated to receive pilgrims, the emotionally stirred helmsman promised that on landing he would at once give a lad a three-penny piece to conduct them to that distant location. To be sure, he added confidentially, they would find little comfort there; the institution, although laid out on a grand scale for the reception of I do not know how many pilgrims, had at present rather deteriorated, and its revenue was being turned to other uses.

Entertained thus, we had come down the beautiful Brenta, passing many a magnificent garden, many a magnificent palace, viewing with a hasty glance the wealthy, busy towns along the shore. As we now sailed into the lagoons, our ship was immediately surrounded by a swarm of gondolas. A Lombard quite familiar with Venice bade me keep him company so as to get into town more speedily and escape the misery of the Dogana. With a moderate gratuity he was able to fend off some people who tried to detain us, and so in the bright sunset we floated quickly to our goal.

THE 29TH, MICHAELMAS, EVENING.

So much has already been told and printed about Venice that instead of a detailed description I shall just give my personal impressions. What again claims my attention above all else is the populace, a great mass, a necessary, instinctive existence.

This race did not flee frivolously to these islands, it was not caprice that prompted subsequent settlers to unite with them; necessity taught them to seek their security in this most disadvantageous location, which later became so advantageous for them and made them wise when the whole northern world still lay captive in darkness; their increase, their riches, were a necessary result. Now their dwellings crowded together ever more closely, sand and swamp were replaced with rocks, the houses sought the air, like trees that stand close to each other, and had to gain in height what they lacked in width. Niggardly with every span of ground and compressed into narrow spaces from the very outset, they allowed the lanes no more breadth than was required for separating two opposite rows of houses and preserving scanty passageways for the citizen. Furthermore water served as their streets, squares, and promenades. The Venetian had to become a new species of creature, just as Venice can only be compared with itself. The great serpentine canal is second to no other street in the world, and nothing can really match the expanse before St. Mark's square: I mean the great watery surface which on this side is embraced in a crescent shape by the main part of Venice. To the left across the water one sees the island of San Giorgio Maggiore, somewhat more to the right the Giudecca and its canal, still farther to the right the Dogana and the entrance to the Grand Canal, where immediately several huge marble temples gleam at us. There, with a few strokes, are the chief objects that catch our eye when we step out from between the two columns of St. Mark's square. All the views and prospects have been engraved so often that anyone who likes prints can easily get a vivid idea of them.

After dinner, I first hastened to obtain a general impression and, without a companion, noting only the points of the compass, plunged into the labyrinth of the city, which, although thoroughly cut up by larger and smaller canals, is connected again by larger and smaller bridges. One cannot imagine the narrowness and density of the whole without having seen it. Usually the width of the lanes can be nearly or completely measured by stretching out one's arms; in the narrowest, a person walking with arms akimbo will hit against the walls with his elbows. There are indeed wider lanes, even an occasional little square, but everything can be called relatively narrow.

I easily found the Grand Canal and the Rialto, the principal bridge; it consists of a single arch of white marble. The view down from it is grand, the canal thickly dotted with boats that bring in all the necessities from the mainland and dock and unload chiefly here, in between them a swarm of gondolas. Especially today, it being Michaelmas, the view was lively and very beautiful; but in order to describe it to some degree I must give a few more details.

The two main sections of Venice, which are divided by the Grand Canal, are connected by a single bridge, the Rialto, but rowboats provide additional communication at specific crossing points. It looked very good today when well-dressed but black-veiled women, in large groups, had themselves rowed over to reach the church of the feted archangel.

I left the bridge and approached one of those crossing points to get a close look at the disembarking women. I found some very lovely faces and figures among them.

Having grown tired, I got into a gondola and left the narrow lanes. To enjoy the spectacle on the opposite side properly, I rode through the northern part of the Grand Canal, around the island of Santa Clara in the lagoons, into the canal of the Giudecca, up toward St. Mark's square, and was now suddenly a co-sovereign of the Adriatic sea, like every Venetian when he reclines in his gondola. At this point I thought respectfully of my good father, whose greatest pleasure was to tell about these things. Will I not do the same? Everything around me is estimable, a great, venerable accomplishment of collective human strength, a magnificent monument, not of a ruler, but of a people. And even if their lagoons are gradually filling up, evil vapors hover over the swamp, their trade is weakened, their power diminished, yet the whole structure and substance of this republic will not for a moment seem less honorable to the observer. It is succumbing to time, like everything that has a visible existence.

SEPTEMBER 30.

Toward evening, again without a guide, I lost my way in the remotest quarters of the city. The bridges here are all fitted with steps, so that gondolas and probably also larger boats can pass comfortably under the arch. I tried to find my way in and out of this labyrinth without asking anyone, again only directing myself by the points of the compass. Finally one does disentangle oneself, but it is an incredible maze, and my method, which is to acquaint myself with it directly through my senses, is the best. Also, up to the last inhabited tip of land I have noted the residents' behavior, manners, customs, and nature; these are differently constituted in every quarter. Dear Lord! what a poor, good-natured beast man is!

A great many small houses stand right in the canals, but here and there are found beautifully paved embankments on which people can stroll back and forth very pleasantly between water, churches, and palaces. The long embankment on the north side is bustling and pleasant; the islands are visible from there, especially Murano, which is Venice in miniature. The lagoons in between are busy with gondolas.

SEPTEMBER 30, EVENING.

Today I again increased my knowledge of Venice by procuring a map of the city. After having studied it for a while, I climbed the tower of St. Mark's, where a unique spectacle meets the eye. It was noon and the sunshine was bright, so that I could clearly recognize places near and far without a telescope. Floodtide covered the lagoons, and when I turned my gaze to the so-called Lido (it is a narrow strip of land closing off the lagoons), I saw the sea, with some sails on it, for the first time. In the lagoons themselves lie galleys and frigates that were supposed to join up with Cavaliere Emo, who is waging war against the Algerians, but that are idled by unfavorable winds. The Paduan and Vicenzian mountains and the Tyrolean range conclude the picture most admirably between west and north.

OCTOBER I.

I went out to view various aspects of the city, and since it was Sunday was struck by the great uncleanliness of the streets, which started me reflecting. There is indeed a type of policing of this material, for the people shove the refuse into the corners, and I see large boats plying back and forth which stop at many places and load the refuse—these are people from the surrounding islands who need fertilizer. But these arrangements lack both regularity and strictness; and since this city was completely planned for cleanliness, just as much as any city in Holland, its uncleanliness is the more inexcusable.

All the streets are paved with flagstones. Even in the remotest quarters, wherever necessary, at least bricks are laid in them, set lengthwise and upright, a little raised in the middle, with depressions at the side to catch the water and conduct it into covered drains. Some other architectural devices in the well-considered original design also testify to the fact that its excellent builders intended to make Venice the cleanest city, just as it is the most extraordinary one. As I strolled along, I could not resist drafting a set of regulations for this purpose, preparing the way, in my thoughts, for a sanitary supervisor who would take his task seriously. Thus one is always ready and eager to sweep before someone else's door.

OCTOBER 2.

First of all I hurried into the Carità; in Palladio's works I had read that he had proposed to build a monastery here which would depict how rich and hospitable ancients lived at home. I was greatly delighted with his plan, which was admirably designed both as a whole and in its individual parts, and I expected to find a marvel. But alas, scarcely a tenth part has been built, though even this is worthy of his genius, having a perfection of arrangement and an exactness of execution that are beyond anything known to me. Years should be spent in contemplating such a work. I think that I have never seen anything more sublime or more perfect, and I believe I am not mistaken. Let us imagine this excellent artist, born with an inner sense of the grand and gracious, who first, with incredible effort, attains to the cultural level of the ancients, so that he may reestablish them by himself. This man is given the opportunity to carry out a favorite idea, to erect a monastery, designated as a dwelling for many monks and a shelter for many strangers, in the form of an ancient private residence.

The church was already standing; one steps out of it into an atrium with Corinthian columns, which is charming and dispels any air of priestliness. On one side is the sacristy, on the other a chapter room, next to this the most beautiful spiral staircase in the world, with a broad, open newel and stone steps that are fixed into the wall and layered in such a way that each supports the other; I could not get enough of climbing up and down it. How well it turned out can be deduced from the fact that Palladio himself declares it well done. From the forecourt one steps out into the great inner court. Unfortunately, only the left wing of the building that was supposed to surround it has been erected: three orders of columns placed one above the other, large rooms on the ground floor, on the second a colonnade along the cells, the upper story a wall with windows. But this description must be supplemented by a look at the plans. Now a word about the construction.

Only the bases and capitals of the columns and the keystones of the arches are of hewn stone, everything else is not exactly of brick, but terra-cotta. Such bricks are quite new to me. The frieze and cornice are also made of them, likewise the members of the arches, everything partially fired, and in the final analysis the building is held together only with a bit of lime. It stands there as though all of one piece. If the whole edifice had been completed, and it could be seen cleanly rubbed down and colored, it would surely be a glorious sight.

However, the plan was too grand, as is the case with so many buildings in recent times. The artist had not only assumed that the existing monastery would be razed, but also that the adjacent houses would be bought; and then funds and interest may have dwindled away. Dear Destiny, why have you favored and immortalized so many stupid follies instead of allowing this great work to be completed?

OCTOBER 3.

Il Redentore church, a great, beautiful work by Palladio, its facade more praiseworthy than that of San Giorgio. Many copperplate engravings have been made of them, but these works have to be actually seen before my statement can be appreciated. Just a few words here.

Palladio was thoroughly imbued with antiquity and reacted to the petty narrowness of his own times like a great man, not surrendering but determined to remodel everything in accord with his noble ideas, as far as possible. He was, as I gather from a hint in his book, dissatisfied because Christian churches continued to be built in the old basilica form; therefore he tried to make his sacred buildings approximate the form of ancient temples. This resulted in certain inappropriate features which I think were successfully avoided in Il Redentore but are all too evident in San Giorgio. Volkmann mentions this, but does not hit the nail on the head.

The interior of Il Redentore is also exquisite, everything by Palladio, even the design of the altars. Unfortunately the niches, which were meant to hold statues, can only boast flat, cut-out, painted board figures.

OCTOBER 3.

The *Patres Capucini* had richly decorated a side altar in honor of St. Francis; the only stone objects left visible were the Corinthian capitals; everything else seemed to be covered with a magnificent but tasteful embroidery in the arabesque style, as nicely as one could wish to see. I was particularly taken with the broad, gold-embroidered tendrils and foliage; but when I went nearer, I discovered a very pretty fraud. Everything I had imagined to be gold was actually straw, pressed flat, glued to paper in beautiful designs, and the background painted in vivid colors. This amusing thing, of totally worthless materials and probably made right in the monastery, was so varied and tasteful that it would have cost several thousand thalers if genuine. We could certainly imitate it if the occasion arose.

On an embankment overlooking the water I had already noticed more than once a plebeian fellow who told stories in the Venetian dialect to larger or smaller numbers of listeners. Unfortunately I cannot understand a word of it, but no one laughs, indeed the audience, which is mostly drawn from the lowest class, rarely smiles. Nor is there anything striking or ridiculous in the storyteller's manner, rather, something very sober, while the admirable variety and precision of his gestures indicates conscious artistry.

OCTOBER 3.

Map in hand, I tried to find my way through the strangest labyrinth to the church of the Mendicanti. The conservatory there is at present considered the best one. The young women were performing an oratorio behind the choir screen, the church was full of listeners, the music very lovely, and the voices magnificent. An alto sang King Saul, the main personage of the poem. I had never before experienced such a voice; some passages in the music were infinitely beautiful, the text perfectly singable, such Italianate Latin that I found some passages laughable; but music has great latitude here.

It would have been a choice pleasure, if the wretched choir director had not beaten time on the screen with a roll of music, as unconcernedly as if he had been instructing schoolboys. The girls had often rehearsed the piece, so that his slapping was quite unnecessary and spoiled the whole impression, just as if someone had tried to explain a beautiful statue by pasting scarlet patches on its joints. The alien sound destroys all the harmony. This man is a musician, and he does not hear that? More likely, he wants to make us aware of his presence by means of an impropriety, when he would be better off letting us surmise his worth from the perfection of the performance. I know the French are capable of that, I would not have believed it of the Italians, and the audience seems accustomed to the noise. This would not be the first time it has been deluded into thinking that something is contributing to enjoyment when it is actually ruining enjoyment.

OCTOBER 3.

Yesterday evening, opera at St. Moses (for theaters are named after the nearest church); not very good! The libretto, the music, the singers—everything lacked that certain inner energy which is the only thing that can lend excitement to such a presentation. No one part of it could be called poor, but only the two women made an effort both to act well and project themselves agreeably. That is at least something. The two have beautiful figures and good voices, and are charming, sprightly, appealing little persons. As for the men, however, not a trace of inner strength or any desire to create an illusion for the audience, and no particularly fine voices.

The ballet was very poorly conceived and was generally hissed at; however, there was enthusiastic applause for several excellent male and female acrobats, the latter of whom felt an obligation to acquaint the spectators with every detail of their physical charms.

OCTOBER 3.

But today I saw a different sort of comedy, which pleased me more. I heard a legal case being tried in public in the ducal palace; it was an important one and, luckily for me, undertaken during the council recess. One of the lawyers was everything any exaggerated *buffo* should be. Portly figure, short but agile, a monstrously aquiline profile, a voice of brass, and a vehemence implying that what he said was meant from the bottom of his heart. I call this a comedy, because no doubt everything is settled before these public presentations take place; the judges already know the verdict, and the litigants know what to expect. However, this method pleases me a great deal more than the way we crouch in small rooms and lawyers' offices. And now I shall try to describe the circumstances and how agreeably, unpretentiously, and naturally everything proceeds.

In a spacious hall of the palace the judges sat at one side in a semicircle. Opposite them the lawyers for both parties, on a rostrum capable of holding several persons side by side, and on a bench directly in front of them, the plaintiff and defendant in person. The plaintiffs lawyer had stepped down from the rostrum, for today's session was not scheduled to include any controversy. All the documents, pro and contra, although already printed, were to be read aloud.

A haggard clerk in a wretched black robe, a thick pad of paper in his hand, readied himself to perform the duty of reader. Moreover the hall was crowded with spectators and listeners. The legal question itself, as well as the persons it concerned, could not but seem significant to the Venetians.

Entailments are distinctly favored in this nation; once a possession is stamped with this character, it keeps it forever. Even if by some twist or circumstance it was sold several hundred years ago, and has passed through many hands, finally, when the case comes up, the descendants of the original family have the last word, and the estates must be handed over.

This time the lawsuit was extremely important, for the complaint was against the doge himself, or rather, against his wife, who accordingly, veiled by her *zendale*, was sitting there in person on the little bench, only a short distance away from the plaintiff. A lady of a certain age, noble figure, comely face, on which a serious, nay, if you will, somewhat irritated expression was to be seen. The Venetians were very proud of the fact that their sovereign lady had to appear before them and the court in her own palace.

The clerk began to read, and only now did I grasp the significance of a little man sitting on a low stool behind a small table in view of the judges, not far from the lawyers' rostrum, and especially of the hourglass he had laid down in front of him. Namely, as long as the clerk reads, the sand does not run; but the lawyer, when he wants to comment, is generally allowed only a certain time period. The clerk reads, the hourglass is recumbent, the little man has his hand on it. When the lawyer opens his mouth, the hourglass is immediately set upright, but is lowered again the moment he is silent. The great skill here resides in interrupting the flow of reading, in making fleeting comments, in arousing and demanding attention. Now the little Saturn gets into the most embarrassing difficulties. He is required to change the horizontal and vertical positions of the hourglass every moment, he sees himself in the situation of the evil spirits in the puppet play, who, when the mischievous harlequin quickly alternates his "berlique! berloque!" do not know whether they should come or go.

Anyone who has heard lawyers collating documents in their chanceries can imagine this reading aloud—rapid, monotonous, but still enunciated with sufficient clarity. A skillful lawyer knows how to interrupt the tedium with jokes, and the audience shows its delight in them with most immoderate laughter. I must mention one joke, the most memorable among those I understood. The clerk was just reciting a document in which one of these owners deemed unlawful was disposing of the estates in question. The lawyer bade him read more slowly, and when he distinctly pronounced the word, "I give, I bequeath!" the orator vehemently attacked him, shouting, "*What* do you intend to give? bequeath *what*? You poor hungry devil! You know that nothing in this world belongs to you. But," he continued, seeming to reflect on the matter, "that illustrious owner was in the very same situation, what he meant to give, to bequeath, belonged to him as little as to you." There was a tremendous burst of laughter, but the hourglass immediately resumed its horizontal position. The reader hummed on, making an angry face at the lawyer; but those jests were all prearranged.

OCTOBER 4.

Yesterday I saw a comedy at the San Luca theater which greatly delighted me; it was an extemporized play with masks, performed with much temperament, energy, and bravura. To be sure, they are not all on a par; the Pantalone very good, one of the women, strong and well built, no extraordinary actress, speaks excellently, and knows how to conduct herself. A nonsensical subject matter, similar to what is treated in Germany under the title *The Partition*. It was three hours of incredibly varied entertainment. But here again the folk is the basis on which everything rests, the spectators join in the action, and the crowd merges with the stage to make a single whole. All day long on the square and at the shore, in the gondolas and the palace, buyers and sellers, the beggar, the boatman, the neighbor woman, the lawyer and his opponent, they are all lively and bustling and interested, speak and assert, cry wares and shout, sing and play, curse and make noise. And in the evening they go to the theater to see and hear their daily life artfully structured, more neatly shaped, interwoven with fairy tales, removed from reality by masks, brought closer by manners. They take a childish delight in this, cry out again, clap, and yell. From morning to night, indeed from midnight to midnight, everything is always just the same.

I doubt that I have ever seen more natural acting than that done by these maskers, which can only be attained by rather long practice and with an especially fortunate natural disposition.

As I write this, they are making a tremendous racket on the canal below my window, and it is past midnight. They are always involved with each other, whether for good or evil.

OCTOBER 4.

I have now heard public speakers: three fellows on the square and the stone embankment at the shore, each telling tales in his own fashion; then two lawyers, two preachers, the actors, among whom I must especially praise the Pantalone; all these have something in common, not only because they belong to one and the same nation, which, always living in public, is always engaged in passionate speaking, but also because they imitate each other. In addition, there is a definite language of gestures, with which they accompany the expression of their intentions, sentiments, and feelings.

Today, on the festival of St. Francis, I was in his church alle Vigne. The Capuchin's loud voice was accompanied, as though with an antiphon, by the shouting of the vendors in front of the church. I stood at the church door between them both, and it was certainly a strange thing to hear.

OCTOBER 5.

This morning I was at the Arsenal, which is always very interesting to me since as yet I am ignorant of maritime affairs and have been attending a lower school in the subject here. For truly the place reminds me of an old family which is still active although the best season of blossoms and fruit is past. Since I also investigate what the workmen are doing, I have seen many remarkable things and climbed up on the finished framework of a ship with forty-eight guns.

A similar one burned down to the waterline six months ago at the Riva de' Schiavoni, its powder magazine was not very full, and when it exploded no great damage was done. The neighboring houses lost their windowpanes.

I have watched the finest oak, from Istria, being processed, meanwhile reflecting quietly about the growth of this worthy tree. I cannot state strongly enough how my hard-won knowledge of natural things, which, after all, man needs as materials and uses for his benefit, constantly helps me to understand the procedures of artists and artisans. Thus, for example, my knowledge of mountains and the minerals taken from them has been of great advantage to me in art.

To sum up the *Bucentaur* in two words, I shall call it a state galley. The older one, of which we still have pictures, deserves this appellation even more than the present one, whose splendor blinds us to its origin.

I keep returning to my old theme: Give the artist a genuine subject, and he can accomplish something genuine. In this case the assignment was to build a galley worthy of taking the leaders of the republic, on the most festive day, to the sacrament of Venice's traditional mastery of the sea; and this task has been superbly executed. One cannot say that the ship is overladen with decoration, because it is *all* decoration, all gilded carving, otherwise useless, a true monstrance for displaying the nation's leaders to it in great magnificence. For well we know: just as the people like to decorate their hats, so they also want to see their superiors splendidly adorned. This ornate ship is a real bit of stage property, which tells us what the Venetians were and considered themselves to be.

I have just come from the tragedy, still laughing, and I must set this amusing experience down on paper right away. The play was not bad, the author had gathered together all the tragic heroes, and the actors had good roles. Most of the situations were familiar, some were new and quite felicitous. Two fathers who hate each other, sons and daughters from the divided families passionately in love with one another, one pair even secretly married. The action was wild and cruel, and in the end the only way left to make the young people happy was for the two fathers to stab each other to death, whereupon the curtain fell amid lively applause. Then, however, the clapping grew louder, they shouted "Fuora," and kept it up until the two leading couples consented to creep out from behind the curtain, make their bows, and leave on the other side.

The audience was still not satisfied, it continued clapping and shouted "I morti." That went on until the two dead men also came out and bowed, whereupon several voices shouted, "Bravi i morti!" They were held captive a long time by the clapping, until finally they too were allowed to go off. This nonsense seems much funnier to an eye- and earwitness who, like me, has his ears full of the "Bravo! Bravi!" which the Italians always have on their lips, and then suddenly hears even the dead summoned with this verbal tribute.

"Good night!" we Northerners can say, at whatever hour after dark we may be parting; but there is only one time when the Italian says "Felicissima notte!" and that is when a lamp is brought into the room as day is passing into night; and then it means something quite different. Thus the idiomatic expressions of one language cannot be translated into another; for, from the basest to the most sublime, every word relates to the nation's peculiarities, whether of character, sentiments, or conditions.

OCTOBER 6.

Yesterday's tragedy taught me some things. First, I heard how the Italians manage their eleven-syllable iambics when declaiming them; second, I saw how cleverly Gozzi combined the masked figures with the tragic ones. That is the right sort of drama for these people, for they want to be moved in a crude way and do not take a heartfelt, affectionate interest in an unfortunate person. They are only pleased when the hero speaks well, for they put a high value on speaking; but then they want to laugh or see something silly.

They can only react to a drama as though it were reality. When the tyrant handed his son the sword and ordered the youth to kill his own wife, who stood opposite him, the people began loudly showing their displeasure at this unreasonable command, and very nearly interrupted the play. They insisted that the old man take back his sword, which of course would have invalidated the subsequent situations in the play. Finally the harried son took courage, stepped into the proscenium, and humbly asked them to have just a moment's patience and the affair would end exactly as they wished. But from an artistic standpoint, it was an absurd and unnatural situation under the circumstances, and I praised the people for their feelings.

Now I can understand better why there are such long speeches and back-and-forth discussions in Greek tragedy. The Athenians were still fonder of hearing speeches than the Italians, and were even sounder judges of them; they had learned a great deal from lounging around all day in the law courts.

OCTOBER 6.

In Palladio's finished works, especially the churches, I have found many objectionable features side by side with the choicest ones. When I meditated about how much justice or injustice I was doing to this extraordinary man, I felt as if he were standing beside me and saying: "That and that I did unwillingly, but did it nevertheless, because under the existing circumstances it was the only way in which I could come very close to my most sublime idea."

After much thought on the subject, it seems to me that when he contemplated the height and width of an already existing church or an older house, for which he was supposed to erect facades, he would just reflect, "How can you give the greatest form to these spaces? In the details, as necessity dictates, you will have to displace or botch something, here or there something unsuitable will result, but never mind, the thing as a whole will have a sublime style and you will be satisfied with your work."

And so the magnificent vision he cherished in his soul was applied even where it was not quite suitable, where he was forced to compress and stunt it in its details.

The wing in the Carità, on the contrary, must necessarily be of very great value to us because there the artist had a free hand and was allowed to carry out his intentions unconditionally. If the monastery had been completed, it would probably be the most perfect work of architecture in the whole modern world.

How he thought and worked becomes increasingly clear to me as I read on in his book and observe how he deals with the ancients. For although he uses very few words, they are all weighty. The fourth volume, which describes the ancient temples, is the right introduction for anyone who wishes to view the ancient remains with understanding.

OCTOBER 6.

Yesterday evening I saw Crébillon's *Electra* at the San Crisostomo theater, that is, in translation. I cannot tell you how tasteless the play seemed to me and how frightfully boring it was.

Generally speaking, the actors were good and were able to please the audience in individual passages. Orestes alone had three separate narrative speeches, poetically formed, in a single scene. Electra, a pretty little woman of medium height and girth, and of almost French vivaciousness, of good decorum, spoke the verses beautifully; only, as unfortunately the role demanded, she acted mad from beginning to end. Meanwhile I have again learned something. The Italian iambic verse with its invariable eleven syllables lends itself poorly to declamation, because the last syllable is quite short and rises in pitch, against the will of the declaimer.

This morning I was at high mass in the church of St. Justina, which the doge must attend annually on this day because of a long-ago victory over the Turks. The gilded barques land at the little square, bringing the sovereign and a portion of the nobility; strangely garbed boatmen busy themselves with the red-painted oars, on the shore stand the monks and clerics, crowding, surging, and waiting, with lighted candles stuck onto poles and portable silver candlesticks; then carpeted bridges are laid from the vessels onto the land. First the

801

long violet garments of the *savii* display themselves on the pavement, then the long red ones of the senators; finally the old man, adorned with his golden Phrygian cap, emerges in a golden robe, the longest of all, and an ermine cloak, and three servants take charge of his train—all of this, as it takes place on a little square facing the portal of a church before whose door the Turkish flags are held, suddenly made me think I was seeing an old, but very well-designed and colored, woven tapestry. To me, the refugee from the north, this ceremony was a great delight. In our country, where all festivities have short coats, and the greatest one imaginable is celebrated with shouldered muskets, something like this might not be in place. But here these dragging garments and peaceful processions are appropriate.

The doge is a very handsome, well-built man, who, in spite of being ill, for dignity's sake holds himself erect under his heavy robe. Aside from that, he looks like the grandpapa of the whole nation and is very gracious and genial. His clothing becomes him very well, the little skullcap under his head covering does not offend, because it is fine and transparent and rests on the whitest, cleanest hair in the world.

Some fifty *nobili* in long, dark, trailing garments were with him, mostly handsome men, not one deformed figure, several of them tall, with large heads that looked well in the blond, curly wigs; jutting features, flesh that is soft and white without looking bloated and repulsive, calm, self-confident, at ease in life, and overall a certain cheerfulness.

When everyone had taken his proper place in the church, the monks came in at the main door and left again by the one at the right side, after having, by pairs, received holy water and bowed to the high altar, the doge, and the nobles.

OCTOBER 6.

For this evening I had commissioned the much-discussed song of the boatmen, the ones who sing Tasso and Ariosto to their own melodies. This must actually be ordered, it does not normally occur, rather it is one of the half-faded legends of olden times. In moonlight I got into a gondola, one singer was in the prow, the other at the stern; they began their song, alternating it verse for verse. The melody, which we know from Rousseau, is a cross between chorale and recitative, always keeping the same cadence without having any rhythm; the modulation is also unvaried, except that, in accord with the content of the verse, both tone and measure are changed with a kind of declamation; but the spirit, the life, of it can be grasped, as follows.

I shall not inquire into the origin of the melody, suffice it to say that it is exactly right for an idle person who chants in different tonalities and imposes this kind of singing on poems he knows by heart.

With a penetrating voice—the common people prize strength above everything else—he sits on a barque at the shore of an island or canal and lets his song resound as far as he can. It spreads out over the quiet surface of the water. In the distance another man hears it; he knows the melody, understands the words, and answers with the next verse. The first man responds to this, and thus one is constantly the echo of the other. The song goes on for several nights, without their growing weary of this entertainment. The farther they are apart, the more charming the song can become; then if the listener stands between them both he is at the right place.

In order to let me hear this, they went ashore on the Giudecca and took up separate positions along the canal. I walked back and forth between them, always retreating from the one who was supposed to begin singing and approaching the one who had stopped. Thus the sense of the song was first revealed to me. Coming as a voice out of the distance it sounds very strange, like a lament without grief; there is something incredibly moving about it, even bringing tears. I ascribed this to my mood, but my old servant said, "È singolare, come quel canto intenerisce, e molto più, quando è più ben cantato." He wished that I might hear the women of the Lido, especially those of Malamocco and Pelestrina, who also sang Tasso to the same and similar melodies. He said further: "It is their custom, when their husbands are off in the sea, fishing, to sit down at the shore and let those songs ring out in the evening with penetrating voices, until from afar they hear the voices of their men and thus converse with them." Is that not very lovely? And yet it is quite likely that an auditor standing nearby would find little pleasure in listening to these voices compete with the waves of the sea. However, the idea of the song becomes human and true, and the melody, which was formerly a dead letter for us to rack our brains about, comes to life. It is a song sent out into the distance by a lonely individual, in the hope that someone else in the same mood will hear and answer.

I visited the Pisani Moretta palace in order to see an exquisite painting by Paul Veronese: the women of Darius's family are kneeling before Alexander and Hephaestion, the mother kneeling in front takes the latter to be the king, he denies it and points to the right one. According to legend, the artist was well received in this palace and worthily entertained there for some time; in return he secretly painted the picture as a gift, rolled it up, and shoved it under the bed. Truly, it deserves to have had a special origin, for it gives one an idea of this master's whole worth. His great artistry in producing the most exquisite harmony, not by spreading a universal tone over the whole piece, but by skillfully distributing light and shadow, and equally wisely alternating the local colors, is very visible here, since we see the picture in a perfect state of preservation, as fresh as if done yesterday. For to be sure, when a picture of this kind has decayed, our enjoyment of it is immediately marred, without our knowing the reason.

If anyone wanted to remonstrate with the artist about the costuming, let him just tell himself that the painting is supposed to depict a story of the sixteenth century, and that will settle the whole matter. The gradation from the mother to the wife and daughters is very true and felicitous; the youngest princess, kneeling at the very end, is a pretty little mouse, with a pleasing, head-strong, defiant little face; she does not seem at all ready to accept her situation.

ADDENDUM TO OCTOBER 8.

My old gift for seeing the world with the eyes of any painter whose pictures have recently made an impression on me has led me onto a peculiar thought. Obviously the eye is formed by the objects it beholds from childhood on, and so the Venetian painter must see everything more clearly and brightly than other people. We who live on ground that is either dirty and muddy or dusty, that is colorless and dims reflections, and who perhaps even live in narrow rooms, cannot independently develop such a cheerful eye.

As I rode through the lagoons in the midday sunlight and watched the gondoliers on the rims of their gondolas, gently rocking, colorfully dressed, rowing, and sharply delineated in the blue air above the bright-green surface of the water, what I was seeing was the best, freshest picture of the Venetian school. The sunshine dazzlingly accentuated the local colors, and even the shadowed portions were so luminous that they, relatively speaking, could have served as highlights. The same was true of the sea-green water. Everything was painted bright on bright, and the foaming waves with flashes of light on them put the necessary dot on the i.

Titian and Paolo Veronese had this clarity to the highest degree, and wher-ever it is not found in their works, the picture has decayed or been painted over.

The dome and vaulted ceilings of St. Mark's church, along with its side areas, abound in pictures, colorful figures against a golden ground are every-where, mosaic work is everywhere. Some things are very good, others inferior, according to which master prepared the designs.

It was brought home to me that everything really depends on the original conception, which must have the right proportions and true spirit; for with square bits of glass both the bad and the good can be reproduced, and here not even in the neatest way. The art which gave the ancients their floors and the Christians their vaulted church ceilings is now wasted on boxes and bracelets. These times are worse than one thinks.

OCTOBER 8.

In the Farsetti palace there is a valuable collection of plaster casts of the best ancient sculptures. I shall pass over the ones I already know from Mannheim and elsewhere, and mention only the newer acquaintances. A Cleopatra in co-lossal repose, with the asp wound around her arm as she slumbers into death, also Niobe, the mother shielding her youngest daughter from Apollo's arrows with her cloak, then some gladiators, a genius resting in his wings, philosophers both seated and standing.

These are works that can give the world enjoyment and culture for thousands of years, without the merits of the artists ever being fully comprehended.

The many significant busts carry me back into those splendid ancient times. But unfortunately I feel how far behind I am in this field of knowledge; yet I shall go forward, for at least I know my way now. The way to it, and to all art and life, has been opened for me by Palladio. This may sound a little odd, but surely not as paradoxical as Jakob Böhme's being enlightened about the universe after having receiving an influx of Jovian radiance from the sight of a pewter bowl! Included in this collection is a piece of the entablature of the temple of Antoninus and Faustina in Rome. The conspicuous presence of this magnificent architectural creation reminded me of the Pantheon capital in Mannheim. How very different these are from our Gothic decoration with its cowering saints stacked up over one another on little consoles, little painted towers, and crockets; thank God, I am rid of these now forever!

I want to mention a few more works of sculpture I have seen in the last few days, actually only in passing by, but with astonishment and edification nevertheless: two huge white marble lions before the gate of the Arsenal, one sitting upright, supported on its front paws, the other one reclining—splendid contrasts, lively and diverse. They are so large that they dwarf everything around them, and we ourselves would be nullified, were it not that sublime objects exalt us. They are said to be from the best Greek period and to have been brought here from Piraeus in the republic's days of glory.

Likewise of possible Athenian origin are a couple of bas-reliefs embedded in the wall of the temple of St. Justina, who was victorious over the Turks; but unfortunately they are somewhat obscured by the pews. The sacristan pointed them out to me, because legend has it that Titian used them as models for the superbly beautiful angels in his picture portraying the murder of St. Peter the Martyr. They are genii toiling along under a burden of divine attributes, but truly of an unimaginable beauty.

Next, with quite a strange feeling, I viewed the colossal nude statue of Marcus Agrippa in the courtyard of a palace; a dolphin twisting up against his side indicated that he was a naval hero. Amazing how such a heroic representation can make a mere man resemble the gods!

I took a close look at the horses on St. Mark's church. From below it is easy to see that they are spotted, and in part have a beautiful yellow metallic sheen, in part are tarnished to a copper green. Nearby one sees and discovers that they were once completely overlaid with gold; and one sees that they are covered over and over with weals, because the barbarians did not want to file off the gold, but to cut it off. However, even that is all right, since at least the form remained.

A magnificent team of horses! I would like to hear a real expert on horses discuss them. What amazes me is that up close they look heavy, while from below in the square they seem as light as stags.

OCTOBER 8.

This morning I went to the Lido with my guardian angel, to the tongue of land that closes off the lagoons and separates them from the sea. We got out of the boat and crossed over the tongue. I heard a mighty sound, it was the sea, and I soon saw it beating high against the shore as the tide went out; it was noon, the time of ebb. So now I have also seen the sea with my own eyes, and have followed after it on the beautiful smooth floor that is left behind when it recedes. I wish the children could have been here, on account of the shells; childish myself, I picked up a supply of them, which, however, I devote to a curious use, namely to dry out some of the secretion of the cuttlefish, which flows away so copiously here.

On the Lido, not far from the sea, is where English people are buried, along with the Jews, for both are prohibited from resting in hallowed ground. I found the grave of the noble Consul Smith and his first wives; I owe my copy of Palladio to him, and I thanked him for it, standing at his unconsecrated grave.

And the grave is not only unconsecrated, but half covered with rubble. The Lido must be considered a mere dune; the sand is conveyed here, the wind drives it back and forth, it is piled up and pushed against everything. In a short time the monument, although quite elevated, will hardly be visible.

The sea is really a grand sight! I want to arrange for a ride in a fishing boat; the gondolas do not venture out there.

OCTOBER 8.

At the seaside I have also found various plants whose similar character has led me to a better understanding of their nature. All of them are both plump and rigid, juicy and tough, and evidently it is the ancient salt of the sandy soil, and even more so the salty air, that give them these qualities; they are brimming with juices like water plants, they are firm and tough like mountain plants; in cases where the ends of the leaves have a tendency to become prickly, like thistles, these prickles are extremely pointed and strong. I found a cluster of such leaves, which seemed to me like our harmless coltsfoot, but armed here with sharp weapons, and the leaf was like leather, also the seedpods and stems, everything plump and fat. I am taking along seeds and some leaves preserved in brine *(Eryngium maritimum)*.

The fish market and the endless number of marine products give me much pleasure; I often go over there and inspect those unlucky creatures that have been snatched out of their home in the sea.

OCTOBER 9.

A delightful day from morning to night! I went to Pelestrina, opposite Chiozza, where the republic is having great structures called *murazzi* raised up against the sea. They are made of hewn stones, and it is really the long tongue of land called the Lido, which divides the lagoons from the sea, that they are supposed to shield from this wild element.

The lagoons are an ancient work of nature. First, ebb and flood and earth acting in opposition to each other, then the gradual subsidence of the primeval waters, were responsible for the existence, at the upper end of the Adriatic sea, of a considerable stretch of swamp which is covered by the flood tide and partly relinquished by the ebb tide. Human ingenuity took over the highest spots, and so Venice is situated on a hundred islands grouped together and is surrounded by hundreds more. In conjunction with this, deep channels were dug into the swamp at incredible cost of money and labor, so that warships could get to the chief locations even at ebb tide. What human intelligence and hard work planned and executed in olden times must now be preserved by intelligence and hard work. The Lido, a long strip of earth, separates the lagoons from the sea, which can enter only at two points, namely at the fort and near Chiozza, at the opposite end. The flood tide normally comes in twice a day, and the ebb tide carries the water out twice, always by the same path in the same directions. The flood tide covers the inner marshy spots and leaves the more elevated ones, if not dry, at least visible.

It would be quite another matter if the sea were to seek new paths, attack the tongue of land, and surge in and out at will. Aside from the fact that the little settlements on the Lido, Pelestrina, San Pietro, and others, would be submerged, those communication channels would also be filled up; and while the water was making havoc of everything, the Lido would be transformed into islands, and the islands now lying behind it into tongues of land. To prevent this, the Lido has to be secured as well as possible, so that the element cannot arbitrarily attack and destroy what humans have already taken possession of and given form and alignment to, for a certain purpose.

In extraordinary cases, when the sea rises excessively, it is especially good that it can enter only at two places, while the rest remains closed; for it cannot penetrate with its full force and in a few hours must submit to the law of ebb tide and moderate its fury.

In other respects Venice has nothing to fear. The slow subsidence of the sea gives her millenia of time, and certainly they try to keep in possession of their city by cleverly improving the canals.

If only they kept their city cleaner, which is as necessary as it is easy, and really of great consequence for the centuries to come! Now it is true there is a heavy penalty for pouring anything into the canals or throwing rubbish into them. However, nothing prevents a hard rain from stirring up all the rubbish shoved into corners and dragging it into the canals, indeed what is worse, conducting it into the drains, which are designed only to carry off water, and clogging them so badly that the main squares are in danger of standing under water. I have even seen a few drains stopped up and full of water on the smaller St. Mark's square, although they are as cleverly installed there as on the large one.

A rainy day causes an intolerable mess; everybody curses and grumbles; while going up and down the bridges people soil their coats and the *tabarri* they trail around in throughout the year; and since they all go about in shoes and stockings, these get spattered, and then they scold, for they have not been stained with ordinary, but with caustic filth. Once the weather is fine again, nobody thinks about cleanliness. How truly it is said: the public always complains about being badly served and does not know how to go about being served better. Here, if the sovereign so willed, everything could be done immediately.

OCTOBER 9.

This evening I climbed up St. Mark's tower; having seen the lagoons in their flood-tide splendor from up there, I also wanted to see them in their ebb-tide lowliness, and these two images must be combined if one wishes to get an accurate idea. It looks strange to see land appearing all around where earlier there was an expanse of water. The islands are no longer islands, only spots of higher elevation in a large gray-greenish marsh, which is intersected by beautiful canals. The swampy part can come into view only gradually because it is profusely overgrown with aquatic plants that thrive in spite of being constantly agitated by ebb and flood, which give the vegetation no rest.

I shall turn once more to the sea in my narrative: Today I saw there the activities of sea snails, limpets, and common crabs, which thoroughly pleased me. What an exquisite, splendid thing a living creature is! How adapted to its condition, how genuine, how existent! How much profit I derive from my little bit of nature study, and how happy I am to continue it! But it can be described, and so I shall not tantalize my friends with mere exclamations.

The masonry raised against the sea consists first of several steep steps, then comes a gently upward-sloping surface, then another step, and a second gently upward-sloping surface, then a steep wall with an overhanging ledge above. Up these steps and surfaces the flooding sea now rises, until, in extraordinary cases, it finally crashes against the wall and its projection.

The sea is followed by its denizens, little edible snails, limpets, and whatever else is capable of movement, especially the common crabs. However, hardly have these animals taken possession of the smooth wall when the sea recedes again, yielding and swelling, just as it came. At first the swarm is at a loss, and keeps hoping that the salty flood will return; but it does not, the sun scorches and dries them out, and now their retreat begins. At this juncture the crabs

808

seek their prey. There is nothing odder and more comical than the gestures of these creatures, which consist of a round body with two long scissors; for their spidery feet are not perceptible. They stalk along as though on stilt-like arms, and as soon as a limpet, hidden under its shield, starts to move away they rush up to stick their scissors into the narrow space between the shell and the masonry, upset the little roof, and dine on the meat. The limpet proceeds on its way slowly, but immediately adheres fast to the stone when it notices the approach of its enemy. The latter now makes strange gestures around the little roof, very dainty and monkey-like; but it lacks the strength to overcome the powerful muscle of the soft little animal. It abandons this prey, hurries off to another one that is wandering along, and the first one cautiously continues on its course. I did not see a single crab attain its goal, although I watched for hours as the swarm retreated, creeping down the two surfaces and the steps located between.

OCTOBER 10.

Now I can say that I have also seen a comedy! Today at the San Luca theater they gave *Le Baruffe Chiozzotte*, which might possibly be translated as "The Noisy Brawls of Chiozza." The characters are all seamen living in Chiozza, with their wives, sisters, and daughters. The usual clamor of these people in joy or anger, their quarrels, vehemence, good nature, banality, wit, humor, and informal manners are well imitated. The play is an old one of Goldoni's, and since I had been in this area only yesterday, and the voices and behavior of the sea and harbor people were still reverberating in my ears and reflecting in my eyes, I was most delighted with it. Although many an individual reference escaped me, I could get the gist of things quite well. The plot of the play is as follows: The women of Chiozza are sitting on the wharf in front of their houses, spinning, knitting, sewing, making pillow lace, as usual; a young man walks past and greets one of the women in a friendlier way than the others; immediately the teasing begins, does not stay within bounds, gets more intense and becomes mockery, rises to reproaches, one rude remark outdoes the other; then one vehement neighbor woman blurts out the truth, and now there is general, unrestrained scolding, reviling, and shouting, there are some downright insults, and finally the officers of the law must interfere.

The second act takes place in the courtroom; the clerk of the court, in place of the absent *podestà*—who as a *nobile* would not be permitted to appear on stage—the clerk, then, has the women summoned individually. This becomes a dubious matter, because he himself is in love with the female lead and, being very happy to talk to her alone, makes a declaration of love instead of interrogating her. Another woman, who is in love with the clerk, dashes in jealously, as does the excited lover of the first woman; the rest follow, new reproaches multiply, and now there is pandemonium in the courtroom, as earlier in the harbor.

809

In the third act the jest reaches a climax, and the whole affair ends with a hasty, makeshift denouement. The most felicitous idea, however, was to introduce a character who presents himself as follows:

An old seaman, whose limbs—but especially his organs of speech—have become halting because of the hard life he has led from youth on, comes on stage as a foil to the active, chattering, clamorous populace. He always starts out by moving his lips, and helps this along with hands and arms, until finally he is able to utter his thoughts. However, because he only succeeds in producing short sentences, he has taken on a laconic earnestness, so that everything he says sounds proverbial or sententious, and this nicely offsets the rest of the wildly emotional action.

But I have never experienced anything like the pleasure the people expressed at seeing themselves and their families represented so naturally. Uninterrupted laughter and jubilation from beginning to end. But I must also acknowledge that the actors performed excellently. According to the nature of the character portrayed, each of them had assumed one of the various voices that are typically heard among the folk. The main actress was charming, much better than she was recently in a passionate role and heroic garb. The women in general, but this one in particular, imitated the voices, gestures, and ways of the people most winningly. The author merits great praise for having created a most pleasant entertainment out of nothing. That can only be done, however, in direct contact with one's own vivacious people. It was certainly written by an expert hand.

Of the Sacchi troupe that Gozzi wrote for, and which, by the way, is disbanded, I have seen the Smeraldina, a stout little figure full of life, versatility, and good humor. With her I saw the Brighella, a lean, well-built actor especially good at gestures and facial expressions. The masked characters, who in Germany seem almost like mummies, since they have neither life nor significance for us, are very much at home here as creatures of this landscape. The ages, characters, and conditions singled out for attention have been typified with strange clothing; and people who themselves run about in masks for the greatest part of the year find it quite natural to have black faces appear on stage as well.

OCTOBER II.

And since in the final analysis solitude is really not possible amid such a great mass of humanity, I have taken up with an old Frenchman who knows no Italian and feels himself betrayed and deceived because, in spite of all his letters of recommendation, he does not rightly know where he stands with people. A man of rank, very well mannered, but he cannot lower his reserve; he may be in his late fifties, and he has a seven-year-old son at home, news of whom he awaits anxiously. I have shown him some kindnesses; he is traveling through Italy comfortably but swiftly, in order to have seen it at last. He likes to learn as much as he can along the way, and I give him information about many things. When I spoke to him about Venice he asked me how long I had been here. Hearing that it had only been for a fortnight and was my first visit, he replied: "Il parait que vous n'avez pas perdu votre temps." That is the first testimony to my good conduct that I can point to. He has been here for a week now and leaves tomorrow. I was much amused to see a truly genuine Versailles courtier abroad. So that sort is traveling now too! And I am amazed to see that a person can travel without becoming aware of his surroundings, and yet in his way he is a very cultured, worthy, respectable man.

OCTOBER 12.

Yesterday a new play was presented at San Luca, *L'Inglicismo in Italia.* Since many English people live in Italy it is natural for their manners to be noticed, and I hoped to learn here how the Italians view these rich and very welcome guests; but it amounted to nothing at all. A few successful clown scenes, as always, but the rest too heavy and seriously meant, and then actually not a trace of English feeling, just the customary Italian moral commonplaces, moreover only directed at the most commonplace matters.

Nor was it well received, and was on the verge of being hissed off; the actors did not feel in their element, they were not on the square in Chiozza. Since this is the last play I shall see here, it would seem that my enthusiasm for that national play was meant to be increased still more by the comparison.

After I have, in conclusion, gone through my journal and inserted little remarks from my notebook, the documents shall be referred to a higher court, namely, sent to my friends for their judgment. I have already found much in these pages that I could state more explicitly, amplify, and improve; but let them stand as a monument to first impressions, which we continue to delight in and treasure, even if they are not always true. If only I could send my friends a breath of this easier kind of life! Indeed the Italians have only a dim notion of the ultramontane, and to me too the other side of the Alps now seems dark; but friendly figures keep beckoning from the mist. Only the climate would tempt me to give preference to these regions over those; for birth and custom are strong ties. I would not care to live here or any other place where I would be idle; but at the moment I am very much occupied with new experiences. The architecture rises up out of its grave like an ancient ghost and bids me study its principles like the rules of a dead language, not so that I can practice it or enjoy it as something living, but only that I may, with a quiet spirit, honor the venerable, forever departed existence of past ages. Since Palladio relates everything to Vitruvius, I have procured the Galiani edition for myself; but this folio volume weighs down my luggage as heavily as the study of it does my brain. Palladio, through his words and works, his manner of thought and action, has already brought Vitruvius closer to me and interpreted him better than the Italian translation can do. Vitruvius is not very easy to read; the book in itself is obscurely written and requires judicious study. Nevertheless I am glancing through it, and am left with many a valuable impression. Or better: I read it like a breviary, more out of piety than for instruction. Night is already falling earlier, which gives me more time for reading and writing.

God be thanked, how dear to me again is everything I have esteemed since childhood! How happy I am that I dare again to approach the ancient writers! For now I may say it, may confess my morbid foolishness. For some years I could not look at any Latin author or contemplate anything that revived in me the image of Italy. If it chanced to happen, I would suffer the most dreadful pain. Herder often taunted me with having learned all my Latin from Spinoza, for he had noticed that this was the only Latin book that I read; but he did not know how wary I had to be of the ancients and that it was only out of fear of them that I fled into those abstruse generalities. Finally I was made very unhappy by Wieland's translation of the *Satires*; I had scarcely read two before I grew confused.

If I had not made the resolution I am now carrying out I would simply have perished, so ripe had the desire become in my heart to see these sights with my own eyes. Historical knowledge was of no benefit to me, for while the things stood there only a hand's breadth away, I was separated from them by an impenetrable wall. Even now I really do not feel that I am seeing the objects for the first time, but as if I were seeing them again. I have only been in Venice a short while, but I have adequately assimilated the local way of life and know that I am taking away a very clear and true, if incomplete, impression.

VENICE, OCTOBER 14, 2 HOURS AFTER SUNDOWN.

Written in my last moments of being here: for I am going at once by courier ship to Ferrara. I am glad to leave Venice, for if I wanted to stay here with pleasure and profit, other steps would have to be taken, which are not in my plan. Also, everyone is leaving the city for his gardens and estates on the mainland. Meanwhile I have packed up well and shall carry the rich, strange, unique picture away with me.

Ferrara to Rome

OCTOBER 16, MORNING, ON THE SHIP.

My traveling companions, men and women, quite tolerable and natural people, are all still asleep in the cabin. But I have spent both nights on deck, wrapped in my cloak. It only grew cool toward morning. Now I have actually entered the forty-fifth degree of latitude and I repeat my old song: the inhabitants of this country could keep everything else if only, like Dido, I could lay thongs around enough of this climate to surround our dwellings at home. Really, it is a different world. It was a very pleasant trip in splendid weather, the sights and views simple but charming. The Po, a friendly river, flows through great plains here, and only its bush- and forest-covered banks are visible, no distant places. Here, as along the Adige, I saw some absurd dikes, as childish and detrimental as those along the Saale.

FERRARA, THE 16TH, NIGHT.

Having arrived here this morning at seven by the German clock, I am preparing to leave again tomorrow. In this large and beautiful, levelly situated, but depopulated town I am for the first time overcome by a sort of aversion. These same streets were once enlivened by a brilliant court, Ariosto lived here discontentedly, Tasso unhappily, and are we to believe ourselves edified by visiting this place? Ariosto's tomb contains a great deal of marble, poorly distributed. For Tasso's prison they show a woodshed or coalshed, where he was certainly not kept. Moreover there is hardly anyone in the house who knows what the visitor wants. Finally, for a gratuity, they do remember. It puts me in mind of Doctor Luther's inkspot, which the castellan freshens up from time to time. Most travelers seem to have a touch of the journeyman about them and like to look around for such marks. I had become quite disgruntled and took little interest in a fine academic institute that had been founded and enriched by a cardinal born in Ferrara, but some old monuments in the courtyard restored my spirits.

Then I was cheered by a painter's clever idea: John the Baptist before Herod and Herodias. The prophet in his customary desert costume points vehemently at the lady. She looks quite calmly at the sovereign sitting beside her, and the sovereign looks quietly and shrewdly at the enthusiast. In front of the king stands a white dog of medium size, while a little Bolognese dog peeps out from under Herodias's skirt, and both of them bark at the prophet. In my opinion, that is a most happy thought.

CENTO, THE 17TH, EVENING.

I am writing from Guercino's native town, in a better mood than yesterday. But the situation is also quite different. A friendly, attractive little town of approximately five thousand inhabitants, productive, clean, in a vast cultivated plain. As is my custom, I immediately climbed up the tower. A sea of pointed poplar trees, among which I saw little farmsteads close at hand, each surrounded by its own field. Excellent soil, a mild climate. It was an autumn evening, but of a kind we can seldom enjoy even in our summertime. The sky, overcast all day, brightened, the clouds scudded north and southwards to the mountains, and I am in hopes of a beautiful day tomorrow.

Here for the first time I saw the Apennines, which I am coming closer to. The winter here lasts only through December and January, April is rainy, otherwise the weather is good, in relationship to the season. Never a prolonged rain; yet this September was warmer and better than their August. I nodded a friendly greeting to the Apennines in the south, for I am tiring of level country. Tomorrow I shall be writing over there at their foot.

Guercino loved his native town, and the Italians in general nurture local patriotism in a very high-minded way. This beautiful sentiment has given rise to many fine institutions, and indeed also the throng of local saints. Here, for example, an academy of painting was founded under that master's auspices. He left behind several pictures which still delight the townspeople and are certainly worthy of doing so.

Guercino is a sacred name, and is on the lips of children as well as adults.

I very much liked the picture showing the risen Christ when He appears to His mother. Kneeling before Him, she looks up at Him with ineffable tenderness. Her left hand touches His body just below the wretched wound, which is a blot on the whole picture. He has placed His left hand around her neck and bends His body back slightly, so as to look at her more easily. This gives the figure a quality that is, if not forced, in any case odd, in spite of which it remains extremely pleasant. The quietly sad expression with which He looks at her is unique, as if the memory of their mutual sufferings, not immediately healed by the resurrection, were hovering before His noble soul.

Strange has engraved this picture; I wish my friends could at least see that copy.

Next to win my affection was a Madonna. The Child demands her breast, she modestly hesitates to bare her bosom. Natural, noble, charming, and beautiful.

Furthermore a Mary, the Child standing in front of her and facing the spectators; she guides His arm, so that He may, with raised fingers, bestow the blessing. A very felicitous and often repeated idea, in the spirit of Catholic mythology.

Guercino is a profoundly good, wholesomely manly painter, without crudeness. Rather, his things have a delicate moral grace, a calm freedom and grandeur, and at the same time something unique, so that his works are unmistakable, once the eye has become accustomed to them. The lightness, purity, and perfection of his brushwork are astonishing. For the drapery he uses especially beautiful, subdued brownish-red pigments. These harmonize very well with the blue he also likes to apply.

The subjects of the remaining pictures are more or less unfortunate. The good artist did his utmost, but still his inventiveness and brushwork, his spirit and hand, were expended in vain. But I am surely very glad that I have also seen this beautiful group of paintings, even though there is little pleasure or instruction in racing past them so quickly.

BOLOGNA, OCTOBER 18, NIGHT.

This morning, before daybreak, I rode away from Cento and arrived here in fairly good time. A nimble and well-informed hired servant, upon hearing that I did not plan to stay long, hurried me through all the streets and so many palaces and churches that I could hardly check them all off in my Volkmann; and who knows whether in the future these marks will help me remember all these places? Now, however, I shall mention a few high spots, where I felt a true satisfaction.

First, then, Raphael's *Cecilia!* It is what I already knew it would be, but now I have seen it with my own eyes; he always *did*, what other artists only *wished* to do, and now all I would like to say is that it is by *him*. Five saints next to each other, none of whom concerns us, but of such consummate existence that we hope the picture may last forever, even though we ourselves must accept disintegration. However, if we want to know him truly, appreciate him correctly, and also not honor him as a god who came into being, like Melchizedek, without father or mother, we must look at his precursors, his masters. These men based themselves on the solid ground of truth, laid the broad foundations diligently, indeed meticulously, and, in competition with each other, built up the pyramid step by step, until at last, benefiting from all these new techniques and inspired by his heavenly genius, he put the topmost stone in place, over and beside which no other can stand.

It especially awakens my historical interest to look at the works of older masters. Francesco Francia is a very respectable artist, Pietro of Perugia such a worthy man that I was tempted to call him an honest German fellow. If only it had been Albrecht Dürer's good luck to have gone down farther into Italy! In Munich I saw a few works by him that were of incredible grandeur. The poor man, how he miscalculated in Venice, making an agreement with the priests that cost him weeks and months! How, on his trip to the Netherlands, he bartered magnificent artworks, with which he had hoped to make his fortune, for parrots and, to save gratuities, made a portrait of the servants who brought him a plate of fruit! I find such a poor fool of an artist infinitely touching, because basically this is also my fate, except that I am somewhat better able to take care of myself.

Toward evening I finally escaped from this venerable, scholarly old town, from the crowds of people who can amble back and forth, gape, buy, and carry on their affairs, protected from sun and weather by the arcades that are seen lining almost all the streets. I climbed up the tower and enjoyed the open air. The view is splendid! In the north I saw the Paduan mountains, then the Swiss, Tyrolean, and Friulian Alps, in short, the whole northern chain, now covered by mist. Toward the west a limitless horizon, broken only by the towers of Modena. Toward the east a similar plain, up to the Adriatic sea, which can be glimpsed at sunrise. Toward the south the foothills of the Apennines, cultivated up to their summits and covered with growth, studded with churches, palaces, garden houses, like the Vicenzian hills. The sky was perfectly clear, without a wisp of cloud, only a sort of haze on the horizon. The warder asserted that this mist had been there in the distance for the last six years. Before that he had always been able, with the aid of his spyglass, to clearly make out the mountains of Vicenza with their houses and chapels, but now only rarely, even on the brightest days. And this mist clings mainly to the northern chain and makes our dear fatherland seem like a truly Cimmerian realm. The man also pointed out to me that the healthful location and air of the city were evident from the fact that its roofs looked like new, with none of the tiles attacked by damp and moss. It must be admitted that the roofs are all in fine condition, but the excellence of the tiles themselves may also be a contributing factor, at any rate in ancient times splendid tiles were manufactured in these regions.

The leaning tower is an ugly sight, and yet in all likelihood it was built like this intentionally. I explain this foolishness to myself as follows: During the period of civil unrest every large building became a fortress, over which every powerful family raised a tower. Gradually this became a matter of pride and pleasure, everybody wanted to show off with a tower, and when straight towers became all too commonplace, a leaning one was built. And indeed the architect and the owner achieved their goal, for we look past the many straight, slim towers and seek out the crooked one. The bricks are laid in horizontal rows. Good, quick-setting cement and iron braces can be used to make some very absurd things!

BOLOGNA, OCTOBER 19, EVENING.

I have used this day to the best of my ability, looking, and looking again, but art is like life; the farther we advance into it, the broader it grows. New constellations that I cannot assess and that confuse me keep emerging in this sky, namely, the Caraccis, Guido, Domenichino, who arose during a later, happier artistic era. Really to enjoy them, however, one needs knowledge and judgment, which I lack and can gain only gradually. The absurdity of their subjects is a great hindrance to pure contemplation and direct understanding of the pictures, which I would like to love and revere, but instead they drive me to distraction.

It is the same as when the children of God married the daughters of men, with the result that various monsters were born. While you are attracted by Guido's beatific intent, by his brush, which should have painted only the most perfect things that can be gazed upon, at the same time you want to avert your eyes from the disgustingly stupid subjects, for which there are no words bad enough, and thus it is throughout. We cannot get away from the dissecting room, the gallows, the abattoir, and the sufferings of the hero; there is never any action, never any immediate interest, always some fantastic expectation from outside. Either sinners or ecstatics, criminals or fools, while the painter tries to save the situation by dragging in some naked fellow or a pretty female onlooker, or perhaps by treating his religious heroes as though they were lay figures to be draped with cloaks arranged in lovely folds. Nothing is there to suggest humanity! Ten subjects, not one of which should have been painted, and one that the artist was not permitted to treat in the right way.

Guido's large picture in the church of the Mendicanti meets every painterly requirement, but nothing could be more nonsensical than the commission the artist was expected to carry out. It is a votive picture. I believe the whole senate praised it and also conceived the idea. The two angels, who would be worthy of consoling Psyche in her misfortune, here must—

St. Proclus, a beautiful figure; but the others, the bishops and priests! At the bottom are some cherubs playing with attributes. The painter, who had a knife at his throat, tried his best, he exerted himself to the utmost, just to show that it was not he who was the barbarian. Two nude figures by Guido: a John in the wilderness, a Sebastian. How exquisitely they are painted! And what do they say? One has his mouth wide open, and the other writhes.

If I look at history in this bad humor I am tempted to say: faith gave renewed prominence to the arts, but superstition took them over and destroyed them again.

After dinner I was in a somewhat milder and less arrogant mood than this morning, and I noted down the following on my writing pad: In the Tanari palace there is a famous painting by Guido which depicts Mary nursing, larger than lifesize, the head as if painted by a god; her expression as she looks down on the child at her breast is indescribable. To me it seems quiet, profound endurance, as if this were not a child of joy and love but a supposititious divine changeling that she only allows to nibble at her because the situation must simply be accepted, and in her deep humility she does not have the slightest idea why she was selected. The remaining space is filled with an enormous drapery, which is much praised by connoisseurs: I really did not know what to make of it. Besides, the colors have darkened; and the room and the day were not the brightest.

In spite of my current confusion I already feel that practice, acquaintance, and inclination are coming to my aid. Thus a *Circumcision* by Guercino strongly appealed to me, because I already know and love the man. I excused the intolerable subject and took pleasure in the execution.—Painted with all imaginable skill, everything in it estimable and as perfect as if made of enamel.

And so I share the fate of Bileam, the confused prophet, who blessed when he intended to curse, and this would be the case still oftener if I were to stay here longer.

If, then, I come again upon a work of Raphael's, or at any rate one ascribed to him with some probability, I am at once completely healed and happy. Thus I have found a *St. Agatha*, a precious, although not very well preserved picture. The artist has given her a wholesome, secure virginity, but without coldness and crudity. I have observed the figure well and in spirit will read my *Iphigenia* aloud to her, not letting my heroine say anything that this saint would not utter.

Now that I have once again mentioned the dear burden that I am carrying with me on my wanderings, I cannot conceal that in addition to having to work my way through great artistic and natural sights a remarkable series of poetic figures is moving through my mind and disturbing me. On my way here from Cento I wanted to continue my work on *Iphigenia*, but what happened? The spirit moved me to think of the plot of "Iphigenia of Delphi," and I had to develop it. Let me sketch it here as briefly as possible:

Electra, certain in her hope that Orestes will bring the image of the Tauric Diana to Delphi, appears in the temple of Apollo and dedicates the cruel axe, which has wrought such havoc in the family of Pelops, as her final sacrifice to propitiate the god. Unfortunately one of the Greeks approaches her and tells how he accompanied Orestes and Pylades to Tauris, saw the two friends led to their deaths, and luckily escaped. The passionate Electra is beside herself and does not know whether to direct her fury at men or the gods.

Meanwhile Iphigenia, Orestes, and Pylades have likewise arrived in Delphi. Iphigenia's saintly calm contrasts quite remarkably with Electra's earthly passion when the two figures meet without recognizing each other. The fugitive Greek sees Iphigenia, recognizes her as the priestess who sacrificed the friends, and reveals this to Electra. The latter is on the point of murdering Iphigenia with the axe she has snatched away again from the altar, when a fortunate turn of events averts this last terrible evil from the sisters. If this scene works out well, then it will very likely be as great and touching as anything ever seen on the stage. But where shall my hands find the time, even though the spirit were willing?

Now, while fretting because too many good and desirable things are claiming my attention, I must remind my friends of a seemingly quite significant dream I had just a year ago. Namely, I dreamt I was in a rather large boat that was landing at a fertile, opulently overgrown island where I knew that the finest pheasants were available. And so I immediately bargained with the islanders for this fowl, of which they promptly brought me many, already killed. They were pheasants, to be sure, but since dreams alter everything, their long tails were studded with colored eyes, like the tails of peacocks or rare birds of paradise. The birds were now laid down in the boat like sheaves of wheat, and piled up so neatly, with heads to the inside and long, varicolored tail feathers hanging outside, that they made the most splendid stack imaginable, and indeed such an ample one that little space was left before or behind it for the helmsman and the oarsmen. In this fashion we plowed the quiet waters, and I was already going over the names of the friends with whom I would share these colorful treasures. Finally arriving at a large harbor, I got lost among high-masted ships and clambered from the deck of one to the other, seeking a secure landing place for my smaller craft.

We delight in such phantoms, which, since they arise out of ourselves, must surely have some analogy with the rest of our life and fortunes.

Now I have also visited the famous scholarly establishment called the Institute or "the Studies." The big building and especially its inner court look quite impressive in a solemn way, although the architecture is not of the best. The stairs and corridors are ornamented with stucco and frescos; everything is decorous and worthy, and I was duly amazed by the manifold beautiful and remarkable objects that have been collected here; nevertheless, Germans are accustomed to a freer method of study, and so the place made me feel uncomfortable.

An earlier observation came back to mind here, about how difficult it is, as time passes and alters everything, for human beings to sacrifice the original appearance of a thing even after its intended purpose has changed. Christian churches still adhere to the basilica form, although the temple form might be better suited to the ritual. Scholarly institutions still have a monastic appearance because it was in those pious precincts that studies found their first peaceful accommodation. The courtrooms in Italy are as spacious and lofty as a community's means permit; it is like being in those marketplaces where trials used to be held under the open sky. And do we not continue to build our largest theaters, with all their appurtenances, under a roof like those of the original kermess stalls, which were made of boards and not expected to last more than a short time? Because of the immense crowds of knowledge seekers at the time of the Reformation, students were forced to live in townspeople's houses, and yet how long it has taken us to open up our orphanages and provide those poor children with the same very necessary worldly education!

BOLOGNA, THE 20TH, EVENING.

I have spent this whole bright, beautiful day in the open air. As soon as I come near to mountains I am attracted to their minerals again. I see myself as Antaeus, who always feels newly strengthened, the more forcefully he is brought into contact with his mother, the earth.

I rode on horseback to Paderno, where the so-called Bolognese heavy spar is found. Little cakes are made from it which, when calcined and then exposed to the light, will afterwards glow in the dark. Here they are called simply *fosfori*.

After passing some sandy clay hills on the way there, I soon found whole masses of selenite showing on the surface. A watery fissure descends near a brick kiln, with many smaller ones emptying into it. At first I supposed this was a soggy hill eroded by the rain, but on closer inspection I could detect the following about its nature: the solid rock composing this part of the range is a very thinly laminated shale alternating with gypsum. The shale is so intimately mixed with pyrites that it undergoes a complete change when in contact with air and moisture. It becomes distended, the strata disappear, a kind of clay is formed, conchoidal, crumbled, with gleaming surfaces like coal. The transition, or transformation, can only be convincingly demonstrated in large pieces; after cracking open several of them I clearly perceived both forms. At the same time it can be seen that the conchoidal planes are covered with white dots and sometimes have yellow parts; so the whole surface is gradually decaying, and in general the hill looks like weathered pyrites. Also, some of the strata are harder, green and red. I frequently found pyrites encrusted on the rocks too.

Then I ascended the crumbling, disintegrating mountains through ravines washed out by the last downpours, and to my delight found large amounts of the heavy spar I was seeking, mostly in imperfect ovoid form, showing on the surface at several spots where the mountains were in the process of falling to bits, some of it quite loose, some still tightly gripped by the shale in which it was situated. One glance sufficed to convince me that these were not detritus. Whether they originated simultaneously with the stratum of shale, or only when the latter swelled up and decomposed, merits closer investigation. The pieces I found, whether larger or smaller, come close to having an imperfectly ovoid shape, while the smallest are actually passing over into an indistinctly crystalline form. The heaviest piece I found weighs eight and a half ounces. In the same shale I also found loose, perfect gypsum crystals. When experts see the pieces I am taking along they will know how to define them more accurately. And so here I am, burdened with rocks again! I have packed up an eighth hundredweight of this heavy spar.

OCTOBER 20, AT NIGHT.

How much more there would be to say if I wanted to tell everything that went through my mind on this beautiful day! But my longing is stronger than my thoughts. I feel myself drawn irresistibly onwards, and I have to force myself to concentrate on what is at hand. And it seems that Heaven has heard my prayers. A *vetturino* has announced his intention of going straight to Rome, and so the day after tomorrow I shall set out in that direction without stopping along the way. Then today and tomorrow I must see to my affairs, attend to various matters, and dispose of them.

LOJANO IN THE APENNINES, OCTOBER 21, EVENING.

Whether I drove myself out of Bologna today, or was chased out, I cannot say. In any case I impulsively grasped an opportunity to leave earlier. Now here I am in a miserable inn together with a papal officer who is going to his native town. When I seated myself next to him in the two-wheeled carriage I commented politely, just to make conversation, that I, being a German who was accustomed to associate with soldiers, found it very agreeable to be traveling now in the company of a papal officer.—"Do not take offence," he replied, "but I am not surprised you like the military, since I hear that in Germany everyone is a soldier. As for me, however, although our service is very easy and I have a perfectly comfortable life in Bologna, where I am garrisoned, still I wish I were rid of this jacket and were managing my father's little farm. But I am the younger son and so I have to put up with it."

THE 22ND, EVENING.

Giredo, another little village high in the Apennines, where I feel quite happy because I am coming closer to my desires. Today we were joined by a lady and gentleman on horseback, an Englishman with his so-called sister. They have fine horses, but are traveling without servants, and it seems that the gentleman serves as both valet and groom. They have found something to complain about everywhere, it is like reading some pages out of Archenholz.

I find the Apennines a remarkable part of the world. Upon the great plain of the Po basin there follows a mountain range that rises from the depths, between two seas, to end the continent on the south. If it were not so steep, so high above sea level, and so strangely tortuous, it would have been affected more and longer in primeval times by the ebb and flood, which would have washed over it and formed larger expanses of flat land. Then it would be one of the most beautiful regions in this most splendid latitude, somewhat higher than the other land. In actual fact, however, it is a curious web of mountain ridges facing each other; often it is not possible to find the point toward which the water is trying to drain. If the valleys were filled in more and the flat surfaces smoother and better watered, the region could be compared to Bohemia, except that these mountains have an entirely different character. Still, one must not imagine a high wasteland, but a countryside mostly cultivated, even though mountainous. Chestnuts develop beautifully here, and the wheat is excellent, the crop already a pretty green. Evergreen oaks with small leaves stand by the roadside, but the churches and chapels are surrounded by slim cypresses.

Yesterday evening the weather was gloomy, today it is bright and beautiful again.

THE 25TH, EVENING. PERUGIA.

For two evenings I have not written anything. The inns were so bad that there was nowhere to lay down a sheet of paper. Things are also beginning to get a bit tangled for me, because ever since my departure from Venice my travel distaff has not been spinning off as well and smoothly as before.

On the morning of the twenty-third, at ten o'clock German time, we came out of the Apennines and saw Florence lying in a wide valley, which is cultivated to an unbelievable degree and dotted with innumerable villas and houses.

I went through the city, the cathedral, the baptistery very hastily. Another new and unfamiliar world has opened up before me here, but I do not intend to linger in it. The Boboli garden has a choice location. I hurried out of it as fast as I went in.

The city shows the municipal wealth that built it; obviously it enjoyed a series of good governments. In Tuscany generally, one is immediately struck by the fine, grandiose appearance of public works such as roads and bridges. Everything here is both sturdy and well kept, the intention is to combine use and advantage with attractiveness, a spirit of precision is noticeable everywhere. In contrast, the papal state seems to survive only because the earth refuses to swallow it.

When I recently described what the Apennines *could* be, that is what Tuscany actually *is*. Owing to the much lower elevation, the primeval sea could perform its duty properly and heaped up a deep clay soil. It is bright yellow and easily tilled. They plow deeply, but still in the primitive way: their plow has no wheels and the plowshare is immovable. So the peasant has to shove it along, bent over behind his oxen, as he digs up the earth. Plowing is done as much as five times, and fertilizer is strewn by hand, very lightly. Finally they sow the wheat, then pile up narrow ridges with deep furrows between them, everything aimed at draining away rainwater. Now the crop grows up on the ridges, and they walk up and down in the furrows to weed. It would be an understandable procedure where there is danger of wetness; but I cannot see why they do it on the finest flat land. I carried out this inspection in the vicinity of Arezzo, where a magnificent plain unfolds. No field could be neater than this one, nowhere even a clod of earth, everything is as finely ground as if it were sifted. Wheat thrives very well here, apparently finding all the conditions appropriate to its nature. The second year they raise beans for the horses, which are not fed oats here. Lupines are also sown and have already grown up splendid and green; they will bear fruit in March. The flax has come up already too; it survives the winter, and the frost only makes the fiber more durable.

The olive trees are curious plants; they closely resemble willows, losing their heartwood in the same way, and the bark splits. But in spite of that they have a fairly solid appearance. One can see that the wood grows slowly and has an incredibly delicate organic structure. The leaf is willow-like, but with fewer leaves to the branch. The hills around Florence are planted all over with olive trees and grapevines, the ground between them is used for grain. Near Arezzo and beyond it the fields are left freer. It seems to me that not enough is done to combat ivy, which is injurious to olive and other trees and could so easily be destroyed. One sees no meadows at all. They say that Indian corn exhausts the soil, and that other crops have suffered since its introduction. I can well believe that, in view of the meager fertilizer.

This evening I took leave of my captain with assurances and promises that I would visit him in Bologna on my return trip. Now a few things that particularly characterize him: Since I was often quiet and reflective, he once said, "Che pensa! non deve mai pensar l'uomo, pensando s'invecchia." Translated, that means: "Why do you think so much! A man must never think, thinking ages him." And after some conversation: "Non deve fermarsi l'uomo in una sola cosa, perchè allora divien matto; bisogna aver mille cose, una confusione nella testa." Translated: "A man must not concentrate on just a single thing, because that will drive him mad, he must have a thousand things, a confusion, in his head."

Of course the good man could not know that I was quiet and reflective for the very reason that my head *was* whirling with a confusion of old and new things. The cultural level of an Italian like him will be seen still more clearly from the following: Noticing of course that I was a Protestant, he eventually got up the courage to say I should please permit him certain questions, for he had heard so many curious things about us Protestants and finally wanted some reliable information on this subject. "May you really," he asked, "have an intimate relationship with a pretty girl without actually being married to her?—Do your priests allow you to do that?" I answered: "Our priests are clever men, who take no notice of such trifling matters. Of course, if we asked their permission, they would not give it."—"So you do not need to ask?" he exclaimed, "Oh, you lucky fellows! And since you do not confess to them, they do not find out about it." Hereupon he began a tirade against his priests and praised our blessed freedom.—"However, with respect to confession," he continued, "what is the situation there? We are told that all the people, even if they are not Christians, still must confess. But because they are too hardened to do it properly, they will confess to an old tree, which of course is very absurd and impious, but nevertheless it shows that they recognize the necessity of confession." Hereupon I explained our notions of confession to him, and how we went about it. That sounded very convenient to him, but he said it was approximately the same as confessing to an old tree. After some hesitation he besought me very earnestly for honest information on another point; that is to say, he had heard from the lips of one of his priests, who was a truthful man, that we were permitted to marry our sisters, which was certainly a great impropriety. When I denied this charge and tried to give him some sympathetic understanding of our doctrine, he did not pay any particular heed, for it seemed too ordinary to him, and he turned to another question:—"We are assured," he said, "that Frederick the Great, who has won so many victories even over the true believers and become famous throughout the world, that he, whom everyone considers a heretic, is actually a Catholic and has a papal dispensation to keep this a secret. For he does not go into any of your churches, as is well known; instead, he worships in a subterranean chapel, broken-hearted that he may not publicly confess the sacred religion. For if he did so, his Prussians, who are a bestial people and raging heretics, would kill him on the spot, which would not help the cause. Therefore the Holy Father has given him this dispensation, in return for which he quietly spreads and favors the only true religion as much as possible." I let all of that pass and merely answered: since it was a great secret, naturally no one could prove it. Our further conversation was in much the same vein, and I could not help feeling amazed at the clever clergy, who try to dismiss and distort everything that might penetrate and confound the dark realm of their traditional teachings.

I left Perugia on a splendid morning and felt the bliss of being alone again. The location of the town is beautiful, the view of the lake most delightful. I have impressed these pictures deeply on myself. First the road went down, then through a pleasant valley enclosed on both sides by distant hills. Finally I saw Assisi lying before me.

I knew from Palladio and Volkmann that a perfectly preserved, beautiful temple of Minerva, built in Augustan times, was still standing there. At Madonna del Angelo I left my *vetturino*, who continued on his way to Foligno, while I climbed up to Assisi in a strong wind; for I longed to wander on foot through what seemed to me a very isolated world. To my left were the enormous substructures over which, piled on top of each other in Babylonian fashion, are the churches where St. Francis rests; but I turned away from them with repugnance, thinking to myself that the minds I found there would bear the same stamp as that of my captain. Then I asked a handsome lad about the Maria della Minerva, and he led me up to the town, which is built on a mountainside. Finally we arrived in the actual old part of the town, and behold, there before my eyes stood the first complete monument from ancient times that I have seen. A modest temple, as befitted such a small town, and yet so perfect, so beautifully conceived, that it would stand out anywhere. Now, first of all, concerning its position! I have great respect for such matters after having read in Vitruvius and Palladio how towns should be built and temples and public buildings placed. In this regard too the ancients understood the grandeur of naturalness. The temple stands at the beautiful halfway point of the mountain, just where two hills meet, on the square which is still just called "the Square." The latter itself slopes upwards a little, and four streets come together on it, forming a very compressed St. Andrew's cross, two coming up from below, two down from above. The houses built opposite the temple were probably not standing in ancient times because they now block the view. If we could imagine them gone, we would look southwards into the most opulent region, and Minerva's temple would be visible from all sides. The layout of the streets may be ancient, for it is determined by the form and slope of the mountain. The temple does not stand in the middle of the square but is aligned in such a way that it is visible in very beautiful perspective to anyone coming up from Rome. Someone ought to draw not only the building but also its felicitous position.

In looking at the facade I became fascinated with the brilliant logic of the artist's procedure here too. The order is Corinthian, the space between the columns somewhat more than two column diameters. The tori and the plinths under them seem to stand on pedestals, but that is an illusion; for the socle is cut through five times, and each time five steps go up between the columns, and then one arrives at the surface on which the columns really stand, and from which one enters the temple. The bold decision to cut through the socle was appropriate here, for since the temple is situated on the mountainside, the steps leading up to it would have had to be placed too far in front and would have narrowed the square. It cannot be determined how many more steps were situated underneath; with few exceptions they are buried and paved over. Reluctantly I tore myself away from this sight and resolved to bring the building to the attention of all architects, so that we may obtain an exact plan of it. For in this instance I was struck again by how poorly things are transmitted. Palladio, in whom I had complete confidence, of course includes a picture of this temple, but he cannot have seen it himself, for he actually puts pedestals on the flat surface. This makes the columns disproportionately high, so that the result is an ugly Palmyric monstrosity, whereas in reality one enjoys a serene, lovely sight that satisfies both eye and intellect. Contemplation of this work awakens feelings in me that I cannot put into words, but they will bear lasting fruit.

It was the most beautiful evening, and I was walking downhill on the Roman road, wonderfully calm in spirit, when behind me I heard rough, vehement voices raised in a quarrel. I supposed it might be the *sbirri* whom I had noticed earlier in the town. I coolly went on my way, but kept listening to them in back of me. Then I soon realized that their discussion was about *me*. Four such men, of unpleasant appearance, two of them armed with muskets, walked past me, muttered something, returned after a few steps, and surrounded me. They asked who I was and what I was doing here. I said I was a foreigner passing through Assisi on foot, while my *vetturino* was driving on to Foligno. They could not conceive of anyone's paying for a carriage and then walking. They asked whether I had been in the Gran Convento. I said no, and assured them that this building had long been familiar to me. But since I was an architect, this time I had inspected only the Maria della Minerva, which, as they knew, was a model building. They did not deny that but were much offended that I had not paid my respects to the saint, and aired their suspicion that my trade might be the smuggling of contraband. I pointed out to them how absurd it was to imagine that a man walking alone down the road, with empty pockets and no knapsack, could be a smuggler. I offered to accompany them back to town to see the *podestà* and show him my papers, whereupon he would acknowledge me to be a respectable foreigner. They muttered at this, saying it would not be necessary; and finally, while I maintained a decidedly serious demeanor, they retreated towards the town again. I watched them go. There in the foreground I saw those coarse fellows walking, while behind them the lovely Minerva gazed at me again in a very friendly and consoling manner. Then I looked to my left at the mournful cathedral of St. Francis and was about to continue on my way when one of the unarmed men detached himself from the group and came up to me quite amicably. Greeting me, he said at once: "My dear foreign sir, you should at least give *me* a gratuity, for I assure you that I took you for an honest man right away and declared this loudly to my companions. But they are hotheads who immediately get angry, and they are ignorant of the world. You will also have noticed that it was I who first applauded and accepted your words." I praised him for this and asked him to safeguard respectable foreigners who came to Assisi in pursuit of religion and art, especially architects, for they would bring fame to the town by measuring and drawing the Minerva temple, which had not as yet been properly drawn and engraved. I said he should be of service to them, for then they would certainly show their gratitude—and with that I pressed several silver coins into his hand, more than he expected. Very much delighted, he asked me to be sure to return, and especially not to miss the saint's festival, where I would most certainly enjoy myself and be edified. In fact, if a handsome man like me should be interested in meeting a handsome woman, as was only right and proper, he could assure me that on his recommendation the most beautiful and respectable woman in all of Assisi would gladly receive me. Then he departed, swearing that he would mention me in his devotions at the saint's grave this very evening, and would pray for my subsequent journey. Thus we parted, and I was much relieved to be alone again with nature and myself. The road to Foligno afforded one of the most charming and beautiful walks I have ever taken. Four full hours along a mountainside, with a richly cultivated valley on my right.

One rides tolerably well with the *vetturini*; but the best part is that one can follow them easily on foot. I have had myself dragged along by them all the way here from Ferrara. This Italy, which enjoys nature's richest favor, has lagged very badly behind other countries with respect to mechanics and technology, which after all are the basis of a more modern and comfortable way of life. The carriage of the *vetturini*, which is still called *sedia*, or seat, is surely descended from the old sedan chairs in which women, or older and more aristocratic persons, had themselves drawn by mules. Two wheels were set underneath to replace the rear mule, which was then harnessed in front next to the tongue, and no further improvements were undertaken. The passenger is still rocked along as he was centuries ago, and they are like this in their dwellings and everything else.

If anyone wants to see the earliest poetic idea still existing in reality, namely, that people lived mostly under the open sky and withdrew into their caves only when necessary, let him enter the buildings here, especially those out in the countryside, which are altogether cave-like in spirit and taste. The Italians are so incredibly insouciant because they do not want reflection to age them! With outrageous frivolity they neglect to prepare for winter and its longer nights, and consequently suffer like dogs for a good part of the year. Here I am in Foligno, in a truly Homeric domestic situation, where everyone assembles around a fire burning on the earthen floor of a great hall and, amidst shouting and clamor, dines at a long table, as in paintings of the marriage at Cana. Under the circumstances I would not have thought of inkwells, but somebody has had one brought in, and so I seize the opportunity to write this. But the page reveals how cold and uncomfortable my writing table is.

Now I surely feel how rash it was to come to this country unprepared and unaccompanied. Because of the various currencies, the *vetturini*, the prices, and the inferior inns there is no way for someone like me, traveling alone for the first time and looking hopefully for uninterrupted pleasure, to avoid feeling very unhappy day in, day out. But my one desire has been to see this land, cost what it may, and although they are dragging me to Rome on Ixion's wheel, I shall not complain.

TERNI, OCTOBER 27, EVENING.

Here I sit in another "cave," one that was damaged in an earthquake a year ago. The little town lies in a delectable region, which I happily surveyed while making the circuit of the walls. It starts off with a lovely plain between mountains, which all still consist of limestone. Terni is located at the foot of the range on this side, like Bologna on the other side.

The papal soldier having left me, I now have a priest as my traveling companion. He seems much more content with his situation than the former, and is very willing to instruct me, whom of course he recognizes as a heretic, when I ask him about the rituals and other matters of that kind. Truly, I am achieving my goal by constantly associating with different persons; and what a vivid picture of the whole country can be gained from just hearing the people converse among themselves! In the most remarkable way they are all adversaries, they feel the strangest fanatical loyalty to their province and town, are all very intolerant of one another, the classes are eternally at war, and all of this to the accompaniment of invariably lively, spontaneous emotion. All day long they perform a comedy for me and make fools of themselves; and yet at the same time they take the situation in and immediately notice when a foreigner is bewildered by their general behavior.

I climbed up to Spoleto and was on the aqueduct, which also serves as a bridge between two mountains. The ten arches of brickwork have stood there so calmly during the centuries, and water still gushes forth everywhere in Spoleto. This, now, is the third ancient structure I have seen, all of them with the same grandeur of design. A second Nature, one that serves civic goals, that is what their architecture is, and thus arose the amphitheater, the temple, and the aqueduct. Only now do I feel how right I was to loathe all capricious edifices, like the Winterkasten on the Weissenstein for example, a nothing built for nothing, a huge decorative confection, and it is the same with a thousand other things. They all stand there stillborn, for whatever has no inner validity has no life, and can neither be nor become great.

How much pleasure and understanding I have derived from the last eight weeks! But they have also cost me considerable effort. I make sure to keep my eyes open all the time and let the sights impress themselves on me deeply. Even if it were possible, I would definitely not care to make judgments.

San Crocefisso, a bizarre chapel next to the road, is in my opinion not the remains of any temple that stood on this spot. On the contrary, some columns, pillars, and pieces of entablature were found and patched together, not stupidly, but crazily. It beggars description, but surely there is an engraving of it somewhere.

And so it is disconcerting to us who are striving to acquire a concept of antiquity that we meet with nothing but ruins, on the basis of which we must try, with poor success, to reconstruct something we do not yet understand.

The situation is quite different with what is called classical soil. If, instead of losing oneself in fantasy here, one accepts the region as reality, just as it lies there, then it is still the definitive scene of action, which calls for the greatest deeds; and therefore up till now I have always made use of my interest in geology and topography to suppress my imagination and sentiment, and to preserve a free, clear view of the locality for myself. Then, in a remarkable fashion, history vividly links itself up with this, and I do not know what comes over me, but I feel the greatest longing to read Tacitus in Rome.

Nor must I entirely neglect the weather. When I was coming up the Apennines from Bologna the clouds were still moving northwards; later, they changed direction and moved toward Lake Trasimeno. Here they hung, then probably moved southwards. The great plain of the Po, which during the summer sent all its clouds to the Tyrolean mountains, now sends some of them to the Apennines, which may explain the rainy weather.

They are beginning to pick olives. It is done by hand here, in other places the trees are beaten with sticks. If winter comes prematurely, the remaining fruit continues to hang nearly until spring. Today I saw some of the largest, oldest trees on very stony ground.

The Muses' favor, like that of the demons, is not always bestowed on us at the proper time. Today I was inspired to work on a subject that is totally unsuited to the circumstances. Here I am, approaching the very heart of Catholicism, surrounded by Catholics, confined in a *sedia* with a priest, and also trying, with the purest of intentions, to observe and comprehend true nature and noble art, and what flashes through my mind very vividly is that all traces of original Christianity have been expunged. Indeed, when I visualized it in its pure form, as we see it in the Acts of the Apostles, I could not help shuddering at the deformed, nay, bizarre heathenism that now weighs upon those agreeable beginnings. Then I thought again of the Wandering Jew, who had witnessed all those curious, complicated developments and had experienced conditions so strange that when

Christ Himself returned to inspect the fruits of His teachings, He was put in danger of being sacrificed a second time. That legend entitled *"Venio iterum crucifigi"* was to provide me with the material for this catastrophe.

Such are the dreams I indulge in. For I am so impatient to be on my way that I sleep with my clothes on, and nothing pleases me more than to be waked before dawn, to sit down quickly in the carriage, and to ride into the morning in a state between sleeping and waking, letting my imagination create whatever images it wishes.

CITTÀ CASTELLANA, OCTOBER 28.

I shall not omit the last evening. It is not yet eight o'clock but everyone has already retired; so, to sum things up, I can recall the recent past and anticipate the near future. It was a very bright and splendid day today, the morning very chilly, the day clear and warm, the evening a little windy, but very beautiful.

We left Terni very early in the morning; we came up to Narni before daybreak, and so I did not see the bridge. Valleys and gorges, places near and far, exquisite regions—all of limestone, and not even a trace of any other rock.

Otricoli is situated on one of the gravel hills deposited by the ancient currents, and consists of lava brought from the other side of the river.

As soon as the bridge is crossed, one is in volcanic terrain, composed either of true lavas or of earlier rock that has been altered through roasting and smelting. One ascends a mountain that would seem to be of gray lava. This contains many white crystals formed like artillery shells. The highway leading from the summit to Città Castellana is of the same stone, worn nicely smooth by vehicles; the town is built on volcanic tufa, in which I thought I glimpsed ash, pumice, and pieces of lava. The view from the castle is very beautiful; Mount Soracte stands alone very picturesquely, probably a limestone mountain of the Apennine chain. The volcanic stretches are much lower than the Apennines, and have only been carved into mountains and cliffs by the waters rushing through them, resulting in the formation of some magnificently picturesque objects, overhanging crags, and other incidental topographical features.

So tomorrow evening I shall be in Rome. I can still hardly believe it, and if this wish is fulfilled, what shall I ever wish for afterwards? Nothing more that I can think of, except to land safely at home in my pheasant boat, and to find my friends healthy, happy, and kindly disposed to me.

Rome

ROME, NOVEMBER 1, 1786.

At last I can open my mouth and send greetings to my friends with a light heart. May they forgive my secrecy and my, as it were, underground journey here! I scarcely dared admit to myself where I was going, even during the trip I was still fearful, and not until I passed under the Porta del Populo was I certain that Rome was mine.

And now let me also say that I think of you again and again, indeed constantly, here in proximity to these sights that I never imagined I would have to see alone. Only when I saw that every one of you was chained body and soul in the north, and that all your interest in these regions had faded away, did I resolve to start out on this long, solitary journey in search of the focal point toward which I was drawn by an irresistible desire. Indeed, for the last few years this was becoming a kind of illness, which could only be cured by the sight and presence of Rome. I can confess it now: finally I could no longer bear to look at a Latin book or the picture of an Italian scene. My longing to see this land was more than ripe. Only now that it is satisfied have my friends and fatherland truly become dear to me again. Now I look forward to my return, indeed all the more so because I feel very certain that I shall not be bringing all these treasures back just for my own possession and private use, but so that they may serve both me and others as guidance and encouragement for an entire lifetime.

ROME, NOVEMBER 1, 1786.

Yes, I have finally arrived in this city, the capital of the world! I wish I had been in the fortunate position of seeing it fifteen years ago with good companions and some really intelligent man as guide. But since I was destined to visit it alone and see it through my own eyes, it is well that this joy was granted to me so late.

I have flown, so to speak, over the Tyrolean mountains, have seen Verona, Vicenza, Padua, and Venice well, Ferrara, Cento, Bologna superficially, and Florence scarcely at all. My desire to reach Rome was so great and increased so much with every passing moment that I could no longer stay anywhere, and stopped in Florence for only three hours. Now I am here and calm—calmed, it would seem, for the rest of my life. For it may well be said that a new life begins when something previously known inside and out, but still only in parts, is beheld in its entirety. Now I see all my childhood dreams come to life; I see now in reality the first engravings that I remember (my father had hung the prospects of Rome in a corridor); and everything long familiar to me in paintings and drawings, copperplates and woodcuts, in plaster and cork, now stands together before me. Wherever I go I find something in this new world I am acquainted with; it is all as I imagined, and yet new. And the same can be said of my observations, my thoughts. I have had no entirely new thought, have found nothing entirely unfamiliar, but the old thoughts have become so precise, so alive, so coherent that they can pass for new.

When Pygmalion's Elisa, whom he had formed completely in accordance with his wishes and given as much truth and life as an artist can, finally came up to him and said: "It is I!" how different the living woman was from the sculpted stone!

It is also morally very beneficial to me to live among these entirely sensual people, who have been the subject of so much talk and writing, whom every foreigner judges by the standards he brings along from home. I excuse everyone who criticizes and chides them; they are too unlike us, and a foreigner finds it tiresome and expensive to deal with them.

ROME, NOVEMBER 3.

Among the chief reasons I imagined I had for hurrying to Rome was the All Saints' festival, the first of November. For I thought, if so much honor is accorded to an individual saint, what will it be like for all of them together? But how I deceived myself! The Roman church had not elected to have any conspicuous universal festival, and every order could celebrate the memory of its special patron quietly; for the name day and the day of honor assigned to him are really when each one shines in his glory.

Yesterday, however, on All Souls' day, I had better success. The memory of these is celebrated by the pope in his private chapel in the Quirinal palace. Everyone is permitted to attend. I hurried to Monte Cavallo with Tischbein. The square before the palace has a very particular, individual quality, and is as irregular as it is grandiose and charming. Now I caught sight of the two colossi! Neither eye nor mind is adequate to grasp them. We hurried with the crowd through the splendidly spacious courtyard and up a more than spacious staircase. In the anteroom opposite the chapel, with a view of the series of rooms, one feels strange to be under the same roof with the vicar of Christ.

The service had begun, pope and cardinals were already in the church. The holy father, a very handsome, dignified figure of a man, cardinals of various ages and countenances.

I was seized by a strange desire to see the supreme head of the church open his golden lips and enrapture us by rapturously describing the ineffable bliss of the souls in heaven. But when I saw that he was just moving back and forth before the altar, turning now to this side, now to that, gesturing and murmuring like an ordinary priest, then the Protestant original sin raised its head, and I was by no means pleased to see the familiar, usual mass celebrated here. Christ even as a boy, after all, had orally interpreted the Scriptures, and as a youth surely did not teach and persuade in silence; for He spoke gladly, wisely, and well, as we know from the Gospels. What would He say, I wondered, if He should enter and find His earthly counterpart mumbling and swaying back and forth? The words, *"Venio iterum crucifigi!"* came into my mind, and I plucked my companion's sleeve, so that we might get out into the openness of the painted and vaulted halls.

Here we found a crowd of persons intently contemplating the exquisite paintings, for this festival of All Souls is simultaneously the festival of all the artists in Rome. Like the chapel, the whole palace with all its rooms is accessible to everyone, and on this day is open free of charge for many hours; one does not need to give any gratuity and is not pestered by the castellan.

The wall paintings occupied my attention, and I met and learned to love and appreciate some additional excellent artists hardly known to me even by name, like the cheerful Carlo Maratti, for example.

But the masterpieces of artists whose style I had already impressed upon my mind were especially welcome. I looked at Guercino's *St. Petronilla* with admiration; it was formerly in St. Peter's, where now a mosaic copy has been installed to replace the original. The saint's corpse is being lifted out of the grave, and the same person, revived, is being received in the celestial heights by a divine youth. Whatever may be said against this double action, it is an inestimable picture.

I was still more amazed by a picture of Titian's. It outshines all the others I have seen. Whether my faculties have already become sharper, or whether it really is the most superb one, I cannot tell. A huge chasuble, stiff with embroidery, indeed with figures of embossed gold, envelops a stately episcopal figure. His left hand on the massive crozier, he gazes upwards in rapture; in his right hand he holds a book out of which he seems just to have received a divine inspiration. Behind him is a lovely virgin, holding a palm branch and looking into the open book with sweet interest. However, a grave old man at his right, quite near to the book, seems to pay no attention to it; holding keys in his hand, he may well be confident about making his own interpretations. Opposite this group is a well-built nude youth, bound, and wounded by arrows, looking straight ahead with modest submissiveness. In the space between, holding a cross and a lily, are two monks who turn devoutly toward the heavenly beings, for the semicircular masonry that surrounds them all is open on top. There in the highest glory the mother turns to look down sympathetically. The lively, active Child on her lap with a cheerful gesture extends a wreath, indeed seems to be throwing it down. Angels, ready with more wreaths, hover on both sides. But over all these and above the threefold nimbus the heavenly Dove holds sway as both central point and keystone.

We tell ourselves: some underlying sacred old tradition must be the explanation for having brought these diverse, ill-assorted personages together in such an artistic and significant way. We do not inquire why and how, we accept it and admire the inestimable artistry.

A fresco by Guido in his chapel is less incomprehensible but still mysterious. The most naively lovely, pious virgin sits quietly and demurely sewing, while two angels wait at her side for any sign that they should serve her. The dear picture tells us that youthful innocence and diligence are guarded and honored by the heavenly angels. No legend is needed here, no interpretation.

But now a cheerful adventure to temper this artistic seriousness: I could plainly see that several German artists, coming up to Tischbein because they were acquainted with him, looked at me and then walked back and forth.

After having left me for a few moments, Tischbein returned and said: "I have a good joke for you! Everyone has heard the rumor about your being in Rome, and the artists have not failed to notice the only unknown foreigner present here today. But one of them has claimed for a long time that he associated with you, in fact was your friend, something we found difficult to believe. When we challenged this man to take a look and resolve the doubt about you, he flatly asserted it was not you, and that the stranger's face and figure did not resemble yours in the least. So your incognito is safe for the moment, at any rate, and afterwards we shall have something to laugh about."

I now circulated with less reserve among the group of artists, and inquired about the painters of various pictures whose artistic style was as yet unfamiliar to me. At last I found myself particularly attracted to a picture showing St. George, the dragon-slayer and liberator of virgins. No one could name the painter for me. Then a small, modest, previously silent man stepped forward and informed me that it was by Pordenone, the Venetian, one of his best pictures, which revealed all his merits. Now I understood my preference very well: the picture had appealed to me because I was already quite well acquainted with the Venetian school and better able to appreciate the virtues of its masters.

The informative artist is Heinrich Meyer, a Swiss, who has been studying here for several years along with a friend named Cölla. He makes excellent copies in sepia of ancient busts and is very well versed in the history of art.

ROME, NOVEMBER 7.

I have been here seven days now, and a general concept of this city is gradually forming in my mind. We walk diligently here and there, I acquaint myself with the street plans of ancient and modern Rome, view the ruins, the buildings, visit this and that villa, and deal quite unhurriedly with the main objects of interest. I just keep my eyes open, look, and go, and come again, for only *in* Rome can one prepare oneself for Rome.

Let us admit, nevertheless, that it is hard, sad work to sort out the old Rome from the new, but one has to do it and hope for inestimable satisfaction at the end. We encounter traces of a magnificence and a destruction that are both beyond our comprehension. What the barbarians left standing, the builders of new Rome have ravaged.

When one looks at something that has existed for more than two thousand years and has been altered so diversely and thoroughly by the changing times, yet is still the same soil, the same hill, indeed often the same column and wall, and in the people still some vestiges of their ancient character, one becomes a participant in the great decisions of fate. And such conditions make it difficult from the outset for the observer to decipher how Rome follows on Rome, and not only the new on the old, but also the various epochs within the old and new Rome on one another. First I am just trying by myself to get the feel of the half-buried places, as only then can one make full use of the fine preliminary studies. For since the fifteenth century and up to the present day excellent artists and scholars have spent their whole lives working on these objects.

And the immensity of all this affects us very quietly as we hurry back and forth in Rome to get to the most outstanding sights. In other places one has to search for what is significant, here we are overwhelmed and surfeited with it. Go where we will, there is always a scene of some kind to look at, palaces and ruins, gardens and wilderness, vistas and confined areas, little houses, stables, triumphal arches and columns, often so close together that they could be drawn on one sheet of paper. A pen is useless here, one needs to write with a thousand slate pencils! And then in the evening I am tired out and exhausted from looking and marveling.

NOVEMBER 7, 1786.

Do forgive me, my friends, if you find me to be laconic from now on. The traveler gathers what he can along the way, every day brings something new, and he hastily thinks about it and evaluates it. Here, however, I have entered a great school indeed, where one day says so much that I dare say nothing about the day. Yes, a person would be well advised to linger here for years while preserving a Pythagorean silence.

ON THE SAME DATE.

I feel quite well. The weather is *brutto*, as the Romans say. There is a wind from the south, the sirocco, which brings varying amounts of rain every day; but I do not find such atmospheric conditions unpleasant, for the air remains warm, unlike rainy days in our country, even in the summer.

NOVEMBER 7.

I am steadily becoming better acquainted with Tischbein's talents, as well as with his plans and artistic goals, and am learning to esteem them more and more. He showed me his drawings and sketches, which include, and also promise, very many good things. His sojourn with Bodmer turned his thoughts to the early times of the human race, when it found itself set on the earth and was faced with the task of becoming lord of the world.

As an ingenious introduction to the whole he has striven to present the great age of the world in a striking manner. Mountains covered with splendid forests, gorges dug out by streams of water, extinct volcanos emitting scarcely the faintest smoke. In the foreground, the mighty stump of an aged oak tree left in the ground, on whose half-exposed roots a stag tests the strength of his antlers, as well conceived as it is beautifully executed.

Then in a very remarkable drawing he has presented man both as a tamer of horses and also as superior in cunning, if not in strength, to all the animals of the earth, air, and water. The composition is extraordinarily beautiful, and it would make a very effective oil painting. We must surely get a copy of that for Weimar. Then he is planning a group of old, wise, and time-tested men, in which he will take the opportunity to depict real persons. With the greatest enthusiasm, however, he is now sketching a battle in which two detachments of cavalry are attacking each other with equal ferocity at a place where they are separated by an enormous rocky gorge, over which a horse can jump only with the greatest effort. Defensive action is unthinkable here. Bold attack, wild resolve, success—or a plunge into the abyss. This picture will give him the opportunity to display in a very significant way his knowledge of horses and their anatomy and movements.

He would now like to see these pictures, and a series of subsequent and interpolated ones, linked together by some poems. The latter could serve to explain what was being depicted, and in exchange he would lend them substance and charm by means of specific figures.

It is a fine idea, but of course the execution of such a work would require us to be together for several years.

NOVEMBER 7.

Just now, at last, I have seen Raphael's loggias and the great paintings, *The School of Athens*, etc., and it is like studying Homer in a partly obliterated, damaged manuscript. The first impression is not altogether pleasant, and one's enjoyment is complete only after everything has been gradually inspected and properly studied. Best preserved are the painted ceilings of the loggias, which depict stories from the Bible, as fresh as if painted yesterday, to be sure very little of it by Raphael's own hand, but most excellently done from his drawings and under his supervision.

NOVEMBER 7.

In earlier years I sometimes had the odd notion that nothing could please me more than to be taken to Italy by some knowledgeable man, say, an Englishman well versed in art and history; and now in the meantime all that has turned out much better than I could ever have imagined. Tischbein has lived such a long time here as my affectionate friend, has lived here wishing to show me Rome; our relationship is old through letters, new with respect to physical presence; where could I have found a more valuable guide? My time here may be limited, but I shall enjoy and learn everything possible.

And, for all that, I see in advance that when I leave I shall wish I were just arriving.

NOVEMBER 8.

My curious and perhaps capricious semi-incognito brings me unexpected advantages. Since everyone has pledged to pretend not to know who I am, and therefore no one may talk to me about myself, people have no alternative but to speak about themselves or the subjects that interest them. Consequently I get detailed information about what each of them is doing, or about whatever remarkable event occurs. Aulic Councilor Reiffenstein put up with this whim; but since for a particular reason he could not abide the name I had assumed, he quickly dubbed me Baron, and now I am called the Baron vis-à-vis Rondanini. That is designation enough, especially since the Italians only address people by their Christian name or their nickname. Suffice it to say, I have my way, and I avoid the constant inconvenience of having to give an account of myself and my works.

NOVEMBER 9.

Sometimes I stand still for perhaps a moment, and survey the highest peaks I already have behind me. With great pleasure I look back at Venice, that great entity sprung from the depths of the sea like Pallas from the head of Jupiter. Here in Rome, the Rotonda, both inside and outside, has filled me with joyful respect for its magnitude. In St. Peter's, I have come to understand how art, as well as nature, can render all comparisons of size futile. And, in like manner, the *Apollo Belvedere* has taken me out beyond reality. For just as even the most exact drawing does not give a real concept of those buildings, so it is here with the marble original as opposed to the plaster casts, although earlier I have known some very fine ones.

NOVEMBER 10, 1786.

I am living here now with a feeling of clarity and calm that I have not had for a long time. My practice of seeing and taking all things just as they are, my constancy in keeping a clear eye, and my complete rejection of all pretensions are proving very useful again, and make me quietly very happy. Every day a new remarkable object, every day some new great, extraordinary pictures, and a totality that is past imagining, however long one might think and dream.

Today I was at the pyramid of Cestius, and on the Palatine in the evening, up there on the ruins of the imperial palaces, which stand like rocky cliffs. I confess that I cannot describe any of this to you! Truly, there is nothing small here, although a few things may be objectionable and tasteless; but even they reflect the general grandeur.

Returning now to myself, as one so gladly does at every opportunity, I discover a feeling that infinitely delights me, and that I shall even venture to put into words. No one can take a serious look around this city, if he has eyes to see, without becoming solid, without forming a more vivid concept of solidity than he has ever had before.

His mind becomes certified as capable, it achieves seriousness without growing prosaic, and a steadiness combined with joy. I, at any rate, feel as if I had never appreciated the things of this world as properly as here. I look forward to the beneficial effect this will have on my whole life.

So let me gather up whatever comes, and it will put itself in order. I am not here to enjoy in my usual way; I want to apply my mind to the great objects, learn, and educate myself before I reach the age of forty.

NOVEMBER II.

Today I visited the nymph Egeria, then the racetrack of Caracalla, the ruined sepulchers along the Via Appia, and the tomb of Metella, which shows me for the first time what solid masonry is. These people built for eternity, their calculations took everything into account except the madness of the ravagers, before which everything had to bow. With all my heart, Charlotte, I wished that you were here with me. The remains of the great aqueduct merit the highest respect. What a fine, great plan it was to give the people water by means of such an enormous installation! In the evening we arrived at the Coliseum when it was already twilight. When one looks at it, everything else seems small. It is so huge that one cannot keep the image of it in mind; it is remembered as smaller, and when one goes back there it seems larger again.

FRASCATI, NOVEMBER 15.

The company has gone to bed, but I am still writing, dipping into the shell full of India ink that has been used for drawing. We have had a few beautiful, rain-free days here, warm and friendly sunshine, almost like summer. The district is very pleasant, the town is situated on a hill, or rather, on a mountainside, and every step offers the sketcher the most magnificent subjects. The view is unlimited, one sees Rome lying there, and the sea beyond it, the mountains of Tivoli to the right side, and so on. In this cheerful region the country houses are truly designed for pleasure, and just as the ancient Romans formerly had their villas here, so for over a hundred years rich and haughty Romans have also established theirs on the most beautiful spots. We have already been walking around here for two days, and there is always something new and charming.

And yet it is a question whether the evenings are not passed even more pleasurably than the days. As soon as our stately hostess has set the three-branched brass lamp on the big round table and said "Felicissima notte!" we all gather in a circle and display the drawings and sketches made during the day. We discuss whether the subject should have been approached from a more favorable angle, whether its character has been captured, and anything else of a similar, elementary, general nature that can be demanded even of a preliminary design. Aulic Councilor Reiffenstein has the discernment and authority to be able to regulate and guide these meetings. However, this laudable society was actually founded by Philipp Hackert, who could draw and finish the real views in a very tasteful fashion. Artists and amateurs, men and women, old and young were given no peace by him, he urged them individually to try out their own talents and abilities also, and he led with his good example. This manner of assembling and entertaining a group was faithfully continued by Aulic Councilor Reiffenstein after his friend's departure, and we think it is very commendable to rouse each person to active participation. The nature and peculiar qualities of the various society members emerge in a pleasant way. Tischbein, for example, as a historical painter, looks at the landscape quite differently from the landscape artist. He finds significant groups and other charming, meaningful subjects where someone else would perceive nothing. Thus he succeeds in catching many a naive human feature, be it in children, countryfolk, beggars, and other such natural creatures, or even in animals. He knows how to depict the latter very successfully with a few characteristic strokes, and in this way always supplies pleasant new material for our entertainment.

If conversation falters, then, as another legacy from Hackert, we read from Sulzer's *Theory*; and even though from a higher point of view this work is not completely satisfactory, still one notices with pleasure its good influence on persons who are at a middle stage of cultural development.

ROME, NOVEMBER 17.

We are back! During the night there was a terrible rainstorm with thunder and lightning, now it is still raining and yet the air is warm.

However, I can describe the happiness of this day in just a few words. I saw Dominichino's fresco paintings in Andrea della Valle, as well as Carracci's Farnese gallery. Actually too much for months, let alone for one day.

NOVEMBER 18.

The weather is fine again, a bright, warm, friendly day.

In the Farnesina I saw the story of Psyche, colored copies of which have brightened my rooms for such a long time. Then at St. Peter's in Montorio, Raphael's *Transfiguration*. All old acquaintances, like friends I have made at a distance through correspondence, and who now are seen face to face. Living together is, after all, something very different; every true affinity and lack of affinity immediately become evident.

Everywhere there are also superb things which are not talked about so much, which are not so often distributed throughout the world in prints and copies. I am taking along some of these, drawn by good young artists.

NOVEMBER 18.

The fact that I have been on the best terms with Tischbein for such a long time by letter, and that I so often told him of my desire to come to Italy (hopeless as that seemed), at once made our meeting pleasant and productive. He had always kept me in mind and planned for me. He is perfectly familiar even with the types of stones used by the ancients and the moderns for building; he has studied them thoroughly, and here his artist's eye and artist's delight in physical objects stand him in good stead. Not long ago he sent a collection of specimens to Weimar especially selected for me, which will welcome me on my return. In the meantime a significant supplement to it has been found. A priest, who is now in France, intended to complete a work on ancient minerals and through the good offices of the Propaganda acquired some quite large pieces of marble from the island of Paros. These were cut up into specimens here, and twelve different pieces were set aside for me, ranging from the finest to the coarsest grain, from the greatest purity to varying admixtures of mica, the former usable for sculpture, the latter for architecture. It is quite obvious that in judging the arts it is very helpful to have exact knowledge of the material used in them.

There is plenty of opportunity here to amass a collection of such things. On the ruins of Nero's palace we walked through freshly dug-up artichoke fields and could not refrain from filling our pockets with small slabs of granite, porphyry, and marble, which lie around here by the thousands and still act as an inexhaustible supply of witnesses to the ancient splendor of the walls they formerly covered.

ADDENDUM TO NOVEMBER 18.

Now, however, I must speak of a strangely problematical picture, which nevertheless bears comparison with those excellent paintings I have seen. Quite some years ago a Frenchman, well known as an art lover and collector, was living here. He came into possession, no one knows from what source, of an ancient painting on limestone. He had Mengs restore the picture and kept it in his collection as an esteemed work. Winckelmann speaks of it somewhere with enthusiasm. It depicts Ganymede as he extends a wine bowl to Jupiter and receives a kiss in return. The Frenchman died and bequeathed the picture to his landlady as an ancient work. Mengs died and said on his deathbed that it was *not* an ancient work, he had painted it himself. And now everyone is arguing with everyone else. One side claims that Mengs just tossed it off as a joke, the other side says that Mengs could never have painted such a thing, indeed that it is almost too beautiful for Raphael. I saw it yesterday and must say that I too know nothing more beautiful than the figure of Ganymede, head and back. The rest is much restored. Meanwhile the picture is discredited, and no one wants to relieve the poor woman of her treasure.

NOVEMBER 20, 1786.

Since experience amply teaches us that drawings and engravings are desired for all sorts of poems, and since indeed the painter himself will dedicate even his best executed pictures to a passage from some poem, Tischbein's idea of having poet and artist work together, thus achieving unity from the outset, merits the highest approbation. Of course the difficulty would be greatly diminished if the poems were short and could be easily produced and taken in at a glance.

Tischbein also has some very pleasant idyllic ideas for this, and it is really remarkable that the subjects he wants treated in this fashion are of a kind that neither the art of poetry nor of painting, by itself, could adequately depict. He has told me about them on our walks, hoping to interest me in becoming involved in this. He has already designed the frontispiece to our joint work; if I was not afraid of entering into something new, I might well let him prevail on me.

ROME, NOVEMBER 22, 1786, ON ST. CECILIA'S DAY.

I must jot down a few lines to preserve a vivid memory of this happy day and to give at least a factual description of what I enjoyed. It was the finest, calmest weather, a perfectly clear sky and warm sun. I went with Tischbein to St. Peter's square, where first we strolled up and down, then, when it got too warm for us, walked in the shadow of the great obelisk, which is just wide enough for two people, and ate the grapes we had bought nearby. Then we entered the Sistine chapel, which we also found to be bright and cheerful, the paintings well lighted. *The Last Judgment* and the manifold ceiling paintings by Michelangelo shared our admiration equally. I could do nothing but gaze and marvel. The manliness and inner certainty of this master, and his grandeur, are beyond all words. After we had looked at everything again and again, we left this holy place and walked towards St. Peter's church, which was most beautifully illuminated by the sunny skies, every part of it looking bright and clearly defined. We, who were only seeking enjoyment, took delight in its great size and splendor, and did not let ourselves be perplexed this time by overnice and oversophisticated questions of taste. We suppressed all keener judgment and simply took pleasure in something pleasurable.

Finally we climbed up to the roof of the church, where one finds what looks like a well-built town in miniature. Houses and storehouses, fountains, churches (to judge from their appearance), and a big temple, all of this high in the air, with beautiful paths in between. We climbed to the top of the dome and viewed the bright and cheerful Apennine region, Mount Soracte, the volcanic hills toward Tivoli, Frascati, Castel Gandolfo, the Campagna, and beyond that the sea. Directly at our feet lay the city of Rome in its whole length and breadth, with its palace-crowned hills, its domes, etc. Not a breeze was stirring, and inside the copper lantern it was as hot as in a greenhouse. After we had absorbed all of that, we climbed down and asked to have the doors opened that lead to the cornices of the dome, the drum, and the nave. One can walk around them to view these parts and the church itself from above. While we were standing on the cornice of the drum, the pope went past below us to say his afternoon prayers. So we missed nothing in St. Peter's. We climbed all the way down again, dined merrily and frugally at a nearby tavern, and continued on our way to the church of St. Cecilia.

I would need many words to describe the ornamentation of this church, which was completely filled with people. There was not a stone of the architecture to be seen. The columns were covered with red velvet and wound about with golden braid, their capitals covered with embroidered velvet approximately imitating their form, and all the cornices and pillars were thus draped and concealed. All the wall spaces between were hung with vividly painted pieces, so that the whole church seemed veneered with mosaic; and over two hundred wax candles burned around and beside the high altar, in such a manner that one whole wall was lined with lights and the church fully illuminated. The side aisles and side altars were similarly decorated and lighted up. Opposite the high altar, under the organ, were two platforms, also draped in velvet, on one of which stood the singers, on the other the instrumentalists, continuously making music. The church was packed full.

I heard a lovely type of musical presentation here. Just as there are concertos for violins or other instruments, so they perform vocal concertos in which one voice, for example the soprano, dominates and sings solo, while the chorus breaks in from time to time and accompanies it, always with the full orchestra, of course. It makes a good effect.—The day had to end, and I must close also. In the evening we still managed to reach the opera house, where the *Litiganti* was being given. But we had enjoyed so many good things already that we walked past without entering.

NOVEMBER 23.

But to save my beloved incognito from the fate of the ostrich, which believes itself hidden when it buries its head, I make certain compromises, while still asserting my old thesis. I was glad to meet the Prince of Liechtenstein, the brother of my very dear Countess Harrach, and dined with him several times. Then I soon became aware that my complaisance would take me a step farther, and so it happened. The prelude had been made by telling me about an abbé named Monti and his tragedy entitled *Aristodemus*, which was soon going to be performed. The author, it was said, wanted to read his work aloud to me and hear my opinion of it. I let the matter drop without actually refusing, but in the end I encountered the poet and one of his friends in the prince's lodgings, and the play was read aloud.

The hero, as is well known, is a king of Sparta, who commits suicide on account of various qualms of conscience; and I was given to understand in a courteous way that the author of *Werther* would probably not be offended to see that several passages from his excellent book were used in this play. And so even within the walls of Sparta I could not escape the angry shade of that unhappy youth.

The play has a very simple, quiet action, both sentiments and language are in keeping with the subject, powerful and yet gentle. The work bespeaks a very fine talent.

In my own way, not the Italian one, to be sure, I proceeded to emphasize all of the play's good and laudable points, which pleased the author well enough, but with southern impatience he demanded something more. I was especially asked to predict how good an effect the play might be expected to have on the audience. I pleaded ignorance of local taste and ways of presentation, but was frank enough to add that I did not quite see how the pampered Romans, who were used to seeing a complete three-act comedy with an interlude consisting of a two-act opera, or a grand opera with very odd ballets as an intermezzo, could find pleasure in the noble, quiet action of an uninterrupted tragedy. Besides, the subject of suicide seemed to me quite foreign to the Italian mind. The killing of other people was something I heard about almost every day; but so far it had not come to my attention that anyone had taken his own dear life, or even considered such a possibility.

Hereupon I gladly listened to whatever objections were raised against my disbelief, and I yielded very willingly to those plausible arguments. I also asserted that nothing would please me more than to see the play performed, and that I, with a chorus of friends, would applaud it most sincerely and loudly. This declaration was most amicably received, and this time I had every reason to be happy about my complaisance—and of course Prince Liechtenstein is the soul of kindness and has arranged opportunities for me to go along with him and see quite a number of artistic treasures for which one needs the owner's special permission and therefore the influence of a high personage.

On the other hand my good humor failed when the Pretender's daughter also expressed a desire to see the foreign marmot. I refused that request and very definitely submerged again.

And yet that is not quite the right behavior either, and I feel very strongly here what I have perceived earlier in life, namely that the well-intentioned person must be just as active and nimble in his dealings with other people as the selfish, small, or wicked person. It is one thing to see this; quite another to act accordingly.

NOVEMBER 24.

The only thing I can say about this nation is that it is made up of primitive people who, under all their splendid trappings of religion and the arts, are not a whit different from what they would be if they lived in caves or forests. What particularly strikes foreigners, and today again is the talk of the entire city—but only talk—is the homicides that take place so routinely. Just in the last three weeks four persons have been murdered in our district. Today a fine artist named Schwendimann, a Swiss, a maker of medallions, Hedlinger's last pupil, was attacked, exactly like Winckelmann. He struggled with the murderer, who inflicted some twenty stab wounds on him; and when the police arrived, the scoundrel stabbed himself to death. That is not the usual style here. The murderer manages to reach a church, and that ends the matter.

And so, in order also to introduce shaded areas into my paintings, I ought to report something about crimes and calamities, earthquakes and floods; indeed, the current eruption of fire from Vesuvius has most of the foreign visitors here on the move, and it is difficult to keep from being swept along with the tide. This natural phenomenon really has something of the rattlesnake about it and irresistibly attracts people. At this moment all of Rome's art treasures go for naught; the foreigners in a body are interrupting the course of their contemplations and rushing off to Naples. I, however, shall stand fast, hoping that the mountain will still keep something in reserve for me.

DECEMBER I.

Moritz, who has attracted our attention with his *Anton Reiser* and *Journey to England,* is here. He is a pure, excellent man, whom we enjoy very much.

DECEMBER I.

Many foreigners are seen here in Rome, not all of whom visit this capital of the world for the sake of higher art. On the contrary, they seek other kinds of entertainment, and the Romans are prepared with a variety of such. There are certain demiarts, which require dexterity and a delight in handicraft. These have been highly developed here, and foreign visitors are encouraged to take an interest in them also.

One of these is encaustic painting. With its preliminaries and preparations and then finally with the firing and whatever else is involved, this can keep anyone who has had any experience with watercolors busy doing mechanical things; and the artistic merit, which is often slight, can seem greater owing to the novelty of the undertaking. There are skilled artists who give instruction in this and, on the pretext of offering guidance, do most of the work themselves. Then, when the picture, gleaming because it has been intensified by encaustic, is seen at last in its golden frame, the fair pupil stands there in complete surprise at her unsuspected talent.

Another pleasant occupation is to make impressions from hollow-cut stones in a fine clay. This is also done with medallions, both sides being reproduced at once.

Lastly, then, there is the process of making the actual glass replicas, which requires more skill, attention, and diligence. Aulic Councillor Reiffenstein has all the implements and arrangements necessary for these things in his house or at least very near at hand.

DECEMBER 2.

By chance I have found Archenholz's *Italy* here. A scribble of that sort certainly shrivels up in the locality itself, just as if one had laid the little book on hot coals, so that it gradually became brown and black, and the leaves curled and went up in smoke. He has seen the things, to be sure; but he has far too little knowledge to support his pompous, contemptuous manner, and he blunders both in his praise and his censure.

ROME, DECEMBER 2, 1786.

It is something quite new to me to have beautiful, warm, calm weather, only occasionally interrupted by a few rainy days, at the end of November. We spend the nice days in the open, the bad ones in our rooms, and there is always something to enjoy, learn, and do.

On November 28th we returned to the Sistine chapel and had the gallery opened, where one has a closer view of the ceiling. It is admittedly very narrow, and one squirms along past the iron bars with some difficulty and seeming danger, for which reason those prone to vertigo do not go up. But it is all repaid by the sight of this supreme masterpiece. And at the moment I am so captivated by Michelangelo that even nature, compared to him, has lost its charm for me, since I cannot see it with his great eyes, after all. If there were only some means of truly fixing such pictures in my mind! At least I am taking along as many engravings and drawings of his works as I can lay my hands on.

From there we went to Raphael's loggias, and I hardly dare admit it, but we could not look at them. Our eyes were so dilated and so spoiled for anything else by those huge forms and the superb perfection of all the parts that we did not care to view the clever, playful arabesques; and the Biblical stories, as beautiful as they are, did not bear comparison with those others. It must be a great joy to contrast these works more frequently, and to compare them at greater leisure and without prejudice; for indeed interest always starts out as one-sided.

From there we strolled, in sunshine that was almost too warm, to the Villa Pamfili, where there are very beautiful gardens, and we stayed until evening. A large level meadow bordered with live oaks and tall pines was entirely planted with oxeye daisies, all with their little faces turned to the sun. Now my botanical speculations started in, and I continued to indulge in them the next day on a walk to Monte Mario, the Villa Melini, and the Villa Madama. It is most interesting to observe the workings of a vegetation that is never dormant and is uninterrupted by severe cold; there are no buds here, and only now do I begin to understand what a bud really is. The strawberry tree *(arbutus unedo)* is blooming again now while its last fruits are ripening, and the orange tree also displays blossoms along with ripe and half-ripe fruits (yet the latter trees, if they do not stand between buildings, are now covered). The cypress, the most stately tree of all when quite old and well grown, gives me a great deal to think about. Very soon I shall visit the botanical garden and hope to learn many things there. Nothing can compare with the new life a reflective individual receives from contemplating a new country. Although I am still the same person, I think I am changed to the very marrow of my bones.

I close for this time and shall fill up my next pages with calamities, murders, earthquakes, and misfortunes, so that some shadows also get into my paintings.

DECEMBER 3.

So far, the atmospheric conditions have changed mostly in six-day cycles. Two quite splendid days, one that is gloomy, two or three rainy days, and then fine ones again. I try to make the best use of each one in its own way.

But these magnificent objects still seem like new acquaintances to me. I have not lived with them, have not determined their characteristics. Some of them seize us by force, so that for a while we are indifferent, nay, unjust to the others. Thus, for example, the Pantheon, the *Apollo Belvedere*, some colossal heads, and recently the Sistine chapel have so captivated my mind and heart that I see almost nothing anymore but them. But how can we, as small as we are and used to what is small, place ourselves on the same level with something so noble, so huge, so refined? And even if I could put it into some sort of order, I am beset again on all sides by another huge mass of things that meet me at every step, and each demands the tribute of attention for itself. And how will I extricate myself? The only way is patiently to let it grow and have its effect, and diligently to take note of what others have done to assist us.

The new edition of Winckelmann's history of art, in Fea's translation, is a very useful work, which I obtained right away. Here on the spot, in the good company of people who can interpret and instruct, I find it very helpful.

The Roman antiquities are also beginning to delight me. History, inscriptions, coins, which I formerly neglected, all are thronging up to me. What I experienced in natural history is happening to me again, for the whole history of the world is linked with this city, and I count the day when I entered Rome as my second natal day, a true rebirth.

DECEMBER 5.

In the few weeks that I have been here I have already seen many foreign visitors come and go, and I am amazed at how lightly most of them take these noble sights. I thank God that from now on none of these birds of passage will be able to impress me at home in the north when he speaks to me about Rome; not one will stir my heart again. For I have seen it too, after all, and already know fairly well what to make of it.

DECEMBER 8.

Now and then we have the most beautiful days. The occasional rains that fall make the grass and potherbs green. Evergreen trees also stand here and there, so that the fallen leaves of the others are scarcely missed. Orange trees, full of fruit, stand in the gardens, growing right out of the ground and uncovered.

I was going to give a detailed account of a very pleasant excursion we made to the sea, and about the catch of fish, but then in the evening poor Moritz broke his arm while riding back, when his horse slipped on the smooth Roman pavement. That spoiled all our pleasure and badly disturbed the peace of our little circle.

ROME, DECEMBER 13.

How sincerely pleased I am that you all have taken my disappearance entirely as I wished. Now reconcile me also with every heart that might have been offended by it. I did not want to hurt anyone, and cannot say anything to vindicate myself now, either. God forbid that I should ever grieve a friend by telling my reasons for this decision.

Now I am gradually recuperating from my *salto mortale*, and devote myself more to study than to pleasure. Rome is a world, and one needs years just to find one's place in it. How fortunate those travelers are who merely look and leave!

This morning I happened to get hold of the letters Winckelmann wrote from Italy. With what emotion I began to read them! He came here thirty-one years ago, at the same season, a still poorer fool than I, and he took the same serious German approach to a thorough and certain knowledge of the art and antiquities. How worthily and well he worked his way through! And how much the memory of this man means to me in this place!

Except for objects in nature, which is true and consistent in all its parts, nothing really speaks as loudly as the trail left by a good, intelligent man, or as genuine art, which is just as logical as nature. One can truly feel that here in Rome, where willfulness has run so wild, where money and power have perpetuated so many absurdities.

I was especially pleased with a passage in Winckelmann's letter to Franke: "One has to be somewhat phlegmatic about looking for all the things in Rome, or else one is taken for a Frenchman. Rome, I believe, is all the world's university, and I too have been tested and purified."

These words correspond exactly with my way of investigating things here, and certainly, before coming to Rome, no one has a notion of how he will be schooled here. He must be, so to speak, reborn, and will look back on his former ideas as though they were children's shoes. The most ordinary person becomes something here, at least he gets an idea of the extraordinary, even if it cannot become a part of his nature.

This letter will be my greeting to you for the new year, and I wish all of you much happiness at its beginning; before its end we shall see each other again, and that will be no small pleasure. The past year has been the most important one in my life; it does not matter whether I die now or last a while longer, in either case I am content. Now, in closing, a word to the little ones.

You can read or relate the following to the children: It does not seem like winter, the gardens are planted with evergreen trees, the sunshine is bright and warm, snow can be seen only on the most distant mountains to the north. The lemon trees, which are planted next to the garden walls, are gradually being covered over with reed matting, but the orange trees remain without cover. Many hundreds of the most beautiful fruits hang on such a tree, which is not trimmed and planted in a tub, as in Germany, but stands glad and free in the earth in a row with its brothers. There is no prettier sight imaginable. One can eat as many of the oranges as one likes for a small gratuity. They are very good already, but will be still better in March.

Recently we were at the seaside and had a net put down for fish. It brought up the most oddly shaped creatures, fish, crabs, and curious monstrosities, also the fish that gives an electric shock to anyone who touches it.

And yet all that is more trouble and worry than enjoyment. The rebirth, which is remolding me from within, is still in progress. I certainly expected to learn something worthwhile here; but I did not imagine that I would have to go so far back in school and unlearn, indeed relearn, so much in a thoroughly different way. Now, however, I am truly convinced and have submitted totally; and the more of myself I must renounce, the happier it makes me. I am like an architect who wants to raise a tower but has laid a poor foundation for it; he perceives that just in time and gladly pulls down what he has already erected, tries to expand and ennoble his plan, to become surer of his base, and rejoices beforehand in the more reliable solidity of the future edifice. May God grant that when I return, the moral consequences of having lived in a wider world will also be manifest in me. Yes, along with my artistic sense my moral one is undergoing a great renovation.

Doctor Münter is here, having returned from his trip to Sicily. He is an energetic, vehement man; I do not know what his goals are. In May he will go to Germany and have much to tell all of you. He has traveled in Italy for two years. He is unhappy with the Italians because they have not sufficiently honored the significant letters of recommendation he brought with him, and which were supposed to give him access to many an archive, many a private library. And so he has not fully accomplished what he desired.

He has collected beautiful coins and owns a manuscript, so he told me, that explains numismatics on the basis of well-defined distinguishing marks, like those of Linné. Herder will probably make further inquiries about it, and perhaps a copy will be permitted. Such a thing is possible to make, good, once it is made, and, after all, we must delve into this subject more seriously sooner or later.

DECEMBER 25.

I am already beginning to see the best things for the second time, and find my first amazement giving way to a feeling of companionship with the object and to a purer sense of its worth. In order for the mind to absorb the highest concept of what these people have accomplished, it must first attain absolute freedom.

Marble is a remarkable material, which is why the *Apollo Belvedere* is so immensely pleasing. For the finest bloom of this living, youthfully free, eternally young being fades at once even in the best plaster cast.

Across from us in the Rondanini palace stands a Medusa mask which expresses the anxious stare of death with ineffable precision in the nobly beautiful form of its larger than life-size face. I already possess a good cast of it, but the spell of the marble has been lost. The elegant semitransparency of the yellowish, nearly flesh-colored stone has disappeared. The plaster always looks chalky and dead in comparison.

And yet what a joy it is to enter a cast maker's workshop, where one sees the magnificent limbs of the statues issue individually from the molds and so obtains entirely new views of the figures. Things that are scattered all over Rome are seen here side by side, which is an invaluable aid to comparison. I was not able to resist purchasing a colossal head of Jupiter. It stands opposite my bed, in a good light, so that I can immediately direct my devotions to it in the morning. For all its grandeur and dignity, however, it has provided us with a most amusing little story.

When our old landlady comes in to make the bed, her beloved cat usually slinks in after her. I was sitting in our big room and heard the woman going about her work in there. All at once, and with unaccustomed haste and vehemence, she opened the door and shouted that I should come in quickly to see a miracle. When I asked what it was, she replied that the cat was worshipping God the Father. She said that she had long since noticed that this animal had the intelligence of a Christian, but this was really a great miracle. I hurried to see this with my own eyes, and it truly was quite remarkable. The bust stands on a high base, and the body is cut off much below the chest, so that the head accordingly juts into the air. Now the cat had leapt on the table, had placed her paws on the god's chest, and, stretching her limbs to the utmost, had stuck her muzzle right into the sacred beard. This she was licking with the greatest daintiness, and was not disturbed in the least either by the landlady's exclamations or my interference. I allowed the good woman her amazement, but my own explanation for this curious feline worship was that the animal with its acute sense of smell probably detected the grease from the mold that had settled into the recesses of the beard and been preserved there.

DECEMBER 29, 1786.

There is still much to tell in praise of Tischbein, how he developed himself, on his own, into something entirely original and German; then I must declare my gratitude to him because during his whole second sojourn in Rome he very kindly saw to my interests by having a series of copies of the best masters made for me, some in black chalk, others in sepia and watercolors. These will attain their true value once I am back in Germany and far removed from the originals, for then they will bring the best things back to mind.

In the course of his artistic career, since he at first intended to be a portrait painter, Tischbein came into contact with significant men, especially in Zurich, and that helped him to strengthen his feeling and broaden his understanding.

I was made doubly welcome for bringing the second part of *Scattered Leaves* along with me here. Herder ought to have the reward of hearing in great detail about the impact this little book has even after repeated readings. Tischbein could not fathom how anyone could have written something like it without having been in Italy.

DECEMBER 29.

Living in this artistic milieu is like being in a room full of mirrors, where there is no way to avoid seeing oneself and others reflected many times. I noticed that Tischbein was often closely observing me, and now it comes out that he plans to paint my portrait. His design is finished, he has already stretched the canvas. I am to be presented life-size as a traveler wrapped in a white cloak, sitting in the open air on a fallen obelisk and surveying the ruins of the Campagna, which are located far in the background. That makes a beautiful picture, but one too large for our northern houses. No doubt I shall creep back into their shelter, but there will be no room for the portrait.

849

DECEMBER 29.

Moreover, I do not waver, in spite of all the attempts that are made to draw me out of my obscurity, and the poets who read their works aloud to me or have them read, and the fact that I would merely have to express the wish if I wanted to play a role in affairs; and it rather amuses me, because I have now observed enough to know how things operate in Rome. For the many little social circles at the feet of the mistress of the world now and then betray a certain provincialism.

Yes, it is the same here as everywhere, and I am bored with whatever might be done with me and through me, even before it happens. One must join a party, help to defend their enthusiasms and cabals, praise artists and dilettantes, belittle competitors, and agree with everything said by the rich and great. On account of this whole litany one would like to run from the world, and I am expected to join in and chant it here, to no purpose whatever?

No, I shall only go in deeply enough to be sure of that, and then stay at home satisfied in this regard also, and disabuse myself and others of all desire for the great wide world. I want to see the enduring Rome, not the one that passes away every ten years. Even if I had the time, I would want to make better use of it. From this vantage point, history especially is read differently from anywhere else in the world. In other places one reads from the outside in, here we imagine we are reading from the inside out, everything lies spread around us and also extends out from us. And that holds true not only of Roman history, but also of all world history. From here I can accompany the conquerors as far as the Weser and the Euphrates. Or, if I am content merely to gape, I can await the returning conquerors in the Sacred Street and partake of all this magnificence in comfort, having been supported meanwhile by gifts of grain and money.

JANUARY 2, 1787.

Say what one will in favor of written and oral communication, it is very rarely adequate, for it cannot transmit the actual character of any entity, not even in intellectual matters. But if one first has taken a careful look, then one is glad to read and hear, for that joins itself to the living impression; now one can think and judge.

You have all often scoffed and wanted to pull me back when, with special fondness, I observed stones, plants, and animals from certain definite points of view; now I am directing my attention to architects, sculptors, and painters, and shall learn to find my way here also.

JANUARY 6.

I have just been to see Moritz, whose arm is healed and was unbound today. He is getting along quite well. What I have seen and learned in the past forty days, while serving this patient as nurse, confessor, and confidant, as finance minister and privy secretary, may subsequently be of advantage to us. During this time, the most wretched suffering always went hand in hand with the noblest pleasures.

Yesterday, for my edification, I set up the cast of a colossal head of Juno in our salon; its original stands in the Villa Ludovisi. This was my first love in Rome, and now I own it. No words can give an idea of it. It is like a song of Homer's.

But surely I have earned the right to have such good company near me in the future, for now I can announce that *Iphigenia* is finished at last. That is to say, two fairly identical copies are lying before me on my table, one of which will soon be on its way to you. Be kind to it, for admittedly what you will find on this paper is not what I was supposed to write; but no doubt you will be able to divine what I was trying to do.

You have all complained several times about obscure passages in my letters which indicate that in the midst of these most splendid sights I was oppressed by a burden. My Grecian traveling companion had no little part in this, for she kept urging me to work, when I should have been looking at things.

I was reminded of that excellent friend of mine who had made arrangements for a long journey; indeed it could have been called a voyage of exploration. After he had studied and economized for several years in preparation for it, finally he took it into his head to elope with the daughter of an eminent family, thinking that he could kill two birds with one stone.

I resolved just as wantonly to take *Iphigenia* along to Carlsbad. I shall briefly record at which places I especially passed my time with her.

When I left the Brenner, I withdrew her from the largest packet and put her in my pocket. At Lake Garda, while the powerful noonday wind was driving the waves onto the shore, and where I was at least as alone as my heroine was on the shore of Tauris, I drafted the first lines of the new version, which I continued in Verona, Vicenza, Padua, but most diligently of all in Venice. Then, however, the work came to a standstill, and I was led to invent something new, namely, to write "Iphigenia on Delphi." Moreover I would have done so at once, if I had not been hindered by distractions and a sense of duty towards the older play.

But in Rome the work went on with due persistence. In the evening before going to sleep I would prepare for the next morning's task, which I would attack immediately upon awakening. My method was quite simple: I would calmly transcribe the play and read it aloud in a regular rhythm, line for line, period for period. What resulted from that is for you to judge. The process was more one of learning than of doing. Several additional comments are being sent along with the play.

JANUARY 6.

That I may speak once again on ecclesiastical subjects, I shall relate that we roamed around on Christmas Eve and visited the churches where services are held. One in particular is very well attended, where the organ and the music in general are structured in such a way that none of the typical sounds of pastoral music are missing, neither the shepherds' shawms, nor the twittering of the birds, nor the bleating of the sheep.

On Christmas day I saw the pope and the whole clergy in St. Peter's, where he celebrated high mass partly in front of his throne, partly while sitting on it. The spectacle is unique in its way, splendid and quite dignified, but I am such a long-time Protestant Diogenist that I find this magnificence more repellent than attractive. Like my pious predecessor I would wish to say to these ecclesiastical world conquerors: "Do not hide the sun of higher art and pure humanity from me."

Today being Epiphany, I have seen and heard the mass celebrated according to the Greek ritual. The ceremonies seemed to me more stately, more austere, more thought-provoking, and yet of a more popular nature than the Latin ones.

But even there I felt again that I am too old for anything except truth. Their ceremonies and operas, their processions and ballets, all of that runs off me like water off an oilcloth cloak. On the other hand, a natural phenomenon, like the sunset seen from the Villa Madama, or an artwork like my much-honored Juno, make a deep and lasting impression on me.

Now I am already shuddering to think of the theater season. Next week seven theaters will be opened. Anfossi himself is here and is giving *Alexander in India*; a *Cyrus* will be given too, and *The Conquest of Troy* as a ballet. The children would enjoy that.

JANUARY 10.

So, then, this letter will be followed by my child of sorrows, for *Iphigenia* deserves this sobriquet in more than one respect. While reading it aloud to our artists I marked several lines, some of which I have improved to the best of my ability; others I have let stand, hoping that perhaps Herder will want to insert a few strokes of his pen. I have grown quite dull working on it.

The real reason that I have preferred to work in prose for the last several years is that our prosody is in an extremely uncertain condition. Accordingly, my discerning, learned friends and colleagues have relied on their feeling and taste to decide many questions, a procedure lacking in all guiding principles.

I would never have ventured to transpose *Iphigenia* into iambs, if a guiding star had not appeared to me in the form of Moritz's *Prosody*. My association with the author, especially during the time he was confined to bed, enlightened me still more, and I entreat my friends to give it their favorable consideration.

It is a striking fact that we find only a few syllables in our language that are definitely short or long. The rest are treated according to our taste or caprice. Now Moritz has puzzled out a certain order of precedence among syllables, according to which a syllable with more significant meaning, juxtaposed to another of lesser meaning, becomes long, while making the latter short. The former, however, will become short again if it happens to be near a syllable of still greater intellectual weight. Here, then, at least we have a basis, and even if it is not definitive, surely for the time being it provides a guideline that one can cling to. I have frequently consulted this maxim and found it in agreement with my instincts.

Having spoken earlier about a reading, I must briefly describe how it went. These young men, being accustomed to my earlier vehement, vigorous works, had expected something in the *Berlichingen* style, and could not immediately become reconciled to the calm pace; but the pure and noble passages did not fail to make their effect. Although Tischbein could hardly accept this almost total abandonment of vehement emotion, he created an appropriate image or symbol for it. He compared it to a sacrifice whose smoke, kept from rising by a gentle atmospheric pressure, travels along the ground, thus giving the flame more liberty to shoot upwards. He drew this very prettily and significantly. I am enclosing the page from his sketchbook.

And so this work, which I intended to put behind me quickly, has for a full three months claimed and delayed me, occupied and tormented me. This is not the first time I have neglected what was most important, and let us not worry and argue about it any further.

I am enclosing a prettily carved stone, a little lion with a gadfly buzzing at its nose. The ancients loved this subject and used it repeatedly. I want you all in future to seal your letters with this little trinket, so that by means of it a kind of artistic echo will resound from you over to me.

JANUARY 13, 1787.

How much I could have written every day, and how greatly I am held back by exertions and distractions from putting an intelligent word down on paper! Moreover, there are some cool days, when it is better to be anywhere than in our rooms, which have neither stoves nor fireplaces, so that they are only comfortable for sleeping in. Nevertheless I must not pass over a few happenings of the last week.

In the Giustiniani palace stands a Minerva that I profoundly revere. Winckelmann scarcely mentions it, at least not in the right place, and I do not feel myself worthy enough to say anything about it. When we viewed the statue, taking a long time to do so, the custodian's wife told us that this used to be a sacred image, and the *Inglesi*, who followed this religion, still were accustomed to honor it by kissing one of its hands. And actually this hand was completely white, whereas the rest of the statue was brownish. She added that a lady of this religion had recently been there, had kneeled down, and worshipped the statue. She, as a Christian, had not been able to look at such a curious action without laughing, and had run from the room so as not to explode. Since I could not tear myself away from the statue either, she asked me if I by any chance had a sweetheart who resembled this marble image, to make it attract me so strongly. The good woman knew only worship and love, and had no notion about the pure admiration of a magnificent work, or of one's fraternal respect for a human spirit. We were pleased about the English girl, and left, hoping to return; and I certainly shall go there soon again. If my friends want to be informed in greater detail, they should read what Winckelmann says about the *high* style of the Greeks. Unfortunately, he does not adduce this Minerva. If I am not mistaken, however, she belongs to that high, austere style just as it is merging into the beautiful style, the opening bud, and a Minerva besides, whose character is so very suitable for this transition!

Now about a spectacle of a different kind! On Epiphany, the festival of the salvation proclaimed to the heathen, we were in the Propaganda. There, in the presence of three cardinals and a large audience, the first item was a discourse on the subject: where did Mary receive the three Magi, in the stable or elsewhere? Then, after the reading of several Latin poems on the same subject, some thirty seminarians stepped up, one after the other, and read short poems, each in his native language: Malabaric, Epirotic, Turkish, Moldavian, Elenic, Persian, Colchian, Hebrew, Arabic, Syrian, Coptic, Saracenic, Armenian, Hibernian, Madagascarian, Icelandic, Bohemian, Egyptian, Greek, Isaurian, Ethiopian, etc., and several whose names I could not catch. The little poems, mostly in the respective national meters, seemed to be recited in the respective national styles of declamation, for barbaric rhythms and sounds came forth. The Greek rang out like a star appearing at night. The audience laughed loudly at the foreign voices, and so this presentation too turned into a farce.

One more little story about how frivolously holy things are treated in holy Rome. The late Cardinal Albani was in a festive assembly of the kind I have just described. One of the schoolboys, turning to the cardinals, began to say "Gnaja! gnaja!" ("Worship! worship!") in such a strange dialect that it sounded approximately like "Canaglia! canaglia!" Albani turned to his fellow cardinals and said, "That one obviously knows us!"

JANUARY 13.

How much Winckelmann left undone, and how much he left us to wish for! The reason he built so swiftly with the materials he had acquired was to get them under roof. Were he still living—and he could still be vigorous and healthy—he would be the first one to give us a revision of his work. How much more he would have observed and corrected, how much he would have used of what others, following his principles, have done, observed, newly excavated, and discovered. And then too, Cardinal Albani, for whose sake he wrote, and perhaps withheld, so much, would be dead.

JANUARY 15, 1787.

And so at last *Aristodemus* has been performed, and indeed very successfully, to the greatest applause. Since Abbé Monti has a family connection with the *Nepote* and is highly esteemed by the upper classes, a good reception was to be expected from them—and indeed the loges did not spare their applause. The parterre was won over right from the start by the poet's beautiful diction and the actors' excellent recitation, and missed no opportunity to make its satisfaction evident. The German artists' bench distinguished itself particularly, since it is always a little boisterous; but this time that was quite appropriate.

The author had remained at home, full of worry about the success of his play, but gradually his apprehensiveness turned into the greatest joy, as favorable reports came in from act to act. Now the performance will surely be repeated, and everything is proceeding very well. Thus the most disparate things, provided that each has its own distinct merit, can please both the crowd and the connoisseurs.

But the performance was also very commendable, and the principal actor, who dominates the whole play, spoke and acted superbly; I thought I was seeing one of the ancient emperors on the stage. They had done very well at creating a splendid theatrical version of the costume that impresses us so much on the statues, and it was evident that the actor had studied the antiquities.

JANUARY 16.

Rome faces a great artistic loss. The King of Naples is having the *Farnese Hercules* brought to his capital. All the artists are grieving, but meanwhile this will be an opportunity for us to see something that was concealed from our predecessors.

The statue in question, that is to say, from the head to the knees, plus the feet below and the base on which they stand, were found on Farnese property; but the lower legs were missing. These were replaced by Guglielmo Porta, and it has stood on them up to the present day. In the meantime the genuine ancient legs had been found on Borghese property, whereupon, of course, they were displayed in the Villa Borghese.

Now Prince Borghese has brought himself to present these choice remains to the King of Naples. The Porta legs are being removed and replaced by the genuine ones, and although the former were previously found quite satisfactory, we now expect an entirely new perception and more harmonious enjoyment.

JANUARY 18.

Yesterday being the festival of St. Anthony the Abbot, we made a merry day for ourselves; it was the finest weather in the world, there had been frost during the night, but the day was warm and bright.

It can be observed that all religions which have expanded either their public worship or their theological speculations eventually have had to grant a certain participation in ecclesiastical favors even to animals. St. Anthony, the abbot or bishop, is the patron of four-footed creatures, his festival a saturnalian holiday for the usually burdened animals and for their keepers and drivers as well. All gentlefolk must stay at home on this day or go on foot. Invariably, dubious stories are told concerning aristocratic unbelievers who obliged their coachmen to drive on this day and were punished with very serious accidents.

The church is built on a square so vast that it could almost be called desolate, but on this day it is very busy and cheerful. Horses and mules, their manes and tails beautifully, indeed gorgeously interwoven with ribbons, are led before a little chapel somewhat removed from the church. There a priest armed with a large whisk sprinkles holy water unsparingly on the gaily decorated beasts, from the butts and tubs that stand before him. He does this roughly, sometimes even roguishly, to provoke them. Devout coachmen bring along larger or smaller candles, their masters send alms and presents, so that their useful, expensive animals may be kept safe from all accidents for the coming year. Donkeys and horned cattle, equally useful and valuable to their owners, likewise receive their allotted share of this blessing.

Afterwards we diverted ourselves with a long walk under such a happy sky, surrounded by the most interesting sights, to which we now paid slight attention, preferring to let joking and merriment reign completely.

JANUARY 19.

So the great king, whose fame carried throughout the world, whose deeds would even make him worthy of the Catholic Paradise, has also finally departed this life and is conversing with heroes of his ilk in the realm of the shades. How willing one is to observe a moment of silence when such a man has been laid to rest.

Today we gave ourselves a good time: we viewed a part of the Capitol that I had neglected until now, then we crossed the Tiber and drank Spanish wine on a ship that just landed. It is claimed that Romulus and Remus were found in this area, and so, as though this were a doubled and tripled Pentecost festival, we could become intoxicated simultaneously with the sacred spirit of art, the mildest weather, antiquarian memories, and Spanish wine.

JANUARY 20.

Something that in the beginning provided pure enjoyment, when it was approached superficially, later becomes a troublesome burden on the mind, when one sees that without thorough knowledge there can be no true enjoyment.

I am fairly well trained in anatomy and, not without effort, have acquired a certain degree of knowledge about the human body. Here, as a result of endlessly contemplating statues, my attention is constantly drawn to it, but in a loftier manner. In our medical-surgical anatomy it is just a question of recognizing a part, and even a wretched muscle will serve. In Rome, however, parts mean nothing unless they go together to make a noble, beautiful form.

In the great San Spirito hospital a very beautiful écorché figure has been set up for the use of artists. The beauty of it is amazing; it could really be looked upon as a flayed demigod, a Marsyas.

Thus, guided by the ancients, we are accustomed to study the skeleton complete with its musculature, not as just a mass of bones artificially strung together, and so it acquires life and movement.

If I now mention that in the evening we also study perspective, that is surely proof we are not idle. But, for all that, we always intend to do more than we actually accomplish.

JANUARY 22.

It can well be said of artistic sense and artistic life in Germany: one hears ringing, but no chiming. When I think now of the magnificent things in our vicinity and of the scant use I made of them, I could almost despair; and then I look forward again to my return home, when I can expect to understand those masterpieces I merely groped around on.

But even in Rome too little provision is made for someone who seriously wants to study his way into the total concept. He must piece it all together from innumerable, although extremely valuable ruins. Admittedly, few foreign visitors are truly serious about seeing and learning anything worthwhile. They follow their own whims, their own notions, and of course that fact is not lost on those who have to do with them. Every guide has particular ends in view, each one tries to recommend some tradesman or promote some artist, and why not? Does not the inexperienced visitor spurn the most superb things that are offered him?

It would have been a tremendous advantage to study, indeed a special museum would have come into being, if the government, which has to grant permission before any ancient relic can be exported, had firmly demanded that a plaster cast of the item always be furnished. But even if a pope had had such an idea, there would have been general opposition, for in a few years people would have been appalled at the value and importance of the things that had been exported, since permission to do so in individual cases can be obtained secretly and by various means.

JANUARY 22.

Even before the performance of *Aristodemus*, but especially then, the patriotism of our German artists awoke. They did not leave off praising my *Iphigenia*, individual passages were asked for again, and finally I found myself required to repeat the whole play for them. Then I discovered again that many a passage came more smoothly from my lips than it was written down on paper. Of course, poetry is not made for the eye.

Its good reputation now reached the ears of Reiffenstein and Angelica, and I was bidden to perform my work again for them. I requested some delay, but at once explained the plot and action of the play in some detail. This presentation won greater approval from the persons mentioned than I thought it would, and even Mr. Zucchi, from whom I expected it least, was very openly and sensitively interested in it. However, this can be explained very well by the fact that the play approaches the form that has long been familiar in Greek, Italian, and French drama, and which still remains the most appealing one to a person who has not yet become accustomed to the English audacities.

ROME, JANUARY 25, 1787.

Now it is constantly getting harder for me to give an account of my Roman sojourn; for just as the sea is found to be ever deeper, the farther one goes into it, so it is with me in my inspection of this city.

The present cannot be understood without the past, and comparison of the two requires more time and leisure. The very location of this capital of the world leads us back to the building of it. We soon see that it was not a large, competently led, nomadic tribe which settled here and wisely established the hub of a realm; no powerful prince chose this as the appropriate place for a colony to dwell. No, shepherds and riffraff were the first to take up their abode here, and a pair of robust youths laid the foundation for the palaces of the rulers of the world on a hill at whose foot they had once been deposited, between swamps and reeds, by the caprice of an obedient servant. Accordingly, the seven hills of Rome do not rise toward the land lying behind them, but toward the Tiber and the primeval bed of the Tiber, which became the Campus Martius. If further excursions are possible for me in the spring, I shall describe the unfortunate location more extensively. I already feel a cordial sympathy with the sorrows of the Alban women, wailing and lamenting as they saw their town destroyed. They had to forsake a place selected by a clever leader, in order to live among the fogs of the Tiber and dwell on the miserable hill Coelius, from which they could look back at their lost paradise. As yet, I know little of the region, but I am convinced that no other town of the ancient world is situated as poorly as Rome. And when the Romans had at last used up all their land, they had to move outside with their country villas, back to the sites of the ruined towns, in order to live and enjoy life.

JANUARY 25.

The many people who live here quietly, each of them occupied in his own fashion, offer a subject for very peaceful meditations. At the house of a cleric who, though without great native talent, has devoted his whole life to art, we saw very interesting copies he has done in miniature of some excellent paintings. His choicest one was of Leonardo da Vinci's *Last Supper* in Milan. The moment seized is when Christ, sitting happily and amicably at table with the disciples, declares and says: "Verily I say unto you, that one of you shall betray me."

There is hope that a print will be made either from this copy or from others that are being worked on. It will be the greatest gift to the general public, if a faithful copy is published.

A few days ago I visited Pater Jacquier, a Franciscan, at Trinità de' Monti. He is a Frenchman by birth, known for his mathematical writings, advanced in years, very pleasant and intelligent. He knew the best men of his time, and even spent a few months with Voltaire, who had great affection for him.

And so I have met still other good, solid men, who are here in vast numbers, but are kept apart by priestly mistrust. The book trade provides no connections, and new literary productions rarely bring any benefit.

And so it befits the solitary person to seek out the hermits. For after the performance of *Aristodemus*, which we had really been instrumental in furthering, I was led into temptation again. But it was only too obvious that the interest was not in me personally, but in strengthening a party, in using me as an instrument; and if I had been willing to step forward and declare myself, I could have played a brief phantom role. Now, however, since they see that I am not to be swayed, they let me alone, and I continue to walk my sure path.

Yes, my existence has taken on ballast, which gives it the proper weight; now I am no longer afraid of the ghosts that so often played with me. Be of good cheer, you will hold me above water and pull me back to you.

JANUARY 28, 1787.

Since they have become clear to me, I shall not fail to indicate two meditative thoughts, which permeate everything and to which I am bidden to return at every moment.

First, then, this city possesses enormous riches, but they are all in ruins, and in the case of every object I feel called upon to determine the era which produced it. Winckelmann urgently spurs us on to separate the epochs, to recognize the various national styles, which in the course of time were gradually developed and eventually spoiled. Every true art lover became convinced of this. We all acknowledge the justice and importance of the demand.

But how to obtain this insight! Little preliminary work has been done. While the concept has been correctly and magnificently put forward, the individual details are obscure and uncertain. It requires years of thoroughly training the eye, and one must learn before one can ask. It is useless to waver and hesitate, for attention is now actively being given to this important point, and everyone who takes the matter seriously can see that no judgment is possible in this field unless it can be developed historically.

The second thought is concerned exclusively with the art of the Greeks and aims at discovering how those incomparable artists went about developing their circle of godly figures—which is perfectly complete and lacking neither any main features nor the transitions and intermediate stages—out of the human form. My supposition is that they proceeded according to the same laws by which nature proceeds, and which I am tracking down. But something else is involved that I cannot put into words.

FEBRUARY 2, 1787.

Unless a person has walked through Rome in the light of the full moon he cannot imagine the beauty of it. All individual details are swallowed up in the great masses of light and shadow, and only the largest, most general images present themselves to the eye. For three days we have been thoroughly enjoying the brightest and most splendid nights. The Coliseum offers a particularly beautiful sight. It is closed at night, a hermit lives there in his tiny little church, and beggars nest in the dilapidated archways. They had laid a fire on the level floor, and a quiet breeze drove the smoke first toward the arena, so that the lower part of the ruins was covered and the huge walls above jutted out over it darkly. We stood at the grating and watched the phenomenon, while the moon stood high and clear in the sky. Gradually the smoke drifted through the walls, holes, and openings, looking like fog in the moonlight. It was an exquisite sight. This is how one must see the Pantheon, the Capitol, the forecourts of St. Peter's, and other great streets and squares illuminated. And so the sun and the moon, just like the human spirit, are quite differently employed here than in other places, here, where their gaze meets huge and yet refined masses.

FEBRUARY 13.

I must mention a stroke of luck, albeit a minor one. But all good fortune, large or small, is of a kind, and always welcome. The foundation for a new obelisk is being dug at Trinità de' Monti, up there where the ground is composed of fill from the ruins of the gardens of Lucullus, which later became the property of the emperors. My wigmaker went by there this morning and in the rubble found a flat pottery shard with some figures, washed it, and showed it to us. I immediately appropriated it. Not quite as big as my hand, it seems to have come from the rim of a large bowl. Two griffons are standing at an altar table; they are most beautifully done and delight me very much. If they were on a carved stone, how gladly I would seal letters with it!

Many other items are being added to my collection, none of them pointless or empty, for that would be impossible here; they are all instructive and significant. But dearest to me is what I am taking along in my mind, an amount that is growing and can be constantly increased.

Before my departure for Naples I could not avoid giving one last additional reading of my *Iphigenia*. Madame Angelica and Aulic Councilor Reiffenstein were the auditors, and even Mr. Zucchi had insisted on attending, because his wife wanted to. Meanwhile he kept working on a large architectural drawing, something he knows how to do exceedingly well in a decorative style. He was in Dalmatia with Clérisseau, had actually entered into partnership with him, and drew the illustrations for the latter's edition of the buildings and ruins. While doing this, he learned so much about perspective and effects that in his old age he can still worthily amuse himself by using his skills on paper.

The play made an incredibly deep impression on Angelica's tender soul. She promised to create a drawing from it, which I should keep as a souvenir. And now, just as I am preparing to leave Rome, I am forming affectionate bonds with these kind people. It is at once a pleasant and a painful feeling to be certain that they do not like to see me go.

FEBRUARY 16, 1787.

The safe arrival of *Iphigenia* was announced to me in a surprising and pleasant manner. On my way to the opera I was brought a letter written in a well-known hand, doubly welcome this time because it was sealed with the little lion, as a token, for the time being, of the safe arrival of the packet. I pushed my way into the opera house and in the midst of this crowd of strangers tried to find a seat under the big chandelier. Here I felt myself brought so close to my friends that I would have liked to jump up and embrace them. My cordial thanks for reporting the bare arrival, and may you accompany your next letter with a kind word of approval!

Here follows the list of how I want the copies that I expect to receive from Göschen divided among my friends. For while the public's opinion of these things is a matter of complete indifference to me, I nevertheless hope that they may give my friends some pleasure.

But a person tends to undertake too much. When I think of my last four volumes as a whole, I almost grow dizzy; I must attack them individually, and then it will be all right.

Would I not have done better to stay with my first resolve, which was to send these things out into the world in fragmentary form, after which, with fresh courage and energy, I could have undertaken new subjects, in which I had a fresher interest? Would I not do better to write "Iphigenia on Delphi" than to struggle with the melancholy fancies of *Tasso*? And yet I have also put too much of my own self into this for me to leave it unfinished.

I have sat down by the fireplace in the vestibule, where the warmth of what is, for once, a well-fueled fire gives me fresh courage to begin a new page. For it is really very wonderful indeed that one can reach so far into the distance with one's newest thoughts, indeed can remove one's immediate surroundings, by means of words, to that distant point.

The weather is quite splendid, the days are growing markedly longer, laurels and box trees are in bloom, also the almond trees. This morning I was surprised by a remarkable sight: I saw from a distance high, pole-like trees densely covered in the most beautiful violet. Closer investigation revealed that it was the tree known in our hothouses by the name Jew tree, but called *cercis siliquastrum* by botanists. Its violet papilionacious flowers are produced right on the trunk. The poles I saw before me had been stripped of twigs last winter, and now the well-formed, colorful flowers were bursting forth from the bark by the thousands. Oxeye daisies are emerging from the ground like hordes of ants; crocuses and adonises appear more rarely, but look all the daintier and more decorative.

What joys and revelations are no doubt in store for me in the more southerly land, and what results these will bring me! It is the same with natural things as with art: so much is written about them, and yet anyone who sees them can arrive at new conclusions in regard to them.

When I think of Naples, indeed also of Sicily, what I hear and what I see in pictures impresses me with the fact that these paradises of the world are also where a volcanic hell violently opens up, and for thousands of years has startled and dismayed those who live there so enjoyably.

But I am glad to banish all thought of those very significant scenes from my mind, so that I may make proper use of this ancient capital of the world once more before my departure.

For two weeks I have been on my feet from morning to night; what I have not yet seen, I go to see. The very best things are being viewed for the second and third time, and now some sort of order is emerging. For as the principal objects assume their correct positions, sufficient room is left between them for many lesser things. My affections are being purified and determined, and only now can my spirit rise to meet what is greater and most genuine with calm interest.

Yet I envy the artist, who, by imitating and reproducing, comes closer in every way to those great intentions, and understands them better, than the mere viewer and thinker. But in the last analysis everyone must do what he is able to, and so I unfurl the sails of my spirit and try to navigate these coasts.

The fireplace is really thoroughly warmed now, heaped up with the finest coals, a rare event at our place because no one is likely to have the time or desire to devote a few hours of attention to the fire; and so I shall take advantage of this lovely atmosphere to rescue some already half-obliterated remarks from my slate.

On February second we went to the Sistine chapel for a service held to consecrate the candles. I immediately felt uncomfortable and soon left again with my friends. For I thought: those are the very candles that have darkened these magnificent paintings for three hundred years, and that is the same incense which, with holy impudence, has not only clouded this unique artistic sun, but from year to year has made it dimmer, and will finally plunge it into darkness.

After that we sought the open air and at the end of a long walk reached San Onofrio, in a corner of which Tasso lies buried. His bust stands in the monastery library. The face is of wax, and I am willing to believe that it is an actual death mask. Although not quite sharply defined, and decayed in places, on the whole it still suggests, more than any other of his portraits, a talented, sensitive, subtle, self-contained man.

So much for this time. Now I shall consult Part Two of honest Volkmann, which contains Rome, to extract from it what I have not yet seen. Before I travel to Naples, the harvest must at least be reaped; surely some good days will also come for binding it into sheaves.

FEBRUARY 17.

The weather is incredibly and inexpressibly fine, with a clear, bright sky throughout February except for four rainy days, almost too warm toward noon. Now we seek the open air, and whereas previously we only cared to deal with gods and heroes, now the countryside is suddenly coming into its own again, and we frequent the environs, which are enlivened by the most splendid daylight. Sometimes I recall how artists in the north try to make something out of thatched roofs and ruined castles, how they dawdle at brook and bush and crumbled rock to capture a picturesque effect; and then I feel quite strange, especially since those things still cling to me from long habit. But two weeks ago I plucked up my courage and, equipped with a small sketch pad, began walking out among the villas, uphill and down, where without much reflection I have been sketching small, striking, truly southern and Roman objects and now am trying, with the help of some good luck, to give them lights and shadows. It is quite peculiar that we can clearly see and know what is good and better, but when we try to make use of this, it withers in our hands, as it were, and we do not reach for what is correct but for what we are accustomed to hold. Only through regular practice would it be possible to make progress, but where am I to find the time and concentration for that? Meanwhile, nevertheless, I feel myself considerably improved by my two weeks of passionate endeavor.

The artists like to instruct me, for I grasp things quickly. But what I have grasped is not immediately put into effect. To grasp something quickly is, moreover, what the mind is fitted for; but to do something worthwhile, for *that* one needs a lifetime of practice.

And yet the amateur, feeble though his efforts at emulation may be, should not let himself be deterred. The few lines I draw on my paper are often overhasty and seldom correct, but they make it easier for me to form each of my ideas of material things, for one can more readily proceed to a general concept if one observes individual objects more closely and precisely.

Only one must not compare oneself with the artists, but work along in one's own way; for nature has provided for its children, and the least of them has as much right to exist as the most excellent one: "A little man is also a man!" And there we shall let the matter rest.

I have seen the sea twice, first the Adriatic, then the Mediterranean, but only, as it were, to pay a call. In Naples we shall become better acquainted. Everything is suddenly falling into place for me: why not sooner, why not more cheaply! How many thousand things, many of them entirely new and unfamiliar, I could tell you!

FEBRUARY 17, 1787.

IN THE EVENING, THE CARNIVAL FOLLY HAVING DIED AWAY.

I do not like to go away and leave Moritz alone. He is on the right path, but when he walks alone, he immediately looks for popular hiding places. I have encouraged him to write to Herder, the letter is enclosed here, and I hope for an answer containing something appropriate and helpful. He is an unusually good man, and he would have advanced much further if from time to time he had found persons capable of explaining his situation to him, and kind enough to do it. If Herder would permit him to write occasionally, that would be the most beneficial connection Moritz could make at present. He is engaged in a laudable antiquarian undertaking, which certainly merits support. Friend Herder could scarcely find his efforts better expended anywhere, or plant his teachings in a more fertile soil.

The big portrait of me that Tischbein has undertaken is already sprouting from the canvas. The artist has had an accomplished sculptor make him a little clay model, which has been very elegantly draped with a cloak. He paints diligently from that, for of course he was to have progressed to a certain point before our departure for Naples, and it takes time just to cover such a large canvas with paint.

FEBRUARY 19.

The weather continues to be so fine that it is beyond words. This was a day I spent painfully among the fools. At nightfall I recuperated at the Villa Medici; the new moon is just past, and next to the slender crescent moon I could see the whole dark disk dimly with the naked eye, and quite distinctly through the telescope. Hovering over the ground all day is a vapor which is familiar to us only from the drawings and paintings of Claude Lorrain; but in nature the phenomenon is rarely seen as beautifully as here. Now flowers that I do not yet know are appearing on the ground, and new blossoms on the trees; the almonds are blooming and are an airy new presence among the dark-green oaks; the sky is like a piece of light-blue taffeta shone on by the sun. To think how it will be in Naples! We find that almost everything is already green. My odd botanical notions are reinforced by all this, and I am on the way to discovering beautiful new conditions under which nature—that invisible immensity—develops the greatest variations from a simple entity.

Vesuvius is spewing out rocks and ash, and at night they see its summit glowing. May active nature give us a lava flow! Now I can scarcely wait for those great sights to be mine also.

FEBRUARY 20, ASH WEDNESDAY.

Now the foolishness is at an end. The innumerable lights yesterday evening were another sad spectacle. To have seen the carnival in Rome completely rids one of the wish ever to see it again. It offers nothing whatever to write about, but an oral presentation of it might possibly be entertaining. While it was going on I had the unpleasant feeling that the people lacked inner joy and did not have enough money to indulge the slight inclination they may still feel. Persons of rank are economical and hold back, the middle class is without means, and the common folk are impotent. There was incredible noise in the last days, but little real gaiety. The sky, so infinitely clear and beautiful, looked down so nobly and innocently at these antics.

However, since I cannot keep from working at art here, to please the children I have drawn some carnival masks and characteristic Roman costumes, and then colored them. These may compensate our dear little ones for a chapter left out of the *Orbis pictus*.

I shall use the moments while I pause from packing to catch up with a few things. Tomorrow we are going to Naples. I look forward to that new place, which is said to be inexpressibly beautiful, and in that paradisiacal natural environment I hope to regain my freedom and desire to return to the study of art in solemn Rome.

Packing is easy for me, I am doing it with a lighter heart than half a year ago, when I was separating myself from everything that was so dear and valuable to me. Yes, it is already a half year, and not a moment of the four months I have spent in Rome has been wasted, which is indeed saying a great deal, but not too much.

I know that my *Iphigenia* has arrived; may I hear at the foot of Vesuvius that it got a good reception!

It is of the greatest importance for me to make this journey with Tischbein, who has as magnificent an insight into nature as into art; but, being true Germans, we cannot exist without plans and prospects for work. We are buying the finest drawing paper, although the great number, beauty, and brilliance of the sights will most probably set limits to our good intentions.

I have controlled myself in one respect, and of all my poetic works am taking along only *Tasso*, the one I have best hopes for. If I knew what all of you are saying about *Iphigenia*, it would guide me, for *Tasso* is a similar work, its subject matter almost even narrower than that of *Iphigenia*, and needing even more elaboration of detail. But I do not yet know what it can become, and I must discard everything I have already written, for it has been neglected too long. Neither the characters, nor the plot, nor the tone have the slightest relationship to my present views.

While clearing up I have come upon some of your dear letters, and in reading through them I see that you reproach me with having contradicted myself in mine. Of course I cannot see that, for what I write I always immediately send off. But I believe that it is very likely, since I am tossed about by tremendous forces, and so it is only natural that I do not always know where I stand.

They tell of a boatman who, being overtaken at night by a storm on the sea, tried to steer homewards. His small son, clinging to him in the darkness, asked: "Father, what is that odd little light over there, that I see first above us, then below us?" The father promised that he would explain it the following day, and it turned out that this had been the flame of the lighthouse, which seemed now below, now above to the eye of someone rocked up and down by the wild waves.

I too am steering to port on a tempestuous sea, and I just keep a close watch on the glow of the lighthouse; even if it seems to change its position, nevertheless I shall at last arrive safely on shore.

Somehow, leaving for a trip always brings every past departure spontaneously to mind, as well as the future final one. And at the same time, more forcefully now than usual, the thought is welling up in me that we encumber our lives with far too many things. For here we are, Tischbein and I, turning our backs not only on these many splendors, but even on our well-stocked private museum. Three Junos are standing there now in a row, for comparison with each other, and we are leaving them as if none was there at all.

On Literature and Art

ON GERMAN ARCHITECTURE
(1772)

On a pilgrimage to your grave, noble Erwin, I searched for the tombstone with the inscription, *Anno Domini 1318. XVI Kal. Febr. Obiit Magister Ervinus, Gubernator Fabricae Ecclesiae Argentinensis.* But I could not find it, nor were any of your countrymen able to help me. And I was saddened to the depth of my soul, for I had come to pour out my veneration for you at that hallowed place. My heart, younger then, warmer, more foolish and better than now, solemnly vowed that once in due possession of my inheritance, I would build you a memorial of marble or of sandstone, whichever I could afford.

Yet you need no memorial! You erected your own, a magnificent one. And though the throngs crawling about it like ants know nothing of your name, you are like the Great Architect who piled up mountains into the clouds.

Few have been blessed with a mind capable of conceiving a Babel-like vision—whole, great, inherently beautiful to the last detail, like God's trees—and even fewer with the good fortune to encounter a thousand willing hands, to excavate the rocky foundations, to conjure up towering structures and, with their dying breath, tell their sons: I will remain with you in the works of my spirit. Complete what is begun, until it reaches into the clouds.

You need no memorial! Certainly not mine! When the rabble utter sacred names, it is superstition or blasphemy. The feeble esthete will feel forever giddy in the presence of your colossus, robust sensibilities will understand you without an interpreter.

Now then, worthy Erwin, before I venture back to sea in my fragile bark, more likely to encounter death than prosperity, behold this grove where I engraved the names of beloved friends, there I will cut yours into a beech tree slender and soaring like your tower, and in its branches I will hang by its four corners this handkerchief full of gifts. It resembles the sheet that was let down from the clouds to the holy apostle, full of clean and unclean beasts. So mine will be filled with flowers, blossoms, leaves, but also dry grass and moss and toadstools sprung up over night—everything I gathered while walking through an uninteresting region, collecting specimens simply to pass the time. I now commit them to decay as an offering in your honor.

"What immature taste," says the Italian and walks on. "Childish nonsense," parrots the Frenchman and triumphantly flicks open his snuffbox à la Grècque. What right have you to show contempt?

Did not the genius of the ancients rise from the grave and fetter your own, Italian? You crept among the mighty remains like a beggar, hoping to learn of proportion, you patched together villas from sacred rubble, and you consider yourself the custodian of the secrets of art because you are able to give an account of the measurements of gigantic buildings, down to the last inch! Had you felt more and measured less, had you been inspired and not simply overawed by these massive structures, you would not have merely imitated them because they were created by the ancients and are beautiful. You would have created your own plans with their own inherent truth, and natural living beauty would have emanated from them.

Instead you applied a thin veneer of truth and beauty to your buildings. You were struck by the magnificent effect of columns, so you wanted to put them to use and embedded them in walls. You wanted colonnades too, so you encircled St. Peter's Square with marble walks which lead nowhere. And mother nature, who despises the inappropriate and hates the superfluous, drove your rabble to prostitute all that splendor by transforming it into a public sewer. Now everyone averts his eyes and holds his nose when approaching this wonder of the world.

And so things go: the artist's fancy serves the rich man's caprice, the travel writer gapes, our esthetes, called philosophers, always fashion principles and histories of art from the stuff of fairytales, while their evil genius murders true human beings at the threshold of revelation.

Principles are even more damaging to the genius than examples. Individual artists may have worked on individual parts before him, but he is the first from whose soul the parts emerge grown together into an everlasting whole. Yet school and principle fetter all powers of perception and activity. Of what use to us is the knowledge, you philosophizing expert of the new French school, that the first man, inventive in his need for shelter, rammed four stakes into the ground, joined them with four poles and made a roof of branches and moss? From this you derive the appropriateness of our own buildings, as if you wanted to rule your new Babylon with a simplistically patriarchal attitude!

And it is wrong to boot. This hut of yours was not the first in the world. Two poles crossed at the top in front, two in the back and a fifth as a ridgepole, as we can see every day from huts in fields and vineyards, that is clearly a far earlier invention, from which you could not even derive a principle for your pigsties.

Thus none of your conclusions are able to ascend to the realm of truth, but merely float in the atmosphere of your own system. You want to teach us what we should use, because what we do use cannot be justified according to your principles.

The column is very dear to your heart, and in another part of the world you would be a prophet. You say: "The column is the first, essential component of a building, and the most beautiful. What exquisite elegance of form! What pure and varied grandeur when they stand in a row! But beware of using them inappropriately; their nature is to stand free. Woe to those wretches who welded their slender shape onto bulky walls!"

And yet it seems to me, dear Abbé, that you should have been concerned when you encountered the unseemliness of walled-in columns so often, and saw that moderns even walled up the intercolumniations of antique temples. If your ears were not deaf to the truth, these stones would have preached the truth to you.

The column is by no means a natural component of our dwellings, on the contrary, it contradicts the character of all our buildings. Our houses did not develop from four columns in four corners, but from four walls on four sides. The walls are in place of columns and exclude columns, and where columns are tacked on, they are a superfluous encumbrance. This is also true of our palaces and churches, with a few exceptions, on which I need not elaborate.

Your buildings present mere surfaces which, the further they extend and the bolder they soar to the sky, inevitably oppress the soul with ever more unbearable monotony. Fortunately, Genius came to our aid and inspired Erwin von Steinbach, saying: Diversify the immense wall, raise it toward heaven so that it soars like a towering, widespreading tree of God. With its thousands of branches and millions of twigs and as many leaves as sand by the sea, it shall proclaim to the land the glory of the Lord, its master.

When I first came to visit the cathedral, my head was filled with general notions of good taste. Based on what I had heard others say, I praised the harmony of mass, the purity of form, and I was a sworn enemy of the confused arbitrariness of Gothic adornment. Under the heading 'Gothic,' as in an entry in the dictionary, I listed all the synonymous misconceptions that I had ever encountered, such as indefinite, disorganized, unnatural, patched-together, tacked-on, overladen. No wiser than a nation which calls the world it does not know barbaric, I called everything which did not fit into my system Gothic: from the elaborate figures and colorful ornaments on the houses of our would-be nobility to the somber remains of early German architecture. A few bizarre curlicues prompted me to join in the general chorus: "Smothered by ornamentation!" So I shuddered, anticipating a misshapen, grotesque monster.

But what unexpected emotions seized me when I finally stood before the edifice! My soul was suffused with a feeling of immense grandeur which, because it consisted of thousands of harmonizing details, I was able to savor and enjoy, but by no means understand and explain. They say it is thus with the joys of heaven, and how often I returned to savor such joys on earth, to embrace the gigantic spirit expressed in the work of our brothers of yore! How often I returned to view its dignity and magnificence from all sides, from every distance, at different times of day! It is hard for the mind of man when his brother's work is so sublime that he can only bow his head and worship. How often the gentle light of dusk, as it fused the countless parts into unified masses, soothed my eyes weary from intense searching. Now all stood before my soul, simple and great, and I, full of bliss, felt develop in me the power at the same time to enjoy and understand. Then I sensed the genius of the great builder. "Why are you so amazed?" he whispered, "All these masses were necessary. Don't you see them in all the older churches of my city? I have merely elevated the arbitrary vastness to harmonious proportions. Above the main portal dominating the two smaller ones on either side, see the broad circular window! Once there was only a small hole to let in light, and now it harmonizes with the nave of the church. See the belltower high above—it demanded smaller windows. That was all necessary, and I lent it beauty. But oh, when I float through these dark and sublime side apertures which appear to be empty and useless! In these bold, slender forms I have concealed the mysterious forces which were to raise two towers high into the air. Alas! but one stands there forlorn, without the five crowning pinnacles I had planned, so that the surrounding provinces would do homage to it and its royal brother!" And so he departed from me, and my heart was filled with sympathy and melancholy, until the birds of the morning who live in the thousands of openings greeted the sun with jubilant songs and awakened me from my slumber. How fresh was its radiance in the misty shimmer of morning light, how happily I stretched out my arms toward it and looked at the vast, harmonious masses animated by countless components! As in the works of eternal nature, down to the smallest fiber, all is form, all serves the whole. How lightly the immense, firmly-grounded edifice soars into the air, how like filigree everything is, yet made for eternity! I owe it to your instruction, noble genius, that I no longer reel when confronting your profundities, that my soul is touched by the blissful calm of a spirit who can look down on such a creation and say, as did God, "It is good!"

And should I not grow angry, divine Erwin, when a German scholar, on the word of envious neighbors, fails to see his advantage and belittles your work with the misunderstood term Gothic, when he ought to thank God for being able to proclaim: This is German architecture! Our architecture! The Italians cannot boast one of their own, much less the French. And if, Professor, you are not willing to admit this advantage, then show us that the Goths really built in this style, which will prove quite difficult. And in the end, if you cannot establish that there was a Homer before Homer, we will gladly grant you your theory of minor trial-and-error efforts, and approach with reverence the work of the master who first created a living whole out of scattered elements. And you, my dear brother in the quest of truth and beauty, close your ears to all pretentious prattle about art—come, enjoy, behold! Beware of profaning the name of your noblest artist and hasten here to see his magnificent work. If you feel repelled, or feel nothing at all, then farewell, harness your horses and be on your way to Paris.

But I will gladly join you, worthy youth, who stands there moved, unable to reconcile the contradictions clashing within your soul, now feeling the irresistible power of the great whole, now calling me a dreamer for seeing beauty where you see only strength and roughness. Do not let a misunderstanding separate us. Do not let the effete doctrine of our modern esthetizisers so enfeeble you that you can no longer bear what is meaningful but rough, lest in the end your sickly sensibility can tolerate only what is polished but meaningless. They would have you believe that the fine arts sprang from our supposed inclination to beautify, to refine, the things around us. That is not true! For it is the common man and the artisan who use these words in the only sense they could be true—not the philosopher.

Art is creative long before it is beautiful. And yet, such art is true and great, perhaps truer and greater than when it becomes beautiful. For in man there is a creative force which becomes active as soon as his existence is secure. When he is free from worry and fear, this demigod, restless in tranquility, begins to cast about for matter to inspire with his spirit. And thus savages decorate their coconut-fiber mats, their feathers, their bodies, with bizarre patterns, ghastly forms and gaudy colors. And even if this creative activity produces the most arbitrary shapes and designs, they will harmonize despite the apparent lack of proportion. For a single feeling created them as a characteristic whole.

This characteristic art is in fact the only true art. If it springs from a sincere, unified, original, autonomous feeling, unconcerned, indeed unaware of anything extraneous, then it will be a living whole, whether born of coarse savagery or cultured sensitivity. You see endless variations of this in different nations and individuals. The more the soul develops a feeling for proportion, which alone is beautiful and eternal, whose fundamental harmony we can prove but whose mysteries we can only feel, in which alone the life of the god-like genius dances to blissful melodies, and the more deeply this beauty penetrates the mind so that both seem to have originated as one and the mind can be satisfied with nothing but beauty and produces nothing but beauty— then the more fortunate is the artist, the more glorious is he, and the deeper we bow before him and worship God's anointed one.

No one will dislodge Erwin from his pedestal. His work stands before you. Approach it and experience the profoundest feeling of truth and beauty of proportion, sprung from a strong, rough-hewn German soul in the setting of the gloomy petty-clericism of the Middle Ages.

And our own age? It has renounced its genius, sent forth its sons to collect foreign produce at their peril. The flighty Frenchman, who borrows even more heavily, has at least ingenuity enough to lend his meager pickings a semblance of oneness. He is building a magic temple to his Sainte Madeleine with Greek columns and German vaults. One of our own artists was asked to create a portal for an old German church, and I saw the model he proposed: stately antique columns.

I will not dwell on how much I detest our dainty doll-painters. Through theatrical poses, fake complexions and colorful costumes they have caught the eye of women. Manly Albrecht Dürer, the neophyte sneers at you—but to me, even the crudest of your woodcut figures is more welcome!

And you yourselves, the privileged, to whom it was given to enjoy the highest beauty and who now come among us to proclaim your revelations, even you do harm to the genius. He does not want to be borne up and carried off on wings not his own, though they be the wings of morning. He must provide his own strength, developed in childhood dreams and honed during youth, until, strong and lithe like a mountain lion, he can hasten forth to seek prey. Nature above all must be his teacher, since you pedagogues will never devise a setting diverse enough to challenge and delight him as his abilities develop.

Hail to thee child who art born with an eye for proportion, ready to practice your talent on all nature's forms. When you gradually awaken to the joyful life around you and share the jubilant pleasure man feels after toil and fear and hope—the vintager's lusty song as the riches of autumn swell his vats, the reaper's lively dance after he has hung his idle sickle high on the beam—when the powerful forces of desire and suffering guide your brush in manlier strokes, when you have striven and suffered enough and have enjoyed enough, and when you are sated with earthly beauty and worthy to rest in the arms of the goddess, worthy to feel in her embrace the sensation which gave birth to the deified Hercules—then receive him, heavenly beauty, you mediator between gods and humans! And then, more than Prometheus, may he bring down the bliss of the gods upon our earth.

SHAKESPEARE: A TRIBUTE
(1771)

It seems to me that the noblest of our sentiments is the hope of continuing to exist even after destiny has apparently returned us to a state of non-existence. This life, gentlemen, is too short. Proof of this is the fact that man, whether prince or pauper, sage or simpleton, will tire of everything but living, and the fact that no one attains the goal he has so ardently sought. Even if things go well for a time along the way, finally, often within reach of one's objective, one stumbles into a trap set by God knows who—and counts for nothing.

Count for nothing? I, who mean everything to myself! Everything I know, I know only through myself! Thus exclaim those who have self-awareness, striding briskly along life's path in preparation for the unending path beyond. Of course, each advances at his own speed. While the one sallies forth at a lively pace, the other dons seven-league boots and overtakes him, and two steps bring him as far as a day's journey the first. Be this as it may, this persevering wanderer remains our friend and companion while we observe and admire the other's gigantic strides, following his trail and comparing his stride with our own.

Let's set out on our journey, gentlemen! Examining a single footprint of that kind excites and inspires us more than gawking at a royal parade of thousands.

Today we honor the memory of the greatest wanderer, and in so doing we honor ourselves. For we carry within us the seeds of the achievements we value in others.

Do not expect me to write much or in an orderly way. Peace of mind is no festive robe. And as yet, I have not thought much about Shakespeare. Vague notions and feelings are the most I have been capable of. The first page I read made me a slave to Shakespeare for life. And when I had finished reading the first drama, I stood there like a man blind from birth whom a magic hand has all at once given light. I realized and felt intensely that my life was infinitely expanded. Everything seemed new to me, unfamiliar, and the unaccustomed light hurt my eyes. Gradually I learned to see, and, thanks to my awakened spirit, I still feel intensely what I have gained.

I never doubted for a moment that I would renounce the traditional theater. The unity of place seemed to me an oppressive prison, the unities of action and time burdensome fetters on our imagination. I struggled free—and knew for the first time that I had hands and feet. And now when I saw what harm the keepers of the rules had done me in their dungeon, and how many free spirits were still cowering there—my heart would have burst had I not declared war on them, had I not tried daily to destroy their prison towers.

The Greek theater, which the French took as their model, was so constituted internally and externally that it would have been easier for a marquis to imitate Alcibiades than for Corneille to follow Sophocles.

First in the service of religion, then solemnly political, the tragedy presented to the people with the simplicity of perfection great individual deeds of their forefathers. It aroused feelings of wholeness and greatness in the soul, for it was itself whole and great.

And in what souls!

Greek souls! I cannot find words to describe what that means, but I can feel it, and for brevity's sake I refer to Homer and Sophocles and Theocritus, who taught me to feel what it means.

Now I hasten to add: "Little Frenchman, why are you wearing Greek armor? It is much too big and heavy for you."

That is why all French tragedies are parodies of themselves.

How regulated everything is! They resemble each other like shoes and are not without their boring spots, typically in the fourth act—but sad to say, you gentlemen know that from your own experience, and I say no more.

I don't know who first had the idea of putting historical-political spectacles on the stage; that is a good question for anyone interested in writing a scholarly treatise. Whether or not the honor of being the originator falls to Shakespeare, it was he who raised this type of drama to a level that we must still take to be the highest, totally beyond the imagination of most. And so there is little chance that anyone will match, much less surpass him.

Shakespeare, my friend, if you were still among us, I would want to be nowhere but in your company. How happy I would be playing the supporting role of Pylades to your Orestes, rather than that of the most venerated high priest in the temple of Delphi.

I will stop now, gentlemen, and continue writing tomorrow, for I have struck an emotional chord which you may not find edifying.

Shakespeare's theater is a colorful gallery where the history of the world passes before our eyes on the invisible thread of time. The structure of his plays, in the accepted sense of the word, is no structure at all. Yet each revolves around an invisible point which no philosopher has discovered or defined and where the characteristic quality of our being, our presumed free will, collides with the inevitable course of the whole. Our corrupted taste, however, so beclouds our vision that we almost require a new Creation to escape the Darkness.

No Frenchmen, or Germans infected by their tastes, not even Wieland, have come off very honorably in this regard, or in others either. Voltaire, who has always specialized in lese majesty, has proved himself here as well to be a veritable Thersites. If I were Ulysses, he would cringe under the blows of my scepter.

Most of these gentlemen take particular offense at Shakespeare's characters. But I cry: Nature! Nature! Nothing is so like Nature as Shakespeare's figures.

Now they're coming at me from all sides!

If they would only give me room so that I can breathe and speak!

Shakespeare competes with Prometheus, imitating him by forming human beings feature by feature, but on a colossal scale—that is why we don't recognize them as our brothers. Then he brings them to life by breathing his spirit into them. He speaks through them all, and we recognize the kinship.

And how can our century dare judge Nature? How should we know Nature, we who from childhood have felt in ourselves and seen in others nothing but restraint and artificiality? I often feel shamed by Shakespeare, for it sometimes happens that at first glance I think, "I would have done that differently." Later I recognize that I am a poor wretch, that Nature proclaims her wisdom through Shakespeare, and that my characters are mere soap bubbles whafted about by fanciful whims.

Now let me finish—though I haven't even started yet.

874

What noble philosophers have said about the world applies to Shakespeare too: What we call evil is only the other side of good; evil is necessary for good to exist and is part of the whole, just as the tropics must be torrid and Lapland frigid for there to be a temperate zone. He guides us through the entire world, yet we pampered novices cry out at the sight of a grasshopper: "Master, it's going to eat us alive!"

To work, gentlemen! Take your trumpets and drive forth those noble souls from the Elysium of so-called good taste, where, drowsy in monotonous twilight, they live, yet do not live; have passions in their hearts but no marrow in their bones, and, because they are not tired enough to rest and yet too lazy to act, they stroll aimlessly among the myrtles and laurels, idling and yawning away their shadowy lives.

SIMPLE IMITATION, MANNER, STYLE
(1789)

It seems advisable to give a clear indication of what we mean by these terms, for we will refer to them frequently. They have long been in use, and although they seem to have been sufficiently defined in theoretical works, everyone employs them according to his own understanding. What these terms mean to the individual will depend on the clarity or vagueness of the idea he wishes to express.

Simple Imitation of Nature

Assume that an aspiring artist with some talent begins to paint natural objects after only brief preliminary training in basic techniques. He copies forms with care and diligence and imitates colors as closely as he can, taking pains never to deviate from nature, beginning and completing every picture with an eye to nature. This person will always be an estimable artist because he will necessarily achieve an incredible degree of accuracy, and his works will be assured, vital and diverse.

If we analyze such a course of development carefully, we are led to the conclusion that this method is suitable for a capable but limited talent in treating pleasant but limited subjects.

Such subjects must be easily available at all times. The artist must be able to observe them at his convenience and copy them at his leisure. Whoever engages in such activity must be tranquil, introspective and satisfied with modest rewards.

This type of imitation would, then, be pursued by calm, conscientious persons of moderate talent who paint still-lifes. Within its limits, this procedure does not preclude a high level of excellence.

Manner

However, such a technique is usually too pedantic or inadequate for the artist. He perceives in a multitude of objects a unifying harmony which he can only reproduce in painting by sacrificing details. He is impatient with drawing letter by letter what nature spells out for him. He invents his own method, creates his own language to express in his own way what he has grasped with his soul. As a result he gives a distinctive form to an object that he has often copied, without now actually seeing it before him or even recalling exactly what it looked like in nature.

Now his art has become a language that expresses his spirit directly and characteristically. And just as anyone who thinks for himself will order and formulate his ideas on moral issues differently from others, so any such artist will see, apprehend and imitate the world differently. He will approach the things of the world with a greater or lesser degree of deliberateness or spontaneity and will accordingly recreate them with circumspection or with casualness.

We can see that this kind of imitation is best suited for subjects which constitute a totality made up of many subordinate elements. These elements must be sacrificed if the general character of the whole is to be adequately expressed, as for example in landscapes, where one would miss the point completely by adhering pedantically to detail rather than trying to do justice to the overall concept.

Style

Through imitation of nature, through the effort of creating a general language, through painstaking and thorough study of diverse subject matter, the artist finally reaches the point where he becomes increasingly familiar with the characteristic and essential features of things. He will now be able to see some order in the multiplicity of appearances and learn to juxtapose and recreate distinct and characteristic forms. Then art will have reached its highest possible level, which is style and equal to the highest achievement of mankind.

While simple imitation therefore depends on a tranquil and affectionate view of life, manner is a reflection of the ease and competence with which the subject is treated. Style, however, rests on the most fundamental principle of cognition, on the essence of things—to the extent that it is granted us to perceive this essence in visible and tangible form.

A more detailed discussion of the above would fill volumes. One can already find a number of books on the subject, but the concept itself can be studied only in nature and in works of art. We would like to add a few observations, and we will take an opportunity to refer to this matter in future discussions of the visual arts.

It is quite obvious that the three ways of producing works of art described here as separate categories are closely related and can sometimes overlap imperceptibly.

Imitation of simple subjects such as flowers and fruits can be developed to a high level. It is natural that someone who paints roses will soon be able to distinguish the most beautiful and freshest, and choose only those from among the thousands which summer has to offer. The act of selecting begins at this point, without the artist having formed a definite concept of the beauty of a rose. He is dealing with tangible forms, and everything depends on the varied texture and the color of the surfaces. The fuzzy peach, the finely bloomed plum, the smooth apple, the glossy cherry, the dazzling rose, the bouquet of carnations, the brightly colored tulips—the artist will have perfect specimens of everything he desires available in his studio. He will place his objects in the most favorable light, and without conscious effort his eyes will learn to see the harmony of the brilliant colors. Every year he will be able to find similar objects, and by calmly observing and copying their simple existence, he will recognize and grasp the characteristics of these objects without laborious attempts at abstraction. In this way, the masterpieces of a Huysum and Rachel Ruysch will be produced—artists who we may say achieved the impossible. It is apparent that such an artist will be even more accomplished and self-assured in his work if he is also something of a botanist. Being thoroughly familiar with the structure of plants, he will know the influence of the various parts on the health and growth of the whole as well as the function and interaction of those parts, and he will study and reflect on the successive development of leaves, flowers, pollen, fruit and seed. He will not only show his taste by what he selects but will amaze and instruct us through the correct representation of the characteristic features. Here we could say that he has formed his own style. But it is also obvious that if such a master were not so conscientious and only concerned with the easy expression of the striking and dazzling, he would soon become a mannerist.

Thus simple imitation operates in the vestibule of style. If the artist works faithfully, carefully and purposefully, if his response to what he sees is controlled, if he imitates with deliberateness and develops an awareness of what he his doing, that is, if he learns to distinguish the similar from the dissimilar and to categorize individual objects according to general concepts—then imitation will eventually be worthy of crossing the threshold to the inner sanctum of style.

If we now consider manner, we see that it can be, in the true sense of the word, a composite of simple imitation and style. If a mannerist approaches exact imitation, yet retains some degree of his more casual technique, while at the same time grasping and expressing in tangible form what is characteristic, and if he combines both these approaches and lends the product a distinct, vigorous, active individuality—then his art will be noble, great and admirable. But

877

if such an artist fails to adhere to and respect nature, he will move further away from the foundations of art, and his manner will become the more vacuous and insignificant the further he moves away from simple imitation and from style.

It should be clear that we use the word 'manner' positively and in a respectful sense; therefore, artists whose works in our opinion belong to this category need not feel slighted. Our only concern is to assure the word 'style' a position of the highest honor in order to have available a term to designate the highest level that art has ever reached or can reach. Merely recognizing this level is a great reward, and discussing it with knowledgeable people a rare pleasure which we trust we will have many opportunities to repeat in the future.

RESPONSE TO A LITERARY RABBLE-ROUSER
(1795)

In this year's March issue of the *Berlinisches Archiv der Zeit und ihres Geschmacks*, an article appeared on German prose and rhetoric, which the editors—as they themselves confess—were reluctant to publish. We for our part do not criticize their decision to accept this immature effort; if it is a journal's responsibility to preserve material that is representative of an era, it must also include the era's improprieties. To be sure, adopting an authoritative tone and certain mannerisms thought to be characteristic of a well-informed mind is anything but unusual among our critics; but individual lapses into more primitive behavior must also be noted, as they do occur. However, we, the editors of the journal *Die Horen*, would like to state for the record what has been frequently and perhaps more eloquently expressed by others: Besides those who make unreasonable and exaggerated demands on our writers, there are also reasonable and grateful minds who quietly support these men who reap such meager rewards for their efforts.

The author of the *Archiv* article deplores the scarcity of first-rate classical prose works in Germany; then he passes with one giant step over almost a dozen of our best authors. He does not even refer to them by name, subjects them to lukewarm praise and sharp criticism and characterizes them in a manner which makes it almost impossible to identify them from his caricatures.

We are convinced that no German author thinks of himself as a writer of classics. We are likewise convinced that the requirements every German author sets for himself are stricter than those muddled and presumptuous demands of a crude troublemaker who attacks a respected group of writers, who certainly do not expect unqualified praise for their every effort but who are entitled to respect.

It is certainly not our intention to comment on the poorly conceived and poorly written text. We are confident that after reading the pages in question, our readers will react with indignation and repudiate the rude arrogance with which the author tries to invade the territory of his betters with the intent to usurp their places; they will agree with our calling this piece a blatant case of literary rabble-rousing. Only a few remarks shall be made in reply to this insolence.

People who consider it indispensable that their spoken or written words express specific concepts rarely use terms such as "classical work" or "classical writer." When and under what circumstances, in any nation, does one become a writer of classics? There are a number of preconditions: If the writer finds in the history of his nation great events which together with their consequences form a harmonious and significant whole; if his countrymen exhibit nobility in their attitudes, depth in their feelings, and strength and consistence in their actions; if he himself is permeated with the spirit of his nation and if he, because of an intuitive understanding of this spirit, feels capable of identifying with the past as well as with the present; if his native country has attained a high cultural level, thus facilitating his own educational process; if he has collected sufficient material and is aware of the perfect and not so perfect attempts of his predecessors; and if enough favorable external and internal circumstances coincide to make his apprenticeship less arduous so that in his mature years he is in a position to conceive a great work, organize it, and produce finally a coherent and unified whole.

These are the preconditions which are absolutely essential for a writer, especially a prose writer, to become "classical." If an unbiased and fair critic were to compare them with the conditions under which the best German writers of our century have in fact labored, their successes would fill him with awed admiration and their failures with sincere regret.

An outstanding piece of writing, just like an outstanding speech, is only a product of the author's life. Neither the writer nor the practical man of affairs can be held responsible for the circumstances and conditions into which he is born and under which he must work. Everyone, even the greatest genius, suffers from his century in some respects, just as he profits from it in others. And only a mature nature can produce an excellent national writer.

We cannot criticize the German nation because it is politically splintered despite its representing a geographic unit. We do not wish for the political turmoil that would pave the way for classical works in Germany.

The most unfair criticism is the one based on a distorted perspective. We should look objectively at past and present conditions and at the individual circumstances which formed our German writers; then it will be easy to find the criteria by which to judge them. There is no real cultural center in Germany where writers can gather and find a common guideline to aid their development and individual fields of interest. Born in various parts of the country, educated in very different ways, they are usually isolated and exposed to the impact of quite varied circumstances; they are inspired by their predilection for this or that model in German or foreign literature; without guidance, they have to work by trial and error to test their abilities. Only gradually, after a long process of soul-searching, do they become sure of what they *should* do, and then, only experimentation tells them what they *can* do. Again and again, the budding writer is bewildered by the demands of a mass public without taste that devours the good and the bad with equal relish. Then again, he receives encouragement from contact with the educated, who unfortunately are scattered all over the country, and he gains reassurance from the knowledge that there are contemporaries who labor and struggle as he does. Finally, the German writer reaches the stage in life where he has to support himself and his family and is forced to work in a field that is alien to his calling. Greatly discouraged and saddened, he must often perform work for which he has no respect, in order to produce the means that would allow him to pursue what his mind has been trained to do, the only thing he considers worthwhile. What respected German writer would not recognize himself in this portrait? Which of them would not admit with some regret that in the beginning of his career he often enough pined for an opportunity to place the unique gifts of his individual genius at the service of a common national culture which unfortunately did not exist? To be sure, the education of the higher classes through foreign customs and literature was quite beneficial, but it also prevented the Germans from developing sooner as Germans.

Consider now the achievements of German poets and prose writers of note! With what scrupulousness, with what devotion they have followed the path prescribed by their clear and well-defined convictions! It is no exaggeration to suggest that any capable, diligent literary scholar could develop a complete theory of style by comparing all editions of our Wieland and merely noting, stage by stage, his successive corrections. Wieland is indefatigable in his pursuit of excellence, and we may take great pride in him, notwithstanding the grumblings of Smelfungi. If every conscientious librarian sees to it that a collection such as this is assembled while it is still possible, the coming century will make use of it with gratitude.

In a future issue of our journal, we hope to present a study of the development of our best writers as revealed in their works. Perhaps the writers will want to contribute information. They may be assured that we are not interested in intimate personal confessions. We would leave it to their discretion to tell us which factors have contributed most to their development and which have presented the greatest obstacles. Their personal participation would be invaluable; it would add new dimensions to what can be gleaned from their works.

Such a study would prove quite helpful because there is one fact which inept critics disregard almost completely. Nowadays, a talented young man has the good fortune to be able to develop his talent earlier and find a lucid style appropriate to his subject. To whom does he owe that but to his predecessors, who in the last half of this century persevered in their own development in the face of all sorts of obstacles, each in his own way? As a result, a kind of school was founded, and the young man who enters in now enjoys a much larger and better defined circle than the writer of earlier times, who only after groping his way in the faint light of dawn was able to expand the circle, and that only gradually and as it were by chance. The would-be critic who wants to help us find the way with his feeble torch arrives too late—daybreak is here, and we will not close the shutters again.

It is not proper to vent one's bad humor in good society. Only a case of very bad humor can make a man deny the existence of excellent writers in Germany at a time when almost everyone writes well. It does not require much effort to find a pleasing novel, a well-told tale, or a lucid essay on this or that subject. Our critical publications, journals, compendia—they prove again and again that a uniformly good style *does* exist. The Germans are gaining more and more expertise and a clearer perspective. A worthy philosophy, in spite of the resistance of doubting minds, helps them to become more aware of their intellectual potential and make use of it. The numerous examples of style, the previous labors and endeavors of so many accomplished writers enable the beginner at an earlier stage to present in an appropriate style and with lucidity and grace what he has received from the outside world and developed further within himself. Thus any kindly disposed and fairminded German will see the writers of his nation at an encouraging stage of development. He is furthermore bound to be convinced that the public will not be misled by an ill-tempered, small-minded critic, who should be excluded from literary society, as should everyone whose destructive efforts only make active members irritated, supporters less interested, and onlookers distrustful and indifferent.

WINCKELMANN AND HIS AGE
(1805)

Introduction

The memory of remarkable men, no less than the presence of significant works of art, causes us from time to time to reflect. Both represent a legacy for every generation, the former by virtue of immortal deeds, the latter as ineffable but tangible presences. The perceptive person knows full well that only contemplating their uniqueness is of real value; yet, we keep on trying to deepen our understanding through thoughts and words.

We are especially encouraged to do so if new information concerning such eminent men or their works is discovered and publicized. Thus, we trust that our present consideration of Winckelmann, his character and his accomplishments, will be found appropriate at a time when newly published letters should shed further light on his thinking and the circumstances of his life.

Early Years

Nature presents human beings at birth with a precious gift: the strong urge to take hold of the world and experience it, find a place in it and become a harmonious part of it. Some excellent minds, on the other hand, tend to shy away from real life, withdraw into themselves, create a special world within and achieve excellence which is inwardly directed.

However, if a highly gifted human being is capable of combining both tendencies, that is, if he seeks to complement his natural abilities with corresponding experiences in the outer world and hence develop his gifts to their utmost potential, then we can be assured that his existence will delight his contemporaries and generations to come.

Winckelmann was such a person. Already richly endowed by nature, he nevertheless spent his life seeking in man and in art—which is primarily concerned with man—those qualities of excellence and nobility he most admired.

As did others, Winckelmann endured a humble childhood, insufficient schooling as a youth, an irregular and unsystematic course of studies as a young man, and the burden of a schoolmaster's job with the familiar difficulties and worries that go with such a career. He turned thirty without fate having once smiled on him; but within him he carried the seed of his future happiness.

Even during those sad years we detect a desire to get firsthand experience of life and the world. Although his urge was unfocused and confused, it was strongly expressed. A few ill-planned attempts to visit foreign countries failed. He dreamed of a journey to Egypt, and he did set out to visit France, but unforeseen obstacles forced him to return. Better counseled by an inner voice, he finally decided that he must get to Rome at all costs. He felt that Rome was his true destination. This was more than a whim or mere idea, it was a definite plan which he sought to realize with shrewdness and perseverance.

Spirit of Antiquity

Man can achieve much through the appropriate use of his individual abilities, and can achieve extraordinary things if several of his talents are combined. But he can only accomplish the unique, the wholly unexpected, if all his qualities unite within him and work together as one. This was the happy lot of the ancients, especially the Greeks in their golden age. We moderns are forced by fate to content ourselves with the first two possibilities.

When man's nature functions soundly as a whole, when he feels that the world of which he is part is a huge, beautiful, admirable and worthy whole, when this harmony gives him pure and uninhibited delight, then the universe, if it were capable of emotion, would rejoice at having reached its goal and admire the crowning glory of its own evolution. For, what purpose would those countless suns and planets and moons serve, those stars and milky ways, comets and nebulae, those created and evolving worlds, if a happy human being did not ultimately emerge to enjoy existence?

Modern man often loses himself in the infinite before finally returning if possible to a limited point of reference—as we seem just now to have demonstrated. The ancients, however, immediately felt completely at home within the pleasant boundaries of this beautiful world. Here was their natural habitat, here was the setting for their activities and here the focal point of their passions.

Why are their poets and historians the object of admiration to the discerning and a cause of despair to their emulators? Because the figures they put before us restrict themselves in the range of their interest to such subjects as themselves, their nation, their own lives and those of their fellow citizens. Because they concentrate all their thoughts and desires and energy on immediate reality. Hence it was not difficult for the like-minded poet to immortalize this reality.

For them, actuality had the unique significance that the imagination and emotions have for us today.

The ancient poet lived in his imagination, just as the ancient historian lived in the political world, and the ancient scientist in the world of nature. They all adhered to the immediate, the true, the real; even the products of their imagination have bones and marrow. Among all things, man and human nature enjoyed the highest respect, and man's inner and outer relationship to the world was observed and represented with profound understanding. Emotions and thinking were not yet fragmented, and the all but irreparable rift in the healthy oneness of man had not yet occurred.

The ancients knew as well how to savor happiness as to endure misfortunes. Just as a healthy organism resists sickness and recovers quickly after an attack, their soundness of mind was easily restored after emotional or physical distress. Winckelmann was the reincarnation of ancient man—insofar as that may be said of anyone in our time. The first thirty years of his life provide overwhelming evidence, for neither his lowly existence, nor discomfort, nor worries could subdue, defeat or wear him down, and as soon as he obtained the necessary freedom, he became, in the sense of the ancients, a whole and complete human being. He was compelled to work, and he experienced joy and deprivation, happiness and sorrow, gain and loss, honor and humiliation in the course of his life. Although tossed between extremes, he was content on this beautiful earth where we are all at the mercy of fate.

The spirit of antiquity which accompanied him in life did not abandon him in his studies. To be sure, even the ancients were in a somewhat difficult situation in those branches of knowledge where the comprehension of the various subjects not pertaining to man required a division of strengths and capabilities that meant an almost unavoidable fracturing of the whole. Modern man runs the even greater risk of losing his focus by his specialized studies in the many fields of knowledge, of becoming lost in disconnected expertise, and, unlike the ancients, he does not have the resources of a unified personality to compensate for the shortcoming.

Motivated partly by inclination, partly by necessity, Winckelmann broadly explored various areas of knowledge. But sooner or later he inevitably returned to the study of antiquity, especially Greek antiquity, as the subject for which he felt so close an affinity, and to which he was to devote himself so completely in the happiest period of his life.

Pagan Spirit

Our description of the spirit of antiquity, a spirit focused on the world and what it has to offer, leads us directly to the consideration that such features are only compatible with a pagan spirit. Trust in oneself, concentration on immediate reality, worship of gods purely as ancestors, admiration of them only as works of art as it were, submission to a supreme fate, and the concept that the future, due to the high value placed on fame after death, is dependent on the here and now—those elements are so interconnected, constitute such an indivisible whole, form a human condition so obviously intended by nature herself, that we perceive in ancient man an imperishable state of health, in moments of sublime joy no less than in abject misery and even death.

This pagan spirit permeates Winckelmann's activities and writings and is most obvious in his early letters, where he is still struggling to come to grips with modern religious views. If we want to understand his so-called conversion, we must remember this attitude of his, this incompatibility of his thinking with, even his aversion to, Christianity. The various factions into which the Christian faith is divided were a matter of total indifference to him, so that, in spirit, he never really belonged to any of its denominations.

Friendship

Since the ancients, as we claim, were truly complete personalities in harmony with themselves and the world, they also had to experience the full scope of human relationships. They did not want to deny themselves the delight that results from the bond between people of similar temperament.

Even in this respect there is a remarkable difference between ancient and modern times. The relationship to women, which in our time has become so tender and spiritual, scarcely rose above the level of physical need. The relationship of parent and child seems to have been somewhat more loving. But friendship among men was for them the only genuine emotional relationship—although two women, Chloris and Thyia, remained inseparable friends even in Hades.

We react with astonishment when, with regard to two young men, we hear of passionate fulfillment of love's desire, the bliss of being inseparable, lifelong devotion, or the need to follow the other into death. Indeed, we feel embarrassed when poets, historians, philosophers, orators inundate us with stories, events, sentiments and opinions pertaining to the subject.

Winckelmann felt born for friendship of that kind. He felt not only capable, but greatly in need of it. He experienced his real self only in the context of friendship and could perceive himself as a whole only if he was complemented by another. Early in life he found a perhaps unworthy object of his feelings. He was utterly devoted to him, and even in his poverty he found the means to be generous, to give, to sacrifice for the friend; indeed, he did not hesitate to mortgage his existence, his life. It is here that Winckelmann, himself in great need, felt noble, rich, magnanimous and happy because he could be of service to the one he loved most, the one for whom he could make the greatest sacrifice, that of forgiving ingratitude.

No matter how times and circumstances changed, Winckelmann modeled all his friendships on the pattern of the first. And although many of these idealized relationships faded, his idealistic attitude nevertheless ensured him the affection of many a good man. Thus he had the good fortune to establish excellent relations with some of the best people of his time.

Beauty

Granted that a latter-day Greek in his intense need for friendship actually creates the object of his affections, he would still gain only a one-sided, an emotional benefit from it and little from the external world, unless there emerged a different, yet related and similar need and a satisfactory object for this need. We are referring to the need for physical beauty, and the incarnation of beauty itself. For the ultimate goal of evolving nature is the beautiful human being. To be sure, nature only rarely succeeds in producing him because there are numerous obstacles to her plans, and even her omnipotence cannot linger long with perfection and lend permanence to the beauty she produces. We are justified in saying that a beautiful human being is beautiful only for one brief moment.

At this point, art enters. Since man represents the pinnacle of nature, he sees himself as a complete being who in turn has to produce a pinnacle. To that end, he strives upward, imbuing himself with all perfection and virtue, and calls to his aid his ability to select, to create order and harmony, to lend significance. Finally he reaches the level where he can produce art, which will now occupy a preeminent place next to his other deeds and works. Once produced, the work of art stands before the world as an ideal reality, producing a lasting, indeed, the ultimate effect. For by developing from a totality of strengths, it absorbs everything magnificent, admirable and agreeable, and, by giving life to the human figure, it elevates man above himself, rounds out the circle of life and deeds, deifies him for a present which comprises past and future. Those who saw the *Olympian Jupiter* were seized by such feelings, as we can gather from ancient descriptions, reports and testimony. A god had become man in order to make man into a god. They saw supreme majesty and were inspired by supreme beauty. In this sense we can agree with those ancients who were fully convinced that it was a misfortune to die without having seen this work.

Winckelmann, by nature, was receptive to such beauty. He first became acquainted with it in ancient literature, but he encountered beauty more intimately in the visual arts, where one learns to recognize it before perceiving and appreciating its manifestations in nature.

If the need for friendship and for beauty are both satisfied by the same object, then man's happiness and gratitude seem to know no limit. He will gladly give all he owns as a token of his devotion and admiration.

Hence we often find Winckelmann in the company of beautiful young men. He never seems more alive and likable than in these often only fleeting moments.

Catholicism

With such a disposition, such needs and desires, Winckelmann was for a long time a slave to the interests of others. Nowhere around him did he see the slightest hope for aid and support.

If Count Bünau, a man of independent means, had bought one important book less, it would have been possible for Winckelmann to go to Rome. As secretary to the court, Bünau also had enough influence to help this deserving man out of any difficulty. Yet he may not have wanted to lose such an efficient assistant or simply did not realize how great a service he would have rendered by relinquishing so capable a man to the world. Furthermore, the court at Dresden, where Winckelmann had some hope for receiving adequate support, was of the Catholic faith. There was only one way of obtaining the court's favor, and that was through father confessors and other clergy.

The example of a prince in manner and morals has immense influence and tacitly requires all his subjects to conduct themselves in a similar way in their private lives. The prince's religion is almost always the predominant one, and Catholicism, like an eternal whirlpool, pulls the calmly passing ripple into its eddy.

So Winckelmann came to the conclusion that in order to be a Roman among the Romans, to become an integral part of that community and enjoy the confidence of its members, he had to adapt to the community, adopt its faith and its customs. His later success proved that he would not have realized his ambition so completely, had it not been for this earlier decision, which was made immeasurably easier by the fact that, being a pagan at heart, his Protestant baptism had not been able to turn him into a true Christian.

Yet his conversion did not come about without intense struggle. A person may, in accordance with his conviction and after due thought, finally make a decision which is in complete harmony with his intentions, desires and needs, which indeed seems so essential for the maintaining and furthering of his very existence that he has no reservations at all about such a step. However, the decision can be in opposition to the general attitude and conviction of many others. Then begins a new conflict which, to be sure, does not cause him uncertainty, but does cause discomfort, impatience and annoyance, because he finds himself in disharmony with the world while he believes he is in harmony with himself.

Hence Winckelmann was torn when he contemplated his conversion. He was anxious, depressed and emotionally wrought when he thought of the effect it would have, especially on the Count, his first patron. How beautiful, profound and candid are the remarks in his letters regarding this matter!

As we know, everyone who changes his religion remains somehow tainted, and it seems impossible to cleanse him. This suggests that people value constancy above all else, not least because, divided into factions as they are, they must forever be concerned with the security and permanence of their group. Neither feelings nor convictions are the issue here. We must endure where fate, rather than choice, has placed us. To remain loyal to a nation, a city, a prince, a friend, a woman, and to focus everything on that relationship, to work and sacrifice and suffer for it—that is valued. Disloyalty, on the other hand, remains odious, and fickleness is ridiculed.

This is a harsh, very serious view of the matter; but we can look at it from another perspective which permits a more kindly and lenient view. Certain character traits we by no means approve of, certain moral blemishes in others we find especially titillating. If we may be allowed an analogy, we would say that it is the same as with venison roast which the gourmet much prefers slightly gamy. We find a divorced woman or a renegade especially fascinating. Persons who otherwise would perhaps seem merely interesting and charming suddenly appear wondrous. It cannot be denied that Winckelmann's conversion heightens the romantic aspects of his life and character in our imagination.

As for Winckelmann himself, the Catholic faith had no profound meaning. He saw it only as a disguise to be worn, and his remarks in this regard are frank enough. It seems that later on he did not observe the practices of his new faith closely enough, and perhaps even aroused the suspicions of zealots through his loose remarks. At least here and there we detect a slight fear of the Inquisition.

Interest in Greek Art

It is difficult, if not impossible, to make the transition from the purely literary, even in its most highly evolved forms of poetry and rhetoric, to the visual arts. Literature and art are separated by a wide chasm which only a very special talent can help bridge. We now have sufficient documentation to judge how well Winckelmann succeeded in this regard.

His love of pleasure first drew him to art treasures. However, for understanding and critical judgment he still needed artists as intermediaries, whose more or less professional opinions he was able to absorb, revise and put into writing. This practice led to the essay he published while still in Dresden, 'Reflections on the Imitation of Greek Works in Painting and Sculpture,' and two supplements.

In this work Winckelmann certainly seems on the right path. The essay contains some superb passages of fundamental importance, and the ultimate goal of art is correctly indicated. However, in subject matter and form, the discussion is so baroque and strange that it would seem impossible to make sense of it without knowing the personalities of the art experts and critics in Saxony at the time and without being aware of their expertise, opinions, inclinations and whims. The work will be incomprehensible to later generations, unless older art lovers who lived closer to the period soon decide to write a description of the conditions which then prevailed, to the extent that such an undertaking is still feasible.

Men like Lippert, Hagedorn, Oeser, Dietrich, Heinecken and Österreich loved, practiced and promoted art, each in his own way. Their goals were limited, their principles one-sided, and quite often peculiar. Their writings abounded with stories and anecdotes that were meant to be entertaining as well as instructive. Winckelmann adopted this method and style, but he himself soon found what he wrote inadequate, a fact he readily admitted to his friends.

Finally, though insufficiently prepared but with some practical experience, he made his way to Italy, the land where true education begins for the truly receptive. It is an experience which suffuses one's entire being and produces effects that are not only harmonizing but tangible as well, because subsequently it can form a strong common bond among people of quite different character.

Rome

Now Winckelmann was in Rome, and who could have been more receptive to the impact of that great experience! His wishes were fulfilled, his happiness established, his hopes more than realized. He saw his ideas embodied in the sculptures around him. In amazement he walked among the remains of an age of splendor. Here the most magnificent works of art of all time stood in the open, and he beheld these miracles as if gazing at the stars, free of charge. And for a token fee every private treasure opened up for him. Like a pilgrim, the new arrival walked around quietly and unnoticed; humbly dressed, he approached the most magnificent and most sacred works. He did not yet pay attention to the impact of individual objects, but their overall effect was endlessly varied, and he already anticipated the harmony that would ultimately and inevitably grow out of their many, often seemingly incompatible elements. He examined and contemplated everything, and was taken for an artist, an error which made his enjoyment even greater and which, after all, flatters anyone.

Instead of continuing our observations, we would like to share with our readers the impressive words which a friend used to describe the powerful effect of his own experience in Rome:

"Rome is the place where all of antiquity converges into one, for us to see. What we feel when we read ancient literature or hear about ancient forms of government, we believe, in Rome, not merely to sense but to experience directly. Just as Homer cannot be compared to other poets, so Rome cannot be compared to any other city, the Roman countryside to any other landscape. For the most part, however, this impression is subjective, not objective. And yet it is more than the sentimental notion of standing at the spot where some great man stood. A powerful force is pulling us into the past which we perceive as nobler and more sublime, though that might simply be a necessary delusion. Even if we wanted, we could not resist this force because the desolation, which the present inhabitants do nothing to prevent, and the unbelievable amount of rubble make us take refuge in imagination. In these surroundings the past appears to our mind with a greatness that makes envy impossible and which we are overjoyed at perceiving, in the only way we can, in our imagination. At the same time, our eyes actually see with absolute clarity the lovely forms, the grandeur and simplicity of the figures, the rich vegetation (though not as luxuriant as further south), the clean outlines in the clear air, and the beauty of the colors. Thus enjoyment of nature is here pure enjoyment of art, perfect and complete. Anywhere else, modern associations interfere with this enjoyment, and it becomes sentimental or intellectual. To be sure, this impression is also subjective. Horace thought Tibur more modern than we find Tivoli today, as is shown by his words: 'Happy he who is far from the throng.' But it is only a delusion to want to be inhabitants of Athens and Rome. We should experience antiquity only from a distance, as isolated from everything ordinary and as something irrevocably past—a feeling a friend and I have when we see ruins. We are always annoyed when a half-buried ruin is excavated. At most, that may benefit scholarship, but at the expense of imagination. There are only two things I dread: if they cultivate the Campagna di Roma, and if they make Rome into an orderly city where no one would carry a knife anymore. If ever

889

such a strict pope comes along (which, I pray, the seventy-two cardinals will prevent!), I shall leave. Only if Rome remains a city of divine anarchy and the area around it such a heavenly wilderness will there be room for the shadows of the past, one of which is worth more than this whole present generation."

Mengs

If Winckelmann had not had the good fortune to meet Mengs so soon, he would have groped for a long time among the ancient remnants in search of works most worthy of study. Mengs' great talent was concentrated on ancient works, and especially those of great beauty, and he immediately acquainted his friend with outstanding examples meriting particular attention. From them Winckelmann learned about beauty of form and style and was immediately inspired to write a treatise, 'On the Taste of Greek Artists.'

If we are at all seriously concerned with works of art, we soon become aware that they are not only produced by different artists, but also in different periods, and that we have to study location, age and the individual talent simultaneously. Hence Winckelmann with his direct way of thinking came immediately to the conclusion that here was the crucial point in the consideration of all art. At first, he addressed works of the highest order, examples of which he intended to present in a study, "On the Style of Sculpture During the Age of Phidias." But he soon went beyond the particular and developed the concept of a history of art. Like a new Columbus, he discovered a new world, long surmised, interpreted and discussed—a world, we can say, which was previously known and had been lost.

It is always saddening to realize that the disorder caused first by the Romans and later by the invasion of peoples from the north, brought the human race to such a pass that the growth of genuine culture was long stunted and even came close to being destroyed for all time.

No matter which branch of art or knowledge we look at, we find that the logical, right perception of the ancient mind had already discovered many things which were later lost because of barbarism and the barbaric means used to free oneself from this barbarism. The things thus lost will remain so to most people for years to come, since high culture in the modern age needs time to make its impact generally felt.

We are not speaking of skills, which mankind fortunately uses without asking where they came from or where they lead.

Our observations are prompted by passages in some ancient authors, where we find preliminary thinking about, and even suggestions for, a history of art which they evidently considered possible and necessary.

Velleius Paterculus noted with great interest a similar pattern of rise and fall in all the arts. As a man who knew about life he was especially intrigued by the observation that the arts are able to remain only a short time at the peak of their development. From the perspective of his time he was not able to see art as a living organism *(zōon)* which has imperceptible beginnings, slow growth, a brilliant moment of perfection, and gradual decline, and that in this respect, art as a whole is like any other being, except that its various stages can only be found separately. Hence Paterculus cites just human factors as a cause in the process, which of course cannot be excluded, but which did not satisfy his keen intelligence because he was quite aware that a pattern was involved which could not be assembled from random pieces.

"That grammarians, painters and sculptors have shared the fate of orators will be discovered by anyone who examines the evidence through the ages. Excellence in any branch of art is found within a very short span of time. I have often wondered why a number of similar-minded, talented artists appear during the same period and gravitate towards the same type of art. I can find no reasons that I consider convincing, but among likely reasons the following are the most important. Emulation serves as nourishment for artists; envy or admiration induces them to imitate; soon what they have produced with such diligence attains the highest level. Yet it is difficult to remain there for long, and whatever cannot progress, must regress. Thus in the beginning we try to catch up with those ahead of us; but when we give up hope of surpassing or even catching up with them, effort fades together with hope. What we cannot obtain we no longer want to pursue, nor do we strive to possess what others have already laid hold of. We look for something new, we abandon what we cannot excel in and seek a different goal. This vacillation, it seems to me, is the greatest obstacle to producing great works."

A passage in Quintilian containing a succinct outline for a history of ancient art also deserves to be singled out as an important contribution to the subject.

Quintilian too, from his conversations with Roman art lovers, may very well have discovered that there was a striking resemblance between the character of Greek artists and of Roman orators, and he may, therefore, have sought more information from experts and connoisseurs. As a result of his studies, and given his comparative approach which made clear that the character of an art coincided with the character of its time, he ended up outlining a history of art, but without knowing or planning to do so.

"It is said that the first painters whose works were admired not solely for their antiquity were Polygnotos and Aglaphon. Their simple colors are still much valued by some who prefer primitive works and the rudimentary stages of a developing art to the greatest masters of the following period—a curious preference, in my opinion.

"Later, Zeuxis and Parrhasius, near contemporaries at the time of the Peloponesian War, did much for the progress of art. Zeuxis is said to have introduced the use of highlights and shading, Parrhasius to have undertaken an intensive study of line. In addition, Zeuxis gave the limbs more substance, made them fuller and more distinctive. It is believed that he followed Homer's example in this, who liked ample forms in women. Parrhasius defined everything meticulously: they call him the lawmaker because his gods and heroes are considered models to be followed now and in the future.

"Painting flourished from the time of Philip of Macedon to the time of Alexander's successors, but was practiced by artists with varied talents. Protogenes excelled in meticulousness, Pamphilus and Melanthius in organization, Antiphilus in lightness of touch, Theon the Samian in strange creations called phantasies, and Apelles in wit and grace. Euphranor is still highly regarded because he was among the best in general artistic ability and was outstanding in painting as well as sculpture.

"We find the same differences in sculpture. Kalon and Hegesias worked with harder lines, similar to the Tuscans; Kalamis had less severe lines, and Myron's were even softer.

"Polyclitus surpasses others in diligence and elegance. Many consider him the best, although some detractors claim that he lacks substance, for by portraying the human form more delicately than it is in reality, he does not seem to do complete justice to the dignity of the gods. He is even said to have avoided depicting old people and not to have ventured beyond smooth cheeks.

"What Polyclitus lacks, Phidias and Alcamenes purportedly possess. Phidias is supposed to have formed gods and humans superbly and, especially in ivory, to have far surpassed his rival. This would be the opinion had he created nothing but his *Minerva* at Athens or his *Olympian Jupiter* in Elis, a statue whose beauty is said to have benefited the adopted religion, so closely did the majesty of the work approximate that of the god it portrayed.

"It is generally held that Lysippus and Praxiteles reached a high degree of verisimilitude in their works. Demetrius, however, is criticized for going too far and preferring likeness to beauty."

Librarian

It happens rarely that a man is fortunate enough to find selfless patrons who are willing to provide the means to further his education. Even those who believe they want the best can only promote what they themselves love and know or, more often, what is useful to them. And so it was Winckelmann's competence in the literary-bibliographical field which drew first Count Bünau's and later Cardinal Passionei's attention to him.

A bibliophile is welcome anywhere, and was so even more at that time, when the desire to collect unusual or rare books was keener and library science not yet a common pursuit. A large German library resembled a large Roman library and was comparable in the size of its holdings. The librarian of a German count was a welcome companion for a cardinal, and the companion in turn felt at ease with his host. Libraries then were veritable treasure troves, whereas today, with the rapid advance of the sciences and the both purposeful and purposeless piling up of material, they are more in the nature of useful storerooms or useless attics. As a result, a librarian, much more than formerly, has reason to stay abreast of developments in the sciences and be aware of the relative value of what is published. Furthermore, a German librarian has to have knowledge that would be of no use in a foreign country.

But only for a short time, and only as long as it was necessary to earn a modest living, did Winckelmann pursue his occupation in the world of books. He also soon lost interest in doing research projects and no longer wanted to compare manuscripts or give information to German scholars who turned to him for advice.

However, his store of knowledge had already earlier helped open up opportunities for him. In their private lives, most Italians, and especially those living in Rome, are for various reasons quite secretive. This secretiveness, this fondness for seclusion, if we may call it that, also prevailed in their literary activities. Unbeknownst to others, many a scholar devoted his life to the study of an important work, without wanting or being able to make his findings public. Also, more frequently than in any other country, there were men who could not be persuaded to commit their opinions and considerable knowledge to writing, much less to publish them. Winckelmann soon found access to such men. Among them he mentions especially Giacomelli and Baldani, and he expresses his pleasure about his ever-widening circle of acquaintances and his growing influence.

Cardinal Albani

Winckelmann was especially fortunate to become companion to Cardinal Albani who, because of his considerable wealth and influence, was in a position to satisfy his great love for collecting art, a passion he had acquired early in life and which, together with almost miraculous good fortune as a collector, had resulted in an outstanding collection. In his later years he took great pleasure in arranging it for exhibition, hoping to emulate those Roman families who in former times had been aware of the worth of such treasures. He even followed the ancient custom of filling the exhibition area with a superabundance of art works. In building after building, wing after wing and hall after hall there were fountains and obelisks, caryatids and bas-reliefs; statues and vessels filled every corner in court and garden, and small and large rooms, galleries and cabinets contained the most unusual artifacts from all periods.

We mentioned that the ancients filled their public places in much the same way. For example, the Romans overloaded the Capitol in a manner we find hard to believe, and the Via Sacra, the Forum, the Palatine were so overcrowded with buildings and monuments that it is difficult to imagine how great numbers of people also found room to live there. But the excavated cities make the true picture clear and let us see with our own eyes how narrow, small, almost model-sized the buildings were. This applies as well to Hadrian's villa, although he had enough space and means to build something on a larger scale.

When Winckelmann left the Cardinal's villa, the place which furthered his education in a most gratifying manner, it displayed similar superabundance. It remained this way long after the Cardinal's death, an object of pleasure and admiration until it was robbed of every treasure during that time of upheaval and disruption. The statues were taken from their niches and pedestals, the bas-reliefs were torn from the walls, and the huge collection was packed for transport. Due to some unexpected change of fortune, these treasures only got as far as the Tiber. After a short while they were returned to the owner, and most of them, except for a few jewels, are again at the original site. Had he lived, Winckelmann might have witnessed this dismantling of an art paradise and its restoration caused by a strange turn of events. But fortunately he was already beyond earthly suffering, and earthly joy, which is not always sufficient compensation.

Good Fortune

Winckelmann met with much good fortune during his life. Not only was he in Rome when the excavation of ancient artifacts was at its height, but there were also the discoveries at Herculaneum and Pompeii, some of which were new, some of which did not become known until then because of professional envy, secrecy and delay. Thus Winckelmann benefitted from a rich harvest which challenged him intellectually and provided an outlet for his scholarly interests.

It is sad to have to think of anything as final and complete. Old armories, galleries and museums to which nothing is added are like mausoleums haunted by ghosts. Such a limited circle of art limits our thinking. We get accustomed to regarding such collections as complete, instead of being reminded through ever new additions that in art, as in life, we have nothing that remains finished and at rest, but rather something infinite in constant motion.

Winckelmann found himself in such a fortunate situation. The earth relinquished its treasures, and a lively trade in art objects brought many old possessions to light which aroused his interest, excited his mind and increased his knowledge as they filed past his eyes.

Of no small advantage to him was his relationship with the heir to the great Stosch estate. Only after Stosch's death did Winckelmann get to know this little empire of art, and he ruled there according to his wisdom and convictions. To be sure, not the same degree of concern was shown for all parts of this extremely valuable collection, the whole of which deserved to be catalogued for the enjoyment and use of later generations. Some items were sold off cheaply. However, in order to publicize the superb collection of engraved gems and attract potential buyers, Winckelmann and the Stosch heir started cataloguing that part. The letters pertaining to this undertaking give interesting testimony of the hasty and yet always intelligent way the project was handled.

Our friend took an active part in breaking up this collection, just as he had done in increasing and assembling the Albani collection. Whether his task was to gather or dispose of works of art, everything passing through his hands expanded the treasure accumulating in his mind.

Writings

At that time in Dresden when Winckelmann first came into contact with art and artists and was a novice in this field, he was already an accomplished writer. He had a good grasp of history and the sciences in many respects. Even in his lowly position, he had a sense and understanding of antiquity and recognized what was of value in his own time, in life and in the individual. He had developed his own style, and when he entered the domain of art he was not merely an eager student but already a learned disciple of his masters. He absorbed their special knowledge quickly and soon found ways of putting it to practical use.

Even later, in a setting artistically richer than in Dresden, when a higher intellectual plane had become accessible to him, he did not change. The things he heard from Mengs, or learned from his new environment, he did not keep to himself for long, did not let the new wine ferment and become clear. He exemplified the saying that you learn by doing, and learned by drafting projects and by writing. How many titles has he left for us, how many subjects he named about which he intended to write! His whole antiquarian career resembled this beginning. We always find him active, occupied with the moment, seizing and holding on to it, as if to something complete and satisfying. And he approached the next moment in a similar way. Knowing this, we are in a better position to evaluate his works.

That they appear in the form we have them today, either in manuscript or fixed in print for posterity, is due to numerous minor circumstances. Had Winckelmann been able to work one month longer on any one of them, we would have a somewhat different work, more correct in content, more definite in form, perhaps something altogether different. For this very reason we regret his premature death, since he would always have revised his writings, incorporating his most recent experiences.

And so, everything he wrote is alive and meant for the living, not for worshippers of the written word. His works, in conjunction with his letters, are a portrayal of life, a living thing. Like the lives of most people, they resemble a first draft, not a finished work. They fill us with hopes, wishes, presentiments. If we attempt to improve them we realize that we ourselves have to improve. If we attempt to criticize them we realize that the same criticism, perhaps on a different level, might apply to us. For limitation is our lot everywhere.

Philosophy

As culture progresses, not all human endeavors and activities concerned with the various fields of learning thrive equally. Rather, depending on a favorable disposition of individuals and on circumstances, one discipline may outpace the other and stimulate more general interest, which causes a certain displeasure among the members of this elaborate family who often get on less well the more closely related they are.

It is usually a baseless complaint of scholars in this or that discipline who bemoan the fact that their field is neglected by their contemporaries. For a capable master need only show himself to attract attention. If Raphael were to appear today he would be assured an abundance of honors and wealth. A capable master draws good students, and their activities in turn branch out indefinitely.

Yet philosophers have always been the special object of hatred, not only of their fellow scholars but also of the more practical people of the world, a hatred for which their situation is perhaps more to blame than they are themselves. For since philosophy by nature addresses itself to the ordinary as well as the sublime, it has to treat worldly things as part of, indeed as subordinate to, itself.

One does not explicitly deny philosophy this presumptuous claim, but everyone believes himself entitled to share in its discoveries, to apply its principles and use whatever else it may have to offer. However, in order to become universal, philosophy has to employ its own terms, strange correlations and peculiar preambles, which do not quite coincide with the current circumstances of people in general or their needs of the moment. Philosophy is then reviled by those who cannot immediately find a means of grasping it.

On the other hand, if one were inclined to make a case against philosophers, one could say that they are themselves unsure of finding the transition to life, and that precisely where they wish to put their convictions into practice they are most prone to error, thereby diminishing their credibility with the world. There is certainly no lack of evidence as grounds for such accusations.

Winckelmann complained bitterly about the philosophers of his time and their extensive influence. But surely one can avoid influences simply by withdrawing into one's own specialty. It strikes us as curious that Winckelmann did not enroll in the Leipzig Academy where, under the guidance of Professor

Christ, he would have found it easier to pursue his major field without paying heed to any philosophers.

But in the light of events in modern times, an observation confirmed by experience is appropriate here, namely that no scholar has been able to reject or oppose or scorn with impunity the great philosophical movement initiated by Kant. The only exception is perhaps the true scholar of antiquity, who because of the peculiar quality of his specialty seems specially privileged.

By occupying himself exclusively with the best the world has produced and by comparing humbler, even inferior things to those excellent achievements alone, his erudition reaches such a high level, his judgment becomes so authoritative, his taste develops such consistency, that within his own area of competence he appears admirably, even astonishingly well trained.

Winckelmann was fortunate to become one of these scholars; of course, life and art had aided him immeasurably on his way.

Poetry

Although Winckelmann did not neglect the poets when he read ancient writers, upon closer examination of his studies and his life we detect no real inclination for poetry. On the contrary, we may say that here and there an actual dislike is noticeable. His fondness for traditional Lutheran hymns and his desire to have an authentic collection of them, even in Rome, suggest a good solid German but hardly a genuine lover of poetry.

The ancient poetic works seem to have interested him at first as documents of old languages and literature, later as source material for his study of the plastic arts. It is all the more surprising and gratifying then to see him emerge as a poet himself, and one with unmistakable talent, in his descriptions of statues and in almost all his later writings. He saw with his eyes, and grasped with his mind, works of art that defy description, and yet he felt the irresistible urge to reveal their essence in words. The utter perfection of a work, the idea which gave birth to its artistic form, the feeling its presence aroused in him—all this he wanted to convey to listener and reader. And in surveying his store of capabilities he saw himself compelled to reach for the most powerful and most effective available. He had to be a poet, whether he was aware of it, whether he wanted to, or not.

Insight Gained

Although Winckelmann was eager to gain the respect of the world, longed for literary fame, sought to make his works attractive and lend them dignity through a certain solemnity of style, he was by no means blind to their shortcomings. Indeed, he noticed them immediately, as was to be expected of anyone bent on improvement and impatient to involve himself in ever new aspects of a subject. The more didactic and dogmatic he had been in an essay, the more he had insisted on this or that elucidation of a monument, the surer he had been of a particular interpretation or meaning of a passage, then the more obvious an error seemed to him, if such was indicated by new data, and the more eager he was to correct it in some way.

If the manuscript was still in his hands, he rewrote it; if it had been sent to the printer, he sent him emendations and addenda. He made no attempt to conceal all these second thoughts from his friends, for his character was rooted in truthfulness, rectitude, directness and sincerity.

Later Works

The *Monumenti Inediti* proved to be a productive project, as Winckelmann came to realize, not all at once but in the course of working on it.

It is quite evident that he was initially motivated by his desire to introduce new subjects and explain them clearly, and to expand the horizons of archeology. In addition, he was interested in testing the method he had already established in his *History of Art* on works which he presented to the reader here. But since he had already gone beyond his *History*, he finally came to the wise decision to make the first part of the *Monumenti* a corrected, edited and condensed version of the *History*, in which he would even refute some of his former views.

Conscious of earlier errors, about which non-Romans had been in no position to offer critical comment, he wrote in Italian so that the work could be judged in Rome. No only did he proceed with great caution, he also consulted experts among his friends with whom he examined the text carefully, making prudent use of their insight and judgment, and so produced a work that will be a legacy for all time. He not only wrote it, he edited it and attended to all the details of publication, including that of cost. An impecunious private citizen accomplished what would have stood a well-established publisher or a number of academicians in good stead.

The Pope

Since we have said so much about Rome, how can we omit mention of the Pope, who was of great help to Winckelmann, at least indirectly?

Winckelmann's stay in Rome coincided with the papacy of Benedict XIV, a cheerful, easygoing man who preferred to let others rule rather than rule himself. It is possible, therefore, that the various positions which Winckelmann held were obtained more through the good offices of his friends in high position than because of the Pope's awareness of his merits.

But on one occasion Winckelmann had an important audience with the head of the Church: he was granted the special distinction of being allowed to read the Pope passages from his *Monumenti Inediti*. And so from this quarter too, Winckelmann gained the highest honor that can accrue to a writer.

Character

Achievement, much more than character, appears to be what is most significant about many people, especially scholars. In Winckelmann, however, the opposite was true. Everything he produced is noteworthy and estimable mainly because his character inevitably revealed itself in the process. In the sections entitled Spirit of Antiquity, Pagan Spirit, Beauty and Friendship, we offered a few general, preliminary remarks on this topic. A closer consideration seems appropriate now as we near the end of our essay.

Winckelmann was a person who was thoroughly honest with himself and others. His innate love of truth increased as he became more self-reliant and independent, until finally he came to see the polite indulgence of error, so common in life and literature, as a crime.

Such an individual could no doubt feel at ease with himself. Yet here too we find that characteristic trait of the ancients: always being occupied with oneself without actually observing oneself. Winckelmann thought only *of* himself, not *about* himself. He was absorbed by the things he intended to do, he was interested in his whole being, the entire scope of his being, and was also confident that his friends shared these interests. We find, therefore, that everything is discussed in his letters, from the highest moral concerns to the most common physical needs. He even admitted he would rather talk about personal trifles than important matters. For all that, he remained a riddle to himself, and was sometimes amazed at his own development, especially when he compared what he had been and what he had become. But then, we may look upon all human beings as elaborate puzzles, able themselves to assemble their picture only in part, whereas outsiders can easily complete it.

Nor do we find in Winckelmann any clearly enunciated principles. In moral and aesthetic matters he was guided by his intuition and his education. He envisioned a sort of natural religion in which God, however, is only the source of beauty and has no other relation to humanity. In matters of duty and gratitude Winckelmann behaved very properly.

While his attention to personal needs was not excessive, and not always consistent, he worked very hard to provide for his old age. The means he employed in the pursuit of his goals were irreproachable, and he showed himself to be honest, upright, even stubborn, yet at the same time prudent and persevering. He never worked according to plan, but on impulse and with passion. The intensity of his joy at every discovery led inevitably to errors, which, given his lively pace of work, he eliminated as quickly as he detected them. Here we have another indication of the antique cast of his character: certainty about the point of departure and uncertainty about the goal, as well as loss of completeness and perfection in the attempt to obtain breadth.

Society

Although Winckelmann was initially not quite at ease in society—ill-prepared as he was by his early years—a sense of dignity soon made up for lack of breeding and manners, and he quickly learned to adapt to circumstances. It is evident everywhere in his letters that he enjoyed the company of elegant, rich and distinguished people and delighted in their esteem. And for easy access to society, he could not have been better off than in Rome.

He himself remarked that people of high standing in Rome, especially the clergy, no matter how ceremonious they might appear in public, were in private informal and comfortable with their companions. However, Winckelmann did not realize that behind this informality lay the oriental relationship of master and servant. Southern peoples would suffer boredom without end if they had to maintain permanently formal relations with members of their circle, as is customary in the north. Travelers have observed that slaves behave much more casually toward their Turkish masters than northern courtiers toward their princes, and, in our own country, subordinates toward their superiors. But upon closer examination we realize that these expressions of respect were actually introduced for the benefit of subordinates, who, by showing respect, always remind their superior of what he owes them.

The southerner, on the other hand, likes to have times when he can be at ease, and that is beneficial to those around him. Winckelmann describes such scenes with great relish. They made it easier for him to bear his dependence, and they encouraged his sense of freedom which was wary of fetters that might threaten it.

Visitors

Winckelmann was very happy in his dealings with the local inhabitants, but he experienced considerable pain at the hands of visitors from abroad. To be sure, nothing is worse than the ordinary tourist in Rome. In any other place, the traveler can go his own way; however those who fail to do as the Romans do are a horror to the true Roman.

The English are ridiculed because they take along their teapots everywhere and even tote them up Mount Etna. But don't all nations take their own teapots along on travels to brew the herbs they brought from home?

Such provincial sightseers—narrow-minded, unobservant, always in a hurry, arrogant—Winckelmann cursed more than once and swore never again to act as their guide, only to relent on the next occasion. He joked about his having to employ schoolmarmish methods to inform and persuade them. Yet he also benefitted considerably from serving as a guide to persons of position and reputation. We mention only the Prince of Dessau, the Hereditary Princes of Mecklenburg-Strelitz and Brunswick, and Baron Riedesel, who in his appreciation of art and antiquity proved completely worthy of our friend.

Achievement

We notice in Winckelmann a relentless striving for esteem and respect, yet he wanted recognition based on accomplishment. He always insisted on substance in subject matter, in expression and in treatment, which explains his strong antipathy for the emphasis of the French on appearances.

Having found opportunity in Rome to associate with visitors of various nationalities, he cultivated these connections with skill and energy. The honors he was awarded by academies and learned societies pleased him, indeed he actively sought them out.

His reputation was enhanced most by a work, written with quiet care, that stands as testimony to his great achievement. I refer to his *History of Ancient Art*, which was immediately translated into French and made its author famous far and wide.

What such a work accomplishes is perhaps best recognized when it first appears. We feel its effect, we enthusiastically embrace what is new and are amazed at how much we benefit from it. Subsequent, less enthusiastic generations, on the other hand, pick critically at the works of their masters and teachers and make demands it would never have occurred to them to make had not those predecessors, of whom ever more is now demanded, achieved so much themselves.

Winckelmann became known to the educated nations of Europe at a moment when he enjoyed sufficient confidence in Rome to be honored with the not unimportant post of Prefect of Antiquities.

Restiveness

Despite that intense happiness which he himself frequently mentioned, he was always plagued by a restlessness which, because it was fundamental in his nature, manifested itself in various ways.

In earlier years he had eked out an existence. Later he lived from the generosity of the court and the favor of many a benefactor, always restricting himself to the most basic needs in order not to become dependent, or more dependent than he already was. Yet he made strenuous efforts to earn his live-lihood and provide for his future, a goal which finally his splendid edition of the *Monumenti* seemed most likely to help him attain.

But the precariousness of his situation had accustomed him to looking here and there for ways of supporting himself, now accepting a minor position in the house of a cardinal, in the Vatican or elsewhere, now grandly resigning if a better prospect was in the offing, all the while looking for other employment and remaining open to various offers.

Furthermore, anyone living in Rome is constantly tempted to travel to other parts of the world. One feels at the center of the ancient world and that the countries of interest to the scholar of antiquity are nearby. Greece, Sicily, Dalmatia, the Peloponnesus, Ionia and Egypt are all there as it were for the taking if one lives in Rome, and arouse from time to time in anyone an im-mense desire to visit them, if like Winckelmann he is born with an urge for visual experience. One's wanderlust is intensified by the many travelers stop-ping over in Rome to prepare for a journey to those lands, sometimes with a purpose in mind, sometimes not. And upon their return, they never weary of telling and writing about the wonders they have experienced in faraway places.

It was natural then for Winckelmann to want to visit all these places, either on his own or in the company of a well-to-do traveler sufficiently able to ap-preciate an informed and gifted companion.

Another cause of this inner restlessness and discontent does honor to his heart: his irresistible desire to be with distant friends. Here we seem to find the focal point of the longing in a man who otherwise was content with his im-mediate surroundings. He saw his friends before his mind's eyes, he conversed with them in letters, he longed for their embrace and wished to relive the days spent in their company.

His longing for those friends in the North intensified when peace was re-stored. He felt pride at the thought of being presented to the great king who had honored him earlier with an invitation to serve him, and he was eager for a reunion with the Prince of Dessau, a serene man of noble character whom Winckelmann considered God's emissary on earth. He wanted to pay his re-spects to the Duke of Brunswick whose great qualities he valued, to personally offer his thanks to the Minister von Münchhausen, a patron of the sciences, and to admire his immortal creation in Göttingen. He also anticipated with pleasure a lively and intimate reunion with his Swiss friends. Such were the allurements that filled his heart and imagination. He had long occupied and entertained himself with such dreams when, at last, he unfortunately yielded to his desires and set out on the journey which was to end in his death.

But he was already so completely devoted to Italian life that any other life seemed unbearable. When he had first traveled to Rome, the rocky, mountain-ous terrain of Tyrol had interested and even delighted him. Now, on the way back he felt as if he were being dragged to his fatherland through a Cimmerian gate. He became so beset with anxiety that he found the idea of continuing his trip impossible.

Last Journey

When Winckelmann departed this earth, he had reached the highest level of happiness he could have wished for. His fatherland awaited him, his friends eagerly anticipated his arrival; the expressions of love and friendship which he needed so much and the bestowal of public honors he valued so highly—all that was about to be lavished on him. In this sense we may perhaps consider him fortunate to have gone on to Elysium from the pinnacle of human existence, to have been taken from us after only momentary shock and brief pain. He did not have to experience the decrepitude of age and the waning of his mental powers, did not have to actually witness the dispersal of art treasures which he had predicted, although in a different sense. He lived like a man and departed a complete human being. Now he has the advantage of being remembered by posterity as one eternally enterprising and vigorous. For a human being wanders among the shades in the form in which he left this world, just as Achilles remains for us the eternally striving youth. Yet we too derive benefit from Winckelmann's untimely departure. From his grave comes a reminder of his strength which fortifies us and arouses the urgent need to continue forever with love and dedication what he has begun.

MYRON'S COW
(1818)

About 400 B.C., a Greek sculptor named Myron made a bronze cast of a cow. Cicero reports having seen the statue in Athens, and in the seventh century Procopius saw it in Rome. Thus, for over a thousand years the work had attracted attention. Although considerable information concerning this statue has come down to us, none of it is of much help in forming a clear idea of the original. Even more surprising is the fact that some thirty-six epigrams on the subject are not more useful in this respect either and are only worthy of note as examples of the kind of confusion which poetically inclined viewers can cause. These epigrams are dull and neither descriptive nor informative, and for this reason tend to be more misleading than helpful when used as a basis for visualizing and defining the lost bronze. The named and unnamed authors seemingly tried to outdo each other in producing rhythmic pleasantries rather than address themselves seriously to the work itself. The best they can say is that they feel compelled to extol the statue's remarkable realism. But such praise by dilettantes is highly suspect.

It was certainly not Myron's goal to achieve a realism that vies with nature. As a direct successor of Phidias and Polyclitus, he had loftier aspirations. He portrayed athletes, and even Hercules, and was no doubt able to lend a style to his works which set them apart from anything found in nature.

It is safe to assume that in antiquity no work gained fame which did not reveal superior creativity. For it is creativity that delights the connoisseur as well as the general public. How then did Myron manage to turn a cow into an important and significant work of art which attracted and fascinated so many through the centuries?

To be sure, all epigrams praise the statue's realism and naturalness, and the poets rival each other in assuring us that it would be easy to mistake the bronze cow for a real one. A lion is tempted to attack it, a bull to mount it, a calf to nurse from it, a herd to follow it. A herdsman tries to drive it on by throwing a stone and whipping it and blowing his horn. A peasant gets harness and plow for the cow to work in the field. A thief wants to steal it, a horsefly alights on it, and even Myron himself cannot distinguish it from the other cows in the herd.

Obviously the poets were trying to surpass each other in empty rhetorical flourishes. What the cow actually looked like and what it did remains obscure. It is even described as lowing—the very thing to make it realistic! Yet a lowing cow, if it were possible to portray it as a piece of sculpture, is such a base and, what is more, undefined motif that the high-minded Greek could not possibly have used it.

That it is a base subject is obvious to everyone. But it is also undefined and insignificant, for the cow may low yearning for the pasture, the herd, the bull, its calf, the stable, the milkmaid, and who knows what else. To be sure, the epigrams do not say that it actually lowed, only that it would low if it had lungs, just as it would move if it were not cast in bronze on a pedestal.

Perhaps we can reach our goal of visualizing the work despite these obstacles if we disregard all the misleading assumptions the epigrams make about the cow, and try to focus on the actual sculpture.

Either as complement or as contrast to the cow, it is impossible to imagine a lion, a bull, a herdsman, the rest of the herd, a peasant, a thief or a horsefly. But there is one living creature the artist could have permitted to associate with the cow, indeed the only suitable one—a calf. It was a nursing cow because only a nursing cow has significance for the herdowner, as a symbol of propagation and nourishment, as a provider of milk and calves.

If we eliminate all the misleading attributes with which the poets tried to embellish the statue (perhaps without ever having seen it), we are still left with some epigrams which explicitly mention that it was a cow with a calf, a nursing cow.

> Myron the wanderer created a cow; a calf, upon seeing her
> Approached to be nursed, believing that she was its mother.

Poor calf! Why come you to me with such pitiful bleating?
Art did not furnish my udder with milk.

Were we to doubt the specific description in these two epigrams and maintain that the calf, just like the other fictitious companions, was only a poetic adornment, we could find irrefutable confirmation in the following:

O herdsman, shun the cow and let your flute be still,
So that her calf may nurse in peace.

The word flute probably refers to the horn the herdsman sounds to move his herd, but he is not to sound it near this cow, for she must not be disturbed. The calf is not imaginary, but actually perceived by the poet and addressed as a living being, like the cow.

If all doubts are now eliminated and we are on the right track, having separated the true attributes from the fanciful ones, the sculptural adornments from the poetic ones, how much more delighted we are to see our theory confirmed and our efforts crowned by the existence of an illustration handed down from antiquity. It has been frequently reproduced on coins from Dyrrhachium and is identical in its major features on all of them. We enclose a sketch and would wish that a skillful artist would create the relief portrait once again as a statue.

Since the magnificent work is now accessible, even though as an inexact reproduction, I need not point out the excellence of the composition at length. The cow, sturdy on her legs as if on pillars, provides with her splendid body protection for the nursing calf. The hungry young creature is sheltered as if in a niche, a cell, a sanctuary, and occupies with utmost grace the space that is organically defined by the cow's body. The half-kneeling position is reminiscent of a supplicant. The upturned head, both pleading and receiving, the gentle effort, the restrained vigor—everything is faintly suggested in the best of these copies, but it must have been perfect beyond imagination in the original. And now the mother turns her head towards the center, and the whole composition is perfectly rounded and complete. It attracts our attention and holds our interest, so that we do not want to, and indeed cannot, imagine anything else outside or next to it. For, like any true work of art, it excludes and momentarily eliminates anything extraneous.

The compositional talent revealed in this work—the balance to be found in apparent imbalance, the contrast to be found in things which are similar, the harmony to be found in things which are dissimilar, and everything which defies expression in words—that is what the sculptor should strive for. But here we dare say that it was the naiveté of the concept, and not naturalism in execution, which delighted all of antiquity.

Nursing is animal behavior, and in four-footed animals a very graceful act. The passive, uncomprehending amazement of the nursing mother and the vigorous, purposeful activity of the offspring offer a magnificent contrast. A foal, already grown to considerable size, still kneels down to be able to obtain the desired nourishment by energetic sucking. The mare, half irritated, half relieved, turns her head, and this movement results in the most intimate scene. City dwellers rarely have the opportunity to see a cow nursing her calf or a mare her foal. Yet during a walk on a spring day we may observe this act with delight in ewes and lambs, and I urge every art and nature lover to pay more attention to such scenes in pastures and fields.

But to return to our sculpture. I think we can generalize and say that animals, individually or in groups, are effective as artistic subjects if the artist depicts them from the side to which the head is turned, because our attention is focused there. For this reason, such portrayals are suited for statues and paintings, as well as bas-reliefs. That explains why Myron's cow could be so perfectly reproduced even on coins.

From animal statuary, rightly held in high esteem, we turn to the gods. It would have been impossible for a Greek sculptor to represent a goddess in the act of nursing a child. The poet, on the other hand, who describes Juno suckling Hercules is not to be censured, since he produces such a superb effect by having the Milky Way created from the milk the divine mother has spilled. The sculptor, however, must reject such subjects. To have Juno or Pallas Athena in marble, bronze or ivory together with a baby son would have demeaned their divine majesty. In high antiquity, Venus, because of her girdle the eternal virgin, has no son. To be sure, Eros, Amor and Cupid, products of an earlier time, appear in the company of Aphrodite, yet they do not seem closely related to her.

At most, beings of lower rank in the mythological hierarchy, such as mortal heroines, nymphs and fauns, who were assigned the roles of nursemaids and tutors, may be portrayed tending a child. For example, Jupiter himself was nursed by a nymph or, as was sometimes said, by a goat, and other gods and heroes were similarly raised in a remote wilderness. Amalthea and Chiron and many others come to mind as examples.

Sculptors have best demonstrated their fine artistic sense and taste by portraying the animal activity of nursing in semihuman subjects. Zeuxis' centaur family is a splendid example. The centaur woman is reclining on the grass, suckling her youngest hybrid offspring while another is being nursed by a mare, and the father in the background displays his prey, a young lion. A family portrait of water-gods, a lovely engraved gem, has also been preserved, probably an imitation of one of Skopa's famous groups.

A triton couple calmly wades through the waves, with one of their offspring, half fish, half boy, cavorting in the water in front of them. Another, disliking perhaps the taste of salty water after having nursed, clamors for his mother to pick him up, which she does while clasping the youngest to her breast. We can hardly imagine anything more graceful, in concept and in execution.

We pass over many similar examples by which the ancients have taught us what excellent subjects nature provides on all levels, whether her head touches the heavens where the gods reside, or her feet the earth where the animals dwell.

There is still one other subject that we must not omit: the Roman she-wolf. No matter how it is depicted, even in the crudest imitation, it is always a source of great pleasure. Two children of heroes receive their nourishment from the full teats of the wild beast, and the savage creature of the forest gazes maternally at her adopted children. Human beings in most intimate contact with a wild animal, a ferocious monster as their mother and nurse—we can certainly expect a miraculous effect on the world from such a miracle. It may well be that the legend was first conceived by an artist who recognized the sculptural potential of such a scene.

But how weak, in comparison with such a grandiose concept, appears a madonna and child. . . .

The Greeks' goal is to deify man, not humanize gods—it is theomorphism, not anthropomorphism! Furthermore, the animal in man is not to be ennobled, but rather the human element in animals emphasized, so that we can delight in them in a higher, artistic sense. After all, we already do this with real animals which, following an irresistible instinct, we are fond of choosing as our companions and servants.

Returning once more to Myron's cow, we would like to mention our speculation that the sculptor portrayed a young cow who has calved for the first time, and furthermore, that the statue may have been less than life-size.

We repeat what we said above, namely that an artist like Myron would not have attempted to outdo nature for the purpose of crude deception, but rather that he knew how to perceive the essence of nature and express it. Because his work communicates itself in an absolutely natural way, we can forgive the ordinary viewer or the dilettante, the orator or the poet, if they see as pure nature what in reality is the product of the highest, deliberate art, namely the harmonious effect which makes the viewer's mind and senses focus on one point. But it would be unforgivable if we maintained even for one moment that the high-minded artist Myron, the successor of Phidias and the predecessor of Praxiteles, lacked artistic insight and grace of expression in creating his statue.

In conclusion we take the liberty of quoting some modern epigrams which refer to this work. The first is by Ménage, who describes Juno as being jealous of this cow because she sees in it a second Io. This worthy poet of modern times was the first to notice how many idealized animal figures there were in antiquity and, what with all the love affairs and metamorphoses, how well they were suited to facilitate encounters between gods and humans. This is an important artistic concept which we should note in judging works from that period. Ménage's lines are as follows:

ON LITERATURE AND ART

When she observed your small cow, the bronze one, O Myron, Juno
grew jealous, believing her Inachus' daughter.

And lastly, a few rhythmic lines which may give a summary of our view:

That you are most splendid and could be the jewel of Admetos' herd;
That you seem to come from the drove of the sungod himself:—All this
fills me with wonder and moves me to praise of the artist. But that you
can also show motherly feelings—that touches my soul.

ON WORLD LITERATURE

1. National literature is no longer of importance; it is the time for world
literature, and all must aid in bringing it about.

2. Everywhere we read and hear about the progress of the human race, of
good prospects for the future regarding relations among nations and human
beings. Whatever the situation may be in this respect—which is beyond my
province to judge or investigate—I wish nonetheless to point out to my friends
that I am convinced that a world literature is beginning to develop, in which
an honorable role is reserved for us Germans. All nations are paying attention
to us; they praise and criticize, accept and reject, imitate and distort, understand or misunderstand us and open or close their hearts to our concerns. We
must accept this with equanimity because it is of great value to us.

3. If we have dared proclaim the beginning of a European, indeed a world
literature, this does not merely mean that the various nations will take note
of one another and their creative efforts, for in that sense a world literature
has been in existence for some time, and is to some extent continuing and developing. We mean, rather, that contemporary writers and all participants in
the literary scene are becoming acquainted and feel the need to take action as
a group because of inclination and public-spiritedness. However, visits more
than correspondence will bring this about, since only personal contact can
establish and solidify true relationships.

4. Every nation has idiosyncracies which differentiate it from others and
make it feel isolated from, attracted to or repelled by them. The outward
manifestations of these idiosyncracies usually seem strikingly repugnant, or
at best ridiculous, to another nation. They also are the reason why we tend
to respect a nation less than it deserves. The true character of a nation, on
the other hand, is seldom recognized or understood, not by outsiders or even
the nation itself. Nations, like human beings, are unaware of the workings of
their inner nature, and ultimately we are surprised, even astounded at what
emerges.

I do not pretend to know these secrets, nor would I have the courage to
define them if I did. I wish only to say that in my opinion the characteristic

traits are now most evident in the French nation, and for that reason it will again exert a great influence on the civilized world.

5. [In reply to a letter from a recently founded literary society in Berlin]

That a group of Germans gathered to take note specifically of German literature was completely proper and highly desirable because all of them, as educated men well-informed about other kinds of writings and public affairs in Germany, were indeed qualified to identify and select literature for their intellectual pleasure.

One can say therefore that the literature of another nation cannot be understood and felt without being aware at the same time of its general social conditions.

We can achieve such awareness in part by reading newspapers, which tell us in great detail about public affairs. But that is not enough. We must also discover what attitudes and opinions, what views and judgment critical journals and reviews express regarding their own nation as well as others, especially the German nation. For example, if we wanted to become acquainted with current French literature, we would have to read lectures delivered and published during the last two years, such as Guizot's "Cours de l'histoire moderne," Villemain's "Cours de la littérature française," and Cousin's "Cours de l'histoire de la philosophie." Their views about themselves and about us emerge most clearly there. Even more helpful, perhaps, are the newspapers and journals that appear more frequently, such as *Le Globe, La Revue Française* and the recent daily, *Le Temps*. They are all indispensible if we wish to have a clear picture of the ebb and flow of the ever-shifting tides of opinion in France, and their subsequent impact.

German literature, as can be seen from our own dailies and the two latest literary magazines, offers only exclamations, sighs and interjections produced by well-meaning individuals. Views are expressed according to temperament and education. There is hardly any concern for more universal or loftier matters. Almost no mention is made of social conditions, not much of the national state of mind and none of the concerns of church and state. We do not wish to criticize these practices, but draw attention to them for what they are. I mention them to point out that French literature, like all forms of French writing, does not for one instant isolate itself from the life and passions of the whole nation: in recent times this appears as an encounter of opposing forces, mustering all talent to assert themselves and defeat the other side. It stands to reason that the established power need not be very imaginative in its response.

But if we follow the course of these lively exchanges of views, we gain an insight into French affairs. And from the way they speak about us, whether favorably or unfavorably, we learn to judge ourselves; it can certainly do no harm if for once someone makes us think about ourselves.

Frankly, I believe more is gained by this than by entering into correspondence with foreign poets. The best of them still remain individuals limited by their particular circle, and if we like their work, they can do little more than say a gracious thank-you. If we should criticize their writings, our relationship is immediately severed.

But if we follow the course proposed above, we will soon be well informed of everything that has been or will be published. Considering the efficiency of today's book trade, any work is readily obtainable. It happens frequently that I have read a book long before I receive a courtesy copy from the author.

Anyone will agree that gaining a real understanding of modern French literature is obviously no small task. The literature of England and Italy would in turn require special approaches, for the conditions there are quite different.

6. But if such a world literature develops in the near future—as appears inevitable with the ever-increasing ease of communication—we must expect no more and no less than what it can and in fact will accomplish.

The world at large, no matter how vast it may be, is only an expanded homeland and will actually yield in interest no more than our native land. What appeals to the multitude will spread endlessly and, as we can already see now, will be well received in all parts of the world, while what is serious and truly substantial will be less successful. However, those who have devoted themselves to higher and more fruitful endeavors will become more easily and more intimately acquainted. Everywhere in the world there are men who are concerned with what has already been achieved and, using that as a basis, with working toward the true progress of mankind. But the course they take and the pace they maintain is not to everyone's liking. The more forceful members of society want to move faster and therefore reject and prevent the furtherance of the very things which could aid their own advancement. The seriousminded must therefore form a silent, almost secret congregation, since it would be futile to oppose the powerful currents of the day. But they must maintain their position tenaciously until the storm has subsided.

Such men will find their main consolation, even their ultimate encouragement in the fact that what is true is at the same time useful. Once they themselves have discovered this connection and can demonstrate it convincingly, they will not fail to have a strong impact, and what is more, for years to come.

7. Although it may be appropriate not to present our thoughts to the reader directly, but rather indirectly to awaken and stimulate his own thinking, it may be advisable to re-examine the above remarks, written some time ago.

The question whether this or that occupation is truly useful is often asked. It is especially relevant at the present when people are no longer permitted to live as they like, quietly, contented, with moderation and free from pressure. The world is in such a turbulent state that every individual is in danger of being sucked into its vortex. In order to satisfy his own need, he finds himself compelled to attend directly and promptly to the needs of others. The question remains whether he has adequate skills to fulfill these pressing obligations.

At this point, all we can do is tell ourselves that only egotism pure and simple can save us. But this egotism requires a confident, considered and calmly formulated decision.

Everyone should ask himself for what he is best suited and develop this talent with the utmost diligence. He should consider himself first an apprentice, later a journeyman, a foreman, and only in the very end and most tentatively, a master.

If with prudent modesty he increases his demands on the world in strict conjunction with the growth of this abilities and thus ingratiates himself by being useful, he will step by step attain his purpose, and once he succeeds in reaching the top will be able to lead a comfortable, productive life.

If he is attentive, life will teach him about the opportunities and obstacles offered and created by the empirical world. But this much the practical individual should always bear in mind: to drive oneself frantically in order to gain the approval of the day brings no advantage for the morrow or the day after.

8. The extravagances to which the theaters of the great and vast city of Paris feel themselves driven prove harmful to us too, although we have by no means reached that point yet. But there we have also the results of an advancing world literature, and our only consolation is that although the general effect is harmful, certain individuals will derive great benefit from it. I have seen convincing evidence of that already.

9. The phenomenon which I call world literature will come about mainly when the disputes within one nation are settled by the opinions and judgments of others.

10. For some time there has been talk of world literature, and properly so. For it is evident that all nations, thrown together at random by terrible wars, then reverting to their status as individual nations, could not help realizing that they had been subject to foreign influences, had absorbed them and occasionally become aware of intellectual needs previously unknown. The result was a sense of goodwill. Instead of isolating themselves as before, their state of mind has gradually developed a desire to be included in the free exchange of ideas.

11. Poetry is cosmopolitan, and the more interesting the more it shows its nationality.

On Philosophy and Science

ON GRANITE
(1784)

Even in antiquity granite was recognized as a mineral worthy of note and it has drawn increased attention in modern times. The ancients knew it under another name; they called it *syenite* after Syene, a town located on the border of Ethiopia. The colossal masses of this stone served to inspire the Egyptians with the idea of creating monumental works. Their kings erected obelisks of it to honor the Sun, and because of its variegated red color it was soon named "the stone with flecks of fire." Today the sphinxes, the statues of Memnon, the enormous columns still strike travelers with awe, and in our own time the powerless lord of Rome is even setting up the relics of an ancient obelisk which his omnipotent predecessors brought intact from foreign soil.

Modern observers have given this mineral its present name because of its granular appearance. In the recent past it was subjected to a moment of degradation before attaining the esteem in which informed scientists now hold it: the tremendous masses of those obelisks and the extraordinary variations in their granularity misled an Italian scientist into believing that the Egyptians had molded them artificially from a fluid mass.

But that view was soon abandoned, and the honor of this mineral was finally restored by a number of observant travelers. Every journey into uncharted mountains reaffirmed the long-standing observation that granite is the loftiest and deepest-lying substance, that this mineral, which modern research has made easier to identify, forms the fundament of our earth, a fundament upon which all other mountains rest. It lies unshakably in the deepest bowels of the earth; its high ridges soar in peaks which the all-surrounding waters have never risen to touch. This much we know of granite, and little else. Composed of familiar materials, formed in mysterious ways, its origins are as little to be found in fire as they are in water. Extremely diverse in the greatest simplicity, its mixtures are compounded in numberless variety. The position and relationship of its elements, its durability and its color vary from peak to peak, and the rock masses of each peak often exhibit variations every few feet although the whole remains homogeneous. And thus anyone who knows the fascination natural mysteries hold for man will understand why I have departed from my usual realm of observation and turned with passionate fervor to this one. I do not fear the accusation that a contrary spirit has led me away from my consideration and depiction of the human heart, the youngest, most diverse, most fluid, most changeable, most vulnerable part of creation, and has brought me to the observation of the oldest, firmest, deepest, most unshakable son of nature. It is evident that all things in nature have a clear relationship to one another, and that the questing spirit resists being denied what it can attain. I have suffered and continue to suffer much through the inconstancy of human opinion, through its sudden changes in me and in others, and I may be forgiven my desire for that sublime tranquillity which surrounds us when we stand in the solitude and silence of nature, vast and eloquent with its still voice. Let those who are aware of this feeling follow me on my journey.

Filled with these thoughts I approach you, the most ancient and worthiest monuments of time. As I stand high atop a barren peak and survey the wide expanse below, I can say to myself: "Here you stand upon ground which reaches right down into the deepest recesses of the Earth; no younger strata, no pile of alluvial debris comes between you and the firm foundation of the primal world. What you tread here is not the perpetual grave of those beautiful, fruitful valleys; these peaks have never given birth to a living being and have never devoured a living being, for they are before all life and above all life."

In this moment, when the inner powers of the Earth seem to affect me directly with all their forces of attraction and movement, and the influences of heaven hover closer about me, I am uplifted in spirit to a more exalted view of nature. The human spirit brings life to everything, and here, too, there springs to life within me an image irresistible in its sublimity.

"This mood of solitude," I say to myself as I gaze down from the barren peak and glimpse a faint patch of low-growing moss far below, "this mood of solitude will overcome all who desire to bring before their souls only the deepest, oldest, most elemental feeling for the truth. Such a one may truly say to himself: 'Here, on this primal and everlasting altar raised directly on the ground of creation, I bring the being of all beings a sacrifice. I feel the first and most abiding origin of our existence; I survey the world with its undulating valleys and its distant fruitful meadows, my soul is exalted beyond itself and above all the world, and it yearns for the heavens which are so near.'"

But soon the burning sun will bring back thirst and hunger, the human necessities. Our observer's gaze will seek out the very valleys over which his spirit had soared. He will envy the dwellers in those more abundant and plentifully watered plains, the inhabitants who have built their happy homes on the debris and ruin of error and opinion, who scratch in the dust of their ancestors and quietly meet the modest needs of their daily existence within those narrow confines. With these thoughts as an overture his soul will make its way into centuries past and recall all that was noted by careful observers, all that was imagined by fiery spirits.

"This crag," I tell myself, "rose more steeply, more sharply, higher into the clouds when its summit still stood as a sea-girt isle in the ancient waters. Round about it streamed the spirit which moved on the face of the waters; in the vast depths the taller peaks were shaped from the debris of primeval mountains, while newer and more distant mountains were formed from the ruins of those peaks and the remains of what lived in the depths. Now the moss has started to spread, the shell-covered creatures of the sea become fewer, the water recedes, the taller peaks grow green, everywhere life begins to burgeon.

"But soon new scenes of devastation clash with this life. Raging volcanoes rise up in the distance, seeming to threaten the world with destruction. Yet the bedrock of my refuge remains unshaken, while those who live on distant shores and islands are buried beneath the faithless land."

I return from these far-ranging thoughts and view the very rocks which have brought exaltation and assurance to my soul by their presence. I see their bulk shot through with cracks, here rising straight up, there askew, sometimes sharply layered, sometimes in formless heaps as though thrown together. At first glance I am tempted to exclaim: "Nothing here is in its primal, ancient state; everything is ruin, chaos, and destruction!" This is exactly the opinion we will meet when we turn from direct observation of these mountains and retreat to the library to delve into the books of our predecessors. Here we will find it asserted that the primeval mountains are an indivisible whole, seemingly cast in a single piece, or that they are divided by fissures into layers and strata which are crisscrossed by innumerable veins of rock; sometimes it is said that this mineral is not stratified, but occurs in individual masses which are intermixed in a completely irregular fashion, while another observer claims to have found strong stratification alternating with muddled confusion. How can we harmonize all these contradictions and find a guidepost for our further investigations?

This is a task which I presently intend to undertake. Though I may not be as fortunate in this as I would hope, my efforts will afford others the opportunity to go further—even errors in observation can serve to cultivate the quality of alertness and give those with sharp eyes reason to use them. Here, however, an admonition may be warranted, less for Germans than for those in other lands to whom this treatise might find its way. Learn how to distinguish this mineral clearly from other varieties. To this day the Italians confuse fine-grained granite with a type of lava, and the French confuse it with gneiss, which they call foliated granite or second-order granite. In fact even we Germans, as conscientious as we usually are in such things, have until recently confused granite with a useless rock chiefly found among layers of schist, a conglomerate of quartz and varieties of hornstone, as well as with the graywacke of the Harz mountains, a younger mixture of quartz and schist particles.

A STUDY BASED ON SPINOZA
(c. 1785)

The concepts of being and totality are one and the same; when pursuing the concept as far as possible, we say that we are conceiving of the infinite.

But we cannot think of the infinite, or of total existence.

We can conceive only of things which are finite or made finite by our mind; i.e., the infinite is conceivable only insofar as we can imagine total existence—but this task lies beyond the power of the finite mind.

The infinite cannot be said to have parts.

Although all finite beings exist within the infinite, they are not parts of the infinite; instead, they partake of the infinite.

We have difficulty believing that something finite might exist through its own nature. Yet everything actually exists through its own nature, although conditions of existence are so linked together that one condition must develop from the other. Thus it seems that one thing is produced by another, but this is not so—instead, one living being gives another cause to be, and compels it to exist in a certain state.

Therefore being is within everything that exists, and thus also the principle of conformity which guides its existence.

The process of measuring is a coarse one, and extremely imperfect when applied to a living object.

A living thing cannot be measured by something external to itself; if it must be measured, it must provide its own gauge. This gauge, however, is highly spiritual, and cannot be found through the senses. Even in the circle the gauge of the diameter may not be applied to the periphery. There have been attempts to measure the human being mechanically: painters have chosen the head as the best portion to use for a unit of measurement. But this cannot be done without creating tiny, indefinable distortions in the other parts of the body.

The things we call the parts in every living being are so inseparable from the whole that they may be understood only in and with the whole. As we stated above, a finite living being partakes of infinity, or rather, it has something infinite within itself. We might better say: in a finite living being the concepts of existence and totality elude our understanding; therefore we must say that it is infinite, just as we say that the vast whole containing all beings is infinite.

The things which enter our consciousness are vast in number, and their relations—to the extent the mind can grasp them—are extraordinarily complex. Minds with the inner power to grow will begin to establish an order so that knowledge becomes easier; they will begin to satisfy themselves by finding coherence and connection.

Thus all of existence and totality must be made finite in our minds so that it conforms to our nature and our way of thinking and feeling. Only then will we say that we understand something, or enjoy it.

The mind may perceive the seed, so to speak, of a relation which would have a harmony beyond the mind's power to comprehend or experience once the relation is fully developed. When this happens, we call the impression sublime; it is the most wonderful bestowed on the mind of man.

When we find a relation our mind is almost able to follow or grasp as it unfolds, we call the impression great.

We said above that all living things in existence have their relation within themselves; thus we call the individual or collective impression they make on us true—so long as it springs from the totality of their existence. We call the object beautiful when this existence is partially finite so that we grasp it easily, when it is related to our nature so that we grasp it with pleasure.

A similar thing may occur when a person (within the limits of his ability) has formed a whole—be it extensive or scanty—from the relationship of things, when he has finally closed the circle. He then believes that what is most comfortable to think, what brings pleasure, is also what is most sure and certain. Indeed, we often find him gazing with self-satisfied pity on those less easily contented, those who strive to discover and understand further relationships between things divine and human. At every opportunity he lets us know with self-deprecating arrogance: in the realm of truth he has found a certainty exalted beyond any need for proof and understanding. He cannot do enough in proclaiming the enviable peace and joy he feels, and in calling attention to this bliss as the ultimate goal for all. But because he can show neither how he arrived at this conviction nor what its real basis is, he offers little comfort to those seeking instruction. Instead, they will hear repeatedly that their minds must grow ever simpler, that they must focus on one point alone and dismiss all thought of complex and confusing relationships. Only then—but all the more certainly—will they find happiness in a state given freely by God as a gift and special boon.

Indeed, to our way of thinking this limitation is no boon, for a defect cannot be viewed as a boon. But we might see a blessing of nature in the fact that man, who is usually able to achieve only partial concepts, may nonetheless find such satisfaction in his narrowness.

THE METAMORPHOSIS OF PLANTS
(1790)

Introduction

1. Anyone who has paid even a little attention to plant growth will readily see that certain external parts of the plant undergo frequent change and take on the shape of the adjacent parts—sometimes fully, sometimes more, and sometimes less.

2. Thus, for example, the single flower most often turns into a double one when petals develop instead of stamens and anthers; these petals are either identical in form and color to the other petals of the corolla, or still bear visible signs of their origin.

3. Hence we may observe that the plant is capable of taking this sort of backward step, reversing the order of growth. This makes us all the more aware of nature's regular course; we will familiarize ourselves with the laws of metamorphosis by which nature produces one part through another, creating a great variety of forms through the modification of a single organ.

4. Researchers have been generally aware for some time that there is a hidden relationship among various external parts of the plant which develop one after the other and, as it were, one out of the other (e.g., leaves, calyx, corolla, and stamens); they have even investigated the details. The process by which one and the same organ appears in a variety of forms has been called *the metamorphosis of plants.*

5. This metamorphosis appears in three ways: *regular, irregular* and *accidental.*

6. *Regular* metamorphosis may also be called *progressive* metamorphosis: it can be seen to work step by step from the first seed leaves to the last formation of the fruit. By changing one form into another, it ascends—as on a spiritual ladder—to the pinnacle of nature: propagation through two genders. I have observed this carefully for several years, and now propose to explain it in the present essay. Hence, in the following discussion we will consider only the annual plant which progresses continuously from seed to fruiting.

7. *Irregular* metamorphosis might also be called *retrogressive* metamorphosis. In the previous case nature pressed forward to her great goal, but here it takes one or more steps backward. There, with irresistible force and tremendous effort, nature formed the flowers and equipped them for works of love; here it seems to grow slack, irresolutely leaving its creation in an indeterminate, malleable state often pleasing to the eye but lacking in inner force and effect. Our observations of this metamorphosis will allow us to discover what is hidden in regular metamorphosis, to see clearly what we can only infer in regular metamorphosis. Thus we hope to attain our goal in the most certain way.

8. We will, however, leave aside the third metamorphosis, caused *accidentally* and from without (especially by insects). It could divert us from the simple path we have to follow, and confuse our purpose. Opportunity may arise elsewhere to speak of these monstrous but rather limited excrescences.

9. I have ventured to develop the present essay without reference to illustrations, although they might seem necessary in some respects. I will reserve their publication until later; this is made easier by the fact that enough material remains for further elucidation and expansion of this short preliminary treatise. Then it will be unnecessary to proceed in the measured tread required by the present work. I will be able to refer to related matters, and several passages

gleaned from like-minded writers will be included. In particular, I will be able to use comments from the contemporary masters who grace this noble science. It is to them that I present and dedicate these pages.

I. Of the Seed Leaves

10. Since we intend to observe the successive steps in plant growth, we will begin by directing our attention to the plant as it develops from the seed. At this stage we can easily and clearly recognize the parts belonging to it. Its coverings (which we will not examine for the moment) are left more or less behind in the earth, and in many cases the root establishes itself in the soil before the first organs of its upper growth (already hidden under the seed sheath) emerge to meet the light.

11. These first organs are known as *cotyledons*; they have also been called seed lobes, nuclei, seed laps, and seed leaves in an attempt to characterize the various forms in which we find them.

12. They often appear unformed, filled with a crude material, and as thick as they are broad. Their vessels are unrecognizable and scarcely distinguishable from the substance of the whole; they have little resemblance to a leaf, and we could be misled into considering them separate organs.

13. In many plants, however, they are more like the leaf in form. They become flatter; their coloration turns greener when they are exposed to light and air; and their vessels become more recognizable, more like the ribs of a leaf.

14. In the end they appear as real leaves: their vessels are capable of the finest development, and their resemblance to the later leaves prevents us from considering them separate organs. Instead, we recognize them as the first leaves of the stem.

15. But a leaf is unthinkable without a node, and a node is unthinkable without an eye. Hence we may infer that the point where the cotyledons are attached is the first true node of the plant. This is confirmed by those plants which produce new eyes directly under the wings of the cotyledons, and develop full branches from these first nodes (as, for example, in *Vicia faba*).

16. The cotyledons are usually double, and here we must make an observation which will become more important later. The leaves of this first node are often paired whereas the later leaves of the stem alternate; i.e., here parts are associated and joined which nature later separates and scatters. Even more noteworthy is the appearance of the cotyledons as a collection of many small leaves around a single axis, and the gradual development of the stem from its center to produce the later leaves singly; this can be seen quite clearly in the growth of the various kinds of pines. Here a circle of needles forms something like a calyx—we will have occasion to remember this when we come to similar phenomena.

17. We will ignore for the moment the quite unformed, individual nuclei of those plants which sprout with but a single leaf.

18. We will, however, note that even the most leaflike cotyledons are always rather undeveloped in comparison to the later leaves of the stem. Their periphery is quite uniform, and we are as little able to detect traces of serration there as we are to find hairs on their surfaces, or other vessels peculiar to more developed leaves.

II. Development of the Stem Leaves from Node to Node

19. Now that the progressive effects of nature are fully visible, we can see the successive development of the leaves clearly. Often one or more of the following leaves were already present in the seed, enclosed between the cotyledons; in their closed state they are known as plumules. In different plants their form varies in relation to that of the cotyledons and the later leaves; most often they differ from the cotyledons simply in being flat, delicate, and generally formed as true leaves. They turn completely green, lie on a visible node, and are undeniably related to the following stem leaves, although they usually lag behind in the development of their periphery, their edge.

20. But further development spreads inexorably from node to node through the leaf: the central rib lengthens, and the side ribs along it reach more or less to the edges. These various relationships between the ribs are the principal cause of the manifold leaf forms. The leaves now appear serrated, deeply notched, or composed of many small leaves (in which case they take the shape of small, perfect branches). The date palm presents a striking example of such successive and pronounced differentiation in the most simple leaf form. In a sequence of several leaves, the central rib advances, the simple fanlike leaf is torn apart, divided, and a highly complex leaf is developed which rivals a branch.

21. The development of the leaf stalk keeps pace with that of the leaf itself, whether the leaf stalk is closely attached to the leaf or forms a separate, small, easily-severed stalk.

22. In various plants we can see that this independent leaf stalk has a tendency to take on the form of a leaf (e.g., in the orange family). Its structure will give rise to certain later observations, but for the moment we will pass them by.

23. Neither can we enter here into further consideration of the stipules; we will simply note in passing that they share in the later transformation of the stalk, particularly when they form a part of it.

24. Although the leaves owe their initial nourishment mainly to the more or less modified watery parts which they draw from the stem, they are indebted to the light and air for the major part of their development and refinement. We found almost no structure and form, or only a coarse one, in those cotyledons produced within the closed seed covering and bloated, as it were, with a crude sap. The leaves of underwater plants likewise show a coarser

structure than those of plants exposed to the open air; in fact, a plant growing in low-lying, damp spots will even develop smoother and less refined leaves than it will when transplanted to higher areas, where it will produce rough, hairy, more finely detailed leaves.

25. In the same way, more rarefied gases are very conducive to, if not entirely responsible for, the anastomosis of the vessels which start from the ribs, find one another with their ends, and form the leaf skin. The leaves of many underwater plants are threadlike, or assume the shape of antlers; we are inclined to ascribe this to an incomplete anastomosis. This is shown at a glance by the growth of *Ranunculus aquaticus*, where the leaves produced underwater consist of threadlike ribs, although those developed above water are fully anastomosed and form a connected surface. In fact, we can see the transition clearly in the half-anastomosed, half-threadlike leaves found in this plant.

26. Experiments have shown that the leaves absorb different gases, and combine them with the liquids they contain; there is little doubt that they also return these refined juices to the stem, and thereby help greatly in the development of the nearby eyes. We have found convincing evidence for this in our analysis of gases developed from the leaves of several plants, and even from the hollow stems.

27. In many plants we find that one node arises from another. This is easy to see in stems closed from node to node (like the cereals, grasses, and reeds), but not so easy to see in other plants which are hollow throughout and filled with a pith or rather, a cellular tissue. This substance, previously called *pith*, was considered to occupy an important position among the inner parts of the plant, but its importance has recently been disputed, and with good cause in my opinion (Hedwig, *Leipzig Magazine*, no. 3). Its supposed influence on growth has been flatly denied; the force for growth and reproduction is now ascribed wholly to the inner side of the second bark, the so-called liber. Since the upper node arises from the node below, and receives sap from it, we can easily see that the node above must receive a sap which is finer and more filtered; it must benefit from the effect of the earlier leaves, take on a finer form, and offer its own leaves and eyes even finer juices.

28. As the coarser liquids are continually drawn off and the purer ones introduced, as the plant refines its form step by step, it reaches the point ordained by nature. We finally see the leaves in their maximum size and form, and soon note a new phenomenon which tells us that the previous stage is over and the next is at hand, the stage of the flower.

III. Transition to Flowering

29. The transition to flowering may occur quickly or slowly. In the latter case we usually find that the stem leaves begin to grow smaller again, and lose their various external divisions, although they expand somewhat at the base

where they join the stem. At the same time we see that the area from node to node on the stem grows more delicate and slender in form; it may even become noticeably longer.

30. It has been found that frequent nourishment hampers the flowering of a plant, whereas scant nourishment accelerates it. This is an even clearer indication of the effect of the stem leaves discussed above. As long as it remains necessary to draw off coarser juices, the potential organs of the plant must continue to develop as instruments for this need. With excessive nourishment this process must be repeated over and over; flowering is rendered impossible, as it were. When the plant is deprived of nourishment, nature can affect it more quickly and easily: the organs of the nodes are refined, the uncontaminated juices work with greater purity and strength, the transformation of the parts becomes possible, and the process takes place unhindered.

IV. Formation of the Calyx

31. We often find this transformation occurring rapidly. In this case the stem, suddenly lengthened and refined, shoots up from the node of the last fully formed leaf and collects several leaves around the axis at its end.

32. The leaves of the calyx are the same organs which appeared previously as the leaves of the stem; now, however, they are collected around a common center, and often have a very different form. This can be demonstrated in the clearest possible way.

33. We already noted a similar effect of nature in our discussion of the cotyledon, where we found several leaves, and apparently several nodes, gathered together around one point. As the various species of pine develop from the seed, they display a rayed circle of unmistakable needles which, unlike other cotyledons, are already well developed. Thus in the earliest infancy of this plant we can already see a hint, as it were, of the power of nature which is to produce flowering and fruiting in later years.

34. In several flowers we find unaltered stem leaves collected in a kind of calyx right under the flower. Since they retain their form clearly, we can rely on the mere appearance in this case, and on botanical terminology which calls them *folia floralia* (flower leaves).

35. We must now turn our attention to the instance mentioned above, where the transition to flowering occurs slowly as the stem leaves come together gradually, transform, and gently steal over, as it were, into the calyx. This can be observed quite clearly in the calyxes of the compositae, especially in sunflowers and calendulas.

36. Nature's power to collect several leaves around one axis can create still closer connections, rendering these clustered, modified leaves even less recognizable, for it may merge them wholly or in part by making their edges grow

together. The crowded and closely packed leaves touch one another everywhere in their tender state, anastomose through the influence of the highly purified juices now present in the plant, and produce a bell-shaped or (so-called) single-leaf calyx which betrays its composite origins in its more or less deep incisions or divisions. We can see this if we compare a number of deeply incised calyxes with multi-leaved ones, and especially if we examine the calyxes of several compositae. Thus, for example, we will find that a calendula calyx (noted in systematic descriptions as *simple* and *much divided*) actually consists of many leaves grown into one another and over one another, with the additional intrusion, so to speak, of contracted stem leaves (as noted above).

37. In many plants, the arrangement of individual or merged sepals around the axis of the stalk is constant in number and form; this is also true of the parts which follow. Biological science, which has developed significantly in recent years, has relied heavily on this consistency for its growth, stability, and reputation. The number and formation of these parts is not as constant in other plants, but even this inconsistency has not deceived the sharp eyes of the masters in this science; through exact definition they have sought to impose stricter limits, so to speak, on these aberrations of nature.

38. This, then, is how nature formed the calyx: it collected several leaves (and thus several nodes) around a central point, frequently in a set number and order; elsewhere on the plant these leaves and nodes would have been produced successively and at a distance from one another. If excessive nourishment had hampered flowering, they would have appeared in separate locations and in their original form. Thus, nature does not create a new organ in the calyx; it merely gathers and modifies the organs we are already familiar with, and thereby comes a step closer to its goal.

V. *Formation of the Corolla*

39. We have seen that the calyx is produced by refined juices created gradually in the plant itself. Now it is destined to serve as the organ of a further refinement. Even a simple mechanical explanation of its effect will convince us of this. For how delicate and suited for the finest filtration must be those tightly contracted and crowded vessels we have seen!

40. We can note the transition from the calyx to the corolla in several ways. Although the calyx is usually green like the stem leaves, the color of one or another of its parts often changes at the tip, edge, back, or even on the inner surface of a part where the outer surface remains green. We always find a refinement connected with this coloration. In this way, ambiguous calyxes arise which might equally well be called corollas.

41. In moving up from the seed leaves, we have observed that a great expansion and development occurs in the leaves, especially in their periphery; from

here to the calyx, a contraction takes place in their circumference. Now we note that the corolla is produced by another expansion; the petals are usually larger than the sepals. The organs were contracted in the calyx, but now we find that the purer juices, filtered further through the calyx, produce petals which expand in a quite refined form to present us with new, highly differentiated organs. Their fine structure, color, and fragrance would make it impossible to recognize their origin, were we not able to get at nature's secret in several abnormal cases.

42. Within the calyx of a carnation, for example, there is often a second calyx: one part is quite green, with a tendency to form a single-leaf, incised calyx; another part is jagged, with tips and edges transformed into the delicate, expanded, colored, true beginnings of petals. Here we can again recognize the relationship between corolla and calyx.

43. The relationship between the corolla and the stem leaves is also shown in more than one way, for in several plants the stem leaves show some color long before the plant approaches flowering; others take on full coloration when flowering is near.

44. Sometimes nature skips completely over the organ of the calyx, as it were, and goes directly to the corolla. We then have the opportunity to observe how stem leaves turn into petals. Thus, for example, an almost fully formed and colored petal often appears on tulip stems. It is even more remarkable when half of this leaf is green and attached as part of the stem, while its other, more colorful half rises up as part of the corolla, thereby dividing the leaf in two.

45. It is probable that the color and fragrance of the petals are attributable to the presence of the male germ cell. Apparently it is still insufficiently differentiated in these petals, where it is combined and diluted with other juices. The beautiful appearance of the colors leads us to the notion that the material filling the petals has attained a high degree of purity, but not yet the highest degree (which would appear white and colorless).

VI. Formation of the Stamens

46. This becomes even more probable when we consider the close relationship between the petals and the stamens. Were the relationship between the other parts so striking, well-known, and undeniable, there would be no need for this discourse.

47. Sometimes nature shows us this transition in an orderly way (e.g., in the canna and other plants of this family). A true petal, little changed, contracts at its upper border, and an anther appears, with the rest of the petal serving in place of the filament.

48. In flowers which frequently become double we can observe every step of this transition. Within the fully formed and colored petals of several rose

species there appear others which are partly contracted in the middle and partly at the side. This contraction is the result of a small thickened wale which somewhat resembles a perfect anther; the leaf likewise begins to assume the simpler form of a stamen. In some double poppies, fully formed anthers rest on almost unaltered petals in the corolla (which is completely double); in others, the petals are more or less contracted by antherlike wales.

49. If all the stamens are transformed into petals, the flowers will be seedless; but if stamens develop even when a flower becomes double, fructification may occur.

50. Thus a stamen arises when the organs, which earlier expanded as petals, reappear in a highly contracted and refined state. This reaffirms the observation made above: we are made even more aware of the alternating effects of contraction and expansion by which nature finally attains its goal.

VII. Nectaries

51. However rapid the transition from corolla to stamens in many plants, we nonetheless find that nature cannot always achieve this in a single step. Instead, it produces intermediate agents which sometimes resemble the one part in form and purpose, and sometimes the other. Although they take on quite different forms, almost all may be subsumed under one concept: they are gradual transitions from the petals to the stamens.

52. Most of these variously formed organs (which Linnaeus calls nectaries) may be subsumed under this concept. Here we are again bound to admire the intelligence of that extraordinary man: without any clear understanding of their purpose, he followed his intuition and ventured to use one name for such seemingly different organs.

53. Some petals show their relationship to the stamens without any perceptible change in form: they contain tiny cavities or glands which secrete a honeylike juice. In the light of our previous discussion, we may infer that this is an undeveloped and incompletely differentiated fluid of fertilization; our inference will be further justified in the discussion to follow.

54. The so-called nectaries may also appear as independent parts; these sometimes resemble the petals in form, and sometimes the stamens. Thus, for example, the thirteen filaments (each with a tiny red ball) on the nectaries of *Parnassia* have a striking resemblance to stamens. Other nectaries appear as stamens without anthers (as in *Val-lisneria* or *Fevillea*); in *Pentapetes* we also find them, in leaf form, alternating with the stamens in a whorl; in addition, systematic descriptions describe them as *filamenta castrata petaliformia*. We find equally unclear formations in *Kiggelaria* and the passion flower.

55. The word *nectary* (in the sense indicated above) seems equally applicable to the distinctive secondary corolla. The formation of petals occurs by

expansion, but secondary corollas are formed by contraction (i.e., in the same way as the stamens). Within full, expanded corollas we therefore find small, contracted secondary corollas, as in the narcissus, *Nerium*, and *Agrostemma*.

56. We see even more striking and remarkable changes in the leaves of other species. At the base of the leaf in some flowers we find a small hollow filled with a honeylike juice. This little cavity is deeper in other species and types; it creates a projection shaped like a spur or horn on the back of the leaf, thus producing an immediate modification in the form of the rest of the leaf. We can observe this clearly in different types and varieties of the columbine.

57. This organ is most transformed in the aconite and *Nigella*, for example, but even here its resemblance to the leaf is not hard to see. In *Nigella*, especially, it has a tendency to form again as a leaf, and the flower becomes double with the transformation of the nectaries. Careful examination of the aconite will show the similarity between the nectaries and the arched leaf under which they are hidden.

58. We said above that the nectaries are transitional forms in the change from petal to stamen. Here we can make a few observations about irregular flowers. Thus, for example, the five outer leaves of *Melianthus* might be called true petals, but the five inner leaves could be described as a secondary corolla consisting of six nectaries; the upper nectary is closest to the leaf in form, while the lower one (now called a nectary) is least like the leaf. In the same sense, we might say that the carina of the papilionaceous flowers is a nectary: of all the flower's leaves, it most resembles the stamens in form, and is quite unlike the leaf form of the so-called vexilla. This also explains the brushlike appendages attached to the end of the carina in some species of *Polygala*, and thus it gives us a clear idea of the purpose these parts serve.

59. It should be unnecessary to state here that these remarks are not intended to confuse the distinctions and classifications made by earlier observers and taxonomists. Our only purpose is to help explain variations in plant form.

VIII. Further Remarks on the Stamens

60. Microscopic examination has shown beyond a doubt that the plant's reproductive organs are brought forth by spiral vessels, as are the other organs. We will use this to support the argument that the different plant parts with their apparent variety of forms are nonetheless identical in their inner essence.

61. The spiral vessels lie amid the bundles of sap vessels, and are enclosed by them. We can better understand the strong force of contraction mentioned earlier if we think of the spiral vessels (which really seem like elastic springs) as extremely strong, so that they predominate over the expansive force of the sap vessels.

62. Now the shortened vessel bundles can no longer expand, join one another, or form a network by anastomosis; the tubular vessels which usually

fill the interstices of the network can no longer develop, and there is nothing left to cause the expansion of stem leaves, sepals, and petals; thus a frail, very simple filament arises.

63. The fine membranes of the anther are barely formed, and the extremely delicate vessels terminate between them. Previously the vessels grew longer, expanded, and joined one another, but now we will assume that these same vessels are in a highly contracted state. We see a fully formed pollen emerge from them; in its activity this pollen replaces the expansive force taken from the vessels which produced it. Now released, it seeks out the female parts which the same effect of nature brings to meet it; it attaches itself to these parts, and suffuses them with its influence. Thus we are inclined to say that the union of the two genders is anastomosis on a spiritual level; we do so in the belief that, at least for a moment, this brings the concepts of growth and reproduction closer together.

64. The fine matter developed in the anthers looks like a powder, but these tiny grains of pollen are just vessels containing a highly refined juice. We therefore subscribe to the view that this juice is absorbed by the pistils to which the pollen grains cling, thereby causing fructification. This is made even more likely by the fact that some plants produce no pollen, but only a liquid.

65. Here we recall the honeylike juice of the nectaries, and its probable relationship to the fully developed liquid of the pollen grains. Perhaps the nectaries prepare the way; perhaps their honeylike liquid is absorbed by the pollen grains, and then further differentiated and developed. This opinion is made more plausible by the fact that this juice can no longer be seen after fructification.

66. We will not forget to mention in passing that the filaments grow together in a variety of ways, as do the anthers. They offer the most wonderful examples of what we have often discussed: the anastomosis and union of plant parts which were, at first, strictly separate.

IX. Formation of the Style

67. Earlier I tried to make as clear as possible that the various plant parts developed in sequence are intrinsically identical despite their manifold differences in outer form. It should come as no surprise that I also intend to explain the structure of the female parts in the same way.

68. We will first examine the style apart from the fruit (as often found in nature). This will be all the easier since it is distinct from the fruit in this form.

69. We observe, then, that the style is at the same stage of growth as the stamens. We noted that the stamens are produced by a contraction; this is also true of the styles, and we find that they are either the same size as the stamens, or only a little longer or shorter in form. In many instances the style looks almost like a filament without anthers; the two resemble one another in external form more

than any of the other parts. Since both are produced by spiral vessels, we can see plainly that the female part is no more a separate organ than the male part. When our observation has given us a clearer picture of the precise relationship between the female and male parts, we will find that the idea of calling their union an anastomosis becomes even more appropriate and instructive.

70. We often find the style composed of several individual styles which have grown together; its parts are scarcely distinguishable at the tip, and sometimes not even separate. This is the most likely stage for this merger to occur; we have often mentioned its effects. Indeed, it must occur because the delicate, partially developed parts are crowded together in the center of the blossom, where they can coalesce.

71. In various cases of regular metamorphosis, nature gives a more or less clear indication of the close relationship between the style and the previous parts of the blossom. Thus, for instance, the pistil of the iris, with its stigma, appears in the full form of a flower leaf. The umbrella-shaped stigma of *Sarracenia* shows (although not so clearly) that it is composed of several leaves, and even the green color remains. With the aid of the microscope we will find the stigma of several flowers formed as full single-leaved or multi-leaved calyxes (e.g., the crocus; or *Zannichellia*).

72. In retrogressive metamorphosis nature frequently shows us instances where it changes the styles and stigmas back into flower leaves. *Ranunculus asiaticus*, for example, becomes double by transforming the stigmas and pistils of the fruit vessel into true petals, while the anthers just behind the corolla are often unchanged. Several other noteworthy cases will be discussed later.

73. Here we will repeat our earlier observation that the style and the stamens are at the same stage of growth; this offers further evidence for the basic principle of alternation in expansion and contraction. We first noted an expansion from the seed to the fullest development of the stem leaf; then we saw the calyx appear through a contraction, the flower leaves through an expansion, and the reproductive parts through a contraction. We will soon observe the greatest expansion in the fruit, and the greatest concentration in the seed. In these six steps nature steadfastly does its eternal work of propagating vegetation by two genders.

X. Of the Fruits

74. Now we come to the fruits. We will soon realize that these have the same origin as the other parts, and are subject to the same laws. Here we are actually speaking of the capsules formed by nature to enclose the so-called covered seeds, or, more precisely, to develop a small or large number of seeds by fructification within these capsules. It will not require much to show that these containers may also be explained through the nature and structure of the parts discussed earlier.

75. Retrogressive metamorphosis again makes us aware of this natural law. Thus, for example, in the pinks—these flowers known and loved for their irregularity—we often find that the seed capsules are changed back into leaves resembling those in the calyx, and the styles are accordingly shortened. There are even pinks in which the fruit capsule is completely transformed into a true calyx. The divisions at the tips of the calyx still bear delicate remnants of the styles and stigmas; a more or less full corolla develops instead of seeds from the very center of this second calyx.

76. Even in regular and constant formations, nature has many ways of revealing the fruitfulness hidden in a leaf. Thus an altered but still-recognizable leaf of the European linden produces a small stalk from its midrib, and grows a complete flower and fruit on this stalk. The disposition of blossoms and fruits on the leaves of *Ruscus* is even more remarkable.

77. In the ferns we see still stronger—we might even say enormous—evidence of the sheer fruitfulness inherent in the stem leaves: these develop and scatter innumerable seeds (or rather, germs) through an inner impulse, and probably without any well-defined action by two genders. Here the fruitfulness of a single leaf rivals that of a wide-spreading plant, or even a large tree with its many branches.

78. With these observations in mind, we will not fail to recognize the leaf form in seed vessels—regardless of their manifold formations, their particular purpose and context. Thus, for example, the pod may be viewed as a single, folded leaf with its edges grown together; husks, as consisting of leaves grown more over one another; and compound capsules may be understood as several leaves united round a central point, with their inner sides open toward one another and their edges joined. We can see this for ourselves when these compound capsules burst apart after maturation, for each part will then present itself as an open pod or husk. We may also observe a similar process taking place regularly in different species of the same genus: the fruit capsules of *Nigella orientalis*, for instance, are partially merged pods grouped around an axis; but in *Nigella damascena* they are fully merged.

79. Nature masks the resemblance to the leaf mainly by forming soft, juicy seed vessels, or hard, woody ones. But this similarity will not escape our attention if we know how to follow it carefully through all its transitions. Here we will have to be content with having given a description of the general concept along with several examples of nature's consistent behavior. The great variety in seed capsules will provide material for a great many other observations in the future.

80. The relationship between the seed capsules and the previous parts also appears in the stigma, situated right on top of the seed capsule and inseparably joined to it. We have already demonstrated the relationship of the stigma to the leaf form, and here we may note it again: in double poppies we find that the stigmas of the seed capsules are changed into delicate, colored leaflets which look exactly like petals.

81. The last and most pronounced expansion in the growth of the plant appears in the fruit. This expansion is often very great—even enormous—in inner force as well as outer form. Since it usually occurs after fertilization, it seems likely that as the developing seed draws juices from the entire plant for its growth, the flow of these juices is directed into the seed capsule. The vessels of the seed capsule are thereby nourished and expanded, often becoming extremely gorged and swollen. It can be inferred from our earlier discussion that purer gases play a part in this, an inference supported by the discovery that the distended pods of *Colutea* contain a pure gas.

XI. Of the Coverings Lying Next to the Seed

82. By way of contrast, the seed is in the most extreme state of contraction and inner development. In various plants we can observe that the seed transforms leaves into an outer covering, adapts them more or less to its shape, and often has the power to annex them fully, completely changing their form. We saw above that many seeds can develop in and from a single leaf; hence it will come as no surprise to find a single embryo clothed in a leaf covering.

83. We can see the traces of such incompletely adapted leaf forms in many winged seeds (e.g., the maple, the elm, the ash, and the birch). The calendula's three distinct rings of differently formed seeds offer a remarkable example of how the embryo pulls broad coverings together, gradually adapting them to its shape. The outer ring is still related to the petals in form, except that a rudimentary seed swells the rib, causing a fold in the leaf; a small membrane also runs lengthwise along the inside of the crease, dividing the leaf in two. The next ring shows further changes: the broad form of the leaf has entirely disappeared, along with the membrane; but its shape is somewhat less elongated, while the rudimentary seed on the back has become more visible, and the small raised spots on the seed have grown more distinct. These two rows appear to be either unfructified or only partially fructified. They are followed by a third row of seeds in their true form: strongly curved, and with a tightly fitted involucre which is fully developed in all its ridges and raised portions. Here we again see a powerful contraction of broad, leaflike parts, a contraction produced by the inner power of the seed, just as we earlier saw the flower leaf contracted by the power of the anthers.

XII. Review and Transition

84. Thus we have sought to follow as carefully as possible in the footsteps of nature. We have accompanied the outer form of the plant through all its transformations, from the seed to the formation of a new seed; we have investigated

the outer expression of the forces by which the plant gradually transforms one and the same organ, but without any pretense of uncovering the basic impulses behind the natural phenomena. So as not to lose the thread which guides us, we have limited our discussion entirely to annual plants; we have noted only the transformation of the leaves accompanying the nodes, and have derived all the forms from them. But to lend our discussion the required thoroughness, we must now speak of the eyes hidden beneath each leaf; under certain circumstances these develop, and under others they seem to disappear entirely.

XIII. Of the Eyes and their Development

85. Nature has given each node the power to produce one or more eyes; this process takes place near its companion leaves, which seem to prepare the way for the formation and growth of the eyes, and help in their production.

86. The primary, simple, slow process of plant reproduction is based on the successive development of one node from the other, and the growth of an eye close to it.

87. We know that such an eye is similar to the ripe seed in its effect; in fact, we can often recognize the whole shape of the potential plant more easily in the eye than in the seed.

88. Although the root point is hard to find in the eye, it is just as much there as in the seed, and will develop quickly and easily, especially in the presence of moisture.

89. The eye needs no cotyledon because it is connected to the fully-developed parent plant, and receives adequate nourishment as long as the connection remains. Once separated, it will draw nourishment from the plant to which it is grafted, or from the roots developed as soon as a branch is planted in the earth.

90. The eye consists of more or less developed nodes and leaves which have the task of enhancing the future growth of the plant. Thus the side branches growing from the nodes of the plant may be considered separate small plants placed on the parent in the same way that the parent is attached to the earth.

91. The two have often been compared and contrasted, most recently in such an intelligent and exact way that we will simply refer to it here with our unqualified admiration (Gaertner, *De fructibus et seminibus plantarum*, Chapt. I).

92. We will say only the following on this point. Nature makes a clear distinction between eyes and seeds in plants with a highly differentiated structure. But if we descend to plants with a less differentiated structure, the two become indistinguishable, even for the sharpest observer. There are seeds which are clearly seeds, and gemmae which are clearly gemmae, but it takes an act of reason rather than observation to find the connection between the seeds, which are actually fertilized and separated from the parent plant by the

reproductive process, and the gemmae, which simply grow out of the plant and detach without apparent cause.

93. With this in mind, we may conclude that the seeds are closely related to the eyes and gemmae, although they differ from the eyes in being enclosed, and from the gemmae in having a perceptible cause for their formation and separation.

XIV. Formation of Composite Flowers and Fruits

94. Thus far we have focused on the transformation of nodal leaves in our attempt to explain the development of simple flowers, as well as the production of seeds enclosed in capsules. Closer examination will show that no eyes form in these cases, and moreover, that the formation of such eyes is utterly impossible. We must look to the formation of eyes, however, to explain the development of composite flowers or compound fruit arranged around a single cone, a single spindle, a single disk, etc.

95. Certain stems do not gradually prepare the way for a single flower by saving their energies; instead, they produce their flowers directly from the nodes, and frequently continue this process without interruption to their very tip. This phenomenon may be explained, however, through the theory presented earlier. All flowers developed from the eyes must be considered whole plants situated on the parent, just as the parent is situated on the earth. Since they now receive purer juices from the nodes, even the first leaves of the tiny twig appear much more fully developed that the first leaves (following the cotyledons) of the parent; in fact, it is often possible to develop the calyx and flower immediately.

96. With an increase in nourishment, the flowers developed from the eyes would become twigs; they are necessarily subject to the same conditions as the parent stem, and share in its fate.

97. As these flowers develop from node to node, we also find that the stem leaves undergo the same changes seen previously in the gradual transition to the calyx. They contract more and more, finally disappearing almost completely, and they are called bracts when their form has become somewhat different from a leaf. The stem likewise grows thinner, the nodes crowd closer together, and all the phenomena noted earlier take place, but there is no decisive formation of a flower at the end of the stem because nature has already exercised its rights from node to node.

98. Having examined the stem adorned with a flower at every node, we will soon arrive at an explanation of the *composite flower*, especially if we recall what was said before about the creation of the calyx.

99. Nature forms a composite calyx out of many leaves compacted around a single axis. Driven by the same strong growth impulse, it suddenly develops

an endless stem, so to speak, with all its eyes in the form of flowers and compacted as much as possible; each small flower fertilizes the seed vessel standing ready below. The nodal leaves are not always lost in this enormous contraction; in the thistles, the little leaves faithfully accompany the floret developed from the eye next to them (compare the form of *Dipsacus laciniatus*). In many grasses, each flower is accompanied by such a little leaf (called a glume).

100. Thus we now realize that the seeds developed around a composite flower are true eyes created and formed by the reproductive process. With this concept firmly in mind, we may compare a variety of plants, their growth and their fruits, and find convincing evidence in what we see.

101. Hence, it will not be hard to explain the covered or uncovered seeds produced in the center of a single flower, often in a group around a spindle. For it is all the same, whether a single flower surrounds a common ovary where the merged pistils absorb the reproductive juices from the flower's anthers and infuse them into the ovules, or whether each ovule has its own pistil, its own anthers, and its own petals around it.

102. We are convinced that with a little practice the observer will find it easy to explain the various forms of flowers and fruits in this way. To do so, however, requires that he feel as comfortable working with the principles established above—expansion and contraction, compaction and anastomosis—as he would with algebraic formulas. Here it is crucial that we thoroughly observe and compare the different stages nature goes through in the formation of genera, species, and varieties, as well as in the growth of each individual plant. For this reason alone, it would be both pleasant and useful to have a collection of properly arranged illustrations labeled with the botanical terms for the different parts of the plant. In connection with the above theory, two kinds of proliferous flowers would serve as especially useful illustrations.

XV. Proliferous Rose

103. The proliferous rose offers a very clear example of everything we sought earlier through our power of imagination and understanding. The calyx and corolla are arranged and developed around the axis, but the seed vessel is not contracted in the center with the male and female organs arranged around it. Instead, the stem, half reddish and half greenish, continues to grow, developing a succession of small, dark red, folded petals, some of which bear traces of anthers. The stem grows further; thorns reappear on it; one by one, the colored leaves which follow become smaller; and finally we see them turn into stem leaves, partly red and partly green. A series of regular nodes forms, and from their eyes small but imperfect rosebuds once again appear.

104. This example also gives visible evidence of another point made earlier; i.e., that all calyxes are only contracted *folia floralia*. Here the regular

calyx gathered around the axis consists of five fully developed, compound leaves with three or five leaflets, the same sort of leaf usually produced by rose branches at their nodes.

XVI. *Proliferous Carnation*

105. After spending some time with this phenomenon, we may turn to another which is still more remarkable: the proliferous carnation. We see a perfect flower equipped with a calyx as well as a double corolla and completed in the center with a seed capsule, although this is not fully developed. Four perfect new flowers develop from the sides of the corolla; these are separated from the parent flower by stalks having three or more nodes. They have their own calyxes, and double corollas formed not so much by individual leaves as by leaf crowns merged at the base, or more often by flower leaves which have grown together like little twigs around a stem. Despite this extreme development, filaments and anthers are found in some. We see fruit capsules with styles, and seed receptacles which have grown back into leaves; in one such flower the seed envelopes had joined to create a full calyx containing the rudiments of another perfect double flower.

106. In the rose we have seen a partially defined flower, as it were, with a stem growing again from its center, and new leaves developing on this stem. But in this carnation, with its well-formed calyx, perfect corolla, and true seed capsules in the center, we find that eyes develop from the circle of petals, producing real branches and blossoms. Thus both instances illustrate that nature usually stops the growth process at the flower and closes the account there, so to speak; nature precludes the possibility of growth in endless stages, for it wants to hasten toward its goal by forming seeds.

XVII. *Linnaeus' Theory of Anticipation*

107. If I have stumbled here and there on the path which a predecessor described as terrifying and dangerous, even though he attempted it under the guidance of his great teacher (Ferber, *Diss. de prolepsi plantarum*); if I have not done enough to pave the way for those who follow; if I have not cleared every obstacle from the path—nonetheless, I hope that this effort will not prove altogether fruitless.

108. It is now time to consider a theory proposed by Linnaeus to explain these phenomena. The things discussed here could not have escaped his sharp eyes; if we have made progress where he faltered, it is only because of a concerted effort by other observers and thinkers to clear the way and eliminate prejudice. A full comparison between his theory and the above discussion

would be too time-consuming here. The knowledgeable reader can make the comparison himself, but it would require too much detailed explanation to clarify it here for those who have not yet studied these things.

109. He started with an observation of trees, those complex and long-lived plants. He observed that a tree planted in a wide pot and overfertilized would produce branch after branch for several years, while the same tree in a smaller pot would quickly bear blossoms and fruits. He saw that the successive development of the first tree was suddenly compressed in the second. He called this effect of nature *prolepsis* (anticipation) since the plant seemed to anticipate six years' growth in the six steps noted above. He therefore developed his theory from tree buds; he did not pay much attention to annual plants, for he could see that these did not fit his theory as well. His theory would have us assume that nature really intended every annual plant to grow for six years, but the plant forestalled this maturation period by quickly blossoming, bearing fruit, and then dying.

110. We, however, began by following the growth of annual plants. Our approach is readily applicable to longer-lived plants, for a bud opening on the oldest tree may be considered an annual plant even though it develops on a long-existent stem and may itself last for a longer time.

111. There was a second reason for Linnaeus' lack of progress: he mistakenly viewed the various concentric parts of the plant (the outer bark, the inner bark, the wood, the pith) as similar in their effect, similar in the way they participated in the life of the plant. He identified the various rings of the stem as the source of blossom and fruit because the latter, like the former, enclose one another and develop out of one another. But this was merely a superficial observation which closer examination shows to be false. The outer bark is unsuited to yield anything further; in the long-lived tree it is too separate and too hardened on the outside, just as the wood becomes too hard on the inside. In many trees the outer bark drops away, and in others it can be peeled without causing damage; thus it produces neither calyx nor any other living part of the tree. It is the second bark that contains all the power of life and growth; to the extent it is damaged, the tree's growth is also hindered. After examining all the external parts of the tree, we will discover that this is the part which brings growth gradually in the stem, and quickly in the flower and fruit. Linnaeus assigned it the mere secondary task of producing petals. By contrast, he assigned to the wood the important job of producing stamens, although we can see that the wood is rendered inactive by its solidity; it is durable but too dead to produce life. He supposed the pith to have the most important function: production of the pistils and numerous offspring. Yet doubts about the great importance of the pith seem to me significant and conclusive, as do the reasons for raising them. The style and fruit merely appear to develop from the pith because our first impression is of soft, ill-defined, pithlike, parenchymatous formations gathered together in the center of the stem where we usually see only the pith.

XVIII. Recapitulation

112. I hope that this attempt to explain the metamorphosis of plants may contribute something to the resolution of these doubts, and lead to further findings and conclusions. The observations which serve as the basis for my work were made at various times, and have already been collected and organized (Batsch, *Introduction to the Identification and History of Plants,* Part I, Chapt. 19). It should not be long before we discover whether the step taken here brings us any closer to the truth. We will summarize the principal results of the foregoing treatise as briefly as possible.

113. If we consider the plant in terms of how it expresses its vitality, we will discover that this occurs in two ways: first, through growth (production of stem and leaves); and secondly, through reproduction (culminating in the formation of flower and fruit). If we examine this growth more closely, we will find that as the plant continues from node to node, growing vegetatively from leaf to leaf, a kind of reproduction also takes place, but a reproduction unlike that of flower and fruit; whereas the latter occurs all at once, the former is successive and appears as a sequence of individual developments. The power shown in gradual vegetative growth is closely related to the power suddenly displayed in major reproduction. Under certain circumstances a plant can be made to continue its vegetative growth, and under others the production of flowers can be forced. The former occurs when cruder juices accumulate; the latter, when more rarefied juices predominate.

114. In saying that vegetative growth is successive reproduction, while flowering and fruiting are simultaneous reproduction, we are also describing how each occurs. A vegetating plant expands to some extent, developing a stalk or stem; the intervals between nodes are usually perceptible, and its leaves spread out on all sides. A blossoming plant, on the other hand, shows a contraction of all its parts; the dimensions of length and breadth are canceled out, as it were; all its organs develop in a highly concentrated state and lie next to one another.

115. Whether the plant grows vegetatively, or flowers and bears fruit, the same organs fulfill nature's laws throughout, although with different functions and often under different guises. The organ which expanded on the stem as a leaf, assuming a variety of forms, is the same organ which now contracts in the calyx, expands again in the petal, contracts in the reproductive apparatus, only to expand finally as the fruit.

116. This effect of nature is accompanied by another: the gathering of different organs in set numbers and proportions around a common center. Under certain conditions, however, some flowers far exceed these proportions, or vary them in other ways.

117. Anastomosis also plays a part in the formation of flowers and fruits; the extremely crowded and delicate organs of fructification are merged during the whole of their existence, or at least some part of it.

118. The phenomena of convergence, centering, and anastomosis are not peculiar to flower and fruit alone. We can discover something similar in the cotyledons, and ample material will be found in other parts of the plant for further observations of this sort.

119. We have sought to derive the apparently different organs of the vegetating and flowering plant from one organ; i.e., the leaf normally developed at each node. We have likewise ventured to find in the leaf form a source for the fruits which completely cover their seed.

120. Here we would obviously need a general term to describe this organ which metamorphosed into such a variety of forms, a term descriptive of the standard against which to compare the various manifestations of its form. For the present, however, we must be satisfied with learning to relate these manifestations both forward and backward. Thus we can say that a stamen is a contracted petal or, with equal justification, that a petal is a stamen in a state of expansion; that a sepal is a contracted stem leaf with a certain degree of refinement, or that a stem leaf is a sepal expanded by an influx of cruder juices.

121. We might likewise say of the stem that it is an expanded flower and fruit, just as we assumed that the flower and fruit are a contracted stem.

122. At the conclusion of the treatise I also took the development of eyes into account, and attempted thereby to explain composite flowers as well as uncovered fruits.

123. Thus I have tried to be as clear and thorough as I could in presenting a view I find rather convincing. Nonetheless, the evidence may still seem insufficient, objections may still arise, and my explanations may sometimes not seem pertinent. I will be all the more careful to note any suggestions in the future, and will discuss this material in a more precise and detailed way so that my point of view becomes clearer; perhaps then it will be more deserving of applause than at present.

TOWARD A GENERAL COMPARATIVE THEORY
(1790–94)

When a science falters and comes to a standstill despite the best efforts of many researchers, it can often be seen that the fault lies in a certain traditional concept of things, a conventional terminology, which the great majority accepts and follows unconditionally, and from which even thoughtful people depart only occasionally and under limited circumstances.

To be as clear as possible I will proceed from this general observation directly to the point: the progress of natural philosophy has been obstructed for many centuries by the conception that a living being is created for certain external purposes and that its form is so determined by an intentional primal force. This idea still holds us back, although some have voiced vehement opposition to it and drawn attention to the stumbling blocks it creates.

In itself this way of thinking may be full of piety, give pleasure to people of a certain temperament, and be indispensable for certain ways of thought. I find it neither advisable nor possible to refute it as a whole. It is, if I may say so, a trivial idea; like all such things it is trivial precisely because human nature finds it comfortable and satisfying.

Man is in the habit of valuing things according to how well they serve his purposes. It lies in the nature of the human condition that man must think of himself as the last stage of creation. Why, then, should he not also believe that he is its ultimate purpose? Why should his vanity not be allowed this small deception? Given his need for objects and his use for them, he draws the conclusion that they have been created to serve him. Why should he not resolve the inner contradictions here with a fiction rather than abandon the claims he holds so dear? Why should he not ignore a plant which is useless to him and dismiss it as a weed, since it really does not exist for him? When a thistle springs up to increase his toil in the fields he blames it on the curse of an angry god or the malice of a spiteful demon rather than considering it a child sprung from all of nature, one as close to her heart as the wheat he tends so carefully and values so highly. Indeed it may be noted that even the most just of men, those who believe they are the most selfless, are often able to rise only to the point of expecting all things to benefit man in some indirect form rather than directly, e.g., through the discovery of a natural force which has applications in medicine or some other area.

Moreover, in himself and others he justifiably puts the greatest value on actions and deeds which are intentional and purposeful. It follows that he will attribute intent and purpose to nature, for he will be unable to form a larger concept of nature than of himself.

He further believes that everything that exists is there for him, is there only as a tool and aid to his own existence. It follows as a matter of course that when nature provides tools for him, it acts with an intention and purpose equal to his own in manufacturing them. The sportsman who has a hunting rifle made will praise the forethought shown by Mother Nature in preparing the dog to fetch his prey.

There are other reasons for man's general difficulty in abandoning this concept. However, the simple example of botany will show that the scientist must leave this view behind if he wishes to make progress in thinking about things in general. The brightest and fullest flowers, the most delicious and attractive fruits, have no more value to the science of botany than a lowly weed in its natural setting or a dried and useless seed capsule, and may even be of less value in a certain sense.

Thus the scientist will have to rise above this trivial concept. Even if he cannot rid himself of it as a human being, he must at least make every effort to shed it as a scientist.

Here this observation about the scientist has only a general application. However, another observation based on the first will have a more specific application. In relating all things to himself man is forced to lend these things an inner purpose which is manifested externally, and all the more so because nothing alive can be imagined as existing without a complete structure. Since this complete structure develops inwardly in a fully specialized and specific way, it needs an external environment which is just as specialized. It can only exist in the outer world under certain conditions and in certain contexts.

Thus we find the most varied forms of animal life stirring on the earth, in the water, and in the air. The common view is that these creatures have received their appendages for the purpose of making various movements and thereby supporting their particular form of existence. But will we not show more regard for the primal force of nature, for the wisdom of the intelligent being usually presumed to underlie it, if we suppose that even its power is limited, and realize that its forms are created by something working from without as well as from within? The statement "The fish exists for the water" seems to me to say far less than "The fish exists in the water and by means of the water." The latter expresses more clearly what is obscured in the former; i.e., the existence of a creature we call "fish" is only possible under the conditions of an element we call "water," so that the creature not only exists in that element, but may also evolve there.

The same principle holds true of all other creatures. An initial and very general observation on the outer effect of what works from within and the inner effect of what works from without would therefore be as follows: the structure in its final form is, as it were, the inner nucleus molded in various ways by the characteristics of the outer element. It is precisely thus that the animal retains its viability in the outer world: it is shaped from without as well as from within. And this is all the more natural because the outer element can shape the external form more easily than the internal form. We can see this most clearly in the various species of seal, where the exterior has grown quite fishlike even though the skeleton still retains all the features of a quadruped.

We show disrespect neither for the primal force of nature nor for the wisdom and power of a creator if we assume that the former acts indirectly, and that the latter acted indirectly at the beginning of all things. Is it not fitting that this great force should bring forth simple things in a simple way and complex things in a complex way? Do we disparage its power if we say it could not have brought forth fish without water, birds without air, other animals without earth, that this is just as inconceivable as the continued existence of these creatures without the conditions provided by each element? Will we not attain a more satisfactory insight into the mysterious architecture of the formative process, now widely recognized to be built on a single pattern, by examining and comprehending this single pattern more fully and then looking into the following question: how does a surrounding element, with its various specific characteristics, affect the general form we have been studying? How does the form, both determined and a determinant, assert itself against these elements? What manner of hard parts, soft parts, interior parts, and exterior parts are created in the form by this effect? And, as indicated before, what is wrought by the elements through all their diversity of height and depth, region and climate?

Much research has already been done on these points. This needs only to be brought together and applied, but in accordance with the method described above.

How admirable that nature must use the same means to produce a creature as it does to sustain it! We progress on our path as follows: first we viewed the unstructured, unlimited element as a vehicle for the unstructured being, and now we will raise our observation to a higher level to consider the structured world itself as an interrelationship of many elements. We will see the entire plant world, for example, as a vast sea which is as necessary to the existence of individual insects as the oceans and rivers are to the existence of individual fish, and we will observe that an enormous number of living creatures are born and nourished in this ocean of plants. Ultimately we will see the whole world of animals as a great element in which one species is created, or at least sustained, by and through another. We will no longer think of connections and relationships in terms of purpose and intention. This is the only road to progress in understanding how nature expresses itself from all quarters and in all directions as it goes about its work of creation. As we find through experience, and as the advance of science has shown, the most concrete and far-reaching benefits for man come from an intense and selfless effort which neither demands its reward at week's end like a laborer, nor lies under any obligation to produce some useful result for mankind after a year, a decade, or even a century.

THE EXPERIMENT AS MEDIATOR
BETWEEN OBJECT AND SUBJECT
(1792)

As the human being becomes aware of objects in his environment he will relate them to himself, and rightly so since his fate hinges on whether these objects please or displease him, attract or repel him, help or harm him. This natural way of seeing and judging things seems as easy as it is essential, although it can lead to a thousand errors—often the source of humiliation and bitterness in our life.

A far more difficult task arises when a person's thirst for knowledge kindles in him a desire to view nature's objects in their own right and in relation to one another. On the one hand he loses the yardstick which came to his aid when he looked at things from the human standpoint; i.e., in relation to himself. This yardstick of pleasure and displeasure, attraction and repulsion, help and harm, he must now renounce absolutely; as a neutral, seemingly godlike being he must seek out and examine what is, not what pleases. Thus the true botanist must remain unmoved by beauty or utility in a plant; he must explore its formation, its relation to other plants. Like the sun which draws forth every plant and shines on all, he must look upon each plant with the same quiet gaze; he must find the measure for what he learns, the data for judgment, not in himself but in the sphere of what he observes.

The history of science teaches us how difficult this renunciation is for man. The second part of our short essay will discuss how he thus arrives (and must arrive) at hypotheses, theories, systems, any of the modes of perception which help in our effort to grasp the infinite; the first part of the essay will deal with how man sets about recognizing the forces of nature. Recently I have been studying the history of physics and this point arose frequently—hence the present brief discourse, an attempt to outline in general how the study of nature has been helped or hindered by the work of able scientists.

We may look at an object in its own context and the context of other objects, while refraining from any immediate response of desire or dislike. The calm exercise of our powers of attention will quickly lead us to a rather clear concept of the object, its parts, and its relationships; the more we pursue this study, discovering further relations among things, the more we will exercise our innate gift of observation. Those who understand how to apply this knowledge to their own affairs in a practical way are rightly deemed clever. It is not hard for any well-organized person, moderate by nature or force of circumstance, to be clever, for life corrects us at every step. But if the observer is called upon to apply this keen power of judgment to exploring the hidden relationships in nature, if he is to find his own way in a world where he is seemingly alone, if he is to avoid hasty conclusions and keep a steady eye on the goal while noting every helpful or harmful circumstance along the way, if he must be his own sharpest critic where no one else can test his work with ease, if he must question himself continually even when most enthusiastic—it is easy to see how harsh these demands are and how little hope there is of seeing them fully satisfied in ourselves or others. Yet these difficulties, this hypothetical impossibility, must not deter us from doing what we can. At any rate, our best approach is to recall how able men have advanced the sciences, and to be candid about the false paths down which they have strayed, only to be followed by numerous disciples, often for centuries, until later empirical evidence could bring researchers back to the right road.

It is undeniable that in the science now under discussion, as in every human enterprise, empirical evidence carries (and should carry) the greatest weight. Neither can we deny the high and seemingly creative independent power found in the inner faculties through which the evidence is grasped, collected, ordered, and developed. But how to gather and use empirical evidence, how to develop and apply our powers—this is not so generally recognized or appreciated.

We might well be surprised how many people are capable of sharp observation in the strictest sense of the word. When we draw their attention to objects, we will discover that such people enjoy making observations, and show great skill at it. Since taking up my study of light and color I have often had opportunity to appreciate this. Now and then I discuss my current interests with people unacquainted with the subject: once their attention is awakened they frequently make quick note of phenomena I was unaware of or had neglected to observe. Thus they may be able to correct ideas developed in haste, and even produce a breakthrough by transcending the inhibitions in which exacting research often traps us.

Thus what applies in so many other human enterprises is also true here: the interest of many focused on a single point can produce excellent results. Here it becomes obvious that the researcher will meet his downfall if he has any feeling of envy which seeks to deprive others of the discoverer's laurels, any overwhelming desire to deal alone and arbitrarily with a discovery.

I have always found the cooperative method of working satisfactory, and I intend to continue with it. I am aware of the debts I have incurred along the way, and it will give me great pleasure later to acknowledge these publicly.

If man's natural talent for observation can be of such help to us, how much more effective must it be when trained observers work hand in hand. In and of itself, a science is sufficient to support the work of many people, although no one person can carry an entire science. We may note that knowledge, like contained but living water, rises gradually to a certain level, and that the greatest discoveries are made not so much by men as by the age; important advances are often made by two or more skilled thinkers at the same time. We have already found that we owe much to the community and our friends; now we discover our debt to the world and the age we live in. In neither case can we appreciate fully enough our need for communication, assistance, admonition, and contradiction to hold us to the right path and help us along it.

Thus in scientific matters we must do the reverse of what is done in art. An artist should never present a work to the public before it is finished because it is difficult for others to advise or help him with its production. Once it is finished, however, he must consider criticism or praise, take it to heart, make it a part of his own experience, and thereby develop and prepare himself for new works. In science, on the other hand, it is useful to publish every bit of empirical evidence, even every conjecture; indeed, no scientific edifice should be built until the plan and materials of its structure have been widely known, judged and sifted.

I will now turn to a point deserving of attention; namely, the method which enables us to work most effectively and surely.

When we intentionally reproduce empirical evidence found by earlier researchers, contemporaries, or ourselves, when we re-create natural or artificial phenomena, we speak of this as an experiment.

The main value of an experiment lies in the fact that, simple or compound, it can be reproduced at any time given the requisite preparations, apparatus, and skill. After assembling the necessary materials we may perform the experiment as often as we wish. We will rightly marvel at human ingenuity when we consider even briefly the variety of arrangements and instruments invented for this purpose. In fact, we can note that such instruments are still being invented daily.

As worthwhile as each individual experiment may be, it receives its real value only when united or combined with other experiments. However, to unite or combine just two somewhat similar experiments calls for more rigor and care than even the sharpest observer usually expects of himself. Two phenomena may be related, but not nearly so closely as we think. Although one experiment seems to follow from another, an extensive series of experiments might be required to put the two into an order actually conforming to nature.

Thus we can never be too careful in our efforts to avoid drawing hasty conclusions from experiments or using them directly as proof to bear out some theory. For here at this pass, this transition from empirical evidence to judgment, cognition to application, all the inner enemies of man lie in wait: imagination, which sweeps him away on its wings before he knows his feet have left the ground; impatience; haste; self-satisfaction; rigidity; formalistic thought; prejudice; ease; frivolity; fickleness—this whole throng and its retinue. Here they lie in ambush and surprise not only the active observer but also the contemplative one who appears safe from all passion.

I will present a paradox of sorts as a way of alerting the reader to this danger, far greater and closer at hand than we might think. I would venture to say that we cannot prove anything by one experiment or even several experiments together, that nothing is more dangerous than the desire to prove some thesis directly through experiments, that the greatest errors have arisen just where the dangers and shortcomings in this method have been overlooked. I will explain this assertion more clearly lest I merely seem intent on raising a host of doubts. Every piece of empirical evidence we find, every experiment in which this evidence is repeated, really represents just one part of what we know. Through frequent repetition we attain certainty about this isolated piece of knowledge. We may be aware of two pieces of empirical evidence in the same area; although closely related, they may seem even more so, for we will tend to view them as more connected than they really are. This is an inherent part of man's nature; the history of human understanding offers thousands of examples of this, and I myself make this error almost daily.

This mistake is associated with another which often lies at its root. Man takes more pleasure in the idea than in the thing; or rather, man takes pleasure in a thing only insofar as he has an idea of it. The thing must fit his character, and no matter how exalted his way of thinking, no matter how refined, it often remains just a way of thinking, an attempt to bring several objects into an intelligible relationship which, strictly speaking, they do not have. Thus the tendency to hypotheses, theories, terminologies, and systems, a tendency altogether understandable since it springs by necessity from the organization of our being.

Every piece of empirical evidence, every experiment, must be viewed as isolated, yet the human faculty of thought forcibly strives to unite all external objects known to it. It is easy to see the risk we run when we try to connect a single bit of evidence with an idea already formed, or use individual experiments to prove some relationship not fully perceptible to the senses but expressed through the creative power of the mind.

Such efforts generally give rise to theories and systems which are a tribute to their author's intelligence. But with undue applause or protracted support they soon begin to hinder and harm the very progress of the human mind they had earlier assisted.

We often find that the more limited the data, the more artful a gifted thinker will become. As though to assert his sovereignty he chooses a few agreeable favorites from the limited number of facts and skillfully marshals the rest so they never contradict him directly. Finally he is able to confuse, entangle, or push aside the opposing facts and reduce the whole to something more like the court of a despot than a freely constituted republic.

So deserving a man will not lack admirers and disciples who study this fabric of thought historically, praise it, and seek to think as much like their master as possible. Often such a doctrine becomes so widespread that anyone bold enough to doubt it would be considered brash and impertinent. Only in later centuries would anyone venture to approach such a holy relic, apply common sense to the subject, and—taking a lighter view—apply to the founder of the sect what a wag once said of a renowned scientist: "He would have been a great man if only he hadn't invented so much."

It is not enough to note this danger and warn against it. We need to declare our own views by showing how we ourselves would hope to avoid this pitfall, or by telling what we know of how some predecessor avoided it.

Earlier I stated my belief that the direct use of an experiment to prove some hypothesis is detrimental; this implies that I consider its indirect use beneficial. Here we have a pivotal point, one requiring clarification.

Nothing happens in living nature that does not bear some relation to the whole. The empirical evidence may seem quite isolated, we may view our experiments as mere isolated facts, but this is not to say that they are, in fact, isolated. The question is: how can we find the connection between these phenomena, these events?

Earlier we found those thinkers most prone to error who seek to incorporate an isolated fact directly into their thinking and judgment. By contrast, we will find that the greatest accomplishments come from those who never tire in exploring and working out every possible aspect and modification of every bit of empirical evidence, every experiment.

It would require a second essay to describe how our intellect can help us with this task; here we will merely indicate the following. All things in nature, especially the commoner forces and elements, work incessantly upon one another; we can say that each phenomenon is connected with countless others just as we can say that a point of light floating in space sends its rays in all directions. Thus when we have done an experiment of this type, found this or that piece of empirical evidence, we can never be careful enough in studying what lies next to it or derives directly from it. This investigation should concern us more than the discovery of what is related to it. To follow every single experiment through its variations is the real task of the scientific researcher. His duty is precisely the opposite of what we expect from the author who writes to entertain. The latter will bore his readers if he does not leave something to the imagination, while the former must always work as if he wished to leave nothing for his successors to do. Of course, the disproportion between our intellect and the nature of things will soon remind us that no one has gifts enough to exhaust the study of any subject.

In the first two parts of my *Contributions to Optics* I sought to set up a series of contiguous experiments derived from one another in this way. Studied thoroughly and understood as a whole, these experiments could even be thought of as representing a single experiment, a single piece of empirical evidence explored in its most manifold variations.

Such a piece of empirical evidence, composed of many others, is clearly of a higher sort. It shows the general formula, so to speak, that overarches an array of individual arithmetic sums. In my view, it is the task of the scientific researcher to work toward empirical evidence of this higher sort—and the example of the best men in the field supports this view. From the mathematician we must learn the meticulous care required to connect things in unbroken succession, or rather, to derive things step by step. Even where we do not venture to apply mathematics we must always work as though we had to satisfy the strictest of geometricians.

In the mathematical method we find an approach which by its deliberate and pure nature instantly exposes every leap in an assertion. Actually, its proofs merely state in a detailed way that what is presented as connected was already there in each of the parts and as a consecutive whole, that it has been reviewed in its entirety and found to be correct and irrefutable under all circumstances. Thus its demonstrations are always more exposition, recapitulation, than argument. Having made this distinction, I may now return to something mentioned earlier.

We can see the great difference between a mathematical demonstration which traces the basic elements through their many points of connection, and the proof offered in the arguments of a clever speaker. Although arguments may deal with utterly separate matters, wit and imagination can group them around a single point to create a surprising semblance of right and wrong, true and false. It is likewise possible to support a hypothesis or theory by arranging individual experiments like arguments and offering proofs which bedazzle us to some degree.

But those who wish to be honest with themselves and others will try by careful development of individual experiments to evolve empirical evidence of the higher sort. These pieces of evidence may be expressed in concise axioms and set side by side, and as more of them emerge they may be ordered and related. Like mathematical axioms they will remain unshakable either singly or as a whole. Anyone may examine and test the elements, the many individual experiments, which constitute this higher sort of evidence; it will be easy to judge whether we can express these many components in a general axiom, for nothing here is arbitrary.

The other method which tries to prove assertions by using isolated experiments like arguments often reaches its conclusions furtively or leaves them completely in doubt. Once sequential evidence of the higher sort is assembled, however, our intellect, imagination and wit can work upon it as they will; no harm will be done, and, indeed, a useful purpose will be served. We cannot exercise enough care, diligence, strictness, even pedantry, in collecting basic empirical evidence; here we labor for the world and the future. But these materials must be ordered and shown in sequence, not arranged in some hypothetical way nor made to serve the dictates of some system. Everyone will then be free to connect them in his own way, to form them into a whole which brings some measure of delight and comfort to the human mind. This approach keeps separate what must be kept separate; it enables us to increase the body of evidence much more quickly and cleanly than the method which forces us to cast aside later experiments like bricks brought to a finished building.

The views and examples of the best men give me reason to hope that this is the right path, and I trust my explanation will satisfy those of my friends who ask from time to time what I am really seeking to accomplish with my optical experiments. My intention is to collect all the empirical evidence in this area, do every experiment myself, and develop the experiments in their most manifold variations so that they become easy to reproduce and more accessible. I will then attempt to establish the axioms in which the empirical evidence of a higher nature can be expressed, and see if these can be subsumed under still higher principles. If imagination and wit sometimes run impatiently ahead on this path, the method itself will fix the bounds to which they must return.

APRIL 28, 1792

THE EXTENT TO WHICH THE IDEA "BEAUTY IS PERFECTION IN COMBINATION WITH FREEDOM" MAY BE APPLIED TO LIVING ORGANISMS
(C. 1794)

An organic being is so multifaceted in its exterior, so varied and inexhaustible in its interior, that we cannot find enough points of view nor develop in ourselves enough organs of perception to avoid killing it when we analyze it. I will attempt to apply the idea "Beauty is perfection in combination with freedom" to living organisms.

The members of every creature are formed so that it may enjoy its existence, and maintain and propagate itself; in this sense everything alive deserves to be called perfect. Here I will turn immediately to the so-called more perfect animals.

If the members of an animal are so formed that the creature can give expression to its being only in a limited way, we will find the animal ugly; limitation of organic nature to a single purpose will produce a preponderance of one or another of its members, rendering the free use of the remaining members difficult.

When I look at this animal my attention will be drawn to the parts which predominate—the creature cannot make a harmonious impression because it has no harmony. Thus the mole is perfect but ugly because its form permits only a few, limited actions, and the preponderance of certain parts renders him misshapen.

Therefore, if an animal is to satisfy even its most limited basic needs without difficulty, it must be perfectly organized. After satisfying its needs, however, it may have enough strength and power left to initiate voluntary actions which are somewhat without purpose; in this case its exterior will also yield an impression of beauty.

Thus if I say this animal is beautiful I am unable to prove my assertion by using some proportion of number or measure. Instead I am stating only: in this animal all the members are so related that none hinders the action of another; compulsion and need are entirely hidden from my sight by a perfect balance so that the animal seems free to act and work just as it chooses. We may recall the sight of a horse using its limbs in freedom.

If we now rise to man, we will find that he is at last almost free of the fetters of animality; his limbs are in a delicate state of subordination and coordination, governed by his will more than those of any other animal, and suited not only to any application but also an expression of the mind. Here I allude to the language of gesture which is restrained in well-bred people, and which, I believe, does as much as the language of words to elevate man above the animal.

To develop the concept of a beautiful human in this manner would require that we take countless matters into consideration; there is clearly much to be done before the exalted concept of freedom can crown human perfection, even in the physical sense.

Here I must note a further point. We call an animal beautiful when it gives the impression that it *could* use its limbs at will, but when it really uses them as it chooses, the idea of the beautiful is immediately lost in feelings of the pretty, the pleasant, the easy, the splendid, etc. Thus we see that beauty actually calls for *repose* together with *strength, inaction* together with *power*.

If the notion of asserting the power of a body or some limb is too closely associated with the being's physical existence, the spirit of the beautiful seems to take flight immediately: the ancients depicted even their lions in the greatest degree of repose and neutrality in order to draw forth the feeling with which we grasp beauty.

I would say that we consider a perfectly organized being beautiful if, in beholding it, we can believe it *capable of manifold and free use of all its members whenever it wishes*. Thus the most intense feeling of beauty is connected with feelings of trust and hope.

It seems to me that an essay on the animal and human form viewed in this way might yield agreeable insights and show some interesting relationships.

In particular, this would elevate the concept of proportion (which we usually try to express through number or measure, as mentioned above) to more spiritual principles, and it is my hope that these spiritual principles might at last come to agree with the approach used by the great artists whose works have come down to us, and also encompass those beautiful products of nature which appear among us from time to time in living form.

Especially interesting would be a discussion of how distinctive features could be generated without going beyond the bounds of beauty, how limitation and specialization could appear without impairing freedom.

To be unique and truly helpful to future friends of nature and art, this treatise would have to be based on anatomy and physiology. However, it is not easy to imagine a form of discourse suitable for the presentation of such a varied and wondrous whole.

OBSERVATION ON MORPHOLOGY IN GENERAL
(C. 1795)

Morphology may be viewed as a theory in and of itself, or as a science in the service of biology. As a whole it is based on natural history, drawing from it the phenomena with which it works. It is also based on the anatomy of all living bodies, and especially on zootomy.

Since its intention is to portray rather than explain, it draws as little as possible on the other sciences ancillary to biology, although it ignores neither the relationships of force and place in physics nor the relationships of element and compound in chemistry. Through its limitations it becomes, in fact, a specialized set of principles. Without exception it considers itself the handmaiden of biology, working together with other subsidiary sciences.

In morphology we propose to establish a science new not because of its subject matter, which is already well known, but because of its intention and method, which lends its principles their unique form and gives it a place among the other sciences. Since this is a new science we will start with a discussion of the latter point, the connection of morphology with other related sciences. We will then set forth its content and the method used in presenting this content.

Morphology may be said to include the principles of structured form and the formation and transformation of organic bodies; thus it belongs to a particular group of sciences, each of which has its own purpose. We will now review these sciences.

Natural history assumes that the variety of forms in the organic world is a known phenomenon. It recognizes that this great variety also shows a certain consistency which is partly universal and partly specific. It not only records the bodily structures known to it, but it arranges them, sometimes in groups and sometimes in sequence, according to the forms that are observed and the characteristics that are sought out and recognized. Thus it enables us to survey an enormous mass of material. Its work has two goals: partly to pursue the discovery of new subjects, and partly to arrange these subjects more in conformity with nature and their own characteristics, eliminating all that is arbitrary insofar as possible.

While natural history concentrates on the surface appearance of forms and views them as a whole, anatomy requires a knowledge of the inner structure; it treats the human body as the most worthy subject for dissection, and the one most in need of the aid only a thorough knowledge of structure can offer. A certain amount of work has been done on the anatomy of other living structures, but this is so scattered, so incomplete, and even so erroneous in many cases, that the collection of material remains almost useless to the scientific researcher.

In seeking to pursue and broaden the empirical observations of natural history, or draw them together for use, researchers have called on other areas of science, turned to closely related fields, or even formulated their own approaches. All this has been done and is still being done to fulfill the need for a general overview in biology (although, as human nature would have it, in a manner which is too one-sided). Nonetheless, an excellent foundation has been laid for the biologist of the future.

From the physicist (in the strictest sense of the word) the theory of organic nature has been able to acquire only a knowledge of the general relationship between forces, and the location and orientation of these forces in the particular area under study. The application of mechanical principles to organisms has merely made us all the more aware of the perfection of living beings, and we might almost say that the less applicable mechanical principles become, the more an organism grows in perfection.

In this area, as in others, we owe much to the chemist who sets form and structure aside and simply observes the character of materials and how they form compounds. Our debt to him will increase in the future, for recent discoveries have made the most refined analyses and syntheses possible, thus holding out the hope that we will be able to approximate the infinitely subtle processes of the living organism itself. Just as we have already created an anatomical biology through careful observation of structure, we may also look forward to a physical-chemical biology in the course of time. We may hope that these two sciences will progress so that each becomes capable of achieving this goal independently.

However, since both sciences are altogether analytical in character, and chemical compounds are based only on processes of separation, it is natural that these approaches to the study and understanding of organisms do not satisfy everyone. Many will prefer to start with a unified whole, develop the parts from it, and then retrace the parts directly to the whole. The nature of the organism supplies us with the best reason for doing this: the most perfect organism appears before us as a unified whole, discrete from all other beings. We know that we ourselves are such a whole; we experience the fullest sense of well-being when we are unaware of our parts and conscious only of the whole itself. The existence of organic nature is possible only insofar as organisms have structure, and these organisms can be structured and maintained as active entities solely through the condition we call "life." Thus it was natural that a science of physiology should be established in an attempt to discover the laws an organism is destined to follow as a living being. For the sake of argument this life was quite properly viewed as derived from a force, an assumption justified and even necessary because life in its wholeness is expressed as a force not attributable to any individual part of an organism.

In thinking of an organism as a whole, or of ourselves as a whole, we will shortly find two points of view thrust upon us. At times we will view man as a being grasped by our physical senses, and at times as a being recognized only through an inner sense or understood only through the effects he produces.

Thus physiology falls into two parts which are not easily separated, i.e., into a physical part and a spiritual part. In reality these are inseparable, but the researcher in this field may start out from one side or the other and thus lend the greater weight to one *or* the other.

However, any of the sciences listed here would require our full attention; indeed, the pursuit of a specific area in just one of them would take an entire lifetime. An even greater difficulty lies in the fact that these sciences are cultivated almost exclusively by physicians, and although they address a certain aspect of their science by adding to its store of empirical observation, the need for application prevents them from extending its frontiers.

Thus we realize that much remains to be done before the biologist who seeks to combine all these views can consolidate them into one and achieve an understanding commensurate with his grand subject, insofar as this is permitted to the human spirit. To achieve this requires a focused activity on all sides, an activity which has been and continues to be in evidence. Progress in this activity would be more rapid and certain if each researcher would pursue it in his own way (but not one-sidedly), if he would joyfully acknowledge his colleagues' every accomplishment instead of putting his own views uppermost, as is usually the case.

Now that we have presented the various sciences contributing to the work of the biologist, and shown their relationship, it is time for morphology to prove its legitimacy as a science in its own right.

Others agree with this. It must prove its legitimacy as an independent science by choosing a subject other sciences deal with only in passing, by drawing together what lies scattered among them and establishing a new standpoint from which the things of nature may be readily observed. The advantages of morphology are that it is made up of widely recognized elements, it does not conflict with any theory, it does not need to displace something else to make room for itself, and it deals with extremely significant phenomena. Its arrangement of phenomena calls upon activities of the mind so in harmony with human nature, and so pleasant, that even its failures may prove both useful and charming.

POLARITY
(C. 1799)

Two needs arise in us when we observe nature: to gain complete knowledge of the phenomena themselves, and then to make them our own by reflection upon them. Completeness is a product of order, order demands method, and method makes it easier to perceive the concept. When we are able to survey an object in every detail, grasp it correctly, and reproduce it in our mind's eye, we can say that we have an intuitive perception of it in the truest and highest sense. We can say that it belongs to us, that we have attained a certain mastery of it. And thus the particular always leads us to the general, the general to the particular. The two combine their effects in every observation, in every discourse.

We will begin with some general notions.

Duality of the phenomenon as opposites:
   We and the objects
   Light and dark

Body and soul
Two souls
Spirit and matter
God and world
Thought and extension
Ideal and real
Sensuality and reason
Fantasy and practical thought
Being and yearning
Two halves of the body
Right and left
Breathing.
Physical experiment:
Magnet.

Our ancestors admired the economy of nature. She was thought to have a practical character, inclined to do much with small means where others produce little with great means. As mere mortals, we stand even more in admiration of the skill with which she is able to produce the widest variety of things while restricted to only a few basic principles.

To do this she uses the principle of life, with its inherent potential to work with the simplest phenomenon and diversify it by intensification into the most infinite and varied forms.

Whatever appears in the world must divide if it is to appear at all. What has been divided seeks itself again, can return to itself and reunite. This happens in a lower sense when it merely intermingles with its opposite, combines with it; here the phenomenon is nullified or at least neutralized. However, the union may occur in a higher sense if what has been divided is first intensified; then in the union of the intensified halves it will produce a third thing, something new, higher, unexpected.

FROM *THEORY OF COLOR*
(1791–1807)

Part Five: Relationship to Other Fields

RELATIONSHIP TO PHILOSOPHY

716. We cannot require a physicist to be a philosopher, but we can expect him to have enough philosophical knowledge to make a fundamental distinction between himself and the world, and then come to terms with the world again in a higher sense. He ought to shape a method consistent with intuitive perception; he must avoid turning the perception into concepts, the concept

into words, avoid using and treating these words as if they were objects. He should be familiar with the philosopher's task so that he can pursue phenomena to the borders of the philosophical realm.

717. We cannot ask a philosopher to be a physicist, and yet his influence on the area of physics is necessary and desirable. Knowledge of every detail is not required, only an insight into the end point where the details converge.

718. Earlier (§§175 ff.) we mentioned this important observation in passing, and we are now at an appropriate place to repeat it. There is no worse mistake in physics or any other science than to treat secondary things as basic and (since basic things cannot be derived from what is secondary) to seek an explanation for the basic things in secondary ones. This gives birth to endless confusion, jargon, and a constant effort to find a way out when the truth begins to emerge and assert itself.

719. Here the observer, the scientific researcher, will be bothered by the fact that the phenomena always contradict his notions. The philosopher, however, can continue to operate with a false conclusion in his own sphere, for no conclusion is so false that it could not somehow be valid as a form without content.

720. But the physicist who can come to an understanding of what we have called an archetypal phenomenon will be on safe ground, and the philosopher with him. The physicist will find safety in the conviction that he has reached the limit of his science, the empirical summit from which he can look back over the various steps in empirical observation, and glance forward into the realm of theory, if not enter it. The philosopher finds safety in accepting from the hand of the physicist results which can serve as his starting point. He will now be justifiably indifferent to phenomena insofar as they are secondary effects organized by science or scattered and disorganized in the empirical state. If he wishes, he may easily examine these phenomena in detail instead of conducting his own research, lingering too long in the intermediate realm, or touching upon the phenomena superficially and without exact knowledge.

721. It has been the author's wish to present the principles of color to the philosopher in this way. For various reasons he may not have succeeded in the discourse itself, but he will pursue this in his revision of the work, in his summary of the discussion, and in the polemic and historical sections. Later, in stating several points more clearly, he will return to this observation.

RELATIONSHIP TO MATHEMATICS

722. Since the physicist deals with the principles of nature as a whole, we can expect him to be a mathematician. In the Middle Ages mathematics was the principal means for seeking mastery over the secrets of nature, and even today geometry properly has an important place in certain areas of natural science.

723. The author cannot boast of any accomplishment in this field, and therefore restricts himself to those areas which involve no geometry; in recent times such areas have been opened up far and wide.

724. Who would deny that mathematics, one of the most splendid of human gifts, has served physics well in its way? But the false application of the mathematical method has undoubtedly harmed this science as well; here and there we will find this fact grudgingly admitted.

725. The theory of color, in particular, has been hurt and greatly hindered in its progress by being lumped with the area of optics dependent on geometry. It may, in fact, be considered entirely separate from geometry.

726. Another problem arose because a fine mathematician had adopted a completely false concept of the physical origin of color; his great accomplishments as a geometrician long served to sanction his scientific error in a world ruled by constant prejudice.

727. The author of the present work has sought throughout to keep the principles of color apart from mathematics, although at certain points the help of geometry would obviously have been desirable. Had other matters not kept unprejudiced mathematicians of the author's acquaintance from working with him, his discussion would not lack merit in this regard. But this failing might be turned to good advantage if the gifted mathematician will discover where his help is needed in the theory of color, and how he can contribute to the perfection of this branch of science.

728. In general, Germans have achieved much while accepting the achievements of other nations—it would be well if they could also become accustomed to working together. We live, however, in an age altogether opposed to this aspiration. Each wishes to be original in his views and independent of other efforts in his life and work, or at least think that he is. We often find that those who have, in fact, accomplished something quote only themselves, their own writings, journals and compendiums, although it would be much better for them and the world if others were called upon to join in the work. The conduct of our neighbors, the French, is exemplary in this regard, as we may note with pleasure in the instance of Cuvier's preface to his *Tableau élémentaire de l'Histoire naturelle des animaux*.

729. Close observers of the sciences and their progress might even ask whether it is advantageous for such disparate (but related) efforts and goals to be united in one person. Given the limitations of human nature would it not be more appropriate, for example, to make a distinction between those who pursue and discover phenomena, and those who work with them in an applied way? In recent times astronomers who observe the heavens in the search for stars have been somewhat separate from those who calculate orbits, consider the laws of the universe, and formulate them more precisely. We will return to these points often in the history of the theory of color.

RELATIONSHIP TO THE TECHNOLOGY OF DYEING

730. Our research has given the mathematician wide berth, but we have sought to meet the practical needs of the dyer. Although our section on the chemical aspect of colors is not fully detailed, it and our general observations on color will say far more to the dyer than the earlier theory which offered him nothing at all.

731. Treatises on dyeing are remarkable in this regard. The Catholic may enter his temple, sprinkle himself with holy water, kneel before the priest, and then with no special piety conduct a business discussion with friends or pursue affairs of the heart. Similarly, every treatise on dyeing begins with respectful mention of color theory without any later evidence that something has come of this theory, that this theory has explained or clarified anything, or yielded anything of value for practical application.

732. Those who fully understand the practical needs of dyeing, however, are forced to disagree with the traditional theory, to expose some of its weaknesses and seek a general approach more in keeping with nature and empirical observation. We will say more about this in the historical section when we come to the work of Castel and Gülich. This will also allow us to show how an expanded empiricism comprehending every accident of nature may actually go beyond its own limits and be taken up and used as a highly developed whole by the theoretician who is clear-sighted and honest of character.

RELATIONSHIP TO PHYSIOLOGY AND PATHOLOGY

733. Although almost all the phenomena in the section dealing with the physiological and pathological aspects of color are well known, there are some new views which the physiologist will welcome. In particular, we hope to have satisfied him by connecting certain isolated phenomena with similar and like phenomena, thus laying part of the groundwork for his further studies.

734. The pathological supplement is admittedly scanty and disconnected. However, we have outstanding experts who are quite experienced and knowledgeable in this area, and so respected intellectually that they would have little difficulty in revising my discussion, completing what I began, and connecting it with higher levels of insight into organisms.

RELATIONSHIP TO NATURAL HISTORY

735. The author hopes to have done some preliminary work for natural history insofar as we expect this field gradually to become the study of how natural phenomena derive from phenomena of a higher type. Color in all its

variety shows on the surface of living beings as a significant outer sign of what is happening within.

736. In one respect, of course, it is not altogether trustworthy because of its uncertainty and changeability, but to the extent it appears as a constant effect, this mutability will itself serve as a criterion for the mutable qualities of life. The author could wish for nothing more than to be given the time to develop his observations on this subject, although this is not the place for such a discussion.

RELATIONSHIP TO GENERAL PHYSICS

737. The present state of general physics seems especially favorable for our work; constant and wide-ranging research have brought natural philosophy to such a high level that it now seems possible to relate the endless realm of empirical phenomena to one central method.

738. Without going too far afield, we will find a certain common tendency in the formulas used—if not dogmatically, then at least for didactic purposes as an expression of elementary natural phenomena. This accord in the outward signs must point to an accord in their inner sense.

739. No matter how different their opinions, faithful observers of nature will agree that anything that appears and meets us as phenomenon necessarily implies an original division capable of union or an original unity capable of division, and that the phenomenon must present itself accordingly. To make two of what is one, to unify what is divided—this is the life of nature, the eternal systole and diastole, the eternal syncrisis and diacrisis, the inhaling and exhaling of the world in which we live, weave, and exist.

740. It should be obvious that what we express here through number, through *one* and *two*, must be understood as a higher process, just as the appearance of a third or fourth stage of development is always to be taken in a higher sense. It is especially important, however, that true intuitive perceptions underlie all these expressions.

741. Although we recognize iron as a separate and individual substance, it is neutral, worthy of note only in certain situations and applications. But how little is needed to transform this neutrality! A division takes place; in seeking to reunite and find itself, it develops an almost magical connection to its own kind. This division, in reality a reuniting, spreads throughout its species. Here we recognize the neutral substance, iron; we see the division arise in it, spread and disappear, only to begin again. In our opinion this is an archetypal phenomenon which borders upon the idea and acknowledges nothing earthly above it.

742. Electricity has its own peculiarities. We know nothing of electricity's essence, for it is neutral. To us it is nothing, a zero, a zero point, a neutral point, but one present in every corporeal substance, a point of origin for a

double phenomenon which will emerge at the least provocation and appear only as it disappears again. The conditions under which this appearance occurs are endlessly varied, and depend on the character of the particular bodies involved. From the grossest mechanical friction between altogether different bodies to the subtlest proximity of two similar bodies only slightly unalike in quality, the phenomenon is present and active, even striking and powerful. Its definition and form are such that we properly and naturally apply the formulas of polarity, plus and minus, in the terms north and south, glass and resin.

743. Although this phenomenon takes place especially on the surface, it is by no means superficial. It influences the characteristics of objects, and in its effect it has a direct relationship to the great double phenomenon so prevalent in chemistry, oxidation and deoxidation.

744. It has been our goal to relate the effects of color to this series, this circle, this garland of phenomena, and make a place for it there. Where we have failed, others will succeed. We found a tremendous, primal opposition between light and dark, or to put it more generally, between light and non-light. We sought to mediate this opposition and thus to build the visible world out of light, shadow, and color. As we developed these phenomena we made use of various formulas drawn from the principles of magnetism, electricity, and chemistry. We had to go beyond these principles, however, for we found ourselves in a higher sphere where the relationships requiring expression were more complex.

745. As general forces, electricity and galvanism are superior to magnetic effects, which are more specialized. We may say likewise that color is governed by the same laws, but rises much higher in displaying its qualities to good advantage through its effect on the eye, a noble sensory organ. Compare the various qualities created in the intensification of yellow and blue in red, the union of the two higher extremes in purple, and the mixture of the two lower extremes in green. This system is far more complex than that for magnetism and electricity. There is another reason these latter phenomena are at a lower level: although they permeate and quicken the world as a whole, they are unable to rise to the level of man in a higher sense, for they cannot be used esthetically. A general, simple, physical system must itself reach a higher level and become more complex if it is to serve loftier purposes.

746. In this sense the reader may recall what we have set forth generally as well as in detail about color; he will then be able to expand and develop for himself the slight indications found here. It would greatly benefit knowledge, science, technology, and art if the beautiful subject of color theory could be freed from its traditional atomistic restraints and isolation, and returned to the general, dynamistic flow of life and activity in which the present age takes such delight. These sentiments will be strengthened when our historical section introduces us to many a brave and insightful man who failed to persuade his contemporaries of his convictions.

RELATIONSHIP TO THE THEORY OF TONE

747. We will proceed to the sensory-moral effects of color, and the esthetic effects arising from them, but this is an appropriate place to say something of their relationship with tone.

It has long been felt that color is related in a certain way to tone; this is shown by the frequent comparisons, some in passing and some in great detail. For the following simple reason, this is an error.

748. Color and tone may in no wise be compared to one another, but both may be related to a higher formula, both may be derived from a higher formula, each in its own way. Color and tone are like two rivers which arise on a single mountain but flow differently through completely opposite regions, so that no two points are comparable as we follow their separate courses. Both are general, basic effects acting in accord with universal law (separation and tendency to union, rising and falling, weight and counterweight), but in quite different directions, in different ways, through different media, on different senses.

749. If some researcher could really take hold of the method we have used in connecting the theory of color with general natural philosophy, and if he could correct our omissions and errors by chance or by insight, we are convinced that the theory of tone could be incorporated fully into general physics; at present its separation is only historical.

750. But herein lies the greatest difficulty: should we destroy the special character of present-day music with its odd practical, accidental, mathematical, esthetic, and creative impulses, could we dissolve it into its basic physical elements and treat it in a purely physical way? This might be possible because of the point we have reached in science and art, and the fine preliminary studies already available.

CONCLUDING OBSERVATION ON LANGUAGE AND TERMINOLOGY

751. We are insufficiently aware that a language is, in fact, merely symbolic, merely figurative, never a direct expression of the objective world, but only a reflection of it. This is especially so when we speak of things which only touch lightly upon our empirical observation, things we might call activities rather than objects. In the realm of natural philosophy such things are in constant motion. They cannot be held fast and yet we must speak of them; hence we look for all sorts of formulas to get at them, at least metaphorically.

752. Metaphysical formulas have great breadth and depth, but a rich content is required to fill them in a worthy way; otherwise they remain empty. Mathematical formulas are often convenient and useful, but they always have a certain stiffness and awkwardness; we soon feel their inadequacy, for even in

elementary instances we will quickly recognize the presence of an incommensurable quality. Furthermore, they are intelligible only to a narrow circle of specially trained minds. Mechanical formulas speak more to ordinary understanding, but are themselves ordinary and always retain a touch of crudity. They transform living things into dead ones; they kill the inner life in order to apply an inadequate substitute from without. Corpuscular formulas are similar; they have the effect of rigidifying things in motion, coarsening idea and expression. In contrast, moral formulas express more delicate relationships but take the form of simple metaphors, and may finally lose themselves in a display of wit.

753. However, the scientist might make conscious use of all these modes of thought and expression to convey his views on natural phenomena in a multifold language. If he could avoid becoming one-sided, and give living expression to living thought, it might be possible to communicate much that would be welcome.

754. How difficult it is, though, to refrain from replacing the thing with its sign, to keep the object alive before us instead of killing it with the word. In recent times this danger has been heightened as expressions and terms are drawn from all areas of knowledge and science to express perceptions of simple natural phenomena. We call on the aid of astronomy, cosmology, geology, natural history, even religion and mysticism; and often the particular, the derived, will hide and obscure the general, the elementary, instead of illuminating and revealing it. We are quite aware of the necessity responsible for such a language and its widespread use, and we know that it has made itself indispensable in a certain sense. But this language will be of service only when more moderately and modestly applied in a conscious and sure way.

755. It would be most desirable, however, to base the language for the details of a particular area on the area itself, to treat the simplest phenomenon as the basic formula and develop the more complex formulas out of it.

756. Scientists have obviously felt that it would be necessary and suitable to use a figurative language in which the basic sign expresses the phenomenon itself, for the formula of polarity has been borrowed from magnetism and extended to electricity, etc. The concepts of *plus* and *minus*, which represent this formula, have found suitable application to many a phenomenon. Even the musician, apparently unconcerned with other fields, has been led by nature to express the principal difference between keys as *major* and *minor*.

757. We, too, have long wished to introduce the term *polarity* into the theory of color, and the present work will show our justification and purpose in doing so. Later we may have an opportunity to link the elementary phenomena of nature in our own way by using this approach, this symbolism always accompanied by the intuitive perception belonging to it. Thus we will be able to clarify and define more adequately the general indications given here.

Part Six: Sensory-Moral Effect of Color

758. Color is ranked high among the primal natural phenomena, for it fills out its own unique sphere in the most various ways. Color is chiefly meant for the sense of vision, the eye; in its most general and basic form, without regard to the character or shape of the surface on which it appears, it acts on man's inner nature through the mediation of the eye. Hence we will not be surprised to find that its effect has a direct connection with the moral realm. A single color acts specifically, while a combination of colors has an effect which is partly harmonious, partly individual, even inharmonious, but always distinct and significant. Thus color, as an element of art, may serve the highest esthetic purposes.

759. People generally take great pleasure in color. The eye needs color as it needs light. We may recall our feeling of refreshment when the sun breaks through the clouds to flood a part of the landscape with light and make its colors visible. The belief that colored jewels have healing powers may be a result of the deep feelings aroused by this inexpressible delight.

760. The colors seen in objects are not entirely external to the eye, are not imprinted on the eye from without. No—the eye itself has a constant predisposition to bring forth colors, and feels pleasure when something in harmony with its own nature comes to it, when its ability to respond is evoked strongly in a certain direction.

761. The idea of opposition between phenomena, and what we now know of particular modifications in this opposition, will lead us to conclude that the impressions made by individual colors are not interchangeable, that they have specific effects and must produce decidedly specific states in the living organ which is the eye.

762. They have a similar effect on man's inner nature. Observation will tell us that each color brings its particular mood. It is told of a witty Frenchman: "Il prétendoit que son ton de conversation avec Madame étoit changé depuis qu'elle avoit changé en cramoisi le meuble de son cabinet qui étoit bleu."

763. To experience these specific, strong effects the eye must be entirely surrounded by one color; e.g., we must be in a room of one color, or look through a colored piece of glass. We will then identify ourselves with the color; our eye and spirit will be brought into unison with it.

764. The colors on the plus side are yellow, red-yellow (orange), and yellow-red (minium, cinnabar). They bring on an active, lively, striving mood.

YELLOW

765. Yellow is the color nearest light. It arises from very slight moderation of light, whether through turbid media or weak reflection from a white surface. In prismatic experiments it extends far into the bright area, where it can

be seen in its greatest purity when the two poles are still separate and yellow is not yet mixed with blue to create green. We have already described in detail how the chemical yellow develops in and across the white.

766. In its greatest purity it always conveys the quality of brightness, and has a cheerful, vivacious, mildly exciting character.

767. In this form it makes a pleasant surrounding, whether in clothing, curtains, or wallpaper. Gold in its unalloyed state brings us a new and exalted idea of this color, especially when enhanced by the metal's gleam. Similarly, a strong yellow on lustrous silk (e.g., satin) has a magnificent and noble effect.

768. We also experience a very warm and cozy impression with yellow. Thus in painting, too, it belongs among the luminous and active colors.

769. This warming effect is most vivid when we look at a landscape through a piece of yellow glass, especially on a gray wintery day. The eye is gladdened, the heart expands, the feelings are cheered, an immediate warmth seems to waft toward us.

770. In its pure and bright state this color is pleasurable and cheering, with an element of vivacity and nobility in the force with which it works. It is extremely delicate, however, and makes a very unpleasant impression when muddied or drawn a little toward the minus side; hence the unpleasant quality in the color of sulfur, which tends toward green.

771. On impure and coarse surfaces, like woolen cloth, felt, etc., where it cannot appear with its full energy, yellow creates an unpleasant effect of this sort. A tiny, imperceptible shift changes the beautiful impression of fire and gold into a muddy one. The color of honor and joy becomes the color of shame, loathing, and disquiet. This may explain the yellow hat of the bankrupt and the yellow circles on the Jew's mantle; even the so-called cuckold's color is actually just a muddy yellow.

RED-YELLOW

772. No color may be considered fixed; it is quite easy to intensify and heighten yellow to a reddish hue by condensing and darkening it. As red-yellow, the color increases in energy and seems to grow in power and magnificence.

773. What was said about yellow will be even more applicable here. Red-yellow brings the eye a strong feeling of warmth and joy, for it represents the intense glow of fire as well as the softer refulgence of the setting sun. Hence it also gives pleasure in our surroundings and is rather joyous or magnificent in clothing. A slight reddish cast immediately lends a different appearance to yellow; as Father Castel has noted, the English and Germans are content with bright pale yellow tones in leather, but the French love yellow intensified to red. In fact, the French generally take pleasure in any color on the active side.

YELLOW-RED

774. Pure yellow passes very easily into red-yellow, and the intensification of the latter to yellow-red is equally inevitable. The pleasant, cheerful feeling created by red-yellow is intensified in deep yellow-red to a feeling of unbearable power.

775. Here the active side displays its highest degree of energy, and it is no wonder that robust, healthy, rough people take special pleasure in this color. A preference for it has frequently been noted in primitive peoples. And when children are left to paint on their own, they make lavish use of cinnabar and minium.

776. If we stare at a uniformly yellow-red surface, the color will actually seem to bore its way into our eye. It produces an incredible shock, and retains its effect even in a degree of darkness.

The sight of a yellow-red cloth upsets and maddens animals. I have also known educated people who could not bear to meet someone wearing a scarlet cloak on a gray day.

777. The colors on the minus side are blue, red-blue, and blue-red. They bring an anxious, tender, longing mood.

BLUE

778. Just as yellow always conveys something of light, we can also say that blue always conveys something of darkness.

779. This color has a strange and almost inexpressible effect on the eye. As color it has its own energy, but on the negative side; in its purest form it is like a stimulating nullity. Its appearance brings a sense of contradiction between stimulation and ease.

780. We see the heights of heaven and the distant mountains as blue. Likewise, a blue surface seems to recede from us.

781. Just as we like to pursue a pleasant object retreating into the distance, we also like to look at blue—not because it attacks us but because it draws us along.

782. Blue brings a feeling of cold and reminds us of shadow. We have already learned how it is derived from black.

783. Rooms decorated only in blue seem rather expansive but quite empty and cold.

784. Blue glass shows objects in a sad light.

785. Blue mixed to some extent with the plus side has an agreeable effect. In fact, sea green is a lovely color.

RED-BLUE

786. We found that yellow intensifies easily, and we will note the same characteristic with blue.

787. Blue intensifies delicately toward the red, thus gaining somewhat in power even though it belongs on the passive side. Its effect, however, is quite different from that of red-yellow. It does not enliven so much as it unsettles.

788. Just as the intensification itself is inexorable, so, too, will we feel a need to make our way through this color—not, as with red-yellow, because we wish to take active strides, but because we seek a resting point.

789. In a very dilute form this color is called lilac; even in this form it has an element of liveliness but lacks gaiety.

BLUE-RED

790. The unsettling effect increases with further intensification, and we can say that wallpaper in a very pure, saturated blue-red would seem unbearable. This is why a very dilute and light form of this color is used in clothing, ribbons, and other ornamentation; there it has a special charm in keeping with its nature.

791. The higher clergy has taken this uneasy color as its own; we might say that it seeks to climb the unsteady ladder of incessant intensification to achieve the cardinal's purple.

RED

792. Under this heading we must exclude anything which leaves an impression of yellow or blue in red. We may think of a very pure red, a perfect carmine dried on a white porcelain saucer. Because of its exalted nature we have frequently called this color purple, although we know that the purple of the ancients tended more to the blue side.

793. Those familiar with the origin of prismatic purple will find no paradox in the statement that this color contains all other colors, in part manifest, in part latent.

794. With yellow and blue we noted an incessant intensification to red, and we observed our feelings as this took place. It will come as no surprise that a genuine resolution occurs in the union of the intensified poles, a satisfaction in the ideal realm. Among physical colors, then, this most exalted of color phenomena arises from the merger of two opposites which have been gradually prepared for union.

795. As a pigment, however, it seems fixed, and appears in cochineal as the most perfect red. Although it is possible to shift this material chemically to the plus or minus side, we may consider it fully balanced in the best carmine.

796. The effect of this color is as unique as its character. It may make a serious and dignified impression, or one of grace and charm; the first effect arises when it is dark and condensed, the second when light and dilute. Thus the dignity of age and the charm of youth may be clad in a single color.

797. History provides many examples of how rulers have coveted the purple. Surroundings in this color are always serious and magnificent.

798. Purple glass shows a well-lit landscape in an awe-inspiring and terrible light. This must be the color cast over heaven and earth on the day of judgment.

799. The two materials used to produce this color in dyeing, kermes and cochineal, have a certain tendency toward the plus and minus sides; by treating them with acids and alkalis we can shift them back and forth. Thus we will find that the French prefer the active side (e.g., French scarlet), while the Italians remain on the passive side with a scarlet retaining a hint of blue.

800. A similar treatment with alkalis produces crimson, a color apparently despised by the French since they apply the expressions *sot en cramoisi* and *méchant en cramoisi* to things they find extremely silly or bad.

GREEN

801. We have characterized yellow and blue as the simplest and most basic colors. The color called green arises when yellow and blue are joined where they first appear and create their impression.

802. The eye finds a physical satisfaction in green. When the mixture of the two colors which yield green is so evenly balanced that neither color predominates, the eye and the soul come to rest on the mixture as if it were something simple. We cannot and will not go beyond it. Thus green is often chosen for rooms where we spend all our time.

TOTALITY AND HARMONY

803. For the purposes of discussion we have assumed it is possible to force the eye to identify itself with a single color, but this identification will last but an instant.

804. When a color around us creates its characteristic effect in the eye and forces us by its presence to remain identified with it, we are under a compulsion which the eye will not willingly accept.

805. Upon perceiving a color the eye immediately becomes active; by nature it unconsciously and necessarily produces another color on the spot, and the two colors together will contain the whole circle of colors. The specific sensation aroused by one color will stimulate the eye to seek a totality.

806. To perceive this totality and find satisfaction, the eye looks around each colored space for a colorless one where it can produce the complementary color.

807. Here we find the basic law governing all harmony of colors. The reader may discover this for himself by becoming thoroughly familiar with the experiments described in the section on physiological colors.

808. When presented with the totality of colors in an external object, the eye will rejoice because the result of its own activity stands before it as a reality. Hence we will begin with a discussion of this harmonious juxtaposition.

809. To understand this most easily we may think of the diameter of our color circle as a movable line; when rotated through the entire circle the two ends will eventually indicate all the complementary colors. These, of course, may be reduced to the three simple opposite pairs:

810. Yellow demands red-blue,

Blue demands red-yellow,

Purple demands green,

and vice versa.

811. As we move our imaginary pointer away from the midpoint in this natural order of colors, the other end will also move, but along the opposite series of colors. Such an arrangement will make it possible to find the required complement of every color. We have shown the colors and their transitions as discrete, but for this purpose it would be helpful to construct a color circle with continuous gradations. Here we have arrived at an important point, one deserving our fullest attention.

812. Previously we were affected in a somewhat pathological way when viewing single colors, for we were swept up in specific sensations: we felt lively and active, passive and anxious, lifted to exalted heights, or reduced to the mundane. But the eye's inborn need for totality allows us to escape this limitation; it finds its freedom by creating the opposite of the color forced on it, thus producing a satisfying whole.

813. These truly harmonious opposites are simple but important as evidence that nature is inclined to set us free through totality, for here we are the direct beneficiaries of a natural phenomenon with esthetic implications.

814. Now we can say that our color circle will have a pleasing effect, if only because of the colors it contains. Here we may note that past observers have mistakenly used the rainbow as an example of color totality although a major color—pure red or purple—is missing; this color cannot appear because, as in the usual prismatic image, yellow-red and blue-red cannot merge.

815. In fact, no general phenomenon in nature manifests the totality of colors. We can produce this totality in all its beauty by experiments, but pigments on paper serve best to show how the phenomenon as a whole forms a circle—at least until our natural gifts, a multitude of observations, and much practice imbue us with the idea of this harmony so that it stands before our mind's eye.

COMBINATIONS WITH CHARACTER

816. Besides the purely harmonious, self-generated combinations which always contain a totality, we can identify arbitrary combinations produced along the chords rather than the diameters of our color circle, i.e., so that the color lying between any two other colors is skipped.

817. We say these combinations have character because they possess a distinctive quality: they make a certain impression without satisfying us. Character

appears only when the part stands out from the whole, when it is related to the whole without being lost in it.

818. Based on our knowledge of how colors arise and are related through harmony, we will expect to find a particular impression associated with the character of each arbitrary combination. We will review them one by one.

YELLOW AND BLUE

819. This is the simplest of these combinations. We might say it lacks content, for there is no trace of red and therefore too little of the totality. In this sense we may call it impoverished; it is also mundane since the two poles are at their lowest level. Nonetheless, it has the advantage of being close to green and thus close to a physical satisfaction.

YELLOW AND PURPLE

820. This is rather one-sided, although it has an element of brightness and magnificence. We see the two extremes of the active side together, but without any sense of progressive development.

Since mixing yellow and purple pigments yields yellow-red, they may to some extent represent this color.

BLUE AND PURPLE

821. These are the two extremes of the passive side, but with the upper extreme's tendency toward the active side predominant. Mixing the two yields blue-red; the combination will resemble blue-red in its effect.

YELLOW-RED AND BLUE-RED

822. These are the intensified extremes of the two sides and have a somewhat exciting, exalted quality in combination. They hint at the purple created by their merger in prismatic experiments.

823. When mixed, any of these four combinations would produce the color between them on the color circle; combinations composed of small bits of color viewed from afar will also produce this intermediate color. A surface with narrow blue and yellow stripes will look green at a distance.

824. Looking at blue and yellow together, however, will involve the eye in a futile struggle to produce green; i.e., it will never come to rest in one color or reach a sense of totality in the whole.

825. Thus we can say with justification that these combinations have character; the character of each is related to the character of the single colors in the combination.

COMBINATIONS WITHOUT CHARACTER

826. Now we will turn to the last set of combinations. These are easy to find on the circle: they are indicated by the lesser chords formed by passing over the point of transition between each color rather over than an entire intermediate color.

827. We may say that these combinations are without character because they lie too close to one another to make a particular impression. Yet several deserve attention as indicators of a certain progressive development, even though the steps in this development remain almost imperceptible.

828. Thus yellow and yellow-red, yellow-red and purple, blue and blue-red, blue-red and purple, contain successive stages of intensification and culmination. In certain proportions their effect will not be unpleasant.

829. Yellow with green is always mundane but cheerful, while blue with green is always mundane but disagreeable; this is why our forebears called the latter "fool's colors."

RELATIONSHIP OF THE COMBINATIONS TO LIGHT AND DARK

830. We can vary these combinations greatly by using a light shade of each color, or a dark shade, or a light shade of one and a dark shade of the other. In each case, however, the general impression will remain the same. We will mention only the following among the infinite variety of effects possible.

831. With black, the active side becomes more energetic and the passive side less so. With white and bright shades, the active side loses power and the passive side becomes more lively. With black, purple and green look dark and somber; with white, they look more cheerful.

832. A color may also be muddied or rendered somewhat unrecognizable and then combined with its own kind or with pure colors. Although this will create infinite degrees of variety, the principles found with the pure colors remain generally valid.

HISTORICAL OBSERVATIONS

833. We dealt with the principles of color harmony above, but it will be useful to add several observations and examples to that discussion.

834. These principles were derived from man's own nature and the relationships we have recognized in color phenomena. Empirical observation brings us many things in accord with these principles and some things which are not.

835. Aborigines, uncivilized nations, and children favor color at its most energetic, hence yellow-red in particular. They also like brightly variegated colors; i.e., combinations of colors at their most energetic but without

harmonic balance. If, however, such a balance is found by instinct or accident, a pleasant effect will result. I recall a Hessian officer back from America who painted his face with pure colors like the Indians, thus producing a totality of sorts which was not unpleasant in its effect.

836. The people of southern Europe dress in very lively colors; the easy availability of silk fabrics favors this tendency. Especially the women with their vivid bodices and ribbons seem always to be in harmony with the landscape, although they cannot outshine the brilliance of the sky and earth.

837. The history of dyeing shows that certain technical considerations and advantages have greatly influenced the costume of various nations. Thus the Germans often wear blue because of its durability in cloth. In many regions the country folk wear green twill because twill takes green well. Any alert traveler will soon observe such things to his amusement and edification.

838. Just as colors create moods, they may also fit moods and situations. Lively nations (the French, for example) love intensified colors, especially those on the active side. More subdued nations (the English or Germans, for example) prefer straw yellow or leather yellow, which they wear with dark blue. Nations which cultivate dignity (like the Italians and Spanish) wear cloaks in a red which tends more to the passive side.

839. In clothing we associate the character of the color with the character of the person. Thus we can observe how single colors and combinations of color are related to complexion, age, and social class.

840. Young women prefer rose and sea-green, older women like violet and dark green. Blonds tend toward violet and light yellow, brunets toward blue and yellow-red; in both cases with good reason.

The Roman emperors were extremely jealous of their purple. The robe of the Chinese emperor is orange embroidered with purple. His servants and members of religious orders are allowed to wear lemon-yellow.

841. Cultivated people tend to shy away from color. This may result partly from weakness of the eye and partly from a lack of certainty in taste which prefers to take refuge in no color at all. In our day women almost always choose white, and men wear black.

842. Here it would not be inappropriate to observe that although people like to be noticed they also like to blend in with their own kind.

843. Black was supposed to remind the Venetian nobleman of republican equality.

844. The extent to which the gray Northern skies have gradually banished colors might be a matter for further research.

845. Absolute colors are naturally quite limited in their use, but muddied, quenched colors (the so-called fashionable colors) create endless varieties of degree and shade, most of which are not without charm.

846. We must also note that ladies wearing absolute colors risk making a rather somber complexion even plainer, and that women who must hold their

own in brilliant surroundings generally need to heighten the color of their complexion with cosmetics.

847. Here it would be amusing to apply the above principles to a critique of uniforms, liveries, cockades, and other insignia. In general we might say that these forms of dress or insignia should not consist of harmonious colors. Uniforms ought to have character and dignity; liveries could strike us as common. It would not be hard to find examples both good and bad, since the circle of colors is limited and has been used often enough.

ESTHETIC EFFECT

848. Above we presented the sensory and moral effect of individual colors and color combinations; on that basis we will now develop their esthetic effect for the artist. We will indicate the most essential points of this effect after first discussing the general requirements for pictorial representation, i.e., light and shadow, which bring us directly to the appearance of color.

CHIAROSCURO

849. Chiaroscuro (light-dark) is the term applied to the appearance of physical objects observed solely through the effect of light and shadow.

850. In a narrower sense this term is often applied to a dark area lit by reflection, but here we will use the word in its original and broader sense.

851. It is possible—and necessary—to separate chiaroscuro from any color effect. The artist will more easily resolve the riddle of depiction by thinking of chiaroscuro as independent of color, and becoming thoroughly familiar with it.

852. Chiaroscuro brings out substance as substance, for light and shadow tell us something about density.

853. Here we must consider the highlight, the neutral tint, and the shadow; in connection with the latter we must also consider the shadow belonging to the object itself, the shadow cast on other objects, and the illuminated shadow (or reflex).

854. The sphere might serve as a natural example on which to base a general understanding of chiaroscuro, but it is inadequate for esthetic purposes. The flowing unity of such a round form creates a nebulous quality. To achieve an artistic effect, surfaces must be brought out so that the sections in shadow and light take on more definition within the whole.

855. The Italians call this *il piazzoso*; in German we could say *das Flächenhafte* [quality of surface]. Thus, although the best example of natural chiaroscuro is the sphere, artistic chiaroscuro would be represented by a polyhedron in which all kinds of lights, half-lights, shadows, and reflexes were seen.

856. A bunch of grapes is considered a good model for artistic composition in chiaroscuro, especially since its shape can produce an excellent grouping;

but this subject is suitable only for a master who knows how to find what he can use in it.

857. To understand our basic concept more fully—for it is difficult to grasp even in a polyhedron—we would suggest considering the cube: its three visible sides bring together a clear representation of light, neutral tint, and shadow.

858. But to proceed to a more complex figure in chiaroscuro, we would select an open book as an example offering more diversity.

859. We will find that antique statuary from the classical age is worked quite skillfully to produce such effects. The parts that catch the light are treated simply while the sections in shadow are more broken up so they can receive a variety of reflections—here we may recall the example of the polyhedron.

860. The paintings from Herculaneum and the Aldobrandini Marriage offer examples of this in antique painting.

861. Modern examples are found in single figures by Raphael, and in complete paintings by Correggio and the Flemish School, especially Rubens.

TENDENCY TO COLOR

862. We seldom find pictures done in black and white. A few works by Polidoro offer examples, as do our copperplate engravings and mezzotints. This style has some value insofar as it deals with form and position, but offers little to please the eye for it depends upon forced abstraction.

863. An element of color will assert itself when the artist lets his feelings guide him. The instant black picks up a bit of blue, there will arise a need for yellow to which the artist will instinctively respond. To enliven the whole he will add yellow as he deems best: pure yellow in the highlights, yellow reddened and muddied to brown in the shadows.

864. All types of camaïeu or monochrome lead ultimately to the introduction of a complementary opposite or some sort of color effect. Thus Polidoro often added a yellow vase or the like to his black and white frescoes.

865. People have always striven instinctively for color in their practice of art. We see every day how amateur artists begin drawing in ink or black crayon on white paper, progress to colored paper, then various crayons, and finally pastels. In our own time we have seen portraits drawn in silverpoint with cheeks touched with red and clothing in color, and even silhouettes with brightly colored uniforms. Paolo Uccello painted colored landscapes with monochrome figures.

866. Even ancient sculpture was unable to resist this urge. The Egyptians painted their bas-reliefs. Statues were given eyes of colored stones. Marble heads and limbs were draped in porphyry garments, and busts were placed on pedestals of calcite in variegated colors. The Jesuits did not miss this opportunity in fashioning their St. Aloysius in Rome, and modern sculpture uses a stain to differentiate flesh from clothing.

POSITION

867. Linear perspective shows the effect of distance through a progressive gradation in the apparent size of objects; aerial perspective likewise lets us see the effect of distance through a gradation in the clarity of objects.

868. Although the eye, by its nature, sees nearby objects more clearly than distant ones, aerial perspective is actually based on the important principle that all transparent media are somewhat turbid.

869. Thus the atmosphere is always more or less turbid. It shows this characteristic especially well in southern regions when the barometric pressure is high, the weather dry, and the sky clear; then we may note a distinct gradation between objects which are not very far from one another.

870. In general this phenomenon is familiar to everyone, but the painter sees the gradation even when the separation is quite small—or at least has the impression that he sees it. In practice he represents it by a progressive gradation in the parts of an object (a completely frontal face, for example). Here lighting requires attention; this has an effect from the side just as position does from foreground to background.

COLORATION

871. In proceeding to the matter of coloring we will assume that the painter is generally acquainted with our theory of color in outline, and has familiarized himself thoroughly with the sections and principles most pertinent to him. He will then find it easy to deal with the theoretical elements as well as the practical ones as he studies them in nature and applies them to his art.

COLORATION OF PLACEMENT

872. In nature, coloration first appears in connection with position, for aerial perspective depends on the principle of turbid media. We see the sky, distant objects, and even nearby shadows as blue. At the same time, sources of illumination and illuminated objects appear in gradations from yellow to purple. In many cases, a physiological need for color will immediately arise, and an entirely colorless landscape will seem fully colored because these effects act both with and against one another in the eye.

COLORATION OF OBJECTS

873. Local colors are basic and general colors, but defined by the characteristics of an object and its surfaces. This definition can be endlessly varied.

874. Colored silk looks quite different from colored wool. Each type of preparation and weaving produces its own variation. Roughness, smoothness, and sheen play a role.

875. Thus it is prejudicial to good art to say that the painter should ignore the material in garments and merely paint something like abstract folds. Doesn't this deny all characteristic variation? Is the portrait of Leo X any less excellent because velvet, satin, and moreen are depicted together?

876. In products of nature, the colors appear more or less modified, defined, even individualized; this may be observed in stones and plants, as well as bird feathers and animal fur.

877. The painter's art lies mainly in imitating the actual appearance of particular materials, thus eliminating the general and basic element in color phenomena. In doing so, he will find the greatest difficulty lies in the surface of the human body.

878. Flesh is generally on the active side, but a bluish tinge plays into it from the passive side. The color is completely changed from its basic state, neutralized by the high degree of structure in the human organism.

879. After some reflection on what has been said in this theory of color, the skillful artist will find it easier to bring coloration of placement and coloration of objects into harmony; he will be in a position to depict things infinitely beautiful, varied, and true as well.

CHARACTERISTIC COLORATION

880. The juxtaposition of colored objects as well as the coloration of the space around them should conform to the artist's purpose. This requires knowledge of how our feelings are affected by colors, both singly and in combination. Hence the painter should become thoroughly familiar with the general dualism of color and the colors of each individual object; he should also be familiar with what we have said about the qualities of the colors.

881. We can divide characteristic coloration into three categories, which we may call the powerful, the gentle, and the brilliant.

882. The first of these is produced by a predominance of the active side; the second, by a predominance of the passive side; and the third, by a totality, a balanced presentation of the color circle.

883. The powerful effect is produced by yellow, yellow-red, and purple (when the latter is still on the plus side). Very little violet or blue may be used, and even less green. The gentle effect is created by blue, violet, and purple (when shifted to the minus side). Little yellow or yellow-red should be present, but large amounts of green may be used.

884. To achieve these two effects in their purest form we should keep the complementary colors to a minimum, using only what is absolutely required to satisfy our sense for the totality.

HARMONIOUS COLORATION

885. The two characteristic qualities noted above may be called harmonious to some extent, but the true effect of harmony arises only when all the colors are brought together in a balanced way.

886. This allows us to create an effect both brilliant and pleasant, but rather general and thus somewhat characterless.

887. This is why most modern painters use coloration lacking in character. They follow only their instinct, and the goal to which it leads them is a totality; they attain their goal with varying degrees of success, thereby losing the character the picture might otherwise have had.

888. But with our earlier principles in mind, we see how we can be confident in choosing a different color mood for every subject. Of course, the application of these principles demands endless modifications which our creative spirit can achieve only when it is permeated by these principles.

GENUINE TONE

889. We may wish to continue borrowing the word *tone* (or rather *tonality*) from music and apply it to coloration; now we can make better use of the term than earlier.

890. We would be justified in drawing a comparison between a picture with a powerful effect and a musical work in a major key, or a painting with a gentle effect and a work in a minor key. We might also find other comparisons to describe modifications of these two basic effects.

FALSE TONE

891. Until now, the word *tone* has been used to describe a veil in a single color spread over the whole picture. This is usually done in yellow, since we instinctively try to shift the picture to the powerful side.

892. We will see a painting in this tone if we look at it through yellow glass. It is worthwhile to do this repeatedly, for the experiment shows the exact effect of such a process: a kind of nocturnal illumination, an intensification, but with the plus side darkened and the minus side muddied.

893. This false tone arose instinctively out of uncertainty about how to proceed; it produces uniformity instead of totality.

WEAK COLORATION

894. This very uncertainty led to such broken use of colors in the painting that the painter simply paints out of gray and into gray, treating colors as delicately as possible.

973

ON PHILOSOPHY AND SCIENCE

895. The harmonic contrasts in such a painting are often successful, but they lack boldness because the painter is afraid of producing a multicolored effect.

THE MULTICOLORED EFFECT

896. A painting may easily become multicolored if the painter has an uncertain impression and merely paints an empirical juxtaposition of the colors in their full force.

897. On the other hand, a juxtaposition of weak colors, even ugly ones, will not have a particularly striking effect. The painter transfers his uncertainty to the viewer, who can then offer neither praise nor criticism.

898. It is also important to note that a multicolored effect will be created if properly arranged colors are misused in regard to light and shadow.

899. This is all the more likely to happen because light and shadow are prescribed by the drawing—they are a part of it, so to speak—but color is still subject to choice and caprice.

FEAR OF THE THEORETICAL

900. Until now painters have shown a dread of any theoretical consideration of color and the like; they have even exhibited a decided aversion to it. This was not altogether unjustified, for up to now so-called theoretical considerations have been without foundation, ill-defined, and rather empirical. We hope that our efforts may somewhat allay these fears, inspiring the artist to test our principles in a practical way and call them to life.

ULTIMATE GOAL

901. For it is impossible to attain the ultimate goal without an overview of the whole. Let the artist familiarize himself thoroughly with what we have discussed. Given what we have said, it is only the agreement of light and shadow, position, and true and characteristic coloration that will lend the painting the appearance of perfection.

GROUNDS

902. Earlier artists made a practice of painting on a light ground. It consisted of gesso thickly applied to canvas or wood and then smoothed. An outline was drawn and the picture was given a blackish or brownish wash. We still have pictures prepared in this way for the addition of color by Leonardo da Vinci, Fra Bartolommeo, and also several by Guido.

903. When the artist was adding color and needed to depict white clothing, he sometimes left this ground untouched. Titian did this in his later years,

when he was quite sure of himself and knew how to accomplish much with lit-tle effort. The whitish ground was treated as a middle shade; then the shadows were added and the highlights brushed on.

904. Even after color was added, the underlying picture (washed on, as it were) continued to have an effect. A garment, for instance, was painted in a transparent color so that the white shone through and enlivened the color, while the section prepared for shadow muted the color without contaminating or muddying it.

905. This method had many advantages. The lighter parts of the picture had a light ground; and the shaded parts, a dark ground. The entire picture was already prepared; the artist could paint with thin colors, certain that the light and the colors would be in agreement. In our time, water color painting is based on these principles.

906. In any case, modern oil painting always uses a light ground. Middle shades are more or less transparent and therefore enlivened by a light ground; even the shadows are less apt to become dark.

907. Dark grounds were also used for a time; apparently Tintoretto intro-duced these. It is not known whether Giorgione used them, but Titian's best pictures were not painted on a dark ground.

908. Such a ground was reddish brown, and when the picture was sketched on it the darkest shadows were laid on. The light colors were heavily im-pasted on the brighter sections, and thinned out toward the shadows; the dark ground then shone through the thinner color as a middle shade. The final ef-fect was achieved by painting over the light sections several times and further adding highlights.

909. Although this method helps speed the work, its results are not ben-eficial. The energetic ground becomes darker and more prominent; as the light colors lose their clarity, the shadow side grows more overpowering. The middle shades turn darker and darker, and the shadows finally become quite black. Only the thickly applied highlights remain bright, and these bright spots are all that remains to be seen in the picture. The paintings of the school of Bologna and of Caravaggio offer many examples of this.

910. Perhaps it would be well to conclude by mentioning painting with glazes. In such painting the previously applied color is considered a light ground. This method can yield an impression of color mixture, intensifica-tion, or so-called tone, but the colors darken in the process.

PIGMENTS

911. We receive these from the hand of the chemist and the scientist. Much has already been said and published about this subject, but it deserves to be reconsidered from time to time. Meanwhile, the master passes his knowledge of it down to the student, and one artist shares it with another.

912. The longest-lasting pigments are preferable, but the way they are used also has a great effect on the longevity of the picture. Thus the fewest possible coloring materials should be used, and the simplest method of application is highly recommended.

913. The large number of pigments has led to many harmful results in coloration. Each pigment has its own way of affecting the eye, and also its own peculiarities in regard to technical application. The former explains why it is harder to achieve harmony with many pigments than with few; and the latter, why chemical reactions occur among coloring materials.

914. Let us recall some other false paths which may seduce the artist. Painters are always looking for new coloring materials, and believe it represents progress in art when they find them. They also long to master the mechanical techniques of earlier periods, thus wasting much time; e.g., our lengthy and laborious efforts to learn wax painting at the end of the last century. Others set out to invent new techniques, which also accomplishes nothing. It is, after all, only the spirit which brings life to any technique.

ALLEGORICAL, SYMBOLIC, MYSTICAL USE OF COLOR

915. We have shown in detail that each color makes its own impression on the human being, thereby revealing its nature to the eye as well as to the spirit. It follows that color may be used for certain sensory, moral, and esthetic purposes.

916. When this use is completely consistent with nature, we may call it symbolic; the color's function would correspond with its effect, and its true quality would give direct expression to the intended meaning. For instance, the use of purple to represent majesty no doubt represents the right form of expression (as noted earlier).

917. Closely related is another use which could be called allegorical. This is more fortuitous and capricious; we might even say conventional, for the significance of the emblem must be learned before its meaning is clear. This is the case, for instance, with green, which has been assigned the meaning of hope.

918. We can also sense that color is open to mystical interpretation. The scheme depicting the multiplicity of colors points to archetypal relationships which are as much a part of human intuitive perception as they are of nature. These associations could no doubt be used as a language to express archetypal relationships which are not so powerful and diverse in their effect on us. The mathematician values the worth and utility of the triangle, but the mystic venerates it. Much may be schematized in the triangle, and in the phenomena of color as well, for by pairing and converging we may derive the ancient and mystical hexagram.

919. We must grasp how yellow and blue diverge, and should reflect especially on the intensification in red where the opposites incline to one another

and merge to create a third element. Then we will certainly arrive at the mystical and intuitive perception that a spiritual meaning can be found in these two separate and opposite entities. When we see them bring forth green below and red above, it will be hard to resist the thought that the green is connected with the earthly creation of the Elohim, and the red with their heavenly creation.

920. But we had best not expose ourselves to suspicions of fantastic imaginings at the end; all the more so since a favorable reception of our color theory will enable allegorical, symbolic, and mystical applications and interpretations to emerge in keeping with the spirit of our age.

FROM *ON MORPHOLOGY*
(1807–17)

The Enterprise Justified

When in the exercise of his powers of observation man undertakes to confront the world of nature, he will at first experience a tremendous compulsion to bring what he finds there under his control. Before long, however, these objects will thrust themselves upon him with such force that he, in turn, must feel the obligation to acknowledge their power and pay homage to their effects. When this mutual interaction becomes evident he will make a discovery which, in a double sense, is limitless; among the objects he will find many different forms of existence and modes of change, a variety of relationships livingly interwoven; in himself, on the other hand, a potential for infinite growth through constant adaptation of his sensibilities and judgment to new ways of acquiring knowledge and responding with action. This discovery produces a deep sense of pleasure and would bring the last touch of happiness in life if not for certain obstacles (within and without) which impede our progress along this beautiful path to perfection. The years, providers at first, now begin to take; within our limits we are satisfied with what we have gained and enjoy it all the more quietly since it seldom meets with any genuine, open and cordial expression of interest from without.

How few are those who feel themselves inspired by what is really visible to the spirit alone! Our senses, our feelings, our temperament exercise far greater power over us—and rightly so, since life is our lot rather than reflection.

Unfortunately, however, even those devoted to cognition and knowledge rarely display the degree of interest we would hope to find. Anything arising from an idea and leading back to it is viewed as something of an encumbrance by the man of a practical mind who notes details, observes precisely, and draws distinctions. In his own way he feels at home in his labyrinth and has no interest in a thread that might more quickly lead him through it; a substance uncoined and uncountable seems a burdensome possession to such a person.

On the other hand, one who has a higher vantage point is quick to disdain detail and create a lethal generality by lumping together things which live only in separation.

We have long found ourselves in the midst of this conflict, in the course of which much has been accomplished, much destroyed. Had the hour of danger just past not brought home to us the value of the written record, I would never have been tempted to entrust my views on nature to this fragile vessel on the ocean of opinion.

Therefore let what I often dreamt of as a book when I was filled with the high hopes of youth now appear as an outline, as a fragmentary collection. May it work and serve as such.

This, in brief, is what I would say in seeking the good will of my contemporaries for these partially finished sketches which date back many years. Anything further will best be introduced as our enterprise unfolds.

JENA, 1807

The Purpose Set Forth

In observing objects of nature, especially those that are alive, we often think the best way of gaining an insight into the relationship between their inner nature and the effects they produce is to divide them into their constituent parts. Such an approach may, in fact, bring us a long way toward our goal. In a word, those familiar with science can recall what chemistry and anatomy have contributed toward an understanding and overview of nature.

But these attempts at division also produce many adverse effects when carried to an extreme. To be sure, what is alive can be dissected into its component parts, but from these parts it will be impossible to restore it and bring it back to life. This is true even of many inorganic substances, to say nothing of things organic in nature.

Thus scientific minds of every epoch have also exhibited an urge to understand living formations as such, to grasp their outward, visible, tangible parts in context, to see these parts as an indication of what lies within and thereby gain some understanding of the whole through an exercise of intuitive perception. It is no doubt unnecessary to describe in detail the close relationship between this scientific desire and our need for art and imitation.

Thus the history of art, knowledge, and science has produced many attempts to establish and develop a theory which we will call "morphology." The historical part of our discourse will deal with the different forms in which these attempts have appeared.

The Germans have a word for the complex of existence presented by a physical organism: *Gestalt* [structured form]. With this expression they exclude what is changeable and assume that an interrelated whole is identified, defined, and fixed in character.

But if we look at all these *Gestalten*, especially the organic ones, we will discover that nothing in them is permanent, nothing is at rest or defined—everything is in a flux of continual motion. This is why German frequently and fittingly makes use of the word *Bildung* [formation] to describe the end product and what is in process of production as well.

Thus in setting forth a morphology we should not speak of *Gestalt*, or if we use the term we should at least do so only in reference to the idea, the concept, or to an empirical element held fast for a mere moment of time.

When something has acquired a form it metamorphoses immediately to a new one. If we wish to arrive at some living perception of nature we ourselves must remain as quick and flexible as nature and follow the example she gives.

In anatomy, when we dissect a body into its parts, and further separate these parts into their parts, we will at last arrive at elementary constituents called "similar parts." These will not concern us here. Instead we will concentrate on a higher principle of the organism, a principle we will characterize as follows.

No living thing is unitary in nature; every such thing is a plurality. Even the organism which appears to us as individual exists as a collection of independent living entities. Although alike in idea and predisposition, these entities, as they materialize, grow to become alike or similar, unlike or dissimilar. In part these entities are joined from the outset, in part they find their way together to form a union. They diverge and then seek each other again; everywhere and in every way they thus work to produce a chain of creation without end.

The less perfect the creation, the more its parts are alike or similar and the more they resemble the whole. The more perfect the creation the less similar its parts become. In the first instance the whole is like its parts to a degree, in the second the whole is unlike its parts. The more similar the parts, the less they will be subordinated to one another. Subordination of parts indicates a more perfect creation.

No matter how well thought out, generalities always contain an element of incomprehensibility if we find no application for them or are unable to supply illustrative examples. Since our entire treatise is devoted to presenting and developing ideas and principles of this type, we will begin by indicating only a few such examples.

Although a plant or tree seems to be an individual organism, it undeniably consists only of separate parts which are alike and similar to one another and to the whole. How many plants are propagated by runners! In the least variety of fruit tree the eye puts forth a twig which in turn produces many identical eyes; propagation through seeds is carried out in the same fashion. This propagation occurs through the development of innumerable identical individuals out of the womb of the mother plant.

Here it is immediately apparent that the secret of propagation by seeds is already present in the principle cited above, and upon closer consideration we will find that even the seed, seemingly a single unity, is itself a collection of identical and similar entities. The bean is usually offered as a good example of the process of germination. If we take a bean in its completely undeveloped state prior to germination, and cut it open, we will first find two seed leaves. These are not to be compared to a placenta, for they are two genuine leaves: though distended and stuffed with a mealy substance, they also turn green when given light and air. In addition we will discover the presence of plumules which are again two leaves capable of further and more extensive development. We may also observe that behind every leaf stalk there is an eye, if not actual then at least in latent form. Thus even in the seed, seemingly simple, we find a collection of several individual parts which we may characterize as alike in idea and similar in appearance.

What is alike in idea may manifest itself in empirical reality as alike, or similar, or even totally unalike and dissimilar: this gives rise to the ever-changing life of nature. It is this life of nature which we propose to outline in these pages.

By way of further introduction we will cite an example from the lowest level of the animal kingdom. There are infusoria which we perceive as fairly simple in form when they move about through moisture. When the moisture evaporates, however, they burst and pour forth a number of spores. Apparently this dispersion into spores would have occurred naturally in the moisture, thereby producing descendants without number.

Plants and animals in their least perfect state are scarcely to be differentiated. Hardly perceptible to our senses, they are a pinpoint of life, mutable or semimutable. Are these beginnings—determinable in either direction—destined to be transformed by light into plant, or by darkness into animal? This is a question we would not trust ourselves to answer no matter how well we are supplied with relevant observations and analogies. We can say, however, that the creatures which gradually emerge from this barely differentiated relationship of plant and animal pursue diametrically opposite paths in their development toward perfection. Thus plants attain their final glory in the tree, enduring and rigid, while the animal does so in man by achieving the highest degree of mobility and freedom.

The above axiom concerning the coexistence of multiple identical and similar entities leads to two further cardinal principles of the organism: propagation by bud and propagation by seed. In fact, these principles are simply two ways of expressing the same axiom. We will seek to trace these two paths through the entire realm of organic nature and in the process will find that many things fall vividly into place.

When considering the vegetative model we are presented immediately with a vertical orientation. The lower position is occupied by the root which works into the earth, belongs to the moisture and to the darkness. The stem, the trunk, or whatever may serve in its place, strives upward in exactly the opposite direction, toward the sky, the light, and the air.

When we then consider this miraculous structure and become familiar with how it rises upward, we will once more meet an important principle of structure: life is unable to work at the surface or express its generative powers there. The whole activity of life requires a covering which protects it against the raw elements of its environment, be they water or air or light, a covering which preserves its delicate nature so that it may fulfill the specific purpose for which it is inwardly destined.

Whether the covering takes the form of bark, skin, or shell, anything that works in a living way must be covered over. And thus everything turned toward the external world gradually falls victim to an early death and decay. The bark of trees, the skin of insects, the hair and feathers of animals, even the epidermis of man, are coverings forever being shed, cast off, given over to non-life. New coverings are constantly forming beneath the old, while still further down, close to this surface or more deeply hidden, life brings forth its web of creation.

JENA, 1807

The Content Prefaced

Of the present collection only the essay on the metamorphosis of plants has been in print before. Appearing alone in 1790, it met with a cold, almost hostile reception. This resistance, however, was entirely natural: the theory of encasement, the concept of preformation, of successive development undergone by things dating from the time of Adam, had by and large captivated even the best minds. Moreover Linnaeus, focusing on plant formation in particular, had decisively and authoritatively initiated a brilliant conceptual approach more suited to the spirit of the time.

Thus my honest effort remained entirely without effect. Content to have found a direction for my own quiet path, I simply made more careful note of the relationship and interaction between normal and abnormal phenomena and, at the same time, paid close attention to the detail so generously provided by empirical observation. In addition I spent an entire summer in a series of experiments to find out how fruiting may be prevented by too much nourishment or accelerated by deprivation.

I availed myself of the opportunity to illuminate or darken a greenhouse at will to learn about the effect of light on plants; my principal concern was with the phenomena of fading and bleaching. I also did experiments with panes of colored glass.

After acquiring enough skill in judging most instances of organic change and transformation in the plant world, and discerning and deducing the sequence of forms, I felt further obliged to learn more about the metamorphosis of insects.

No one will dispute that this metamorphosis is a fact: the life of such creatures is a continual transformation, one which is clear and obvious. I had retained my earlier knowledge of this subject, based on years of raising silkworms. I now broadened it by observation of various genera and species from egg to moth; I also had drawings made, the most worthwhile of which I still possess.

Here I found no conflict with what is stated in treatises on the subject. I needed only to work out a schematic table whereby the individual observations could be arranged in sequence and the wonderful life of these creatures surveyed with clarity.

I will also seek to give an account of these efforts, one which is unconstrained since my view is not in contradiction to any other.

In the pursuit of these studies I turned my attention to the comparative anatomy of animals, especially mammals. There was already great interest in this area. Buffon and Daubenton achieved much. Camper appeared in a meteoric blaze of intelligence, science, talent and industry, Sömmerring showed himself to be worthy of admiration, and Merck brought his always active endeavors to bear on this subject. I had an excellent relationship with all three, with Camper by letter and with the other two in person (a contact which continued even after we parted).

The study of physiognomy required attention to both definition and mutability of form; this point also stimulated much work and discussion with Lavater.

Later, during my frequent and extended visits in Jena, Loder's inexhaustible talents as a teacher quickly provided me the pleasure of some insight into animal and human formation.

The method I had adopted in the observation of plants and insects served to guide me on this path as well, for in distinguishing and comparing forms it was also necessary to discuss formation and transformation, each in their turn.

Nonetheless, that era was more confused than can be imagined today. It was maintained, for example, that if man could learn to walk about comfortably on all fours, bears might become human after standing upright for a time. The audacious Diderot ventured certain suggestions about how goat-footed fauns could be bred to sit in livery atop the coaches of the great and wealthy as a special mark of pomp and distinction.

The distinction between man and animal long eluded discovery. Ultimately it was believed that the definitive difference between ape and man lay in the placement of the ape's four incisors in a bone clearly and physically separate from other bones. Thus the whole of science, in jest or in earnest, vacillated between attempts to prove what was half true and attempts to lend the semblance of truth to what was false—but all with the purpose of keeping itself occupied and sustaining itself through whimsical and willful activity. The greatest confusion, however, arose from the controversy over whether beauty was something real and inherent in objects, or relative, determined by convention, even individually ascribable to the one who beholds and recognizes it.

Meanwhile I had devoted my full energies to the study of osteology, for in the skeleton the unmistakable character of every form is preserved conclusively and for all time. I surrounded myself with a collection of older and more recent remains, and on trips I carefully looked through museums and small collections for creatures whose formation as a whole, or in part, could prove instructive to me.

In the process I was soon obliged to postulate a prototype against which all mammals could be compared as to points of agreement or divergence. As I had earlier sought out the archetypal plant I now aspired to find the archetypal animal; in essence, the concept or idea of the animal.

My laborious and painstaking research was made easier, even sweetened, when Herder undertook to set down his ideas on the history of mankind. Our daily conversation was concerned with the primal origins of the water-covered earth and the living creatures which have evolved on it from time immemorial. Again and again we discussed the primal origin and its ceaseless development; through mutual sharing and debate we daily refined and enriched our store of scientific knowledge.

This topic which occupied me so intensely was also the subject of lively discussions with other friends, and such conversations had a mutually beneficial effect. Indeed, it is perhaps not presumptuous to think that much of what grew out of those discussions and spread in the sciences as tradition is now bearing fruit. We may now enjoy these fruits even though the garden from which the grafts were taken is not always given credit.

With the more frequent application of empirical observation and deepened philosophical approach of today many things have become common knowledge which were inaccessible to me and my colleagues when the following essays were written. Thus, although their contents may now seem superfluous, they should be considered in the light of history as witness to a quiet, consistent, and unrelenting effort.

THE INFLUENCE OF MODERN PHILOSOPHY
(1817)

I had no sense for philosophy in the real meaning of the word; I had only the continuing response brought by my need to resist the intrusions of the world and take hold of it. This response necessarily led me to a way of seizing upon philosophers' opinions as if they were objects from which something might be learned. As a youth I loved to read in Brucker's history of philosophy, yet I read it like a man whose life is spent looking up at the circling of the stars in heaven, a man who sees the most obvious constellations, but without any understanding of astronomy; one with knowledge of the Big Dipper but not of the North Star.

I had often discussed art and its theoretical requirements with Moritz in Rome; the evidence of our fruitful perplexity can be found even today in one short publication. Moreover, in describing plant metamorphosis I found it necessary to develop a method which conformed to nature. There was no latitude for error as the vegetation revealed its processes to me step by step. Without interfering, I had to recognize the ways and means the plant used as it gradually rose from a state of complete encapsulation to one of perfection. In my physics experiments I became convinced that any observation of physical objects required above all that I be thorough in my search for every condition under which a phenomenon may arise, and that I be as comprehensive as possible in collecting phenomena. In the end, the phenomena must form a series, or rather, overlap; thus they give the scientist a picture of some organization by which the inner life of the phenomena become manifest as a whole. All the while I was only dimly aware of these things; nowhere did I find any enlightenment suited to my nature, for ultimately no man can be enlightened in a way not his own.

Kant's *Critique of Pure Reason* had long since appeared, but it lay entirely beyond my ken. I heard a few discussions of the work, however, and I could see that an old issue was being revived: i.e., what role do we ourselves play in our intellectual life, and what part is played by the external world. I had never separated the two, and when I philosophized about things in my own way I did so with unconscious naiveté; I truly believed that my eyes beheld what my mind thought true. But when this dispute arose I found myself on the side of those who put the human being in the best light. I applauded my friends who said with Kant: although all knowledge may be prompted by experience, it does not therefore follow that it arises wholly from experience. I liked the ideas of knowledge *a priori* and synthetic judgments *a priori*. All my life, whether in poetry or research, I had alternated between a synthetic approach and an analytic one—to me these were the systole and the diastole of the human mind, like a second breathing, never separated, always pulsing. I had no words (much less, concepts) to describe these things; but now, for the first time, theory seemed to smile on me. I found pleasure in the portal but I dared not set foot in the labyrinth itself; sometimes my gift for poetry got in my way, sometimes common sense, and I felt that I made little progress.

Actually, Herder was a student of Kant, but, unfortunately, also his opponent; now I was in an even worse state, for I could not agree with Herder, nor could I follow Kant. In the meantime I was intent on continuing my studies of the formation and transformation of organisms, and here the method I had applied to plants proved to be a reliable guide. I could not help but notice that nature always follows an analytic course—development out of a living, mysterious whole—but then seems to act synthetically in bringing together apparently alien circumstances and joining them into one. Thus I returned again and again to Kant's teachings, thought that I understood a few of the principles, and learned much that was useful.

Then the *Critique of Judgment* fell into my hands, and with this book a wonderful period arrived in my life. Here I found my most disparate interests brought together; products of art and nature were dealt with alike, esthetic and teleological judgment illuminated one another. I did not always agree with the author's way of thinking, and occasionally something seemed to be missing, but the main ideas in the book were completely analogous to my earlier work and thought. The inner life of nature and art, their respective effects as they work from within—all this came to clear expression in the book. The products of these two infinitely vast worlds were shown to exist for their own sake; things found together might be there *for* one another, but not *because* of one another (at least not intentionally).

The antipathy I felt toward ultimate causes was now put in order and justified. I could make a clear distinction between purpose and effect, and I saw why our human understanding so often confuses the two. I was glad to find poetry and comparative science related so closely: both are subject to the same faculty of judgment. Now passionately enthusiastic, I was all the more eager to pursue my own paths because I had no idea where they led, and because the what and how of my discoveries met with little approval among the Kantians. After all, I was only expressing what had stirred in me, and not what I had read. Thrown back on my own devices, I read the book again and again. I still have my old copy, and turn with pleasure to the sections I marked at the time. I also find marked sections in the *Critique of Reason* which I seem to have understood more deeply than before, for two works sprung from one mind always shed light on one another. I did not have the same success in approaching the Kantians: they listened to me, but were unable to respond or help in any way. It happened several times that one or the other of them would admit with a bemused smile: this is indeed an analogue to Kantian thought, but a peculiar one.

It did not become clear just how extraordinary the situation was until I established my connection with Schiller. Our discussions were quite productive or theoretical, and usually both. He preached the gospel of freedom, while I defended the rights of nature. Perhaps more out of friendship to me than any belief of his own, he described Mother Nature in his esthetic letters without those rough expressions I found so distasteful in his essay "On Grace and Dignity." For my part, I stubbornly insisted on the superiority of Greek poetry (or poetry based on it), and even held this up as the only kind of poetry to be deemed proper and worthy of pursuit. Thus he was forced to consider the point more carefully; to this dispute we owe the essays on naive and sentimental poetry. Here it is argued that both modes of poetry should exist side by side, that each must accord the other equal standing.

With this thought he broke ground for a whole new esthetics: *hellenic, romantic,* and all other concepts of this sort may be traced back to his discussion of whether a style is primarily real or ideal.

And thus I slowly grew accustomed to a language which had been totally foreign to me. This was made easier by the fact that it encouraged a higher level of thinking about art and science. I felt much nobler and richer than I had when we were subjected to the indignities of the popular philosophers, and philosophers of another sort for whom I can find no name.

For my further progress I am particularly grateful to Niethammer, who worked patiently with me to unravel the principal riddles, and to develop and explain individual concepts and expressions. My debt then and later to Fichte, Schelling, Hegel, the Humboldt brothers, and Schlegel will be repaid with thanks when I am able to describe—or at least indicate, even sketch— this most important period, the final decade of the last century, from my own point of view.

COLORS IN THE SKY
(1817–20)

These colors correlate closely with meteorological conditions.

We must make careful note of the following observation, for it demonstrates the principle underlying every appearance of color in the atmosphere.

A turbid glass held before a dark background and illuminated from the front will appear bluish. The less turbid the glass, the bluer it will look; the least turbid glass will seem violet. Conversely, the same glass held before something bright will look yellow. The denser the glass, the redder it will seem, so that in the end even the sun will appear ruby red.

The air, even at its clearest, is a vehicle for moisture and must therefore be considered a turbid medium. This is why the sky opposite the sun and around it looks blue: the darkness of space creates this effect through the veiling. This is also why mountains in the middle distance seem darker blue than those in the far distance.

On the highest mountain peaks the air will seem deep blue because of the purity of the atmosphere there; ultimately it will take on a reddish tinge. In the plains, where the air becomes increasingly dense and filled with turbidity, the blue will grow ever paler, finally vanishing and assuming a completely white appearance.

Seen through an atmosphere thick with haze, the sun and the bright area around it will seem to have a yellow-red to red color.

Before sunrise and after sunset, when the sun shines through the thick haze on the horizon, the clouds will be lit with a glow which is yellow or even red.

When there is a heavy layer of haze in the upper atmosphere the sun will appear blood red, as through a very turbid glass.

[The blue scale is] combined with the scale of yellow and red. The former has only half its steps, but not even all these will be found in our part of the world. The latter contains the whole range, but the deepest red is rarely found here. In Italy it appears at the time of the sirocco.

PROBLEMS
(1823)

Natural system: a contradictory expression.

Nature has no system; she has—she is—life and development from an unknown center toward an unknowable periphery. Thus observation of nature is limitless, whether we make distinctions among the least particles or pursue the whole by following the trail far and wide.

The idea of metamorphosis deserves great reverence, but it is also a most dangerous gift from above. It leads to formlessness; it destroys knowledge, dissolves it. It is like the *vis centrifuga*, and would be lost in the infinite if it had no counterweight; here I mean the drive for specific character, the stubborn persistence of things which have finally attained reality. This is a *vis centripeta* which remains basically untouched by any external factor. We may recall the genus *Erica*.

But since both forces operate at the same time, any didactic description would have to show them simultaneously—which seems impossible.

There may be no escape from this difficulty without recourse once more to artifice.

Compare the natural sequence of musical notes with the equal temperament within the confines of the octaves. It is actually the temperament which makes truly satisfying music of a higher kind possible, nature notwithstanding.

It would be necessary to introduce a method of discoursing by artifice. A symbolism would have to be established! But who is to do this? And who is to recognize it, once accomplished?

Regarding what botany calls "genera" (in the usual sense of the word), I have always held it impossible to treat one genus like another. I would say there are genera with a character which is expressed throughout all their species; we can approach them in a rational way. They rarely dissolve into varieties, and thus they deserve to be treated with respect. I will mention the gentians, but the observant botanist may add several more.

On the other hand, there are characterless genera in which species may become hard to distinguish as they dissolve into endless varieties. If we make a serious attempt to apply the scientific approach to these, we will never reach an end; instead, we will only meet with confusion, for they elude any definition, any law. I have occasionally ventured to call these the wanton genera, and have even applied this epithet to the rose, although this in no way detracts from its graceful quality. *Rosa canina* may especially deserve this reproach.

Wherever the human being plays a significant role, he acts as a lawgiver: in morality, through his recognition of duty; in the area of religion, by declaring his adherence to a particular conviction about God and things divine, and then by connecting certain analogous outer ceremonies with his conviction. The same thing occurs in government, whether peaceful or warlike: actions and deeds are meaningful only if prescribed by the human being for himself and others. The same is true of art: we have described above how music has yielded to man's spirit; in our own time it is an open secret that the greatest epochs saw the human spirit actively at work in the plastic arts through the most talented artists. In the sciences we find an indication of this in the innumerable attempts to systemize, to schematize. But our full attention must be focused on the task of listening to nature to overhear the secret of her process, so that we neither frighten her off with coercive imperatives, nor allow her whims to divert us from our goal.

EXCERPT FROM
"TOWARD A THEORY OF WEATHER"
(1825)

General Introduction

We can never directly see what is true, i.e., identical with what is divine; we look at it only in reflection, in example, in the symbol, in individual and related phenomena. We perceive it as a life beyond our grasp, yet we cannot deny our need to grasp it.

This applies primarily to phenomena of the tangible world, but here we will speak only of the less tangible principles of weather.

Weather manifests itself to the active human being mainly through heat and cold, through humidity and dryness, and through moderate and immoderate degrees of these conditions. We experience all this in a direct way, without further thought and research.

988

Many instruments have been invented to measure in degrees these phenomena that affect us daily. The thermometer engages everyone's attention: whether we are sweating or freezing, we seem somewhat more content when able to express our suffering in degrees Reaumur or Fahrenheit.

Less attention is paid the hygrometer. Daily and monthly, we simply accept humidity and dry air as they come. But the wind is everyone's concern: the ubiquitous wind vane lets everyone know whence it blows and whither it goes, although what this means in a larger sense remains as much a mystery as the other phenomena.

It is remarkable, however, that the most important effect on atmospheric conditions is the least noted by the common man: a sickly constitution is needed to feel those atmospheric changes shown by the barometer, and a more advanced education to observe them.

These were long hidden from us because they manifested themselves as various degrees of pressure—in succession at one place, or simultaneously at several places, and at different altitudes. In our time, this aspect of the atmosphere plays a leading role in weather observations; we will also give it special importance.

Above all we must remember that nothing that exists or comes into being, lasts or passes, can be thought of as entirely isolated, entirely unadulterated. One thing is always permeated, accompanied, covered, or enveloped by another; it produces effects and endures them. And when so many things work through one another, where are we to find the insight to discover what governs and what serves, what leads the way and what follows? This creates great difficulty in any theoretical statement; here lies the danger of confusion between cause and effect, illness and symptom, deed and character.

The serious observer has no choice but to choose some midpoint and then see how he can deal with what is left on the periphery. This is what we have attempted to do, as the following will show.

Thus it is actually the atmosphere in which and with which we will now be occupied. We dwell in it as inhabitants of the seashore. We gradually ascend to the highest peak where it is difficult to live, but in thought we climb further. We have ventured to think of the moon, the other planets and their moons, and finally the fixed stars, as collaborating in the whole; and the human being, who necessarily refers everything to himself, goes on to flatter himself with the notion that the universe, of which he is but a part, really exerts a special and noticeable effect on him.

In the face of reason he may have given up his astrological whimsey; i.e., that the starry heavens rule the fate of man. Nonetheless, he could not drop the conviction that the planets (if not the fixed stars), or the moon (if not the planets), determine and define the weather in a regular way.

But we will reject any such effect and consider weather phenomena on the earth to be neither cosmic nor planetary; it is our premise that they may be explained in purely tellurian terms.

Resumption

Accordingly, we will assume two basic movements of the earth's living body, and will consider all barometric effects as symbolic expressions of these.

First, the so-called oscillation of the earth directs us to a regular movement around the axis which produces the rotation of the earth, and thus day and night. This moving element falls twice in twenty-four hours, and rises twice; this has been shown by a variety of earlier observations. We can imagine it as a living spiral, a living helix without end. Its effect of attraction and release appears in the daily rise and fall of the barometer in relation to its normal level. This must be most pronounced where the greatest mass revolves, and must diminish toward the pole, finally disappearing altogether; observers have already shown this to be true. The rotation has a decided effect on the atmosphere, for clear skies and rain appear in daily succession. . . .

The second generally recognized movement is one which causes an increase and decrease in gravity; we can compare it to an inhaling and exhaling from the center toward the periphery. We have considered the rise and fall of the barometer as a symptom of this.

Control and Release of the Elements

In continuing to consider, apply, and test the above, we will be led further by events around us; let us therefore add the following about what was discussed earlier.

It is obvious that what we call the elements have a constant urge to go their own wild and brutal way. Where man has taken possession of the earth and is obliged to keep it, he must be forever vigilant and ready to resist. But these individual defenses are not nearly so effective as the use of a law to counter the unruly. Here nature has prepared the way for us in a most wonderful fashion by setting an alive, formed existence against the formless.

Thus the elements are to be viewed as colossal opponents with whom we must forever do battle; in each case we can overcome them only through the highest powers of the mind, by courage and cunning.

We may say that the elements are willfulness itself; the earth continually strives to seize the water and force it to solidify, annex it as earth, rock, or ice.

With equal turbulence the water would hurl the earth once more into its abyss, the earth it so reluctantly left behind. The air, supposedly an enlivening and protective friend, suddenly races down upon us as a storm to smash us and choke us. The fire relentlessly attacks everything in reach which is flammable or meltable. These observations depress us when we realize how often we must make them after a great and irretrievable catastrophe. It elevates our hearts and minds, however, when we realize how man has armed himself against the elements, defended himself, and even used the enemy as his slave.

In such instances we reach the highest level of thought with a perception of what nature bears within itself as law and rule to impose on those unbridled, lawless forces. Although we have learned much about this, we can consider only the most obvious point here.

The intensified attraction of the earth (indicated by a rise in the barometer) is the force which regulates the state of the atmosphere and controls the elements; it resists excessive water formation and the strongest movements of air; it even seems to keep electricity in a state of perfect neutrality.

Lower barometric pressure, on the other hand, releases the elements; here we should first note that the lower region of the continental atmosphere has a tendency to flow from west to east. Moisture, rain showers, waves, billows—mild or stormy, they all travel eastward, and where these phenomena are created along the way, they are born with the tendency to press eastward.

Here we will mention another point worth considering: after the barometric pressure has been low for a long time and the elements have grown unaccustomed to obeying, they will not return immediately to their bounds when the barometer rises. They remain on the same track for a time; the turbulence in the lower levels regains the desired balance only gradually, long after the upper atmosphere has reached a quiet resolution. Unfortunately we are also affected by this last period—coastal dwellers and sailors are especially hurt by it. The end of 1824 and the beginning of this year give the saddest evidence of this; westerlies and southwesterlies produce and accompany the most tragic happenings at sea and on the coast.

Once off in a general direction, our thinking hardly knows where to stop. We might be inclined to view the earthquake as earth's electricity unbound, the volcano as the element of fire aroused, and to relate these things to barometric effects. But empirical observation does not support this, for these movements and events seem to be localized, with some effect over a wider area.

Analogy

When seduced into venturing a larger or smaller scientific construct, we are well advised to look for analogies to test it. In following this advice here, I find the preceding description resembles the one I use in the *Theory of Color*.

In chromatics I oppose light and darkness to one another; these would never have any connection if matter did not intervene. Whether matter is opaque, transparent, or even alive, the quality of light and dark will manifest in it, and color in all its nuances will be created forthwith.

We have likewise put the *force of attraction* and its effect, *gravity*, on the one side, and the *force of warmth* and its effect, *expansion*, on the other; we have treated them as independent of one another. Between the two we put the atmosphere, empty of any so-called corporality, and we see that what we call "weather" arises in accordance with the effects of these two forces on the rarefied matter of the air. Thus the element in which and by which we live is organized in various but regular ways.

Recognition of Law

It can be seen that this is a highly complicated matter. In dealing with it, we think it right to start with its clearest aspect, i.e., the aspect most frequently repeated under similar conditions, the one which points to a constant regularity. Here we must not allow ourselves to be confused by the fact that what we thought mutually productive and consistent may sometimes seem to deviate and contradict itself. This is especially important in cases like this, where cause and effect are so easily confused in the midst of such complexity, and where correlates are viewed as mutually determining. To be sure, we will assume a basic law of weather. But we will also pay close attention to the endless physical, geological, and topographical differences, so that we can understand deviations in the phenomena as far as possible. If we hold fast to the regularity we will always find ourselves led back to it by our observations; anyone who fails to recognize the law will doubt the phenomenon, for, in the highest sense, every exception is included in the rule.

Self-Examination

In working on a venture like the present essay, the author must never forget to test himself in a variety of ways. This is done best and most certainly by looking back into history.

Even if we consider only those researchers who strove to restore the sciences, we will find that each was forced to make do with what empirical observation provided. The sum of what was actually known left many a gap across its breadth; various scientists sought to fill these gaps by reason or the power of imagination, for every scientist seeks the whole. With the growth of empirical knowledge, these inventions of imagination, these premature conclusions of reason, were set aside; a pure fact replaced them, and the phenomena took on more and more reality and harmony. A single example will serve for all.

I well remember: from my earliest school days to the present, the great and disproportionate space between Mars and Jupiter has interested every observer, and produced a variety of explanations. We may recall the efforts made by Kant, the great philosopher, to reach some degree of satisfaction about this phenomenon.

Here, if we may say so, a problem came to light—the light of day itself hid the fact that many small asteroids were circling one another, replacing a larger celestial body in the most extraordinary way.

Thousands of such problems may be found in the realm of scientific research: they would be solved more quickly if we did not so hastily dispose of them or obscure them by opinions.

Meanwhile, what we call *hypothesis* continues to assert its old claims, especially when it brings some movement in an apparently insoluble problem and puts us in a position to see things more easily. Such credit belongs to antiphlogistic chemistry: the same subjects were dealt with, but rearranged in a different order so that we could grasp them in a new way, and from a different angle.

In a similar vein, I have attempted to find a tellurian explanation for the principles governing our weather, and in some sense to ascribe atmospheric phenomena to the changing, pulsating gravity of the earth. Day by day I have come to feel the complete inadequacy of the notion that such constant phenomena as planets and moon cause a mysterious ebb and flow in the atmosphere. If I have simplified our concept in this regard, it is in the hope of bringing the time closer when we will discover the true underlying principles of the matter.

Although I am under no illusion that this explains and settles everything, I am still convinced that we should continue our research in this way, and look at the details of the matter as they emerge. This will bring us to a point I have neither imagined, nor can imagine; a point which will bring the solution of this problem and related ones.

ANALYSIS AND SYNTHESIS
(C. 1829)

In this year's third lecture on the history of philosophy Mr. Victor Cousin bestows high praise on the eighteenth century for its emphasis on the analytic method in science and for the care it took to avoid premature synthesis, i.e. hypotheses. However, after giving almost unqualified approval to this approach, he notes that synthesis should not be excluded entirely since its use—albeit with caution—is sometimes necessary.

Consideration of these statements quickly led us to the thought that this is an area where the nineteenth century needs to do more: the friends and followers of science must note that we have failed to test, develop, and clarify false syntheses, i.e., hypotheses handed down to us from the past. We have failed to restore to the human spirit its ancient right *to come face to face with nature.*

Here we will cite two of these false syntheses by name: the decomposition of light and the polarization of light. Although often repeated by men of science, these two empty phrases say nothing to the thoughtful observer.

It is not enough that we apply the analytic approach to the observation of nature; i.e., that we refine as many details as possible out of a given object and thereby familiarize ourselves with it. We should go on to apply the same analysis to existing syntheses so that we may discover whether a valid method has been applied in creating them.

Thus we have subjected Newton's approach to intensive analysis. He made the mistake of using a single phenomenon, and an overrefined one at that, as the foundation for a hypothesis supposed to explain the most varied and far-reaching events in nature.

To develop our theory of color we used the analytic approach; insofar as possible we presented every known phenomenon in a certain sequence so that we could determine the degree to which all might be governed by a general principle. It is our hope that this will help point the way for the nineteenth century as it carries out the duty we mentioned above.

We used a like approach in presenting the various phenomena created in double reflection. We bequeath both these efforts to some distant future in the knowledge that we have redirected our experiments to nature and thus truly set them free.

Let us proceed to another more general observation. A century has taken the wrong road if it applies itself exclusively to analysis while exhibiting an apparent fear of synthesis: the sciences come to life only when the two exist side by side like exhaling and inhaling.

A false hypothesis is better than none at all, for the mere fact that it is false does no harm. But when such a hypothesis establishes itself, when it finds general acceptance and becomes something like a creed open to neither doubt nor test, it is an evil under which centuries to come will suffer.

Here Newton's theory may serve as an example. Objections to its shortcomings arose during Newton's own lifetime, yet these objections were smothered under the weight of his great accomplishments in other areas and his standing in social and learned circles. But the French are most to blame in disseminating and rigidifying this theory. It will be their task in the nineteenth century to rectify their error by encouraging a fresh analysis of that tangled and ossified hypothesis.

An important point is apparently overlooked when analysis is used alone: every analysis presupposes a synthesis. A pile of sand cannot be analyzed, but if the pile contains grains of different materials (sand and gold for instance), an analysis might be made by washing it: then the light grains will wash away and the heavy ones remain.

Thus modern chemistry depends largely on separating what nature has united. We do away with nature's synthesis so that we may learn about nature through its separate elements.

What higher synthesis is there than a living organism? Why would we submit ourselves to the torments of anatomy, physiology, and psychology if not to reach some concept of the whole, a concept which can always restore itself to wholeness no matter how it is torn to pieces?

———————

Therefore a great danger for the analytical thinker arises when he *applies his method where there is no underlying synthesis.* In that case his work will be a true labor of the Danaids, and we can find the saddest examples of this. For in essence he is simply working to return to the synthesis. But if no synthesis underlies the object of his attention he will labor in vain to discover it. All his observations will only prove more and more an obstruction as their number increases.

Thus the analytical thinker ought to begin by examining (or rather, by noting) whether he is really working with a hidden synthesis or only an aggregation, a juxtaposition, a composite, or something of the sort. The areas of knowledge which have ceased to develop raise such doubts. It might be possible to make some useful observations of this sort about the fields of geology and meteorology.

A MORE INTENSE CHEMICAL ACTIVITY IN PRIMORDIAL MATTER
(1826)

In speaking of primal beginnings we should speak primally, i.e., poetically. Of those things to which our everyday language pertains—experience, understanding, judgment—none is adequate to the task. Upon entering deep into these barren, rocky chasms I felt for the first time that I envied the poets.

We must suppose that all primordial matter had greater energy, more intense chemical activity, and a stronger gravitational pull. Projecting rocks attracted the heavy particles suspended in the water to form a deposit, not below, but on their flanks. Parts of this solution may also have sunk to the bottom, thus producing the ambiguous quality of many formations. It is important to note that the solidification was always accompanied by seismic shocks.

The oldest epochs were altogether more uniform and homogeneous in nature, the newer ones more diverse, more or less dissimilar.

EXCERPT FROM "THE SPIRAL TENDENCY IN VEGETATION"
(1829-31)

When something in our observation of nature takes us aback, when we find our usual way of thought inadequate for its comprehension, we are well advised to look about for parallels in the history of thought and understanding.

Here we were simply reminded of Anaxagoras' homoeomeries, although a man of his day had to be satisfied with explaining a thing only through itself. Supported by empirical observation, however, we might venture to consider such a notion.

We may leave aside the fact that these homoeomeries are applicable mainly to simple primitive phenomena. But on a higher level, we have actually discovered that spiral organs extend throughout the plant in the most minute form, and we are equally sure there is a spiral tendency whereby the plant lives out its life, finally reaching full development.

Thus let us not completely reject Anaxagoras' idea as inadequate, for we should remember that there is always something to what a gifted man can formulate in thought, even though the formulation may be difficult to accept and apply.

In light of this new insight, we will venture to state the following. Having grasped the concept of metamorphosis fully, we may go on to examine the development of the plant in more detail, and will begin by noting a *vertical* tendency. We can think of this as a spiritual staff supporting the plant's existence and maintaining it over long periods of time. This vital principle manifests itself in the longitudinal fibers which yield flexible strands for a variety of uses. It forms the wood in trees and keeps annuals or biennials upright; even in climbing or creeping plants it works to create the extension from node to node.

Thus we must observe the spiral forms which wind about these plants.

The system which rises vertically in the plant produces the enduring element, the solid, the lasting (the fibers in short-lived plants, most of the wood in long-lived ones).

The spiral system is the element that develops, expands, nourishes; as such it is short-lived and different from the vertical. Where its effect predominates, it soon grows weak and begins to decay; where it joins the vertical system, the two grow together to form a lasting unity as wood or some other solid part.

Neither of the two systems can be considered as working alone; they are always and forever together. In complete balance they produce the most perfect development of vegetation.

The spiral system is really the nourishing element through which eye after eye is developed, and we can therefore see that an excess of nourishment will make it predominant over the vertical system. Thus the whole will be robbed of its support, of its skeletal structure, so to speak; it will lose itself in the rush to develop an excessive number of eyes. In tall, fully formed ash trees, for example, I have never found those flattened, twisted branches which look something like crosiers when the effect is pronounced. But I have found them

996

on trees where the top has been lost and the new twigs receive an excess of nourishment from the old trunk.

Other monstrosities (to be discussed later) arise when the vertical growth no longer balances the spiral system, when it is overshadowed by the spiral system. The vertical structure (whether fibrous or woody) is weakened and undermined in such a plant; it is brought to ruin, as it were. But the spiral system (on which eyes and buds depend) is accelerated, the tree branch flattened, the stem of the plant (which lacks wood) is bloated, and its interior destroyed. In the process, the spiral tendency appears, showing itself in twists, turns and curves. Examination of a branch will give us a full and thorough text for interpretation.

The spiral *vessels* have long been recognized, and their existence is freely acknowledged, but we must really think of them as individual organs subordinated to the spiral tendency. They have been sought in all parts of the plant and found almost everywhere, especially in sapwood where they even exhibit certain signs of life. It is quite in keeping with nature that its large-scale intentions are realized in the smallest detail.

As the basic law of life, this spiral tendency must first appear in the development from the seed. We will start with an observation of its appearance in the dicotyledons where the first seed leaves are clearly paired. The pair of cotyledons in these plants is often followed by a second pair of small but more developed leaves arranged crosswise, an arrangement which may continue for a time. But in many such plants it becomes obvious that the leaves growing higher on the stem do not subscribe to this social order, nor do the potential or actual eyes located behind them. One always tries to rush ahead of the other, causing the strangest placements; when all the parts in such a series finally gather together, the time of fructification in the flower draws near, and the development of the fruit follows.

In the *Calla* the leaf ribs quickly develop into leaf stems, and gradually grow round until they finally appear, completely rounded, as flower stalks. The flower is apparently a leaf end which has lost its green color; its vessels run from socket to periphery without branching, and curve inward around the spike which now represents the vertical position where flowering and fruiting take place.

The vertical tendency expresses itself from the moment of sprouting; it is how the plant takes root in the earth and grows upward at the same time. Perhaps we could observe how long this tendency remains predominant in the growth process, for we might assume it to be entirely responsible for the alternating placement of dicotyledonous leaf pairs at right angles to one another; this may seem problematic, however, since a certain spiral effect in any upward growth is not to be denied. In any case, as recessive as the vertical tendency may become, it reappears in blossoming where it creates the axis for the formation of each flower, manifesting itself most clearly in the spike and the spathe.

Research in plant anatomy has gradually clarified the matter of the spiral vessels found throughout the plant organism, as well as the aberrations in their form. This is not the place to go into detail; the beginning botanist can learn about them from a handbook, and the more advanced observer can turn to one of the larger works, or even look at nature itself.

It has long been thought that these vessels bring life to the plant organism, although their actual effect has not been sufficiently explained.

In our time, researchers have insisted that these vessels themselves should be recognized as alive, and described as such.

SELECTIONS FROM
MAXIMS AND REFLECTIONS

Whoever wishes to deny nature as an organ of the divine must begin by denying all revelation.

———

"Nature conceals God!" But not from everyone!

———

Archetypal phenomena: ideal, real, symbolic, identical.

Empirical realm: endless proliferation of these, thus hope of succor, despair of perfection.

Archetypal phenomenon:

> ideal as the ultimate we can know,
> real as what we know,
> symbolic, because it includes all instances,
> identical with all instances.

———

The direct experience of archetypal phenomena creates a kind of anxiety in us, for we feel inadequate. We enjoy these phenomena only when they are brought to life through their eternal interplay in the empirical.

———

When archetypal phenomena stand unveiled before our senses we become nervous, even anxious. Sensory man seeks salvation in astonishment, but soon

998

that busy matchmaker, Understanding, arrives with her efforts to marry the highest to the lowliest.

———————

The magnet is an archetypal phenomenon; this is clear the instant we say it. Thus it also comes to symbolize all else for which no words or names must be sought.

———————

Basic characteristic of an individual organism: to divide, to unite, to merge into the universal, to abide in the particular, to transform itself, to define itself, and, as living things tend to appear under a thousand conditions, to arise and vanish, to solidify and melt, to freeze and flow, to expand and contract. Since these effects occur together, any or all may occur at the same moment. Genesis and decay, creation and destruction, birth and death, joy and pain, all are interwoven with equal effect and weight; thus even the most isolated event always presents itself as an image and metaphor for the most universal.

———————

It is not easy for us to grasp the vast, the supercolossal, in nature; we have lenses to magnify tiny objects but none to make things smaller. And even for the magnifying glass we need eyes like Carus and Nees to profit intellectually from its use.

However, since nature is always the same, whether found in the vast or the small, and every piece of turbid glass produces the same blue as the whole of the atmosphere covering the globe, I think it right to seek out prototypal examples and assemble them before me. Here, then, the enormous is not reduced; it is present within the small, and remains as far beyond our grasp as it was when it dwelt in the infinite.

———————

The most sublime metamorphosis in the inorganic realm occurs when the amorphous takes on structure as it comes into being. Every material has the inclination and right to do this. Micaceous schist turns into garnets, often forming minerals with almost no mica; it is found only between the crystals of garnet as a minor formative element of the whole.

———————

The nature with which *we* must work is no longer nature—it is an entity quite different from that dealt with by the Greeks.

———————

The history of science is a great fugue in which the voices of nations are heard one after the other.

Four epochs of science:

> *childlike,*
> poetic, superstitious;
> *empirical,*
> searching, curious;
> *dogmatic,*
> didactic, pedantic;
> *ideal,*
> methodical, mystical.

Sciences destroy themselves in two ways: by the breadth they reach and by the depth they plumb.

A crisis must necessarily arise when a field of knowledge matures enough to become a science, for those who focus on details and treat them as separate will be set against those who have their eye on the universal and try to fit the particular into it. Now, however, an ideal, more comprehensive scientific approach is attracting an ever wider circle of friends, patrons, and colleagues; at this higher stage the division is no longer so marked, although still noticeable enough.

Those I would call *universalists* hold firm to the conviction that everything is present everywhere and may be discovered there, although in forms endlessly divergent and varied. The others, whom I will call *singularists*, agree with this principle, and even follow it in their observations, definitions, and teachings. But they claim to find exceptions wherever the prototype is not fully expressed, and rightly so. Their only error lies in failing to recognize the basic form where it is disguised, and denying it where it is hidden. Yet both ways of thought are authentic. They stand in eternal opposition with no prospect of joining forces or defeating one another: hence we must avoid engaging in controversy and simply state our convictions clearly and openly.

I will therefore restate mine: at this higher level we cannot *know*, but must *act*, just as we need little knowledge but much skill in a game. Nature has given us the chess board; we cannot and should not work beyond its limits. She has carved our pieces; gradually we will learn their value, their moves, and their powers. Now it will be our task to find the moves we think best; each seeks this in his own way regardless of any advice. Leave well enough alone, then. Let us merely observe the distance between us and the others, finding our allies in those who declare themselves on our side. We should also recall that we are dealing with an insoluble problem. We must be ready to attend to anything we may hear, especially anything opposed to our own view, for here we will recognize the problematic character of things and, especially, of people. I am not sure I will continue my work in this well-tilled field, but I reserve my right to note and point out certain new directions of study or individual research.

We may use Lichtenberg's writings as a wonderful divining rod: wherever he jests, a problem lies hidden.

He set one of his witticisms in the vast empty space between Mars and Jupiter. Kant had carefully demonstrated that all matter in this area must have been swept up by the two planets. Here Lichtenberg says in his humorous way: "Why should there not be unseen worlds as well?" And wasn't his comment absolutely true? Aren't the newly discovered planets invisible to everyone in the world except a few astronomers whose word we must trust?

Content without method leads to fantasy; method without content to empty sophistry; matter without form to unwieldly erudition, form without matter to hollow speculation.

The worthiest professor of physics would be one who could show the inadequacy of his text and diagrams in comparison to nature and the higher demands of the mind.

Germans—and they are not alone in this—have the knack of making the sciences unapproachable.

Those books which bring us the truths and falsehoods of the day in encyclopedic form have a special role in perpetuating error. There is no application of scientific method here; our knowledge, our beliefs, our assumptions—all are included. This is why after fifty years such works look strange indeed.

In general the sciences put some distance between themselves and life, and make their way back to it only by a roundabout path.

To be popularized, theoretical things must be presented in an absurd manner: the theoretical matter must be shown in practical application before the world at large will accept it.

———————

A scientific researcher must always think of himself as a member of a jury. His only concern should be the adequacy of the evidence and the clarity of the proofs which support it. Guided by this, he will form his opinion and cast his vote without regard for whether he shares the author's view.

———————

In doing this he should be unconcerned with the question of whether he is in the majority or the minority—he has accomplished his task, he has expressed his convictions, and he cannot command the minds or feelings of others.

———————

The history of philosophy, science, and religion all show that opinions may be circulated en masse, but the one which predominates is the one which is most concrete, i.e., comfortably tailored to the human mind at its most ordinary. In fact, anyone who learns to think in the higher sense may assume that he will find the majority opposed to him.

———————

The ultimate goal would be: to grasp that everything in the realm of fact is already theory. The blue of the sky shows us the basic law of chromatics. Let us not seek for something behind the phenomena—they themselves are the theory.

———————

Weak minds make the mental error of leaping straight from the particular to the general when, in fact, the general is to be found only within the whole.

———————

Nature will reveal nothing under torture; its frank answer to an honest question is "Yes! Yes!—No! No!" More than this comes of evil.

———————

He who beholds a phenomenon will often extend his thinking beyond it; he who merely hears about the phenomenon will not be moved to think at all.

———————

There is a delicate empiricism which makes itself utterly identical with the object, thereby becoming true theory. But this enhancement of our mental powers belongs to a highly evolved age.

The manifestation of a phenomenon is not detached from the observer—it is caught up and entangled in his individuality.

———

In observing nature on a scale large or small, I have always asked: Who speaks here, the object or you? I also take this approach in regard to my predecessors and colleagues.

———

There is a secret element of regularity in the object which corresponds to a secret element of regularity in the subject.

———

. . . Thus when making observations it is best to be fully conscious of objects, and when thinking to be fully aware of ourselves.

———

When we try to recognize the idea inherent in a phenomenon we are confused by the fact that it frequently—even normally—contradicts our senses. The Copernican system is based on an idea which was hard to grasp; even now it contradicts our senses every day. We merely echo something we neither see nor understand.

The metamorphosis of plants contradicts our senses in this way.

———

Reason is applied to what is developing, practical understanding to what is developed. The former does not ask, What is the purpose? and the latter does not ask, What is the source? Reason takes pleasure in development; practical understanding tries to hold things fast so that it can use them.

———

Thinking man has a strange trait: when faced with an unsolved problem he likes to concoct a fantastic mental image, one he can never escape even when the problem is solved and the truth revealed.

———

Throughout the history of scientific investigation we find observers leaping too quickly from phenomenon to theory; hence they fall short of the mark and become theoretical.

———

The Greeks spoke of neither cause nor effect in their descriptions and stories—instead, they presented the phenomenon as it was.

In their science, too, they did not perform experiments, but relied on experiences as they occurred.

The animal is instructed by his sensory organs; man instructs his organs and governs them.

The present age has a bad habit of being abstruse in the sciences. We remove ourselves from common sense without opening up a higher one; we become transcendent, fantastic, fearful of intuitive perception in the real world, and when we wish to enter the practical realm, or need to, we suddenly turn atomistic and mechanical.

Our most basic and necessary concept—that of *cause* and *effect*—leads to numerous and repeated errors in application.

We can grasp immediate causes and thus find them easiest to understand; this is why we like to think mechanistically about things which really are of a higher order.

. . . Thus mechanistic modes of explanation become the order of the day when we ignore problems which can only be explained dynamistically.

A careful review of physics will show that not all the phenomena it studies are of equal value, nor are all the experiments on which it relies.

Primary, archetypal experiments are pivotal, and work based on them has a sure and firm foundation. But there are also secondary experiments, tertiary experiments, etc.; when we give them equal weight we only confuse what was clarified through the primary experiment.

Someday someone will write a pathology of experimental physics and bring to light all those swindles which subvert our reason, beguile our judgment and, what is worse, stand in the way of any practical progress. The phenomena must be freed once and for all from their grim torture chamber of empiricism, mechanism, and dogmatism; they must be brought before the jury of man's common sense.

Few people have the gift of grasping nature and using it directly; between knowledge and application they prefer to invent a phantom which they develop in great detail; doing so, they forget both object and purpose.

The mathematician relies on the element of quantity, on all that is defined by number and size, and thus to some degree on the universe in its external form. But if we set out to apply the full measure of mind and all its powers to this universe, we will realize that *quantity* and *quality* must be viewed as two poles of material existence. This is why the mathematician refines his language of formula so highly; as far as possible he wants to incorporate the incalculable world into the realm of measure and number. Everything will then seem graspable, comprehensible, and mechanical, and he may be accused of an underlying atheism for supposedly he has included the most incalculable element of all (which we call God), and thus has eliminated its special, over-riding presence.

An important task: to banish mathematical-philosophical theories from those areas of physics where they impede rather than advance knowledge, those areas where a one-sided development in modern scientific education has made such perverse use of them.

A strict separation must be maintained between physics and mathematics. Physics must remain quite independent; it must use all its powers of love, respect, and reverence to find its way into nature and the sacred life of nature irrespective of what mathematics does. The latter, on the other hand, must declare itself independent of all externalities, take its own path of intellect, and develop in a purer way than it now does in working with the physical world to gain something from it or impose something on it.

Like dialectics, mathematics is an organ for a higher kind of inner sense; in practice it is an art like rhetoric. Both value nothing but form—the content is unimportant. It does not matter whether mathematics counts pennies or guineas, whether rhetoric defends what is true or what is false.

Here, however, the character of the person doing these things, practicing these arts, is most important. An effective advocate with a just cause, an able mathematician before the starry heavens—both seem equally godlike.

What except for its exactitude is exact about mathematics? And this exactitude—does it not flow from an inner feeling for the truth?

Mathematics cannot eliminate prejudice, prevent willfulness, or resolve partisan differences. It has no power over anything in the moral realm.

A mathematician is perfect only to the degree that he is a perfect human being, to the degree that he can experience the beauty in what is true. Only then will his work be complete, transparent, comprehensive, pure, clear, graceful—even elegant. All this is needed to become a Lagrange.

To escape the endless profusion, fragmentation, and complication of modern science and recover the element of simplicity, we must always ask ourselves: What approach would Plato have taken to a nature which is both simple in essence and manifold in appearance?

Insofar as he makes use of his healthy senses, man himself is the best and most exact scientific instrument possible. The greatest misfortune of modern physics is that its experiments have been set apart from man, as it were; physics refuses to recognize nature in anything not shown by artificial instruments, and even uses this as a measure of its accomplishments.

The Newtonian experiment which forms the basis for the traditional theory of color is extremely complicated; it requires the following:

For the spectral colors to appear we need:

1. a glass prism
2. which has three sides
3. and is small;
4. a window shutter
5. with an opening
6. which is quite small;
7. the sun's form entering
8. and falling on the prism at a certain distance
9. from a certain angle;
10. an image formed on a surface
11. placed a certain distance behind the prism.

ON PHILOSOPHY AND SCIENCE

If conditions 3, 6, and 11 are not met, if we enlarge the opening, use a large prism, or bring the surface closer, the desired spectrum can and will not appear.

The battle with Newton is actually being conducted at a very low level. It is directed against a phenomenon which was poorly observed, poorly developed, poorly applied, and poorly explained in theory. He stands accused of sloppiness in his earlier experiments, prejudice in his later ones, haste in forming theories, obstinacy in defending them, and generally of a half-unconscious, half-conscious dishonesty.

In New York there are ninety different Christian sects, each acknowledging God and our Lord in its own way without interference. In scientific research—indeed, in any kind of research—we need to reach this goal; for how can it be that everyone demands open-mindedness while denying others their own way of thinking and expressing themselves?